THE LAW RELATING TO

INTERNATIONAL COMMERCIAL DISPUTES

By

JONATHAN HILL

Reader in Law, University of Bristol

LLP

LONDON NEW YORK HAMBURG HONG KONG

LLOYD'S OF LONDON PRESS LTD.

1994

Lloyd's of London Press Ltd.
Legal Publishing Division
27 Swinton Street
London WC1X 9NW

USA AND CANADA
Lloyd's of London Press Inc.
Suite 308, 611 Broadway
New York, NY 10012 USA

GERMANY
Lloyd's of London Press GmbH
59 Ehrenbergstrasse
2000 Hamburg 50, Germany

SOUTH EAST ASIA
Lloyd's of London Press (Far East) Ltd.
Room 1101, Hollywood Centre
233 Hollywood Road
Hong Kong

First published in Great Britain, 1994

British Library Cataloguing in Publication Data
A catalogue record for this book is
available from the British Library

ISBN 1-85044-596-6

Text set in 10pt on 12pt Postscript Times by
Mendip Communications Ltd., Frome, Somerset
Printed in Great Britain by
Bell & Bain Limited, Glasgow

PREFACE

The major part of this book is concerned with the branch of English law which is known by one of two equally unsatisfactory labels: private international law or the conflict of laws. Although private international law straddles the whole of the legal system, this book deals with only the most important aspects relating to commercial disputes. The focus is on the legal problems which arise out of cross-border trade. However, the chapters which follow are concerned with the legal framework for the resolution of disputes, rather than the substantive law which determines their outcome.

Recent years have seen both a significant increase in the volume of international transactions and rapid changes in the law which aims to provide the framework for the resolution of the disputes which arise out of them. In the last twenty years nearly all facets of the law relating to international commercial disputes have been transformed either by new judicial attitudes or, more significantly, by legislation (often implementing international conventions to which the United Kingdom has become a party). There can be little doubt that recent developments have rendered the law considerably more complex.

The primary purpose of this work is to provide an accessible guide for lawyers who are coming into contact for the first time with the legal problems of international business. The aim is to provide a clear and comprehensible account of the rules and principles which are relevant to the mainstream of commercial disputes. Considerations of space have meant that some of the more esoteric aspects of the law have had to be excluded or considered in outline only.

It would be misleading to suggest either that the current state of the law is always certain or that, where it is certain, it is always commendable. Accordingly, areas of ambiguity and controversy are identified. For those readers who are interested in delving more deeply into the arcane mysteries of private international law references to further material have been provided.

Much of the law which provides the framework for the resolution of international commercial disputes is derived from international instruments as a consequence of which English law is very similar to—or the same as—the laws of the other parts of the United Kingdom and the laws of other countries in Europe and beyond. Nevertheless, the text is written from an English perspective and no attempt has been made to draw attention systematically to differences between English law and the laws of other countries.

Writing is a solitary business. My thanks go to Sheila for her support and understanding. Thanks are also due to Chris Clarkson who read parts of the manuscript and to the publishers who prepared the tables and index.

I have attempted to state the law as on 1 October 1993, although it has been possible to refer to some more recent material.

For the sake of simplicity, throughout the text, "England" is used to signify "England and Wales" and "he", "his" and "him" to signify "he or she", "his or her" and "him or her".

Bristol
21 November 1993

JONATHAN HILL

THE LAW
RELATING TO
INTERNATIONAL
COMMERCIAL
DISPUTES

CONTENTS

Preface v
Table of Cases xxvii
Table of Legislation, Rules, Conventions etc. xliii

CHAPTER 1: INTRODUCTION 1
1.1: Preliminary remarks 1
1.2: Jurisdiction and the recognition and enforcement of foreign judgments 3
1.2.1: Basic concepts 3
1.2.1.1: Jurisdiction 3
1.2.1.1.1: Two aspects to jurisdiction 3
1.2.1.1.2: Actions *in personam* and actions *in rem* 3
1.2.1.2: Recognition and enforcement 4
1.2.2: The traditional regime 4
1.2.3: The Brussels and Lugano Conventions 6
1.2.4: Jurisdiction and the recognition and enforcement of judgments within the United Kingdom 7
1.3: Choice of law 7
1.4: Bibliographical note 10

PART I. JURISDICTION AND THE RECOGNITION AND ENFORCEMENT OF FOREIGN JUDGMENTS

CHAPTER 2: PERSONS WHO CAN AND CANNOT SUE OR BE SUED 15
2.1: Legal capacity to sue or be sued 15
2.1.1: Foreign corporations 15
2.1.2: Other foreign juristic entities 15
2.1.3: Corporations established under the laws of territories which are not States 16
2.1.4: International corporations 17
2.1.4.1: Introduction 17
2.1.4.2: The *Tin Council* case 19
2.1.4.3: *Arab Monetary Fund* v. *Hashim (No 3)* 20
2.1.5: Foreign States 22
2.1.6: Foreign governments 23
2.2: Persons who cannot sue: enemy aliens 24
2.3: State immunity 25
2.3.1: Background 25
2.3.2: What is a State? 26
2.3.3: The Scheme of the Act 26
2.3.3.1: The principles of immunity 26
2.3.3.2: Exceptions to immunity 26

2.3.3.3: The burden of proof 27
2.3.4: Immunity from adjudicative jurisdiction 27
2.3.4.1: Submission 27
2.3.4.2: Arbitration 28
2.3.4.3: Ships 29
2.3.4.4: Commercial activities 31
2.3.4.5: Contracts of employment 32
2.3.4.6: Tort 32
2.3.4.7: Ownership, possession and use of property 32
2.3.4.8: Intellectual property rights 33
2.3.4.9: Membership of organisations 34
2.3.4.10: Taxes 34
2.3.5: Immunity from enforcement jurisdiction 34
2.3.5.1: Preliminary remarks 34
2.3.5.2: Immunity under section 13(1) and (2) 34
2.3.5.3: Waiver of immunity 35
2.3.5.4: No immunity in respect of property used for commercial purposes 36
2.3.5.5: Enforcement against separate entities 38
2.3.5.5.1: The general rule 38
2.3.5.5.2: The special position of a State's central bank 38
2.3.6: Service of process in proceedings against States 39
2.3.6.1: Instituting proceedings 39
2.3.6.2: Entering appearance 40
2.3.6.3: Judgments in default 40
2.4: Diplomatic immunity 41
2.4.1: Diplomatic officers 41
2.4.1.1: Diplomatic agents 41
2.4.1.2: Members of the administrative and technical staff 42
2.4.1.3: Members of the service staff 42
2.4.1.4: Waiver 42
2.4.1.5: The temporal scope of immunity 42
2.4.2: Consular agents 43
2.5: International organisations 43

CHAPTER 3: THE BRUSSELS AND LUGANO CONVENTIONS: GENERAL CONSIDERATIONS 45
3.1: Introduction 45
3.2: Interpretation of the Conventions 50
3.2.1: Interpretation of the Brussels Convention 50
3.2.1.1: References to the European Court of Justice under the Luxembourg Protocol 50
3.2.1.2: Methods of interpretation 51
3.2.1.3: Interpretation by national courts 53
3.2.2: Interpretation of the Lugano Convention 54
3.2.2.1: Protocols and declarations 54
3.2.2.2: Domestic legislation 55
3.2.2.3: Can the courts of EC Member States refer questions of interpretation to the Court of Justice? 55
3.2.3: Practical problems in cases which are not referred to the Court of Justice 56
3.3: Scope of the Conventions 56
3.3.1: Introductory remarks 56
3.3.2: Civil and commercial matters 57
3.3.3: Exceptions 58

3.3.3.1: Family law 59
3.3.3.2: Bankruptcy and insolvency 59
3.3.3.3: Social security 60
3.3.3.4: Arbitration 60
3.3.3.4.1: Legal proceedings relating to arbitration 61
3.3.3.4.2: Legal proceedings relating to arbitration in which the validity of the arbitration agreement arises as a preliminary question 61
3.3.3.4.3: Legal proceedings relating to the validity of an arbitration agreement 62
3.3.3.4.4: Legal proceedings in which the jurisdiction of the court is contested on the basis of an arbitration agreement 63
3.3.3.4.5: The recognition and enforcement of judgments given in breach or disregard of an arbitration agreement 63
3.4: The relationship between the Brussels and Lugano Conventions 66
3.5: The relationship between the Brussels and Lugano Conventions and other international conventions 67

CHAPTER 4: JURISDICTION IN PERSONAM UNDER THE BRUSSELS AND LUGANO CONVENTIONS: INTRODUCTION 69
4.1: Domicile under the Conventions 69
4.1.1: The domicile of individuals 69
4.1.1.1: Introduction 69
4.1.1.2: Domicile in the United Kingdom 70
4.1.1.3: Domicile in other States 71
4.1.2: The domicile of corporations 71
4.1.2.1: Introduction 71
4.1.2.2: Domicile in the United Kingdom 71
4.1.2.3: Domicile in another State 72
4.1.3: Multiple domiciles 73
4.1.4: Special definitions 73
4.2: The basic structure of the jurisdiction rules 74
4.2.1: Jurisdiction rules applicable to defendants domiciled in a Contracting State: Articles 2 and 3 74
4.2.2: Jurisdiction rules applicable to persons who are not domiciled in a Contracting State: Article 4 75
4.2.3: The standard of proof 75
4.2.3.1: The merits of the dispute 76
4.2.3.2: Questions of jurisdiction 76
4.3: Service abroad in cases falling within the scope of the Conventions 78
4.3.1: Service abroad without leave 78
4.3.2: Methods of service 79
4.4: Procedural safeguards 80

CHAPTER 5: JURISDICTION IN PERSONAM UNDER THE BRUSSELS AND LUGANO CONVENTIONS: JURISDICTION RULES 83
5.0: Introduction 83
5.1: Exclusive jurisdiction: Article 16 84
5.1.1: Article 16(1) 84
5.1.1.1: Preliminary remarks 84
5.1.1.2: Article 16(1)(a): rights *in rem* 85
5.1.1.2.1: General principles 85
5.1.1.2.2: Proceedings relating to contracts for the sale of land 86
5.1.1.2.3: Proceedings relating to trusts of land 86

5.1.1.3: Article 16(1)(a): tenancies of immovable property 87
5.1.1.4: Proceedings concerning immovable property in more than one Contracting State 89
5.1.2: Certain proceedings relating to corporations 90
5.1.3: Certain proceedings concerning entries in public registers 90
5.1.4: Certain proceedings concerning intellectual property 91
5.1.5: Enforcement proceedings 91
5.1.6: Examination of jurisdiction 92
5.2: Submission: Article 18 92
5.3: Jurisdiction agreements: Article 17 94
5.3.1: Preliminary considerations 94
5.3.1.1: The text 94
5.3.1.2: The relationship between the two Conventions 94
5.3.2: Article 17(1): basic conditions 95
5.3.2.1: An agreement on jurisdiction 95
5.3.2.2: Choosing the courts of a Contracting State 95
5.3.2.3: Choice of the courts of a non-contracting State 96
5.3.3: Article 17(1): formal requirements 97
5.3.3.1: In writing or evidenced in writing 97
5.3.3.1.1: In writing 97
5.3.3.1.2: Evidence in writing 99
5.3.3.2: In a form which accords with practices which the parties have established between themselves 99
5.3.3.3: Trade usages 100
5.3.3.4: Article 17(1) and third parties 100
5.3.3.5: The formal requirements of Article 17 and national law 101
5.3.4: Material validity and interpretation 102
5.3.5: Alternative fora 103
5.3.6: Non-exclusive jurisdiction clauses 103
5.3.7: Article 17(4): clauses for the benefit of one party only 104
5.3.8: Article 17(5): jurisdiction clauses in employment contracts 104
5.4: The domicile rule: Article 2 105
5.5: Alternative fora I: Article 5 106
5.5.1: Introduction 106
5.5.2: Jurisdiction in matters relating to contract and tort: introduction 107
5.5.2.1: Methods of interpretation 107
5.5.2.2: Are paragraphs (1) and (3) all-embracing? 108
5.5.2.3: Are paragraphs (1) and (3) mutually exclusive? 109
5.5.3: Jurisdiction in matters relating to a contract 110
5.5.3.1: Matters relating to a contract 110
5.5.3.2: The obligation in question 111
5.5.3.2.1: The general rule 111
5.5.3.2.2: Multiple obligations 111
5.5.3.3: Place of performance 113
5.5.3.4: Employment contracts 114
5.5.3.4.1: Background 114
5.5.3.4.2: The scope of the rules relating to individual contracts of employment 115
5.5.3.4.3: The Lugano Convention 116
5.5.3.4.4: The Brussels Convention 116
5.5.3.5: Agreements on the place of performance: The relationship between Article 5(1) and Article 17 117
5.5.4: Jurisdiction in matters relating to tort 117

5.5.4.1: Matters relating to tort, delict or quasi-delict 117
5.5.4.2: The place where the harmful event occurred 118
5.5.5: Branch, agency or other establishment 120
5.5.5.1: Branch, agency or other establishment 120
5.5.5.2: Relations between a branch and the parent body 121
5.5.5.3: Operations 122
5.5.6: Trusts 122
5.6: Alternative fora II: Article 6 123
5.6.1: Introduction 123
5.6.2: Multiple defendants 123
5.6.3: Third party proceedings 124
5.6.4: Counterclaims 126
5.6.5: Contractual claims involving matters relating to rights *in rem* in immovable property 126
5.7: Insurance and consumer contracts: Articles 7 to 15 127
5.7.1: Insurance: Articles 7 to 12A 127
5.7.1.1: Proceedings brought against insurers 128
5.7.1.1.1: Article 8 128
5.7.1.1.2: Article 9 128
5.7.1.1.3: Article 10 128
5.7.1.1.4: Article 5(5) 129
5.7.1.1.5: Jurisdiction agreements 129
5.7.1.2: Proceedings brought against the policy-holder, the insured or a beneficiary 129
5.7.1.3: Jurisdiction agreements 130
5.7.1.3.1: Paragraph 1 131
5.7.1.3.2: Paragraph 2 131
5.7.1.3.3: Paragraph 3 131
5.7.1.3.4: Paragraph 4 132
5.7.1.3.5: Paragraph 5 132
5.7.2: Consumer contracts: Articles 13 to 15 134
5.7.2.1: The scope of Section 4 134
5.7.2.2: Proceedings brought against the consumer 135
5.7.2.3: Proceedings brought against the other party 135
5.7.2.4: Jurisdiction agreements 136
5.8: Provisional, including protective, measures 137
5.9: *Lis pendens* and related actions: Articles 21 to 23 137
5.9.1: General considerations 138
5.9.1.1: Section 8 and the scope of the Conventions 138
5.9.1.2: Parties not domiciled in a Contracting State 138
5.9.1.3: Section 8 and enforcement proceedings 139
5.9.1.4: The court first seised 139
5.9.2: *Lis pendens*: Article 21 140
5.9.2.1: The same cause of action 140
5.9.2.2: The same parties 142
5.9.2.3: The relationship between the court first seised and the court second seised 144
5.9.2.3.1: The general rule 144
5.9.2.3.2: Article 21 and jurisdiction under Sections 3 to 5 144
5.9.2.3.3: Article 21 and jurisdiction agreements 145
5.9.2.3.4: The relationship between Article 21 and Article 22 146
5.9.2.3.5: The relationship between Article 21 and Article 24 146
5.9.3: Related proceedings: Article 22 146
5.9.4: Rival exclusive jurisdictions: Article 23 148

5.10: Discretion to stay English proceedings 149
5.10.1: *Forum non conveniens* 149
5.10.2: Foreign jurisdiction clauses 151
5.10.3: Disputes relating to foreign land 152

CHAPTER 6: JURISDICTION IN PERSONAM UNDER TRADITIONAL RULES 153
6.1: Presence 153
6.1.1: Individuals 153
6.1.1.1: Personal service: RSC, Order 10, rule 1(1) 153
6.1.1.2: Postal service and letter box service: RSC, Order 10, rule 1(2) 155
6.1.2: Corporations 156
6.1.2.1: British companies 156
6.1.2.2: Oversea companies: introduction 157
6.1.2.3: Section 690A: what is a branch? 158
6.1.2.4: Section 691: what is an established place of business? 159
6.1.2.5: Section 694A: service of process on an oversea company with a branch in England 160
6.1.2.6: Section 695: service of process of an oversea company with a place of business in England 162
6.1.3: Partnerships: RSC, Order 81 163
6.1.4: Discretion to stay: *forum non conveniens* 164
6.2: Submission 164
6.2.1: Jurisdiction agreements 164
6.2.2: Agreements to submit 165
6.2.3: Voluntary appearance 165
6.3: Service out of the jurisdiction under RSC, Order 11, rule 1(1) 167
6.3.1: Introduction 167
6.3.1.1: Three issues 167
6.3.1.2: Procedure 169
6.3.2: A serious question to be tried 169
6.3.3: The heads of RSC, Order 11, rule 1(1) 170
6.3.3.1: Jurisdiction based on domicile 170
6.3.3.2: Injunctions 171
6.3.3.3: Multiple defendants 171
6.3.3.4: Contract 172
6.3.3.4.1: General scope 172
6.3.3.4.2: Made within the jurisdiction 173
6.3.3.4.3: Whose agent? 174
6.3.3.4.4: Contracts governed by English law 174
6.3.3.4.5: Jurisdiction clauses in favour of the English courts 175
6.3.3.5: Breach of contract within the jurisdiction 175
6.3.3.6: Tort 175
6.3.3.7: Restitution 176
6.3.3.8: Other heads of jurisdiction 177
6.3.3.9: Interpretation and standard of proof 177
6.3.4: *Forum conveniens* 179
6.4: The importance of discretion 179
6.4.1: Forum shopping 179
6.4.2: The development of English law 180
6.4.3: The test of appropriateness 182
6.4.4: The application of the test: factors to be taken into account 186

6.4.4.1: Convenience and expense 186
6.4.4.2: *Lis alibi pendens* 186
6.4.4.3: Multiple defendants 187
6.4.4.4: The "Cambridgeshire factor" 188
6.4.4.5: Time bars 189
6.4.4.6: Delay 189
6.4.4.7: Costs 189
6.4.4.8: Damages 190
6.4.4.9: Procedural fairness 190
6.4.4.10: The applicable law 191
6.4.4.11: Language 191
6.4.4.12: Preference for the choice of law rules of the forum 192
6.4.5: The weighing of factors 193
6.4.6: Appeals against the exercise of discretion 194
6.5: Cases involving jurisdiction clauses 195
6.5.1: Preliminary remarks 195
6.5.2: Cases involving a foreign jurisdiction clause 196
6.5.3: Cases involving an English jurisdiction clause 198
6.6: Jurisdiction in cases involving foreign land 198

CHAPTER 7: THE ALLOCATION OF JURISDICTION WITHIN THE UNITED KINGDOM 201
7.1: Jurisdiction in civil and commercial matters: the Modified Convention 201
7.1.1: The scope of the Modified Convention 201
7.1.2: Interpretation 202
7.2: Bases of jurisdiction under the Modified Convention 203
7.2.1: Exclusive jurisdiction: Article 16 203
7.2.2: Prorogation of jurisdiction 204
7.2.2.1: Article 18 204
7.2.2.2: Article 17 204
7.2.3: Special jurisdiction 205
7.2.3.1: Article 5 205
7.2.3.2: Articles 6 and 6A 206
7.2.4: Consumer contracts 206
7.2.5: Procedural matters and provisional measures 207
7.3: Staying proceedings in cases under the Modified Convention 207
7.3.1: *Lis pendens* 207
7.3.2: Discretion to stay proceedings under the Modified Convention 208
7.3.2.1: Internal disputes 208
7.3.2.2: Discretion in cases governed by one of the Conventions and the Modified Convention 208

CHAPTER 8: JURISDICTION IN ADMIRALTY PROCEEDINGS 211
8.0: Introduction 211
8.1: Jurisdiction under the Supreme Court Act 1981 212
8.1.1: The Admiralty jurisdiction of the High Court: section 20 212
8.1.1.1: Section 20(1)(a) and (b) 212
8.1.1.2: Section 20(1)(c) 216
8.1.1.3: Section 20(1)(d) 217
8.1.2: Jurisdiction *in rem*: section 21(2) to (8) 217
8.1.2.1: Section 21(2): cases falling within section 20(2)(a)–(i) and (s) 217
8.1.2.2: Section 21(3): maritime liens 217

8.1.2.2.1: Maritime liens 218
8.1.2.2.2: "Or other charge" 218
8.1.2.3: Section 21(4): cases falling within section 20(2)(e) to (r) 218
8.1.2.3.1: The relevant person 219
8.1.2.3.2: The particular ship: section 21(4)(b)(i) 219
8.1.2.3.3: Other ship: section 21(4)(b)(ii) 219
8.1.2.3.4: Beneficial owner 220
8.1.2.4: The relationship between section 21(3) and (4) 221
8.1.3: Jurisdiction in actions *in personam*: section 21(1) and section 22 221
8.1.4: Commencing Admiralty proceedings 221
8.1.4.1: Actions *in rem* 222
8.1.4.2: Actions *in personam* 223
8.1.4.3: Staying Admiralty proceedings 223
8.2: The impact of the Brussels and Lugano Conventions 224
8.2.1: Introduction 224
8.2.1.1: The basic scheme of the Conventions 224
8.2.1.2: Do the Conventions apply to actions *in rem*? 224
8.2.1.3: The preservation of special conventions 225
8.2.2: The combined effect of Title II and Article 57 226
8.2.3: Staying proceedings 228
8.2.3.1: Articles 21 and 22 228
8.2.3.2: *Forum non conveniens* 228
8.2.4: Limitation and salvage 229
8.2.4.1: Salvage of cargo or freight 229
8.2.4.2: Limitation of liability 229

CHAPTER 9: THE RECOGNITION AND ENFORCEMENT OF FOREIGN JUDGMENTS 231
9.1: Introduction 232
9.1.1: Why recognise foreign judgments? 232
9.1.2: Which foreign judgments should be entitled to recognition and enforcement? 232
9.1.3: "Merger" 233
9.2: Recognition and enforcement at common law 234
9.2.1: The basic framework of recognition and enforcement 234
9.2.2: Final and conclusive 236
9.2.3: For a fixed sum 236
9.2.4: On the merits 237
9.2.5: The jurisdiction of the original court 238
9.2.5.1: Introductory remarks 238
9.2.5.2: Submission 239
9.2.5.3: A sufficient territorial connection: individuals 242
9.2.5.4: A sufficient territorial connection: corporations 243
9.2.5.5: A sufficient territorial connection: the problem of federal States 245
9.2.5.6: No other bases of jurisdiction 246
9.2.6: Cause of action estoppel and issue estoppel 246
9.2.6.1: Identity of the parties 247
9.2.6.2: Cause of action estoppel: identity of the cause of action 248
9.2.6.3: Issue estoppel: identity of the issue 249
9.2.7: Defences to recognition and enforcement 250
9.2.7.1: Natural justice 251
9.2.7.1.1: Traditional categories 251
9.2.7.1.2: Substantial justice 251

9.2.7.2: Fraud 253
9.2.7.2.1: General principles 253
9.2.7.2.2: The application of the principles to different types of fraud 254
9.2.7.3: Public policy 255
9.2.7.4: *Res judicata* 256
9.2.7.5: Civil Jurisdiction and Judgments Act 1982, section 32 257
9.2.7.6: Multiple damages 258
9.2.8: Recognition and enforcement of judgments *in rem* 259
9.2.8.1: Jurisdiction of the original court 259
9.2.8.2: Defences 259
9.2.8.3: Enforcement 259
9.3: Recognition and enforcement under statutory regimes based on the common law 260
9.3.1: Enforcement under Part II of the Administration of Justice Act 1920 261
9.3.2: Recognition and enforcement under the Foreign Judgments (Reciprocal Enforcement) Act 1933 262
9.3.2.1: Enforcement: conditions and procedure 262
9.3.2.2: Resisting enforcement 264
9.3.2.2.1: Improper registration 264
9.3.2.2.2: Lack of jurisdiction 264
9.3.2.2.3: Lack of notice of the proceedings 265
9.3.2.2.4: Fraud 265
9.3.2.2.5: Public policy 265
9.3.2.2.6: Irreconcilability 266
9.3.2.2.7: When an appeal is pending abroad 266
9.3.2.2.8: Protection of Trading Interests Act 1980 266
9.3.2.3: Recognition 266
9.4: Recognition and enforcement under the Brussels and Lugano Conventions 267
9.4.1: Basic conditions for recognition and enforcement under Title III 267
9.4.1.1: The scope of the Conventions 267
9.4.1.2: What is a "judgment"? 268
9.4.1.2.1: Article 25 268
9.4.1.2.2: Interlocutory orders 268
9.4.1.2.3: Penalties 269
9.4.1.2.4: Partial enforcement 269
9.4.1.3: The relationship between Title II and Title III 270
9.4.2: The principle of automatic recognition 271
9.4.3: Defences to recognition 271
9.4.3.1: No review of the merits: Article 29 271
9.4.3.2: Limited review of jurisdiction: Article 28 272
9.4.3.3: Public policy: Article 27(1) 274
9.4.3.3.1: The proper approach to public policy 274
9.4.3.3.2: Limits on public policy 275
9.4.3.3.3: Public policy and fraud 275
9.4.3.4: Safeguarding the rights of the defendant: Article 27(2) 276
9.4.3.4.1: The relationship between Article 20 and Article 27(2) 277
9.4.3.4.2: One defence or two? 277
9.4.3.4.3: "In default of appearance" 279
9.4.3.4.4: Due service 279
9.4.3.4.5: In sufficient time 280
9.4.3.5: Irreconcilability: Article 27(3) 282
9.4.3.6: Irreconcilability: Article 27(5) 284
9.4.3.7: Irreconcilability: Article 27(4) 284

9.4.3.8: Appeals in the State of origin: Article 30 284
9.4.3.8.1: Article 30(1): what is an "ordinary appeal"? 285
9.4.3.8.2: Article 30(2): the special position of appeals in Ireland and the United Kingdom 285
9.4.3.8.3: The exercise of discretion 286
9.4.4: Enforcement of judgments 286
9.4.4.1: Introduction 286
9.4.4.2: Application for enforcement 287
9.4.4.2.1: The application 287
9.4.4.2.2: Formalities 287
9.4.4.2.3: Security for costs 289
9.4.4.3: The decision 289
9.4.4.4: Appeals against registration 291
9.4.4.4.1: The first appeal 291
9.4.4.4.2: The effect of an appeal pending before the court of the State of origin 291
9.4.4.4.3: Limitations on enforcement 293
9.4.4.4.4: A further appeal on a point of law 295
9.4.4.5: Appeals against a decision to refuse enforcement 296
9.4.4.5.1: An appeal against a refusal to register 296
9.4.4.5.2: A further right to appeal on a point of law 296
9.4.4.6: Legal aid 297
9.4.5: Authentic instruments and court settlements 297
9.4.5.1: Authentic instruments 297
9.4.5.2: Court settlements 298
9.4.6: The relationship between national law and Titles III and IV 298
9.4.6.1: The exclusivity and autonomy of the Conventions 298
9.4.6.2: Enforcement and execution 299
9.5: Recognition and enforcement of judgments within the United Kingdom 300
9.5.1: Introduction 300
9.5.2: Recognition 301
9.5.3: Enforcement 302
9.5.3.1: Introduction 302
9.5.3.2: Money judgments: Schedule 6 302
9.5.3.3: Non-money judgments: Schedule 7 303
9.6: Judgments against States and European Community judgments 304
9.6.1: Recognition of judgments given against the United Kingdom 304
9.6.2: Recognition and enforcement of judgments given against other States 305
9.6.3: European Community judgments 305

PART II. OBLIGATIONS

CHAPTER 10: CHOICE OF LAW IN CONTRACT: INTRODUCTION 309
10.1: The common law 309
10.2: The Contracts (Applicable Law) Act 1990 311
10.2.1: Background and commencement 311
10.2.2: Opposition to the Rome Convention 312
10.3: Interpretation of the Rome Convention 313
10.3.1: The jurisdiction of the Court of Justice 313
10.3.2: Interpretation in cases where there is no reference 315
10.4: The scope of the Convention 316
10.4.1: Material scope 316
10.4.1.1: Choice of law relating to contractual obligations 316

10.4.1.2: Exceptions 317
10.4.1.2.1: Status and family law matters 318
10.4.1.2.2: Insurance contracts 318
10.4.1.2.3: Jurisdiction and arbitration agreements 318
10.4.1.2.4: Negotiable instruments 319
10.4.1.2.5: Agency 320
10.4.1.2.6: Questions governed by company law 320
10.4.1.2.7: Evidence and procedure 320
10.4.2: Territorial scope 321
10.4.2.1: Universal application 321
10.4.2.2: "Internal" conflicts 321
10.4.3: Temporal scope 321
10.5: Exclusion of the doctrine of renvoi 321

CHAPTER 11: CHOICE OF LAW IN CONTRACT: GENERAL CHOICE OF LAW RULES 323
11.1: The applicable law in cases of choice 323
11.1.1: Introduction 323
11.1.1.1: The principle of party autonomy 323
11.1.1.2: The existence and validity of choice 324
11.1.1.3: Choice and incorporation 324
11.1.2: Express choice 325
11.1.3: "Implied" choice 326
11.1.3.1: Standard forms 326
11.1.3.2: Previous course of dealing 328
11.1.3.3: Jurisdiction clause 328
11.1.3.4: Reference to provisions of domestic law 329
11.1.3.5: Related transactions between the same parties 329
11.1.3.6: Arbitration clauses 330
11.1.3.7: Concluding remarks 330
11.1.4: Splitting the applicable law 331
11.1.5: Changing the chosen law 332
11.1.6: Mandatory rules 333
11.2: The applicable law in the absence of choice 333
11.2.1: Introductory remarks 333
11.2.2: Closest connection 334
11.2.3: The presumption in paragraph 2 334
11.2.3.1: Introduction 335
11.2.3.2: Characteristic performance 335
11.2.3.3: The connecting factor 338
11.2.3.3.1: Habitual residence 338
11.2.3.3.2: Central administration 339
11.2.3.3.3: Place of business 339
11.2.3.3.4: Principal place of business 340
11.2.3.4: The presumption 341
11.2.3.5: The presumption does not apply 342
11.2.3.6: Rebuttal of the presumption 342
11.2.3.7: Scission 343
11.2.4: Mandatory rules 343
11.3: Mandatory rules and public policy 344
11.3.1: Introduction 344
11.3.2: The application of mandatory rules 345

11.3.3: The application of "overriding rules" 346
11.3.3.1: "Overriding rules" under Article 7(1) 346
11.3.3.2: "Overriding rules" of the forum: Article 7(2) 347
11.3.4: Public policy: Article 16 348
11.4: Particular aspects of the contract 349
11.4.1: Preliminary remarks 349
11.4.2: Material validity: Article 8 350
11.4.2.1: Introduction 350
11.4.2.2: The general principle 351
11.4.2.3: The problem of consent 351
11.4.3: Formal validity: Article 9 352
11.4.3.1: What are questions of form? 352
11.4.3.2: Choice of law rules 353
11.4.4: Capacity 354
11.4.4.1: Individuals 354
11.4.4.1.1: General principles 354
11.4.4.1.2: Article 11 356
11.4.4.2: Corporations 356
11.4.5: Performance 356
11.4.5.1: The applicable law 356
11.4.5.2: Performance and manner of performance 357
11.4.6: Interpretation 358
11.4.7: Consequences of breach 358
11.4.8: Discharge 359
11.4.9: Nullity 360
11.4.10: Illegality 360
11.4.10.1: Initial illegality 361
11.4.10.2: Subsequent illegality 362

CHAPTER 12: CHOICE OF LAW IN CONTRACT: SPECIFIC CONTRACTS 365
12.1: Certain consumer contracts 365
12.1.1: The scope of Article 5 365
12.1.1.1: General scope 366
12.1.1.2: The qualifying conditions 367
12.1.2: Three special rules 367
12.1.2.1: The applicable law in the absence of choice 367
12.1.2.2: The application of mandatory rules in cases where the parties have chosen a law 368
12.1.2.3: Formal validity 368
12.1.3: "Overriding rules" of the forum 368
12.2: Individual employment contracts 369
12.2.1: What is an individual employment contract? 369
12.2.2: The applicable law in cases where the parties have not made a choice of law 370
12.2.2.1: The common law 370
12.2.2.2: Article 6(2) 371
12.2.3: The application of mandatory rules in cases where the parties have made a choice of law 372
12.2.4: "Overriding rules" of the forum 373
12.3: Carriage of goods 374
12.3.1: The applicable law 374
12.3.2: "Overriding rules" of the forum 375

12.4: Contracts relating to immovables 376
12.4.1: The applicable law 376
12.4.2: Formal validity 377
12.4.3: Capacity 377
12.5: The sale of tangible movables 378
12.5.1: The transfer of tangible movables 378
12.5.2: Retention of title agreements 379
12.6: Voluntary assignment of intangibles 380
12.6.1: Introduction 380
12.6.2: The assignor–assignee relationship 381
12.6.2.1: The contract between the assignor and the assignee 381
12.6.2.2: The transfer of property from the assignor to the assignee 381
12.6.3: The assignee–debtor relationship 382
12.7: Agency 382
12.7.1: Introduction 382
12.7.2: Formal validity 383
12.7.3: Is the principal bound? 383
12.8: Insurance and reinsurance 383
12.8.1: Introduction 383
12.8.2: Insurance Companies Act 1982 385
12.8.2.1: General policies 385
12.8.2.2: Long-term policies 386
12.8.3: The Friendly Societies Act 1992 386
12.9: Negotiable instruments 387
12.9.1: Introduction 387
12.9.1.1: What is a negotiable instrument? 387
12.9.1.2: Which law governs whether a particular instrument is negotiable? 388
12.9.1.3: The Contracts (Applicable Law) Act 1990 389
12.9.2: Choice of law rules 389
12.9.2.1: Questions of form 389
12.9.2.2: Interpretation 390
12.9.2.3: Presentment 392
12.9.2.4: The date of payment 393
12.9.2.5: Contractual capacity 393
12.9.2.6: Transfer of the instrument 394
12.10: Quasi-contract and restitution 394
12.10.1: Classification 394
12.10.2: Choice of law rules 395

CHAPTER 13: CHOICE OF LAW IN TORT 397
13.1: The place of the tort 397
13.1.1: Introduction 397
13.1.2: Various theories 398
13.1.2.1: The place of acting and the place of result 398
13.1.2.2: The substance of the tort 398
13.1.3: The test formulated by the English courts 399
13.1.3.1: The use of authorities 399
12.1.3.2: Evolution of the common law 399
13.1.3.3: Specific torts 400
13.1.3.3.1: Negligence 400
13.1.3.3.2: Misrepresentation 401
13.1.3.3.3: Economic torts 402

13.1.3.3.4: Libel 403
13.1.3.4: The Law Commission's proposals 403
13.2: Approaches to choice of law in tort 404
13.2.1: Introduction 404
13.2.1.1: *Lex fori* 404
13.2.1.2: *Lex loci delicti* 404
13.2.1.3: Alternative approaches 405
13.2.2: Alternative approaches to choice of law in tort 405
13.2.2.1: The proper law of the tort 405
13.2.2.2: Governmental interest analysis 406
13.2.3: Alternative approaches in practice 407
13.2.3.1: *Babcock* v. *Jackson*: an easy starting-point 407
13.2.3.2: Subsequent developments: harder cases 408
13.2.4: Problems with governmental interest analysis 410
13.3: The English cases 411
13.3.1: Background to the English choice of law rules 411
13.3.2: *Boys* v. *Chaplin*: outline 412
13.3.3: Lord Wilberforce's speech and its application 414
13.3.3.1: The general rule 414
13.3.3.2: The exception 416
13.3.3.3: Quantification: substance and procedure 420
13.4: The interaction of contract and tort choice of law rules 420
13.4.1: Introduction 420
13.4.1.1: The nature of the problem 420
13.4.1.2: Contract or tort? 421
13.4.1.3: The position if the plaintiff advances the claim in contract 422
13.4.2: The position if the plaintiff advances the claim in tort 422
13.4.2.1: Preliminary remarks 422
13.4.2.2: The basic approach 423
13.4.2.2.1: The simple analysis 423
13.4.2.2.2: The developed analysis 424
13.4.2.2.3: Further preliminary choice of law questions 424
13.4.2.3: The application of the developed analysis 425
13.5: Reform of the English choice of law rules 427

CHAPTER 14: FOREIGN CURRENCY OBLIGATIONS AND JUDGMENTS IN A FOREIGN CURRENCY 431
14.1: Nominalism 431
14.1.1: The general principle 431
14.1.2: The importance of the law governing the obligation 432
14.1.2.1: Revalorisation under the law applicable to the transaction 433
14.1.2.2: Damages for late payment 434
14.1.3: Avoiding the effects of nominalism: gold clauses 435
14.1.3.1: Gold-coin clauses and gold-value clauses 435
14.1.3.2: The role of the applicable law 436
14.2: The money of account and the money of payment 436
14.2.1: Introduction 436
14.2.2: Determining the money of account 437
14.2.2.1: Debts 437
14.2.2.2: Damages 438
14.2.3: Discharging foreign currency obligations 441
14.3: Judgments in a foreign currency 442

14.3.1: Background 442
14.3.2: The *Miliangos* case 443
14.4: Problems arising out of exchange control legislation 444
14.4.1: General principles 444
14.4.2: "Exchange contracts" 446
14.4.2.1: What is an "exchange contract"? 446
14.4.2.2: The effect of Article VIII(2)(b) 447

CHAPTER 15: FOREIGN LIMITATION PERIODS 449
15.1: The Foreign Limitations Periods Act 1984 449
15.1.1: The general principle 449
15.1.2: Public policy and undue hardship 451
15.1.2.1: Undue hardship: section 2(2) 451
15.1.2.2: Public policy 452
15.1.2.3: The effects of disapplying the foreign limitation period under section 2 452
15.2: The Rome Convention 453

PART III. ARBITRATION

CHAPTER 16: ARBITRATION: INTRODUCTION 457
16.1: What is arbitration? 457
16.2: Outline of English arbitration law 457
16.2.1: What is arbitration law? 457
16.2.2: The sources of English arbitration law 458
16.2.3: The powers of the court 458
16.2.3.1: Assistance and support 458
16.2.3.1.1: Enforcing the agreement to arbitrate 458
16.2.3.1.2: The constitution of the arbitral tribunal 458
16.2.3.1.3: Extending time limits 459
16.2.3.1.4: The conduct of proceedings 460
16.2.3.1.5: Enforcement of the award 461
16.2.3.2: Supervision and control 461
16.2.3.2.1: The problem of delay 461
16.2.3.2.2: Intervention during the conduct of an arbitration 463
16.2.3.2.3: Costs and fees 464
16.2.3.2.4: Recourse against the award 464
16.3: Various types of arbitration 466
16.3.1: Domestic and international 466
16.3.2: Ad hoc and institutional 466
16.3.3: Specialised arbitrations 467
16.4: Trends in commercial arbitration 468
16.4.1: Encouragement 468
16.4.2: Harmonisation 469
16.4.2.1: The Geneva Protocol 1923 and the Geneva Convention 1927 469
16.4.2.2: The New York Convention 1958 469
16.4.2.3: UNCITRAL Arbitration Rules 469
16.4.2.4: The UNCITRAL Model Law 470

CHAPTER 17: ARBITRATION: THE APPLICABLE LAW AND JURISDICTION 473
17.1: The law governing the arbitration agreement 473
17.2: The curial law 475

17.2.1: Introduction: The "delocalisation" theory 475
17.2.2: Internal and external procedures 476
17.2.3: Choice of law principles and the seat of arbitration 477
17.2.4: Severing the link between the curial law and the seat of arbitration 477
17.2.5: The internal conduct of an arbitration 478
17.2.5.1: The sources of the rules 478
17.2.5.2: Conflicts between the curial law and the agreement of the parties 480
17.3: The law applicable to the merits of the dispute 480
17.3.1: Types of choice of law clause 480
17.3.2: Legal introduction 481
17.3.3: Choice of law of a particular country 482
17.3.4: The applicable law in the absence of express choice 482
17.3.5: Public international law 485
17.3.6: Arbitration *extra legem* 485
17.3.6.1: Introduction 485
17.3.6.2: Equity and good conscience: *aimable composition* and arbitration *ex aequo et bono* 487
17.3.7: The *lex mercatoria* 488
17.3.8: The impact of mandatory rules 491
17.3.9: Remedies in cases where the arbitrator fails to apply the conflicts rules of the forum 492
17.3.9.1: Appeals on a point of law and exclusion agreements 492
17.3.9.2: Where there is no valid exclusion agreement 492
17.3.9.3: Where there is a valid exclusion agreement 493
17.4: Arbitration and EC law 494
17.5: Jurisdiction 496
17.5.1: Jurisdiction *in personam* 496
17.5.1.1: The scope of the Brussels and Lugano Conventions 496
17.5.1.2: Traditional rules: general principles 497
17.5.1.3: Enforcement proceedings 498
17.5.2: The scope of the court's powers 498
17.5.2.1: Typical cases 498
17.5.2.2: Potential problems 500

CHAPTER 18: THE AGREEMENT TO ARBITRATE 503
18.1: Introduction 503
18.1.1: What is an arbitration agreement? 503
18.1.2: The doctrine of separability 503
18.1.3: Validity and scope of the arbitration agreement 505
18.1.4: The enforcement of domestic arbitration agreements 505
18.2: The enforcement of arbitration agreements under the Arbitration Act 1975 506
18.2.1: The statutory framework 506
18.2.2: Conditions for the grant of a stay under section 1 507
18.2.2.1: An arbitration agreement within the scope of section 1 507
18.2.2.1.1: Foreign element 507
18.2.2.1.2: In writing 508
18.2.2.1.3: Capable of settlement by arbitration 510
18.2.2.2: Scope of the clause 510
18.2.2.3: Before appearance 511
18.2.2.4: Null and void, inoperative or incapable of being performed 511
18.2.2.4.1: Null and void 511
18.2.2.4.2: Inoperative or incapable of being performed 512

18.2.2.5: Dispute 513
18.2.3: The effect of a stay under section 1 515
18.3: Inherent jurisdiction 516

CHAPTER 19: APPEALS UNDER THE ARBITRATION ACT 1979 517
19.1: Preliminary remarks 517
19.2: What is an award? 519
19.3: Leave of the court for the purpose of an appeal to the High Court 520
19.4: Appeals to the Court of Appeal 521
19.4.1: Appeals under section 1(6A) 521
19.4.2: Appeals under section 1(7) 522
19.4.2.1: The requirement of a certificate under section 1(7)(b) 522
19.4.2.2: Leave 522
19.5: Exclusion agreements 523
19.5.1: What is an exclusion agreement? 523
19.5.2: When can the right of appeal be excluded? 524
19.5.2.1: Domestic and non-domestic arbitration agreements 524
19.5.2.2: Exclusion agreements in cases involving domestic arbitration agreements 524
19.5.2.3: Exclusion agreements in cases involving non-domestic arbitration agreements 524
19.5.2.4: Exclusion agreements in special category cases involving non-domestic arbitration agreements 524
19.5.2.5: The effect of a valid exclusion agreement 526
19.5.2.6: The future 526

CHAPTER 20: THE ENFORCEMENT OF ARBITRAL AWARDS 527
20.1: Preliminary issues 527
20.1.1: The relationship between enforcement and setting aside 527
20.1.2: The enforcement of domestic awards 527
20.1.3: The enforcement of foreign arbitral awards 528
20.2: Recognition and enforcement of foreign awards under the Arbitration Act 1975 529
20.2.1: The scope of the Arbitration Act 1975 529
20.2.1.1: The arbitration agreement 529
20.2.1.2: Territorial scope 529
20.2.1.2.1: Introduction 529
20.2.1.2.2: Where is an award made? 530
20.2.1.3: Temporal scope 531
20.2.2: Conditions for obtaining enforcement 531
20.2.2.1: The relevant documents 531
20.2.2.2: Procedural steps 532
20.2.3: Grounds for refusing enforcement 533
20.2.3.1: The statutory framework 533
20.2.3.2: Lack of capacity: section 5(2)(a) 533
20.2.3.3: Invalidity of the arbitration agreement: section 5(2)(b) 534
20.2.3.4: Procedural unfairness: section 5(2)(c) 535
20.2.3.5: Excess of jurisdiction: section 5(2)(d) and section 5(4) 536
20.2.3.6: Failure to comply with the relevant procedural rules: section 5(2)(e) 537
20.2.3.7: Invalid award: section 5(2)(f) 538
20.2.3.7.1: Not binding 538
20.2.3.7.2: Set aside or suspended 539
20.2.3.8: Non-arbitrability 540
20.2.3.9: Public policy 540
20.2.3.9.1: Awards based on the *lex mercatoria* or arbitration *extra legem* 541

20.2.3.9.2: Illegality and comity 541
20.2.3.10: No review of the merits 542
20.2.4: Discretion to stay enforcement proceedings 543
20.3: Recognition and enforcement of foreign awards at common law 544
20.3.1: The relationship between the Arbitration Act 1975 and the common law 544
20.3.2: Methods of enforcement 544
20.3.3: Conditions for enforcement at common law 545
20.3.4: Defences at common law 546
20.3.4.1: Matters which are not defences 546
20.3.4.2: Valid defences 547
20.3.4.2.1: Excess of jurisdiction 547
20.3.4.2.2: Breach of the principles of natural justice 547
20.3.4.2.3: Public policy 548
20.3.4.2.4: Fraud 548
20.4: Recognition and enforcement of foreign awards under Part II of the Arbitration Act 1950 548
20.4.1: The relationship between Part II of the 1950 Act and other regimes 548
20.4.2: Conditions for recognition and enforcement 549
20.4.3: Defences to enforcement 550
20.5: Other regimes for the recognition and enforcement of foreign arbitral awards 550
20.5.1: Part II of the Civil Jurisdiction and Judgments Act 1982 550
20.5.2: Part II of the Administration of Justice Act 1920 551
20.5.3: Part I of the Foreign Judgments (Reciprocal Enforcement) Act 1933 551
20.5.4: Arbitration (International Investment Disputes) Act 1966 552
20.5.5: Recognition of awards made by the Iran–US Claims Tribunal 552
20.6: Awards judgments and the cause of action 553
20.6.1: Conflicting judgments and awards 553
20.6.2: The effect of a foreign judgment on the award 555
20.6.3: The effect of a foreign arbitral award on the cause of action 556

PART IV. PROCEDURAL MATTERS

CHAPTER 21: PROVISIONAL MEASURES 559
21.1: Different types of provisional measure 559
21.1.1: Introduction 559
21.1.2: Interlocutory injunctions 561
21.1.3: Mareva injunctions 562
21.1.3.1: Background 562
21.1.3.2: Obtaining a Mareva injunction 562
21.1.3.3: The effect of a Mareva injunction 564
21.1.3.3.1: Injunctions operate *in personam* 564
21.1.3.3.2: Third parties 565
21.1.3.3.3: Mareva injunctions and the provision of security 565
21.1.3.4: Ancillary and related orders 565
21.1.3.4.1: Disclosure orders 565
21.1.3.4.2: Receivership orders 566
21.1.4: Anton Piller orders 567
21.2: Jurisdiction to grant provisional measures: proceedings *in rem* 567
21.3: Jurisdiction to grant provisional measures: proceedings *in personam* 570
21.3.1: Jurisdiction to grant provisional measures in aid of foreign proceedings 570
21.3.1.1: The position at common law 570
21.3.1.2: Section 25 of the Civil Jurisdiction and Judgments Act 1982 572

21.3.1.2.1: Jurisdiction under section 25 572
21.3.1.2.2: Provisional measures and Article 21 573
21.3.1.2.3: Post-judgment provisional measures and Article 16(5) 574
21.3.1.2.4: Discretion? 575
21.3.1.3: Jurisdiction to grant provisional measures in cases involving an exclusive jurisdiction clause 575
21.3.2: Jurisdiction to grant provisional measures in support of arbitration proceedings 576
21.3.2.1: Section 12(6)(h) of the Arbitration Act 1950 576
21.3.2.2: Section 37(1) of the Supreme Court Act 1981 577
21.4: Extraterritorial provisional measures 578
21.4.1: Introduction 578
21.4.2: Extraterritorial Mareva injunctions 580
21.4.2.1: The necessary conditions 580
21.4.2.2: Factors relevant to the exercise of discretion 581
21.4.2.3: Practice 582
21.4.2.4: The protection of the defendant and third parties 582
21.4.2.4.1: Protecting the defendant against a multiplicity of proceedings and the misuse of information 583
21.4.2.4.2: The protection of third parties: the *Babanaft* proviso 583
21.4.2.5: The dangers of extraterritorial Mareva injunctions 585
21.5: Enforcement of foreign provisional measures 586
21.5.1: Introduction 586
21.5.2: Title III and provisional measures 587
21.5.2.1: Procedural orders 587
21.5.2.2: Measures granted *ex parte* 587

CHAPTER 22: ANTISUIT INJUNCTIONS 589
22.1: Preliminary remarks 589
22.2: The basis on which an injunction may be granted 591
22.2.1: Unconscionable conduct 591
22.2.2: Infringement of a legal or equitable right 593
22.3: The Brussels and Lugano Conventions 595

CHAPTER 23: PROOF OF FOREIGN LAW 597
23.1: Foreign law: a question of fact 597
23.2: Cases in which foreign law does not have to be proved 598
23.3: Mode of proof 599
23.3.1: The requirement of evidence 599
23.3.2: Uncontradicted evidence 599
23.3.3: Conflicting evidence 600
23.3.4: Who is an expert? 600
23.3.5: Decisions on points of foreign law in subsequent cases 601
23.3.6: Seeking outside help 602
23.4: Appeals 602

APPENDICES

Appendix 1: Civil Jurisdiction and Judgments Act 1982 (c27) 605
Appendix 2: Supreme Court Act 1981 (c54) 661
Appendix 3: Contracts (Applicable Law) Act 1990 (c36) 667
Appendix 4: Arbitration Act 1975 (c3) 681
Appendix 5: Arbitration Act 1979 (c42) 685
Index 689

TABLE OF CASES

[European Court cases appear in the main table and are also listed separately]

A *v.* C [1981] QB 956 .... 21.1.3.4.1.1
A Co Ltd *v.* Republic of X [1990] 2 Lloyd's Rep 520 .... 2.3.5.3.2
AB Bofors-Uva CAV Ltd *v.* AB Skandia Transport [1982] 1 Lloyd's Rep 410 .. 17.1.4, 18.2.2.4.1.3, 20.5.3.2
AB Götaverken *v.* General National Maritime Transport Co (Sup Ct of Sweden), reported in (1981) 6 YB Comm Art 237 ....20.2.3.7.1.3
ALG Incorporated *v.* Uganda Airlines Corporation, *The Times*, 31 July 1992 .... 21.4.2.3
A/S Tallinna Laevauhisus *v.* Estonian State Steamship Line (1947) 80 Ll L Rep 99 .... 23.3.2
Abidin Daver, The [1984] AC 398 .... 6.4.1.4, 6.4.2.4, 6.4.3, 6.4.4.2.2, 6.4.4.9
Abouloff *v.* Oppenheimer & Co (1882) 10 QBD 295 .... 9.2.7.2.1.1, 9.2.7.2.2.2, 9.2.7.2.2.3
Acrux, The [1965] P 391 .... 8.1.1.1.2, 8.1.1.1.8
Adams *v.* Cape Industries Plc [1990] Ch 433 .... 9.1.1, 9.2.5.1.2, 9.2.5.2.4, 9.2.5.2.7, 9.2.5.2.8, 9.2.5.3.1, 9.2.5.3.2, 9.2.5.3.3, 9.2.5.3.4, 9.2.5.4.3, 9.2.5.4.4, 9.2.5.5.1, 9.2.5.5.2, 9.2.7.1.2.1, 9.2.7.1.2.2, 9.2.7.1.2.3, 9.3.2.2.2.2, 20.2.3.4.3
Adelaide Electric Supply Co Ltd *v.* Prudential Assurance Co Ltd [1934] AC 122 .... 14.2.2.1.1, 14.2.2.1.3
Agia Skepi, The [1992] 2 Lloyd's Rep 467 .... 6.3.3.4.1.3
Aifanourios, The, 1980 SC 346 .... 8.1.1.1.5
Aiglon Ltd *v.* Gau Shan Co Ltd [1993] 1 Lloyd's Rep 164 .... 5.6.1.2, 5.10.1.2
Al Battani, The [1993] 2 Lloyd's Rep 219 .... 6.4.4.6, 6.4.4.11, 6.5.2.4, 8.1.4.1.4
Albaforth, The [1984] 2 Lloyd's Rep 91 .... 6.4.3, 13.1.3.3.2.3
Alcock *v.* Smith [1892] 1 Ch 238 .... 12.9.2.2.2., 12.9.2.2.4, 12.9.2.6
Alcom Ltd *v.* Republic of Colombia [1984] AC 580 .... 2.3.5.4.4, 2.3.5.4.9
Allied Arab Bank Ltd *v.* Hajjar [1988] QB 787 ....21.1.3.4.1.2
Allied Marine Transport Ltd *v.* Vale do Rio Doce Navegacao SA [1985] 1 WLR 925 .... 16.2.3.2.1.3
Allison (Kenneth) Ltd *v.* AE Limehouse & Co [1992] 2 AC 105 .... 6.1.1.1.3
Alltrans Inc *v.* Interdom Holdings Ltd [1991] 4 All ER 458 ....21.3.1.2.1.3
Altertext Inc *v.* Advanced Data Communications Ltd [1985] 1 WLR 457 .... 21.4.1.2
American Cyanamid Co *v.* Ethicon Ltd [1975] AC 396 .... 21.1.2.1, 21.1.2.2
Amin Rasheed Shipping Corporation *v.* Kuwait Insurance Co [1984] AC 50 . 6.3.3, 6.4.3, 6.4.4.9, 6.4.4.10.1, 10.1.4, 10.1.5, 10.5, 11.1.3.1.1, 12.8.1.1, 13.4.2.2.3.2, 17.2.1.3
Anderson *v.* Equitable Assurance Society of The United States (1926) 134 LT 557 .... 14.1.2.1.2, 14.2.3.3
Andrea Ursula, The [1973] QB 265 .... 8.1.2.3.4.1
Andria, The (now renamed Vasso) [1984] QB 477 .... 21.2.2, 21.2.3, 21.2.5
Angelic Grace, The [1980] 1 Lloyd's Rep 288 .... 19.2.2
Anglo-Austrian Bank, *Re* [1920] 1 Ch 69 .... 11.4.8.1
Antaios, The. See Antaios Compania Naviera SA *v.* Salen Rederierna AB (The Antaios)
Antaios Compania Naviera SA *v.* Salen Rederierna AB (The Antaios) [1985] AC 191 .... 19.3.1, 19.3.2, 19.4.1
Anterist *v.* Crédit Lyonnais: Case 22/85 [1986] ECR 1951 .... 5.3.7
Anton Piller KG *v.* Manufacturing Processes Ltd [1976] Ch 55 .... 21.1.1.1, 21.1.4.2
Antonis P Lemos, The [1985] AC 711 .... 8.1.1, 8.1.1.1.5
Anziani, *Re* [1930] 1 Ch 407 .... 12.5.1.2
Arab African Energy Corporation Ltd *v.* Olieprodukten Nederland BV [1983] 2 Lloyd's Rep 419 .... 18.2.2.1.2.2, 19.5.1.2
Arab Monetary Fund *v.* Hashim [1993] 1 Lloyd's Rep 543 .... 2.5.3, 12.10.2, 13.3.3.1.4, 15.1.1.3, 15.1.2.1.1, 15.1.2.1.2, 15.1.2.1.3, 15.1.2.3
Arab Monetary Fund *v.* Hashim (No. 3) [1990] 3 WLR 139; [1991] 2 AC 114 .... 2.1.4.1.2, 2.1.4.3, 2.1.4.3.3, 2.1.4.3.4, 2.1.4.3.6
Arab Monetary Fund *v.* Hashim (No. 6), *Financial Times*, 24 July 1992 .... 22.2.1.3

Arkwright Mutual Insurance Co *v.* Bryanston Insurance Co Ltd [1990] 2 QB 649 .... 5.3.2.3.2, 5.10.1.1, 5.10.2.2
Armadora Occidental SA *v.* Horace Mann Insurance Co [1977] 1 WLR 1098 .... 12.8.1.2
Armagas Ltd *v.* Mundogas SA [1985] 1 Lloyd's Rep 1; reversed on other grounds [1986] AC 717 .. 13.1.3.1, 13.1.3.3.2.3, 13.3.2.7, 13.3.3.1.2
Armar Shipping Co Ltd *v.* Caisse Algérienne d'Assurance et de Réassurance [1981] 1 WLR 207 .... 11.1.5.3
Armour *v.* Thyssen Edelstahlwerke AG, 1986 SLT 94, affirmed 1989 SLT 182; reversed [1991] 2 AC 339 .... 12.5.2.1
Arnold *v.* National Westminster Bank Plc [1989] Ch 63 .... 19.4.2.1
Ashtiani *v.* Kashi [1987] QB 888 .... 21.1.3.2.2, 21.4.1.3, 21.4.1.4, 21.4.1.5
Ashville Investments Ltd *v.* Elmer Contractors Ltd [1989] QB 488 .... 18.1.2.3
Aspen Trader, The [1981] 1 Lloyd's Rep 273 .... 15.1.2.1.2, 16.2.3.1.3.3
Assunzione, The [1954] P 150 .... 12.3.1.4
Assurances Générales de France *v.* Chiyoda Fire and Marine Co (UK) Ltd [1992] 1 Lloyd's Rep 325 .... 5.9.1.4.3, 5.9.2.2.1, 5.9.2.3.4.2
Atlantic Emperor, The. See Rich (Marc) & Co AG *v.* Società Italiana Impianti PA
Atlantic Star, The [1974] AC 436; [1973] QB 364 .... 6.4.1.3, 6.4.2.2, 6.4.2.4
Atlantic Underwriting Agencies Ltd *v.* Compagnia di Assicurazione di Milano SpA [1979] 2 Lloyd's Rep 240 .... 6.3.3.9.4
Attock Cement Co Ltd *v.* Romanian Bank for Foreign Trade [1989] 1 WLR 1147 .... 6.3.1.1.2, 6.3.3.9.2
Attorney General *v.* Times Newspapers Ltd [1992] 1 AC 191 .... 21.1.3.3.1.1
August 8, The [1983] 2 AC 450 .... 8.0.2
Auckland Corporation *v.* Alliance Assurance Co Ltd [1937] AC 587 .... 14.2.2.1.1, 14.2.2.1.3
Avant Petroleum Inc *v.* Gatoil Overseas Inc [1986] 2 Lloyd's Rep 236 .... 21.1.3.3.1.2
Aventicum, The [1978] 1 Lloyd's Rep 184 .... 8.1.2.3.4.1, 8.1.2.3.4.2

BP Exploration Co (Libya) Ltd *v.* Hunt [1976] 1 WLR 788 .... 6.3.3.4.1.2, 6.3.3.4.1.3, 6.3.3.4.2.3
BP Exploration Co (Libya) Ltd *v.* Hunt (No. 2) [1979] 1 WLR 783 .... 14.3.2.3
Babanaft International Co SA *v.* Bassatne [1990] Ch 13 .... 5.8.2, 21.1.3.3.1.2, 21.3.1.2.1.2, 21.3.1.2.3.2, 21.4.1.5, 21.4.2.2.1, 21.4.2.2.2, 21.4.2.4.1, 21.4.2.4.2.2, 21.4.2.4.2.3
Babcock *v.* Jackson [1963] 2 Lloyd's Rep 286 .... 13.2.3.1, 13.2.3.1.1, 13.2.3.1.2, 13.2.3.1.3, 13.2.3.1.4, 13.2.3.2.1, 13.2.3.2.2, 13.2.3.2.3, 13.2.4.2, 13.3.3.2.3, 13.3.3.2.5
Bachchan *v.* India Abroad Publications Inc, *Financial Times*, 14 May 1992 .... 9.2.7.3.1
Bain Clarkson Ltd *v.* Owners of "Sea Friends" [1991] 2 Lloyd's Rep 322 .... 8.1.1.1.9
Banco Atlantico *v.* British Bank of the Middle East [1990] 2 Lloyd's Rep 504 .... 5.10.1.5, 6.4.4.12.4, 12.9.2.2.2
Bank Mellat *v.* GAA Development & Construction Co [1988] 2 Lloyd's Rep 44 ...... 16.2.3.2.4.6, 17.3.9.3.2, 20.2.2.2.2
Bank Mellat *v.* Helliniki Techniki SA [1984] QB 291 .... 17.2.1.4, 17.2.5.1.4, 17.5.2.1.2, 21.3.2.1.1
Bank of Africa Ltd *v.* Cohen [1909] 2 Ch 129 .... 12.4.3
Bank of Crete SA *v.* Koskotas [1991] 2 Lloyd's Rep 587 .... 21.1.3.4.1.2
Bank of Scotland *v.* Seitz, 1990 SLT 584 .... 5.5.3.3.3
Bankers & Shippers Insurance Co of New York *v.* Liverpool Marine & General Insurance Co Ltd (1926) 24 Ll L Rep 85 .... 20.3.3.3
Banku Polskiego *v.* Mulder (KJ) & Co [1941] 2 KB 266 .... 12.9.2.3.3
Banque des Marchands de Moscow (Koupetschesky), *Re* [1958] Ch 182 .... 23.3.2
Banque des Marchands de Moscow (Koupetschesky) (No. 2), *Re* [1954] 1 WLR 1108 .... 12.9.2.2.3, 14.4.1.1
Banque Paribas *v.* Cargill International SA [1992] 2 Lloyd's Rep 19 .... 6.3.1.1.2, 6.3.2.4
Barclay-Johnson *v.* Yuill [1980] 1 WLR 1259 .... 21.1.3.2.2
Barclays Bank International Ltd *v.* Levin Brothers (Bradford) Ltd [1977] QB 270 .... 14.2.3.3
Barclays Bank Plc *v.* Glasgow City Council [1993] QB 429 .... 5.5.2.2.2, 5.5.3.1.2, 5.5.4.1
Barclays Bank Plc *v.* Homan, *The Times*, 13 October 1992 .... 22.2.1.4
Barclays Bank of Swaziland *v.* Hahn [1989] 1 WLR 506 .... 6.1.1.2.3, 6.1.1.2.5
Baroda (Maharanee of) *v.* Wildenstein [1972] 2 QB 283 .... 1.1.6, 4.2.1.4, 6.1.1.1.3, 6.4.2.2, 9.2.5.3.3
Bata *v.* Bata [1948] WN 366 .... 13.1.3.3.3.3
Bazias 3, The, The Bazias 4 [1993] QB 673 .... 21.2.6, 21.2.7
Beatty *v.* Beatty [1924] 1 KB 807 .... 9.2.3.1, 23.2.3
Bekhor (AJ) & Co Ltd *v.* Bilton [1981] QB 923 .... 21.1.3.4.1.2
Beldis, The [1936] P 51 .... 8.1.1.1.5
Benaim & Co *v.* Debono [1924] AC 514 .... 6.3.3.4.2.1
Berghöfer (F) GmbH & Co KG *v.* ASA SA: Case 221/84 [1985] ECR 2699 .... 5.3.3.1.1.4
Berisford (S & W) Plc *v.* New Hampshire Insurance Co [1990] 2 QB 631 .... 5.10.1.1, 5.10.1.5
Bernhard *v.* Harrah's Club, 16 Cal 3d 313, 546 P 2d 719 (1976) 13.2.3.2.4

Berny, The [1979] QB 80 .... 8.1.4.1.4
Bibby Bulk Carriers Ltd *v.* Cobelfret NV [1989] QB 155 .... 6.4.4.4.1, 6.4.4.4.2
Black *v.* Yates [1992] QB 526 .... 9.1.3.3
Black-Clawson International Ltd *v.* Papierwerke Waldhof-Aschaffenburg AG [1975] AC 591; [1981] 2 Lloyd's Rep 446 .... 17.1.4, 9.2.4.2, 9.3.2.3
Blanckaert & Willems PVBA *v.* Trost: Case 139/80 [1981] ECR 819 .... 5.5.5.1.2, 5.5.5.2
Blohn *v.* Desser [1962] 2 QB 116 .... 9.2.5.2.7
Bodley Head Ltd *v.* Flegon [1972] 1 WLR 680 .... 11.4.4.1.1.4
Boissevain *v.* Weil [1950] AC 327 .... 14.4.1.5
Boissière & Co *v.* Brockner & Co (1889) 6 TLR 85 .... 9.2.5.2.3
Bonacina, *Re* [1912] 2 Ch 394 .... 10.4.1.1.3, 12.10.1.1
Bonython *v.* Commonwealth of Australia [1951] AC 201 .... 10.1.3, 10.1.4, 14.2.2.1.1, 14.2.2.1.2, 14.2.2.1.3, 14.2.2.1.4
Boocock *v.* Hilton International Co [1993] 1 WLR 1065 .... 6.1.2.2.5
Boys *v.* Chaplin [1971] AC 356 .... 6.4.1.1, 13.3.1.5, 13.3.2.1, 13.3.2.4, 13.3.2.7, 13.3.3, 13.3.3.1.2, 13.3.3.1.4, 13.3.3.1.5, 13.3.3.2.1, 13.3.3.2.2, 13.3.3.2.3, 13.3.3.2.4, 13.3.3.2.5, 13.3.3.2.6, 13.3.3.2.7, 13.3.3.2.8, 13.3.3.3.2, 13.4.1.2.3, 13.4.2.2, 13.4.2.2.3.3, 13.4.2.3.3, 13.4.2.3.4
Bremer Oeltransport GmbH *v.* Drewry [1933] 1 KB 753 .... 8.1.1.1.5
Bremer Vulkan Schiffbau und Maschinenfabrik *v.* South India Shipping Corporation Ltd [1981] AC 909 .... 16.2.3.2.1.1, 16.2.3.2.1.2, 16.2.3.2.1.3, 18.1.2.1
Brinkibon Ltd *v.* Stahag Stahl und Stahlwarenhandelsgesellschaft mbH [1983] 2 AC 34 .... 6.3.3.4.2.1
Brink's-Mat Ltd *v.* Elcombe [1988] 1 WLR 1350 .... 21.1.3.2.3
British Aerospace Plc *v.* Dee Howard Co [1993] 1 Lloyd's Rep 368 .... 5.3.4.2, 6.4.4.4.2
British Airways Board *v.* Laker Airways Ltd [1985] AC 58 .... 22.2.2.1
British South Africa Co *v.* Companhia de Moçambique [1893] AC 602 .... 5.10.3, 6.6.3
Brodin *v.* A/R Seljan, 1973 SLT 198 .... 12.2.4.2, 13.4.2.3.2, 13.4.2.3.3, 13.4.2.3.6
Broken Hill Proprietary Co Ltd *v.* Latham [1933] Ch 373 .... 14.2.2.1.3
Broken Hill Proprietary Co Ltd *v.* Xanakis [1982] 2 Lloyd's Rep 304 .... 11.1.3.5
Brunsden *v.* Humphrey (1884) 14 QBD 141 .... 9.2.6.2.2, 9.2.6.2.3
Buckland *v.* Palmer [1984] 1 WLR 1109 .... 9.2.6.2.3
Buerger *v.* New York Life Assurance Co (1927) 96 LJKB 930 .... 23.3.1, 23.3.2
Bulk Oil (Zug) Ltd *v.* Sun International Ltd [1984] 1 WLR 147 .... 17.4.5, 18.2.2.1.3.2
Bumper Development Corporation *v.* Commissioner of Police of the Metropolis [1991] 1 WLR 1362 .... 2.1.2.2, 23.1.1, 23.3.1, 23.3.3

CFEM Façades SA *v.* Bovis Construction Ltd [1992] ILPr 561 .... 9.4.1.2.2.1, 9.4.3.3.1, 9.4.4.3.2, 21.1.1.1, 21.5.2.1
Callwood *v.* Callwood [1960] AC 659 .... 23.1.1
Calzaturificio Brennero sas *v.* Wendel GmbH Schuhproduktion International: Case 258/83 [1984] ECR 3971 .... 9.4.4.4.2.1, 9.4.4.4.4.2
Cambridge Nutrition Ltd *v.* British Broadcasting Corporation [1990] 3 All ER 523 .... 21.1.2.1
Cammell *v.* Sewell (1860) 5 H & N 728 .... 12.5.1.3, 12.5.1.4
Campbell Connelly & Co Ltd *v.* Noble [1963] 1 WLR 252 .... 12.6.2.2
Canadian Pacific Railway Co *v.* Parent [1917] AC 195 .... 13.4.2.3.5
Capelloni *v.* Pelkmans: Case 119/84 [1985] ECR 3147 .... 9.4.4.4.3.2, 9.4.4.4.3.3, 9.4.4.4.3.4, 9.4.6.2.1, 21.3.1.2.4.2
Carl Zeiss Stiftung *v.* Rayner & Keeler Ltd (No. 2) [1967] 1 AC 853 .... 2.1.5.4, 2.1.5.5, 9.2.2, 9.2.6.1.1, 9.2.6.1.2, 9.2.6.3.1, 9.2.6.3.2
Carrick *v.* Hancock (1895) 12 TLR 59 .... 6.1.1.1.1, 9.2.5.3.1
Carron *v.* Federal Republic of Germany: Case 198/85 [1986] ECR 2437 .... 9.4.4.2.2.1, 9.4.4.2.2.3
Carvalho *v.* Hull, Blyth (Angola) Ltd [1979] 1 WLR 1228 .... 6.4.4.9
Case of Mixt Moneys, The. See Gilbert *v.* Brett (The Case of Mixt Moneys)
Castanho *v.* Brown & Root (UK) Ltd [1981] AC 557 .... 6.4.1.2, 22.1.3
Castle Alpha, The [1989] 2 Lloyd's Rep 383 .... 17.1.3
Castree *v.* ER Squibb & Sons Ltd [1980] 1 WLR 1248 .... 13.1.3.2.4, 13.1.3.3.1.1
Castrique *v.* Imrie (1870) LR 4 HL 414 .... 8.1.4.1.1, 9.2.8.1, 9.2.8.3
Chambers *v.* Starkings. *See* Sage *v.* Double A Hydraulics Ltd; Chambers *v.* Starkings
Channel Tunnel Group Ltd *v.* Balfour Beatty Construction Ltd [1993] AC 334; [1992] QB 656 (CA) 17.2.3.1, 17.5, 17.5.2.1.3, 17.5.2.2.2, 18.2.1.2, 18.2.2.5.2, 18.2.2.5.7, 18.2.3.1, 18.2.3.2, 18.3.1, 18.3.2, 21.1.1.1, 21.3.1.1.4, 27.3.1.1.5, 21.3.1.3.3, 21.3.2.1.2, 21.3.2.2
Chaparral, The [1968] 2 Lloyd's Rep 158 .... 6.5.3.2
Chappell *v.* North [1891] 2 QB 252 .... 18.2.2.3.2
Charm Maritime Inc *v.* Kyriakou [1987] 1 Lloyd's Rep 433 .... 9.2.6
Charman *v.* WOC Offshore BV [1993] 1 Lloyd's Rep 378 .... 5.7.1.3.5.1, 5.7.1.3.5.4

Chartered Bank *v.* Daklouche [1980] 1 WLR 107 .... 21.1.3.2.2
Chesterman's Trusts, *Re* [1923] 2 Ch 466 .... 11.1.1.2, 14.1.1.2, 14.1.2
Chiron Corporation *v.* Organon Teknika Ltd (No. 2) [1993] FSR 567 .... 11.3.1.5
Church of Scientology of California *v.* Commissioner of Metropolitan Police (1976) 120 Sol J 690 .... 13.1.3.3.3.3, 13.3.2.7, 13.3.3.1.3, 13.4.2.2.3.2
Citadel Insurance Co *v.* Atlantic Union Insurance Co SA [1982] 2 Lloyd's Rep 543 .... 12.8.1.2
City of Mecca, The (1879) 5 PD 28; reversed (1881) 6 PD 106 .... 8.1.1.2.2, 9.2.8.3
Clara Killam (1870) LR 3 A & E 161 .... 8.1.1.1.4
Cleveland Museum of Art *v.* Capricorn Art International SA [1990] 2 Lloyd's Rep 166 .... 6.1.2.4.3, 6.1.2.4.4, 6.4.4.2.2, 6.4.4.2.3, 6.4.4.3.3
Coast Lines Ltd *v.* Hudig & Veder Chartering NV [1972] 2 QB 34 .... 6.4.4.10.2
Colt Industries Inc *v.* Sarlie (No. 1) [1966] 1 WLR 440 .... 6.1.1.1.2, 9.2.5.3.2
Colt Industries Inc *v.* Sarlie (No. 2) [1966] 1 WLR 1287 .... 9.2.2
Columbia Picture Industries *v.* Robinson [1987] Ch 38 .... 21.1.4.2
Comdel Commodities Ltd *v.* Siporex Trade SA (No. 2) [1991] 1 AC 148 .... 16.2.3.1.3.3
Commercial Bank of the Near East Plc *v.* A, B, C & D [1989] 2 Lloyd's Rep 319 .... 6.5.3.3
Compagnie Tunisienne de Navigation SA *v.* Compagnie d'Armement Maritime SA [1971] AC 572 .... 10.1.4, 11.1.2.1, 11.1.2.4, 11.1.3.6.1, 17.3.4.2, 19.5.2.4.4
Concha *v.* Murrieta (1889) 40 ChD 543 .... 23.3.3
Conquer *v.* Boot [1928] 2 KB 336 .... 9.2.6.2.3
Continental Bank NA *v.* Akakos Compania Naviera SA, *The Times*, 26 November 1993 .... 5.9.2.3.3.1, 22.3.5, 22.3.6
Cook Industries Inc *v.* Galliher [1979] Ch 439 .... 21.4.1.1
Cooper-King *v.* Cooper-King [1900] P 65 .... 23.3.4
Cordova Land Co Ltd *v.* Victor Brothers Inc [1966] 1 WLR 793 .... 13.1.3.2.1, 13.1.3.3.2.1
Coupland *v.* Arabian Gulf Oil Co [1983] 1 WLR 1136 .... 5.5.2.3, 13.3.2.7, 13.3.3.1.5, 13.4.1.2.2, 13.4.2.2.1.1, 13.4.2.2.1.3
Cretanor Maritime Co Ltd *v.* Irish Marine Management Ltd [1978] 1 WLR 966 .... 21.1.3.3.1.1
Cruse *v.* Chittum [1974] 2 All ER 940 .... 11.2.3.3.1.1
Czarnikow *v.* Roth, Schmidt & Co [1922] 2 KB 478 .... 17.3.2.2, 17.3.4.4, 17.3.6.1.1, 19.1.2

Dagmara, The [1988] 1 Lloyd's Rep 431 .... 8.1.1.1.4
Dallal *v.* Bank Mellat [1986] 1 QB 441 .... 20.5.5.2
D'Almeida Araujo Lda *v.* Sir Frederick Becker & Co Ltd [1953] 2 QB 329 .... 11.4.7.1
Dalmia Cement Ltd *v.* National Bank of Pakistan [1975] QB 9 .... 17.5.2.2.2, 20.2.2.2.2, 20.3.2
Dalmia Dairy Industries Ltd *v.* National Bank of Pakistan [1978] 2 Lloyd's Rep 223 .... 17.1.4, 18.1.2.3, 20.2.3.4.3, 20.2.3.5.3, 20.2.3.9.2.1, 20.3.3.2, 20.3.3.5, 20.3.4.1, 20.3.4.2.1, 20.3.4.2.2, 23.4
Daniel *v.* Foster, 1989 SLT 90 (Sh Ct) 4.1.3.2, 11.2.3.3.1.3
Davenport *v.* Corinthian Motor Policies at Lloyd's, 1991 SLT 774 .... 5.5.2.2.2, 7.2.3.1.1
David Taylor & Son Ltd *v.* Barnett Trading Co. *See* Taylor (David) & Son Ltd *v.* Barnett Trading Co.
De Beéche *v.* South American Stores (Gath & Chaves) Ltd [1935] AC 148 .... 14.4.1.1, 23.3.4
de Bloos SPRL (Ets A) *v.* Société en commandite par actions Bouyer: Case 14/76 [1976] ECR 1497 .... 5.5.3.2.1.1, 5.5.3.3.4, 5.5.5.1.1, 5.5.5.2
de Cavel *v.* de Cavel: Case 143/78 [1979] ECR 1055 .... 9.4.1.2.1, 21.5.1.2
de Dampierre *v.* de Dampierre [1988] AC 92 .... 6.4.4.2.2
de Wolf *v.* Harry Cox BV: Case 42/76 [1976] ECR 1759 .... 9.4.6.1.1
De Wutz *v.* Hendricks (1824) 2 Bing 314 .... 11.4.10.1.1
Debaecker *v.* Bouwman: Case 49/84 [1985] ECR 1779 .... 9.4.3.4, 9.4.3.4.1.3, 9.4.3.4.5.4, 9.4.3.4.5.5, 9.4.3.4.5.6
Decision of 27 February 1969 (1969) 22 NJW 978 (German Bundesfinanzhof) 20.2.3.9
Deichland, The [1990] 1 QB 361 (CA); [1988] 2 Lloyd's Rep 494 .... 3.5.4, 4.1.3.3, 5.9.2.1.4, 5.9.2.2.3, 8.1.4.1.3, 8.2.1.2, 8.2.2.1, 8.2.2.4, 8.2.2.5
Denilauler *v.* Snc Couchet Frères: Case 125/79 [1980] ECR 1553 .... 9.4.1.2.2.2, 9.4.4.3.2, 21.5.2.2
Derby & Co Ltd *v.* Weldon [1990] Ch 48 .... 21.4.1.6, 21.4.2.1.2, 21.4.2.2.1, 21.4.2.4, 21.4.2.4.1, 21.4.2.4.2.4
Derby & Co Ltd *v.* Weldon (Nos 3 & 4) [1990] Ch 65 .... 21.1.3.2.2, 21.1.3.4.1.2, 21.1.3.4.2, 21.4.1.3, 21.4.1.6, 21.4.2.1.1, 21.4.2.1.2, 21.4.2.2.1, 21.4.2.4.1, 21.4.2.4.2.4, 21.4.2.5
Derby & Co Ltd *v.* Weldon (No. 6) [1990] 1 WLR 1139 .... 21.4.1.6, 21.4.2.1.2, 21.4.2.1.3, 21.4.2.2.1
Despina GK, The [1983] QB 214 .... 8.1.1.2.2, 9.2.8.3
Despina R, The. See Services Europe Atlantique Sud (SEAS) *v.* Stockholms Rederiaktiebolag (The Despina R)
Deutsche Genossenschaftsbank *v.* SA Biasserie du Pêcheur: Case 148/84 [1985] ECR 1981 .... 9.4.2.4, 9.4.4.4.2.1, 9.4.5.1.2, 9.4.6.1.2, 9.4.6.2.1

Deutsche Schachtbau- und Tiefbohrgesellschaft mbH *v.* R'As al-Khaimah National Oil Co [1990] 1 AC 295 .... 11.1.1.1.2, 17.1.2, 17.3.4.7, 17.3.4.8, 17.3.7.6, 20.2.3.9, 20.2.3.9.1, 20.2.3.9.2.2
Di Sora (Duchess) *v.* Phillips (1863) 10 HL Cas 624 .... 23.3.1
Diamond *v.* Bank of London & Montreal Ltd [1979] QB 333 .... 13.1.3.3, 13.1.3.3.2.2
Dimskal Shipping Co SA *v.* International Transport Workers Federation (The Evia Luck) (No. 2) [1989] 1 Lloyd's Rep 166; reversed on other grounds [1990] 1 Lloyd's Rep 319 (CA); [1992] 2 AC 152 (HL) 12.10.2, 13.1.3.3.3.3, 13.3.2.7
Distillers Co (Biochemicals) Ltd *v.* Thompson [1971] AC 458 .... 13.1.3.2.2, 13.1.3.2.4, 13.1.3.3.1.2
Dobell (GE) & Co *v.* Steamship Rossmore Co Ltd [1895] 2 QB 408 .... 11.1.1.3.2
Dost Aly Khan, *In the goods of* (1880) 6 PD 6 .... 23.3.4
Dresser UK Ltd *v.* Falcongate Freight Management Ltd [1992] 1 QB 502 .... 5.9.1.4.3
Dubai Bank Ltd *v.* Galadari (No. 5), *The Times*, 26 June 1990 .... 23.3.3
Duchess Di Sora *v.* Phillips. *See* Di Sora (Duchess) *v.* Phillips
Duder *v.* Amsterdamsch Trustees Kantoor [1902] 2 Ch 132 .... 21.4.1.1
Duijnstee *v.* Goderbauer: Case 288/82 [1983] ECR 3663 .... 5.1.4, 5.1.6
Dumez France SA *v.* Hessische Landesbank: Case 228/88 [1990] ECR I–49 .... 5.5.4.2.4, 5.5.4.2.5
Dunbee Ltd *v.* Gilman & Co (Australia) Pty Ltd [1968] 2 Lloyd's Rep 394 .... 9.2.5.2.6
Dunlop Pneumatic Tyre Co Ltd *v.* Aktien-Gesellschaft für Motor und Motorfahrzeugbau Vorm Cudell & Co [1902] 1 KB 342 .... 6.1.2.4.5
Dynamit AG *v.* Rio Tinto Co [1918] AC 260 .... 23.1.1

ED & F Man (Sugar) Ltd *v.* Haryanto (No. 2). *See* Man (ED & F) (Sugar) Ltd *v.* Haryanto (No. 2)
EMI Records Ltd *v.* Modern Music Karl-Ulrich Walterbach GmbH [1992] QB 115 ..... 9.4.1.2.2.2, 9.4.4.3.2, 21.5.2.2
Eagle Star Insurance Co Ltd *v*. Yuval Insurance Co Ltd [1978] 1 Lloyd's Rep 357 ..... 17.3.6.2.4, 17.3.6.2.5, 18.2.2.3.2
East & West India Dock Co *v.* Kirk (1887) 12 App Cas 738 .... 17.2.5.1.6
East India Trading Co Inc. *v.* Carmel Exporters and Importers Ltd [1952] 2 QB 439 .... 20.6.2.3
Effer SpA *v.* Kantner: Case 38/81 [1982] ECR 825 .... 3.3.3.4.3, 4.2.3.2.2, 4.2.3.2.3, 4.2.3.2.4, 5.5.3.1.2
El Amria, The [1981] 2 Lloyd's Rep 119 .... 5.10.2.1, 5.10.2.2, 6.4.3, 6.5.2.3, 6.5.2.4
El du Pont de Nemours & Co *v.* Agnew [1987] 2 Lloyd's Rep 585 .... 6.4.4.2.1, 6.4.4.2.3, 6.4.4.2.4, 6.4.4.10.3
Elefanten Schuh GmbH *v.* Jacqmain: Case 150/80 [1981] ECR 1671 .... 5.2.1, 5.2.3, 5.3.3.5, 5.9.3.2
Eleftheria, The [1970] P 94 .... 5.10.2.1, 5.10.2.2, 6.5.2.2, 6.5.2.3, 6.5.2.4
Ellis *v.* M'Henry (1871) LR 6 CP 228 .... 9.2.7, 11.4.8.1
Elwyn (Cottons) Ltd *v.* Pearle Designs Ltd [1990] ILPr 40 .... 9.4.4.4.3.4
Emanuel *v.* Symon [1908] 1 KB 302 .... 9.2.5.1.1, 9.2.5.1.2, 9.2.5.6
Embiricos *v.* Anglo-Austrian Bank [1905] 1 KB 677 .... 12.9.2.6
Employers' Liability Assurance Corporation Ltd *v.* Sedgwick, Collins & Co Ltd [1927] AC 95 ... 9.2.5.3.1
Emre II, The [1989] 2 Lloyd's Rep 182 .... 21.2.4
Enoch and Zaretzky, Bock & Co's Arbitration, *Re* [1910] 1 KB 327 .... 20.2.3.4.3
Entores Ltd *v.* Miles Far East Corporation [1955] 2 QB 327 .... 6.3.3.4.2.1
Eschersheim, The [1976] 1 WLR 430 .... 8.1.1.1.4, 8.1.1.1.5
Estatsis Salotti di Colzani Aimo *v.* RÜWA Polstereimaschinen GmbH: Case 24/76 [1976] ECR 1831 .... 5.3.3, 5.3.3.1.1.1
Etri Fans Ltd *v.* NMB (UK) Ltd [1987] 1 WLR 1110 .... 18.3.2
Ets A de Bloos SPRL *v.* Société en Commandite par actions Bouyer. *See* de Bloos SPRL (Ets A) *v.* Société en commandite par actions Bouyer
European Asian Bank AG *v.* Punjab & Sind Bank [1982] 2 Lloyd's Rep 356 .... 6.4.3
European Asian Bank AG *v.* Punjab & Sind Bank (No. 2) [1983] 1 WLR 642 .... 18.2.2.5.6
Evans Marshall & Co Ltd *v.* Bertola SA [1973] 1 WLR 349 .... 5.3.2.3.1, 5.3.4.2, 6.5.2.5
Evia Luck, The. See Dimskal Shipping Co SA *v.* International Transport Workers Federation (The Evia Luck) (No. 2)
Evpo Agnic, The [1988] 1 WLR 1090 .... 8.1.1, 8.1.2.3.1.1, 8.1.2.3.4.4

Fagin's Bookshop, *Re* [1992] BCLC 118 .... 5.1.3.2
Father Thames, The [1979] 2 Lloyd's Rep 364 .... 8.1.1.1.3, 8.1.2.3.4.1
Faure, Fairclough Ltd *v.* Premier Oil & Cake Mills Ltd [1968] 1 Lloyd's Rep 237 .... 16.3.3.2
Federal Huron, The [1985] 3 All ER 378 .... 14.2.2.2.1, 14.2.2.2.8
Fehmarn, The [1958] 1 WLR 159 .... 6.5.2.3
Feist *v.* Société Intercommunale Belge d'Eléctricité [1934] AC 161 .... 14.1.3.1.2, 14.1.3.2
Fidelitas Shipping Co Ltd *v.* V/O Exportchleb [1966] 1 QB 630 .... 9.2.6
Fillite (Runcorn) Ltd *v.* Aqua-Lift (a firm) (1989) 45 BLR 27 .... 18.2.2.2
Finnish Marine Insurance Co Ltd *v.* Protective National Insurance Co [1990] 1 QB 1078 .... 6.3.3.4.1.1, 6.3.3.4.1.2

Firma P *v.* Firma K: Case 178/83 [1984] ECR 3033 .... 9.4.4.5.1.2
First National Bank of Boston *v.* Union Bank of Switzerland [1990] 1 Lloyd's Rep 32 .... 6.4.4.3.3
Food Corporation of India *v.* Antclizo Shipping Corporation [1988] 1 WLR 603 .... 16.2.3.2.1.3
Foster *v.* Driscoll [1929] 1 KB 470 .... 11.3.4.1, 11.4.10.1.1, 11.4.10.1.2, 14.2.3.5, 14.4.1.2
Franklin *v.* Westminster Bank (1931) (unreported) 14.1.1.3
Freccia del Nord, The [1989] 1 Lloyd's Rep 388 .... 5.9.1.4.2, 8.1.4.1.4
Freights Queen, The [1977] 2 Lloyd's Rep 140 .... 11.1.3.5

G & H Montage GmbH *v.* Irrani. *See* Montage (G & H) GmbH *v.* Irrani
GUR Corporation *v.* Trust Bank of Africa Ltd [1987] QB 559 .... 2.1.5.2, 2.1.5.4, 2.1.5.5
Galaxias Steamship Co Ltd *v.* Panagos Christofis (1948) 81 Ll L Rep 499 .... 13.4.1.1.1, 13.4.1.1.2
Galéries Segoura SPRL *v.* Bonakdarian: Case 25/76 [1976] ECR 1851 .... 5.3.3, 5.3.3.1.1.4, 5.3.3.2
Gascoine *v.* Pyrah, *The Times*, 26 November 1991 .... 4.3.1.3, 5.5.2.3, 5.5.4.2.2, 5.6.2.3
Gatoil International Inc *v.* Arkwright-Boston Manufacturers Mutual Insurance Co [1985] AC 255 .... 8.1.1, 8.1.1.1.5
Geogas SA *v.* Trammo Gas Ltd [1991] 2 QB 139; [1991] 1 WLR 776 .... 19.4.2.2.1, 19.4.2.2.2, 19.4.2.2.3
George Monro Ltd *v.* American Cyanamid & Chemical Corporation. *See* Monro (George) Ltd *v.* American Cyanamid & Chemical Corporation
George Veflings Rederi A/S *v.* President of India [1979] 1 WLR 59 .... 14.2.3.4
Gerling Konzern Speziale Kreditversicherungs-AG *v.* Amministrazione del Tesoro dello Stato: Case 201/82 [1983] ECR 2503 .... 5.3.3.1.1.4, 5.3.3.4.1
Ghoth *v.* Ghoth [1992] 2 All ER 920 .... 21.4.2.4.2.3
Gibbon *v.* Commerz und Creditbank AG [1958] 2 Lloyd's Rep 113 .... 6.3.3.4.2.2
Gibraltar (Government of) *v.* Kenney. *See* Government of Gibraltar *v.* Kenney
Gilbert *v.* Brett (The Case of Mixt Moneys) (1604) Davis 18 .... 14.1.1.1
Glider Standard Austria SH, *Re*, 1964 [1965] P 463 .... 8.1.2
Godard *v.* Gray (1870) LR 6 QB 139 .... 9.2.7, 9.4.3.1, 20.3.4.1
Goldean Mariner, The [1989] 2 Lloyd's Rep 390, affirmed [1990] 2 Lloyd's Rep 215 .... 6.3.3.3.1, 6.4.4.3.2, 6.4.4.3.3, 6.4.4.4.2
Golden Acres Ltd *v.* Queensland Estates Pty Ltd [1969] Qd R 378 .... 1.3.5, 10.1.2
Goodwin *v.* Robarts (1876) 1 App Cas 476 .... 12.9.1.2.1
Goring, The [1988] AC 831 .... 8.1.1.1.5
Gourdain *v.* Nadler: Case 133/78 [1979] ECR 733 .... 3.3.3.2.4
Government of Gibraltar *v.* Kenney [1956] 2 QB 410 .... 18.1.2.2
Government of India *v.* Taylor [1955] AC 491 .... 9.2.3.1
Greer *v.* Poole (1880) 5 QBD 272 .... 12.8.1.1
Grehan *v.* Medical Inc [1988] ECC 6 .... 13.5.1
Guaranty Trust Co of New York *v.* Hannay & Co [1918] 1 KB 43 .... 12.9.2.1.3
Guaranty Trust Co of New York *v.* Hannay & Co [1918] 2 KB 623 .... 23.1.1
Guatemala Republica *v.* Nunez. *See* Republica de Guatemala *v.* Nunez
Gubisch Maschinenfabrik KG *v.* Palumbo: Case 144/86 [1987] ECR 4861 .... 5.9, 5.9.2.1.1, 5.9.2.1.2, 5.9.2.1.3, 5.9.2.1.4, 5.9.2.1.5, 5.9.2.1.6
Gulf Bank KSC *v.* Mitsubishi Heavy Industries Ltd, *The Times*, 24 August 1993 .... 6.3.3.4.1.2

Habourdin International SA *v.* SpA Italocremona: Case 80/83 [1983] ECR 3639 .... 3.2.1.1.4
Hacker *v.* Euro-Relais GmbH: Case C-280/90 [1992] ILPr 515 .... 5.1.1.3.4
Hagen, The [1908] P 189 .... 6.3.1.2, 6.3.3.9.4
Haiti (Republic of) *v.* Duvalier. *See* Republic of Haiti *v.* Duvalier
Halcyon Skies, The [1977] QB 14 .... 8.1.1.1.8
Halley, The (1868) LR 2 PC 193 .... 13.3.1.3, 13.3.3.2.6
Hamlyn & Co *v.* Talisker Distillery [1894] AC 202 .... 5.3.4.1, 17.1.2, 17.3.4.2
Hammer & Sohne *v.* HWT Realisations Ltd, 1985 SLT (Sh Ct) 21 .... 12.5.2.1
Handelskwekerij GJ Bier BV *v.* Mines de Potasse d'Alsace SA: Case 21/76 [1976] ECR 1735 .... 3.2.1.2.3, 5.5.4.2.2, 13.1.1.2
Handte (Jakob) & Co GmbH *v.* Société Traitements Mécano-chimiques des Surfaces: Case C-26/91 [1993] ILPr 5 .... 5.5.1.4, 5.5.2.1.1, 5.5.2.1.2, 5.5.2.2.1, 5.5.2.3, 5.5.3.1.1, 5.5.4.1, 13.4.1.2.3
Harbour Assurance Co (UK) Ltd *v.* Kansa General International Insurance Co Ltd [1992] 1 Lloyd's Rep 81; [1993] QB 701 .... 18.1.2.4, 18.2.2.4.1.2
Harrods (Buenos Aires) Ltd, *Re* [1992] Ch 72 .... 4.1.2.2.2, 5.3.2.3.2, 5.9.3.5, 5.10.1.2, 5.10.1.3, 5.10.1.4, 5.10.1.5, 5.10.1.6, 5.10.1.9, 5.10.2.2., 6.4.6, 7.3.2.2.1, 8.2.3.2
Havhelt, The [1993] 1 Lloyd's Rep 523 .... 21.2.4, 21.2.7
Hayter *v.* Nelson [1990] 2 Lloyd's Rep 265 .... 18.1.3.1, 18.1.4.1, 18.2.2.5.5, 18.2.2.5.7
Heidberg, The [1993] 2 Lloyd's Rep 324 .... 1.3.5
Heisler *v.* Anglo-Dal Ltd [1954] 1 WLR 1273 .... 14.2.3.3

Helbert Wagg & Co Ltd's Claim, *Re* [1956] Ch 323 .... 11.4.8.1, 14.4.1.1, 14.4.1.4
Helene Roth, The [1980] QB 273 .... 8.1.4.1.4
Henderson *v.* Henderson (1843) 3 Hare 100 .... 9.2.6, 9.4.3.3.3.3
Henry *v.* Geoprosco International Ltd [1967] QB 726 .... 9.2.5.2.2, 9.3
Hesperides Hotels Ltd *v.* Aegean Turkish Holidays Ltd [1979] AC 508 .... 6.6.4
Heyman *v.* Darwins Ltd [1942] AC 356 .... 18.1.2.2, 18.1.2.3
Hiscox *v.* Outhwaite [1992] 1 AC 562 ... 20.2.1.2.2.2, 20.2.3.3.2, 20.2.3.3.3, 20.2.3.7.2.3, 20.2.3.7.2.4, 20.2.3.10
Hitachi Shipbuilding and Engineering Co Ltd *v.* Viafiel Compania Naviera SA [1981] 2 Lloyd's Rep 498 .... 21.1.3.3.1.1
Hobbs *v.* Australian Press Association [1933] 1 KB 1 .... 6.1.3.2
Hoffmann *v.* Krieg: Case 145/86 [1988] ECR 645 ...... 9.4.2.3, 9.4.3.3.1, 9.4.3.3.2, 9.4.3.5.1, 9.4.3.5.2, 9.4.6.2.1, 9.4.6.2.3
Hollandia, The [1983] 1 AC 565 .... 5.3.4.3, 6.5.1.3, 12.3.2.1
Home & Overseas Insurance Co Ltd *v.* Mentor Insurance Co (UK) Ltd [1990] 1 WLR 153 .... 17.3.6.2.4, 17.3.6.2.5, 17.3.6.2.6, 18.2.2.5.4, 18.2.2.5.7
Houlditch *v.* Donegal (1834) 8 Bligh NS 301 .... 9.2.6.3.2
House of Spring Gardens Ltd *v.* Waite [1991] 1 QB 241 .... 9.2.7.2.1.2, 20.3.4.2.4
Hunter *v.* Chief Constable of the West Midlands Police [1982] AC 529 .... 9.2.7.2.1.1
Huntington *v.* Attrill [1893] AC 150 .... 9.2.3.1
Hutton (EF) & Co (London) Ltd *v.* Monfarrij [1989] 1 WLR 488 .... 6.3.3.4.1.3, 6.3.3.9.4

I Congreso del Partido [1978] QB 500 .... 8.1.2.3.4.1
IP Metal Ltd *v.* Ruote OZ SpA [1993] 2 Lloyd's Rep 60 .... 5.9.3.4
ISC Technologies Ltd *v.* Guerin [1992] 2 Lloyd's Rep 430 .... 6.3.1.2, 6.3.3.3.4, 6.3.3.6, 6.3.3.7, 6.4.3
India (Government of) *v.* Taylor. *See* Government of India *v.* Taylor
India (Republic of) *v.* India Steamship Co Ltd. *See* Republic of India *v.* India Steamship Co Ltd
India Videogram Association *v.* Patel [1991] 1 WLR 173 .... 6.1.1.2.4, 6.1.1.2.5
Industrial Diamond Supplies *v.* Riva: Case 43/77 [1977] ECR 2175 .... 9.4.3.8.1, 9.4.3.8.2, 9.4.4.4.2.3
Industrie, The (1871) LR 3 A & E 303 .... 8.1.1.1.4
Industrie Tessili Italiana Como *v.* Dunlop AG: Case 12/76 [1976] ECR 1473 .... 3.2.1.2.3, 5.5.3.3.1
Interdesco SA *v.* Nullifire Ltd [1992] 1 Lloyd's Rep 180 .... 9.4.3.3.3.2
International Minerals & Chemical Corporation *v.* Karl O Helm AG [1986] 1 Lloyd's Rep 81 .... 14.1.2.2.2
International Tank & Pipe SAK *v.* Kuwait Aviation Fuelling Co KSC [1975] QB 224 .... 17.1.3
Interpool Ltd *v.* Galani [1988] QB 738 .... 21.4.1.4
Interview Ltd, *Re* [1975] IR 382 .... 12.5.2.1, 12.5.2.3
Intpro Properties (UK) Ltd *v.* Sauvel [1983] QB 1019 .... 2.3.4, 2.3.4.7.2, 2.4.1.1
Ipswich BC *v.* Fisons Plc [1990] Ch 709 .... 19.3.1, 19.3.2
Iraqi Ministry of Defence *v.* Arcepey Shipping Co [1981] QB 65 .... 21.1.3.3.1.1, 21.1.3.3.1.2
Irish Shipping Ltd *v.* Commercial Union Co Plc [1990] 2 WLR 117 .... 6.4.4.12.3
Isabelle Lancray SA *v.* Peters und Sickert KG: Case 305/88 [1990] ECR I-2725 .... 9.4.3.4.2.1, 9.4.3.4.4.2
Israel Discount Bank of New York *v.* Hadjipateras [1984] 1 WLR 137 .... 9.2.7, 9.2.7.3.2
Iveco Fiat SpA *v.* Van Hool NV: Case 313/85 [1986] ECR 337 .... 5.3.3.1.1.3
Ivenel *v.* Schwab: Case 133/81 [1982] ECR 1891 .... 5.5.3.4.1.1, 5.5.3.4.1.2, 5.5.3.4.3.1

J (A Minor), *Re* (Abduction: Custody Rights) [1990] 2 AC 562 .... 11.2.3.3.1.1, 11.2.3.3.1.2
Jacobs, Marcus & Co *v.* Crédit Lyonnais (1884) 12 QBD 589 .... 11.4.5.1.2, 11.4.8.1
Jacobson *v.* Frachon (1928) 138 LT 386 .... 9.2.7.1.1
Jakob Handte & Co GmbH *v.* Société Traitements Mécano-chimiques des Surfaces. *See* Handte (Jakob) & Co GmbH *v.* Société Traitements Mécano-chimiques des Surfaces
Jalamatsya, The [1987] 2 Lloyd's Rep 164 .... 21.2.4, 21.2.6
James Miller & Partners Ltd *v.* Whitworth Street Estates (Manchester) Ltd. *See* Miller (James) & Partners Ltd *v.* Whitworth Street Estates (Manchester) Ltd
Jenkins & Sons *v.* Coomber [1898] 2 QB 168 .... 12.9.2.2.5
Jet Holdings Inc *v.* Patel [1990] 1 QB 335 .... 9.2.7.1.1, 9.2.7.2.1.1, 9.2.7.2.2.2
Jet West Ltd *v.* Haddican [1992] 1 WLR 487 .... 21.1.3.1.3
Jeyaretnam *v.* Mahmood, *The Times*, 21 May 1992 .... 6.4.4.9
Jogia (A Bankrupt), *Re* [1988] 1 WLR 484 .... 12.10.2
John C Helmsing, The [1990] 2 Lloyd's Rep 290 .... 17.5.1.2.4, 18.2.2.5.7
Johnson *v.* Coventry Churchill International Ltd [1992] 3 All ER 14 .... 13.3.2.7, 13.3.3.2.1, 13.3.3.2.2, 13.3.3.2.4, 13.4.2.2.3.3
Johnstone *v.* Pedlar [1921] 2 AC 262 .... 2.2.2
Jones *v.* Trollope Colls Cementation Overseas Ltd, *The Times*, 26 January 1990 .... 15.1.2.1.2, 15.1.2.1.4, 15.1.2.2
Jugoslavenska Oceanska Plovidba *v.* Castel Investment Co Inc [1974] QB 292 .... 14.3.1

K/S A/S Admiral Shipping *v.* Portlink Ferries Ltd [1984] 2 Lloyd's Rep 166 ....21.1.3.3.1.1
K/S A/S Bani *v.* Korea Shipbuilding & Engineering Corporation [1987] 2 Lloyd's Rep 445 .... 17.5.2.1.2
Kalfelis *v.* Bankhaus Schröder, Münchmeyer, Hengst & Co: Case 189/87 [1988] ECR 5565 .... 5.5.1.4, 5.5.2.1.1, 5.5.2.2.1, 5.5.2.2.2, 5.5.2.3, 5.5.4.1, 5.6.2.1, 5.6.2.2, 5.6.2.3, 13.4.1.2.3
Kapetan Georgis, The [1988] 1 Lloyd's Rep 352 .... 6.4.4.3.2, 6.4.4.4.2
Kapur *v.* Kapur [1984] FLR 920 .... 11.2.3.3.1.1
Kefalonia Wind, The [1986] 1 Lloyd's Rep 273 .... 14.2.2.2.8
Kelly *v.* Selwyn [1905] 2 Ch 117 .... 12.6.3
Kenneth Allison Ltd *v.* AE Limehouse & Co. *See* Allison (Kenneth) Ltd *v.* AE Limehouse & Co
Kherson, The [1992] 2 Lloyd's Rep 261 .... 5.9.2.1.4, 5.9.2.2.2, 8.0.2, 21.2.5
Kianta Osekeyhtio *v.* Britain & Overseas Trading Co Ltd [1954] 1 Lloyd's Rep 247 .... 20.2.3.5.2, 20.3.4.2.1
King *v.* Thomas McKenna Ltd [1991] 2 QB 480 .... 16.2.3.2.4.5, 16.2.3.2.4.6
Kleinwort, Sons & Co *v.* Ungarische Baumwolle Industrie Aktiengesellschaft [1939] 2 KB 678 .... 11.4.10.2.1, 20.2.3.9.2.2
Klöckner & Co AG *v.* Gatoil Overseas Inc [1990] 1 Lloyd's Rep 177 .... 3.2.1.1.4, 5.9.1.4.2, 5.9.2.3.3.1
Klomps *v.* Michel: Case 166/80 [1981] ECR 1593 .... 4.4.3, 9.4.3.4.1.3, 9.4.3.4.2.1, 9.4.3.4.3.1, 9.4.3.4.4.1, 9.4.3.4.4.2, 9.4.3.4.5.1, 9.4.3.4.5.3, 9.4.3.4.5.8
Koechlin et Cie *v.* Kestenbaum Brothers [1927] 1 KB 889 .... 12.9.2.6, 23.3.2
Kolsky *v.* Mayne Nickless Ltd [1970] 3 NSWR 511 .... 13.3.3.1.4
Komninos S, The [1990] 1 Lloyd's Rep 541; [1991] 1 Lloyd's Rep 370 .... 7.1.1.3, 10.1.4, 11.1.3.3.1, 11.1.3.3.3, 15.1.2.1.4, 15.1.2.3
Kongress Agentur Hagen GmbH *v.* Zeehaghe BV: Case C-365/88 [1990] ECR I-1845 .... 5.6.3.2, 5.6.3.3
Kornatzki *v.* Oppenheimer [1937] 4 All ER 133 .... 14.1.2.1.3
Kruppstaal AG *v.* Quitmann Products Ltd [1982] ILRM 551 .... 12.5.2.1
Kruse *v.* Questier & Co Ltd [1953] 1 QB 669 .... 18.1.2.2
Kurz *v.* Stella Musical Veranstaltungs GmbH [1992] Ch 196 .... 5.2.4, 5.3.6.2, 7.2.2.2.3
Kuwait Airways Corporation *v.* Iraqi Airways, *The Times*, 27 October 1993; *Financial Times*, 17 July 1992 .... 2.3.2.2, 2.3.4.1.2, 2.3.6.1.4

LTU Lufttransportunternehmen GmbH & Co KG *v.* Eurocontrol: Case 29/76 [1976] ECR 1541 .... 3.2.3, 3.3.2.2, 3.3.2.4
Ladd *v.* Marshall [1954] 1 WLR 1489 .... 9.2.7.2.1.1
Ladenimor SA *v.* Intercomfinanz SA: Case C-314/92 .... 5.10.1.2, 7.3.2.2.1
Lakhta, The [1992] 2 Lloyd's Rep 269 .... 6.4.4.1
Lazard Brothers & Co Ltd *v.* Midland Bank Ltd [1933] AC 289 .... 2.1.1, 23.3.1, 23.3.5.1
Lebel *v.* Tucker (1867) LR 3 QB 77 .... 12.9.2.2.4
Lee *v.* Abdy (1886) 17 QBD 309 .... 12.6.2.1.2
Leisure Data *v.* Bell [1988] FSR 367 .... 21.1.2.2
Lemeda Trading Co Ltd *v.* African Middle East Petroleum Co Ltd [1988] QB 448 ....11.4.10.1.1
Leoborg, The [1962] 2 Lloyd's Rep 146 .... 8.1.1.1.6
Leroux *v.* Brown (1852) 12 CB 801 .... 11.4.3.1.2, 11.4.3.1.3
Letang *v.* Cooper [1965] 1 QB 232 .... 9.2.6.2.2
Liberian Shipping Corporation "Pegasus" *v.* A King & Sons Ltd [1967] 2 QB 86 .... 15.1.2.1.2
Libyan Arab Foreign Bank *v.* Bankers Trust Co [1989] QB 720 ....11.4.10.2.3
Linda, The [1988] 1 Lloyd's Rep 388; [1988] 1 Lloyd's Rep 175 .... 5.9.2.2.2, 8.0.2.
Lisboa, The [1980] 2 Lloyd's Rep 546 .... 6.5.1.3, 21.3.1.3.3, 22.2.1.4, 22.2.2.5
Littauer Glove Corporation *v.* FW Millington (1920) Ltd (1928) 44 TLR 746 .... 9.2.5.4.2
L'Office Cherifien des Phosphates *v.* Yamashita-Shinnihon Steamship Co Ltd [1993] 3 WLR 266 ....16.2.3.2.1.4
Lonrho Ltd *v.* Shell Petroleum Co Ltd, *The Times*, 1 February 1978 .... 18.2.2.2
Lord Nelson *v.* Earl Bridport. *See* Nelson (Lord) *v.* Earl Bridport
Lysaght Ltd *v.* Clark & Co [1891] 1 QB 552 .... 6.1.3.2

M'Elroy *v.* M'Allister, 1949 SC 110 .... 13.2.1.1.2, 13.3.2.4, 13.3.3.1.3, 13.3.3.2.1
Machado *v.* Fontes [1897] 2 QB 231 .... 13.3.2.4, 13.3.2.5, 13.3.2.6, 13.3.3.1.5
Maciej Rataj, The [1991] 2 Lloyd's Rep 458, reversed on other grounds [1992] 2 Lloyd's Rep 552 .... 5.9.2.1.5, 5.9.2.1.6, 5.9.2.2.1, 5.9.2.2.2, 5.9.3.4, 5.9.3.5, 8.0.2
Mackender *v.* Feldia AG [1967] 2 QB 590 .... 5.3.2.3.1, 6.5.2.5, 18.1.2.2
MacKinnon *v.* Iberia Shipping Co Ltd, 1955 SC 20 .... 13.3.2.4
Maclaine Watson & Co Ltd *v.* International Tin Council (No. 2) [1989] Ch 286 .... 21.4.1.4
MacShannon *v.* Rockware Glass Ltd [1978] AC 795 .... 6.4.2.4, 6.4.3
Magnum, The [1989] 1 Lloyd's Rep 47 .... 6.4.4.11, 6.4.4.12.2
Maharanee of Baroda *v.* Wildenstein. *See* Baroda (Maharanee of) *v.* Wildenstein

Man (ED & F) (Sugar) Ltd *v.* Haryanto (No. 2) [1991] 1 Lloyd's Rep 429; [1991] 1 Lloyd's Rep 161 .... 9.2.6, 9.2.7.4.2, 22.1.2, 22.2.1.6
Mansouri *v.* Singh [1986] 1 WLR 1393 .... 14.4.2.2
Marc Rich & Co AG *v.* Società Italiana Impianti PA. *See* Rich (Marc) & Co AG *v.* Società Italiana Impianti PA
Marc Rich & Co AG *v.* Società Italiana Impianti PA (No. 2). *See* Rich (Marc) & Co AG *v.* Società Italiana Impianti PA (No. 2)
Mareva Compania Naviera SA *v.* International Bulk Carriers SA [1975] 2 Lloyd's Rep 509 .... 21.1.1.1, 21.1.3.2.2
Margaret, The (1881) 6 PD 76 .... 8.1.1.1.4
Marine Contractors Ltd *v.* Shell Petroleum Development Co of Nigeria Ltd [1984] 2 Lloyd's Rep 77 .... 19.5.1.2
Maritime Trader, The [1981] 2 Lloyd's Rep 153 .... 8.1.2.3.4.3
Marrache *v.* Ashton [1943] AC 311 .... 14.2.3.4
Marsden *v.* Kingswell Watts (a firm) [1992] 2 All ER 239 .... 6.1.3.2
Martin Peters Bauunternehmung GmbH *v.* Zuid Nederlandse Aannemers Vereniging. *See* Peters (Martin) Bauunternehmung GmbH *v.* Zuid Nederlandse Aannemers Vereniging
Mattar & Saba *v.* Public Trustee [1952] 3 DLR 399 .... 9.2.5.2.6
Matthews *v.* Kuwait Bechtel Corporation [1959] 2 QB 57 .... 5.5.2.3, 13.4.1.2.1, 13.4.1.2.2
Maudslay, Sons & Field, *Re* [1900] 1 Ch 602 .... 21.4.1.1
Mavani *v.* Ralli Bros Ltd [1973] 1 WLR 468 .... 17.5.2.1.2
Mawan, The [1988] 2 Lloyd's Rep 459 .... 8.1.2.3.4.5
May & Hassell Ltd *v.* Vsesojuznoje Objedinenije "Exportles" (1940) 66 Ll L Rep 103 .... 18.2.2.2
Meadows Indemnity Co Ltd *v.* Insurance Corporation of Ireland Plc [1989] 1 Lloyd's Rep 181; [1989] 2 Lloyd's Rep 298 .... 6.4.4.2.3, 6.4.4.3.2, 6.4.6
Medway Packaging Ltd *v.* Meurer Maschinen GmbH [1990] 2 Lloyd's Rep 112 .... 4.2.3.2.3, 5.5.3.2.1.1, 5.5.3.3.4
Meeth *v.* Glacetal: Case 23/78 [1978] ECR 2133 .... 5.3.5.1, 5.3.6.2
Merak, The [1965] P 223 ....18.2.2.4.2.3
Mercury Publicity Ltd *v.* Wolfgang Loerke GmbH [1993] ILPr 142 .... 4.2.3.2.3, 5.5.3.4.2
Merker *v.* Merker [1963] P 283 .... 9.2.7
Merle, The (1874) 31 LT 447 .... 8.1.1.1.4
Merrifield, Ziegler & Co *v.* Liverpool Cotton Association (1911) 105 LT 97 .... 20.3.4.1
Messiniaki Tolmi, The [1984] 1 Lloyd's Rep 266 .... 6.2.3.2
Metal Scrap Trade Corporation Ltd *v.* Kate Shipping Co Ltd [1988] 1 WLR 767; reversed on other grounds [1990] 1 WLR 115 (HL) 18.1.3.2, 18.2.2.3.2
Metall und Rohstoff AG *v.* Donaldson Lufkin & Jenrette Inc [1990] 1 QB 391 ..... 6.3.1.1.4, 6.3.2.4, 6.3.3.6, 6.3.3.9.2, 6.4.4.4.2, Chap. 13, preamble, 13.1.3.1, 13.1.3.2.4, 13.1.3.3, 13.1.3.3.1.3, 13.1.3.3.3.1, 13.3.3.2.2, 15.1.1.3
Middlemiss & Gould *v.* Hartlepool Corporation [1972] 1 WLR 1643 .... 20.1.2.2
Midland Bank Plc *v.* Laker Airways Ltd [1986] QB 689 .... 22.2.1.7
Miliangos *v.* George Frank (Textiles) Ltd [1976] AC 443 .... 14.3.2, 14.3.2.1, 14.3.2.3
Miller (James) & Partners Ltd *v.* Whitworth Street Estates (Manchester) Ltd [1970] AC 583 .... 10.1.4, 11.1.3.1.3, 11.2.2, 17.2.3.1
Minalmet GmbH *v.* Brandeis Ltd: Case C-123/91 [1993] ILPr 132 .... 9.4.3.4.2.2
Minister of Public Works of the Government of the State of Kuwait *v.* Sir Frederick Snow & Partners [1984] AC 426 .... 20.2.1.3
Minster Investments Ltd *v.* Hyundai Precision & Industry Co Ltd [1988] 2 Lloyd's Rep 621 .... 5.5.4.2.2
Mitsubishi Corporation *v.* Alafouzos [1988] 1 Lloyd's Rep 191 .... 6.4.4.10.3, 11.1.3.5
Mölnlycke AB *v.* Procter & Gamble Ltd [1992] 1 WLR 1112 .... 4.2.3.1.2, 4.2.3.2.3, 5.1.4
Monro (George) Ltd *v.* American Cyanamid & Chemical Corporation [1944] 1 KB 432 .... 13.1.3.2.1, 13.1.3.2.4, 13.1.3.3.1.1
Montage (G & H) GmbH *v.* Irvani [1990] 1 WLR 667 .... 12.9.2.2.6, 12.9.2.3.1
Moschanthy, The [1971] 1 Lloyd's Rep 37 .... 21.2.7
Moulis *v.* Owen [1907] 1 KB 746 .... 12.9.2.2.3, 23.3.1
Mount Albert Borough Council *v.* Australasian Temperance & General Mutual Life Assurance Society Ltd [1938] AC 224 .... 11.4.8.1
Mulox IBC Ltd *v.* Geels: Case C-125/92, OJ 1993 C211/18 .... 5.5.3.4.1.1, 5.5.3.4.1.2
Multinational Gas & Petrochemical Co *v.* Multinational Gas & Petrochemicals Services Ltd [1983] Ch 258 .... 6.3.3.3.1, 13.1.3.2.4
Myrto, The [1977] 2 Lloyd's Rep 243 .... 8.1.2

National Mortgage and Agency Co of New Zealand Ltd *v.* Gosselin (1922) 38 TLR 832 .... 6.3.3.4.3.1

National Mutual Life Association of Australasia Ltd *v.* Attorney-General for New Zealand [1956] AC 369 .... 14.2.2.1.4
National Westminster Bank Plc *v.* Arthur Young McLelland Moores & Co (No. 2) [1991] 1 WLR 1256 .... 19.4.2.1
Naviera Amazonica Peruana SA *v.* Compania Internacional de Seguros del Peru [1988] 1 Lloyd's Rep 116 .... 17.2.1.4, 17.2.3.1, 17.2.3.3, 17.2.4.1, 17.2.4.3, 17.5.2.2.2, 18.2.2.1.1.3, 21.3.2.1.2
Nelson (Lord) *v.* Earl Bridport (1845) 8 Beav 527 .... 12.4, 23.3.3
Nema, The. See Pioneer Shipping Ltd *v.* B.T.P Tioxide Ltd (The Nema)
Netherlands State *v.* Rüffer: Case 814/79 [1980] ECR 3807 .... 3.3.2.4, 3.3.2.5
Neumeier *v.* Kuehner, 31 NY 2d 121; 286 NE 2d 454 (1972) 13.2.4.2
New Brunswick Railway Co *v.* British & French Trust Corporation Ltd [1939] AC 1 .... 14.1.3.2
New England Reinsurance Corporation *v.* Messoghios Insurance Co SA [1992] 2 Lloyd's Rep 251 .... 4.2.3.2.3
New Hampshire Insurance Co *v.* Strabag Bau AG [1992] 1 Lloyd's Rep 361 .... 5.3.3.3.2, 5.7.1
Newtherapeutics Ltd *v.* Katz [1991] Ch 226 .... 4.2.3.1.3, 4.3.1.2, 5.1, 5.1.2.2, 6.3.3.4.1.1
Nile Rhapsody, The [1992] 2 Lloyd's Rep 399 .... 6.4.4.10.2, 6.4.4.11, 6.5.2.3
Ninemia Maritime Corporation *v.* Trave Schiffahrtsgesellschaft mbH und Co KG [1983] 1 WLR 1412 .... 21.1.3.2.1, 21.1.3.2.2, 21.4.2.1.1
Nippon Yusen Kaisha *v.* Karageorgis [1975] 1 WLR 1093 .... 21.1.1.1, 21.1.3.2.2
Njegos, The [1936] P 90 .... 11.1.3.5
Noirhomme *v.* Walklate [1992] 1 Lloyd's Rep 427 .... 4.3.2.2, 9.4.4.4.2.1, 9.4.6.2.2
Nordglimt, The [1988] 1 QB 183 .... 3.5.4, 5.9.2.2.2, 8.2.1.3.2, 8.2.2.3, 8.2.2.4, 21.2.3, 21.2.4, 21.2.6
Nordsee Deutsche Hochseefischerei GmbH *v.* Reederei Mond Hochseefischerei AG & Co KG: Case 102/81 [1982] ECR 1095 .... 16.1.1, 17.4.1, 17.4.2
Norske Atlas Insurance Co Ltd *v.* London General Insurance Co Ltd (1927) 28 Ll L Rep 104 .... 17.3.2.2, 17.3.6.1.2, 20.2.3.9.1, 20.3.3.2
North London Railway Co *v.* Great Northern Railway Co (1883) 11 QBD 30 .... 21.3.1.1.1
Nouvion *v.* Freeman (1889) 15 App Cass 1 .... 9.2.2
Nova (Jersey) Knit Ltd *v.* Kammgarn Spinnerei [1977] 1 WLR 713 .... 17.1.3

Ochsenbein *v.* Papelier (1873) LR 8 Ch App 695 .... 9.2.7.2.2.2
Oinoussin Pride, The [1991] 1 Lloyd's Rep 126 .... 6.4.4.3.2, 6.4.4.7
Oppenheim & Co *v.* Mahomed Haneef [1922] 1 AC 482 .... 20.3.4.2.4
Oriel Ltd, *Re* [1986] 1 WLR 180 .... 6.1.2.4.2, 6.1.2.4.4, 6.1.2.4.5
Orion Compania Espanola de Seguros *v.* Belfort Maatschappij voor Algemene Verzekgringeen [1962] 2 Lloyd's Rep 257 .... 17.3.2.2, 17.3.5
Overseas Union Insurance Ltd *v.* AA Mutual International Insurance Co Ltd [1988] 2 Lloyd's Rep 63 .... 17.3.6.2.3, 18.2.2.4.1.2
Overseas Union Insurance Ltd *v.* Incorporated General Insurance Ltd [1992] 1 Lloyd's Rep 439 .... 6.3.1.1.2, 6.3.1.1.6
Overseas Union Insurance Ltd *v.* New Hampshire Insurance Co: Case C-351/89 [1991] ECR I-3317 .... 5.7.1, 5.9.1.2.1, 5.9.2.2.3, 5.9.2.3.1, 5.9.2.3.2.2, 5.9.2.3.3.3, 5.9.2.3.4.2, 22.3.4, 22.3.6
Owens Bank Ltd *v.* Bracco: Case C-129/92 (unreported); [1992] 2 AC 443 (CA and HL) 5.1.5.2, 5.1.5.3, 5.9.1.3, 6.4.4.4.2, 9.0.1, 9.2.7.2.1.1, 9.2.7.2.1.2, 9.2.7.2.2.1, 9.2.7.2.2.2, 9.3.1.3
Ozalid Group (Export) Ltd *v.* African Continental Bank Ltd [1979] 2 Lloyd's Rep 231 .... 14.1.2.2.2

Paal Wilson & Co A/S *v.* Partenreederei Hannah Blumenthal [1983] 1 AC 854 .... 16.2.3.2.1.3
Paczy *v.* Haendler & Nattermann GmbH [1981] 1 Lloyd's Rep 302 .... 18.2.2.4.2.3
Palmer *v.* Caledonian Railway Co [1892] 1 QB 823 .... 11.2.3.3.4.1
Paris Air Crash of March 13, 1974, *Re*, 399 F Supp 732 (1975) 6.4.1.2
Parkasho *v.* Singh [1968] P 233 .... 23.4
Parouth, The [1982] 2 Lloyd's Rep 351 .... 11.4.2.1.1, 17.1.5
Parsons & Whittemore Overseas Co Inc *v.* Société Générale de l'Industrie du Papier, 508 F 2d 969 (2d Cir, 1974) 20.2.3.9
Partenreederei ms Tilly Russ *v.* NV Haven- & Vervoerbedriff Nova: Case 71/83 [1984] ECR 2417 .... 5.3.3.1.1.1, 5.3.3.2, 5.3.3.4.1, 5.3.3.4.2
Paul Smith Ltd *v.* H & S International Holding Inc. *See* Smith (Paul) Ltd *v.* H & S International Holding Inc
Pemberton *v.* Hughes [1899] 1 Ch 781 .... 9.2.7
Penn *v.* Lord Baltimore (1750) 1 Ves Sen 444 .... 6.6.3
Petereit *v.* Babcock International Holdings Ltd [1990] 1 WLR 350 .... 9.4.4.4.2.4
Peters (Martin) Bauunternehmung GmbH *v.* Zuid Nederlandse Aannemers Vereniging: Case 34/82 [1983] ECR 987 .... 5.5.2.1.1
Petrofina SA *v.* AOT Ltd [1992] QB 571 .... 8.1.1.1.5

Philippine Republic Case, The (1977) 46 BVerfGE 342 .... 2.3.5.4.9
Phillips *v.* Eyre (1870) LR 6 QB 1 .... 13.3.1.2, 13.3.1.4, 13.3.1.5, 13.3.2.4, 13.3.2.6, 13.3.3.1.1, 13.3.3.1.5, 13.3.3.2.6, 13.4.2.3.5, 13.5.1, 13.5.2
Phosphate Sewage Co Ltd *v.* Molleson (1879) 4 App Cass 801 .... 9.2.7.2.1.1
Pia Vestra, The [1984] 1 Lloyd's Rep 169 .... 8.1.1.1.4
Pick *v.* Manufacturers' Life Insurance Co [1958] 2 Lloyd's Rep 93 .... 12.8.1.1
Picker *v.* London and County Banking Co (1887) 18 QBD 515 .... 12.9.1.2.2
Pioneer Shipping Ltd *v.* BTP Tioxide Ltd (The Nema) [1982] AC 724 .... 19.3.1, 19.3.2, 19.4.2.2.2
Plendy Plastic Products BV *v.* Pluspunkt Handelsgesellschaft mbH: Case 228/81 [1982] ECR 2723 .... 9.4.3.4.1.1, 9.4.3.4.1.2
PO, The [1991] 2 Lloyd's Rep 206 .... 3.5.3, 3.5.4, 5.10.1.2, 6.4.6, 7.3.2.2.1, 8.2.1.3.2, 8.2.2.2, 8.2.3.2
Polly Peck International Ltd *v.* Citibank NA, *The Times*, 20 October 1993 .... 5.9.1.4.3
Polly Peck International Plc *v.* Nadir [1992] 2 Lloyd's Rep 238; *The Independent*, 2 September 1992 .... 6.3.3.7, 21.1.3.3.1.1, 21.1.3.3.1.2
Polzeath, The, [1916] P 241 .... 11.2.3.3.4.1, 11.2.3.3.4.4
Porter *v.* Freudenberg [1915] 1 KB 857 .... 2.2.2
Pospischal *v.* Phillips, *The Times*, 20 January 1988 .... 21.1.3.3.1.1
Powell Duffryn Plc *v.* Petereit: Case C-214/89 [1992] ILPr 300 .... 5.3.2.1, 5.3.3.1.1.2
Practice Statement (Judicial Precedent) [1966] 1 WLR 1234 .... 14.3.2.1
Pratt *v.* Swanmore Builders Ltd [1980] 2 Lloyd's Rep 504 .... 16.2.3.2.2.1
President of India *v.* La Pintada Compania Navigacion SA [1985] AC 104 .... 14.1.2.2.2
President of India *v.* Lips Maritime Co [1988] AC 395 .... 14.1.2.2.3
President of India *v.* Jadranska Slobodna Plovidba [1992] 2 Lloyd's Rep 274 .... 16.2.3.2.4.6, 17.3.9.3.2
Prevese, The [1973] 1 Lloyd's Rep 202 .... 8.1.4.1.4
Price *v.* Dewhurst (1837) 8 Sim 279 .... 9.2.7.2.2.2
Prins Bernhardt, The [1964] P 117 .... 8.1.4.1.1
Prinsengracht, The [1993] 1 Lloyd's Rep 41 .... 3.5.4, 8.1.4.1.3, 8.2.2.5
Prodexport State Co for Foreign Trade *v.* ED & F Man Ltd [1973] 1 QB 389 .... 18.1.2.2
Protector Alarms Ltd *v.* Maxim Alarms Ltd [1978] FSR 442 .... 21.4.1.1
Prowse *v.* European & American Steam Shipping Co (1860) 13 Moo PC 484 .... 23.3.1

Queen of the South, The [1968] P 449 .... 8.1.1.1.5

R *v.* Barnet LBC *ex parte* Shah [1983] 2 AC 309 .... 11.2.3.3.1.1, 11.2.3.3.1.2
R *v.* International Trustee for the Protection of Bondholders Aktiengesellschaft [1936] WN 325; [1937] AC 500 .... 14.1.3.1.1
Rahman (Prince Abdul) bin Turk; al Sudairy *v.* Abu-Taha [1980] 1 WLR 1258 .... 21.1.3.2.2
Ralli Brothers *v.* Compania Naviera Sota y Aznar [1920] 2 KB 287 .... 11.4.10.2.1, 11.4.10.2.3, 14.4.1.3
Rank Film Distributors Ltd *v.* Lanterna Editrice Srl [1992] ILPr 58 .... 4.2.3.2.3, 5.9.2.3.3.1
Rayner (JH) (Mincing Lane) Ltd *v.* Department of Trade and Industry [1990] 2 AC 418; [1989] Ch 72; [1987] BCLC 667 .... 2.1.4.1.2, 2.1.4.2, 2.1.4.3.2, 2.1.4.3.3, 2.1.4.3.4, 2.1.4.3.6, 2.3.3.3, 2.3.4.4.1
Regazzoni *v.* KC Sethia (1944) Ltd [1958] AC 301 .... 11.3.4.1, 11.4.10.1.1, 14.4.1.2
Reich *v.* Purcell, 67 Cal 2d 551, 432 P 2d 727 (1967) 13.2.3.2.3
Reichert *v.* Dresdner Bank: Case C-115/88 [1990] ECR I-27 .... 5.1.1.1.2, 5.1.1.1.3, 5.1.1.2.1.2, 5.1.1.2.3.4, 12.4.1.3
Reichert *v.* Dresdner Bank (No. 2): Case C-261/90 [1992] ILPr 404 .... 5.1.5.1, 5.5.2.1.1, 5.5.2.2.2, 5.5.4.1, 5.8.1, 21.3.1.2.1.1
Rena K, The [1979] QB 377 .... 18.2.2.4.2.2, 18.2.3.2, 21.1.3.1.3, 21.3.2.1.1
Republic of Haiti *v.* Duvalier [1990] 1 QB 202 .... 5.8.2, 5.9.2.3.5, 6.3.3.2, 21.3.1.2.1.3, 21.3.1.2.2, 21.3.1.2.4.1, 21.4.1.6, 21.4.2.2.1, 21.4.2.2.2, 21.4.2.4.1, 21.4.2.4.2.4
Republic of India *v.* India Steamship Co Ltd [1992] 1 Lloyd's Rep 124 (CA); reversed on other grounds [1993] AC 410 (HL) 9.1.3.2, 9.1.3.4, 9.2.6.2.4
Republic of Somalia *v.* Woodhouse Drake & Carey (Suisse) SA [1993] QB 54 .... 2.1.6.2
Republica de Guatemala *v.* Nunez [1927] 1 KB 669 .... 12.6.2.1.2
Rewia, The [1991] 1 Lloyd's Rep 69, reversed on other grounds [1991] 2 Lloyd's Rep 325 .... 4.2.3.2.3, 5.3.2.3.2, 5.10.2.2, 6.5.2.4, 11.2.3.3.4.1, 11.2.3.3.4.2, 11.2.3.3.4.4
Rich (Marc) & Co AG *v.* Società Italiana Impianti PA (The Atlantic Emperor) [1989] 1 Lloyd's Rep 548; Case C-190/89 [1991] ECR I-3855 .... 3.3.3.4, 3.3.3.4.2.1, 3.3.3.4.2.2, 3.3.3.4.2.3, 3.3.3.4.3, 3.3.3.4.4, 3.3.3.4.5.2, 3.3.3.4.5.3, 5.9.1.1, 9.4.3.2.8, 11.4.2.1.1, 17.1.5, 17.5.1.1.2, 17.5.1.2.4, 20.6.2.4
Rich (Marc) & Co AG *v.* Società Italiana Impianti PA (No. 2) [1992] 1 Lloyd's Rep 624 .... 3.3.3.4.5.4, 9.2.5.2.3, 9.2.7.5.4, 9.4.3.2.8
River Rima, The [1988] 1 WLR 758 .... 8.1.1.1.7
Roachbank, The [1988] 2 Lloyd's Rep 337 .... 19.4.2.2.1
Robinson & Co *v.* Continental Insurance Co of Mannheim [1915] 1 KB 155 .... 2.2.2

Rome *v.* Punjab National Bank (No. 2) [1989] 1 WLR 1211 .... 6.1.2.6.3
Roneleigh Ltd *v.* MII Exports Inc [1989] 1 WLR 619 .... 6.4.3, 6.4.4.7
Rosler *v.* Hilbery [1925] Ch 250 .... 6.4.2.1
Rösler *v.* Rottwinkel: Case 241/83 [1985] ECR 99 ... 5.1.1.1.1, 5.1.1.3.1, 5.1.1.3.2, 5.1.1.3.3, 5.1.1.3.4, 5.1.1.3.5
Rossano *v.* Manufacturers' Life Insurance Co [1963] 2 QB 352 .... 12.8.1.1
Rosseel NV *v.* Oriental Commercial & Shipping Co (UK) Ltd [1991] 2 Lloyd's Rep 625; [1990] 1 WLR 1387 .... 17.5.1.3, 20.2.3.1.3, 20.2.3.10, 21.4.2.2.2
Roussel-Uclaf *v.* G.D. Searle & Co Ltd [1978] 1 Lloyd's Rep 225 .... 18.3.2
Royal Bank of Scotland *v.* Cassa di Risparmio delle Provincie Lombardi, *Financial Times*, 21 January 1992 .... 5.5.3.2.2.6, 5.5.3.3.3
Royal Exchange Assurance Corporation *v.* Sjoforsakrings Aktiebolaget Vega [1902] 2 KB 384 .. 12.8.1.2

SA Consortium General Textiles *v.* Sun & Sand Agencies Ltd [1978] QB 279 ..... 9.2.3.3, 9.2.5.2.5, 9.2.7.3.1
SAR Schotte GmbH *v.* Parfums Rothschild SARL: Case 218/86 [1987] ECR 4905 .... 5.5.5.1.2
SPRL Acardo *v.* SA Haviland: Case 9/87 [1988] ECR 1539 .... 5.5.2.1.1
Sadler *v.* Robins (1808) 1 Camp 253 .... 9.2.3.1
Sage *v.* Double A Hydraulics Ltd; Chambers *v.* Starkings, *The Times*, 2 April 1992 .... 6.2.3.2, 6.2.3.5
Saint Anna, The [1983] 1 WLR 895 .... 8.1.1.1.5
St. Elefterio, The [1957] P 179 .... 8.1.1.1.5
St. Merriel, The [1963] P 247 .... 8.1.1.1.2, 8.1.2.2.2
St. Pierre *v.* South American Stores (Gath & Chaves) Ltd [1936] 1 KB 382 .... 6.4.2.2, 6.4.2.4, 11.4.6
Sanders *v.* Van Der Putte: Case 73/77 [1977] ECR 2383 .... 5.1.1.3.1, 5.1.1.3.2, 5.1.1.3.3
Sanicentral GmbH *v.* Collin: Case 25/79 [1979] ECR 3423 .... 3.3.2.3
Sargasso, The [1993] 1 Lloyd's Rep 424 .... 5.9.1.4.3
Saudi Prince, The [1982] 2 Lloyd's Rep 255 .... 8.1.2.3.4.1
Saxby *v.* Fulton [1909] 2 KB 208 .... 23.2.2
Sayers *v.* International Drilling Co NV [1971] 1 WLR 1176 .... 12.2.2.1.1, 12.2.2.2.3, 12.2.4.2, 13.3.2.3, 13.4.2.2.1.1, 13.4.2.2.1.2, 13.4.2.2.3.3, 13.4.2.3.4
Scherrens *v.* Maenhout: Case 158/87 [1988] ECR 3791 .... 5.1.1.4
Schibsby *v.* Westenholz (1870) LR 6 QB 155 .... 9.1.2.1, 9.2.5.6
Schorsch Meier GmbH *v.* Hennin [1975] QB 416 .... 14.3.1
Scott *v.* Avery (1856) 5 HL Cas 811 .... 18.1.1
Seaconsar Far East Ltd *v.* Bank Markazi Jomhouri Islami Iran [1993] 1 Lloyd's Rep 236; [1993] 3 WLR 756; [1993] 4 All ER 456 .... 4.2.3.1.2, 4.2.3.2.4, 6.3.1.1.1, 6.3.1.1.5, 6.3.2.3, 6.3.2.4, 6.3.2.5, 6.3.3.9.1, 6.3.3.9.2, 6.3.3.9.3
Seaward *v.* Paterson [1897] 1 Ch 545 .... 21.1.3.3.2
Securities and Investments Board *v.* Lloyd-Wright [1993] 4 All ER 210 .... 21.1.3.2.3
Securities and Investments Board *v.* Pantell SA [1990] Ch 426 .... 21.4.2.4.2.5
Sengupta *v.* Republic of India [1983] ICR 221 .... 2.3.4.5.2
Senna, The (No. 2) [1985] 1 WLR 490 .... 9.2.1.2, 9.2.4.3
Services Europe Atlantique Sud (SEAS) *v.* Stockholms Rederiaktiebolag Svea (The Despina R) [1979] AC 685 .... 14.2.2.2.1, 14.2.2.2.2, 14.2.2.2.6, 14.2.2.2.8, 14.3.2.3
Sethia Liners Ltd *v.* State Trading Corporation of India Ltd [1985] 1 WLR 1398 .... 18.2.2.5.3, 18.2.2.5.7
Sfeir & Co *v.* National Insurance Co of New Zealand [1964] 1 Lloyd's Rep 330 .... 9.3.1.3
Shah, *ex parte*. *See* R *v.* Barnet LBC *ex parte* Shah
Sharif *v.* Azad [1967] 1 QB 605 .... 14.4.2.1, 23.3.2
Shearson Lehmann Hutton Inc *v.* TVB Treuhandgesellschaft für Vermögensverwaltung und Beteiligungen mbH: Case C-89/91 [1993] ILPr 199 .... 5.7.2.1
Shenavai *v.* Kreischer: Case 266/85 [1987] ECR 239 .... 5.1, 5.5.3.2.2.2, 5.5.3.4.2
Shevill *v.* Presse Alliance SA [1992] 2 WLR 1 .... 5.5.4.2.3
Silver Athens, The (No. 2) [1986] 2 Lloyd's Rep 583 .... 21.2.6
Sim *v.* Robinow (1892) 19 R 665 .... 6.4.2.5, 6.4.3
Simonin *v.* Mallac (1860) Sw & Tr 67 .... 11.4.4.1.1.1
Sirdar Gurdyal Singh *v.* Rajah of Faridkoke [1894] AC 670 .... 5.3.3.3.2, 9.2.5.3.1, 9.2.5.6
Siskina, The. See Siskina (Owners of cargo lately laden on board) *v.* Distos Compania Naviera SA (The Siskina)
Siskina (Owners of cargo lately laden on board) *v.* Distos Compania Naviera SA (The Siskina) [1979] AC 210 .... 5.8.2, 6.3.3.2, 6.3.3.9.4, 21.1.1.1, 21.3.1.1.1, 21.3.1.1.2, 21.3.1.1.3, 21.3.1.1.4, 21.3.1.1.5, 21.3.1.2.1.2, 21.3.1.3.3
Sisters, The (1876) 1 PD 117 .... 8.1.1.1.4
Six Constructions Ltd *v.* Humbert: Case 32/88 [1989] ECR 341 .... 5.5.2.2.3, 5.5.3.4.1.1, 5.5.3.4.1.2
Skylark, The [1965] P 474 .... 8.1.1.1.9
Smith (Paul) Ltd *v.* H & S International Holding Inc [1991] 2 Lloyd's Rep 127 .... 17.2.2.1, 17.2.5.1.2, 18.1.2.4, 18.2.2.5.2, 18.2.2.5.7

Smith, Coney & Barrett *v.* Becker, Gray & Co [1916] 2 Ch 86 .... 18.1.2.4
Smith, Kline & French Laboratories Ltd *v.* Bloch [1983] 1 WLR 730 .... 6.4.1.2
Société Commerciale de Réassurance *v.* ERAS (International) Ltd [1992] 1 Lloyd's Rep 570 (CA) 6.3.1.1.3, 6.3.1.1.6, 6.3.3.3.1, 15.1.1.3
Société des Hôtels Le Touquet *v.* Cummings [1922] 1 KB 451 .... 14.1.2.2.2
Société d'Informatique Service Réalisation Organisation *v.* Ampersand Software Ltd BV, *The Times*, 29 July 1993 .... 9.4.3.3.3.3
Société du Gaz de Paris *v.* Société Anonyme de Navigation "Les Armateurs Français," 1926 SC (HL) 13 .... 6.4.2.5
Société Générale de Paris *v.* Dreyfus Brothers (1885) 29 ChD 239 .... 6.4.2.1
Société Nationale Industrielle Aérospatiale *v.* Lee Kui Jak [1987] AC 871 .... 22.1.3, 22.1.4, 22.2, 22.2.1.1, 22.2.1.5
Sohio Supply Co *v.* Gatoil (USA) Inc [1989] 1 Lloyd's Rep 588 .... 5.3.4.2, 6.4.1.2, 22.2.2.4
Soleh Boneh International Ltd *v.* Government of the Republic of Uganda [1993] 2 Lloyd's Rep 208 .... 2.3.5.2.2, 20.2.4.4
Somafer SA *v.* Saar-Ferngas AG: Case 33/78 [1978] ECR 2183 .... 3.2.1.2.1, 5.5.1.4, 5.5.5, 5.5.5.1.2, 5.5.5.3.1, 5.5.5.3.2, 6.1.2.3.2
Somalia (Republic of) *v.* Woodhouse Drake & Carey (Suisse) SA. *See* Republic of Somalia *v.* Woodhouse Drake & Carey (Suisse) SA
Sonia S, The [1983] 2 Lloyd's Rep 63 .... 8.1.1.1.5
Sonntag *v.* Waidmann: Case C-172/91 [1993] ILPr 466 .... 3.3.2.1, 3.3.2.4, 3.3.2.5, 9.4.3.4.3.1, 9.4.3.4.3.2, 9.4.4.4.4.2
South Carolina Insurance Co *v.* Assurantie Maatschappij "De Zeven Provincien" NV [1987] AC 24 .... 21.3.1.1.5, 22.1.4, 22.2, 22.2.1.1, 22.2.2.1
South India Shipping Corporation Ltd *v.* Export-Import Bank of Korea [1985] 1 WLR 585 .... 6.1.2.4.1, 11.2.3.3.3
Sovfracht (V/O) *v.* Van Udens Scheepvaart en Agentuur Maatschappij (NV Gebr) [1943] AC 203 .... 2.2.2
Span Terza, The [1982] 1 Lloyd's Rep 225 .... 8.1.2.3.1.1, 8.1.2.3.3
Spiliada Maritime Corporation *v.* Cansulex Ltd [1987] AC 460 .... 6.3.3.4.1.3, 6.4.2.5, 6.4.3, 6.4.4.2.1, 6.4.4.2.2, 6.4.4.4.1, 6.4.4.5, 6.4.4.7, 6.4.4.10.1, 6.4.4.12.3, 6.4.5.1, 6.4.6, 6.5.1.2, 6.5.2.3, 6.5.3.2, 17.5.1.2.4
Spurrier *v.* La Cloche [1902] AC 446 .... 5.3.4.1
Standard Steamship Owners' Protection & Indemnity Association (Bermuda) Ltd *v.* Gann [1992] 2 Lloyd's Rep 528 .... 6.4.4.10.2, 6.5.3.3
Star Texas, The 17.2.3.2
Steele *v.* M'Kinlay (1880) 5 App Cass 754 .... 12.9.2.2.5
Stevens *v.* Head (1993) 67 ALJR 343 .... 13.3.3.3.2
Sumitomo Heavy Industries Ltd *v.* Oil & Natural Gas Commission 16.2.3.2.1.4
Sussex Peerage Case (1844) 11 Cl & Fin 85 .... 23.3.1
Swift, The [1901] P 168 .... 8.1.1.1.4
Syal *v.* Heyward [1948] 2 KB 443 .... 9.2.7.2.1.1
Szalatnay-Stacho *v.* Fink [1947] KB 1 .... Chap. 13, preamble

TDK Tape Distributor UK Ltd *v.* Videochoice Ltd [1986] 1 WLR 141 .... 21.1.3.3.1.1
Tacoma City, The [1991] 1 Lloyd's Rep 330 .... 8.1.1.1.8
Talbot *v.* Berkshire County Council [1993] 3 WLR 708 .... 9.2.6.2.3
Tate Access Floors Inc *v.* Boswell [1991] Ch 512 .... 21.1.3.2.3
Taylor (David) & Son Ltd *v.* Barnett Trading Co [1953] 1 WLR 562 .... 18.1.2.4
Tesaba, The [1982] 1 Lloyd's Rep 397 .... 8.1.1.1.6
Tesam Distribution Ltd *v.* Schuh Mode Team GmbH [1990] ILPr 149 .... 4.2.3.2.3, 4.2.3.2.4, 5.5.3.1.2
Texaco Melbourne, The [1993] 1 Lloyd's Rep 471 .... 14.2.2.2.9
Thoday *v.* Thoday [1964] P 181 .... 9.2.6
Tolten, The [1946] P 135 .... 6.6.3
Tooker *v.* Lopez, 24 NY 2d. 569, 249 N.E. 2d. 394 (1969) 13.2.3.2.2, 13.2.4.3
Toprak Mahsulleri Ofisi *v.* Finagrain Compagnie Commerciale Agricole et Financière SA [1979] 2 Lloyd's Rep 98 .... 14.4.1.4
Tracomin SA *v.* Sudan Oil Seeds Ltd (No. 1) [1983] 1 WLR 662; affirmed [1983] 1 WLR 1026 .... 9.2.5.2.2, 9.2.7.5.3
Tracomin SA *v.* Sudan Oil Seeds (No. 2) [1983] 1 WLR 1026 .... 22.2.2.3
Trade Fortitude, The [1992] 1 Lloyd's Rep 169 .... 19.2.2
Trendtex Trading Corporation *v.* Central Bank of Nigeria [1977] QB 529 .... 2.3.1.3, 23.1.1
Trendtex Trading Corporation *v.* Crédit Suisse [1980] 3 All ER 721; [1982] AC 679 .... 6.4.4.10.2, 12.6.3
Tubantia, The [1924] P 78 .... 8.1.1.2.2
Turkiye Is Bankasi AS *v.* Bank of China [1993] 1 Lloyd's Rep 132 .... 11.1.3.5

Tuyuti, The [1984] QB 838 .... 21.2.3

Uhla, The (1867) 37 LJ Adm 16n 8.1.1.1.4
Union International Insurance Co Ltd *v.* Jubilee Insurance Co Ltd [1991] 1 WLR 415 .... 6.3.3.4.3.2
Union Nationale des Coopératives Agricoles de Céréales *v.* Robert Catterall & Co Ltd [1959] 2 QB 44 .... 17.3.2.2, 20.3.3.4, 20.3.3.5, 20.3.4.1, 20.6.2.1
Union of India *v.* McDonnell Douglas Corporation [1993] 2 Lloyd's Rep 48 .... 17.2.2.2, 17.2.4.2, 17.2.5.1.5, 17.2.5.2.1, 17.5.2.2.3, 17.5.2.2.4
Union Transport Plc *v.* Continental Lines SA [1991] 2 Lloyd's Rep 48 (CA); [1992] 1 WLR 15 (HL) 5.5.3.2.2.4
Unisys International Services Ltd *v.* Eastern Counties Newspapers Ltd [1991] 1 Lloyd's Rep 538 .... 16.2.3.2.1.3
Unit Construction Co Ltd *v.* Bullock [1960] AC 351 .... 4.1.2.2.1, 11.2.3.3.2
United City Merchants (Investments) Ltd *v.* Royal Bank of Canada [1983] 1 AC 168 .... 14.4.2.1, 14.4.2.2
United Railways of Havana and Regla Warehouses Ltd, *Re* [1961] AC 1007 .... 14.3.1, 14.3.2.1
United States of America *v.* Inkley [1989] QB 255 .... 9.2.3.2, 9.2.3.3
Universal Thermosensors Ltd *v.* Hibben [1992] 1 WLR 840 .... 21.1.4.2
Upcerne, The [1912] P 160 .... 8.1.1.1.3

V *v.* B (A Minor) (Abduction) [1991] 1 FLR 266 .... 11.2.3.3.1.1
Vaassen *v.* Management of the Beambtenfonds voor het Mijnbedriff: Case 61/65 [1966] ECR 261 .... 17.4.2
Vadala *v.* Lawes (1890) 25 QBD 310 .... 9.2.7.2.1.1, 9.2.7.2.2.2
Van Dalfsen *v.* Van Loon: Case C-183/90 [1992] ILPr 5 .... 9.4.3.8.3, 9.4.4.3.2, 9.4.4.4.2.2, 9.4.4.4.2.3, 9.4.4.4.2.4, 9.4.4.4.4.2
Vanessa Ann, The [1985] 1 Lloyd's Rep 549 .... 8.1.1.1.1
Varna, The [1993] 2 Lloyd's Rep 253 .... 21.2.5
Veracruz I, The [1992] 1 Lloyd's Rep 353 .... 21.3.1.1.3
Vervaeke *v.* Smith [1983] 1 AC 145 .... 9.2.7.4.2
Virgin Aviation Services Ltd *v.* CAD. Aviation Services [1991] ILPr 79 .... 5.9.3.4, 5.9.3.5
Vishva Abha, The [1990] 2 Lloyd's Rep 312 .... 6.4.3, 6.4.4.8
Vishva Ajay, The [1989] 2 Lloyd's Rep 558 .... 6.4.4.6, 6.4.4.7
Vishva Prabha, The [1989] 2 Lloyd's Rep 286 .... 6.5.2.4
Vita Food Products Inc *v.* Unus Shipping Co Ltd [1939] AC 277 .... 10.1.2, 10.1.4
Vitovice Horni a Hutni Tezirstvo *v.* Korner [1951] AC 869 .... 6.3.2.5
Vogel *v.* R & A Kohnstamm Ltd [1973] QB 133 .... 9.2.5.2.7, 9.2.5.4.2
Volvox Hollandia, The [1988] 2 Lloyd's Rep 361 .... 5.9.2.1.6, 6.4.4.2.3
Von Gallera *v.* Maître: Case 56/84 [1984] ECR 1769 .... 3.2.1.1.4

Watkins *v.* North American Land & Timber Co Ltd (1904) 20 TLR 534 .... 6.1.1.1.2
Waverley SF Ltd *v.* Carnand Metalbox Engineering Plc 16.2.3.2.1.4
Webb *v.* Webb [1991] 1 WLR 1410; [1992] ILPr 374 (CA) 5.1.1.2.3.2, 5.1.1.2.3.3, 5.1.1.2.3.4
West of England Steamship Owners' Protection and Indemnity Association Ltd *v.* John Holman & Sons [1957] 1 WLR 1164 .... 6.1.3.3
Westminster City Council *v.* Government of The Islamic Republic of Iran [1986] 1 WLR 979 .... 2.3.6.1.3
Williams & Glyn's Bank Plc *v.* Astro Dinamico Compania Naviera SA [1984] 1 WLR 438 .... 6.2.3.2
Wilson, Smithett & Cope Ltd *v.* Terruzzi [1976] QB 683 .... 14.4.2.1
Winkworth *v.* Christie, Manson & Woods Ltd [1980] Ch 496 .... 12.5.1.5
Woodhouse AC Israel Cocoa Ltd SA *v.* Nigerian Produce Marketing Co Ltd [1971] 2 QB 23 .... 14.2.1.1
Worcester City & County Banking Co *v.* Firbank, Pauling & Co [1894] 1 QB 784 .... 6.1.3.2
World Star, The [1986] 2 Lloyd's Rep 274 .... 21.2.4

X *v.* Y [1990] 1 QB 220 .... 5.8.2, 5.9.2.3.5, 6.3.3.2, 21.3.1.2.1.3

Yukon Consolidated Gold Corporation Ltd *v.* Clark [1938] 2 KB 241 .... 9.3.1.1

Z Ltd *v.* A–Z & AA–LL [1982] QB 558 .... 21.1.3.3.1.1, 21.1.3.3.2, 21.4.2.4.2.1
Zahnrad Fabrik Passau GmbH *v.* Terex Ltd, 1986 SLT 84 .... 12.5.2.1
Zambia Steel & Building Supplies Ltd *v.* James Clark & Eaton Ltd [1986] 2 Lloyd's Rep. 225 .... 18.2.2.1.2.4, 18.2.2.1.2.6
Zelger *v.* Salinitri: Case 56/79 [1980] ECR 89 .... 5.5.3.5
Zelger *v.* Salinitri (No. 2): Case 129/83 [1984] ECR 2397 .... 3.2.1.2.3, 5.9.1.4.1
Zeta, The [1893] AC 469 .... 8.1.1.1.3
Zivonstenska Banka National Corporation *v.* Frankman [1950] AC 57 .... 14.4.1.1
Zoersch *v.* Waldock [1964] 1 WLR 675 .... 2.5.2
Zucker *v.* Tyndalls Holdings Plc [1992] 1 WLR 1127 .... 21.3.1.1.3

European Court Cases

Case 61/65: Vaassen *v.* Management of the Beambtenfonds voor het Mijnbedriff [1966] ECR 261 ... 17.4.2
Case 12/76: Industrie Tessili Italiana Como *v.* Dunlop AG [1976] ECR 1473 ... 3.2.1.2.3, 5.5.3.3.1
Case 14/76: Ets A de Bloos SPRL *v.* Société en commandite par actions Bouyer [1976] ECR 1497 ... 5.5.3.2.1.1, 5.5.3.3.4, 5.5.5.1.1, 5.5.5.2
Case 21/76: Handelskwekerij GJ Bier BV *v.* Mines de Potasse d'Alsace SA [1976] ECR 1735 ... 3.2.1.2.3, 5.5.4.2.2, 13.1.1.2
Case 24/76: Estasis Salotti di Colzani Aimo *v.* RÜWA Polstereimaschinen GmbH [1976] ECR 1831 ... 5.3.3, 5.3.3.1.1.1
Case 25/76: Galéries Seyoura SPRL *v.* Bonakdarian [1976] ECR 1851 ... 5.3.3, 5.3.3.1.1.4, 5.3.3.2
Case 29/76: LTU Lufttransportunternehmen GmbH & Co KG *v.* Eurocontrol [1976] ECR 1541 ... 3.2.3, 3.3.2.2, 3.3.2.4
Case 42/76: de Wolf *v.* Harry Cox BV [1976] ECR 1759 ... 9.4.6.1.1
Case 43/77: Industrial Diamond Supplies *v.* Riva [1977] ECR 2175 ... 9.4.3.8.1, 9.4.3.8.2, 9.4.4.4.2.3
Case 73/77: Sanders *v.* Van Der Putte [1977] ECR 2383 ... 5.1.1.3.1, 5.1.1.3.2, 5.1.1.3.3
Case 23/78: Meeth *v.* Glacetal [1978] ECR 2133 ... 5.3.5.1, 5.3.6.2
Case 33/78: Somafer SA *v.* Saar-Ferngas AG [1978] ECR 2183 ... 3.2.1.2.1, 5.5.1.4, 5.5.5, 5.5.5.1.2, 5.5.5.3.1, 5.5.5.3.2, 6.1.2.3.2
Case 133/78: Gourdain *v.* Nadler [1979] ECR 733 ... 3.3.3.2.4
Case 143/78: de Cavel *v.* de Cavel [1979] ECR 1055 ... 9.4.1.2.1, 21.5.1.2
Case 25/79: Sanicentral GmbH *v.* Collin [1979] ECR 3423 ... 3.3.2.3
Case 56/79: Zelger *v.* Salinitri [1980] ECR 89 ... 5.5.3.5
Case 125/79: Denilauler *v.* Snc Couchet Frères [1980] ECR 1553 ... 9.4.1.2.2.2, 9.4.4.3.2, 21.5.2.2
Case 814/79: Netherlands State *v.* Rüffer [1980] ECR 3807 ... 3.3.2.4, 3.3.2.5
Case 139/80: Blanckaert & Willems PVBA *v.* Trost [1981] ECR 819 ... 5.5.5.1.1, 5.5.5.2
Case 150/80: Elefanten Schuh GmbH *v.* Jacqmain [1981] ECR 1671 ... 5.2.1, 5.2.3, 5.3.3.5, 5.9.3.2
Case 166/80: Klomps *v.* Michel [1981] ECR 1593 ... 4.4.3, 9.4.3.4.1.3, 9.4.3.4.2.1, 9.4.3.4.3.1, 9.4.3.4.4.1, 9.4.3.4.4.2, 9.4.3.4.5.1, 9.4.3.4.5.3, 9.4.3.4.5.8
Case 38/81: Effer SpA *v.* Kantner [1982] ECR 825 ... 3.3.3.4.3, 4.2.3.2.2, 4.2.3.2.3, 4.2.3.2.4, 5.5.3.1.2
Case 102/81: Nordsee Deutsche Hochseefischerei GmbH *v.* Reederei Mond Hochseefischerei AG & Co KG [1982] ECR 1095 ... 16.1.1, 17.4.1, 17.4.2
Case 133/81: Ivenel *v.* Schwab [1982] ECR 1891 ... 5.5.3.4.1.1, 5.5.3.4.1.2, 5.5.3.4.3.1
Case 228/81: Plendy Plastic Products BV *v.* Pluspunkt Handelsgesellschaft mbH [1982] ECR 2723 ... 9.4.3.4.1.1, 9.4.3.4.1.2
Case 34/82: Martin Peters Bauunternehmung GmbH *v.* Zuid Nederlandse Aannemers Vereniging [1983] ECR 987 ... 5.5.2.1.1
Case 201/82: Gerling Konzern Speziale Kreditversicherungs-AG *v.* Amministrazione del Tesoro dello Stato [1983] ECR 2503 ... 5.3.3.1.1.4, 5.3.3.4.1
Case 288/82: Duijnstee *v.* Goderbauer [1983] ECR 3663 ... 5.1.4, 5.1.6
Case 71/83: Partenreederei ms Tilly Russ *v.* NV Haven- & Vervoerbedriff Nova [1984] ECR 2417 ... 5.3.3.1.1.1, 5.3.3.2, 5.3.3.4.1
Case 80/83: Habourdin International SA *v.* SpA Italocremona [1983] ECR 3639 ... 3.2.1.1.4
Case 129/83: Zelger *v.* Salinitri (No. 2) [1984] ECR 2397 ... 3.2.1.2.3, 5.9.1.4.1
Case 178/83: Firma P *v.* Firma K [1984] ECR 3033 ... 9.4.4.5.1.2
Case 241/83: Rösler *v.* Rottwinkel [1985] ECR 99 ... 5.1.1.1.1, 5.1.1.3.1, 5.1.1.3.2, 5.1.1.3.3, 5.1.1.3.4, 5.1.1.3.5
Case 258/83: Calzaturificio Brennero sas *v.* Wendel GmbH Schuhproduktion International [1984] ECR 3971 ... 9.4.4.4.2.1, 9.4.4.4.4.2
Case 49/84: Debaecker *v.* Bouwman [1985] ECR 1779 .. 9.4.3.4, 9.4.3.4.1.3, 9.4.3.4.5.4, 9.4.3.4.5.5, 9.4.3.4.5.6
Case 56/84: Von Gallera *v.* Maître [1984] ECR 1769 ... 3.2.1.1.4
Case 119/84: Capelloni *v.* Pelkmans [1985] ECR 3147 ... 9.4.4.4.3.2, 9.4.4.4.3.3, 9.4.4.4.3.4, 9.4.6.2.1, 21.3.1.2.4.2
Case 148/84: Deutsche Genossenschaftsbank *v.* SA Brasserie du Pêcheur [1985] ECR 1981 ... 9.4.2.4, 9.4.4.4.2.1, 9.4.5.1.2, 9.4.6.1.2, 9.4.6.2.1
Case 221/84: F Berghöfer GmbH & Co KG *v.* ASA SA [1985] ECR 2699 ... 5.3.3.1.1.4
Case 22/85: Anterist *v.* Crédit Lyonnais [1986] ECR 1951 ... 5.3.7
Case 198/85: Carron *v.* Federal Republic of Germany [1986] ECR 2437 ... 9.4.4.2.2.1, 9.4.4.2.2.3
Case 266/85: Shenavai *v.* Kreischer [1987] ECR 239 ... 5.1, 5.5.3.2.2.2, 5.5.3.4.2
Case 313/85: Iveco Fiat SpA *v.* Van Hool NV [1986] ECR 3337 ... 5.3.3.1.1.3
Case 144/86: Gubisch Maschinenfabrik KG *v.* Palumbo [1987] ECR 4861 .. 5.9, 5.9.2.1.1, 5.9.2.1.2, 5.9.2.1.3, 5.9.2.1.4, 5.9.2.1.5, 5.9.2.1.6
Case 145/86: Hoffmann *v.* Krieg [1988] ECR 645 ... 9.4.2.3, 9.4.3.3.1, 9.4.3.3.2, 9.4.3.5.1, 9.4.3.5.2, 9.4.6.2.1, 9.4.6.2.3

Case 218/86: SAR Schotte GmbH *v.* Parfums Rothschild SARL [1987] ECR 4905 .... 5.5.5.1.2
Case 9/87: SPRL Acardo *v.* SA Haviland [1988] ECR 1539 .... 5.5.2.1.1
Case 158/87: Scherrens *v.* Maenhout [1988] ECR 3791 .... 5.1.1.4
Case 189/87: Kalfelis *v.* Bankhaus Schröder, Münchmeyer, Hengst & Co [1988] ECR 5565 .... 5.5.1.4, 5.5.2.1.1, 5.5.2.2.1, 5.5.2.2.2, 5.5.2.3, 5.5.4.1, 5.6.2.1, 5.6.2.2, 5.6.2.3, 13.4.1.2.3
Case 32/88: Six Constructions Ltd *v.* Humbert [1989] ECR 341 .... 5.5.2.2.3, 5.5.3.4.1.1, 5.5.3.4.1.2
Case C-115/88: Reichert *v.* Dresdner Bank [1990] ECR I-27 .... 5.1.1.1.2, 5.1.1.1.3, 5.1.1.2.1.2, 5.1.1.2.3.4, 12.4.1.3
Case C-228/88: Dumez France SA *v.* Hessische Landesbank [1990] ECR I-49 .... 5.5.4.2.4, 5.5.4.2.5
Case C-305/88: Isabelle Lancray SA *v.* Peters und Sickert KG [1990] ECR I-2725 ...... 9.4.3.4.2.1, 9.4.3.4.4.2
Case C-365/88: Kongress Agentur Hagen GmbH *v.* Zeehaghe BV [1990] ECR I-1845 .... 5.6.3.2, 5.6.3.3
Case C-190/89: Marc Rich & Co AG *v.* Società Italiana Impianti PA [1991] ECR I-3855 .... 3.3.3.4, 3.3.3.4.2.1, 3.3.3.4.2.2, 3.3.3.4.2.3, 3.3.3.4.3, 3.3.3.4.4, 3.3.3.4.5.2, 3.3.3.4.5.3, 5.9.1.1, 9.4.3.2.8, 11.4.2.1.1, 17.5.1.1.2, 17.5.1.2.4, 20.6.2.4
Case C-214/89: Powell Duffryn Plc *v.* Petereit [1992] ILPr 300 .... 5.3.2.1, 5.3.3.1.1.2
Case C-351/89: Overseas Union Insurance Ltd *v.* New Hampshire Insurance Co [1991] ECR I-3317 .... 5.7.1, 5.9.1.2.1, 5.9.2.2.3, 5.9.2.3.1, 5.9.2.3.2.2, 5.9.2.3.3.3, 5.9.2.3.4.2, 22.3.4, 22.3.6
Case C-183/90: Van Dalfsen *v.* Van Loon [1992] ILPr 5 .... 9.4.3.8.3, 9.4.4.3.2, 9.4.4.4.2.2, 9.4.4.4.2.3, 9.4.4.4.2.4, 9.4.4.4.4.2
Case C-261/90: Reichert *v.* Dresdner Bank (No. 2) [1992] ILPr 404 .... 5.1.5.1, 5.5.2.1.1, 5.5.2.2.2, 5.5.4.1, 5.8.1, 21.3.1.2.1.1
Case C-280/90: Hacker *v.* Euro-Relais GmbH [1992] ILPr 515 .... 5.1.1.3.4
Case C-26/91: Jakob Handte & Co GmbH *v.* Société Traitements Mécano-chimiques des Surfaces [1993] ILPr 5 .... 5.5.1.4, 5.5.2.1.1, 5.5.2.1.2, 5.5.2.2.1, 5.5.2.3, 5.5.3.1.1, 5.5.4.1, 13.4.1.2.3
Case C-89/91 Shearson Lehmann Hutton Inc *v.* TVB Treuhandgesellschaft für Vermögensverwaltung und Beteiligungen mbH [1993] ILPr 199 .... 5.7.2.1
Case C-123/91: Minalmet GmbH *v.* Brandeis Ltd [1993] ILPr 132 .... 9.4.3.4.2.2
Case C-172/91: Sonntag *v.* Waidmann [1993] ILPr 466 .... 3.3.2.1, 3.3.2.4, 3.3.2.5, 9.4.3.4.3.1, 9.4.3.4.3.2, 9.4.4.4.4.2
Case C-125/92: Mulox IBC Ltd *v.* Geels, OJ 1993 C211/18 .... 5.5.3.4.1.1, 5.5.3.4.1.2
Case C-129/92: Owens Bank Ltd *v.* Bracco (unreported); [1992] 2 AC 443 (CA and HL) 5.1.5.2, 5.1.5.3, 5.9.1.3
Case C-314/92: Ladenimor SA *v.* Intercomfinanz SA 5.10.1.2, 7.3.2.2.1

TABLE OF LEGISLATION, RULES, CONVENTIONS ETC.

[Paragraph numbers printed in **bold** indicate where text is quoted]

Statutes, Rules and Regulations

Administration of Justice Act 1920 .... 9.3, 9.3.1.1, 9.3.1.2, 9.3.1.4, 9.3.2, 21.5.1.1
s.9 .... 9.3.1.1
(1) 9.3.1.2, 9.3.1.4
(2) **9.3.1.3**
(3)(a)(5) 9.3.1.1
12(1) 9.3.1.2, 20.5.2
Part II 9.0.1, 9.1.2.1, 9.3, 9.3.1, 9.3.2, 20.1.3.3, 20.5.2, 20.5.3.1, 20.6.2.1
Administration of Justice Act 1956 .... 8.1.2.3.1.1
s.1 .... 8.1.1.2.1
(1) 8.1.1.1.1
Administration of Justice Act 1969—
Part II 9.4.4.4.4.1
Admiralty Act 1840 .... 8.1.1.2.1, 8.1.1.2.2
Admiralty Court Act 1861 .... 8.1.1.2.1, 8.1.1.2.2
Appellate Jurisdiction Act 1876—
s.3 .... 19.4.2.2.3
Arbitration Act 1950 .... 1.2.1.1.2.1, 16.2.2, 16.2.3.1.3.3, 17.5.1.2.3
s.4 .... 16.3.1.3
(1) **18.1.4.2**, 18.2.2.1.1.2, 18.2.2.5.4
(2) 18.2.2.5.1
10 .... 16.2.3.1.2
(3) 3.3.3.4.2.1, 17.5.1.2.4
12(1) 16.2.3.1.4.3
(h) 21.3.2
(2) 17.2.5.2.2
(6) **16.2.3.1.4.1**, 16.2.3.1.4.3, 21.3.2.1.1, 21.3.2.1.2
(a) 17.5.2.1.2
(h) 16.2.3.1.4.2, 17.5.2.1.3, 18.2.3.2, 21.3.2.1, 21.3.2.1.1, 21.3.2.1.2, 21.3.2.2
13(3) 16.2.3.2.2.2
13A **16.2.3.2.1.4**
14 .... **19.2.2**
ss.18(1)(2), 19(1) 16.2.3.2.3
s.22 .... 20.2.1.2.2.2
(1) **16.2.3.2.4.2**
23 .... 17.3.9.3.2, 17.3.9.3.3, 17.5
(1) 16.2.3.2.2.2
(2) **16.2.3.2.4.2**
24(1) 16.2.3.2.2.2
(2) 16.2.3.2.2.1, 18.2.2.4.2.1
(3) 19.5.2.2, 19.5.2.5
25 .... 16.2.3.2.2.2
(2)(b) 16.2.3.2.2.1
Arbitration Act 1950—*cont.*
s.26 .... 16.2.3.1.5, 20.1.2.2, 20.2.2.2.1, 20.2.2.2.2, 20.3.2, 20.4.2.3, 20.5.1.2, 20.5.1.4, 20.5.3.1
(1) **20.1.2.1**
27 .... 15.1.2.1.2, **16.2.3.1.3.3**, 17.1.3
32 .... 18.1.1
35 .... 20.4.1.2
(1) 20.4.2.1
36(1) 20.4.2.3
37(1) **20.4.2.2**
(a)(b)(c) 20.4.2.3
(d) 20.2.3.7.1.1
(2) 20.4.2.3, **20.4.3**
38(1) **20.4.2.3**
(2) 20.4.2.3
40 .... 20.4.1.2
Part I 17.5.2.2.2
II 20.1.3.3, 20.2.3.5.2, 20.2.3.9, 20.3.3.5, 20.3.4.2.1, 20.4, 20.4.1, 20.4.1.1, 20.4.1.2, 20.4.2.1, 20.4.3
Arbitration Act 1975 .. 3.3.3.4.5.7, 16.2.2, 16.2.3.1.5, 16.4.1, 17.3.7.6, 18.2, 18.2.1.1, 18.2.2.1.2.2, 18.2.2.1.2.3, 18.2.2.1.2.4, 18.2.2.1.3.1, 18.2.2.4.1.1, 18.2.2.5.5, 20.1.3.1, 20.1.3.2, 20.1.3.3, 20.2, 20.2.1, 20.2.1.1, 20.2.1.2.1.2, 20.2.1.2.2.2, 20.2.1.2.2.4, 20.2.1.3, 20.2.3.1.2, 20.2.3.7.1.3, 20.2.3.10, 20.3.1, 20.3.4.2.3, 20.4.1.2, 20.4.2.1, 20.5.5.2, 20.6.1.1, 20.6.1.3, 20.6.2.1, **Appendix 4**
s.1 .... 8.1.4.3, 16.3.1.3, 18.2.1.2, 18.2.2, 18.2.2.1, 18.2.2.1.1.1, 18.2.2.1.2.4, 18.2.2.4.1.3, 18.2.2.4.2.4, 18.2.2.5.2, 18.2.2.5.3, 18.2.2.5.4, 18.2.3, 18.2.3.2, 18.3.1, 21.2.4
(1) 3.3.3.4.4, 17.5.2.1.3, **18.2.1.2**, 18.2.2.1, 18.2.2.3.1, 18.2.2.5.1
(2) 18.2.2.1.1.1
(4) **18.2.2.1.1.1**
2 .... 20.2.1.1, 20.2.1.2.1.2, 20.4.1.2, 20.4.2.1
3(1)(a) 20.2.2.2.1
(2) 20.2
4 .... **20.2.2.1**, 20.3.4.2.1
5 .... 20.2.3.1.3
(1) 20.2.3.1.3
(2) .. 20.2.3.1.1, 20.2.3.1.2, 20.2.3.3.3, 20.2.3.4.4, 20.2.3.6.3, 20.2.3.7.2.4

Arbitration Act 1975—*cont.*
s.5(2)(a) 20.2.3.1.1, 20.2.3.2, 20.2.3.2.1, 20.2.3.2.2, 20.2.3.8
(b) ... 18.1.3.2, 20.2.3.1.1, 20.2.3.3, 20.2.3.3.1, 20.2.3.3.2
(c) 20.2.3.1.1, 20.2.3.4, 20.2.3.4.1, 20.2.3.4.2, 20.2.3.4.3, 20.3.4.2.2
(d) ... 18.1.3.2, 20.2.3.1.1, 20.2.3.5, 20.2.3.5.1, 20.2.3.5.2, 20.3.4.2.1
(e) 20.2.3.1.1, 20.2.3.6, 20.2.3.6.1, 20.2.3.6.2, 20.2.3.6.3
(f) 16.4.2.4.2, 20.1.1.2, 20.2.3.1.1, 20.2.3.6.2, 20.2.3.7, 20.2.3.7.1.2, 20.2.3.7.2.1, 20.2.3.7.2.3, 20.2.3.8, 20.2.4.1
(3) 20.2.3.1.1, 20.2.3.1.2, 20.2.3.8, 20.2.3.9
(4) 20.2.3.1.1, 20.2.3.5, **20.2.3.5.4**
(5) .. 20.2.1.2.2.3, 20.2.3.1.1, 20.2.3.1.3, **20.2.4.1**, 20.2.4.2, 20.2.4.4
6 .... 20.3.1
7(1) 18.2.2.1.2.1, 18.2.2.1.3.1, 20.2.1.1, 20.2.1.2.1.2, 20.2.3.3.2
Arbitration Act 1979 .... 1.2.1.1.2.1, 14.1.2.2.4, 16.2.2, 16.2.3.2.4.2, 16.2.3.2.4.6, 16.4.1, 16.4.2.4.4, 17.3.6.1.1, 17.3.9.1, 17.3.9.2, 17.3.9.3.2, 17.4.5, 17.5.1.2.3, 17.5.2.2.4, 19.1.4, 19.1.5, 19.2.2, 19.3.3, 19.5.1.1, 19.5.2.4.4, 20.2.3.7.1.3, 20.2.3.10, **Appendix 5**
s.1 ..... 19.3.1, 19.4.2.2.2, 19.5, 19.5.1.2, 20.2.1.2.2.2
(1) 19.1.4
(2) 17.3.9.2, **19.1.7**, 19.4
(3) **19.1.7**
(b) 19.4.2.2.2, 19.5.2.5
(4) **19.1.7**, 19.3.1
(5) **19.1.7**
(b) 19.5.2.5
(6) **19.1.7**
(6A) **19.1.7**, 19.4, 19.4.1
(7) **19.1.7**, 19.4, 19.4.2, 19.4.2.1, 19.4.2.2.1
(b) 19.4.2.1
(8) **19.1.7**
2 .... 19.1.6
(1)(a) 19.5.2.5
3 .... 19.1.7, 19.5
(1) 19.5.1.1, **19.5.2.5**
(3) 19.5.2.2, 19.5.2.5
(6) 17.3.8.3, 19.5.2.2
(7) **19.5.2.1**, 19.5.2.2
4 .... 19.5
(1) **19.5.2.4.1**, 19.5.2.6.1
(ii) 19.5.2.4.3
(2) 19.5.2.4.1
5(2) 16.2.3.2.1.4
Arbitration Clauses (Protocol) Act 1924 .... 18.2.2.5.1
Arbitration (Commodity Contracts) Order 1979 (S.I. 1979 No. 754) 19.5.2.4.1
Arbitration (Foreign Awards) Act 1930 ..... 20.4.1.1
s.8 .... 18.2.2.5.1
Arbitration (International Investment Disputes) Act 1966 .... 20.1.3.3, 20.5.4, 20.5.4.1
ss.1, 2(1) 20.5.4.3
Banking Act 1987 .... 6.3.3.8
Bills of Exchange Act 1882 .... 10.4.1.2.4.1, 12.9.2
s.2 .... 12.9.2.1.1

Bills of Exchange Act 1882—*cont.*
s.3(1) 12.9.1.1.2
4 .... **12.9.2.2.1**
21 .... 12.9.2.1.1
22 .... **12.9.2.5**
ss.48, 51(2) 12.9.2.3.1
s.72 .... 6.4.4.12.5, 12.9.2, 12.9.2.2.3
(1) **12.9.2.1.1**, 12.9.2.1.2, 12.9.2.1.3, 12.9.2.6
(2) **12.9.2.2.1**, 12.9.2.2.3, 12.9.2.2.4, 12.9.2.2.6, 12.9.2.3.1, 12.9.2.6
(3) **12.9.2.3.2**, 12.9.2.3.3
(5) **12.9.2.4**
ss. 73, 83(1), 89(2) 12.9.1.1.3
Bretton Woods Agreement Act 1945 .... 14.4.2
Bretton Woods Agreements Order in Council 1946 (SR & O 1946 No. 36) .. 14.4.2
British Law Ascertainment Act 1859 .... 23.3.6.1
Carriage by Air Act 1961 .... 1.2.1.1.2.1
Carriage of Goods by Road Act 1965 .... 1.2.1.1.2.1, 18.2.2.4.1.3, 20.5.3.2
Carriage of Goods by Sea Act 1971 .... 5.3.4.3, 11.3.3.2.1, 12.3.2.1, 12.3.2.2
Child Abduction and Custody Act 1985 .... 11.2.3.3.1.1
Sched. 1 .... 11.2.3.3.1.1
Civil Aviation Act 1982—
s.87 .... 8.1.1.1.5
Civil Evidence Act 1972—
s.4(1) **23.3.4**
(2) **23.3.5.2**, 23.3.5.3
(4) 23.3.5.2, **23.3.5.3**
Civil Jurisdiction and Judgments Act 1982 .. 1.2.2.1, 1.2.4.2, 3.1.11, 3.2.1.3.1, 3.3.3.4.5.7, 4.1.3.2, 4.2.3.1.2, 4.3.1.1, 4.3.1.2, 9.4.4.1.2, 9.4.5, 9.5.1.1, 9.5.1.2, 9.5.3.3.1, 20.6.1.3, 20.6.3, 21.3.1.1.2
ss.1–3 .... **Appendix 1**
s.1 .... 9.3
2 .... 3.1.7., 8.2.1.3.2
3 .... **3.2.1.3.1**, 3.2.2.2, 10.3.2.3
(3) 3.1.9, 3.2.1.3.2, 7.1.2.3
3A .... **Appendix 1**
3B .... **3.2.2.2**, **Appendix 1**
4 . **9.4.4.2.1**, 9.4.4.2.3, 9.4.4.3.3, 9.4.4.4.1, 9.4.4.4.3.1, 9.4.4.4.3.4, 9.4.6.2.2, **Appendix 1**
(3) 9.4.6.2.2
5 .... 9.4.4.2.1
6 .... 9.4.4.4.4.1, 9.4.4.5.2, **Appendix 1**
7 .... 9.4.4.2.1, **Appendix 1**
ss.9–11 .... **Appendix 1**
s.9 .... 3.5.3
(1) **3.5.3**
(1A) **3.4.1**
10(2) 7.2.3.1.1
(3) 7.2.4
ss. 16–19 .... **Appendix 1**
s.16(1) **7.1.1.2**
(a) 7.2.2.1, 7.2.2.2.1
(b) 7.1.1.3, 7.2.1.1, 7.2.3.1.1, 7.2.4
(2) 7.1.2.1
(3) **7.1.2.3**
17 .... 7.1.1.3, 7.2.1.2
18 .... 9.5.1.1, 9.5.1.2, 9.5.3.1, 9.5.3.3.2, 20.5.1.3
(1) **9.5.3.1**
(2)(a)(d) 9.5.1.2

Civil Jurisdiction and Judgments Act 1982—*cont.*
s.18(2)(e) 9.5.3.1, **20.5.1.2**
(3)(b) 9.5.1.2
(4)(b) 9.5.1.2
(5)(d) 9.5.1.2, 21.5.1.2
(8) 9.5.3.1, 20.5.1.4
19 .... 9.5.1.1, 9.5.1.2, 9.5.3.1, 20.5.1.3
(1) **9.5.2.1**, 9.5.2.2
(2) 9.5.1.2
(3) 9.5.1.2
(b) 20.5.1.3
25 .... 5.8.2, 5.9.2.3.5, 21.3.1.1.5, 21.3.1.2, 21.3.1.2.1, 21.3.1.2.1.2, 21.3.1.2.1.3, 21.3.1.2.2, 21.3.1.2.4.1, 21.3.1.3.2, 21.3.1.3.3, **Appendix 1**
(1) 6.3.3.2, 7.2.5, **21.3.1.2.1.2**, 21.3.1.2.1.3, 21.3.1.2.2, 21.4.2.2.2
(2) **21.3.1.2.1.2**
(3) 21.3.1.2.1.2
26 .... 8.1.4.3, 18.2.3.2, **21.2.2**, 21.2.3, 21.2.6, 21.2.7, **Appendix 1**
(1) 21.3.1.3.3
(a)(b) 21.2.4
(2) 21.2.7
ss. 30–34 .... **Appendix 1**
s.30 .... **6.6.4**
31(1) **9.6.2**
(3) 9.6.2
32 .... 3.3.3.4.5.2, 3.3.3.4.5.7, 9.2.7.5, **9.2.7.5.1**, 9.2.7.5.4, 9.3.1.4, 9.3.2.2.2.3, 9.4.3.2.7, 9.5.2.1, 20.6.1.2, 20.6.1.3, 20.6.1.4
(1) 9.4.3.2.7, 9.4.3.2.8, 22.2.2.6
(a) 9.2.7.5.2, 9.2.7.5.3
(2) 9.2.7.5.2, 9.4.3.2.7
(3) 9.2.7.5.3, 9.4.3.2.7
(4) 9.4.3.2.7
(a)(b) 9.2.7.5.4
33 .... **9.2.5.2.1**, 9.2.5.2.2, 9.2.5.2.3
34 .... **9.1.3.1**, 9.1.3.2, 9.1.3.3, 9.1.3.4, 9.2.6.2.1, 20.6.2.3, 20.6.3
ss. 41–46 .... 1.2.3, 6.3.3.1, **Appendix 1**
s.41 .... 4.1.1.1.2, 4.1.1.3
(2) **4.1.1.2.1**, 4.1.1.3
(3)(4)(5) 4.1.1.2.2
(6) 4.1.1.2.1, 4.1.1.2.2
(7) **4.1.1.3**
42 .... 4.1.3.3, 7.2.1.2, 11.2.3.3.2
(1) 4.1.2.1
(3) 4.1.2.1, **4.1.2.2.1**, 4.1.2.2.2
(4)(5)(6)(7) 4.1.2.1, **4.1.2.2.3**
43 .... 4.1.4, 5.1.2.1, 7.2.1.2
44 .... 4.1.4, 5.7.1.1, 5.7.2.3.2
45 .... 7.2.3.1.1
(3) 5.5.6.2
ss. 49–51 .... **Appendix 1**
s.49 .... 5.9.3.5, **5.10**, 7.3, **7.3.2**, 7.3.2.1, 7.3.2.2.1, 8.1.4.3
50 .... 9.2.7.5.4, 9.5.1.2, 9.5.2.1
54 .... 9.3.2.2.2.3
Part I 9.0.2
II 9.0.3, 9.5.1.1, 9.5.2.2, 9.5.2.3, 9.5.3.1, 20.1.3.3, 20.5.1, 20.5.1.1, 20.5.1.2, 20.5.1.4, 20.6.2.1, 21.5.1.2

Civil Jurisdiction and Judgments Act 1982—*cont.*
Sched. 1 .... **Appendix 1**
Arts. 16, 17 .... 4.3.1.1
Sched. 2 .... 3.2.1.1.1, **Appendix 1**
3C .... **Appendix 1**
4 .... 3.3.1.2, 4.3.1.1, 6.6.4, 7.1.1.2, 7.1.2.3, **Appendix 1**
5 .... 7.1.1.3, **Appendix 1**
para. 2 .... 7.2.12
6 .... 9.5.1.1, 9.5.3.1, 9.5.3.2, 9.5.3.3.1, 20.5.1.2, **Appendix 1**
para. 1 .... 9.5.3.2.1
para. 2 .... 9.5.3.2.1
(2)(e) 20.5.1.2
para. 3 .... 9.5.3.2.2, 9.5.3.3.2
para. 4 .... 9.5.3.2.2
paras. 5, 6 .... 9.5.3.2.3, 20.5.1.2
paras. 7, 8 .... 9.5.3.2.3
para. 9 .... 9.5.3.2.4
para. 10 .... 9.5.3.2.4
(b) 9.5.2.1
7 .... 9.5.1.1, 9.5.3.1, 9.5.3.3, 9.5.3.3.1, 20.5.1.2, **Appendix 1**
para. 1 .... 9.5.3.3.1
para. 2 .... 9.5.3.3.2
(2)(e) 20.5.1.2
paras. 3, 4 .... 9.5.3.3.2
para. 5 .... 9.5.3.3.2, 20.5.1.2
(5) 9.5.3.3.3
para. 6 .... 9.5.3.3.2, 20.5.1.2
para. 7 .... 9.5.3.3.2
para. 8 .... 9.5.3.3.3
para. 9 .... 9.5.3.3.3
(b) 9.5.2.1
14 .... 9.3.2.2.2.3
Civil Jurisdiction and Judgments Act 1982 (Amendment) Order 1989 (SI 1989 No. 1346) 3.1.8
Civil Jurisdiction and Judgments Act 1982 (Amendment) Order 1990 (SI 1990 No. 2591) 3.1.8
Civil Jurisdiction and Judgments Act 1991 3.1.11
Civil Jurisdiction and Judgments Act 1991 (Commencement Order) 1992 (SI 1992 No. 745) 3.1.11
Civil Jurisdiction and Judgments (Authentic Instruments and Court Settlements) Order 1993 (SI 1993 No. 604) 9.4.5
Companies Act 1985 .... 5.10.1.3, 6.1.2.1, 6.1.2.2.3, 6.1.2.2.5, 6.1.2.4.1, 6.1.2.4.2, 6.1.3.1
s.690A 2.1.4.1.1, 6.1.2.2.3, 6.1.2.3, 6.1.2.3.3, 6.1.2.5.1, 6.1.2.5.2, 6.1.2.5.3, 6.1.2.5.5, 6.1.2.6.1, 6.1.2.6.3
(1) 6.1.2.2.3
(2) 6.1.2.5.1, 6.1.2.5.3
B 6.1.2.2.4
691 .... 2.1.4.1.1, 6.1.2.2.3, 6.1.2.4, 6.1.2.5.1, 6.1.2.6.1, 6.1.2.6.2, 6.1.2.6.3
(1) 6.1.2.2.3, **6.1.2.6.1**
692A 6.1.2.2.4
(4) 6.1.2.5.1

Companies Act 1985—*cont.*
s.694A 6.1.2.2.3, 6.1.2.5, 6.1.2.5.4, 6.1.2.6.3
(2) **6.1.2.5.2**, 6.1.2.5.3
(3) 2.1.4.1.1, **6.1.2.5.2**, 6.1.2.5.3
(4) 6.1.2.5.5
695 .... 6.1.2.2.3, 6.1.2.6, 6.1.2.6.1, **6.1.2.6.2**, 6.1.2.6.3, 6.1.2.6.4, 11.2.3.3.3
(1) 6.1.2.6.3, 6.1.2.6.4
(2) 2.1.4.1.1, 6.1.2.6.3
698(2)(b) 6.1.2.3.1
725(1)(2)(3) 6.1.2.1
744 .... **6.1.2.2.2**
Part XXIII 6.1.2.2.1, 6.1.2.2.3, 6.1.2.3.1, 11.2.3.3.3
Sched. 21A 6.1.2.5.1
para. 1 .... 6.1.2.5.1, 6.1.2.5.2
para. 3(e) 6.1.2.5.1, 6.1.2.5.2
21B 6.1.2.5.1
Consular Relations Act 1968 .... 2.4.2.1, 2.4.2.2
Consumer Protection Act 1987 .... 13.3.3.1.3
Contracts (Applicable Law) Act 1990 .... 1.3.3, 6.3.3.4.4.1, 10.0.1, 10.2, 10.2.1.2, 10.2.2.1, 10.3.2.1, 10.4.1.1.4, 11.4.10.2.3, 12.3.2.1, 12.9.1.3, 13.4.1.3, 23.1.3, **Appendix 3**
s.2(1) 10.2.1.3
(2) 10.2.1.3, 11.3.3.1, 11.4.9
(3) 10.4.2.2
3 .... **10.3.2.3**
Contracts (Applicable Law) Act 1990 (Commencement No. 1) Order 1991 (SI 1991 No. 707) 10.3.1.2
Copyright, Designs and Patents Act 1988—
s.90(3) 12.6.2.2
Criminal Justice Act 1988—
Part VI 6.3.3.8
Diplomatic Privileges Act 1964 .... 2.4.1, 2.4.1.4, 2.4.1.5, 2.5.1
s.2(1) 2.4.1
(3) 2.4.1.4
(6) 2.4.1.1
Sched. 1 .... 2.4.1
Domicile and Matrimonial Proceedings Act 1974 .... 11.2.3.3.1.1
Drug Trafficking Offences Act 1986 .... 6.3.3.8
Employment Protection (Consolidation) Act 1978 .... 11.3.3.2.1, 12.2.4.1
ss.33, 140(1)(2), 141 .... 12.2.4.1
European Communities Act 1972—
s.3 .... 23.1.1
European Communities (Enforcement of Community Judgments) Order 1972 (SI 1972 No. 1590) 9.6.3
Evidence (Colonial Statutes) Act 1907 .... 23.3.6.1
Exchange Control Act 1947 .... 14.4.1.1
Family Law Act 1986 .... 11.2.3.3.1.1
Financial Services Act 1986 .... 6.3.3.8
Foreign Corporations Act 1991 .... 2.1.3.2
s.1 .... **2.1.3.2**
(1)(b) 2.1.3.3
Foreign Judgments (Reciprocal Enforcement) Act 1933 .... 9.0.1, 9.0.2, 9.1.2.1, 9.2.7.5.4, 9.3, 9.3.2, 9.3.2.1.1, 9.3.2.2.2.2, 9.3.2.2.3, 9.3.2.2.6, 9.3.2.2.7, 9.3.2.2.8, 9.6.2, 20.5.3.1, 20.5.3.2, 20.6.2.1, 21.5.1.1
Foreign Judgments (Reciprocal Enforcement) Act 1993—*cont.*
s.1(2)(a)(b)(c)(2A)(3) 9.3.2.1.1
2(1) 9.3.2.1.2
provisos (a)(b) 9.3.2.1.3
(2)(4) 9.3.2.1.3
4 .... 9.3.2.2
(1) 20.5.3.1
(a)(i) 9.3.2.2.1
(ii) 9.3.2.2.2.1
(iii) **9.3.2.2.3**
(iv) 9.3.2.2.4
(v) 9.3.2.2.5
(vi) 9.3.2.2.1
(b) 9.3.2.2.6
(2) **9.3.2.2.2.1**, 9.3.2.2.2.3
(a) 9.3.2.2.2.2
(3) 9.3.2.2.2.1, 9.3.2.2.2.3
(b) 9.3.2.2.2.3
5(1)(2) 9.3.2.2.7
6 .... **9.3.2**, 20.5.3.3
8(1) 9.3.2.3
10A 20.5.3.3
Part I 9.3.2.2.1, 20.1.3.3, 20.5.3, 20.5.3.1
Foreign Limitation Periods Act 1984 .... 1.3.5, 13.3.3.1.4, Chap. 15
s.1 .... 11.4.8.3, **15.1.1.1**, 15.1.1.2, 15.1.1.5, 15.1.2.1.1, 15.1.2.1.3, 15.1.2.1.4, 15.2
(1) 15.2
(a) 15.1.1.4, 15.1.1.5
(2) 15.1.1.3
(3)(4)(5) 15.1.1.2
2 ..... **15.1.1.5**, 15.1.2.1.2, 15.1.2.1.3, 15.1.2.3, 15.2
(1) 15.1.2.2
(2) 13.3.3.1.4, 15.1.2.1, 15.1.2.1.1, 15.1.2.1.3, 15.1.2.1.4, 15.1.2.2
3 .... **9.2.4.2**
4 .... **15.1.1.4**
(2) 15.1.1.2
(3) 15.1.1.5
ss.5, 6, 7(3)(a)(b) 15.1
Friendly Societies Act 1992 .... 12.8.3
s.101 .... 12.8.1.3, 12.8.3
116 .... 12.8.3
Sched. 20 .... 12.8.1.3, 12.8.3
GAFTA Arbitration Rules—
r.8 .... 19.1.1
8.2 .... 20.2.3.7.1.3
Hague-Visby Rules 5.3.4.3, 12.3.2.1, 12.3.2.2
Art. III, para. 8 .... **12.3.2.2**
Hovercraft Act 1968—
s.2(1) 8.0.2
ICC Rules 17.2.1.4, 17.2.5.1.4, 18.2.2.1.1.3, 18.2.2.1.2.2, 19.5.1.2, 20.2.3.5.3, 20.2.3.9.2.1, 20.3.4.2.2
Art. 13(3) **17.3.4.7**
22 .... 20.2.1.2.2.1
24(1) 19.5.1.1
(2) **19.5.1.1**
Insolvency Act 1986—
s.426 .... 9.5.1.2
Insurance Companies Act 1982 .... 12.8.2
s.94B 12.8.1.3
96A(3) 10.4.1.2.2.2

Insurance Companies Act 1982—*cont.*
Sched. 2, Pt. I 12.8.2.1
3A 12.8.1.3, 12.8.2, 12.8.3
para. 1(1) 12.8.2.1
para. 1(2) 12.8.2.1
para. 1(3) 12.8.2.1
para. 1(4) 12.8.2.1
para. 1(5) 12.8.2.1
para. 1(6) 12.8.2.1
para. 2(1) 12.8.2.1
para. 2(2) 12.8.2.1
para. 2(4) 12.8.2.1
para. 3(1) 12.8.2.1
para. 6 .... 12.8.2.2
para. 7 .... 12.8.2.2
para. 8 .... 12.8.2.2
International Organisations Act 1968 .... 2.1.4.1.2, 2.5.1, 2.5.3
s.1 .... 2.1.4.2.2
International Organisations Act 1981 .... 2.5.1
International Tin Council (Immunities and Privileges Order 1972) (SI 1972 No. 120) 2.1.4.2.2, 2.1.4.2.3
Art. 5 .... 2.1.4.2.2
Judgments Extension Act 1868 .... 9.5.1.1
LCIA Arbitration Rules—
Art. 5(2) **20.2.3.4.3**
7(2) 17.2.4.3
16(8) 19.5.1.2
Landlord and Tenant Act 1985—
ss.11(1)(a), 12(1), 13(1) 11.3.1.4
Law of Property (Miscellaneous Provisions) Act 1989—
s.2 .... 11.4.3.1.1
Law Reform (Miscellaneous Provisions) (Scotland) Act 1990—
s.66 .... 16.4.2.4.4
Sched. 7 .... 16.4.2.4.4
Law Reform (Personal Injuries) Act 1948—
s.1(3) 12.2.2.1.1, **12.2.4.2**, 13.4.2.3.2, 13.4.2.3.4
Limitation Act 1980—
s.5 .... 16.2.3.1.3.2
34(1)(3)(4) 16.2.3.1.3.1
35 .... 15.1.1.1
Maintenance Orders Act 1950—
s.22(2) 23.2
Marine Insurance Act 1906 .... 11.1.3.1.2
Sched. 1 .... 11.1.3.1.1
Matrimonial Causes Act 1973 .... 11.2.3.3.1.1
Merchant Shipping Act 1894 .... 8.1.1.1.10
s.1 .... 11.2.3.3.4.1
55 .... 8.1.1.1.10
ss.544–546 .... 8.1.1.1.6
Merchant Shipping Act 1974—
Part I 8.1.1.1.4
Merchant Shipping Act 1979 .... 8.1.1.1.10
Merchant Shipping (Oil Pollution) Act 1971 .... 1.2.1.1.2.1, 8.1.1.1.4
Nuclear Installations Act 1965 .... 6.3.3.8
Overseas Companies and Credit and Financial Institutions (Branch Disclosure) Regulations 1992 (SI 1992 No. 3179) 6.1.2.2.3
Patents Act 1977—
s.44(1) 11.3.1.5
Police Act 1964—
s.48(1) 13.3.3.1.3
Protection of Trading Interests Act 1980 .... 9.2.7.6.1, 9.3.1.4, 9.3.2.2.8
s.5 .... 9.2.7.6.1, 9.2.7.6.2, 9.3.2.1.2, 9.3.2.2.8
(1)(a)(b)(3)(4) 9.2.7.6.2
6 .... 9.2.7.6.2
Protection of Trading Interests (Australian Trade Practices) Order 1988 (SI 1988 No. 569) 9.2.7.6.2
Road Traffic Act 1988—
s.151 .... 5.7.1.1.3.3
Sale of Goods Act 1979—
s.12(1) 11.3.1.4
Social Security Act 1975 .... 6.3.3.8
State Immunity Act 1978 .... 2.3.1.3, 2.3.3. *et seq*, 2.5.1, 9.6.1.1, 9.6.2
s.1(1) **2.3.3.1**, 2.3.4.6
ss.2–11 .... 2.3.3.2, 2.3.4, 9.6.1.1, 9.6.2
2 .... 2.3.4.3.5, 2.3.5.3.2
(1)(2) 2.3.4.1.1
(3)(4)(a)(b)(5) 2.3.4.1.2
(6)(7) 2.3.4.1.3
ss.3–5 .... 2.3.4.3.5
s.3(1) **2.3.4.4.1**, 2.3.4.4.2
(2) **2.3.4.4.1**
(3) 2.3.4.3.3, **2.3.4.4.2**, 2.3.5.4.6
4(1) 2.3.4.5.1
(2) **2.3.4.5.1**
(a) 2.3.4.5.2
(3) **2.3.4.5.1**, 2.3.4.5.2
(4) **2.3.4.5.1**
5 .... 2.3.4.6
6 .... 2.3.4.7.2
(1) **2.3.4.7.1**
(b) 2.3.4.7.2, 2.3.4.7.3
(4) 2.3.4.7.4
7 .... 2.3.4.8
8 .... 2.3.4.9
9 .... 2.3.4.2, 2.3.4.3.5
(1) **2.3.4.2**
(2) 2.3.4.2
10 .... 2.3.4.3.1, 2.3.4.3.3, 2.3.4.3.4, 2.3.5.4.1
(1) 2.3.4.3.1, 2.3.4.3.5
(2) **2.3.4.3.2**, 2.3.4.3.4
(3) 2.3.4.3.2
(4) **2.3.4.3.3**, 2.3.4.3.4
(5) 2.3.4.3.3
(6) 2.3.4.3.5
11 .... 2.3.4.10
12 .... 2.3.3.2, 2.3.6, 9.6.1.2
(1) **2.3.6.1.1**, 2.3.6.1.2, 2.3.6.1.3, 2.3.6.1.5, 2.3.6.1.6, 2.3.6.2, 2.3.6.3
(2) **2.3.6.2**, 2.3.6.3
(3) 2.3.6.1.2
(4)(5) **2.3.6.3**
(6) 2.3.6.1.1., 2.3.6.2, 2.3.6.3
(7) 2.3.6, 2.3.6.1.6
13 .... 2.3.3.2, 2.3.4.2, 2.3.5.1.1, 2.3.5.1.2
(1) 2.3.5.2, **2.3.5.2.1**, 2.3.5.5.1, 2.3.5.5.2
(a) 2.3.5.2.2

State Immunity Act 1978—*cont.*
s.13(2) 2.3.5.2, **2.3.5.2.2**, 2.3.5.3.1, 2.3.5.3.2, 2.3.5.4.1, 2.3.5.5.1, 2.3.5.5.2
(a) 2.3.4.7.2
(b) 2.3.5.4.1, 2.3.5.4.5
(3) 2.3.5.2.2, **2.3.5.3.1**, 2.3.5.3.2, 2.3.5.5.1, 2.3.5.5.2
(4) 2.3.5.2.2, **2.3.5.4.1**, 2.3.5.4.3, 2.3.5.4.4, 2.3.5.4.5, 2.3.5.4.7, 2.3.5.5.1, 2.3.5.5.2
(5) 2.3.5.3.1, 2.3.5.4.3, 2.3.5.4.4
14 .... 2.3.2.1, 2.3.3.2, 2.3.5.1.1, 2.3.5.1.2
(1) **2.3.2.1**, 2.3.5.5.1
(2) 2.3.2.1, 2.3.5.5.1, 2.3.5.5.2
(3) **2.3.5.5.1**
(4) **2.3.5.5.2**
16 .... 2.3.4.7.1, 2.3.4.7.2, 2.3.4.7.3
17(1) 2.3.4.3.3, 2.3.5.4.6, 2.3.5.4.7
18 .... 9.6.1.1
(1) 9.6.1.1
(b) 2.3.5.4.1, 2.3.5.4.2
19(1) 9.6.1.2
(2) 9.6.1.3
21(c) 2.3.5.4.2
23(3) 2.3.1.3
Statute of Frauds 1677 .... 11.4.3.1.2
s.4 .... 11.4.3.1.2, 11.4.3.1.3
Supreme Court of Judicature Act 1873 .... 8.1.1.2.1
Supreme Court Act 1981 .... 2.3.4.3.1, 8.0.1, 8.1, 8.1.1.2.1, 8.2.1.3.1, 8.2.2.1, 8.2.2.2, 8.2.2.3, 8.2.2.4, 21.2.3
s.18(1) 6.3.1.2
ss.20–24 .... 8.1.1, 8.2.2.1
s.20 .... 8.1.1, **Appendix 2**
(1)(a)(b) 8.1.1.1, 8.1.1.1.1
(c) 8.1.1.2, 8.1.1.2.1, 8.1.1.3
(d) 8.1.1.3
(2) 8.1.1.1.1
(a)(b) **8.1.1.1.2**, 8.1.2.1
(c) **8.1.1.1.2**, 8.1.2.1, 8.1.2.2.2
(d) **8.1.1.1.2**, 8.1.1.1.3, 8.1.3.1
(e) **8.1.1.1.3**, 8.1.1.1.4, 8.1.2.2.1, 8.1.2.3, 8.1.2.4, 8.1.3.2, 8.1.4.1.4
(f) **8.1.1.1.4**, 8.1.2.3, 8.1.3.2, 8.1.4.1.4
(g) **8.1.1.1.4**, 8.1.2.3, 8.1.4.1.4
(h) **8.1.1.1.4**, 8.1.1.1.5, 8.1.2.3, 8.1.4.1.4
(j) **8.1.1.1.5**, 8.1.1.1.6, 8.1.2.2.1, 8.1.2.3, 8.1.2.4, 8.1.4.1.4, 8.2.4.1
(k)(l) **8.1.1.1.6**, 8.1.2.3, 8.1.4.1.4
(m) **8.1.1.1.6**, 8.1.1.1.7, 8.1.2.3, 8.1.4.1.4
(n) **8.1.1.1.7**, 8.1.2.3, 8.1.4.1.4
(o) **8.1.1.1.7**, 8.1.1.1.8, 8.1.2.2.1, 8.1.2.3, 8.1.2.4, 8.1.4.1.4
(p) **8.1.1.1.8**, 8.1.1.1.9, 8.1.2.2.1, 8.1.2.3, 8.1.2.4, 8.1.4.1.4
(q) 8.1.1.1.9, 8.1.2.3, 8.1.4.1.4
(r) 8.1.1.1.9, 8.1.2.2.1, 8.1.2.3, 8.1.2.4, 8.1.4.1.4
(s) 8.1.1.1.9, 8.1.2.1
(3) 8.1.1.1.1, **8.1.1.1.10**, 8.1.3.1
(b)(c) 8.1.3.1
(4) 8.1.1.1.2
(5) 8.1.1.4
(6) 8.1.1.1.5
(7) 8.1.1

Supreme Court Act 1981—*cont.*
s.21 .... 8.1.1.1.3, 8.2.2.3, **Appendix 2**
(1) 2.3.4.3.1, 8.1.3, 8.1.3.1
(2) 8.1.2, 8.1.2.1, 8.1.2.2.2, 8.1.2.3, 8.1.4.1.4
(3) 8.1.2, 8.1.2.2, 8.1.2.2.2, 8.1.2.3, 8.1.2.4, 8.1.4.1.4
(4) 8.1.2, **8.1.2.3**, 8.1.2.3.1.1, 8.1.2.3.3, 8.1.2.3.4.2, 8.1.2.3.4.4, 8.1.2.3.4.5, 8.1.2.4, 8.1.3.2, 8.1.4.1.4
(b) 8.1.2.3.4.1
(i) 8.1.2.3.2
(ii) 8.1.2.3.3
(5) 8.0.2, 8.1.2
(6) 8.1.2
(7) 8.1.2.3.1.2
(8) 8.1.2, 8.1.4.1.4
22 .... 2.3.4.3.1, 8.1.3, 8.1.3.1, 8.2.2.3, **Appendix 2**
(2) 8.1.3.1
23 .... 8.1.1, **Appendix 2**
24 .... **Appendix 2**
37(1) 16.2.3.1.4.3, 17.5.2.1.3, 18.2.3.2, **21.1.1.2**, 21.1.3.2.1, 21.1.3.2.2, 21.1.3.4.2, 21.3.1.1.3, 21.3.1.1.4, 21.3.1.1.5, 21.3.1.3.1, 21.3.2, 21.3.2.2, 21.4.1.1
(3) **21.1.3.2.2**, 21.4.1.3, 21.4.1.5
69(5) **23.1.2**
Third Parties (Rights Against Insurers) Act 1930 .... 5.7.1.1.3.3
UNCITRAL Arbitration Rules 16.3.2.1, 16.4.2.3, 16.4.2.3.2, 16.4.2.3.3, 17.2.5.1.5, 17.3.4.5, 17.3.4.6, 19.5.1.2, 20.5.5.1
Arts. 15–30 .... 17.2.5.1.2
16–30 .... 17.2.5.1.3
Art. 15(1) **17.2.5.1.2**
16(4) 20.2.1.2.2.1
23 .... **17.2.5.1.3**
26(1) **16.2.3.1.4.2**
33(1) **17.3.4.5**
(2) **17.3.6.1.1**
Unfair Contract Terms Act 1977 .... 11.3.3.2.1, 11.3.3.2.2, 12.1.2.2.1, 12.1.3.3
ss.2–7 .... 11.3.3.2.2
s.2 .... 13.2.4.2
(1) 11.3.3.2.3
6(1)(a) 11.3.1.4
26 .... 11.3.3.2.2
27 .... 11.3.3.2.2
(1) 11.3.3.2.2
(2) 11.3.3.2.2, 11.3.3.2.3, 12.1.3.1, 12.1.3.2, 12.1.3.3
(b) 12.1.3.3

AUSTRALIA
Trade Practices Act 1974—
s.81(1A) 9.2.7.6.2

FRANCE
Civil Code 11.1.3, 11.1.3.4
Art. 14 .... 1.1.6, 4.2.2.3, 9.4.1.3.2
Code of Civil Procedure—
Arts. 1496, 1497 .... 17.3.2.2

GERMANY
Basic Law—
Art. 34 .... 13.3.3.1.3

Civil Code—
para. 242 .... 14.1.2.1.1
Code of Civil Procedure—
para. 1035 .... 17.2.5.2.2
Social Security Act—
s.636 .... 13.3.3.2.4

INDIA
Arbitration Act 1940 .... 17.2.4.2

NETHERLANDS, THE
Code of Civil Procedure 9.4.6.1.1
Art. 1054(2) 17.3.2.2, 17.3.4.1
(3) 17.3.2.2

REPUBLIC OF SOUTH AFRICA
Status of Ciskei Act 1981 .... 2.1.5.6
s.1 .... 2.1.5.2

SWITZERLAND
Code des obligations 17.3.9.3.3
Private International Law Act—
Art. 187(2) 17.3.2.2

UNITED ARAB EMIRATES
Federal Decree No 35 .... 2.1.4.3.3

USA
Clayton Act 22.2.1.7
Sherman Act 22.2.1.7

Directives

Dir. 76/308 EEC, 15 March 1976 .... 6.3.3.8
Dir. 88/357 EEC, OJ 1988 L172/1 (Second Non-life Directive)—
Art. 7 .... 12.8.1.3
Dir. 89/666 EEC, OJ 1989 L395/36 (Eleventh Company Law Directive) 6.1.2.2.3, 6.1.2.3.1, 6.1.2.3.2, 6.1.2.5.4
Art. 2(1)(e) 6.1.2.5.4
Dir. 90/619 EEC, OJ 1990 L330/50 (Second Life Directive)—
Art. 4 .... 12.8.1.3

Rules of the Supreme Court

Ord. 2, r.1 .... 6.1.2.2.5
6, r.7 .... 4.3.1.3
(1)(b) 4.3.1.3
Ords. 10–12 .... 1.2.1.1.2.1
Ord. 10 .... 6.1.1.2.4
r.1 .... 6.1.3.2
(1) 6.1.1.1, 6.1.1.1.1, 6.1.1.1.3
(2) 6.1.1.2, **6.1.1.2.1**, 6.1.1.2.2, 6.1.1.2.4, 6.1.1.2.5, 6.1.3.2, 6.2.1.2
(3) **6.1.1.2.1**
(a)(b)(i) 6.1.1.2.5
(4) 6.1.1.1.3
(5) 6.1.1.1.3, 6.2.3.3
r.3 .... 6.1.1.1.3, 6.3.3.4.5
(1) 6.2.2
(a) 6.1.1.2.4, 6.1.3.2
(2) 6.2.2
r.5 .... Chap. 6, preamble
Ord. 11 .. 6.1.3.2, 6.1.3.3, 6.3.1, 6.3.1.1.1, 6.3.1.1.2, 6.3.3.2, 6.3.3.4.1.3, 6.3.3.4.4.1, 6.3.3.6, 6.3.3.9.1, 6.3.3.9.3, 6.3.3.9.4, 6.4, 6.4.2.1, 6.4.2.3, 6.4.2.5, 6.4.3, 6.4.4.2.3, 6.4.4.4.1, 6.4.4.7, 6.4.4.8, 6.4.4.12.3, 6.5.2.1, 6.6.3, 8.1.4.2, 13.1.3.1, 13.4.1.2.1, 17.5.1.2.2, 17.5.1.2.4, 21.3.1.1.2, 21.4.1.2, 21.4.2.2.1
r.1 ... 2.3.6.1.6, 5.9.1.4.3, 21.3, 21.3.1.2.1.3
(1) 1.2.2.1, 1.2.2.2, 4.2.2.3, 4.2.3.1.2, 4.2.3.2.4, 5.5.1.3, 5.6.1.2, 5.6.2.4, 6.3, 6.3.1, 6.3.1.1.3, 6.3.3, 6.3.3.9.1, 6.3.3.9.2, 9.2.5.2.2, 9.2.5.6, 9.4.1.3.2, 13.1.1.1, 13.1.3.1, 17.5.1.2.1, 17.5.1.2.2, 21.3.1.1.2, 21.4.1.2
(a) 6.3.2.4, **6.3.3.1**, 17.5.1.2.2
(b) **6.3.3.2**, 9.2.5.2.2, 17.5.1.2.2, 21.3, 21.3.1.1.1, 21.3.1.1.2, 21.3.1.2.1.3
(c) .. 5.6.1.2, 5.6.2.4, 6.1.3.3, 6.3.1.2, **6.3.3.3**, 6.3.3.3.1, 6.3.3.3.2, 6.3.3.3.3, 6.3.3.3.4, 6.4.4.3.1, 6.4.4.3.2, 6.4.4.3.3, 17.5.1.2.2
(d) 4.2.3.2.4, **6.3.3.4**, 6.3.3.4.1.1, 6.3.3.4.1.2, 6.3.3.4.1.3, 17.5.1.2.2
(i) 6.3.2.3, 6.3.3.4.2.2, 6.3.3.4.2.3, 6.3.3.4.3.1, 6.3.3.9.1, 17.5.1.2.2
(ii) 6.3.3.4.3.1
(iii) 5.3.2.3.1, 6.3.3.4.4.2, 6.4.4.10.1, 6.4.4.12.2, 11.1.3.1.1, 13.4.1.2.1, 17.5.1.2.2
(iv) 4.2.3.2.4, 5.3.3.5, 6.2.1.3, 6.3.3.4.5, 6.5.3.1, 6.5.3.2, 6.5.3.3
(e) **6.3.3.5**, 6.3.3.9.1
(f) 4.2.3.2.4, **6.3.3.6**, 13.1.1.1
(g)–(s) **6.3.3.8**
(m) 17.5.1.3, 20.2.2.2.2
(t) **6.3.3.7**
(2) 4.2.3.1.2, 4.3.1.2, 5.3.3.5, 6.3.3.1, 6.3.3.4.5, 6.5.1.1, 7.2.5, 21.3.1.2.1.3
(a) **4.3.1.1**
(i) 7.3.1.1, 7.3.1.2
(b) 1.2.1.1.2.1
(4) 6.3.3.1
r.3(3) 6.2.2
r.4(1) 6.3.12
(a)(b)(c)(d) 6.3.3.3.3
(2) 6.3.1.1.1, 8.1.4.2
r.7(4) 2.3.6.1.1, 2.3.6.1.2
r.9 .... 2.3.6.1.1, Chap. 6, preamble
12 .... 6.2.3.4
r.1(1) 5.2.4, 6.2.3.3
r.8 .... 6.2.3.4, 6.2.3.5, 6.3.1.2
(1) 5.2.4
r.9 .... Chap. 6, preamble
(1) 21.3.1.2.1.3
r.10 .... 5.2.4, 18.2.2.3.1
13 .... 5.2.4
14 .... 18.2.2.5.2, 18.2.2.5.4, 18.2.2.5.6, 18.2.2.5.7
r.1(1) 18.2.2.5.2
16, r.3(4) 6.3.3.3.1
23 .... 9.4.4.2.3
28, r.8 .... 20.1.2.2

Ord. 29, r.2(1) 21.1.1.1
38, r.7 .... 23.3.5.3
39, r.13 .... 23.3.6.2
47, r.1 .... 9.4.6.2.2
48 .... 21.1.3.4.1.4, 21.4.1.4
r.1 .... 21.1.3.4.1.4, 21.3.1.2.3.2
58, r.1 .... 6.3.1.2
65, r.3 .... 6.1.2.1
r.4 .... 6.1.1.1.3
71 .... 9.4.4.1.2
rr.1–13 .... 9.3.1.2
rr.2(1), 3(1), 5(1), 7(1)(2)(3), 9(1) 9.3.2.12
rr.15–24 .... 9.6.3
r.27 .... 9.4.4.2.1
r.28 .... 9.4.4.2.2.6
r.29 .... 9.4.4.2.3
rr.30(1)(2), 32 .... 9.4.4.3.3
r.33(1) 9.4.4.4.1, 9.4.4.5.1.1
(2) 9.4.4.4.1
(b) 9.4.4.5.1.1
(3) 9.4.4.4.1
r.34 .... 9.4.4.4.3.1
(3) 9.4.4.4.3.5
(4) 9.4.4.4.3.4
r.37(1)(2) 9.5.3.2.3
r.38(1)(2) 9.5.3.3.2
r.39 .... 9.5.3.2.1
73 .... 1.2.1.1.2.1, 17.5.1.2.4
r.7 .... 17.5.1.2.4
(1) 17.5.1.2.3
(1A) 17.5.1.3, 20.2.2.2.1
r.10(1)(5)(6)(7) 20.2.2.2.1
75 .... 8.1.4
r.2(2) 8.1.4.2
r.4 .... 8.1.3.1
(1) 8.1.3.1
r.5 .... 21.2.1, 21.2.5
r.8(1) 8.1.4.1.1, 8.1.4.1.2
(a) 8.1.4.1.1
(b) 8.1.4.1.2
r.10 .... 21.2.1
(2) 8.1.4.1.3
(5) 8.1.4.1.2
r.11 .... 8.2.2.4
(1)(2) 8.1.4.1.2
76 .... 6.3.3.8
81 .... 6.1.3
r.1 .... 6.1.3.1, 6.1.3.3
r.3(1) **6.1.3.1**, 6.1.3.3
(a)(b)(c) 6.1.3.2

Conventions, Protocols, Agreements etc.

Accession Convention of 1978 ..... 3.1.6, 3.1.7, 3.1.9, 3.2.1.3.1, 3.3.3.4.5.2, 5.1.1.3.3, 5.3.3.3.1, 5.5.1.2, 5.6.1.1, 5.7.1, 5.7.1.3, 5.7.1.3.5.3, 8.2.4.1, 9.4.3.8.2, 12.4.1.3
Accession Convention of 1982 3.1.8, 3.1.9, 3.2.1.3.1
Accession Convention of 1989 (The San Sebastian Convention) 3.1.8, 3.1.9, 3.2.1.3.1, 5.1.1.1.1, 5.1.1.3.5, 5.3.3.3.1, 5.3.8.2, 5.5.3.4.1.2, 5.5.3.4.4, 5.6.5.1, 5.7.1.3.3.2
Algiers Declaration of 1981 .... 20.5.5.1
Arrest Convention of 1952 (International Convention for the Unification of Certain Rules relating to the Arrest of Seagoing Ships) 3.5.3, 8.0.1, 8.2.1.3.1, 8.2.1.3.2, 8.2.2.1, 8.2.2.3, 8.2.2.4, 8.2.4.1
Art. 3 .... 8.1.2.3
7 .... 8.2.2.4
(1)(b) 8.2.4.1
Bretton Woods Agreement 14.4.2.1
Art. VIII(2)(b) 14.4.2, 14.4.2.2
Brussels Convention of 1926 on Immunity of State-Owned Ships 2.3.4.3.5
Brussels Convention of 1968 (Convention on Jurisdiction and the Enforcement of Judgments in Civil and Commercial Matters) .... **Appendix 1**
General .... 1.1.6, 1.2.1.1.2.1, 1.2.2.1, 1.2.3, 1.2.4.1, 1.2.4.2, 1.3.5, Chap. 3, Chap. 4, Chap. 5, 6.1.2.1, 6.6.4, 7.1.1.1, 7.1.1.3, 7.1.2.1, 7.1.2.3, 7.3.2, 8.0.1, 8.2 *et seq*, 9.0.1, 9.1.2.2, 9.2.5.2.1, 9.2.7.2.1.2, 9.4. *et seq*, 10.2.1.1, 10.3.1.1, 10.3.1.4, 10.3.2.3, 10.4.1.1.3, 11.2.3.3.1.3, 11.2.3.3.2, 11.2.3.3.3, 17.5, 17.5.1.1.1, 20.4.2.1, 20.6.1.1, 20.6.1.3, 22.3 *et seq.*
Preamble 3.3.1.2, 5.3.2.2.5
Title I (Art. 1) ... 1.2.3, 3.2.1.2.3, 3.3.1.1, 6.1.1.1.3, 6.2.1.3, 9.4, 9.4.1.1, 9.4.1.2.3.2, 9.4.1.3.1, 9.4.1.3.2, 9.4.3.2.8, 9.4.4.3.2, 20.6.1.4
Art. 1 .... **3.3.1.3**, 3.3.2.2, 3.3.2.5, 3.3.3, 3.3.3.2.2, 3.3.3.4.2.1, 3.3.3.4.4, 3.3.3.4.5.4, 5.8.2, 5.9.1.1, 5.9.3.5, 5.10.2.2, 6.3.3.1, 6.6.1, 6.6.2, 7.1.1.2, 7.1.1.3, 7.2.5, 8.2.2.3, 9.3, 9.4.3.5.1, 10.4.1.2.1, 17.5.1.1.2, 21.3.1.2.1.2, 21.5.2.1
(1) 3.3.3
(2) 3.3.3.2.4, 9.4.3.7
(h) 6.3.3.4.4.2
(4) 3.3.3.4, 3.3.3.4.1, 3.3.3.4.2.2, 3.3.3.4.3, 3.3.3.4.5.1, 3.3.3.4.5.5, 20.6.1.3
Title II (Arts. 2–24) .... 1.2.3, 1.2.4.1, 3.3.1.1, 3.3.3.2.2, 3.3.3.4.4, 3.5.4, 4.1.1.1.2, 4.2.1.1, 4.2.1.2, 4.2.1.4, 4.2.2.1, 4.2.3, 4.2.3.1.1, 4.2.3.2.2, 4.2.3.2.4, 4.3.1.1, 4.3.1.2, 4.3.1.3, 4.3.2.2, 4.4.2, 5.0.1, 5.1.4, 5.1.5.2, 5.1.6, 5.2.1, 5.2.4, 5.3.2.3.2, 5.3.3.5, 5.3.6.2, 5.3.7, 5.5.2.1.1, 5.5.5.2, 5.6.1.1, 5.6.3.1, 5.6.3.2, 5.6.4, 5.7, 5.7.1.3.4, 5.9.1.2.2, 5.9.2.3.2.1, 5.9.3.2, 5.9.3.4, 5.10, 5.10.1.4, 5.10.1.8, 5.10.1.9, 5.10.2.2, 5.10.3, 6.1.2.1, 6.6.2, Chap. 7, preamble, 7.1.1.2, 7.1.2.1, 7.1.2.3, 7.3.2.2.1, 8.1.4.2, 8.2.1.1, 8.2.1.2, 8.2.1.3.1, 8.2.2., 8.2.2.1., 9.1.2.2, 9.4, 9.4.1.3, 9.4.1.3.1, 9.4.1.3.2, 9.4.1.3.3, 9.4.3.2.1, 9.4.3.2.2, 9.4.3.3.1, 9.4.4.3.2, 13.4.1.2.3, 21.3.1.2.1.3, 22.3.2, 22.3.3, 22.3.6
secs. 2–6 .... 4.2.1.2, 5.4.2

Brussels Convention of 1968 (Convention on Jurisdiction and the Enforcement of Judgments in Civil and Commercial Matters)—*cont.*
Title II—*cont.*
secs. 3–5 .... 5.9.2.3.2, 5.9.2.3.2.2, 5.9.2.3.3.2
sec. 3 ..... 5.7.1, 5.7.1.2.2, 5.7.1.3, 5.7.1.3.2, 5.7.1.3.3.2, 5.7.1.3.5.3, 5.7.2, 5.7.2.4.1, 7.1.2.2, 9.4.3.2.4, 9.4.3.2.6, 9.4.3.2.7
sec. 4 ..... 5.7.2, 5.7.2.1, 5.7.2.3.2, 5.7.2.3.3, 5.7.2.4.1, 9.4.3.2.4, 9.4.3.2.6, 9.4.3.2.7
sec. 5 .... 9.4.3.2.4, 9.4.3.2.5, 9.4.3.2.7
sec. 6 .... 5.9.2.3.3.2, 9.4.3.2.7
sec. 8 .... 5.5.1.2, 5.9, 5.9.1.1, 5.9.1.2.2, 5.9.1.3, 5.9.1.4.1, 5.9.2.3.3.1, 7.3.2.2.1, 7.3.2.2.2, 9.4.3.5.1
Arts. 2–4 .... 5.7.2.3.2
2–6 .... 5.0.1, 8.2.4.2.2
2–18 .... 5.0.2
Art. 2 .... 4.1.1.1.1, 4.2.1, 4.2.1.2, 4.2.1.3, 5.3.8.3, 5.4, **5.4.1**, 5.4.2, 5.5.1.4, 5.5.2.2.3, 5.5.4.2.1, 5.5.4.2.4, 5.5.4.2.5, 5.5.6.2, 5.6.1.1, 5.6.2.2, 5.6.3.2, 5.6.5.1, 5.9.2.2.3, 5.10.1.1, 5.10.1.6, 7.1.1.1, 7.3.2.2.1, 8.2.1.2, 8.2.2.2, 22.3.2
(1) 5.4.2
3 .... 4.1.4, 4.2.1, 4.2.1.2, 4.2.1.3, 4.2.1.4, 5.4.2, 5.5.2.2.3, 5.9.2.2.3, 6.3.1, 8.2.1.2, 8.2.2.2, 9.4.1.3.3
(2) 4.2.2.3
4 .... 4.1.4, 4.2.2, 4.2.2.1, 5.3.2.3.1, 5.3.3.5, 5.7.1, 5.7.2, 5.9.1.2.2, 5.9.2.3.1, 5.10.1.1, 5.10.1.4, 17.5.1.1.1, 22.3.3
(1) **4.2.2.1**
(2) 4.2.2.3
5 .... 4.2.1.3, 5.4.2, 5.5, 5.5.1.1, 5.5.1.3, 5.5.1.4, 5.5.2.2.3, 5.6.1.1, 5.6.3.2, 5.6.5.1, 7.2.3.1.1, 7.2.3.1.2, 13.4.1.2.3
(1) 3.2.1.2.3, 3.3.3.4.3, 4.2.3.2.2, 4.2.3.2.3, 4.2.3.2.4, 5.3.1.1, 5.3.8.1, 5.3.8.3, 5.5.1.2, 5.5.2, 5.5.2.1.1, 5.5.2.1.2, 5.5.2.2, 5.5.2.2.1, 5.5.2.2.2, 5.5.2.2.3, 5.5.2.3, 5.5.3, 5.5.3.1.1, 5.5.3.1.2, 5.5.3.2.1.1, 5.5.3.2.1.2, 5.5.3.2.2.1, 5.5.3.2.2.3, 5.5.3.2.2.4, 5.5.3.3.1, 5.5.3.3.2, 5.5.3.4.1.1, 5.5.3.4.1.2, 5.5.3.4.2, 5.5.3.4.4, 5.5.3.5, 5.5.4.1, 5.5.5, 5.6.3.3, 5.6.5.1, 7.3.2.2.2, 9.4.3.2.9, 13.4.1.2.3, 22.3.2
(2) 3.3.3, 5.5.1.2
(3) 3.2.1.2.3, 3.2.2.3, 4.2.3.2.4, 5.5.1.2, 5.5.2, 5.5.2.1.1, 5.5.2.1.2, 5.5.2.2, 5.5.2.2.1, 5.5.2.2.2, 5.5.2.2.3, 5.5.2.3, 5.5.4, 5.5.4.1, 5.5.4.2.1, 5.5.4.2.2, 5.5.4.2.3, 5.5.4.2.4, 6.3.3.6, 7.1.1.1, 7.3.2.2.1, 13.1.1.1, 13.1.1.2
(4) 5.5.1.2
(5) 5.5.1.2, 5.5.5, 5.5.5.1.1, 5.5.5.2, 5.5.5.3.1, 5.5.5.3.3, 5.7.1, 5.7.1.1.4, 5.7.2, 5.7.2.3.4, 6.1.2.3.2
(6) 5.5.1.2, 5.5.6.1, 5.5.6.2, 5.5.6.3, 7.2.3.1.1
(7) 5.5.1.2, **8.2.4.1**

Brussels Convention of 1968 (Convention on Jurisdiction and the Enforcement of Judgments in Civil and Commercial Matters)—*cont.*
Art. 6 .... 4.2.1.3, 5.4.2, 5.5.2.2.3, 5.6, 5.6.1.1, 5.6.1.2, 5.6.3.2, 5.9, 5.9.3.2, 9.4.3.5.1
(1) ... 5.6.2.1, 5.6.2.2, 5.6.2.3, 5.6.2.4, 5.6.3.1, 5.6.3.2, 5.7.1.1.1
(2) 5.6.3.1, 5.6.3.2, 5.6.3.3
(3) 5.6.4
(4) 5.6.5.1, 5.6.5.2
6A ... 4.2.1.3, 5.4.2, 5.6.1.1, **8.2.4.2.1**, 8.2.4.2.2
Arts. 7–12A 5.7.1
7–15 .... 4.2.1.3, 4.2.2.2, 5.4.2, 5.7
Art. 7 .... 5.7.1.1.3.2, 5.7.1.1.4
Arts. 8–10 .... 5.7.1.1, 5.7.1.1.5, 5.7.1.2.2
8–11 .... 5.7.1.3
Art. 8 .... **5.7.1.1.1**, 5.7.1.1.3.1, 5.7.1.1.3.2
(2) 5.7.2.3.2
9 .... **5.7.1.1.2**, 5.7.1.1.3.2
10 .... 5.6.3.1, 5.7.1.1.3, 5.7.1.1.3.1
(1) 5.7.1.1.3.1, 5.7.1.3.3.1, 5.7.1.3.3.2
(2) 5.7.1.1.3.2, 5.7.1.1.3.3, 5.7.1.2.2
(3) 5.7.1.2.2
11(1) 5.7.1.2.1, 5.7.1.2.2
(2) 5.7.1.2.2
12 .... 5.3.1.1, 5.3.8.1, 5.7.1.3, 5.7.1.3.2, 5.7.2.4.1, 5.7.2.4.2
(1) 5.7.1.3.1, 5.7.1.3.5.1
(2) 5.7.1.3.2
(3) 5.7.1.3.3, 5.7.1.3.3.2, 5.7.2.4.2
(4) 5.7.1.3.4
(5) 5.7.1.3.5, 5.7.1.3.5.1, 5.7.1.3.5.2, 5.7.1.3.5.3
12A 5.7.1.3, 5.7.1.3.5.1, **5.7.1.3.5.2**, 5.7.1.3.5.3, 5.7.1.3.5.4
Arts. 13–15 .... 5.7.2
Art. 13 .... 5.7.2.1, 5.7.2.3.2, 12.1.1.1.1
(1) 5.7.2.1, 5.7.2.3.4
(2) 5.7.2.3.2
(3) 5.7.2.1
14 .... 5.7.2.3.3, 7.2.4
(1) **5.7.2.3.1**
(2) **5.7.2.2**, 9.4.3.2.6
(3) 5.7.2.2
15 .... 5.3.1.1, 5.3.8.1, 5.7.2.4.1, **5.7.2.4.2**, 9.4.3.2.6
Arts. 16–18 .... 5.0.1
Art. 16 ..... 1.2.3, 3.4.3, 4.2.1.3, 4.2.2.1, 4.2.2.2, 5.1, 5.1.1.1.3, 5.1.1.3.2, 5.1.1.3.3, 5.1.6, 5.2.1, 5.3.1.1, 5.4.2, 5.9.2.3.2.1, 5.9.2.3.2.2, 5.9.2.3.3.1, 5.9.2.3.3.2, 5.9.2.3.3.3, 5.9.4.1, 5.9.4.2, 6.6.2, 7.1.1.2, 7.1.1.3, 7.2.1.1, 9.4.3.2.5
(1) 3.2.1.2.3, 4.2.3, 5.1, 5.1.1, 5.1.1.2.1.1, 5.1.1.2.1.2, 5.1.1.2.3.1, 5.1.1.2.3.2, 5.1.1.3.2, 5.1.1.3.3, 5.1.1.3.4, 5.1.1.3.5, 5.6.5.1, 5.9.4.1, 5.10.3, 6.6.1, 12.4.1.3
(a) **5.1.1.1.1**, 5.1.1.2, 5.1.1.2.1.1, 5.1.1.2.2, 5.1.1.2.3.1, 5.1.1.2.3.4, 5.1.1.3, 5.1.1.3.3
(b) **5.1.1.1.1**, 5.1.1.3.5, 9.4.3.2.9

Brussels Convention of 1968 (Convention on Jurisdiction and the Enforcement of Judgments in Civil and Commercial Matters)—*cont.*

Art. 16(2) 3.3.3.2.2, 4.1.4, 4.2.3.1.3, 4.3.1.2, 5.1.2.1, 5.1.2.2, 5.9.4.1, 7.2.1.1, 7.2.1.2
(3) 5.1.3.1, 5.1.3.2
(4) 5.1.4, 7.2.1.1, 7.2.1.2
(5) 5.1.5.1, 5.1.5.2, 5.1.5.3, 5.1.5.4, 5.9.1.3, 21.3.1.2.3, 21.3.1.2.3.1, 21.3.1.2.3.2
17 .... 1.2.3, 3.4.3, 4.2.1.3, 4.2.2.2, 4.2.3, 4.2.3.2.4, 5.2.2, 5.3, **5.3.1.1**, 5.3.1.2, 5.3.2.1, 5.3.2.2.1, 5.3.2.2.2, 5.3.2.2.3, 5.3.2.2.5, 5.3.2.3.1, 5.3.3, 5.3.3.1.1.3, 5.3.3.1.1.4, 5.3.3.2, 5.3.3.3.1, 5.3.3.3.2, 5.3.3.4.1, 5.3.3.4.2, 5.3.3.5, 5.3.4.1, 5.3.4.3, 5.3.5.1, 5.3.5.2, 5.3.6.1, 5.3.6.2, 5.4.2, 5.5.3.5, 5.5.6.2, 5.7.2.4.1, 5.9.2.3.3.1, 5.9.2.3.3.2, 5.9.2.3.3.3, 5.9.4.2, 5.10.2.2, 6.2.1.2, 6.2.1.3, 6.3.3.4.5, 6.5.1.1, 6.5.1.2, 7.1.1.3, 7.2.2.2.1, 7.2.2.2.3, 8.2.2.1, 9.4.3.2.7, 10.4.1.2.3.1, 21.3.1.3.2, 22.3.5, 22.3.6
(1) 5.3.2, 5.3.2.1, 5.3.2.2.4, 5.3.3, 5.3.3.4, 5.5.3.5, 5.7.1.3, 5.9.3.4, 7.2.2.2.3
(a) 5.3.3, 5.3.3.1.1.1, 5.3.3.1.1.4
(b) 5.3.3, 5.3.3.2
(c) 5.3.3, 5.3.3.3.1, 5.3.3.3.2
(4) 5.3.7
(5) 5.3.8, 5.3.8.1, 5.3.8.2, 5.3.8.3
18 ..... 1.2.3, 4.2.1.3, 4.2.2.2, **5.2.1**, 5.2.2, 5.2.3, 5.2.4, 5.4.2, 5.7.1, 5.7.2, 6.2.3.1, 7.1.1.3, 7.1.1.4
19 .... **5.1.6**
20 ..... 3.5.4, **4.4.1**, 4.4.2, 4.4.3, 4.4.5, 8.2.1.3.1, 9.4.1.3.3, 9.4.3.2.1, 9.4.3.4.1, 9.4.3.4.1.1, 9.4.3.4.1.2, 9.4.3.4.1.3, 9.4.4.5.1.1
(1) 4.4.2
(2) 9.4.3.4.1.1
Arts. 21–23 .... 5.9, 5.9.1.1, 7.1.2.2, 7.3.2.2.2
Art. 21 .... 1.2.3, 3.2.1.2.3, 3.3.3.4.2.1, 4.2.2.2, 5.1.5.4, 5.3.5.2, 5.9.1.2.1, 5.9.1.2.2, 5.9.1.3, 5.9.1.4.3, **5.9.2**, 5.9.2.1.1, 5.9.2.1.2, 5.9.2.1.3, 5.9.2.1.4, 5.9.2.1.5, 5.9.2.1.6, 5.9.2.2.1, 5.9.2.2.2, 5.9.2.2.3, 5.9.2.3.1, 5.9.2.3.2, 5.9.2.3.2.2, 5.9.2.3.3, 5.9.2.3.3.1, 5.9.2.3.3.2, 5.9.2.3.3.3, 5.9.2.3.4, 5.9.2.3.4.1, 5.9.2.3.4.2, 5.9.2.3.5, 5.9.4.1, 6.4.4.2.1, 7.3.1.1, 7.3.1.2, 7.3.2.2.1, 8.2.3.1, 9.4.3.5.1, 9.4.3.6.2, 21.2.4, 21.3.1.2.2, 22.3.2, 22.3.4, 22.3.5, 22.3.6
22 ... 1.2.3, 4.2.2.2, 5.9.1.3, 5.9.1.4.3, 5.9.2.1.6, 5.9.2.2.1, 5.9.2.2.2, 5.9.2.3.4, 5.9.2.3.4.1, 5.9.2.3.4.2, 5.9.3, **5.9.3.1**, 5.9.3.2, 5.9.3.4, 5.9.3.5, 7.3.2.2.1, 8.2.3.1
(2) 5.9.3.3
(3) 5.6.2.3, 5.9.3.4
23 ...... 1.2.3, 4.2.2.2, 5.9.1.3, 5.9.2.3.2.1, 5.9.4, **5.9.4.1**, 5.9.4.2

Brussels Convention of 1968 (Convention on Jurisdiction and the Enforcement of Judgments in Civil and Commercial Matters)—*cont.*

Art. 24 .... 1.2.3, 4.2.2.2, **5.8.1**, 5.8.2, 5.9.2.3.5, 6.3.3.2, **21.3.1.2.1.1**, 21.3.1.2.1.2, 21.3.1.2.2, 21.3.1.2.3.2, 21.3.1.2.4.1, 21.3.1.3.2, 21.3.1.3.3
Title III (Arts. 25–49) 1.2.3, 3.3.1.1, 3.3.3.4.4, 3.3.3.4.5.1, 3.3.3.4.5.3, 3.5.2, 5.1.5.2, 5.9.1.3, 5.9.2.3.2.2, 5.9.2.3.3.2, 5.9.4.2, 9.2.7.5.4, 9.4, 9.4.1, 9.4.1.1, 9.4.1.2.1, 9.4.1.2.2.1, 9.4.1.2.2.2, 9.4.1.2.2.3, 9.4.1.2.3.1, 9.4.1.2.3.2, 9.4.1.2.4, 9.4.1.3, 9.4.1.3.1, 9.4.1.3.2, 9.4.1.3.3, 9.4.3.2.7, 9.4.3.2.9, 9.4.3.3.3.3, 9.4.3.4, 9.4.3.5.2, 9.4.4.1.1, 9.4.4.2.2.5, 9.4.4.3.2, 9.4.4.4.2.3, 9.4.4.4.3.4, 9.4.6, 9.4.6.1.1, 9.4.6.1.2, 21.3.1.2.4.2, 21.5.1.2, 21.5.2, 21.5.2.1, 21.5.2.2, 22.3.4
sec. 3 .... 9.4.5.1.2
Art. 25 .... 5.1.5.3, 9.4, **9.4.1.2.1**, 9.4.1.3.1, 9.4.4.3.2
26 .... **9.4.2.2**, 9.4.2.3
27 .... 9.4.2.3, 9.4.3.3.3.1, 9.4.3.4.1.2, 9.4.4.3.1, 9.4.4.3.2
(1) ... 9.4.3.2.1, 9.4.3.3, 9.4.3.3.1, 9.4.3.3.3.3
(2) 4.3.2.2, 4.4.3, 9.3.2.2.3, 9.4.3.4, 9.4.3.4.1, 9.4.3.1.1, 9.4.3.4.1.2, 9.4.3.4.1.3, 9.4.3.4.2.1, 9.4.3.4.2.2, 9.4.3.4.3.1, 9.4.3.4.3.2, 9.4.3.4.4.1, 9.4.3.4.5.1, 9.4.3.4.5.3, 9.4.3.4.5.7, 9.4.3.4.5.8
(3) .. 3.3.3.4.5.8, 9.4.3.3.2, 9.4.3.5, 9.4.3.5.1, 9.4.3.5.2, 9.4.3.5.3, 20.6.1.4
(4) **9.4.3.7**
(5) 9.2.7.4.2, 9.4.3.5.3, 9.4.3.6, 9.4.3.6.1, 9.4.3.6.2
28 .... 9.4.2.3, 9.4.3.2, 9.4.3.2.1, 9.4.3.2.2, 9.4.3.2.4, 9.4.3.3.1, 9.4.4.3.1, 9.4.4.3.2
(1) 5.9.2.3.2.2, 5.9.2.3.3.2, 5.9.4.2, 9.4.3.2.3, 9.4.3.2.4, 9.4.3.2.6, 9.4.3.2.7
(2) 9.4.3.2.4
(3) 5.9.2.3.2.2
29 .... 9.4.3.1, 9.4.3.2.2, 9.4.4.3.2
30 .... **9.4.3.8**, 9.4.3.8.1, 9.4.3.8.2, 9.4.3.8.3
(2) 9.4.3.8.2
Arts. 31 *et seq* 9.4.5.1.2
Art. 31 .... 9.4.4.2.1
(1) **9.4.4.2.1**
(2) 9.4.4.1.2, 9.4.4.2.1
32 .... 9.4.4.2.1, 9.4.4.6
(1) 3.2.1.1.5, 9.4.4.2.1, 9.4.4.5.1.2
33 .... 9.4.4.2.2.3, 9.4.4.2.2.6, 9.4.4.6
(1) 9.4.4.2.2.1
(2) 9.4.4.2.2.2
(3) 9.4.4.2.2.4, 9.4.4.3.2
34 .... 9.4.4.6
(1) 9.4.4.3.1
(2) **9.4.4.3.1**, 9.4.4.3.2
(3) **9.4.4.3.1**, 9.4.4.3.2, 9.4.4.4.2.3
35 .... 9.4.4.6
36 .... 9.4.4.4.1, 9.4.4.4.3.1, 9.4.4.4.3.5

Brussels Convention of 1968 (Convention on Jurisdiction and the Enforcement of Judgments in Civil and Commercial Matters)—*cont.*
Art. 36(1)(2) 9.4.4.4.1
37 .... 3.2.1.1.2, 21.3.1.2.4.2
(1) 3.2.1.1.5, 9.4.4.4.1, 9.4.4.4.2.1, 9.4.4.4.4.2, 9.4.4.5.2
(2) 3.2.1.1.5, 9.4.4.4.2.2, 9.4.4.4.4.1, 9.4.4.4.4.2, 9.4.4.5.2
38 .... 9.4.4.4.4.2, 9.4.6.2.2
(1) 9.4.3.8.3, 9.4.4.4.2.1, 9.4.4.4.2.2, 9.4.4.4.2.3, 9.4.4.4.2.4
(2)(3) 9.4.4.4.2.1
39 .... 9.4.4.2.1, 9.4.4.4.3.1, 9.4.4.4.3.2, 9.4.4.4.3.3, 9.4.4.4.3.4, 9.4.4.4.3.5, 21.3.1.2.3.1, 21.3.1.2.4.2
(1) 9.4.4.4.3.1, 9.4.4.4.3.4
(2) 9.4.4.4.3.1
40 .... 9.4.4.5.1.1, 9.4.4.5.1.2, 9.4.4.5.2
(1) 3.2.1.1.5, 9.4.4.5.1.1
(2) 9.4.4.5.1.1
41 .... 3.2.1.1.2, 3.2.1.1.5, 9.4.4.5.2
42(1)(2) 9.4.1.2.4
43 .... 9.4.1.2.3.1
44(1) **9.4.4.6**
45 .... 9.4.4.2.3
46 .... 9.4.4.2.2.4, 9.4.4.2.2.6, 9.4.4.5.1.2
(1) 9.4.2.3, 9.4.4.2.2.4, 9.4.4.2.2.5
(2) 9.4.2.3, 9.4.4.2.2.4, 9.4.4.2.2.6
47 .... 9.4.4.2.2.4, 9.4.4.2.2.6, 9.4.4.5.1.2
(1) 9.4.4.2.2.4, 9.4.4.2.2.5
(2) 9.4.4.2.2.4, 9.4.4.2.2.6
48 .... 9.4.4.2.2.6
(1) 9.4.2.3, 9.4.4.2.2.6
(2) 9.4.4.2.2.6
49 .... 9.4.4.2.2.6
Title IV (Arts. 50, 51) 9.4.5, 9.4.6
Art. 50 .... 9.4.5, **9.4.5.1.2**, 9.4.5.1.3
51 .... 9.4.5, **9.4.5.2**
52 .... 3.2.1.2.3, **4.1.1.1.1**, 4.1.1.3
53 .... 3.2.1.2.3, **4.1.2.1**
Title VII (Arts. 55–59) 3.5.1, 3.5.3
Arts. 55, 56 .... 3.5.1
Art. 57 .... 3.5.3, 3.5.4, 4.2.1.5, 8.1.4.2, 8.2.1.3.2, 8.2.2, 8.2.2.1, 8.2.2.2, 8.2.2.3, 8.2.2.4, 8.2.4.1
(1) **3.5.1**, 3.5.2, 8.2.1.3.1
(2) 8.2.1.3.1
(a) 4.2.1.5
(3) 3.5.2
59 .... 4.1.2.1
CMR Convention 18.2.2.4.1.3, 20.5.3.2
Collision Convention of 1952 (International Convention for the Unification of Certain Rules concerning Civil Jurisdiction in matters of Collision) 3.5.3, 8.0.1, 8.1.3.1, 8.2.1.3.1, 8.2.2.1, 8.2.2.2, 8.2.2.5
Art. 1(1)(b) 8.2.2.2
European Convention of 1968 on Information on Foreign Law 23.3.6.2
European Convention of 1972 on State Immunity 2.3.1.3, 2.3.4.2, 2.3.5.4.1, 2.3.5.4.2, 9.6.1.1, 9.6.1.3
European Convention of 1972 on State Immunity—*cont.*
Art. 12 .... 2.3.4.2
24 .... 2.3.5.4.1, 2.3.5.4.2
First Protocol of 1988 on interpretation of the Rome Convention (Brussels Protocol) .... 10.3.1.2, 10.3.2.3, **Appendix 3**
Art. 2 .... 10.3.1.3, 10.3.1.4
3 .... 10.3.1.4
6 .... 10.3.1.2
Geneva Convention of 1927 on the Execution of Foreign Arbitral Awards 16.4.2.1, 20.1.3.3, 20.4.1.1, 20.4.2.1
Art. I(d) 20.2.3.7.1.1
II(1)(b) 20.2.3.2.1
Geneva Convention on the International Carriage of Goods by Road 20.5.3.2
Geneva Protocol of 1923 on Arbitration Clauses 16.4.2.1, 20.1.3.3, 20.4.2.1
Hague Convention 1965 .... 9.4.3.4.4.2
Art. 15 .... 4.4.1, 4.4.5
19 .... 4.3.2.2
Hague Convention of the Civil Aspects of International Abduction—
Art. 3 .... 11.2.3.3.1.1
Hague Service Convention 4.3.2.1, 4.4.5
Art. 5 .... 4.3.2.2
10 .... 4.3.2.2
(b) 4.3.2.3
Istanbul Convention of 1990 (European Convention on Certain International Aspects of Bankruptcy) 3.3.3.2.1
Lugano Convention (Convention on Jurisdiction and the Enforcement of Judgments in Civil and Commercial Matters). *See also* Brussels Convention of 1968—
General .... 1.1.6, 1.2.1.1.2.1, 1.2.2.1, 1.2.3, 1.2.4.1, 1.2.4.2, 1.3.5, Chap. 3, Chap. 4, Chap. 5, 7.1.1.1, 7.3.2, 8.0.1, 8.2 *et seq*, 9.0.1, 9.1.2.2, 9.2.5.2.1, 9.4 *et seq*, 11.2.3.3.1.3, 11.2.3.3.2, 11.2.3.3.3, 17.5, 17.5.1.1, 20.6.1.1, 22.3 *et seq*
Art. 3 .... **Appendix 1**
5(1) .... 5.5.1.1, 5.5.3.4.3.1, 5.5.3.4.3.2, **Appendix 1**
(3) 3.2.2.3
Arts. 7–12A 5.7.1.3.3.2
Art. 12(3) .... **Appendix 1**
16 .... 3.4.2, 3.4.3, 5.1
(1)(b) .... **5.1.1.1.2**, 5.1.1.3.5, **Appendix 1**
17 .... 3.4.2, 3.4.3, 5.3.1.2
(5) .... **5.3.1.1**, **Appendix 1**
21 .... 3.4.2, 3.4.3
22 .... 3.4.2, 3.4.3
28 .... **Appendix 1**
(2) 9.4.3.2.3, 9.4.3.2.9
(3) 9.4.3.2.4
(4) 5.9.2.3.2.2
Arts. 32, 37, 40, 41 .... **Appendix 1**
Art. 50 .... 9.4.5.1.2
Arts. 54, 54A .... **Appendix 1**
Art. 54B .... 3.4.1, 3.5.3, 9.4.3.2.9, **Appendix 1**
(1) 3.4.2, 5.3.1.2

Lugano Convention (Convention on Jurisdiction and the Enforcement of Judgments in Civil and Commercial Matters)—*cont.*
Art. 54B(2) 3.4.2
(a) 3.4.3, 5.1, 5.3.1.2
(b) 3.4.2, 3.4.3
(c) 3.4.2
(3) **9.4.3.2.9**
Arts. 55, 56 .... **Appendix 1**
Art. 57(1) 9.4.3.2.10
(2)(3) .... **Appendix 1**
(4) .... 9.4.3.2.9, **9.4.3.2.10**, 9.4.3.2.11, **Appendix 1**
(5) .... **Appendix 1**
Arts. 60–68 .... **Appendix 1**
Luxembourg Protocol of 1971 .... **Appendix 1**
General 3.1.5, 3.1.6, 3.1.8, 3.1.9, 3.2.1.1.1, 3.2.1.1.4, 3.2.1.1.6, 3.2.1.2.4, 3.2.1.3.1, 3.2.2.1.1, 3.2.2.3, 3.2.3, 9.4.3.2.2
Art. 1 .... 3.2.1.1.2
2 .... **3.2.1.1.2**, 3.2.1.1.3, 3.2.1.1.4
(1) 3.2.1.1.3, 3.2.1.1.6
(2) 3.2.1.1.6
3 .... 3.2.1.1.3, 3.2.1.1.5
4 .... 3.2.1.1.6, 10.3.1.4
Modified Convention .... 1.2.1.1.2.1, 1.2.4.1, 3.3.1.2, 5.5.6.3, 5.10.1.1, 6.1.2.1, Chap. 7, 11.2.3.3.1.3
Art. 2 .... 7.2, 7.3.2.2.1, **Appendix 1**
3 .... 7.2, **Appendix 1**
5 .... 7.2, 7.2.3.1, 7.2.3.1.1, 7.2.3.1.2, **Appendix 1**
(1) 5.5.3.1.2, 7.2.2.2.2, 7.2.2.2.3
(3) 7.2.3.1.2
(6) 7.2.3.1.1, 7.2.3.2
(8) **7.2.3.1.2**
5A .... 4.1.4, 7.2, **7.2.1.2**, **Appendix 1**
6 .... 7.2, 7.2.3.2, **Appendix 1**
(4) 7.2.3.2
6A .... 7.2, 7.2.3.2, **Appendix 1**
Arts. 13–15 .... 7.2, 7.2.4, **Appendix 1**
Art. 13(2) 7.2.4
15 .... 7.2.2.2.2
16 .... 7.2, 7.2.1, 7.2.1.1, 7.2.1.2, 7.2.2.1, 7.2.2.2.2, **Appendix 1**
(2) 4.1.4, 7.2.1.2
17 .... 6.2.1.2, 7.2, 7.2.2.2, 7.2.2.2.1, 7.2.2.2.3, 7.3.2.2.2, **Appendix 1**
(1) **7.2.2.2.1**, 7.2.2.2.3
(2)(3) 7.2.2.2.2
18 .... 7.2, 7.2.2.1, **Appendix 1**
19 .... 7.2.1.1, 7.3, **Appendix 1**
20 .... 7.3, **Appendix 1**
(1)(2) 7.2.5
24 .... 7.2.5, **Appendix 1**
New York Convention of 1958 on the Recognition and Enforcement of Foreign Arbitral Awards 10.4.1.2.3.1, 16.2.2, 16.4.1, 16.4.2.2, 16.4.2.4.1, 17.4.4, 18.2.1.1, 18.2.2.1.2.2, 18.2.2.1.2.4, 18.2.2.1.3.1, 18.2.2.5.1, 20.1.3.1, 20.2.1.2.1.1, 20.2.1.2.1.2, 20.2.3.1.2, 20.2.3.7.1.3, 20.6.1.3

New York Convention of 1958 on the Recognition and Enforcement of Foreign Arbitral Awards—*cont.*
Art. I(1) 20.2.1.2.1.1
II(2) 18.2.2.1.2.1, 18.2.2.1.2.3, 18.2.2.1.2.5
V(1)(a) 18.1.3.2, 20.2.3.1.1, 20.2.3.2.1, 20.2.3.2.2
(b) 20.2.3.1.1
(c) 18.1.3.2, 20.2.3.1.1
(d) 17.5.2.2.5, 20.2.3.1.1, 20.2.3.6.3
(e) 16.4.2.4.2, 20.1.1.2, 20.2.3.1.1
(2) 20.2.3.1.1, 20.2.3.8
VI 20.2.3.1.1
VII(1) 18.2.2.1.2.6, 20.3.1
Protocol to the Brussels Convention—
Art. I 5.3.3, 5.5.3
IV(1) **4.3.2.1**, 4.3.2.2
(2) **4.3.2.3**
V 5.6.3.1, 5.7.1.1.3.1
Protocol No. 1 to the Lugano Convention—
Art. I 5.3.3, 5.5.3
Arts. Ia, Ib .... 9.4.3.2.9, **Appendix 1**
IV .... **Appendix 1**
(1) **4.3.2.1**
(2) **4.3.2.3**
V .... 5.6.3.1, 5.7.1.1.3.1, **Appendix 1**
Arts. Va, Vb, VI .... **Appendix 1**
Protocol No 2 on the Uniform Interpretation of the Lugano Convention .... **Appendix 1**
General 3.2.2.1.3, 3.2.2.2
Art. 1 .... **3.2.2.1.1**
Arts. 2, 3, 4 .... 3.2.2.1.1
Protocol No 3 on the Application of Article 57 of the Lugano Convention .... **Appendix 1**
Rome Convention of 1980 on the Law Applicable to Contractual Obligations .... 1.3.3, 1.3.5, 6.3.3.4.4.1, 10.0.1, 10.0.2, 10.0.3, 10.2.1.2, 10.2.2, 10.2.2.1 *et seq*, Chap. 11, preamble, 11.1.1.1.1, 11.1.3, 11.1.3.7.1, 11.2.3.3, 11.3.1.1, 11.3.1.2, 11.4.3.2.1 *et seq*, Chap. 12, preamble, 12.7.3, 12.9.2.6, 13.3.1.1, 13.4.1.3, 15.2, 17.1.1, 17.3.4.6, 23.1.3, **Appendix 3**
Art. 1(1) **10.4.1.1.1**, 10.4.1.1.3, 23.1.3
(a) 11.4.4
(2) **10.4.1.2**
(a) 10.4.1.2.1, 12.4.3, 12.6.2.1.2
(b) 10.4.1.2.1
(c) 10.4.1.2.4.1, 12.9.1.3
(d) 5.3.4.1, 17.1.1
(e) 11.4.4
(f) 12.7.1
(h) 10.4.1.1.4, 11.4.3.1.3, 11.4.7.2, 23.1.3
(3) 10.4.1.2, 10.4.1.2.2.2, 10.4.1.2.2.3, 12.8.1.2
(4) 10.4.1.2, 12.8.1.2
2 .... **10.4.2.1**, 23.1.3
Arts. 3–6 .... 11.4.1
Art. 3 .... Chap. 11, preamble, 11.1.5.3, 11.2.1, 11.2.3.7, 11.4.2.2.3, 12.1.1.1.5, 12.1.2.1, 12.2.2.2.1, 12.2.3.1, 12.3.1.1, 12.6.3

Rome Convention of 1980 on the Law Applicable to Contractual Obligations—*cont.*
Art. 3(1) 11.1.1.1.1, 11.1.2.4, 11.1.3, 11.1.3.3.3, 11.1.3.4, 11.1.3.6.2, 11.1.4.2, 11.1.4.3, 11.2.4, 12.1.2.2.1, 12.1.2.2.2, 12.4.1.1, 12.5, 12.6.2.1.1, 12.8.1.2, 12.8.2.1, 17.3.3, 17.3.4.2
(2) 10.4.1.1.4, **11.1.5.1**, 11.1.5.2, 11.1.5.3, 23.1.3
(3) 11.3.1.3, **11.3.2.1**, 11.3.2.2, 11.3.2.3, 11.3.2.4, 11.3.3.2.1, 12.1.3.2, 12.1.3.3, 12.5, 12.8.1.2, 12.8.2.1, 17.3.4.8, 17.3.8.3
(4) 11.1.1.2
4 .... Chap. 11, preamble, 11.1.3, 11.1.4.2, 11.1.4.3, 11.1.5.3, **11.2.1**, 11.2.2, 11.2.3, 11.2.3.1.2, 11.2.3.6.1, 11.2.3.7, 11.2.4, 11.3.1.1, 11.3.3, 11.4.2.2.1, 11.4.2.2.3, 12.1.1.1.5, 12.2.2.2.1, 12.2.2.2.2, 12.3.1.4, 12.5, 12.6.2.1.1, 12.6.3, 12.8.1.2, 17.3.9.2
(1) .. 11.2.2, 11.2.3.3.1.3, 11.2.3.5, 11.2.3.6.1, 11.2.3.7, Chap. 12, preamble, 12.3.1.3, 17.3.4.2
(2) .. 11.2.3, 11.2.3.1.1, 11.2.3.1.2, 11.2.3.2.1, 11.2.3.2.3, 11.2.3.2.4, 11.2.3.2.5, 11.2.3.2.6, 11.2.3.3, 11.2.3.3.1.3, 11.2.3.3.2, 11.2.3.3.4.4, 11.2.3.4.1, 11.2.3.4.3, 11.2.3.4.4, 11.2.3.6.1, 11.2.3.6.2, 11.2.3.6.3, 12.1.2.1, 12.2.2.2.3, 12.3.1.1, 12.3.1.2, 12.4.1.1, 12.7.1, 12.8.1.2, 17.3.4.2
(3) 11.2.3, 11.2.3.6.1, **12.4.1.1**, 12.4.1.3
(4) .. 11.2.3, 11.2.3.6.1, Chap. 12, preamble, **12.3.1.1**, 12.3.1.2, 12.3.1.3, 12.3.1.4
(5) ...... 11.2.3.5, 11.2.3.6.1, 11.2.3.6.3, Chap. 12, preamble, 12.2.2.2.3, 12.3.1.3, 12.4.1.2, 12.8.1.2, 17.3.4.2
5 .... 5.7.2.1, 11.2.3, 11.3.3.2.3, 12.1, 12.1.1, 12.1.1.1.1, 12.1.1.1.2, 12.1.1.1.3, 12.1.1.1.4, 12.1.1.1.5, 12.1.2.3, 12.1.3.1, 12.1.3.2, 12.1.3.3
(1) 12.1.1, **12.1.1.1.1**
(2) 12.1.1, 12.1.1.1.5, 12.1.1.2, 12.1.2.2.1, 12.1.2.2.2, 12.1.2.3, 12.1.3.2, 12.1.3.3, 12.2.3.1, 17.3.4.8
(3) 12.1.2.1, 12.1.3.2
(4) .. 11.3.3.2.3, 12.1.1, **12.1.1.1.1**, 12.1.1.1.4, 12.1.1.1.5, 12.1.3.3
(a) 12.1.1.1.4
(b) 12.1.1.1.4, 12.1.1.1.5
(5) 12.1.1, 12.1.1.1.1, 12.1.1.1.4
6 .... 5.5.3.4.3.2, 11.2.3, 12.2.1.1, 12.2.1.2
(1) **12.2.3.1**, 17.3.4.8
(2) 12.2.2.2, **12.2.2.2.1**, 12.2.2.2.2, 12.2.2.2.3, 12.2.3.1, 12.2.3.2, 13.4.1.3
(a) 12.2.2.2.2, 12.2.2.2.3
(b) 12.2.2.2.2, 12.2.2.2.3, 12.2.3.1
7 .... 11.3.1.3, 11.3.3.2.1, 12.5, 12.8.1.2, 17.3.4.8, 17.3.8.3
(1) 10.2.1.3, **11.3.3.1**, 11.4.10.2.1, 11.4.10.2.2, 17.3.8.3

Rome Convention of 1980 on the Law Applicable to Contractual Obligations—*cont.*
Art. 7(2) 11.3.3.2, **11.3.3.2.1**, **11.3.3.2.2**, 11.3.3.2.3, 11.3.4.2, 11.4.10.2.2, 11.4.10.2.3, 12.1.3.1, 12.1.3.3, 12.2.4.1, 12.2.4.2, 12.3.2.1, 12.8.2.1, 13.4.1.3, 14.4.1.5, 14.4.2.2, 17.3.8.3
8 .... 11.1.1.2, 11.4.1, 11.4.2, 11.4.2.1.2, 12.6.2.1.1
(1) 11.1.5.2, **11.4.2.1.2**, 11.4.2.2.1, 11.4.2.2.3, 11.4.2.2.4, 11.4.2.3.1, 11.4.10.1.1, 13.4.1.3
(2) **11.4.2.1.2**, 11.4.2.3.1, 11.4.2.3.2
9 .... 10.4.1.2.7, 11.1.1.2, 11.1.5.1, 11.4.1, 11.4.2.1.2, 11.4.3, 11.4.3.1.1, 11.4.3.1.3, 11.4.3.2.1, 12.6.2.1.1
(1)(2) 11.4.3.2.1, **11.4.3.2.2**, 11.4.3.2.4, 11.4.3.2.5, 12.4.2, 12.7.2
(3) 11.4.3.2.1, 11.4.3.2.4, 12.4.2, 12.7.2
(4) 11.4.3.2.1, **11.4.3.2.5**, 12.4.2
(5) 11.4.3.2.1, 12.1.2.3
(6) 11.4.3.2.1, **12.4.2**
10(1) **11.4.1**, 11.4.10.2.3, 14.1.2, 14.2.3.2
(a) 11.4.6, 14.2.2.1.1
(b) **11.4.5.1.1**, 11.4.5.2.2, 11.4.5.2.3
(c) 10.4.1.2.7, 11.4.7.2, 11.4.7.3, 14.2.2.2.1
(d) 11.4.8.1, 11.4.8.2, 11.4.10.2.1, 14.4.1.1, 15.2
(e) 10.2.1.3, 11.4.9
(2) 11.4.5.2.1, 11.4.5.2.2, 11.4.5.2.3, 14.2.3.1, 14.2.3.2
11 .... 10.4.1.2, 10.4.1.2.1, 11.1.1.2, 11.4.4, **11.4.4.1.2**, 12.4.3
12 .... 11.4.1, **12.6.1.2**
(1) 12.6.2.1.2, 12.6.2.2
(2) 12.6.3
14 .... 10.4.1.2
(1) **10.4.1.2.7**
(2) 10.4.1.2.7
15 .... **10.5**, 13.4.2.2.3.2
16 .... 11.3.4, **11.3.4.2**, 11.3.4.3, 11.4.8.2, 11.4.10.1.2, 11.4.10.2.2, 11.4.10.2.3, 11.4.10.2.4, 14.2.3.5, 14.4.1.2, 15.2, 17.3.4.8
17 .... 10.4.3
18 .... **10.3.2.2**, 11.2.3.3, 11.4.3.1.3
19(2) 10.4.2.2
22 .... **10.2.1.3**, 11.4.9
(1)(a) 11.3.3.1
29 .... 10.2.1.2
33 .... 10.3.2.2
Second Protocol of 1988 on Interpretation of the Rome Convention 10.3.1.2
Arts. 1, 3 .... 10.3.1.2
Sixth International Tin Agreement (1982) 2.1.4.2.2
Art. 16 .... **2.1.4.2.1**
Treaty of Rome (Treaty establishing the European Economic Community), 25 March 1957 .... 3.1.1, 3.2.1.2.1, 17.4.1
Art. 7 .... 9.4.4.2.3
85 .... 20.2.3.9
(1) 20.2.3.9

Treaty of Rome (Treaty establishing the European Economic Community), 25 March 1957—*cont.*
Art. 85(3) 18.2.2.1.3.2
177 .... 3.1.5, 3.2.1.1.1, 3.2.1.1.4, 17.4.2, 17.4.5
220 .... 3.1.3, 10.3.1.1
UNCITRAL Model Law on International Commercial Arbitration 16.4.2.4, 16.4.2.4.3, 16.4.2.4.4, 16.4.2.4.5
Vienna Convention of 1961 on Diplomatic Relations 2.4.1
Art. 1(d) 2.4.1.1
(f) 2.4.1.2
(g) 2.4.1.3
31(1) 2.4.1.1
(a)(c) 2.4.1.1
Vienna Convention of 1961 on Diplomatic Relations—*cont.*
Art. 32(1)(2)(3)(4) 2.4.1.4
37(1) 2.4.1.1
(2) 2.4.1.2
(3) 2.4.1.3
38(1) 2.4.1.1
39(1)(2)(3) 2.4.1.5
Vienna Convention of 1963 on Consular Relations 2.4.2.1
Arts. 5, 43 .... 2.4.2.1
Art. 45 .... 2.4.2.2
Vienna Convention of 1969 on the Law of Treaties—
Art. 30(3)(4)(a) 3.3.3.4.5.7
Washington Convention of 1965 .. 20.1.3.3, 20.5.4.1, 20.5.4.3

CHAPTER 1

INTRODUCTION

1.1 PRELIMINARY REMARKS

1.1.1 Where all the elements relevant to a situation are connected with England, a dispute which cannot be settled amicably may be resolved in England by litigation; the plaintiff may apply for provisional measures from the court, the judge will apply English law and if the plaintiff is successful the judgment will be enforceable against the assets of the defendant. If parties agree such a dispute may be resolved by arbitration.

1.1.2 A variety of complications arise in international cases—that is, cases with a foreign element. In this context "foreign" is not to be understood in a political sense. A State which has a unified legal system contains only one country or law district and legal relations operating exclusively within that State are domestic. So, a dispute arising out of a road accident in Limoges involving a Parisian motorist and a local cyclist is a domestic French dispute. However, in a State which comprises two or more legal systems, such as the United States of America or the United Kingdom, it is important to distinguish the State as a political unit from the separate countries or law districts within it. The United Kingdom contains three law districts—England, Scotland and Northern Ireland—and from the perspective of English private international law a dispute concerning a contract between an Englishwoman and a Scotsman is as much a case involving a foreign element as a dispute arising out of a contract between an Englishwoman and a Frenchman.

1.1.3 Although disputes arising out of international commercial transactions take a myriad of different forms and involve a wide variety of different issues, the basic legal framework for their resolution is uniform. Broadly speaking, this framework can be broken down into three stages: (i) jurisdiction, (ii) choice of law and (iii) the recognition and enforcement of judgments and awards.

1.1.4 The first issue is to identify the forum (or fora) in which the dispute may be resolved. In cases involving contractual disputes the parties may have agreed in advance to refer any dispute arising out of the transaction to the courts of a particular country or to arbitration. Where the dispute does not arise out of a contract, it is unusual for there to be an advance agreement between the parties and, even in cases involving international contracts, it is surprising how often the agreement does not include a dispute resolution clause. Whether or not the parties have agreed to litigation in a particular country or to arbitration, the first stage of an international commercial dispute involves questions of jurisdiction: which court or tribunal is competent in relation to the claim?

1.1.5 Where judgment is given by the court of a country in which the defendant has assets, a successful plaintiff may proceed to enforcement of the judgment immediately.

However, the courts of the country where the defendant's assets are located may not be competent to determine the plaintiff's claim, or—even if those courts are competent—the plaintiff may seek procedural or other advantages by bringing proceedings against the defendant in another competent forum. Two problems arise in this situation. First, if the defendant does not have sufficient assets to satisfy the judgment in the country where the judgment is given, in what circumstances, if any, will the plaintiff be able to enforce the judgment in the country where sufficient assets are located? Secondly, can the courts of the country where the assets are located (or the courts of another country) grant provisional measures to ensure that the rights of the parties are not irreparably harmed pending the final judgment?

1.1.6 In the fields of jurisdiction and the recognition and enforcement of judgments two very different types of regime have evolved. The traditional approach, which is reflected in the common law, is for the law to embrace the "twin vices" of "exorbitant national jurisdictional rules,[1] and extremely narrow judgment recognition practices resulting in a sort of 'law of the jungle' in transnational enforcement".[2] Of course, the narrowness of one country's rules for the recognition and enforcement of judgments given by the courts of other countries results—at least in part—from the breadth of other countries' jurisdiction rules. The alternative approach—which in practice can be achieved only by international agreement—is to limit the grounds on which jurisdiction can be assumed in international cases, as a result of which rules concerning the recognition and enforcement of foreign judgments can be less restrictive. This alternative approach is found in the Brussels and Lugano Conventions and in the system which operates within the United Kingdom.

The third important aspect of international commercial disputes involves choice of law. In an entirely domestic case it seems obvious that, as a general rule, the court should apply the law of the forum. However, in cases with a significant foreign element, the question arises as to the law which should govern the substance of the dispute.

1.1.7 Litigation is not the only method of resolving international disputes. On the international plane arbitration is a dispute resolution mechanism of increasing importance. Many of the questions which arise in the context of arbitration are similar to those which are central to international litigation: can the claimant obtain provisional measures? which law governs the merits of the dispute? can a successful claimant enforce an award in a country other than that in which the award is given? There are, however, various problems which are particular to arbitration—notably, with regard to the relationship between the courts and the arbitral process.[3]

1. For example, Article 14 of the French Civil Code, which enables the French court to assume jurisdiction on the basis of the plaintiff's French nationality, or the rule according to which the English court may assume jurisdiction on the basis of the defendant's fleeting presence within the jurisdiction when the writ is served (as in *Maharanee of Baroda* v. *Wildenstein* [1972] 2 QB 283).

2. Borchers, "Comparing Personal Jurisdiction in the United States and the European Community: Lessons for American Reform" (1992) 40 Am J Comp L 121, 128.

3. Part III, Chapters 16 to 20.

1.2 JURISDICTION AND THE RECOGNITION AND ENFORCEMENT OF FOREIGN JUDGMENTS

1.2.1 Basic concepts

1.2.1.1 Jurisdiction[4]

The word "jurisdiction" is employed in a number of different senses. For example, a rule which refers to a contract "made within the jurisdiction" uses the term "jurisdiction" to signify a geographical area. On the other hand, a rule which provides that, in certain circumstances, the courts of a particular country are to have "exclusive jurisdiction", employs the term "jurisdiction" to mean adjudicatory competence. An English court has jurisdiction, in the latter sense, if it will "hear and determine an issue upon which its decision is sought".[5]

1.2.1.1.1 TWO ASPECTS TO JURISDICTION

The issue of jurisdiction is to be approached from two different angles.

(i) There are questions relating to the characteristics of the parties.[6] For example, there may be doubts as to whether a particular plaintiff or defendant is recognised by English law as having legal capacity to take part in proceedings in England. There may also be arguments as to whether the defendant is entitled to immunity from suit.

(ii) There are general rules which circumscribe the jurisdiction of the courts in international cases (for example, where the defendant is resident in a foreign country or where the cause of action arose abroad or where the parties agreed to submit their disputes to the courts of another country).[7] Although it is possible to imagine a legal system with no rules limiting the jurisdiction of the courts in international cases, in practice, the English courts are subject to a variety of limitations as to their jurisdiction.

1.2.1.1.2 ACTIONS IN PERSONAM AND ACTIONS IN REM

1.2.1.1.2.1 When considering questions of jurisdiction it is important to draw a distinction between actions *in personam* and actions *in rem*. An action *in personam*, which is directed against a named individual, is begun by service of the document instituting the proceedings on the defendant in accordance with the Rules of the Supreme Court. The purpose of an action *in personam* is to make the defendant do something—such as perform a contract, or pay damages for breach—or to prevent the defendant from doing something. If the plaintiff succeeds in his action the judgment is directed against the defendant who is bound by it. The judgment does not, however, directly affect the legal position of third parties. The rules governing the jurisdiction *in personam* of the English courts fall into three broad categories: (i) rules derived from international conventions, most notably the Brussels and Lugano Conventions,[8] (ii)

4. Chapters 2 to 8.
5. Cheshire & North, *Private International Law* (12th ed, 1992), p. 179.
6. Chapter 2.
7. Chapters 4 to 8.
8. Chapters 4 and 5. The United Kingdom is party to a large number of international conventions which

traditional rules, based primarily on the rules contained in RSC, Orders 10 to 12,[9] and (iii) the rules contained in the so-called Modified Convention, which in various circumstances allocates jurisdiction within the United Kingdom.[10]

1.2.1.1.2.2 An action *in rem* is not directed against an individual, but against a thing (*res*). An action *in rem*, which in the commercial sphere is most commonly directed against a ship, is commenced by serving the writ on the *res* in connection with which the claim arises.[11] It is impossible to commence an action *in rem* unless the *res* is physically within the jurisdiction of the court. If an action *in rem* proceeds as such to judgment, the effect of the judgment *in rem* is to determine rights in the *res*, including the rights of third parties. In the commercial sphere, proceedings *in rem* fall within the Admiralty jurisdiction of the High Court.[12]

1.2.1.2 Recognition and enforcement[13]

Recognition of a foreign judgment is passive in the sense that it does not require any positive action by the court of the country in which recognition is sought. Enforcement, on the other hand, requires the court of the country in which enforcement is sought to take the active step of authorising enforcement of the foreign judgment against the defendant's assets. Whereas there can be recognition without enforcement, there can be no enforcement without recognition. So, for example, where A obtains a foreign judgment ordering B to pay damages for breach of contract, A may apply to enforce the judgment against B's assets in England. If the English court authorises enforcement, this necessarily entails recognition of the judgment. If, however, the foreign court dismisses A's claim on the basis that B was not guilty of breach and A starts proceedings against B in England on the same cause of action B may seek to rely on the foreign judgment by way of defence. In this situation, the English court is asked to recognise the judgment as creating a bar to A's action in England, but no question of enforcement is raised.

1.2.2 The traditional regime

1.2.2.1 In English law the traditional jurisdiction rules are relatively simple.[14] There are two key features: the rules are largely procedural in character—in that the essence of the

seek to regulate the jurisdiction of the courts of the Contracting States in specific areas, such as carriage by air, carriage by road and oil pollution. Legislation has been passed in order to discharge the United Kingdom's international obligations (for example, the Carriage by Air Act 1961, the Carriage of Goods by Road Act 1965, and the Merchant Shipping (Oil Pollution) Act 1971). For a list of the implementing legislation and a discussion of the relevant provisions see Dicey & Morris, *The Conflict of Laws* (12th ed, 1993) pp. 550–572. Generally speaking, under these legislative regimes, if the necessary jurisdictional requirements are met, the plaintiff is permitted to serve a writ on the defendant out of the jurisdiction without leave of the court: RSC, Order 11, r. 1(2)(b).

9. Chapter 6. There are additional bases of jurisdiction in particular circumstances (for example, RSC, Order 73, applies to cases concerning applications under the Arbitration Act 1950 or the Arbitration Act 1979): para. 17.5.1.2.

10. Chapter 7.

11. Where the claim arises in connection with a ship, there are various circumstances in which an action *in rem* may be brought against a ship other than that in relation to which the claim arose: para. 8.1.2.3.

12. Chapter 8. The Admiralty Court also has jurisdiction *in personam*: para. 8.1.3.

13. Chapter 9.

14. Chapter 6.

court's jurisdiction is the service of a writ on the defendant; and the limits of the court's jurisdiction are determined by reference to the exercise of a number of discretions. Broadly speaking, under the traditional rules, an English court has jurisdiction in actions *in personam* in three situations. (i) A defendant may submit to the jurisdiction of the court. (ii) An English court has jurisdiction over a defendant who is properly served with a writ within the jurisdiction. In such a case, however, the court has a discretion to stay the proceedings on the basis that there is some more appropriate forum abroad (*forum non conveniens*). (iii) The court may assume jurisdiction over an absent defendant by giving the plaintiff leave to serve a writ on the defendant out of the jurisdiction under RSC, Order 11, rule 1(1). Leave, which is discretionary, depends on the plaintiff being able to satisfy certain conditions, one of which is that the court must be the most appropriate forum for the trial of the action (*forum conveniens*). Although the traditional rules continue to apply in many cases, their scope has been significantly curtailed, most notably by the Civil Jurisdiction and Judgments Act 1982 (as amended) which implements the Brussels and Lugano Conventions. The traditional rules are residual in the sense that if jurisdiction is determined by either of the Conventions the plaintiff is unable to invoke any of the traditional bases of jurisdiction.

1.2.2.2 In theory, it is possible to imagine a situation where all foreign judgments are entitled to recognition and enforcement. Not surprisingly, however, there is no legal system which adopts this approach in practice. There are various reasons why, under the traditional regime,[15] the automatic recognition and enforcement of foreign judgments is not a practical possibility.

(i) The original court may have assumed jurisdiction over the defendant on a basis which the court in which recognition or enforcement is sought does not regard as legitimate. In situations where the jurisdiction of the English court is based on the presence or submission of the defendant, a judgment given in the plaintiff's favour will normally be enforceable abroad. However, in cases where the plaintiff invokes the jurisdiction of the court under RSC, Order 11, rule 1(1) it is quite likely that, should the plaintiff have to seek enforcement abroad on account of the defendant having insufficient assets within the jurisdiction to satisfy the judgment, a foreign court will refuse enforcement on the ground that the judgment resulted from proceedings in which jurisdiction was assumed on an exorbitant basis. By the same token, at common law, a foreign judgment will not be recognised or enforced in England unless there was a sufficient connection between the defendant and the foreign court which, according to the standards imposed by English law, justified the assumption of jurisdiction.

(ii) A foreign judgment is not entitled to recognition or enforcement in England if the foreign proceedings involved some substantial injustice. So, an English court will refuse to recognise or enforce a foreign judgment if the defendant was not given a proper opportunity to present his case in the foreign proceedings or if the defendant was given insufficient time to prepare a defence or if the plaintiff acted fraudulently (for example, by seeking to mislead the court with forged evidence) or if the foreign judgment offends against English public policy.

15. Para. 9.2.

(iii) Situations arise in which the courts of different countries reach incompatible decisions on the same or related issues. Where two foreign judgments conflict, the court in which recognition or enforcement is sought cannot respect both of them. Equally, the court of the country in which recognition or enforcement is sought cannot be expected to recognise or enforce a foreign judgment which conflicts with one of its own judgments.

1.2.3 The Brussels and Lugano Conventions

The primary purpose of the Brussels and Lugano Conventions is to facilitate the recognition and enforcement of foreign judgments in civil and commercial matters within the Contracting States. The parties to the Brussels Convention are the Member States of the European Community (EC); the parties to the Lugano Convention are the EC Member States and the countries which are members of the European Free Trade Association (EFTA). The core of the Conventions is to be found in the first three titles: Title I (scope),[16] Title II (jurisdiction)[17] and Title III (recognition and enforcement).[18] The Jenard-Möller Report, the explanatory report which accompanies the Lugano Convention, identifies the following nine principles which are common to both Conventions[19]:

> First principle: The scope of the two Conventions as determined ratione materiae is confined to civil and commercial matters relating to property.[20] ...
> Second principle: Both Conventions fall into the "double treaty" category, that is to say they contain rules of direct jurisdiction. These rules are applicable in the State in which the initial proceedings are brought and serve to determine the court vested with jurisdiction, whereas "simple treaties" merely contain rules of indirect jurisdiction which do not apply until the stage of recognition and enforcement has been reached.
> Third principle: A defendant's domicile[21] is the point on which the rules on jurisdiction hinge.[22] ...
> Fourth principle: Both Conventions contain precise and detailed rules of jurisdiction specifying the instances in which a person domiciled in a Contracting State may be sued in the courts of another Contracting State.[23] ...
> Fifth principle: The defendant's rights must have been respected in the State of origin.[24] ...
> Sixth principle: Grounds for refusing recognition and enforcement are limited.[25] ...
> Seventh principle: The enforcement procedure is unified and simplified.[26] ...

16. Para. 3.3.
17. Chapters 4 and 5.
18. Para. 9.4.
19. Jenard-Möller Report, OJ 1990 C189/65-67, para. 13.
20. Para. 3.3.
21. In English law "domicile" for the purposes of the Conventions is defined by sections 41 to 46 of the Civil Jurisdiction and Judgments Act 1982: para. 4.1.
22. Although, as a general rule, the courts of the Contracting States may continue to apply traditional bases of jurisdiction as against defendants who are not domiciled in a Contracting State, the third principle must be read subject to a variety of provisions which apply regardless of domicile: Article 16 (exclusive jurisdiction); Article 18 (submission); Article 17 (jurisdiction agreements); Articles 21 and 23 (*lis pendens*); Article 22 (related actions); Article 24 (provisional, including protective measures). See para. 4.2.
23. Chapter 5.
24. Para. 4.4.
25. Para. 9.4.3.
26. Para. 9.4.4.

Eighth principle: The Conventions govern relations with other international conventions.[27] ...

Ninth principle: Steps are taken to ensure that interpretation of the two Conventions is uniform.[28] ...

1.2.4 Jurisdiction and the recognition and enforcement of judgments within the United Kingdom

1.2.4.1 Whereas some of the jurisdiction rules contained in the Brussels and Lugano Conventions allocate jurisdiction to the courts of a "place", others confer jurisdiction on the courts of a Contracting State. Since the United Kingdom is a Contracting State made up of three different law districts, some mechanism is required to allocate jurisdiction between the courts of England, Scotland and Northern Ireland. Moreover, the Conventions do not allocate jurisdiction in cases which are entirely internal to the United Kingdom. The Modified Convention—which is based on Title II of the Brussels Convention—is the mechanism for allocating jurisdiction in civil and commercial matters within the United Kingdom.[29]

1.2.4.2 The Brussels and Lugano Conventions are also not concerned with the recognition and enforcement within the United Kingdom of judgments given by the courts of England, Scotland and Northern Ireland. A simplified system for the recognition and enforcement of judgments within the United Kingdom was introduced by the Civil Jurisdiction and Judgments Act 1982.[30]

1.3 CHOICE OF LAW

1.3.1 Every legal system must—either expressly or impliedly—contain choice of law rules for determining the substantive law to be applied to the merits of the dispute between the parties (*lex causae*). At the most simple level a legal system may contain the rule that the law of the forum (*lex fori*) should be applied to all aspects of disputes coming before the courts, regardless of whether the dispute is domestic or international. While the application of the *lex fori* can be justified in certain cases with a foreign element, the application of the *lex fori* is often likely to defeat the legitimate expectations of foreign litigants. It is not difficult to envisage examples in which the application of the *lex fori* seems inappropriate or unjust; where, for example, parties enter a contract to be performed in France and agree that French law should govern their relations, the application of English law—if materially different from French law—may upset the economic balance of the contract. Similarly, where a plaintiff is injured in an accident abroad by a local resident, the natural expectation is that the defendant's liability should be governed by the law of the place where the tort was committed.

1.3.2 In view of the fact that there are significant differences between the systems of private law of different countries, a choice of law rule which requires the application of the *lex fori* to international disputes leads to a situation where the outcome of a dispute

27. Para. 3.5.
28. Para. 3.2.
29. Chapter 7.
30. Para. 9.5.

may depend entirely upon where the litigation takes place. Although forum shopping can be restricted through the application of jurisdiction rules, it is hardly discouraged by different legal systems giving different answers to the same legal questions. It is to be expected that, if the courts of more than one country are competent to entertain an action, one of the factors which is relevant to the plaintiff's choice of forum is the likelihood of the substantive claim being successful.

1.3.3 Although it is almost impossible in practice to bring about a situation where the result of a dispute is the same irrespective of the forum in which it is litigated, a step can be taken in that direction by the harmonisation of choice of law rules. The Rome Convention on the Law Applicable to Contractual Obligations, which was implemented in the United Kingdom by the Contracts (Applicable Law) Act 1990, introduces an (almost) uniform code for contractual choice of law questions throughout the Member States of the EC.[31] So, where a dispute arises out of an international contract, the courts of each of the Contracting States apply the same rules for determining the law to govern the substantive rights and obligations of the parties.[32] Although it was originally intended that the Rome Convention should apply to both contractual and non-contractual obligations, the final text governs only contractual obligations. The English approach to choice of law in tort is still conditioned by its historical origins and the courts seem largely incapable of escaping from an anachronistic straitjacket of their own creation.[33]

1.3.4 It should not be thought that the application of the law of a foreign country is somehow incompatible with territorial sovereignty. Choice of law rules form part of the private international law of the forum. So, where an English choice of law rule directs the court to apply the law of a foreign country to the merits of the dispute, the foreign law is the applicable law by virtue of the application of English conflicts rules, not because English law is subordinate to the law of the foreign country in question. It follows, therefore, that there are limits on the extent to which the forum will give effect to the laws of foreign countries, limits which are set by the forum itself.

1.3.5 Within any legal system, whereas some rules of law are optional others are mandatory. Since mandatory rules are almost invariably designed to advance certain economic or social policies (such as restrictions on exchange control or consumer protection), each country has a legitimate interest in seeing that its mandatory rules are applied to situations which are intended to fall within their scope. For example, in *Golden Acres Ltd* v. *Queensland Estates Pty Ltd*,[34] a well known decision of the Supreme Court of Queensland, the defendant, a local company, appointed a Hong Kong company as agent to sell land in Queensland. The contract, which included an express choice of the law of Hong Kong, provided that the agent was to receive commission in excess of the limit imposed by Queensland law. The agent brought proceedings in Queensland to recover the commission stipulated by the contract, relying on the law of Hong Kong as the applicable law. As a general rule, where the parties have made a choice of law, the court is prepared to uphold that choice and apply the chosen law. However, the judge thought that "the selection of a law other than that

31. Chapters 10 to 12.
32. Certain issues and certain types of contract which are excluded from the Convention's scope continue to be governed by the common law: para. 10.4.
33. Chapter 13.
34. [1969] Qd R 378.

of Queensland was made for the specific purpose of avoiding the consequences of illegality which would or might have followed if the Queensland law applied".[35] The court concluded that the law of Queensland prevailed over the law chosen by the parties on the basis that "it would be contrary to public policy for the legislative intention to be stultified by parties to a contract, of which the proper law would be Queensland, selecting some other law for the purpose of avoiding the application of Queensland law".[36]

By way of conclusion four points should be noted:

(i) The distinction between substance and procedure is a crucial one. It is an almost universal principle that matters of procedure are governed by the *lex fori*. Where a dispute concerning an international contract is litigated in England, English rules of evidence and procedure are applied, irrespective of the law applicable to the merits of the dispute.[37] So, English law governs questions such as whether a plaintiff in English proceedings is entitled to provisional measures (such as a Mareva injunction)[38] or whether the court can grant an injunction restraining a litigant from proceeding abroad[39] or give judgment in a foreign currency.[40] The dividing line between substance and procedure turns on the classification of the issue by the law of the forum. Having said that, the precise location of the border is not always easy to find. The Foreign Limitation Periods Act 1984 establishes, however, that questions of limitation are to be determined by reference to the applicable law rather than the *lex fori*.[41]

(ii) Even as regards substantive matters, it should not be assumed that the effect of choice of law rules is necessarily to refer all aspects of a particular legal relationship to the same law. For example, in a case relating to an international contract, issues such as formal validity, material validity and contractual capacity may be referred to the laws of different countries.

(iii) When a dispute is litigated in England the fact that, according to English choice of law rules, the law of a foreign country is the applicable law does not necessarily mean that the foreign law is applied to determine the rights and obligations of the parties. The general rule is that an English court does not have judicial notice of the laws of other countries. Accordingly, rules of foreign law have to be pleaded and proved by the party seeking to rely upon them. If the foreign law is not pleaded or cannot be proved, English law is applied by default.[42]

(iv) Finally, something should be said about the relationship between jurisdiction rules and choice of law rules. Historically, choice of law rules have formed the heartland of private international law. Until relatively recently English law permitted the assumption of jurisdiction in cases which had only a limited connection with England. The more distant the connection between the

35. Hoare J, [1969] Qd R 338, 384.
36. Hoare J, [1969] Qd R 338, 385.
37. For a recent example see *The Heidberg* [1993] 2 Lloyd's Rep 324.
38. Chapter 21.
39. Chapter 22.
40. Para. 14.3.
41. Chapter 15.
42. Chapter 23.

litigation and the forum, the more likely it is that the choice of law rules of the forum will direct that the law of a foreign country should be the applicable law. However, the trend in recent years has been to use jurisdiction rules to steer legal proceedings towards a forum which is appropriate for the resolution of the dispute in question. In England this trend can be seen in the development of the doctrine of *forum non conveniens* by the courts and the implementation of the Brussels and Lugano Conventions. Although there is no necessary connection between the allocation of jurisdiction and the determination of the applicable law, if the effect of jurisdiction rules is to direct litigation to an appropriate forum, there is an increased likelihood that the *lex fori* will also be the applicable law. The development of more sophisticated techniques for handling jurisdiction disputes has, therefore, reduced the importance of choice of law rules. Instead of private international law being concerned primarily with choice of law questions, the focus has shifted to jurisdiction and the recognition and enforcement of judgments.

1.4 BIBLIOGRAPHICAL NOTE

Throughout the text there are references to articles, notes and comments in the periodical literature. In addition there is a range of works which may be consulted.

(i) The standard works which deal with the whole field of private international law are Cheshire & North, *Private International Law* (12th ed, 1992) and Dicey & Morris, *The Conflict of Laws* (12th ed, 1993). It is also appropriate to mention Morris, *The Conflict of Laws* (4th ed, 1993). For discussion of the impact of the European Community on English private international law see Fletcher, *Conflict of Laws and European Community Law* (1982) and Lasok & Stone, *Conflict of Laws in the European Community* (1987).

(ii) In the field of jurisdiction and the recognition and enforcement of judgments the following works (which vary considerably in size) may be noted: Briggs & Rees, *Norton Rose on Civil Jurisdiction and Judgments* (1993); Collins, *The Civil Jurisdiction and Judgments Act 1982* (1983); Dashwood, Hacon & White, *A Guide to the Civil Jurisdiction and Judgments Convention* (1986); Hartley, *Civil Jurisdiction and Judgments* (1984); Jacob, *Private International Litigation* (1988); Kaye, *Civil Jurisdiction and Enforcement of Judgments* (1987) and O'Malley & Layton, *European Civil Practice* (1989). Tebbens, Kennedy & Kohler (eds), *Civil Jurisdiction and Judgments in Europe* (1992) contains the proceedings of a colloquium on the Brussels and Lugano Conventions held under the auspices of the Court of Justice in Luxembourg in 1991. Jurisdiction in Admiralty proceedings is treated by Jackson, *Enforcement of Maritime Claims* (1985) and *Civil Jurisdiction and Judgments: Maritime Claims* (1987) and Meeson, *Admiralty Jurisdiction and Practice* (1993). For consideration of jurisdictional immunity see Lewis, *State and Diplomatic Immunity* (3rd ed, 1989).

(iii) The English rules on choice of law in contract were revolutionised by the implementation of the Rome Convention on the Law Applicable to Contractual Obligations. A series of essays on various aspects of the Convention is to be found in North (ed), *Contract Conflicts* (1982). A guide to the Convention and the implementing legislation is provided by Kaye, *The New Private International Law of Contract of the*

European Community (1993) and Plender, *The European Contracts Convention* (1991). Choice of law in tort is examined by Kaye, *Private International Law of Tort and Product Liability* (1991) and Morse, *Torts in Private International Law* (1978).

(iv) The law dealing with foreign currency obligations and judgments in a foreign currency is analysed authoritatively and exhaustively by Mann, *The Legal Aspect of Money* (5th ed, 1992). It would be difficult to exaggerate the influence of this work, the first edition of which appeared in 1938.

(v) Arbitration law is discussed from a domestic perspective by Merkin, *Arbitration Law* (1991), Mustill & Boyd, *Commercial Arbitration* (2nd ed, 1989) and *Russell on Arbitration* (20th ed, 1982). International aspects are considered by Redfern & Hunter, *Law and Practice of International Commercial Arbitration* (2nd ed, 1991). Also of interest is Bernstein & Wood (eds), *Handbook of Arbitration Practice* (2nd ed, 1993).

(vi) For a discussion of the law relating to provisional measures (with particular emphasis on Mareva injunctions and Anton Piller orders): Gee, *Mareva Injunctions* (2nd ed, 1990); Hoyle, *Mareva Injunctions and Related Orders* (2nd ed, 1989) and Ough & Flenley, *The Mareva Injunction and Anton Piller Order* (2nd ed, 1993).

PART I

JURISDICTION AND THE RECOGNITION AND ENFORCEMENT OF FOREIGN JUDGMENTS

CHAPTER 2

PERSONS WHO CAN AND CANNOT SUE OR BE SUED

In order to be able to take part in legal proceedings in England—whether as plaintiff or defendant—the party in question must have legal capacity in the eyes of English law (para. 2.1). Although there are no general limitations on the types of person who can sue or be sued, at common law enemy aliens cannot in a time of war invoke the jurisdiction of the English courts (para. 2.2). More importantly, there are certain categories of defendant who may have the benefit of immunity from suit in England—notably, foreign States, international organisations (such as the United Nations) and their officers and employees (paras. 2.3–2.5).

2.1 LEGAL CAPACITY TO SUE OR BE SUED

2.1.1 Foreign corporations

The recognition of foreign corporations is normally relatively straightforward. It is a well established principle of English private international law that the existence or dissolution of a foreign corporation duly created or dissolved under the law of a foreign country is recognised in England.[1] As a consequence of this principle, a foreign association which has legal personality under the law of the place where it is constituted can sue or be sued in England, even if a similar English association would not have legal personality under English law.

2.1.2 Other foreign juristic entities

2.1.2.1 In English law there are essentially only two types of legal person: (i) individuals and (ii) corporations or other personified groups of individuals. Other legal systems, however, may confer legal personality on entities which do not fall within these two categories. Can such foreign juristic entities take part in proceedings in England?

2.1.2.2 In *Bumper Development Corporation* v. *Commissioner of Police of the Metropolis*[2] the plaintiff purchased a bronze sculpture which was later seized by the police as part of a campaign of returning stolen religious artefacts to their owners. It was

1. Dicey & Morris, *The Conflict of Laws* (12th ed, 1993) p. 1107 (Rule 155). See, for example, *Lazard Brothers & Co* v. *Midland Bank Ltd* [1933] AC 289.
2. [1991] 1 WLR 1362. Collier, [1992] CLJ 39; Carter, (1991) 62 BYIL 452.

alleged that the sculpture had been stolen from a ruined temple in India. According to Indian law the temple was regarded as a legal person. When the plaintiff brought an action against the police for the return of the sculpture, the temple, acting through a representative, sought to assert its claim to the sculpture. The issue was "whether a foreign legal person which would not be recognised as a legal person by our own law can sue in the English courts".[3] Purchas LJ, who gave the judgment of the Court of Appeal, noted that English law's "insistence on an essentially animate content in a legal person leads to a formidable conceptual difficulty in recognising as a party entitled to sue in our courts something which on one view is little more than a pile of stones".[4] Nevertheless, the Court of Appeal held that the temple was capable of being recognised as a juristic entity with capacity to sue in England. Relying on the principle of comity, Purchas LJ thought that in the circumstances of the case there would not be "any offence to English public policy in allowing a Hindu religious institution to sue in our courts".[5]

2.1.2.3 Three points should be made about this decision: (i) there is no reference in the judgment to any judicial authority on the question of capacity to sue; (ii) Purchas LJ thought that it was undesirable to go further than was necessary for the decision in the particular case; (iii) it was essential for the decision that the constitution of the temple empowered its representative to take all necessary steps in the proceedings on its behalf.[6]

2.1.3 Corporations established under the laws of territories which are not States

2.1.3.1 Foreign corporations are entitled to recognition in England at common law because they are properly constituted and have legal personality according to the law of the place where they are constituted. A potential problem arises in relation to a business which is incorporated in a territory which is not recognised by HM Government as a State. Can such an organisation be recognised as having legal personality for the purposes of English law?

2.1.3.2 The Foreign Corporations Act 1991 is designed to provide a simple answer to this question. The purpose of the 1991 Act is to ensure that a foreign corporation which operates under the law in force in a territory which is not recognised as a State by the United Kingdom is nevertheless treated in the same way as foreign corporations from recognised States. Section 1 of the Act provides:

> (1) If at any time—
> (a) any question arises whether a body which purports to have or, as the case may be, which appears to have lost corporate status under the laws of a territory which is not at that time a recognised State should or should not be regarded as having legal personality as a body corporate under the law of any part of the United Kingdom, and
> (b) it appears that the laws of that territory are at that time applied by a settled court system in that territory,
>
> that question and any other material question relating to the body shall be determined (and account shall be taken of those laws) as if that territory were a recognised State.

3. Purchas LJ, [1991] 1 WLR 1362, 1371.
4. [1991] 1 WLR 1362, 1371.
5. [1991] 1 WLR 1362, 1372.
6. Purchas LJ, [1991] 1 WLR 1362, 1373.

(2) For the purposes of subsection (1) above—

(a) "a recognised State" is a territory which is recognised by Her Majesty's Government in the United Kingdom as a State;

(b) the laws of a territory which is so recognised shall be taken to include the laws of any part of the territory which are acknowledged by the federal or other central government of the territory as a whole; and

(c) a material question is a question (whether as to capacity, constitution or otherwise) which, in the case of a body corporate, falls to be determined by reference to the laws of the territory under which the body is incorporated.

(3) Any registration or other thing done at a time before the coming into force of this section shall be regarded as valid if it would have been valid at that time, had subsections (1) and (2) above then been in force.

2.1.3.3 The essential condition for the recognition of a corporation which originates in a territory which is not recognised as a State is that "it appears that the laws of that territory are at that time applied by a settled court system in that territory". This deceptively simple formula is surrounded by a penumbra of uncertainty. In the situation where a previously recognised State disintegrates into a number of break-away territories, it may well be difficult to determine the moment at which, for the purposes of section 1(1)(b), the court system becomes "settled" in the new territories.

2.1.4 International corporations[7]

2.1.4.1 Introduction

2.1.4.1.1 The term "international corporation" is often used loosely to mean one of three different types of organisation.

(i) In the modern world there are numerous national corporations which have international business. International banks and other so-called multinational companies fall within this category. With regard to these corporations the international angle poses no special problems. Depending on their place of incorporation English law treats such corporations quite simply as domestic or foreign legal persons. Multinational corporations of this type may take one of two forms. A national company may establish subsidiary companies in other countries. In such a case, the parent and the subsidiaries are separate legal persons and each subsidiary can own property, enter contracts on its own behalf and litigate. Because of the independent legal personality of each of the subsidiaries no special legal problems are posed by dealings between a subsidiary and the parent or between the subsidiaries *inter se* or between a subsidiary and third parties. The alternative organisational structure is where a multinational company merely establishes a presence in various countries. For example, a bank may set up branches in foreign countries, while remaining a single legal entity. Normally, a company which operates outside the frontiers of the country where it is incorporated is required by the laws of the territories

7. Jenks, "The Legal Personality of International Organisations" (1945) 22 BYIL 267; Mann, "International Corporations and National Law" (1967) 42 BYIL 145; Collier, "The Status of an International Corporation" in Feuerstein & Parry (eds), *Multum Non Multa: Festschrift für Kurt Lipstein* (1980) 20–29; Hill, "International Corporations in the English Courts" (1992) 12 OJLS 135.

where it carries on business to register its presence. For example, under English law an oversea company which establishes a branch or place of business in England is required to deliver various documents to the registrar of companies for registration.[8] However, an oversea company which is registered in England or which has a branch or a place of business in England is not a separate legal entity; English law simply recognises the company's legal personality under the law of the place where it is incorporated. Where this second form of organisation is adopted, the multinational company is one legal person operating in several countries.

(ii) There are also corporations which are created under national law, but whose formation is contemplated in a treaty concluded between States. In such cases the conception of the company is international, but its birth is not. The corporation is national in character and is treated by English law in the same way as any other foreign corporation.

(iii) The only legal entities which are truly international corporations, rather than national corporations with an international dimension, are those organisations which are established by treaties concluded between States and which owe their creation and existence to public international law. It is this third category which has posed problems in English law.

2.1.4.1.2 If the United Kingdom is a member of an international corporation (in the sense of a corporation formed by a treaty) and an Order in Council is made under the International Organisations Act 1968 the organisation is treated as having legal personality as an English corporation. The problem cases concern international organisations which are not the subject of an Order under the 1968 Act. There are three possible ways of dealing with the question of whether such organisations have legal capacity in England.

(i) It may be decided as a matter of English private international law that the existence of a legal person constituted under public international law can be recognised in the same way as legal persons constituted under foreign systems of domestic law.

(ii) The court may refuse recognition to an international corporation unless English law has conferred legal personality on it.

(iii) An international corporation may be recognised as a national corporation under the domestic law of one or more of the States who were party to the treaty establishing it.

Each of these possibilities gained some measure of support in *Arab Monetary Fund* v. *Hashim (No. 3)*.[9] Ultimately, however, the House of Lords decided—on the basis of its

8. Companies Act 1985, ss. 690A and 691. The information which must be filed with the registrar includes the name and address of at least one person who is authorised to accept service of process on behalf in the company. Even if a company which has a "branch" or an "established place of business" in England does not register, it is still amenable to the jurisdiction of the English courts: Companies Act 1985, ss. 694A(3) and 695(2). See para. 6.1.2.

9. [1990] 3 WLR 139. Greenwood, (1989) 60 BYIL 475.

decision in *JH Rayner (Mincing Lane) Ltd* v. *Department of Trade and Industry*[10]—that the third solution was the appropriate one.

2.1.4.2 The Tin Council case: JH Rayner (Mincing Lane) Ltd *v.* Department of Trade and Industry[11]

2.1.4.2.1 The International Tin Council was established by a treaty after the Second World War for the purpose of regulating the market in relation to tin. The ITC, whose headquarters were in London, dealt on the London Metal Exchange, buying and selling tin with a view to supporting the world price. The Sixth International Tin Agreement, to which the United Kingdom was a party, was signed in New York in 1982. Article 16 of that agreement provided:

> The Council shall have legal personality. It shall in particular have the capacity to contract, to acquire and dispose of movable and immovable property and to institute legal proceedings.

2.1.4.2.2 In order that the ITC could function properly in England the International Tin Council (Immunities and Privileges) Order 1972[12] was made pursuant to section 1 of the International Organisations Act 1968. Article 5 of the Order stated that the "Council shall have the legal capacities of a body corporate". In 1985 the ITC announced that it could not meet the liabilities which it had incurred through its operations. At this time its debts stood at something in excess of £750 million. In the complex litigation which ensued—the main purpose of which was to seek to establish the liability of the parties to the Sixth International Tin Agreement for the debts of the ITC—one of the questions which the courts had to consider was the status of the ITC in English law.

2.1.4.2.3 The starting-point for the decision was stated by Lord Oliver in the following terms: "as a matter of the constitutional law of the United Kingdom, the Royal Prerogative, whilst it embraces the making of treaties, does not extend to altering the law or conferring rights upon individuals or depriving individuals of rights which they enjoy in domestic law without the intervention of Parliament".[13] Both Lord Templeman and Lord Oliver emphasised that the status of the ITC in English law depended on the International Tin Council (Immunities and Privileges) Order 1972 and not the treaty: "Without the Order in Council the ITC had no existence in the law of the United Kingdom and no significance save in the name of an international body created by a treaty between sovereign States which was not justiciable by municipal courts."[14]

2.1.4.2.4 The *ratio* of the case is clear: because of the doctrine of non-justiciability, an international corporation of which the United Kingdom is a member has no status to sue or be sued in England unless English law has conferred on it the characteristics of a body corporate. The House of Lords was not required to, and did not, consider the position of an international corporation established by a treaty to which the United Kingdom is not a party. This was the issue which arose in the litigation concerning the Arab Monetary Fund.

10. [1990] 2 AC 418.
11. [1990] 2 AC 418. Greenwood, [1990] CLJ 8 and (1989) 60 BYIL 461.
12. SI 1972 No. 120.
13. [1990] 2 AC 418, 500.
14. Lord Oliver, [1990] 2 AC 418, 510.

2.1.4.3 Arab Monetary Fund *v.* Hashim (No. 3)[15]

2.1.4.3.1 The Arab Monetary Fund was established by an agreement between twenty Arab States and Palestine in 1976. The purpose of the AMF, whose head office was located in Abu Dhabi (UAE), was to lay the monetary foundations of Arab economic integration and to accelerate the process of economic development throughout the Arab world. Article 2 of the agreement provided that the AMF was to have "an independent juridical personality" and "in particular, the right to own, contract and litigate". The various signatories to the agreement subsequently took the steps necessary to bestow juridical personality on the AMF in their domestic systems. In the UAE, in accordance with the constitution, the treaty establishing the AMF was confirmed by the council of ministers and ratified by decree. The decree had the effect of conferring on the AMF independent legal personality and the capacity to sue and be sued under the law of the UAE. It was alleged that the defendant, the AMF's former director-general, had embezzled $50 million. When litigation was commenced in England to recover these sums the defendant sought to have the claim struck out on the basis that the AMF did not have capacity to sue in England.

2.1.4.3.2 At first instance the judge inclined towards the recognition of the AMF in English law on the basis that it had legal personality under public international law.[16] The advantages of this solution (which had gained some acceptance in the Court of Appeal in *JH Rayner (Mincing Lane) Ltd* v. *Department of Trade and Industry*[17]) were clearly set out in Hoffmann J's judgment:

> Extending our conflicts rule to international organisations seems to me sensible and practical. The rule as it applies to entities created by foreign domestic laws is based on the inconvenience of having legal entities which exist in one country but not in another. International organisations set up by foreign States do exist in fairly substantial numbers, trade with this country and bank in the City of London. They are invariably recognised as juridical entities by the domestic systems of the parties to the treaty as well as by many other countries. . . . It is difficult to see why an entity created by a treaty between two or more foreign States should be less entitled to recognition than an entity created under the sovereign authority of a single foreign State within its domestic system.[18]

2.1.4.3.3 Following the House of Lords' decision in the *Tin Council* case counsel for the AMF dropped the argument that the AMF should be recognised as an international organisation with personality under public international law.[19] Hoffmann J decided that the proper approach was to "ignore the treaty and regard the AMF as constituted under Abu Dhabi law as a separate *persona ficta*".[20] As such the AMF was entitled to recognition as a domestic entity under ordinary conflicts rules. This analysis was adopted by Lord Templeman in the House of Lords: "when sovereign States enter into an agreement by treaty to confer legal personality on an international organisation, the treaty does not create a corporate body. But when the AMF Agreement was registered in the UAE by means of Federal Decree No. 35 that registration conferred on the

15. [1991] 2 AC 114. Mann, "International Organisations as National Corporations" (1991) 107 LQR 357; Marston, [1991] CLJ 218.
16. [1990] 3 WLR 139, 143.
17. [1989] Ch 72. Greenwood, [1989] CLJ 46.
18. [1990] 3 WLR 139, 144.
19. Strictly speaking, this was not necessary: the *Tin Council* case concerned an organisation of which the United Kingdom was a member; *Arab Monetary Fund* v. *Hashim (No. 3)* did not.
20. [1990] 3 WLR 139, 147.

international organisation legal personality and thus created a corporate body which English courts can and should recognise".[21]

2.1.4.3.4 This analysis achieves a practical result which is clearly more sensible than refusing recognition to the AMF altogether—the solution which had been favoured by the majority of the Court of Appeal. However, problems result from choosing to recognise an organisation created by treaty as a national corporation, rather than as an international corporation. Although it has only one domicile and residence (in the UAE), the effect of the decision of the House of Lords is that the AMF has multiple nationality and multiple personality because it is incorporated in numerous States. The corporate body which had been created in the UAE was merely one of a number of different emanations of the same international body—a situation which Hoffmann J had recognised as giving rise to "questions of trinitarian subtlety".[22] Furthermore, the doctrine according to which international organisations are recognised as national corporations means that, if neither the United Kingdom nor any foreign country takes legislative steps to recognise or give effect to an international organisation established by treaty, it has no legal status in England; it is not able to sue or be sued, enter into contracts or hold property. Although the better approach to the problem which arose in *Arab Monetary Fund* v. *Hashim (No. 3)* is to recognise an organisation established by treaty as an international corporation, this route was effectively blocked off by "some ill-considered and unnecessary observations"[23] by members of the House of Lords in the *Tin Council* case.

2.1.4.3.5 It seems that the British Government, conscious of the economic implications of denying legal status to international bodies, is interested in keeping an eye on the law in this area. In correspondence between the Bank of England and the Lord Chancellor, the latter welcomed the decision of the House of Lords on the basis that it would "encourage banks and other entities to do business in the United Kingdom in the continuing expectation that the courts will be able to recognise their legal personality and capacity".[24]

2.1.4.3.6 Nevertheless, since the doctrine established by the House of Lords—that an international organisation can be recognised only as a national corporation—leads to the conclusion that an international organisation is denied legal capacity if it has not been recognised by legislation (whether in the United Kingdom or abroad), it seems unlikely that the last chapter of this particular saga has been written. It has been suggested that, while the opinion of Lord Oliver in the *Tin Council* case was of sufficient weight to cause the abandonment of an alternative line of argument before Hoffmann J in *Arab Monetary Fund* v. *Hashim (No. 3)*, it may not be impregnable to a future attack at the level of the House of Lords.[25] Should further problems concerning the legal capacity of international organisations arise, legislative intervention might be thought appropriate.[26]

21. [1991] 2 AC 114, 160.
22. [1990] 3 WLR 139, 148.
23. Collier, CLJ 39, 41.
24. Cited by Mercer, "The Arab Monetary Fund and the Courts: The Status of Foreign Entities Established by Treaty—Official Moves to Reassure the Markets" (1992) 13 Bus LR 159–160.
25. Marston, "The Origin of the Personality of International Organisations in United Kingdom Law" (1991) 40 ICLQ 403, 424.
26. See the correspondence between the Bank of England and the Lord Chancellor, cited by Mercer, "The Arab Monetary Fund and the Courts: The Status of Foreign Entitles Established by Treaty—Official Moves to Reassure the Markets" (1992) 13 Bus LR 159, 160.

2.1.5 Foreign States

2.1.5.1 There is no doubt that a foreign State which is recognised by the United Kingdom has capacity to sue and—subject to various immunities[27]—be sued in England. It is equally well established that an unrecognised State cannot sue or be sued in an English court. Although the two questions are not unrelated, from the perspective of English private international law, the crucial legal issue is not whether a territory is entitled to recognition as a State as a matter of public international law, but whether the State should be recognised by the English courts. It is possible that a territory is recognised as a State by the general international community, but not by the United Kingdom. Such was the position of Southern Rhodesia following the declaration of independence in 1965. The current view is that the English courts regard Foreign Office certificates as conclusive. Accordingly, if the Foreign Office does not recognise a State, the English courts will not recognise it as an independent State with capacity to sue or be sued in England.

2.1.5.2 In *GUR Corporation* v. *Trust Bank of Africa Ltd*[28] the Court of Appeal introduced an exception to this general principle. The factual background to this case was the establishment of tribal homelands by the Republic of South Africa. In 1981 the Republic of South Africa declared, by section 1 of the Status of Ciskei Act 1981, that the territory of Ciskei constituted a sovereign and independent State. The international community—including the United Kingdom—took no notice of this statutory provision and continued to regard the territory of Ciskei as subject to the sovereignty of South Africa. In 1983 the plaintiff contracted with the Republic of Ciskei's Department of Works to build a hospital and two schools in Ciskei. The plaintiff obtained from the defendant bank a guarantee in favour of Ciskei in return for a deposit of $300,000. In due course Ciskei demanded payment under the guarantee, but the defendant refused. When the plaintiff started proceedings to recover the security, the defendant sought to join Ciskei as third party.

2.1.5.3 At first instance the issue was raised as to whether Ciskei had *locus standi* to sue or be sued. Steyn J held that since Ciskei had not received official recognition as a State by the United Kingdom it could not be a party to litigation in England. The Court of Appeal took a different view. Although Ciskei could not be a party to litigation as an independent State this did not preclude the possibility of treating Ciskei's Department of Works as an emanation of the Republic of South Africa, which was regarded by the international community as still having sovereignty over the territory of Ciskei.

2.1.5.4 The approach adopted by the Court of Appeal was derived from *Carl Zeiss Stiftung* v. *Rayner & Keeler Ltd (No. 2)*[29] in which the House of Lords was required to consider the validity of administrative acts of the GDR. Although the USSR had purported to establish the GDR as an independent State it was not officially recognised as such by the United Kingdom. As far as the Foreign Office was concerned the USSR

27. See para. 2.3.

28. [1987] QB 559. Beck, "A South African Homeland Appears in the English Courts: Legitimation of the Illegitimate?" (1987) 36 ICLQ 350; Crawford, (1986) 57 BYIL 405; Lloyd Jones, [1987] CLJ 7; Mann, "The Judicial Recognition of an Unrecognised State" (1987) 36 ICLQ 348; Warbrick, "Unrecognised States and Domestic Law" (1987) 50 MLR 84.

29. [1967] 1 AC 853. Grieg, "The Carl-Zeiss Case and the Position of Unrecognised Governments in English Law" (1967) 83 LQR 96.

was *de jure* entitled to exercise governing authority in respect of the territory which was known at the end of the Second World War as the Eastern Zone of Germany. Nevertheless, the House of Lords was prepared to recognise the administrative acts of the public authorities of the GDR as acts done by a subordinate body set up by the USSR to act on its behalf. In *GUR Corporation* v. *Trust Bank of Africa Ltd* the Court of Appeal—applying the same reasoning—concluded that the Government of the Republic of Ciskei was a subordinate body set up by the Republic of South Africa to act on its behalf and that it had *locus standi* as such in this country.

2.1.5.5 The decision of the Court of Appeal has been the subject of criticism. From the point of view of precedent it might be questioned whether the decision of the House of Lords in *Carl Zeiss Stiftung* v. *Rayner & Keeler Ltd (No. 2)* was relevant in *GUR Corporation* v. *Trust Bank of Africa Ltd*. In the *Carl Zeiss* case the issue was whether the administrative acts of the GDR were effective; there was no question of the standing of the GDR to sue or be sued in England. The policy of the decision may also be questioned. The case raised competing policies: on the one hand, it is reasonable that the courts should seek to do their best to meet the needs and wishes of litigants; on the other, it is desirable that the courts should speak in terms which are not inconsistent with the foreign policy of the British Government. By effectively conferring status on the Republic of Ciskei the court undermined the stand taken by the international community against the policy of apartheid in South Africa, of which the creation of the tribal homelands was a part. The effect of the decision was that the party before the court was not the Republic of South Africa, but the unrecognised Republic of Ciskei, represented by its Department of Works. To deny recognition to the Republic of Ciskei would undoubtedly cause inconvenience to parties who contracted with the Republic of Ciskei, since they would be unable to have their rights determined in England. However, such contracting parties would presumably be able to bring proceedings against the Republic of Ciskei either in South Africa or in the territory of Ciskei itself.

2.1.5.6 There is a certain illogicality in the Court of Appeal's decision. What, for example, would have been the position if Ciskei had declared its independence from South Africa, repudiated the Status of Ciskei Act 1981 and begun a campaign for the destruction of apartheid? It is hard to believe that in these circumstances the English courts would continue to treat Ciskei as a subordinate authority of South Africa. However, by denying Ciskei's status in these circumstances, the courts would be giving Ciskei more status as an engine of apartheid than as an opponent of it.[30]

2.1.6 Foreign governments

2.1.6.1 The fact that a State is recognised does not in itself determine who is entitled to sue on behalf of that State. In cases of unconstitutional usurpation of power or the disintegration of constitutional authority there may be disagreement as to who is entitled—as the government of a State—to litigate on behalf of that State and to enforce the rights which are vested in it. Before April 1980 the position of foreign governments was similar to that of foreign States; the right of a foreign government to litigate in England depended on its being recognised by the British Government. In April 1980 the

30. See Crawford, (1986) 57 BYIL 405, 409.

Foreign Secretary announced that HM Government would no longer accord recognition to foreign governments. It has, therefore, been left to the courts to formulate a test for determining whether or not an authority should be regarded as a foreign government of a particular State.

2.1.6.2 This important issue was considered in *Republic of Somalia* v. *Woodhouse Drake & Carey (Suisse) SA.*[31] The crucial facts may be stated briefly: a cargo had been purchased by the Republic of Somalia; the captain of the ship on which the cargo was loaded refused to enter the port of Mogadishu; the cargo was sold and the proceeds were paid into court. The issue facing the court was whether the so-called "Interim Government" was entitled to the sum which had been paid into court. Hobhouse J thought that in view of the state of relative chaos in Somalia, the claim of the "Interim Government" should fail. The relevant test for deciding whether to recognise a government was formulated in the following terms:

> [T]he factors to be taken into account in deciding whether a government exists as the government of a State are: (a) whether it is the constitutional government of the State; (b) the degree, nature and stability of administrative control, if any, that it of itself exercises over the territory of the State; (c) whether Her Majesty's Government has any dealings with it and if so what is the nature of those dealings; and (d) in marginal cases, the extent of international recognition that it has as the government of the State.[32]

Paragraphs (a) and (b) are alternative tests of being a government, although constitutionality and effectiveness normally coincide; paragraphs (c) and (d) are matters of evidence on which a court will rely to see if the test in paragraph (a) and/or paragraph (b) is satisfied.[33]

2.2 PERSONS WHO CANNOT SUE: ENEMY ALIENS

2.2.1 As a general rule a plaintiff is entitled to commence proceedings in England regardless of nationality, residence or domicile. However, at common law an alien enemy is not entitled to invoke the jurisdiction of the English courts. In order for someone to be an enemy alien there must be a state of war between the United Kingdom and the enemy country in question. It is quite rare for a state of war to arise; most situations in which an armed conflict arises do not constitute a state of war from the legal point of view.

2.2.2 The alien status of a person depends not on nationality, but on physical location. A British subject who voluntarily resides or carries on business in a foreign country which is at war with the United Kingdom is an enemy alien.[34] Similarly, a citizen of a country which is at war with the United Kingdom, but who resides in the United Kingdom with the permission of the Crown is not an enemy alien for the purposes of

31. [1993] QB 54. Kingsbury, "Judicial Determination of Foreign 'Government' Status" (1993) 109 LQR 377; Warbrick, "Recognition of Governments" (1993) 56 MLR 92.
32. Hobhouse J, [1993] QB 54, 68.
33. Warbrick, "Recognition of Governments" (1993) 56 MLR 92, 96.
34. *Porter* v. *Freudenberg* [1915] 1 KB 857; *Sovfracht (V/O)* v. *Van Udens Scheepvaart en Agentuur Maatschappij (NV Gebr)* [1943] AC 203.

English jurisdiction rules.[35] Furthermore, it should be noted that there is nothing to prevent a plaintiff from invoking the jurisdiction of the English courts against an enemy alien.[36]

2.3 STATE IMMUNITY

2.3.1 Background

2.3.1.1 The purpose of the doctrine of sovereign immunity is to promote the functioning of all governments by protecting States from the burden of defending litigation abroad. In the nineteenth century foreign States were entitled to absolute immunity. The doctrine of absolute immunity was justified by the fact that state activities were limited to the public sphere. As regards both internal matters (such as law and order) and external matters (such as foreign policy and defence) it is reasonable that within the public sphere States should not be required to litigate in a foreign court against their will.

2.3.1.2 During the twentieth century governments have become involved in commercial activities which are scarcely any different in nature from the activities of private individuals and companies. When a foreign State enters the marketplace or when it acts as a private party would act, there is no justification for allowing the foreign State to avoid the economic costs of its actions. If, for example, an English company enters a contract to build a hospital in a foreign country, it is not obvious that, from a jurisdictional point of view, it should be regarded as legally relevant whether the other contracting party is a foreign company or a foreign government. The law should not permit the foreign State to shift the everyday burdens of the marketplace onto the shoulders of private parties. Accordingly, a distinction has to be drawn between those state activities which are public—and in relation to which a State may reasonably expect to be immune from legal proceedings in a foreign court—and those state activities which are private or commercial in nature—in relation to which a State cannot reasonably expect to be immune from litigation.[37] These different types of activity are given Latin labels: *acta jure imperii* and *acta jure gestionis*.

2.3.1.3 Following the Second World War the English courts began to develop a doctrine of restrictive immunity at common law.[38] However, the law in this area was placed on a statutory footing by the State Immunity Act 1978[39] (which implements the European Convention on State Immunity of 1972[40]). The State Immunity Act 1978 is to a large extent based on the distinction between *acta jure imperii* and *acta jure gestionis*.

35. *Johnstone* v. *Pedlar* [1921] 2 AC 262.

36. *Robinson & Co* v. *Continental Insurance Co of Mannheim* [1915] 1 KB 155; *Porter* v. *Freudenberg* [1915] 1 KB 857.

37. See Crawford, "International Law and Foreign Sovereigns: Distinguishing Immune Transactions" (1983) 54 BYIL 75.

38. See, in particular, the decision of the Court of Appeal in *Trendtex Trading Corporation* v. *Central Bank of Nigeria* [1977] QB 529. Markesinis, [1977] CLJ 211.

39. Bowett, [1978] CLJ 193; Lewis, [1980] LMCLQ 1; Mann, (1979) 50 BYIL 43; G White, [1979] JBL 105; R White, (1979) 42 MLR 72.

40. Sinclair, "The European Convention on State Immunity" (1973) 22 ICLQ 254.

The statutory rules do not apply to proceedings in respect of matters that occurred before 22 November 1978, the date on which the Act came into force.[41]

2.3.2 What is a State?

2.3.2.1 Section 14(1) defines what is meant by a State for the purposes of the Act:

> The immunities and privileges conferred by this Part of this Act apply to any foreign or commonwealth State other than the United Kingdom; and references to a State include references to:
> (a) the sovereign or other head of that State in his public capacity;
> (b) the government of that State; and
> (c) any department of that government,
> but not to any entity (hereafter referred to as a "separate entity") which is distinct from the executive organs of the government of the State and is capable of suing or being sued.

2.3.2.2 The purpose of the last part of this subsection is to try to distinguish government departments from state-owned and state-managed organisations. A separate entity is not generally entitled to immunity, except with regard to proceedings relating to anything done by it in the exercise of sovereign authority and in circumstances in which a State would have been immune.[42] Of course, there is the question as to what constitutes "sovereign authority". It must be expected, however, that it is extremely unusual for an entity which is "distinct from the executive organs of the State" to "exercise sovereign authority"; accordingly, for most practical purposes a separate entity within the meaning of the Act does not have any immunities. Having said that, in *Kuwait Airways Corporation* v. *Iraqi Airways*[43] the Court of Appeal held that the confiscation of the plaintiff's aircraft in August 1990 by the defendant at the direction of the government of Iraq was an activity carried out in the exercise of sovereign authority for the purposes of section 14 of the 1978 Act. Furthermore, it should be noted that a State's central bank—which, depending on the circumstances, may or may not be a separate entity—is subject to special rules.[44]

2.3.3 The scheme of the Act

2.3.3.1 The principle of immunity

The structure of the 1978 Act derives from the nineteenth century position. The starting-point is the principle of immunity. Section 1(1) provides: "A State is immune from the jurisdiction of the courts of the United Kingdom except as provided in the following provisions of this Part of this Act."

2.3.3.2 Exceptions to immunity

The major part of the 1978 Act is concerned with the various exceptions to the principle of immunity. The legislation draws a distinction between adjudicative jurisdiction and enforcement jurisdiction: sections 2 to 11 deal with adjudicative jurisdiction; sections 13

41. State Immunity Act 1978, s. 23(3).
42. State Immunity Act 1978, s. 14(2).
43. *The Times*, 27 October 1993.
44. See para. 2.3.5.5.2.

and 14 regulate enforcement jurisdiction; section 12 is concerned with procedural issues. The boundaries of immunity from adjudicative jurisdiction and from enforcement jurisdiction are drawn differently, with the consequence that it is perfectly possible for a State to be held liable for a debt but for there to be no means available to the creditor to enforce the judgment in England.

2.3.3.3 The burden of proof

Is the court to presume that a State is entitled to immunity unless it is proved by the plaintiff to the contrary or should the burden of proof be on the party invoking immunity? It has been argued that, notwithstanding the way in which the Act is structured, the burden of proof should be on the defendant to establish that it is entitled to immunity.[45] Judicial opinion, however, is that the burden of proof falls on the plaintiff to show that the defendant is not entitled to immunity.[46] Furthermore, it is not enough that the plaintiff establishes a good arguable case. Even in those cases where the defendant does not seek to challenge the jurisdiction of the court, preferring to take no part at all in the proceedings, the question of whether the defendant is entitled to immunity "must be decided as a preliminary issue in favour of the plaintiff, in whatever form and by whatever procedure the court may consider appropriate".[47]

2.3.4 Immunity from adjudicative jurisdiction

Sections 2 to 11 list the ten areas in which States are not entitled to immunity from adjudicative jurisdiction. These ten areas are not mutually exclusive; there are certain points of overlap between them. Although it is thought that the exclusions from immunity are, for the most part, cumulative rather than alternative,[48] the Court of Appeal declined to express a concluded opinion on this point when it arose in *Intpro Properties (UK) Ltd* v. *Sauvel.*[49]

2.3.4.1 Submission

2.3.4.1.1 Section 2(1) provides that a State is not immune "as respects proceedings in respect of which it has submitted to the jurisdiction of the courts of the United Kingdom". A State may submit after the dispute has arisen or by prior written agreement.[50] A choice of English law is not to be regarded as a submission to the jurisdiction of the English courts.[51]

2.3.4.1.2 As a general rule a State is deemed to have submitted if it institutes proceedings or if it has intervened or taken any step in the proceedings.[52] However, a State is not regarded as having submitted, notwithstanding the fact that it has taken part in proceedings, in a number of situations:

45. Mann, "The State Immunity Act 1978" (1979) 50 BYIL 43, 62.
46. *JH Rayner (Mincing Lane) Ltd* v. *Department of Trade and Industry* [1987] BCLC 667, 678.
47. Kerr LJ in *JH Rayner (Mincing Lane) Ltd* v. *Department of Trade and Industry* [1989] Ch 72, 194.
48. See Crawford, (1983) 54 BYIL 283, 284.
49. [1983] QB 1019.
50. State Immunity Act 1978, s. 2(2).
51. State Immunity Act 1978, s. 2(2).
52. State Immunity Act 1978, s. 2(3).

(i) where the State takes part in proceedings in order to claim immunity[53];

(ii) where the steps taken in the proceedings are in substance objections to the court's jurisdiction (such as applying for a stay of execution, contesting the validity of service, or applying for a stay of proceedings on the basis of *forum non conveniens*) and are alternative to a claim to immunity[54];

(iii) where the State intervenes in proceedings to assert an interest in property in circumstances in which the State would have been entitled to immunity had the proceedings been brought against it[55];

(iv) where the State intervenes in proceedings in ignorance of facts entitling it to immunity if those facts could not reasonably have been ascertained and immunity is claimed as soon as reasonably practicable.[56]

2.3.4.1.3 A State can be regarded as submitting only by virtue of acts performed by its representatives. The head of a State's diplomatic mission in the United Kingdom (or the person for the time being performing those functions) is deemed to have the authority to submit to the jurisdiction of the courts. Furthermore, where proceedings arise out of a contract, any person who has entered the contract on behalf of and with the authority of the State in question is deemed to have the necessary authority to submit.[57] Once a State has submitted to proceedings that submission extends to any appeal or any counterclaim which arises out of the same legal relationship or facts as the claim.[58]

2.3.4.2 Arbitration

Section 9(1) provides:

> Where a State has agreed in writing to submit a dispute which has arisen, or may arise, to arbitration, the State is not immune as respects proceedings in the courts of the United Kingdom which relate to the arbitration.

This provision does not apply where both the parties to the agreement are States or where the parties have agreed that immunity is to apply.[59]

(i) Article 12 of the European Convention on State Immunity of 1972—on which section 9 is based—is restricted to court proceedings relating to civil and commercial matters. There would seem to be no such restriction in the law of the United Kingdom.

(ii) What is meant by the word "relate" in the context of section 9(1)? Of particular importance is the question of whether the Act permits proceedings in England to enforce an award against a State. The wording of the European Convention on State Immunity and the structure of the 1978 Act—which draws a clear distinction between adjudicative jurisdiction and enforcement jurisdiction—indicate that the enforcement of awards is not within the scope of section 9, but falls to be determined by section 13.[60]

53. State Immunity Act 1978, s. 2(4)(a).
54. *Kuwait Airways Corporation* v. *Iraqi Airways*, *Financial Times*, 17 July 1992.
55. State Immunity Act 1978, s. 2(4)(b).
56. State Immunity Act 1978, s. 2(5).
57. State Immunity Act 1978, s. 2(7).
58. State Immunity Act 1978, s. 2(6).
59. State Immunity Act 1978, s. 9(2).
60. Fox, "States and the Undertaking to Arbitrate" (1988) 37 ICLQ 1, 14–15.

(iii) Does an agreement to arbitrate in country X amount to a waiver of immunity with regard to court proceedings relating to the arbitration in any forum or only to proceedings brought before the courts of country X? Academic opinion is divided. One view is that section 9 applies regardless of the seat of arbitration[61]; the alternative view is that section 9 removes immunity only in respect of proceedings relating to arbitrations conducted in the United Kingdom.[62] In practice the only proceedings relating to arbitration which are likely to be brought in a country other than that in which the seat of arbitration is located are proceedings concerning either the availability of provisional measures or the enforcement of arbitral awards. State immunity in these contexts is to be determined by the provisions of the 1978 Act dealing with enforcement immunity rather than those dealing with adjudicative immunity.

(iv) What is the effect of an arbitration agreement which is entered into by a state official who does not have authority to do so under the law of the State in question? It has been suggested that in this case the waiver is *ultra vires* and the court should not assume jurisdiction.[63] The alternative, and preferable view is that the waiver should be regarded as effective as long as the official who entered the agreement with the private party had the apparent authority to do so.[64]

2.3.4.3 Ships

2.3.4.3.1 Many States own or operate fleets of merchant ships. In practice, therefore, one of the most important areas where the issue of immunity may be relevant is in the context of shipping. Section 10 applies to Admiralty proceedings and proceedings on any claim which could be made the subject of Admiralty proceedings.[65] Although the most usual way in which Admiralty proceedings are commenced is by service of a writ on a ship, an action *in rem* is based on a claim *in personam* and the Supreme Court Act 1981—which defines the court's Admiralty jurisdiction—makes it clear that, subject to section 22 of that Act, "an action *in personam* may be brought in the High Court in all cases within the Admiralty jurisdiction of that court".[66] The exceptions to immunity contained in section 10 apply equally to proceedings *in rem* and *in personam*.[67]

2.3.4.3.2 Section 10(2) provides:

> A State is not immune as respects:
> (a) an action *in rem* against a ship belonging to that State; or
> (b) an action *in personam* for enforcing a claim in connection with such a ship,
> if, at the time when the cause of action arose, the ship was in use or intended for use for commercial purposes.

61. Mann, "The State Immunity Act 1978" (1979) 50 BYIL 43, 58.
62. Fox, "States and the Undertaking to Arbitrate" (1988) 37 ICLQ 1, 14.
63. Sornarajah, "Problems of Applying the Restrictive Theory of Sovereign Immunity" (1982) 31 ICLQ 661, 685.
64. Oparil, "Waiver of Sovereign Immunity in the United States and Great Britain by an Arbitration Agreement" (1986) 4 J Int Arb (4) 61, 72.
65. State Immunity Act 1978, s. 10(1).
66. Supreme Court Act 1981, s. 21(1).
67. For a discussion of jurisdiction in Admiralty proceedings see Chapter 8.

This subsection is qualified by subsection (3), which deals with the situation where the plaintiff starts proceedings *in rem* against a sister ship (S2), rather than the ship in connection with which the claim arose (S1). The effect of subsection (3) is that both S1 and S2 must have been in use or intended for use for commercial purposes at the time when the claim arose in connection with S1.

2.3.4.3.3 Subsection (4) provides special rules for cargoes:

> A State is not immune as respects:
> (a) an action *in rem* against a cargo belonging to that State if both the cargo and the ship carrying it were, at the time when the cause of action arose, in use or intended for use for commercial purposes; or
> (b) an action *in personam* for enforcing a claim in connection with such a cargo if the ship carrying it was then in use or intended for use as aforesaid.

Although the exclusions from immunity in section 10 refer to ships and cargoes "belonging to" a State, subsection (5) provides that "references to a ship or cargo belonging to a State include references to a ship or cargo in its possession or control or in which it claims an interest". "Commercial purposes" is defined by section 17(1) as "purposes of such transactions or activities as are mentioned in section 3(3)".[68]

2.3.4.3.4 Although the idea behind section 10 is relatively straightforward—States should not be able to claim immunity in respect of commercial shipping activity—the statutory provisions are rather complex. In particular, the distinction between ships and cargoes gives rise to some subtleties. The effect of subsections (2) and (4) can be illustrated by the following examples:

> A warship which happens to be used for carrying motor cars for civilian use cannot be immune, but if a trading ship carries ammunition for military purposes both the ship and the cargo are immune, at least if there is no commercial cargo on board. Cement carried in a trading ship may be immune: the result depends on the purpose for which it will be used. If the consignee intends to sell the cement to the military administration, but is not contractually bound to do so, the non-commercial purpose does not in any legally relevant sense exist. If the consignee has sold an identifiable quantity being part of the cargo of cement for the building of military barracks, immunity extends to such quantity and it would probably be no counter-argument that one must not look beyond the consignee; what matter are the ultimate purposes in so far as they can be proven. Shoes for the army (to revert to an often-discussed example) are a cargo for a non-commercial purpose, but if they are consigned to a private merchant who only hopes to sell them to the army, the purpose remains commercial.[69]

2.3.4.3.5 Whereas normally the various exceptions to immunity can be applied cumulatively, where a situation falls within the scope of section 10(1) (ie the plaintiff's claim is within the Admiralty jurisdiction of the court) the exceptions from immunity contained in sections 3 to 5 (commercial transactions, contracts of employment and tort) do not apply if the following two requirements, provided by section 10(6), are met: (i) the State is a party to the Brussels Convention of 1926 on Immunity of State-Owned Ships; and (ii) the claim relates to the operation of a ship owned or operated by that State, or to the carriage of cargo or passengers on any such ship, or to the carriage of

68. The definition of "commercial transaction" for the purpose of section 3(3) is broadly drafted to include: contracts for the supply of goods and services; loans and other transactions for the provision of finance; and other transactions and activities (of a commercial or analogous nature) into which a State enters or engages otherwise than in the exercise of sovereign authority. See para. 2.3.4.4.2.

69. Mann, "The State Immunity Act 1978" (1979) 50 BYIL 43, 58–59.

cargo owned by that State on any other ship. Although the plaintiff cannot rely on sections 3 to 5 if both these requirements are satisfied, the other exceptions to immunity—notably section 2 (submission) and section 9 (arbitration) are not excluded by section 10(6). Of course, if either of the requirements set out in section 10(6) is not satisfied, the general provisions of sections 3, 4 and 5 may be relied upon by the plaintiff.

2.3.4.4 Commercial activities

2.3.4.4.1 One of the most important exceptions to immunity is contained in section 3 which provides:

> (1) A State is not immune as respects proceedings relating to—
> (a) a commercial transaction entered into by the State; or
> (b) an obligation of the State which by virtue of a contract (whether a commercial transaction or not) falls to be performed wholly or partly in the United Kingdom.
> (2) This section does not apply if the parties to the dispute are States or have otherwise agreed in writing; and subsection (1)(b) above does not apply if the contract (not being a commercial transaction) was made in the territory of the State concerned and the obligation in question is governed by its administrative law.

Section 3(1)(b) has been given a broad interpretation by the English courts. Whereas section 3(1)(a) refers to a transaction "entered into by the State", there is no similar reference in section 3(1)(b). The requirements of section 3(1)(b) are that the proceedings in question relate to obligations of the State, that those obligations are to be performed in the United Kingdom and that they have arisen by virtue of a contract. Section 3(1)(b) does not require that the contract should have been entered into by the State.[70]

2.3.4.4.2 Section 3(3) defines what is meant by "commercial transaction" in the following terms:

> (a) any contract for the supply of goods or services;
> (b) any loan or other transaction for the provision of finance or any guarantee or indemnity in respect of any such transaction or of any other financial obligation; and
> (c) any other transaction or activity (whether of a commercial, industrial, financial, professional or other similar character) into which a State enters or in which it engages otherwise than in the exercise of sovereign authority;
> but neither paragraph of subsection (1) above applies to a contract of employment between a State and an individual.

As regards paragraphs (a) and (b) it is the nature of the transaction not its purpose which is important. Accordingly, a contract for the sale of goods is a commercial transaction regardless of the purpose for which the goods are acquired and regardless of whether the State is engaged in the exercise of sovereign authority. The sale of boots or the borrowing of money on which interest is payable are commercial transactions, notwithstanding the fact that the boots are for the army and the money is for munitions. However, as regards paragraph (c), the transaction or activity cannot be "commercial" if the State enters into it in the exercise of sovereign authority.

70. *JH Rayner (Mincing Lane) Ltd* v. *Department of Trade and Industry* [1989] Ch 72.

2.3.4.5 *Contracts of employment*

2.3.4.5.1 Section 4, which contains special rules relating to contracts of employment, is drafted in a very complex manner. Subsection (1) provides that a State is not immune as regards "proceedings relating to a contract of employment between the State and an individual where the contract was made in the United Kingdom or the work is to be wholly or partly performed there". This exception to the principle of immunity is itself subject to exceptions in subsection (2), which in turn are subject to further exceptions in subsections (3) and (4):

(2) Subject to subsections (3) and (4) below, this section does not apply if—
(a) at the time when the proceedings are brought the individual is a national of the State concerned; or
(b) at the time when the contract was made the individual was neither a national of the United Kingdom nor habitually resident there; or
(c) the parties to the contract have otherwise agreed in writing.

(3) Where the work is for an office, agency or establishment maintained by the State in the United Kingdom for commercial purposes, subsection 2(a) and (b) above do not exclude the application of this section unless the individual was, at the time when the contract was made, habitually resident in that State.

(4) Subsection (2)(c) above does not exclude the application of this section where the law of the United Kingdom requires the proceedings to be brought before a court of the United Kingdom.

2.3.4.5.2 In *Sengupta* v. *Republic of India*[71] the plaintiff, an Indian national, was employed by the Indian High Commission. When the plaintiff was dismissed he sued his employer in England. In these circumstances the State was entitled to immunity since the employee was "a national of the State concerned" for the purposes of section 4(2)(a) and the High Commission was not an "establishment maintained by the State in the United Kingdom for commercial purposes" within the meaning of section 4(3).

2.3.4.6 *Tort*

Section 5 provides that a State is "not immune as respects proceedings in respect of (a) death or personal injury, or (b) damage to or loss of tangible property, caused by an act or omission in the United Kingdom". The wording of section 5 means that a State is immune in the United Kingdom in cases where a wrongful act performed wholly outside the United Kingdom gives rise to damage within the United Kingdom. Similarly, in cases where as a result of a tort—whether committed in the United Kingdom or abroad—the plaintiff suffers pure economic loss the general principle of immunity in section 1(1) applies.

2.3.4.7 *Ownership, possession and use of property*

2.3.4.7.1 Section 6(1) provides that a State is not immune as respects proceedings relating to "(a) any interest of that State in, or its possession or use of, immovable

71. [1983] ICR 221. Crawford, (1983) 54 BYIL 279. Although the case was decided under the common law which was applicable before the entry into force of the 1978 Act Browne-Wilkinson J considered the position under the legislation.

property in the United Kingdom; or (b) any obligation of the State arising out of its interest in, or its possession or use of, any such property". Although the basic principle in section 6(1) is clear, it is subject to an exception in section 16 which provides that section 6(1) "does not apply to proceedings concerning a State's title to or its possession of property used for the purposes of a diplomatic mission".

2.3.4.7.2 The relationship between sections 6 and 16 was considered by the courts in *Intpro Properties (UK) Ltd* v. *Sauvel.*[72] In 1979 the plaintiff let a house in London to the third defendant, the French Government. The house was occupied by the first defendant, who was a financial counsellor at the French embassy in London. In 1983 dry rot was discovered in the house, but the plaintiff was unable to gain access to effect the necessary repairs. The plaintiff started proceedings with a view to recovering damages for the third defendant's refusal to allow the plaintiff entry to the premises. Counsel for the plaintiff relied on the exception to immunity contained in section 6(1)(b). Although it was accepted on the basis of section 13(2)(a) that it was not possible to obtain an injunction or an order for possession against the third defendant, the plaintiff argued that this did not bar the claim for damages for breach of covenant. Since the action was plainly covered by section 6(1)(b) the question facing the court was whether the plaintiff's claim was excluded by section 16.

2.3.4.7.3 The Court of Appeal decided that section 16 did not apply. (i) The premises were not used for the purposes of a diplomatic mission. Although it was true that the first defendant used the premises for social functions associated with his employment, this was not enough to bring the case within the scope of the provision. (ii) The Court of Appeal thought that the proceedings in the present case did not concern the State's title to the premises or their possession of them within the meaning of section 16. Accordingly, the situation fell within the scope of section 6(1)(b) and the third defendant was not entitled to immunity.

2.3.4.7.4 Where proceedings are brought in relation to state-owned property which is in the possession of a third party, the State is being indirectly impleaded. In these circumstances section 6(4) allows the third party to raise immunity as a defence to the extent that the defence would have been available to the State in a direct action. As a result of section 6(4) a bank may be able to resist claims against funds belonging to a State which are deposited with it.

2.3.4.8 Intellectual property rights

Three points emerge from section 7:

(i) a State is not immune as respects proceedings relating to patents, trademarks and other intellectual property rights registered or protected in the United Kingdom;

(ii) there is no immunity in cases where a person alleges that a State has infringed his intellectual property rights in the United Kingdom;

(iii) there is no immunity in proceedings relating to the right to use a business name in the United Kingdom.

72. [1983] QB 1019. Crawford, (1983) 54 BYIL 283.

2.3.4.9 Membership of organisations

Section 8 deals with proceedings relating to an organisation—whether "a body corporate, an unincorporated body or a partnership"—of which a State is a member. The State does not enjoy immunity as regards proceedings arising between the State and the organisation or between the State and the other members of the organisation if two conditions are satisfied: (i) the organisation has members which are not States; and (ii) the organisation is incorporated under United Kingdom law or is controlled from or has its principal place of business in the United Kingdom.

2.3.4.10 Taxes

A State is not immune as respects proceedings relating to its liability for value added tax, customs and excise duties and agricultural levies and business rates.[73]

2.3.5 Immunity from enforcement jurisdiction

2.3.5.1 Preliminary remarks

2.3.5.1.1 As regards adjudicative jurisdiction, the exceptions to the general principle of immunity are extremely wide. In most cases of a commercial nature States and state entities (whether government departments or separate entities) are unable to invoke the doctrine of immunity in their favour. However, immunity from adjudicative jurisdiction is only one side of the coin. It is not enough that a plaintiff is able to sue a State in England in respect of a commercial transaction; it is just as important that a successful plaintiff should be able to have recourse to the courts to enforce a judgment or award in his favour. It is in this regard that the 1978 Act might be thought to be lacking; the immunity from enforcement jurisdiction provided by sections 13 and 14 goes further than is necessary.

2.3.5.1.2 The general point which emerges from sections 13 and 14 is that arbitration or litigation against a State is a far from secure process. A judgment or award against a State may prove to be no more than a Pyrrhic victory. It is not sufficient that the State submits to the adjudicative jurisdiction of national courts or to arbitration; to be sure of being able to enforce a judgment or award against a State private parties need to bargain also for a waiver of immunity against enforcement jurisdiction.[74]

2.3.5.2 Immunity under section 13(1) and (2)

2.3.5.2.1 Section 13(1) provides:

> No penalty by way of committal or fine shall be imposed in respect of any failure or refusal by or on behalf of a State to disclose or produce any document or other information for the purposes of proceedings to which it is a party.

This subsection does not mean, however, that a State can refuse to co-operate in discovery with impunity. The judge is entitled to draw the appropriate inference from a State's refusal to produce a relevant document.

73. State Immunity Act 1978, s. 11.
74. Delaume, "Sovereign Immunity and Transnational Arbitration" (1987) 3 Arb Int 28, 44–45.

2.3.5.2.2 The general principle of immunity from enforcement jurisdiction is extremely wide. Section 13(2) provides that "(a) relief shall not be given against a State by way of injunction or order for specific performance or for the recovery of land or any other property; and (b) the property of a State shall not be subject to any process for the enforcement of a judgment or arbitration award or, in an action *in rem*, for its arrest, detention or sale". Although the Act does not define what is meant by "injunction or order for specific performance" it is clear that an order directed at a State to provide security for the other party's costs does not fall within the scope of section 13(1)(a): "a simple order for the payment of money from no specified source" is not an injunction.[75]

The enforcement immunity conferred by section 13(2) is subject to two exceptions: (i) there is a general exception in cases where the defendant has waived immunity[76]; and (ii) there is a more specific exception to section 13(2)(b) in relation to property used for commercial purposes.[77]

2.3.5.3 Waiver of immunity

2.3.5.3.1 Section 13(3) provides:

> Subsection (2) above does not prevent the giving of any relief or the issue of any process with the written consent of the State concerned; and any such consent (which may be contained in a prior agreement) may be expressed so as to apply to a limited extent or generally; but a provision merely submitting to the jurisdiction of the courts is not to be regarded as a consent for the purposes of this subsection.

Subsection (5) goes on to provide that "[t]he head of a State's diplomatic mission in the United Kingdom, or the person for the time being performing his functions, shall be deemed to have authority to give on behalf of the State any such consent as is mentioned in subsection (3)".

2.3.5.3.2 Subsection (3) was considered in *A Co Ltd* v. *Republic of X*,[78] a case concerning the effect of the following terms contained in contracts for the sale of coffee and cocoa:

> 6. Sovereign Immunity
> The Ministry of Finance hereby waives whatever defence it may have of sovereign immunity for itself or its property (present or subsequently acquired).
>
> 7. Governing Law & Arbitration
> (a) This agreement shall be governed and construed in accordance with the laws of England without reference to conflict of the laws, and A Co and the Ministry of Finance hereby submit to the jurisdiction of the English courts.

It was clear that, as regards adjudicative jurisdiction, clause 7 of the contract was effective as a submission for the purposes of section 2 of the 1978 Act. In the course of proceedings the plaintiff applied for a Mareva injunction to prevent the Republic from disposing of assets up to $12 million—which was the sum owed under the contracts. The question was whether clause 6 constituted "written consent" for the purpose of section 13(2), thereby enabling the English court to grant the relief sought by the plaintiff. It

75. Staughton LJ in *Soleh Boneh International Ltd* v. *Government of the Republic of Uganda* [1993] 2 Lloyd's Rep 208, 213.
76. State Immunity Act 1978, s. 13(3).
77. State Immunity Act 1978, s. 13(4).
78. [1990] 2 Lloyd's Rep 520. Mann, "Waiver of Immunity" (1991) 107 LQR 362.

was held that by expressly waiving "whatever defence it may have of sovereign immunity for itself or its property" the Republic had waived its enforcement immunity. Accordingly, the fact that the defendant was a State did not inhibit the court's jurisdiction.

2.3.5.4 No immunity in respect of property used for commercial purposes

2.3.5.4.1 Section 13(4) provides:

Subsection (2)(b) above does not prevent the issue of any process in respect of property which is for the time being in use or intended for use for commercial purposes; but, in a case not falling within section 10 above, this subsection applies to property of a State party to the European Convention on State Immunity only if—

(a) the process is for enforcing a judgment which is final within the meaning of section 18(1)(b) below and the State has made a declaration under Article 24 of the Convention; or

(b) the process is for enforcing an arbitration award.

The structure of subsection (4) is somewhat complex. The principle in subsection (2) is that a State's property cannot be the subject of an order for enforcement. Subsection (4) provides a general exception: an order for enforcement may be made against a State's commercial property—that is, property which is for the time being in use or intended for use for commercial purposes. There are, however, specific exceptions to the general exception.

2.3.5.4.2 The effect of these provisions is as follows:

(i) there can be no enforcement against a State's property which is not commercial property (unless there has been an express waiver of enforcement immunity);

(ii) an award can be enforced against the commercial property of a State;

(iii) in a situation which falls within the Admiralty jurisdiction of the court, a judgment can be enforced against the commercial property of a State;

(iv) in a situation which does not fall within the Admiralty jurisdiction of the court, a judgment can be enforced against the commercial property of a State which is not a party to the European Convention on State Immunity;

(v) in a situation which does not fall within the Admiralty jurisdiction of the court, a judgment cannot be enforced against the commercial property of a State which is a party to the European Convention on State Immunity unless the judgment is final[79] and the State in question has made a declaration under Article 24 of the Convention.[80]

2.3.5.4.3 In determining whether or not property is intended for commercial purposes within the meaning of section 13(4), subsection (5) provides that the certificate of the head of a State's diplomatic mission in the United Kingdom, or the person for the

79. A judgment is final if it "is not or is no longer subject to appeal or, if given in default of appearance, liable to be set aside": State Immunity Act, s. 18(1)(b).

80. The certificate of the Secretary of State as to whether a State is a party to the Convention and has made a declaration under Article 24 is conclusive: State Immunity Act 1978, s. 21(c).

time being performing his functions, to the effect that any property is not in use or intended for use by or on behalf of the State for commercial purposes "shall be accepted as sufficient evidence of that fact unless the contrary is proved".

2.3.5.4.4 Subsections (4) and (5) were considered by the House of Lords in *Alcom Ltd* v. *Republic of Colombia.*[81] The plaintiff, having obtained a default judgment against the Republic of Colombia, applied for a garnishee order to freeze the Republic's bank account to a specified amount which would be sufficient to satisfy the judgment. The account in question was the account used for the day-to-day running of the Republic's diplomatic mission in the United Kingdom. Since the Colombian ambassador had certified that the funds deposited at the bank were not used or intended for use for commercial purposes, section 13(5) placed the onus on the plaintiff to establish that the account was used for commercial purposes.

2.3.5.4.5 Two questions arose for decision by the House of Lords. (i) Was the debt owed by the bank to the defendant—ie the positive bank balance—"property" within the meaning of section 13(2)(b) and (4)? The House of Lords had no hesitation in answering this question in the affirmative. (ii) If the positive balance was property, was this property "for the time being in use or intended for use for commercial purposes"? Lord Diplock said:

> To speak of a debt as "being used or intended for use" for any purposes by the creditor to whom the debt is owed involves employing ordinary English words in what is not their natural sense. . . . What is clear beyond all question is that, if the expression "commercial purposes" in section 13(4) bore what would be its ordinary and natural meaning in the context in which it there appears, a debt representing the balance standing to the credit of a diplomatic mission in a current bank account used for meeting the day-to-day expenses of running the mission would fall outside the subsection.[82]

2.3.5.4.6 The problem of interpretation flows from the definition of "commercial purposes" in section 17(1). The expression "commercial purposes" is defined by reference to "commercial transaction" in section 3(3), which includes "any contract for the supply of goods and services" irrespective of the purpose of the contract in question. This was the aspect of the case which had been regarded as crucial by Lord Donaldson MR in the Court of Appeal: "The purpose of money in a bank account can never be 'to run an embassy'. It can only be to pay for goods and services or to enter into other transactions which enable the embassy to be run."[83]

2.3.5.4.7 This interpretation did not find favour in the House of Lords. Notwithstanding the definition in section 17(1) Lord Diplock said:

> Unless it can be shown by the judgment creditor who is seeking to attach the credit balance by garnishee proceedings that the bank account was earmarked by the foreign State solely (save for *de minimis* exceptions) for being drawn on to settle liabilities incurred in commercial transactions, as for example by issuing documentary credits in payment of the price of goods sold to the State, it cannot in my view, be sensibly brought within the crucial words of the exception for which section 13(4) provides.[84]

2.3.5.4.8 Lord Diplock's analysis was that, since the balance in an account cannot be

81. [1984] AC 580. Crawford, (1984) 55 BYIL 340; Fox, "Enforcement Jurisdiction, Foreign State Property and Diplomatic Immunity" (1985) 34 ICLQ 115; Ghandi, "Sovereign Immunity" (1984) 47 MLR 597; Lloyd Jones, [1984] CLJ 222.
82. [1984] AC 580, 602–603.
83. [1984] AC 580, 558–589.
84. [1984] AC 580, 604.

dissected into the various uses to which the money drawn might be put in the future, it cannot be said that it is in use or intended for use for commercial purposes unless it is solely intended for use for commercial purposes. If it can be shown that an account is used solely for commercial purposes, the account is not immune from enforcement jurisdiction. In practice, however, embassy funds—which are invariably held in a general bank account either for mixed purposes or for general unallocated purposes—will always be exempt from execution.

2.3.5.4.9 The result achieved in *Alcom Ltd* v. *Republic of Colombia* is entirely justified on policy grounds. If it were possible to take enforcement measures against the bank account of a diplomatic mission in extreme cases the mission of a friendly foreign State might be required to close. Furthermore, the decision of the House of Lords is consistent with public international law and the decision of the German Constitutional Court in a similar case.[85]

2.3.5.5 Enforcement against separate entities

2.3.5.5.1 THE GENERAL RULE

For the purposes of the 1978 Act a separate entity within the meaning of section 14(1)[86] is, to the extent that it is entitled to immunity, to be treated in the same way as a State.[87] Section 14(3) provides:

> If a separate entity (not being a State's central bank or other monetary authority) submits to the jurisdiction in respect of proceedings in the case of which it is entitled to immunity by virtue of subsection (2) above, subsections (1) to (4) of section 13 above shall apply to it in respect of those proceedings as if references to a State were references to that entity.

Where a separate entity has immunity—by virtue of the fact that the proceedings relate to something it has done in the exercise of sovereign authority—the mere fact of submission to the jurisdiction of the court does not entitle an English court to issue injunctions or allow enforcement against any of the separate entity's property. Conversely, where a separate entity is not entitled to immunity under section 14(2) it is treated in the same way as a private corporation—in the sense that there are no special restrictions on enforcement procedures.

2.3.5.5.2 THE SPECIAL POSITION OF A STATE'S CENTRAL BANK

A judgment given against a State's central bank is of little comfort to the plaintiff if the judgment cannot be enforced against funds held by the bank. Nevertheless, section 14(4) places central banks in a privileged position:

> Property of a State's central bank or other monetary authority shall not be regarded for the purposes of subsection (4) of section 13 above as in use or intended for use for commercial purposes; and where any such bank or authority is a separate entity subsections (1) to (3) of that section shall apply to it as if references to a State were references to the bank or authority.

A result of this subsection is to render the assets of a central bank inviolable by making it effectively impossible to take enforcement measures in England: "The legislator has . . . rendered proceedings against a central bank almost wholly illusory, notwithstanding the

85. *The Philippine Republic Case* (1977) 46 BVerfGE 342.
86. See para. 2.3.2.1.
87. State Immunity Act 1978, s. 14(2).

fact that by virtue of section 14(2) a central bank which is a separate entity will be subject to jurisdiction as such in cases in which the proceedings relate to matters of a commercial character and the State itself would not be immune."[88] It goes without saying that the position adopted by the State Immunity Act 1978 represents a triumph of economic expediency over commercial justice: "The mercenary attitude to central banks . . . remains a matter for great regret. It is no doubt due to the wish to attract foreign funds to the City of London by assuring their owners that they have nothing to fear from their creditors."[89]

2.3.6 Service of process in proceedings against States

Section 12 lays down procedural requirements in relation to proceedings brought against States. These requirements do not apply "to proceedings against a State by way of counterclaim or to an action *in rem*".[90]

2.3.6.1 Instituting proceedings

2.3.6.1.1 Once it has been established that a State is not substantively immune there are still questions concerning the assumption of jurisdiction and service of process. There are two valid methods whereby a writ[91] may be served on a foreign State. (i) There is nothing to stop "the service of a writ or other document in any manner to which the State has agreed".[92] (ii) There is the method of service laid down by section 12(1), which provides:

> Any writ or other document required to be served for instituting proceedings against a State shall be served by being transmitted through the Foreign and Commonwealth Office to the Ministry of Foreign Affairs of the State and service shall be deemed to have been effected when the writ or document is received at the Ministry.

2.3.6.1.2 Section 12(1) is drafted in mandatory terms; unless the foreign State has agreed to some other method of service, the writ "shall be served" in the manner prescribed by the Act. Even where the parties have agreed on a method of service the plaintiff may choose to make use of the statutory procedure instead.[93] Although there is nothing in the Rules of the Supreme Court to permit the court to dispense with service, a State "which appears in proceedings cannot thereafter object that subsection (1) above has not been complied with".[94]

2.3.6.1.3 As a result of the mandatory nature of section 12(1), where diplomatic relations between the United Kingdom and a foreign country have broken down, there may be no effective mechanism for service of a writ. In this situation the plaintiff is unable to proceed in England, notwithstanding the fact that the court has jurisdiction over the claim and the State party is not entitled to immunity under the 1978 Act.[95]

88. Mann, "The State Immunity Act 1978" (1979) 50 BYIL 43, 61–62.
89. Mann, "The State Immunity Act 1978" (1979) 50 BYIL 43, 62.
90. State Immunity Act 1978, s. 12(7).
91. The same rules apply to proceedings commenced by originating summons: RSC, Order 11, r. 9.
92. State Immunity Act 1978, s. 12(6); RSC, Order 11, r. 7(4).
93. RSC, Order 11, r. 7(4).
94. State Immunity Act 1978, s. 12(3).
95. See, for example, *Westminster City Council* v. *Government of the Islamic Republic of Iran* [1986] 1 WLR 979. Crawford, (1986) 57 BYIL 423.

2.3.6.1.4 In *Kuwait Airways Corporation* v. *Iraqi Airways*[96] fifteen aircraft belonging to the plaintiff had been seized by the Iraqi military forces on the invasion of Kuwait in 1991. Five were removed by the Iraqi airforce and the remaining ten were handed over to the first defendant. The plaintiff brought proceedings for the recovery of the aircraft which had not been destroyed and for damages. The defendant was properly served with a writ within the jurisdiction and on 11 January 1992 the plaintiff obtained leave to serve a concurrent writ on the second defendant, the Republic of Iraq. The British embassy in Baghdad was closed on 12 January 1992 and Iraq broke off diplomatic relations as from 6 February 1992. The documents instituting the proceedings against the second defendant were served at the Iraqi embassy in London and were received by an accredited diplomat. When the plaintiff obtained a default judgment the second defendant applied to have the judgment set aside on the basis of improper service.

2.3.6.1.5 Evans J held that, as regards the second defendant, service had not been properly effected and, therefore, that the judgment which the plaintiff had obtained against the second defendant should be set aside. Section 12(1) makes it clear that service is to be effected by transmission "to" the Ministry of Foreign Affairs and takes effect when the document is received "at" the Ministry. Service of the writ at the embassy in London was ineffective.

2.3.6.1.6 It must be stressed that subsection (1) deals only with the method of service, it does not spell out the circumstances in which an English court may assume jurisdiction. In cases where the defendant does not have immunity but is not prepared to submit to the jurisdiction of the court, the writ must be served out of the jurisdiction. Section 12(1) does not affect "any rules of court whereby leave is required for the service of process outside the jurisdiction".[97] In order to be able to serve a writ out of the jurisdiction the plaintiff has to satisfy the requirements of RSC, Order 11, rule 1.[98]

2.3.6.2 Entering appearance

Section 12(2) provides that "[a]ny time for entering an appearance (whether prescribed by rules of court or otherwise) shall begin to run two months after the date on which the writ or document is received" in accordance with the procedure laid down in subsection (1). This provision does not apply in those cases where the parties have agreed an alternative method of service.[99]

2.3.6.3 Judgments in default

Section 12 contains special provisions dealing with judgments against States given in default of appearance:

> (4) No judgment in default of appearance shall be given against a State except on proof that subsection (1) above has been complied with and that the time for entering an appearance as extended by subsection (2) above has expired.[100]
>
> (5) A copy of any judgment given against a State in default of appearance shall be transmitted

96. *Financial Times*, 17 July 1992.
97. State Immunity Act 1978, s. 12(7).
98. See paras. 5.1–5.8 and 6.3–6.4.
99. State Immunity Act 1978, s. 12(6).
100. Subsection (4) does not apply in cases where the parties have agreed on a method of service different from that laid down in section 12(1): State Immunity Act 1978, s. 12(6).

through the Foreign and Commonwealth Office to the Ministry of Foreign Affairs of that State and any time for applying to have the judgment set aside (whether prescribed by rules of court or otherwise) shall begin to run two months after the date on which the copy of the judgment is received at the Ministry.

2.4 DIPLOMATIC IMMUNITY

2.4.1 Diplomatic officers

It is a long established principle that the representatives of foreign States should be immune from suit in England. Whereas diplomats used to enjoy absolute immunity, immunity under the Diplomatic Privileges Act 1964 is qualified. The 1964 Act implements certain provisions of the Vienna Convention on Diplomatic Relations of 1961,[101] the relevant parts of which are set out in Schedule 1 to the Act. The Act divides persons who are entitled to immunity into three categories: diplomatic agents; members of the administrative and technical staff; and members of the service staff.

2.4.1.1 Diplomatic agents

The Vienna Convention on Diplomatic Relations provides that diplomatic agents include the head of the mission and members of the diplomatic staff.[102] Diplomatic agents are, generally, immune from suit, subject to three limitations, two of which are potentially important in the commercial context.[103]

(i) A diplomatic agent is not immune in "a real action relating to private immovable property . . . unless he holds the property on behalf of the sending State for the purposes of the mission".[104]
(ii) A diplomatic agent has no immunity as regards "an action relating to any professional or commercial activity exercised by the diplomatic agent in the receiving State outside his official functions".[105]

These privileges and immunities are extended to members of the family of a diplomatic agent as long as they form part of the agent's household and they are not citizens of the United Kingdom.[106] Any diplomatic agent who is a citizen of or permanently resident in the United Kingdom has immunity from civil jurisdiction only "in respect of official acts performed in the exercise of his functions".[107]

101. Diplomatic Privileges Act 1964, s. 2(1).
102. Article 1(d).
103. Article 31(1).
104. Article 31(1)(a). A diplomatic agent's private residence is not held for the purposes of the mission: *Intpro Properties (UK) Ltd* v. *Sauvel* [1983] QB 1019.
105. Article 31(1)(c).
106. Article 37(1).
107. Article 38(1). This limited immunity may be extended by Order in Council under section 2(6) of the Diplomatic Privileges Act 1964.

2.4.1.2 Members of the administrative and technical staff

Members of the administrative and technical staff are "the members of the staff of the mission employed in the administrative and technical service of the mission".[108] Clerical staff fall within this classification. Broadly speaking, the immunity of members of the administrative and technical staff—together with members of their families forming part of their households who are not citizens of or permanently resident in the United Kingdom—enjoy the same immunities as diplomatic agents. There is, however, a significant restriction; the immunity of members of the administrative and technical staff does not extend to acts performed outside the course of their duties.[109]

2.4.1.3 Members of the service staff

Members of the service staff are staff "in the domestic service of the mission"[110] (such as cooks and cleaners). Members of the service staff who are not citizens of or permanently resident in the United Kingdom "enjoy immunity in respect of acts performed in the course of their duties".[111]

2.4.1.4 Waiver

Privileges conferred by the 1964 Act may be waived by the sending State.[112] Such a waiver must be express.[113] A waiver by the head of the diplomatic mission is deemed to be a waiver by the sending State.[114] A diplomatic officer who invokes the jurisdiction of the court by commencing proceedings in England cannot claim immunity in respect of any counterclaim directly connected with the principal claim.[115] A waiver of immunity from adjudicative jurisdiction is not sufficient to render any subsequent judgment enforceable against a diplomatic officer. There can be no enforcement unless there has been a separate waiver of immunity from enforcement jurisdiction.[116]

2.4.1.5 The temporal scope of immunity

Any person who is entitled to immunities and privileges "shall enjoy them from the moment he enters the territory of the receiving State on proceeding to take up his post or, if already in its territory, from the moment when his appointment is notified to the Ministry for Foreign Affairs".[117] Once a diplomatic officer's functions have come to an end, the immunities conferred by the Act cease at the moment when he leaves the

108. Article 1(f).
109. Article 37(2).
110. Article 1(g).
111. Article 37(3).
112. Article 32(1).
113. Article 32(2).
114. Diplomatic Privileges Act 1964, s. 2(3).
115. Article 32(3).
116. Article 32(4).
117. Article 39(1).

country or on expiry of a reasonable period in which to do so.[118] If a diplomatic officer dies, members of his family retain their immunities until the expiry of a reasonable period in which to leave the country.[119]

2.4.2 Consular agents

2.4.2.1 The position of consular agents is governed by the Consular Relations Act 1968, which gives effect to certain provisions of the Vienna Convention on Consular Relations of 1963. Consular agents do not enjoy any immunity in relation to their private acts. Although immunity does extend to the acts of consular agents performed in the exercise of their consular functions,[120] there is no immunity in relation to (i) a civil action on a contract, unless the agent expressly or impliedly contracted on behalf of the State in question, or (ii) a civil action by a third party for damage arising from an accident in the United Kingdom caused by a vessel, vehicle or aircraft.[121]

2.4.2.2 The immunity conferred by the Consular Relations Act 1968 may be waived by the sending State.[122] Such waiver must be express and in writing. The institution of proceedings by a consular agent prevents the agent from claiming immunity in relation to a counterclaim directly connected with the claim. A waiver of immunity from adjudicative jurisdiction does not amount to a submission to execution, for which a separate waiver is required.

2.5 INTERNATIONAL ORGANISATIONS

2.5.1 By virtue of the International Organisations Act 1968, as amended by the International Organisations Act 1981, certain types of international organisation and their representatives may be granted immunities similar to those enjoyed by foreign States and their representatives. The 1968 Act does not, however, grant blanket immunity in the same way as the State Immunity Act 1978 or the Diplomatic Privileges Act 1964. The organisations which are entitled to immunity and the particular immunities they enjoy are specified by Orders in Council made under the 1968 Act or under the legislation which it replaced.

2.5.2 In cases where the legislation does not apply a defendant may, nevertheless, be entitled to immunity under public international law. In *Zoersch* v. *Waldock*[123] the Court of Appeal decided, *obiter*, that the former President of the European Commission of Human Rights was entitled to immunity in England as a matter of customary international law. Accordingly, in relation to acts performed in an official capacity immunity may continue to apply notwithstanding the fact that the defendant no longer holds office.

2.5.3 *Arab Monetary Fund* v. *Hashim*[124] involved a claim to immunity in the context

118. Article 39(2).
119. Article 39(3).
120. The words "consular functions" are defined by Article 5 of the Vienna Convention on Consular Relations.
121. Article 43.
122. Article 45.
123. [1964] 1 WLR 675.
124. [1993] 1 Lloyd's Rep 543.

of proceedings brought by the AMF—an international organisation in relation to which no Order in Council has been made under the 1968 Act—against its former director-general. Evans J thought that "the English courts should give effect to an immunity which is shown to exist under customary international law".[125] However, to the extent that the immunity of officials of international organisations exists under customary international law it exists for the benefit of the organisation rather than the official. It follows that if the immunity is waived by the organisation there is no further bar to the proceedings against the official in England.[126]

125. [1993] 1 Lloyd's Rep 543, 573.
126. [1993] 1 Lloyd's Rep 543, 574.

CHAPTER 3

THE BRUSSELS AND LUGANO CONVENTIONS: GENERAL CONSIDERATIONS

In the commercial sphere the most important conventions which regulate jurisdiction and the recognition and enforcement of foreign judgments are the Brussels and Lugano Conventions ("the Conventions") (para. 3.1).[1] These parallel Conventions establish a regime for the allocation of jurisdiction in civil and commercial matters and for the reciprocal recognition and enforcement of judgments within the territories of the European Community (EC) and the European Free Trade Association (EFTA). To ensure the uniform interpretation of the Brussels Convention references may be made by national courts to the Court of Justice. Although no similar mechanism was created in relation to the Lugano Convention, steps have been taken to foster uniform interpretation (para. 3.2). The material scope of the Conventions is limited to civil and commercial matters (para. 3.3). The Lugano Convention contains provisions concerning the relationship between the Brussels and Lugano Conventions (para. 3.4) and both Conventions expressly regulate their relationship with other conventions in the areas of jurisdiction and the recognition and enforcement of judgments (para. 3.5).

3.1 INTRODUCTION

3.1.1 Central to the operation of the European Community is the free movement of goods, services, workers and capital. Free movement on the scale envisaged by the Treaty of Rome entails a vast network of international contracts for the sale of goods and the supply of services throughout the Community. A massive increase in cross-border trade inevitably leads to an increase in international litigation. International trade depends in some measure on mutual trust and confidence derived from the availability of effective legal remedies in cases where disputes arise. Those who framed the Treaty of Rome were aware that traditional approaches to conflicts problems would not achieve the co-operation which was required to bring about the level of economic integration which was envisaged. The nature of the problem can be illustrated by the following example. Suppose that the plaintiff, who is resident in country X, contracts to buy goods from the defendant, who is resident in country Y. A dispute follows and the plaintiff proceeds against the defendant in country X. The courts of country X assume jurisdiction, notwithstanding the fact that the defendant has no connection with country X and takes no part in the proceedings. Having obtained a judgment in his favour in country X the plaintiff seeks to enforce it against the

1. In this chapter it is to be assumed that the provisions of the Brussels and Lugano Conventions are identical unless the contrary is indicated.

defendant's assets in country Y. The courts of country Y refuse to enforce the judgment on the ground that the courts of country X assumed jurisdiction over the defendant on an exorbitant basis.

3.1.2 This example illustrates that the primary obstacles to the mutual recognition and enforcement of judgments are exorbitant jurisdiction rules. In order for a foreign judgment to be entitled to recognition and enforcement it must have been pronounced by a court having jurisdiction in the private international law sense. Once it is appreciated that international jurisdiction and the enforcement of foreign judgments "should be recognised as branches of the same tree"[2] the obvious solution is to harmonise jurisdiction rules. If national courts are entitled to assume jurisdiction over a foreign defendant on only a limited number of agreed bases, the recognition and enforcement of foreign judgments can be simplified. This is the approach adopted by the Conventions.

3.1.3 Article 220 of the Treaty of Rome—which established the European Economic Community—provides that Member States "shall, so far as necessary, enter into negotiations with each other with a view to securing for the benefit of their nationals . . . the simplification of formalities governing the reciprocal recognition and enforcement of judgments of courts or tribunals and of arbitration awards". In a note sent to the Member States on 22 October 1959 inviting them to commence negotiations, the Commission of the EEC pointed out that:

> As jurisdiction in both civil and commercial matters is derived from the sovereignty of Member States, and since the effect of judicial acts is confined to each national territory, legal protection and, hence, legal certainty in the common market are essentially dependent on the adoption by the Member States of a satisfactory solution to the problem of recognition and enforcement of judgments.[3]

3.1.4 In 1960 a committee of experts, consisting of representatives of the six Member States, was set up. The work of this committee culminated in the Convention on Jurisdiction and the Enforcement of Judgments in Civil and Commercial Matters (the Brussels Convention) which was signed by the original six Member States (Belgium, Germany, France, Italy, Luxembourg, the Netherlands) in 1968.

3.1.5 In 1971 the six Contracting States signed the Luxembourg Protocol which provides a mechanism for questions of interpretation arising out of the Brussels Convention to be referred to the Court of Justice. Although the Protocol is similar in purpose to Article 177 of the Treaty of Rome, the list of courts which are entitled to refer questions to the Court of Justice is somewhat restricted. The Brussels Convention came into force between the original Contracting States on 1 February 1973; the Protocol came into force on 1 September 1975.

3.1.6 When Denmark, Ireland and the United Kingdom joined the EC they undertook to accede to the Brussels Convention and the Luxembourg Protocol. The 1978 Accession Convention introduced a number of amendments to the 1968 Convention. Some amendments were necessitated by the distinctive features of the legal systems of the new Member States (such as the trust in English and Irish law);

2. Mann, "The Doctrine of Jurisdiction in International Law" [1964] I Hag Rec 1, 75.
3. Cited by the Jenard Report, OJ 1979 C59/3.

others were thought desirable in view of the traditional role played by the English courts in certain areas of commercial activity (notably insurance and shipping); other amendments were thought appropriate in the light of uncertainties surrounding the original text.

3.1.7 Section 2 of the Civil Jurisdiction and Judgments Act 1982—which provides that the Conventions shall have the force of law in the United Kingdom—was brought into force on 1 January 1987.[4] From that date the Accession Convention came into force between the United Kingdom, on the one hand, and the original six Contracting States and Denmark, on the other. The Accession Convention did not come into force as between the United Kingdom and Ireland until 1 June 1988.

3.1.8 Greece acceded to the Brussels Convention and Luxembourg Protocol in 1982. The 1982 Accession Convention, which made only technical changes, was brought into force in the United Kingdom on 1 October 1989[5] (it having already come into force as regards the other Contracting States on 1 April). Spain and Portugal acceded to the Brussels Convention by the 1989 Accession Convention (the San Sebastian Convention). The accession of Spain and Portugal provided an opportunity to make some substantive changes to the text, besides making the necessary technical amendments. The 1989 Accession Convention was brought into force in most of the Contracting States on various dates in the period 1991 to 1993.[6]

3.1.9 Notwithstanding the fact that the text of the Brussels Convention has been altered on two occasions the basic structure has remained unchanged. Each of the Conventions is accompanied by an official report which may be used as a guide to interpretation.[7]

The evolution of the Brussels Convention is summarised below:

i Brussels Convention 1968
parties: Belgium, Germany, France, Italy, Luxembourg, the Netherlands (the Six)
signed: 27 September 1968
at: Brussels
entry into force: 1 February 1973
report: Jenard Report, OJ 1979 C59/1

ii Luxembourg Protocol 1971
parties: the Six
signed: 3 June 1971
at: Luxembourg
entry into force: 1 September 1975
report: Jenard Report, OJ 1979 C59/66

iii Accession Convention 1978
parties: the Six, Denmark, Ireland, United Kingdom (the Nine)
signed: 9 October 1978
at: Luxembourg

4. Mathers, "The Brussels Convention of 1968: Its Implementation in the United Kingdom" (1983) 3 YBEL 49.

5. Civil Jurisdiction and Judgments Act 1982 (Amendment) Order 1989, SI 1989 No. 1346.

6. For entry into force in the United Kingdom: Civil Jurisdiction and Judgments Act 1982 (Amendment) Order 1990, SI 1990 No. 2591.

7. Civil Jurisdiction and Judgments Act 1982, s. 3(3). See para. 3.2.1.3.

entry into force:
— between the Six and Denmark: 1 November 1986
— between the Six + Denmark and the United Kingdom: 1 January 1987
— between the Six + Denmark + the United Kingdom and Ireland: 1 June 1988
report: Schlosser Report, OJ 1979 C59/77

iv Accession Convention 1982
parties: the Nine and Greece (the Ten)
signed: 25 October 1982
at: Luxembourg
entry into force:
— between the Six + Denmark + Ireland and Greece: 1 April 1989
— between the Six + Denmark + Ireland + Greece and the United Kingdom: 1 June 1989
report: Evrigenis–Kerameus Report, OJ 1986 C298/1

v Accession Convention 1989
parties: the Ten, Spain, Portugal (the Twelve)
signed: 26 May 1989
at: San Sebastian
entry into force:

Belgium	
Denmark	
Germany	
Greece	1 July 1992
Spain	1 February 1991
France	1 February 1991
Ireland	1 December 1993
Italy	1 May 1992
Luxembourg	1 February 1992
Netherlands	1 February 1991
Portugal	1 July 1992
United Kingdom	1 December 1991

report: Almeida Cruz–Desantes Real–Jenard Report, OJ 1990 C189/35

3.1.10 In 1988 the EC Member States negotiated a parallel convention, in almost identical terms to the Brussels Convention, with the countries which are members of EFTA.[8] It is envisaged that the Lugano Convention might be extended beyond its current geographical scope. A country which is a member neither of the EC nor of EFTA may be invited to accede, as long as the invitation has the unanimous agreement of the EC Member States and the EFTA countries.

3.1.11 The Lugano Convention was implemented into English law by the amendments to the Civil Jurisdiction and Judgments Act 1982 introduced by the Civil Jurisdiction and Judgments Act 1991. The Lugano Convention came into force between the United Kingdom and a number of the EFTA countries in 1992 and 1993.[9] The Convention has not yet been ratified by all the Contracting States.

8. Iceland, Norway, Austria, Switzerland, Finland, Sweden.
9. Civil Jurisdiction and Judgments Act 1991 (Commencement Order) 1992, SI 1992 No. 745.

3.1.12 As between the EC Member States the Brussels Convention continues to apply. However, judgments granted by the courts of the EFTA countries are entitled to recognition and enforcement in EC Member States and in the other EFTA countries under the Lugano Convention. Moreover, the jurisdiction rules contained in the Lugano Convention are applicable by EC Member States as regards defendants domiciled in an EFTA country.[10]

3.1.13 Although the basic scheme of the Lugano Convention is the same as the Brussels Convention, there are certain specific differences between the two Conventions (both in terms of jurisdiction rules and recognition and enforcement rules). Furthermore, there is no protocol to the Lugano Convention which makes provision for the reference of questions of interpretation to the Court of Justice. Although various measures have been taken to encourage the courts of the Contracting States to interpret identical provisions in the Conventions in an identical way,[11] it is not possible to guarantee that divergences will not occur.

3.1.14 The details of the Lugano Convention are set out below:

parties: the Twelve, Iceland, Norway, Austria, Switzerland, Finland, Sweden
opened for signature: 16 September 1988
at: Lugano
entry into force:

Belgium	
Denmark	
Germany	
Greece	
Spain	
France	1 January 1992
Ireland	1 December 1993
Italy	1 December 1992
Luxembourg	1 February 1992
Netherlands	1 January 1992
Portugal	1 July 1992
United Kingdom	1 May 1992
Iceland	
Austria	
Finland	1 July 1993
Norway	1 April 1993
Switzerland	1 January 1992
Sweden	1 January 1993

report: Jenard–Möller Report, OJ 1990 C189/57

10. See para. 3.4.
11. See para. 3.2.2.

3.2 INTERPRETATION OF THE CONVENTIONS

3.2.1 Interpretation of the Brussels Convention

3.2.1.1 References to the European Court of Justice under the Luxembourg Protocol

3.2.1.1.1 The Luxembourg Protocol of 1971[12] is the primary instrument for ensuring that the Brussels Convention is interpreted uniformly. The 1971 Protocol provides a mechanism whereby national courts may refer questions of interpretation to the Court of Justice.[13] Although the basic idea behind the 1971 Protocol and Article 177 of the Treaty of Rome is the same, the details are different.

3.2.1.1.2 Article 1 of the Protocol provides that the Court of Justice of the European Communities shall have jurisdiction to give rulings on the interpretation of the 1968 Convention as well as on the 1971 Protocol and subsequent Accession Conventions. Article 2 provides:

> The following courts may request the Court of Justice to give preliminary rulings on questions of interpretation—
>
> 1. . . .
>
> — in the United Kingdom: the House of Lords and courts to which application has been made under the second paragraph of Article 37 or under Article 41 of the Convention.
>
> 2. The courts of the Contracting States when sitting in an appellate capacity.
>
> 3. In the cases provided for in Article 37 of the Convention, the courts referred to in that Article.

3.2.1.1.3 The approach adopted by the Protocol is to divide cases into (i) those situations where the court in question shall request a ruling from the Court of Justice and (ii) those situations in which the court may request a ruling. Article 3 provides that where a question of interpretation of the Convention is raised in a case pending before one of the courts listed in Article 2(1) that court "shall, if it considers that a decision on the question is necessary to enable it to give judgment, request the Court of Justice to give a ruling thereon". As regards the courts listed in the second and third paragraphs of Article 2, it is provided that where a question of interpretation is raised "that court may . . . request the Court of Justice to give a ruling thereon".

3.2.1.1.4 As regards civil proceedings other than proceedings for the enforcement of a foreign judgment, the position is very simple: the House of Lords "shall", and the Court of Appeal (or any other court sitting in an appellate capacity) "may" request a ruling from the Court of Justice if the court "considers that a decision on the question is necessary to enable it to give judgment". Unlike Article 177 of the Treaty of Rome, the 1971 Protocol does not allow a court of first instance to refer questions of interpretation to the Court of Justice. The exclusion of courts of first instance, the wisdom of which may be questioned,[14] is "designed mainly to prevent the interpretation of the court

12. See Civil Jurisdiction and Judgments Act 1982, Schedule 2.

13. For a discussion of the procedure adopted in relation to references under the Luxembourg Protocol see Jung, "The Brussels and Lugano Conventions: The European Court's Jurisdiction; its Procedures and Methods" (1992) 11 CJQ 38.

14. See, for example, Hirst J in *Klöckner & Co AG* v. *Gatoil Overseas Inc* [1990] 1 Lloyd's Rep 177, 187.

being requested in too many cases, and particularly in trivial matters".[15] A reference from a court which is not listed in Article 2 is inadmissible.[16]

3.2.1.1.5 The position in relation to proceedings concerning the enforcement of judgments under the Brussels Convention is more complex. In order to explain the distinction drawn by the first and second paragraphs of Article 3 it is necessary to outline briefly the procedure for the enforcement of judgments.[17] The procedure—as it applies in England—can be broken down into three stages.

(i) The judgment creditor applies *ex parte* to the High Court for registration of the judgment.[18]

(ii) There is a right of appeal against the decision taken at the *ex parte* stage. If registration is granted, the judgment debtor may appeal to the High Court against registration[19]; if registration is refused, the judgment creditor may appeal to the High Court against the refusal to register the judgment.[20]

(iii) A further appeal lies to the Court of Appeal on points of law against a decision of the High Court at the second stage of the procedure.[21]

Under Article 3 of the Luxembourg Protocol if the court "considers that a decision on the question is necessary to enable it to give judgment" the High Court, at the second stage of the procedure, "may" request a ruling from the Court of Justice and the Court of Appeal, at the third stage of the procedure, "shall" request a ruling.

3.2.1.1.6 The 1971 Protocol also makes provision for questions of interpretation to be referred to the Court of Justice by the "competent authority of a Contracting State". The first paragraph of Article 4 sets out the conditions which must be satisfied: "if judgments given by courts of that State conflict with the interpretation given by the Court of Justice or in a judgment of one of the courts of another Contracting State referred to in Article 2(1) or (2)". The procedure under Article 4 has not yet been used.

3.2.1.2 Methods of interpretation[22]

3.2.1.2.1 The style of interpretation employed by the Court of Justice is teleological, rather than literal. The Court of Justice has taken the view that the Brussels Convention must be interpreted "having regard both to its principles and objectives and to its

15. Jenard Report, OJ 1979 C59/68, para. 11(1).
16. Case 80/83 *Habourdin International SA* v. *SpA Italocremona* [1983] ECR 3639; Case 56/84 *Von Gallera* v. *Maître* [1984] ECR 1769.
17. The procedure for the enforcement of foreign maintenance orders is outside the scope of the present work. For further discussion of the recognition and enforcement of judgments under the Conventions see para. 9.4.
18. Article 32(1).
19. Article 37(1).
20. Article 40(1).
21. Article 37(2) and Article 41.
22. For a review of the case law of the Court of Justice see: McClellan, "The Convention of Brussels of September 27, 1968 on Jurisdiction and the Recognition and Enforcement of Judgments in Civil and Commercial Matters" (1978) 15 CMLRev 228; McClellan, "Jurisdiction and the Recognition and Enforcement of Judgments in Civil and Commercial Matters in the European Communities" (1979) 16 CMLRev 268; McClellan & Kremlis, "The Convention of September 27, 1968 on Jurisdiction and Enforcement of Judgments in Civil and Commercial Matters" (1983) 20 CMLRev 529; Pieri, "The 1968 Brussels Convention on Jurisdiction and Enforcement of Judgments in Civil and Commercial Matters Four Years' Case Law of the European Court of Justice" (1987) 24 CMLRev 635.

relationship within the Treaty [of Rome]".[23] Each of the different language versions of the Brussels Convention is equally authoritative; no single language version of the Convention is to be regarded as self-sufficient. What appears to be an ambiguity in the English text may be resolved by having regard to other language versions. Since it may be impossible to interpret the Convention in a manner which is consistent with all the different language versions the proper interpretation of a provision of the Convention may fly in the face of the English text.

3.2.1.2.2 In private international law, the traditional approach is for questions of classification to be determined by the *lex fori*. So, whether a particular issue raises a question of contractual or tortious liability, substance or procedure, formal or essential validity is to be decided by the classificatory scheme of the forum. If this traditional approach were applied to all aspects of the Convention its uniform application could be seriously compromised. It makes sense, therefore, to approach the interpretation of many of the concepts which are employed in the Convention from a supranational perspective rather than from a purely national one. Of course, the Court of Justice is uniquely placed to formulate autonomous or independent interpretations which take account of the different legal traditions of the various Contracting States.

3.2.1.2.3 There is no simple answer to the question of whether a particular rule or concept is to be given a national or autonomous interpretation.[24] Often the objectives of the Brussels Convention require that a particular concept should be given an independent interpretation; ultimately, however, the Court of Justice is faced by a question of policy. The practice of the Court of Justice has been to favour an autonomous interpretation in relation to the terms used in Title I, which defines the material scope of the Convention, and the conceptual categories which determine the scope of the specific jurisdiction provisions (for example, "matters relating to a contract" in Article 5(1) and "rights *in rem* in immovable property" in Article 16(1)). The Court of Justice has also gone further and defined terms which might conceivably have been left to the *lex fori* (such as "the place where the harmful event occurred" for the purposes of Article 5(3)[25]). Nevertheless, the Convention makes it clear that certain elements are to be defined by the internal law of the various Contracting States. For example, Articles 52 and 53, which deal with the domicile of individuals and corporations, provide that it is for the law of the Contracting State in question to determine whether a person is domiciled in that State. Moreover, the Court of Justice has taken the view that matters which relate to procedural consequences or the detailed operation of legal concepts are to be interpreted by reference to the national law. For example, it is for the procedural law of the country in question to decide when a court is seised of proceedings for the purposes of Article 21[26]; in the context of Article 5(1) "the place of performance" is referred to the *lex causae* as determined by the conflicts rules of the forum.[27]

3.2.1.2.4 There is a tendency for English lawyers to deprecate the efforts of the Court of Justice. It has, for example, been said that the Court of Justice is "a tribunal which has

23. Case 33/78 *Somafer SA* v. *Saar-Ferngas AG* [1978] ECR 2183, 2190 (para. 4).
24. For a discussion of this question see Kohler, "The Case Law of the European Court on the Judgments Convention" (1982) 7 ELRev 3, 7–13; Layton, "The Interpretation of the Brussels Convention by the European Court and English Courts" (1992) 11 CJQ 28, 32–35.
25. Case 21/76 *Handelskwekerij GJ Bier BV* v. *Mines de Potasse d'Alsace SA* [1976] ECR 1735.
26. Case 129/83 *Zelger* v. *Salinitri (No. 2)* [1984] ECR 2397.
27. Case 12/76 *Industrie Tessili Italiana Como* v. *Dunlop AG* [1976] ECR 1473.

proved to be singularly unsuited for the decision of matters of practical and commercial implications".[28] There can be little doubt that the burden placed on the Court of Justice is an onerous one: "The task of interpreting [the Brussels Convention] . . . requires a broad knowledge of the private and procedural law of the Member States. A special expertise is called for, not needed otherwise in administering Community law."[29] Accordingly, there is much to be said in favour of the creation of a special chamber of the Court of Justice to deal with references made under the 1971 Protocol.

3.2.1.3 Interpretation by national courts

3.2.1.3.1 The Civil Jurisdiction and Judgments Act 1982 sets out the way in which an English court should approach questions relating to the interpretation of the Brussels Convention in cases where no reference is made to the Court of Justice. Section 3 of the 1982 Act provides:

> (1) Any question as to the meaning or effect of any provision of the Brussels Conventions shall, if not referred to the European Court in accordance with the 1971 Protocol, be determined in accordance with the principles laid down by and any relevant decision of the European Court.
> (2) Judicial notice shall be taken of any decision of, or any expression of opinion by, the European Court on any such question.
> (3) Without prejudice to the generality of subsection (1), the following reports (which are reproduced in the Official Journal of the Communities), namely—
> (a) the reports by Mr P Jenard on the 1968 Convention and the 1971 Protocol[30]; and
> (b) the report by Professor Peter Schlosser on the Accession Convention[31]; and
> (c) the report by Professor Demetrios I Evrigenis and Professor K D Kerameus on the 1982 Accession Convention[32]; and
> (d) the report of Mr Mertinho de Almeida Cruz, Mr Manuel Desantes Real and Mr P Jenard on the 1989 Accession Convention,[33]
> may be considered in ascertaining the meaning or effect of any provision of the Brussels Conventions and shall be given such weight as is appropriate in the circumstances.

3.2.1.3.2 In general terms, a national court should approach the interpretation of the Brussels Convention as would the Court of Justice. The terse style in which the Convention is drafted means that many important questions are left open. There are, for example, no provisions in the Convention which seek to define any of the key concepts. The Reports of the working parties which negotiated the 1968 Convention and the subsequent Accession Conventions, which are mentioned in subsection (3), are a useful starting-point for fleshing out the provisions of the Convention. Although the Reports have an official status and are helpful in providing answers to some of the questions which are not answered by the wording of the Convention itself, their importance must not be overstated. The Reports are far from comprehensive; they do not attempt to solve all the questions of interpretation which may arise under the

28. Mann, "The Proper Law of the Contract—An Obituary" (1991) 107 LQR 353, 354.
29. Lipstein, "Enforcement of Judgments under the Jurisdiction and Judgments Convention: Safeguards" (1987) 36 ICLQ 873, 878.
30. OJ 1979 C59/1.
31. OJ 1979 C59/71.
32. OJ 1986 C298/1.
33. OJ 1990 C189/35.

Convention. Furthermore, the Reports are in no sense binding on the Court of Justice or national courts.

3.2.2 Interpretation of the Lugano Convention

3.2.2.1 Protocols and declarations

3.2.2.1.1 Although there are a number of differences between the wording of the Brussels Convention and the Lugano Convention the majority of the provisions are identical. Whereas the Luxembourg Protocol provides for the courts of the Contracting States to refer questions of interpretation of the Brussels Convention to the Court of Justice, there is no such mechanism for the Lugano Convention—since not all the parties to the Lugano Convention are Member States of the EC. It would, however, be extremely unfortunate if provisions in the Lugano Convention were to be given a different interpretation from identical provisions in the Brussels Convention. With this in mind, the parties to the Lugano Convention took steps designed to encourage the uniform interpretation of the parallel Conventions.[34] The various instruments concluded by the Contracting States have two objectives: the uniform interpretation of the Lugano Convention by the courts of EC and EFTA States; and the consistent interpretation of identical provisions of the Brussels and Lugano Conventions.

3.2.2.1.2 The first issue is addressed by Protocol No. 2 on the Uniform Interpretation of the Lugano Convention. Article 1 provides:

> The courts of each Contracting State shall, when applying and interpreting the provisions of the Convention, pay due account to the principles laid down by any relevant decision delivered by courts of the other Contracting States concerning provisions of this Convention.

In Article 2 the Contracting Parties agree to set up a system of exchange of information concerning judgments delivered pursuant to the Lugano Convention as well as under the Brussels Convention; Article 3 provides for the establishment of a Standing Committee to assist in the exchange of information; Article 4 concerns the meetings of the Standing Committee.

3.2.2.1.3 Article 1 of Protocol No. 2 concerns uniformity only; it does not offer a solution to the problem posed by the existence of the same provisions in two separate Conventions. This problem is tackled by means of declarations. The Declaration of the Representatives of the Governments of the States Signatories to the Lugano Convention which are members of the European Communities provides:

> The Representatives of the Governments of the Member States of the European Communities *declare* that they consider as appropriate that the Court of Justice of the European Communities, when interpreting the Brussels Convention, pay due account to the rulings contained in the case law of the Lugano Convention.[35]

3.2.2.1.4 There is also a declaration by the EFTA countries that "they consider as appropriate that their courts when interpreting the Lugano Convention, pay due account to the rulings contained in the case law of the Court of Justice of the European Communities and of courts of Member States of the European Communities in respect

34. See Minor, "The Lugano Convention: Some Problems of Interpretation" (1990) 27 CMLRev 507.
35. OJ 1988 L319/37.

of provisions of the Brussels Convention which are substantially reproduced in the Lugano Convention".[36]

3.2.2.1.5 Notwithstanding the absence of a supranational system for achieving the uniform interpretation of the Conventions, a serious effort has been made to ensure that as far as possible divergences do not arise. However, the requirements imposed by Protocol No. 2 and the declarations are weak in the sense that national courts are called upon to do no more than "pay due account" to various matters. Accordingly, the system put in place by the Contracting States falls well short of a guarantee that uniformity and consistency will be achieved.

3.2.2.2 Domestic legislation

Section 3B of the Civil Jurisdiction and Judgments Act 1982 provides:

(1) In determining any question as to the meaning or effect of a provision of the Lugano Convention, a court in the United Kingdom shall, in accordance with Protocol No. 2 to that Convention, take account of any principles laid down in any relevant decision delivered by a court of any other Lugano Contracting State concerning provisions of the Convention.

(2) Without prejudice to any practice of the courts as to the matters which may be considered apart from this section, the report on the Lugano Convention by Mr P Jenard and Mr G Möller (which is reproduced in the Official Journal of the Communities of 28th July 1990)[37] may be considered in ascertaining the meaning or effect of any provision of the Convention and shall be given such weight as is appropriate in the circumstances.

This section is drafted differently from section 3, which deals with the interpretation of the Brussels Convention. Nevertheless, in view of the desirability of ensuring that the identical provisions of the Conventions are interpreted in the same way, the general approach to questions of interpretation should be the same under both sections. Accordingly, when faced with a question of interpretation under the Lugano Convention it would not be appropriate for the court to have regard only to the literal meaning of the provision in question. The court may refer to the Jenard–Möller Report to assist in the interpretation of the provisions of the Lugano Convention.

3.2.2.3 Can the courts of EC Member States refer questions of interpretation to the Court of Justice?

It has been suggested that it may be possible for the courts of EC Member States to refer questions of interpretation to the Court of Justice under the Luxembourg Protocol even in cases where the proceedings fall within the scope of the Lugano Convention:

While such a court can make no reference on the applicable provisions of the Lugano Convention, it might be arguable that it can refer to the Court of Justice a question on the interpretation of parallel provisions of the Brussels Convention. Indeed, the court may consider that the interpretation of the Brussels Convention is necessary in order to enable it to ensure, in accordance with the preamble of the Lugano Convention, the uniform interpretation of both the Brussels and the Lugano Convention.[38]

According to this argument, if an English court is required to consider a novel point

36. OJ 1988 L319/40.
37. OJ 1990 C189/57.
38. Jung, "The Brussels and Lugano Conventions: The European Court's Jurisdiction; its Procedures and Methods" (1992) 11 CJQ 38, 50.

arising under, say, Article 5(3) of the Lugano Convention in the context of proceedings brought against a Swiss domiciliary, the court may refer to the Court of Justice under the 1971 Protocol a question concerning the interpretation of Article 5(3) of the Brussels Convention. Were an English court to make such a reference in these circumstances it is far from clear that the Court of Justice would be prepared to accept it.

3.2.3 Practical problems in cases which are not referred to the Court of Justice

A court of first instance is not able to refer questions of interpretation to the Court of Justice under the Luxembourg Protocol of 1971 and in relation to the Lugano Convention the Court of Justice has no jurisdiction. Nevertheless, if a new point arises in circumstances where a reference to the Court of Justice is not possible, the national court must consider, *inter alia*, whether a particular rule or concept should be given a national or independent interpretation. If an autonomous interpretation is appropriate it will be necessary for the court to refer, "firstly, to the objectives and scheme of the Convention and, secondly, the general principles which stem from the corpus of national legal systems".[39] The difficulty of such a task is not to be underestimated. Whereas the Court of Justice is a multilingual institution with the resources to undertake the necessary inquiries, a national court is in a less advantageous position. It is not clear how "a national court, whether in the Community or in an EFTA State, when working with the procedures and methods of its domestic legal system, could come to . . . an independent interpretation which also fits in with the different context of other legal systems and can therefore persuade judges from all Member States".[40]

3.3 SCOPE OF THE CONVENTIONS

3.3.1 Introductory remarks

3.3.1.1 The scope of the Conventions may be relevant to two stages of a dispute.

(i) When the plaintiff invokes the jurisdiction of the courts of a Contracting State in circumstances in which the court does not have jurisdiction under Title II the defendant may seek to contest jurisdiction on the basis that the subject matter of the dispute falls within the material scope of the Convention.

(ii) When a party seeks to rely on a judgment given by the courts of one Contracting State in another Contracting State under Title III the party against whom the judgment is invoked may seek to resist recognition or enforcement of the judgment on the basis that the subject matter of the judgment does not fall within the Convention's scope. In these circumstances the court of the Contracting State in which recognition or enforcement is sought is not bound by a decision taken by the court of the State of origin as to the scope of Title I.

39. Case 29/76 *LTU Lufttransportunternehmen GmbH & Co KG* v. *Eurocontrol* [1976] ECR 1541, 1552 (para. 3).

40. Jung, "The Brussels and Lugano Conventions: The European Court's Jurisdiction; its Procedures and Methods" (1992) 11 CJQ 38, 49.

3.3.1.2 The Conventions apply only "where an international element is involved".[41] This is made clear in the Preamble to each Convention which states that in order to achieve their objectives it is necessary for the Contracting States "to determine the international jurisdiction of their courts". A case which is internal to the United Kingdom does not, therefore, fall within the scope of the Conventions, even if the forum would regard it as being of a non-domestic character; the fact that a dispute involves elements which are connected with Scotland or Northern Ireland does not bring the Conventions into play. Such a situation may, however, fall within the scope of the Modified Convention which is contained in Schedule 4 to the Civil Jurisdiction and Judgments Act 1982.[42]

3.3.1.3 The material scope of the Conventions is determined by Article 1—the only provision in Title I—which provides:

This Convention shall apply in civil and commercial matters whatever the nature of the court or tribunal. It shall not extend, in particular, to revenue, customs or administrative matters.

The Convention shall not apply to:

1. the status or legal capacity of natural persons, rights in property arising out of a matrimonial relationship, wills and succession;
2. bankruptcy, proceedings relating to the winding-up of insolvent companies or other legal persons, judicial arrangements, compositions and analogous proceedings;
3. social security;
4. arbitration.

3.3.2 Civil and commercial matters

3.3.2.1 The first paragraph establishes that what is relevant for the purposes of the Conventions' material scope is the subject matter of the proceedings; the nature of the court in which those proceedings are brought is irrelevant. The Conventions cover civil claims brought before criminal courts[43] and apply to civil and commercial matters brought before administrative tribunals.[44]

3.3.2.2 The basic formula "civil and commercial matters" is not defined. The Schlosser Report notes that "[t]he distinction between civil and commercial matters on the one hand and matters of public law on the other is well recognised in the legal systems of the original Member States and is, in spite of some important differences, on the whole arrived at on the basis of similar criteria".[45] The Court of Justice has added that the phrase "civil and commercial matters" is to be given an autonomous meaning; it is not for the courts of the Contracting States to determine the scope of Article 1 according to the conceptions of their own legal system.[46]

3.3.2.3 From the perspective of a legal system which belongs to the common law tradition the Conventions are drafted in a foreign legal vocabulary. Although the public law/private law dichotomy has reared its head in English jurisprudence, the distinction does not permeate the thinking of common lawyers. Nevertheless, in practice the phrase "civil and commercial matters" presents few problems in the majority of cases. For example, it is obvious that litigation between private individuals or corporations (such

41. Jenard Report, OJ 1979 C59/8.
42. See Chapter 7.
43. Case C-172/91 *Sonntag* v. *Waidmann* [1993] ILPr 466, 484 (para. 16).
44. Jenard Report, OJ 1979 C59/9.
45. OJ 1979 C59/82, para. 23.
46. Case 29/76 *LTU Lufttransportunternehmen GmbH & Co KG* v. *Eurocontrol* [1976] ECR 1541.

as a dispute relating to a contract of employment[47]) falls within the Conventions' material scope.

3.3.2.4 Problems are most likely to arise in cases in which one of the parties to the litigation is a public authority. The Court of Justice has taken the view that the dividing line between civil and commercial matters, on the one hand, and public law matters, on the other, is to be determined by a functional test, rather than an institutional one.[48] The fact that one of the parties is a public authority does not necessarily mean that the situation falls outside the scope of the Conventions. By the same token, litigation involving a claim brought by a public authority is not to be regarded as a civil and commercial matter simply by virtue of the fact that the claim is brought in the ordinary courts and is not based on administrative law.[49] The decisive factor is whether proceedings involve "a public authority acting in the exercise of its public authority powers".[50]

3.3.2.5 In *Netherlands State* v. *Rüffer*,[51] for example, the defendant, who was domiciled in Germany, owned a boat which sank in a public waterway for which the plaintiff, the Netherlands State, was responsible. The plaintiff removed the wreck and sold it. As the proceeds were insufficient to cover the full costs incurred, the plaintiff sued the defendant in the Dutch courts for the balance. Although the subject matter of the proceedings was tortious according to Dutch law, the litigation fell outside the scope of Article 1 since, in recovering the wreck, the plaintiff had been acting in the exercise of its public powers pursuant to an international convention. Conversely, in *Sonntag* v. *Waidmann*[52] the plaintiffs' son was killed in an accident on a school excursion in Italy. The plaintiffs, having obtained an award of damages in proceedings in Italy against the teacher who had been in charge of the excursion, sought to enforce the judgment in Germany. The question arose as to whether the judgment fell within the scope of the Brussels Convention. The Court of Justice decided that "the right to obtain redress for harm suffered as a result of an act punishable by criminal law is generally recognised as being civil in nature".[53] In supervising pupils a teacher who works in the public sector acts on behalf of the State but does not exercise public authority powers. Accordingly, the Italian judgment was to be regarded as falling within the scope of Article 1.

3.3.3 Exceptions

Matters falling outside the scope of the Conventions do so only if they constitute the principal subject matter of the proceedings; they are thus not excluded when they come before the court as a subsidiary matter either in the main proceedings or in preliminary proceedings.[54]

47. Case 25/79 *Sanicentral GmbH* v. *Collin* [1979] ECR 3423.
48. Case 29/76 *LTU Lufttransportunternehmen GmbH & Co KG* v. *Eurocontrol* [1976] ECR 1541.
49. Case 814/79 *Netherlands State* v. *Rüffer* [1980] ECR 3807. Hartley, (1981) 6 ELRev 215.
50. Case C-172/91 *Sonntag* v. *Waidmann* [1993] ILPr 466, 485 (para. 20).
51. Case 814/79 [1980] ECR 3807.
52. Case C-172/91 [1993] ILPr 466.
53. Case C-172/91 [1993] ILPr 466, 485 (para. 19).
54. Jenard Report, OJ 1979 C59/10.

3.3.3.1 Family law

It emerges from the Jenard Report that the purpose of the exception in Article 1(1) is to exclude all questions of family law other than matters relating to maintenance.[55] Two particular problems arise out of the wording of the first exception. (i) A distinction has to be drawn between "rights in property arising out of a matrimonial relationship" which fall outside the scope of Article 1 and maintenance obligations which are covered by the Conventions.[56] (ii) As far as the English legal system is concerned, there is a difficult dividing line to be drawn between property issues in general which fall within the scope of the Conventions and "rights in property arising out of a matrimonial relationship" which do not. Whereas legal systems derived from Roman law include matrimonial property regimes—particular rules which govern the property relations of spouses—in English law the general law (albeit with certain modifications) applies. Further consideration of these problems is beyond the scope of this work.

3.3.3.2 Bankruptcy and insolvency

3.3.3.2.1 When the original Brussels Convention was being negotiated the Member States were also starting work on a Draft Convention on Bankruptcy, Winding Up, Arrangements, Compositions and Similar Proceedings.[57] Accordingly, bankruptcy was excluded from the Brussels Convention's scope. It seems, however, that the proposals contained in the Draft Bankruptcy Convention have fallen on stony ground.[58] Under the auspices of the Council of Europe a European Convention on Certain International Aspects of Bankruptcy (the Istanbul Convention) was signed on 5 June 1990.[59] Unlike the Draft EC Convention, the Istanbul Convention does not seek to lay down direct rules of jurisdiction. Accordingly, the assumption of jurisdiction in bankruptcy matters is governed by national law.

3.3.3.2.2 The scope of the exception is straightforward as regards the bankruptcy of individuals. More difficult is the position of companies. There are clearly many issues relating to companies which fall squarely within the Conventions. For example, Title II expressly allocates jurisdiction in respect of proceedings which have as their object the validity of the constitution, the nullity or the dissolution of companies or the decisions of their organs.[60] Obviously, civil and commercial contracts entered into by companies also fall within Article 1.

3.3.3.2.3 As regards the winding-up of companies, a number of distinctions need to be made.

(i) Legal proceedings incidental to the voluntary winding-up of a company under the law of the United Kingdom are normal civil or commercial disputes within

55. OJ 1979 C59/10.
56. Article 5(2) provides special jurisdiction rules "in matters relating to maintenance".
57. Reaction to the Draft Bankruptcy Convention was mixed: Farrar, "The EEC Draft Convention on Bankruptcy and Winding Up" [1977] JBL 320; Fletcher, "The Proposed Community Convention on Bankruptcy and Related Matters" (1977) 2 ELRev 15; Hunter, "The Draft Bankruptcy Convention of the European Economic Communities" (1972) 21 ICLQ 682; Hunter, "The Draft EEC Bankruptcy Convention—A Further Examination" (1976) 25 ICLQ 310.
58. For a review of the history of the Draft Bankruptcy Convention see Aminoff, "The EEC Draft Bankruptcy Convention—An Exercise in Harmonising Private International Law" [1990] 1 LIEI 121.
59. Güneysu, "The New European Bankruptcy Convention" (1991) 11 YBEL 295.
60. Article 16(2).

the scope of the Conventions; this is also the position in cases involving winding-up subject to the supervision of the court.

(ii) In relation to winding-up by the court, if the company is insolvent, the proceedings are outside the scope of the Conventions; if the company is solvent the proceedings fall within the Conventions' scope. In cases where a company is wound up by the court what is important is not the legal ground on which the company is wound up, but whether the company is in fact solvent or insolvent.[61]

3.3.3.2.4 There has been only one reference to the Court of Justice on the scope of this exception. In *Gourdain* v. *Nadler*[62] the French court had, on the application of a company's liquidator, ordered the *de facto* manager of a French company to pay a certain sum into the assets of the company. The liquidator then sought to enforce the French judgment in Germany. The Court of Justice decided that if the decision of the court of origin is given in the context of bankruptcy or analogous proceedings it falls within the scope of the exception in Article 1(2). It should be noted that the decision of the French court was derived directly from the bankruptcy or winding-up; it is implicit in the Court of Justice's analysis that proceedings which are incidental to the bankruptcy or winding-up, rather than directly derived from it, do not fall within the exception. This would also be consistent with the general approach to the exceptions advocated by the Jenard Report.[63]

3.3.3.3 Social security

An explanation of the scope of the exception concerned with matters relating to social security is to be found in the Jenard Report: "the litigation on social security which is excluded from the scope of the Convention is confined to disputes arising from relationships between the administrative authorities concerned and employers or employees. On the other hand the Convention is applicable when the authority concerned relies on a direct right of recourse against a third party responsible for injury or damage, or is subrogated as against a third party to the rights of an injured party insured by it, since, in doing so, it is acting in accordance with ordinary legal rules".[64]

3.3.3.4 Arbitration

The precise scope of Article 1(4) has provoked considerable controversy. In *Marc Rich & Co AG* v. *Societa Italiana Impianti PA* the Court of Appeal referred various questions concerning the scope of Article 1(4) to the Court of Justice.[65] In its judgment the Court of Justice went a long way towards clarifying the position.[66]

61. Schlosser Report, OJ 1979 C59/91, para. 55.
62. Case 133/78 [1979] ECR 733.
63. OJ 1979 C59/10.
64. Jenard Report, OJ 1979 C59/13.
65. [1989] 1 Lloyd's Rep 548 (also referred to by the name *The Atlantic Emperor*). For a discussion of the case following the reference by the Court of Appeal, but prior to the decision of the Court of Justice, see Kaye, "The Judgments Convention and Arbitration: Mutual Spheres of Influence" (1991) 7 Arb Int 289; Thomas, "The Arbitration Exclusion in the Brussels Convention 1968: An English Perspective" (1990) 7 J Int Arb (2) 43; Davidson, "Civil Jurisdiction and Arbitration", 1992 SLT 267.
66. Case C-190/89 [1991] ECR I-3855. Audit, "Arbitration and the Brussels Convention" (1993) 9 Arb Int 1; Briggs, (1991) 11 YBEL 527; Hartley, (1991) 16 ELRev 529; Kaye, "The EEC and Arbitration: The Unsettled Wake of *The Atlantic Emperor*" (1993) 9 Arb Int 27.

A wide variety of disputes may arise out of arbitration. The question is whether all court proceedings which raise any issue relating to arbitration fall outside the scope of the Conventions. There are five different situations which need to be considered:

(i) legal proceedings relating to arbitration;
(ii) legal proceedings relating to arbitration in which the validity of the arbitration agreement arises as a preliminary question;
(iii) legal proceedings relating to the validity of an arbitration agreement;
(iv) legal proceedings in which the jurisdiction of the court is contested on the basis of an arbitration agreement;
(v) legal proceedings for the recognition or enforcement of a foreign judgment given in defiance of an arbitration agreement.

3.3.3.4.1 LEGAL PROCEEDINGS RELATING TO ARBITRATION

Although there are some commentators who have suggested that the arbitration exception in Article 1(4) applies only to arbitral proceedings themselves—with the consequence that all court proceedings relating to arbitration fall within the Conventions' scope[67]—the orthodox view is that the Conventions do not apply "for the purpose of determining the jurisdiction of courts and tribunals in respect of litigation relating to arbitration".[68] The Conventions do not cover "court proceedings which are ancillary to arbitration proceedings, for example the appointment or dismissal of arbitrators, the fixing of the place for arbitration, the extension of the time limit for making awards or the obtaining of a preliminary ruling on questions of substance as provided by English law".[69] Nor do they cover "proceedings and decisions concerning applications for the revocation, amendment, recognition and enforcement of arbitration awards".[70]

3.3.3.4.2 LEGAL PROCEEDINGS RELATING TO ARBITRATION IN WHICH THE VALIDITY OF THE ARBITRATION AGREEMENT ARISES AS A PRELIMINARY QUESTION

3.3.3.4.2.1 The question which arose in *Marc Rich & Co AG* v. *Societa Italiana Impianti PA* was whether legal proceedings which are ancillary to arbitration proceedings are still outside the scope of the Brussels Convention if the existence or validity of the arbitration agreement is challenged. In this case, the plaintiff, a Swiss company, offered by telex to buy a quantity of crude oil from the defendant, an Italian company. The defendant accepted the offer subject to certain further conditions. The plaintiff telexed again setting out the terms in greater detail; these terms included a clause which provided for English law to govern the contract and for disputes to be referred to arbitration in London. The plaintiff alleged that the cargo of oil was contaminated and claimed damages. The defendant commenced legal proceedings in Italy with a view to obtaining a declaration of non-liability; the plaintiff subsequently started arbitration proceedings in England. When the defendant failed to appoint an arbitrator in

67. See, for example, Schlosser, "The 1968 Convention and Arbitration" (1991) 7 Arb Int 227.
68. Jenard Report, OJ 1979 C59/13.
69. Schlosser Report, OJ 1979 C59/93, para. 64(b).
70. Schlosser Report, OJ 1979 C59/93, para. 65(c).

accordance with the terms of the arbitration clause the plaintiff applied to the court under section 10(3) of the Arbitration Act 1950 asking the court to appoint an arbitrator on the defendant's behalf. The defendant contested the jurisdiction of the court, contending (i) that there was no arbitration agreement, (ii) that the case fell within the scope of Article 1 of the Brussels Convention, and (iii) that—in view of the earlier proceedings in Italy—the English court was obliged to decline jurisdiction under Article 21.[71]

3.3.3.4.2.2 On a reference for a preliminary ruling from the Court of Appeal, the Court of Justice accepted that the purpose of Article 1(4) is to exclude from the scope of the Convention all court proceedings relating to arbitration:

> It follows that, by excluding arbitration from the scope of the Convention on the ground that it was already covered by international conventions, the Contracting Parties intended to exclude arbitration in its entirety, including proceedings brought before national courts. More particularly, it must be pointed out that the appointment of an arbitrator by a national court is a measure adopted by the State as part of the process of setting arbitration proceedings in motion. Such a measure therefore comes within the sphere of arbitration and is thus covered by the exclusion contained in Article 1(4) of the Convention.[72]

3.3.3.4.2.3 Was this conclusion affected by the fact that the validity of the arbitration clause was challenged by the defendant? The defendant argued that a plaintiff should not be able to side-step the provisions of the Convention merely by alleging the existence of an arbitration agreement. The Court of Justice did not accept this argument:

> In order to determine whether a dispute falls within the scope of the Convention, reference must be made solely to the subject matter of the dispute. If, by virtue of its subject matter, such as the appointment of an arbitrator, a dispute falls outside the scope of the Convention, the existence of a preliminary issue which the court must resolve in order to determine the dispute cannot, whatever that issue may be, justify the application of the Convention. . . . It follows that, in the case before the Court, the fact that a preliminary issue relates to the existence or validity of the arbitration agreement does not affect the exclusion from the scope of the Convention of a dispute concerning the appointment of an arbitrator.[73]

The scope of the Conventions does not extend to "litigation pending before a national court concerning the appointment of an arbitrator, even if the existence or validity of an arbitration agreement is a preliminary issue in that litigation".[74]

3.3.3.4.3 LEGAL PROCEEDINGS RELATING TO THE VALIDITY OF AN ARBITRATION AGREEMENT

What is the position where the main issue in the legal proceedings is the existence of an arbitration agreement? This issue would arise where, for example, a party to a contract seeks a declaration from the court that an alleged arbitration clause is invalid. In *Marc Rich & Co AG* v. *Societa Italiana Impianti PA* Advocate-General Darmon took the view that "a dispute as to the existence of an arbitration agreement falls outside the scope of the Convention".[75] This conclusion is supported by the decision of the Court of

71. For discussion of the third point see para. 5.9.2.
72. Case C-190/89 [1991] ECR I-3855, 3900–3901 (paras. 18–19).
73. Case C-190/89 [1991] ECR I-3855, 3902–3903 (paras. 26 and 28).
74. Case C-190/89 [1991] ECR I-3855, 3903 (para. 29).
75. Case C-190/89 [1991] ECR I-3855, 3876 (para. 35).

Justice in *Effer SpA* v. *Kantner*[76] in which it was decided that a dispute as to the existence of a contract is a matter "relating to a contract" for the purposes of Article 5(1).[77] By the same process of reasoning, a dispute over the existence of an arbitration agreement relates to arbitration within Article 1(4).

3.3.3.4.4 LEGAL PROCEEDINGS IN WHICH THE JURISDICTION OF THE COURT IS CONTESTED ON THE BASIS OF AN ARBITRATION AGREEMENT

In a case where the defendant contests the jurisdiction of the court of a Contracting State on the basis of an arbitration agreement, does the court have jurisdiction to determine the validity or existence of the arbitration agreement? It does not follow from the fact that Title II confers jurisdiction as regards the main issue, which falls within the scope of the Conventions, that the court with jurisdiction over the main issue also has jurisdiction to deal with an incidental question falling outside the Conventions; whether a court has jurisdiction to determine the existence or validity of an arbitration clause is a matter for the law of the court seised, not a matter to be determined by the Conventions.[78] Having said that, in the context of proceedings commenced in England, it seems clear that once the plaintiff has invoked the jurisdiction of the court, the court would—on the basis of the plaintiff's submission—have jurisdiction to determine the validity or existence of an arbitration clause invoked by the defendant in order to contest the court's jurisdiction. If the court rules that the arbitration clause is "null and void"[79] the subject matter of the dispute is not arbitration and therefore the proceedings fall within the scope of Article 1. (The question then arises as to whether the decision holding that the alleged arbitration agreement is invalid is a judgment which is entitled to recognition in other Contracting States under Title III.)

3.3.3.4.5 THE RECOGNITION AND ENFORCEMENT OF JUDGMENTS GIVEN IN BREACH OR DISREGARD OF AN ARBITRATION AGREEMENT

3.3.3.4.5.1 The final questions surrounding Article 1(4) arise in the context of the recognition and enforcement of foreign judgments. There are two issues which need to be considered.

(i) Where the court of a Contracting State grants a declaration that an arbitration agreement is "null and void" is that declaratory judgment entitled to recognition in other Contracting States under Title III? In these circumstances the judgment should be regarded as concerning arbitration and therefore as falling outside the scope of the Conventions.[80]

(ii) More problematical is the case where a national court adjudicates on the subject matter of a dispute, because it overlooked an arbitration agreement or considered it inapplicable. Can recognition and enforcement of that judgment be refused in another Contracting State on the ground that the arbitration

76. Case 38/81 [1982] ECR 825.
77. See para. 5.5.3.1.
78. Advocate-General Darmon in Case C-190/89 *Marc Rich & Co AG* v. *Societa Italiana Impianti PA* [1991] ECR I-3855, 3878 (para. 44).
79. Arbitration Act 1975, s. 1(1).
80. Audit, "Arbitration and the Brussels Convention" (1993) 9 Arb Int 1, 12.

agreement was after all valid and therefore pursuant to Article 1(4), the judgment falls outside the scope of the Conventions?[81]

3.3.3.4.5.2 The Schlosser Report reveals that at the time of the negotiation of the 1978 Accession Convention there was disagreement as to the precise scope of the arbitration exception in this area.[82] The 1978 Accession Convention, however, made no amendment to the original text of the Convention. In the Evrigenis–Kerameus Report the view is expressed that "the verification as an incidental question of an arbitration agreement which is cited by a litigant in order to contest the jurisdiction of the court before which he is being sued pursuant to the Convention, must be considered as falling within its scope".[83] This passage has been interpreted as supporting the view that the Convention applies "to recognition and enforcement of a judgment which disposes of a dispute within the scope of the Convention after giving a decision on the validity of an arbitration agreement".[84] The alternative interpretation—that a judgment on the merits following a decision on the validity of an arbitration agreement concerns "arbitration" and therefore falls outside the scope of the Conventions—means that the recognition and enforcement of a foreign judgment given in breach or disregard of an arbitration agreement can be refused in England on the basis of section 32 of the Civil Jurisdiction and Judgments Act 1982.[85]

3.3.3.4.5.3 The decision of the Court of Justice in *Marc Rich & Co AG* v. *Societa Italiana Impianti PA* does not directly address this question and opinion as to its significance is divided.[86] On the one hand, it has been suggested that the decision of the Court of Justice supports a wide interpretation of the arbitration exception:

> If the court of a Contracting State has given judgment in breach of an arbitration agreement, it now appears that there will be no obligation upon an English court to recognise it. If the recognition of the judgment would, in national law, otherwise depend upon whether there had been breach of (or compliance with) an arbitration agreement, the Convention cannot properly, and does not, impose an obligation upon a court to disregard its law on arbitration, for arbitration falls outside the Convention.[87]

On the other hand, it has been argued that the decision of the Court of Justice "strongly suggests that judgments in cases where there has been a breach of an agreement to go to arbitration are, nonetheless, within the scope of the Convention".[88] On the basis of this view, the only grounds on which such a judgment can be refused recognition and enforcement are those contained in Title III itself.

3.3.3.4.5.4 The only English case in which the issue has arisen is inconclusive. In *Marc Rich & Co AG* v. *Societa Italiana Impianti PA (No. 2)*[89] the Court of Appeal was required to consider whether an Italian judgment given in breach of an alleged arbitration clause was entitled to recognition under the Brussels Convention. In the Italian proceedings—which had been commenced before the plaintiff started

81. The question is posed by the Schlosser Report, OJ 1979 C59/92, para. 62.
82. OJ 1979 C59/92, para. 61.
83. OJ 1986 C298/10, para. 35.
84. Advocate-General Darmon in Case C-190/89 *Marc Rich & Co AG* v. *Societa Italiana Impianti PA* [1991] ECR I-3855, 3878 (para. 45).
85. See para. 9.2.7.5.
86. The issue was mentioned but expressly left open by Advocate-General Darmon: Case C-190/89 *Marc Rich & Co AG* v. *Societa Italiana Impianti PA* [1991] ECR I-3855, 3878 (para. 45).
87. Briggs, (1991) 11 YBEL 527, 529.
88. Cheshire & North, *Private International Law* (12th ed, 1992) p. 436.
89. [1992] 1 Lloyd's Rep 624. Kaye, "Forensic Submission as a Bar to Arbitration" (1993) 12 CJQ 359.

arbitration proceedings in England—the Italian court held that the arbitration agreement was invalid. Although the plaintiff had contested the jurisdiction of the Italian court, a defence on the merits had also been advanced. The position was, therefore, that, although the Court of Justice had decided (in the plaintiff's favour) that the plaintiff's application to the court for the appointment of an arbitrator was outside the scope of the Brussels Convention (with the consequence that the English court had the necessary jurisdiction), the Italian court had decided (in the defendant's favour) that the arbitration clause was invalid. In reliance on the Italian judgment the defendant sought to resist the appointment of an arbitrator in England. If the Italian judgment was entitled to recognition in England the arbitration could not proceed. Logically, the first issue was whether the Italian judgment fell within the scope of Article 1 of the Brussels Convention. The Court of Appeal, however, side-stepped this important issue. Neill LJ (with whom the other members of the Court of Appeal agreed) decided the case on the basis that by putting forward a defence on the merits the plaintiff had submitted to the jurisdiction of the Italian court, with the consequence that—whether or not the case fell within the scope of Article 1—there was no basis on which the plaintiff could resist recognition of the judgment in England.

3.3.3.4.5.5 When the implications of the rival interpretations of Article 1(4) are considered, the broader interpretation of the exception appears preferable. Two examples illustrate the extent to which a narrow interpretation of Article 1(4) not only has the effect of undermining arbitration as a method of resolving international commercial disputes but also leads to the subordination of English conflicts rules to those of other Contracting States.

3.3.3.4.5.6 The first example involves the following situation:

> [A] Belgian company and an Italian company are parties to a contract. Difficulties arise as to performance and the former party alleges breach on the part of the latter. The Belgian party invokes an arbitration clause in the contract, under which any dispute is to be submitted to arbitration in Belgium under Belgian law. The Italian party, nevertheless, contends that the alleged clause is not part of the contract and refuses to participate in the arbitral proceedings which continue in his absence. An award is ultimately made in favour of the Belgian party. Meanwhile, the Italian party has gone to an Italian court contending that there is no agreement to arbitrate and asking the court for a declaration that he has not committed a breach of contract. The court agrees with him on both counts and issues the declaration.[90]

If the arbitration exception is interpreted broadly, the Italian judgment falls outside the scope of the Brussels Convention and—if the arbitration clause is valid in English law—recognition should be refused on the basis of section 32 of the Civil Jurisdiction and Judgments Act 1982.[91] If, however, the Italian judgment is regarded as falling within the scope of the Brussels Convention both the Belgian award and the Italian judgment are *prima facie* entitled to recognition in England (under the Civil Jurisdiction and Judgments Act 1982 and the Arbitration Act 1975 respectively[92]). In a case of conflict between treaties the general principle of international law is that the earlier convention applies only to the extent that it is consistent with the latter.[93] It would follow, therefore, that the judgment would take precedence over the award.

90. Davidson, "Civil Jurisdiction and Arbitration" 1992 SLT 267, 269.
91. See para. 9.2.7.5.
92. For a discussion of the recognition and enforcement of foreign arbitral awards under the Arbitration Act 1975 see para. 20.2.
93. Vienna Convention on the Law of Treaties 1969, Article 30(3) and (4)(a).

3.3.3.4.5.7 The second example concerns the possible conflict between an English award and a judgment given by the courts of another Contracting State. Article 27(3) of the Conventions provides that a foreign judgment shall not be recognised "if the judgment is irreconcilable with a judgment given in a dispute between the parties in the State in which recognition is sought". It seems highly unlikely that an award could be regarded as a "judgment" for the purposes of Article 27(3).[94] If a judgment given in defiance of an arbitration clause falls within the material scope of the Conventions, an Italian judgment which declares an arbitration agreement to be null and void will take precedence over an English award—even though as far as English law is concerned the arbitration agreement and the award are unimpeachable.

3.4 THE RELATIONSHIP BETWEEN THE BRUSSELS AND LUGANO CONVENTIONS

3.4.1 Section 9(1A) of the Civil Jurisdiction and Judgments Act 1982 provides:

> Any question arising as to whether it is the Lugano Convention or any of the Brussels Conventions which applies in the circumstances of a particular case falls to be determined in accordance with the provisions of Article 54B of the Lugano Convention.

3.4.2 Article 54B(1) provides that the Lugano Convention shall not prejudice the application by the Member States of the European Communities of the Brussels Convention. The second paragraph of Article 54B provides that the Lugano Convention shall in any event be applied:

(a) in matters of jurisdiction, where the defendant is domiciled in a territory of a Contracting State which is not a member of the European Communities, or where Article 16 or 17 of this Convention confers a jurisdiction on the courts of such a Contracting State;
(b) in relation to a *lis pendens* or to related actions as provided for in Articles 21 and 22, when proceedings are instituted in a Contracting State which is not a member of the European Communities and in a Contracting State which is a member of the European Communities;
(c) in matters of recognition and enforcement, where either the State of origin or the State addressed is not a member of the European Communities.

Article 54B(2)(c) requires little explanation; judgments given by the courts of EFTA countries are entitled to recognition and enforcement in England under the Lugano Convention. Subparagraphs (b) and (c), however, require further consideration.

3.4.3 Various jurisdiction rules contained in the Conventions do not depend on the defendant being domiciled in a Contracting State. Article 16, for example, allocates jurisdiction "regardless of domicile". The effect of Article 54B(2)(a) is that where proceedings are brought in England against a defendant who is domiciled in a Lugano Contracting State which is not a member of the EC the relevant jurisdiction rule is Article 16 of the Lugano Convention. Article 16 of the Brussels Convention applies only in relation to defendants who are domiciled in a Brussels Contracting State or in a non-contracting State. The position is the same *mutatis mutandis* in relation to Article

94. Hartley, (1991) 16 ELRev 529, 532.

17. The effect of Article 54B(2)(b) is to confirm that where parallel proceedings are brought in an EC Member State and a country which is a member of EFTA, the relevant rules concerning *lis pendens* and related actions are Articles 21 and 22 of the Lugano Convention.

3.5 THE RELATIONSHIP BETWEEN THE BRUSSELS AND LUGANO CONVENTIONS AND OTHER INTERNATIONAL CONVENTIONS

3.5.1 Title VII concerns the relationship between the Brussels and Lugano Conventions and other conventions. Article 55 lists certain conventions which are overridden by the Brussels and Lugano Conventions; Article 56 provides, however, that those conventions continue to apply to matters to which the Brussels and Lugano Conventions do not apply.

The most important provision in Title VII is Article 57, the first paragraph of which provides:

> This Convention shall not affect any conventions to which the Contracting States are or will be parties and which, in relation to particular matters, govern jurisdiction or the recognition or enforcement of judgments.

3.5.2 The second paragraph provides that the Conventions shall not prevent a court of a Contracting State which is a party to a convention referred to in Article 57(1) from assuming jurisdiction in accordance with that convention "even where the defendant is domiciled in a Contracting State which is not a party to that convention". Furthermore, Article 57(3) provides that judgments given in a Contracting State by a court in the exercise of jurisdiction provided for in a convention referred to in Article 57(1) shall be recognised and enforced in other Contracting States in accordance with Title III.

3.5.3 Article 57 is of particular importance for the United Kingdom because of the significance of other conventions in the field of maritime law, in particular the International Convention for the Unification of Certain Rules relating to the Arrest of Seagoing Ships (the Arrest Convention) and the International Convention for the Unification of Certain Rules concerning Civil Jurisdiction in matters of Collision (the Collision Convention) both of which date from 1952. Article 57 is supplemented in English law by section 9(1) of the Civil Jurisdiction and Judgments Act 1982, which provides:

> The provisions of Title VII of the 1968 Convention and, apart from Article 54B, of Title VII of the Lugano Convention (relationship between the Convention in question and other conventions to which Contracting States are or may become parties) shall have effect in relation to—
> (a) any statutory provision, whenever passed or made, implementing any such other convention in the United Kingdom; and
> (b) any rule of law so far as it has the effect of so implementing any such other convention, as they have effect in relation to that other convention itself.

The effect of section 9 of the 1982 Act is that the principle in Article 57 applies not only to special conventions, but also to domestic legislation which translates the substance of special conventions into English law.[95]

3.5.4 A number of points concerning the operation of Article 57 should be noted.

95. *The Po* [1991] 2 Lloyd's Rep 206.

(i) Article 57 allows the Conventions to be displaced only by special conventions which "govern jurisdiction or the recognition or enforcement of judgments". A convention which governs substantive matters cannot override the Conventions.

(ii) If the convention in question concerns jurisdiction, the terms of the convention itself determine whether its jurisdiction rules override, or are additional to, or are alternative to the rules in the Conventions.

(iii) The court of a Contracting State may, relying on a special convention, assume jurisdiction over a defendant who is domiciled in a Contracting State which is not a party to the convention in question. In any event, the court hearing the action must apply Article 20.[96]

(iv) The operation of Article 57 does not depend on it being shown that the Contracting State in which proceedings are brought has expressly implemented the special convention. Where jurisdiction is assumed under a special convention the crucial elements are that the Contracting State in which proceedings are brought is a party to the special convention in question; that the forum has jurisdiction in accordance with its municipal law; and that the assumption of jurisdiction is consistent with the terms of the special convention in question. If these three conditions are satisfied, a defendant who is domiciled in a Contracting State may be sued in another Contracting State, notwithstanding the fact that the court in which the proceedings are brought does not have jurisdiction under Title II.[97]

96. For a discussion of Article 20, see para. 4.4.

97. See *The Nordglimt* [1988] 1 QB 183; *The Deichland* [1990] 1 QB 361; *The Po* [1991] 2 Lloyd's Rep 206; *The Prinsengracht* [1993] 1 Lloyd's Rep 41. For consideration of these cases see para. 8.2.

CHAPTER 4

JURISDICTION IN PERSONAM UNDER THE BRUSSELS AND LUGANO CONVENTIONS: INTRODUCTION

The main focus of Title II of the Brussels and Lugano Conventions ("the Conventions") is the allocation of jurisdiction between the Contracting States as regards proceedings brought against defendants domiciled in a Contracting State.[1] Accordingly, although the application of the Conventions is not restricted to proceedings in which the defendant is domiciled in a Contracting State, in many circumstances a defendant's domicile is "the point on which the rules on jurisdiction hinge"[2] (para. 4.1). The basic structure of Title II is to distinguish those bases of jurisdiction which apply regardless of the defendant's domicile from those which apply only to defendants who are domiciled in a Contracting State (para. 4.2). As regards the service of documents abroad the Conventions are supplemented by the Rules of the Supreme Court (para. 4.3). Although the Conventions aim to simplify the recognition and enforcement of foreign judgments, this should not be at the cost of imposing procedural unfairness on the defendant (para. 4.4).

4.1 DOMICILE UNDER THE CONVENTIONS

4.1.1 The domicile of individuals

4.1.1.1 Introduction

4.1.1.1.1 Article 52 states:

> In order to determine whether a party is domiciled in the Contracting State whose courts are seised of a matter, the court shall apply its internal law.
>
> If a party is not domiciled in the State whose courts are seised of the matter, then, in order to determine whether the party is domiciled in another Contracting State, the court shall apply the law of that State.

Under Article 2 a person domiciled in a Contracting State may be sued in the courts of the State in which he is domiciled. The efficacy of this provision depends on the Contracting States sharing a broadly similar concept of domicile. Whereas on the continent domicile means something akin to ordinary residence, at common law domicile is a technical and artificial concept which approximates to a person's permanent home.

4.1.1.1.2 The application of the common law concept of domicile in the United

1. In this chapter it is to be assumed that the provisions of the Brussels and Lugano Conventions are identical unless the contrary is indicated.

2. Jenard–Möller Report, OJ 1990 C189/65, para. 13.

Kingdom would have seriously distorted the operation of Title II; the English courts would have been deprived of jurisdiction in cases where the defendant had made his home in England without establishing an intention to reside there permanently and jurisdiction would have been conferred on the English courts in certain cases even though under the laws of nearly all the other Contracting States the defendant would have been regarded as domiciled in a country other than England.[3] For this reason the implementing legislation in the United Kingdom includes a special definition of domicile for the purposes of Title II. As regards individuals, the definition of domicile is to be found in section 41 of the Civil Jurisdiction and Judgments Act 1982.

4.1.1.2 Domicile in the United Kingdom

4.1.1.2.1 Section 41(2) of the 1982 Act provides:

An individual is domiciled in the United Kingdom if and only if—
- (a) he is resident in the United Kingdom; and
- (b) the nature and circumstances of his residence indicate that he has a substantial connection with the United Kingdom.

Subsection (6) provides that where an individual has been resident in the United Kingdom for "the last three months or more" it is to be presumed that subsection (2)(b) is fulfilled "unless the contrary is proved". Of course, the Act does not stipulate that a person who has resided in a particular country for less than three months is not to be regarded as having a substantial connection with that country. So, for example, an Italian student who comes to England intending to reside here for twelve months may be regarded as domiciled in England on his arrival.[4]

4.1.1.2.2 In certain circumstances it is not sufficient to know simply that a person is domiciled in the United Kingdom; some jurisdiction rules require the "place" where a person is domiciled or the part of the United Kingdom in which a person is domiciled to be identified. As a general rule a person is domiciled in a particular part of the United Kingdom if and only if he is resident in that part and the nature and circumstances of his residence indicate that he has a substantial connection with that part.[5] A person who is resident in a part of the United Kingdom for the last three months or more is presumed to have a substantial connection with that part.[6] If an individual is domiciled in the United Kingdom but does not have a substantial connection with any part of the United Kingdom he is to be regarded as domiciled in the part of the United Kingdom where he is resident.[7] An individual is domiciled in a particular "place" in the United Kingdom if he is domiciled in the part of the United Kingdom in which that place is situated and he is resident in that place.[8]

3. Schlosser Report, OJ 1979 C59/96, para. 73(c).
4. Mathers, "The Brussels Convention of 1968: Its Implementation in the United Kingdom" (1983) 3 YBEL 49, 54.
5. Civil Jurisdiction and Judgments Act 1982, s. 41(3).
6. Civil Jurisdiction and Judgments Act 1982, s. 41(6).
7. Civil Jurisdiction and Judgments Act 1982, s. 41(5).
8. Civil Jurisdiction and Judgments Act 1982, s. 41(4).

4.1.1.3 Domicile in other States

If the application of section 41(2) leads to the conclusion that a person is not domiciled in the United Kingdom, the method for ascertaining whether that person is domiciled in another Contracting State is to apply the law of that Contracting State. For instance, to determine whether a person is domiciled in Greece, Greek law must be applied.

If a person is domiciled neither in the United Kingdom nor in another Contracting State, for the purposes of the Conventions that person must be regarded as domiciled in a non-contracting State. Generally speaking, it is not important to determine the particular non-contracting State in which a person is domiciled.[9] Nevertheless, section 41(7) of the 1982 Act provides:

> An individual is domiciled in a State other than a Contracting State if and only if—
> (a) he is resident in that State; and
> (b) the nature and circumstances of his residence indicate that he has a substantial connection with that State.

The combination of Article 52 and section 41 may lead to the conclusion that a person who is physically present within the Contracting States is not to be regarded as domiciled in any of them. In such a case, the Conventions are relevant only to the extent that they lay down rules which apply regardless of domicile.

4.1.2 The domicile of corporations

4.1.2.1 Introduction

Article 53 provides:

> For the purposes of this Convention, the seat of a company or other legal person or association of natural or legal persons shall be treated as its domicile. However, in order to determine that seat, the court shall apply its rules of private international law.

It was noted in the Schlosser Report that there is no equivalent in the law of the United Kingdom to the concept of the "seat" of a company in continental legal systems.[10] In terms of the location of companies the connecting factors with which English law is most familiar are the place of incorporation and the place of business. The implementing legislation in the United Kingdom includes provisions for determining the domicile of a company. Section 42(1) provides that for the purposes of the 1982 Act "the seat of a corporation or association . . . shall be treated as its domicile". The seat of a corporation is determined by reference to subsections (3) to (7).

4.1.2.2 Domicile in the United Kingdom

4.1.2.2.1 To determine if a corporation's seat is in the United Kingdom section 42(3) provides:

> A corporation or association has its seat in the United Kingdom if and only if—
> (a) it was incorporated or formed under the law of a part of the United Kingdom and has its registered office or some other official address in the United Kingdom; or
> (b) its central management and control is exercised in the United Kingdom.

9. See, however, Article 59 of the Conventions.
10. OJ 1979 C59/96, para. 75(e).

Whereas it is easy enough to determine the place of incorporation, "central management and control"—which refers to a company's administrative centre as opposed to its main business centre—is a more fluid concept. Where central management and control is divided a corporation ought to be regarded as domiciled wherever "some portion of controlling power and authority can be identified".[11]

4.1.2.2.2 The effect of subsection (3)—which lays down alternative connecting factors—is that a corporation may be regarded as domiciled in England, notwithstanding the fact that it has effectively severed all meaningful links with England. In *Re Harrods (Buenos Aires) Ltd*,[12] for example, a company which had been incorporated in England in 1913 was domiciled in England even though its business was exclusively carried on in Argentina and its central management and control was exercised there.[13]

4.1.2.2.3 Section 42 of the 1982 Act also contains provisions for identifying the part of the United Kingdom in which a corporation is domiciled and the place of domicile. Subsections (4) and (5) provide:

> (4) A corporation or association has its seat in a particular part of the United Kingdom if and only if it has its seat in the United Kingdom and—
> (a) it has its registered office or some other official address in that part; or
> (b) its central management or control is exercised in that part; or
> (c) it has a place of business in that part.
> (5) A corporation or association has its seat in a particular place in the United Kingdom if and only if it has its seat in the part of the United Kingdom in which that place is situated and—
> (a) it has its registered office or some other official address in that place; or
> (b) its central management or control is exercised in that place; or
> (c) it has a place of business in that place.

4.1.2.3 Domicile in another State

Subsections (6) and (7) determine whether or not a company is to be regarded as domiciled in another State:

> (6) Subject to subsection (7), a corporation or association has its seat in a State other than the United Kingdom if and only if—
> (a) it was incorporated or formed under the law of that State and has its registered office or some other official address there; or
> (b) its central management and control is exercised in that State.
> (7) A corporation or association shall not be regarded as having its seat in a Contracting State other than the United Kingdom if it is shown that the courts of that State would not regard it as having its seat there.

The effect of these subsections is that a company will be regarded as domiciled in a particular Contracting State only if (i) it is regarded by the law of that State as having its seat there and (ii) it was incorporated under the law of that State or it has an official address in that State or its central management and control is exercised in that State.

11. Lord Radcliffe in *Unit Construction Co Ltd* v. *Bullock* [1960] AC 351, 366 (albeit in a somewhat different context).
12. [1992] Ch 72.
13. For discussion of some of the problems to which this case gave rise see para. 5.10.1.2.

4.1.3 Multiple domiciles

4.1.3.1 It is implicit within the Conventions that it is possible for a person to be domiciled in more than one Contracting State. The Schlosser Report considers the possibility of a company "having a 'domicile' in the United Kingdom in accordance with legislation in the United Kingdom and a 'seat' in a continental State in accordance with the legislation of that State".[14] Although the question has not been considered by the Court of Justice the United Kingdom courts have accepted that both an individual and a company may have more than one domicile.

4.1.3.2 In *Daniel* v. *Foster*,[15] a Scottish case, it was decided that the defendant was domiciled in Scotland for the purposes of the Civil Jurisdiction and Judgments Act 1982 even though his main home was in England. The approach adopted by the court in this case is equally applicable to cases involving two Contracting States rather than two parts of the same Contracting State. Given that a person may have more than one residence and that "domicile" in the 1982 Act is based on a residential test, it follows that a person may have more than one domicile for the purposes of the Conventions. The common law doctrine of domicile—under which a person can have only one domicile at any one time—is not relevant in this context.

4.1.3.3 In *The Deichland*[16] the Court of Appeal held that a company which was incorporated in Panama, but whose central management and control was exercised in Germany, was domiciled in Germany for the purposes of the Brussels Convention. Since the connecting factors were with a non-contracting State as regards the place of incorporation and a Contracting State as regards the place where central management and control was exercised it was not necessary to decide whether a company could be domiciled in more than one Contracting State. However, although in section 42 the seat of a company is referred to only in the singular, it is quite clear that a corporation might satisfy the statutory test in relation to more than one Contracting State.[17] Moreover, there is no fundamental objection to two Contracting States having jurisdiction as a consequence of a corporation being regarded as domiciled in more than one Contracting State.[18]

4.1.4 Special definitions

There are special provisions in the Civil Jurisdiction and Judgments Act 1982 for determining the seat of companies for the purposes of Article 16(2) of the Conventions and Articles 5A and 16(2) of the Modified Convention (jurisdiction in matters relating to the validity of the constitution and dissolution of companies and of decisions of their organs)[19] as well as for the purposes of Articles 3 and 4 of the Conventions (consumer and insurance contracts).[20]

14. OJ 1979 C59/96-97, para. 75(e).
15. 1989 SLT 90 (Sh Ct).
16. [1990] 1 QB 361.
17. Neill LJ, [1990] 1 QB 361, 375.
18. Stuart-Smith LJ, [1990] 1 QB 361, 379.
19. Civil Jurisdiction and Judgments Act 1982, s. 43.
20. Civil Jurisdiction and Judgments Act 1982, s. 44.

4.2 THE BASIC STRUCTURE OF THE JURISDICTION RULES

4.2.1 Jurisdiction rules applicable to defendants domiciled in a Contracting State: Articles 2 and 3

4.2.1.1 As regards proceedings which fall within the scope of Title I—by virtue of the fact that the proceedings concern civil and commercial matters and do not fall within the scope of any of the exceptions—a person who is domiciled in a Contracting State may generally be sued in the courts of a Contracting State only in accordance with the rules laid down in Title II.

4.2.1.2 The first paragraph of Article 2 provides that "persons domiciled in a Contracting State shall, whatever their nationality, be sued in the courts of that State". This provision—which enshrines the principle *actor forum sequitur rei* (the plaintiff must sue the defendant in the jurisdiction to which the defendant is subject)—is in many respects the foundation of Title II as it applies to defendants domiciled in a Contracting State.[21] Notwithstanding the use of the word "shall", Article 2 must be read in conjunction with the first paragraph of Article 3 which provides: "Persons domiciled in a Contracting State may be sued in the courts of another Contracting State only by virtue of the rules set out in Sections 2 to 6 of this Title."

4.2.1.3 The effect of the first paragraph of Article 3 is twofold:

(i) Article 2 is subordinate to the general jurisdiction rules contained in Articles 16 to 18 and the specific jurisdiction rules applicable to insurance and consumer contracts in Articles 7 to 15;

(ii) a plaintiff is often given the option of proceeding against a person who is domiciled in a Contracting State either in the courts of the Contracting State in which the defendant is domiciled under Article 2 or in the courts of another Contracting State designated by Article 5, Article 6 or Article 6A.

4.2.1.4 The second paragraph of Article 3 lists the various exorbitant bases of jurisdiction which cannot be applied against defendants who are domiciled in a Contracting State. This list includes the English rule which enables jurisdiction to be founded on the document instituting the proceedings having been served on the defendant during his temporary presence in England.[22] Strictly speaking, the second paragraph adds nothing to the first, which makes the point that the courts of Contracting States may assume jurisdiction over defendants who are domiciled in a Contracting State only according to the rules set out in Title II.

4.2.1.5 It is important to note the operation of Article 57, which provides that the Conventions "shall not affect any conventions to which the Contracting States are or will be parties and which, in relation to particular matters, govern jurisdiction or the recognition or enforcement of judgments". The courts of a Contracting State which is a party to a convention on a particular matter may assume jurisdiction in accordance with that convention, even where the defendant is domiciled in another Contracting State which is not a party to that convention.[23]

21. For a discussion of "domicile" for the purposes of Title II see para. 4.1.
22. See, for example, *Maharanee of Baroda* v. *Wildenstein* [1972] 2 QB 283.
23. Article 57(2)(a). See paras. 3.5 and 8.2.

4.2.2 Jurisdiction rules applicable to persons who are not domiciled in a Contracting State: Article 4

4.2.2.1 The first paragraph of Article 4 provides:

If the defendant is not domiciled in a Contracting State, the jurisdiction of the courts of each Contracting State shall, subject to the provisions of Article 16, be determined by the law of that State.

The text of Article 4 is potentially misleading since it suggests that the only jurisdictional bases under Title II which may be applied to persons who are not domiciled in a Contracting State are those to be found in Article 16. This is not the case. In addition to the expressly identified exception, there are within Title II various implicit exceptions to the general principle set out in Article 4.

4.2.2.2 The following provisions do not depend for their application on the defendant being domiciled in a Contracting State: Article 16 (exclusive jurisdiction); Article 17 (prorogation of jurisdiction); Article 18 (submission); various provisions within the special jurisdiction rules which govern insurance and consumer contracts (Articles 7 to 15); Articles 21 to 23 (*lis pendens* and related actions); Article 24 (provisional, including protective, measures).

4.2.2.3 The second paragraph of Article 4 provides that, as regards a defendant who is not domiciled in a Contracting State, "any person domiciled in a Contracting State may, whatever his nationality, avail himself in that State of the rules of jurisdiction there in force, and in particular those specified in the second paragraph of Article 3, in the same way as the nationals of that State". So, a plaintiff who is domiciled in England may bring proceedings in France against a defendant who is not domiciled in a Contracting State under Article 14 of the French Civil Code, even though the jurisdiction provisions of the Civil Code were originally enacted solely for the benefit of French nationals. Article 4(2) of the Conventions makes no difference to practice in England, since under English law the bases of jurisdiction under RSC, Order 11, rule 1(1) have always been available to plaintiffs regardless of nationality.

4.2.3 The standard of proof

When a plaintiff invokes the jurisdiction of the courts of a Contracting State under Title II, what is the standard of proof that the plaintiff must satisfy? It is important to distinguish two different issues: (i) the standard of proof which the plaintiff must establish as regards the merits of the dispute and (ii) the standard of proof as regards the jurisdiction of the court. Questions of jurisdiction may arise in one of two forms. First, certain circumstances give rise to a pure question of jurisdiction. For example, in relation to proceedings which have as their object rights *in rem* in immovable property Article 16(1) confers exclusive jurisdiction on the courts of the Contracting State in which the property is situated. Where proceedings are brought in country X for a declaration that the defendant holds certain immovable property situated in country Y on bare trust for the plaintiff and the defendant contests jurisdiction on the basis that Article 16(1) confers exclusive jurisdiction on the courts of country Y, the pure question of jurisdiction is whether the object of the proceedings is "rights *in rem* in immovable property". Secondly, a question of jurisdiction may be inextricably linked with questions relating to the merits of the plaintiff's claim. For example, if the plaintiff starts proceedings for breach of contract in country X in reliance on Article 17 (which confers exclusive jurisdiction on the courts of the Contracting State agreed by the parties) and the defendant contests jurisdiction on the ground that the contract containing the jurisdiction agreement is void, the court must investigate—at least to some extent—the merits of the claim in order to determine whether it has jurisdiction.

4.2.3.1 The merits of the dispute

4.2.3.1.1 It has been suggested that the strength of the plaintiff's claim is totally irrelevant for the purposes of jurisdiction under the Conventions.[24] Moreover, there is nothing in the Conventions or the accompanying Reports to suggest that for jurisdiction to be founded on the terms of Title II the plaintiff's claim as to the merits must satisfy any particular standard of proof.

4.2.3.1.2 In the context of RSC, Order 11, rule 1(1) the House of Lords held in *Seaconsar Far East Ltd* v. *Bank Markazi Jomhouri Islami Iran*[25] that one of the conditions for leave to serve a writ out of the jurisdiction is that, as regards the merits, there is a serious question to be tried. It would be strange if a stricter test were applicable in cases in which service of the writ is to be effected under RSC, Order 11, rule 1(2) (which applies to claims which "by virtue of the Civil Jurisdiction and Judgments Act 1982 the court has power to hear and determine"),[26] rather than under rule 1(1). Accordingly, any suggestion that, in cases falling within the scope of the Conventions, the plaintiff should have a good arguable case on the merits[27] is to be regarded as unsound in principle.

4.2.3.1.3 This does not mean, however, that the court should ignore entirely the strength of the plaintiff's claim. It would, for example, be absurd if a court were unable to strike out an action which is vexatious or frivolous or otherwise an abuse of the process of the court. In *Newtherapeutics Ltd* v. *Katz*,[28] a case in which the plaintiff brought proceedings in England in reliance on Article 16(2) of the Brussels Convention, service of the writ on one of the defendants was set aside on the basis that the action was so hopeless it was bound to fail.

4.2.3.2 Questions of jurisdiction

4.2.3.2.1 The proper approach to cases involving questions of jurisdiction is outlined by the Schlosser Report, which states that:

> [A] court may assume jurisdiction only if it is completely satisfied of all the facts on which such jurisdiction is based; if it is not so satisfied it can and must request the parties to provide the necessary evidence, in default of which the action will be dismissed as inadmissible. In such circumstances the lack of jurisdiction would be declared by the court of its own motion, and not as a result of a challenge by one of the parties. Whether a court is itself obliged to investigate the facts relevant to jurisdiction, or whether it can, or must, place the burden of proof in this respect on the party interested in the jurisdiction of the court concerned, is determined solely by national law.[29]

24. Kohler, "Practical Experience of the Brussels Jurisdiction and Judgments Convention in the Six Original Contracting States" (1985) 34 ICLQ 563, 570–571.
25. [1993] 3 WLR 756. See para. 6.3.2.
26. See para. 4.3.1.1.
27. See, for example, *Mölnlycke AB* v. *Procter & Gamble Ltd* [1992] 1 WLR 1112.
28. [1991] Ch 226.
29. OJ 1979 C59/82, para. 22.

4.2.3.2.2 In *Effer SpA* v. *Kantner*[30] the plaintiff commenced proceedings for breach of contract in Germany on the basis that Germany was "the place of performance of the obligation in question" for the purposes of Article 5(1). The defendant contested the jurisdiction of the court on the ground that no contract had been concluded between the parties. The nature of the problem facing the court in this type of case is obvious: the plaintiff should not be allowed to invoke the jurisdiction of the court simply by alleging the existence of a contract; by the same token, the defendant should not be allowed to circumvent the provisions of Title II simply by denying a contract's existence. The Court of Justice stated that:

> [R]espect for the aims and spirit of the Convention demands that [Article 5(1)] should be construed as meaning that the court called upon to decide a dispute arising out of a contract may examine, of its own motion even, the essential preconditions for its jurisdiction, having regard to conclusive and relevant evidence adduced by the party concerned, establishing the existence or the inexistence of the contract.[31]

4.2.3.2.3 In *Tesam Distribution Ltd* v. *Schuh Mode Team GmbH*[32] the Court of Appeal decided that the decision of the Court of Justice in *Effer SpA* v. *Kantner* justifies the assumption of jurisdiction on the basis of a good arguable case.[33] So, in a situation where the plaintiff invokes the jurisdiction of the English court under Article 5(1) the court must be satisfied that the plaintiff has a good arguable case not only that a contract was concluded by the parties but also that England is the place of performance of the obligation in question.

4.2.3.2.4 In the context of cases falling within the scope of the Conventions the Court of Appeal has interpreted "a good arguable case" as meaning "a serious question which calls for a trial for its proper determination".[34] Two points should be noted.

(i) Any suggestion that the decision in *Effer SpA* v. *Kantner* requires the plaintiff to satisfy the court at the interlocutory stage that the claim will succeed goes too far.[35] Nevertheless, it is far from certain that the decision in *Effer SpA* v. *Kantner* authorises a test as open-textured as that adopted by the Court of Appeal.

(ii) In *Seaconsar Far East Ltd* v. *Bank Markazi Jomhouri Islami Iran*[36] the House of Lords held that one of the conditions for leave to be given for service of a writ out of the jurisdiction under RSC, Order 11, rule 1(1) is that the plaintiff should have a good arguable case that the claim falls within the jurisdiction rule relied upon. It is clear from this decision that the requirement of a good arguable case imposes a stricter standard of proof than the requirement that there should be a serious question to be tried.[37]

30. Case 38/81 [1982] ECR 825.
31. [1982] ECR 825, 834 (para. 7).
32. [1990] ILPr 149.
33. This test has been applied in a number of subsequent cases: *Medway Packaging Ltd* v. *Meurer Maschinen GmbH* [1990] 2 Lloyd's Rep 112; *The Rewia* [1991] 2 Lloyd's Rep 325; *Mercury Publicity Ltd* v. *Wolfgang Loerke GmbH* [1993] ILPr 142; *New England Reinsurance Corporation* v. *Messoghios Insurance Co SA* [1992] 2 Lloyd's Rep 251; *Rank Film Distributors Ltd* v. *Lanterna Editrice Srl* [1992] ILPr 58; *Mölnlycke AB* v. *Procter & Gamble Ltd* [1992] 1 WLR 1112.
34. Nicholls LJ in *Tesam Distribution Ltd* v. *Schuh Mode Team GmbH* [1990] ILPr 149, 158.
35. Nicholls LJ in *Tesam Distribution Ltd* v. *Schuh Mode Team GmbH* [1990] ILPr 149, 158.
36. [1993] 3 WLR 756.
37. See para. 6.3.3.9.

Some of the issues under Title II are very similar to those which are relevant in the context of applications under RSC, Order 11, rule 1(1): for example, under Article 5(1) and rule 1(1)(d) the question may arise as to whether a contract was concluded between the parties; under Article 17 and rule 1(1)(d)(iv) the existence of an agreement on jurisdiction may be disputed; under Article 5(3) and rule 1(1)(f) the parties may disagree as to where the damage was sustained. Quite apart from the decision of the Court of Justice in *Effer SpA* v. *Kantner* there is no obvious reason why the standard of proof for establishing jurisdiction under Title II should be any lower than that required by RSC, Order 11, rule 1(1).

4.3 SERVICE ABROAD IN CASES FALLING WITHIN THE SCOPE OF THE CONVENTIONS

4.3.1 Service abroad without leave

4.3.1.1 The Rules of the Supreme Court determine the circumstances in which a defendant who is not present within the jurisdiction may be served with a writ out of the jurisdiction. The general rule is that a defendant may only be served with the leave of the court.[38] However, RSC, Order 11, rule 1(2)(a) creates a considerable exception in cases falling within the scope of Title II:

> Service of a writ out of the jurisdiction is permissible without the leave of the court provided that each claim made by the writ is either—
> (a) a claim which by virtue of the Civil Jurisdiction and Judgments Act 1982 the court has power to hear and determine, made in proceedings in which the following conditions apply—
> (i) no proceedings between the parties concerning the same cause of action are pending in the courts of any other part of the United Kingdom or of any other Convention territory, and
> (ii) either the defendant is domiciled in any part of the United Kingdom or in any other Convention territory, or
> the proceedings begun by the writ are proceedings to which Article 16 of Schedule 1 or Schedule 4 refers, or the defendant is a party to an agreement conferring jurisdiction to which Article 17 of Schedule 1 or of Schedule 4 to that Act applies...

4.3.1.2 These rules are generally simple to apply; if the English court has jurisdiction under Title II the defendant may be served out of the jurisdiction without the leave of the court.[39] There are, however, uncertainties surrounding the requirement that "each claim made by the writ" should fall within the jurisdiction of the court by virtue of the operation of the 1982 Act. The problem results from the fact that Title II is concerned with "proceedings" whereas RSC, Order 11, rule 1(2) refers to "claims". What is the correct course of action for the plaintiff to take in a case where one or more of the claims falls within rule 1(2) and the others do not? As regards the claims not falling within rule 1(2) should the plaintiff seek leave to serve out on the basis that Title II does not

38. See para. 6.3.
39. Although this principle is clear, the courts have not always applied it correctly. See, for example, *Newtherapeutics Ltd* v. *Katz* [1991] Ch 226.

allocate jurisdiction to the English court over "each claim made by the writ", or can the plaintiff dispense with leave on the basis that the proceedings are within the jurisdiction of the court? The wording of RSC, Order 11, rule 1(2) suggests that, in these circumstances, leave is required as regards those claims in relation to which jurisdiction is not allocated by Title II. This was not, however, the approach taken in *Newtherapeutics Ltd* v. *Katz*.[40] The first defendant, who was believed to be domiciled in New York, was a director of the plaintiff, an English company. The plaintiff alleged various breaches of duty on the part of the directors. It was alleged not only that the directors had entered a transaction which was *ultra vires*, but also that the transaction was so detrimental that no reasonable director could possibly have entered it. The claim based on *ultra vires* was clearly within the jurisdiction of the court by virtue of Article 16(2); the claim based on unreasonableness, however, was not. Knox J held that the court had jurisdiction in relation to both claims on the basis that the proceedings were principally concerned with matters falling within the exclusive jurisdiction of the court.

4.3.1.3 It is also provided by RSC, Order 6, rule 7(1)(b) that a writ should contain an endorsement that the court has power under the Civil Jurisdiction and Judgments Acts to hear and determine the claim and that no proceedings involving the same cause of action are pending between the same parties in another part of the United Kingdom or in another Contracting State. The effect of a writ which is irregular—in the sense of not including the necessary endorsement—was considered in *Gascoine* v. *Pyrah*.[41] Although failure to include the required endorsement is a substantial irregularity, generally it is not so serious as to bar the plaintiff's action. In the normal course of events, the plaintiff will issue a summons for leave to amend the writ by inserting the endorsement required by RSC, Order 6, rule 7 and, on the judge being satisfied that Title II allocates jurisdiction to the court, leave will be given.

4.3.2 Methods of service

4.3.2.1 The Conventions do not seek to harmonise the laws of the Contracting States regarding the various ways in which originating process may be served on the defendant. Bilateral conventions between Contracting States and the Hague Service Convention are unaffected by the Conventions. The first paragraph of Article IV of the Protocol to the Brussels Convention provides:

> Judicial and extrajudicial documents drawn up in one Contracting State which have to be served on persons in another Contracting State shall be transmitted in accordance with the procedures laid down in the conventions and agreements concluded between the Contracting States.[42]

4.3.2.2 The wording of this paragraph is potentially misleading. It would seem, on the face of it, that as between Contracting States the methods of service specified by international conventions are mandatory. According to a literal interpretation, it would not be possible to effect service in another Contracting State simply by complying with the law of the place where service is effected. The better view, however, is that the effect

40. [1991] Ch 226.
41. *The Times*, 26 November 1991.
42. The first paragraph of Article IV of Protocol No. 1 to the Lugano Convention is identical.

of the first paragraph of Article IV is that any of the methods of service created or preserved by multilateral or bilateral conventions between the various Contracting States are permissible in relation to proceedings falling within the scope of Title II. This was the view adopted by the High Court in *Noirhomme* v. *Walklate*.[43] In this case the plaintiff sought to enforce a Belgian judgment in England against the defendant, an English domiciliary. The defendant had not taken part in the Belgian proceedings and resisted enforcement on the basis that he had not been duly served with the document which instituted the proceedings.[44] The plaintiff had served the originating process on the defendant by sending the relevant document by post to the defendant's address. The defendant's argument was that, as a result of the first paragraph of Article IV of the Protocol, to effect due service the relevant document has to be served in accordance with the procedure laid down by Article 5 of the Hague Service Convention. Judge Kershaw QC took the view that "the phrase 'laid down' in Article IV of the Protocol to the Brussels Convention means the same as the phrase 'provided for' in Article 19 of the Hague Convention and both phrases cover procedures which are preserved as well as those which are provided anew".[45] Since English law permits postal service of an originating process coming from abroad—and this method of service is preserved by Article 10 of the Hague Service Convention—the defendant had been duly served.

4.3.2.3 The Conventions do, however, provide a further method for serving documents abroad. The second paragraph of Article IV of the Protocol to the Brussels Convention provides that, unless the Contracting State in question objects:

> [D]ocuments may also be sent by the appropriate public officers of the State in which the document has been drawn up directly to the appropriate public officers of the State in which the addressee is to be found. In this case the officer of the State of origin shall send a copy of the document to the officer of the State applied to who is competent to forward it to the addressee. The document shall be forwarded in the manner specified by the law of the State applied to. The forwarding shall be recorded by a certificate sent directly to the officer of the State of origin.[46]

Although the Jenard Report states that this provision "simply adds a new method of transmission to those already provided for",[47] the procedure in Article IV corresponds to Article 10(b) of the Hague Service Convention. Germany has declared that service may not take place in Germany by this method.

4.4 PROCEDURAL SAFEGUARDS

4.4.1 Article 20 provides:

> Where a defendant domiciled in one Contracting State is sued in a court of another Contracting State and does not enter an appearance, the court shall declare of its own motion that it has no jurisdiction unless its jurisdiction is derived from the provisions of this Convention.
>
> The court shall stay the proceedings so long as it is not shown that the defendant has been able to receive the document instituting the proceedings or an equivalent document in sufficient time to enable him to arrange for his defence, or that all necessary steps have been taken to this end.

43. [1992] 1 Lloyd's Rep 427.
44. Article 27(2). See para. 9.4.3.4.
45. [1992] 1 Lloyd's Rep 427, 430.
46. The second paragraph of Article IV of Protocol No. 1 to the Lugano Convention is identical.
47. OJ 1979 C59/40.

The provisions of the foregoing paragraph shall be replaced by those of Article 15 of the Hague Convention of 15 November 1965 on the service abroad of judicial and extrajudicial documents in civil or commercial matters, if the document instituting the proceedings or notice thereof had to be transmitted abroad in accordance with that Convention.

Article 20 is one of the most important provisions of the Conventions.[48] It applies where a defendant, who is domiciled in a Contracting State, does not enter an appearance; Article 20 does not, however, provide any protection for a defendant who is not domiciled in a Contracting State.

4.4.2 Article 20(1) provides that where a defendant—who is domiciled in a Contracting State—does not enter an appearance, the court must of its own motion examine whether it has jurisdiction. If the court does not have jurisdiction under Title II it must decline jurisdiction. It is not sufficient for the court to accept the submissions of the plaintiff as regards jurisdiction; the court must itself ensure that the plaintiff proves that it has international jurisdiction.[49] Article 20 introduced a fundamental change in England, since traditionally English courts are able to reach a decision only on the basis of submissions of fact or law made by the parties.[50] It does not, however, follow from Article 20 that the court must, of its own motion, investigate the facts relevant to deciding the question of jurisdiction. The only essential factor is that the uncontested assertions by the parties should not bind the court. As a result of Article 20, a court of a Contracting State may assume jurisdiction only if it is completely satisfied of all the facts on which such jurisdiction is based; if it is not so satisfied it can and must request the parties to provide the necessary evidence, in default of which the action will be dismissed as inadmissible.[51]

4.4.3 Article 20 is designed to ensure that a default judgment cannot be given against a defendant who is domiciled in a Contracting State unless appropriate steps to notify the defendant of the proceedings have been taken. Where the second paragraph applies, Article 20 does not require that the defendant was actually notified of the proceedings in sufficient time: "The defendant must be responsible for any delay caused by his own negligence or by that of his relations or servants. The critical time is thus the time at which service was properly effected, and not the time at which the defendant received actual knowledge of the institution of proceedings."[52]

4.4.4 The court may give judgment in default "even if no affidavit can be produced to confirm service on the defendant of the document instituting proceedings, provided it is shown that all the necessary approaches have been made to the competent authorities of the State in which the defendant is domiciled in order to reach him in sufficient time. Where necessary, it must also be shown that 'all investigations required by good conscience and good faith have been undertaken to discover the defendant' ".[53]

4.4.5 In those cases in which the third paragraph applies, a default judgment may be given in cases where the defendant has been served in accordance with the Hague Service Convention. The words "in accordance with" are not free from ambiguity. The Hague Service Convention does two things: it lays down a new method of serving

48. Jenard Report, OJ 1979 C59/39.
49. Jenard Report, OJ 1979 C59/39.
50. Schlosser Report, OJ 1979 C59/81, para. 22.
51. Schlosser Report, OJ 1979 C59/82, para. 22.
52. Jenard Report, OJ 1979 C59/40. But see, however, Case 166/80 *Klomps* v. *Michel* [1981] ECR 1593 for consideration of the similar requirements of Article 27(2). This is discussed at para. 9.4.3.4.
53. Jenard Report, OJ 1979 C59/40.

documents abroad; and it preserves various other methods of serving documents abroad which pre-date it. It would seem that for the purposes of Article 20, a default judgment may be given by the courts of a Contracting State if the defendant was served with the document instituting the proceedings by any of the methods created or preserved by the Hague Service Convention. As regards the relationship between the second and third paragraphs, the Jenard Report states that the second paragraph is transitional and that where the State of the forum and the State in which the document is to be transmitted have both ratified the Hague Service Convention the court seised of the matter will be exclusively bound by Article 15 of the Hague Convention.[54]

54. Jenard Report, OJ 1979 C59/40.

CHAPTER 5

JURISDICTION IN PERSONAM UNDER THE BRUSSELS AND LUGANO CONVENTIONS: JURISDICTION RULES

5.0 INTRODUCTION

5.0.1 The direct jurisdiction rules of the Brussels and Lugano Conventions ("the Conventions") are to be found in Title II.[1] Title II contains a patchwork of rules whereby jurisdiction is conferred on the courts of the Contracting States. Within the bases of jurisdiction established by Articles 2 to 6 and 16 to 18 some bases of jurisdiction are not dependent on where the defendant is domiciled; others apply only as regards defendants who are domiciled in a Contracting State. In the first category there are three general bases of jurisdiction which apply both to defendants who are not domiciled in a Contracting State as well as to defendants who are so domiciled: Article 16 confers exclusive jurisdiction in certain circumstances (para. 5.1); Article 18 confers jurisdiction in cases where the parties submit to the jurisdiction of the court (para. 5.2); Article 17 gives effect to jurisdiction agreements in favour of the courts of a Contracting State (para. 5.3). The remaining general bases of jurisdiction apply only in relation to defendants who are domiciled in a Contracting State: the general principle laid down in Article 2 is that a defendant who is domiciled in a Contracting State shall be sued in the courts of that Contracting State (para. 5.4); Articles 5 and 6, however, define circumstances in which a defendant who is domiciled in a Contracting State may be sued in the courts of another Contracting State (paras. 5.5 and 5.6). Of course, as regards a defendant who is domiciled in a Contracting State the bases of jurisdiction set out in Articles 2, 5 and 6 are in addition to those to be found in Articles 16 to 18. The Conventions also contain provisions which allocate jurisdiction with regard to proceedings relating to insurance and consumer contracts (para. 5.7) and which enable the courts of one Contracting State to grant provisional measures in aid of proceedings in another Contracting State (para. 5.8). As regards a defendant who is not domiciled in a Contracting State, if the provisions of Title II do not allocate jurisdiction, Article 4 provides that "the jurisdiction of the courts of each Contracting State shall . . . be determined by the law of that State".

5.0.2 Since the main purpose of the Conventions is to facilitate the free flow of judgments it is important that the risks of irreconcilable judgments should be minimised. Accordingly, there are circumstances in which, although the courts of a Contracting State have *prima facie* jurisdiction under one of the bases set out in Articles 2 to 18, it is provided that jurisdiction must be declined; in other cases the courts of a Contracting State have a discretion as to whether to allow proceedings to continue

1. In this chapter it is to be assumed that the provisions of the Brussels and Lugano Conventions are identical unless the contrary is indicated.

(para. 5.9). From an English perspective, questions arise concerning the powers of the court to stay proceedings, particularly under the doctrine of *forum non conveniens* (para. 5.10).

5.1 EXCLUSIVE JURISDICTION: ARTICLE 16

Article 16 is the predominant provision of Title II. The jurisdiction rules in Article 16 are mandatory and exclusive; they "may not be departed from either by an agreement purporting to confer jurisdiction on the courts of another Contracting State or by an implied submission to the jurisdiction".[2] The matters referred to in Article 16 are normally the subject of exclusive jurisdiction only if they constitute the principal subject matter of the proceedings.[3] Where, however, litigation involves two related claims, if the principal claim falls within the scope of Article 16, it is reasonable to suppose that the court which has exclusive jurisdiction over the principal claim by virtue of Article 16 should also have jurisdiction over the other claim.[4] The five paragraphs of Article 16 concern matters which are thought to be unsuited to adjudication by a foreign court:

(1) proceedings relating to immovable property;
(2) certain proceedings concerning the formation and dissolution of companies and the decisions of their organs;
(3) certain proceedings concerning entries in public registers;
(4) certain proceedings concerning intellectual property;
(5) proceedings concerning the enforcement of judgments.

As regards paragraphs 2 to 5 the two Conventions are identical. There are, however, differences in relation to Article 16(1). Article 16 of the Brussels Convention is applicable to defendants domiciled in a Brussels Contracting State or in a non-contracting State; Article 16 of the Lugano Convention is applicable in cases where the defendant is domiciled in an EFTA country which has ratified the Lugano Convention.[5]

5.1.1 Article 16(1)

5.1.1.1 Preliminary remarks

5.1.1.1.1 The first paragraph of Article 16 has had a chequered history. Article 16(1) of the Brussels Convention provides that the following courts shall have exclusive jurisdiction regardless of domicile:

(a) in proceedings which have as their object rights *in rem* in immovable property or tenancies of immovable property, the courts of the Contracting State in which the property is situated;
(b) however, in proceedings which have as their object tenancies of immovable property concluded for temporary private use for a maximum period of six consecutive months, the courts of the Contracting State in which the defendant is domiciled shall also have jurisdiction, provided that the landlord and the tenant are natural persons and are domiciled in the same Contracting State.

2. Jenard Report, OJ 1979 C59/34.
3. Jenard Report, OJ 1979 C59/34.
4. *Newtherapeutics Ltd* v. *Katz* [1991] Ch 226. Some support for this analysis is to be found in the decision of the Court of Justice in Case 266/85 *Shenavai* v. *Kreischer* [1987] ECR 239. See para. 5.5.3.2.2.
5. Lugano Convention, Article 54B(2)(a).

As originally drafted Article 16(1) comprised the text which is now subparagraph (a); subparagraph (b) was added by the 1989 Accession Convention with a view to reversing the effect of the decision of the Court of Justice in *Rösler* v. *Rottwinkel*.[6]

5.1.1.1.2 Article 16(1)(a) of the Lugano Convention is identical to the equivalent provision of the Brussels Convention. The second subparagraph reads as follows:

> (b) however, in proceedings which have as their object tenancies of immovable property concluded for temporary private use for a maximum period of six consecutive months, the courts of the Contracting State in which the defendant is domiciled shall also have jurisdiction, provided that the tenant is a natural person and neither party is domiciled in the Contracting State in which the property is situated.

5.1.1.1.3 In relation to disputes concerning immovable property, there are a number of reasons which justify the allocation of exclusive jurisdiction to the courts of the country in which the property is situated.[7] (i) An action concerning immovable property frequently entails a whole series of procedural acts which have to be carried out on the spot. There may be enquiries, verifications or surveys which, by definition, can only be carried out at the place where the property is situated. (ii) Local customs familiar only to the court of the particular place may be relevant. (iii) Disputes relating to immovable property may concern entries in land registers at the place where the property is situated.

5.1.1.1.4 In *Reichert* v. *Dresdner Bank* the Court of Justice indicated that "the essential reason for conferring exclusive jurisdiction on the courts of the Contracting State in which the property is situated is that the courts of the *locus rei sitae* are the best placed, for reasons of proximity, to ascertain the facts satisfactorily and to apply the rules and practices which are generally those of the State in which the property is situated".[8] Nevertheless, "Article 16 must not be given a wider interpretation than is required by its objective".[9]

5.1.1.2 Article 16(1)(a): rights in rem

5.1.1.2.1 GENERAL PRINCIPLES

5.1.1.2.1.1 A fundamental question concerning Article 16(1)(a) is whether the words "rights *in rem*" are to be interpreted as an autonomous concept or by reference to the *lex situs*. The Schlosser Report expressed a clear preference for the latter approach: "If an action relating to immovable property is brought in a particular State and the question whether the action is concerned with a right *in rem* within the meaning of Article 16(1) arises, the answer can hardly be derived from any law other than that of the *situs*."[10]

5.1.1.2.1.2 However, the Court of Justice has decided that "in order to ensure that the rights and obligations arising from the Convention for Contracting States and for

6. Case 241/83 [1985] ECR 99.
7. See the opinion of Advocate-General Mischo in Case C-115/88 *Reichert* v. *Dresdner Bank* [1990] ECR I-27, 36 (para. 23).
8. Case C-115/88 [1990] ECR I-27, 41 (para. 10).
9. Case C-115/88 *Reichert* v. *Dresdner Bank* [1990] ECR I-27, 41 (para. 9).
10. OJ 1979 C59/121, para. 168(c).

individuals concerned are as equal and as uniform as possible, an independent definition must be given in Community law to the phrase 'proceedings which have as their object rights *in rem* in immovable property' ".[11] Furthermore, the Court of Justice has provided the following definition:

> Article 16(1) must be interpreted as meaning that the exclusive jurisdiction of the Contracting State in which the property is situated does not encompass all actions concerning rights *in rem* in immovable property but only those which both come within the scope of the Brussels Convention and are actions which seek to determine the extent, content, ownership or possession of immovable property or the existence of other rights *in rem* therein and to provide the holders of those rights with the protection of the powers which attach to their interest.[12]

This ruling has been criticised, on the basis that it is too narrow, by one commentator who suggests that an action "should fall within Article 16(1) if it seeks to establish that a party has or does not have rights to immovable property, or that the rights he has are or are not subject to the rights of another in respect of that property".[13]

5.1.1.2.2 PROCEEDINGS RELATING TO CONTRACTS FOR THE SALE OF LAND

According to the Schlosser Report, actions based on contracts for the transfer of ownership or other rights *in rem* affecting immovable property do not have as their object rights *in rem* and therefore do not fall within the exclusive jurisdiction rules.[14] Difficult borderline problems can arise, however. For example, does Article 16(1)(a) apply where the vendor sues the purchaser for specific performance of the contract and the purchaser defends by questioning the vendor's title?

5.1.1.2.3 PROCEEDINGS RELATING TO TRUSTS OF LAND

5.1.1.2.3.1 Article 16(1)(a) poses particular problems in England since it reflects the conceptual structure of the civil law systems of the original Contracting States. In the context of the English legal system the first question is whether the expression "rights *in rem* in immovable property" includes only legal estates and interests in land or whether an interest under a trust of land is a right *in rem* in immovable property for the purposes of Article 16(1)(a). The Schlosser Report suggests that since equitable interests can fulfil the same functions as rights *in rem* under continental legal systems they should be treated as such under Article 16(1).[15]

5.1.1.2.3.2 In *Webb* v. *Webb*,[16] however, the English courts took the contrary view. In this case the plaintiff acquired an apartment in the south of France. The apartment was put in the name of the defendant, the plaintiff's son. Subsequently, proceedings were commenced in England with a view to establishing that the defendant held the apartment on trust for the plaintiff. The defendant contested the jurisdiction of the court, arguing that, by virtue of Article 16(1) of the Brussels Convention, the proceedings fell within the exclusive jurisdiction of the French courts. The outline of the

11. Case C-115/88 *Reichert* v. *Dresdner Bank* [1990] ECR I-27, 41 (para. 8). Hartley, (1991) 16 ELRev 69; Briggs, (1990) 10 YBEL 481.
12. Case C-115/88 *Reichert* v. *Dresdner Bank* [1990] ECR I-27, 41–42 (para. 11).
13. Briggs, (1990) 10 YBEL 481, 483.
14. OJ 1979 C59/122, para. 172.
15. OJ 1979 C59/121, para. 167.
16. [1991] 1 WLR 1410; [1992] ILPr 374 (CA).

defendant's argument was as follows: the plaintiff was bringing the action in order to establish his rights of ownership of the property; rights of ownership are rights *in rem*; the property was immovable property; the action was covered by Article 16(1). The plaintiff's argument was based, first, on the fact that his claim was derived from the nature and content of the arrangements made between the plaintiff and the defendant when the property was purchased and, secondly, on the principle that equity acts *in personam*. According to this argument, the plaintiff's rights had nothing to do with French land law; they were analogous to rights derived from a contract for the sale of land.

5.1.1.2.3.3 The plaintiff's argument found favour at first instance; since the orders sought by the plaintiff "[did] not seek to disturb the title of the defendant otherwise than by his own act . . . the proceedings [did] not have as their object rights *in rem*".[17] In the Court of Appeal the majority, comprising Taylor and Scott LJJ, was inclined to adopt the same reasoning. However, since Nourse LJ thought that the proceedings fell within the exclusive jurisdiction of the French courts, it was decided to refer a number of questions to the Court of Justice.[18]

5.1.1.2.3.4 There is, of course, no simple solution to the problem posed in *Webb* v. *Webb*. Two points should, however, be noted. (i) Since the concept "rights *in rem*" is to be given an independent interpretation the fact that, as far as English law is concerned, equity acts *in personam* is not, in itself, the crucial issue. (ii) Although a declaration by the court that the defendant holds the property on trust for the plaintiff does not effect a transfer of legal ownership, once such a declaration is made, the plaintiff is entitled to call for a conveyance. In reality, the object of the proceedings is "to determine . . . ownership . . . of immovable property"[19] and therefore they should be regarded as falling within the scope of Article 16(1)(a).

5.1.1.3 Article 16(1)(a): tenancies of immovable property

5.1.1.3.1 In relation to disputes arising out of leases of immovable property the rationale for giving exclusive jurisdiction to the courts of the Contracting State in which the property is situated is "the fact that tenancies are closely bound up with the law of immovable property and with the provisions, generally of a mandatory character, governing its use, such as legislation controlling the level of rents and protecting the rights of tenants, including tenant farmers".[20] Tenancies of immovable property "are generally governed by special rules and it is preferable, in the light of their complexity, that they be applied only by the courts of the States in which they are in force".[21]

5.1.1.3.2 In *Sanders* v. *Van Der Putte*[22] the Court of Justice decided that the words "tenancies of immovable property" must be given an independent meaning, having regard to the purpose of Article 16(1). Although Article 16 should not be given a wider

17. Judge Baker QC, [1991] 1 WLR 1410, 1419.
18. The docket number of the reference is C-294/92.
19. Case C-115/88 *Reichert* v. *Dresdner Bank* [1990] ECR I-27, 41–42 (para. 11).
20. Case 241/83 *Rösler* v. *Rottwinkel* [1985] ECR 99, 126 (para. 19).
21. Case 73/77 *Sanders* v. *Van Der Putte* [1977] ECR 2383, 2391 (para. 14).
22. Case 73/77 [1977] ECR 2383. Hartley, (1978) 3 ELRev 164.

interpretation than is required by its objective,[23] the Court of Justice has taken a broad view of "proceedings which have as their object . . . tenancies of immovable property". In *Rösler* v. *Rottwinkel*[24] the Court of Justice held that "any dispute concerning the existence of tenancies or the interpretation of the terms thereof, their duration, the giving up of possession to the landlord, the repair of damage caused by the tenant or the recovery of rent and of incidental charges payable by the tenant, such as charges for the consumption of water, gas and electricity, falls within the exclusive jurisdiction conferred by Article 16(1)".[25]

5.1.1.3.3 So, although Article 16 does not cover a dispute arising out of agreement in relation to carrying on a business in a building rented by the landlord from a third party,[26] disputes arising out of short term holiday lets fall within Article 16(1)(a). In *Rösler* v. *Rottwinkel*[27] the plaintiff, who owned a villa in Italy, let it to the defendant for three weeks for a holiday. When disputes arose between the parties, both of whom were domiciled in Germany, the plaintiff sued the defendant in Germany. Notwithstanding the view expressed in the Schlosser Report that the underlying principle of Article 16(1) "quite clearly does not require its application to short term agreements for use and occupation such as, for example, holiday accommodation,"[28] the Court of Justice decided that Article 16(1) applies to all lettings of immovable property, even for a short term and even where they relate only to the use and occupation of a holiday home.[29] Furthermore, even though the Jenard Report states that Article 16(1) "was not intended by the committee to apply to proceedings concerned only with the recovery of rent",[30] the Court of Justice thought that a claim by the plaintiff for the recovery of charges payable under the lease was within the scope of Article 16(1).[31] Nevertheless, the Court of Justice explained that "disputes which are only indirectly related to the use of the property let, such as those concerning the loss of holiday enjoyment and travel expenses, do not fall within the exclusive jurisdiction conferred" by Article 16.[32]

5.1.1.3.4 The conclusion reached by the Court of Justice in *Rösler* v. *Rottwinkel* received little support from commentators[33] and its impact has been significantly reduced by subsequent developments. First, Article 16(1) does not apply to holiday contracts which include not only accommodation, but also other services, such as information and advice, the reservation of transport, reception on arrival and insurance against cancellation. In *Hacker* v. *Euro-Relais GmbH*[34] the Court of Justice held that "[a] complex contract of that type, which concerns a range of services in return for a lump sum paid by the customer, is outside the scope within which the exclusive

23. Case 73/77 *Sanders* v. *Van Der Putte* [1977] ECR 2383, 2391 (para. 18).
24. Case 241/83 [1985] ECR 99.
25. Case 241/83 [1985] ECR 99, 128 (para. 29).
26. Case 73/77 *Sanders* v. *Van Der Putte* [1977] ECR 2383.
27. Case 241/83 [1985] ECR 99.
28. OJ 1979 C59/120, para. 164.
29. Case 241/83 [1985] ECR 99, 127 (para. 25).
30. OJ 1979 C59/35.
31. It is, perhaps, worth noting that the working party for the 1978 Accession Convention had been unable to agree whether Article 16(1) applied to proceedings concerned only with the recovery of rent: Schlosser Report, OJ 1979 C59/120, para. 164.
32. Case 241/83 [1985] ECR 99, 128 (para. 29).
33. See, for example, Hartley, (1985) 10 ELRev 361; Mann, "Exclusive Exotic Jurisdiction" (1985) 101 LQR 329.
34. Case C-280/90 [1992] ECR-I 1111. Hartley, (1993) 17 ELRev 550.

jurisdiction laid down by Article 16(1) finds its *raison d'être* and cannot constitute a 'tenancy agreement' within the meaning of that Article".[35]

5.1.1.3.5 Secondly, the effects of the decision in *Rösler* v. *Rottwinkel* are curtailed by the addition of subparagraph (b) to Article 16(1). In the negotiations leading up to the conclusion of the Lugano Convention the EFTA Member States insisted on the inclusion of a special provision dealing with short term lettings.[36] A similar provision was then added to the Brussels Convention by the 1989 Accession Convention. There are three points which should be made about Article 16(1)(b).

(i) The effect of subparagraph (b) is not to deprive the courts of the Contracting State in which the property is situated of jurisdiction in cases concerning short term lettings; the courts of the *situs* have jurisdiction by virtue of subparagraph (a). So, were the facts of *Rösler* v. *Rottwinkel* to arise again, the plaintiff would be able to bring proceedings against the defendant in Italy. However, assuming that the conditions of subparagraph (b) are satisfied, in cases involving short term lettings, there are "two exclusive jurisdictions, which might be described as alternative exclusive jurisdictions".[37]

(ii) The amendment does not reverse the decision of the Court of Justice in *Rösler* v. *Rottwinkel* that actions solely for the recovery of rent fall within the scope of Article 16(1).

(iii) The Lugano Convention version of Article 16(1)(b) is less restrictive than the equivalent provision of the Brussels Convention. Article 16(1)(b) of the Brussels Convention is limited to the pattern of facts which arose in *Rösler* v. *Rottwinkel* itself; not only must both parties be individuals, but they must also be domiciled in the same Contracting State. Article 16(1)(b) of the Lugano Convention applies as long as the tenant is an individual (even if the landlord is a corporation) and neither party is domiciled in the Contracting State where the property is situated.

5.1.1.4 Proceedings concerning immovable property in more than one Contracting State

In *Scherrens* v. *Maenhout*[38] the plaintiff claimed to be entitled under a single lease of a farm which consisted of twelve hectares in the Netherlands and five hectares in Belgium. The two plots were about seven kilometres apart. The Court of Justice held that "in a dispute as to the existence of a lease relating to immovable property situated in two Contracting States, exclusive jurisdiction over the immovable property situated in each Contracting State is held by the courts of that State".[39] However, the result might be different in a dispute relating to a single plot of land which straddles a national boundary, especially if nearly all the plot is situated in one State only. In such a situation it might be appropriate for the courts of the Contracting State in which the greater part of the plot is situated to have exclusive jurisdiction in relation to the entirety of the dispute.[40]

35. Case C-280/90 [1992] ECR-I 1111, 1132 (para. 15).
36. Jenard–Möller Report, OJ 1990 C189/75, para. 51.
37. Jenard–Möller Report, OJ 1990 C189/75, para. 52.
38. Case 158/87 [1988] ECR 3791. Briggs, (1988) 8 YBEL 271.
39. Case 158/87 [1988] ECR 3791, 3805 (para. 13).
40. Case 158/87 *Scherrens* v. *Maenhout* [1988] ECR 3791, 3805 (para. 14).

5.1.2 Certain proceedings relating to corporations

5.1.2.1 Article 16(2) provides that "in proceedings which have as their object the validity of the constitution, the nullity or the dissolution of companies or other legal persons or associations of natural or legal persons, or the decisions of their organs, the courts of the Contracting State in which the company, legal person or association has its seat" shall have exclusive jurisdiction regardless of domicile. Section 43 of the Civil Jurisdiction and Judgments Act 1982 sets out a special definition of "seat" for the purposes of this provision.

5.1.2.2 The English version of the text is not entirely unambiguous: does Article 16(2) cover proceedings which have as their object the decisions of the organs of companies or is it limited to proceedings which have as their object the validity of the decisions of the organs of companies? In view of other language versions, especially the German text, the correct interpretation would appear to be that Article 16(2) is limited to proceedings concerning the validity of decisions and does not cover proceedings concerning decisions as such.[41]

5.1.3 Certain proceedings concerning entries in public registers

5.1.3.1 As regards "proceedings which have as their object the validity of entries in public registers" Article 16(3) confers exclusive jurisdiction, regardless of domicile, on "the courts of the Contracting State in which the register is kept". Although it seems clear that Article 16(3) is limited to proceedings concerning the validity of entries in registers, the Jenard Report suggests that Article 16(3) covers "proceedings relating to the validity *or effects* of entries" in public registers.[42]

5.1.3.2 There is little guidance in the Reports as to what is to be understood by the words "public register". There would appear to be two possible interpretations: (i) the narrow view is that a register should be regarded as public only if it is owned by a public authority; (ii) the broader view is that any register which is open to public inspection should be regarded as public, even if it is privately owned. The broader view derives some support from the Jenard Report which states that Article 16(3) applies not only to entries in land registers and land charges registers, but also to entries in commercial registers.[43] Although commercial registers are hardly known in England they are very important in many continental systems. Their purpose is to provide a clear means of enabling anyone to find out who is a trader; they are usually maintained by the local chamber of commerce and they list the names and addresses of persons entitled to trade. The broader view has also been endorsed by the High Court; in *Re Fagin's Bookshop Plc*[44] it was held that a public limited company's register of shareholders is a public register for the purposes of Article 16(3).

41. *Newtherapeutics Ltd* v. *Katz* [1991] Ch 226. Kaye, "Corporate Jurisdiction under the European Judgments Convention" (1990) 11 CJQ 221; Carter, (1990) 61 BYIL 397.
42. OJ 1979 C59/35. (Emphasis added.)
43. OJ 1979 C59/35.
44. [1992] BCLC 118.

5.1.4 Certain proceedings concerning intellectual property[45]

Article 16(4) provides that "in proceedings concerned with the registration or validity of patents, trade marks, designs, or other similar rights required to be deposited or registered, the courts of the Contracting State in which the deposit or registration has been applied for, has taken place or is under the terms of an international convention deemed to have taken place" shall have exclusive jurisdiction, regardless of domicile. Since the grant of a national patent is the exercise of national sovereignty, Article 16(4) provides for exclusive jurisdiction in proceedings concerned with patents. The phrase "proceedings concerned with the registration or validity of patents, trade marks, designs, or other similar rights" should be given a uniform interpretation, independent of national law. Furthermore, Article 16(4) should be interpreted in such a way that it creates no greater exception to the general rules contained in Title II than necessary.[46] Accordingly, passing-off actions and actions relating to the infringement of patents do not fall within the scope of Article 16(4).[47]

5.1.5 Enforcement proceedings

5.1.5.1 With regard to "proceedings concerned with the enforcement of judgments", Article 16(5) provides that "the courts of the Contracting State in which the judgment has been or is to be enforced" shall have exclusive jurisdiction, regardless of the defendant's domicile. Article 16(5) applies only in relation to proceedings which are directly concerned with the enforcement of judgments already delivered. In *Reichert* v. *Dresdner Bank (No. 2)* the Court of Justice confirmed that Article 16(5) applies to "disputes which may arise from 'the use of force or constraint, or the dispossession of movables and immovables in order to obtain the physical implementation of judgments and measures' and that 'the difficulties to which these procedures give rise are within the exclusive jurisdiction of the court of the place where the judgment is to be enforced' ".[48]

5.1.5.2 Article 16(5) does not fit very comfortably with the other provisions of Title II; it is basically a self-evident rule whose proper place would appear to be in Title III. The only reason for the incorporation of Article 16(5) in Title II seems to have been a wish on the part of those who drafted the Brussels Convention to itemise exhaustively in Title II all matters of jurisdiction.[49]

5.1.5.3 Article 25 defines "judgment" for the purposes of the Conventions as "any judgment given by a court or tribunal of a Contracting State".[50] Accordingly, Article 16(5) does not apply to a judgment given by the court of a non-contracting State[51]: "the reciprocal recognition and enforcement of the judgments of non-contracting State A in Contracting States B and C must depend wholly on the arrangements between State A and States B and C respectively. It has nothing whatever to do with anyone else".[52]

5.1.5.4 In cases involving the enforcement of a judgment given by the courts of a

45. Wadlow, "Intellectual Property and the Judgments Convention" (1985) 10 ELRev 305.
46. Case 288/82 *Duijnstee* v. *Goderbauer* [1983] ECR 3663.
47. Jenard Report, OJ 1979 C59/36. See, for example, *Mölnlycke AB* v. *Procter & Gamble Ltd* [1992] 1 WLR 1112.
48. Case C-261/90 [1992] ILPr 404, 424 (para. 28). See also Jenard Report, OJ 1979 C59/36.
49. Advocate-General Lenz in Case C-129/92 *Owens Bank Ltd* v. *Bracco* [1994] 1 All ER 336, 362 (para. 46).
50. See para. 9.4.1.2.
51. Case C-129/92 *Owens Bank Ltd* v. *Bracco* [1994] 1 All ER 336, 373 (para. 25).
52. Parker LJ in *Owens Bank Ltd* v. *Bracco* [1992] 2 AC 443, 452. Briggs, "Foreign Judgments, Fraud and the Brussels Convention" (1991) 107 LQR 531.

Contracting State, where enforcement proceedings are pending in two other Contracting States the effect of Article 16(5) is that each court in which enforcement proceedings are brought has exclusive jurisdiction over the proceedings within that Contracting State. In these circumstances, the court of neither Contracting State is required to stay its proceedings or decline jurisdiction under Article 21.[53]

5.1.6 Examination of jurisdiction

As a general rule it is for the defendant in proceedings to raise all the points which are relevant to his defence—whether these points are procedural or substantive. Title II produces an exception to this principle by requiring the court of a Contracting State whose jurisdiction is invoked to consider whether Article 16 confers exclusive jurisdiction on the courts of another Contracting State—even if the defendant does not contest jurisdiction. Article 19, which is the corollary of the rule that submission by the defendant cannot override Article 16, provides:

> Where a court of a Contracting State is seised of a claim which is principally concerned with a matter over which the courts of another Contracting State have exclusive jurisdiction by virtue of Article 16, it shall declare of its own motion that it has no jurisdiction.

The court's duty to declare that it has no jurisdiction whenever it finds that a court of another Contracting State has exclusive jurisdiction under Article 16 arises even where the procedural rules of the court limit the court's enquiry to the grounds raised by the parties.[54]

5.2 SUBMISSION: ARTICLE 18

5.2.1 Nearly all systems of law accept that submission by the defendant is a basis on which a court is entitled to assume jurisdiction—even if the defendant has no other connection with the forum. If, once the dispute has arisen, the defendant agrees to make a voluntary appearance to defend the plaintiff's claim on the merits, there is no reason why the litigation should not go ahead in that forum. As regards the Conventions the principle of jurisdiction based on submission is found in Article 18:

> Apart from jurisdiction derived from other provisions of this Convention, a court of a Contracting State before whom a defendant enters an appearance shall have jurisdiction. This rule shall not apply where appearance was entered solely to contest the jurisdiction, or where another court has exclusive jurisdiction by virtue of Article 16.

The terms of Article 18 make it clear that submission by the defendant cannot override the exclusive jurisdiction provisions in Article 16. Apart from that, however, Article 18 overrides all other jurisdictional rules contained in Title II. Submission has the effect of superseding an earlier jurisdiction agreement between the parties.[55]

5.2.2 There is some doubt as to whether Article 18 applies regardless of the defendant's domicile. The Jenard Report seems to contemplate Article 18 being

53. For a discussion of Article 21 see para. 5.9.
54. Case 288/82 *Duijnstee* v. *Goderbauer* [1983] ECR 3663.
55. Case 150/80 *Elefanten Schuh GmbH* v. *Jacqmain* [1981] ECR 1671.

applicable only in cases where the defendant is domiciled in a Contracting State.[56] However, the text of Article 18 makes no reference to the domicile of the parties. Since Article 18 appears in Section 6 of Title II—the section which includes Article 17, the application of which is not restricted to defendants domiciled in a Contracting State—Article 18 should also be regarded as applying regardless of domicile.

5.2.3 Under the procedural laws of some Contracting States a defendant who restricts his argument to questions of jurisdiction is not permitted to defend on the merits at a later stage if the court assumes jurisdiction. In these circumstances, it is better, from a practical point of view, to allow a party not only to contend that the court has no jurisdiction, but also to argue that if the court rejects the jurisdiction defence it should decide in his favour on the merits. Although the English language version states that where the defendant takes part in proceedings this amounts to submission unless the defendant entered an appearance "solely to contest the jurisdiction" of the court, other language versions are formulated differently; the French text, for example, does not include the equivalent of the word "solely". In *Elefanten Schuh GmbH* v. *Jacqmain*[57] the Court of Justice held that the fact that the defendant has put forward a defence on the merits does not necessarily mean that he should be regarded as having submitted for the purposes of Article 18. Article 18 must be interpreted as meaning that a defendant should not be regarded as having submitted "where the defendant not only contests the court's jurisdiction but also makes submissions on the substance of the action, provided that, if the challenge to jurisdiction is not preliminary to any defence as to the substance, it does not occur after the making of the submissions which under national procedural law are considered to be the first defence addressed to the court seised".[58] A challenge to the jurisdiction of the court is effective to negative submission "only if the plaintiff and the court seised of the matter are able to ascertain from the time of the defendant's first defence that it is intended to contest the jurisdiction of the court".[59]

5.2.4 In the context of English procedural law, a defendant who wishes to defend proceedings, whether on the basis of jurisdiction or on the merits of the case, must acknowledge service of the writ and give notice of intention to defend.[60] Failure to give notice of intention to defend within the stipulated time entitles the plaintiff to proceed to judgment in default.[61] An "acknowledgment of service of the writ or other process" amounts to "the entry of appearance" for the purposes of Article 18.[62] However, the defendant's acknowledgment of service and notice of intention to defend is treated as "solely to contest the jurisdiction of the court" for the purposes of Article 18 if, within the period limited for defence, a summons is issued under RSC, Order 12, rule 8(1). Procedural steps taken by the defendant before the expiry of the period for service of defence (such as an application for discovery of documents or even for an extension of time for service of defence) do not amount to submission under Title II.[63]

56. OJ 1979 C59/38.
57. Case 150/80 [1981] ECR 1671.
58. Case 150/80 [1981] ECR 1671, 1686 (para. 17).
59. Case 150/80 [1981] ECR 1671, 1685 (para. 15).
60. RSC, Order 12, r. 1(1).
61. RSC, Order 13.
62. RSC, Order 12, r. 10.
63. *Kurz* v. *Stella Musical Veranstaltungs GmbH* [1992] Ch 196. Thomas, "Non-Exclusive Jurisdiction Clauses and Submission by Appearance" [1992] LMCLQ 292.

5.3 JURISDICTION AGREEMENTS: ARTICLE 17

5.3.1 Preliminary considerations

5.3.1.1 The text

It is not uncommon for an international commercial agreement to include a jurisdiction clause. A contractual jurisdiction clause is an agreement by the parties to refer any dispute arising under the contract to the courts of a particular country. Article 17 concerns the formal requirements for agreements conferring jurisdiction and the effects of such agreements. Article 17 of the Brussels Convention provides:

1. If the parties, one or more of whom is domiciled in a Contracting State, have agreed that a court or the courts of a Contracting State are to have jurisdiction to settle any disputes which have arisen or which may arise in connection with a particular legal relationship, that court or those courts shall have exclusive jurisdiction. Such an agreement conferring jurisdiction shall be either:
   (a) in writing or evidenced in writing, or
   (b) in a form which accords with practices which the parties have established between themselves, or
   (c) in international trade or commerce, in a form which accords with a usage of which the parties are or ought to have been aware and which in such trade or commerce is widely known to, and regularly observed by, parties to contracts of the type involved in the particular trade or commerce concerned.

Where such an agreement is concluded by parties, none of whom is domiciled in a Contracting State, the courts of other Contracting States shall have no jurisdiction over their disputes unless the court or courts chosen have declined jurisdiction.

2. The court or courts of a Contracting State on which a trust instrument has conferred jurisdiction shall have exclusive jurisdiction in any proceedings brought against a settlor, trustee or beneficiary, if relations between these persons or their rights or obligations under the trust are involved.

3. Agreements or provisions of a trust instrument conferring jurisdiction shall have no legal force if they are contrary to the provisions of Articles 12 or 15, or if the courts whose jurisdiction they purport to exclude have exclusive jurisdiction by virtue of Article 16.

4. If an agreement conferring jurisdiction was concluded for the benefit of only one of the parties, that party shall retain the right to bring proceedings in any other court which has jurisdiction by virtue of this Convention.

5. In matters relating to individual contracts of employment an agreement conferring jurisdiction shall have legal force only if it is entered into after the dispute has arisen or if the employee invokes it to seise courts other than those for the defendant's domicile or those specified in Article 5(1).

The text of the first four paragraphs of Article 17 of the Lugano Convention is identical. The fifth paragraph of Article 17 of the Lugano Convention, however, reads as follows:

In matters relating to individual contracts of employment an agreement conferring jurisdiction shall have legal force only if it is entered into after the dispute has arisen.

5.3.1.2 The relationship between the two Conventions

Article 54B(2)(a) of the Lugano Convention provides that where the defendant is domiciled in a Contracting State which is not a Member State of the EC Article 17 of the Lugano Convention must be applied. So, if a plaintiff seeks to rely on an English jurisdiction clause against a defendant domiciled in Switzerland the relevant provision is Article 17 of the Lugano Convention; if, however, the Swiss party is the plaintiff and the defendant is domiciled in an EC State, Article 17 of the Brussels Convention applies.[64] If the plaintiff is domiciled in Switzerland and the defendant is not domiciled in a Contracting State, Article 17 of the Lugano Convention applies.

5.3.2 Article 17(1): basic conditions

5.3.2.1 An agreement on jurisdiction

Article 17(1) deals with the situation where the parties "have agreed" that the courts of a Contracting State are to have jurisdiction over disputes arising in connection with a legal relationship. The concept of an agreement conferring jurisdiction should be regarded as an independent concept.[65] Although a jurisdiction agreement normally takes the form of a contractual clause, the scope of Article 17 is not limited to simple contracts. In *Powell Duffryn Plc* v. *Petereit*[66] the defendant, an English company, had purchased shares in a German company. Subsequently, the shareholders amended the company's articles of association. Under the amended articles of association, disputes between the shareholders and the company were to be submitted to the court which normally had jurisdiction over the company. When the German company became bankrupt, the liquidator brought an action against the defendant in the German court designated by the articles of association. The defendant contested the German court's jurisdiction on the basis that the articles of association did not constitute an agreement within Article 17 of the Brussels Convention. The Court of Justice ruled that, regardless of the applicable law, the company's articles of association were—for the purposes of Article 17—to be regarded as "a contract governing at one and the same time relationships between the shareholders and between them and the company".[67] For the purposes of Article 17 an agreement on jurisdiction is an autonomous concept which includes a clause conferring jurisdiction which appears in the articles of association of a limited company. Such a clause is, therefore, binding on the shareholders and it is irrelevant whether the shareholder against whom the jurisdiction clause is invoked opposed the adoption of the clause or became a shareholder after the clause was adopted.

5.3.2.2 Choosing the courts of a Contracting State

5.3.2.2.1 If the parties choose a particular court in a Contracting State, the effect of Article 17 is to confer jurisdiction on that court, but not on other courts in the same country. So, if the parties agree that disputes are to be referred to the courts in Rome, this is not sufficient to confer jurisdiction on the courts of Milan.

5.3.2.2.2 Where parties, at least one of whom is domiciled in a Contracting State, agree to refer their disputes to the courts of a Contracting State, the effect of such an agreement is twofold. (i) Article 17 confers mandatory jurisdiction on the courts chosen. The courts chosen by the parties cannot stay the proceedings on a discretionary basis (such as *forum non conveniens*). (ii) Article 17 prevents the courts of all the other Contracting States from assuming jurisdiction.

64. Lugano Convention, Article 54B(1).
65. Case C-214/89 *Powell Duffryn Plc* v. *Petereit* [1992] ILPr 300, 327 (para. 14).
66. Case C-214/89 [1992] ILPr 300. Hartley, (1993) 18 ELRev 225; Polak, (1993) 30 CMLRev 406; Robinson, "Articles of Association and Article 17 of the Brussels Convention" (1992) 13 Bus LR 260.
67. Case C-214/89 [1992] ILPr 300, 327 (para. 16).

5.3.2.2.3 In the situation where parties, none of whom is domiciled in a Contracting State, agree to refer their disputes to the courts of a Contracting State, the courts chosen may, applying national law, decline jurisdiction. If the chosen courts decline jurisdiction the courts of other Contracting States may then assume jurisdiction on the basis of national rules outside the Conventions. However, until the chosen courts have declined jurisdiction, the effect of Article 17 is to prevent the courts of the other Contracting States from assuming jurisdiction.

5.3.2.2.4 There is the possibility for disagreement as to the moment at which the domicile of the parties is relevant for the purposes of Article 17(1). Where, for example, one of the parties is domiciled in a Contracting State at the time when the agreement is concluded, but neither is domiciled in a Contracting State when proceedings are commenced, does the situation fall within the first sentence of Article 17(1) or the last sentence? The Court of Justice has not been required to rule on this question. The relevant time should be the time of contracting; by entering an agreement on jurisdiction the parties assume reciprocal obligations, the nature and content of which should not be dependent on changes in circumstances following the conclusion of the agreement.

5.3.2.2.5 A question arises as to whether Article 17 applies in a situation where both parties are domiciled in the same Contracting State. The crucial issue is not whether the parties are domiciled in different Contracting States, but whether the case concerns the "international jurisdiction" of the courts.[68] Where two parties domiciled in Germany agree to refer disputes to the English courts, Article 17 applies; equally Article 17 applies in a situation where two French domiciliaries agree to refer to the French courts disputes arising out of a contract which is to be performed in Germany.

5.3.2.3 Choice of the courts of a non-contracting State

5.3.2.3.1 What is the situation where the parties agree to refer their disputes to the courts of a non-contracting State? If the defendant is not domiciled in a Contracting State, Article 4 authorises the courts of each Contracting State to apply their own national jurisdiction rules. So, if A (an English company) and B (a New York company) enter an agreement which includes an English choice of law clause and a jurisdiction clause in favour of the courts of New York, A may seek leave to serve a writ on B out of the jurisdiction under RSC, Order 11, rule 1(1)(d)(iii).[69] In this situation Article 17 is wholly irrelevant. While the court, applying traditional rules, will generally refuse leave to serve out in a case where the parties have agreed to the jurisdiction of a foreign court,[70] in exceptional circumstances leave may be given where the case is closely connected with England.[71]

5.3.2.3.2 More difficult is the situation where the defendant is domiciled in a Contracting State. The question arises as to whether an English court may stay proceedings brought against an English domiciliary on the basis that the parties agreed to refer their dispute to the courts of a non-contracting State. In this type of case the court has jurisdiction by virtue of the defendant's domicile in England and there is nothing in Title II to suggest that the court has any discretion. Nevertheless, the

68. Preamble to the Conventions. See para. 3.3.1.2.
69. See para. 6.3.3.4.
70. *Mackender* v. *Feldia AG* [1967] 2 QB 590.
71. *Evans Marshall & Co Ltd* v. *Bertola SA* [1973] 1 WLR 349. For further discussion see para. 6.5.

authorities indicate that the court retains its inherent jurisdiction to stay the proceedings in these circumstances.[72]

5.3.3 Article 17(1): formal requirements

The problem which Article 17 is intended primarily to address is that posed by a jurisdiction clause in standardised general conditions of trade which may go unnoticed by one of the parties.[73] In a standard contract where the terms are not freely negotiated by the parties on the basis of equality, there is "the danger of [one of the parties] inadvertently finding himself bound by standard forms of agreement containing jurisdiction clauses without realising it".[74] Article 17 is premised on the consensus between the parties being "clearly and precisely demonstrated".[75] The formal requirements of Article 17 have the function of ensuring that the consensus between the parties is in fact established.[76] The Court of Justice has emphasised the importance of strict compliance with the formal requirements, so that there is "certainty that the clause conferring jurisdiction was in fact part of the subject matter of the contract properly so-called".[77]

In a number of cases the Court of Justice has had to consider the formal requirements of Article 17 and some aspects of the case law of the Court of Justice have been incorporated in the amended text of Article 17(1). It should be stressed that the requirements set out in subparagraphs (a), (b) and (c) of Article 17(1) are alternative; the fact that a clause is not in writing or evidenced in writing for the purposes of Article 17(1)(a) does not necessarily mean that it is ineffective. Indeed, in view of the relaxation of the formal requirements in recent years it should be relatively rare for an agreement referring disputes to the courts of a Contracting State not to be effective under Article 17.[78]

5.3.3.1 In writing or evidenced in writing[79]

5.3.3.1.1 IN WRITING

5.3.3.1.1.1 For a jurisdiction agreement to be "in writing" for the purposes of Article 17(1)(a) it is not sufficient that the contractual clause in question is in a written or printed form; it is the consent of each party to the clause in question which must be in writing. Accordingly, the requirement of writing is fulfilled if the jurisdiction clause is contained in a document which is signed by both parties.[80] Where a clause conferring

72. Schlosser Report, OJ 1979 C59/124, para. 176. *Arkwright Mutual Insurance Co* v. *Bryanston Insurance Co Ltd* [1990] 2 QB 649; *The Rewia* [1991] 1 Lloyd's Rep 69, 75, reversed on other grounds [1991] 2 Lloyd's Rep 325; *Re Harrods (Buenos Aires) Ltd* [1992] Ch 72. For further discussion see para. 5.10.
73. Jenard Report, OJ 1979 C59/37.
74. Schlosser Report, OJ 1979 C59/124, para. 179.
75. Case 24/76 *Estatis Salotti di Colzani Aimo* v. *RÜWA Polstereimaschinen GmbH* [1976] ECR 1831, 1841 (para. 7); Case 25/76 *Galeries Segoura SPRL* v. *Bonakdarian* [1976] ECR 1851, 1860 (para. 6).
76. Case 24/76 *Estatis Salotti di Colzani Aimo* v. *RÜWA Polstereimaschinen GmbH* [1976] ECR 1831, 1841 (para. 7); Case 25/76 *Galeries Segoura SPRL* v. *Bonakdarian* [1976] ECR 1851, 1860 (para. 6).
77. Case 24/76 *Estasis Salotti di Colzani Aimo* v. *RÜWA Polstereimaschinen GmbH* [1976] ECR 1831, 1842 (para. 12).
78. It is provided, however, that a jurisdiction agreement shall be valid with respect to a person domiciled in Luxembourg only if that person has expressly and specifically agreed: Protocol to the Brussels Convention, Article I; Protocol No. 1 to the Lugano Convention, Article I.
79. Hartley, (1977) 2 ELRev 148.
80. Case 71/83 *Partenreederei ms Tilly Russ* v. *NV Haven- & Vervoerbedrijf Nova* [1984] ECR 2417, 2432 (para. 16).

jurisdiction is included among the general conditions of sale of one of the parties, printed on the back of the contract, the requirement of writing is not fulfilled unless the contract signed by both parties contains an express reference to those general conditions.[81] Similarly, where a contract is concluded by reference to a prior document which contains a jurisdiction clause, the requirement of writing is satisfied only if the reference is express and can be checked by a party exercising reasonable care.[82] This means that the document containing the clause must have been communicated to the other contracting party; an indirect reference to earlier correspondence is not sufficient.

5.3.3.1.1.2 An exception to these strict rules has been formulated by the Court of Justice in relation to a jurisdiction agreement contained in the articles of association of a company. In *Powell Duffryn Plc* v. *Petereit* the Court of Justice decided that "if the articles contain a jurisdiction clause, every shareholder is deemed to be aware of the clause and to have given actual consent to the conferment of jurisdiction upon the court in question, provided that the company's articles of association are lodged at a place which is accessible to the shareholders, such as the company's registered office, or are kept in a public register".[83]

5.3.3.1.1.3 *Iveco Fiat SpA* v. *Van Hool NV*[84] concerned a jurisdiction clause in an agreement which had been concluded for a limited period. After the period had elapsed, the agreement was not formally renewed. Nevertheless, the parties continued dealing with each other for many years on the basis of the original agreement. The question was whether, in these circumstances, the parties could continue to rely on the jurisdiction clause. The Court of Justice held that where the expired agreement continued to serve as the legal basis for the contractual relations between the parties, whether the jurisdiction clause satisfied the formal requirements of Article 17 depended on the applicable law. If, for example, under the applicable law, the parties could validly renew the contract otherwise than in writing, the formal requirements of Article 17 would be met. If, however, under the applicable law, the parties could only validly renew the contract in writing, Article 17 would not be satisfied unless either of the parties had confirmed in writing the jurisdiction clause or the group of clauses of which the jurisdiction clause formed a part without any objection from the other party to whom the written confirmation had been notified.[85]

5.3.3.1.1.4 Where a contract containing a jurisdiction clause has not been signed by the party against whom it is invoked, it is clear that the clause is not to be regarded as being in writing for the purposes of Article 17(1)(a). What is the position, however, where A contracts with B on A's standard terms and B, who has not signed the contract, seeks to invoke the jurisdiction clause in the written contract against A? There is no obvious reason in this case why the jurisdiction clause should not be regarded as satisfying the requirements of Article 17(1)(a).[86]

81. Case 24/76 *Estasis Salotti di Colzani Aimo* v. *RÜWA Polstereimaschinen GmbH* [1976] ECR 1831, 1842 (para. 10).
82. Case 24/76 *Estasis Salotti di Colzani Aimo* v. *RÜWA Polstereimaschinen GmbH* [1976] ECR 1831, 1842 (para. 13).
83. Case C-214/89 [1992] ILPr 300, 328–329 (para. 28).
84. Case 313/85 [1986] ECR 3337.
85. Case 313/85 [1986] ECR 3337, 3355–3356 (paras. 7–8).
86. See Case 201/82 *Gerling Konzern Speziale Kreditversicherungs-AG* v. *Amministrazione del Tesoro dello Stato* [1983] ECR 2503.

5.3.3.1.2 EVIDENCED IN WRITING

The alternative requirement in subparagraph (a)—that a jurisdiction clause be evidenced in writing—has been interpreted by the Court of Justice as referring to the situation where a contract, which is concluded orally, is later confirmed in writing. Two different situations should be distinguished.

(i) The first situation arises where the contract is concluded orally and there is no express oral agreement on jurisdiction. In *Galeries Segoura SPRL* v. *Bonakdarian*[87] a contract of sale—which was concluded orally—was later confirmed by the seller in writing. The confirmation included the seller's standard terms and conditions, which incorporated a jurisdiction clause. The Court of Justice decided that the mere fact that the buyer does not raise any objections to the seller's written confirmation (which contains the jurisdiction clause) does not in itself constitute acceptance of the clause. The jurisdiction clause satisfies Article 17(1)(a) only if the buyer accepts the seller's standard terms and conditions in writing.[88]

(ii) The second situation arises where there is an express oral agreement on jurisdiction which is subsequently confirmed in writing. In *F Berghöfer GmbH & Co KG* v. *ASA SA*[89] the Court of Justice decided that where jurisdiction is conferred by an express oral agreement the formal requirements of Article 17 are satisfied if one party sends written confirmation of that agreement to the other and the latter raises no objection.[90] In this situation it does not matter which party sends the written confirmation. The decision of the Court of Justice has been criticised on the basis that "[i]t would have been more logical to distinguish between confirmation by the party who stood to lose, which provides real proof of consent, since approval by the party who stood to gain may be presumed, and confirmation by the party who stood to gain, which provides no real evidence of agreement between the parties".[91]

5.3.3.2 *In a form which accords with practices which the parties have established between themselves*

Article 17(1)(b) reflects the case law of the Court of Justice. In *Galeries Segoura SPRL* v. *Bonakdarian* the Court of Justice decided that where a contract has been concluded orally the requirements of Article 17 are satisfied if the "oral agreement forms part of a continuing trading relationship between the parties, provided also that it is established that the dealings taken as a whole are governed by the general conditions of the party giving confirmation, and these conditions contain a clause conferring jurisdiction".[92] This ruling was confirmed and applied in *Partenreederei ms Tilly Russ* v. *NV Haven- & Vervoerbedrijf Nova*,[93] a case concerning a contract of carriage which had been

87. Case 25/76 [1976] ECR 1851.
88. Case 25/76 [1976] ECR 1851, 1861 (para. 8).
89. Case 221/84 [1985] ECR 2699.
90. Case 221/84 [1985] ECR 2699, 2708–2709 (para. 15).
91. Pieri, "The 1968 Brussels Convention on Jurisdiction and Enforcement of Judgments in Civil and Commercial Matters: Four Years' Case Law of the European Court of Justice" (1987) 24 CMLRev 635, 644.
92. Case 25/76 [1976] ECR 1851, 1862 (para. 11).
93. Case 71/83 [1984] ECR 2417.

concluded orally between the parties and then confirmed in writing when the carrier issued a bill of lading. The bill of lading, which included a jurisdiction clause, was signed by the carrier but not by the shipper. The Court of Justice held that the requirements of Article 17 were satisfied, notwithstanding the absence of express written agreement by the shipper, as long as the carrier and the shipper had a continuing business relationship which was governed as a whole by the carrier's general conditions which contained the jurisdiction clause.[94]

5.3.3.3 Trade usages

5.3.3.3.1 According to the original 1968 text a jurisdiction agreement did not satisfy the formal requirements of Article 17 unless it was in writing or evidenced in writing; anything less was insufficient. Experience soon showed, however, that the strictness of Article 17 did not cater adequately for the customs and needs of international trade. Accordingly, the 1978 Accession Convention provided that from the point of view of form a clause would be valid if, in international trade or commerce, the agreement was "in a form which accords with practices in that trade or commerce of which the parties are or ought to have been aware". Since the amended text of the Brussels Convention did not satisfy the representatives of the EFTA countries Article 17 was amended again. The new formula which is contained in Article 17(1)(c) is part of the text of the Brussels Convention as amended by the 1989 Accession Convention and the Lugano Convention.

5.3.3.3.2 The effect of Article 17(1))(c) is that:

> [E]ven in international trade or commerce, it is not sufficient that an agreement conferring jurisdiction be in a form which accords with practices (or a usage) in such trade or commerce of which the parties are or ought to have been aware. It is moreover required that the usage shall be, on the one hand, widely known in international trade or commerce and, on the other, regularly observed by parties to contracts of the type involved in the particular trade or commerce concerned.[95]

It should be stressed that paragraph (c) does not obviate the need for an agreement on jurisdiction.[96] It seems inconceivable that an implied choice of jurisdiction could satisfy the formal requirements of Article 17. Furthermore, it is clear that a choice of jurisdiction cannot be implied into a contract governed by English law; under English law a choice of jurisdiction must be express.[97]

5.3.3.4 Article 17(1) and third parties

5.3.3.4.1 In view of the way in which the formal requirements of Article 17 have been interpreted by the Court of Justice, potential problems arise in cases where the party to the litigation was not a party to the original agreement which incorporates the jurisdiction clause. There are two factual situations which should be distinguished.

(i) The first situation arises where a third party beneficiary wishes to rely on a contractual agreement on jurisdiction. In *Gerling Konzern Speziale*

94. Case 71/83 [1984] ECR 2417, 2433 (para. 18).
95. Jenard–Möller, OJ 1990 C189/77, para. 58.
96. See Schlosser Report, OJ 1979 C59/125, para. 179.
97. *Sirdar Gurdyal Singh* v. *Rajah of Faridkoke* [1894] AC 670; *New Hampshire Insurance Co* v. *Strabag Bau AG* [1992] 1 Lloyd's Rep 361.

Kreditversicherungs-AG v. *Amministrazione del Tesoro dello Stato*[98] the Court of Justice ruled that a third party beneficiary (in this case a beneficiary of a contract of insurance) can invoke a jurisdiction clause even if he has not signed it. The purpose of Article 17 is to ensure that the consent of the parties against whom the clause may be invoked is clearly and precisely expressed. From this point of view, there can be no reason for requiring a third party beneficiary to have signed the jurisdiction agreement.

(ii) The second situation arises where the person against whom the jurisdiction clause is invoked is not an original party to the contract containing the clause. The Court of Justice has taken the view that where a contract which includes a jurisdiction clause is concluded between A and B, A may invoke the clause against C, a third party, if two conditions are met: the jurisdiction clause is valid under Article 17 as between A and B; and under the applicable law C has succeeded to B's rights and obligations under the original contract.[99]

5.3.3.4.2 In *Partenreederei ms Tilly Russ* v. *NV Haven- & Vervoerbedrijf Nova*[100] timber was shipped on board a vessel which was owned by the defendant, a German company. The bill of lading included an exclusive jurisdiction clause in favour of the German courts. In due course the bill was transferred to the plaintiff, as purchaser of the cargo. When the plaintiff, alleging damage to the timber and short delivery, started proceedings against the carrier in Belgium, the defendant sought to rely on the jurisdiction agreement, notwithstanding the fact that the plaintiff had not been an original party to the bill of lading. In this type of dispute, it is to be expected that the jurisdiction clause will be enforceable against the third party. As a general rule the original bill of lading will comply with the formal requirements of Article 17 and the holder, on acquiring the bill of lading, will normally succeed to the shipper's rights and obligations.

5.3.3.5 The formal requirements of Article 17 and national law

It is quite possible for there to be divergences between the formal requirements of Article 17 and the requirements imposed by the applicable law.

(i) It is possible that a jurisdiction clause, which is valid under the applicable law, is formally invalid under Article 17. It should not be concluded, however, that in this situation the jurisdiction clause is entirely without effect. Of course, a jurisdiction clause which is invalid under Article 17 cannot be invoked against a person who is domiciled in a Contracting State. However, the position may be different as regards a person who is not domiciled in a Contracting State. Article 4 provides that, as a general rule, a defendant who is not domiciled in a Contracting State may be sued in a Contracting State in accordance with traditional jurisdiction rules. If a plaintiff issues English proceedings against a New York company on the basis of an English jurisdiction clause, the

98. Case 201/82 [1983] ECR 2503.

99. Case 71/83 *Partenreederei ms Tilly Russ* v. *NV Haven- & Vervoerbedrijf Nova* [1984] ECR 2417, 2435 (para. 26). North, "Jurisdiction Clauses in Bills of Lading and the European Judgments Convention" [1985] LMCLQ 177; Wilderspin, (1984) 9 ELRev 456.

100. Case 71/83 [1984] ECR 2699.

invalidity of the clause under Article 17 means simply that the writ does not fall within RSC, Order 11, rule 1(2) and, therefore, cannot be served on the defendant without the leave of the court. However, RSC, Order 11, rule 1(1)(d)(iv) provides that a plaintiff may apply for leave to serve the defendant out of the jurisdiction on the ground that the contract "contains a term to the effect that the High Court shall have jurisdiction".[101] As regards a defendant who is not domiciled in a Contracting State, if the jurisdiction clause is valid according to its proper law, the fact that the clause is formally invalid under Article 17 is no obstacle to leave to serve out being given under RSC, Order 11, rule 1(1)(d)(iv).

(ii) The applicable law may impose formal requirements which are more severe than those contained in Article 17. In *Elefanten Schuh GmbH* v. *Jacqmain*[102] the Court of Justice held that the formal requirements of Article 17 are both necessary and sufficient. Accordingly, a national law which lays down more stringent requirements than Article 17 is incompatible with Title II and cannot render formally invalid a jurisdiction agreement which satisfies the requirements of Article 17.

5.3.4 Material validity and interpretation

5.3.4.1 Article 17 is concerned with formal validity only. To be enforceable, a jurisdiction clause must also be materially valid according to its proper law.[103] Since agreements on jurisdiction are excluded from the scope of the Rome Convention on the Law Applicable to Contractual Obligations[104] the common law choice of law rules are relevant for determining the proper law. If a contract which contains a jurisdiction clause also contains an express choice of law clause, the chosen law is the proper law of the jurisdiction agreement. If there is no express choice, the law of the forum chosen by the parties is generally the governing law.[105]

5.3.4.2 The proper law governs questions of interpretation of a jurisdiction clause.[106] So, for example, in a clause whereby the parties agree to refer disputes to "British courts" it is for the proper law to determine what is meant by "British" in this context. Similarly, whether a jurisdiction agreement is exclusive or non-exclusive is an issue which should be referred to the proper law of the agreement. In an ordinary commercial contract which is governed by English law a clause which refers disputes to "the jurisdiction of the English court" is normally interpreted as conferring exclusive jurisdiction, notwithstanding the fact that the word "exclusive" is not used.[107]

5.3.4.3 A clause which is materially invalid under the proper law (for example, because it is voidable for duress) is ineffective, regardless of whether the formal requirements of Article 17 are satisfied. The proper law may, in certain circumstances,

101. See para. 6.3.3.4.
102. Case 150/80 [1981] ECR 1671.
103. *Hamlyn & Co* v. *Talisker Distillery* [1894] AC 202; *Spurrier* v. *La Cloche* [1902] AC 446.
104. Article 1(2)(d). See para. 10.4.1.2.3.
105. *Hamlyn & Co* v. *Talisker Distillery* [1894] AC 202.
106. *Evans Marshall & Co Ltd* v. *Bertola SA* [1973] 1 WLR 349. See, Kahn-Freund, "Jurisdiction Agreements: Some Reflections" (1977) 26 ICLQ 825.
107. *Sohio Supply Co* v. *Gatoil (USA) Inc* [1989] 1 Lloyd's Rep 588; *British Aerospace Plc* v. *Dee Howard Co* [1993] 1 Lloyd's Rep 368.

be overridden by mandatory rules of the forum. So, for example, a foreign jurisdiction clause in a bill of lading is rendered "null and void" by the Hague-Visby Rules—incorporated into English law by the Carriage of Goods by Sea Act 1971—if according to the substantive law applied by the chosen forum the carrier's liability would be less than his liability under the Rules.[108]

5.3.5 Alternative fora

5.3.5.1 Article 17 refers to agreements conferring jurisdiction on a court or the courts of a single Contracting State. In *Meeth* v. *Glacetal*[109] the Court of Justice decided that, notwithstanding the literal wording of Article 17, a clause conferring jurisdiction on alternative fora is valid for the purposes of Article 17. So, where a contract between A and B contains a jurisdiction clause which provides that if A sues B the courts of Germany are to have jurisdiction, but if B sues A the courts of France are to have jurisdiction, the jurisdiction clause falls within the scope of Article 17. Furthermore, if A sues B in Germany in accordance with the terms of the jurisdiction clause and B raises a set-off in the context of those proceedings, the German court has jurisdiction to consider "a set-off connected with the legal relationship in dispute if such court considers that course to be compatible with the letter and spirit of the clause conferring jurisdiction".[110]

5.3.5.2 The liberal approach adopted by the Court of Justice suggests that a clause which provides that either party may bring proceedings against the other in the courts of two or more Contracting States would be effective under Article 17. So, if a contract includes a term stating that "all disputes arising under the contract shall be decided by the courts of England or France", either party would have a choice whether to bring proceedings in the English or French courts. If, in such a case, proceedings were commenced in more than one of the chosen fora on the same cause of action Article 21 would require any court other than the court first seised to decline jurisdiction.[111]

5.3.6 Non-exclusive jurisdiction clauses

5.3.6.1 Whether a jurisdiction clause is exclusive or non-exclusive is a matter of construction to be determined by reference to its proper law.[112] Where a jurisdiction clause states that the courts of a particular country are to have jurisdiction, but that such jurisdiction is not to be exclusive, is the effect of Article 17 to confer exclusive jurisdiction, non-exclusive jurisdiction or no jurisdiction at all?

5.3.6.2 Article 17 would on the face of it appear to confer exclusive jurisdiction on the chosen courts, since it states that where parties have agreed that "the courts of a Contracting State are to have jurisdiction ... those courts shall have exclusive jurisdiction". Such a literal interpretation—which would defeat the intentions of the parties—has little to recommend it. An alternative—but equally unattractive—interpretation is to regard non-exclusive jurisdiction clauses as falling outside the scope

108. *The Hollandia* [1983] 1 AC 565. See further para. 12.3.2.
109. Case 23/78 [1978] ECR 2133. Hartley, (1979) 4 ELRev 125.
110. Case 23/78 [1978] ECR 2133, 2143 (para. 8).
111. See para. 5.9.
112. See para. 5.3.4.

of Article 17 altogether. A more reasonable approach is to seek to give the clause the impact intended by the parties and to regard the agreement as being effective to confer jurisdiction on the chosen court, but not so as to derogate from the jurisdiction of other courts under other provisions of Title II. Although this interpretation is almost impossible to reconcile with the actual wording of Article 17, it was favoured by Hoffmann J in *Kurz* v. *Stella Musical Veranstaltungs GmbH.*[113] In view of the case law of the Court of Justice any other conclusion would lead to illogical distinctions. The decision in *Meeth* v. *Glacetal*[114] establishes that, if parties to a contract wish to confer jurisdiction on the courts of more than one Contracting State, they may expressly do so. A jurisdiction agreement, concluded between two parties who are domiciled in Germany, purporting to confer non-exclusive jurisdiction of the English courts is designed to have largely the same effect as a clause which purports to confer exclusive jurisdiction on the courts of Germany and England. It would make little sense to give effect to the parties' intentions in relation to the latter agreement, while refusing to do so in relation to the former.

5.3.7 Article 17(4): clauses for the benefit of one party only

Article 17(4) provides that where a jurisdiction agreement is concluded for the benefit of one party to the agreement, the person in whose favour the clause is concluded may choose not to rely on it and rely instead on other jurisdictional bases in Title II. In *Anterist* v. *Crédit Lyonnais*[115] the Court of Justice held that an agreement conferring jurisdiction is not to be regarded as having been concluded for the benefit of only one of the parties where all that is established is that the parties have agreed that the courts of the Contracting State in which that party is domiciled are to have jurisdiction. So, where an English domiciliary and a Spanish company enter an agreement conferring exclusive jurisdiction on the Spanish courts, it cannot simply be assumed that the clause is for the sole benefit of the Spanish company. According to the Court of Justice a clause is to be regarded as being for the benefit of only one party where there is an express and specific mention to that effect or where the clause allows one of the parties a greater choice of jurisdictions. It has been suggested that the interpretation adopted by the Court of Justice has effectively emptied Article 17(4) of all substance "as clauses stating expressly that they are to the advantage of one or other party and clauses giving to one party a wider choice of jurisdictions than to the other are practically non-existent".[116]

5.3.8 Article 17(5): jurisdiction clauses in employment contracts

5.3.8.1 In relation to consumer contracts and matters relating to insurance there are limitations on the effectiveness of jurisdiction agreements.[117] As originally drafted the Brussels Convention did not include any provisions dealing expressly with contracts of employment, notwithstanding the fact that from the point of view of inequality of

113. [1992] Ch 196. Fentiman, [1992] CLJ 234; Thomas, "Non-Exclusive Jurisdiction Clauses and Submission by Appearance" [1992] LMCLQ 292.
114. Case 23/78 [1978] ECR 2133.
115. Case 22/85 [1986] ECR 1951.
116. Pieri, "The 1968 Brussels Convention on Jurisdiction and Enforcement of Judgments in Civil and Commercial Matters: Four Years' Case Law of the European Court of Justice" (1987) 24 CMLRev 635, 646.
117. Article 12 (insurance) and Article 15 (consumer contracts). For further discussion of these provisions see para. 5.7.

bargaining power contracts of employment give rise to problems similar to those raised by consumer contracts and insurance contracts. When the Lugano Convention was being negotiated the EFTA countries proposed the addition of a fifth paragraph to Article 17, which provides that, in relation to an individual contract of employment, an agreement conferring jurisdiction shall have legal force only if it is entered into after the dispute has arisen. The motivation for this provision is the desire to give protection to the employee, who from the socio-economic point of view is the weaker party in the contractual relationship.[118]

5.3.8.2 The 1989 Accession Convention also added a fifth paragraph to Article 17, but in a slightly different form:

> [T]he solution incorporated in the Lugano Convention was considered too radical: this would be the case in particular where the agreement conferring jurisdiction, while entered into prior to the dispute arising, could in the employee's own view be favourable to him. For this reason the new paragraph 5 in Article 17 of the [Brussels] Convention provides that the agreement conferring jurisdiction may only take effect where it is entered into after the dispute has arisen—as in the Lugano Convention—or if "the employee invokes it to seise courts other than those for the defendant's domicile or those specified in Article 5(1)", which moderates the radicality of the Lugano Convention.[119]

5.3.8.3 As a result of Article 17(5) of the Brussels Convention, where an individual contract of employment contains a jurisdiction clause, the employee has, in his capacity as plaintiff, a free choice between the courts of the State of the defendant's domicile (Article 2) or the courts for the place of performance of the contract of employment (Article 5(1)) or the courts to which prorogation has been made (Article 17(5)).[120] The employer, however, cannot rely on the jurisdiction clause in the contract of employment.

5.4 THE DOMICILE RULE: ARTICLE 2

5.4.1 Article 2 provides:

> Subject to the provisions of this Convention, persons domiciled in a Contracting State shall, whatever their nationality, be sued in the courts of that State.
>
> Persons who are not nationals of the State in which they are domiciled shall be governed by the rules of jurisdiction applicable to nationals of that State.

The second paragraph makes it clear that national courts cannot discriminate against plaintiffs on grounds of nationality. Traditionally, English jurisdiction rules have treated foreign plaintiffs—with the exception of enemy aliens[121]—on exactly the same basis as English plaintiffs. This provision, therefore, makes no change to English practice in this area.

5.4.2 The first paragraph of Article 2 must be read in conjunction with Article 3, which provides that a person domiciled in a Contracting State may be sued in another Contracting State in accordance with the provisions set out in Sections 2 to 6 of Title II.

(i) In cases where jurisdiction is allocated by the general rules in Articles 16, 17 and 18 or by the specific rules relating to insurance and consumer contracts in

118. Jenard–Möller Report, OJ 1990 C189/77, para. 60.
119. Almeida Cruz–Desantes Real–Jenard Report OJ 1990 C189/47–48, para. 27(d).
120. Almeida Cruz–Desantes Real–Jenard Report, OJ 1990 C189/48, para. 27(f).
121. See para. 2.2.

Articles 7 to 15, jurisdiction cannot be based on Article 2.

(ii) In cases where—on the basis of Article 2—the defendant may be sued in the courts of the Contracting State in which he is domiciled, the plaintiff often has the choice of invoking the jurisdiction of the courts of another Contracting State under Article 5, Article 6 or Article 6A.

5.5 ALTERNATIVE FORA I: ARTICLE 5

5.5.1 Introduction

5.5.1.1 Article 5 provides a number of situations in which a person domiciled in a Contracting State may be sued in another Contracting State. Article 5 contains seven paragraphs relating to the following matters:

(1) "matters relating to a contract";
(2) "matters relating to maintenance";
(3) "matters relating to tort, delict or quasi-delict";
(4) "a civil claim for damages or restitution which is based on an act giving rise to criminal proceedings";
(5) "a dispute arising out of the operations of a branch, agency or other establishment";
(6) certain proceedings relating to trusts;
(7) "a dispute concerning the payment of remuneration claimed in respect of the salvage of a cargo or freight".

Paragraphs (2) to (7) of the Lugano Convention are the same as the equivalent provisions of the Brussels Convention; as regards jurisdiction concerning individual contracts of employment within paragraph (1) the two Conventions diverge to some extent.

5.5.1.2 Paragraph (2) does not concern commercial matters and is beyond the scope of this work; paragraph (4) is of very limited application in England since under English law civil claims for damages in criminal proceedings are relatively unimportant in practice; paragraph (7), which was added to the Brussels Convention by the 1978 Accession Convention, is discussed in a subsequent chapter.[122] In the present context, therefore, the most important elements of Article 5 are paragraphs (1), (3), (5) and (6).

5.5.1.3 The connecting factors which justify jurisdiction under Article 5 are not factors which connect the defendant to the forum; the relevant factors are the factual connections between the cause of action and the forum. In this sense Article 5 is not unlike RSC, Order 11, rule 1(1) in inspiration.[123] Its operation is, however, very different, since in cases where the plaintiff relies on the jurisdiction rules contained in Article 5, the court may not decline jurisdiction (unless authorised by the provisions of Section 8 of Title II[124]).

5.5.1.4 Article 5 is a derogation from the general principle contained in Article 2; it gives the plaintiff the opportunity to proceed against the defendant in a court of a

122. See para. 8.2.4.1.
123. See para. 6.3.3.
124. See para. 5.9.

Contracting State in which the defendant is not domiciled. The Court of Justice has taken the view that the derogations from the principle *actor forum sequitur rei* must be interpreted restrictively.[125] In *Somafer SA* v. *Saar-Ferngas AG* the Court of Justice sought to justify the narrow interpretation of Article 5:

> Multiplication of the bases of jurisdiction in one and the same case is not likely to encourage legal certainty and the effectiveness of legal protection throughout the territory of the Community, and therefore it is in accord with the objective of the Convention to avoid a wide and multifarious interpretation of the exceptions to the general rule of jurisdiction contained in Article 2.[126]

Moreover, "the objective of the legal protection of persons established in the Community which the Convention seeks, *inter alia*, to attain means that the jurisdiction rules which derogate from the general principle of the Convention must be interpreted in such a way as to enable a normally well-informed defendant to make a reasonable prediction as to the court in which he may be sued, apart from the courts of the State in which he is domiciled".[127]

5.5.2 Jurisdiction in matters relating to contract and tort: introduction

Article 5(1) confers jurisdiction as regards "matters relating to a contract"; Article 5(3) deals with "matters relating to tort, delict or quasi-delict". A number of issues should be addressed by way of introduction.

(i) How should the interpretation of "contract" and "tort, delict or quasi-delict" be approached?
(ii) Are paragraphs (1) and (3) all-embracing or are there cases in which the plaintiff seeks to establish the liability of the defendant which fall within neither paragraph (1) nor paragraph (3)?
(iii) Are paragraphs (1) and (3) mutually exclusive?

5.5.2.1 Methods of interpretation

5.5.2.1.1 There is clearly a potential problem surrounding the dividing line between "contract", on the one hand, and "tort, delict or quasi-delict", on the other. Different legal systems draw that dividing line in different places; what is a breach of contract in one legal system may be regarded as a tort in another. There are three possible ways of deciding whether proceedings are concerned with matters relating to a contract or matters relating to tort: (i) classify the issue according to the *lex fori*; (ii) classify the issue according to the *lex causae*; (iii) formulate an independent or autonomous interpretation. It is not surprising that the Court of Justice has adopted the third of these approaches. According to the case law of the Court of Justice the phrase "matters relating to a contract" is "an independent concept which for the purpose of the application of the Convention, must be interpreted by reference principally to the system and objectives of the Convention in order to ensure that it is fully effective".[128] The scope of Article 5(1) depends neither on the *lex fori* nor the law governing the

125. Case 189/87 *Kalfelis* v. *Bankhaus Schröder, Münchmeyer, Hengst & Co* [1988] ECR 5565, 5585 (para. 19).
126. Case 33/78 [1978] ECR 2183, 2191 (para. 6).
127. Case C-26/91 *Jakob Handte & Co GmbH* v. *Société Traitements Mécano-chimiques des Surfaces* [1993] ILPr 5, 22–23 (para. 18).
128. Case 9/87 *SPRL Acardo* v. *SA Haviland* [1988] ECR 1539, 1554 (para. 11). Briggs, (1988) 8 YBEL 269.

alleged contract.[129] For example, in *Jakob Handte & Co GmbH* v. *Société Traitements Mécano-chimiques des Surfaces*[130] A (a German company) manufactured a component which was sold by B (a French company) to C (a Swiss company) who fitted it into a machine which was sold to D (another French company). When D brought proceedings in France against A, B and C one of the questions facing the court was whether jurisdiction could be assumed against A. According to French law D's claim against A was contractual in nature and France was the place of performance of the obligation in question. In most Contracting States a manufacturer's liability towards a subsequent purchaser for defects in the product sold is considered to be non-contractual. The Court of Justice explained that the "classification given by the relevant national law to the legal relationship in question before the national court" was not relevant.[131] Similarly, in *Kalfelis* v. *Bankhaus Schröder, Münchmeyer, Hengst & Co* the Court of Justice decided that for the purposes of Title II the term "tort, delict or quasi-delict" in Article 5(3) must be regarded as an autonomous concept.[132]

5.5.2.1.2 It follows from the approach adopted by the Court of Justice that, in certain circumstances, a claim—which, for jurisdictional purposes, has to be classified as contractual—is, from the point of view of the substantive law to be applied by the forum, to be regarded as tortious. The classification for jurisdictional purposes has no bearing on the substance of the case:

> A court that acquires jurisdiction under Article 5(1) is not prevented by the Convention from proceeding with the action on the basis that it is delictual and a court that acquires jurisdiction under Article 5(3) is not prevented by the Convention from proceeding with the action on the basis that it is contractual.[133]

5.5.2.2 Are paragraphs (1) and (3) all-embracing?

5.5.2.2.1 A consideration of this question must take as its starting-point the decision in *Kalfelis* v. *Bankhaus Schröder, Münchmeyer, Hengst & Co.*[134] In the course of its judgment the Court of Justice stated that Article 5(3) must be regarded as covering "all actions which seek to establish the liability of a defendant and which are not related to 'contract' within the meaning of Article 5(1)".[135] On the face of it, this passage would appear to endorse the view that Article 5(1) and Article 5(3), taken together, cover all situations in which the plaintiff seeks to establish the civil liability of the defendant. In *Jakob Handte & Co GmbH* v. *Société Traitements Mécano-chimiques des Surfaces* Advocate-General Jacobs expressed the view that "[d]elictual liability is . . . a residual category encompassing liability that is not contractual".[136] According to this view Article 5(3) covers claims which are based on unjust enrichment.

5.5.2.2.2 The expansive interpretation of Article 5(3) may be legitimately

129. Case 34/82 *Martin Peters Bauunternehmung GmbH* v. *Zuid Nederlandse Aannemers Vereniging* [1983] ECR 987 (Hartley, (1983) 8 ELRev 262); Case 9/87 *SPRL Acardo* v. *SA Haviland* [1988] ECR 1539; Case C-26/91 *Jakob Handte & Co GmbH* v. *Société Traitements Mécano-chimiques des Surfaces* [1993] ILPr 5.

130. Case C-26/91 [1993] ILPr 5. Decker, "Contract or Tort: A Conflict of Classification" (1993) 42 ICLQ 366.

131. Case C-26/91 [1993] ILPr 5, 19 (para. 10).

132. Case 189/87 [1988] ECR 5565, 5585 (para. 16). Briggs, (1988) 8 YBEL 272. See also Case C-261/90 *Reichert* v. *Dresdner Bank (No. 2)* [1992] ILPr 404.

133. Advocate-General Jacobs in Case C-26/91 *Jakob Handte & Co GmbH* v. *Société Traitements Mécano-chimiques des Surfaces* [1993] ILPr 5, 14–15 (para. 24).

134. Case 189/87 [1988] ECR 5565. Briggs, (1988) 8 YBEL 272.

135. Case 189/87 [1988] ECR 5565, 5585 (para. 17).

136. Case C-26/91 [1993] ILPr 5, 10 (para. 11).

questioned. It has been suggested that, looking at the decision in *Kalfelis* v. *Bankhaus Schröder, Münchmeyer, Hengst & Co* as a whole, the Court of Justice accepted the possibility that there may be situations in which an obligation is excluded from the scope of Article 5(3) if it is not tortious, but is not covered by Article 5(1) either, if its contractual nature cannot be established.[137] In *Reichert* v. *Dresdner Bank (No. 2)* Advocate-General Gulmann noted that "it may be difficult to distinguish actions for liability which may be covered either by Article 5(1) or Article 5(3) from actions which cannot be regarded as actions for contractual liability or liability in tort, delict or quasi-delict. In such cases, the distinction may have the result that there is no forum with special jurisdiction for the matter in question and that the action can only be brought before the court of the defendant's domicile".[138] Furthermore, both the Court of Session[139] and the English High Court[140] have taken the view—albeit in the context of the Modified Convention—that proceedings which raise questions of the defendant's liability may be regarded as concerning neither matters relating to a contract nor matters relating to tort, delict or quasi-delict.

5.5.2.2.3 Indeed, the proposition that paragraphs (1) and (3) of Article 5 are not all-embracing is more consistent with the Court of Justice's view that "the provisions on 'special jurisdiction' in Articles 5 and 6 of the Convention constitute derogations from the principle that jurisdiction is vested in the courts of the State of the defendant's domicile, laid down in the general provisions of Articles 2 and 3 and, therefore, those provisions on special jurisdiction must be interpreted restrictively".[141] It must always be remembered that the conclusion that, in specific circumstances, the proceedings fall neither within Article 5(1) nor Article 5(3) does not entail the consequence that there is no forum in which the plaintiff's claim can be brought; the plaintiff may proceed in the Contracting State in which the defendant is domiciled.

5.5.2.3 Are paragraphs (1) and (3) mutually exclusive?

From the decision of the Court of Justice in *Kalfelis* v. *Bankhaus Schröder, Münchmeyer, Hengst & Co* it is clear that paragraphs (1) and (3) are to be regarded as mutually exclusive.[142] This is in marked contrast to the traditional English approach which regards tort and contract as overlapping categories.[143] From the point of view of jurisdiction, Article 5 does not give the plaintiff a choice as to whether to frame the action in contract or in tort. If the proceedings concern "matters relating to a contract" jurisdiction cannot be derived from Article 5(3), even if the plaintiff's action is regarded as being in tort by the *lex fori*; similarly, if the proceedings concern "matters relating to tort, delict or quasi-delict" the court may not assume jurisdiction under Article 5(1) on

137. Pocar, "Jurisdiction in Matters Relating to Tort or Delict" in Tebbens, Kennedy & Kohler (eds), *Civil Jurisdiction and Judgments in Europe* (1992) 109, 111.

138. Case C-261/90 [1992] ILPr 404, 415.

139. *Davenport* v. *Corinthian Motor Policies at Lloyd's*, 1991 SLT 774 (an action for recovery of a statutory indemnity).

140. *Barclays Bank Plc* v. *Glasgow City Council* [1993] QB 429 (a claim for reimbursement arising from the nullity of transactions known as "interest rate swaps"). Briggs, "Jurisdiction over Restitutionary Claims" [1992] LMCLQ 283.

141. Case 32/88 *Six Constructions Ltd* v. *Humbert* [1989] ECR 341, 364 (para. 18).

142. Case 189/87 [1988] ECR 5565, 5585 (para. 19). The decision of Judge Southwell QC in *Gascoine* v. *Pyrah, The Times*, 26 November 1991 is inconsistent with this proposition and in this respect cannot be supported. This issue was not considered by the Court of Appeal: [1994] ILPr 82.

143. *Matthews* v. *Kuwait Bechtel Corporation* [1959] 2 QB 57; *Coupland* v. *Arabian Gulf Oil Co* [1983] 1 WLR 1136.

the basis that the plaintiff's action is regarded by the *lex fori* as contractual.[144] Furthermore, in *Kalfelis* v. *Bankhaus Schröder, Münchmeyer, Hengst & Co* the Court of Justice decided that where a plaintiff has a claim against a defendant part of which is based in contract and another part of which is based in tort "a court which has jurisdiction under Article 5(3) over an action in so far as it is based on tort or delict does not have jurisdiction over that action in so far as it is not so based".[145]

5.5.3 Jurisdiction in matters relating to a contract

The general rule in Article 5(1) is that a person domiciled in a Contracting State may be sued in another Contracting State "in matters relating to a contract, in the courts for the place of performance of the obligation in question".[146] This general rule is qualified in relation to "individual contracts of employment".[147]

5.5.3.1 Matters relating to a contract

5.5.3.1.1 In most instances there will be few problems in determining whether or not the proceedings relate to a contract. Article 5(1) "should be understood to cover a situation where there is an obligation freely entered into by one party to another".[148] Because, for the purposes of Article 5(1) "contract" must be given an autonomous interpretation, particular aspects of domestic law—such as the English doctrine of consideration—cannot be used to determine the boundaries of Article 5(1). For example, a dispute relating to a promise to make a gift would almost certainly fall within the scope of Article 5(1). Conversely, the potential liability of a manufacturer of goods to a subbuyer is not to be regarded as contractual regardless of the characterisation of the *lex fori.*[149]

5.5.3.1.2 The Court of Justice has decided that a denial of the existence of an alleged contract by the defendant does not, in itself, deprive the court of jurisdiction under Article 5(1).[150] If there is evidence establishing a genuine dispute as to the existence of the contract and there is a serious question which calls for a trial for its determination jurisdiction may be assumed under Article 5(1).[151] If, however, "there is no evidence of the existence of a contract, and therefore no real dispute as to its existence, the court has no jurisdiction under Article 5(1)".[152] On the basis of these developments it has been suggested that "as long as the existence or non-existence, or performance or non-performance of a contractual (or consensual?) obligation is at the bottom of the claim made, the matter will be held to relate to a contract within Article 5(1)".[153]

144. Case C-26/91 *Jakob Handte & Co GmbH* v. *Société Traitements Mécano-chimiques des Surfaces* [1993] ILPr 5.
145. Case 189/87 [1988] ECR 5565, 5585 (para. 19).
146. Article 5(1) does not confer jurisdiction over a defendant domiciled in Luxembourg unless that person enters an appearance: Protocol to the Brussels Convention, Article I; Protocol No. 1 to the Lugano Convention, Article I.
147. See para. 5.5.3.4.
148. Case C-26/91 *Jakob Handte & Co GmbH* v. *Société Traitements Mécano-chimiques des Surfaces* [1993] ILPr 5, 22 (para. 15).
149. Case C-26/91 *Jakob Handte & Co GmbH* v. *Société Traitements Mécano-chimiques des Surfaces* [1993] ILPr 5.
150. Case 38/81 *Effer SpA* v. *Kantner* [1982] ECR 825. Hartley, (1982) 7 ELRev 235.
151. *Tesam Distribution Ltd* v. *Schuh Mode Team GmbH* [1990] ILPr 149.
152. Hirst J in *Barclays Bank Plc* v. *Glasgow City Council* [1993] QB 429, 440. (This case was decided under Article 5(1) of the Modified Convention.)
153. Briggs, (1988) 8 YBEL 269, 270.

5.5.3.2 The obligation in question

5.5.3.2.1 THE GENERAL RULE

5.5.3.2.1.1 The connecting factor which determines jurisdiction for the purposes of Article 5(1) is "the place of performance of the obligation in question". As regards the determination of "the obligation in question" the general rule laid down by the Court of Justice is that, for the purposes of Article 5(1), "the obligation to be taken into account is that which corresponds to the contractual right on which the plaintiff's action is based".[154] This is the obligation which the contract imposes on the defendant, the non-performance of which is relied upon by the plaintiff in support of his claim. Furthermore, Article 5(1) refers to the original obligation, not any subsidiary obligation which may arise on breach of the original obligation.[155]

5.5.3.2.1.2 According to the analysis of the Court of Justice the identification of the obligation in question depends, in many situations, on which party is plaintiff and which party is defendant. Consider, for example, the situation where A (an English company) delivers apples to B (an Italian company) and B, alleging that the subject matter of the contract was pears, refuses to accept the goods or to pay for them. If B sues A for damages for breach of contract the obligation which forms the basis of the proceedings is A's obligation to deliver goods in Italy; but if A sues B for recovery of the purchase price, the obligation on which the proceedings are based is B's obligation to pay for the goods. Although in each situation, for the purposes of Article 5(1), "the obligation in question" is different, in both cases the same fundamental issues are involved.

5.5.3.2.2 MULTIPLE OBLIGATIONS

5.5.3.2.2.1 In many cases proceedings arising out of a contractual dispute involve breaches of different obligations under the contract. What is the correct approach to the situation where, for example, the defendant is in breach of two obligations, one to be performed in England and the other to be performed in Belgium? There are three possibilities.

(i) Article 5(1) could be interpreted simply as allocating jurisdiction to the English courts for the first claim and to the Belgian courts for the second claim. According to this view, the only way in which the plaintiff could have both claims resolved by the same forum would be to bring proceedings in the Contracting State in which the defendant is domiciled.

(ii) Article 5(1) could be interpreted as allocating jurisdiction in relation to both claims to the courts for the place where the characteristic obligation under the contract is to be performed.

(iii) Article 5(1) could be interpreted as allocating jurisdiction in relation to both claims to the courts for the place where the principal obligation in dispute is to be performed.

Of course, there is no requirement that the same approach should be adopted in all cases. Indeed, the case law of the Court of Justice has applied different approaches in different situations.

154. Case 14/76 *Ets A de Bloos SPRL* v. *Société en commandite par actions Bouyer* [1976] ECR 1497, 1508 (para. 13).

155. See, for example, *Medway Packaging Ltd* v. *Meurer Maschinen GmbH* [1990] 2 Lloyd's Rep 112.

5.5.3.2.2.2 In *Shenavai* v. *Kreischer*[156] the Court of Justice took the opportunity to confirm the general rule that the obligation in question is the contractual obligation which forms the actual basis of the legal proceedings. However, in a passage which was not strictly necessary for the decision, the Court of Justice considered the problem posed by a dispute concerned with a number of obligations arising under the same contract and forming the basis of proceedings commenced by the plaintiff: "in such a case the court before which the matter is brought will, when determining whether it has jurisdiction, be guided by the maxim *accessorium sequitur principale*; in other words, where various obligations are at issue, it will be the principal obligation which will determine its jurisdiction".[157]

5.5.3.2.2.3 One must be careful not to read too much into this passage; the mere fact that one obligation is more important than another does not necessarily mean that the less important obligation is ancillary to the more important one. It is important to draw a distinction between (i) a contract which contains a number of independent obligations and (ii) a contract which contains a principal obligation and one or more ancillary obligations. In the first case, Article 5(1) allocates jurisdiction in respect of each independent obligation to the courts for the place where the particular obligation is to be performed; in the second situation Article 5(1) allocates jurisdiction—in relation to claims concerning both the principal obligation and the ancillary obligation or obligations—to the courts for the place where the principal obligation is to be performed.

5.5.3.2.2.4 In *Union Transport Plc* v. *Continental Lines SA*[158] it was alleged that as a result of an exchange of telexes the parties had concluded a contract for the charter of a vessel to be nominated by the defendant to load a cargo of telegraph poles in Florida for carriage to Bangladesh. The defendant, a Belgian company, argued that there was no contract. When the defendant failed to nominate a vessel the plaintiff started proceedings in England. On the assumption that the parties had concluded a contract the defendant was in breach of two obligations—to nominate and to provide a vessel. Since the second obligation was to be performed in Florida, the only basis on which the English court might have jurisdiction was that the obligation to nominate was to be performed in England. The defendant argued that, even though the obligation to nominate was to be performed in England, the court did not have jurisdiction under Article 5(1) since the obligation to provide a vessel was the primary obligation to which the obligation to nominate was ancillary.

5.5.3.2.2.5 Both the Court of Appeal and the House of Lords concluded, in the plaintiff's favour, that the obligation to nominate was the principal obligation. In deciding which obligation is principal and which one is ancillary a number of points should be considered.

(i) The precise terms of the contract are crucial. Had the vessel been named in the charter the failure to tender the vessel would have been the principal obligation.[159]

(ii) The time sequence does not determine which obligation is principal and which

156. Case 266/85 [1987] ECR 239. Allwood, (1988) 13 ELRev 60.
157. Case 266/85 [1987] ECR 239, 256 (para. 19).
158. [1991] 2 Lloyd's Rep 48 (CA); [1992] 1 WLR 15 (HL). Briggs, "The Brussels Convention Reaches the House of Lords" (1992) 108 LQR 186.
159. See Lord Goff, [1992] 1 WLR 15, 22.

obligation is ancillary; the first obligation breached by the defendant is not necessarily the principal obligation.

(iii) If the breach of the particular obligation does not, in itself, give rise to a complete cause of action that obligation is unlikely to be the principal obligation. In the Court of Appeal Lloyd LJ noted that "[t]he very fact that a complete cause of action could have been based on the failure to nominate a vessel without referring to the provision of a vessel goes a long way to show that the failure to nominate was the principal obligation".[160]

5.5.3.2.2.6 In *Royal Bank of Scotland* v. *Cassa di Risparmio delle Provincie Lombard*[161] the Court of Appeal considered the problems which may arise in a case where the plaintiff has more than one cause of action arising out of the same facts. Although, as a general rule, the plaintiff cannot abandon one cause of action simply to improve his position on jurisdiction, if a plaintiff, who has two related—but separate—causes of action, abandons one of them, he "may be able to rely on the localised status of the sole remainder to found jurisdiction for that one alone".[162]

5.5.3.3 Place of performance

5.5.3.3.1 Should the place of performance be determined by reference to the *lex fori*, the *lex causae* or an independent interpretation? In *Industrie Tessili Italiana Como* v. *Dunlop AG*[163] the Court of Justice held that the place of performance of the obligation in question is to be determined by the law which governs that obligation according to the conflicts rules of the court before which the matter is brought. If English jurisdiction is invoked under Article 5(1) and the place of performance is disputed, the court must, first, decide, by reference to English choice of law rules, which law is applicable to the contractual obligation in question and, then, determine the place of performance by reference to the applicable law (which may or may not be English law).

5.5.3.3.2 The significance of the applicable law to questions of jurisdiction may be considerable, especially where proceedings relate to a contractual obligation to pay. For example, in a situation where an English seller delivers goods to a German buyer, who refuses to pay for them, the question as to which court has jurisdiction in relation to the seller's action for the purchase price is likely to turn on the law governing the contract. Whereas under English law the debtor must, as a general rule, seek out the creditor at his place of business and pay him there,[164] under German law the general rule is that an obligation to pay is to be discharged at the debtor's place of business. Accordingly, if English law is the applicable law Article 5(1) makes provision for English jurisdiction; if German law governs, there is no basis on which proceedings against the German buyer may be brought in England.

5.5.3.3.3 As far as English law is concerned, determining the place of performance of an obligation to make payment is not always straightforward. There is, for example, the problem of ascertaining where an obligation to pay money to an international bank or other corporation with branches worldwide is to be performed. As a general

160. [1991] 2 Lloyd's Rep 48, 51.
161. *Financial Times*, 21 January 1992.
162. Mustill LJ. (Lexis transcript.)
163. Case 12/76 [1976] ECR 1473.
164. *Chitty on Contracts* (26th ed, 1989) pp. 968–969, para. 1530.

proposition, it is reasonable to suppose that if the place of payment is not stipulated, the creditor's principal place of business should be regarded as the place of performance. However, where an obligation to pay a sum of money (for example, under a guarantee) is intimately connected with a bank account which is held at a particular branch, the place of performance should be the location of the branch where the account is held.[165] It should also be noted that it is not an immutable rule of English law that, in the absence of any express provision in the contract, a debtor's obligation to pay is to be performed at the creditor's place of business. Specific types of contract contain special rules. For example, in a contract of reinsurance premiums are payable in cash at the insurer's principal place of business and claims are payable at the address of the reinsured, unless the contract provides expressly or by implication to the contrary[166]; in *Royal Bank of Scotland* v. *Cassa di Risparmio delle Provincie Lombard*[167] the Court of Appeal held, in the context of a dispute relating to letters of credit governed by the Uniform Customs and Practice for Documentary Credits, that the place of performance of the defendant's obligation to reimburse the plaintiff is where claims for reimbursement by the plaintiff were to be made, rather than where the plaintiff's principal place of business was located.

5.5.3.3.4 One issue which seems to arise quite frequently in practice involves the determination of the place of performance of an obligation to give notice (such as notice of termination of an agreement).[168] In English law it seems that, in the absence of an agreement to the contrary, an obligation to give notice is to be performed at the place of business of the party who is to be notified.[169]

5.5.3.4 Employment contracts

5.5.3.4.1 BACKGROUND[170]

5.5.3.4.1.1 The Brussels Convention of 1968 did not contain special jurisdiction rules for employment contracts, although rules designed to protect the weaker party in insurance and consumer contracts were agreed by the original Contracting States. The preliminary draft of the 1968 Convention had included special provisions concerned with employment contracts, but after prolonged consideration by the committee they were not inserted into the final text.[171] However, in its interpretation of Article 5(1) the Court of Justice treated employment contracts differently from other contracts. In *Ivenel* v. *Schwab*[172] the Court of Justice held that, in a case of claims based on different obligations arising under a contract of employment, the obligation to be taken into account for the purposes of Article 5(1) is the obligation which characterises the contract—namely, the employee's obligation to perform his duties under the contract. The effect of this ruling is that if an employee habitually works in a Contracting State the

165. *Bank of Scotland* v. *Seitz*, 1990 SLT 584.

166. Hunter, "Reinsurance Litigation and the Civil Jurisdiction and Judgments Act 1982" [1987] JBL 344, 347.

167. *Financial Times*, 21 January 1992.

168. See, for example, Case 14/76 *Ets A de Bloos SPRL* v. *Société en commandite par action Bouyer* [1976] ECR 1497.

169. *Medway Packaging Ltd* v. *Meurer Maschinen GmbH* [1990] 2 Lloyd's Rep 112.

170. Allwood, "Characteristic Performance and Labour Disputes under the Brussels Convention: Pandora's Box" (1987) 7 YBEL 131.

171. The reasons for their exclusion are to be found in the Jenard Report, OJ 1979 C59/24.

172. Case 133/81 [1982] ECR 1891.

courts for the place where the work is carried out have jurisdiction. More problematical is the situation where the employee habitually works in more than one Contracting State or in a number of non-contracting States. In *Mulox IBC Ltd* v. *Geels*[173] it was held that where an employee works in more than one Contracting State, the place of performance of the obligation in question is the place where, or from which, the employee mainly performs his obligations *vis-à-vis* his employer. In *Six Constructions Ltd* v. *Humbert*,[174] a case involving a contract under the terms of which the employee was employed to carry out work in a number of non-contracting States, the Court of Justice decided that:

> [W]hen the court finds that claims made before it are based on obligations arising from a contract of employment and that the employee's obligation to carry out the agreed work was and must be fulfilled outside the territory of the Contracting States, it has no choice but to conclude that the place provided for in Article 5(1) of the Convention cannot serve as a basis for attributing jurisdiction to a court within that territory and that Article 5(1) cannot therefore be applicable.[175]

5.5.3.4.1.2 During negotiation of the Lugano Convention the EFTA Member States requested that employment contracts should be the subject of separate provisions.[176] In the 1989 Accession Convention the opportunity was taken to amend Article 5(1) of the Brussels Convention. Both Conventions contain a special rule which determines jurisdiction in relation to "individual contracts of employment". Both Conventions effectively adopt the rule in *Ivenel* v. *Schwab*, while taking different approaches to the problems which arose in *Mulox IBC Ltd* v. *Geels* and *Six Constructions Ltd* v. *Humbert*.

5.5.3.4.2 THE SCOPE OF THE RULES RELATING TO INDIVIDUAL CONTRACTS OF EMPLOYMENT

Although it is reasonable to assume that the words "individual contracts of employment" are to be given an autonomous interpretation, until the matter is referred to the Court of Justice the precise scope of the employment contract rules will remain a matter for speculation. Nevertheless, a number of points are relevant in this context.

(i) It is clear that collective agreements between employers and workers' representatives are not individual contracts of employment for the purposes of the second part of Article 5(1).[177]
(ii) Similarly, a contract for work on a self-employed basis should not fall within the scope of the employment contract rules.
(iii) A contract of employment "presupposes a relationship of subordination of the employee to the employer".[178]
(iv) In *Shenavai* v. *Kreischer*,[179] a case decided under the original text of Article 5(1) of the Brussels Convention, the Court of Justice stated that the significant characteristics of contracts of employment are that "they create a lasting bond which brings the worker to some extent within the organisational framework of the business of the undertaking or employer, and they are linked to the place where the activities are pursued, which determines the application

173. Case C-125/92 [1993] ILPr 668.
174. Case 32/88 [1989] ECR 341. Briggs, (1989) 9 YBEL 323; Hartley, (1989) 14 ELRev 236.
175. Case 32/88 [1989] ECR 341, 364 (para. 19).
176. Jenard–Möller Report, OJ 1990 C189/72, para. 37.
177. Jenard–Möller Report, OJ 1990 C189/73, para. 42.
178. Jenard–Möller Report, OJ 1990 C189/73, para. 41.
179. Case 266/85 [1987] ECR 239.

of mandatory rules and collective agreements".[180]

(v) The special rules which apply to individual contracts of employment should not be applied by analogy to other types of contract which share some of the same characteristics. In *Mercury Publicity Ltd* v. *Wolfgang Loerke GmbH*[181] the Court of Appeal refused to apply the employment contract rules to a contract under the terms of which the plaintiff employed the defendant company as a commercial agent. The Court of Appeal rejected the idea that the special jurisdiction rules could be extended to a contract between two independent corporations.

5.5.3.4.3 THE LUGANO CONVENTION

5.5.3.4.3.1 Article 5(1) of the Lugano Convention provides that "in matters relating to individual contracts of employment" a person domiciled in a Contracting State may be sued in another Contracting State in the courts for the place "where the employee habitually carries out his work, or if the employee does not habitually carry out his work in any one country . . . the place of business through which he was engaged". Where the employee habitually works in a Contracting State, the effect of Article 5(1) is to endorse the decision of the Court of Justice in *Ivenel* v. *Schwab*: the employee may sue the employer in the courts for the place where the employee habitually carries out his work. However, the text of Article 5(1) of the Lugano Convention goes further than this, since if the employee is domiciled in Belgium, but habitually carries out his work in France, the employer may sue the employee in France.

5.5.3.4.3.2 Where the employee does not habitually work in one Contracting State, Article 5(1) of the Lugano Convention allows either the employer or employee to sue the other party in the courts for the place of business through which the employee was engaged. This solution is different from that produced by the case law of the Court of Justice under the original text of the Brussels Convention. The approach adopted by Article 5(1) of the Lugano Convention was suggested by Article 6 of the Rome Convention on the Law Applicable to Contractual Obligations which provides that, in relation to a contract of employment, if the parties have not chosen the applicable law and the employee does not habitually work in one particular country, the applicable law is normally the law of the country in which the place of business through which he was engaged is situated.[182] According to the Jenard–Möller Report, the term "place of business" is to be understood in a broad sense; in particular, it covers any entity such as a branch or an agency with no legal personality.[183]

5.5.3.4.4 THE BRUSSELS CONVENTION

The solution adopted by the 1989 Accession Convention "attempts to improve on that adopted by the Lugano Convention without departing from it too greatly".[184] As amended, Article 5(1) provides that "in matters relating to individual contracts of employment" a person domiciled in a Contracting State may be sued in another

180. Case 266/85 [1987] ECR 239, 255–256 (para. 16).
181. [1993] ILPr 142.
182. See para. 12.2.2.2.
183. OJ 1990 C189/73, para. 43.
184. Almeida Cruz–Desantes Real–Jenard Report, OJ 1990 C189/45, para. 23(c).

Contracting State in the courts for the place "where the employee habitually carries out his work, or if the employee does not habitually carry out his work in any one country, the employer may also be sued in the courts for the place where the business which engaged the employee was or is now situated". Where the employee habitually carries out his work in a single country, the position under the two Conventions is the same: either party may sue the other in the courts for the place where the employee works. However, where the employee does not habitually work in a single country, Article 5(1) of the Brussels Convention gives the employee the option of suing the employer in the courts for the place where the business which engaged the employee was or is now situated—rather than in the courts for the place where the employer is domiciled. The employer does not have this option, however, and must proceed against the employee in the courts of the Contracting State in which the defendant is domiciled.

5.5.3.5 Agreements on the place of performance: the relationship between Article 5(1) and Article 17

To be effective a jurisdiction agreement must satisfy the formal requirements of Article 17(1).[185] What is the position if parties to a contract expressly agree the place of performance of their obligations? If, for example, an Italian domiciliary expressly agrees to perform a contractual obligation in England, does the English court have jurisdiction in relation to proceedings affecting that obligation notwithstanding the fact that the agreement does not comply with the formal requirements of Article 17(1)? In *Zelger* v. *Salinitri*[186] the Court of Justice decided that if the place of performance of a contractual obligation has been specified by the parties in a clause which is valid according to the law applicable to the contract, the court for that place has jurisdiction in relation to disputes relating to that obligation under Article 5(1), irrespective of whether the formal conditions provided under Article 17(1) have been observed.

5.5.4 Jurisdiction in matters relating to tort

Article 5(3) provides that "in matters relating to tort, delict or quasi-delict" a person domiciled in a Contracting State may be sued in another Contracting State "in the courts for the place where the harmful event occurred".

5.5.4.1 Matters relating to tort, delict or quasi-delict

The Court of Justice has not been required to provide a positive definition of what constitutes matters relating to "tort, delict or quasi-delict". What emerges from the cases is that to fall within the scope of Article 5(3) the action must "seek to establish the liability of the defendant"[187] and that proceedings relating to an obligation which has been freely entered into by one party to another cannot fall within the scope of Article 5(3).[188] Although the question is not free from doubt,[189] it seems unlikely that Article 5(3) is to be regarded as a residual category which includes all claims seeking to establish

185. See para. 5.3.3.
186. Case 56/79 [1980] ECR 89. Hartley, (1981) 6 ELRev 61.
187. Case C-261/90 *Reichert* v. *Dresdner Bank (No. 2)* [1992] ILPr 404, 423 (para. 20).
188. Case 189/87 *Kalfelis* v. *Bankhaus Schröder, Münchmeyer, Hengst & Co* [1988] ECR 5565; Case C-26/91 *Jakob Handte & Co GmbH v. Société Traitements Mécano-chimiques des Surfaces* [1993] ILPr 5.
189. See para. 5.5.2.2.

liability which do not fall within Article 5(1). At the very least Article 5(3) is premised on the existence of two elements: "The first is that there must be 'wrongful' conduct and the second is that such conduct must have caused 'a harmful event'".[190] The use of the words "harmful event" in Article 5(3), while entirely appropriate for claims in tort, "seems most inappropriate for restitutionary claims".[191] A claim based on unjust enrichment does not fall within the scope of Article 5(3).

5.5.4.2 The place where the harmful event occurred

5.5.4.2.1 In a road accident case there can be little doubt as to where the harmful event occurs. If, as a result of the negligence of an English motorist, a person is injured in France the victim may bring proceedings against the driver either in England (Article 2) or in France (Article 5(3)). The road accident case is simple because the defendant's act and the plaintiff's damage occur in the same Contracting State. More difficult is the case where the defendant acts in one Contracting State and the plaintiff suffers injury in another. A somewhat fanciful, but nonetheless illuminating example is where the defendant, in France, shoots with a gun and injures the plaintiff, who is standing on the other side of the border in Germany. In such a case, where does the harmful event occur?

5.5.4.2.2 The answer given by the Court of Justice to this problem is that the harmful event occurs either where the act which gives rise to the damage was performed or where the damage occurred. In *Handelskwekerij GJ Bier BV* v. *Mines de Potasse d'Alsace SA*[192] the defendant, a French corporation, discharged effluent into the Rhine in France; the pollution flowed down-river and the plaintiff, a Dutch horticulturist, suffered loss as a result of the pollution of the water supply. The plaintiff invoked the jurisdiction of the Dutch courts, relying on Article 5(3). The defendant contested jurisdiction on the basis that the harmful event occurred in France rather than in the Netherlands. The Court of Justice decided that "the place of the event giving rise to the damage no less than the place where damage occurred can, depending on the case, constitute a significant connecting factor from the point of view of jurisdiction".[193] Accordingly, notwithstanding the fact that Article 5(3) refers to the "place" in the singular, the Court of Justice held that Article 5(3) must be interpreted as giving the plaintiff the option of proceeding "either at the place where the damage occurred or the place of the event giving rise to it".[194] So, in a case where A gives negligent advice to B in France and B relies on that advice to his detriment in England B may bring proceedings either in France (on the basis that France is the place of the event giving rise to the damage[195]) or in England (on the basis that England is the place where the damage occurred[196]).

5.5.4.2.3 The interpretation of Article 5(3) in the context of a libel action raises a particular problem since liability does not depend proof of damage. On the basis

190. Advocate-General Gulmann in Case C-261/90 *Reichert* v. *Dresdner Bank (No. 2)* [1992] ILPr 404, 415.
191. Hirst J in *Barclays Bank Plc* v. *Glasgow City Council* [1993] QB 429, 443.
192. Case 21/76 [1976] ECR 1735. Hartley, (1977) 2 ELRev 143.
193. Case 21/76 [1976] ECR 1735, 1746 (para. 15).
194. Case 21/76 [1976] ECR 1735, 1747 (para. 19).
195. *Gascoine* v. *Pyrah*, *The Times*, 26 November 1991.
196. *Minster Investments Ltd* v. *Hyundai Precision & Industry Co Ltd* [1988] 2 Lloyd's Rep 621. Hartley, (1988) 13 ELRev 217.

of the decision of the Court of Appeal in *Shevill* v. *Presse Alliance SA*[197] each defamatory statement is to be treated as a separate "harmful event" for the purposes of Article 5(3). So, if a defamatory statement is published in both England and France, the plaintiff may rely on Article 5(3) to sue the defendant in England as regards the publication in England and in France as regards the publication in France. There must be some doubt as to whether this interpretation will appeal to the Court of Justice.[198] It has been suggested that the Court of Justice will probably "regard all publications of the same statement as a single 'harmful event' and adopt some principle designed to locate that event in the country with which the tort is most closely connected".[199]

5.5.4.2.4 Although the Court of Justice seems to have taken a relatively liberal view of Article 5(3), it is important to remember that Article 5(3) is a derogation from Article 2 which must be interpreted restrictively. In *Dumez France SA* v. *Hessische Landesbank*[200] the plaintiff was a French company which owned two German subsidiaries. The plaintiff alleged that as a result of tortious acts by the defendant, a German bank, the German subsidiaries had become insolvent. The plaintiff claimed damages for the loss suffered as a consequence and started proceedings in France. The defendant contested the jurisdiction of the French courts on the basis that France was not "the place where the harmful event occurred". Although Germany was obviously the place where the event giving rise to the damage had occurred, the plaintiff's argument was that France was the place where the damage had occurred, since it was in France that the plaintiff suffered the loss. The Court of Justice thought that the fallacy of the plaintiff's argument was to equate the place where the damage occurred with the place where the injury was suffered. Although the plaintiff suffered loss in France—it was in France that the plaintiff's assets were located—the injury suffered by the plaintiff was only an indirect consequence of harm inflicted on the German subsidiaries; the damage occurred in Germany—where the defendant's action caused injury to the immediate victim. For the purposes of Article 5(3) the place where the damage occurs is "the place where the event giving rise to the damage, and entailing tortious, delictual or quasi-delictual liability, directly produced its harmful effects upon the person who is the immediate victim of the event".[201] So, where A (a French domiciliary) negligently kills B (the husband of C, a German domiciliary) in England, C may bring proceedings against A in France (on the basis of Article 2) or in England (on the basis of Article 5(3)), but not in Germany.

5.5.4.2.5 Despite the superficial attraction of the plaintiff's argument in *Dumez France SA* v. *Hessische Landesbank*, the Court of Justice could hardly have reached any other conclusion. Had the Court of Justice accepted the plaintiff's argument, the effect would have been to undermine Article 2 in the context of claims relating to economic loss by allowing the defendant to be sued in the home forum of the indirect victim of a tortious act.

197. [1992] 2 WLR 1.
198. The House of Lords has referred a number of questions to the Court of Justice. The docket number of the reference is C-68/93.
199. Hartley, (1992) 17 ELRev 274, 276.
200. Case 228/88 [1990] ECR I-49. Briggs, (1990) 10 YBEL 484; Hartley, (1991) 16 ELRev 71.
201. Case 228/88 [1990] ECR I-49, 80 (para. 20).

5.5.5 Branch, agency or other establishment[202]

Article 5(5) provides that "as regards a dispute arising out of the operations of a branch, agency or other establishment" a person domiciled in a Contracting State may be sued in another Contracting State "in the courts for the place in which the branch, agency or other establishment is situated". So, where a French company sets up a branch in England, those who deal with the company through the branch can sue in England in relation to any dispute which arises out of the operations of the branch. In many situations Article 5(5) overlaps with Article 5(1). Not surprisingly the Court of Justice has held that the concepts "operations" and "a branch, agency or other establishment" must be given autonomous interpretations.[203]

5.5.5.1 Branch, agency or other establishment

5.5.5.1.1 As regards the words "other establishment", the Court of Justice has decided that "[i]t is clear from both the object and wording of this provision that the spirit of the Convention requires that the concept of 'establishment'. . . shall be based on the same essential characteristics as a branch or agency".[204] A number of general criteria are relevant when considering the characteristics which a branch, agency or other establishment must display in order to fall within Article 5(5).

5.5.5.1.2 The Court of Justice has said that "one of the essential characteristics of the concepts of branch or agency is the fact of being subject to the direction and control of the parent body".[205] In *Blanckaert & Willems PVBA* v. *Trost*[206] it was held that the requirement of "direction and control" is not satisfied where the agent is an independent commercial agent who is free to arrange his own work, may represent several firms at the same time, and merely passes orders to the parent body, being involved neither in the terms of orders nor with their execution. The subsequent case law of the Court of Justice establishes that the requirement of direction and control is not of universal application. In *SAR Schotte GmbH* v. *Parfums Rothschild SARL*[207] the defendant was the French subsidiary of a German company. The plaintiff, a German company, sold goods to the defendant, having corresponded and negotiated with the German parent. When a dispute arose as to the quality of the products, the plaintiff started proceedings in Germany. The question facing the court was whether the German parent could be regarded as a "branch, agency or other establishment" of the French subsidiary. The Court of Justice laid particular emphasis on the impression given by the arrangement between parent and the subsidiary: "third parties doing business with the establishment which acts as an extension of another company must be able to

202. Fawcett, "Methods of Carrying on Business and Article 5(5) of the Brussels Convention" (1984) 9 ELRev 326; March Hunnings, "Agency and Jurisdiction in the EEC Conflict of Laws" [1982] JBL 244.
203. Case 33/78 *Somafer SA* v. *Saar-Ferngas AG* [1978] ECR 2183.
204. Case 14/76 *Ets A de Bloos SPRL* v. *Société en commandite par action Bouyer* [1976] ECR 1497, 1510 (para. 21).
205. Case 14/76 *Ets A de Bloos SPRL* v. *Société en commandite par action Bouyer* [1976] ECR 1497, 1510 (para. 20).
206. Case 139/80 [1981] ECR 819. Hartley, (1981) 6 ELRev 481.
207. Case 218/86 [1987] ECR 4905. Allwood, (1988) 13 ELRev 213.

rely on the appearance thus created and regard that establishment as an establishment of the other company even if, from the point of view of company law, the two companies are independent of each other".[208] Although the test of direction and control is a useful one, it yields to "the way in which these two undertakings behave in their business relations and present themselves *vis-à-vis* third parties in their commercial dealings".[209] This decision has been criticised on the ground that the doctrine of "appearance"—which finds no support in the Conventions or the accompanying Reports—is inherently vague.[210] For example, is the simple fact that one company appears to be acting on behalf of another sufficient or is it important that the companies have the same name—as was the case in *SAR Schotte GmbH* v. *Parfums Rothschild SARL* itself?

5.5.5.1.3 A branch, agency or other establishment must have "a place of business which has the appearance of permanency".[211]

5.5.5.1.4 A branch, agency or other establishment has "a management and is materially equipped to negotiate business with third parties so that the latter, although knowing that there will if necessary be a legal link with the parent body, the head office of which is abroad, do not have to deal directly with such parent body but may transact business at the place of business constituting the extension".[212]

5.5.5.2 Relations between a branch and the parent body

One of the issues surrounding Article 5(5) is whether, in a case where a dispute arises between an agent and the parent body, the agent may rely on Article 5(5) to bring proceedings against the parent body in the courts for the place where the agent is situated. Although this question has not been considered by the Court of Justice, in two references concerning the scope of Article 5(5) Advocate-General Reischl expressed the view that "Article 5(5) . . . has the sole purpose of facilitating legal proceedings for *third parties* who are involved with a subsidiary establishment in that they are not obliged to lodge their application where the parent company is situate. Thus it was solely for their benefit that jurisdiction was established in a place nearer to that in which the cause of action arose."[213] This analysis is clearly correct.[214] One of the fundamental objectives of the Conventions is to eliminate the categories of exorbitant jurisdiction based in particular on the plaintiff's domicile. Since there is no reason why Title II should contain a general basis of jurisdiction which enables an agent to sue the parent body in the agent's home forum, the scope of Article 5(5) should be limited to disputes in which third parties are involved.[215]

208. Case 218/86 [1987] ECR 4905, 4920 (para. 15).
209. Case 218/86 [1987] ECR 4905, 4920 (para. 16).
210. Schultsz, "Jurisdiction in Matters Relating to Tort and Delict" in Tebbens, Kennedy & Kohler (eds), *Civil Jurisdiction and Judgments in Europe* (1992) 99, 106–108.
211. Case 33/78 *Somafer SA* v. *Saar-Ferngas AG* [1978] ECR 2183, 2192 (para. 12).
212. Case 33/78 *Somafer SA* v. *Saar-Ferngas AG* [1978] ECR 2183, 2192 (para. 12).
213. Case 14/76 *Ets A de Bloos SPRL* v. *Société en commandite par action Bouyer* [1976] ECR 1497, 1519. (Emphasis in original.) See also Case 139/80 *Blanckaert & Willems PVBA* v. *Trost* [1981] ECR 819.
214. Hartley, (1977) 2 ELRev 57, 61.
215. McClellan, "The Convention of Brussels of September 27, 1968 on Jurisdiction and the Recognition and Enforcement of Judgments in Civil and Commercial Matters" (1978) 15 CMLRev 228, 237.

5.5.5.3 Operations

5.5.5.3.1 In *Somafer SA* v. *Saar-Ferngas AG*[216] the defendant, a French demolition company, was engaged to blow up a bunker in Germany. In Germany the defendant dealt with its customers through a representative. The plaintiff, a German enterprise, undertook safety measures to protect the gas supply in the vicinity of the demolition work and alleged that the defendant's German representative had agreed to reimburse the plaintiff for the cost of the safety precautions. The plaintiff brought proceedings against the defendant in Germany with a view to recovering its expenses. One of the questions was whether, for the purposes of Article 5(5), the dispute arose out of the "operations" of the representative.

5.5.5.3.2 The Court of Justice took the view that operations includes three things:

(i) "actions relating to rights and contractual or non-contractual obligations concerning the management properly so-called of the agency, branch or establishment itself such as those concerning the situation of the building where such entity is established or the local engagement of staff to work there";

(ii) actions relating to obligations which have been undertaken at the place of business of the entity in the name of the parent body and which must be performed in the Contracting State where the place of business is established;

(iii) "actions concerning non-contractual obligations arising from the activities in which the branch, agency or other establishment has engaged at the place in which it is established on behalf of the parent body".[217]

5.5.5.3.3 It has been suggested that this narrow definition excludes from the scope of Article 5(5) the situation where a manufacturer, domiciled in one Contracting State, uses a branch office to sell in another Contracting State goods which are defective, if the branch does no more than enter into the contract of sale on behalf of the parent; if, however, the branch office gives undertakings as to delivery of the goods and the action concerns delivery the dispute clearly arises out of the operations of the branch.[218]

5.5.6 Trusts

5.5.6.1 Article 5(6), which was added on the accession of the United Kingdom and Ireland to the Brussels Convention, provides that a person domiciled in a Contracting State may be sued in another Contracting State "as settlor, trustee or beneficiary of a trust created by the operation of a statute, or by a written instrument, or created orally and evidenced in writing, in the courts of the Contracting State in which the trust is domiciled".

5.5.6.2 The rule in paragraph (6) is based on the argument that trusts, even though they have no legal personality, may be said to have a geographical centre of operation.[219] For the purposes of English law the domicile of a trust is to be determined by section 45 of the Civil Jurisdiction and Judgments Act 1982, subsection (3) of which provides that a trust "is domiciled in a part of the United Kingdom only if the system of law of that part

216. Case 33/78 [1978] ECR 2183. Hartley, (1979) 4 ELRev 127.

217. Case 33/78 [1978] ECR 2183, 2192–2193 (para. 13).

218. Fawcett, "Methods of Carrying on Business and Article 5(5) of the Brussels Convention" (1984) 9 ELRev 326, 334.

219. Schlosser Report, OJ 1979 C59/106–107, para. 114(a).

is the system of law with which the trust has its closest and most real connection". It must be remembered that Article 5(6) provides an alternative forum to that directed by Article 2; a trustee who has gone to Corsica can also be sued in the courts there.[220] Furthermore, jurisdiction under Articles 2 and 5(6) can be ousted by the stipulation of an exclusive jurisdiction by the settlor in accordance with Article 17.[221]

5.5.6.3 Unlike the other paragraphs of Article 5, paragraph (6) allocates jurisdiction to the courts of a Contracting State rather than to the courts for a "place". Where the courts of the United Kingdom have jurisdiction by virtue of Article 5(6) the Modified Convention allocates jurisdiction between the various parts of the United Kingdom.[222]

5.6 ALTERNATIVE FORA II: ARTICLE 6

5.6.1 Introduction

5.6.1.1 The primary objective of the Conventions is not the harmonisation of jurisdiction rules for its own sake, but the free movement of judgments between the Contracting States. A simplified system for the recognition and enforcement of judgments depends, at least in part, on the avoidance of conflicting judgments. However, the direct jurisdiction rules contained in Title II often give the plaintiff a choice of fora in relation to a particular claim. Moreover, Article 5, as interpreted by the Court of Justice, creates situations in which courts of various Contracting States have jurisdiction over different claims arising out of one set of facts. Article 6 counteracts the jurisdiction rules contained in Title II which generate a multiplicity of proceedings in different Contracting States by enabling related actions to be heard together. Article 6 achieves this—rather paradoxically—by providing alternatives to the courts stipulated by Articles 2 and 5. Article 6A, which was added to the Brussels Convention by the 1978 Accession Convention, is considered in a subsequent chapter.[223]

5.6.1.2 Although in many respects Article 6 is similar in its purpose to RSC, Order 11, rule 1(1)(c),[224] its operation is very different. Whereas the assumption of jurisdiction under RSC, Order 11, rule 1(1) depends on England being the most appropriate forum, there is no element of discretion under Article 6, which "gives the plaintiff an unfettered right of choice".[225]

5.6.2 Multiple defendants

5.6.2.1 Article 6(1) provides that a person domiciled in a Contracting State may be sued "where he is one of a number of defendants in the courts for the place where any one of them is domiciled". The key questions concerning this provision were referred to the Court of Justice in *Kalfelis* v. *Bankhaus Schröder, Münchmeyer, Hengst & Co.*[226]

220. Schlosser Report, OJ 1979 C59/107, para. 118.
221. See para. 5.3.1.1.
222. See para. 7.2.3.1.1.
223. See para. 8.2.4.2.
224. See para. 6.3.3.3.
225. Hirst J in *Aiglon Ltd* v. *Gau Shan Co Ltd* [1993] 1 Lloyd's Rep 164, 174.
226. Case 189/87 [1988] ECR 5565. Briggs, (1988) 8 YBEL 272; Hartley, (1989) 14 ELRev 172.

(i) Should Article 6(1) be interpreted as meaning that there must be a connection between the actions against the various defendants?
(ii) If so, what sort of connection is required? The Jenard Report states merely that in order for Article 6(1) to be applicable "there must be a connection between the claims made against each of the defendants, as for example in the case of joint debtors".[227]

5.6.2.2 In considering the first question the Court of Justice noted that Article 6(1) constitutes an exception to the principle set out in Article 2, and therefore "[i]t follows that an exception of this kind must be treated in such a manner that there is no possibility of the very existence of that principle being called into question".[228] Accordingly, the Court of Justice had no hesitation in concluding that it is necessary for a connection to exist between the actions against each defendant.[229] Furthermore, it is necessary to determine the nature of the connection independently—rather than by reference to the *lex fori* or the *lex causae*.

5.6.2.3 As regards the second question the Court of Justice decided that for Article 6(1) to apply there must exist between various actions brought by the same plaintiff against different defendants "a connection of such a kind that it is expedient to determine those actions together in order to avoid the risk of irreconcilable judgments resulting from separate proceedings".[230] It should stressed that it does not follow from the fact that claims against two defendants arise out of the same set of facts that the claims should necessarily be heard together. The crucial question is whether there is a danger of irreconcilable judgments: "It is for the national court to verify in each individual case whether that condition is satisfied".[231]

5.6.2.4 In cases concerning multiple defendants, some of whom are domiciled in Contracting States and some of whom are not, the combined effect of Article 6(1) and RSC, Order 11, rule 1(1)(c) will often be to allow the plaintiff to proceed against all the defendants in England. Where, for example, D1 is domiciled in England, D2 is domiciled in New York and D3 is domiciled in Germany the plaintiff may obtain leave to serve D2 out of the jurisdiction under RSC, Order 11, rule 1(1) and D3 can be joined as a party to the English proceedings under Article 6(1). However, in a situation where D1 is domiciled in New York and D2 is domiciled in Germany, in order to proceed in England the plaintiff must have an independent basis of jurisdiction against D2. The fact that the English court is prepared to give leave to serve out as against D1 does not mean that D2 can be sued in England under Article 6(1).

5.6.3 Third party proceedings

5.6.3.1 Whereas Article 6(1) concerns the situation where the plaintiff wishes to proceed against two or more defendants, Article 6(2) deals with the situation where a defendant wishes, in the event of being found liable, to pass liability on to a third party. Third party proceedings provide an important procedural device for related

227. OJ 1979 C59/26.
228. Case 189/87 [1988] ECR 5565, 5583 (para. 8).
229. Case 189/87 [1988] ECR 5565, 5583 (para. 9).
230. Case 189/87 [1988] ECR 5565, 5584 (para. 13). The inspiration for the formula adopted by the Court of Justice is Article 22(3) which defines what is meant by "related actions". See para. 5.9.3.
231. Case 189/87 [1988] ECR 5565, 5584 (para. 13). See, for example, *Gascoine* v. *Pyrah* [1994] ILPr 82.

proceedings to be resolved together, thereby preventing separate proceedings being conducted in different countries. The rule in Title II which allows third parties to be joined to the original proceedings is Article 6(2), which provides that a person domiciled in a Contracting State may be sued "as a third party in an action on a warranty or guarantee or in any other third party proceedings, in the court seised of the original proceedings, unless these were instituted solely with the object of removing him from the jurisdiction of the court which would be competent in his case".[232]

5.6.3.2 The Jenard Report provides a clear example of the importance of this provision:

> A German exporter delivers goods to Belgium and the Belgian importer resells them. The purchaser sues the importer for damages in the court for the place of his domicile, for example in Brussels. The Belgian importer has a right of recourse against the German exporter and consequently brings an action for breach of warranty against that exporter in the court in Brussels, since it has jurisdiction over the original action.[233]

Whereas Article 6(1) applies only if one of the defendants is sued in the courts of his domicile there is no such limitation in Article 6(2). The purpose of Article 6 is to enable the entire dispute to be heard by a single court; it is not important, for example, whether jurisdiction over the first defendant is based on Article 2 or Article 5.[234] The wording of Article 6(2) does not appear to rule out the possibility of a third party who is domiciled in a Contracting State being joined to proceedings even where the first defendant is not domiciled in a Contracting State and the basis of jurisdiction in the original proceedings is an exorbitant one. However, this interpretation of Article 6(2) conflicts with the general framework of Title II; a more plausible interpretation is that Article 6(2) is limited to cases where jurisdiction in the original proceedings is derived from the jurisdictional code set out in Title II.

5.6.3.3 In *Kongress Agentur Hagen GmbH* v. *Zeehaghe BV*[235] the plaintiff, relying on Article 5(1), started proceedings in the Netherlands against the first defendant, a German company, claiming damages for breach of contract. The first defendant sought leave to join the second defendant, another German company, under Article 6(2). One of the questions which arose was whether the Dutch court was entitled to assess the admissibility of the application for leave in the light of the procedural rules of its national law (and to refuse to allow the second defendant to be joined, for example, on the ground that this would delay and complicate the proceedings). The Court of Justice drew a distinction between jurisdiction and procedure: "With regard to an action on a warranty or guarantee, Article 6(2) . . . merely determines which court has jurisdiction and is not concerned with conditions for admissibility properly so called."[236] However, although national courts will apply national procedural rules to the question of admissibility, "an application for leave to bring an action on a warranty or guarantee may not be refused expressly or by implication on the ground that the third parties sought to be joined reside or are domiciled in a Contracting State other than that of the court seised of the original proceedings".[237] Accordingly, Article 6(2) does not require

232. It is provided that Article 6(2) in actions on a warranty or guarantee or in any third party proceedings may not be resorted to in the Federal Republic of Germany: Protocol to the Brussels Convention, Article V. Third party proceedings against insurers are dealt with by Article 10.
233. OJ 1979 C/59/27.
234. Case C-365/88 *Kongress Agentur Hagen GmbH* v. *Zeehaghe BV* [1990] ECR I-1845.
235. Case C-365/88 [1990] ECR I-1845. Briggs, (1990) 10 YBEL 487; Hartley, (1991) 16 ELRev 73.
236. Case C-365/88 [1990] ECR I-1845, 1865 (para. 18).
237. Case C-365/88 [1990] ECR I-1845, 1866 (para. 21).

the national court to accede to the request for leave to bring third party proceedings; the court may apply the procedural rules of its national law in order to determine whether that action is admissible, provided that the effectiveness of the Convention is not impaired.

5.6.4 Counterclaims

As a general principle, a plaintiff who invokes the jurisdiction of a court cannot legitimately complain if the same court assumes jurisdiction over a counterclaim which arises out of the same facts. This principle forms part of the jurisdictional regime contained in Title II; Article 6(3) provides that a person domiciled in a Contracting State may be sued "on a counterclaim arising from the same contract or facts on which the original claim was based, in the court in which the original claim is pending". So, if A sues B in England, B may raise a counterclaim against A, even though A is not domiciled in England. The only condition for the application of Article 6(3) is that the counterclaim should arise from the contract or from the facts on which the original claim was based.

5.6.5 Contractual claims involving matters relating to rights in rem in immovable property

5.6.5.1 The fourth paragraph of Article 6 was drafted during the negotiations leading to the Lugano Convention and was added to the Brussels Convention by the 1989 Accession Convention. As regards proceedings which have as their object rights *in rem* in immovable property, Article 16(1) allocates exclusive jurisdiction to the courts of the Contracting State in which the property is situated.[238] Jurisdiction in matters relating to a contract is governed by Articles 2 and 5(1). This division of jurisdiction could lead to actions arising out of the same set of facts being heard in different courts. The Jenard–Möller Report draws attention to a situation where the division of jurisdiction between Article 16(1), on the one hand, and Articles 2 and 5, on the other, may be significant:

> When a person has a mortgage on immovable property the owner of that property is quite often also personally liable for the secured debt. Therefore it has been made possible in some States to combine an action concerning the personal liability of the owner with an action for the enforced sale of the immovable property. This presupposes of course that the court for the place where the immovable property is situated also has jurisdiction as to actions concerning the personal liability of the owner.[239]

5.6.5.2 Article 6(4) provides that a person domiciled in a Contracting State may be sued "in matters relating to a contract, if the action may be combined with an action against the same defendant in matters relating to rights *in rem* in immovable property, in the court of the Contracting State in which the property is situated". The effect of this provision is that an action concerning the personal liability of the owner of immovable property can be combined with an action for the enforced sale of the property in those States where such a combination of actions is possible.[240]

238. See para. 5.1.
239. OJ 1990 C189/74, para. 46.
240. Jenard–Möller Report, OJ 1990 C189/74, para. 46.

5.7 INSURANCE AND CONSUMER CONTRACTS: ARTICLES 7 TO 15

Title II contains detailed provisions dealing with jurisdiction in matters relating to insurance and to consumer contracts. Three general points should be made by way of introduction.

(i) The basic aim of Articles 7 to 15 is to protect the party who from the socio-economic point of view is weaker. In the context of insurance the weaker party may be the policy-holder, the insured or the beneficiary; in a consumer contract, the consumer is in a weaker position than the supplier. The effect of these provisions is that, regardless of whether he is the defendant or the plaintiff, the weaker party generally has the option of requiring the litigation to take place in his home forum.

(ii) The requirements for jurisdiction agreements in insurance and consumer contracts are very strict, with the consequence that only in limited circumstances may such agreements be enforced against the weaker party.

(iii) An insurer or supplier who has a branch, agency or other establishment in a Contracting State is deemed to be domiciled in that Contracting State as regards disputes arising out of the operations of the branch, agency or other establishment.

5.7.1 Insurance: Articles 7 to 12A

Article 7 provides that, in matters relating to insurance, jurisdiction is to be determined by Section 3 of Title II. Although, generally speaking, Section 3 applies independently of the rest of Title II, Article 7 also provides that the operation of Section 3 shall not prejudice Article 4 or Article 5(5). Furthermore, the special jurisdiction rules contained in Section 3 yield to Article 18 if the defendant voluntarily puts in an appearance to contest the plaintiff's claim on the merits.

The provisions of Title II do not define what is meant by "insurance" for the purposes of Section 3. The Schlosser Report takes the view that, since reinsurance contracts cannot be equated with insurance contracts, Articles 7 to 12A do not apply to reinsurance contracts.[241] However, in *Overseas Union Insurance Ltd* v. *New Hampshire Insurance Co*[242] the Court of Justice left open the question as to whether Section 3 applies to quota share reinsurance.

Even though Section 3 was intended to protect the small policy-holder against the more powerful insurer, the scope of Section 3 is not limited to cases in which it can be shown that the policy-holder is weak and in need of protection.[243] When the 1978 Accession Convention was being negotiated the United Kingdom attempted to have policy-holders who were commercially strong excluded from the protective ambit of Section 3. Although the insurance provisions were amended by the 1978 Accession Convention, the amendments were less extensive than the United Kingdom delegation might have liked. Section 3 goes considerably further than is necessary in order to achieve its intended goal.

241. OJ 1979 C59/117, para. 151.
242. Case C-351/89 [1991] ECR I-3317.
243. *New Hampshire Insurance Co* v. *Strabag Bau AG* [1992] 1 Lloyd's Rep 361.

5.7.1.1 Proceedings brought against insurers

The rules for determining jurisdiction over insurers who are domiciled in a Contracting State are set out in Articles 8 to 10. For the purposes of these rules an insurer "who is not domiciled in a Contracting State but has a branch, agency or other establishment in one of the Contracting States shall, in disputes arising out of the operations of the branch, agency or other establishment, be deemed to be domiciled in that State".[244] The effect of Articles 8 to 10 is to give the policy-holder a wide choice of fora in which to bring proceedings against the insurer.

5.7.1.1.1 ARTICLE 8

Article 8 provides that an insurer domiciled in a Contracting State may be sued:

1. in the courts of the State where he is domiciled, or
2. in another Contracting State, in the courts for the place where the policy-holder is domiciled, or
3. if he is a co-insurer, in the courts of a Contracting State in which proceedings are brought against the leading insurer.

For the purposes of paragraph 2 "policy-holder" should be taken to mean the party to the contract of insurance other than the insurer. Where the insured or the beneficiary is not the same person as the policy-holder, their place of domicile is not taken into consideration.[245] The domicile of the policy-holder which is relevant for the purposes of this provision is the domicile existing at the time when the proceedings are instituted.[246] The third paragraph of Article 8 reflects the same policy considerations as those behind Article 6(1).[247]

5.7.1.1.2 ARTICLE 9

Article 9 provides:

In respect of liability insurance or insurance of immovable property, the insurer may in addition be sued in the courts for the place where the harmful event occurred. The same applies if movable and immovable property are covered by the same insurance policy and both are adversely affected by the same contingency.

The effect of Article 9 is that if a cottage in the Lake District and its contents are insured on the same policy, the insurer can be sued in England in relation to a claim arising out of a fire which causes damage to both the cottage and the contents. Article 9 also applies if "the movables are covered by an endorsement to the policy covering the immovable property".[248]

5.7.1.1.3 ARTICLE 10

5.7.1.1.3.1 From a practical perspective, Article 10 is likely to be of greatest significance in road accident cases.[249] Article 10(1) provides that in respect of liability insurance "the

244. Article 8. This provision is implemented in the United Kingdom by section 44 of the Civil Jurisdiction and Judgments Act 1982.
245. Jenard Report, OJ 1979 C59/31.
246. Jenard Report, OJ 1979 C59/31.
247. See para. 5.6.2.
248. Jenard Report, OJ 1979 C59/32.
249. Jenard Report, OJ 1979 C59/32.

insurer may also, if the law of the court permits it, be joined in proceedings which the injured party has brought against the insured". So, where the victim of a road accident sues the driver in the courts of a Contracting State which would not have jurisdiction over the driver's insurer by virtue of Article 8, the effect of Article 10(1) is to permit the driver to join the insurer as third party, but only "if the court seised of the matter has jurisdiction in such a case under its own law".[250]

5.7.1.1.3.2 Article 10(2) goes on to say that the provisions of Articles 7, 8 and 9 "shall apply to actions brought by the injured party directly against the insurer, where such direct actions are permitted". The Jenard Report states that the phrase "where such direct actions are permitted" has been used "specifically to include the conflict of laws rules of the court seised of the matter",[251] and suggests that the "rules of conflict must be used to decide whether the law to be applied is the law of the place where the harmful event occurred, the law governing the contract of insurance or the *lex fori*".[252]

5.7.1.1.3.3 How is Article 10(2) to be applied in a situation where a plaintiff is injured in a road accident in Belgium as a result of the negligence of a driver who is insured with an English insurance company? Which law determines whether the plaintiff may bring a direct action against the insurer in England? It is submitted that the traditional English approach would be to regard this question as procedural rather than substantive, with the consequence that English law, as the *lex fori*, would determine the question. Under English law direct actions against insurers are allowed in limited circumstances.[253]

5.7.1.1.4 ARTICLE 5(5)

It should be remembered that the provisions concerned with matters relating to insurance are without prejudice to Article 5(5).[254] Accordingly, an insurer who is domiciled in a Contracting State may be sued in the courts of another Contracting State "as regards a dispute arising out of a branch, agency or other establishment, in the courts for the place in which the branch, agency or other establishment is situated".[255]

5.7.1.1.5 JURISDICTION AGREEMENTS

The jurisdiction rules set out in Articles 8 to 10 must be read in conjunction with the provisions relating to jurisdiction agreements. In various circumstances a jurisdiction agreement may authorise the bringing of proceedings against an insurer in a Contracting State which is not designated by Articles 8 to 10.

5.7.1.2 Proceedings brought against the policy-holder, the insured or a beneficiary

5.7.1.2.1 Where the defendant in proceedings concerning matters relating to insurance is not the insurer, the general principle is that the courts of the defendant's domicile have jurisdiction. Article 11(1) provides that "an insurer may bring proceedings only in

250. Jenard Report, OJ 1979 C59/32.
251. OJ 1979 C59/32.
252. OJ 1979 C59/32, n. 4.
253. See Third Parties (Rights Against Insurers) Act 1930 and Road Traffic Act 1988, s. 151.
254. Article 7.
255. See para. 5.5.5.

the courts of the Contracting State in which the defendant is domiciled, irrespective of whether he is the policy-holder, the insured or a beneficiary".

5.7.1.2.2 There are, however, exceptions to this general principle.

(i) It is expressly provided that Article 11(1) is without prejudice to Article 10(3) which states that where, in accordance with Article 10(2), an injured party brings a direct action against the insurer in the courts of a Contracting State "[i]f the law governing such direct actions provides that the policy-holder or the insured may be joined as a party to the action, the same court shall have jurisdiction over them". The Jenard Report justifies this exception to the general rule in the following terms: "In the interests of the proper administration of justice, it must be possible for the actions to be brought in the same court to prevent different courts from giving judgments which are irreconcilable. The procedure will in addition protect the insurer against fraud."[256]

(ii) Article 11(2) provides that the provisions of Section 3 "shall not affect the right to bring a counterclaim in the court in which, in accordance with this Section, the original claim is pending". If, for example, the policy-holder, in accordance with Articles 8 to 10, starts proceedings against the insurer in the courts of a Contracting State in which the policy-holder is not domiciled, the insurer may bring a counterclaim in those courts.

(iii) In limited circumstances, a jurisdiction agreement between the parties will enable proceedings to be brought against the policy-holder in a Contracting State in which the defendant is not domiciled.

5.7.1.3 Jurisdiction agreements

The general jurisdiction rules contained in Articles 8 to 11 must be read in conjunction with Articles 12 and 12A which deal with the validity of jurisdiction agreements in matters relating to insurance. Article 12 provides that the provisions of Section 3 may be departed from only by an agreement on jurisdiction which satisfies one of the conditions set out in paragraphs 1 to 5.

Before the five alternative conditions are considered, a few general points should be noted.

(i) The purpose of Article 12 is to prevent parties from limiting the choice offered to the policy-holder and to prevent the insurer from avoiding the restrictions imposed by Article 11.[257]

(ii) The Schlosser Report indicates that jurisdiction agreements in consumer contracts must, in so far as they are permitted at all, comply with the formal requirements of Article 17(1).[258] Since on this question there is no obvious reason why a distinction should be made between consumer contracts and matters relating to insurance, jurisdiction agreements under Article 12 should comply with the formal requirements of Article 17(1).

(iii) The jurisdiction agreement provisions were amended by the 1978 Accession Convention. The major purpose of the amendments was to uphold the validity

256. OJ 1979 C59/32.
257. Jenard Report, OJ 1979 C59/33.
258. OJ 1979 C59/120, para. 161a.

of exclusive jurisdiction clauses in certain types of insurance policy (such as policies of marine insurance) in which the policy-holder is unlikely to require the protection given by the provisions in Section 3 of Title II.

(iv) Whether a particular jurisdiction agreement is permitted by Article 12 depends on a number of factors, including whether it was concluded before or after the dispute arose, whether the jurisdiction clause is exclusive or non-exclusive, the domicile of the policy-holder and the nature of the risk involved.

5.7.1.3.1 PARAGRAPH 1

By virtue of Article 12(1), a jurisdiction clause "which is entered into after the dispute has arisen" is permissible: "After a dispute has arisen, that is to say as soon as the parties disagree on a specific point and legal proceedings are imminent or contemplated, the parties completely regain their freedom."[259] If the condition in paragraph 1 is satisfied, the clause will be upheld whether it is exclusive or non-exclusive.

5.7.1.3.2 PARAGRAPH 2

Article 12(2) refers to a jurisdiction agreement "which allows the policy-holder, the insured or a beneficiary to bring proceedings in courts other than those indicated in this Section". A jurisdiction clause in a contract of insurance which purports to confer exclusive jurisdiction on the courts of a single Contracting State is not valid under Article 12(2) (although it may be permissible under one of the other paragraphs of Article 12). The main purpose of Section 3 is to give the policy-holder a choice of fora in which to sue the insurer. A jurisdiction clause which gives the policy-holder more choice is perfectly valid; a clause which limits that choice is not compatible with the general aims of Title II.

5.7.1.3.3 PARAGRAPH 3

5.7.1.3.3.1 Article 10(1) provides that in an action brought by the injured party against the insured, the insured may join the insurer as a third party. The Jenard Report raises the problem of the situation where the insured and the insurer are domiciled in the same Contracting State: "For example, where an accident is caused in France by a German domiciled in Germany who is insured with a German company, should third party proceedings, which are recognised under French law, be possible even though the litigation concerns a contract of insurance between a German insured person and a German insurer? As it is subject to German law, should this contract not be litigated in a German court?"[260]

5.7.1.3.3.2 Article 12(3), which was inserted to deal with this situation, provides that the rules in Section 3 may be departed from by an agreement "which is concluded between a policy-holder and an insurer, both of whom are [at the time of the conclusion of the contract] domiciled [or habitually resident] in the same Contracting State, and which has the effect of conferring jurisdiction on the courts of that State even if the

259. Jenard Report, OJ 1979 C59/33.
260. OJ 1979 C59/32.

harmful event were to occur abroad, provided that such agreement is not contrary to the law of that State".[261]

Accordingly, in the example given by the Jenard Report, if the contract of insurance between the insurer and the insured contains an exclusive jurisdiction clause in favour of the German courts, the French courts have no jurisdiction over the insurer, notwithstanding the terms of Article 10(1).

5.7.1.3.4 PARAGRAPH 4

One of the general purposes of Title II is to provide jurisdictional safeguards for defendants who are domiciled in a Contracting State. Article 12 takes a less protective attitude towards parties who are not domiciled in a Contracting State. Paragraph (4) allows effect to be given to a jurisdiction agreement "which is concluded with a policy-holder who is not domiciled in a Contracting State, except in so far as the insurance is compulsory or relates to immovable property in a Contracting State".

5.7.1.3.5 PARAGRAPH 5

5.7.1.3.5.1 The final paragraph of Article 12 refers to a jurisdiction agreement "which relates to a contract of insurance in so far as it covers one or more of the risks set out in Article 12A".

In *Charman* v. *WOC Offshore BV* Hirst J decided that the phrase "in so far as" in Article 12(5) should be given a literal interpretation, so that a jurisdiction agreement is valid under Article 12(5) only to the extent that it relates to risks referred to in Article 12A.[262] As a result of this interpretation litigation arising out of a contract which covers some risks within the scope of Article 12A and other risks falling outside its scope might be split between two jurisdictions. It is, however, open to the parties in this type of situation to enter a second jurisdiction agreement after the dispute has arisen. Such an agreement is valid under Article 12(1), regardless of the nature of the risk.

5.7.1.3.5.2 The risks referred to in Article 12(5) are set out in Article 12A:

1. any loss or damage to:
   (a) sea-going ships, installations situated offshore or on the high seas, or aircraft, arising from perils which relate to their use for commercial purposes;
   (b) goods in transit other than passengers' baggage where the transit consists of or includes carriage by such ships or aircraft;
2. any liability, other than for bodily injury to passengers or loss of or damage to their baggage:
   (a) arising out of the use or operation of ships, installations or aircraft as referred to in (1)(a) above in so far as the law of the Contracting State in which such aircraft are registered does not prohibit agreements on jurisdiction regarding insurance of such risks;
   (b) for loss or damage caused by goods in transit as described in (1)(b) above;
3. any financial loss connected with the use or operation of ships, installations or aircraft as referred to in (1)(a) above, in particular, loss of freight or charter-hire;
4. any risk or interest connected with any of those referred to in (1) to (3) above.

261. Although the Jenard–Möller Report states that the Lugano Convention makes no amendments to Articles 7 to 12A (OJ 1990 C189/74, para. 48) the words in parentheses appear in the text of the Lugano Convention (OJ 1988 L319/12) but not in the Brussels Convention as amended by the 1989 Convention (OJ 1990 C189/6).

262. [1993] 1 Lloyd's Rep 378, 384. This issue was expressly left open by the Court of Appeal: [1993] 2 Lloyd's Rep 551.

5.7.1.3.5.3 Article 12(5) and Article 12A were added to the Brussels Convention by the 1978 Accession Convention in response to the United Kingdom's request for special rules for the insurance of large risks. Section 3 (as originally drafted) was focused on the problems posed by domestic insurance contracts in which there is a disparity in economic power between the policy-holder and the insurer. The concept of social protection underlying a restriction on the admissibility of provisions conferring jurisdiction in insurance matters was not thought to be justified in situations where the policy-holder is a powerful undertaking.[263] As a result of the amendments made by the 1978 Accession Convention agreements on jurisdiction are in principle given special treatment in marine insurance and some sectors of aviation insurance. Nevertheless, in certain circumstances the effect of Section 3 is to give protection to a policy-holder whose position is no weaker than that of the insurer. There are no special provisions in the case of risks relating to transport by land.

5.7.1.3.5.4 The Schlosser Report gives some guidance as to the scope of Article 12A.

(i) Article 12A(1)(a) applies only to hull insurance and not to liability insurance, and the term "sea-going ships" means all vessels intended to travel on the sea.[264]

(ii) Article 12A(1)(b) covers the value of goods destroyed or lost in transit, but not liability insurance for any loss or damage caused by those goods[265]; it is irrelevant during which section of the transport the circumstances causing liability occurred.[266]

(iii) An example of insurance against ancillary risks within Article 12A(4) would be shipowner's disbursements consisting of exceptional operation costs, eg harbour dues accruing while the ship remains disabled.[267] For the purposes of Article 12A(4) the words "connected with" are to be given a liberal or generous interpretation. Where a contract of insurance covers marine risks (within Article 12A(1) to (3)) and non-marine risks, the non-marine risks will fall within Article 12A as long as the extra risks or interests covered by paragraph (4) are not disproportionately large compared with those covered by paragraphs (1) to (3).[268] However, the tail must not be allowed to wag the dog; a contract relating to the insurance of land-based property will not fall within Article 12A simply by the inclusion of some trivial marine risk

(iv) There is uncertainty as to the scope of Article 12A(2)(a): "Whether these provisions also cover all liability arising in connection with the construction, modification and repair of a ship; whether therefore the provision includes all liability which the shipyard incurs towards third parties and which was caused by the ship; or whether the expression 'use or operation' has to be construed more narrowly as applying only to liability arising in the course of a trial voyage—all these are questions of interpretation which still await an answer".[269]

263. Schlosser Report, OJ 1979 C59/114, para. 140.
264. OJ 1979 C59/115, para. 141.
265. OJ 1979 C59/115, para. 142.
266. OJ 1979 C59/115, para. 145.
267. OJ 1979 C59/115–116, para. 147.
268. *Charman* v. *WOC Offshore BV* [1993] 2 Lloyd's Rep 551.
269. OJ 1979 C59/115, para. 144.

5.7.2 Consumer contracts: Articles 13 to 15

Section 4 of Title II contains the jurisdiction provisions which apply to certain consumer contracts. Like Section 3, Section 4 is largely independent from the rest of Title II; the jurisdiction rules which apply to contracts generally do not apply to consumer contracts within the scope of Section 4. However, Section 4 operates without prejudice to Articles 4 and 5(5) and it should be assumed that Section 4 can be overridden by Article 18 in cases where the defendant appears to contest the plaintiff's claim on the merits. In its basic aim, Section 4 is no different from Section 3; its purpose is to protect the weaker party, which—in the context of Section 4—is the consumer.

5.7.2.1 The scope of Section 4

Not all proceedings involving consumers fall within the scope of Section 4. For the consumer provisions to apply four conditions must be satisfied.[270]

5.7.2.1.1 The proceedings must concern a contract.

5.7.2.1.2 The first sentence of Article 13 provides that the contract must have been concluded by "a person for a purpose which can be regarded as being outside his trade or profession, hereinafter called 'the consumer'". The concept "consumer" must be given an independent interpretation.[271] The Court of Justice has been unwilling to extend the consumer provisions to persons for whom the protection provided by Section 4 is not required. In *Shearson Lehmann Hutton Inc* v. *TVB Treuhandgesellschaft für Vermögensverwaltung und Beteiligungen mbH*[272] a German national had instructed the defendant to carry out currency futures transactions on a commission basis. The original contracting party assigned his rights under the contract to the plaintiff, a German company, which brought proceedings against the defendant. The plaintiff was not a consumer, but sought to rely on the consumer provisions on the basis that the original contracting party had dealt with the defendant as a consumer. The Court of Justice held that Section 4 provides protection only to the extent that the consumer is personally involved in the proceedings as plaintiff or defendant.[273] A plaintiff who acts in the exercise of his trade or profession rather than in his private capacity is not a consumer for the purposes of Section 4 of Title II and, therefore, cannot invoke the special rules on jurisdiction laid down as regards consumer contracts.[274]

5.7.2.1.3 The contract must fall within one of the three categories set out in Article 13:

1. a contract for the sale of goods on instalment credit terms,[275] or
2. a contract for a loan repayable by instalments, or for any other form of credit, made to finance the sale of goods, or
3. any other contract for the supply of goods or a contract for the supply of services, and
   (a) in the State of the consumer's domicile the conclusion of the contract was preceded by a specific invitation addressed to him or by advertising, and
   (b) the consumer took in that State the steps necessary for the conclusion of the contract.

270. A number of the concepts which are used to fix the boundaries of Section 4 are derived from the provisions of the draft treaty which ultimately became Article 5 of the Rome Convention on the Law Applicable to Contractual Obligations. Article 5 of the Rome Convention is discussed at para. 12.1.

271. Case C-89/91 *Shearson Lehmann Hutton Inc* v. *TVB Treuhandgesellschaft für Vermögensverwaltung und Beteiligungen mbH* [1993] ILPr 199.

272. Case C-89/91 [1993] ILPr 199.

273. Case C-89/91 [1993] ILPr 199, 221 (para. 23).

274. Case C-89/91 [1993] ILPr 199, 221 (para. 22).

275. Article 13(1) covers hire purchase: Schlosser Report, OJ 1979 C59/118, para. 157.

5.7.2.1.4 The contract must not be a contract of transport.[276]

5.7.2.2 Proceedings brought against the consumer

Article 14(2) states:

Proceedings may be brought against a consumer by the other party to the contract only in the courts of the Contracting State in which the consumer is domiciled.

The relevant time for determining the consumer's domicile is when the proceedings are instituted, rather than when the contract was concluded.[277] It should also be noted that Article 14(3) makes it clear that the other party has "the right to bring a counterclaim in the court in which, in accordance with this Section, the original claim is pending". So, if the consumer sues the other party in the courts of that party's domicile, the latter may bring a counterclaim against the consumer, even though the consumer is not domiciled in that Contracting State.

5.7.2.3 Proceedings brought against the other party

5.7.2.3.1 The consumer is given a choice of fora in which to proceed against the other party. Article 14(1) provides:

A consumer may bring proceedings against the other party to a contract either in the courts of the Contracting State in which that party is domiciled or in the courts of the Contracting State in which he is himself domiciled.

5.7.2.3.2 The other party may be deemed, for certain purposes, to be domiciled in a Contracting State, even though for the purposes of Articles 2 to 4 he is not domiciled in a Contracting State. The second sentence of Article 13(2)—which corresponds to Article 8(2)—provides:

Where a consumer enters into a contract with a party who is not domiciled in a Contracting State but has a branch, agency or other establishment in one of the Contracting States, that party shall, in disputes arising out of the operations of the branch, agency or establishment, be deemed to be domiciled in that State.[278]

Article 13 provides that the consumer contract provisions are without prejudice to Article 4. Accordingly, if the other party is not domiciled in a Contracting State, and is not deemed to be so domiciled for the purposes of Article 13(2), Section 4 does not apply and jurisdiction must be determined by reference to traditional rules.

5.7.2.3.3 The effect of Article 14 is that a consumer may sue in the courts of his new domicile if he moves to another Contracting State after concluding the contract out of which an action subsequently arises. However, as the Schlosser Report indicates, this only becomes practical in the case of instalment sales and credit contracts: "For actions arising out of other consumer contracts . . . Section 4 will in virtually all cases cease to be applicable if the consumer transfers his domicile to another State after conclusion of the

276. Article 13(3).
277. Jenard Report, OJ 1979 C59/33.
278. This provision is implemented in the United Kingdom by section 44 of the Civil Jurisdiction and Judgments Act 1982.

contract. This is because the steps necessary for the conclusion of the contract will almost always not have been taken in the new State of domicile".[279]

5.7.2.3.4 The consumer contract provisions are expressed to be without prejudice to Article 5(5).[280] This means that a defendant who is domiciled in a Contracting State may be sued in the courts of another Contracting State "as regards a dispute arising out of a branch, agency or other establishment, in the courts for the place in which the branch, agency or other establishment is situated".[281]

5.7.2.4 Jurisdiction agreements

5.7.2.4.1 Article 15 deals with the validity of jurisdiction agreements in consumer contracts within the scope of Section 4. In its basic format and approach Article 15 is similar to Article 12, which is the equivalent provision in Section 3 of Title II. As regards formal requirements, the Schlosser Report notes that "the working party was unanimously of the opinion that agreements on jurisdiction must, in so far as they are permitted at all, comply with the formal requirements of Article 17. Since the form of such agreements is not governed by Section 4, it must be governed by Article 17."[282]

5.7.2.4.2 Article 15 provides:

The provisions of this Section may be departed from only by an agreement—

1. which is entered into after the dispute has arisen, or
2. which allows the consumer to bring proceedings in courts other than those indicated in this Section, or
3. which is entered into by the consumer and the other party to the contract, both of whom are at the time of conclusion of the contract domiciled or habitually resident in the same Contracting State, and which confers jurisdiction on the courts of that State, provided that such an agreement is not contrary to the law of that State.

The first two paragraphs have the same effect as the equivalent provisions of Article 12.[283] Article 15(3) is similar to Article 12(3), but its underlying rationale is different:

In actions brought by a seller or a lender, it is rather difficult to determine jurisdiction where the buyer or borrower establishes himself abroad after the contract has been concluded. To protect these persons, they should ideally be sued only in the courts of the State where they have established their new domicile. For reasons of equity the committee has however provided that where a seller and a buyer, or a lender and a borrower, are both domiciled or at least habitually resident in the same State when the contract is concluded, they may confer on the courts of that State jurisdiction over all disputes arising out of the contract, on condition that such agreements are not contrary to the law of that State.[284]

By employing domicile and habitual residence as alternative connecting factors, Article 15(3) has the effect that "a seller or a lender need not sue the defendant abroad in the courts of the State in which the defendant is domiciled, if, when the proceedings are instituted, the defendant is still resident in the State in which the contract was concluded".[285]

279. OJ 1979 C59/119, para. 161.
280. Article 13(1).
281. For a discussion of Article 5(5) see para. 5.5.5.
282. Schlosser Report, OJ 1979 C59/120, para. 161a.
283. See para. 5.7.1.3.
284. Jenard Report, OJ 1979 C59/33.
285. Jenard Report, OJ 1979 C59/34.

5.8 PROVISIONAL, INCLUDING PROTECTIVE, MEASURES[286]

5.8.1 Article 24 provides:

> Application may be made to the courts of a Contracting State for such provisional, including protective, measures as may be available under the law of that State, even if, under this Convention, the courts of another Contracting State have jurisdiction as to the substance of the matter.

Article 24 applies to "measures which, in matters coming within the ambit of the Convention, are intended to maintain a legal or factual situation in order to safeguard rights an application for the recognition of which has been made to the court with jurisdiction as to the substance of the matter".[287] The English Mareva injunction is one of the types of measure falling within the scope of Article 24.

5.8.2 Article 24 does not in itself confer jurisdiction on an English court to grant provisional measures in support of foreign proceedings; the effect of *Siskina (Owners of cargo lately laden on board)* v. *Distos Compania Naviera SA*[288] is to deprive the court of jurisdiction to grant interim relief except where the court is "properly seised of the substance of the claim".[289] Section 25 of the Civil Jurisdiction and Judgments Act 1982, however, provides that the High Court may grant interim relief in cases where the subject matter of the litigation falls within the scope of Article 1 of the Brussels Convention and the proceedings have been commenced or are to be commenced in a Brussels or Lugano Contracting State other than the United Kingdom, whether or not the defendant is otherwise amenable to the *in personam* jurisdiction of the court. Where, for example, proceedings have been commenced in France, the plaintiff may obtain in England a Mareva injunction freezing the defendant's assets, even though the court has no jurisdiction in relation to the plaintiff's substantive claim.[290] The power to grant interim relief in support of proceedings in another Contracting State is not dependent on the defendant's domicile in a Contracting State.[291]

5.9 LIS PENDENS AND RELATED ACTIONS: ARTICLES 21 TO 23

The primary aim of the Conventions is to achieve the simplification of the recognition and enforcement of judgments. The attainment of this goal depends, to a considerable extent, on reducing the situations in which the courts of different Contracting States may render conflicting judgments.[292] The jurisdiction rules contained in Article 6 are designed to facilitate the consolidation of related actions in a single forum. Of at least equal significance are the provisions in Section 8 of Title II which are "intended, in the interests of the proper administration of justice within the Community, to prevent parallel proceedings before the courts of different Contracting States and to avoid conflicts between decisions which might result therefrom".[293] Article 21 is concerned with proceedings in two or more Contracting States between the same parties and

286. For further discussion see para. 21.3.1.2.
287. Case C-261/90 *Reichert* v. *Dresdner Bank (No. 2)* [1992] ILPr 404, 426 (para. 34).
288. [1979] AC 210.
289. See Kerr LJ in *Babanaft International Co SA* v. *Bassatne* [1990] Ch 13, 30.
290. *Republic of Haiti* v. *Duvalier* [1990] 1 QB 202.
291. *X* v. *Y* [1990] 1 QB 220.
292. Case 144/86 *Gubisch Maschinenfabrik KG* v. *Palumbo* [1987] ECR 4861, 4874 (para. 8).
293. Case 144/86 *Gubisch Maschinenfabrik KG* v. *Palumbo* [1987] ECR 4861, 4874 (para. 8).

involving the same cause of action; Article 22 deals with situations where related actions are pending in the courts of different Contracting States; Article 23 addresses the problem where a dispute falls within the exclusive jurisdiction of more than one Contracting State. Before the specific provisions of Section 8 are examined, a number of general points need to be considered.

5.9.1 General considerations

5.9.1.1 Section 8 and the scope of the Conventions

The provisions of Section 8 are limited to proceedings which fall within the material scope of the Conventions; Articles 21 to 23 should be regarded as applicable only in cases where the proceedings in both Contracting States fall within the scope of Article 1. Where, for example, A starts proceedings in Italy in breach of an arbitration agreement and B applies to the English court for the appointment of an arbitrator, on the assumption that the English court regards the arbitration agreement as valid, Articles 21 and 22 are inapplicable because the English proceedings fall outside the scope of the Brussels Convention.[294]

5.9.1.2 Parties not domiciled in a Contracting State

5.9.1.2.1 In *Overseas Union Insurance Ltd* v. *New Hampshire Insurance Co*[295] the plaintiff was a company incorporated in Singapore; the defendant was a company incorporated in New Hampshire, but with business in France. The dispute between the parties was whether the plaintiff was bound by a reinsurance contract. The defendant started proceedings against the plaintiff in France to enforce the contract; the plaintiff disputed the jurisdiction of the French court and started proceedings against the defendant in England with a view to obtaining a declaration that it was no longer bound by the contract; the defendant sought a stay of the English proceedings on the basis of Article 21 of the Brussels Convention. One of the questions facing the court was whether Article 21 applies in a situation where neither party is domiciled in a Contracting State.

The purpose of Article 21 "is best served if Article 21 of the Convention is interpreted as broadly as possible to enable it to be applied in principle . . . in all cases of proceedings pending before the courts of different Contracting States which are capable of leading to irreconcilable decisions".[296]

5.9.1.2.2 The Court of Justice noted that Article 21:

> makes no reference to the domicile of the parties to the proceedings. Moreover, Article 21 does not draw any distinction between the various heads of jurisdiction provided for in the Convention. In particular, it does not provide for any derogation to cover a case where, in accordance with the provisions of Article 4 of the Convention, a court of a Contracting State exercises its jurisdiction by virtue of the law of that State over a defendant who is not domiciled in a Contracting State.[297]

294. Audit, "Arbitration and the Brussels Convention" (1993) 9 Arb Int 1, 23. This matter was referred by the Court of Appeal in Case C-190/89 *Marc Rich & Co AG* v. *Societa Italiana Impianti PA* [1991] ECR I-3855, but was not addressed by the Court of Justice.

295. Case C-351/89 [1991] ECR I-3317. Briggs, (1991) 11 YBEL 521; Hartley, (1992) 17 ELRev 75.

296. Advocate-General Van Gerven in Case C-351/89 *Overseas Union Insurance Ltd* v. *New Hampshire Insurance Co* [1991] ECR I-3317, 3338 (para. 9).

297. [1991] ECR I-3317, 3348 (para. 13).

Article 21 must be applied regardless of the domicile of the parties and regardless of whether the jurisdiction of the courts is determined by Title II or is derived from the law of the Contracting State in question in accordance with Article 4. The principles formulated by the Court of Justice in relation to Article 21 apply equally to the other provisions of Section 8.

5.9.1.3 Section 8 and enforcement proceedings

In *Owens Bank Ltd* v. *Bracco*[298] the Court of Appeal decided, albeit *obiter*, that Articles 21 and 22 apply only to "proceedings which may lead to a judgment, ie original proceedings, and not to proceedings to enforce a judgment which has been obtained in original proceedings, such enforcement proceedings being expressly dealt with under Title III and expressly committed by Article 16(5) to the courts of the Contracting State in which the original judgment has been or is to be enforced".[299] It follows that if the plaintiff, having obtained a judgment against the defendant in France, starts enforcement proceedings in Italy and England, both the Italian and English courts have exclusive jurisdiction under Article 16(5), but Article 23 does not require the English court to decline jurisdiction. Article 23 applies only where the courts of different Contracting States have jurisdiction over the same dispute.[300] Although the decision of the Court of Appeal in *Owens Bank Ltd* v. *Bracco* was criticised,[301] the proposition that the provisions of Section 8 do not apply to enforcement proceedings gains support from the opinion of Advocate-General Lenz in the same case.[302]

5.9.1.4 The court first seised

5.9.1.4.1 A concept which is central to the operation of each of the provisions of Section 8 is "the court first seised". It is clear from the jurisprudence of the Court of Justice that the proper way of determining when a court is seised is to apply the procedural law of the forum in question. In *Zelger* v. *Salinitri (No. 2)*[303] the Court of Justice decided that the court first seised is "the one before which the requirements for proceedings to become definitively pending are first fulfilled, such requirements to be determined in accordance with the national law of each of the courts concerned".[304] So, if proceedings are commenced in England and France it is for English law to determine when the English court is seised and for French law to determine when the French court is seised.

5.9.1.4.2 As far as English law is concerned, it is now firmly established that, as a general rule, proceedings become definitively pending when the writ is served on the defendant. As regards an action *in rem* the court is not seised until the plaintiff has not only made his mind up as to which ship he will arrest, but also has served the writ upon the ship or arrested it.[305] It used to be thought that in an action *in personam* the court was

298. [1992] 2 AC 443 (CA and HL).
299. [1992] 2 AC 443, 455.
300. Advocate-General Lenz in Case C-129/92 *Owens Bank Ltd* v. *Bracco* [1994] 1 All ER 336, 367 (para. 65).
301. Briggs, "Foreign Judgments, Fraud and the Brussels Convention" (1991) 107 LQR 531.
302. Case C-129/92 *Owens Bank Ltd* v. *Bracco* [1994] 1 All ER 336, 367 (para. 65).
303. Case 129/83 [1984] ECR 2397. Hartley, (1985) 10 ELRev 56.
304. Case 129/83 [1984] ECR 2397, 2408 (para. 16).
305. *The Freccia del Nord* [1989] 1 Lloyd's Rep 388.

seised when the writ was issued, rather than when the writ was served. The Schlosser Report notes that in England "proceedings become pending as soon as the originating document has been issued".[306] There is no suggestion in the Report that this rule is incompatible with the operation of the Brussels Convention and in *Klöckner & Co* v. *Gatoil Overseas Inc* Hirst J decided that "the critical moment when an action has been brought in this country, and therefore becomes pending, is the moment of the issue of the writ".[307]

5.9.1.4.3 The Court of Appeal, however, rejected this analysis in *Dresser UK Ltd* v. *Falcongate Freight Management Ltd.*[308] Bingham LJ thought that "procedural idiosyncrasy is not (like national costume or regional cuisine) to be nurtured for its own sake and in answering the question before us we must have regard to the realities of litigation in this country and the purpose of the Convention, not to tradition, nomenclature or rules developed for other purposes".[309] Taking as its starting-point the principle that national courts should interpret conventions in accordance with the international purpose which they are intended to achieve, the Court of Appeal decided that it is "artificial, far-fetched and wrong to hold that the English court is seised of proceedings, or that proceedings are decisively, conclusively, finally or definitely pending before it, upon mere issue of proceedings".[310] Whether service is to be effected in England or abroad under RSC, Order 11, rule 1,[311] in the ordinary, straightforward case, service of proceedings is the moment at which the English court becomes seised.[312] It should be noted, however, that this is not an invariable rule; the court is seised if, prior to service of the writ, there is an actual exercise of jurisdiction (for example, where the court makes an interlocutory order, such as a Mareva injunction or an Anton Piller order, or orders the arrest of a vessel in the context of proceedings *in rem*).[313]

5.9.2 *Lis pendens*: Article 21

Article 21 provides:

> Where proceedings involving the same cause of action and between the same parties are brought in the courts of different Contracting States, any court other than the court first seised shall of its own motion stay its proceedings until such time as the jurisdiction of the court first seised is established.
>
> Where the jurisdiction of the court first seised is established, any court other than the court first seised shall decline jurisdiction in favour of that court.

5.9.2.1 The same cause of action

5.9.2.1.1 Although the English and German versions of Article 21 refer to the "same cause of action", the duty to stay or dismiss proceedings under Article 21 does not arise

306. OJ 1979 C59/125, para. 182.
307. [1990] 1 Lloyd's Rep 177, 204.
308. [1992] 1 QB 502. Briggs, "Get Your Writs Out?" [1992] LMCLQ 150; Hogan, (1992) 17 ELRev 555. Although the decision of the Court of Appeal was concerned with the meaning of the words "first seised" in the context of Article 22, the same interpretation should be applied in Article 21.
309. [1992] 1 QB 502, 522.
310. Bingham LJ, [1992] 1 QB 502, 523.
311. Sheen J in *The Sargasso* [1993] 1 Lloyd's Rep 424, 427.
312. See, for example, *Assurances Générales de France* v. *Chiyoda Fire and Marine Co (UK) Ltd* [1992] 1 Lloyd's Rep 325; *Polly Peck International Ltd* v. *Citibank NA, The Times*, 20 October 1993.
313. Bingham LJ in *Dresser UK Ltd* v. *Falcongate Freight Management Ltd* [1992] 1 QB 502, 522.

unless the proceedings involve "the same cause of action" and "the same subject matter". This interpretation results from the fact that other language versions of Article 21 draw a distinction between the cause of action and the subject matter of the proceedings.[314]

5.9.2.1.2 *Gubisch Maschinenfabrik KG* v. *Palumbo*[315] concerned a dispute relating to the validity of a contract for the sale of goods. The German "seller" started proceedings in Germany against an Italian "buyer" to enforce the terms of the disputed contract. When the "buyer" started proceedings in Rome with a view to obtaining a declaration that the alleged contract was not binding on him the "seller" contested the jurisdiction of the Italian courts on the basis of Article 21. The main question facing the court was whether the German and Italian proceedings could be said to have the same cause of action and the same subject matter "when the first seeks to enforce the contract and the second seeks its rescission or discharge"[316] or whether the two sets of proceedings merely involved related actions.

5.9.2.1.3 Advocate-General Mancini thought that the two sets of proceedings did not involve either the same subject matter or the same cause of action since the Italian action was "for a *declaration* that a contract of sale is *inoperative* because the offer was revoked, whilst the action before the German court assumes the validity of the contract and seeks to *obtain judgment* for the amount of the price".[317] According to the Advocate-General Article 21 should be interpreted strictly since "the broad interpretation according to which the provision should also be applicable in the case of actions which are different, although based on the same legal circumstances, ultimately confuses matters which the Convention was designed to keep apart, namely related actions and *lis pendens*".[318] The Court of Justice did not agree with the Advocate-General's analysis and decided, first, that the German and Italian proceedings involved the same cause of action, because the proceedings arose out of the same contractual relationship, and, secondly, that they involved the same subject matter, since the question whether the contract was binding between the parties lay at the heart of the two actions.[319]

5.9.2.1.4 The scope of Article 21 is not limited to claims which are entirely identical.[320] It follows that parallel proceedings *in personam* and *in rem* in different Contracting States may be regarded as involving the same cause of action and the same subject matter. Although there are differences in character between an action *in rem* and an action *in personam* there are no differences between the essential elements of the cause of action in the two types of proceedings. Whether an action is brought *in personam* or *in rem* the underlying complaint is the same and the essential facts which the plaintiff must establish to support his right to the judgment of the court are the same.[321] (This still leaves the question of whether the parties to the two actions are the same.[322])

5.9.2.1.5 The logic of the decision in *Gubisch Maschinenfabrik KG* v. *Palumbo* is

314. Case 144/86 *Gubisch Maschinenfabrik KG* v. *Palumbo* [1987] ECR 4861, 4875 (para. 14).
315. Case 144/86 [1987] ECR 4861. Hartley, (1988) 13 ELRev 216.
316. Case 144/86 [1987] ECR 4861, 4875 (para. 15).
317. Case 144/86 [1987] ECR 4861, 4869 (para. 4). (Emphasis in original.)
318. Case 144/86 [1987] ECR 4861, 4869 (para. 3).
319. Case 144/86 [1987] ECR 4861, 4876 (para. 16).
320. Case 144/86 [1987] ECR 4861, 4876 (para. 17).
321. *The Deichland* [1990] 1 QB 361; *The Kherson* [1992] 2 Lloyd's Rep 261.
322. See para. 5.9.2.2.

perhaps rather surprising; if proceedings for a negative declaration are started first this will have the effect of paralysing any subsequent action in another forum. In *The Maciej Rataj*[323] a dispute arose concerning a cargo of soya bean oil; the shipowners started proceedings in the Netherlands with a view to obtaining a declaration to the effect that the cargo owners were not entitled to the remedy of damages against them; subsequently, the cargo owners claimed damages in proceedings brought against the shipowners in England. One of the bases on which the shipowners contested the jurisdiction of the English court was Article 21. At first instance, Sheen J decided that in the Dutch proceedings the defendant did not have a cause of action against the cargo owners at all and refused to decline jurisdiction.[324] The Court of Appeal, however, decided—on the basis of the decision of the Court of Justice in *Gubisch Maschinenfabrik KG* v. *Palumbo*—that Article 21 was applicable, since both sets of proceedings involved the same contractual relationship. Nevertheless, the Court of Appeal thought that it was appropriate to refer a number of questions to the Court of Justice.[325]

5.9.2.1.6 Claims for negative declarations of the type which arose in this case are "a novel type of pre-emptive forum shopping with novel implications".[326] A simple rule which requires all courts other than the court first seised to decline jurisdiction is not a very satisfactory way of dealing with the problems posed by proceedings for a negative declaration, since in a case such as *The Maciej Rataj* it leads to the result that the natural forum for the trial of the action is displaced in favour of the forum in which the negative declaration is sought, even if the proceedings for a negative declaration are not brought *bona fide*. There are, therefore, some advantages to the analysis proposed by Advocate-General Mancini in *Gubisch Maschinenfabrik KG* v. *Palumbo*; if parallel proceedings are regarded as being related—rather than concerned with the same cause of action and the same subject matter—the court which is not the first seised has a discretion under Article 22 whether or not to stay the proceedings instead of being required to do so by Article 21. Of course, the disadvantage of the Advocate-General's approach is that it increases the risks of irreconcilable judgments.

5.9.2.2 The same parties

5.9.2.2.1 There is little authority on how the words "the same parties" should be interpreted. In *The Maciej Rataj* Neill LJ suggested that in multiparty cases there are three possible interpretations: "(1) it could mean a situation where there is an exact correspondence of the parties; (2) it could mean a situation where at least one party is common to both actions; or (3) it could mean a situation where the parties in the two actions are *substantially* the same".[327] None of these approaches is entirely satisfactory, however. The proper approach in multiparty proceedings is to break down the litigation into the various pairs of plaintiffs and defendants and apply Articles 21 and 22 accordingly.[328] So, in a situation where disputes arise out of a joint venture agreement

323. [1992] 2 Lloyd's Rep 552. Carter, (1991) 62 BYIL 455; Collins, "Negative Declarations and the Brussels Convention" (1992) 108 LQR 545.
324. [1991] 2 Lloyd's Rep 458, 463.
325. The docket number of the reference is C-406/92.
326. Kerr LJ in *The Volvox Hollandia* [1988] 2 Lloyd's Rep 361, 364.
327. [1992] 2 Lloyd's Rep 552, 560. (Emphasis in original.)
328. See, for example, *Assurances Générales de France* v. *Chiyoda Fire and Marine Co (UK) Ltd* [1992] 1 Lloyd's Rep 325.

involving four parties (A, B, C, and D), if A and B start proceedings against D in France, and C and D start proceedings against A and B in Germany, the German courts are required to apply Article 21 to the A-D and B-D litigation, but as far as the German courts are concerned the C-A and C-B proceedings are related proceedings falling within the scope of Article 22.

5.9.2.2.2 The application of Article 21 to parallel proceedings *in rem* and *in personam* in different Contracting States presents particular problems. Where, for example, the plaintiff commences an action *in personam* against the defendant in one Contracting State and then starts an action *in rem* by arresting a ship which is owned by the defendant (or in which the defendant has an interest) in another Contracting State are the parties to the two sets of proceedings the same? A technical approach to this question was favoured in *The Nordglimt*.[329] Hobhouse J noted that, in principle, the parties to an action *in rem* are the plaintiff and the vessel; accordingly, where an action *in personam* is brought abroad and an action *in rem* is brought in England, Article 21 cannot apply while the English action proceeds *in rem*. Even on the assumption that this analysis is correct, two points should be noted.

(i) The proceedings *in rem* and the proceedings *in personam* are "related actions" for the purposes of Article 22.[330]
(ii) Where the foreign proceedings are *in personam* and the English proceedings are commenced *in rem*, if the defendant shipowner acknowledges service of the writ in England, the action in England takes on a hybrid character; the action becomes *in personam* but does not lose its character of being an action *in rem*.[331] Where an English action takes on this hybrid character it would be reasonable to suppose that Article 21 becomes applicable.[332]

5.9.2.2.3 There is, however, an alternative approach to Article 21—which is suggested by the analysis of Article 2 by the Court of Appeal in *The Deichland*.[333] In this case the plaintiff commenced an action *in rem* in England by serving a writ on a vessel chartered by the defendant, who was domiciled in Germany. The question arose as to whether the English court had jurisdiction or whether Article 2 of the Brussels Convention obliged the plaintiff to bring proceedings in Germany. The Court of Appeal rejected the argument that while the action was solely *in rem* the defendant was not being sued and therefore Article 2 did not apply. Neill LJ thought that "looking at the reality of the matter it is [the defendant] who is interested in contesting liability and against whom the plaintiffs would wish to proceed *in personam* if an appearance is entered . . . In these circumstances I find it impossible to conclude that on the proper construction of Articles 2 and 3 of the 1968 Convention [the defendant] is not being 'sued' in these proceedings even though at this stage the proceedings are solely *in*

329. [1988] QB 183.
330. *The Nordglimt* [1988] 1 QB 183.
331. Neill LJ in *The Maciej Rataj* [1992] 2 Lloyd's Rep 552, 558. Although in *The Linda* [1988] 1 Lloyd's Rep 388 and *The Kherson* [1992] 2 Lloyd's Rep 261 Sheen J asserted that an action which is commenced *in rem* becomes an action *in personam* (and loses its *in rem* character entirely) if the owner (i) acknowledges service of the writ *in rem* and (ii) obtains release of the vessel by putting up security, the Court of Appeal has taken the view that the action does not lose its *in rem* character for all purposes: Neill LJ in *The Maciej Rataj* [1992] 2 Lloyd's Rep 552, 561.
332. *The Kherson* [1992] 2 Lloyd's Rep 261.
333. [1990] 1 QB 361.

rem".[334] This approach suggests that if the defendant is sued *in personam* in one Contracting State and is "sued" *in rem* in another Contracting State the two sets of proceedings involve the same parties for the purposes of Article 21. This interpretation would be consistent with the objective of preventing parallel proceedings in different Contracting States and avoiding conflicting judgments. The Court of Justice has stressed that the purpose of Article 21 is best served if it is interpreted broadly, since this reduces the risks of conflicting judgments.[335] If an action *in personam* is brought against a shipowner in one Contracting State and an action *in rem* is brought against the ship for the same claim in another Contracting State, it goes without saying that conflicting judgments could result.[336]

5.9.2.3 The relationship between the court first seised and the court second seised

5.9.2.3.1 THE GENERAL RULE

In *Overseas Union Insurance Ltd* v. *New Hampshire Insurance Co*[337] the Court of Justice was asked to answer the following question: in a case where Article 21 applies, is the court second seised restricted either to staying its proceedings or declining jurisdiction, or may the court second seised examine whether the court first seised has jurisdiction? The Court of Justice decided that the second court seised may not, as a general rule, investigate whether the foreign court assumed jurisdiction on a proper basis:

> [I]n no case is the court second seised in a better position than the court first seised to determine whether the latter has jurisdiction. Either the jurisdiction of the court first seised is determined directly by the rules of the Convention, which are common to both courts and may be interpreted and applied with the same authority by each of them, or it is derived, by virtue of Article 4 of the Convention, from the law of the State of the court first seised, in which case that court is undeniably better placed to rule on the question of its own jurisdiction.[338]

5.9.2.3.2 ARTICLE 21 AND JURISDICTION UNDER SECTIONS 3 TO 5

5.9.2.3.2.1 Where more than one Contracting State has exclusive jurisdiction under Article 16, any court other than the court first seised must decline jurisdiction under Article 23.[339] This provision requires the court second seised to consider the basis on which the court first seised assumed jurisdiction. What is the situation, however, where the English court has exclusive jurisdiction under Article 16, but before the English writ is served proceedings are commenced in another Contracting State which does not have exclusive jurisdiction under Title II?

5.9.2.3.2.2 The framework of the Conventions, if not the wording of Article 21 itself, supports the view that where the court second seised has exclusive jurisdiction and the court first seised does not, Article 21 should not apply so as to require the court with exclusive jurisdiction to stay its proceedings or decline jurisdiction. Although, as a general rule, where the recognition of a judgment given in one Contracting State is sought in another Contracting State the jurisdiction of the court of the State of origin

334. [1990] 1 QB 361, 374.
335. Case C-351/89 *Overseas Union Insurance Ltd* v. *New Hampshire Insurance Co* [1991] ECR I-3317, 3348 (para. 16).
336. Hartley, "The Effect of the 1968 Brussels Judgments Convention on Admiralty Actions in Rem" (1989) 105 LQR 640, 656.
337. Case C-351/89 [1991] ECR I-3317.
338. Case C-351/89 [1991] ECR I-3317, 3350 (para. 23).
339. For the text of Article 23 and a discussion of this provision see para. 5.9.4.

may not be reviewed,[340] Article 28(1) provides that a judgment given by the courts of a Contracting State shall be refused recognition if it conflicts with the jurisdiction rules contained in Sections 3 to 5 of Title II.[341] Where, for example, the court which is second seised has exclusive jurisdiction under Section 5 (Article 16) and the court first seised does not, it makes no sense for the court second seised to decline jurisdiction, since by virtue of Article 28(1) the judgment of the court first seised is not, in any event, entitled to recognition under Title III.[342] Since Article 28(1) provides also that recognition of a judgment may be refused on the basis that the court of the State of origin misapplied the jurisdiction provisions in Sections 3 and 4 of Title II, the foregoing analysis applies equally, *mutatis mutandis*, to cases concerning insurance and consumer contracts.

5.9.2.3.3 ARTICLE 21 AND JURISDICTION AGREEMENTS

5.9.2.3.3.1 *Klöckner & Co AG* v. *Gatoil Overseas Inc*[343] concerned parallel proceedings in Germany and England. It was alleged by the plaintiff that the contract in relation to which the dispute had arisen contained a clause conferring exclusive jurisdiction on the English courts. On the assumption that the German courts were the first seised, was the English court required to stay or dismiss the proceedings, notwithstanding the English jurisdiction clause? Hirst J accepted the argument that Articles 16 and 17 should be treated equally; since Article 16 provides an exception to Article 21, so should Article 17—with the consequence that where the parties have entered an English jurisdiction agreement, the English court does not have to stay the proceedings or decline jurisdiction, even if proceedings concerning the same cause of action are pending in the courts of another Contracting State.[344] In *Continental Bank NA* v. *Akakos Compania Naviera SA*[345] the Court of Appeal accepted the argument that Article 17 takes precedence over the provisions of Section 8 of Title II.

5.9.2.3.3.2 It is, however, erroneous to draw too close a parallel between Article 16 and Article 17. The justification for treating Article 16 as an exception to Article 21 is Article 28(1)—which provides that a judgment shall not be recognised if it conflicts with Sections 3, 4 or 5 of Title II. Whereas Article 16 is in Section 5 (Exclusive Jurisdiction), Article 17 is to be found in Section 6 (Prorogation of Jurisdiction); there is nothing in Title III which allows the courts of a Contracting State to refuse to recognise or enforce a judgment given by the courts of another Contracting State on the basis that, by virtue of Article 17, the court of the State of origin did not have jurisdiction.

5.9.2.3.3.3 In view of the fact that the Court of Justice has indicated that the purpose of Article 21 is to avoid, as far as possible, conflicting judgments[346] the better view is that Article 17 (unlike Article 16) does not provide an exception to Article 21. If it were otherwise it is possible that different courts would reach divergent conclusions about the effect of a jurisdiction clause. It is preferable in the interests of the administration of justice that only one court expresses a view on the point.[347]

340. Brussels Convention, Article 28(3); Lugano Convention, Article 28(4).
341. For further discussion of Article 28(1) see para. 9.4.3.2.
342. In *Overseas Union Insurance Ltd* v. *New Hampshire Insurance Co* the Court of Justice admitted of the possibility that there is an exception to Article 21 in cases where the court second seised has exclusive jurisdiction under Article 16: Case C-351/89 [1991] ECR I-3317, 3349 (para. 20).
343. [1990] 1 Lloyd's Rep 177.
344. See also *Rank Film Distributors Ltd* v. *Lanterna Editrice Srl* [1992] ILPr 58.
345. *The Times*, 26 November 1993.
346. Case C-351/89 *Overseas Union Insurance Ltd* v. *New Hampshire Insurance Co* [1991] ECR I-3317.
347. Briggs, (1991) 11 YBEL 521, 526–527.

5.9.2.3.4 THE RELATIONSHIP BETWEEN ARTICLE 21 AND ARTICLE 22

5.9.2.3.4.1 Multiparty litigation may generate problems surrounding the relationship between Article 21 and Article 22. The following example illustrates the nature of the problem. Disputes arise between A, B, C, and D out of a joint venture in which all four parties are involved: (i) A and B commence proceedings against C in England; (ii) C commences proceedings against D in Italy; (iii) D commences proceedings in England against C and B. If the Italian court stays the proceedings between C and D or declines jurisdiction under Article 22, the English court may assume jurisdiction over the proceedings brought by D against B and C. If, however, the Italian court does not stay the proceedings or decline jurisdiction, the main question, as regards Article 21, is this: in relation to D's action against C in England, must the English court stay or dismiss the proceedings under Article 21 in favour of the Italian courts on the basis that the proceedings are between the same parties and involve the same cause of action as the Italian proceedings?

5.9.2.3.4.2 The case law of the Court of Justice is of some assistance. In *Overseas Union Insurance Ltd* v. *New Hampshire Insurance Co* the Court of Justice stressed that "in no case is the court second seised in a better position than the court first seised to determine whether the latter has jurisdiction".[348] The decision to stay proceedings or decline jurisdiction under Article 22 is a discretionary one; it is not for the courts of one Contracting State to review the exercise of discretion by the courts of another Contracting State.[349] Accordingly, as regards the proceedings commenced by D against C in England, the English court must stay the proceedings or decline jurisdiction under Article 21. The fact that there is not complete identity between the parties to the litigation as a whole in England and Italy is not relevant; all that is required is that the particular actions in two jurisdictions are between the same parties and involve the same cause of action and the same subject matter.

5.9.2.3.5 THE RELATIONSHIP BETWEEN ARTICLE 21 AND ARTICLE 24

Article 24 provides that the courts of a Contracting State may grant provisional, including protective measures, even though the courts of another Contracting State have jurisdiction as to the substance of the matter. Article 24 was implemented in England by section 25 of the Civil Jurisdiction and Judgments Act 1982.[350] Article 21 does not in any way restrict the operation of Article 24. So, if the plaintiff commences proceedings against the defendant in France, the English court may, in support of those proceedings, grant a Mareva injunction freezing the defendant's assets and Article 21 is not applicable.[351]

5.9.3 Related proceedings: Article 22

5.9.3.1 Article 22 provides:

Where related actions are brought in the courts of different Contracting States, any court other than the court first seised may, while the actions are pending at first instance, stay its proceedings.

348. Case C-351/89 [1991] ECR I-3317, 3350 (para. 23).
349. *Assurances Générales de France* v. *Chiyoda Fire and Marine Co (UK) Ltd* [1992] 1 Lloyd's Rep 325.
350. See paras. 5.8 and 21.3.1.2.
351. *Republic of Haiti* v. *Duvalier* [1990] 1 QB 202; *X* v. *Y* [1990] 1 QB 220.

A court other than the court first seised may also, on the application of one of the parties, decline jurisdiction if the law of that court permits the consolidation of related actions and the court first seised has jurisdiction over both actions.

For the purposes of this Article, actions are deemed to be related where they are so closely connected that it is expedient to hear and determine them together to avoid the risk of irreconcilable judgments resulting from separate proceedings.

5.9.3.2 Article 22 deals with the problem where related actions are brought in the courts of different Contracting States. Its purpose is to confer a discretion on a court other than the court first seised to stay its proceedings or to decline jurisdiction. It should be stressed, however, that where the courts of a Contracting State have jurisdiction under Title II in relation to a particular action, the effect of Article 22 is not to confer jurisdiction as regards related actions. The specific provision which addresses the problems of multiple defendants is Article 6.[352] In *Elefanten Schuh GmbH* v. *Jacqmain* the Court of Justice made it clear that "Article 22 of the Convention is intended to establish how related actions which have been brought before courts of different Member States are to be dealt with. It does not confer jurisdiction; in particular, it does not accord jurisdiction to a court of a Contracting State to try an action which is related to another action of which that court is seised pursuant to the rules of the Convention".[353]

5.9.3.3 The literal wording of Article 22(2) indicates that jurisdiction may be declined if the court first seised has jurisdiction over both actions and the court second seised permits consolidation of the actions. Surely, Article 22(2) contains a drafting error; logically, it should refer to the consolidation of actions under the law of the court first seised.[354] Notwithstanding the literal wording it is to be hoped that this provision is interpreted as enabling the court second seised to decline jurisdiction in a situation where the court first seised allows the actions to be consolidated. Any other solution is hard to defend from the point of view of policy or principle.

5.9.3.4 Although Article 22(3) indicates the criterion which determines whether actions are related ("they are so closely connected that it is expedient to hear and determine them together to avoid the risk of irreconcilable judgments resulting from separate proceedings") Title II does not give any suggestion of the basis on which the discretion conferred by Article 22 should be exercised. Although there is no relevant case law from the Court of Justice, the Jenard Report states that where actions are related "the first duty of the court is to stay its proceedings".[355] It would seem, therefore, that where an application for a stay under Article 22 is made, a strong presumption lies in favour of the applicant.[356] Where, however, the risk of irreconcilable judgments is small, the court second seised may legitimately decline to stay the proceedings.[357] Furthermore, even in cases where there is a more serious risk of irreconcilable judgments, the English court may choose not to stay its proceedings under Article 22 if the parties have agreed to the exclusive jurisdiction of the English courts and one of the parties has started proceedings in another Contracting State in breach of the terms of

352. See para. 5.6.2.
353. Case 150/80 [1981] ECR 1671, 1687 (para. 19).
354. See Schockweiler, "Lis Alibi Pendens and Related Actions" in Tebbens, Kennedy & Kohler (eds), *Civil Jurisdiction and Judgments in Europe* (1992) 157, 160.
355. OJ 1979 C59/41.
356. Ognall J in *Virgin Aviation Services Ltd* v. *CAD Aviation Services* [1991] ILPr 79, 88.
357. *The Maciej Rataj* [1991] 2 Lloyd's Rep 458, reversed on other grounds [1992] 2 Lloyd's Rep 552.

the agreement.[358] Where the jurisdiction of the other Contracting State has been challenged, but not yet established, the English court is entitled to assume that the court first seised will reach the same conclusion on the question of the validity of the jurisdiction agreement. If, however, the court first seised, having decided that the jurisdiction agreement does not satisfy the requirements of Article 17(1), has assumed jurisdiction the English court should be prepared to grant a stay under Article 22.

5.9.3.5 The English courts have been troubled by the relationship between Article 22 and the doctrine of *forum non conveniens*.[359] (i) Are all the factors which an English court takes into account when considering whether to stay proceedings on the basis of *forum non conveniens* relevant when considering an application for a stay under Article 22? Although the High Court is divided on this issue,[360] there would appear to be no basis on which the traditional English approach to the staying of actions under the doctrine of *forum non conveniens* can be imported into Article 22.[361] (ii) If the proceedings fall within the scope of Article 1 and the court first seised is the court of a Contracting State, but a stay is not granted under Article 22, may the English court, nevertheless, stay the proceedings on the basis of *forum non conveniens*? Although section 49 of the Civil Jurisdiction and Judgments Act 1982 preserves the court's inherent jurisdiction to stay proceedings in circumstances in which to do so is not inconsistent with the Conventions, if there is a conflict of jurisdiction between two Contracting States the doctrine of *forum non conveniens* is inconsistent with the Conventions and is therefore inapplicable.[362]

5.9.4 Rival exclusive jurisdictions: Article 23

5.9.4.1 Article 23 provides:

> Where actions come within the exclusive jurisdiction of several courts, any court other than the court first seised shall decline jurisdiction in favour of that court.

The basic rule in Article 23 is the same as in Article 21: first come, first served. Although it is not likely that Article 23 will be frequently invoked, it is possible for the courts of more than one Contracting State to have exclusive jurisdiction under Article 16. For example, the courts of two Contracting States may have exclusive jurisdiction under Article 16(1) (where a dispute between two parties who are domiciled in Belgium arises in relation to a short term letting of immovable property situated in Italy) or under Article 16(2) (where a company's seat is in France under French law but is in Germany under German law).

5.9.4.2 Article 23 is applicable only where the rival courts have exclusive jurisdiction under Article 16. If the court first seised assumes jurisdiction under Article 17, but the second court has exclusive jurisdiction under Article 16, the court second seised should not be required to decline jurisdiction. It would make no sense for the court second seised to decline jurisdiction, since by virtue of Article 28(1) the judgment of the court first seised is not entitled to recognition under Title III in these circumstances.[363]

358. *IP Metal Ltd* v. *Ruote OZ SpA* [1993] 2 Lloyd's Rep 60.
359. For a discussion of *forum non conveniens* see para. 6.4.
360. Compare *Virgin Aviation Services Ltd* v. *CAD Aviation Services* [1991] ILPr 79 and *The Maciej Rataj* [1991] 2 Lloyd's Rep 458.
361. Schlosser Report, OJ 1979 C59/125, para. 181.
362. *Re Harrods (Buenos Aires) Ltd* [1992] Ch 72. See para. 5.10.
363. See para. 9.4.3.2.

5.10 DISCRETION TO STAY ENGLISH PROCEEDINGS

It is clear that the philosophy of the jurisdictional code contained in Title II is fundamentally different from that which lies behind traditional English jurisdiction rules. The provisions of Title II are, in the main, mechanical and formalistic, whereas the assumption of English jurisdiction in international cases has traditionally been based on open-textured rules which allow the judges considerable discretion.

Section 49 of the Civil Jurisdiction and Judgments Act 1982 provides:

> Nothing in this Act shall prevent any court in the United Kingdom from staying, . . . striking out or dismissing any proceedings before it, on the ground of *forum non conveniens* or otherwise, where to do so is not inconsistent with the 1968 Convention or, as the case may be, the Lugano Convention.

The question, therefore, arises: when, if at all, is it consistent with the Conventions to stay proceedings on a discretionary basis?

5.10.1 *Forum non conveniens*

5.10.1.1 The greatest area of controversy surrounds whether the court may stay proceedings on the basis of the doctrine of *forum non conveniens* in a case where the defendant is domiciled in England. One view is that, in these circumstances, the doctrine of *forum non conveniens* is generally incompatible with the Conventions.[364] (It is not, however, incompatible with the Modified Convention which allocates jurisdiction between the different parts of the United Kingdom.[365]) The rejection of the doctrine of *forum non conveniens* was favoured by the High Court in *S & W Berisford Plc* v. *New Hampshire Insurance Co*[366] and *Arkwright Mutual Insurance Co* v. *Bryanston Insurance Co Ltd.*[367] In the former case Hobhouse J succinctly stated the rationale for the exclusion of the doctrine of *forum non conveniens* in cases where the English court has jurisdiction over the defendant under Article 2:

> It is clear that the Convention is designed (subject to Article 4) to achieve uniformity and to "harmonise" the relevant procedural and jurisdictional rules of the courts of the Contracting States. The Convention leaves no room for the application of any discretionary jurisdiction by the courts of this country; the availability of such a discretion would destroy the framework of the Convention and create lack of uniformity in the interpretation and implementation of the Convention.[368]

5.10.1.2 It has been suggested, however, that "[t]o argue that the power of the English court to stay on grounds of *forum non conveniens* should be limited by the Convention even in cases in which there is no Community interest in protecting the plaintiff is surely going too far".[369] The view that the doctrine of *forum non conveniens* is not necessarily incompatible with the Conventions was accepted by the Court

364. Cheshire & North, *Private International Law* (12th ed, 1992) pp. 331–334.
365. See para. 7.3.
366. [1990] 2 QB 631.
367. [1990] 2 QB 649. Briggs, "Spiliada and the Brussels Convention" [1991] LMCLQ 10; Collins, "Forum Non Conveniens and the Brussels Convention" (1990) 106 LQR 535.
368. [1990] 2 QB 631, 645.
369. Hartley, (1992) 17 ELRev 553, 555. See also Kaye, *Civil Jurisdiction and Enforcement of Foreign Judgments* (1987) pp. 1244–1245; Collins, "Forum Non Conveniens and the Brussels Convention" (1990) 106 LQR 535.

of Appeal in *Re Harrods (Buenos Aires) Ltd.*[370] While it is clear that it is inconsistent with the Conventions to apply the doctrine of *forum non conveniens* in any case where the conflict is between the jurisdiction of the English court and the jurisdiction of the courts of another Contracting State,[371] the Court of Appeal held that if the conflict is between the English court and the courts of a non-contracting State the English court retains its inherent jurisdiction to stay the proceedings.[372]

5.10.1.3 In *Re Harrods (Buenos Aires) Ltd* the defendant, a company which was incorporated in England, conducted its business exclusively in Argentina. Since 1979 the company's only shareholders were two Swiss companies. The minority shareholder started proceedings in England by the presentation of a petition under the Companies Act 1985; the defendant applied for a stay of proceedings on the basis of *forum non conveniens*—notwithstanding the fact that the court had jurisdiction by virtue of the company's domicile in England.

5.10.1.4 In concluding that the Brussels Convention does not restrict the power of the court to stay proceedings on the basis of *forum non conveniens* in cases where the conflict of jurisdiction is between England and a non-contracting State, the Court of Appeal laid particular emphasis on the fact that Title II is intended to regulate jurisdiction as between the Contracting States. Dillon LJ said:

> For the English court to refuse jurisdiction, in a case against a person domiciled in England, on the ground that the court of some non-contracting State is the more appropriate court to decide the matters in issue does not in any way impair the object of the Convention of establishing an expeditious, harmonious, and, I would add, certain, procedure for securing the enforcement of judgments, since *ex hypothesi* if the English court refuses jurisdiction there will be no judgment of the English court to be enforced in the other Contracting States. Equally and for the same reason such a refusal of jurisdiction would not impair the object of the Convention that there should, subject to the very large exception of Article 4, be a uniform international jurisdiction for obtaining the judgments which are to be so enforced.[373]

5.10.1.5 How is the doctrine of *forum non conveniens* to be applied in cases where the English court has jurisdiction on the basis that the defendant is domiciled in England? *Re Harrods (Buenos Aires) Ltd* was a somewhat unusual case in the sense that the fact that the company was incorporated in England was "an anomalous historical survival".[374] As a general rule, a company which is domiciled in England has a substantial connection with England. It is not very common for a corporation to resist suit in its domiciliary forum and it is rare for the English court to refuse jurisdiction in such a case.[375] Furthermore, as Hobhouse J indicated in *S & W Berisford Plc* v. *New Hampshire Insurance Co* since "the Convention is, and is intended to be, a codified scheme to make provision for cases to be tried in appropriate fora, if . . . the Convention does leave room for a relevant discretion, there nevertheless must be some very weighty factor to displace the jurisdiction provided for by the Convention and considered by the Convention to be the appropriate jurisdiction".[376]

370. [1992] Ch 72. Briggs, "Forum Non Conveniens and the Brussels Convention Again" (1991) 107 LQR 180; Hartley, (1992) 17 ELRev 553; Kaye, "The EEC Judgments Convention and the Outer World: Goodbye to Forum Non Conveniens?" [1992] JBL 47. See also *The Po* [1991] 2 Lloyd's Rep 206.

371. *Aiglon Ltd* v. *Gau Shan Co Ltd* [1993] 1 Lloyd's Rep 164.

372. The case was appealed to the House of Lords which referred a number of questions to the Court of Justice. The docket number of the reference is C-314/92 (*sub nom Ladenimor SA* v. *Intercomfinanz SA*).

373. [1992] Ch 72, 97.

374. Bingham LJ, [1992] Ch 72, 125.

375. See Bingham LJ in *Banco Atlantico* v. *British Bank of the Middle East* [1990] 2 Lloyd's Rep 504, 510.

376. [1990] 2 QB 631, 645–646.

5.10.1.6 Indeed, *Re Harrods (Buenos Aires) Ltd* shows how difficult it may be to apply the doctrine of *forum non conveniens* in cases where the English court has jurisdiction under Article 2. At first instance, Harman J had thought it was "blindingly obvious" that England was the most appropriate forum.[377] The majority in the Court of Appeal thought that the judge had erred sufficiently to entitle the Court of Appeal to substitute its own decision. Dillon LJ, however, "could not say that the conclusion the judge reached, by whatever route, was as a conclusion obviously wrong", and therefore thought that the Court of Appeal could not interfere with the judge's exercise of discretion.[378]

5.10.1.7 It seems clear that the distinction made by the Court of Appeal between conflicts of jurisdiction between Contracting States, on the one hand, and conflicts of jurisdiction between a Contracting State and a non-contracting State is too simplistic. A mistake made by the Court of Appeal is to assume that the Conventions have only one purpose, namely, the reciprocal recognition and enforcement of judgments between the Contracting States. The Conventions have other objectives: for example, "[a] plaintiff must be sure which court has jurisdiction. He should not have to waste his time and money risking that the court concerned may consider itself less competent than another".[379]

5.10.1.8 If one of the objectives of the Conventions is to benefit plaintiffs from other Contracting States, it would follow that the doctrine of *forum non conveniens* should normally be excluded whenever the plaintiff is domiciled in a Contracting State and the ground of jurisdiction is one of those laid down in Title II.[380] So, if a Frenchman is injured by an Englishman in a car accident in Ontario and the victim proceeds against the tortfeasor in England, the defendant should not be able to plead that Ontario is the natural forum and that, as the courts of only Ontario and England are interested, the doctrine of *forum non conveniens* may be applied.[381]

5.10.1.9 In view of these problems, one might legitimately question whether there is any benefit—except of the most marginal kind—to be had from the application of the doctrine of *forum non conveniens* in cases where a plaintiff invokes the jurisdiction of the court of a Contracting State on one of the bases provided for by Title II. At the very least some qualification will have to be made to the broad principle formulated by the Court of Appeal in *Re Harrods (Buenos Aires) Ltd.*

5.10.2 Foreign jurisdiction clauses

5.10.2.1 The discretionary powers of the English courts are not limited to those conferred by the doctrine of *forum non conveniens*. At common law the court may stay proceedings in cases where the parties have agreed to refer their dispute to the jurisdiction of the courts of another country.[382]

5.10.2.2 Whereas the application of the doctrine of *forum non conveniens* in the situation which arose in *Re Harrods (Buenos Aires) Ltd* is relatively controversial, fewer uncertainties surround the exercise of the discretion to stay proceedings in cases where

377. [1992] Ch 72, 83.
378. [1992] Ch 72, 118.
379. Schlosser Report, OJ 1979 C59/97, para. 78.
380. Hartley, (1992) 17 ELRev 553, 555.
381. Briggs, "Forum Non Conveniens and the Brussels Convention Again" (1991) 107 LQR 180, 181.
382. *The Eleftheria* [1970] P 94; *The El Amria* [1981] 2 Lloyd's Rep 119.

the parties have agreed to the jurisdiction of a foreign court. Of course, if the subject matter of the proceedings falls within the scope of Article 1 and the parties have agreed to refer disputes to the courts of another Contracting State, the English court must decline jurisdiction if the agreement on jurisdiction satisfies the requirements of Article 17. Where, however, an action is brought in England in breach of a jurisdiction clause in favour of the courts of a non-contracting State, Article 17 has no application. The Schlosser Report makes it clear that, although Title II does not contain any rules as to the validity of an agreement to refer disputes to the courts of a non-contracting State, the court of a Contracting State which is applied to despite such an agreement has a right to decide on its validity (and hence whether to exercise jurisdiction under Title II) under its own conflicts rules.[383] It would appear that the Conventions do not preclude the court of a Contracting State from applying principles such as those stated in *The Eleftheria*[384] and *The El Amria*[385] where its jurisdiction is being sought to be excluded in favour of a non-contracting State,[386] regardless of whether the defendant is domiciled in a Contracting State.[387] So, where proceedings are brought against an English domiciliary in England, the defendant may apply for a stay on the basis that the parties agreed to refer their dispute to the courts of a non-contracting State.

5.10.3 Disputes relating to foreign land

The rigid application of the jurisdiction rules contained in Title II might lead to unsatisfactory results in certain cases involving claims to immovable property. As regards immovable property which is situated within a Contracting State, Article 16(1) provides that in relation to "proceedings which have as their object rights *in rem* in, or tenancies of immovable property" the courts of the State in which the property is situated shall have exclusive jurisdiction. The provisions of Title II do not, however, regulate claims relating to immovable property situated in non-contracting States. What is the position where proceedings are brought in England against an English domiciliary in relation to a right *in rem* in immovable property situated in a non-contracting State? At common law the court has no jurisdiction to entertain an action for the determination of the title to, or the right to possession of, any immovable property situated outside England.[388] This rule is eminently sensible. Since it is an almost universal principle that claims relating to immovable property should be determined by the courts of the country in which the immovable property is situated section 49 of the 1982 Act should be interpreted as enabling the court to stay proceedings in cases involving title to, or the possession of immovable property situated in a non-contracting State, notwithstanding the fact that the court has jurisdiction under Title II.

383. OJ 1979 C59/124, para. 176.
384. [1970] P 94.
385. [1981] 2 Lloyd's Rep 119.
386. Potter J in *Arkwright Mutual Insurance Co* v. *Bryanston Insurance Co Ltd* [1990] 2 QB 649, 659.
387. *The Rewia* [1991] 1 Lloyd's Rep 69, 75, reversed on other grounds [1991] 2 Lloyd's Rep 325.
388. *British South Africa Co* v. *Companhia de Moçambique* [1893] AC 602. There are limited exceptions to this general principle. See para. 6.6.3.

CHAPTER 6

JURISDICTION IN PERSONAM UNDER TRADITIONAL RULES

Under traditional English jurisdiction rules there are three situations in which the court may assume jurisdiction: (i) where the defendant is present within the jurisdiction, (ii) where the defendant submits to the jurisdiction of the court and (iii) where the case is a proper one for the court to give leave for service of a writ[1] on the defendant out of the jurisdiction (paras. 6.1–6.3). In the first and third of these situations the limits of jurisdiction are fixed by the exercise of the court's discretion (para. 6.4). Special considerations arise in cases where the parties have agreed to refer their disputes to the courts of a particular country (para. 6.5) or to arbitration.[2] Finally, it should be noted that the courts have formulated rules limiting their jurisdiction in cases involving foreign land (para. 6.6). The traditional rules must, of course, be read subject to the provisions of the Brussels and Lugano Conventions ("the Conventions") which allocate jurisdiction to the courts of the Contracting States.[3] The traditional bases of jurisdiction do not apply if jurisdiction is determined by one or other of the Conventions.

6.1 PRESENCE

6.1.1 Individuals

6.1.1.1 Personal service: RSC, Order 10, rule 1(1)

6.1.1.1.1 The most straightforward method of invoking the jurisdiction of the court is to serve the writ personally on the defendant. RSC, Order 10, rule 1(1) states simply that a writ "must be served personally on each defendant by the plaintiff or his agent". If the defendant is present within the jurisdiction personal service presents no problems; the plaintiff or his agent simply hands a copy of the relevant document to the defendant. The rationale behind this jurisdictional rule is said to be allegiance. In *Carrick* v. *Hancock*[4] Lord Russell of Killowen CJ said "that the jurisdiction of a court was based upon the principle of territorial dominion, and that all persons within territorial

1. As a general rule the principles relating to actions begun by writ apply equally to actions commenced by originating summons: RSC, Order 10, r. 5; Order 11, r. 9; Order 12, r. 9.
2. The effect of an arbitration clause on the court's jurisdiction is discussed in Chapter 18.
3. See Chapters 3 to 5.
4. (1895) 12 TLR 59.

dominion owe their allegiance to its sovereign power and obedience to all its laws and to the lawful jurisdiction of its courts".[5]

6.1.1.1.2 When jurisdiction is founded on the defendant's presence in England it is wholly irrelevant that the cause of action arose abroad and that the writ was served while the defendant was present within the jurisdiction only for a short period.[6] However, if the plaintiff, through fraud, induces the defendant to enter the jurisdiction the action may be struck out as an abuse of process.[7]

6.1.1.1.3 A classic illustration of the assumption of jurisdiction on the basis of the defendant's presence is *Maharanee of Baroda* v. *Wildenstein.*[8] In this case a contractual dispute arose between two French residents who happened to share an interest in horse racing. The plaintiff issued a writ against the defendant and, on 20 June 1970, the writ was served on him at the racecourse at Ascot during his temporary presence in England. The validity of the service was upheld:

> [U]nless the plaintiff knows full well that she has no cause of action (and that is not suggested), she did no wrong in taking out a High Court writ in the first place (foreigner though she is) and serving it here at the first available opportunity upon the defendant (foreigner though *he* also is). Both in taking it out and serving it (albeit when the defendant was fleetingly on British soil) she was doing no more than our law permits, even though it may have ruined his day at the races. Some might regard her action as bad form; none can legitimately condemn it as an abuse of legal process.[9]

(i) Notwithstanding the mandatory language of RSC, Order 10, rule 1(1) there are numerous situations where personal service is not possible. For example, many defendants in commercial disputes are limited companies or partnerships for which different rules apply.[10] There are also special rules for service in Admiralty actions *in rem*[11] and in cases where the defendant is a foreign State.[12]

(ii) There are many alternatives to personal service. For example, in cases where the defendant's connections with England are reasonably substantial the plaintiff may serve the writ by post (postal service) or place it through the defendant's letter box (letter box service).[13] A defendant will also be regarded as having been duly served if the defendant's solicitor indorses on the writ a statement that he accepts service of the writ on behalf of that defendant[14]; or if the defendant acknowledges service of the writ before it has actually been served[15]; or if the court makes an order for substituted service[16]; or if the plaintiff serves the writ in accordance with the terms of a contract between the parties[17]; or if one party, knowing that another wishes to serve process upon him, requests or authorises the other to do so in a particular way (provided

5. (1895) 12 TLR 59, 60.
6. *Colt Industries Inc* v. *Sarlie (No. 1)* [1966] 1 WLR 440. Carter, (1965–66) 41 BYIL 447.
7. *Watkins* v. *North American Land & Timber Co Ltd* (1904) 20 TLR 534.
8. [1972] 2 QB 283.
9. Edmund-Davies LJ, [1972] 2 QB 283, 294.
10. See paras. 6.1.2 and 6.1.3.
11. See Chapter 8.
12. See para. 2.3.6.
13. See para. 6.1.1.2.
14. RSC, Order 10, r. 1(4).
15. RSC, Order 10, r. 1(5).
16. RSC, Order 65, r. 4.
17. RSC, Order 10, r. 3. See para. 6.2.2.

that the Rules of the Supreme Court do not prohibit consensual service).[18]

(iii) Jurisdiction based merely on the presence of the defendant within the jurisdiction at the time of service of the writ is subject to the discretion of the court to stay the proceedings on the ground that there is a more appropriate forum for the trial of the action.[19]

(iv) In civil and commercial matters falling within the scope of Title I of the Conventions jurisdiction based merely on the presence of the defendant in England at the time of service of the writ cannot be invoked against a defendant domiciled within a Contracting State.[20]

6.1.1.2 Postal service and letter box service: RSC, Order 10, rule 1(2)

6.1.1.2.1 RSC, Order 10, rule 1 provides:

(2) A writ for service on a defendant within the jurisdiction may, instead of being served personally on him, be served—

(a) by sending a copy of the writ by ordinary first-class post to the defendant at his usual or last known address, or

(b) if there is a letter box for that address, by inserting through the letter box a copy of the writ enclosed in a sealed envelope addressed to the defendant. . . .

(3) Where a writ is served in accordance with paragraph (2)—

(a) the date of service shall, unless the contrary is shown, be deemed to be the seventh day . . . after the date on which the copy was sent to or, as the case may be, inserted through the letter box for the address in question;

(b) any affidavit proving due service of the writ must contain a statement to the effect that—

(i) in the opinion of the deponent (or, if the deponent is the plaintiff's solicitor or an employee of that solicitor, in the opinion of the plaintiff) the copy of the writ, if sent to, or, as the case may be, inserted through the letter box for, the address in question, will have come to the knowledge of the defendant within seven days thereafter; and

(ii) in the case of service by post, the copy of the writ has not been returned to the plaintiff through the post undelivered to the addressee.

6.1.1.2.2 The purpose of postal service and letter box service is not to provide for a general method of service on a defendant who is not within the jurisdiction. This is made clear by the wording of rule 1(2) which refers to service "on a defendant within the jurisdiction"; postal service and letter box service are alternatives to personal service within the jurisdiction. Accordingly, as a general rule, if at the time of service the defendant is not within the jurisdiction, the defendant has not been properly served.

6.1.1.2.3 There is, however, an exception to this general rule. In *Barclays Bank of Swaziland* v. *Hahn*[21] the plaintiff issued a writ against the defendant claiming £12 million under a guarantee executed in Swaziland. The defendant, who enjoyed a peripatetic lifestyle, spent on average three months per year in England. When in England he lived in a flat in London which was rented by his wife. The plaintiff, having failed to serve the writ on the defendant in South Africa, tried to serve the defendant in England by inserting a copy of the writ through the letter box of the flat at a time when the plaintiff

18. *Kenneth Allison Ltd* v. *AE Limehouse & Co* [1992] 2 AC 105.
19. See para. 6.4.
20. See para. 4.2.1.
21. [1989] 1 WLR 506. Beck, "Letter Box Service and Errant Defendants" (1990) 106 LQR 47; Fallon, "Physical Presence and Jurisdiction" (1989) 8 CJQ 297; Kaye, "International Letter Box or Postal Jurisdiction—Not a Second Class Service" (1990) 9 CJQ 330.

believed that the defendant was there. In fact, the defendant arrived at Heathrow airport shortly after the time of purported service and, having been warned that the writ had been put through the letter box, he left the country without visiting the flat.

6.1.1.2.4 The House of Lords accepted the defendant's contention that RSC, Order 10 requires that the defendant should be physically within the jurisdiction at the time of service. However, the moment when the writ was inserted through the letter box was not the moment of service; rule 3(1)(a) provides that the date of service is deemed to be the seventh day after the date on which the writ was inserted through the letter box, unless the contrary is shown; the contrary is shown if the defendant acquires knowledge of the writ within seven days of its being inserted through the letter box. In the present case, the defendant was served within the jurisdiction for the purposes of rule 1(2) when, being within the jurisdiction, he was made aware of the writ: "The intervening moment when presence in England and knowledge of the writ coincided was . . . the date on which service was actually shown to have taken place."[22]

6.1.1.2.5 It does not automatically follow from *Barclays Bank of Swaziland* v. *Hahn*[23] that where postal or letter box service is relied upon by the plaintiff it is a requirement of rule 1(2) that the defendant should be physically present within the jurisdiction at some point during the seven day period following postage of the writ or its insertion through the letter box. What is important is that the affidavit proving due service contains a statement that in the opinion of the plaintiff the writ will come to the knowledge of the defendant within seven days of the writ being posted or inserted through the letter box; service then takes place at the moment when the defendant enters the jurisdiction—even if this is after the expiry of the seven day period.[24] So, for example:

> [A]ssume that the defendant lives in London but is away on business in Scotland at the time when the writ is put through his letter box, there is no difficulty about contacting him in Scotland and the plaintiff has every expectation that within a period of seven days someone in the defendant's house will have acquainted him with the fact that the writ has been served. Assume further that he was in fact told on the telephone by his wife, or some other occupant of the house, that service had taken place, but that he does not return within the jurisdiction for a fortnight after insertion through the letter box. In those circumstances [there is] no reason why the plaintiff should not be able to make an affidavit under rule 1(3)(b)(i) stating his opinion that the writ will have come to the knowledge of the defendant within seven days. But because the service can take place only when the defendant is within the jurisdiction, the presumption as to the date of service in rule 1(3)(a) will have been rebutted and service will be regarded as having been effected only when he returned.[25]

6.1.2 Corporations[26]

6.1.2.1 British companies

In the absence of any relevant legislation service of a writ on a body corporate can be effected in England either by personal service on one of the officers of the corporation or by sending a copy of the writ to its registered office.[27] These rules are displaced by the

22. Hoffmann J in *India Videogram Association* v. *Patel* [1991] 1 WLR 173, 175.
23. [1989] 1 WLR 506.
24. *India Videogram Association* v. *Patel* [1991] 1 WLR 173.
25. Hoffmann J in *India Videogram Association* v. *Patel* [1991] 1 WLR 173, 175–176.
26. For a critical assessment of the current law see Fawcett, "A New Approach to Jurisdiction over Companies in Private International Law" (1988) 37 ICLQ 645.
27. RSC, Order 65, r. 3.

provisions of the Conventions, the Modified Convention and the Companies Act 1985. In cases where proceedings are brought against companies which are incorporated in the United Kingdom, the overwhelming majority concern civil and commercial matters falling within the scope of the Conventions. In these cases jurisdiction has to be determined by reference to Title II of the Conventions and to the Modified Convention.[28] When jurisdiction is not determined by the Conventions, the Companies Act 1985 applies.

(i) In relation to a company registered in England, the plaintiff may serve a writ at the company's registered office in England.[29] This is true even if the company carries on business abroad and conducts no business in England.
(ii) A company which is registered in Scotland, but which carries on business in England, may be served by sending the writ to the company's principal place of business in England with a copy to the registered office in Scotland.[30]
(iii) A company which is registered in Scotland, but which does not carry on business in England, may be served in Scotland only in accordance with the rules which apply to extraterritorial jurisdiction.[31]
(iv) A company which is incorporated in Northern Ireland is an "oversea company" for the purposes of the Companies Act 1985.

6.1.2.2 Oversea companies: introduction

6.1.2.2.1 A corporation is a legal person, but it has no physical existence. Accordingly, the rule which states that jurisdiction may be assumed on the basis of the defendant's physical presence in England could apply to corporations only by analogy. The common law evolved various tests to determine whether a foreign corporation was "here"—so that it could be served within the jurisdiction. These rules have, however, been superseded by legislation.

6.1.2.2.2 Subject to the provisions of the Conventions, the jurisdiction of the English courts over companies which are not incorporated in Great Britain is regulated by Part XXIII of the Companies Act 1985. An "oversea company", as defined by section 744 of the 1985 Act, is:

(a) a company incorporated elsewhere than in Great Britain which, after the commencement of this Act, establishes a place of business in Great Britain, and
(b) a company so incorporated which has, before that commencement, established a place of business and continues to have an established place of business in Great Britain at that commencement.

6.1.2.2.3 The rules for the service of process on oversea companies have been complicated by the implementation in the United Kingdom of the Eleventh Company Law Directive.[32] Since 1 January 1993 the Companies Act 1985 has contained two registration regimes for oversea companies: a branch registration regime and a place of business registration regime. It is clear that "branch" is a narrower concept than "place

28. See para. 4.2.1.
29. Companies Act 1985, s. 725(1).
30. Companies Act 1985, s. 725(2) and (3).
31. See para. 6.3.
32. Directive 89/666 EEC, OJ 1989 L395/36. The Directive was implemented by the Overseas Companies and Credit and Financial Institutions (Branch Disclosure) Regulations 1992 (SI 1992 No. 3179) which made various amendments to Part XXIII of the Companies Act 1985.

of business"; whereas a branch has a place of business, not every place of business is a branch.

(i) The branch registration regime applies to companies covered by section 690A. A company falls within the scope of section 690A if it is "a limited company which (a) is incorporated outside the United Kingdom and Gibraltar, and (b) has a branch in Great Britain".[33] The rules relating to service of process on an oversea company which falls within the branch registration scheme are to be found in section 694A.

(ii) By virtue of section 691 the place of business registration regime applies to "a company incorporated outside Great Britain" which "establishes a place of business in Great Britain".[34] The rules relating to service of process on an oversea company within the scope of section 691 are to be found in section 695.

6.1.2.2.4 The two regimes are mutually exclusive with the branch registration regime taking precedence.[35] The place of business registration regime applies mainly to companies which have a place of business—but not a branch—within the jurisdiction; an oversea company which ceases to have a branch in England but continues to have a place of business shifts from the branch registration regime to the place of business registration regime.[36] It should be noted, however, that the place of business registration regime covers oversea companies which are not limited companies and to companies which are incorporated in Northern Ireland or in Gibraltar.

6.1.2.2.5 The provisions of the 1985 Act lay down the only manner in which a writ can be served on an oversea company; failure to follow the procedure prescribed by the legislation renders service ineffective.[37] However, the court has discretion under RSC, Order 2, rule 1 to cure any irregularity where to do so is in the interests of justice.[38]

6.1.2.3 Section 690A: what is a branch?

6.1.2.3.1 For the purposes of Part XXIII of the Companies Act 1985 a "branch" is "a branch within the meaning of the Council Directive concerning disclosure requirements in respect of branches opened in a Member State by certain types of company governed by the law of another State (the Eleventh Company Law Directive, 89/666/EEC)".[39] This provision is of limited assistance since the Eleventh Company Law Directive does not attempt to define the word "branch".

6.1.2.3.2 Ultimately the Court of Justice will have to determine what is meant by the word "branch" in the context of the Eleventh Company Law Directive. It may be supposed that the Court of Justice will have regard to its jurisprudence concerning the meaning of "branch" for the purposes of Article 5(5) of the Brussels Convention.[40] According to the decision in *Somafer SA* v. *Saar-Ferngas AG* a branch is:

33. Companies Act 1985, s. 690A(1).
34. Companies Act 1985, s. 691(1).
35. Companies Act 1985, s. 690B.
36. Companies Act 1985, s. 692A.
37. Neill LJ in *Boocock* v. *Hilton International Co* [1993] 1 WLR 1065, 1073.
38. *Boocock* v. *Hilton International Co* [1993] 1 WLR 1065.
39. Companies Act 1985, s. 698(2)(b).
40. See para. 5.5.5.

a place of business which has the appearance of permanency, such as the extension of a parent body, has a management and is materially equipped to negotiate business with third parties so that the latter, although knowing that there will if necessary be a legal link with the parent body, the head office of which is abroad, do not have to deal directly with such parent body but may transact business at the place of business constituting the extension.[41]

6.1.2.3.3 Two important consequences flow from the approach adopted by the Court of Justice.

(i) A place of business which performs operations which are ancillary or incidental to the company's business—such as an office which merely undertakes promotional activities—is not a branch within the meaning of section 690A.
(ii) Where there is a unified management structure a single branch may include more than one place of business. Where, however, each establishment in Great Britain has its own management structure, with distinct reporting lines to the parent, each establishment should be regarded as a separate branch.

6.1.2.4 Section 691: what is an established place of business?

For the purposes of section 691 it is not enough that the oversea company has a place of business, the place of business must be established within the jurisdiction.

6.1.2.4.1 The courts have taken a flexible approach to the phrase "place of business". In *South India Shipping Corporation Ltd* v. *Export-Import Bank of Korea*[42] the question was whether the office which a Korean bank rented in London amounted to a place of business within the meaning of the Companies Act. No business transactions were conducted from the London office, which was used solely for the purpose of gathering information and maintaining public relations with other banking and financial institutions in the United Kingdom and Europe. The Court of Appeal rejected the contention that for premises in England to constitute a place of business the company must be carrying on a substantial part of its business within the jurisdiction and held that the London office was a place of business for the purposes of the Companies Act. There is no rule of law that activities which might be described as incidental to the defendant's main business cannot establish a presence within the jurisdiction. Ackner LJ said:

The defendant bank is an export–import bank, not a high street bank. It has both premises and staff within the jurisdiction. It conducts external relations with other banks and financial institutions. It carries out preliminary work in relation to granting or obtaining loans. It seeks to give publicity to the foreign bank and encourage trade between Korea and the United Kingdom, and it consults with other banks and financial institutions on the usual operating matters. It has therefore established a place of business within Great Britain and it matters not that it does not conclude within the jurisdiction any banking transactions or have banking dealings with the general public as opposed to other banks or financial institutions.[43]

6.1.2.4.2 Because the Act imposes obligations to deliver documents and make returns by a specified date, the Act is premised on the notion that there is some readily

41. Case 33/78 [1978] ECR 2183, 2192 (para. 12).
42. [1985] 1 WLR 585.
43. [1985] 1 WLR 585, 592.

identifiable point in time at which it can be said that a company has established a place of business within the jurisdiction.[44] Moreover, the word "established", according to Oliver LJ in *Re Oriel Ltd*, "connotes not only the setting up of a place of business at a specific location, but a degree of permanence or recognisability as being a location of a company's business".[45]

6.1.2.4.3 A visible sign or physical indication is not essential, though its absence is to be taken into account. In *Cleveland Museum of Art* v. *Capricorn Art International SA*,[46] for example, proceedings were commenced against art dealers in England. The writ was served on premises which the plaintiff alleged were the defendant's place of business in England. The fact that there was no outward sign of the defendant's presence was not material "since it would surely be uncharacteristic for art dealers in objects of . . . high quality to place conspicuous nameplates or the like on their premises".[47]

6.1.2.4.4 In certain circumstances it may not be clear whether a particular place of business is or is not the defendant's place of business. In a dispute of this kind, the court will have regard to the commercial reality, rather than the formal legal position.[48] So, for example, the fact that the alleged place of business is not owned or leased by the defendant is not decisive, if the impression given to the outside world is that the premises in question constitute the defendant's place of business. What is required is "some more or less permanent location, not necessarily owned or even leased by the company, but at least associated with the company and from which habitually or with some degree of regularity business is conducted".[49]

6.1.2.4.5 In view of the observations of Oliver LJ in *Re Oriel Ltd* many of the pre-Act authorities on corporate presence—such as *Dunlop Pneumatic Tyre Co Ltd* v. *Aktien-Gesellschaft für Motor und Motorfahrzeugbau Vorm Cudell & Co*,[50] in which it was held that a German company which occupied a stand at a trade fair in England for nine days was present within the jurisdiction—must be regarded as having been superseded by the statutory rules.

6.1.2.5 Section 694A: service of process on an oversea company with a branch in England

6.1.2.5.1 A company within the scope of section 690A—that is, a limited company incorporated outside the United Kingdom and Gibraltar which has a branch in Great Britain—is required within one month of having opened a branch in a part of Great Britain to register under paragraph 1 of Schedule 21A to the 1985 Act and to deliver certain information to the registrar.[51] If an oversea company has more than one branch each branch must be registered and the relevant information must be delivered in relation to each branch. By virtue of paragraph 3(e) of Schedule 21A the information

44. Oliver LJ in *Re Oriel* [1986] 1 WLR 180, 187.
45. [1986] 1 WLR 180, 184.
46. [1990] 2 Lloyd's Rep 166.
47. Hirst J, [1990] 2 Lloyd's Rep 166, 172.
48. *Cleveland Museum of Art* v. *Capricorn Art International SA* [1990] 2 Lloyd's Rep 166.
49. Oliver LJ in *Re Oriel Ltd* [1986] 1 WLR 180, 184.
50. [1902] 1 KB 342.
51. Companies Act 1985, s. 690A(2). The information required to be registered is set out in the Companies Act 1985, Schedule 21A. For the transitional arrangements which apply to oversea companies which previously registered a place of business under section 691 and which became subject to the new branch registration regime on 1 January 1993 see Companies Act 1985, s. 692A(4) and Schedule 21B.

which must be delivered includes "a list of the names and addresses of all persons resident in Great Britain authorised to accept on the company's behalf service of process in respect of the business of the branch and of any notices required to be served on the company in respect of the business of the branch".

6.1.2.5.2 Section 694A—which sets out the prescribed methods for serving a writ on a company falling within the scope of section 690A—provides:

> (2) Any process required to be served on a company to which this section applies in respect of the carrying on of the business of a branch registered by it under paragraph 1 of Schedule 21A is sufficiently served if—
> (a) addressed to any person whose name has, in respect of the branch, been delivered to the registrar as a person falling within paragraph 3(e) of that Schedule, and
> (b) left at or sent by post to the address for that person which has been so delivered.
> (3) Where—
> (a) a company to which this section applies makes default, in respect of a branch, in delivering to the registrar the particulars mentioned in paragraph 3(e) of Schedule 21A, or
> (b) all the persons whose names have, in respect of a branch, been delivered to the registrar as persons falling within paragraph 3(e) of that Schedule are dead or have ceased to reside in Great Britain, or refuse to accept service on the company's behalf or for any reason cannot be served,
> a document may be served on the company in respect of the carrying on of the business of the branch by leaving it at, or sending it by post to, any place of business established by the company in Great Britain.

6.1.2.5.3 These provisions are relatively unambiguous. An oversea company which falls within the scope of section 690A is required to register the name and address of at least one person—normally an officer of the company—who is authorised to accept service on the company's behalf. Where an oversea company has complied with this requirement, a plaintiff is normally able to rely on section 694A(2) and may serve the company by serving the writ on the person whose name has been registered. A company which has a branch in England, but which has failed to register in accordance with section 690A, may be served at any place of business within the jurisdiction under section 694A(3).

6.1.2.5.4 It is important to note that section 694A makes provision for service on an oversea company "in respect of the carrying on of the business of" the branch.[52] Where the plaintiff has a claim against an oversea company which has a branch in England service under section 694A may be effected only with regard to proceedings which arise out of the carrying on of the business of the branch; the mere fact that an oversea company has a branch in England does not authorise the assumption of jurisdiction in relation to disputes which are unconnected with the activities of the branch. In this respect the regime introduced by section 694A is in marked contrast to that which regulates the service of process on a place of business.

6.1.2.5.5 Where a company within the scope of section 690A has more than one branch in Great Britain section 694A(4) provides that "any notice or process required to be served on the company which is not required to be served in respect of the carrying on of the business of one branch rather than another shall be treated for the purposes of this section as required to be served in respect of carrying on the business of each of its branches". The significance of this somewhat opaque provision is not immediately clear.

52. This restriction is derived from Article 2(1)(e) of Council Directive 89/666 EEC, OJ 1989 L395/36.

It would seem, however, that where a company has, for example, two branches in Great Britain and the proceedings do not relate to the business of a single branch—but relate to the businesses carried on by both branches—service on the company is to be effected by satisfying the service requirements in relation to each of the branches.

6.1.2.6 Section 695: service of process on an oversea company with a place of business in England

6.1.2.6.1 If an oversea company does not fall within the scope of section 690A, the relevant rules are those to be found in sections 691 and 695. Section 691(1) contains a requirement that oversea companies which have established a place of business in England should deliver certain information to the registrar:

> When a company incorporated outside Great Britain establishes a place of business in Great Britain, it shall within one month of doing so deliver to the registrar of companies for registration— . . .
> (b) a return in the prescribed form containing— . . .
> (ii) a list of the names and addresses of some one or more persons resident in Great Britain authorised to accept on the company's behalf service of process and any notices required to be served on it.

6.1.2.6.2 Section 695 indicates the way in which an oversea company which falls within section 691 may be served in England:

> (1) Any process or notice required to be served on an oversea company to which section 691 applies is sufficiently served if addressed to any person whose name has been delivered to the registrar under preceding sections in this Part and left at or sent by post to the address which has been so delivered.
> (2) However—
> (a) where such a company makes default in delivering to the registrar the name and address of a person resident in Great Britain who is authorised to accept on behalf of the company service of process or notices, or
> (b) if at any time all the persons whose names and addresses have been so delivered are dead or have ceased so to reside, or refuse to accept service on the company's behalf, or for any reason cannot be served,
> a document may be served on the company by leaving it at, or sending it by post to, any place of business established by the company in Great Britain.

6.1.2.6.3 The basic scheme of sections 691 and 695 are the same as the scheme established by sections 690A and 694A.

(i) An oversea company which has a place of business in England is required to register the name and address of someone who is authorised to accept service on the company's behalf. If the company registers the name of a person authorised to accept service and the address for service, a plaintiff may—in reliance on section 695(1)—serve the writ on the person whose name has been registered. Where the company has complied with section 691 service may be effected under section 695(1) even if the company ceases to have a place of business in England at the time when the proceedings are commenced.[53]

(ii) A company which has established a place of business in England, but which

53. *Rome* v. *Punjab National Bank (No. 2)* [1989] 1 WLR 1211.

fails to register in accordance with section 691, may be served at the place of business under section 695(2).

6.1.2.6.4 It is clear that the plaintiff may rely on section 695 notwithstanding the fact that the dispute has no connection with the English forum; there is no requirement under section 695 that the proceedings should relate to the business conducted in England. If any injustice results from the assumption of jurisdiction under section 695—for example, where the jurisdiction of the court is invoked under section 695(1) in relation to a cause of action which arises after the company has ceased to have a place of business within the jurisdiction—this can be remedied by the exercise of the court's discretion to stay the proceedings on the basis of *forum non conveniens.*[54]

6.1.3 Partnerships: RSC, Order 81

6.1.3.1 A partnership is not a corporate body and therefore does not fall within the scope of the rules contained in the Companies Act 1985. Where a partnership carries on business within the jurisdiction the partners may be sued in England in the name of the firm.[55] RSC, Order 81, rule 3(1) provides that the writ may be served:

> (a) on any one or more of the partners, or
> (b) at the principal place of business of the partnership within the jurisdiction, on any person having at the time of service the control or management of the partnership business there; or
> (c) by sending a copy of the writ by ordinary first-class post . . . to the firm at the principal place of business of the partnership within the jurisdiction.

Where service is effected in accordance with these rules the writ is deemed to have been served on the firm, regardless of whether any member of the firm is out of the jurisdiction.[56]

6.1.3.2 In order to constitute good service for the purposes of rule 3(1)(a), service on the partner in question must be such as would constitute service on him if he were a personal defendant.[57] Accordingly, where a partner is present within the jurisdiction a plaintiff may serve the partner personally or make use of postal or letter box service.[58] If the plaintiff resorts to postal or letter box service the relevant address for service is the defendant's "usual or last known address" within the jurisdiction.[59] To comply with the rule the plaintiff must serve the writ at the place where the partner lives, or is last known to have lived, rather than the address of the partnership; postal or letter box service on a partner at the firm's address is wholly ineffective for the purposes of rule 3(1)(a).[60] If the partner cannot be served within the jurisdiction, the plaintiff may apply for leave to serve out of the jurisdiction, but leave will only be given if the plaintiff can satisfy the requirements of RSC, Order 11.[61] Where partners are sued in the name of the firm, service of the writ on one of the partners is effective as regards all the partners, including

54. See para. 6.4.
55. RSC, Order 81, r. 1.
56. RSC, Order 81, r. 3(1).
57. Leggatt LJ in *Marsden* v. *Kingswell Watts (a firm)* [1992] 2 All ER 239, 242.
58. RSC, Order 10, r. 1.
59. RSC, Order 10, r. 1(2).
60. *Marsden* v. *Kingswell Watts (a firm)* [1992] 2 All ER 239.
61. See paras. 6.3–6.4.

those who are abroad, whether service takes place in England[62] or abroad.[63] If, in reliance on rule 3(1)(b), the writ is served on the person having control or management of the partnership business at the principal place of business, this is effective service on all the partners—even those who are not within the jurisdiction.[64] Although a plaintiff is able to invoke the jurisdiction of the court by sending a copy of the writ by post to the partnership's principal place of business in England, rule 3(1)(c) makes no provision for letter box service.

6.1.3.3 Where service is effected under RSC, Order 81, rule 3(1) the partners are not named as defendants. The plaintiff may, however, choose to make individual partners parties to the action. As regards any partner who cannot be served within the jurisdiction, the plaintiff needs to obtain the leave of the court to serve out of the jurisdiction under RSC, Order 11, rule 1(1)(c) on the basis that the partner in question is "a proper party to the action".[65] In a situation where the partnership has no place of business in England, the partners cannot be sued in the name of the firm under RSC, Order 81.[66] Where the partners are abroad, in an appropriate case, the court may give leave for service of a writ on individual partners out of the jurisdiction under RSC, Order 11.

6.1.4 Discretion to stay: *forum non conveniens*

The fact that jurisdiction is established on the basis of the defendant's presence in England does not automatically mean that the proceedings will be allowed to continue in England. On an application from the defendant, the court may stay the proceedings on the basis that another forum is clearly more appropriate for a trial of the action in the interests of the parties and the ends of justice.[67]

6.2 SUBMISSION

Whereas jurisdiction based on presence is ultimately derived from the State's authority or territorial dominion, jurisdiction based on submission derives from the consent of the defendant. It is important in this context to distinguish three different situations.

6.2.1 Jurisdiction agreements

6.2.1.1 Prior to the issue of the writ the parties may enter an agreement to refer an existing dispute or potential disputes arising from a particular legal relationship to the English courts. Jurisdiction clauses take many different forms. For example, the parties

62. *Lysaght Ltd* v. *Clark & Co* [1891] 1 QB 552.
63. *Hobbs* v. *Australian Press Association* [1933] 1 KB 1.
64. *Worcester City & County Banking Co* v. *Firbank, Pauling & Co* [1894] 1 QB 784.
65. *West of England Steamship Owners' Protection and Indemnity Association Ltd* v. *John Holman & Sons* [1957] 1 WLR 1164. See para. 6.3.3.3.
66. RSC, Order 81, r. 1.
67. See para. 6.4.

to a bill of lading may agree to refer any dispute arising under the contract to the courts of the country where the carrier has its principal place of business.

6.2.1.2 In cases where the parties to a dispute have agreed to English jurisdiction the court is not seised of proceedings simply by virtue of the issue of a writ in England; the writ must be served on the defendant. Where the effect of Article 17 of the Conventions[68] is to confer jurisdiction on the English court leave of the court to serve the defendant out of the jurisdiction is not required; the writ may be served on the defendant as of right.[69]

6.2.1.3 Article 17 is not effective to confer jurisdiction in cases where either the subject matter of the proceedings does not fall within the scope of Title I or neither party is domiciled in a Brussels or Lugano Contracting State. In these situations if the defendant—whether an individual or a corporation—cannot be served within the jurisdiction and declines to put in a voluntary appearance, the plaintiff needs to obtain the leave of the court to serve the writ out of the jurisdiction.[70]

6.2.2 Agreements to submit

An agreement to submit involves an agreement between the parties on the method whereby the writ is to be served. Where parties have agreed to English jurisdiction and the contract specifies the method of service, service of the writ in accordance with the terms of the contract constitutes good service.[71] In cases governed by Article 17, there is no leave requirement, whether service is to be effected in England or abroad.[72] In cases where the agreement between the parties does not provide for service of the writ in England, the plaintiff must obtain the leave of the court to serve the defendant out of the jurisdiction if the subject matter of the proceedings does not fall within the scope of the Conventions or if neither party is domiciled in a Brussels or Lugano Contracting State.[73]

6.2.3 Voluntary appearance

6.2.3.1 In cases where the subject matter of the proceedings falls within the scope of the Conventions, whether the defendant has submitted to the jurisdiction of the court by voluntary appearance falls to be determined by Article 18.[74] In cases not falling within the Conventions' scope regard should be had exclusively to the Rules of the Supreme Court.

6.2.3.2 A defendant who neither is present in England nor has agreed to submit to English jurisdiction may nevertheless confer jurisdiction on the court by appearing to defend the case on the merits. Submission arises where, independently of any prior agreement between the parties, the defendant accepts the jurisdiction of the court by acknowledging service of the writ without challenging the court's jurisdiction.[75] For a

68. Article 17 of the Conventions is discussed at para. 5.3; Article 17 of the Modified Convention is considered at para. 7.2.2.2.
69. RSC, Order 11, r. 1(2).
70. RSC, Order 11, r. 1(1)(d)(iv). For the text of this provision see para. 6.3.3.4.
71. RSC, Order 10, r. 3(1).
72. RSC, Order 11, r. 3(3).
73. RSC, Order 10, r. 3(2).
74. See para. 5.2.
75. *Williams & Glyn's Bank Plc* v. *Astro Dinamico Compania Naviera SA* [1984] 1 WLR 438.

submission to be voluntary it must be directed to determination of the claim which is the subject matter of the proceedings. A challenge to jurisdiction is not a submission:

[A] person voluntarily submits to the jurisdiction of the court if he voluntarily recognises, or has recognised, that the court has jurisdiction to hear and determine the claim which is the subject matter of the relevant proceedings. In particular, he makes a voluntary submission to the jurisdiction if he takes a step in proceedings which in all the circumstances amounts to a recognition of the court's jurisdiction in respect of the claim which is the subject matter of those proceedings.[76]

For example, the issue of a time summons seeking an extension of time in which to lodge a defence is a sufficient step to amount to submission.[77]

6.2.3.3 RSC, Order 12, rule 1(1) provides that a defendant may "acknowledge service of the writ and defend the action by a solicitor or in person". A defendant submits to the jurisdiction if he chooses to acknowledge service and to defend on the merits. A defendant may even choose to acknowledge service before actual service; RSC, Order 10, rule 1(5) provides that "where a writ is not duly served on a defendant but he acknowledges service of it, the writ shall be deemed to have been duly served upon him".

6.2.3.4 The procedure set out in RSC, Order 12 is to allow a defendant who is not otherwise subject to the jurisdiction of the court to agree to litigation in England. The plaintiff, when serving the writ, must serve the defendant with the form for acknowledging service. If the defendant wishes to defend he must return the acknowledgement of service to the court giving notice that he intends to contest the proceedings. (This is called "notice of intention to defend".) If the defendant fails to return the acknowledgement the plaintiff may proceed to obtain a default judgment. A defendant who gives notice of intention to defend has a choice whether to defend on the merits or whether to contest the jurisdiction of the court (or the regularity of the issue or service of the writ). If the defendant wishes to contest the jurisdiction of the court he must issue a summons under RSC, Order 12, rule 8.

6.2.3.5 A defendant who makes an application under rule 8 is not regarded as having submitted even if the application is unsuccessful. However, after acknowledging service and issuing a summons, the defendant is well advised not to take any further steps in the proceedings until after the summons has been heard. If the defendant does anything further after the issue of the summons there is a risk that he might be taken to have waived his right to challenge the court's jurisdiction. A useful test in deciding whether the steps taken by the defendant after the issue of the summons constitute submission is to ask whether a disinterested bystander with knowledge of the case would regard the acts of the defendant or his solicitor as inconsistent with the making and maintaining of his challenge to the court's jurisdiction.[78]

76. Goff LJ in *The Messiniaki Tolmi* [1984] 1 Lloyd's Rep 266, 270.

77. *Sage* v. *Double A Hydraulics Ltd*; *Chambers* v. *Starkings*, *The Times*, 2 April 1992.

78. See Farquharson LJ in *Sage* v. *Double A Hydraulics Ltd*; *Chambers* v. *Starkings*, *The Times*, 2 April 1992.

6.3 SERVICE OUT OF THE JURISDICTION UNDER RSC, ORDER 11, RULE 1(1)

6.3.1 Introduction

There are situations where it is appropriate for proceedings against a foreign defendant to be brought in England notwithstanding the fact that the court cannot assume jurisdiction on the basis of the defendant's presence or submission. For example, England would appear to be the most appropriate forum for dealing with disputes relating to contracts which have a close connection with England or to accidents which occur in England. The purpose of RSC, Order 11 is to enable the court to assume jurisdiction over foreign defendants in circumstances where the subject matter of the dispute has a sufficient connection with England. Nevertheless, RSC, Order 11, rule 1(1) contains bases of jurisdiction which are exorbitant—in the sense that they are not founded on a close connection between the defendant and the forum. In cases falling within the material scope of the Conventions these bases of jurisdiction cannot be invoked against a defendant who is domiciled in a Contracting State.[79]

6.3.1.1 Three issues

6.3.1.1.1 RSC, Order 11, rule 4(2) provides that leave to serve a defendant out of the jurisdiction shall not be granted "unless it shall be made sufficiently to appear to the court that the case is a proper one for service out of the jurisdiction" under the Order. In deciding whether or not to exercise its discretion to allow service on a defendant out of the jurisdiction the court will have regard to three issues.[80]

(i) As regards the merits of the plaintiff's claim, there must be a serious issue to be tried.
(ii) The plaintiff's claim must fall within the paragraph of RSC, Order 11 relied on.
(iii) The court must be satisfied that England is the *forum conveniens*—that is, the forum in which the case can most suitably be tried in the interests of the parties and the ends of justice.

A number of recent decisions of the Court of Appeal are not easy to reconcile, largely because of differences of opinion as to the precise relationship between the three different stages of the enquiry.[81] Three different ways of looking at the three aspects of an application under RSC, Order 11 have been advocated.

6.3.1.1.2 In *Overseas Union Insurance Ltd* v. *Incorporated General Insurance Ltd* Parker LJ concluded that "there is only one requirement, namely that it shall be made sufficiently to appear that the case is a proper one. There is one overall scheme of which the elements are a case on the merits, fulfilment of one or more of the qualifying conditions, and England being the most appropriate forum".[82] The implications of this analysis are spelled out in the following example:

79. Article 3. See para. 4.2.1.2.
80. *Seaconsar Far East Ltd* v. *Bank Markazi Jomhouri Islami Iran* [1993] 3 WLR 756.
81. See *Attock Cement Co Ltd* v. *Romanian Bank for Foreign Trade* [1989] 1 WLR 1147; *Metall und Rohstoff AG* v. *Donaldson Lufkin & Jenrette Inc* [1990] 1 QB 391; *Overseas Union Insurance Ltd* v. *Incorporated General Insurance Ltd* [1992] 1 Lloyd's Rep 439; *Société Commerciale de Réassurance* v. *ERAS (International) Ltd* [1992] 1 Lloyd's Rep 570; *Banque Paribas* v. *Cargill International SA* [1992] 2 Lloyd's Rep 19; *Seaconsar Far East Ltd* v. *Bank Markazi Jomhouri Islami Iran* [1993] 1 Lloyd's Rep 236.
82. [1992] 1 Lloyd's Rep 439, 447–448.

Suppose . . . that it is common ground between the parties, or there is overwhelming evidence that, if the case is to be tried at all, England is the appropriate forum and that, on the merits, the plaintiff's case is worthy of serious consideration, I can see no reason why he should be forced to have his action for breach of contract tried in an inappropriate forum because eg his contention that the contract was governed by English law does not persuade the judge that that is probably the case, or that there is a strong probability that that is the case.[83]

6.3.1.1.3 The second approach was advocated by the Court of Appeal in *Société Commerciale de Réassurance* v. *ERAS (International) Ltd.*[84] Mustill LJ thought that "although the traditional three-stage enquiry is convenient for the purpose of analysis it should not be allowed to disguise the fact that the stages are linked. The exercise does not consist of a series of gates of which the first, once negotiated, can be put entirely out of mind".[85] The basis of the Court of Appeal's analysis was that, whereas the second requirement is derived from the terms of RSC, Order 11 itself—and therefore relates to jurisdiction in the strict sense—the first and third requirements are the creation of precedent and are not concerned directly with formal jurisdiction. According to this approach the first and third requirements are derived ultimately from the existence of the court's discretion to permit service once it is established that the second requirement is fulfilled. As for the relationship between the first and the third requirements, the more obviously England appears to be the natural forum for the action the less the court need concern itself with examining the prospects of the plaintiff's success.[86]

6.3.1.1.4 The third approach is revealed by *Metall und Rohstoff AG* v. *Donaldson Lufkin & Jenrette Inc*[87] in which the Court of Appeal treated each of the three requirements as being distinct from the others. According to this analysis, both the first and second requirements are to be regarded as preconditions for the assumption of jurisdiction, with the consequence that the exercise of the court's discretion to permit service abroad centres on the question of whether England is the *forum conveniens.*

6.3.1.1.5 Most of the confusion surrounding the case law of the Court of Appeal has been resolved by the decision of the House of Lords in *Seaconsar Far East Ltd* v. *Bank Markazi Jomhouri Islami Iran.*[88] Lord Goff, with whom the other members of the House of Lords agreed, indicated that the proper approach to applications under RSC, Order 11, rule 1(1) is to look at each of the three aspects separately:

[A] judge faced with a question of leave to serve proceedings out of the jurisdiction under Order 11 will in practice have to consider both (1) whether jurisdiction has been sufficiently established . . . under one of the paragraphs of rule 1(1), and (2) whether there is a serious issue to be tried, so as to enable him to exercise his discretion to grant leave, before he goes on to consider the exercise of that discretion, with particular reference to the issue of *forum conveniens.*[89]

6.3.1.1.6 In rejecting the approaches advocated by Parker LJ in *Overseas Union Insurance Ltd* v. *Incorporated General Insurance Ltd* and by Mustill LJ in *Société Commerciale de Réassurance* v. *ERAS (International) Ltd* Lord Goff said:

83. Parker LJ in *Overseas Union Insurance Ltd* v. *Incorporated General Insurance Ltd* [1992] 1 Lloyd's Rep 439, 448.
84. [1992] 1 Lloyd's Rep 570.
85. [1992] 1 Lloyd's Rep 570, 588.
86. Mustill LJ, [1992] 1 Lloyd's Rep 570, 588.
87. [1990] 1 QB 391.
88. [1993] 3 WLR 756.
89. [1993] 3 WLR 756, 767.

Suppose that, for example, the plaintiff's case is very strong on the merits. If so, I cannot see that a case particularly strong on the merits can compensate for a weak case on *forum conveniens*. Likewise, in my opinion, a very strong connection with the English forum cannot justify a weak case on the merits, if a stronger case on the merits would otherwise be required. In truth, as I see it, the two elements are separate and distinct.[90]

6.3.1.2 Procedure

Where the plaintiff seeks leave to serve a defendant out of the jurisdiction he must make an *ex parte* application to a master. The application must be supported by an affidavit stating "(a) the grounds on which the application is made, (b) that in the deponent's belief the plaintiff has a good cause of action and (c) in what place or country the defendant is, or probably may be found".[91] The plaintiff must make full and frank disclosure of the material circumstances in the affidavit. If any material fact is omitted, this is sufficient to justify the discharge of the order giving leave.[92] If leave is given *ex parte*, the defendant may apply to have leave set aside.[93] Where the exercise of the court's discretion is challenged, the defendant's application to have service set aside should not be confused with an application for a stay on the basis of *forum non conveniens* in cases where the defendant is served within the jurisdiction as of right. Where the defendant who has been served abroad seeks to have service set aside on the ground that England is not the *forum conveniens*, the burden of proof rests on the plaintiff to show that—on the date on which the order granting leave was given—England was the *forum conveniens.*[94] There is a right of appeal to a judge of the High Court against decisions of the master.[95] Appeals to the Court of Appeal from the High Court may be brought only with leave.[96]

6.3.2 A serious question to be tried

6.3.2.1 A full investigation of the merits of the case at the interlocutory stage would involve an enormous waste of effort and resources. It would, however, be unfair on the defendant if the plaintiff could obtain leave to serve out of the jurisdiction without having to establish that he has a plausible claim. The requirement that the evidence should disclose that there is a serious issue to be tried is an attempt to balance these competing tensions.

6.3.2.2 Some of the confusion in the case law has resulted from the fact that arguments as to the merits may arise in two superficially similar, but crucially different contexts. It is important to distinguish (i) the situation where jurisdiction and the merits

90. [1993] 3 WLR 756, 767.
91. RSC, Order 11, r. 4(1). There is a further requirement in cases where leave to serve out is sought under RSC, Order 11, r. 1(1)(c). See para. 6.3.3.3.
92. *The Hagen* [1908] P 189.
93. RSC, Order 12, r. 8.
94. Hoffmann J in *ISC Technologies Ltd* v. *Guerin* [1992] 2 Lloyd's Rep 430, 434.
95. RSC, Order 58, r. 1.
96. Supreme Court Act 1981, s. 18(1).

are inextricably bound up together and (ii) the situation where the issues which go to jurisdiction and the issues which go to the merits of the case are quite distinct.

6.3.2.3 An example of a situation falling within the first category is where the plaintiff seeks to enforce a contract which was allegedly made in England and applies for leave under RSC, Order 11, rule 1(1)(d)(i) and the defendant challenges the court's jurisdiction by denying the existence of the contract. In this type of case the existence of the contract is relevant both to jurisdiction and to the merits and the same standard of proof must be applied to both issues.[97] Obviously, the proper standard to be applied in this situation is the test which is applicable to questions of jurisdiction.[98]

6.3.2.4 An example of the second type of case is where the plaintiff invokes the court's jurisdiction under RSC, Order 11, rule 1(1)(a) on the basis that the defendant is domiciled in England and the defendant resists jurisdiction on the ground that the plaintiff has no cause of action. In this situation the question of jurisdiction (is the defendant domiciled in England?) is distinct from the question of the merits (has the plaintiff got a cause of action?). It has often been said that, as regards the second question, the relevant test is that the plaintiff should establish a good arguable case on the merits—which has been interpreted as meaning that the plaintiff's case must be "arguable"[99] or "worthy of consideration"[100] or that the court must be satisfied that the plaintiff has "a good chance of success".[101]

6.3.2.5 In *Seaconsar Far East Ltd* v. *Bank Markazi Jomhouri Islami Iran*[102] the House of Lords indicated that the courts have been proceeding on the basis of a misunderstanding—largely, as a result of a misinterpretation of the decision of the House of Lords in *Vitovice Horni a Hutni Tezirstvo* v. *Korner.*[103] There is no requirement that the plaintiff should establish a good arguable case on the merits: "the standard of proof in respect of the cause of action can be broadly stated to be whether, on the affidavit evidence before the court, there is a serious question to be tried".[104]

6.3.3 The heads of RSC, Order 11, rule 1(1)

RSC, Order 11, rule 1(1) lists the circumstances in which "service of a writ is permissible with the leave of the court". The various jurisdictional heads are to be found in paragraphs (a) to (t).

6.3.3.1 Jurisdiction based on domicile

(a) relief is sought against a person domiciled[105] within the jurisdiction;

97. *Seaconsar Far East Ltd* v. *Bank Makazi Jomhouri Islami Iran* [1993] 3 WLR 756.
98. See para. 6.3.3.9.
99. Parker LJ in *Banque Paribas* v. *Cargill International SA* [1992] 2 Lloyd's Rep 19, 25.
100. Stuart-Smith LJ in *Seaconsar Far East Ltd* v. *Bank Markazi Jomhouri Islami Iran* [1993] 1 Lloyd's Rep 236, 248.
101. Lloyd LJ in *Seaconsar Far East Ltd* v. *Bank Markazi Jomhouri Islami Iran* [1993] 1 Lloyd's Rep 236, 243. See also Slade LJ in *Metall und Rohstoff AG* v. *Donaldson Lufkin & Jenrette Inc* [1990] 1 QB 391, 434.
102. [1993] 3 WLR 756.
103. [1951] AC 869.
104. Lord Goff, [1993] 3 WLR 756, 763.
105. For the purposes of this provision "domicile" is to be determined by reference to sections 41 to 46 of the Civil Jurisdiction and Judgments Act 1982: RSC, Order 11, r. 1(4).

Where the proceedings concern civil and commercial matters within the meaning of Article 1 of the Conventions the plaintiff may serve a defendant who is domiciled—but not physically present—in England as of right.[106] However, certain matters—for example, arbitration—are excluded from the scope of the Conventions. In a case concerning one of the excluded matters, a defendant who is domiciled in England but not physically present may be served out of the jurisdiction with the leave of the court.

6.3.3.2 Injunctions[107]

> (b) an injunction is sought ordering the defendant to do or refrain from doing anything within the jurisdiction (whether or not damages are also claimed in respect of a failure to do or the doing of that thing);

In *Siskina (Owners of cargo lately laden on board)* v. *Distos Compania Naviera SA*[108] the House of Lords held that where a plaintiff applies to the court for interim relief against a foreign defendant the claim for an injunction cannot stand alone as a basis of jurisdiction. At common law a plaintiff is entitled to rely on paragraph (b) only if the court is prepared to assume jurisdiction over the absent defendant on another of the heads of RSC, Order 11. The doctrine laid down by the House of Lords has, however, been modified as regards cases in which the plaintiff brings proceedings in a Brussels or Lugano Contracting State.[109] Where, for example, proceedings have been commenced in France, the plaintiff may apply for interim relief in England and the court may give leave to serve the defendant out of the jurisdiction under paragraph (b), even though the court has no jurisdiction in relation to the plaintiff's substantive claim.[110]

6.3.3.3 Multiple defendants

> (c) the claim is brought against a person duly served within or out of the jurisdiction and a person out of the jurisdiction is a necessary or proper party thereto;

6.3.3.3.1 Paragraph (c) is a head of jurisdiction which is extremely important in practice. In a situation where there are two or more potential defendants it is very inconvenient if the plaintiff cannot proceed against them in the same forum.[111] Paragraph (c) provides a mechanism whereby defendants who are not otherwise amenable to the jurisdiction of the court may be served out of the jurisdiction. There are various situations where paragraph (c) may be invoked.

(i) Where the first defendant is sued in England as of right, other defendants may be served out of the jurisdiction under paragraph (c).
(ii) Where the first defendant is served out of the jurisdiction under another of the heads of RSC, Order 11 other defendants may be served out of the jurisdiction under paragraph (c).
(iii) Paragraph (c) may be employed in the context of third party proceedings; the

106. RSC, Order 11, r. 1(2)
107. For further discussion see para. 21.3.
108. [1979] AC 210. Lipstein, [1978] CLJ 241.
109. Article 24 of the Brussels and Lugano Conventions; Civil Jurisdiction and Judgments Act 1982, s. 25(1).
110. *Republic of Haiti* v. *Duvalier* [1990] 1 QB 202; *X* v. *Y* [1990] 1 QB 220.
111. For a good example of a factual situation where the practical value of RSC, Order 11, r. 1(1)(c) is revealed see *The Goldean Mariner* [1990] 2 Lloyd's Rep 215.

first defendant who is sued in England may seek to serve other defendants out of the jurisdiction under this head.[112]

6.3.3.3.2 While paragraph (c) provides advantages for plaintiffs it presents certain risks for defendants. The particular danger is that paragraph (c) is potentially open to abuse by plaintiffs. It would be entirely wrong if a plaintiff were able to start proceedings in England against a "dummy" defendant simply as a means of bringing a foreign defendant before the court; it is for this reason that the courts have approached rule 1(1)(c) with a certain degree of caution.[113]

6.3.3.3.3 The Rules of the Supreme Court provide a measure of protection for defendants in these circumstances. Where the application is made under paragraph (c) the affidavit supporting the application must state "the grounds for the deponent's belief that there is between the plaintiff and the person on whom a writ has been served a real issue which the plaintiff may reasonably ask the court to try".[114] It follows that, if the plaintiff's action against the first defendant is not *bona fide*, the court will refuse to allow other defendants to be served out of the jurisdiction under paragraph (c).

6.3.3.3.4 Nevertheless, to satisfy paragraph (c) all the plaintiff has to show is that the defendant in question is a necessary or proper party; if the defendant is a proper party the fact that he is not also a necessary party is not relevant. Furthermore, a plaintiff may join a defendant to proceedings in England under paragraph (c), notwithstanding the fact that the claim in question could not have been made in a writ for service out of the jurisdiction if the defendant had been the primary defendant.[115]

6.3.3.4 Contract

(d) the claim is brought to enforce, rescind, dissolve, annul or otherwise affect a contract, or to recover damages or obtain other relief in respect of the breach of a contract, being (in either case) a contract which—
   (i) was made within the jurisdiction, or
   (ii) was made by or through an agent trading or residing within the jurisdiction on behalf of a principal trading or residing out of the jurisdiction, or
   (iii) is by its terms, or by implication, governed by English law, or
   (iv) contains a term to the effect that the High Court shall have jurisdiction to hear and determine any action in respect of the contract;

6.3.3.4.1 GENERAL SCOPE

6.3.3.4.1.1 For the purposes of paragraph (d) the contract which is the subject matter of the litigation must be a contract between the plaintiff and the defendant.[116] Also, the word "contract" must be interpreted strictly; paragraph (d) does not extend to the relationship created by the appointment of a company director, even though such a relationship is analogous to a contractual relationship.[117]

112. RSC, Order 16, r. 3(4). See *Société Commerciale de Réassurance* v. *ERAS (International) Ltd* [1992] 1 Lloyd's Rep 570.
113. See *Multinational Gas & Petrochemical Co* v. *Multinational Gas & Petrochemical Services Ltd* [1983] Ch 258. Fawcett, "Jurisdiction over Foreign Companies" (1984) 100 LQR 17.
114. RSC, Order 11, r. 4(1)(d). This is in addition to the information prescribed by RSC, Order 11, r. 4(1)(a) to (c). See para. 6.3.1.2.
115. *ISC Technologies Ltd* v. *Guerin* [1992] 2 Lloyd's Rep 430.
116. *Finnish Marine Insurance Co Ltd* v. *Protective National Insurance Co* [1990] 1 QB 1078.
117. *Newtherapeutics Ltd* v. *Katz* [1990] Ch 226.

6.3.3.4.1.2 Paragraph (d) encompasses a claim for a declaration that a contract has been rescinded for misrepresentation or a claim that a contract has been discharged by frustration,[118] as well as a claim for a declaration that a contractual term remains enforceable between the parties.[119] However, a claim for a declaration that an alleged contract never existed is not within the rule's scope; a distinction has to be drawn between "the case where there has been a contract, which has later been discharged by an accepted repudiation, frustration or rescission, and a 'contract' which has never been entered into at all".[120]

6.3.3.4.1.3 The words "or otherwise affect" "are very wide; indeed, almost as wide as they can be".[121] It has even been held that, in certain circumstances, where there is a direct link between two contracts, a claim arising out of a contract which, viewed in isolation, cannot be the subject of leave to serve out of the jurisdiction under RSC, Order 11, may nevertheless be regarded as falling within the scope of paragraph (d) if that claim affects another contract which is covered by one or more of subparagraphs (i) to (iv).[122] There must, however, be an immediate link between the two contracts:

> [S]uppose that an English company has two contracts with a contractor. The first is a foreign contract for some prefabrication which is entirely outside Order 11. The second is a construction contract to be performed in this country by means of the materials to be prefabricated abroad under the foreign contract. Suppose that there is then a breach of the foreign contract. . . . [I]t could not possibly be right that the company could obtain leave to serve abroad a claim under the foreign prefabrication contract merely on the ground that its breach has had some consequences for, or repercussions upon, the due performance of the English contract.[123]

6.3.3.4.2 MADE WITHIN THE JURISDICTION

6.3.3.4.2.1 It is for English law as the *lex fori* to determine whether or not a contract is made within the jurisdiction. Whereas a contract concluded by exchange of letters is made where the acceptance of the offer is posted,[124] a contract concluded by telephone or telex is made where the offeror receives notification of acceptance.[125] By analogy, a contract concluded by fax is concluded where the acceptance is received.

6.3.3.4.2.2 Potential problems arise in cases where a contract is negotiated in one country but formally signed in another or where a contract is concluded in one country and then amended in another. It has been held that a contract may be regarded as made within the jurisdiction, notwithstanding the fact that it was preceded by a less formal agreement which was made abroad. In *Gibbon* v. *Commerz und Creditbank AG*[126] the parties reached an agreement in Hamburg, but letters were subsequently exchanged in London. The Court of Appeal decided that the agreement was made in London on the

118. *BP Exploration Co (Libya) Ltd* v. *Hunt* [1976] 1 WLR 788.
119. *Gulf Bank KSC* v. *Mitsubishi Heavy Industries Ltd*, *The Times*, 24 August 1993.
120. Judge Hamilton QC in *Finnish Marine Insurance Co Ltd* v. *Protective National Insurance Co* [1990] 1 QB 1078, 1084. Carter, (1990) 61 BYIL 395.
121. Kerr J in *BP Exploration Co (Libya) Ltd* v. *Hunt* [1976] 1 WLR 788, 795. This passage was approved by the House of Lords in *Spiliada Maritime Corporation* v. *Cansulex Ltd* [1987] AC 460. There are, however, limits to the scope of RSC, Order 11, r. 1(1)(d): *The Agia Skepi* [1992] 2 Lloyd's Rep 467.
122. *EF Hutton & Co (London) Ltd* v. *Monfarrij* [1989] 1 WLR 488.
123. Kerr LJ in *EF Hutton & Co (London) Ltd* v. *Monfarrij* [1989] 1 WLR 488, 494.
124. *Benaim & Co* v. *Debono* [1924] AC 514.
125. *Entores Ltd* v. *Miles Far East Corporation* [1955] 2 QB 327; *Brinkibon Ltd* v. *Stahag Stahl und Stahlwarenhandelsgesellschaft mbH* [1983] 2 AC 34.
126. [1958] 2 Lloyd's Rep 113.

basis that the written agreement superseded what was agreed in Hamburg.[127] However, it would follow that in a situation where a written agreement merely evidences a concluded oral contract which was made abroad, the plaintiff should not be able to rely on rule 1(1)(d)(i).

6.3.3.4.2.3 In *BP Exploration Co (Libya) Ltd* v. *Hunt*[128] the parties had entered an agreement in London in 1960. In 1967 this agreement was partly amended in Texas. The 1967 amendment could not, however, stand alone; it merely amended certain provisions of the 1960 agreement. It was argued on behalf of the defendant that, since the contract had been made partly in England and partly in Texas, the situation did not fall within rule 1(1)(d)(i). Two propositions emerge (albeit *obiter*) from Kerr J's judgment: (i) if the effect of the amendment is to discharge completely the original agreement the contract is to be regarded for jurisdictional purposes as having been made at the place where it is amended; (ii) where a contract is made partly within the jurisdiction and partly abroad, "it is sufficient for the purposes of the rule if the contract which is the subject matter of the action was substantially made within the jurisdiction".[129]

6.3.3.4.3 WHOSE AGENT?

6.3.3.4.3.1 Subparagraph (ii) applies to cases where the contract is negotiated by an agent in England, but is concluded by the principal abroad. (If the agent concludes the contract in England on the principal's behalf, the case falls within rule 1(1)(d)(i).) The introduction of this head of jurisdiction is justified on the basis that if foreigners choose to carry on business here by means of agents it is only right and proper to be able to serve them even though they are out of the jurisdiction.[130]

6.3.3.4.3.2 Where it is the plaintiff rather than the defendant who conducts business in England through an agent, there is no justification for the assumption of jurisdiction over a foreign defendant. Accordingly, subparagraph (ii) is relevant only where the agent through whom the contract was made was acting on behalf of the defendant.[131] A foreign plaintiff cannot obtain leave to serve a writ on a defendant outside the jurisdiction on the basis that the contract was made through the former's English agent.

6.3.3.4.4 CONTRACTS GOVERNED BY ENGLISH LAW

6.3.3.4.4.1 Applications for leave to serve out of the jurisdiction under RSC, Order 11 on the ground that the dispute relates to a contract governed by English law have provided numerous opportunities for the formulation and refinement of the proper law doctrine as it applies to contractual obligations.[132] As regards contracts entered into on or after 1 April 1991, the proper law doctrine has given way to the Rome Convention on the Law Applicable to Contractual Obligations, which was implemented into English law by the Contracts (Applicable Law) Act 1990.

6.3.3.4.4.2 The common law choice of law rules continue to apply to those questions

127. See Morris LJ, [1958] 2 Lloyd's Rep 113, 120.
128. [1976] 1 WLR 788. Carter, (1976–77) 48 BYIL 371.
129. [1976] 1 WLR 788, 798.
130. Atkin LJ in *National Mortgage and Agency Co of New Zealand Ltd* v. *Gosselin* (1922) 38 TLR 832, 833.
131. *Union International Insurance Co Ltd* v. *Jubilee Insurance Co Ltd* [1991] 1 WLR 415.
132. For example, *Amin Rasheed Shipping Corporation* v. *Kuwait Insurance Co* [1984] AC 50. See Fawcett, "The Interrelationships of Jurisdiction and Choice of Law in Private International Law" [1991] CLP 38.

falling outside the Convention's scope. One of the excluded matters is "procedure".[133] The question therefore arises as to whether the common law rules continue to determine whether or not a contract is governed by English law for the purposes of subparagraph (iii). Although the Rules of the Supreme Court are procedural, they incorporate issues of substantive law. The law governing a contract for the purposes of subparagraph (iii) is a substantive question, which—as regards any contract falling within the Convention's scope—is to be determined by reference to the rules contained in the Convention.[134]

6.3.3.4.5 JURISDICTION CLAUSES IN FAVOUR OF THE ENGLISH COURTS[135]

Many contracts contain a jurisdiction clause—that is, an agreement to refer disputes arising out of a legal relationship to the courts of a particular country. If the agreement provides a contractual method for the service of the writ within the jurisdiction the plaintiff may employ that agreed method.[136]

In many situations rule 1(1)(d)(iv) is superseded by Article 17 of the Conventions.[137] If the conditions for the application of Article 17 are met the plaintiff may serve a foreign defendant out of the jurisdiction without the leave of the court.[138]

6.3.3.5 Breach of contract within the jurisdiction

> (e) the claim is brought in respect of a breach committed within the jurisdiction of a contract made within or out of the jurisdiction, and irrespective of the fact, if such be the case, that the breach was preceded or accompanied by a breach committed out of the jurisdiction that rendered impossible the performance of so much of the contract as ought to have been performed within the jurisdiction;

For paragraph (e) to apply there must have been a contract between the parties, the defendant must be guilty of breach and the breach must have occurred in England. In principle, where the contract is breached by non-performance, the place where the breach has been committed should be determined by the law which governs the contract. Although there are some English authorities which support this proposition, in the majority of cases the courts seem to apply English law as the *lex fori* to this question.

6.3.3.6 Tort

> (f) the claim is founded on a tort and the damage was sustained, or resulted from an act committed, within the jurisdiction;

Until 1987 leave could be given in tort cases only if the plaintiff's claim was "founded on a tort committed within the jurisdiction". The current verbal formulation, which was inspired by Article 5(3) of the Brussels Convention,[139] avoids the problems associated with having to determine the place of the tort in cases where the wrongful act is

133. Article 1(2)(h).
134. For a discussion of choice of law in contract see Chapters 10 to 12.
135. For further discussion see para. 6.5.
136. RSC, Order 10, r. 3.
137. See para. 5.3.
138. RSC, Order 11, r. 1(2).
139. See para. 5.5.4.

committed in one country and the damage is sustained in another.[140] In order for the plaintiff to be able to rely on paragraph (f) the court must be satisfied that (i) the claim is founded on a tort and either (ii) the damage was sustained within the jurisdiction or (iii) the damage resulted from an act committed within the jurisdiction. These three requirements were considered by the Court of Appeal in *Metall und Rohstoff AG* v. *Donaldson Lufkin & Jenrette Inc.*[141]

(i) To decide whether or not the claim is "founded on a tort" for the purposes of paragraph (f) "the courts will apply exclusively English law".[142] Claims to equitable restitutionary remedies for breach of trust or breach of fiduciary duty are not "founded on a tort" and therefore must be brought within some other paragraph of RSC, Order 11.[143]

(ii) For the purposes of paragraph (f), it is enough that "some significant damage has been sustained in England".[144]

(iii) In the context of RSC, Order 11 the key question is whether there are sufficient links between the defendant and the English forum to justify the assumption of jurisdiction. Accordingly, when considering whether the damage resulted from acts committed within the jurisdiction the acts of the putative defendant are those which are relevant. Paragraph (f) does not require all the acts to have been committed within the jurisdiction; it is not sufficient, however, that the plaintiff can point to some relatively minor or insignificant act committed, perhaps fortuitously, within the jurisdiction. The court is required "to look at the tort alleged in a common sense way and ask whether damage has resulted from substantial and efficacious acts committed within the jurisdiction (whether or not other substantial and efficacious acts have been committed elsewhere): if the answer is yes, leave may (but of course need not) be given".[145]

6.3.3.7 *Restitution*

(t) the claim is brought for money had and received or for an account or other relief against the defendant as constructive trustee, and the defendant's alleged liability arises out of acts committed, whether by him or otherwise, within the jurisdiction.

This paragraph is primarily designed to enable proceedings to be brought in fraud cases against a foreign entity which has not participated in the fraud, but which has been used by the persons who control it as a receptacle for the proceeds of the fraud. The basic factual connection which justifies the assumption of jurisdiction under paragraph (t) is that the defendant committed acts within the jurisdiction. It is not, however, necessary for the plaintiff to show that all the acts in question were committed within the jurisdiction, so long as some of them were.[146] So, for example, it is not essential that the

140. See para. 13.1.
141. [1990] 1 QB 391. Fentiman, [1989] CLJ 191; Carter, (1989) 60 BYIL 485.
142. Slade LJ in *Metall und Rohstoff AG* v. *Donaldson Lufkin & Jenrette Inc* [1990] 1 QB 391, 443.
143. *ISC Technologies Ltd* v. *Guerin* [1992] 2 Lloyd's Rep 430.
144. Slade LJ in *Metall und Rohstoff AG* v. *Donaldson Lufkin & Jenrette Inc* [1990] 1 QB 391, 437.
145. Slade LJ in *Metall und Rohstoff AG* v. *Donaldson Lufkin & Jenrette Inc* [1990] 1 QB 391, 437.
146. *ISC Technologies Ltd* v. *Guerin* [1992] 2 Lloyd's Rep 430.

defendant acquired the knowledge upon which a claim to enforce an alleged constructive trust is based within the jurisdiction.[147]

6.3.3.8 Other heads of jurisdiction

(g) the whole subject-matter of the action is land situate within the jurisdiction (with or without rent or profits) or the perpetuation of testimony relating to land so situate;
(h) the claim is brought to construe, rectify, set aside or enforce an act, deed, will, contract, obligation or liability affecting land situate within the jurisdiction;
(i) the claim is made for a debt secured on immovable property or is made to assert, declare or determine proprietary or possessory rights, or rights of security, in or over movable property, or to obtain authority to dispose of movable property, situate within the jurisdiction;
(j) the claim is brought to execute trusts of a written instrument being trusts that ought to be executed according to English law and of which the person to be served with the writ is a trustee, or for any relief or remedy which might be obtained in such an action;
(k) the claim is made for the administration of the estate of a person who died domiciled within the jurisdiction or for any relief or remedy which might be obtained in any such action;
(l) the claim is brought in a probate action within the meaning of Order 76;
(m) the claim is brought to enforce any judgment or arbitral award[148];
(n) the claim is brought against a defendant not domiciled in Scotland or Northern Ireland in respect of a claim by the Commissioners of Inland Revenue for or in relation to any of the duties or taxes which have been, or are for the time being, placed under their care and management;
(o) the claim is brought under the Nuclear Installations Act 1965 or in respect of contributions under the Social Security Act 1975;
(p) the claim is made for a sum to which the Directive of the Council of the European Communities dated 15th March 1976 No. 76/308/EEC applies, and service is to be effected in a country which is a member State of the European Economic Community;
(q) the claim is made under the Drug Trafficking Offences Act 1986;
(r) the claim is made under the Financial Services Act 1986 or the Banking Act 1987;
(s) the claim is made under Part VI of the Criminal Justice Act 1988;

6.3.3.9 Interpretation and standard of proof

6.3.3.9.1 As regards the merits of the plaintiff's claim, the requirement is that there is a serious question to be tried.[149] What, however, is the relevant test when there is a dispute as to whether the plaintiff's claim falls within the scope of one of the heads of RSC, Order 11?

In *Seaconsar Far East Ltd* v. *Bank Markazi Jomhouri Islami Iran*[150] the House of Lords decided that the plaintiff must establish "a good arguable case" that the claim falls within the paragraph of rule 1(1) relied upon. It is important to note that this test applies not only where the question of jurisdiction is separate from questions as to the merits, but also where these two issues are interrelated. Where, for example, the plaintiff invokes the jurisdiction of the court under RSC, Order 11, rule 1(1)(d)(i)

147. *Polly Peck International Plc* v. *Nadir*, *The Independent*, 2 September 1992.
148. For a discussion of jurisdiction in cases relating to the enforcement of arbitral awards see para. 17.5.1.3.
149. See para. 6.3.2.
150. [1993] 3 WLR 756.

the plaintiff must establish a good arguable case that (i) there was a contract and (ii) such a contract was made within the jurisdiction. It is not enough merely to show that if the contract existed it was made within the jurisdiction.[151] Similarly, where the plaintiff seeks to rely on RSC, Order 11, rule 1(1)(e) there must be a good arguable case that (i) there was a contract, (ii) the contract was broken and (iii) the breach was committed within the jurisdiction. It is not enough for the plaintiff to show that "if there was a contract and it had been broken such breach was committed within the jurisdiction".[152]

6.3.3.9.2. The formula "a good arguable case" is inherently vague. It would seem that a good arguable case may be equated with "a strong argument" or "a strong case for argument".[153] Accordingly, some recent cases which suggest that the plaintiff must show that he is "probably right"[154] or that there is "a strong probability that the claim falls within the letter and the spirit of the subhead . . . of Order 11, rule 1(1) relied upon"[155] go too far.

6.3.3.9.3 It is important to note the limits of the decision in *Seaconsar Far East Ltd* v. *Bank Markazi Jomhouri Islami Iran.* The House of Lords' attention was directed to the case where the dispute between the parties on the question of jurisdiction turns on disputed questions of fact or on disputes as to the legal conclusions which may be drawn from the facts (such as whether the defendant's conduct amounts to a breach of contract). The application of the test of "a good arguable case" in this context is designed to ensure that, as far as possible, Order 11 proceedings are not turned into trials on affidavits—an obviously unsatisfactory procedure.

6.3.3.9.4 The House of Lords did not, however, address the situation in which there is no dispute on the facts of the case, but the parties disagree on the construction of the words of the relevant paragraph of RSC, Order 11. In this type of case—in which the court is faced with a pure question of law which must be determined one way or the other—it is reasonable to expect the plaintiff to establish that "the case comes clearly within one of the heads of RSC, Order 11 and further that it comes not merely within the letter but also within the spirit of the rule".[156] When confronted with a problem concerning the correct construction and application of provisions of RSC, Order 11 to a particular situation the court must decide whether the plaintiff is right or wrong; this type of situation does not involve or require any further investigation and, therefore, it is not enough for the plaintiff to say that, even if he cannot bring himself within both the letter and the spirit of Order 11, he nevertheless has a good arguable case.[157] If there is any ambiguity in the construction of the rules, such ambiguity must be resolved in the defendant's favour.[158]

151. Lord Goff, [1993] 3 WLR 756, 765–766.
152. Lord Goff, [1993] 3 WLR 756, 764–765.
153. *Seaconsar Far East Ltd* v. *Bank Markazi Jomhouri Islami Iran* [1993] 3 WLR 756, 764.
154. Staughton LJ in *Attock Cement Co Ltd* v. *Romanian Bank for Foreign Trade* [1989] 1 WLR 1147, 1155.
155. Slade LJ in *Metall und Rohstoff AG* v. *Donaldson Lufkin & Jenrette Inc* [1990] 1 QB 391, 434.
156. Lloyd J in *Atlantic Underwriting Agencies Ltd* v. *Compagnia di Assicurazione di Milano SpA* [1979] 2 Lloyd's Rep 240, 245.
157. *EF Hutton & Co (London) Ltd* v. *Monfarrij* [1989] 1 WLR 488.
158. *The Hagen* [1908] P 189; *Siskina (Owners of cargo lately laden on board)* v. *Distos Compania Naviera SA* [1979] AC 210.

6.3.4 *Forum conveniens*

The third requirement is that the plaintiff must establish that England is the most appropriate forum.[159]

6.4 THE IMPORTANCE OF DISCRETION

The exercise of the court's discretion is of fundamental importance when considering the boundaries of jurisdiction under traditional English rules. In cases where a writ is served in England as of right, the defendant may apply for a stay of proceedings on the ground that there is another more appropriate forum (*forum non conveniens*). Where the plaintiff seeks leave under RSC, Order 11 leave will be refused unless the court is satisfied that England is clearly the appropriate forum (*forum conveniens*).

6.4.1 Forum shopping

6.4.1.1 The fact that many systems of procedural law include exorbitant jurisdiction rules means that in the context of an international dispute the plaintiff often has a choice between two or more countries in which to proceed against the defendant. The existence of alternative fora gives rise to forum shopping[160]—a practice which has been defined as "a plaintiff by-passing his natural forum and bringing his action in some alien forum which would give him relief or benefits which would not be available to him in his natural forum".[161] Of course, this definition raises more questions than it answers: "What is the natural forum? Is it the forum with which the dispute is most closely connected or the forum in which it can be resolved most conveniently?"[162]

6.4.1.2 Forum shopping is widespread; for example, in more than a quarter of cases heard by the English Commercial Court both parties come from overseas.[163] Of course, forum shopping is not confined to foreign plaintiffs trying to obtain the perceived benefits of English justice. There is a recent history of plaintiffs trying their luck in the United States of America in the hope of obtaining higher damages awards: "As a moth is drawn to the light, so is a litigant drawn to the United States".[164] A striking example is the litigation following the crash near Paris of a DC-10 owned by a Turkish airline in 1974. Eleven hundred plaintiffs from all over the world brought proceedings in California against a number of defendants, including the manufacturers of the aircraft. Having failed to persuade the Californian court to decline jurisdiction on the basis of *forum non conveniens* the defendants agreed not to contest liability. Following proceedings in which the quantum of damages was contested, damages were awarded to two plaintiffs and the remaining claims were settled.[165]

159. See para. 6.4.
160. See Fawcett, "Forum Shopping—Some Questions Answered" (1984) 35 NILQ 141.
161. Lord Pearson in *Boys* v. *Chaplin* [1971] AC 356, 401.
162. Slater, "Forum Non Conveniens: A View from the Shop Floor" (1988) 104 LQR 554, 560.
163. See Staughton LJ in *Sohio Supply Co* v. *Gatoil (USA) Inc* [1989] 1 Lloyd's Rep 588, 592.
164. Lord Denning MR in *Smith, Kline & French Laboratories Ltd* v. *Bloch* [1983] 1 WLR 730, 733. See also *Castanho* v. *Brown & Root (UK) Ltd* [1981] AC 557.
165. *In re Paris Air Crash of March 3, 1974*, 399 F Supp 732 (1975). See Juenger, "Forum Shopping Domestic and International" (1989) 63 Tulane LR 553, 560–562.

6.4.1.3 There is no consensus as to whether forum shopping is an evil which ought to be discouraged or prevented. According to one school of thought, forum shopping is not something which merits condemnation. Forum shopping "is only a pejorative way of saying that, if you offer a plaintiff a choice of jurisdictions, he will naturally choose the one in which he thinks his case can be most favourably presented: this should be a matter neither for surprise nor for indignation".[166] The question may be asked: "Is it necessarily objectionable to bring proceedings in an alien forum if that forum is one of the established centres for the resolution of disputes and offers specialised services or facilities not available in the natural forum?"[167] There is also an economic angle to forum shopping, since international dispute resolution can be a valuable source of invisible exports.

6.4.1.4 On the other hand, there are arguments against allowing plaintiffs to engage in forum shopping. (i) While it would be wrong to deprive prospective plaintiffs of all choice—since there may well be more than one forum which would be suitable for the trial of the action—forum shopping may lead to injustice to the defendant. For example, forum shopping may be used by a plaintiff to put pressure on a defendant to settle a claim on terms which are more favourable to the plaintiff than would have been the case had proceedings been brought in the natural forum. (ii) It is said that forum shopping is contrary to the public interest in the sense that it is wasteful of the time of witnesses and of others. (iii) Forum shopping may be thought to be incompatible with the principle of comity in that to allow foreigners to litigate in England when there is a natural forum elsewhere is in some way derogatory of foreign courts or foreigners generally.[168] Thinking along these lines has given birth to the contrasting expressions "judicial chauvinism" (which is evidenced by a liberal attitude towards forum shopping) and "judicial comity" (which is typified by a commitment to directing litigation to its natural forum). In *The Abidin Daver* Lord Diplock expressed the view that the evolution of English law during the 1970s and 80s was proof of the fact that in England "judicial chauvinism has been replaced by judicial comity".[169]

6.4.2 The development of English law

6.4.2.1 From a doctrinal point of view there are two different strands in the case law. On the one hand, the courts are conscious of the exorbitant nature of jurisdiction under RSC, Order 11. It has long been established that the court will not grant leave to serve a writ on a defendant out of the jurisdiction unless the plaintiff shows that the England is the appropriate forum. Although the phrase "*forum conveniens*" does not seem to have been used regularly until after the decision of the Court of Appeal in *Rosler* v. *Hilbery*[170] in 1925, in English law the concept can be traced back to the late nineteenth century.[171]

166. Lord Simon in *The Atlantic Star* [1974] AC 436, 471.
167. Slater, "Forum Non Conveniens: A View from the Shop Floor" (1988) 104 LQR 554, 560–561.
168. Slater, "Forum Non Conveniens: A View from the Shop Floor" (1988) 104 LQR 554, 562.
169. [1984] AC 398, 411.
170. [1925] Ch 250.
171. *Société Générale de Paris* v. *Dreyfus Brothers* (1885) 29 ChD 239.

6.4.2.2 By contrast, in cases where jurisdiction is invoked as of right—on the basis of the defendant's presence in England at the time of service—the traditional approach of the courts was to decline jurisdiction only in exceptional cases. The basic premise was that "[t]he right of access to the King's court must not be lightly refused".[172] In *St Pierre* v. *South American Stores (Gath & Chaves) Ltd* it was decided that if a defendant who had been served within the jurisdiction requested the court to exercise its inherent jurisdiction to stay the proceedings, a stay would generally be refused unless the defendant could show that "the continuance of the action would work an injustice because it would be oppressive or vexatious to him or would be an abuse of the process of the court in some other way; and . . . the stay [would] not cause an injustice to the plaintiff".[173] Since a mere balance of convenience was not a sufficient ground for depriving a plaintiff of the advantages of prosecuting his action in England, a stay of proceedings would normally be refused even in a case where neither party was resident in or otherwise closely connected with England and the cause of action related to events which had taken place abroad.[174] This endorsement of forum shopping was a reflection of the view that "if the forum is England, it is a good place to shop in, both for the quality of the goods and the speed of service".[175]

6.4.2.3 There was, however, a tension between the approach adopted to applications for leave to serve out under RSC, Order 11 and applications for a stay of proceedings under the court's inherent jurisdiction. The assumption of jurisdiction under RSC, Order 11 undermines the idea that jurisdiction is based on territorial sovereignty. If a writ can be served anywhere in the world on the basis that the litigation has a sufficient connection with the forum, the automatic assumption of jurisdiction on the basis of the defendant's fleeting presence becomes open to question. RSC, Order 11 shows that the theoretical foundation of jurisdiction is not territorial sovereignty and suggests an approach to jurisdiction based on contacts between the case and the forum, whether or not the defendant is served within the jurisdiction.[176]

6.4.2.4 In the 1970s and early 1980s the first steps were taken towards integrating the divergent common law rules. In a trio of cases—*The Atlantic Star*,[177] *MacShannon* v. *Rockware Glass Ltd*[178] and *The Abidin Daver*[179]—the House of Lords dismissed the traditional approach as recalling "the good old days, the passing of which many may regret, when the inhabitants of this island felt an innate superiority over those unfortunate enough to belong to other races"[180] and indicated a far greater willingness

172. Scott LJ in *St Pierre* v. *South American Stores (Gath & Chaves) Ltd* [1936] 1 KB 382, 398.
173. Scott LJ, [1936] 1 KB 382, 398.
174. See, for example, *Maharanee of Baroda* v. *Wildenstein* [1972] 2 QB 283.
175. Lord Denning MR in *The Atlantic Star* [1973] QB 364, 382.
176. See Pryles, "The Basis of Adjudicatory Competence in Private International Law" (1973) 21 ICLQ 61.
177. [1974] AC 436. Bridge, "Changing Attitudes to Jurisdiction" (1973) 36 MLR 649; Carter, (1972–73) 46 BYIL 428; Collier, [1973] CLJ 240; McLean, "Foreign Collisions and Forum Conveniens" (1973) 22 ICLQ 748.
178. [1978] AC 795. Carter, (1978) 49 BYIL 291; Weiler, "Forum Non Conveniens—An English Doctrine?" (1978) 41 MLR 739. For developments immediately after *MacShannon* v. *Rockware Glass Ltd* see Carter, (1979) 50 BYIL 245.
179. [1984] AC 398. Barma & Elvin, "Forum Non Conveniens; Where Do We Go from Here?" (1985) 101 LQR 48; Carter, (1984) 55 BYIL 351; Fawcett, "Lis Alibi Pendens and the Discretion to Stay" (1984) 47 MLR 481.
180. Lord Reid in *The Atlantic Star* [1974] AC 436, 453.

to stay English proceedings in cases where England was not the appropriate forum. In *The Atlantic Star*[181] the House of Lords suggested that the words "vexatious and oppressive" in the *St Pierre* formula should be given a flexible interpretation. In *MacShannon* v. *Rockware Glass Ltd*[182] the House of Lords went further and reformulated the *St Pierre* test. According to the test laid down by Lord Diplock, "[i]n order to justify a stay . . . (a) the defendant must satisfy the court that there is another forum to whose jurisdiction he is amenable in which justice can be done between the parties at substantially less inconvenience or expense, and (b) the stay must not deprive the plaintiff of a legitimate personal or juridical advantage which would be available to him if he invoked the jurisdiction of the English court".[183] In *The Abidin Daver*[184] the more flexible approach which had been advocated in *MacShannon* v. *Rockware Glass Ltd* was extended to the situation where parallel proceedings between the same parties and concerning the same cause of action were brought in England and abroad.

6.4.2.5 Towards the middle of the 1980s it became increasingly clear that similar considerations were relevant both in cases where the defendant applies for a stay of proceedings commenced in England and in cases where the plaintiff seeks leave to serve out of the jurisdiction under RSC, Order 11.[185] The decision of the House of Lords in *Spiliada Maritime Corporation* v. *Cansulex Ltd*,[186] in which English law at last fully embraced the doctrine of *forum non conveniens*,[187] is the logical conclusion of this realisation.

6.4.3 The test of appropriateness

The key features of the test of appropriateness emerge from Lord Goff's speech in *Spiliada Maritime Corporation* v. *Cansulex Ltd*[188]; Lord Templeman gave a short concurring speech; the other members of the House of Lords agreed with both speeches. The basic test has been considered and applied in a significant number of subsequent cases.

(i) The same fundamental principles apply to cases where the defendant seeks a stay of proceedings which have been started as of right in England (*forum non conveniens*) and where the plaintiff seeks leave to serve a writ on the defendant out of the jurisdiction under RSC, Order 11 (*forum conveniens*). In

181. [1974] AC 436.
182. [1978] AC 795.
183. [1978] AC 795, 812.
184. [1984] AC 398.
185. Briggs, "Forum Non Conveniens—Now We Are Ten?" (1983) 3 LS 74 and "The Staying of Actions on the Ground of 'Forum Non Conveniens' Today" [1984] LMCLQ 227; Schuz, "Controlling Forum-Shopping: The Impact of MacShannon v. Rockware Glass Ltd" (1986) 35 ICLQ 374.
186. [1987] AC 460. Briggs, "Forum Non Conveniens—the Last Word?" [1987] LMCLQ 1; Carter, (1986) 57 BYIL 429; Collier, [1987] CLJ 33; Jacob, (1987) 6 CJQ 89. For a policy-based evaluation see Fawcett, "Trial in England or Abroad: The Underlying Policy Considerations" (1989) 9 OJLS 205.
187. This doctrine has long been established in other jurisdictions. For a discussion of the development of the law in the United States see Robertson, "Forum Non Conveniens in America and England: 'A Rather Fantastic Fiction'" (1987) 103 LQR 398, 400–409. The leading Scots cases are *Sim* v. *Robinow* (1892) 19 R 665 and *Société du Gaz de Paris* v. *Société Anonyme de Navigation "Les Armateurs Français"* 1926 SC (HL) 13.
188. [1987] AC 460.

adopting this approach the House of Lords rejected the view expressed by Lord Wilberforce in *Amin Rasheed Shipping Corporation* v. *Kuwait Insurance Co*[189] that the principles which had been formulated as regards the staying of actions were of little assistance in deciding cases under RSC, Order 11.

(ii) The word "*conveniens*" is not to be equated with convenience. Notwithstanding the Latin label "it is most important not to allow it to mislead us into thinking that the question at issue is one of 'mere practical convenience'".[190] In Lord Goff's view "the question is not one of convenience, but of suitability or appropriateness of the jurisdiction".[191]

(iii) Whether the case involves an application for a stay or an application for leave to serve out of the jurisdiction the court's task is to identify the forum "in which the case can be tried more suitably for the interests of the parties and for the ends of justice".[192]

(iv) As regards the staying of proceedings under the court's inherent jurisdiction, the general principle should be applied in the following way:

(a) The basic principle is that a stay will only be granted on the ground of *forum non conveniens* where the court is satisfied that there is some other available forum, having competent jurisdiction, which is the appropriate forum for the trial of the action.[193]

(b) The burden of proof rests on the defendant to persuade the court to exercise its discretion to grant a stay. If, however, the defendant shows that there is some other forum which *prima facie* is the appropriate forum for the trial of the action, the burden shifts to the plaintiff to show that there are special circumstances by reason of which justice requires that trial should nevertheless proceed in England.[194]

(c) The burden on the defendant is not to show that England is not the natural or appropriate forum for the trial, but to establish that there is another available forum which is clearly or distinctly more appropriate than the English forum. (On this point, proper regard must be paid to the fact that jurisdiction has been founded in England as of right.[195])

(d) The first step is to see what factors there are which point in the direction of another forum as that with which the dispute has the most real and substantial connection. Such factors may not only affect convenience and expense (such as the availability of witnesses) but may also relate to the applicable law and the places where the parties reside or carry on business.[196] There are, however, certain situations in which the court is likely to assume that a particular country is the natural forum. For example, "if the substance of an alleged tort is committed within a certain jurisdiction, it is not easy to imagine what other facts could displace the

189. [1984] AC 50, 72.
190. Lord Goff in *Spiliada Maritime Corporation* v. *Cansulex Ltd* [1987] AC 460, 474.
191. [1987] AC 460, 474.
192. Lord Goff, [1987] AC 460, 474; citing Lord Kinnear in *Sim* v. *Robinow* (1892) 19 R 665, 668.
193. Lord Goff, [1987] AC 460, 476.
194. Lord Goff, [1987] AC 460, 476.
195. Lord Goff, [1987] AC 460, 477.
196. Lord Goff, [1987] AC 460, 477–478.

conclusion that the courts of that jurisdiction are the natural forum".[197]

(e) The time for considering whether another forum is more appropriate is the date on which the defendant's application for a stay is heard.[198]

(f) If the court concludes that *prima facie* there is no other forum which is clearly more appropriate for the trial of the action, it will ordinarily refuse a stay.[199] Furthermore, if there is no natural forum for the trial of the action, the court is entitled to refuse to grant a stay.[200] Such cases are likely to occur in commercial disputes, where connecting factors may point to a number of different jurisdictions[201] and in Admiralty cases involving collisions on the high seas.[202]

(g) If, however, the court concludes that there is some available forum which *prima facie* is clearly more appropriate for the trial of the action, it will ordinarily grant a stay unless there are circumstances by reason of which justice requires that a stay should nevertheless be granted. In this enquiry, the court will consider all the circumstances of the case, including circumstances which go beyond those taken into account when considering connecting factors with other jurisdictions. The burden of proof is on the plaintiff to show that justice requires that a stay should not be granted. If the plaintiff can establish that he will not obtain justice in the foreign jurisdiction, that is a very relevant consideration.[203]

(h) In *MacShannon* v. *Rockware Glass Ltd* Lord Diplock had thought that the court should not grant a stay if it would "deprive the plaintiff of a legitimate personal or juridical advantage which would be available to him if he invoked the jurisdiction of the English court".[204] In *Spiliada Maritime Corporation* v. *Cansulex Ltd* Lord Goff was eager to play down the importance of advantages to the plaintiff; the mere fact that the plaintiff has a legitimate personal or juridical advantage in proceeding in England should not be decisive.[205] The court should not be deterred from granting a stay of proceedings simply because the plaintiff will be deprived of such an advantage "provided that the court is satisfied that substantial justice will be done in the available appropriate forum".[206]

(v) In relation to applications for leave to serve out of the jurisdiction under RSC, Order 11 the general principle laid down in *Spiliada Maritime Corporation* v. *Cansulex Ltd* requires the court to exercise its discretion in the following way:

(a) According to Lord Templeman, where the plaintiff seeks leave to serve out of the jurisdiction, the plaintiff must satisfy the court that England is "the most appropriate forum to try the action".[207] Lord Goff thought that

197. Robert Goff LJ in *The Albaforth* [1984] 2 Lloyd's Rep 91, 96; applied in *ISC Technologies Ltd* v. *Guerin* [1992] 2 Lloyd's Rep 430.
198. Hoffmann J in *ISC Technologies Ltd* v. *Guerin* [1992] 2 Lloyd's Rep 430, 434.
199. Lord Goff in *Spiliada Maritime Corporation* v. *Cansulex Ltd* [1987] AC 460, 478.
200. Lord Goff, [1987] AC 460, 477.
201. See, for example, *European Asian Bank AG* v. *Punjab & Sind Bank* [1982] 2 Lloyd's Rep 356.
202. *The Vishva Abha* [1990] 2 Lloyd's Rep 312.
203. Lord Goff in *Spiliada Maritime Corporation* v. *Cansulex Ltd* [1987] AC 460, 478.
204. [1978] AC 795, 812.
205. [1987] AC 460, 482–484.
206. Lord Goff, [1987] AC 460, 482.
207. [1987] AC 460, 465.

the burden of proof on the plaintiff is not simply to persuade the court that England is the appropriate forum for the trial of the action, but "to show that this is clearly so".[208] It is doubtful whether there is a difference of substance between these alternative verbal formulations.

(b) The test of appropriateness must always be applied by reference to the date on which the order granting (or refusing) leave was made. In cases where the decision to grant or refuse leave to serve out is subsequently challenged, events which occur after the decision has been made are relevant only to the extent that they throw light on those factors which were relevant considerations at that time.[209]

(c) In deciding whether the case is a proper one for leave to be given, the court must "take into account the nature of the dispute, the legal and practical issues involved, such questions as local knowledge, availability of witnesses and their evidence and expense".[210] Furthermore, it is necessary to take into account both the residence or place of business of the defendant and the relevant ground of RSC, Order 11 invoked by the plaintiff.

(d) For the purposes of the doctrine of *forum conveniens* the significance of the different grounds under RSC, Order 11 varies greatly from case to case. For example, in some cases the fact that the applicable law is English is of considerable importance; in others it is almost wholly irrelevant.[211]

(e) The court should not be deterred from exercising its discretion against granting leave simply because the plaintiff will be deprived of a legitimate personal or juridical advantage "provided that the court is satisfied that substantial justice will be done in the available appropriate forum".[212] Leave to serve out of the jurisdiction may be granted, notwithstanding the fact that there is an alternative forum abroad which is *prima facie* more appropriate, if the court is satisfied that the plaintiff will not obtain substantial justice abroad.[213]

(vi) A point which is explicit in cases which preceded *Spiliada Maritime Corporation* v. *Cansulex Ltd* should also be noted. When applying the test of appropriateness the court should not be drawn into a consideration of the advantages and disadvantages of the system of administering justice in foreign countries as compared with the system of administering justice in England: "for an English court to investigate such a matter and to pronounce a judgment on it is not consistent with the mutual respect which the courts of friendly States, each of which has a well developed system for the administration of justice, owe, or should owe to each other".[214]

208. [1987] AC 460, 481.
209. Hoffmann J in *ISC Technologies Ltd* v. *Guerin* [1992] 2 Lloyd's Rep 430, 434.
210. Lord Wilberforce in *Amin Rasheed Shipping Corporation* v. *Kuwait Insurance Co* [1984] AC 50, 72.
211. Lord Goff in *Spiliada Maritime Corporation* v. *Cansulex Ltd* [1987] AC 460, 481.
212. Lord Goff, [1987] AC 460, 482.
213. *Roneleigh Ltd* v. *MII Exports Inc* [1989] 1 WLR 619.
214. Brandon LJ in *The El Amria* [1981] 2 Lloyd's Rep 119, 126. See also Lord Diplock and Lord Wilberforce in *Amin Rasheed Corporation* v. *Kuwait Insurance Co* [1984] AC 50, 67–68 & 72 and the speech of Lord Brandon in *The Abidin Daver* [1984] AC 398, 425.

6.4.4 The application of the test: factors to be taken into account

When applying the test of appropriateness there is almost no limit to the range of factors which the court may, in the specific circumstances, consider to be relevant. The decided cases show that regard may be had to procedural factors (such as delay and costs) as well as to substantive factors (such as the applicable law). Of course, not all the factors are relevant in any particular case.

6.4.4.1 Convenience and expense

Although the doctrine of *forum (non) conveniens* is concerned with appropriateness rather than simply practical convenience, it is important not to lose sight of the fact that considerations of convenience and expense are relevant. So, the court should have regard to matters such as the residence and place of business of the parties as well as the availability of witnesses and other evidence.[215]

6.4.4.2 Lis alibi pendens

6.4.4.2.1 It is generally undesirable that the same dispute should be litigated in more than one forum. The additional inconvenience and expense which results from allowing two sets of legal proceedings to be pursued concurrently in two different countries where the same facts are in issue and the testimony of the same witnesses required is considerable. Furthermore, if both sets of proceedings proceed to judgment there is a risk of inconsistent decisions being handed down, which in turn may lead to problems of enforcement. Accordingly, the court should strive earnestly to avoid the risk of inconsistent decisions and should favour the litigation of issues only once, in the most appropriate forum.[216] Where parallel proceedings between the same parties concerning the same cause of action are brought in the courts of two or more Brussels or Lugano Contracting States any court other than the court first seised must stay its proceedings or decline jurisdiction under Article 21.[217] Where, however, parallel proceedings are brought in England and in a non-contracting State the *Spiliada* test confers a discretion on the court.

6.4.4.2.2 Prior to *Spiliada Maritime Corporation* v. *Cansulex Ltd* the leading authority on the staying of proceedings in cases where litigation on the same issue was pending in a foreign country (*lis alibi pendens*) was the House of Lords' decision in *The Abidin Daver.*[218] In *de Dampierre* v. *de Dampierre*, however, Lord Goff indicated that the general principle laid down in *Spiliada Maritime Corporation* v. *Cansulex Ltd* is applicable "whether or not there are other relevant proceedings already pending in the alternative forum".[219] Although there appear to be differences between the approach advocated by Lord Diplock in *The Abidin Daver* and the *Spiliada* test, it has come to be accepted that there is in fact no conflict between the cases.[220]

6.4.4.2.3 In cases concerning applications under RSC, Order 11 the plaintiff must

215. See, for example, *The Lakhta* [1992] 2 Lloyd's Rep 269.
216. Bingham LJ in *EI du Pont de Nemours & Co* v. *Agnew* [1987] 2 Lloyd's Rep 585, 589.
217. See para. 5.9.2.
218. [1984] AC 398.
219. [1988] AC 92, 108.
220. See, for example, *Cleveland Museum of Art* v. *Capricorn Art International SA* [1990] 2 Lloyd's Rep 166.

satisfy the court that England is clearly the appropriate forum, notwithstanding the fact that proceedings have already been started abroad; in cases involving an application for a stay the defendant must show that the existence of parallel proceedings abroad, along with all the other relevant factors, has the effect of making the foreign court the more appropriate forum. The existence of *lis alibi pendens* does not raise a presumption in favour of a stay or refusal to give leave so as to reverse the burden of proof.[221] The undesirability of there being concurrent proceedings in two countries is merely one of the considerations to be weighed as part of the overall assessment; it cannot necessarily lead to a stay or refusal to give leave.[222] The weight to be attached to the existence of *lis alibi pendens* depends on the circumstances of the case, including the stage reached in the proceedings abroad,[223] the connections with the foreign court and the basis on which the foreign court assumed jurisdiction.[224]

6.4.4.2.4 In modern practice, when one who asserts a positive claim has brought—or intends to bring—proceedings in one jurisdiction, it is not uncommon for the other party to bring an action for a negative declaration in another jurisdiction. As a general rule, the court will not allow actions for negative declarations to influence the decision on the question of appropriateness: "whether an action for a negative declaration is brought in England or abroad, it will not assist the plaintiff in displacing the natural forum for the substantive dispute".[225]

6.4.4.3 Multiple defendants

6.4.4.3.1 It is clearly inconvenient in a case where there is more than one defendant if the plaintiff is required to pursue litigation against each defendant in a different jurisdiction. Furthermore, unless multiparty disputes are heard by the same court there is a risk of inconsistent decisions. A plaintiff, therefore, has a legitimate interest in trying to consolidate the claims into one set of proceedings. RSC, Order 11, rule 1(1)(c) enables the plaintiff to serve a writ out of the jurisdiction on a defendant who is a necessary or proper party to litigation being brought against another defendant in England.[226]

6.4.4.3.2 If a foreign court has jurisdiction to determine all the claims in multiparty proceedings this is a factor which points against the assumption of jurisdiction by an English court.[227] Conversely, where all the potential defendants can be sued in England—by virtue of their being served within the jurisdiction as of right or out of the jurisdiction with leave of the court—this is a factor which points towards England as the appropriate forum. Indeed, this factor may be decisive. There are circumstances in which, simply by virtue of the fact that RSC, Order 11, rule 1(1)(c) enables there to be a single trial with all effective parties present and bound by the result, the English court is

221. Hirst J in *Meadows Indemnity Co Ltd* v. *Insurance Corporation of Ireland Plc* [1989] 1 Lloyd's Rep 181, 189.

222. Bingham LJ in *El du Pont de Nemours & Co* v. *Agnew* [1987] 2 Lloyd's Rep 585, 589.

223. *Cleveland Museum of Art* v. *Capricorn Art SA* [1990] 2 Lloyd's Rep 166.

224. *The Volvox Hollandia* [1988] 2 Lloyd's Rep 361.

225. Collins, "Negative Declarations and the Brussels Convention" (1992) 108 LQR 545, 547. See, for example, *El du Pont de Nemours & Co* v. *Agnew* [1987] 2 Lloyd's Rep 585.

226. See para. 6.3.3.3.

227. *The Oinoussin Pride* [1991] 1 Lloyd's Rep 126.

the most appropriate forum even though the factual connections with another forum are stronger.[228]

6.4.4.3.3 In cases where the plaintiff seeks to rely on RSC, Order 11, rule 1(1)(c) there appears to be a certain circularity in the reasoning if the existence of exorbitant jurisdiction is relied upon to justify the exercise of that jurisdiction.[229] Accordingly, the court must exercise caution in cases where the plaintiff attempts "to persuade the courts of one country to arrogate for themselves a jurisdiction which belongs more properly to the courts of another country".[230] The fact that an English court may—by virtue of RSC, Order 11, rule 1(1)(c)—assume a wider and more flexible jurisdiction than the courts of many other countries does not mean that England is always the appropriate forum in cases where the plaintiff is seeking to pursue a number of foreign defendants. Although the court is entitled to make liberal use of English procedural rules whenever it is appropriate in the interests of doing justice between all the parties concerned, these rules "must not be abused by exorbitant uses in international contexts".[231] It must never become the practice to bring foreign defendants to England as a matter of course, on the ground that the only alternative requires more than one suit in more than one jurisdiction.[232]

6.4.4.4 The "Cambridgeshire factor"

6.4.4.4.1 In *Spiliada Maritime Corporation* v. *Cansulex Ltd*[233] very few of the factual connections were with England; neither party was English and the all the events which gave rise to the cause of action occurred abroad. Nevertheless, the House of Lords concluded that England was the *forum conveniens.* The dispute between the parties concerned a cargo of sulphur which had been loaded by the defendant, a company incorporated in British Columbia, on a ship owned by the plaintiff. The plaintiff alleged that the sulphur was wet when loaded, thereby causing corrosion to the hold of the ship. A similar cargo had been loaded at the same time on another ship, the *Cambridgeshire*, which was owned by an English company. When the plaintiff applied for leave to serve out under RSC, Order 11, many of the key elements of the dispute were already the subject of litigation in England in respect of the *Cambridgeshire.*[234]

6.4.4.4.2 The House of Lords decided that it was right to take into account the fact that there would be benefits in terms of efficiency, expedition and economy by having available experienced teams of lawyers and experts who were familiar with the legal and factual issues raised by the case by virtue of their involvement in the *Cambridgeshire* action. Lord Goff noted that:

> [A]nyone who has been involved, as counsel, in very heavy litigation of this kind, with a number of experts on both sides and difficult scientific questions involved, knows only too well what the

228. *The Kapetan Georgis* [1988] 1 Lloyd's Rep 352; *Meadows Indemnity Co Ltd* v. *Insurance Corporation of Ireland Plc* [1989] 2 Lloyd's Rep 298; *The Goldean Mariner* [1990] 2 Lloyd's Rep 215.
229. *The Goldean Mariner* [1990] 2 Lloyd's Rep 215.
230. Sir Michael Kerr in *First National Bank of Boston* v. *Union Bank of Switzerland* [1990] 1 Lloyd's Rep 32, 38. See also *Cleveland Museum of Art* v. *Capricorn International SA* [1990] 2 Lloyd's Rep 166.
231. Sir Michael Kerr in *First National Bank of Boston* v. *Union Bank of Switzerland* [1990] 1 Lloyd's Rep 32, 38.
232. Lloyd LJ in *The Goldean Mariner* [1990] 2 Lloyd's Rep 215, 222.
233. [1987] AC 460.
234. *Bibby Bulk Carriers Ltd* v. *Cobelfret NV* [1989] QB 155.

learning curve is like, how much information and knowledge has to be, and is, absorbed, not only by the lawyers but really by the whole team, including both lawyers and experts, as they learn about the interrelation of law, fact and scientific knowledge, having regard to the contentions advanced by both sides in the case, and identify in their minds the crucial matters on which attention has to be focused, why these are the crucial matters, and how they are to be assessed.[235]

In subsequent cases the so-called "*Cambridgeshire* factor" has been advanced, albeit with very little success, as a relevant consideration both in cases involving an application for a stay of proceedings,[236] as well as in cases concerning an application for leave to serve out of the jurisdiction.[237]

6.4.4.5 Time bars

What significance should the court attach to the fact that the plaintiff's claim is time barred in the alternative forum? This was another of the issues considered by the House of Lords in *Spiliada Maritime Corporation* v. *Cansulex Ltd.*[238] It does not automatically follow that the court will grant leave to serve out or refuse a stay whenever the plaintiff's claim is time barred in the alternative forum. Lord Goff gave the following examples:

[S]uppose that the plaintiff allowed the limitation period to elapse in the appropriate jurisdiction, and came here simply because he wanted to take advantage of a more generous time bar applicable in this country; or suppose that it was obvious that the plaintiff should have commenced proceedings in the appropriate jurisdiction, and yet he did not trouble to issue a protective writ there; in cases such as these, I cannot see that the court should hesitate to stay the proceedings in this country, even though the effect would be that the plaintiff's claim would inevitably be defeated by a plea of the time-bar in the appropriate jurisdiction.[239]

There may, however, be cases where the plaintiff has acted reasonably, but finds that he is time barred in the appropriate jurisdiction. In such a case it would be unjust for the court to deprive the plaintiff of any remedy by staying the proceedings or refusing leave.

6.4.4.6 Delay

Delay in the foreign forum is a factor which the court will take into account when considering the question of appropriateness.[240] If the delay is extreme it may be regarded by the court as decisive.[241]

6.4.4.7 Costs

In principle the court should not assume jurisdiction under RSC, Order 11 or decline to stay the proceedings simply on the basis that there is a costs advantage to the plaintiff if the litigation takes place in England rather than abroad; the issue of costs is but one factor which must be weighed in the balance.[242] Although an advantage to the plaintiff in

235. [1987] AC 460, 485.
236. *Owens Bank Ltd* v. *Bracco* [1992] 2 AC 443; *British Aerospace Plc* v. *Dee Howard Co* [1993] 1 Lloyd's Rep 368.
237. *Metall und Rohstoff AG* v. *Donaldson Lufkin & Jenrette Inc* [1990] 1 QB 391; *The Kapetan Georgis* [1988] 1 Lloyd's Rep 352; *The Goldean Mariner* [1989] 2 Lloyd's Rep 390, affirmed [1990] 2 Lloyd's Rep 215.
238. [1987] AC 460.
239. [1987] AC 460, 483.
240. *The Al Battani* [1993] 2 Lloyd's Rep 219.
241. *The Vishva Ajay* [1989] 2 Lloyd's Rep 558.
242. *The Oinoussin Pride* [1991] 1 Lloyd's Rep 126.

litigating in England is not normally decisive, the *Spiliada* test entitles the court to give leave to serve out or to refuse to grant a stay if substantial justice will not be done in the foreign forum.[243] In *Roneleigh Ltd* v. *MII Exports Inc*[244] the Court of Appeal upheld the judge's decision to give leave to serve out, even though all the relevant connecting factors pointed towards New Jersey as the appropriate forum. The basis of the decision was that, since the law of New Jersey does not allow a successful plaintiff to recover costs, substantial justice would not be done in the foreign forum.[245]

6.4.4.8 Damages

As a general rule, the fact that the plaintiff, if successful, will recover higher damages in England than abroad is not sufficient in itself to justify the granting of leave under RSC, Order 11 or the refusal of a stay of English proceedings. There are, however, certain circumstances in which the difference between the damages which could be recovered in England and abroad is so great that the court may legitimately take the view that it would amount to an injustice if the plaintiff were required to pursue his claim abroad.[246]

6.4.4.9 Procedural fairness

If the defendant asserts that he will not receive a fair hearing in the alternative forum, does this factor tilt the balance in favour of England as the *forum conveniens*? It is important to draw a distinction between two different types of case.

(i) The court is not permitted to embark on a comparison of the respective merits and failings of the English legal system and the legal systems of foreign countries. Accordingly, the party who seeks to invoke the jurisdiction of the English court will not be permitted to bring into the equation perceived defects of the legal system of the alternative forum (such as the competence of the judiciary or the system of civil procedure). It would, for example, be "wholly wrong for an English court, with quite inadequate experience of how it works in practice in a particular country, to condemn as inferior to that of our own country a system of procedure for the trial of issues of fact that has long been adopted by a large number of both developed and developing countries in the modern world".[247] A litigant's fears as to the quality of justice in the alternative forum are not relevant.[248]

(ii) If the litigant can show that he would not receive a fair trial in the alternative forum—for example, for political, racial or religious reasons—this is a factor which the court ought to take into account when considering the question of appropriateness.[249] In *The Abidin Daver* Lord Diplock thought that if a plaintiff who "wishes to resist a stay upon the ground that even-handed justice may not be done to him in that particular foreign jurisdiction, [he] must assert

243. See para. 6.4.3.
244. [1989] 1 WLR 619.
245. See also *The Vishva Ajay* [1989] 2 Lloyd's Rep 558.
246. *The Vishva Abha* [1990] 2 Lloyd's Rep 312.
247. Lord Diplock in *Amin Rasheed Shipping Corporation* v. *Kuwait Insurance Co* [1984] AC 50, 67.
248. *Jeyaretnam* v. *Mahmood, The Times*, 21 May 1992.
249. *Carvalho* v. *Hull, Blyth (Angola) Ltd* [1979] 1 WLR 1228.

this candidly and support his allegations with positive and cogent evidence".[250] It is rare that the party seeking to obtain leave or to resist a stay of proceedings is able to satisfy the court that there are legitimate reasons for thinking that he will not be treated fairly in the alternative forum.

6.4.4.10 The applicable law

6.4.4.10.1 Where a dispute arises out of a contract which is governed by English law, the plaintiff may seek leave to serve the defendant out of the jurisdiction under RSC, Order 11, rule 1(1)(d)(iii). Since in certain sectors of the economy (such as shipping and insurance) it is common for English choice of law clauses to be included in contracts which, from a purely factual point of view, have no meaningful connection with England, the courts traditionally took the view that where reliance is placed on rule 1(1)(d)(iii) the burden on the plaintiff to show that England is the *forum conveniens* is a particularly heavy one.[251] However, more recently it has come to be acknowledged that the importance to be attached to the fact that English law is the applicable law depends on the circumstances of the case.[252]

6.4.4.10.2 In some cases where English law is the applicable law the court is prepared to place very considerable emphasis on the fact that English judges are better placed than others to rule on questions of English law.[253] The English courts are also best equipped to apply English canons of construction in cases where the dispute between the parties requires the court to construe the terms of a contract governed by English law. If the task is undertaken by a foreign court expense and inconvenience results from the court having to rely on the expert evidence of English lawyers.[254] It should be added that the line of reasoning favoured by the English courts suggests that it is also preferable that questions of foreign law should be decided by the relevant foreign court.[255]

6.4.4.10.3 The importance of the applicable law is increased in cases involving questions of public policy. Where an issue of English public policy arises in the context of a dispute concerning a contract governed by English law it is highly desirable that that issue should be decided by an English court.[256] A question of English public policy is not "a question capable of fair resolution in any foreign court, however distinguished and well instructed".[257]

6.4.4.11 Language

In certain circumstances the fact that the dispute between the parties raises questions of construction of documentary material is a factor which strengthens the case for

250. [1984] AC 398, 411.
251. See, for example, Lord Diplock's speech in *Amin Rasheed Shipping Corporation* v. *Kuwait Insurance Co* [1984] AC 50, 68.
252. See Lord Goff in *Spiliada Maritime Corporation* v. *Cansulex Ltd* [1987] AC 460, 481.
253. *Coast Lines Ltd* v. *Hudig & Veder Chartering NV* [1972] 2 QB 34.
254. *Standard Steamship Owners' Protection & Indemnity Association (Bermuda) Ltd* v. *Gann* [1992] 2 Lloyd's Rep 528.
255. See Robert Goff J in *Trendtex Trading Corporation* v. *Crédit Suisse* [1980] 3 All ER 721, 735; *The Nile Rhapsody* [1992] 2 Lloyd's Rep 399.
256. *Mitsubishi Corporation* v. *Alafouzos* [1988] 1 Lloyd's Rep 191.
257. Bingham LJ in *EI du Pont de Nemours & Co* v. *Agnew* [1987] 2 Lloyd's Rep 585, 594.

regarding a particular court as the appropriate forum. Where a decision depends upon the construction of a document in one language and the rival courts are, on the one hand, courts whose native language is that of the document and, on the other, courts whose native language is not that of the document, the matter may be more suitably tried in the former courts.[258] So, in a dispute relating to the interpretation of a document in the English language, if the alternative forum is Egypt, there is a natural inclination to regard England as the *forum conveniens.*[259] However, in cases where the language of the alternative forum is not English, it does not automatically follow from the fact that the dispute relates to documents in English that England is the appropriate forum; the courts of a foreign country may be the *forum conveniens* if the applicable law is the law of that country and it is by reference to that law that the documents have to be interpreted.[260]

6.4.4.12 Preference for the choice of law rules of the forum

6.4.4.12.1 Each legal system has choice of law rules for deciding which substantive rules to apply to disputes which come before the courts. While in certain areas there has been some measure of harmonisation, there are considerable divergences between the choice of law rules applied by different countries. Because different countries have different choice of law rules, a plaintiff may have a claim which will fail if brought in the natural forum, but will succeed if brought in another.

6.4.4.12.2 The nature of the problem which arises from these divergences may be illustrated by *The Magnum,*[261] a case which concerned a dispute arising out of a contract of insurance which contained an express choice of English law. When the plaintiff made a claim under the policy the defendant, a Spanish insurance company, denied liability. The plaintiff's claim would fail if it were pursued in Spain because the Spanish court would disregard the choice of law clause and, applying domestic Spanish law, would disallow the plaintiff's claim on the basis of public policy. The plaintiff, therefore, sought leave to serve the defendant out of the jurisdiction under RSC, Order 11, rule 1(1)(d)(iii). Under English conflicts rules the applicable law was English law according to which the plaintiff had a valid claim under the contract. In this type of case how should the court balance the factual connections in favour of the foreign country against the fact that the choice of law rules applied by the foreign court lead to a result which is the opposite of that reached by the application of English conflicts rules?

6.4.4.12.3 The cases show that in situations where the English choice of law rules and the choice of law rules of a foreign country conflict in this way, the court will regard the conflict as a factor which points towards England as the *forum conveniens.* In *Irish Shipping Ltd* v. *Commercial Union Co Plc,* in which the issue was whether England or Belgium was the appropriate forum,[262] Staughton LJ said:

258. Parker LJ in *The Magnum* [1989] 1 Lloyd's Rep 47, 51.

259. *The Al Battani* [1993] 2 Lloyd's Rep 219; *The Magnum* [1989] 1 Lloyd's Rep 47 (Carter, (1989) 60 BYIL 482).

260. *The Nile Rhapsody* [1992] 2 Lloyd's Rep 399.

261. [1989] 1 Lloyd's Rep 47.

262. Although the case did not concern RSC, Order 11, the action was described by Staughton LJ as "somewhat akin to proceedings under Order 11" ([1990] 2 WLR 117, 133) and the *Spiliada* test was regarded by the Court of Appeal to be relevant.

In an ideal world there would be no difference between the conflict rules applied by all nations. . . . But unfortunately uniformity is far from achieved. It is by no means improbable that the Belgian and English conflict rules differ in their application to this case. In those circumstances, it seems to me fairly arguable that a plaintiff is entitled to claim the benefit of the conflict rules prevailing here. So far as concerns domestic law, it would be wrong to suppose that our system is better than any other. But in the case of conflict rules, which ought to be but are not the same internationally, there is a case for saying that we should regard our rules as the most appropriate.[263]

6.4.4.12.4 The significance of the assumption of jurisdiction by the English court—so that English conflicts rules are applied in preference to those of another country—is illustrated by *Banco Atlantico SA* v. *British Bank of the Middle East.*[264] The plaintiff, a Spanish bank, was the holder of bills of exchange, which were drawn on a third party, but in relation to which the defendant, an English bank, acted as guarantor. When the bills were not paid on presentment, the plaintiff started proceedings in England. The defendant applied for a stay of proceedings on the basis that the courts of Sharjah (UAE) were clearly a more appropriate forum.

6.4.4.12.5 Although there could be no doubt that the underlying factual matrix of the case was most closely connected with the UAE, a stay was refused. Of particular importance was the fact that, because of a lack of symmetry between choice of law rules, the courts of England and Sharjah would be likely to reach different conclusions on the merits of the case. If the litigation took place in England, the court would—on the basis of English conflicts rules[265]—conclude that the applicable law was Spanish law, under which the plaintiff had an arguable claim. However, the evidence before the Court of Appeal indicated that the Sharjah court would apply its own domestic law, rather than Spanish law, and that under the law of Sharjah the plaintiff's claim was bound to fail. The Court of Appeal decided that to grant a stay of proceedings—thereby forcing the plaintiff to pursue the defendant abroad—would not be appropriate; it was not "conducive to justice to require [the plaintiff], as a party with an arguable claim under what we would hold to be the proper law . . . to litigate, if at all, in a jurisdiction where it would be bound on the evidence to face summary rejection of its claims".[266]

It has been questioned whether this approach is the correct one to take. If restraint is to be exercised in adjectival matters—it is not appropriate to embark upon a comparison of the procedures or methods or reputation or standing of the courts of one country as compared to those of another—should not the same restraint be exercised in substantive matters?[267]

6.4.5 The weighing of factors

6.4.5.1 Following the House of Lords' decision in *Spiliada Maritime Corporation* v. *Cansulex Ltd* it was suggested that the legal community could "look forward to some peace and quiet on this front and fewer reported cases".[268] However, the flow of reported cases concerned with *forum (non) conveniens* has continued unabated. What the decided cases show is that there is a vast array of potentially relevant factors, many

263. [1990] 2 WLR 117, 134.
264. [1990] 2 Lloyd's Rep 504.
265. Bills of Exchange Act 1882, s. 72.
266. Bingham LJ, [1990] 2 Lloyd's Rep 504, 509.
267. Carter, (1989) 60 BYIL 482, 484–485.
268. Collier, [1987] CLJ 33, 35.

of which point in different directions, and that it is not always easy to predict the weight which the court, in the exercise of its discretion, will attach to any particular factor. For example, in some cases a costs advantage to the plaintiff is crucial; in others it is of marginal significance. In *Spiliada Maritime Corporation* v. *Cansulex Ltd* Lord Templeman observed:

> The factors which the court is entitled to take into account in considering whether one forum is more appropriate are legion. The authorities do not, perhaps cannot, give any guidance as to how these factors are to be weighed in any particular case.[269]

It seems, therefore, that uncertainty—rather than being an unfortunate by-product—is a central and inevitable feature of the traditional English system of jurisdiction. Perhaps not surprisingly, some remain to be convinced of the virtues of the doctrine of *forum (non) conveniens.*[270]

6.4.5.2 From a practical point of view it is not essential that jurisdiction rules should be simple, but it is highly desirable that they be certain.[271] A system of jurisdiction rules based on the test of appropriateness can lead to certainty only if the natural forum is self-evident in most cases and trial judges apply the test in a consistent and impartial manner. The cases do not suggest that these conditions can be satisfied. In cases where a defendant who is served within the jurisdiction applies for a stay, what is the court to do if the defendant shows that there is another more appropriate forum and the plaintiff shows that a stay would deprive him of a legitimate personal or juridical advantage? In these circumstances the court must apply "the underlying fundamental principle".[272] This, however, requires the court to strike a balance between largely unbalanceable considerations.[273]

6.4.5.3 From a theoretical point of view a system of jurisdiction rules which seeks to locate each international commercial dispute in the most appropriate forum for its resolution has an obvious appeal. However, such a system depends for its realisation on the exercise of discretion, rather than the application of predictable rules. Accordingly, the theoretical attractions of the doctrine of *forum (non) conveniens* are bought at a price—namely, uncertainty, delay and expense—which has to be paid by litigants. It is arguable that the doctrine costs more than its worth.[274]

6.4.6 Appeals against the exercise of discretion

In *Spiliada Maritime Corporation* v. *Cansulex Ltd* Lord Templeman thought that "the solution of disputes about the relative merits of trial in England and trial abroad is pre-eminently a matter for the trial judge. . . . An appeal should be rare and the appellate court should be slow to interfere".[275] The fact that the Court of Appeal

269. [1987] AC 460, 465.
270. Robertson, "Forum Non Conveniens in America and England: 'A Rather Fantastic Fiction'" (1987) 103 LQR 398; Slater, "Forum Non Conveniens: A View from the Shop Floor" (1988) 104 LQR 554; Stone, "The Civil Jurisdiction and Judgments Act 1982: Some Comments" (1983) 32 ICLQ 477.
271. Carter, (1972–73) 46 BYIL 428, 430.
272. Lord Goff, [1987] AC 460, 482.
273. Carter, (1986) 57 BYIL 429, 433.
274. Robertson, "Forum Non Conveniens in America and England: 'A Rather Fantastic Fiction'" (1987) 103 LQR 398, 426.
275. [1987] AC 460, 465.

disagrees with the weight that the trial judge has given to the various relevant factors is not sufficient to justify intervention. Before interfering with the exercise of discretion the appellate court must be satisfied that the trial judge "misdirected himself" or "erred in principle" or "either took into account some irrelevant consideration or ignored a relevant one".[276]

The extent to which the Court of Appeal adheres to the principle that the appellate courts should be "slow to interfere" may be questioned. If the Court of Appeal does not agree with the exercise of discretion it is not difficult to pay lip-service to the principle of non-interference, but to decide that the judge erred in principle, or misdirected himself in some significant manner, or failed to consider a relevant factor, or considered a factor which he should have ignored.

6.5 CASES INVOLVING JURISDICTION CLAUSES

6.5.1 Preliminary remarks

6.5.1.1 In cases falling within the scope of the Conventions a jurisdiction clause in favour of the courts of a Contracting State is effective to confer jurisdiction on the courts of that State—as long as the agreement on jurisdiction satisfies the requirements of Article 17. Where the English courts have jurisdiction under Article 17 the plaintiff may serve the defendant out of the jurisdiction without the leave of the court.[277] If one or more of the parties is domiciled in a Contracting State the effect of Article 17 is mandatory; the chosen courts may not decline jurisdiction and the courts of other Contracting States may not assume jurisdiction. However, if neither party is domiciled in a Contracting State, the courts chosen by the parties may decline jurisdiction.[278]

6.5.1.2 The traditional rules have a residual character; they apply only where the provisions of the Conventions do not determine jurisdiction. In cases which are not governed by Article 17, or in relation to which the effect of Article 17 is not mandatory, it is reasonable to expect that if parties agree to refer their disputes to the courts of a particular country, an English court will, as a general rule, enforce that agreement. However, since at common law a jurisdiction clause in favour of a foreign court does not oust the English court's jurisdiction, it cannot be assumed that jurisdiction clauses will be enforced as a matter of course. Whether a plaintiff is able to proceed in England depends on the exercise of the court's discretion. The special considerations to which situations involving jurisdiction clauses give rise suggest that the general test laid down in *Spiliada Maritime Corporation* v. *Cansulex Ltd* should not apply. To a considerable extent, the case law supports the view that, where parties to a contract have entered a jurisdiction agreement, special rules should govern the way in which the court's discretion is exercised.

6.5.1.3 While the procedural effect of a jurisdiction clause is a matter of English law as the *lex fori*, its existence, validity and interpretation is normally determined by

276. Neill LJ in *Meadows Indemnity Co Ltd* v. *Insurance Corporation of Ireland Plc* [1989] 2 Lloyd's Rep 298, 305. For examples of the problems which the Court of Appeal has in deciding whether or not it is a suitable case for intervention see *Re Harrods (Buenos Aires) Ltd* [1992] Ch 72; *The Po* [1991] 2 Lloyd's Rep 206.

277. RSC, Order 11, r. 1(2).

278. See para. 5.3.2.2.3.

reference to its (putative) proper law.[279] Whether an exclusive jurisdiction agreement is to be regarded as precluding the parties from seeking provisional measures in a court other than the chosen court is also a question of interpretation to be referred to the proper law of the agreement.[280] The proper law may, in certain circumstances, be overridden by mandatory rules of the forum.[281]

6.5.2 Cases involving a foreign jurisdiction clause

6.5.2.1 Where the parties have agreed to the jurisdiction of a foreign court, one of the parties should not generally be able to bring proceedings in England in breach of the terms of the agreement. Where the plaintiff serves a writ on the defendant as of right the court should normally stay the English proceedings on the defendant's application; if the plaintiff seeks leave to serve out under RSC, Order 11 leave should generally be refused.

6.5.2.2 The relevant principles applicable in cases where the defendant applies for a stay of proceedings brought in breach of a jurisdiction clause in favour of a foreign forum were summarised in *The Eleftheria* by Brandon J:

> (1) Where plaintiffs sue in England in breach of an agreement to refer disputes to a foreign court, and the defendants apply for a stay, the English court, assuming the claim to be otherwise within its jurisdiction, is not bound to grant a stay but has a discretion whether to do so or not. (2) The discretion should be exercised by granting a stay unless strong cause for not doing so is shown. (3) The burden of proving such strong cause is on the plaintiffs. (4) In exercising its discretion the court should take into account all the circumstances of the particular case. (5) In particular, but without prejudice to (4), the following matters, where they arise, may properly be regarded: (a) In what country the evidence on the issues of fact is situated, or more readily available, and the effect of that on the relative convenience and expense of trial as between the English and foreign courts. (b) Whether the law of the foreign court applies and, if so, whether it differs from English law in any material respects. (c) With what country either party is connected, and how closely. (d) Whether the defendants genuinely desire trial in the foreign country, or are only seeking procedural advantages. (e) Whether the plaintiffs would be prejudiced by having to sue in the foreign court because they would: (i) be deprived of security for their claim; (ii) be unable to enforce any judgment obtained; (iii) be faced by a time bar not applicable in England; or (iv) for political, racial, religious or other reasons be unlikely to get a fair trial.[282]

The court should give full weight to the *prima facie* desirability of holding plaintiffs to their agreement, and "must be careful not just to pay lip-service to the principle involved, and then fail to give effect to it because of a mere balance of convenience".[283]

6.5.2.3 Although there might once have been a question mark as to whether the test laid down in *The Eleftheria* was entirely consistent with earlier decisions of the Court of Appeal,[284] following *The El Amria*[285] there can be no doubt that the *Eleftheria* test correctly states the law. The leading judgment in *The El Amria* was given by Brandon LJ, who affirmed the principles which he had formulated in *The Eleftheria*. Suggestions that cases involving jurisdiction clauses should be decided by reference to the *Spiliada*

279. See para. 5.3.4.
280. *The Lisboa* [1980] 2 Lloyd's Rep 546.
281. *The Hollandia* [1983] 1 AC 565. See paras. 5.3.4 and 12.3.2.
282. Brandon J in *The Eleftheria* [1970] P 94, 99–100.
283. Brandon J in *The Eleftheria* [1970] P 94, 103.
284. See, in particular, *The Fehmarn* [1958] 1 WLR 159. This decision was widely criticised and is now explained on the basis of its unusual facts.
285. [1981] 2 Lloyd's Rep 119.

test and that the only effect of a foreign jurisdiction clause is to reverse the burden of proof[286] are unsound in principle.

6.5.2.4 Although the application of the *Eleftheria* test should normally lead to the English proceedings being stayed in cases where the parties have entered a jurisdiction agreement in favour of the courts of another country, the court may be prepared to exercise its discretion against the grant of stay if there are parallel proceedings in England involving the same issues and it is thought "essential, in order to avoid the risk of different decisions on the same issues by courts in two different countries, that the two actions should be tried together".[287] On the basis of the decision in *The El Amria* it has been held that whenever "a strong cause for not doing so is shown"[288] a stay may be refused. Indeed, it has been suggested that, notwithstanding the presumption in favour of a stay, since the rules give discretion to the court and virtually every case has factors pointing in opposite directions, in practice, "an English court is about as likely to retain the case as to give effect to the choice of forum clause".[289]

6.5.2.5 Where the parties have agreed to litigate in a foreign forum it does not automatically follow that the court will refuse leave to serve out of the jurisdiction; all depends on whether the court is satisfied that the case is a proper one for service out of the jurisdiction. Although, as a general rule, by refusing leave the court will prevent the plaintiff from going back on his word,[290] there may be circumstances in which the court considers it appropriate to give leave notwithstanding the parties' prior agreement to refer their disputes to another forum. In *Evans Marshall & Co Ltd* v. *Bertola SA*[291] a dispute arose concerning a distribution agreement between the plaintiff, an English wine merchant, and the first defendant, a Spanish company. Under the terms of the agreement the plaintiff was granted sole agency and distribution rights for the first defendant's products in the United Kingdom. Clause 15 of the agreement provided that any claim arising between the two parties "will be submitted to the Barcelona Court of Justice". After a period of nearly twenty years the first defendant terminated the agreement and appointed the second defendant as agent in the United Kingdom in the plaintiff's place. The plaintiff issued proceedings against the defendants in England and sought leave to serve the first defendant out of the jurisdiction.

6.5.2.6 The Court of Appeal concluded that it was "one of those exceptional cases"[292] in which it was proper to give leave, notwithstanding the agreement to refer any dispute to the Spanish courts. Although the issue raised in the case was whether the contract had been properly terminated under Spanish law and the dispute between the plaintiff and the first defendant was the kind of dispute which was likely to have been anticipated when the agreement was signed, four reasons were thought to support the conclusion that England was the appropriate forum: the case was exclusively concerned with events which happened in England; all the essential witnesses were in England; Spanish law did not differ from English law in any relevant respect; the second defendant had been

286. See *The Nile Rhapsody* [1992] 2 Lloyd's Rep 399. Briggs, "Jurisdiction Clauses and Judicial Attitudes" (1993) 109 LQR 382.

287. Brandon LJ in *The El Amria* [1981] 2 Lloyd's Rep 119, 129. See also *The Rewia* [1991] 1 Lloyd's Rep 69 (reversed on other grounds: [1991] 2 Lloyd's Rep 325); *The Vishva Prabha* [1989] 2 Lloyd's Rep 286.

288. Sheen J in *The Al Battani* [1993] 2 Lloyd's Rep 219, 224.

289. Sturley, "Bill of Lading Choice of Forum Clauses: Comparisons between United States and English Law" [1992] LMCLQ 248, 251.

290. *Mackender* v. *Feldia AG* [1967] 2 QB 590.

291. [1973] 1 WLR 349.

292. Cairns LJ, [1973] 1 WLR 349, 385.

served as of right in England and it was preferable to have one set of proceedings in England.

6.5.3 Cases involving an English jurisdiction clause

6.5.3.1 Where parties to a contract have agreed that the English courts are to have jurisdiction the case falls squarely within RSC, Order 11, rule 1(1)(d)(iv) which provides that service out of the jurisdiction is permissible with the leave of the court if the claim is brought to "affect a contract . . . which . . . contains a term to the effect that the High Court shall have jurisdiction to hear and determine any action in respect of the contract".[293]

6.5.3.2 When the plaintiff's claim falls within rule 1(1)(d)(iv) the question arises as to whether the jurisdiction clause is to be weighed in the balance as one of the factors within the *Spiliada* test, or whether some other principle is to be applied. Since in *Spiliada Maritime Corporation* v. *Cansulex Ltd*[294] the House of Lords did not consider the effect of jurisdiction clauses, the principle adopted in *The Chaparral*[295]—a case which pre-dates *Spiliada Maritime Corporation* v. *Cansulex Ltd* by more than twenty years—should be applied. In *The Chaparral* a dispute arose in relation to a contract which provided that any dispute arising "must be treated before the London Court of Justice". When the plaintiff obtained leave to serve the writ out of the jurisdiction, the defendant applied to have leave set aside on the ground that England was not the appropriate forum and that proceedings had already been started in the State of Florida. The Court of Appeal refused to set aside service; although the court retains a discretion, "it is a discretion which, in the ordinary way and in the absence of strong reason to the contrary, will be exercised in favour of holding parties to their bargain".[296]

6.5.3.3 Whether a jurisdiction clause is exclusive or non-exclusive makes little or no difference to the way in which the court's discretion is exercised.[297] There appears to be no reported case in which an English court has stayed proceedings in the face of an English jurisdiction clause or refused to grant leave in a case falling within RSC, Order 11, rule 1(1)(d)(iv) or its predecessors.

6.6 JURISDICTION IN CASES INVOLVING FOREIGN LAND

6.6.1 Article 16(1) of the Conventions provides that, regardless of the defendant's domicile, "in proceedings which have as their object rights *in rem* in, or tenancies of immovable property," the courts of the Contracting State in which the property is situated shall have exclusive jurisdiction. So, where the proceedings are within the scope of Article 1 of the Conventions, and the principal subject matter of the dispute concerns rights *in rem* in, or tenancies of immovable property located in another Contracting State there can be no question of proceedings being brought in England.

6.6.2 In cases where the situation does not fall within the scope of Article 1 of the Conventions, or the immovable property in question is located in a non-contracting

293. For the full text of RSC, Order 11, r. 1(1)(d) see para. 6.3.3.4.
294. [1987] AC 460.
295. [1968] 2 Lloyd's Rep 158.
296. Willmer LJ, [1968] 2 Lloyd's Rep 158, 163.
297. *Commercial Bank of the Near East Plc* v. *A, B, C & D* [1989] 2 Lloyd's Rep 319; *Standard Steamship Owners' Protection & Indemnity Association (Bermuda) Ltd* v. *Gann* [1992] 2 Lloyd's Rep 528.

State, the common law rules are applicable. At least, this is clearly the position if the defendant is not domiciled in a Contracting State. More difficult is the situation where the defendant is domiciled in a Contracting State. Where the immovable property is situated in a non-contracting State and the defendant is domiciled in a Contracting State Article 16 does not apply and there is nothing in Title II to suggest that the courts of a Contracting State cannot assume jurisdiction under the Conventions. However, where an English defendant is sued in England in relation to a dispute concerning immovable property located in a non-contracting State the Brussels Convention should not be regarded as preventing the court from declining jurisdiction. There would be little to recommend a system of jurisdiction rules which obliges the English court to hear and determine a dispute concerning title to land in New York between a French plaintiff and an English defendant. In these circumstances the court should be able to stay the proceedings.

6.6.3 At common law, the general principle is that the court has no jurisdiction to entertain an action for the determination of the title to, or the right to possession of, any immovable property situated outside England.[298] There are three well established exceptions to the general principle.

(i) If the court has jurisdiction *in personam* over a defendant, the court may assume jurisdiction in respect of a contract or an equity affecting foreign land.[299] However, where jurisdiction is founded on presence, the defendant may apply for a stay on the basis of the doctrine of *forum non conveniens*; where the plaintiff seeks to invoke the jurisdiction of the court under RSC, Order 11 leave will be granted only if England is the most appropriate forum.[300]

(ii) In certain cases involving the administration of estates, the court may determine questions of title to foreign land.[301]

(iii) The court may assume jurisdiction *in rem* against a ship to enforce a claim for damage done to foreign land.[302]

6.6.4 It used to be the case that the court could not assume jurisdiction in an action for the recovery of damages for trespass or other torts to immovable property outside England.[303] This rule was, however, reversed by section 30 of the Civil Jurisdiction and Judgments Act 1982, which provides:

> (1) The jurisdiction of any court in England and Wales or Northern Ireland to entertain proceedings for trespass to, or any other tort affecting, immovable property shall extend to cases in which the property in question is situated outside that part of the United Kingdom unless the proceedings are principally concerned with a question of the title to, or the right to possession of, that property.
>
> (2) Subsection (1) has effect subject to the 1968 Convention and the Lugano Convention and to the provisions set out in Schedule 4.

298. *British South Africa Co* v. *Companhia de Moçambique* [1893] AC 602.
299. *Penn* v. *Lord Baltimore* (1750) 1 Ves Sen 444.
300. See para. 6.4.
301. This topic is beyond the scope of the present work.
302. *The Tolten* [1946] P 135. See para. 8.1.1.1.
303. *Hesperides Hotels Ltd* v. *Aegean Turkish Holidays Ltd* [1979] AC 508.

CHAPTER 7

THE ALLOCATION OF JURISDICTION WITHIN THE UNITED KINGDOM

The regime for the allocation of jurisdiction within the United Kingdom mirrors the system which exists on the international plane: (i) in civil and commercial matters jurisdiction is determined by the Modified Convention which—to a significant extent—reflects Title II of the Brussels Convention; (ii) the traditional rules apply in cases not governed by the Modified Convention.[1]

7.1 JURISDICTION IN CIVIL AND COMMERCIAL MATTERS: THE MODIFIED CONVENTION

7.1.1 The scope of the Modified Convention

7.1.1.1 Questions surrounding the allocation of jurisdiction within the United Kingdom in civil and commercial matters can arise in two different contexts.

(i) Although there are certain jurisdiction rules within the Brussels and Lugano Conventions ("the Conventions") which allocate jurisdiction to "the courts for a place" within one of the Contracting States, the Conventions also contain provisions which confer jurisdiction on the courts of the United Kingdom but do not determine whether the courts of England, Scotland or Northern Ireland are competent. Whereas, for example, Article 5(3) provides that in matters relating to tort the "courts for the place where the harmful event occurred" have jurisdiction, Article 2 simply states that a person domiciled in a Contracting State "shall . . . be sued in the courts of that State".

(ii) Cases arise which, from the perspective of other Contracting States, do not involve questions of international jurisdiction—since they are entirely internal to the United Kingdom—but, which from the perspective of English law, are cases with a foreign element since not all the relevant elements are connected with England. Where, for example, an English motorist injures a Scottish pedestrian in Northern Ireland, the Conventions—which are concerned only with international jurisdiction—do not provide an answer to the question as to which courts have jurisdiction.

7.1.1.2 The mechanism for allocating jurisdiction in these two types of case is the

1. See Chapter 6.

Modified Convention, which is to be found in Schedule 4 to the Civil Jurisdiction and Judgments Act 1982. Section 16(1) of the 1982 Act provides:

> The provisions set out in Schedule 4 (which contains a modified version of Title II of the 1968 Convention) shall have effect for determining, for each part of the United Kingdom, whether the courts of law of that part, or any particular court of law in that part, have or has jurisdiction in proceedings where—
>
> (a) the subject matter of the proceedings is within the scope of the 1968 Convention as determined by Article 1 (whether or not that or any other Convention has effect in relation to the proceedings); and
>
> (b) the defendant . . . is domiciled in the United Kingdom or the proceedings are of a kind mentioned in Article 16 of the 1968 Convention (exclusive jurisdiction regardless of domicile).

7.1.1.3 The scope of section 16 is limited in the sense that the rules in the Modified Convention do not apply to all situations where the effect of the Conventions is to allocate jurisdiction to the courts of the United Kingdom, rather than to the courts for a place within the United Kingdom. (i) Some matters which fall within the material scope of Article 1 of the Brussels Convention are excluded from the Modified Convention.[2] (ii) With the exception of Article 16 (which applies regardless of domicile), the Modified Convention applies only where the defendant is domiciled in the United Kingdom.[3] This creates potential problems as regards Articles 17 and 18 of the Conventions. Where, for example, a dispute between a Scotsman and a Brazilian arises under a contract which contains an English jurisdiction clause, if the Brazilian sues the Scotsman for breach of contract in the United Kingdom jurisdiction is determined by the combined effect of the Brussels Convention and the Modified Convention, whereas if the Scotsman sues the Brazilian only the Brussels Convention applies. What, therefore, is the effect of a jurisdiction clause in favour of the English courts in a case falling within the Brussels Convention (or the Lugano Convention) but not within the Modified Convention? In the usual case, where the parties have identified the courts of a part of the United Kingdom, Article 17 should be interpreted as allocating jurisdiction to the courts of that part. There is no obvious solution, however, to the situation where the parties expressly agree to the jurisdiction of "the courts of the United Kingdom" or to the jurisdiction of the "British courts". The indications are that such clauses will be interpreted—at least in England—as agreements in favour of the English courts.[4]

7.1.1.4 Similarly, there is no provision in the Modified Convention dealing with the situation where a defendant who is not domiciled in the United Kingdom submits to the jurisdiction of a court in the United Kingdom. In this type of case the only solution is to interpret Article 18 of the Conventions as conferring jurisdiction on the court of the part of the United Kingdom before which the defendant enters an appearance.

7.1.2 Interpretation

7.1.2.1 Many of the provisions of the Modified Convention reproduce the text of the Brussels Convention, substituting the words "part of the United Kingdom" for "Contracting State" and "part" for "State". There are, however, various provisions of the Modified Convention which differ from the equivalent provisions of Title II; there

2. Civil Jurisdiction and Judgments Act 1982, s. 17 and Schedule 5.
3. Civil Jurisdiction and Judgments Act 1982, s. 16(1)(b).
4. *The Komninos S* [1990] 1 Lloyd's Rep 541. See para. 11.1.3.3.

are also some additions and some omissions. To the extent that the Modified Convention departs from Title II, modifications by way of omission are indicated by dots and words resulting from modifications by way of addition or substitution are indicated by bold type.[5]

7.1.2.2 The major omissions are in two areas. (i) The Modified Convention does not contain any provisions which are equivalent to Articles 21 to 23.[6] (ii) The Modified Convention contains no special jurisdiction rules dealing with matters relating to insurance. Where Section 3 of Title II confers jurisdiction on the courts of the United Kingdom (rather than on the courts for a place within the United Kingdom) or where a dispute relating to insurance is internal to the United Kingdom, the general jurisdiction rules of the Modified Convention have to be applied.

7.1.2.3 To the extent that the provisions of the Brussels Conventions and the Modified Convention are the same they should be interpreted in the same way. Section 16(3) of the 1982 Act provides:

> In determining any question as to the meaning or effect of any provision contained in Schedule 4—
>
> (a) regard shall be had to any relevant principles laid down by the European Court in connection with Title II of the 1968 Convention and to any relevant decision of that court as to the meaning or effect of any provision of that Title; and
>
> (b) without prejudice to the generality of paragraph (a), the reports mentioned in section 3(3)[7] may be considered and shall, so far as relevant, be given such weight as is appropriate in the circumstances.

7.2 BASES OF JURISDICTION UNDER THE MODIFIED CONVENTION

The Modified Convention takes as its starting-point the principle that a person "domiciled in a **part of the United Kingdom** shall . . . be sued in the courts of that **part**".[8] The only circumstances in which a person domiciled in a part of the United Kingdom may be sued in the courts of another part of the United Kingdom are those set out in the other provisions of the Modified Convention: Section 5 (Article 16), Section 6 (Articles 17 and 18), Section 2 (Articles 5, 5A, 6 and 6A) and Section 4 (Articles 13 to 15).[9]

7.2.1 Exclusive jurisdiction: Article 16

7.2.1.1 Article 16 of the Conventions confers jurisdiction on a Contracting State. Where that State is the United Kingdom, Article 16 of the Modified Convention allocates jurisdiction to the courts of part of the United Kingdom.[10] Article 16 of the Modified Convention also allocates jurisdiction in cases which are internal to the United

5. Civil Jurisdiction and Judgments Act 1982, s. 16(2).
6. For further discussion see para. 7.3.1.
7. See para. 3.2.1.3.
8. Article 2.
9. Modified Convention, Article 3.
10. Except in cases coming within Article 16(4) of the Conventions and certain cases coming within Article 16(2).

Kingdom.[11] Where the courts of one part of the United Kingdom have exclusive jurisdiction under Article 16, a court in another part of the United Kingdom must declare of its own motion that it has no jurisdiction.[12]

7.2.1.2 In the main Article 16 of the Modified Convention is in the same form as the equivalent provisions of the Brussels Convention. There are, however, two differences.

(i) The Modified Convention does not reproduce Article 16(4), which deals with certain proceedings relating to intellectual property rights. Indeed, proceedings concerned with the registration or validity of patents, trademarks, designs or other similar rights are excluded from the scope of the Modified Convention altogether.[13] Since all the United Kingdom registers concerned with patents, trademarks and designs are located in England, the practical effect of Article 16(4) of the Conventions is to allocate exclusive jurisdiction to the English courts.

(ii) Article 16(2) of the Conventions allocates exclusive jurisdiction with regard to various proceedings involving companies, including proceedings concerning the validity of decisions taken by the organs of companies. Article 16(2) of the Modified Convention adopts the approach of the Conventions as regards proceedings concerning the constitution, the nullity or the dissolution of companies. However, as regards proceedings concerned with the decisions of the organs of companies Article 5A of the Modified Convention (which has no counterpart in the Brussels Convention) provides:

> **Proceedings which have as their object a decision of an organ of a company or other legal person or an association of natural or legal persons may, without prejudice to the other provisions of this Title, be brought in the courts of the part of the United Kingdom in which that company, legal person or association has its seat.**[14]

7.2.2 Prorogation of jurisdiction

7.2.2.1 Article 18

Article 18 of the Modified Convention, which is in terms similar to the equivalent provision of the Brussels Convention, applies only where the defendant is domiciled in the United Kingdom.[15] So, where a person domiciled in Scotland enters an appearance in England the effect of Article 18 of the Modified Convention is to confer jurisdiction on the English court. This rule does not apply where the defendant appears solely to contest jurisdiction or where another court has exclusive jurisdiction under Article 16.

7.2.2.2 Article 17

7.2.2.2.1 Article 17 of the Modified Convention provides a mechanism for allocating jurisdiction to the courts of England, Scotland or Northern Ireland not only in cases where the dispute is internal to the United Kingdom (for example, where a contractual dispute between a Scotsman and a company domiciled in Northern Ireland arises out of

11. Civil Jurisdiction and Judgments Act 1982, s. 16(1)(b).
12. Modified Convention, Article 19.
13. Civil Jurisdiction and Judgments Act 1982, s. 17 and Schedule 5, para. 2.
14. For the purposes of Article 5A "seat" is to be determined by section 43 of the Civil Jurisdiction and Judgments Act 1982, rather than by section 42.
15. Civil Jurisdiction and Judgments Act 1982, s. 16(1)(a).

an agreement which contains an English jurisdiction clause), but also where Article 17 of the Brussels Convention confers jurisdiction on the courts of the United Kingdom and the defendant is domiciled in a part of the United Kingdom.[16] Article 17(1) of the Modified Convention provides:

> If the parties . . . have agreed that a court or the courts of a **part of the United Kingdom** are to have jurisdiction to settle any disputes which have arisen or which may arise in connection with a particular legal relationship, **and, apart from this Schedule, the agreement would be effective to confer jurisdiction under the law of that part**, that court or those courts shall have . . . jurisdiction . . .

7.2.2.2.2 It is also provided that agreements on jurisdiction "shall have no legal force if they are contrary to the provisions of Article . . . 15, or if the courts whose jurisdiction they purport to exclude have exclusive jurisdiction by virtue of Article 16" and that, in relation to individual contracts of employment, a jurisdiction agreement is effective "only if it is entered into after the dispute has arisen or if the employee invokes it to seise courts other than those for the defendant's domicile or those specified in Article 5(1)".[17]

7.2.2.2.3 The first paragraph of Article 17 of the Modified Convention is drafted differently from Article 17(1) of the Brussels Convention in two respects.

(i) Whereas Article 17 of the Brussels Convention generally confers exclusive jurisdiction on the courts chosen by the parties,[18] Article 17(1) of the Modified Convention states merely that the courts of the part of the United Kingdom chosen by the parties "shall have . . . jurisdiction". So, if a contractual dispute arises between a Scotsman and a German in circumstances in which the English courts have jurisdiction under Article 5(1) (because England is the place of performance of the obligation in question) and the Scots courts have jurisdiction under Article 17, if the German starts proceedings against the Scot in England for breach of contract, neither Article 17 of the Brussels Convention nor Article 17 of the Modified Convention requires the court to stay the proceedings in favour of the courts of Scotland.[19]

(ii) Article 17 of the Modified Convention does not impose any requirements as to form. Instead it is provided that to confer jurisdiction on the courts of a part of the United Kingdom the agreement must be effective under the law of that part.

7.2.3 Special jurisdiction

7.2.3.1 Article 5

7.2.3.1.1 In most cases Article 5 of the Conventions allocates jurisdiction to the courts for a place in a Contracting State. In general, therefore, Article 5 of the Modified

16. Civil Jurisdiction and Judgments Act 1982, s. 16(1)(a).
17. Modified Convention, Article 17(2) and (3).
18. See, however, *Kurz* v. *Stella Musical Veranstaltungs GmbH* [1992] Ch 196 (discussed at para. 5.3.6.2).
19. Whether the court may stay the proceedings under its inherent jurisdiction in these circumstances is discussed at para. 7.3.

Convention is relevant only in cases which are internal to the United Kingdom.[20] However, as regards proceedings concerning trusts which are domiciled in the United Kingdom,[21] because Article 5(6) of the Conventions allocates jurisdiction to a Contracting State rather than a place, Article 5(6) of the Modified Convention applies to cases involving international jurisdiction as well as to internal cases. Article 5(6) of the Modified Convention does not apply, however, in cases where the trust is domiciled in the United Kingdom but the defendant is not.[22] Where Article 5(6) of the Brussels Convention or of the Lugano Convention confers jurisdiction on the courts of the United Kingdom (because the trust is domiciled in the United Kingdom) and Article 5(6) of the Modified Convention does not apply (because the defendant is not domiciled in the United Kingdom) it is provided that the proceedings "shall be brought in the courts of the part of the United Kingdom in which the trust is domiciled".[23]

7.2.3.1.2 Article 5 of the Modified Convention is in most respects in the same form as Article 5 of the Brussels Convention; a person domiciled in a part of the United Kingdom may, in certain circumstances, be sued in the courts for a place identified by various paragraphs of Article 5. Two points should, however, be noted. (i) Article 5(3) refers to "the courts for the place where the harmful event occurred **or in the case of a threatened wrong is likely to occur**". (ii) The Modified Convention has added an eighth paragraph to Article 5, which provides that a person domiciled in a part of the United Kingdom may also be sued:

in proceedings—
- **(a) concerning a debt secured on immovable property; or**
- **(b) which are brought to assert, declare or determine proprietary or possessory rights, or rights of security, in or over movable property, or to obtain authority to dispose of movable property,**

in the courts of the part of the United Kingdom in which the property is situated.

7.2.3.2 Articles 6 and 6A

Articles 6 and 6A of the Modified Convention reproduce as between the different parts of the United Kingdom the equivalent provisions of the Brussels Convention which apply as between the Contracting States. Article 6A and the first three paragraphs of Article 6 of the Modified Convention apply only to internal cases, since the equivalent provisions of the Conventions allocate jurisdiction to particular courts rather than to the courts of a Contracting State in general. Like Article 5(6), Article 6(4) of the Modified Convention plays a dual role in the sense that it not only applies to internal cases, but also supplements the equivalent provisions of the Conventions.

7.2.4 Consumer contracts

Articles 13 to 15 of the Modified Convention are, in general terms, in the same form as the equivalent provisions of the Brussels Convention. They do not apply, however, to

20. See, for example, *Davenport* v. *Corinthian Motor Policies at Lloyd's* 1991 SLT 774.
21. The domicile of a trust is determined by section 45 of the Civil Jurisdiction and Judgments Act 1982.
22. Civil Jurisdiction and Judgments Act 1982, s. 16(1)(b).
23. Civil Jurisdiction and Judgments Act 1982, s. 10(2).

contracts of insurance.[24] Furthermore, the Modified Convention does not apply in cases where a consumer who is domiciled in the United Kingdom brings proceedings against a defendant who is domiciled elsewhere.[25] Where a plaintiff, in reliance of Article 14 of the Brussels Convention or of the Lugano Convention brings proceedings in the United Kingdom on the ground that he is a consumer domiciled in the United Kingdom such proceedings should be brought "in the courts of the part of the United Kingdom in which he is domiciled".[26]

7.2.5 Procedural matters and provisional measures

Where the High Court has jurisdiction under the Modified Convention the plaintiff may serve the originating process out of the jurisdiction on the defendant without leave of the court.[27] However, if the defendant does not enter an appearance, the English court must declare of its own motion that it has no jurisdiction unless jurisdiction is derived from the Modified Convention itself.[28] Furthermore, the court shall stay the proceedings unless it has been shown that the defendant has been able to receive the originating process in sufficient time to enable him to arrange for his defence.[29] Finally, Article 24 provides that the courts of part of the United Kingdom may grant provisional measures in support of proceedings in another part of the United Kingdom. For example, where proceedings within the scope of Article 1 of the Brussels Convention are brought in Scotland, the English court may grant a Mareva injunction in aid of those substantive proceedings.[30]

7.3 STAYING PROCEEDINGS IN CASES UNDER THE MODIFIED CONVENTION

With the exception of Articles 19 and 20 there are no provisions in the Modified Convention which indicate the circumstances in which the courts of the United Kingdom may or must stay proceedings or decline jurisdiction. Although, broadly speaking, whether the court may stay proceedings which fall within the scope of the Modified Convention is a matter to be determined by reference to traditional principles, there are two limits to the court's discretion: the first is imposed by the Rules of the Supreme Court, the second by section 49 of the Civil Jurisdiction and Judgments Act 1982.

7.3.1 *Lis pendens*

7.3.1.1 Article 21 of the Conventions provides that where proceedings involving the same cause of action and between the same parties are brought in the courts of different

24. Modified Convention, Article 13(2).
25. Civil Jurisdiction and Judgments Act 1982, s. 16(1)(b).
26. Civil Jurisdiction and Judgments Act 1982, s. 10(3).
27. RSC, Order 11, r. 1(2).
28. Modified Convention, Article 20(1).
29. Modified Convention, Article 20(2).
30. Civil Jurisdiction and Judgments Act 1982, s. 25(1). See paras. 5.8.2 and 21.3.1.2.

Contracting States, any court other than the court first seised must stay its own proceedings or decline jurisdiction. Although there is no equivalent provision in the Modified Convention the Rules of the Supreme Court provide that, in cases where the English court has jurisdiction in civil and commercial matters, service of a writ out of the jurisdiction is permissible without leave of the court only as long as "no proceedings between the parties concerning the same cause of action are pending in the courts of any other part of the United Kingdom".[31]

7.3.1.2 As a general rule RSC, Order 11, rule 1(2)(a)(i) ensures that the same cause of action will not be litigated in more than one part of the United Kingdom. There is, however, a potential gap created by the fact that the Modified Convention does not contain Article 21. Where, for example, A (domiciled in England) brings proceedings in Northern Ireland against B (domiciled in Northern Ireland) and B subsequently issues proceedings in England against A concerning the same cause of action, there is nothing in the Rules of the Supreme Court to prevent the writ being served on A in England and there is nothing in the Modified Convention to require the English court to stay its proceedings. In these circumstances, the question arises as to whether the English court has discretion to stay the proceedings in the exercise of its inherent jurisdiction.

7.3.2 Discretion to stay proceedings under the Modified Convention

Section 49 of the Civil Jurisdiction and Judgments Act 1982 provides:

> Nothing in this Act shall prevent any court in the United Kingdom from staying, . . . striking out or dismissing any proceedings before it, on the ground of *forum non conveniens* or otherwise, where to do so is not inconsistent with the 1968 Convention or, as the case may be, the Lugano Convention.

When considering the inherent jurisdiction of the English court to stay its proceedings, a distinction needs to be drawn between (i) cases which are entirely internal to the United Kingdom and (ii) situations where the Modified Convention supplements a provision of either of the Conventions which allocates jurisdiction to the courts of the United Kingdom, rather than to the courts for a place.

7.3.2.1 Internal disputes

In cases which are internal to the United Kingdom—where the Modified Convention applies alone—section 49 of the 1982 Act should not operate as a bar to a stay of proceedings in England under the court's inherent jurisdiction. It is not in any way inconsistent with the Conventions—which determine only the international jurisdiction of the courts of the contracting states—for the English court to stay proceedings in an internal case.[31a]

7.3.2.2 Discretion in cases governed by one of the Conventions and the Modified Convention

7.3.2.2.1 The position is more complex in cases where the Modified Convention operates in tandem with one or other of the Conventions. A variety of different

31. RSC, Order 11, r. 1(2)(a)(i).

31a. See, however, the decision of Drake J in *Foxer* v. *Scotsman Publications Ltd*, *The Times*, 17 February 1994.

situations should be considered: where the alternative forum is (i) the court of a non-contracting State or (ii) the court of another Contracting State or (iii) the court of another part of the United Kingdom.

(i) As regards a conflict of jurisdiction between the English court and the court of a non-contracting State, there is clear authority for the proposition that section 49 of the 1982 Act is not to be regarded as an obstacle to the exercise of the court's inherent jurisdiction.[32] Where the parties have agreed to the exclusive jurisdiction of a non-contracting State or where proceedings have already been commenced in a more appropriate foreign forum there are obviously arguments in favour of the exercise of the court's inherent jurisdiction. There are, however, strong arguments against the general application of the doctrine of *forum non conveniens* in situations where jurisdiction is derived from Title II, especially where the plaintiff is domiciled in a Contracting State.[33]

(ii) Where proceedings are started in England and the alternative forum is the court of another Contracting State the position is straightforward and uncontroversial. If there are parallel proceedings in England and another Contracting State, any court other than the court first seised must stay its proceedings or decline jurisdiction if proceedings involve the same parties and the same cause of action; the court may grant a stay if the proceedings are related.[34] In circumstances not covered expressly by Section 8 of Title II, there is no room for the exercise of the court's inherent jurisdiction to stay proceedings, whether on the basis of *forum non conveniens* or on some other basis.[35]

(iii) Perhaps the most difficult situation is where the combined effect of the Modified Convention and one or other of the Conventions is to allocate non-exclusive jurisdiction to more than one part of the United Kingdom. So, for example, where a foreign plaintiff is injured in an accident in Scotland as a result of the negligence of an English defendant, Article 5(3) of the Brussels Convention confers jurisdiction on the courts of Scotland and the combined effect of Article 2 of the Brussels Convention and Article 2 of the Modified Convention is to confer jurisdiction on the English courts. The logic of the decision in *Re Harrods (Buenos Aires) Ltd*[36] would be to allow the English court to grant a stay under its inherent jurisdiction in cases where the alternative forum is another part of the United Kingdom.[37]

7.3.2.2.2 There seems little doubt that cases may arise which cry out for a stay of proceedings. Because the Rules of the Supreme Court may not be entirely effective in preventing parallel proceedings involving the same cause of action from being brought in different parts of the United Kingdom and the Modified Convention does not contain provisions equivalent to those found in Section 8 of Title II, it is important that the

32. *Re Harrods (Buenos Aires) Ltd* [1992] Ch 72; *The Po* [1991] 2 Lloyd's Rep 206. The House of Lords in *Re Harrods (Buenos Aires) Ltd* referred a number of questions to the Court of Justice: Case C-314/92 (*sub nom Ladenimor SA* v. *Intercomfinanz SA*).

33. See para. 5.10.

34. Brussels and Lugano Conventions, Articles 21 and 22.

35. *Re Harrods (Buenos Aires) Ltd* [1992] Ch 72.

36. [1992] Ch 72.

37. Cheshire & North, *Private International Law* (12th ed, 1992) p. 340.

English court should be able to stay proceedings in circumstances where if a stay were refused there would be risk of irreconcilable judgments being given by the courts of different parts of the United Kingdom. Furthermore, in cases where the parties have entered a jurisdiction agreement in favour of the courts of a part of the United Kingdom the court should seek to uphold the parties' agreement. Accordingly, a stay might be appropriate in a case where proceedings are commenced in England—for example under Article 5(1) of the Brussels Convention—notwithstanding the fact that the parties agreed to refer disputes to the exclusive jurisdiction of the courts of another part of the United Kingdom. It should be noted, however, that the position within the United Kingdom would be simpler if (i) Article 17 of the Modified Convention conferred exclusive rather than non-exclusive jurisdiction on the chosen courts and (ii) the Modified Convention included provisions equivalent to Articles 21 to 23 of the Brussels Convention.

CHAPTER 8

JURISDICTION IN ADMIRALTY PROCEEDINGS

8.0 INTRODUCTION

8.0.1 The jurisdiction of the Admiralty Court is based on the scheme established by the Supreme Court Act 1981 (para. 8.1). Some of the bases of jurisdiction set out in the 1981 Act are derived from international conventions, notably the International Convention for the Unification of Certain Rules Relating to the Arrest of Sea-Going Ships (the Arrest Convention) and the International Convention for the Unification of Certain Rules concerning Civil Jurisdiction in matters of Collision (the Collision Convention), both of which date from 1952. While the framework is established by domestic legislation, the Brussels and Lugano Conventions ("the Conventions") have a significant impact on the operation of jurisdiction rules in relation to proceedings falling within their scope (para. 8.2).

8.0.2 An Admiralty action may be brought *in personam* against a named defendant or *in rem* against a *res*. In an action *in rem* the defendant is the *res* itself—which is usually a ship, but may be cargo, freight or, in certain circumstances, other property.[1] A plaintiff may commence both an action *in rem* and an action *in personam* in relation to the same claim. In such a case it is necessary for two writs to be issued. An action *in rem* enables the plaintiff to arrest the ship, so that the ship can be sold and the plaintiff's claim satisfied out of the proceeds. Although where proceedings are commenced *in rem* the ship is notionally the defendant in many cases the owner or charterer of the ship submits to the jurisdiction and puts up security for the plaintiff's claim, thereby preventing the ship's arrest or obtaining its release if it has already been arrested. If a shipowner or charterer acknowledges service of a writ in England, the action in England takes on a hybrid character; the action becomes *in personam* but does not lose its character of being an action *in rem.*[2] Whereas a judgment *in rem* is restricted to the value of the *res*, there is no such restriction as regards a judgment *in personam*; a judgment *in rem*, unlike a judgment *in personam*, determines the status of the *res* and affects third parties.

1. An action *in rem* may be brought against an aircraft (Supreme Court Act 1981, s. 21(5)) or a hovercraft (Hovercraft Act 1968, s. 2(1)). Actions *in rem* against aircraft are very unusual.

2. Although in *The Linda* [1988] 1 Lloyd's Rep 175 and *The Kherson* [1992] 2 Lloyd's Rep 261 Sheen J asserted that an action which is commenced *in rem* becomes an action *in personam* and loses its *in rem* character entirely if the owner (i) acknowledges service of the writ *in rem* and (ii) obtains release of the vessel by putting up security, the authorities do not support this assertion. See Neill LJ in *The Maciej Rataj* [1992] 2 Lloyd's Rep 552, 561 referring, in particular to the speech of Lord Brandon in *The August 8* [1983] 2 AC 450, 456.

8.1 JURISDICTION UNDER THE SUPREME COURT ACT 1981[3]

8.1.1 The Admiralty jurisdiction of the High Court: section 20

The Admiralty jurisdiction of the High Court is defined by sections 20 to 24 of the Supreme Court Act 1981.[4] Jurisdiction does not depend on the nationality of the ship, the residence or domicile of the owners or the place where the event giving rise to the claim occurred.[5] As regards those heads of jurisdiction which are based on the Arrest Convention "a broad and liberal construction should be given to them".[6] Furthermore, the court will have regard to the Convention[7] and, where appropriate, the *travaux préparatoires*[8] to assist in the construction of the Act. The provisions of the 1981 Act are complex and involve a wide range of overlapping bases of jurisdiction.

8.1.1.1 Section 20(1)(a) and (b)

Paragraphs (a) and (b) of section 20(1) refer to various statutory heads of jurisdiction which are listed in subsections (2) and (3) respectively.[9] Since a number of the bases of jurisdiction overlap it is quite common for a claim to fall within more than one head of the court's Admiralty jurisdiction. Subsection (3) sets out three bases of jurisdiction:

(a) any application to the High Court under the Merchant Shipping Acts 1894 to 1979 other than an application under section 55 of the Merchant Shipping Act 1894 for the appointment of a person to act as substitute for a person incapable of acting;
(b) any action to enforce a claim for damage, loss of life or personal injury arising out of—
 (i) a collision between ships; or
 (ii) the carrying out of or omission to carry out a manoeuvre in the case of one or more of two or more ships; or
 (iii) non-compliance, on the part of one or more of two or more ships, with the collision regulations;
(c) any action by shipowners or other persons under the Merchant Shipping Acts 1894 to 1979 for the limitation of the amount of their liability in connection with a ship or other property.

Subsection (2) provides that the Admiralty jurisdiction of the High Court includes the matters set out in paragraphs (a) to (s).

8.1.1.1.1 DISPUTES BETWEEN CO-OWNERS

(b) any question arising between the co-owners of a ship as to possession, employment or earnings of that ship[10];

Paragraph (b) includes "power to settle any account outstanding and unsettled between

3. Jackson, "Admiralty Jurisdiction—The Supreme Court Act 1981" [1982] LMCLQ 236.
4. The court does not have jurisdiction over any claim certified by the Secretary of State to be one which falls to be determined in accordance with the provisions of the Rhine Navigation Convention: Supreme Court Act 1981, s. 23.
5. Supreme Court Act 1981, s. 20(7).
6. Lord Brandon in *The Antonis P Lemos* [1985] AC 711, 725.
7. *The Evpo Agnic* [1988] 1 WLR 1090.
8. *Gatoil International Inc* v. *Arkwright-Boston Manufacturers Mutual Insurance Co* [1985] AC 255.
9. These provisions are largely derived from section 1(1) of the Administration of Justice Act 1956.
10. See, for example, *The Vanessa Ann* [1985] 1 Lloyd's Rep 549.

the parties in relation to the ship, and to direct that the ship, or any share thereof, shall be sold, and to make such other order as the court thinks fit". [11]

8.1.1.1.2 MORTGAGES AND CHARGES

(c) any claim in respect of a mortgage of or charge on a ship or any share therein;

In this context "charge" means a charge in the nature of a mortgage and does not include a maritime lien.[12]

8.1.1.1.3 DAMAGE TO A SHIP

(d) any claim for damages received by a ship[13];

Although many cases which fall within paragraph (d) also fall within paragraph (e), since the damage results from a collision between two ships, paragraph (d) extends to cases where damage is done by something other than a ship—for example, by a pier[14] or a buoy.[15] The 1981 Act makes no provision for the enforcement of a claim within paragraph (d) other than by means of an action *in personam*.[16]

8.1.1.1.4 DAMAGE DONE BY A SHIP

(e) any claim for damage done by a ship;

Damage is a prerequisite for jurisdiction under paragraph (e); where there is a collision between two ships but no damage is inflicted, no cause of action arises.[17] However, there is no requirement that there should be physical contact between the ship by which the damage is done and the property which is damaged.[18] So, the court has jurisdiction in a case where the negligent navigation of a vessel causes two other ships to collide.[19] For the purposes of paragraph (e) what is important is that the damage is the direct result or natural consequence of something done by those engaged in the navigation of the ship and that the ship itself is the actual instrument by which the damage was done.[20] Accordingly, where a ship is deliberately driven off fishing grounds by another vessel the ensuing economic or financial damage is, in principle, within the scope of paragraph (e).[21] Paragraph (e) includes not only damage done to a ship but also damage done to other property such as a breakwater,[22] oyster beds,[23] a pier[24] or an underwater cable.[25] Paragraph (e) also extends to (i) any claim in respect of liability under the Merchant

11. Supreme Court Act, s. 20(4).
12. *The St Merriel* [1963] P 247; *The Acrux* [1965] P 391.
13. *The Father Thames* [1979] 2 Lloyd's Rep 364.
14. *The Zeta* [1893] AC 469.
15. *The Upcerne* [1912] P 160.
16. Supreme Court Act 1981, s. 21. See, however, Jackson, *The Enforcement of Maritime Claims* (1985) pp. 12–13.
17. *The Margaret* (1881) 6 PD 76.
18. *The Industrie* (1871) LR 3 A&E 303.
19. *The Sisters* (1876) 1 PD 117.
20. *The Eschersheim* [1976] 1 WLR 430.
21. *The Dagmara* [1988] 1 Lloyd's Rep 431. The fact that the claim falls within the jurisdiction of the court does not, of course, mean that the plaintiff has a good cause of action.
22. *The Uhla* (1867) 37 LJ Adm 16 n.
23. *The Swift* [1901] P 168.
24. *The Merle* (1874) 31 LT 447.
25. *The Clara Killam* (1870) LR 3 A&E 161.

Shipping (Oil Pollution) Act 1971 and (ii) any claim in respect of a liability falling on the International Oil Pollution Compensation Fund 1984 under Part I of the Merchant Shipping Act 1974.[26]

8.1.1.1.5 CARRIAGE AND HIRE

(h) any claim arising out of any agreement relating to the carriage of goods in a ship or to the use or hire of a ship;

In general the courts have construed paragraph (h) broadly, giving the words "their ordinary wide meaning".[27] There are three aspects to paragraph (h) which have been the subject of judicial consideration.

(i) The phrase "agreement relating to the carriage of goods in a ship" suggests that "the carriage of goods by sea is the central matter to which the agreement relates."[28] On this basis, a claim arising out of a c.i.f. contract for the sale of goods is not within the scope of paragraph (h).[29] Where a contract includes some elements which relate to the use of a ship and others which do not, severance of the contract is possible and a plaintiff may invoke the jurisdiction of the Admiralty Court in relation to claims arising out of that part of the contract involving the use of a vessel; the part of a c.i.f. contract concerning demurrage is not within paragraph (h).[30]

(ii) The words "arising out of" should be construed as meaning "connected with", rather than "arising under".[31] Accordingly, paragraph (h) is wide enough to cover claims based either in contract or tort[32] and extends even to an action in tort by a subcharterer against a shipowner, notwithstanding the fact that the parties in the tort action are not the contracting parties to the agreement out of which the claim arises.[33] It has also been held that paragraph (h) confers jurisdiction on the Admiralty Court in the situation where a dispute arising out of a charterparty has been referred to arbitration and the successful claimant seeks to enforce the award by means of an action *in rem*; since the court has jurisdiction to enforce the charterparty it also has jurisdiction to enforce the award based on it.[34]

(iii) The breadth of paragraph (h) results from the use of the words "any agreement relating to", rather than the narrower expression "any agreement for".[35] It has been held that paragraph (h) includes within its scope an agreement for mooring and unmooring and other services of a ship[36] and an agreement for salvage services (as involving the use of a salvage vessel).[37]

26. Supreme Court Act 1981, s. 20(5).
27. Lord Diplock in *The Eschersheim* [1976] 1 WLR 430, 438.
28. Phillips J in *Petrofina SA* v. *AOT Ltd* [1992] QB 571, 576.
29. *Petrofina SA* v. *AOT Ltd* [1992] QB 571.
30. *Petrofina SA* v. *AOT Ltd* [1992] QB 571.
31. *The Antonis P Lemos* [1985] AC 711.
32. *The St Elefterio* [1957] P 179.
33. *The Antonis P Lemos* [1985] AC 711.
34. In *The Saint Anna* [1983] 1 WLR 895 Sheen J, when faced with two conflicting decisions of the Court of Appeal (*Bremer Oeltransport GmbH* v. *Drewry* [1933] 1 KB 753; *The Beldis* [1936] P 51), decided to follow the earlier case which favoured the wider interpretation.
35. *Gatoil International Inc* v. *Arkwright-Boston Manufacturers Mutual Insurance Co* [1985] AC 255.
36. *The Queen of the South* [1968] P 449.
37. *The Eschersheim* [1976] 1 WLR 430. *Cf. The Tesaba* [1982] 1 Lloyd's Rep 397.

Nevertheless, there are limits to the scope of paragraph (h) since "[i]t would . . . be unreasonable to infer from the expression actually used . . . that it is intended to be sufficient that the agreement in issue should be in some way connected, however remotely, with the carriage of goods in a ship or with the use or hire of a ship."[38] To fall within paragraph (h) there must be "some reasonably direct connection" with the stipulated activities.[39] So, the following are not connected with the carriage of goods in a ship or the use or hire of a ship in a sufficiently direct sense to be capable of coming within paragraph (h): a claim in connection with an agreement for the hire by shipowners of containers to be carried on a ship[40]; a claim for the payment of premiums under a contract of insurance in relation to a cargo of oil[41]; a claim arising out of a contract of marine insurance.[42]

8.1.1.1.6 SALVAGE

(j) any claim in the nature of salvage (including any claim arising by virtue of the application, by or under section 87 of the Civil Aviation Act 1982, of the law relating to salvage of aircraft and their apparel and cargo);

Claims in the nature of salvage include "such claims for services rendered in saving life from a ship or an aircraft or in preserving cargo, apparel or wreck as, under sections 544 to 546 of the Merchant Shipping Act 1894, or any Order in Council made under section 87 of the Civil Aviation Act 1982, are authorised to be made in connection with a ship or an aircraft".[43] Paragraph (j) is concerned with claims for salvage services and does not include a claim against the salvor (for example, for negligent salvage).[44]

8.1.1.1.7 GOODS SUPPLIED TO A SHIP

(m) any claim in respect of goods or materials supplied to a ship for her operation or maintenance;

It is clear that paragraph (m) contemplates a contract of supply, whether by way of sale or hire, between the claimant and a shipowner. It is important to note, however, that the expression used in paragraph (m) is "supplied to a ship" and not "supplied to a shipowner".[45] While paragraph (m) includes within its scope a contract which "expressly provides that the goods or materials are required for the use of a particular ship, the identity of which is specified in the contract or will be specified by the time when the contract comes to be performed", it does not extend to a contract which "contains no

38. Lord Keith in *Gatoil International Inc* v. *Arkwright-Boston Manufacturers Mutual Insurance Co* [1985] AC 255, 270–271.

39. Lord Keith in *Gatoil International Inc* v. *Arkwright-Boston Manufacturers Mutual Insurance Co* [1985] AC 255, 271.

40. This proposition follows from the fact that the House of Lords overruled *The Sonia S* [1983] 2 Lloyd's Rep 63 in *Gatoil International Inc* v. *Arkwright-Boston Manufacturers Mutual Insurance Co* [1985] AC 255.

41. *Gatoil International Inc* v. *Arkwright-Boston Manufacturers Mutual Insurance Co* [1985] AC 255.

42. *The Aifanourios* [1980] SC 346.

43. Supreme Court Act 1981, s. 20(6). There is no cause of action for salvage in respect of services rendered to a ship in danger in navigable non-tidal inland waters: *The Goring* [1988] AC 831.

44. *The Tesaba* [1982] 1 Lloyd's Rep 397.

45. Lord Brandon in *The River Rima* [1988] 1 WLR 758, 763.

reference to a particular ship for the use of which the goods or materials are required, leaving the shipowner to make his own decision about that later."[46]

8.1.1.1.8 WAGES

(o) any claim by a master or member of the crew of a ship for wages (including any sum allotted out of wages or adjudged by a superintendent to be due by way of wages);

Paragraph (o), which arises whether or not the wages are earned on board the ship,[47] covers a claim for unpaid employers' contributions to a pension fund, since the contributions are, in principle, part of the employee's total earnings.[48] However, claims for severance payments[49] or unpaid statutory social insurance benefits[50] are not within the scope of this provision.

8.1.1.1.9 DISBURSEMENTS

(p) any claim by a master, shipper, charterer or agent in respect of disbursements made on account of a ship;

Paragraph (p) does not cover the situation where an insurer seeks to recover from the owner sums paid out by the insurer under a policy of marine insurance.[51]

8.1.1.1.10 OTHER BASES OF JURISDICTION

(a) any claim to the possession or ownership of a ship or to the ownership of any share therein;
(f) any claim for loss of life or personal injury sustained in consequence of any defect in a ship or in her apparel or equipment, or in consequence of the wrongful act, neglect or default of—
  (i) the owners, charterers or persons in possession or control of a ship; or
  (ii) the master or crew of a ship, or any other person for whose wrongful acts, neglects or defaults the owners, charterers or persons in possession or control of a ship are responsible, being an act, neglect or default in the navigation or management of the ship, in the loading, carriage or discharge of goods on, in or from the ship, or in the embarkation, carriage or disembarkation of persons on, in or from the ship;
(g) any claim for loss of or damage to goods carried in a ship[52];
(k) any claim in the nature of towage in respect of a ship or an aircraft[53];
(l) any claim in the nature of pilotage in respect of a ship or an aircraft;
(n) any claim in respect of the construction, repair or equipment of a ship or in respect of dock charges or dues;
(q) any claim arising out of an act which is or is claimed to be a general average act;
(r) any claim arising out of bottomry;
(s) any claim for the forfeiture or condemnation of a ship or of goods which are being or have been carried, or have been attempted to be carried, in a ship, or for the restoration of a ship or any such goods after seizure, or for droits of Admiralty.[54]

46. Lord Brandon in *The River Rima* [1988] 1 WLR 758, 763.
47. *The Tacoma City* [1991] 1 Lloyd's Rep 330.
48. *The Halcyon Skies* [1977] QB 14.
49. *The Tacoma City* [1991] 1 Lloyd's Rep 330.
50. *The Acrux* [1965] P 391.
51. *Bain Clarkson Ltd* v. *Owners of "Sea Friends"* [1991] 2 Lloyd's Rep 322.
52. See, for example, *The Pia Vestra* [1984] 1 Lloyd's Rep 169.
53. See, for example, *The Leoborg* [1962] 2 Lloyd's Rep 146.
54. See, for example, *The Skylark* [1965] P 474.

8.1.1.2 Section 20(1)(c)

8.1.1.2.1 Section 20(1)(c) provides that the High Court has "any other Admiralty jurisdiction which it had immediately before the commencement of [the 1981] Act". This takes one back to section 1 of the Administration of Justice Act 1956 which states that the Admiralty jurisdiction of the High Court extends to "any other jurisdiction which either was vested in the High Court of Admiralty immediately before the date of commencement of the Supreme Court of Judicature Act 1873 . . . or is conferred by or under an Act which came into operation on or after that date on the High Court as being a court with Admiralty jurisdiction". The effect of these provisions is that the Admiralty Court is competent in relation to matters within the Admiralty Act 1840 and the Admiralty Court Act 1861 and in relation to matters within the court's inherent jurisdiction.

8.1.1.2.2 For nearly all practical purposes the jurisdiction conferred by the 1840 and 1861 Acts is fully reflected in the statutory heads of jurisdiction under the 1981 Act.[55] Although it is relatively rare for the court's inherent jurisdiction to be invoked, it may still occasionally be relevant in relation to "injurious acts on the high seas"[56] or in relation to the enforcement of a foreign judgment *in rem*. In *The Despina GK*[57] the plaintiff sought to enforce a Swedish judgment *in rem* by means of proceedings *in rem* in England, reliance being placed on the decision of Sir Robert Phillimore in *The City of Mecca*.[58] It was held that the Admiralty Court's inherent jurisdiction covers proceedings *in rem* for the enforcement of a foreign judgment *in rem* provided that the *res* is still the property of the judgment debtor at the time when it is arrested.

8.1.1.3 Section 20(1)(d)

Whereas section 20(1)(c) looks to the past, section 20(1)(d) looks to the future and provides that the jurisdiction of the Admiralty Court shall include "any jurisdiction connected with ships or aircraft which is vested in the High Court apart from this section and is for the time being by rules of court made or coming into force after the commencement of this Act assigned to the Queen's Bench Division and directed by the rules to be exercised by the Admiralty Court".

8.1.2 Jurisdiction in rem: section 21(2) to (8)

Subsections (2) to (4) of section 21 define the three categories of case in which the various bases of Admiralty jurisdiction may be invoked by way of proceedings *in rem* against a ship.[59] Where the ship or other property which is the subject matter of the action *in rem* is sold in the exercise of the court's Admiralty jurisdiction,[60] the court has

55. For a possible exception see Meeson, *Practice and Procedure of the Admiralty Court* (1987) p. 4.
56. *The Tubantia* [1924] P 78.
57. [1983] QB 214.
58. (1879) 5 PD 28; reversed on appeal on the ground that the foreign judgment was in fact a judgment *in personam*: (1881) 6 PD 106.
59. An action *in rem* may be brought against an aircraft only in the case of claims in the nature of towage or pilotage: Supreme Court Act 1981, s. 21(5). See *Re Glider Standard Austria SH 1964* [1965] P 463.
60. For the circumstances in which the court will order sale see *The Myrto* [1977] 2 Lloyd's Rep 243, 259–260.

the necessary jurisdiction to determine any question arising as to the title to the proceeds of sale.[61]

8.1.2.1 Section 21(2): cases falling within section 20(2)(a) to (c) and (s)

Section 21(2) provides that "[i]n the case of any such claim as is mentioned in section 20(2)(a), (c) or (s) or any such question as is mentioned in section 20(2)(b), an action *in rem* may be brought in the High Court against the ship or property in connection with which the claim or question arises". Actions falling within this provision are truly *in rem* in the sense that they may be brought only against the *res* in connection with which they arose.

8.1.2.2 Section 21(3): maritime liens

Subsection (3) provides that "[i]n any case in which there is a maritime lien or other charge on any ship, aircraft or other property for the amount claimed, an action *in rem* may be brought in the High Court against that ship, aircraft or property". The 1981 Act does not define what is meant by a maritime lien nor the circumstances in which such a lien comes into existence.

8.1.2.2.1 MARITIME LIENS[62]

A maritime lien is a privileged claim upon a ship, which attaches to the ship as soon as the claim arises. Of particular significance is that a maritime lien gives the claimant priority over other creditors and may be enforced against the ship even if the ship is sold to a third party after the cause of action arises. A maritime lien arises in respect of claims for damage caused by a ship and for certain services rendered to a ship (namely, salvage, wages, master's disbursements and bottomry).[63] These claims fall within paragraphs (e), (j), (o), (p) and (r) of section 20(2).

8.1.2.2.2 "OR OTHER CHARGE"

Section 21(3) does not apply to mortgages of ships, which are specifically dealt with by section 21(2).[64] In *The St Merriel*[65] Hewson J decided that the word "charges" includes statutory charges, which are equated to maritime liens, but not a repairer's possessory lien.

8.1.2.3 Section 21(4): cases falling within section 20(2)(e) to (r)

Subsection (4) is rather different from subsections (2) and (3) in that it provides that an action *in rem* may be brought against one of a number of ships, but only if the ship against which the action is brought is owned (or, in certain circumstances, chartered) by the person who would be the defendant were the proceedings brought *in personam*.

61. Supreme Court Act 1981, s. 21(6).
62. Thomas, *Maritime Liens* (1980).
63. Jackson, *Enforcement of Maritime Claims* (1985) pp. 15–33.
64. Referring to section 20(2)(c) of the Supreme Court Act 1981. See Hewson J in *The St Merriel* [1963] P 247, 251–252.
65. [1963] P 247, 254.

Section 21(4), which unlike subsections (2) and (3) does not provide for an action *in rem* to be brought against any property other than a ship, states:

In the case of any such claim as is mentioned in section 20(2)(e) to (r), where—
(a) the claim arises in connection with a ship; and
(b) the person who would be liable on the claim in an action *in personam* ("the relevant person") was, when the cause of action arose, the owner or charterer of, or in possession or in control of, the ship,

an action *in rem* may (whether or not the claim gives rise to a maritime lien on that ship) be brought in the High Court against—
(i) that ship, if at the time when the action is brought the relevant person is either the beneficial owner of that ship as respects all the shares in it or the charterer of it under a charter by demise; or
(ii) any other ship of which, at the time when the action is brought, the relevant person is the beneficial owner as respects all the shares in it.

Section 21(4) introduces a much greater degree of flexibility than subsections (2) and (3) since it provides for an action *in rem* to be brought against either the ship which was directly involved in the events which gave rise to the cause of action in question or, in certain circumstances, against another ship. The operation of section 21(4) is based on four notions: (i) "the relevant person"; (ii) "the particular ship"[66]; (iii) "other ship"; and (iv) the "beneficial owner".

8.1.2.3.1 THE RELEVANT PERSON

8.1.2.3.1.1 The relevant person is a person who would be liable on the claim *in personam* and who at the time when the cause of action arose was the owner or charterer of the ship or was in possession or control of it. In this context owner means registered owner.[67] As regards the expression "charterer" the position is less clear. There is no doubt that "charterer" includes a demise charterer[68]; the question is whether it also covers a time or voyage charterer. The majority of the Court of Appeal in *The Span Terza*[69] indicated that a time charterer was within the scope of the equivalent provision of the Administration of Justice Act 1956. However, in *The Evpo Agnic* Lord Donaldson MR, who had dissented in *The Span Terza*, reiterated his view that "charterer" must mean demise charterer.[70] The expression "in possession or control" refers to a person—such as a salvor—who is in the position of a demise charterer, albeit not under a demise charter.[71]

8.1.2.3.1.2 In determining, for the purpose of subsection (4), whether a person would be liable on a claim in an action *in personam* it should be assumed that he has his habitual residence or a place of business in England.[72] It should be stressed, however, that this provision is relevant only for determining the jurisdiction *in rem* of the court; it does not give the court jurisdiction *in personam* over the relevant person.

66. This is the expression used in Article 3 of the 1952 Arrest Convention.
67. Lord Donaldson MR in *The Evpo Agnic* [1988] 1 WLR 1090, 1096.
68. Lord Donaldson MR in *The Evpo Agnic* [1988] 1 WLR 1090, 1095.
69. [1982] 1 Lloyd's Rep 225.
70. Lord Donaldson MR in *The Evpo Agnic* [1988] 1 WLR 1090, 1095.
71. Lord Donaldson MR in *The Evpo Agnic* [1988] 1 WLR 1090, 1095–1096.
72. Supreme Court Act 1981, s. 21(7).

8.1.2.3.2 THE PARTICULAR SHIP: SECTION 21(4)(B)(I)

The particular ship is the ship in connection with which the claim arises. The plaintiff may bring proceedings *in rem* against the particular ship if at the time when the action is brought the relevant person is either the beneficial owner[73] of all the shares in the ship or a demise charterer.

8.1.2.3.3 OTHER SHIP: SECTION 21(4)(B)(II)

In order for the plaintiff to be able to bring an action *in rem* against any ship other than the particular ship the relevant person must be the beneficial owner[74] of it; that the relevant person is a demise charterer is not sufficient. Generally speaking, where the court has jurisdiction *in rem* over a ship by virtue of section 21(4)(b)(ii) that ship is a sister ship of the particular ship. However, section 21(4) is not limited to cases where the other ship and the particular ship are both owned by the relevant person. Where, for example, the relevant person is the charterer of one ship and the owner of another, if the claim arises in connection with the chartered vessel, the plaintiff may bring proceedings against the ship owned by the relevant person in respect of liabilities incurred by the relevant person as charterer.[75]

8.1.2.3.4 BENEFICIAL OWNER

8.1.2.3.4.1 Although there has been judicial disagreement as to the meaning of the words "beneficial owner",[76] the accepted view is that beneficial ownership means equitable ownership, whether or not accompanied by legal ownership; it does not include possession and control (for example, under a charter by demise) falling short of legal or equitable ownership.[77] As a general rule, the registered owner is also the beneficial owner. However, section 21(4)(b) enables the plaintiff to arrest a ship which has been transferred into different legal ownership, the relevant person retaining beneficial ownership of the ship.[78] It has been said that "where there is a suggestion of a trusteeship or a nominee holding, there is no doubt that the court can investigate it".[79]

8.1.2.3.4.2 The proliferation of one-ship companies and complex corporate structures may make the determination of the beneficial ownership of a ship less than straightforward. Although "the court in all cases can and in some cases should look behind the registered owner to determine the true beneficial ownership",[80] the court is not inclined to pierce the corporate veil unless there is a clear indication that the apparent arrangements are a sham. So, in the absence of special circumstances, section 21(4) does not allow the plaintiff to bring proceedings *in rem* against a ship owned by a subsidiary company of the relevant person or by a sister company.

8.1.2.3.4.3 In *The Maritime Trader*[81] the plaintiff issued a writ *in rem* in relation to a claim arising out of a charter concluded between the plaintiff and a German company.

73. See para. 8.1.2.3.4.
74. See para. 8.1.2.3.4.
75. *The Span Terza* [1982] 1 Lloyd's Rep 225.
76. *The Andrea Ursula* [1973] QB 265; *I Congreso del Partido* [1978] QB 500.
77. The view of Robert Goff J in *I Congreso del Partido* [1978] QB 500 was preferred in *The Father Thames* [1979] 2 Lloyd's Rep 364.
78. See *The Saudi Prince* [1982] 2 Lloyd's Rep 255.
79. Slynn J in *The Aventicum* [1978] 1 Lloyd's Rep 184, 187.
80. Slynn J in *The Aventicum* [1978] 1 Lloyd's Rep 184, 187.
81. [1981] 2 Lloyd's Rep 153.

The writ was served on a ship owned by a subsidiary of the German company. The court had no jurisdiction in these circumstances since, although the German company owned all the shares in the subsidiary, it had no legal or equitable property in the assets of the subsidiary and, therefore, it could not be said that the ship was beneficially owned by the relevant person.

8.1.2.3.4.4 In *The Evpo Agnic*[82] the plaintiffs owned a cargo being carried by a ship belonging to a one-ship Panamanian company. The ship sank and the plaintiffs brought proceedings *in rem* against a ship owned by a second one-ship Panamanian company. Both companies had the same president, vice-president and shareholders. The Court of Appeal held that the court did not have jurisdiction *in rem* under section 21(4) and ordered the unconditional release of the vessel which had been arrested; the two ships were not in the same beneficial ownership, notwithstanding the fact that a number of vessels, including those owned by the two companies, were run as a fleet under the management of a third company.

8.1.2.3.4.5 For an action *in rem* to be maintained under section 21(4) not only must the relevant person have been the owner or charterer of the particular ship at the time when the cause of action arose, that person must also be the beneficial owner (or, in the case of proceedings against the particular ship, the demise charterer) of the ship against which the proceedings are brought at the time when the action is brought. Accordingly, where the ship against which proceedings are brought has changed hands before the action is brought the court has no jurisdiction *in rem* in relation to that ship.[83]

8.1.2.4 The relationship between section 21(3) and (4)

Subsections (3) and (4) overlap in certain respects. For example, in a salvage case in which the salvor has a maritime lien over the salved ship the salvor's claim falls within section 21(4)—on the basis that the court has jurisdiction under section 20(2)(j)—as well as under section 21(3). A similar overlap exists in cases giving rise to a maritime lien which fall within one of paragraphs (e), (o), (p) and (r) of section 20(2). In these cases the plaintiff may proceed under either subsection. If the plaintiff relies on section 21(3) the action *in rem* may be brought only against the ship or other property in connection with which the claim arises. If the appropriate conditions are satisfied, the plaintiff may proceed under section 21(4) against either the particular ship or another ship, but not against other property.

8.1.3 Jurisdiction in actions in personam: section 21(1) and section 22

8.1.3.1 Actions *in personam* may be brought in relation to all cases coming within the Admiralty jurisdiction of the High Court.[84] Indeed, as regards claims falling within section 20(2)(d) and section 20(3), the 1981 Act makes no provision for the plaintiff to enforce the claim otherwise than by an action *in personam*. There are, however, limitations on the court's *in personam* jurisdiction as regards collision actions within the scope of section 20(3)(b)[85] and limitation actions within the scope of section 20(3)(c).[86]

82. [1988] 1 WLR 1090.
83. *The Mawan* [1988] 2 Lloyd's Rep 459.
84. Supreme Court Act 1981, s. 21(1).
85. Supreme Court Act 1981, s. 22.
86. RSC, Order 75, r. 4.

So that English law complies with the Collision Convention, it is provided that jurisdiction cannot be assumed *in personam* in the circumstances set out in section 20(3)(b) unless there is a specific link with England (for example, in terms of the defendant's habitual residence or place of business or of the place where the cause of action arose).[87] As regards a limitation action, a writ *in personam* cannot be served out of the jurisdiction unless there is a similar link with England.[88]

8.1.3.2 It should be noted that the limitations imposed as regards collision actions apply only to actions *in personam*. Paragraphs (e) and (f) of section 20(2) confer jurisdiction on the Admiralty Court in relation to "any claim for damage done by a ship" and certain claims "for loss of life or personal injury". Claims falling within these paragraphs may be enforced by means of proceedings *in rem*.[89]

8.1.4 Commencing Admiralty proceedings

The relevant procedural rules for the commencement of Admiralty proceedings are to be found in RSC, Order 75. Admiralty proceedings *in rem* against a ship are commenced by service of a writ on the ship. In addition, the plaintiff may obtain the arrest of the ship. Admiralty proceedings *in personam* are commenced by service of a writ on the defendant. The tendency is for plaintiffs to prefer to commence the action *in rem* where possible, since this is the most effective way of obtaining security for the claim.

8.1.4.1 Actions in rem

8.1.4.1.1 The High Court's jurisdiction in Admiralty proceedings *in rem* is strictly territorial. A writ *in rem* must be served on the *res* within the jurisdiction of the court—which means in English territorial waters. There is no provision for a writ *in rem* to be served out of the jurisdiction.[90] The basic rule is that "a writ by which an action *in rem* is begun must be served on the property against which the action is brought".[91] It is not enough for the plaintiff to serve the writ on the master on board the ship.[92]

8.1.4.1.2 Service of a warrant of arrest or writ in an action *in rem* is effected by "(a) affixing the warrant or writ for a short time on any mast of the ship or on the outside of any suitable part of the ship's superstructure, and (b) on removing the warrant or writ, leaving a copy of it affixed (in the case of the warrant) in its place or (in the case of the writ) on a sheltered, conspicuous part of the ship".[93] Where the action *in rem* is against cargo which has been discharged or transshipped (or against freight in relation to such cargo) service is effected "(a) by placing the warrant or writ for a short time on the cargo and, on removing the warrant or writ, leaving a copy of it on the cargo, or (b) if the cargo is in the custody of a person who will not permit access to it, by leaving a copy of the warrant or writ with that person".[94] Where, however, the cargo has not been discharged, the general rule is that a writ *in rem* or a warrant of arrest may be served on the ship in

87. Supreme Court Act 1981, s. 22(2).
88. RSC, Order 75, r. 4(1).
89. Supreme Court Act 1981, s. 21(4).
90. *Castrique* v. *Imrie* (1870) LR 4 HL 414.
91. RSC, Order 75, r. 8(1). Where the claim concerns freight service is to be effected on the cargo or the ship in which the cargo is carried: RSC, Order 75, r. 8(1)(a).
92. *The Prins Bernhardt* [1964] P 117.
93. RSC, Order 75, r. 11(1).
94. RSC, Order 75, r. 11(2).

which the cargo was carried or on the cargo itself.[95] The effect of arresting a cargo is to detain the ship until such time as the cargo can be discharged. If the property in relation to which the claim relates has already been sold and the proceeds paid into court, an action *in rem* may be commenced by filing a copy of the writ in the registry.[96]

8.1.4.1.3 A writ and a warrant for arrest may be issued at the same time, whether or not the vessel is physically within the jurisdiction of the English court; either the writ or the warrant for arrest may be served first. Only the Admiralty Marshal (or his substitute) may serve a warrant for arrest.[97] If the owner of the ship puts up security, the plaintiff will generally refrain from arresting the ship. Similarly, the owner of the ship may put up security after arrest in order to obtain the ship's release. Security may take the form of bail, which is an undertaking given to the court, or a guarantee or undertaking given out of court, usually by a bank or insurance company. Bail may be given only after acknowledgment of the writ and, therefore, in these cases the owner of the *res* is taken to have submitted personally to the court's jurisdiction.[98] Contractual security—for example, in the form of a letter of guarantee given out of court by the shipowner's P & I Club—may be given without the owner of the *res* submitting or agreeing to submit to the jurisdiction.[99]

8.1.4.1.4 In cases falling within the scope of section 21(2) and (3) the plaintiff may bring proceedings only against the property in relation to which the claim arises. Under subsection (4), however, the plaintiff may have a choice as to the ship against which to proceed *in rem*. Where the court has jurisdiction *in rem* under section 21(4)—by virtue of the fact that the claim falls within section 20(2)(e) to (r)—the plaintiff may issue a writ *in rem* against a number of ships (for example, the particular ship and one or more sister ships). Indeed, where possible, it is sensible to name in the writ as many of the ships against which proceedings *in rem* may be brought as can be identified, since it may not be possible to add further names to the writ at a later stage.[100] Once a ship has been served with a writ or arrested in an action *in rem* brought to enforce a claim under section 20(2)(e) to (r), no other ship may be served with a writ or arrested in that or any other action *in rem* to enforce that claim[101] and the writ should be amended by deleting all the other names upon it.[102] The position is, therefore, that the plaintiff can keep his options open when the writ is issued, but may proceed *in rem* against only one of the named ships.[103]

8.1.4.2 Actions in personam

Whereas a writ *in rem* may not be served out of the jurisdiction, a writ commencing Admiralty proceedings *in personam* may, in certain circumstances, be served out of the

95. RSC, Order 75, r. 8(1); RSC, Order 75, r. 10(5).
96. RSC, Order 75, r. 8(1)(b).
97. RSC, Order 75, r. 10(2).
98. *The Prinsengracht* [1993] 1 Lloyd's Rep 41.
99. *The Deichland* [1990] 1 QB 361. For consideration of the importance of the form of security see para. 8.2.2.
100. See, for example, *The Prevese* [1973] 1 Lloyd's Rep 202.
101. Supreme Court Act 1981, s. 21(8).
102. *The Al Battani* [1993] 2 Lloyd's Rep 219.
103. *The Berny* [1979] QB 80; *The Helene Roth* [1980] QB 273; *The Freccia del Nord* [1989] 1 Lloyd's Rep 388.

jurisdiction. In cases where the defendant is domiciled in a Brussels or Lugano Contracting State jurisdiction may be assumed only under Title II or under one of the special conventions whose effect is preserved by Article 57.[104] If jurisdiction is not regulated by the Conventions service out of the jurisdiction depends on the leave of the court. The conditions for the granting of leave in cases within the jurisdiction of the Admiralty Court are governed by the principles formulated under RSC, Order 11[105]; leave to serve out will not be given unless "it shall be made sufficiently to appear to the court that the case is a proper one for service out of the jurisdiction".[106] Accordingly, in addition to the claim falling within the jurisdiction of the court, the evidence must reveal a serious question to be tried and the English court must be the *forum conveniens.*[107]

8.1.4.3 Staying Admiralty proceedings

Subject to the provisions of the Conventions, where proceedings are started in England within the Admiralty jurisdiction of the High Court—whether *in rem* or *in personam*—the court may stay the proceedings under its inherent jurisdiction.[108] There are no special principles which apply to actions *in rem*; indeed, many of the cases in which the courts have worked out the general principles upon which a stay should be granted under the court's inherent jurisdiction have involved actions *in rem.* So, a defendant may obtain a stay of proceedings on the basis that there is a more appropriate forum abroad or that the parties have agreed to the exclusive jurisdiction of the courts of another country.[109] Where the parties have agreed to arbitration the court is obliged to grant a stay of proceedings in non-domestic cases under section 1 of the Arbitration Act 1975.[110] Where an action *in rem* is stayed or dismissed on one of these grounds the court may order the retention of the *res* which has been arrested or—in cases where the grant of a stay is discretionary—may order that the stay or dismissal of proceedings be conditional on the provision of security for the award or judgment.[111]

8.2 THE IMPACT OF THE BRUSSELS AND LUGANO CONVENTIONS[112]

8.2.1 Introduction

8.2.1.1 The basic scheme of the Conventions

The Conventions are intended to provide a comprehensive framework for the allocation of jurisdiction between the courts of the Contracting States in matters falling within the Conventions' material scope. The Conventions apply to civil and commercial matters; accordingly matters falling within the jurisdiction of the Admiralty Court are almost invariably within the scope of the Conventions.

104. See para. 8.2.
105. RSC, Order 75, r. 2(2).
106. RSC, Order 11, r. 4(2).
107. See paras. 6.3–6.5.
108. Civil Jurisdiction and Judgments Act 1982, s. 49.
109. See paras. 6.4–6.5.
110. See para. 18.2.
111. Civil Jurisdiction and Judgments Act 1982, s. 26. See para. 21.2.
112. Hartley, "The Effect of the 1988 Brussels Judgments Convention on Admiralty Actions in Rem" (1989) 105 LQR 640.

According to the basic scheme of the jurisdiction rules contained in Title II a defendant domiciled in a Contracting State may be sued either in the courts of the Contracting State in which he is domiciled or in the courts of another Contracting State in accordance with the provisions of Title II but not otherwise. Although, as a general rule, Title II does not allocate jurisdiction with regard to proceedings brought against a defendant who is not domiciled in a Contracting State, a number of the provisions of Title II apply regardless of the defendant's domicile.

8.2.1.2 Do the Conventions apply to actions in rem?

The jurisdiction rules in Title II are clearly drafted with actions *in personam* in mind. For example, Article 2 provides that a person domiciled in a Contracting State may be sued in the courts of his domicile. As regards Admiralty proceedings it is very common for proceedings to be brought *in rem*. What is the impact of Title II in these circumstances? Since in an action *in rem* the ship is the notional defendant, it is arguable that the Conventions have no application because the defendant is not a person domiciled in a Contracting State. Although this argument was accepted by Sheen J in *The Deichland*,[113] it was rejected by the Court of Appeal.[114] The essential facts were very simple: the plaintiff commenced an action *in rem* in England by serving a writ on a vessel chartered by the defendant, a Germany company; the ship was not arrested, but security for the plaintiff's claim was put up on the defendant's behalf in consideration of the plaintiff's refraining from arresting the vessel. The defendant sought a declaration that the English court had no jurisdiction and that, as a result of Article 2 of the Brussels Convention, the plaintiff should have brought the proceedings in Germany. The Court of Appeal decided that, even where proceedings are solely *in rem*, the person who is interested in contesting liability and against whom the plaintiff would wish to proceed *in personam* if an appearance were entered is being "sued" for the purposes of Articles 2 and 3 of the Brussels Convention. So, an action *in rem* is governed by Title II in the same way as an action *in personam* even before the person who is interested in contesting liability has submitted to the jurisdiction.

8.2.1.3 The preservation of special conventions

8.2.1.3.1 Title II does not contain the only bases of jurisdiction authorised by the Conventions. As a general principle, the Conventions preserve the effect of special conventions concerning civil jurisdiction; Article 57(1) provides that the Conventions do "not affect any conventions to which the Contracting States are or will be parties and which, in relation to particular matters, govern jurisdiction". Moreover, the courts of a Contracting State which is party to a special convention may assume jurisdiction in accordance with that convention even against defendants who are domiciled in a Contracting State which is not a party to that convention[115]—although in such a situation the court must apply Article 20 of the Brussels or Lugano Convention, as the

113. [1988] 2 Lloyd's Rep 494.
114. [1990] 1 QB 361. Hogan, (1990) 15 ELRev 81, 82–84.
115. Article 57(2).

case may be.[116] The most important conventions in Admiralty matters are the Arrest and Collision Conventions of 1952. Although attempts have been made to bring English law into line with the treaty obligations assumed by the United Kingdom under these conventions, the Supreme Court Act 1981 does not implement these conventions into English law as such.

8.2.1.3.2 There is some dispute as to the precise effect of Article 57. The Schlosser Report states that as a result of Article 57 "provisions on jurisdiction contained in special conventions are to be regarded as if they were provisions of the 1968 Convention itself".[117] In *The Nordglimt*[118] Hobhouse J seemed to go even further by suggesting that the effect of Article 57 is to achieve "an indirect incorporation of the 1952 [Arrest] Convention into English municipal law through the 1968 Conventions".[119] However, in *The Po*[120] Lloyd LJ cast some doubt on the correctness of Hobhouse J's sweeping statement, noting that "Article 57 provides that the 1968 Convention shall not *affect* the special conventions. It is a long way from that to saying that the conventions have become part of English municipal law by virtue of section 2 of the 1982 Act".[121]

8.2.2 The combined effect of Title II and Article 57

8.2.2.1 Whether or not Article 57 achieves an incorporation of special conventions into the law of the United Kingdom, the impact of the Conventions on the Admiralty jurisdiction of the English court is reasonably clear.

(i) Where the person who is interested in contesting the plaintiff's claim in proceedings *in rem* is not domiciled in a Contracting State, the general rule is that the Admiralty jurisdiction of the English court is based exclusively on the relevant provisions of the 1981 Act. This general principle is subject, however, to the provisions of Title II which apply regardless of domicile. If, for example, the plaintiff starts proceedings *in rem* in England with a view to enforcing a claim under a bill of lading which contains a jurisdiction agreement in favour of the courts of another Contracting State, the owner of the vessel may, in reliance on Article 17, challenge the jurisdiction of the court and apply for a stay of proceedings.

(ii) On the basis of the Court of Appeal's decision in *The Deichland*, the combined effect of Title II and Article 57 is that if the person who is interested in contesting the plaintiff's claim in proceedings *in rem* is domiciled in a Contracting State, the court has jurisdiction under sections 20 to 24 of the 1981 Act only if the assumption of jurisdiction under these sections is consistent either with the terms of the Arrest Convention or the Collision Convention—which are preserved by Article 57[122]—or with one of the heads of jurisdiction set out in Title II. This proposition can be illustrated by a number of cases.

116. See para. 4.4.
117. OJ 1979 C59/140, para. 240(b).
118. [1988] 1 QB 183.
119. [1988] 1 QB 183, 197.
120. [1991] 2 Lloyd's Rep 206.
121. [1991] 2 Lloyd's Rep 206, 211. (Emphasis in original.)
122. Jenard Report, OJ 1979 C59/59.

8.2.2.2 *The Po*[123] concerned a collision in Rio de Janeiro harbour between a vessel owned by the plaintiff and a vessel owned by the defendant, an Italian corporation. As a result of the collision the plaintiff's vessel was a constructive total loss. In September 1988 the plaintiff served a writ *in rem* on the defendant's vessel while she was in Southampton harbour. To prevent arrest security was put up by the defendant's P & I Club. The defendant argued that, since the case was governed by the Brussels Convention, the English court had no jurisdiction and the proceedings should have been brought in Italy. There was no doubt that the English court had jurisdiction under the 1981 Act and under Article 1(1)(b) of the Collision Convention which provides that proceedings in relation to an action for collision occurring between seagoing vessels may be introduced "before the Court of the place . . . where arrest could have been effected and bail or other security has been furnished". Nevertheless, the Collision Convention as such does not form part of English law. The Court of Appeal rejected the defendant's argument that Article 57 does not entitle a plaintiff to rely on a special convention as against a defendant domiciled in a Contracting State unless the convention has been implemented into domestic law:

> Article 57 of the 1968 Convention does not depend for its beneficial operation on showing that the Contracting States have *implemented* the special convention. It is enough that the State is a *party* to the Convention, which the United Kingdom is. The High Court indubitably has jurisdiction in accordance with English municipal law in the present case, since the writ *in rem* was properly served on the vessel when she was at Southampton . . . This assumption of jurisdiction was not only not contrary to the Collision Convention, but was positively authorised by the [Collision] Convention, since the vessel could have been arrested, and security was duly offered and accepted. In those circumstances I cannot see that it matters whether the Collision Convention as such, or the last part of Article 1(1)(b), are part of English municipal law. Since the assumption of jurisdiction was in accordance with the Collision Convention, it is saved from being contrary to Articles 2 and 3 of the 1968 Convention by Article 57.[124]

8.2.2.3 A similar result was arrived at in *The Nordglimt*[125] in the context of the Arrest Convention. Although the United Kingdom is a party to the Arrest Convention, it has never been given the force of law in English municipal law; Parliament has simply given effect to certain of the provisions of the Arrest Convention in sections 21 and 22 of the 1981 Act. In *The Nordglimt* the plaintiff started proceedings *in rem* in England against a vessel which was owned by the defendant, a Danish company. The vessel was arrested and security was put up for her release. The question was whether the plaintiff could rely on the 1981 Act notwithstanding the fact that proceedings fell within the scope of Article 1 of the Brussels Convention and the defendant was domiciled in a Contracting State. Although the court's jurisdiction was based on the 1981 Act, the assumption of jurisdiction was consistent with the terms of the Arrest Convention. Since Article 57 preserves the effect of jurisdiction rules contained in conventions to which the United Kingdom is a party, the court was entitled to assume jurisdiction.

8.2.2.4 *The Nordglimt* should be contrasted with *The Deichland*[126] in which the plaintiff brought proceedings *in rem* against a vessel chartered by the defendant, a German company. Whereas in *The Nordglimt* the vessel was arrested and subsequently

123. [1991] 2 Lloyd's Rep 206. Hartley, "Coming to Terms with the Brussels Jurisdiction and Judgments Convention" [1991] LMCLQ 446.
124. Lloyd LJ, [1991] 2 Lloyd's Rep 206, 211. (Emphasis in original.)
125. [1988] 1 QB 183.
126. [1990] 1 QB 361. Carter, (1989) 60 BYIL 489.

released, in *The Deichland* the ship was not arrested, because security was put up on the defendant's behalf in consideration of the plaintiff's refraining from arresting the vessel. There was no doubt that, had the defendant not been domiciled in a Contracting State, the only relevant rules would have been those contained in the 1981 Act—according to which the court had jurisdiction over the proceedings. However, since the defendant was domiciled in a Contracting State, the question was whether the court had jurisdiction under the Brussels Convention, which in turn depended on whether the court had assumed jurisdiction under a special convention preserved by Article 57. The crucial question was, therefore, whether the court had jurisdiction under the Arrest Convention. Although the terms of the 1981 Act incorporate the substance of the Arrest Convention, they are wider than the terms of the Arrest Convention itself. The 1981 Act is framed in such a way that the jurisdiction of the court is based on the service of the writ on the ship within the jurisdiction[127]; it does not depend on the ship having been arrested. Article 7 of the Arrest Convention, however, is premised on the vessel in question having been arrested and confers jurisdiction on "courts of the country in which the arrest was made". The Court of Appeal held that, since the court did not have jurisdiction under the Arrest Convention, it did not have jurisdiction over the German defendant; by virtue of Article 57 where the defendant is domiciled in a Contracting State, the provisions of the 1981 Act are only to be given effect so far as they implement the Arrest Convention and not otherwise.

8.2.2.5 Accordingly—except in those situations falling within the Collision Convention, in which jurisdiction does not depend on the ship having been arrested—a plaintiff who wishes to proceed in the Admiralty Court *in rem* against a ship owned or chartered by a defendant who is domiciled in a Contracting State must ensure either that the ship is arrested or that the defendant submits or agrees to submit to the jurisdiction. Since in *The Deichland* contractual security was given without the defendant having submitted to the jurisdiction of the court, the plaintiff should have proceeded to arrest the vessel. Where the defendant puts up security in the form of a bail bond the court has jurisdiction over the defendant on the basis of submission—it being impossible for bail to be given unless the defendant has entered an appearance by voluntarily acknowledging the writ—and there is, therefore, no need to obtain an agreement to submit or to arrest the vessel.[128]

8.2.3 Staying proceedings

8.2.3.1 Articles 21 and 22

Under Article 21 where proceedings involving the same cause of action and between the same parties are brought in the courts of different Contracting States, any court other than the court first seised shall of its own motion stay its proceedings until such time as the jurisdiction of the court first seised is established. Under Article 22 where related actions are brought in the courts of different Contracting States, any court other than the court first seised may, while the actions are pending at first instance, stay its proceedings. The interpretation of these provisions has already been considered in the

127. RSC, Order 75, r. 11. See para. 8.1.4.1.
128. *The Prinsengracht* [1993] 1 Lloyd's Rep 41.

context of (i) cases where there are parallel proceedings *in personam* in more than one Contracting State and (ii) situations where an action *in rem* is brought in one Contracting State and an action *in personam* in another.[129] Of course, Articles 21 and 22 also apply where a plaintiff starts proceedings *in rem* against a ship owned by the defendant in one Contracting State and subsequently starts proceedings *in rem* against a sister ship in another Contracting State on the same cause of action.

8.2.3.2 Forum non conveniens

The general principles which are applicable to the staying of actions—whether on the ground of *forum non conveniens* or some other basis—apply equally to actions commenced in the Admiralty Court, whether *in personam* or *in rem*. According to the Court of Appeal the court may stay the proceedings on the basis of *forum non conveniens* in favour of the courts of a non-contracting State even in cases where the person being sued is domiciled in a Contracting State.[130] In *The Po*[131] an action *in rem* was commenced in England against a ship owned by the defendant, an Italian company. The defendant applied for a stay on the basis that, since the dispute concerned a collision in Rio de Janeiro harbour, the Brazilian courts were a more appropriate forum. Although a stay was refused, the Court of Appeal accepted that the doctrine of *forum non conveniens* was, in principle, applicable in these circumstances.

8.2.4 Limitation and salvage

There are two provisions in the Conventions which apply specifically to proceedings within the Admiralty jurisdiction of the High Court.

8.2.4.1 Salvage of cargo or freight

Article 5(7) of the Conventions provides that a person domiciled in a Contracting State may be sued:

> as regards a dispute concerning the payment of remuneration claimed in respect of the salvage of a cargo or freight, in the court under the authority of which the cargo or freight in question—
> (a) has been arrested to secure such payment; or
> (b) could have been so arrested, but bail or other security has been given;
> provided that this provision shall apply only if it is claimed that the defendant has an interest in the cargo or freight or had such an interest at the time of salvage.

Many matters relating to Admiralty jurisdiction are governed by special jurisdiction conventions which are preserved by Article 57 of the Conventions.[132] Although the Arrest Convention allows a claimant to invoke the jurisdiction of a State in which a ship has been arrested on account of a salvage claim,[133] there is no equivalent jurisdiction in relation to salvaged cargo and freight. Under English law, however, the Admiralty Court has jurisdiction in respect of claims connected with salvaged cargo and freight.[134]

129. See para. 5.9.
130. *Re Harrods (Buenos Aires) Ltd* [1992] Ch 72. This decision is discussed at para. 5.10.
131. [1991] 2 Lloyd's Rep 206.
132. See para. 8.1.1.
133. Article 7(1)(b) of the 1952 Arrest Convention.
134. Supreme Court Act 1981, s. 20(2)(j).

In the absence of Article 5(7)—which was added by the 1978 Accession Convention—the English court would no longer have been able to assume Admiralty jurisdiction over defendants domiciled in a Contracting State in relation to such claims. The limitations of Article 5(7) should, however, be noted; it applies only where the defendant had an interest in the cargo or freight at the time of salvage and if the cargo or freight was arrested (or could have been arrested). The purpose of Article 5(7) "is to confer jurisdiction only with regard to those claims which are secured by a maritime lien. If the owner of a ship in difficulties has concluded a contract for its salvage, as his contract with the cargo owner frequently obliges him to do, any disputes arising from the former contract will not be governed by this provision".[135]

8.2.4.2 Limitation of liability

8.2.4.2.1 Article 6A of the Conventions provides:

> Where by virtue of this Convention a court of a Contracting State has jurisdiction in actions relating to liability arising from the use or operation of a ship, that court, or any other court substituted for this purpose by the internal law of that State, shall also have jurisdiction over claims for limitation of such liability.

In English law the limitation of the liability of the owner of a seagoing ship may arise in one of two ways.

(i) Where a claimant starts proceedings against the shipowner, limitation of liability may be raised by the shipowner by way of counterclaim.
(ii) If a shipowner anticipates a liability claim, it may be in his interest to take the initiative, in which case the action takes the form of originating proceedings against one or more of the potential claimants.

8.2.4.2.2 The context in which Article 6A is relevant is where the shipowner brings an independent action against a claimant with a view to limiting his liability.[136] In the situation where the shipowner takes the initiative he may, of course, rely on Articles 2 to 6. However, Articles 2 to 6 do not allow the shipowner to bring limitation proceedings in the courts of his domicile. Since the shipowner could be sued in the courts of his domicile, it is desirable also to allow the shipowner to have recourse to this jurisdiction. It is the purpose of Article 6A to provide for this. The value of Article 6A to the shipowner is that it enables all actions concerning limitation to be concentrated in his home forum.[137]

135. Schlosser Report, OJ 1979, C59/109, para. 123(b).
136. Schlosser Report, OJ 1979 C59/110, para. 127.
137. Schlosser Report, OJ 1979 C59/110, para. 128(a).

CHAPTER 9

THE RECOGNITION AND ENFORCEMENT OF FOREIGN JUDGMENTS

9.0.1 The basic principles underlying the law relating to the recognition and enforcement of foreign judgments are reasonably clear (para. 9.1). Notwithstanding Lord Bridge's view that the enforcement of foreign judgments is now primarily governed by statutory codes,[1] the common law is still of very considerable significance in that it applies to judgments given by the courts of most countries in Eastern Europe and the Middle East as well as to most non-Commonwealth countries in the Americas (including the United States of America), Africa and Asia (para. 9.2). There are, however, statutory regimes which either supplement or supersede the common law: Part II of the Administration of Justice Act 1920 provides a scheme for the enforcement (but not the recognition) of judgments given by various Commonwealth jurisdictions; the Foreign Judgments (Reciprocal Enforcement) Act 1933, which is a virtual codification of the common law rules, introduced a framework for the implementation of bilateral treaties between the United Kingdom and foreign countries (mostly in Western Europe) as well as for the recognition and enforcement of judgments given in proceedings where the original court assumed jurisdiction under the provisions of various international conventions (para. 9.3).

9.0.2 Among the statutory schemes for the recognition and enforcement of judgments, the most important is that contained in Part I of the Civil Jurisdiction and Judgments Act 1982, which implements the Brussels and Lugano Conventions ("the Conventions"). Part I of the 1982 Act introduced a simplified procedure for the recognition and enforcement of judgments given by the courts of Contracting States (para. 9.4). It should be remembered that, since the material scope of the Conventions is limited to civil and commercial matters,[2] the recognition and enforcement in England of judgments given by the courts of a Contracting State in matters which fall outside the scope of the Conventions has to be based on the common law or, where applicable, the Foreign Judgments (Reciprocal Enforcement) Act 1933. So, for example, the 1933 Act determines whether a judgment given by a French court in a social security matter is entitled to recognition or enforcement in England.

9.0.3 Part II of the 1982 Act introduced a mechanism for the mutual recognition and enforcement of judgments given by the courts of the different parts of the United Kingdom (para. 9.5). There are also statutory provisions dealing with the recognition and enforcement of foreign judgments given against the United Kingdom and other

1. *Owens Bank Ltd* v. *Bracco* [1992] 2 AC 443, 489.
2. See para. 3.3.

States and with the recognition and enforcement of judgments of the institutions of the European Community (para. 9.6).

9.1 INTRODUCTION

9.1.1 Why recognise foreign judgments?

In the modern world, where so much commerce is international in nature, the international community has a general interest in ensuring that judgments operate as a form of international currency; if judgments were only valid and enforceable in the country of origin international trade would be an even more hazardous enterprise. In *Adams* v. *Cape Industries Plc*[3] Slade LJ, who delivered the judgment of the Court of Appeal, suggested that underlying the system for the recognition and enforcement of foreign judgments is "an acknowledgement that the society of nations will work better if some foreign judgments are taken to create rights which supersede the underlying cause of action, and which may be directly enforced in countries where the defendant or his assets are to be found."[4] Although this idea may explain why some foreign judgments should be entitled to recognition or enforcement it does not provide an answer to the question of which judgments should—and should not—be recognised or enforced.

9.1.2 Which foreign judgments should be entitled to recognition and enforcement?

9.1.2.1 Broadly speaking, there are two possible theories for the recognition and enforcement of foreign judgments: the doctrine of reciprocity and the doctrine of obligation. Different parts of English law are inspired by different doctrines. Although the English courts have from time to time flirted with the doctrine of reciprocity, it is the doctrine of obligation which underpins the common law. The theory of obligation flows from a jurisdiction-based approach to the recognition and enforcement of foreign judgments. If, on the one hand, there exists between the country of origin and the person against whom the judgment was given a connection which is sufficient to justify the assumption of jurisdiction by the original court, the judgment creates an obligation which the courts of other countries ought to recognise and, where appropriate, enforce; if, on the other hand, the connection is not sufficient the judgment does not create any obligation outside the country of origin. The doctrine of obligation was accepted as part of English common law in *Schibsby* v. *Westenholz*[5] and the statutory schemes which are based on the common law—Part II of the Administration of Justice Act 1920 and the Foreign Judgments (Reciprocal Enforcement) Act 1933—adopt the same underlying approach.

9.1.2.2 The scheme for the recognition and enforcement of judgments established by the Brussels and Lugano Conventions is largely based on the theory of reciprocity, rather than the notion of obligation. The courts of the United Kingdom are required to recognise and enforce the judgments of the courts of the other Contracting States,

3. [1990] Ch 433.
4. [1990] Ch 433, 552.
5. (1870) LR 6 QB 155.

because the courts of the other Contracting States are required *mutatis mutandis* to recognise and enforce judgments given by the courts of the United Kingdom. Of course, this reciprocity is, to a significant extent, made possible because Title II lays down uniform jurisdiction rules which must be applied by the courts of all the Contracting States. However, because many of the jurisdictional safeguards contained in Title II are not extended to parties who are not domiciled in a Contracting State, there are circumstances in which the courts of one Contracting State are required to recognise or enforce a judgment given by the courts of another Contracting State notwithstanding the fact that the original court assumed jurisdiction on an exorbitant basis.[6] The foundation of the system for the recognition and enforcement of foreign judgments in these circumstances is the theory of reciprocity.

9.1.3 "Merger"

9.1.3.1 It used to be the case that in English law a foreign judgment in the plaintiff's favour did not operate to extinguish the cause of action. Accordingly, a judgment creditor who had obtained an award of damages in foreign proceedings might choose between applying to enforce the judgment and suing the judgment debtor in England on the original cause of action in the hope of obtaining a higher award. This rule, which gave a litigant two bites at the cherry, was indefensible. The doctrine of non-merger was abolished by the Civil Jurisdiction and Judgments Act 1982, section 34 of which provides:

> No proceedings may be brought by a person in England or Wales . . . on a cause of action in respect of which a judgment has been given in his favour in proceedings between the same parties, or their privies, in a court in another part of the United Kingdom or in a court of an overseas country, unless that judgment is not enforceable or entitled to recognition in England or Wales . . .

9.1.3.2 Where, following a judgment abroad, proceedings are commenced in England, the burden is on the defendant to show that the three conditions laid down by section 34 are satisfied.

- (i) The cause of action in the English proceedings must be the same as the cause of action in the proceedings leading to the foreign judgment.[7] Where there is any dispute as to whether the causes of action in the two sets of proceedings are the same, this issue must be determined by English law; whether or not the causes of action would be regarded as identical by the domestic law of the country of origin is irrelevant.[8]
- (ii) The proceedings leading to the foreign judgment and the English proceedings must be between the same parties (or their privies).[9]
- (iii) The foreign judgment must be entitled to recognition in England (whether at common law or under one of the statutory schemes).

6. See para. 9.4.1.3.
7. See para. 9.2.6.2.
8. *Republic of India* v. *India Steamship Co Ltd* [1992] 1 Lloyd's Rep 124 (CA), reversed on other grounds: [1993] AC 410 (HL).
9. See para. 9.2.6.1.

9.1.3.3 The operation of section 34 can be illustrated by *Black* v. *Yates*,[10] a case in which the plaintiff's husband had been killed in Spain in a motor accident which had been caused by the defendant's negligence. The defendant was prosecuted and convicted in Spanish criminal proceedings to which the plaintiff joined a civil claim for damages, as permitted by Spanish procedural law. The court, applying the same principles as those which would have been applied by a civil court, awarded the plaintiff the equivalent of £18,000 by way of compensation. When the plaintiff commenced proceedings against the defendant in England—claiming damages under the Fatal Accidents Acts—the defendant sought to rely on section 34. It was held that the plaintiff's action was barred; section 34 "contemplates proceedings of whatever character in the court of an overseas country in which the plaintiff and defendant in English proceedings have previously participated as opposing parties for the purposes of adjudicating a cause of action between them, in respect of which the English plaintiff has obtained a judgment in his favour enforceable or entitled to recognition in England and Wales".[11] There is no requirement that "the English plaintiff should have been the original party in the overseas proceedings or that such proceedings be exclusively civil in character".[12]

9.1.3.4 A crucial question concerning the operation of section 34 is whether it is a mandatory provision limiting the jurisdiction of the court or whether it merely makes available a defence to the person in whose favour the foreign judgment was given. In *Republic of India* v. *India Steamship Co Ltd*[13] the Court of Appeal decided that the effect of section 34 is mandatory and cannot be overridden by the agreement of the parties. This decision was strongly criticised[14] and reversed on appeal by the House of Lords.[15] Having examined the common law prior to the entry into force of section 34 and the purpose behind the legislation, the House of Lords concluded that section 34 does no more than establish a defence which is capable of being defeated by estoppel, waiver or contrary agreement.[16] Accordingly, if a plaintiff, having obtained a judgment in his favour in foreign proceedings, starts proceedings in England on the same cause of action and the defendant consents to the jurisdiction of the English court section 34 does not operate as a bar to the plaintiff's action.

9.2 RECOGNITION AND ENFORCEMENT AT COMMON LAW

9.2.1 The basic framework of recognition and enforcement

9.2.1.1 A foreign judgment is entitled to enforcement in England only if the person seeking to rely on the judgment is able to establish that certain basic requirements are met.

10. [1992] QB 526. Carter, (1991) 62 BYIL 458.
11. Phillips J, [1992] QB 526, 546.
12. Phillips J, [1992] QB 526, 546.
13. [1992] 1 Lloyd's Rep 124.
14. Collins, "Illogical Survivals and Astonishing Results" (1992) 108 LQR 393.
15. [1993] AC 410.
16. Lord Goff, [1993] AC 410, 473.

(i) The judgment must be final and conclusive.[17]
(ii) The judgment must be for a fixed sum of money.[18]
(iii) The original court must have been a court of competent jurisdiction.[19]

If these three conditions are satisfied the judgment is *prima facie* entitled to enforcement.

9.2.1.2 Although the majority of cases concerning foreign judgments involve proceedings commenced by a judgment creditor for the enforcement of a money judgment in England, there are certain situations in which a party seeks recognition of a foreign judgment rather than its enforcement. The paradigm case which involves the recognition of a foreign judgment but not its enforcement arises when the defendant seeks to rely on a foreign judgment as a defence to proceedings in England. Recognition by way of defence is raised where A sues B for breach of contract in a foreign court, the foreign court dismisses A's claim, A starts proceedings on the same cause of action in England and B relies on the foreign judgment as a bar to the proceedings in England. Whether a foreign judgment should be regarded as an effective bar to the subsequent proceedings in England depends on the doctrine of estoppel *per rem judicatam*—which comprises two strands: cause of action estoppel and issue estoppel. A judgment does not create an estoppel unless a number of conditions are satisfied.[20]

(i) The judgment in the earlier action relied on as creating an estoppel must be final and conclusive.[21]
(ii) The judgment must be on the merits.[22]
(iii) The judgment must have been given by a court of competent jurisdiction.[23]
(iv) The parties (or their privies) in the earlier action relied on as creating the estoppel must be the same as those in the later action in which that estoppel is raised as a bar.[24]
(v) The cause of action (or issue) in the later action in which the estoppel is raised must be the same cause of action (or issue) as that decided by the court in the earlier action.[25]

9.2.1.3 The fact that the basic conditions for the recognition or enforcement of a foreign judgment have been satisfied does not guarantee that the judgment will be recognised or enforced. The party against whom the judgment is invoked may resist recognition or enforcement by establishing one of a number of defences; some have been formulated by the courts; others are the creation of Parliament.[26]

17. See para. 9.2.2.
18. See para. 9.2.3.
19. See para. 9.2.5.
20. Lord Brandon in *The Sennar (No. 2)* [1985] 1 WLR 490, 499.
21. See para. 9.2.2.
22. See para. 9.2.4.
23. See para. 9.2.5.
24. See para. 9.2.6.1.
25. See paras. 9.2.6.2 and 9.2.6.3.
26. See para. 9.2.7.

9.2.2 Final and conclusive

A judgment given in interlocutory proceedings between the parties is not entitled to recognition or enforcement at common law. In order for a judgment to be regarded as final and conclusive it must definitively determine the dispute between the parties; if the original court may alter its terms, the judgment is not final and conclusive.[27] However, the existence of the possibility of an appeal to a higher court in the country of origin does not deprive a judgment of its finality.[28] Furthermore, the fact that an appeal is pending in the country of origin at the time when the judgment creditor brings proceedings in England is not a bar to enforcement. However, where an appeal against the judgment is pending abroad, the court will normally stay enforcement proceedings until after the appeal has been heard.[29]

9.2.3 For a fixed sum

9.2.3.1 At common law foreign injunctions or orders for specific performance are not enforceable in England; only judgments for a fixed sum of money are entitled to enforcement.[30] However, where the foreign judgment is in the nature of a fine or other penalty, it will not be enforced.[31] Similarly, since an English court will not enforce, either directly or indirectly, foreign revenue laws a foreign judgment which orders the payment of taxes is not enforceable in England.[32]

9.2.3.2 In *United States of America* v. *Inkley*[33] the Court of Appeal confirmed the common law rule that the English courts will not enforce the penal laws of a foreign State. In the course of his judgment Purchas LJ set out the following principles:

> (1) the consideration of whether the claim sought to be enforced in the English courts is one which involves the assertion of foreign sovereignty, whether it be penal, revenue or other public law, is to be determined according to the criteria of English law; (2) that regard will be had to the attitude adopted by the courts in the foreign jurisdiction which will always receive serious attention and may on occasions be decisive; (3) that the category of the right of action, ie whether public or private, will depend on the party in whose favour it is created, on the purpose of the law or enactment in the foreign State on which it is based and on the general context of the case as a whole; (4) that the fact that the right, statutory or otherwise, is penal in nature will not deprive a person, who asserts a personal claim depending thereon, from having recourse to the courts of this country; on the other hand, by whatever description it may be known if the purpose of the action is the enforcement of a sanction, power or right at the instance of the State in its sovereign capacity, it will not be entertained; (5) that the fact that in the foreign jurisdiction recourse may be had in a civil forum to enforce the right will not necessarily affect the true nature of the right being enforced in this country.[34]

9.2.3.3 The context of the dispute in *United States of America* v. *Inkley* was an action

27. *Nouvion* v. *Freeman* (1889) 15 App Cas 1; *Carl Zeiss Stiftung* v. *Rayner & Keeler Ltd (No. 2)* [1976] 1 AC 853.
28. *Nouvion* v. *Freeman* (1889) 15 App Cas 1.
29. *Colt Industries Inc* v. *Sarlie (No. 2)* [1966] 1 WLR 1287.
30. *Sadler* v. *Robins* (1808) 1 Camp 253; *Beatty* v. *Beatty* [1924] 1 KB 807.
31. *Huntington* v. *Attrill* [1893] AC 150.
32. *Government of India* v. *Taylor* [1955] AC 491.
33. [1989] QB 255. Carter, (1988) 59 BYIL 347.
34. [1989] QB 255, 265.

by the government of the United States to enforce a judgment for the amount of an appearance bond given by the defendant in civil proceedings in Florida. Applying the relevant principles the Court of Appeal concluded that "the general context and background against which the appearance bond was executed was criminal or penal", particularly since "the whole purpose of the bond was to ensure, so far as it was possible, the presence of the executor of the bond to meet justice at the hands of the State in a criminal prosecution".[35] By contrast, in *SA Consortium General Textiles* v. *Sun & Sand Agencies Ltd*[36] the defendants had been ordered by a French judgment to pay in addition to compensatory damages a sum by way of further damages for *résistance abusive*—a head of damage awarded in France where a defendant has unreasonably refused to satisfy an obviously good claim. The Court of Appeal rejected the defendant's argument that the extra head of damage was a penalty. According to Lord Denning MR a penalty is "a sum payable to the State by way of punishment and not a sum payable to a private individual, even though it is payable by way of exemplary damages".[37]

9.2.4 On the merits

9.2.4.1 Since the only judgments which are entitled to enforcement in England are money judgments, there can be no doubt in enforcement proceedings that the foreign judgment is a decision on the merits. The application of the principle that, in order to be entitled to recognition in England, a foreign judgment must be on the merits is more complex in cases which raise the issue of recognition without enforcement. For example, is a judgment a decision on the merits if the original court dismissed the plaintiff's claim on the basis that the court had no jurisdiction or on the basis that the plaintiff's action was time-barred?

9.2.4.2 The Foreign Limitation Periods Act 1984 introduced the rule that a foreign judgment based on limitation is to be regarded as a decision on the merits. Section 3 of the 1984 Act provides:

> Where a court in any country outside England and Wales has determined any matter wholly or partly by reference to the law of that or any other country (including England and Wales) relating to limitation, then, for the purposes of the law relating to the effect to be given in England and Wales to that determination, that court shall, to the extent that it has so determined the matter, be deemed to have determined it on its merits.[38]

9.2.4.3 The decision of the House of Lords in *The Sennar (No. 2)*[39] must be considered. The important facts can be briefly stated. In 1975 the plaintiff, a German company, started proceedings *in rem* against a vessel owned by the defendant, a Sudanese company, in Rotterdam. The plaintiff's claim, which arose out of a bill of lading relating to a cargo of Sudanese groundnuts, was that the master of the ship had

35. Purchas LJ, [1989] QB 255, 265.
36. [1978] QB 279.
37. [1978] QB 279, 299–300.
38. The effect of this section is to reverse *Black-Clawson International Ltd* v. *Papierwerke Waldhof-Aschaffenburg AG* [1975] AC 591. Carter, (1974–75) 47 BYIL 381; Jaffey, "Recognition of a Defendant's Foreign Judgment" (1975) 38 MLR 585.
39. [1985] 1 WLR 490.

committed a tort against the plaintiff by incorrectly dating the bill of lading. The defendant contested the jurisdiction of the Dutch courts on the basis that the bill of lading conferred exclusive jurisdiction on the courts of Sudan.

9.2.4.4 The Dutch courts dismissed the claim on the grounds that, as a party to the bill of lading, the plaintiff was entitled to found the claim only in contract and was bound by the jurisdiction clause. When the plaintiff subsequently started proceedings against the defendant in England with a view to obtaining damages in tort, the defendant sought to rely on the Dutch judgment in support of the application for a stay of the English proceedings. The central question facing the House of Lords was whether the plaintiff's action was barred by the Dutch judgment. The plaintiff's main argument was that the judgment was on a procedural question (namely, the jurisdiction of the Dutch courts) and therefore was not a judgment on the merits; it was the defendant's contention that the Dutch judgment created an issue estoppel[40] on the question of whether the plaintiff's claim fell within the scope of the jurisdiction clause contained in the bill of lading.

9.2.4.5 On the question of whether the Dutch judgment was a decision on the merits Lord Brandon said:

> Looking at the matter negatively a decision on procedure alone is not a decision on the merits. Looking at the matter positively a decision on the merits is a decision which establishes certain facts proved or not in dispute; states what are the relevant principles of law applicable to such facts; and expresses a conclusion with regard to the effect of applying those principles to the factual situation concerned.[41]

It was clear that the Dutch judgment was a decision on the merits in this positive sense as regards two issues: (i) that the plaintiff's only claim against the defendant was for breach of the contract of carriage and (ii) that the effect of the jurisdiction clause was to make any remedy for breach of that contract enforceable only in the Sudanese courts (unless the defendant elected otherwise).[42] Accordingly, the defendant could rely on the Dutch judgment to support the application for a stay of the English proceedings.

9.2.5 The jurisdiction of the original court

9.2.5.1 Introductory remarks

9.2.5.1.1 As a general proposition, an English court which is called upon to recognise or enforce a foreign judgment is not concerned with the internal law of the country of origin. Even if, as a result of a defect, the judgment may be set aside on appeal, the judgment is nevertheless *prima facie* enforceable in England unless and until it is set aside by the courts of the country of origin. As a general rule, whether the original court had jurisdiction over the person against whom the judgment is invoked according to its own rules is irrelevant; the question is whether—as a matter of English law—the original court is to be regarded as a court of competent jurisdiction in the private international law sense. In other words, was the connection between the country of

40. See para. 9.2.6.
41. [1985] 1 WLR 490, 499.
42. Lord Diplock, [1985] 1 WLR 490, 494–495.

origin and the person against whom the judgment is invoked sufficient to create an obligation which the English court should recognise or enforce? The traditional starting-point for a discussion of this question is a passage taken from the judgment of Buckley LJ in *Emanuel* v. *Symon*:

In actions *in personam* there are five cases in which the courts of this country will enforce a foreign judgment: (1) where the defendant is a subject of the foreign country in which the judgment has been obtained; (2) where he was resident in the foreign country when the action began; (3) where the defendant in the character of plaintiff has selected the forum in which he is afterwards sued; (4) where he has voluntarily appeared; and (5) where he has contracted to submit himself to the forum in which the judgment was obtained.[43]

9.2.5.1.2 It is doubtful whether case (1) would still be held to give rise to jurisdiction.[44] The remaining categories effectively boil down to two types of case: first, where the party against whom the judgment is invoked submitted to the jurisdiction of the original court (cases (3), (4) and (5) all being variants of submission); or, secondly, where there is a sufficient territorial connection between the party against whom the judgment is invoked and the country of origin (case (2)). In the second type of case there are three questions to consider.

- (i) What is the appropriate territorial connection in the case of individuals? The traditional view—based on *Emanuel* v. *Symon*—is that residence within the jurisdiction of the original court is necessary. The law was, however, re-examined by the Court of Appeal in *Adams* v. *Cape Industries Plc*.[45]
- (ii) What is the relevant test in cases involving corporations?
- (iii) When considering the connection between the country of origin and the person against whom the judgment is invoked, what is the relevant territorial unit in the case of a political State, such as the United States of America, comprising different law districts which have different rules of law and different legal procedures?

9.2.5.2 Submission

9.2.5.2.1 The original court is regarded as a court of competent jurisdiction if the person against whom the judgment is invoked submitted to the jurisdiction of the court. Section 33 of the Civil Jurisdiction and Judgments Act 1982 provides:

(1) For the purposes of determining whether a judgment given by a court of an overseas country should be recognised or enforced in England and Wales ..., the person against whom the judgment was given shall not be regarded as having submitted to the jurisdiction of the court by reason only of the fact that he appeared (conditionally or otherwise) in the proceedings for all or any one or more of the following purposes, namely—

- (a) to contest the jurisdiction of the court;
- (b) to ask the court to dismiss or stay the proceedings on the ground that the dispute in question should be submitted to arbitration or to the determination of the courts of another country;
- (c) to protect, or obtain the release of, property seized or threatened with seizure in the proceedings.

(2) Nothing in this section shall affect the recognition or enforcement in England and

43. [1908] 1 KB 302, 309.
44. See para. 9.2.5.6.
45. [1990] Ch 433. Carter, (1990) 61 BYIL 402; Collier, [1990] CLJ 416.

Wales ... of a judgment which is required to be recognised or enforced there under the 1968 Convention or the Lugano Convention.

9.2.5.2.2 Section 33, which has the effect of reversing the position at common law,[46] does not provide a positive definition of acts which amount to submission; rather it identifies a range of procedural acts which are not to be regarded as amounting to submission. The effect of section 33 is that a litigant who contests the jurisdiction of the original court, requests the original court to decline jurisdiction (for example, on the basis of *forum non conveniens* or because the parties had agreed to arbitration[47]) or appears to protect his property, is not regarded as having submitted. Presumably, in situations where the procedure of the original court is similar to the procedure under RSC, Order 11, rule 1(1), a litigant is not to be regarded as having submitted by applying to have service out of the jurisdiction set aside, although this situation does not obviously fall within the express wording of paragraph (b).

9.2.5.2.3 A defendant is to be regarded as having submitted to the jurisdiction of the original court if he voluntarily appears in the proceedings to defend the action on the merits or if he counterclaims in those proceedings or if he agrees to submit to the jurisdiction of the court (for example, in a contractual jurisdiction clause). It is clear that contesting the jurisdiction and the merits of the case in the alternative also amounts to submission.[48] The person against whom a foreign judgment was given is able to rely on section 33 only as long as he does not go beyond the range of procedural acts set out in that provision; in a situation where the original court rejects the defendant's challenge to its jurisdiction and the defendant proceeds to fight the case on the merits, the defendant must be regarded as having submitted.[49] If, however, the defendant "makes it clear in his first defence rather than in some subsequent defence that he is contesting the jurisdiction, that will not amount to a submission even though there is some additional material which constitutes a plea to the merits of the case".[50] There may be a difficult dividing line to be drawn between, on the one hand, contesting jurisdiction and the merits in the alternative and, on the other, contesting jurisdiction while reserving the possibility of fighting on the merits should the plea as to jurisdiction fail.

9.2.5.2.4 In complex, multiparty litigation there is a question as to whether submission in one set of proceedings can be regarded as submission (or an agreement to submit) to related proceedings involving the same issues. In *Adams* v. *Cape Industries Plc*[51] an English company, which was involved—through subsidiaries—in the mining and sale of asbestos, was the defendant in two sets of proceedings (the Tyler 1 actions and the Tyler 2 actions) brought by a total of more than 600 asbestos workers in Texas. Although the defendant took part in the Tyler 1 actions, which were settled, as regards the Tyler 2 actions, the defendant contested the jurisdiction of the court but took no

46. In particular, *Henry* v. *Geoprosco International Ltd* [1976] QB 726. Carter, (1974–75) 47 BYIL 379; Collier, [1975] CLJ 219; Solomons, "Enforcement of Foreign Judgments: Jurisdiction of Foreign Court" (1976) 25 ICLQ 665.

47. *Tracomin SA* v. *Sudan Oil Seeds Ltd (No. 1)* [1983] 1 WLR 662, affirmed [1983] 1 WLR 1026 (although the only point raised on appeal was the temporal scope of section 33).

48. *Boissière & Co* v. *Brockner & Co* (1889) 6 TLR 85.

49. *Marc Rich & Co AG* v. *Societa Italiana Impianti PA (No. 2)* [1992] 1 Lloyd's Rep 624. Kaye, "Forensic Submission as a Bar to Arbitration" (1993) 12 CJQ 359.

50. Neill LJ in *Marc Rich & Co AG* v. *Societa Italiana Impianti PA (No. 2)* [1992] 1 Lloyd's Rep 624, 633.

51. [1990] Ch 433.

further part in the proceedings. In enforcement proceedings in England the plaintiffs in the Tyler 2 actions argued that the defendant, by taking part in the Tyler 1 actions, had effectively submitted to the jurisdiction of the court in relation to the Tyler 2 actions. Scott J rejected the argument that the two sets of proceedings in reality constituted "one unit of litigation" and held that the steps taken by the defendant in the Tyler 1 actions could not be regarded as constituting consent to the Tyler 2 actions.[52]

9.2.5.2.5 A defendant who expressly agrees to the jurisdiction of the original court is regarded as having submitted, even if the judgment is given in default. So, if parties agree to refer a dispute to the exclusive jurisdiction of the courts of country X, a judgment given in the plaintiff's favour by the courts of country X in a matter falling within the scope of the jurisdiction agreement is *prima facie* entitled to enforcement in England. However, a jurisdiction agreement in favour of a particular court in a particular country is not to be regarded as amounting to a general submission to all the courts in that country; for example, an agreement to submit to the courts of St Petersburg is not an agreement to submit to any court in Russia and in such circumstances the courts of Moscow are not to be regarded as having jurisdiction in the private international law sense.[53]

9.2.5.2.6 More problematical are cases where it is alleged that the person against whom the judgment is invoked impliedly agreed to submit to the jurisdiction of the original court. The generally accepted view is that an agreement to submit must be express.[54] For example, a contractual choice of the law of country X is not an implied agreement to submit to the jurisdiction of the courts of country X.[55] Whether or not an agreement to submit is express is a question of interpretation which, as a matter of principle, should be determined by the law governing the agreement.

9.2.5.2.7 *Blohn* v. *Desser*[56] is often cited for the proposition that an agreement to submit may be implied. The defendant in that case had been a sleeping partner in a firm which carried on business in Austria. The plaintiff, having obtained a judgment against the firm in Vienna, sought to enforce the judgment in England against the defendant. The defendant, whose name was on the commercial register in Vienna, had taken no part in the Austrian proceedings. Diplock J thought that it was "clear law that [a contract] to submit to the forum in which the judgment was obtained, may be express or implied".[57] This observation was, however, *obiter*. In *Vogel* v. *R & A Kohnstamm Ltd*[58] Ashworth J rejected the notion that an implied agreement to submit could be a sufficient basis of jurisdiction. Further doubt was cast on *Blohn* v. *Desser* in *Adams* v. *Cape Industries Plc*; Scott J took the view that the minimum that is required is "a clear indication of consent to the exercise by the foreign court of jurisdiction".[59]

9.2.5.2.8 In principle, consent to the jurisdiction of the original court—even if it does

52. [1990] Ch 433, 462–463.

53. See Shaw and Goff LJJ in *SA Consortium General Textiles* v. *Sun & Sand Agencies Ltd* [1978] QB 279.

54. Cheshire & North, *Private International Law* (12th ed, 1992), p. 352; Dicey & Morris, *The Conflict of Laws* (12th ed, 1993) p. 483.

55. This principle is supported by Commonwealth authorities: *Mattar & Saba* v. *Public Trustee* [1952] 3 DLR 399; *Dunbee Ltd* v. *Gilman & Co (Australia) Pty Ltd* [1968] 2 Lloyd's Rep 394.

56. [1962] 2 QB 116. Carter, (1962) 38 BYIL 493; Jacob, [1961] CLJ 184; Webb, "Enforcement of Foreign Judgments: Implied Submission" (1962) 25 MLR 96.

57. [1962] 2 QB 116, 123.

58. [1973] QB 133. Carter, (1971) 45 BYIL 415; Cohn, "Submission to Foreign Jurisdiction" (1972) 21 ICLQ 157.

59. [1990] Ch 433, 466.

not form part of a contractually enforceable agreement—should be sufficient to confer jurisdiction in the private international law sense if it gives rise to an estoppel. Accordingly, if it is alleged that the defendant consented to the jurisdiction of the original court otherwise than by a contractual agreement, such consent is "of no legal effect if not acted upon or if withdrawn before being acted on".[60] Similarly, if proceedings in the original court are instituted and brought to judgment against an absent defendant without reliance on the defendant's representation of willingness to submit to the jurisdiction, or in ignorance of it, the representation cannot subsequently be relied on by the plaintiff as a consensual basis for establishing the court's jurisdiction. Furthermore, if a non-contractual representation is to be relied upon as establishing the original court's jurisdiction, it must be a representation intended to be relied upon or, at least, be a representation that the plaintiff believed and had reasonable ground for believing was intended to be acted upon.

9.2.5.3 A sufficient territorial connection: individuals

9.2.5.3.1 Although *Adams* v. *Cape Industries Plc*[61] was concerned with the question of whether the original court had jurisdiction in the private international law sense over a corporation, the decision of the Court of Appeal includes a comprehensive review of the authorities in cases involving foreign judgments given against individuals. In *Carrick* v. *Hancock*,[62] for example, an action had been started in Sweden, the defendant having been served with the document instituting the proceedings during a short visit to Sweden. Although the defendant took part in the proceedings—and therefore the decision of the English court to enforce the judgment can be justified on the basis of the defendant's submission—Lord Russell of Killowen CJ is reported as saying "that the jurisdiction of a court was based upon the principle of territorial dominion, and that all persons within any territorial dominion owe their allegiance to its sovereign power and obedience to all its laws and to the lawful jurisdiction of its courts".[63]

9.2.5.3.2 On the basis of the authorities, the Court of Appeal decided in *Adams* v. *Cape Industries Plc* that, in the absence of any form of submission, the jurisdiction of the original court depends upon the physical presence of the person against whom the judgment is invoked in the country concerned at the date of service of the originating process. The temporary presence of a litigant in the country of origin will not, however, found jurisdiction if it was induced by compulsion, fraud or duress; presence in the country of origin must have been voluntary.[64]

9.2.5.3.3 The acceptance of temporary presence in the foreign country as a basis of jurisdiction in the private international law sense may appear reasonable in view of that fact that, under the Rules of the Supreme Court, the temporary presence of a foreigner in England at the time of service of the writ is regarded as justifying the assumption of English jurisdiction.[65] However, the apparent symmetry between the rules which

60. Scott J in *Adams* v. *Cape Industries Plc* [1990] Ch 433, 466.
61. [1990] Ch 433.
62. (1895) 12 TLR 59.
63. (1895) 12 TLR 59, 60. See also *Sirdar Gurdyal Singh* v. *Rajah of Faridkote* [1894] AC 670; *Employers' Liability Assurance Corporation Ltd* v. *Sedgwick, Collins & Co Ltd* [1927] AC 95.
64. [1990] Ch 433, 518. See also *Colt Industries Inc* v. *Sarlie (No. 1)* [1966] 1 WLR 440. Carter, (1965–66) 41 BYIL 447.
65. *Maharanee of Baroda* v. *Wildenstein* [1972] 2 QB 283. See para. 6.1. This basis of jurisdiction cannot be invoked against a defendant who is domiciled in a Brussels or Lugano Contracting State: para. 4.2.1.

govern English jurisdiction, on the one hand, and those which determine whether a foreign court is a court of competent jurisdiction, on the other, is false. Where the jurisdiction of the English court is invoked on the basis of the defendant's temporary presence in England, the court has a discretion to stay its proceedings on the ground of *forum non conveniens* and "the exercise of the discretion is likely to be an issue when jurisdiction is founded on mere presence".[66] Furthermore, the cases relied upon by the Court of Appeal in *Adams* v. *Cape Industries Plc* pre-date the adoption of the doctrine of *forum non conveniens* in England. It has been suggested that, in view of the development of the doctrine of *forum non conveniens* in England, it would be rational to determine the competence of a foreign court in the private international law sense by the application of a test based on the appropriateness of the foreign forum, rather than on relatively inflexible factors such as presence or residence.[67]

9.2.5.3.4 If temporary presence is an acceptable basis of jurisdiction in the private international law sense residence within the jurisdiction of the original court must also be acceptable—at least where residence is accompanied by presence. What, however, is the position where the person against whom the judgment is invoked is resident within the jurisdiction of the original court but was not physically present when process was served? This question was expressly left open by the Court of Appeal in *Adams* v. *Cape Industries Plc*.[68] There is, however, no obvious reason why residence—which is a more substantial connection than mere presence—should not be sufficient, whether or not accompanied by presence at the moment when the foreign proceedings are commenced.

9.2.5.4 A sufficient territorial connection: corporations

9.2.5.4.1 Whereas, in the context of individuals, presence and residence are relatively straightforward concepts to apply, the presence of a corporation is more metaphysical. In considering the presence of a company the courts have distinguished two types of situation: (i) cases where it is alleged that a company has direct presence in the foreign country; (ii) cases of indirect presence, in which it is alleged that the company is present in the foreign country through a representative.

9.2.5.4.2 In order for direct presence to be established the corporation must be carrying on business in the foreign country at a definite and, to some extent, permanent place at the time when proceedings are commenced.[69] Indirect presence poses greater difficulty. In deciding whether a company is present in a foreign country through a representative, the court has regard to all the circumstances of the case. Of particular significance, however, is whether the representative is empowered to conclude contracts on the company's behalf. If the representative is no more than a channel of communication between the company and third parties the company cannot realistically be regarded as present in the foreign country.[70]

9.2.5.4.3 The question of corporate presence was subjected to an exhaustive review

66. Cheshire & North, *Private International Law* (12th ed, 1992), p. 350.
67. Briggs, "Which Foreign Judgments Should We Recognise Today?" (1987) 36 ICLQ 240.
68. [1990] Ch 433, 518.
69. *Littauer Glove Corporation* v. *FW Millington (1920) Ltd* (1928) 44 TLR 746.
70. *Vogel* v. *R & A Kohnstamm Ltd* [1973] QB 133. Carter, (1971) 45 BYIL 415; Cohn, "Submission to Foreign Jurisdiction" (1972) 21 ICLQ 157.

by the Court of Appeal in *Adams* v. *Cape Industries Plc*.[71] It is worth quoting in full the summary of the Court of Appeal's conclusion:

(1) The English courts will be likely to treat a trading corporation incorporated under the law of one country ("an overseas corporation") as present within the jurisdiction of the courts of another country only if either (i) it has established and maintained at its own expense (whether as owner or lessee) a fixed place of business of its own in the other country and for more than a minimal period of time has carried on its own business at or from such premises by its servant or agents (a "branch office" case), or (ii) a representative of the overseas corporation has for more than a minimal period of time been carrying on the overseas corporation's business in the other country at or from some fixed place of business.

(2) In either of these two cases presence can only be established if it can fairly be said that the overseas corporation's business (whether or not together with the representative's own business) has been transacted at or from the fixed place of business. In the first case, this condition is likely to present few problems. In the second, the question whether the representative has been carrying on the overseas corporation's business or has been doing no more than carry on his own business will necessitate an investigation of the functions which he has been performing and all aspects of the relationship between him and the overseas corporation.

(3) In particular, but without prejudice to the generality of the foregoing, the following questions are likely to be relevant on such investigation: (a) whether or not the fixed place of business from which the representative operates was originally acquired for the purpose of enabling him to act on behalf of the overseas corporation; (b) whether the overseas corporation has directly reimbursed him for (i) the cost of his accommodation at the fixed place of business; (ii) the cost of his staff; (c) what other contributions, if any, the overseas corporation makes to the financing of the business carried on by the representative; (d) whether the representative is remunerated by reference to transactions, eg by commission, or by fixed regular payments or in some other way; (e) what degree of control the overseas corporation exercises over the running of the business conducted by the representative; (f) whether the representative reserves (i) part of his accommodation, (ii) part of his staff for conducting business related to the overseas corporation; (g) whether the representative displays the overseas corporation's name at his premises or on his stationery, and if so, whether he does so in such a way as to indicate that he is a representative of the overseas corporation; (h) what business, if any, the representative transacts as principal exclusively on his own behalf; (i) whether the representative makes contracts with customers or other third parties in the name of the overseas corporation, or otherwise in such manner as to bind it; (j) if so, whether the representative requires specific authority in advance before binding the overseas corporation to contractual obligations.[72]

9.2.5.4.4 In *Adams* v. *Cape Industries Plc* the plaintiffs argued that the defendant, an English company, was carrying on business within the jurisdiction of the original court through subsidiary marketing companies, which were incorporated in Illinois. The Court of Appeal rejected the plaintiffs' argument based on direct presence; although the economic reality of the situation was that the defendant controlled the activities of the group of subsidiary companies involved in the mining and marketing of asbestos, the defendant and the subsidiary companies were separate legal persons. The fact that the defendant organised its affairs so that its potential liability would be limited was not in itself sufficient to justify lifting the corporate veil. The Court of Appeal also rejected the plaintiffs' argument based on indirect presence; although the activities of the subsidiary companies were of assistance to the defendant, the subsidiary companies were not empowered to bind the defendant and were primarily carrying on business on their own account.

71. [1990] Ch 433.
72. [1990] Ch 433, 530–531.

9.2.5.5 A sufficient territorial connection: the problem of federal States

9.2.5.5.1 What is the relevant territorial unit for the purposes of the rule that the original court is to be regarded as a court of competent jurisdiction if the defendant was present when the writ was served? This question was considered, albeit *obiter*, by the Court of Appeal in *Adams* v. *Cape Industries Plc.*[73]

Where the judgment is granted by the courts of a unitary State, there can be no dispute over the relevant territorial jurisdiction; if a judgment creditor seeks to enforce a Japanese judgment in England, the question is whether the judgment debtor was present in Japan at the commencement of proceedings.

9.2.5.5.2 The solution is not so obvious, however, where the judgment is granted by the courts of a political State which is made up of a number of different law districts. In the context of the facts of *Adams* v. *Cape Industries Plc*, the question was this: did the plaintiffs have to establish that the defendant was present within Texas—the state in which the proceedings took place—or was presence somewhere within the United States of America—the federal State—sufficient? The Court of Appeal tentatively concluded that presence somewhere in the United States would have been enough. This conclusion was based, first, on a distinction between state and federal matters and, secondly, on the view that there is a national jurisdiction in federal matters under the law of the United States.

(i) The distinction between state and federal matters seems logical. In proceedings concerning the enforcement of a state judgment, the important question, in the absence of submission by the defendant, is whether the person against whom the judgment is invoked was present in the state in question. It is clear, for example, that a judgment by a Texas court against an English resident who carries on business in France is not entitled to recognition or enforcement in England. The same is true if the English resident establishes himself in Illinois: "The fact that Chicago is in the United States does not make Texas any the less a foreign court for a resident in Illinois than if Chicago were in France."[74]

(ii) As regards federal judgments it would seem reasonable that presence within the federal State should be sufficient—but only if there is a national jurisdiction in federal matters. But, is there a national jurisdiction in federal matters in the United States? Although the three members of the Court of Appeal thought, "albeit with varying degrees of doubt",[75] that there is, the better view is that there is not. Statutory provisions exist for the registration of federal court judgments in other states of the Union and, under the law of the United States, a judgment of a federal court is no different from a judgment of a state court—in the sense that it is regarded as a foreign judgment for enforcement purposes.[76] The view suggested by the Court of Appeal could lead to the unfortunate situation where the judgment of a federal court sitting in Texas would be enforceable in England, even though it would not be enforceable in other parts of the United States.[77]

73. [1990] Ch 433.
74. Slade LJ, [1990] Ch 433, 555.
75. [1990] Ch 433, 557.
76. Collier, [1990] CLJ 416, 418.
77. Carter, (1990) 61 BYIL 402, 404.

9.2.5.6 No other bases of jurisdiction

Although there are dicta to the contrary,[78] it is now generally thought that the mere fact that the person against whom the judgment is invoked is a national of the country where the foreign judgment is obtained is not sufficient to justify the recognition or enforcement of the judgment.[79] Logically, it would follow that the fact that the person against whom the judgment is invoked is domiciled within the jurisdiction of the original court is insufficient. It is also clear that a foreign court is not to be regarded as competent in the private international law sense simply because the party against whom the judgment is invoked owns assets within the jurisdiction of the original court.[80] Similarly, the fact that the cause of action arose within the jurisdiction of the original court is, in itself, irrelevant.[81] Finally, it should be noted that, although the English courts are prepared to assume jurisdiction over a defendant under RSC, Order 11, rule 1(1) in cases where England is thought to be the *forum conveniens*,[82] a foreign judgment is not entitled to recognition or enforcement in England on the ground that the original court assumed jurisdiction over the defendant on a similar basis.[83]

9.2.6 Cause of action estoppel and issue estoppel

In order for a foreign judgment to be an effective bar to subsequent proceedings in England it must create either a cause of action estoppel or an issue estoppel. Cause of action estoppel "prevents a party to an action from asserting or denying, as against the other party, the existence of a particular cause of action, the non-existence or existence of which has been determined by a court of competent jurisdiction in previous litigation between the same parties".[84] Issue estoppel is narrower. Indeed, a cause of action estoppel may involve two or more issue estoppels: "within one cause of action, there may be several issues raised which are necessary for the determination of the whole case. The rule then is that, once an issue has been raised and distinctly determined between the parties, then, as a general rule, neither party can be allowed to fight that issue all over again."[85] A judgment creates a cause of action (or issue) estoppel if (i) the judgment was given on the merits,[86] (ii) the parties in the earlier action were the same as those in the later action, and (iii) the cause of action (or issue) in the earlier action is the same as the cause of action (or issue) in the later action.

The doctrine of estoppel *per rem judicatam* has been developed on two grounds: first, it is in the public interest that there should be an end to litigation and, secondly, justice to the individual requires that a litigant should not be vexed twice for the same cause.[87] Accordingly, as a general rule, where a judgment creates an estoppel the estoppel will

78. In particular, in *Emanuel* v. *Symon* [1908] 1 KB 302.
79. Cheshire & North, *Private International Law* (12th ed, 1992) pp. 359–360; Dicey & Morris, *The Conflict of Laws* (12th ed, 1993) pp. 485–486.
80. *Emanuel* v. *Symon* [1908] 1 KB 302.
81. *Sirdar Gurdyal Singh* v. *Rajah of Faridkote* [1894] AC 670.
82. See paras. 6.3–6.5.
83. This follows from *Schibsby* v. *Westenholz* (1870) LR 6 QB 155.
84. Diplock LJ in *Thoday* v. *Thoday* [1964] P 181, 197.
85. Lord Denning MR in *Fidelitas Shipping Co Ltd* v. *V/O Exportchleb* [1966] 1 QB 630, 640.
86. See para. 9.2.4.
87. Slade LJ in *Charm Maritime Inc* v. *Kyriakou* [1987] 1 Lloyd's Rep 433, 440.

extend "not only to points upon which the court was actually required by the parties to form an opinion and pronounce a judgment, but to every point which properly belonged to the subject of litigation, and which the parties, exercising reasonable diligence, might have brought forward at the time".[88]

9.2.6.1 Identity of the parties

9.2.6.1.1 Whether the plea is based on cause of action estoppel or issue estoppel, it is essential that there is identity between the parties in the earlier action which is relied on as creating the estoppel and the parties in the later action in which the judgment is raised as a bar to the proceedings. The requirement of identity is satisfied if the parties are the same or if there is privity between a party to the earlier litigation and the later proceedings. In this context, privity signifies privity of blood, title or interest.[89] The common feature of these three categories of privity is that privies all have an interest in the subject matter of the action.

9.2.6.1.2 The leading case is *Carl Zeiss Stiftung* v. *Rayner & Keeler Ltd (No. 2)*.[90] Carl Zeiss Stiftung, a foundation which had been established in the Grand Duchy of Saxe-Weimar in 1891, was located at Jena, which at the time of the litigation—prior to German reunification—was in the German Democratic Republic. The English proceedings were started in 1955 by solicitors instructed by the Council of Gera, which, it was alleged, was the legal representative of Carl Zeiss Stiftung (Jena). One of the purposes of the proceedings was to prevent the defendant, a West German corporation known as Carl Zeiss Stiftung (Heidenheim, Brenz), from passing off optical and glass instruments with the name "Carl Zeiss" or "Zeiss". In 1953 the Council of Gera had brought proceedings in West Germany with a view to preventing the defendant from using the name "Carl Zeiss". In 1960 the Federal Supreme Court dismissed the claim. Although the plaintiffs in the English proceedings were the English solicitors, rather than the Council of Gera, the defendant argued that either there was complete identity of the parties in both proceedings or there was, at least, privity of interest between the English plaintiffs and the plaintiffs in the German action.

9.2.6.1.3 The majority of the House of Lords rejected both contentions. There was not complete identity because in the English proceedings the plaintiffs were the solicitors, whereas the West German judgment was pronounced against the Council of Gera. The argument based on privity of interest was rejected on the ground that in each set of proceedings the nominal plaintiff, who had no real interest in the subject matter of the litigation, was seeking to represent Carl Zeiss Stiftung (Jena) so that the foundation might enforce its rights. However, Lord Wilberforce, who dissented on this point, thought that the correct approach is to look to see who in reality is behind the action. In the present case the reality was that the Council of Gera was behind the proceedings both in West Germany and England and in each case on behalf of Carl Zeiss Stiftung

88. Wigram V-C in *Henderson* v. *Henderson* (1843) 3 Hare 100, 115. See also *ED & F Man (Sugar) Ltd* v. *Haryanto (No. 2)* [1991] 1 Lloyd's Rep 429.
89. Lord Reid in *Carl Zeiss Stiftung* v. *Rayner & Keeler Ltd (No. 2)* [1967] 1 AC 853, 910.
90. [1967] 1 AC 853.

(Jena). It is hard to resist Lord Wilberforce's conclusion that to treat the solicitors as the parties to the English action was both lacking in reality and unduly technical.[91]

9.2.6.2 Cause of action estoppel: identity of the cause of action

9.2.6.2.1 The question as to whether the same cause of action is involved in different proceedings may arise in a number of different situations.

(i) Where a plaintiff who has been successful in foreign proceedings—but less successful than he might have hoped—wishes to relitigate the same cause of action in England section 34 of the Civil Jurisdiction and Judgments Act 1982 bars the plaintiff's action.[92]

(ii) The successful party in foreign litigation may wish to rely on the foreign judgment as a defence to proceedings brought by the other party in England on the same cause of action.

(iii) A litigant may seek to rely on a foreign judgment on a cause of action which has already been determined differently by an English court (or by the court of another foreign country).

The same principles are applicable in each of these situations.

9.2.6.2.2 The English authorities are not entirely satisfactory. The general principle is that a cause of action consists of the minimum facts which a plaintiff is required in law to plead and (if necessary) prove in order to obtain the relief which he claims.[93] The doctrine of *res judicata* requires that "damages resulting from one and the same cause of action must be assessed and recovered once [and] for all".[94]

9.2.6.2.3 In cases involving the tort of negligence the cases show that some judges have sought to draw a distinction between, on the one hand, different losses falling within a particular head of damage and, on the other, different heads of damage arising out of a single set of facts. Different losses within a particular head of damage clearly result from the same cause of action; a plaintiff cannot justify an action for the loss of an eye by the defendant's negligence when he has already recovered for the loss of a foot by the same negligence, by saying that in the first action he only gave particulars of the loss of his foot.[95] However, in *Brunsden* v. *Humphrey*[96] the majority of the Court of Appeal thought that is possible to segregate different causes of action by reference to different heads of damage. According to this view, if as a result of an accident a plaintiff suffers both personal injury and property damage he has two distinct causes of action, one for his personal injuries and the other for damage to his property. The decision in *Brunsden* v. *Humphrey*, the logic of which has been questioned,[97] was not followed by the Court of Appeal in *Talbot* v. *Berkshire County Council*.[98] It would seem, therefore, that a cause of action should be regarded as encompassing different heads of damage arising out of a single set of facts.

91. [1967] 1 AC 853, 968–969.
92. See para. 9.1.3.
93. *Letang* v. *Cooper* [1965] 1 QB 232.
94. Bowen LJ in *Brunsden* v. *Humphrey* (1884) 14 QBD 141, 147.
95. Talbot J in *Conquer* v. *Boot* [1928] 2 KB 336, 345.
96. (1884) 14 QBD 141.
97. *Buckland* v. *Palmer* [1984] 1 WLR 1109.
98. [1993] 3 WLR 708.

9.2.6.2.4 With regard to cases involving a breach of contract which gives rise to different losses, the position is made clear by the decision of the House of Lords in *Republic of India* v. *India Steamship Co Ltd.*[99] In this case litigation arose out of bills of lading under which the plaintiff's cargo had been carried from Sweden to India in a ship owned by the defendant. During the course of the voyage there was a fire on board the ship as a result of which some of the plaintiff's cargo was jettisoned and the rest was damaged. In proceedings commenced by the plaintiff in India the court awarded damages for short delivery. When the plaintiff started proceedings for breach of contract in England the defendant applied to strike out the English action. The plaintiff alleged that the cause of action in the English proceedings related to damages for delivery of the cargo in a damaged condition, whereas the Indian judgment concerned only damages for short delivery. The question facing the court was whether the Indian and English proceedings involved two different causes of action or one cause of action resulting in two kinds of damage.

9.2.6.2.5 The House of Lords decided that, since proof of damage is not necessary to establish the cause of action, the cause of action in the Indian and English proceedings was the same: "it is necessary to identify the relevant breach of contract; and if it transpires that the cause of action in the first action is a breach of contract which is the same breach of contract which constitutes the cause of action in the second, then the principle of *res judicata* applies, and the plaintiff cannot escape from the conclusion by pleading in the second action particulars of damage which were not pleaded in the first."[100]

9.2.6.3 Issue estoppel: identity of the issue

Although the basic framework of issue estoppel and cause of action estoppel is the same, issue estoppel creates greater problems.

9.2.6.3.1 Whatever may be the difficulties in determining whether proceedings in two different countries involve the same cause of action, those difficulties are more extreme where the question is whether proceedings in two countries involve the same issue. Some of these difficulties are illustrated by the decision of the House of Lords in *Carl Zeiss Stiftung* v. *Rayner & Keeler Ltd (No. 2)*.[101] In the earlier German proceedings it had been held that the constitution of Carl Zeiss Stiftung (Jena) had been rendered ineffective—as a result of which the Council of Gera did not have authority to act as the foundation's legal representative. One of the questions facing the House of Lords was whether the decision of the Federal Supreme Court created an issue estoppel which determined that the plaintiffs were acting without the authority of Carl Zeiss Stiftung (Jena). On this question it was argued by the plaintiffs that, whereas in the German proceedings the issue was whether the Council of Gera representing Carl Zeiss Stiftung (Jena) could sue in respect of certain matters in Germany, in the English proceedings the issue was whether this could be done in England. This somewhat artificial distinction was rejected by the majority of the House of Lords. As Lord Wilberforce noted, the issue which arose in both the English and the German proceedings was whether Carl

99. [1993] AC 410.
100. Lord Goff, [1993] AC 410, 420.
101. [1967] 1 AC 853. The relevant background facts are set out in para. 9.2.6.1.

Zeiss Stiftung (Jena) had become paralysed or its organs rendered ineffective so that the Council of Gera was not authorised to act on the foundation's behalf.[102]

9.2.6.3.2 Issue estoppel raises practical problems which do not arise in relation to cause of action estoppel:

> Suppose the first case is one of trifling importance but it involves for one party proof of facts which would be expensive and troublesome; and that party can see the possibility that the same point may arise if his opponent later raises a much more important claim. What is he to do? The second case may never be brought. Must he go to great trouble and expense to forestall a possible plea of issue estoppel if the second case is brought? This does not arise in cause of action estoppel: if the cause of action is important, he will incur the expense; if it is not, he will take the chance of winning on some other point.[103]

Not surprisingly, therefore, the English courts have counselled caution in the application of the doctrine of estoppel *per rem judicatam* in cases of issue estoppel. In *Carl Zeiss Stiftung* v. *Rayner & Keeler Ltd (No. 2)* Lord Reid, echoing the observations of Lord Brougham in *Houlditch* v. *Donegal*,[104] provides two important reasons in favour of being cautious. First, the English courts "are not familiar with modes of procedure in many foreign countries, and it may not be easy to be sure that a particular issue has been decided or that its decision was a basis of the foreign judgment and not merely collateral or *obiter*".[105] Secondly, "it might be unjust to hold that a litigant here should be estopped from putting forward his case because it was impracticable for him to do so in an earlier case of trivial character abroad, with the result that the decision in that case went against him".[106]

9.2.7 Defences to recognition and enforcement

The existence of a system of legal rules for the recognition and enforcement of foreign judgments is premised on the idea that, having obtained a judgment on the merits in an appropriate jurisdiction, a litigant should be able to rely on that judgment in another country. Although in English law the basis of the common law rules on recognition and enforcement of foreign judgments is not reciprocity in a strict sense, the basic foundation of private international law in this area is the collective interest of the world's legal systems in the free movement of judgments. Practical common sense, therefore, points towards defences to the recognition and enforcement of foreign judgments being kept to a minimum. As a general rule, under English law the person against whom the judgment is invoked is not allowed to raise defences in the English proceedings which were raised, or could have been raised, in the foreign proceedings.[107] Where, however, new evidence comes to light after judgment in the foreign proceedings has been given, the person against whom the judgment is invoked should be able to rely on such evidence in the context of proceedings in England. An English judgment may be set aside on the basis of fresh evidence and there is no good reason why a foreign judgment should be treated more favourably.

102. [1967] 1 AC 853, 967–968.
103. Lord Reid in *Carl Zeiss Stiftung* v. *Rayner & Keeler Ltd (No. 2)* [1967] 1 AC 853, 917.
104. (1834) 8 Bligh NS 301, 338.
105. [1967] 1 AC 853, 918.
106. [1967] 1 AC 853, 918.
107. *Ellis* v. *M'Henry* (1871) LR 6 CP 228; *Israel Discount Bank of New York* v. *Hadjipateras* [1984] 1 WLR 137. The defences of fraud and natural justice are exceptions to this general rule. See paras. 9.2.7.1 and 9.2.7.2.

Notwithstanding the fact that the grounds for refusing recognition and enforcement should be kept to a minimum an English court should not be obliged to recognise or enforce a foreign judgment which either offends English standards of justice (whether substantive or procedural) or conflicts with an earlier judgment granted by an English court. Nevertheless, the court which is called upon to recognise or enforce a foreign judgment should not act as a court of appeal in respect of the original court. Under English law it is not generally open for the person against whom the judgment was given to attack a foreign judgment on the merits. So, the fact that the original court made an error of fact or an error of law (even of English law) is not a basis for refusing recognition or enforcement.[108] Similarly, lack of internal competence under the domestic law of the country of origin is not a ground for refusing recognition or enforcement,[109] although in the unlikely event of a foreign judgment being a complete nullity under the law of the country of origin—rather than simply irregular—it should not be recognised or enforced in England.[110]

9.2.7.1 Natural justice

9.2.7.1.1 TRADITIONAL CATEGORIES

Until recently it was assumed, on the authority of *Jacobson* v. *Frachon*,[111] that a foreign judgment could be refused recognition or enforcement in England on the ground that the foreign proceedings involved a breach of the principles of natural justice in only two situations: (i) where the defendant was not given notice of the proceedings in the original court; or (ii) where the person against whom the judgment was given was not presented with a proper opportunity to present his case. Whether there has been a breach of natural justice in either of these senses is to be assessed by English standards; the fact that a foreign court might take a different view on whether the principles of natural justice have been observed is irrelevant. Indeed, the person against whom the judgment is invoked should be able to raise the question of natural justice in the context of proceedings in England even if the foreign court ruled on the question in the other party's favour in the original proceedings.[112] The English courts have been loath to refuse to recognise or enforce foreign judgments on these traditional grounds.

9.2.7.1.2 SUBSTANTIAL JUSTICE

9.2.7.1.2.1 Prior to the decision of the Court of Appeal in *Adams* v. *Cape Industries Plc*[113] it was reasonable to suppose that if a foreign judgment was challenged on the basis of a procedural defect which fell within neither of the traditional categories the party seeking to resist recognition or enforcement would have to show that, by virtue of the defect, the foreign judgment was contrary to English public policy. However, in *Adams* v. *Cape Industries Plc* the Court of Appeal decided, albeit *obiter*, that the natural justice

108. *Godard* v. *Gray* (1870) LR 6 QB 139.
109. Lindley LJ in *Pemberton* v. *Hughes* [1899] 1 Ch 781, 791.
110. Morris, *The Conflict of Laws* (4th ed, 1993) p. 121. See, however, *Merker* v. *Merker* [1963] P 283.
111. (1927) 138 LT 386.
112. *Jet Holdings Inc* v. *Patel* [1990] 1 QB 335.
113. [1990] Ch 433.

defence extends to situations involving procedural defects which lead to "a breach of an English court's views of substantial justice".[114]

9.2.7.1.2.2 In *Adams* v. *Cape Industries Plc*—a case involving proceedings for the enforcement of a foreign judgment which had awarded damages to more than 200 plaintiffs for personal injuries—the foreign proceedings had not involved a judicial investigation of the injuries of any of the individual plaintiffs; the judge simply directed that the average award for each of the plaintiffs should be $75,000 and counsel placed the plaintiffs in four bands—according to the seriousness of their injuries. In the view of the Court of Appeal, substantive justice requires that the amount of compensation should not be fixed subjectively by or on behalf of the plaintiff: "the extent of the defendant's obligation is to be assessed objectively by the independent judge upon proof by the plaintiff of the relevant facts".[115] Accordingly, even had the foreign court been regarded as a court of competent jurisdiction,[116] enforcement of the judgment would have been refused on the basis that the procedure adopted was contrary to English notions of substantial justice.

9.2.7.1.2.3 It seems clear that the defence based on the contravention of English notions of substantial justice is different from and more general than the defence of natural justice: "It could almost be seen as an ultimate discretion to withhold recognition simply because in the eyes of the English forum justice was palpably not done."[117] The substantial justice defence formulated by the Court of Appeal in *Adams* v. *Cape Industries Plc* is more analogous to the defence of public policy than the defence of natural justice as traditionally understood.

9.2.7.1.2.4 In considering whether a foreign judgment should be refused enforcement on the basis that it contravenes English notions of substantial justice, the court must consider not only the injustice caused by the procedure adopted by the original court but also any possibilities for the party against whom the judgment is invoked to correct procedural irregularities under the law of the country of origin. The relevance of the existence of a remedy in the country of origin and the weight to be attached to it depend upon factors which include the nature of the procedural defect and the reasonableness in the circumstances of requiring or expecting the party resisting recognition or enforcement to make use of the remedy.[118]

9.2.7.1.2.5 If the person against whom the judgment is invoked had notice of an irregularity in the procedure adopted by the original court and the procedural law of the country of origin offers him a fair opportunity of correcting that error, it would not be appropriate for recognition or enforcement of the foreign judgment to be refused in England in a case where that opportunity was not taken. However, if the party against whom the judgment is invoked is not aware of the procedural defect or if there are no means whereby the original court is able to remedy the defect or if it is not reasonable to expect the party in question to avail himself of the remedies available in the original court the English court may legitimately refuse to recognise or enforce the foreign judgment on the basis that it contravenes English notions of substantial justice.

114. Slade LJ, [1990] Ch 433, 564.
115. Slade LJ, [1990] Ch 433, 567.
116. On this question see para. 9.2.5.
117. Carter, (1988) 59 BYIL 360, 363.
118. [1990] Ch 433, 570.

9.2.7.2 *Fraud*

9.2.7.2.1 GENERAL PRINCIPLES

9.2.7.2.1.1 The defence of fraud is anomalous in a number of respects.

(i) Although, as a general rule, an English court cannot review the decision of the original court as to the merits, an exception is made in cases involving allegations of fraud.

(ii) Whereas it is not normally possible to raise in English proceedings defences which were raised or could have been raised in the foreign proceedings, *Abouloff* v. *Oppenheimer & Co*[119] and *Vadala* v. *Lawes*[120] show that a foreign judgment will not be recognised or enforced in England if it was obtained by fraud—even if the allegation of fraud was investigated and rejected by the original court.

(iii) There is clear authority for the proposition that an English court may investigate the question of fraud even if the person against whom the judgment was given chose not to raise the matter in the course of the foreign proceedings.[121]

(iv) Although as regards the setting aside of an English judgment on the ground of fraud the rule is that the person seeking to set aside the judgment must produce fresh evidence which "entirely changes the aspect of the case"[122] or which "would probably have an important influence on the result of the case",[123] no such requirement applies to cases concerning the setting aside of foreign judgments on the basis of fraud.

Not surprisingly, *Abouloff* v. *Oppenheimer & Co* and *Vadala* v. *Lawes* have been subject to criticism; nevertheless, they have been upheld by recent decisions of the Court of Appeal[124] and the House of Lords.[125]

9.2.7.2.1.2 There is, however, an exception to these rules. In *House of Spring Gardens Ltd* v. *Waite*[126] the plaintiff obtained a judgment in Ireland against the defendant for nearly £3.5 million (the first judgment).[127] After the appeal to the Irish Supreme Court had been dismissed, the defendant started proceedings in the Irish High Court with a view to having the first judgment set aside on the basis of fraud. The defendant's allegation of fraud was rejected (the second judgment). When the plaintiff sought to enforce the first judgment in England the question arose as to whether the defendant could raise the defence of fraud again. The Court of Appeal decided that the facts were clearly distinguishable from the earlier cases and that the scope of the defence of fraud

119. (1882) 10 QBD 295.
120. (1890) 25 QBD 310.
121. *Syal* v. *Heyward* [1948] 2 KB 443.
122. Earl Cairns LC in *Phosphate Sewage Co Ltd* v. *Molleson* (1879) 4 App Cas 801, 814.
123. Denning LJ in *Ladd* v. *Marshall* [1954] 1 WLR 1489, 1491. See also Lord Diplock in *Hunter* v. *Chief Constable of the West Midlands Police* [1982] AC 529, 545.
124. *Jet Holdings Inc* v. *Patel* [1990] 1 QB 335.
125. *Owens Bank Ltd* v. *Bracco* [1992] 2 AC 443. Briggs, "Foreign Judgments: More Surprises" (1992) 109 LQR 549; Collier, [1992] CLJ 441.
126. [1991] 1 QB 241. Carter, (1990) 61 BYIL 405.
127. The Irish judgment was granted before 1 June 1988, the date on which the Brussels Convention came into force between the Republic of Ireland and the United Kingdom.

should not be extended. In the present case the allegation of fraud had been raised in separate proceedings, the purpose of which was to investigate the question of fraud in the original proceedings. The Court of Appeal took the view that, unless the second judgment itself was impeachable for fraud, the second judgment should be regarded as final on the question of whether the first judgment had been obtained by fraud. The result should be the same if the question of fraud is determined in separate proceedings in a country other than that in which the original judgment was given.[128]

9.2.7.2.2 THE APPLICATION OF THE PRINCIPLES TO DIFFERENT TYPES OF FRAUD

9.2.7.2.2.1 At the most general level, fraud may take two forms.[129] First, a party to litigation may raise an allegation of fraud affecting the cause of action upon which the plaintiff based his claim in the foreign proceedings (for example, an allegation that a contract was procured by fraud). Secondly, one of the parties may raise an allegation of fraud affecting the conduct of the proceedings of the original court itself. As regards the first type of case, the general rule applicable to the setting aside of an English judgment is the relevant one[130]—the applicant must produce fresh evidence in support of the allegation that there was fraud relating to the underlying transaction.

9.2.7.2.2.2 As regards allegations of fraud affecting the conduct of the proceedings of the original court the approach of the English courts has been rather unsophisticated, the principle laid down in *Abouloff* v. *Oppenheimer & Co* and *Vadala* v. *Lawes* being applied indiscriminately. A better approach would be to look more closely at different types of fraud affecting the conduct of the proceedings. Three different factual situations emerge from the cases.

(i) The most common cases of fraud involve allegations that the original court was misled by one of the litigants; for example, it may be alleged that the document which was used to prove the existence of a disputed transaction was forged.[131]

(ii) The party against whom the judgment is invoked may allege fraud in cases where he was deprived of an opportunity to take part in the foreign proceedings, whether as a result of a trick by the other party or as a result of threats. For example, in *Ochsenbein* v. *Papelier*[132] the plaintiff, having started proceedings in France, tricked the defendant into thinking that the action would be discontinued by burning the writ in the defendant's presence. The plaintiff, in fact, proceeded with the French action behind the defendant's back and obtained a default judgment in his favour. More recently, in *Jet Holdings Inc* v. *Patel*,[133] it was argued that a Californian judgment should be refused enforcement in England because the defendant, having previously been threatened and attacked by employees of the plaintiff company, had been afraid to visit the United States and take part in the Californian proceedings.

128. *Owens Bank Ltd* v. *Bracco* [1992] 2 AC 443, 471 (CA).
129. See the judgment of the Court of Appeal in *Owens Bank Ltd* v. *Bracco* [1992] 2 AC 443, 459.
130. *Owens Bank Ltd* v. *Bracco* [1992] 2 AC 443, 459 (CA). This aspect of the Court of Appeal's decision was not considered by the House of Lords.
131. See *Owens Bank Ltd* v. *Bracco* [1992] 2 AC 443.
132. (1873) LR 8 Ch App 695.
133. [1990] 1 QB 335.

(iii) Allegations of fraud may concern the conduct of the original court itself.[134] An allegation that the judge was bribed by one of the litigants would be the most extreme example of fraud of this type. There are no recent reported decisions which raise fraud falling within this third category.

9.2.7.2.2.3 The law should draw a distinction between these three types of fraud affecting the conduct of the proceedings of the original court. In relation to category (i) the person against whom the judgment was given will *prima facie* have been given the opportunity to raise the question of fraud before the original court. Since the English court is in no better a position than the original court to assess whether or not one of the parties was attempting to practise deception, a litigant should not be allowed to raise this type of fraud in proceedings in England—except in cases where fresh evidence has come to light after the conclusion of the foreign proceedings. This type of case should be treated in the same way as cases involving allegations of fraud affecting the cause of action. As regards category (ii) it is legitimate to allow the question of fraud to be raised at the stage of recognition or enforcement if the conduct of the party seeking to rely on the judgment has effectively prevented the other party from taking a full part in the proceedings. The rule in *Abouloff* v. *Oppenheimer & Co* is obviously justified in those rare cases falling within category (iii). Where the alleged fraud involves matters such as judicial bias, the opportunity to raise the matter before the original court is effectively meaningless; the party against whom the judgment was given should, therefore, be free to raise the question of fraud in English proceedings.

9.2.7.3 Public policy

9.2.7.3.1 Public policy plays a role in many areas of private international law, including the recognition and enforcement of foreign judgments. It would be unreasonable to expect an English court to enforce a foreign judgment which conflicts with English public policy.[135] Even though the content of public policy is notoriously open-textured, in the civil and commercial sphere it will be only in very exceptional circumstances that a judgment will be refused recognition or enforcement on this basis. Most of the cases cited in the text-books in which public policy has been successfully invoked concern family law matters and the courts seem to have taken an uncharacteristically relaxed view of foreign judgments outside that limited area. For example, there is nothing contrary to English public policy in enforcing an award of exemplary damages.[136] Similarly, although the court will not enforce a domestic wagering contract, enforcement of a foreign judgment based on a wagering contract will not be refused on public policy grounds.

9.2.7.3.2 In *Israel Discount Bank of New York* v. *Hadjipateras*[137] the plaintiff brought

134. *Price* v. *Dewhurst* (1837) 8 Sim 279.

135. Of course, foreign courts refuse to enforce English judgments on similar grounds. The courts of the United States, for example, will not enforce an English judgment which is incompatible with the protection of free speech guaranteed by the First Amendment: *Bachchan* v. *India Abroad Publications Inc*, *Financial Times*, 14 May 1992.

136. Lord Denning MR in *SA Consortium General Textiles* v. *Sun & Sand Agencies Ltd* [1978] QB 279, 300.

137. [1984] 1 WLR 137. Collier, [1984] CLJ 47.

actions in New York against the defendant and his father as guarantors of obligations assumed by a third party. In the New York proceedings the defendant swore an affidavit stating that he had entered the guarantees as a result of undue influence exerted by his father. The New York court gave judgment for the plaintiff, who started enforcement proceedings in England. The defendant sought to defend the English proceedings on the ground that a judgment which is based on an agreement obtained by undue influence is contrary to public policy. Although leave to defend was refused, the Court of Appeal accepted the proposition that a foreign judgment based on an agreement which contravenes public policy may be unenforceable on the ground of public policy.

9.2.7.3.3 The premises on which the decision of the Court of Appeal appears to be based have been subjected to devastating criticism.[138] (i) The traditional view is that the public policy defence relates to the substance of the foreign judgment, not to the underlying cause of action. There is little or no authority for the proposition that a foreign judgment based on an agreement which contravenes public policy is unenforceable on the ground of public policy. Accordingly, the proposition must be regarded as, at best, questionable. (ii) Even if the Court of Appeal is right in thinking that it is contrary to public policy to enforce a foreign judgment which is based on an agreement which contravenes public policy, the Court of Appeal's view that an agreement concluded under undue influence is unenforceable by reason of public policy cannot be supported.

9.2.7.4 Res judicata

9.2.7.4.1 However sophisticated the courts try to be in handling questions of jurisdiction, situations arise in which the same issues are litigated in different jurisdictions. Accordingly, situations arise in which the courts of different countries give inconsistent answers to the same questions. The problem of irreconcilable judgments may arise either where a foreign judgment relates to a matter which has already been decided in England or where there are two foreign judgments on the same issue. The application of the doctrine of estoppel *per rem judicatam* means that a foreign judgment will not be recognised or enforced in England if it conflicts with an earlier judgment—as long as the earlier judgment creates a cause of action estoppel or an issue estoppel.[139]

9.2.7.4.2 Where an English judgment creates an estoppel, the court will not recognise or enforce a later foreign judgment which conflicts with it.[140] More difficult is the problem posed by two irreconcilable foreign judgments. If one judgment is entitled to recognition or enforcement in England and the other is not the solution is obvious. What is the position, however, if both judgments are *prima facie* entitled to recognition or enforcement in England? The only practical solution is to give effect to whichever judgment was rendered first.[141]

138. Collier, [1984] CLJ 47.

139. See para. 9.2.6.

140. *Vervaeke* v. *Smith* [1983] 1 AC 145; *ED & F Man (Sugar) Ltd* v. *Haryanto (No. 2)* [1991] 1 Lloyd's Rep 429. Carter, (1991) 62 BYIL 461.

141. This is the solution favoured by Article 27(5) of the Brussels and Lugano Conventions. See para. 9.4.3.6.

9.2.7.5 Civil Jurisdiction and Judgments Act 1982, section 32

9.2.7.5.1 Where parties to a contract agree to a particular dispute resolution mechanism, be it arbitration or litigation, the general policy of English law is to hold the parties to the agreement.[142] This policy is extended to cases involving the recognition and enforcement of foreign judgments. Section 32 of the Civil Jurisdiction and Judgments Act 1982 provides:

(1) Subject to the following provisions in this section, a judgment given by a court of an overseas country in any proceedings shall not be recognised or enforced in the United Kingdom if—
- (a) the bringing of those proceedings in that court was contrary to an agreement under which the dispute in question was to be settled otherwise than by proceedings in the courts of that country; and
- (b) those proceedings were not brought in that court by, or with the agreement of, the person against whom the judgment was given; and
- (c) that person did not counterclaim in the proceedings or otherwise submit to the jurisdiction of that court.

(2) Subsection (1) does not apply where the agreement referred to in paragraph (a) of that subsection was illegal, void or unenforceable or was incapable of being performed for reasons not attributable to the fault of the party bringing the proceedings in which the judgment was given.

(3) In determining whether a judgment given by a court of an overseas country should be recognised or enforced in the United Kingdom, a court in the United Kingdom shall not be bound by any decision of the overseas court relating to any matters mentioned in subsection (1) or (2).

9.2.7.5.2 In the context of proceedings in which one of the parties seeks to rely on a foreign judgment, the question of whether a contract includes "an agreement under which the dispute in question was to be settled otherwise than by proceedings in the courts of that country" for the purposes of section 32(1)(a) is to be determined by the English court in accordance with English conflicts principles. Where a question arises as to whether, for the purposes of subsection (2), a dispute resolution clause is "illegal, void or unenforceable or . . . incapable of being performed" English private international law prevails over the law of the country of origin.

9.2.7.5.3 In *Tracomin SA* v. *Sudan Oil Seeds (No. 1)*[143] the parties entered a contract, which under English law—the law governing the contract—contained an English arbitration clause. The plaintiff started proceedings in Switzerland with a view to recovering damages for breach of contract. The defendant contested the jurisdiction of the Swiss court on the basis of the arbitration clause, but took no further part on the proceedings. Having decided that the arbitration clause was of no effect the Swiss court assumed jurisdiction and gave judgment in favour of the plaintiff. The plaintiff then sought to enforce this judgment in England. Enforcement of the Swiss judgment was refused on the basis that, for the purposes of section 32(1)(a), the arbitration clause was, according to its proper law, a valid agreement "under which the dispute in question was to be settled otherwise than by proceedings in the [Swiss] courts". By virtue of section 32(3) the fact that the Swiss court had reached a contrary conclusion as to the effectiveness of the arbitration clause was to be ignored.

9.2.7.5.4 The availability of the defence contained in section 32 depends on the party against whom the judgment was given not having taken part in the original proceedings. A defendant who does anything which amounts to submission to the jurisdiction of the

142. See para. 6.5.
143. [1983] 1 WLR 1026.

original court[144] cannot rely on the dispute resolution clause in the context of proceedings in England concerning the recognition or enforcement of the foreign judgment.[145] Furthermore, section 32 does not apply to (i) judgments given by the courts of Scotland and Northern Ireland,[146] (ii) foreign judgments which are entitled to recognition or enforcement under Title III of the Conventions,[147] or (iii) judgments given in proceedings arising under certain international conventions which are entitled to recognition or enforcement under the Foreign Judgments (Reciprocal Enforcement) Act 1933.[148]

9.2.7.6 Multiple damages[149]

9.2.7.6.1 Although the wording of the Protection of Trading Interests Act 1980 does not indicate its particular purpose, its main object is to nullify the extraterritorial effect of the anti-trust laws of the United States of America. The effect of section 5 is that judgments given by the courts of the United States for triple damages under the Clayton and Sherman Acts are not entitled to enforcement in the United Kingdom.

9.2.7.6.2 According to the terms of section 5 of the 1980 Act there are three types of judgment which are not enforceable in the United Kingdom.

(i) The court shall not enforce a foreign judgment for multiple damages,[150] which is defined as "a judgment for an amount arrived at by doubling, trebling or otherwise multiplying a sum assessed as compensation for the loss or damage sustained by the person in whose favour the judgment is given".[151]

(ii) The court shall not enforce a foreign judgment which is based on a provision or rule of law specified or described in an order of the Secretary of State.[152] An order may be made in respect of any provision or rule of law which appears to the Secretary of State "to be concerned with the prohibition or regulation of agreements, arrangements or practices designed to restrain, distort or restrict competition in the carrying on of business of any description or to be otherwise concerned with the promotion of such competition as aforesaid".[153]

(iii) The court shall not enforce a judgment on a claim for contribution in respect of damages awarded by a judgment falling within (i) or (ii).

It should also be noted that section 6 of the 1980 Act provides a mechanism which enables a judgment debtor who has satisfied or partially satisfied a judgment which falls within the scope of section 5 to claw-back any sums paid which are in excess of the amount attributable to compensation.

144. See para. 9.2.5.2.
145. *Marc Rich & Co AG* v. *Societa Italiana Impianti PA (No. 2)* [1992] 1 Lloyd's Rep 624.
146. Civil Jurisdiction and Judgments Act 1982, s. 50.
147. Civil Jurisdiction and Judgments Act 1982, s. 32(4)(a).
148. Civil Jurisdiction and Judgments Act 1982, s. 32(4)(b).
149. Lloyd Jones, "Protection of Trading Interests Act 1980" [1981] CLJ 41; Collins, "Blocking and Clawback Statutes: The United Kingdom Approach" [1986] JBL 372 & 452.
150. Protection of Trading Interests Act, s. 5(1)(a).
151. Protection of Trading Interests Act, s. 5(3).
152. Protection of Trading Interests Act 1980, s. 5(1)(b).
153. Protection of Trading Interests Act 1980, s. 5(4). See Protection of Trading Interests (Australian Trade Practices) Order 1988, SI 1988 No. 569. The effect of this Order is that a judgment based on section 81(1A) of the Australian Trade Practices Act 1974 is not enforceable in the United Kingdom.

9.2.8 Recognition and enforcement of judgments *in rem*

Judgments *in rem* may concern either the legal status of persons or the possession or ownership of property. In the commercial context, it is the second category which is of prime importance. The significant feature of a judgment *in rem* is that it determines not only the rights and duties of the parties to the litigation; a judgment *in rem* determines possession or ownership of the *res* and is conclusive as regards the whole world. Whereas a judgment *in personam* operates *inter partes*, a judgment *in rem* operates *erga omnes*.

The basic framework for the recognition and enforcement of judgments *in rem* is the same as that for the recognition or enforcement of judgments *in personam*: the original court must have been a court of competent jurisdiction; the judgment must be final and conclusive; recognition or enforcement may be refused if one of a number of defences is established. There are, however, differences which should be noted.

9.2.8.1 Jurisdiction of the original court

A foreign court which grants a judgment *in rem* in relation to movable or immovable property is to be regarded as a court of competent jurisdiction only if the property in question was located within the territorial jurisdiction of the country of origin at the time when the proceedings were commenced.[154] No other basis of jurisdiction will suffice.

9.2.8.2 Defences

The extent to which defences which are generally available in the context of proceedings involving foreign judgments *in personam* are also applicable to foreign judgments *in rem* is not free from doubt. If the foreign judgment was procured by fraud or is contrary to public policy it seems that recognition or enforcement will be refused. It has been suggested, however, that the degree of recognition to be accorded to a foreign judgment *in rem*—at least a foreign judgment dealing with movable property—falls to be determined not so much by the rules governing the recognition of foreign judgments, but by the rules governing the validity of assignments of property.[155] On this basis, subject to the defences of public policy and fraud, the recognition of a foreign judgment *in rem* would be governed by the *lex situs*.

9.2.8.3 Enforcement

In practice, the recognition of foreign judgments *in rem* is likely to be of more significance than their enforcement.[156] Indeed, certain foreign judgments *in rem*—for example, a foreign judgment which determines title to foreign land—cannot be enforced in England. There are, however, circumstances in which a judgment creditor

154. *Castrique* v. *Imrie* (1870) LR 4 HL 414.
155. Dicey & Morris, *The Conflict of Laws* (12th ed, 1993) p. 496.
156. *Castrique* v. *Imrie* (1870) LR 4 HL 414.

may wish to enforce a judgment *in rem* in England.[157] There can be no doubt that a judgment *in rem* may be enforced in England by means of proceedings *in personam*. In *The Despina GK*[158] it was decided that a foreign judgment *in rem* may be enforced in England by an action *in rem*:

> A judgment creditor who has obtained a final judgment against a shipowner by proceeding *in rem* in a foreign admiralty court can bring an action *in rem* in this court against that ship to enforce the decree of the foreign court if that is necessary to complete the execution of that judgment, provided that the ship is the property of the judgment debtor at the time when she is arrested.[159]

9.3 RECOGNITION AND ENFORCEMENT UNDER STATUTORY REGIMES BASED ON THE COMMON LAW

Although the common law rules are still extremely important in practice, the recognition of foreign judgments has to some extent been put on a statutory basis. Part II of the Administration of Justice Act 1920 provides for the enforcement of judgments given by the superior courts of Commonwealth countries. The Foreign Judgments (Reciprocal Enforcement) Act 1933 provides for the recognition and enforcement of judgments given by the courts of foreign countries outside the Commonwealth to which the United Kingdom has assumed obligations under bilateral treaties,[160] as well as to foreign judgments given in proceedings under a number of international conventions.[161] It was also intended that the 1933 Act should supersede Part II of the 1920 Act. However, as the law now stands the 1933 Act applies to the judgments of very few Commonwealth countries.[162] The regimes established by the 1920 Act and the 1933 Act exist side by side and are mutually exclusive.

The basic scheme of the legislation is to provide a mechanism for the registration of judgments given by the superior courts of foreign countries. A registered judgment is enforceable in England in the same way as a judgment of an English court. The conceptual structure of the legislation mirrors that of the common law and to a considerable extent the legislation is a codification of common law principles. Accordingly, the meaning of many of the provisions of the 1920 and 1933 Acts is to be gleaned from earlier case law. Nevertheless, it is not appropriate to attempt to ascertain the common law position by reasoning backwards from the statutory provisions.[163]

157. See, for example, *The City of Mecca* (1879) 5 PD 28, reversed by the Court of Appeal on the ground that the foreign judgment was in fact a judgment *in personam*: (1881) 6 PD 106.

158. [1983] QB 214.

159. Sheen J, [1983] QB 214, 219.

160. The Foreign Judgments (Reciprocal Enforcement) Act 1933 applies to judgments given by the superior courts of the following non-Commonwealth countries: Austria, Belgium, the Federal Republic of Germany, France, Israel, Italy, the Netherlands, Norway, Suriname. It should be noted, however, that judgments given by the courts of a Contracting State (as defined by section 1 of the Civil Jurisdiction and Judgments Act 1982) fall within the scope of the Conventions if the judgment in question concerns civil and commercial matters as defined by Article 1.

161. See Dicey & Morris, *The Conflict of Laws* (12th ed, 1993) pp. 550–572.

162. Australian Capital Territories, Bangladesh, Canada, Guernsey, India, Isle of Man, Jersey, Pakistan, Tonga.

163. *Henry* v. *Geoprosco International Ltd* [1976] QB 726.

9.3.1 Enforcement under Part II of the Administration of Justice Act 1920

9.3.1.1 Section 9 of the Administration of Justice Act 1920 sets out the scheme for the registration of various foreign judgments and the defences to registration. Where a judgment is registered under section 9 "the judgment shall, as from the date of registration, be of the same force and effect ... as if it had been a judgment originally obtained or entered upon the date of registration in the registering court".[164] The 1920 Act is concerned only with enforcement, not with recognition. The 1920 Act does not supersede the common law; the fact that a judgment is registrable under the 1920 Act does not deprive the judgment creditor of the right to sue on the obligation created by the foreign judgment.[165] It is provided, however, that where an action is brought at common law on a judgment which is registrable under the Act "the plaintiff shall not be entitled to recover any costs of the action unless the application to register the judgment ... has previously been refused or unless the court otherwise orders".[166]

9.3.1.2 Section 9(1) provides that where a judgment has been obtained in a superior court of a territory to which the Act applies the judgment creditor may apply to the High Court "at any time within twelve months after the date of the judgment, or such longer period as may be allowed by the court, to have the judgment registered in the court, and on any such application the court may, if in all the circumstances of the case they think it is just and convenient that the judgment should be enforced in the United Kingdom ... order the judgment to be registered accordingly".[167] Section 9(1) applies only to judgments "whereby any sum of money is made payable"[168] and confers a discretion on the High Court whether or not to order registration. The 1920 Act does not, however, indicate the basis on which the discretion of the court should be exercised.

9.3.1.3 Section 9(2) lists the circumstances in which registration must be refused:

(a) the original court acted without jurisdiction; or
(b) the judgment debtor, being a person who was neither carrying on business[169] nor ordinarily resident within the jurisdiction of the original court, did not voluntarily appear or otherwise submit or agree to submit to the jurisdiction of that court; or
(c) the judgment debtor, being the defendant in the proceedings, was not duly served with the process of the original court and did not appear, notwithstanding that he was ordinarily resident or was carrying on business within the jurisdiction of that court or agreed to submit to the jurisdiction of that court; or
(d) the judgment was obtained by fraud; or
(e) the judgment debtor satisfies the registering court either that an appeal is pending, or that he is entitled and intends to appeal, against the judgment; or
(f) the judgment was in respect of a cause of action which for reasons of public policy or for some other similar reason could not have been entertained by the registering court.

Many of these provisions are the same as, or roughly equivalent to, defences to enforcement at common law. The defence of fraud provided by paragraph (d) is the same as the defence at common law.[170] It is assumed that reference to lack of

164. Administration of Justice Act 1920, s. 9(3)(a).
165. *Yukon Consolidated Gold Corporation Ltd* v. *Clark* [1938] 2 KB 241.
166. Administration of Justice Act 1920, s. 9(5).
167. The relevant procedure for obtaining registration under this section is to be found in RSC, Order 71, rr. 1–13. See para. 9.3.2.1.
168. Administration of Justice Act 1920, s 12(1).
169. See *Sfeir & Co* v. *National Insurance Co of New Zealand* [1964] 1 Lloyd's Rep 330.
170. *Owens Bank Ltd* v. *Bracco* [1992] 2 AC 443.

jurisdiction in paragraph (a) refers to lack of jurisdiction by the standards of English private international law, rather than under the law of the original court. This interpretation, however, renders paragraph (b) largely redundant. There is no defence based on natural justice as such; paragraph (c) is limited to cases where the defendant has not been duly served. Furthermore, the public policy defence in paragraph (f) refers to the cause of action, rather than the effect of the judgment, and therefore is more limited than the equivalent defence at common law. Paragraph (e) provides a basis for non-registration which is not a defence at common law; at common law a foreign judgment may be regarded as final and conclusive even though an appeal is pending.

9.3.1.4 The list of defences is incomplete—for example, the fact that the foreign judgment is incompatible with an English judgment is not expressly stated as a ground for refusing registration. However, in this type of case it is to be expected that the English court would exercise the discretion conferred by subsection (1) against registration. Presumably, an English court would, in the exercise of its discretion, refuse registration of a foreign judgment which was in the nature of a fine or other penalty. It should be added that the defences to enforcement provided by section 32 of the Civil Jurisdiction and Judgments Act 1982[171] and by the Protection of Trading Interests Act 1980[172] also apply to cases falling within the scope of the 1920 Act.

9.3.2 Recognition and enforcement under the Foreign Judgments (Reciprocal Enforcement) Act 1933

Whereas the registration of foreign judgments under Part II of the Administration of Justice Act 1920 is discretionary, registration is mandatory in relation to foreign judgments which qualify under the Foreign Judgments (Reciprocal Enforcement) Act 1933. Furthermore, whereas the 1920 Act co-exists with the common law rules, the scheme provided by the 1933 Act, where applicable, supersedes the common law. Section 6 of the 1933 Act provides:

> No proceedings for the recovery of a sum payable under a foreign judgment, being a judgment to which this Part of this Act applies, other than proceedings by way of registration of the judgment, shall be entertained by any court in the United Kingdom.

9.3.2.1 Enforcement: conditions and procedure

9.3.2.1.1 The 1933 Act applies to judgments given by a superior court of a foreign country.[173] In order for a judgment to be enforced under the 1933 Act a number of conditions must be satisfied.

(i) The judgment must be final and conclusive between the parties.[174] A judgment is deemed to be final and conclusive even though the judgment may still be the

171. See para. 9.2.7.5.

172. See para. 9.2.7.6.

173. Certain types of judgments are, however, excluded: for example, a judgment given by a superior court on appeal from a court which is not a superior court and a judgment given by the superior court of a foreign judgment for the purposes of the enforcement of another judgment. See Foreign Judgments (Reciprocal Enforcement) Act 1933, s. 1(2A).

174. Foreign Judgments (Reciprocal Enforcement) Act 1933, s. 1(2)(a).

subject of an appeal or even if an appeal is pending.[175]

(ii) The judgment must be a judgment for a sum of money, not being a sum payable in respect of taxes or other charges of a similar nature or in respect of a fine or other penalty.[176]

(iii) The Act must have been extended to the foreign country in question by delegated legislation.[177]

9.3.2.1.2 Where a judgment satisfies these conditions the judgment creditor may apply for registration. A judgment creditor may apply to have the judgment registered in the High Court at any time within six years after the date of the foreign judgment or, where there have been proceedings by way of appeal against the judgment, after the date of the last judgment given in those proceedings.[178] The application for registration may be made *ex parte*.[179] The application must be supported by an affidavit which, *inter alia*, exhibits the judgment or a certified or authenticated copy of it, states the name and address of the judgment creditor and the judgment debtor and that the judgment creditor is entitled to enforce the judgment, specifies the amount of interest, if any, which is payable under the law of the original court and verifies that section 5 of the Protection of Trading Interests Act 1980 does not apply.[180] It is up to the judgment creditor to draw up the order giving leave to register the judgment.[181] Notice of registration must be served on the judgment debtor; service must be effected either personally or at the judgment debtor's last known address.[182] Where the judgment debtor is not present within the jurisdiction, the notice of registration may be served abroad without leave of the court.[183] The notice of registration must state, *inter alia*, full particulars of the judgment, the right of the judgment debtor to have the registration set aside and the period in which an application to set aside may be made.[184] Any application to set aside must be made by summons and supported by affidavit.[185]

9.3.2.1.3 Where a judgment is registered under the 1933 Act the judgment has the same force and effect as a judgment of the High Court: proceedings may be taken on the foreign judgment; the sum of money for which the judgment is registered carries interest; and the High Court has the same control over the execution of a registered judgment as in relation to a judgment of the High Court.[186]

There are two bases on which registration is to be refused. (i) If the foreign judgment has been wholly satisfied it may not be registered.[187] Where the foreign judgment has been partly satisfied, the judgment may be registered only to the extent of the balance

175. Foreign Judgments (Reciprocal Enforcement) Act 1933, s. 1(3).
176. Foreign Judgments (Reciprocal Enforcement) Act 1933, s. 1(2)(b).
177. Foreign Judgments (Reciprocal Enforcement) Act 1933, s. 1(2)(c). See nn. 160 and 162.
178. Foreign Judgments (Reciprocal Enforcement) Act 1933, s. 2(1).
179. RSC, Order 71, r. 2(1).
180. RSC, Order 71, r. 3(1).
181. RSC, Order 71, r. 5(1).
182. RSC, Order 71, r. 7(1).
183. RSC, Order 71, r. 7(2).
184. RSC, Order 71, r. 7(3).
185. RSC, Order 71, r. 9(1).
186. Foreign Judgments (Reciprocal Enforcement) Act 1933, s. 2(2).
187. Foreign Judgments (Reciprocal Enforcement) Act 1933, s. 2(1), proviso (a).

remaining due at the date of the application for registration.[188] (ii) Registration is to be refused if the judgment cannot be enforced by execution in the country of origin.[189]

9.3.2.2 Resisting enforcement

The defences to enforcement under the 1933 Act are contained in section 4, which lists the circumstances in which a registered judgment "shall" or "may" be set aside. Section 4 is drafted in a somewhat convoluted way.

9.3.2.2.1 IMPROPER REGISTRATION

Registration must be set aside if the judgment is not a judgment to which Part I of the 1933 Act applies or if the judgment was registered in contravention of the Act.[190] Furthermore, registration must be set aside if the rights under the judgment are not vested in the person by whom the application for registration was made.[191]

9.3.2.2.2 LACK OF JURISDICTION

9.3.2.2.2.1 If the original court did not have jurisdiction, registration must be set aside.[192] Lack of jurisdiction is extensively defined by section 4(2) and (3). Subsection (2) lists certain circumstances in which the original court will be regarded as having had jurisdiction:

> (a) in the case of an action *in personam*—
>   (i) if the judgment debtor, being a defendant in the original court, submitted to the jurisdiction of that court by voluntarily appearing in the proceedings . . . ; or
>   (ii) if the judgment debtor was plaintiff in, or counterclaimed in, the proceedings in the original court; or
>   (iii) if the judgment debtor, being a defendant in the original court, had before the commencement of proceedings, agreed in respect of the subject matter of the proceedings, to submit to the jurisdiction of that court or of the courts of the country of that court; or
>   (iv) if the judgment debtor, being a defendant in the original court, was at the time when the proceedings were instituted resident in, or being a body corporate had its principal place of business in, the country of that court; or
>   (v) if the judgment debtor, being a defendant in the original court, had an office or place of business in the country of that court and the proceedings in that court were in respect of a transaction effected through or at that office or place;
>
> (b) in the case of a judgment given in an action of which the subject matter was immovable property or in an action *in rem* of which the subject matter was movable property, if the property in question was at the time of the proceedings in the original court situate in the country of that court;
>
> (c) in the case of a judgment given in an action other than any such action as is mentioned in paragraph (a) or paragraph (b) of this subsection, if the jurisdiction of the original court is recognised by the law of the registering court.

9.3.2.2.2.2 To a significant extent this subsection reproduces the common law rules. The first three subparagraphs of paragraph (a) reflect the common law rules on

188. Foreign Judgments (Reciprocal Enforcement) Act 1933, s. 2(4).
189. Foreign Judgments (Reciprocal Enforcement) Act 1933, s. 2(1), proviso (b).
190. Foreign Judgments (Reciprocal Enforcement) Act 1933, s. 4(1)(a)(i).
191. Foreign Judgments (Reciprocal Enforcement) Act 1933, s. 4(1)(a)(vi).
192. Foreign Judgments (Reciprocal Enforcement) Act 1933, s. 4(1)(a)(ii).

submission. Subparagraphs (iv) and (v) define the type of connection between the judgment debtor and the original court which is regarded as sufficient to justify the original court's assumption of *in personam* jurisdiction. Whereas *Adams* v. *Cape Industries Plc*[193] indicates that temporary presence is sufficient at common law, nothing less than residence will suffice under the 1933 Act. As regards corporations, the test is the presence of a place of business in the foreign country.

9.3.2.2.2.3 Subsection (2) is qualified by subsection (3) and by section 32 of the Civil Jurisdiction and Judgments Act 1982.[194] Subsection (3) provides that the original court is deemed not to have had jurisdiction if (i) the subject matter of the proceedings was immovable property not situated within the country of origin or (ii) if the judgment debtor, being a defendant in the original proceedings, was a person who under the rules of public international law was entitled to immunity in the country of origin and did not submit to the jurisdiction of that court. By virtue of section 32 of the 1982 Act recognition or enforcement of a foreign judgment shall be refused if the proceedings before the original court were contrary to an agreement under which the dispute in question was to be settled otherwise than by proceedings in the court of that country and the person against whom the judgment was given did not submit to the jurisdiction of the original court.[195]

9.3.2.2.3 LACK OF NOTICE OF THE PROCEEDINGS

Section 4(1)(a)(iii) provides that registration shall be set aside if the registering court is satisfied:

> that the judgment debtor, being the defendant in the proceedings in the original court, did not (notwithstanding that process may have been duly served on him in accordance with the law of the country of the original court) receive notice of those proceedings in sufficient time to enable him to defend the proceedings and did not appear.

This provision is in substance very similar to Article 27(2) of the Conventions.[196] Of course, the case law of the Court of Justice relating to the interpretation of Article 27(2) of the Brussels Convention is not directly relevant to cases falling within the 1933 Act.

9.3.2.2.4 FRAUD

A foreign judgment which has been obtained by fraud shall not be recognised or enforced under the 1933 Act.[197]

9.3.2.2.5 PUBLIC POLICY

Registration of a foreign judgment shall be set aside if "enforcement of the judgment would be contrary to public policy in the country of the registering court".[198]

193. [1990] Ch 433. See para. 9.2.5.3.
194. See para. 9.2.7.5.
195. Section 32 of the 1982 Act replaced section 4(3)(b) of the 1933 Act: Civil Jurisdiction and Judgments Act 1982, s. 54 and Schedule 14.
196. See para. 9.4.3.4.
197. Foreign Judgments (Reciprocal Enforcement) Act 1933, s. 4(1)(a)(iv). See para. 9.2.7.2.
198. Foreign Judgments (Reciprocal Enforcement) Act 1933, s. 4(1)(a)(v). See para. 9.2.7.3.

9.3.2.2.6 IRRECONCILABILITY

Section 4(1)(b) provides that registration of a judgment may be set aside if the registering court is satisfied that "the matter in dispute in the proceedings in the original court had previously to the date of the judgment in the original court been the subject of a final and conclusive judgment by a court having jurisdiction in the matter".

The effect of this provision is that a foreign judgment which is *prima facie* entitled to registration under the 1933 Act may be denied enforcement if there is an earlier inconsistent judgment—whether an English judgment or the judgment of another foreign country which is entitled to recognition or enforcement in England.

9.3.2.2.7 WHEN AN APPEAL IS PENDING ABROAD

The fact that an appeal against the foreign judgment may be brought or has been commenced in the country of origin does not prevent enforcement under the 1933 Act. However, section 5(1) provides that, where the judgment debtor satisfies the court that he is entitled to appeal against foreign judgment and intends to do so or that an appeal is pending, the court may set aside registration or adjourn the application to set aside registration for a suitable period during which time the foreign appeal can be heard. If registration is set aside under section 5(1) this does not preclude the judgment creditor from re-applying to register the judgment once the foreign appeal has been disposed of.[199]

9.3.2.2.8 PROTECTION OF TRADING INTERESTS ACT 1980

It should be added that the defences to enforcement provided by section 5 of the Protection of Trading Interests Act 1980 also apply to cases falling within the scope of the 1933 Act.[200]

9.3.2.3 Recognition

The 1933 Act provides for the recognition of judgments falling within the scope of the legislation without there being a need for the party in whose favour the judgment was granted to register the judgment.[201] Defences to enforcement are also defences to recognition. Although, as a general rule, a judgment which cannot be registered is not entitled to recognition, recognition shall not be refused on the basis that a sum of money is not payable under the judgment or the judgment has been wholly or partly satisfied or the judgment cannot be enforced by execution in the country of origin.[202] Of course, to qualify for recognition under the 1933 Act the foreign judgment must be a judgment on the merits.[203]

199. Foreign Judgments (Reciprocal Enforcement) Act 1933, s. 5(2).
200. See para. 9.2.7.6.
201. Foreign Judgments (Reciprocal Enforcement) Act 1933, s. 8(1).
202. Foreign Judgments (Reciprocal Enforcement) Act 1933, s. 8(1).
203. *Black-Clawson International Ltd* v. *Papierwerke Waldhof-Aschaffenburg AG* [1975] AC 591. For consideration of what is meant by the phrase "on the merits" see para. 9.2.4.

9.4 RECOGNITION AND ENFORCEMENT UNDER THE BRUSSELS AND LUGANO CONVENTIONS[204]

In comparison with the position at common law, Title III of the Conventions provides a simplified regime for the recognition and enforcement of judgments given by the courts of the Contracting States. In order for a judgment to be entitled to recognition under Title III there are five basic conditions which must be satisfied:

(i) the case must concern international recognition;
(ii) the case must fall within the material scope of Title I;
(iii) the judgment must have been granted by the court of a Contracting State;
(iv) the judgment must fall within Article 25;
(v) the judgment must have been granted after the entry into force of the Brussels or Lugano Convention, as the case may be.

To a significant extent, simplification as regards recognition and enforcement is made possible by the provisions of Title II, which assign jurisdiction in civil and commercial matters to the courts of Contracting States. Whereas, at common law, an important stage of the enquiry is whether the original court was a court of competent jurisdiction, in cases falling within the scope of Title III the court in which recognition or enforcement is sought may not—as a general rule—review the basis on which the court of the State of origin assumed jurisdiction. The grounds on which recognition or enforcement may be refused are limited. Title III also contains detailed provisions which establish a uniform—and mandatory—procedure for the enforcement of judgments given by the courts of Contracting States.

9.4.1 Basic conditions for recognition and enforcement under Title III

9.4.1.1 The scope of the Conventions

In order for a judgment to be entitled to recognition or enforcement under Title III the judgment must fall within the scope of the Conventions. This means, first, that the case must concern the recognition or enforcement of a judgment given in a Contracting State other than the State in which recognition or enforcement is sought. The Conventions do not apply, for example, to the recognition or enforcement in England of judgments given by the courts of Scotland and Northern Ireland.[205] Secondly, the judgment must be in respect of a matter which is within the material scope of the Conventions as circumscribed by Title I.[206] It should be noted that there may be situations in which the question as to whether proceedings fall within the scope of the Conventions arises both at the original stage and at the stage of recognition or enforcement. In this situation, the decision of the court of the State of origin does not bind the court of other Contracting States; the court of the State in which recognition or enforcement is sought must determine for itself whether or not the proceedings fall within the scope of Title I.

204. In this section it is to be assumed that the provisions of the Brussels and Lugano Conventions are identical unless the contrary is indicated.
205. See para. 9.5.
206. See para. 3.3.

9.4.1.2 What is a "judgment"?

9.4.1.2.1 ARTICLE 25

The term judgment is defined by Article 25 which provides:

> For the purposes of this Convention, "judgment" means any judgment given by a court or tribunal of a Contracting State, whatever the judgment may be called, including a decree, order, decision or writ of execution, as well as the determination of costs or expenses by an officer of the court.

Whereas under the common law only final judgments for a fixed sum of money are enforceable in England, there is no such restriction under the Conventions. Accordingly, provisional, interim measures or orders for specific performance are, in principle, entitled to enforcement under Title III.[207] In addition, Title III makes no distinction between judgments *in personam* and judgments *in rem*.

9.4.1.2.2 INTERLOCUTORY ORDERS[208]

9.4.1.2.2.1 The Schlosser Report makes it clear that "interlocutory decisions which are not intended to govern the legal relationships of the parties, but to arrange the further conduct of the proceedings, should be excluded from the scope of Title III".[209] In *CFEM Façades SA* v. *Bovis Construction Ltd*[210] the question was whether a French court order, which appointed experts to examine a building in London, to take evidence from witnesses and to draw conclusions as to the quality of the building, was entitled to recognition and enforcement in England. The judge held that it was not: "interlocutory decisions in the course of civil and commercial litigation which do no more than regulate procedural matters and which neither govern the legal relationships of the parties nor affect their proprietary rights are outside the scope of the recognition and enforcement provisions of Title III".[211]

9.4.1.2.2.2 Even as regards interlocutory orders which *prima facie* fall within the scope of Title III by virtue of the fact that they are intended to govern the legal relationships of the parties, there are certain limits to their recognition and enforcement. In *Denilauer* v. *Snc Couchet Frères* the Court of Justice ruled that "judicial decisions authorising provisional or protective measures, which are delivered without the party against which they are directed having been summoned to appear and which are intended to be enforced without prior service do not come within the system of recognition and enforcement provided for by Title III".[212] On the basis of this decision, a judgment will be entitled to recognition or enforcement under Title III only if either the judgment results from proceedings in which both parties participate or the judgment results from proceedings in relation to which the defendant was summoned, but did not appear; Title III does not extend to the situation where an order is made *ex parte*,

207. Case 143/78 *de Cavel* v. *de Cavel* [1979] ECR 1055.
208. Collins, "Provisional Measures, the Conflict of Laws and the Brussels Convention" (1981) 1 YBEL 249.
209. OJ 1979 C59/127, para. 187.
210. [1992] ILPr 561.
211. Judge Goldblatt QC, [1992] ILPr 561, 577.
212. Case 125/79 [1980] ECR 1553, 1571 (para. 18). Hartley, (1981) 6 ELRev 59; March Hunnings, "Enforceability of Ex Parte Orders in the EEC" [1981] JBL 243.

notwithstanding the fact that the defendant is given a reasonable opportunity to apply in the State of origin for the order to be set aside.[213]

9.4.1.2.2.3 It will, therefore, be extremely unusual for provisional or protective measures (such as Mareva injunctions) to be entitled to recognition under Title III. One of the key features of protective and provisional measures is the element of surprise—which can be achieved only by means of an *ex parte* application. Where, however, protective or provisional measures are granted subsequent to an *inter partes* hearing—rather than on an *ex parte* application—the court's order should be entitled to recognition and enforcement under Title III. It should be noted that the fact that a procedural or *ex parte* order is not entitled to international enforcement does not necessarily mean that the order is rendered ineffective; all it means is that the parties must look to the courts of the State of origin, rather than to the courts of other States, to control the implementation of the order.

9.4.1.2.3 PENALTIES

9.4.1.2.3.1 At common law an English court will not enforce, either directly or indirectly, foreign judgments ordering the payment of taxes, fines or other penalties. It is apparent, however, from Article 43 that "a judgment which orders a periodic payment by way of a penalty" is in principle entitled to enforcement under Title III. However, a judgment of this type is not entitled to enforcement unless "the amount of the payment has been finally determined by the courts of the State of origin".[214]

9.4.1.2.3.2 There is some uncertainty whether a judgment which orders a periodic payment by way of a penalty can be enforced under Title III when the payments accrue to the State, rather than to the judgment creditor.[215] It is to be expected that, as a general rule, a judgment of this type does not relate to civil and commercial matters and, therefore, falls outside the scope of Title I. However, if the judgment is within the scope of Title I, there is no reason why it should be excluded from the enforcement provisions contained in Title III.

9.4.1.2.4 PARTIAL ENFORCEMENT

The Conventions provide that "[w]here a foreign judgment has been given in respect of several matters and enforcement cannot be authorised for all of them, the court may authorise enforcement for one or more of them".[216] It is further provided that "[a]n applicant may request partial enforcement of a judgment".[217] So, where a foreign order involves certain elements which fall within the scope of Title III and other elements which do not, the judgment creditor may apply for enforcement of only those elements which are covered by the provisions of Title III.

213. *EMI Records Ltd* v. *Modern Music Karl-Ulrich Walterbach GmbH* [1992] QB 115.
214. Article 43.
215. Schlosser Report, OJ 1979 C59/132, para. 213(bb).
216. Article 42(1).
217. Article 42(2).

9.4.1.3 The relationship between Title II and Title III

9.4.1.3.1 Title III (recognition and enforcement) is not directly linked to Title II (jurisdiction). The recognition and enforcement provisions in Title III are not limited to judgments which result from proceedings in which the court of the State of origin assumed jurisdiction under the direct jurisdiction rules in Title II; Title III applies whether or not the parties are domiciled in a Contracting State and whatever their nationality.[218] The key questions are whether the judgment falls both within the material scope of the Conventions (Title I) and within Article 25.

9.4.1.3.2 Because the recognition and enforcement provisions do not depend on the court of the State of origin having assumed jurisdiction under the direct jurisdiction provisions of Title II, the combination of Titles I and III may have an oppressive effect on parties who are not domiciled in a Contracting State. If a French court assumes jurisdiction over a defendant who is not domiciled in a Contracting State under Article 14 of the Civil Code and gives judgment against him, the judgment is *prima facie* entitled to recognition and enforcement in England under Title III. Similarly, if proceedings are brought in England against a New York corporation under RSC, Order 11, rule 1(1), the English judgment—if it concerns matters within the material scope of Title I—is enforceable in any of the Contracting States under Title III, even though the English court assumed jurisdiction on an exorbitant basis—which would not have been available had the defendant been domiciled in a Contracting State.

9.4.1.3.3 There can be little doubt that the Conventions endorse the application of double standards. As regards defendants domiciled in a Contracting State, recognition and enforcement under Title III is justified by the fact that the defendant has the benefit of the jurisdictional and procedural safeguards provided by Title II; the list of exorbitant bases of jurisdiction contained in Article 3 cannot be invoked against a person who is domiciled in a Contracting State and Article 20 must be applied in cases where a defendant who is domiciled in a Contracting State is sued in the courts of another Contracting State.[219] However, as regards defendants not domiciled in a Contracting State, the strict recognition and enforcement regime in Title III is applicable, even though the defendant has none of the jurisdictional and procedural safeguards contained in Title II. Perhaps not altogether surprisingly, this aspect of the Conventions has not found favour with American commentators.[220] The Brussels Convention has been criticised for overtly discriminating against outsiders: "Not only does it continue to authorise unreasonable jurisdictional assertions against outsiders; it enhances their effect by requiring unquestioning recognition of such judgments in all of the Contracting States."[221]

218. Jenard Report, OJ 1979 C54/43.
219. See para. 4.4.
220. See, for example, Nadelmann, "The Outer World and the Common Market Experts' Draft of a Convention on Recognition of Judgments" (1967–68) 5 CMLRev 409; Von Mehren, "Recognition and Enforcement of Sister-State Judgments: Reflections on General Theory and Current Practice in the European Economic Community and the United States" (1981) 81 Col LR 1044.
221. Borchers, "Comparing Personal Jurisdiction in the United States and the European Community: Lessons for American Reform" (1992) 40 Am J Comp L 121, 132–133.

9.4.2 The principle of automatic recognition

9.4.2.1 At common law a precondition for the recognition of a foreign judgment is that the original court had jurisdiction in the private international law sense.[222] The absence of internationally approved bases of jurisdiction—and the fact that many countries readily assume jurisdiction over foreign defendants on exorbitant bases—justifies the common law rule that, when called upon to recognise a foreign judgment, the court is entitled to determine for itself whether the original court was a court of competent jurisdiction.

9.4.2.2 The Conventions, however, establish common bases of jurisdiction—at least as regards defendants domiciled in Contracting States. This justifies the (almost) automatic recognition of judgments falling within the scope of the Conventions. Article 26 provides: "A judgment given in a Contracting State shall be recognised in the other Contracting States without any special procedure being required."

9.4.2.3 The principle of automatic recognition means that a foreign judgment which is entitled to recognition under Article 26 must in principle have the same effects in the State in which recognition is sought as it does in the State of origin.[223] It should be noted, however, that the process for recognition under the Conventions is not completely devoid of formalities. The party seeking recognition should normally produce both a copy of the judgment[224] and, in the case of a judgment given in default, the original or a certified true copy of the document which establishes that the party in default was served with the document instituting the proceedings.[225] Furthermore, the principle of automatic recognition is subject to the defences to recognition contained in other provisions, notably Articles 27 and 28.

9.4.2.4 Enforcement, on the other hand, is not automatic, in the sense that the Conventions lay down a detailed procedure for obtaining an enforcement order.[226] Furthermore, since the State in which enforcement is sought is obliged to lend its own remedies by way of execution,[227] the judgment may, in fact, be enforced rather differently from the way in which it would have been enforced in the State of origin.[228]

9.4.3 Defences to recognition

9.4.3.1 No review of the merits: Article 29

At common law a litigant may not challenge a foreign judgment on the basis that a point of fact or law was wrongly decided by the original court.[229] The same principle is to be found in Article 29 which provides that "[u]nder no circumstances may a foreign judgment be reviewed as to its substance".

222. See para. 9.2.5.
223. Case 145/86 *Hoffmann* v. *Krieg* [1988] ECR 645.
224. Article 46(1).
225. Article 46(2). If the person seeking recognition does not produce the documents required by Article 46(2), the court may, by virtue of Article 48(1), specify a time for their production, accept equivalent documents, or dispense with their production.
226. See para. 9.4.4. The same procedure applies where a declaration of recognition is sought.
227. Case 148/84 *Deutsche Genossenschaftsbank* v. *SA Brasserie du Pêcheur* [1985] ECR 1981.
228. Briggs, (1988) 8 YBEL 265, 266.
229. *Godard* v. *Gray* (1870) LR 6 QB 139. This principle is, of course, subject to the defence of fraud. See para. 9.2.7.2.

9.4.3.2 Limited review of jurisdiction: Article 28

9.4.3.2.1 As a general principle the court in which recognition is sought is not entitled to examine the basis on which the court of the State of origin assumed jurisdiction over the defendant. The final paragraph of Article 28 provides not only that "the jurisdiction of the court of the State of origin may not be reviewed", but also that "the test of public policy referred to in Article 27(1) may not be applied to the rules relating to jurisdiction".[230] This principle is justified by the overall structure of the Conventions:

> The very strict rules of jurisdiction laid down in Title II, and the safeguards granted in Article 20 to defendants who do not enter an appearance, make it possible to dispense with any review, by the court in which recognition or enforcement is sought, of the jurisdiction of the court in which the original judgment was given.[231]

9.4.3.2.2 Just as Article 29 implies confidence in the courts of other Contracting States on questions of law and fact, the final paragraph of Article 28 assumes the proper application of the jurisdiction provisions of Title II by the court of the State of origin. Accordingly, if a defendant intends to challenge the jurisdiction of the court of the State of origin he must do so before that court (and, if the case falls within the scope of the Brussels Convention, the matter may be referred to the Court of Justice[232]). The effect of the final paragraph of Article 28 is to prevent a defendant, who chooses not to take part in the proceedings, from being able to challenge the jurisdiction of the court of the State of origin at the stage of recognition or enforcement.

9.4.3.2.3 There are, however, limited exceptions to the general principle that the assumption of jurisdiction by the court of the State of origin may not be reviewed by the court in which recognition is sought. The exceptions in Article 28(1) apply to recognition under both of the Conventions. Further specific exceptions are provided for by Article 28(2) of the Lugano Convention.

9.4.3.2.4 Article 28(1) provides that "a judgment shall not be recognised if it conflicts with the provisions of Sections 3, 4 or 5 of Title II". It is provided, however, that the court of the State in which recognition is sought "shall be bound by the findings of fact on which the court of the State of origin based its jurisdiction".[233] The reason for this exception to the general principle in the final paragraph of Article 28 is not difficult to discern.

9.4.3.2.5 As regards Article 16 (the only provision of Section 5), it is ultimately for the court of the State which has exclusive jurisdiction to determine its own jurisdiction. If the court of one Contracting State wrongly assumes jurisdiction when a court of another Contracting State has exclusive jurisdiction under Article 16, it is right and proper that the court on which Article 16 confers exclusive jurisdiction should refuse to recognise or enforce the foreign judgment.

9.4.3.2.6 As regards judgments which conflict with Section 3 or Section 4 of Title II, the exception to the general principle that there should be no review of jurisdiction by the court of the State in which recognition is sought is justified by the aim of the Conventions to protect the weaker party. Where, for example, a dispute arises in

230. The defence of public policy under the Conventions is discussed at para. 9.4.3.3.
231. Jenard Report, OJ 1979 C59/46.
232. For the terms of the Luxembourg Protocol see para. 3.2.1.1.
233. Brussels Convention, Article 28(2); Lugano Convention, Article 28(3).

relation to a consumer contract concluded between an English consumer and an Italian supplier, Article 14(2) provides that the consumer shall be sued in the country of his domicile.[234] If the supplier sues the consumer in Italy, it hardly seems reasonable to expect the consumer to appear in the Italian proceedings to contest the jurisdiction of the Italian court. The effect of Article 28(1) is that, should the Italian court erroneously assume jurisdiction over the consumer, the consumer is able to ignore the foreign proceedings and defend any subsequent enforcement proceedings in England on the basis that the assumption of jurisdiction by the court of the State of origin was inconsistent with Section 3 of Title II of the Brussels Convention.

9.4.3.2.7 It should be noted that Article 28(1) refers only to Sections 3, 4 and 5. Recognition may not be refused on the basis that the court of the State of origin wrongly assumed jurisdiction in breach of the terms of a jurisdiction agreement which satisfies the requirements of Article 17 (which forms part of Section 6). So, for example, a judgment given by a German court is entitled to recognition in England under Title III even if the English court believes that the subject matter of the dispute litigated in Germany falls within the scope of an English jurisdiction clause which is valid under Article 17. Although section 32 of the Civil Jurisdiction and Judgments Act 1982 provides a defence to recognition or enforcement of a foreign judgment which results from proceedings brought in breach of a dispute resolution clause,[235] the relevant provisions do not apply to judgments which are entitled to recognition or enforcement under the Conventions.[236]

9.4.3.2.8 The position should be different in a case where the court of a Contracting State assumes jurisdiction in defiance of an arbitration clause. Although the law on this question is not free from doubt, where a court assumes jurisdiction and gives judgment notwithstanding the existence of an arbitration clause which, according to English conflicts principles, is valid under its proper law, the judgment should be regarded as falling outside the scope of Title I altogether on the basis that it concerns "arbitration".[237] If the judgment is not within the scope of Title I recognition or enforcement may be refused on the basis that the bringing of the proceedings in the original court was "contrary to an agreement under which the dispute in question was to be settled otherwise than proceedings in the courts of that country".[238]

9.4.3.2.9 Article 28(2) of the Lugano Convention provides that recognition may also be refused in any case provided for by Article 54B or Article 57(4) of the Lugano Convention.[239] Article 54B(3) provides:

234. This general rule must, however, be read subject to Article 15 which allows the parties—albeit in rather limited circumstances—to agree to the exclusive jurisdiction of the courts of a Contracting State other than the State in which the consumer is domiciled. See para. 5.7.2.

235. Civil Jurisdiction and Judgments Act 1982, s. 32(1)–(3). See para. 9.2.7.5.

236. Civil Jurisdiction and Judgments Act 1982, s. 32(4).

237. The potentially relevant case law avoids addressing this issue directly: Case C-190/89 *Marc Rich & Co AG* v. *Societa Italiana Impianti PA* [1991] ECR-I 3855; *Marc Rich & Co AG* v. *Societa Italiana Impianti PA (No. 2)* [1992] 1 Lloyd's Rep 624.

238. Civil Jurisdiction and Judgments Act 1982, s. 32(1). For further discussion of the problems posed by judgments given in defiance of an arbitration agreement see para. 3.3.3.4.5 and para. 20.6.1.

239. There are further grounds for refusing recognition in Protocol No. 1 to the Lugano Convention. Article Ia allowed Switzerland to declare, at the time of ratification, that recognition of a judgment would be refused in cases where Article 5(1) was the only basis on which the court of the State of origin was entitled to assume jurisdiction. Article Ib allows any Contracting State to make a reservation whereby a judgment may be refused recognition if two conditions are satisfied: (i) the jurisdiction of the court of the State of origin is based, pursuant to Article 16(1)(b), exclusively on the domicile of the defendant in the State of origin and (ii) the property is situated in the State in which recognition is being sought.

In addition to the grounds provided for in Title III, recognition or enforcement may be refused if the ground of jurisdiction on which the judgment has been based differs from that resulting from this Convention and recognition or enforcement is sought against a party who is domiciled in a Contracting State which is not a member of the European Communities, unless the judgment may otherwise be recognised or enforced under any rule of law in the State addressed.

This provision is relevant only in the context of the recognition or enforcement of a judgment granted by the court of an EC Member State or an EFTA State.[240]

9.4.3.2.10 The first paragraph of Article 57 provides that the Lugano Convention "shall not affect any conventions to which the Contracting States are or will be parties and which, in relation to particular matters, govern . . . the recognition or enforcement of judgments".[241] Article 57(4) of the Lugano Convention goes on to state:

In addition to the grounds provided for in Title III, recognition or enforcement may be refused if the State addressed is not a contracting party to a convention referred to in the first paragraph and the person against whom recognition or enforcement is sought is domiciled in that State, unless the judgment may otherwise be recognised or enforced under any rule of law in the State addressed.

This ground for refusing recognition or enforcement was introduced into the Lugano Convention at the request of the EFTA countries.[242] This provision does not allow recognition or enforcement to be refused unless (i) the State in which recognition or enforcement is sought is not a party to the convention in question and (ii) the judgment debtor is domiciled in that State.

9.4.3.2.11 Two points should be stressed. (i) The ground for refusal introduced by Article 57(4) does not apply automatically; it confers a discretion on the court in which recognition or enforcement is sought. The Jenard–Möller Report gives no indication of the basis on which this discretion might be exercised. (ii) Even though Article 57(4) was included at the request of the EFTA States, "a judgment delivered in an EFTA Member State on the basis of a rule of jurisdiction provided for in a special convention might be refused recognition or enforcement . . . in a Community Member State".[243]

9.4.3.3 Public policy: Article 27(1)

Article 27(1) provides that recognition of a judgment given by the court of a Contracting State shall not be recognised "if such recognition is contrary to public policy in the State in which recognition is sought".

9.4.3.3.1 THE PROPER APPROACH TO PUBLIC POLICY

The Jenard Report states that Article 27(1) "ought to operate only in exceptional cases".[244] Furthermore, the final paragraph of Article 28 expressly provides that public policy cannot be used as a basis for refusing to recognise a judgment in a situation where the court of the State of origin misapplied the jurisdiction rules contained in Title

240. Jenard–Möller Report, OJ 1990 C189/68, para. 16(5).
241. See para. 3.5 and 8.2.2.
242. Jenard–Möller Report, OJ 1990 C189/82, para. 82.
243. Jenard–Möller Report, OJ 1990 C189/82, para. 82.
244. OJ 1979 C59/44. This view is supported by the Court of Justice in Case 145/86 *Hoffmann* v. *Krieg* [1988] ECR 645.

II. Accordingly, one would expect an objection founded on public policy to be more likely to fail than to succeed.[245]

The restricted approach to questions of public policy is justified by the structure of the Conventions.[246] Some of the areas in which public policy questions often arise are excluded from the Conventions' material scope; the Conventions do not apply to proceedings concerning public law, social security and nearly all aspects of family law. Moreover, the Conventions tackle specific subject areas in which public policy may arise by means of direct jurisdiction rules in Title II. There are, for example, special jurisdiction rules dealing with consumer contracts, employment contracts and matters relating to insurance.

9.4.3.3.2 LIMITS ON PUBLIC POLICY

The fact that specific grounds for refusing recognition are to be found in paragraphs 2 to 5 means that the public policy defence should have no role to play where one of the more specific grounds for refusing recognition applies.[247] In *Hoffmann* v. *Krieg*[248] the Court of Justice took the view that the public policy defence is precluded when the issue is whether a foreign judgment is compatible with a national judgment. In such a case "the issue must be resolved on the basis of the specific provision under Article 27(3), which envisages cases in which the foreign judgment is irreconcilable with a judgment given in a dispute between the same parties in the State in which [recognition or] enforcement is sought".[249] The same approach applies to the other specific grounds for refusing recognition.

9.4.3.3.3 PUBLIC POLICY AND FRAUD

9.4.3.3.3.1 At common law fraud is a basis for refusing to recognise a foreign judgment even if the issue of fraud was raised in the original proceedings and rejected.[250] While fraud is not listed in the defences in Article 27, it is clear that "to obtain a judgment by fraud can in principle constitute an offence against the public policy of the State addressed".[251] In what circumstances is it contrary to public policy to recognise a judgment which has been obtained by fraud?

9.4.3.3.3.2 In *Interdesco SA* v. *Nullifire Ltd*[252] the plaintiff, a French paint manufacturer, entered an agreement with the defendant, an English company, under which the defendant was given exclusive distribution rights in the United Kingdom and Ireland in respect of the plaintiff's products. Before the agreement had expired, it was terminated by the defendant on the basis that the plaintiff's products failed to satisfy United Kingdom standards and were, therefore, unmarketable. The plaintiff brought

245. Judge Goldblatt QC in *CFEM Façades SA* v. *Bovis Construction Ltd* [1992] ILPr 561, 571.
246. Forde, "The 'Ordre Public' Exception and Adjudicative Jurisdiction Conventions" (1980) 29 ICLQ 259, 271.
247. Jenard Report, OJ 1979 C59/44.
248. Case 145/86 [1988] ECR 645.
249. Case 145/86 [1988] ECR 645, 668 (para. 21).
250. See para. 9.2.7.2.
251. Schlosser Report, OJ 1979 C59/128, para. 192(a).
252. [1992] 1 Lloyd's Rep 180.

proceedings in France for wrongful termination of the agreement. The French court, which relied on the results of tests conducted in France by the testing institution appointed by the parties in the distribution agreement and attached little weight to contradictory English tests indicating that the paint was substandard, awarded damages to the plaintiff. When the plaintiff sought to enforce the judgment in England the defendant argued that, as the judgment had been procured by fraud, enforcement would be contrary to English public policy.

9.4.3.3.3.3. The defence based on Article 27(1) was rejected on the basis that the proper approach to fraud under Title III is very different from that adopted by the common law. Three important principles emerge from the case.

(i) Where the court of another Contracting State "has, in its judgment, ruled on precisely the matters that a defendant seeks to raise when challenging the judgment on the ground of fraud, the Convention precludes the court from reviewing the conclusion of the foreign court".[253]

(ii) Where a Convention judgment is "challenged on the ground that the foreign court has been fraudulently deceived, the English court should first consider whether a remedy lies in such a case in the foreign jurisdiction in question. If so it will normally be appropriate to leave the defendant to pursue his remedy in that jurisdiction".[254]

(iii) It is not generally appropriate for the English court to deny recognition to a judgment under the Convention on the ground of public policy except in circumstances where it would permit a challenge to an English judgment.[255]

It follows that, as a general rule, the public policy defence under Article 27(1) cannot be relied upon in cases of fraud unless, first, the party resisting recognition of the foreign judgment produces evidence which could not have been produced with reasonable diligence in the foreign proceedings and which, although not necessarily decisive, would probably have an important influence on the result of the case and, secondly, there is no means of recourse under the law of the State of origin.[256]

9.4.3.4 Safeguarding the rights of the defendant: Article 27(2) [257]

Although the aim of the Conventions is to facilitate the mutual recognition and enforcement of foreign judgments between the Contracting States, Title III cannot be allowed to undermine in any way the defendant's right to a fair hearing.[258] Article 27(2), which is designed to ensure that the procedural rights of the defendant are not compromised, provides that a judgment shall not be recognised "where it was given in default of appearance, if the defendant was not duly served with the document which instituted the proceedings or with an equivalent document in sufficient time to enable him to arrange for his defence". This provision has been considered by the Court of Justice more frequently than the other defences to recognition provided by Title III.

253. Phillips J, [1992] 1 Lloyd's Rep 180, 187.
254. Phillips J, [1992] 1 Lloyd's Rep 180, 188.
255. For example, the principle in *Henderson* v. *Henderson* (1843) 3 Hare 100.
256. See also *Société d'Informatique Service Réalisation Organisation* v. *Ampersand Software Ltd BV* [1994] ILPr 55.
257. Kennett, "Reviewing Service: Double Check or Double Fault?" (1992) 11 CJQ 115.
258. Case 49/84 *Debaecker* v. *Bouwman* [1985] ECR 1779, 1796 (para. 10).

9.4.3.4.1 THE RELATIONSHIP BETWEEN ARTICLE 20 AND ARTICLE 27(2)

9.4.3.4.1.1 Article 20(2) provides that, where a defendant who is domiciled in one Contracting State is sued in another Contracting State, the court should stay the proceedings unless it is shown that "the defendant has been able to receive the document instituting the proceedings ... in sufficient time to enable him to arrange for his defence, or that all necessary steps have been taken to this end".[259] The ground for refusing recognition of a judgment under Article 27(2) overlaps—to a considerable extent—with Article 20(2). The question which, therefore, arises is this: can the person against whom the judgment is invoked rely on Article 27(2) when the court of the State of origin has already decided, in the context of Article 20, that he was given sufficient time to prepare his defence or is the court of the State in which recognition or enforcement is sought bound by the decision of the court of the State of origin on this point? This question was considered by the Court of Justice in *Pendy Plastic Products BV* v. *Pluspunkt Handelsgesellschaft mbH*,[260] a case involving proceedings to enforce in Germany a Dutch judgment which had been given in proceedings brought against a German company. Although the defendant had not put in an appearance, the Dutch court decided that the defendant had received the writ in sufficient time and gave a default judgment in the plaintiff's favour. When the plaintiff sought to enforce the judgment in Germany, the defendant alleged that there had been insufficient time to prepare a defence.

9.4.3.4.1.2 The Court of Justice started from the general principle that "the provisions of the Brussels Convention are designed to ensure that the defendant's rights are effectively protected".[261] Accordingly, the court of the State in which recognition or enforcement is sought is not bound by the decision of the court of the State of origin: "in accordance with the objective of Article 27 of the Convention, the court of the State in which [recognition or] enforcement is sought must examine the question posed by paragraph (2) of that Article, notwithstanding the decision given by the court of the original State on the basis of the second and third paragraphs of Article 20."[262]

9.4.3.4.1.3 It should be noted that there is a very important distinction between the scope of Article 20 and the scope of Article 27(2). Whereas Article 20 applies to cases where proceedings are brought against a defendant who is domiciled in a Contracting State other than the State in which the original proceedings take place, Article 27(2) applies to all defendants regardless of their domicile. Accordingly, Article 27(2) is of particular importance in two sorts of case: (i) where the original proceedings are brought against a defendant who is not domiciled in a Contracting State and (ii) where the original proceedings are brought in the Contracting State in which the defendant is domiciled.[263]

9.4.3.4.2 ONE DEFENCE OR TWO?

9.4.3.4.2.1 The Jenard Report indicates that Article 27(2) is intended to give a double protection: "First, the document must have been duly served. ... Secondly, even where

259. See para. 4.4.
260. Case 228/81 [1982] ECR 2723.
261. Case 228/81 [1982] ECR 2723, 2736 (para. 13).
262. Case 228/81 [1982] ECR 2723, 2736 (para. 13).
263. Although this was implicit in the decision of the Court of Justice in Case 166/80 *Klomps* v. *Michel* [1981] ECR 1593, it was expressly articulated in Case 49/84 *Debaecker* v. *Bouwman* [1985] ECR 1779.

service has been duly effected, recognition can be refused if the court in which recognition is sought considers that the document was not served in sufficient time to enable the defendant to arrange for his defence."[264] There are two questions concerning the relationship between the requirement of due service and the sufficiency of time for preparation of the defence.

(i) If the court of the State of origin rules that the defendant was duly served, does Article 27(2) require a separate examination of the question as to whether the defendant had sufficient time to prepare his defence?

The Court of Justice gave an affirmative answer to this question in *Klomps* v. *Michel*.[265]

(ii) If the defendant has had sufficient time in which to prepare his defence, can recognition be resisted on the ground that service was not duly effected?

In *Isabelle Lancray SA* v. *Peters und Sickert KG*[266] the plaintiff, a French company, and the defendant, a German firm, had entered a contract which contained a clause conferring jurisdiction on the French courts. The plaintiff started proceedings and the defendant was summoned to appear before the French court. The defendant wrote to the French court to contest the validity of the summons and did not appear in the French proceedings. When the plaintiff, having obtained a default judgment in France, sought to enforce it in Germany, the defendant resisted enforcement on the basis that due service had not been effected. The Court of Justice followed the logic of its decision in *Klomps* v. *Michel* that Article 27(2) imposes two independent and cumulative requirements: "If the sole issue was whether the document came to the defendant's attention in sufficient time, plaintiffs would be tempted to ignore the prescribed forms for due service ... That would create considerable uncertainty as to whether documents had actually been served, thus thwarting the uniform application of the provisions of the Convention."[267] Accordingly, on the assumption that, in the present case, service did not comply with French law, the judgment was not enforceable, notwithstanding the fact that the defendant's case "from the procedural point of view, seem[ed] somewhat lacking in merit".[268]

9.4.3.4.2.2 If service of the document instituting the proceedings is defective the fact that the defendant is perfectly well aware of the contents of the document and has plenty of time to prepare the defence is not relevant. Similarly, a defendant can rely on Article 27(2) notwithstanding the fact that, after having become aware of the judgment in default, he failed to avail himself of the opportunity offered by the procedural law of the State of origin to apply to have the judgment set aside on the ground that service of the document instituting the proceedings was defective.[269]

264. OJ 1979 C59/44.
265. Case 166/80 [1981] ECR 1593, 1607 (para. 15). Hartley, (1982) 7 ELRev 419.
266. Case C-305/88 [1990] ECR-I 2725. Briggs, (1990) 10 YBEL 490.
267. Case C-305/88 [1990] ECR-I 2725, 2748 (para. 20).
268. Advocate-General Jacobs, Case 305/88 [1990] ECR-I 2725, 2741 (para. 23).
269. Case C-123/91 *Minalmet GmbH* v. *Brandeis Ltd* [1993] ILPr 132.

9.4.3.4.3 "IN DEFAULT OF APPEARANCE"

9.4.3.4.3.1 Although it has been suggested that the definition of "appearance" should be a matter for the law of the State of origin,[270] the Court of Justice has implicitly accepted that the notion of "appearance" is to be given a Community meaning. In *Klomps* v. *Michel* the Court of Justice held that if, after a judgment has been given, the defendant appears for the first time before the court of the State of origin with a view to having the judgment set aside, the judgment is still to be regarded as having been given in default of appearance.[271] Conversely, if the defendant appears to fight the case on the merits reliance cannot be placed on Article 27(2). Similarly, where a civil claim is joined to criminal proceedings, if the defendant answers the criminal charge and is aware of the civil claim which is being made against him in the criminal proceedings, the plea to the criminal charge will be regarded as an appearance to the proceedings as a whole.[272]

9.4.3.4.3.2 Since the case law of the Court of Justice has explored only some aspects of the word "appearance" for the purposes of Article 27(2) a number of questions remain unresolved. The rationale for the defence in Article 27(2) is to ensure that the defendant has had an opportunity of defending himself.[273] It would seem to follow that the reason for the defendant's appearance is not relevant[274] and that a defendant who appears to challenge the jurisdiction of the court or to request a postponement cannot rely on Article 27(2).[275] There are situations, however, where a broad view of "appearance" may operate harshly. It is not obvious why, for example, a defendant who applies to the court of the State of origin for more time for the preparation of his defence should be placed in a worse position than the defendant who chooses to ignore the proceedings entirely. The second aspect of the double protection offered by Article 27(2) is significantly reduced if a defendant is deprived of the possibility of relying on the defence of insufficient time simply by making an application for an extension of time.

9.4.3.4.4 DUE SERVICE

9.4.3.4.4.1 In considering whether or not the defendant has been duly served, it is important to identify the document instituting the proceedings. In *Klomps* v. *Michel*[276] the plaintiff issued summary proceedings in Germany against the defendant for recovery of a debt. The German court, on the plaintiff's demand, made an "order for payment". This document was served by leaving notice of the order at the defendant's address in Germany. Since the defendant made no objection to the order within the prescribed three days the court made an "enforcement order". This document was served in the same way as the order for payment. Since the defendant raised no objection to the enforcement order within the prescribed period of a week, the enforcement order became enforceable in German law. One of the questions referred to the Court of Justice was the meaning to be ascribed to "the document which instituted the proceedings or ... an equivalent document". The Court of Justice held that Article 27(2) refers to "any document ... service of which enables the plaintiff,

270. Advocate-General Darmon in Case C-172/91 *Sonntag* v. *Waidmann* [1993] ILPr 466, 480.
271. Case 166/80 [1981] ECR 1593, 1607 (paras. 12–13).
272. Case C-172/91 *Sonntag* v. *Waidmann* [1993] ILPr 466, 488 (para. 41).
273. Case C-172/91 *Sonntag* v. *Waidmann* [1993] ILPr 466, 487 (para. 38).
274. Cheshire & North, *Private International Law* (12th ed, 1992) p. 427.
275. Hartley, *Civil Jurisdiction and Judgments* (1984) p. 90.
276. Case 166/80 [1981] ECR 1593.

under the law of the State of the court in which the judgment was given, to obtain, in default of appropriate action taken by the defendant, a decision capable of being recognised and enforced under the provisions of the Convention".[277] According to this test, on the facts of *Klomps* v. *Michel* it was the order for payment rather than the enforcement order which was the relevant document for the purposes of Article 27(2).

9.4.3.4.4.2 The regularity of the service is to be determined by reference to the law of the State whose document it is which is served—that is, "the internal law of the State in which judgment was given and to the international conventions on the service abroad of judicial instruments binding on that State".[278] So, where service is initially defective, the law of the State of origin determines whether any subsequent steps taken by the plaintiff are effective to cure that defect.[279] However, the court of the State in which recognition is sought is not bound by the findings of the court of the State of origin. Accordingly, the court of the State in which recognition is sought may determine for itself whether, on the facts of the case, the defendant was duly served in accordance with the law of the State of origin. Where service is based on a bilateral or multilateral convention (such as the Hague Convention of 15 November 1965 on the Service Abroad of Judicial and Extrajudicial Documents) the interpretation of the provisions of the applicable convention adopted by the court of the State in which recognition is sought may differ from that favoured by the court of the State of origin.

9.4.3.4.5 IN SUFFICIENT TIME

9.4.3.4.5.1 When deciding whether the defendant has been given sufficient time the period which should be considered is "the time ... available to the defendant for the purposes of preventing the issue of a judgment in default which is enforceable under the Convention".[280] On the facts of *Klomps* v. *Michel*,[281] the relevant period for the purposes of Article 27(2) was the period during which the defendant could raise an objection to the order for payment; because the enforcement order operated as a default judgment, the period for raising an objection to the enforcement order was irrelevant.

9.4.3.4.5.2 In the simple situation where the defendant is personally served with the document instituting the proceedings it is obvious that time starts to run from the moment of service. More problematical is the situation where the defendant is not personally served and becomes aware of the document instituting the proceedings at some date after service has been duly effected. This type of situation is likely to arise in cases where the defendant is served by post or where some method of substituted service is used. The essential question in this situation is this: does the period for determining whether the defendant was given sufficient time for the preparation of his defence run from the date of service or the date on which the defendant personally became aware of the document instituting the proceedings?

9.4.3.4.5.3 The general rule is that time runs from the moment of service—determined by reference to the law of the State of origin.[282] However, this general rule should not be applied in all cases. Since due service does not depend on proof that the

277. Case 166/80 *Klomps* v. *Michel* [1981] ECR 1593, 1606 (para. 11).
278. Jenard Report, OJ 1979 C59/44; Case 166/80 *Klomps* v. *Michel* [1981] ECR 1593, 1607 (para. 15).
279. Case C-305/88 *Isabelle Lancray SA* v. *Peters und Sickert KG* [1990] ECR-I 2725.
280. Case 166/80 *Klomps* v. *Michel* [1982] ECR 1593, 1606 (para. 11).
281. See para. 9.4.3.4.4.1.
282. Case 166/80 *Klomps* v. *Michel* [1981] ECR 1593, 1608 (para. 19).

defendant received notification of the commencement of proceedings, there may be "exceptional circumstances which warrant the conclusion that, although service was duly effected, it was, however, inadequate for the purpose of enabling the defendant to take steps for his defence, and, accordingly, could not cause the time stipulated by Article 27(2) to begin to run".[283]

9.4.3.4.5.4 The issue of "exceptional circumstances" arose in *Debaecker* v. *Bouwman*.[284] In this case the defendant, a Dutch national, rented a flat in Antwerp from the plaintiff. Shortly after entering the arrangement the defendant left the premises without giving notice or leaving a forwarding address. The plaintiff started proceedings in Belgium against the defendant for compensation and, because the defendant's whereabouts were not known, the writ was served—in accordance with Belgian procedural law—on the Police Commissariat in Antwerp. A few days later the defendant sent the plaintiff a registered letter repudiating the lease and giving the plaintiff details of a post office box through which he could be contacted. The plaintiff, however, made no attempt to inform the defendant of the pending legal proceedings. The Belgian court gave a default judgment in the plaintiff's favour. In the enforcement proceedings in the Netherlands the question facing the court was whether there were exceptional circumstances which justified the conclusion that, although the writ had been properly served in accordance with Belgian law, the defendant—who had not received any notification of the proceedings—had not been given sufficient time in which to prepare his defence. In answering this question the court was called upon not only to decide whether account is to be taken of events which take place after the writ has been served, but also to consider whether the defendant's behaviour is relevant.

9.4.3.4.5.5 The Court of Justice decided that "if the circumstances to be taken into account were confined to those which were known at the time of service, there would be a danger of interpreting the requirement of service in sufficient time in such a restrictive and formalistic manner that it would in fact coincide with the requirement of due service, thus negating one of the safeguards laid down by the Convention for the protection of the defendant".[285] Accordingly, the court of the State in which recognition or enforcement is sought may, in examining whether service is effected in sufficient time, take account of exceptional circumstances which arise after service is duly effected.[286] However, the Court of Justice was not prepared to go so far as to say that a plaintiff is under an obligation to notify the defendant in person in cases where the plaintiff discovers the defendant's whereabouts after fictitious service has been duly effected. The fact that the plaintiff, after service, learns of the defendant's new address does not compel him to take any further steps, but renders his subsequent behaviour important for the purpose of determining whether service was effected in sufficient time. In a case such as *Debaecker* v. *Bouwman* the plaintiff's failure to inform the defendant at the postal address was "in reality merely a factor which must be taken into account in order to establish whether service was effected in sufficient time".[287] Nevertheless, a plaintiff who—as a result of the defendant's disappearance—starts proceedings by way of fictitious or substituted service would be well advised to inform

283. Case 166/80 *Klomps* v. *Michel* [1981] ECR 1593, 1608–1609 (para. 19).
284. Case 49/84 [1985] ECR 1779. Hartley, (1987) 12 ELRev 220.
285. Case 49/84 [1985] ECR 1779, 1798 (para. 19).
286. Case 49/84 [1985] ECR 1779, 1799 (para. 22).
287. Case 49/84 [1985] ECR 1779, 1800 (para. 27).

the defendant of the proceedings if and when the defendant's whereabouts comes to light. By notifying the defendant at the new address, the plaintiff ensures that the court in which recognition or enforcement is sought cannot decide that the defendant's change of address is an exceptional circumstance.[288]

9.4.3.4.5.6 As regards the relevance, if any, of the defendant's behaviour in deciding whether the defendant had been given sufficient time in which to arrange for his defence, the Court of Justice declined to lay down any hard and fast rules:

> [T]he defendant's behaviour cannot automatically rule out the possibility of taking into account exceptional circumstances which warrant the conclusion that service was not effected in sufficient time. Instead, such behaviour may be assessed by the court in which [recognition or] enforcement is sought as one of the matters in the light of which it determines whether service was effected in sufficient time. It will therefore be for that court to assess ... to what extent the defendant's behaviour is capable of outweighing the fact that the plaintiff was apprised after service of the defendant's new address.[289]

9.4.3.4.5.7 Although the case law of the Court of Justice discusses the factors which are relevant to an assessment of whether the defendant was given sufficient time in which to prepare his defence, there is no indication of the standard by which sufficiency is to be judged. It is reasonable to suppose that the standard cannot simply be that provided by the law of the State of origin, otherwise Article 27(2) would amount to no more than a verification by the court in which recognition is sought that the court of the State of origin correctly applied its own procedural law. Nevertheless, it would hardly seem proper for an English court to refuse recognition of a foreign judgment simply on the ground that the time given to a defendant for the preparation of his defence under the law of the State of origin is less than the time given by English procedural law. Ultimately, the smooth operation of this aspect of Article 27(2) depends on the formulation of a supranational standard—or at least an appreciation that the courts cannot rely on purely national standards.

9.4.3.4.5.8 When applying Article 27(2), national courts are required to make a factual appreciation in the light of the surrounding circumstances. Whether the time given in a particular situation is sufficient will depend on all the circumstances of the case (including matters such as the kind of action involved, the parties to it, the need to obtain a legal adviser, and whether translations are required).[290] It is, accordingly, impossible to lay down fixed periods which are, or are not, sufficient. For example, although the German courts have taken the view that a period of 13 days or even 20 days is insufficient for the preparation of a defence by a German defendant in an action in Belgium, the Italian courts have decided that periods of between 20 and 30 days are sufficient to enable the defendant to arrange his defence in another Contracting State.[291]

9.4.3.5 Irreconcilability: Article 27(3)

9.4.3.5.1 One of the aims of the Conventions is to reduce the incidence of conflicting judgments. The most important provisions in this regard are Article 6 and the provisions

288. Case 49/84 [1985] ECR 1779, 1800 (para. 28).
289. Case 49/84 [1985] ECR 1779, 1801 (para. 32).
290. Advocate-General Reischl in Case 166/80 *Klomps* v. *Michel* [1981] ECR 1593, 1621.
291. Kennett, "Reviewing Service: Double Check or Double Fault?" (1992) 11 CJQ 115, 143.

of Section 8 of Title II.[292] It is, however, impossible to prevent entirely conflicting judgments—especially since the material scope of the Conventions is limited by Article 1. The most important of the provisions dealing with the problem of irreconcilable judgments is contained in Article 27(3) according to which recognition of a judgment shall be refused "if the judgment is irreconcilable with a judgment given in a dispute between the same parties in the State in which recognition is sought". Although for recognition or enforcement to be refused under Article 27(3) the proceedings leading to the irreconcilable judgments must have been between the same parties,[293] there is no requirement that the proceedings should have concerned the same cause of action. In order to ascertain whether the two judgments are irreconcilable within the meaning of Article 27(3) "it should be examined whether they entail legal consequences that are mutually exclusive".[294] This will not always be an easy task for a national court to undertake.

9.4.3.5.2 Article 27(3) applies not only in cases where the courts of two Contracting States have rendered irreconcilable judgments in matters falling within the scope of the Conventions. Where a judgment creditor seeks to enforce a judgment under Title III enforcement will be refused under Article 27(3) if the foreign judgment is irreconcilable with a judgment of the court of the State in which enforcement is sought in a matter falling outside the Conventions' scope. So, for example, a foreign judgment ordering a man to make maintenance payments to his wife by virtue of his conjugal obligations to support her is irreconcilable within the meaning of Article 27(3) with a judgment given by the court of the State in which enforcement is sought pronouncing the divorce of the spouses, notwithstanding the fact that the divorce decree is not a judgment which falls within the material scope of the Conventions.[295]

9.4.3.5.3 Whereas Article 27(3) obviously deals with the situation where a foreign judgment is irreconcilable with a judgment given in the State in which recognition or enforcement is sought (for example, where a judgment creditor seeks to enforce in England a foreign judgment which is irreconcilable with an English judgment), the wording of this paragraph does not appear to cover the situation where the courts of two Contracting States have rendered irreconcilable judgments and recognition or enforcement of one of the judgments is sought in a third Contracting State. Since it is impossible for a English court to recognise or enforce two conflicting judgments—and it would be inappropriate to refuse recognition or enforcement to both—a means has to be found for deciding which judgment is to take priority. In the situation where both judgments are *prima facie* entitled to recognition or enforcement the obvious solution is for the court of the State in which recognition or enforcement is sought to favour the first judgment, rather than any subsequent judgment. This is the rule adopted by Article 27(5) in cases where there is a conflict between a judgment obtained in a Contracting State and a judgment granted in a non-contracting State. While there appears to be consensus as to the appropriate solution its legal basis is less certain. One possibility is to adopt a liberal interpretation of Article 27(3) so that judgments "given" in a Contracting State include not only judgments granted by the courts of that State, but

292. See paras. 5.6 and 5.9.
293. See the discussion of this issue in relation to Article 21 at para. 5.9.2.2.
294. Case 145/86 *Hoffmann* v. *Krieg* [1988] ECR 645, 668 (para. 22).
295. Case 145/86 *Hoffmann* v. *Krieg* [1988] ECR 645. Briggs, (1988) 8 YBEL 265; Hartley, (1991) 16 ELRev 64.

also judgments granted by the courts of other countries which are entitled to recognition in that State. Alternatively, the doctrine of public policy might be pressed into service as the peg on which to hang the applicable principle.

9.4.3.6 Irreconcilability: Article 27(5)

9.4.3.6.1 Article 27(5) provides that a judgment given by the courts of a Contracting State shall be refused recognition "if the judgment is irreconcilable with an earlier judgment given in a non-contracting State involving the same cause of action and between the same parties, provided that this latter judgment fulfils the conditions necessary for its recognition in the State addressed".

9.4.3.6.2 The solution provided by Article 27(5) is relatively straightforward. If, for example, A sues B in New York for breach of contract and obtains a judgment ordering B to pay damages, and B subsequently obtains a declaration of non-liability from the Italian courts, the Italian judgment is not entitled to recognition in England under the Brussels Convention if the earlier New York judgment satisfies the conditions for recognition at common law. In the context of Article 27(5) the words "cause of action" should be interpreted in the same way as under Article 21.[296]

9.4.3.7 Irreconcilability: Article 27(4)

Article 1(2) provides that various family law matters—the status or legal capacity of natural persons, rights in property arising out of a matrimonial relationship, wills and succession—are excluded from the scope of the Conventions. Article 27(4) provides that a judgment shall be refused recognition:

> if the court of the State of origin, in order to arrive at its judgment, has decided a preliminary question concerning the status or legal capacity of natural persons, rights in property arising out of a matrimonial relationship, wills or succession in a way that conflicts with a rule of the private international law of the State in which the recognition is sought, unless the same result would have been reached by the application of the rules of private international law of that State.

It seems unlikely that Article 27(4) will arise frequently in the context of commercial disputes.

9.4.3.8 Appeals in the State of origin: Article 30

At common law a judgment is not entitled to recognition or enforcement in England unless it is final. There is no such requirement under the Conventions. However, Article 30 provides:

> A court of a Contracting State in which recognition is sought of a judgment given in another Contracting State may stay the proceedings if an ordinary appeal against the judgment has been lodged.
>
> A court of a Contracting State in which recognition is sought of a judgment given in Ireland or the United Kingdom may stay the proceedings if enforcement is suspended in the State of origin by reason of an appeal.

296. See para. 5.9.2.1.

Article 30 is concerned with the situation where a party, in the course of litigation, wishes to plead a judgment which has been given in another Contracting State but which has not yet become *res judicata*: "In order to remedy the inconvenience which would result if such judgment were reversed, Article 30 allows the court to stay the proceedings upon the principal issue of which it is seised, until the foreign judgment whose recognition is sought has become *res judicata* in the State in which it was given."[297]

9.4.3.8.1 ARTICLE 30(1): WHAT IS AN "ORDINARY APPEAL"?

While the idea behind Article 30 is apparent, there is a problem of interpretation surrounding the words "ordinary appeal". The Schlosser Report states that a "clearly defined distinction between ordinary and extraordinary appeals is nowhere to be found".[298] In *Industrial Diamond Supplies* v. *Riva*[299] the Court of Justice noted that "although in some States the distinction between 'ordinary' and 'extraordinary' appeals is based on the law itself, in other legal systems the classification is made primarily or even purely in the works of learned authors while in a third group of States this distinction is completely unknown".[300] Not surprisingly, therefore, the Court of Justice thought that the term "ordinary appeal" has to be given a Community meaning within the framework of the Convention itself.[301] The Court of Justice decided that a broad interpretation was appropriate:

> [A]ny appeal which is such that it may result in the annulment or the amendment of the judgment which is the subject matter of the procedure for recognition or enforcement according to the Convention and the lodging of which is bound, in the State in which the judgment was given, to a period which is laid down by the law and starts to run by virtue of that same judgment constitutes an "ordinary appeal" which has been lodged or may be lodged against a foreign judgment.[302]

9.4.3.8.2 ARTICLE 30(2): THE SPECIAL POSITION OF APPEALS IN IRELAND AND THE UNITED KINGDOM

Although the decision of the Court of Justice in *Industrial Diamond Supplies* v. *Riva* pre-dated the 1978 Accession Convention it was decided that the general approach taken in Article 30 was not suitable in relation to judgments given by the courts of Ireland and the United Kingdom. The Schlosser Report notes that no equivalent to the distinction between ordinary and extraordinary appeals can be found in common law systems.[303] So, by virtue of the second paragraph of Article 30, in cases involving the recognition of judgments given in Ireland or the United Kingdom, the court of the State in which recognition is sought may stay its proceedings in any case where an appeal in the State of origin has the effect of suspending enforcement of the judgment in that State.

297. Jenard Report, OJ 1979 C59/46–47.
298. OJ 1979 C59/129, para. 196(a). For a review of the approach adopted by the Contracting States see Schlosser Report, OJ 1979 C59/129–130, paras. 196–202.
299. Case 43/77 [1977] ECR 2175. Hartley, (1978) 3 ELRev 160.
300. Case 43/77 [1977] ECR 2175, 2187–2188 (para. 22).
301. Case 43/77 [1977] ECR 2175, 2188 (para. 27).
302. Case 43/77 [1977] ECR 2175, 2190–2191 (para. 42).
303. OJ 1979 C59/128, para. 195.

9.4.3.8.3 THE EXERCISE OF DISCRETION

The court of the State in which recognition is sought may stay its proceedings under Article 30 on the application of either of the parties or of its own motion. Article 30, however, provides no guidance as to the criteria which the court should apply when deciding whether or not to exercise its discretion to grant a stay. In the context of enforcement proceedings the Court of Justice has indicated that the court of the State in which enforcement is sought may, when considering an application for a stay under Article 38(1), take into account only arguments which the party against whom enforcement is authorised was unable to raise before the court of the State of origin.[304] It would be appropriate for the same approach to be adopted in the context of Article 30.

9.4.4 Enforcement of judgments

9.4.4.1 Introduction

9.4.4.1.1 The basic idea underlying the Conventions is that enforcement should go hand in hand with recognition. Accordingly, enforcement can be refused only if there is a ground for refusing recognition.[305] Nevertheless, within Title III there are detailed rules governing the procedure for the enforcement of judgments granted by the courts of Contracting States in civil and commercial matters. When the original Brussels Convention was being drafted the committee considered a number of possibilities: reference back to national laws, subject to certain rules of the Convention; ordinary contentious procedure; summary contentious procedure; or *ex parte* application. The committee decided to adopt a system for the whole Community based on an *ex parte* application.[306] One of the principles of the Conventions, therefore, is that the enforcement procedure is unified and simplified.[307]

9.4.4.1.2 As far as English law is concerned, the procedure outlined in the Conventions has been supplemented by the Civil Jurisdiction and Judgments Act 1982 and RSC, Order 71 which set out a registration scheme. Since the *exequatur* system for foreign judgments does not exist in the law of the United Kingdom, Article 31(2) provides that a judgment given in another Contracting State shall be enforced in England, Scotland or Northern Ireland where, on the application of any interested party, it has been registered for enforcement in that part of the United Kingdom.[308]

9.4.4.1.3 The basic procedure for enforcement of judgments under the Conventions can be divided into four elements: application for enforcement; the decision of the court whether or not to order enforcement; appeals against enforcement; appeals against a decision to refuse enforcement.[309]

304. Case C-183/90 *Van Dalfsen* v. *Van Loon* [1991] ECR-I 4743. See para. 9.4.4.4.2.3.
305. Jenard Report, OJ 1979 C59/47. See para. 9.4.4.3.
306. Jenard Report, OJ 1979 C59/47.
307. Almeida Cruz–Desantes Real–Jenard Report, OJ 1990 C189/38, para. 4.
308. Jenard–Möller Report, OJ 1990 C189/79, para. 68.
309. See Jenard Report, OJ 1979 C59/48.

9.4.4.2 Application for enforcement

9.4.4.2.1 THE APPLICATION

Article 31(1) provides that "[a] judgment given in a Contracting State and enforceable in that State shall be enforced in another Contracting State when, on the application of any interested party, it has been declared enforceable there". As regards enforcement in England, a judgment given in a Contracting State and enforceable in that State shall be enforced when, on the application of an interested party, it has been registered for enforcement in England.[310] An application for registration is submitted to the High Court.[311] Section 4 the Civil Jurisdiction and Judgments Act 1982 provides:

> (1) A judgment, other than a maintenance order,[312] which is the subject of an application under Article 31 of the 1968 Convention or of the Lugano Convention for its enforcement in any part of the United Kingdom shall, to the extent that its enforcement is authorised by the appropriate court, be registered in the prescribed manner in that court.
>
> In this subsection "the appropriate court" means the court to which the application is made in pursuance of Article 32 (that is to say the High Court . . .)
>
> (2) Where the judgment is registered under this section, the reasonable costs or expenses of and incidental to its registration shall be recoverable as if they were sums recoverable under the judgment.
>
> (3) A judgment registered under this section shall, for the purposes of its enforcement, be of the same force and effect, the registering court shall have in relation to its enforcement the same powers, and proceedings for or with respect to its enforcement may be taken, as if the judgment had originally been given by the registering court and had (where relevant) been entered.
>
> (4) Subsection (3) is subject to Article 39 (restriction on enforcement where appeal pending or time for appeal unexpired),[313] to section 7[314] and to any provision made by rules of court as to the manner in which and conditions subject to which a judgment registered under this section may be enforced.

The application for registration of a judgment under section 4 does not take the form of contentious proceedings; the application "shall be made *ex parte*".[315]

9.4.4.2.2 FORMALITIES

9.4.4.2.2.1 By way of general principle Article 33(1) provides that the procedure for making the application "shall be governed by the law of the State in which enforcement is sought". In commenting on this provision the Jenard Report states that reference must be made to the domestic law of the State in which enforcement is sought "for the particulars which the application must contain, the number of copies which must be submitted to the court, the authority to which the application must be submitted, also, where necessary, the language in which it must be drawn up, and whether a lawyer should be instructed to appear".[316] Indeed, "the law of the State in which enforcement is

310. Article 31(2).
311. Article 32(1).
312. The enforcement of maintenance orders, which is dealt with by section 5 of the 1982 Act, is beyond the scope of this work.
313. See para. 9.4.4.4.3.
314. Section 7 of the 1982 Act provides for the English court to award interest on a money judgment which is registered under the Act.
315. RSC, Order 71, r. 27.
316. OJ 1979 C59/49.

sought governs the entire procedure for making the application".[317] However, "[t]he law of the State in which enforcement is sought must ... conform to the aims of the Convention".[318]

9.4.4.2.2.2 In addition to the requirements of the national law, Article 33(2) provides that, as part of the application for an enforcement order, the applicant must "give an address for service of process within the area of jurisdiction of the court applied to".[319] The purpose of this requirement is twofold: (i) it enables the applicant to be informed quickly of the court's decision on the application; and (ii) it enables the defendant to institute an appeal.[320]

9.4.4.2.2.3 Two points arising out of Article 33 were considered by the Court of Justice in *Carron* v. *Federal Republic of Germany*.[321]

(i) The Court of Justice decided that "[w]here the law of the State in which enforcement is sought does not indicate the exact time at which an address for service is to be given, it must be held, in accordance with the aims of the Convention, that it must be given sufficiently early to ensure that the proceedings are not improperly delayed and that the rights of the party against whom enforcement is sought are safeguarded. At the latest it must be given when the decision authorising enforcement is served".[322]

(ii) The Court of Justice decided that "inasmuch as the Convention provides no sanction for failure to comply with Article 33 the sanction must, like the other procedural rules referred to in that Article, be determined by the law of the State in which enforcement is sought".[323] An important qualification was, however, added to this principle: any sanction imposed by the law of the State in which enforcement is sought "may neither cast doubt on the validity of the enforcement order nor in any way prejudice the rights of the party against whom enforcement is sought".[324]

9.4.4.2.2.4 Article 33(3) requires the applicant to attach to his application the documents required by Articles 46 and 47. These are:

(i) a copy of the judgment which satisfies the conditions necessary to establish its authenticity[325];

(ii) in the case of a judgment given in default, the original or a certified true copy of the document which establishes that the party in default was served with the document instituting the proceedings or with an equivalent document[326];

(iii) documents which establish that, according to the law of the State of origin, the judgment is enforceable and has been served[327];

317. Case 198/85 *Carron* v. *Federal Republic of Germany* [1986] ECR 2437, 2445 (para. 10).
318. Case 198/85 *Carron* v. *Federal Republic of Germany* [1986] ECR 2437, 2446 (para. 14).
319. Because furnishing an address for service is unknown in German law, Article 33(2) provides that "if the law of the State in which enforcement is sought does not provide for the furnishing of such an address, the applicant shall appoint a representative *ad litem*".
320. Jenard Report, OJ 1979 C59/50.
321. Case 198/85 [1986] ECR 2437.
322. Case 198/85 [1986] ECR 2437, 2445 (para. 10).
323. Case 198/85 [1986] ECR 2437, 2445 (para. 13).
324. Case 198/85 [1986] ECR 2437, 2446 (para. 14).
325. Article 46(1).
326. Article 46(2).
327. Article 47(1).

(iv) where appropriate, a document showing that the applicant is in receipt of legal aid in the State of origin.[328]

9.4.4.2.2.5 It would seem from the terms of Title III that if the person seeking an enforcement order is unable to produce a copy of the judgment (as required by Article 46(1)) or documents establishing that the judgment is enforceable in the State of origin (as required by Article 47(1)) the court of the State in which enforcement is sought is simply required to refuse to authorise enforcement. However, the Jenard Report suggests that the court should not refuse the application in this situation—instead "the court may stay the proceedings and allow the applicant time to produce the documents".[329] Only if the documents produced are not sufficient and the court cannot obtain sufficient information should the application be rejected.

9.4.4.2.2.6 Article 48(1) provides that if the documents specified in Articles 46(2) and 47(2) are not produced, "the court may specify a time for their production, accept equivalent documents or, if it has sufficient information before it, dispense with their production". The court may also require a translation of the relevant documents, certified by a person qualified to do so in one of the Contracting States.[330] Finally, Article 49 provides that Contracting States are not permitted to impose a requirement of "legalisation or other similar formality" in respect of the documents referred to in Articles 46 to 48.[331]

9.4.4.2.3 SECURITY FOR COSTS

One of the general principles of European Community law is that Member States should not discriminate against citizens of other Member States on the basis of nationality.[332] RSC, Order 71, rule 29—which implements Article 45—provides that, notwithstanding the provisions of RSC, Order 23, a party making an application under section 4 of the 1982 Act "shall not be required solely on the ground that he is not domiciled or resident within the jurisdiction, to give security for costs of the application". This provision does not, of course, prevent the court from requiring an applicant to give security in cases where there are appropriate reasons other than the applicant's nationality, domicile or residence.

9.4.4.3 The decision

9.4.4.3.1 The court's decision is based entirely on the *ex parte* application of the person seeking enforcement of the foreign judgment: "the party against whom enforcement is sought shall not at this stage of the proceedings be entitled to make any submissions on the application".[333] The insistence on the application for enforcement being *ex parte* is to maintain the element of surprise which is necessary to ensure that the judgment debtor

328. Article 47(2).
329. OJ 1979 C59/50.
330. Article 48(2).
331. The formal requirements of Article 33, and Articles 46 to 49 are translated into English law by means of RSC, Order 71, r. 28.
332. Treaty of Rome, Article 7.
333. Article 34(1).

is not given an opportunity of withdrawing his assets from the jurisdiction.[334] It is also provided that the court applied to shall give its decision without delay.[335] The second and third paragraphs of Article 34 provide:

> The application may be refused only for one of the reasons specified in Articles 27 and 28. Under no circumstances can a judgment be reviewed as to its substance.

9.4.4.3.2 Article 34(3) reiterates the rule contained in Article 29[336] and requires no further comment. The second paragraph is, however, potentially misleading. Since there can be no enforcement of a judgment which is not entitled to recognition, it is entirely unexceptionable that Article 34(2) provides that the grounds in Articles 27 and 28 are an effective bar to enforcement of a foreign judgment under Title III. However, it would be wrong to think that these are the only grounds on which registration in England of judgments granted by the courts of other Contracting States may be refused. Three important points should be recalled.

(i) The material scope of the Conventions is limited to civil and commercial matters as defined by Title I. So, enforcement will be refused if the court of the State in which enforcement is sought decides that the judgment is not within the scope of Title I, whether or not the court of the State of origin assumed jurisdiction over the defendant under the direct jurisdiction provisions contained in Title II.

(ii) Certain court orders (such as procedural orders[337] and *ex parte* injunctions[338]) are not "judgments" for the purposes of Article 25 and therefore are not enforceable.[339]

(iii) It is made clear in Article 33(3) that for a foreign judgment to be enforced under Title III it must be enforceable in the State of origin. So, "[i]f a judgment from which an appeal still lies or against which an appeal has been lodged in the State in which it was given cannot be provisionally enforced in that State, it cannot be enforced in the State in which enforcement is sought".[340] Nevertheless, there is no general requirement that the judgment should be *res judicata* in order to be enforceable.[341] If under the law of the State of origin an appeal does not suspend the enforceability of the judgment, it is enforceable in the other Contracting States.

9.4.4.3.3 If the High Court gives leave for the judgment to be registered under section 4 of the 1982 Act the order for registration must be drawn up by or on behalf of the party making the application for registration[342] in the proper form. The order must state the period within which an appeal may be made against the order and state that the

334. Jenard Report, OJ 1979 C59/50.
335. Article 34(1).
336. See para. 9.4.3.1.
337. *CFEM Façades SA* v. *Bovis Construction Ltd* [1992] ILPr 561.
338. Case 125/79 *Denilauer* v. *Snc Couchet Frères* [1980] ECR 1553; *EMI Records Ltd* v. *Modern Music Karl-Ulrich Walterbach GmbH* [1992] QB 115.
339. See para. 9.4.1.2.
340. Jenard Report, 1979 C59/48.
341. Case C-183/90 *Van Dalfsen* v. *Van Loon* [1991] ECR-I 4743, 4774 (para. 28).
342. RSC, Order 71, r. 30(1).

judgment cannot be executed before the expiry of that period.[343] If registration is ordered the party against whom enforcement is sought must be notified.[344]

9.4.4.4 Appeals against registration

9.4.4.4.1 THE FIRST APPEAL

If a judgment given in a Contracting State is registered under section 4 of the 1982 Act, the judgment debtor may appeal against this decision to the High Court.[345] Since the appeal takes the form of contentious proceedings the applicant must be summoned to appear. The appeal "must be made by summons to a judge".[346] The summons must be served within the period specified by Article 36. The general rule is that an appeal must be lodged within one month of the date of service of the notice of registration.[347] However, if the party against whom enforcement is authorised is domiciled in a Contracting State other than that in which the decision authorising enforcement was given, the time for appealing is two months from the date of service of the notice of registration.[348] In relation to a judgment debtor who is not domiciled in a Contracting State the Jenard Report suggests that a certain amount of flexibility as regards time limits might be appropriate: "if the party is domiciled outside the Community, the period within which an appeal may be lodged runs from the date when the decision is served or is deemed to have been served according to the law of the State in which the decision was given. In this case the period of one month may be extended on account of distance in accordance with the law of that State".[349] English law provides that where the person against whom enforcement is sought is not domiciled in a Contracting State if "an application is made within two months of service of notice of registration, the court may extend the period within which an appeal may be made against the order for registration".[350]

9.4.4.4.2 THE EFFECT OF AN APPEAL PENDING BEFORE THE COURT OF THE STATE OF ORIGIN

9.4.4.4.2.1 Where an appeal is brought under Article 37(1), Article 38(1) provides that the court of the State in which enforcement is sought may stay the proceedings if an "ordinary appeal"[351] has been lodged against the judgment in the State of origin or if the time for such an appeal has not yet expired. If an appeal has not yet been lodged the court of the State in which enforcement is sought may specify the time within which such an appeal is to be lodged.[352] If, however, the time for the bringing of an appeal in the

343. RSC, Order 71, r. 30(2).
344. For details of the notice of registration see RSC, Order 71, r. 32.
345. Article 37(1).
346. RSC, Order 71, r. 33(1). A precedent it to be found in O'Malley & Layton, *European Civil Practice* (1989) pp. 1904–1905, para. A4.4 ("Summons on appeal to the judge against the grant of an order for registration of a judgment given in another Contracting State").
347. Article 36(1); RSC, Order 71, r. 33(2).
348. Article 36(2); RSC, Order 71, r. 33(2).
349. OJ 1979 C59/51.
350. RSC, Order 71, r. 33(3).
351. For the meaning of "ordinary appeal" see para. 9.4.3.8.1. As regards judgments given in Ireland and the United Kingdom Article 38(2) provides that an "ordinary appeal" in this context means "any form of appeal".
352. Article 38(1).

State of origin has expired, there can be no question of a stay being granted under Article 38(1).[353] As the right to bring an appeal pursuant to Article 37(1) vests exclusively in the judgment debtor,[354] it is the judgment debtor who is entitled to apply for a stay. Where an appeal has been brought in the State of origin Article 38(3) permits the court of the State in which enforcement is sought to make enforcement "conditional on the provision of such security as it shall determine". Article 38(3) does not, however, enable a court to order the applicant to provide security pending its own decision on the appeal against enforcement.[355]

9.4.4.4.2.2 So, in cases where an appeal has been lodged against the judgment in the State of origin—or the time for such an appeal has not yet expired—Article 38(1) gives the court of the State in which enforcement is sought a broad range of options: the court may stay the proceedings (unconditionally or subject to terms); or authorise enforcement (with or without conditions); or, in appropriate cases, specify the time within which the defendant must lodge his appeal before the courts of the State of origin.[356] Any decision taken by the court of the State in which enforcement is sought under Article 38(1) is final, there being no right of appeal under Article 37(2).[357]

9.4.4.4.2.3 The purpose of Article 38(1) is to enable the court of the State in which enforcement is sought "to stay the proceedings whenever reasonable doubt arises with regard to the fate of the decision in the State in which it was given".[358] However, the effect of Article 38(1) is that "the court before which recognition or enforcement is sought is not under a duty to stay the proceedings but merely has the power to do so".[359] In *Van Dalfsen* v. *Van Loon*[360] the Court of Justice held that, since it provides an exception to the general principle that a judgment which is enforceable in the State of origin is entitled to enforcement in other Contracting States, Article 38(1) should be interpreted strictly.[361] In view of the fact that in no circumstances may the foreign judgment be reviewed on the merits,[362] the court of the State in which enforcement is sought may not, when considering whether or not to grant a stay of enforcement proceedings under Article 38(1), take account of arguments which were raised before the court of the State of origin,[363] or of the merits of the appeal brought by the judgment debtor in the State of origin.[364] Similarly, the scheme of Title III precludes the court of the State in which enforcement is sought from considering arguments which could have been raised, but which were not raised before the court of the State of origin.[365] The arguments which the court may take into account for the purposes of Article 38(1) are "only such submissions as the appellant was unable to put before the court of the State

353. See *Noirhomme* v. *Walklate* [1992] 1 Lloyd's Rep 427.

354. Case 148/84 *Deutsche Genossenschaftsbank* v. *SA Brasserie du Pêcheur* [1985] ECR 1981.

355. Case 258/83 *Calzaturificio Brennero sas* v. *Wendel GmbH Schuhproduktion International* [1984] ECR 3971. Hartley, (1986) 11 ELRev 95; Lipstein, "Enforcement of Judgments under the Jurisdiction and Judgments Convention: Safeguards" (1987) 36 ICLQ 873.

356. Jenard Report, 1979 C59/52. Kaye, "Stay of Enforcement Proceedings under the European Judgments Convention: Factors Relevant to the Exercise of Discretion" [1991] JBL 261.

357. Case C-183/90 *Van Dalfsen* v. *Van Loon* [1991] ECR-I 4743, 4774 (para. 25).

358. Case 43/77 *Industrial Diamond Supplies* v. *Riva* [1977] ECR 2175, 2189 (para. 33).

359. Case 43/77 *Industrial Diamond Supplies* v. *Riva* [1977] ECR 2175, 2189 (para. 32).

360. Case C-183/90 [1991] ECR-I 4743. Briggs, (1991) 11 YBEL 530.

361. Case C-183/90 [1991] ECR-I 4743, 4775 (para. 30).

362. Article 34(3).

363. Case C-183/90 *Van Dalfsen* v. *Van Loon* [1991] ECR-I 4743, 4775 (para. 33).

364. Case C-183/90 *Van Dalfsen* v. *Van Loon* [1991] ECR-1 4743, 4775 (para. 32).

365. Case C-183/90 *Van Dalfsen* v. *Van Loon* [1991] ECR-I 4743, 4776 (para. 36).

in which the judgment was given".[366] The relevant factors are: (i) the fact that the foreign judgment has been appealed against, (ii) the admissibility or inadmissibility of the appeal lodged before the court of the State of origin, (iii) the nature of the injury which would be inflicted on the judgment debtor in the event of complete enforcement—and whether the injury would be irreversible—and (iv) whether protective measures would be sufficient from the judgment creditor's point of view if the enforcement proceedings were stayed.[367]

9.4.4.4.2.4 It is clear, therefore, that Article 38(1) does not allow judgment debtors to frustrate the enforcement process simply by bringing an appeal against the judgment in the State of origin. Since a judgment obtained in a Contracting State is *prima facie* enforceable, it would be wholly inappropriate for the court of the State in which enforcement is sought to adopt a general practice of depriving a successful plaintiff of the fruits of the judgment by the imposition of a more or less automatic stay, merely on the ground that there is a pending appeal. Following the decision of the Court of Justice in *Van Dalfsen* v. *Van Loon* it is to be expected that a stay of enforcement proceedings under Article 38(1) will be a relatively rare occurrence. Nevertheless, Article 38(1) requires the court of the State in which enforcement is sought to strike a balance between the interests of the judgment creditor and those of the judgment debtor. It would be wrong if, as a result of allowing unconditional enforcement, the court were to place the judgment debtor in a position such that he is unable to reverse the effects of enforcement. If the refusal of a stay would cause extreme hardship to the judgment debtor and the position of the judgment creditor can be protected by the grant of protective measures, the proper course for the court to take is to grant a stay of the enforcement proceedings pending the outcome of the appeal in the State of origin.[368]

9.4.4.4.3 LIMITATIONS ON ENFORCEMENT

9.4.4.4.3.1 Since the application for enforcement is made *ex parte*, it would be unfair if, immediately on registration under section 4 of the 1982 Act, the foreign judgment could be enforced by the judgment creditor without the judgment debtor being given the opportunity of being heard. Article 39, which deals with the period immediately following the determination of the application for enforcement, contains two very important rules which seek to achieve a fair balance between the interests of the parties.[369]

(i) Article 39(1) provides that "[d]uring the time specified for an appeal pursuant to Article 36 and until such an appeal has been determined, no measures of enforcement may be taken other than protective measures taken against the property of the party against whom enforcement is sought". The protective measures which the applicant may obtain are those which are available under the law of the State in which enforcement is sought. It is important that during this initial period no irreversible measures of execution are taken against the judgment debtor.

(ii) Article 39(2) provides that the decision authorising enforcement (which in the

366. Case C-183/90 *Van Dalfsen* v. *Van Loon* [1991] ECR-I 4743, 4777 (para. 37).

367. Advocate-General Van Gerven in Case C-183/90 *Van Dalfsen* v. *Van Loon* [1991] ECR-I 4743, 4763 (para. 19).

368. *Petereit* v. *Babcock International Holdings Ltd* [1990] 1 WLR 350.

369. The substance of Article 39 is translated into English law by RSC, Order 71, r. 34.

English context is the registration of the judgment under section 4 of the 1982 Act) "shall carry with it the power to proceed to ... protective measures [against the property of the party against whom enforcement is sought]". This means that the applicant may obtain protective measures *ex parte* before the defendant is informed of the court's decision to allow registration of the judgment. The Jenard Report stresses the importance of the availability of protective measures at the outset of the enforcement process; the applicant "must be able to take quickly all measures necessary to prevent the judgment debtor from removing the assets on which execution is to be levied".[370]

9.4.4.4.3.2 The relationship between Article 39 and the law of the State in which enforcement is sought was considered by the Court of Justice in *Capelloni* v. *Pelkmans*.[371] It is obvious that Article 39 is far from being a comprehensive code; for example, it does not give a list of the types of protective measures which may be taken, the kind and value of the property to which such measures may relate, the requirements for validity of the measures (such as whether the judgment creditor may carry out the measures himself or whether he is required to act through the medium of an officer of the court or other agent), the procedure for enforcing them and for verifying that they are in due form. Nevertheless, the power to grant protective measures is not a matter which is governed entirely by the procedural rules of the law of the State in which enforcement is sought.

9.4.4.4.3.3 Although the task of settling any matter which is not the subject of specific provisions in the Conventions is left to the procedural law of the court of the State in which enforcement is sought, the application of that law must not have the effect of contravening the principles laid down, whether expressly or by implication, by the Conventions.[372] In certain circumstances, therefore, the procedural law of the State in which enforcement is sought will have to yield to the requirements of the regime established by the Conventions; whether a particular procedural rule is applicable depends on the content of the provision and its compatibility with the principles enshrined in Article 39.[373] For example, "a judgment creditor on an application for protective measures cannot be required to prove or even make out a *prima facie* case on the merits, even if he might otherwise have to do so under national law apart from the Convention".[374]

9.4.4.4.3.4 Under English law equitable remedies, including injunctions, are discretionary. Moreover, the Rules of the Supreme Court do not specify the circumstances in which protective measures under Article 39(1) should be granted; the Rules of the Supreme Court state merely that the fact that an appeal against registration has the effect of suspending execution of the judgment shall not "prevent the court from granting protective measures pending final determination of any issue relating to enforcement of the judgment".[375] Nevertheless, it would appear that the Conventions have created a situation in which the court no longer has a discretion whether to allow

370. OJ 1979 C59/52.
371. Case 119/84 [1985] ECR 3147. Hartley, (1986) 11 ELRev 96.
372. Case 119/84 *Capelloni* v. *Pelkmans* [1985] ECR 3147, 3159–3160 (paras. 20–21).
373. Case 119/84 *Capelloni* v. *Pelkmans* [1985] ECR 3147, 3160 (para. 21).
374. Advocate-General Slynn in Case 119/84 *Capelloni* v. *Pelkmans* [1985] ECR 3147, 3150.
375. RSC, Order 71, r. 34(4).

protective measures.[376] Where a judgment debtor appeals against registration of a judgment under section 4 of the 1982 Act, the logic of the scheme established by Title III is that the English court is obliged by Article 39 to grant a Mareva-type injunction—up to the value of the plaintiff's unsatisfied judgment—in respect of the defendant's assets. This was the solution adopted in Ireland in *Elwyn (Cottons) Ltd* v. *Pearle Designs Ltd*[377] (albeit in a different domestic statutory framework). In this case the plaintiff, having obtained a judgment in England, applied both for its enforcement and for protective measures in the form of an order restraining the defendant from reducing its assets below a sum equivalent to the judgment debt. On an appeal against the decision of the Master refusing to grant the protective measures requested by the plaintiff Carroll J, having considered the Court of Justice's decision in *Capelloni* v. *Pelkmans*, concluded that, since the measure applied for was one which the court had power to grant in respect of proceedings within its jurisdiction, the court was not entitled to refuse the order sought.[378]

9.4.4.4.3.5 If the court determines the appeal brought by the judgment debtor pursuant to Article 36 in the applicant's favour—thereby confirming registration of the foreign judgment—Article 39 ceases to have any limiting effect and the applicant may, on satisfying the relevant procedural requirements,[379] proceed to execution.

9.4.4.4.4 A FURTHER APPEAL ON A POINT OF LAW

9.4.4.4.4.1 Once the High Court has resolved the judgment debtor's appeal against registration there is a further right of appeal, which—depending on the outcome of the first appeal—may be brought either by the judgment debtor or the judgment creditor. Article 37(2) provides that the decision of the High Court in the first appeal, which is referred to as the "judgment given on appeal", may be contested only by a "single further appeal on a point of law" (the final appeal). The mechanics of the final appeal are set out in section 6 of the 1982 Act. The effect of section 6 is that, as a general rule, the final appeal will be heard by the Court of Appeal. However, in exceptional circumstances, the final appeal may be directed to the House of Lords by the leap-frog procedure established by Part II of the Administration of Justice Act 1969.

9.4.4.4.4.2 The scope of the final appeal provided for by Article 37(2) has been strictly limited by the Court of Justice. The final appeal relates only to the judgment given on appeal brought under Article 37(1)—that is, the decision ruling on the merits of an appeal lodged against a decision authorising the enforcement of a foreign judgment.[380] Article 37(2) does not permit an appeal either against interlocutory orders made by the court of the State in which enforcement is sought in the context of the enforcement procedure[381] or against decisions taken by the court of the State in which enforcement is sought under Article 38 (such as a decision to refuse to stay enforcement proceedings

376. Jenard Report, OJ 1979 C59/52.

377. [1990] ILPr 40. See Hogan, "The Judgments Convention and Mareva Injunctions in the United Kingdom and Ireland" (1989) 14 ELRev 191, 200–204.

378. [1990] ILPr 40, 42.

379. RSC, Order 71, r. 34(3)

380. Case C-183/90 *Van Dalfsen* v. *Van Loon* [1991] ECR-I 4743, 4772 (para. 21).

381. Case 258/83 *Calzaturificio Brennero sas* v. *Wendel GmbH Schuhproduktion International* [1984] ECR 3971. Hartley, (1986) 11 ELRev 95; Lipstein, "Enforcement of Judgments under the Jurisdiction and Judgments Convention: Safeguards" (1987) 36 ICLQ 873.

pending the outcome of an appeal in the State of origin).[382] Even if the decision on the application under Article 38 is contained in the same judgment as the decision on the merits of the appeal against authorisation of enforcement, there is no right of appeal under Article 37(2) against the decision taken under Article 38.[383] Moreover, it is only the judgment debtor who can bring the final appeal under Article 37(2); no appeal can be brought by an interested third party.[384]

9.4.4.5 Appeals against a decision to refuse enforcement

9.4.4.5.1 AN APPEAL AGAINST A REFUSAL TO REGISTER

9.4.4.5.1.1 If, on the original *ex parte* application, the court of the State in which enforcement is sought refuses to order enforcement of the foreign judgment, the applicant may appeal to the court specified by Article 40(1); as regards the enforcement of judgments in England the High Court is the specified forum. Article 40(2) provides that the judgment debtor is to be summoned to appear and, if he fails to do so, the second and third paragraphs of Article 20[385] shall apply even if he is not domiciled in a Contracting State. In England an appeal under Article 40 "must be made by summons to a judge".[386] The time limit for bringing such an appeal is one month from the determination of the application for registration.[387]

9.4.4.5.1.2 The requirement that the appeal proceedings under Article 40 must be contentious has been strictly interpreted by the Court of Justice.[388] Even if the judgment creditor's application for enforcement under Article 32(1) is rejected on purely formal grounds (for example, because of the judgment creditor's failure to produce the documents required by Articles 46 and 47) the appeal under Article 40 must be in the form of contentious proceedings, notwithstanding the fact that, by allowing the judgment debtor's participation, the enforcement proceedings are deprived of any element of surprise.

9.4.4.5.2 A FURTHER RIGHT TO APPEAL ON A POINT OF LAW

Just as there is an appeal on a point of law under Article 37(2) against an appeal pursuant to Article 37(1), Article 41 provides for a single further appeal on a point of law against an appeal decided under Article 40. The final appeal may be brought either by the judgment creditor or the judgment debtor—depending on the outcome of the original appeal. As regards enforcement proceedings in England, the Court of Appeal will normally be the forum for appeals under Article 41.[389]

382. Case C-183/90 *Van Dalfsen* v. *Van Loon* [1991] ECR-I 4743.
383. Case C-183/90 *Van Dalfsen* v. *Van Loon* [1991] ECR-I 4743, 4772 (para. 22–25).
384. Case C-172/91 *Sonntag* v. *Waidmann* [1993] ILPr 466, 487–488 (para. 34–35).
385. See para. 4.4.1.
386. RSC, Order 71, r. 33(1).
387. RSC, Order 71, r. 33(2)(b).
388. *Firma P* v. *Firma K* (Case 178/83) [1984] ECR 3033. Hartley, (1985) 10 ELRev 233.
389. Civil Jurisdiction and Judgments Act 1982, s. 6.

9.4.4.6 Legal aid

Article 44(1) provides:

An applicant who, in the State of origin, has benefited from complete or partial legal aid or exemption from costs or expenses, shall be entitled, in the procedures provided for in Articles 32 to 35, to benefit from the most favourable legal aid or the most extensive exemption from costs or expenses provided for by the law of the State addressed.

It should be noted that the extension of legal aid applies only to the original application for enforcement and not to the appeal procedures. This provision is of most significance in cases involving the enforcement of maintenance obligations and is likely to be relatively unimportant in the context of commercial disputes.

9.4.5 Authentic instruments and court settlements

Title IV makes provision for the enforcement of authentic instruments and court settlements in the same way as judgments. Since 1 April 1993 the scheme for the enforcement of judgments contained in the Civil Jurisdiction and Judgments Act 1982 has been applicable to authentic instruments and court settlements falling within the scope of Articles 50 and 51 of the Conventions.[390]

9.4.5.1 Authentic instruments

9.4.5.1.1 The original Brussels Convention broke new ground in formulating rules for the enforcement of authentic instruments.[391] An authentic instrument is a document which is drawn up by a public officer, signed by the parties and witnessed by the public officer. An authentic instrument has a status which is different from an ordinary contract; it is a formal record of the transaction in question and it enables the creditor of the obligations set out in the instrument to proceed to execution without having to obtain a judgment from the court.

9.4.5.1.2 Article 50 provides that the procedure for the enforcement of judgments is equally applicable to the enforcement of authentic instruments:

A document which has been formally drawn up or registered as an authentic instrument and is enforceable in one Contracting State shall, in another Contracting State, be declared enforceable there, on application made in accordance with the procedures provided for in Articles 31 *et seq.* The application may be refused only if enforcement of the instrument is contrary to the public policy of the State addressed.

The instrument produced must satisfy the conditions necessary to establish its authenticity in the State of origin.

The provisions of Section 3 of Title III shall apply as appropriate.

The application of Article 50 of the Brussels Convention appears to be relatively uncommon.[392] Article 50 was, however, included in the Lugano Convention, even though among the EFTA Member States the concept of an authentic instrument is

390. Civil Jurisdiction and Judgments (Authentic Instruments and Court Settlements) Order 1993, SI 1993 No. 604.

391. Jenard Report, OJ 1979 C59/56.

392. Jenard–Möller Report, OJ 1990 C189/80, para. 72. But see Case 148/84 *Deutsche Genossenschaftsbank* v. *SA Brasserie du Pêcheur* [1985] ECR 1981.

found only in Austrian law.[393] There is no equivalent to an authentic instrument in English law.

9.4.5.1.3 The Reports which accompany the Conventions set out the conditions which must be fulfilled by an instrument in order to be regarded as authentic within the meaning of Article 50: (i) the authenticity of the instrument should have been established by a public authority; (ii) this authenticity should relate to the content of the instrument and not only, for example, the signature; (iii) the instrument has to be enforceable in itself in the State of origin.[394]

9.4.5.2 Court settlements

Article 51 applies the regime which governs authentic instruments to court settlements:

> A settlement which has been approved by a court in the course of proceedings and is enforceable in the State in which it was concluded shall be enforceable in the State addressed under the same conditions as authentic instruments.

This provision was included in the original text of the Brussels Convention because under Dutch and German law a settlement which has been approved by a court in the course of proceedings is enforceable without further formality.[395] Settlements occurring outside courts (which are known in Danish law) do not fall within Article 51; likewise, commercial bills and cheques are not covered by Article 51.[396]

9.4.6 The relationship between national law and Titles III and IV

9.4.6.1 The exclusivity and autonomy of the Conventions

9.4.6.1.1 The procedure for enforcement set out in the Conventions is exclusive in the sense that judgments given in Contracting States which fall within the scope of the Conventions may be enforced only under Title III; a judgment creditor may not seek to rely on the common law. In *de Wolf* v. *Harry Cox BV*[397] the defendant had been ordered by the Belgian courts to pay the plaintiff various relatively trivial sums due under a contract. Although the Belgian judgment was entitled to enforcement in the Netherlands, the costs of enforcement under the Brussels Convention were considerably higher than under the Dutch Code of Civil Procedure. Could the judgment creditor side-step the enforcement provisions of the Brussels Convention and rely on Dutch law? The Court of Justice had no hesitation in answering this question in the negative. Neither the Advocate-General nor the Court of Justice was moved by the fact that the procedure laid down by the Convention might be more expensive. The quid pro quo for the advantages of the regime introduced by the Conventions is that the enforcement procedure in Title III must be strictly complied with: "nobody is entitled to invoke the principles of common law on the subject as a means of escaping the system laid down by the Convention, with which all the Contracting States must comply. The effect of the Convention cannot vary according to the Member States, for otherwise its

393. Jenard–Möller Report, OJ 1990 C189/80, para. 72.
394. Jenard–Möller Report, OJ 1990 C189/80, para. 72.
395. Jenard Report, OJ 1979 C59/56.
396. Jenard–Möller Report, OJ 1990 C189/80, para. 72.
397. Case 42/76 [1976] ECR 1759.

effectiveness and the uniformity of its application, which are essential, would be seriously jeopardised".[398]

9.4.6.1.2 In *Deutsche Genossenschaftsbank* v. *SA Brasserie du Pêcheur*[399] the Court of Justice stressed that one of the principal objectives of Title III is to simplify procedures in the State in which enforcement is sought: "In order to obtain that objective the Convention established an enforcement procedure which constitutes an autonomous and complete system, including the matter of appeals."[400] The procedure established by Title III is comprehensive and may not be supplemented by the domestic law of the Contracting State in which enforcement is sought.

9.4.6.2 Enforcement and execution

9.4.6.2.1 The Conventions regulate the procedure for obtaining an order for enforcement but do not deal with execution itself, which continues to be governed by the domestic law of the State in which execution is sought.[401] Consequently, a foreign judgment for which an enforcement order has been issued is executed in accordance with the procedural rules of the law of the country in which execution is sought, including its rules on legal remedies.[402]

9.4.6.2.2 The importance of the distinction between the enforcement and execution is revealed in *Noirhomme* v. *Walklate*.[403] In this case the plaintiff, having obtained a default judgment in Belgium, sought to enforce it in England. When the judgment was duly registered under section 4 of the 1982 Act, the defendant appealed against registration and sought a stay of execution so that he could investigate the possibility of an appeal in Belgium. At the time of the defendant's application for a stay no appeal was pending and it was assumed by the court (in the absence of any contrary evidence from the defendant) that the time for bringing an appeal in Belgium had expired. Accordingly, the defendant could not obtain a stay of enforcement proceedings under Article 38. The question then arose as to whether the court had the power to grant a stay of execution under RSC, Order 47, rule 1. Although the plaintiff argued that a stay could be granted only under Article 38, Judge Kershaw QC noted that by virtue of section 4(3) of the 1982 Act "when a judgment has been registered the English court has in relation to enforcement the same jurisdiction as if the judgment had been given in the registering court".[404] Accordingly, the power to stay under RSC, Order 47, rule 1—which provides that a stay of execution may be ordered if the court is satisfied that there are special circumstances which make enforcement of the judgment inexpedient—was potentially applicable. It was decided, however, that the circumstances in the present case were not such as to justify the grant of a stay.

9.4.6.2.3 The general principle that execution is left to the internal law of the State in which execution is sought is subject to an exception which was formulated in *Hoffmann*

398. Advocate-General Meyras, Case 42/76 [1976] ECR 1759, 1775.
399. Case 148/84 [1985] ECR 1981.
400. Case 148/84 [1985] ECR 1981, 1992 (para. 17).
401. Case 148/84 *Deutsche Genossenschaftsbank* v. *SA Brasserie du Pêcheur* [1985] ECR 1981, 1992 (para. 18); Case 119/84 *Capelloni* v. *Pelkmans* [1985] ECR 3147, 3159 (para. 16).
402. Case 145/86 *Hoffmann* v. *Krieg* [1988] ECR 645, 670 (para. 28).
403. [1992] 1 Lloyd's Rep 427.
404. [1992] 1 Lloyd's Rep 427, 431.

v. *Krieg*.[405] The Court of Justice noted that "the application, for the purposes of the execution of a judgment, of the procedural rules of the State in which enforcement is sought may not impair the effectiveness of the scheme of the Convention as regards enforcement orders".[406] Accordingly, as a general rule, a judgment debtor cannot rely on remedies available under the law of the State in which execution is sought "when an appeal against execution of a foreign judgment for which an enforcement order has been issued is lodged by the same person who could have appealed against the enforcement order and is based on an argument which could have been raised in such an appeal".[407] A judgment debtor should not normally be allowed to use defences to execution under the law of the State in which execution is sought as a way of avoiding the procedures and time limits established by the Conventions.[408]

9.5 RECOGNITION AND ENFORCEMENT OF JUDGMENTS WITHIN THE UNITED KINGDOM

9.5.1 Introduction

9.5.1.1 At common law judgments given by the courts of Scotland and Northern Ireland are foreign judgments. However, since the Judgments Extension Act 1868 there has been in existence a statutory regime designed to facilitate the reciprocal recognition and enforcement of judgments given within the United Kingdom. The Civil Jurisdiction and Judgments Act 1982 repealed all the earlier legislation and established a new regime, which is to be found in Part II of the Act; sections 18 and 19 (supplemented by Schedules 6 and 7 to the 1982 Act) deal with enforcement and recognition respectively.

9.5.1.2 In the context of commercial matters the scope of sections 18 and 19 is very wide. The regime for the recognition and enforcement of judgments given by the courts of the constituent parts of the United Kingdom extends to "any judgment or order (by whatever name called) given or made by a court of law in the United Kingdom,"[409] as well as to "any award or order made by a tribunal in any part of the United Kingdom which is enforceable in that part without an order of a court of law"[410] and to fines for contempt of court.[411] Section 18 also applies to arbitral awards.[412] There are, however, express exclusions from the scope of section 18, of which the most important are judgments given in the exercise of jurisdiction in relation to insolvency law, within the meaning of section 426 of the Insolvency Act 1986,[413] and provisional, including

405. Case 145/86 [1988] ECR 645.
406. Case 145/86 [1988] ECR 645, 670 (para. 29).
407. Case 145/86 [1988] ECR 645, 670 (para. 30).
408. The position is different, however, if—as in *Hoffmann* v. *Krieg* itself—the objection to execution raised by the judgment debtor is based on factors which are outside the material scope of the Conventions.
409. Civil Jurisdiction and Judgments Act 1982, s. 18(2)(a). Section 50 of the 1982 Act provides that a "court of law" includes: (i) in Northern Ireland—the Court of Appeal, the High Court, and a county court; (ii) in Scotland—the Court of Session and a sheriff court; and (iii) the House of Lords.
410. Civil Jurisdiction and Judgments Act 1982, s. 18(2)(d).
411. Civil Jurisdiction and Judgments Act 1982, s. 18(4)(b).
412. The recognition and enforcement of arbitral awards under the 1982 Act is discussed at para. 20.5.1.
413. Civil Jurisdiction and Judgments Act 1982, s. 18(3)(ba).

protective, measures (other than orders for the making of an interim payment).[414] Although the scope of section 19 is broadly the same as section 18,[415] there are a few additional minor exclusions.[416]

9.5.2 Recognition

9.5.2.1 The recognition in England of judgments given by the courts of Scotland and Northern Ireland is dealt with by section 19(1) which provides:

> A judgment to which this section applies given in one part of the United Kingdom shall not be refused recognition in another part of the United Kingdom solely on the ground that, in relation to that judgment, the court which gave it was not a court of competent jurisdiction according to the rules of private international law in force in that other part.

It is far from obvious what the effect of this provision is meant to be. Three points may, however, be noted.

(i) It is clear that the mere fact that the original court did not have jurisdiction in the private international law sense is not a basis of refusing recognition.
(ii) It is also clear that recognition of a judgment given in Scotland or Northern Ireland cannot be refused on the basis of section 32 of the 1982 Act.[417]
(iii) Although section 19(1) makes no reference to the problem of irreconcilable judgments, the 1982 Act provides that enforcement may be refused if the judgment given in another part of the United Kingdom conflicts with an earlier judgment given by a court of the country in which enforcement is sought.[418] There seems no obvious reason why recognition of a judgment should not be refused on the same basis.

9.5.2.2 This still leaves a number of questions unanswered. The literal wording of section 19(1)—in particular, the use of the word "solely"—suggests that a judgment given in Scotland or Northern Ireland may be refused recognition in England if the original court's lack of jurisdiction in the private international law sense is coupled with some other defence (such as fraud).[419] From the point of view of policy, however, this interpretation makes little sense and should be rejected. An alternative view is that, since Part II of the 1982 Act makes no mention of the common law defences other than lack of jurisdiction in the international sense, a judgment given in Scotland or Northern Ireland may be refused recognition if the judgment was procured by fraud or if the original proceedings involved a breach of natural justice or if recognition of the judgment is contrary to English public policy.[420] The somewhat surprising consequence of this alternative view, however, is that a judgment given in Scotland or Northern Ireland is more likely to be refused recognition than a judgment granted by the courts of a Brussels or Lugano Contracting State.

9.5.2.3 Although the present position cannot be regarded as anything other than

414. Civil Jurisdiction and Judgments Act 1982, s. 18(5)(d).
415. Civil Jurisdiction and Judgments Act 1982, s. 19(2).
416. Civil Jurisdiction and Judgments Act 1982, s. 19(3).
417. A judgment given in Scotland or Northern Ireland is not an "overseas judgment": Civil Jurisdiction and Judgments Act 1982, s. 50.
418. Civil Jurisdiction and Judgments Act 1982, Schedule 6, para. 10(b) and Schedule 7, para. 9(b).
419. Cheshire & North, *Private International Law* (12th ed, 1992) p. 395.
420. O'Malley & Layton, *European Civil Practice* (1989) p. 1001.

uncertain, it seems likely that the traditional common law defences based on natural justice, fraud and public policy are not available in cases falling within Part II of the 1982 Act. According to this view, the party against whom a judgment has been given has no alternative but to pursue his remedies, if any, before the courts of the country where the judgment was given.

9.5.3 Enforcement

9.5.3.1 Introduction

Although certain judgments which are enforceable under section 18 are excluded from the scope of section 19,[421] as a matter of general principle any defence which may be invoked against recognition of a judgment should also be available in the context of enforcement proceedings. Accordingly, a judgment given by the courts of Scotland or Northern Ireland should be refused enforcement in England not only in the circumstances expressly identified in section 18 (as supplemented by Schedules 6 and 7) but also to the extent that the judgment is not entitled to recognition.[422]

Section 18(1) provides:

In relation to any judgment to which this section applies—

(a) Schedule 6 shall have effect for the purpose of enabling any money provisions contained in the judgment to be enforced in a part of the United Kingdom other than the part in which the judgment was given; and

(b) Schedule 7 shall have effect for the purpose of enabling any non-money provisions so contained to be enforced.

The regime put in place by the 1982 Act is mandatory and exclusive; as regards those judgments falling within the scope of section 18, the only way in which the judgment of the courts of Scotland and Northern Ireland can be enforced is by registration under Schedule 6 or 7.[423] Where a single judgment contains both money provisions and non-money provisions, the money provisions must be registered under Schedule 6 and the non-money provisions under Schedule 7.

9.5.3.2 Money judgments: Schedule 6

9.5.3.2.1 The enforcement in England of a Scottish or Northern Irish money judgment (which is defined as a "provision for the payment of one or more sums of money"[424]) is effected by a system of registration. The basic scheme is for the person seeking enforcement to obtain a certificate from the court of the country of origin[425] and to register the certificate in the country where enforcement is sought. In England a register of certificates, under the direction of the senior master, is kept in the Central Office.[426]

9.5.3.2.2 The certificate will state the sum or aggregate of sums payable under the

421. Civil Jurisdiction and Judgments Act 1982, s.19(3).
422. See para. 9.5.2.
423. Civil Jurisdiction and Judgments Act 1982, s. 18(8). The regime is not, however, exclusive for arbitral awards within section 18(2)(e) of the Civil Jurisdiction and Judgments Act 1982. See para. 20.5.1.
424. Civil Jurisdiction and Judgments Act 1982, Schedule 6, para. 1.
425. Civil Jurisdiction and Judgments Act 1982, Schedule 6, para. 2.
426. RSC, Order 71, r. 39.

judgment (including interest on the judgment debt).[427] There are various circumstances in which a certificate cannot be issued:

(i) if the time for bringing an appeal has not expired; or
(ii) if an appeal has been brought and has not been finally determined; or
(iii) if enforcement of the judgment is stayed or suspended; or
(iv) if the time for enforcement of the judgment has expired.[428]

9.5.3.2.3 Once a certificate has been issued, any interested party may apply for registration in the High Court.[429] The application should be made by producing at the Central Office, within six months from the date of its issue, a certificate in the form prescribed by the Act along with a copy certified by the applicant's solicitor to be a true copy.[430] When the certificate is filed the certified copy, sealed by an officer of the office in which the certificate is filed, is returned to the applicant's solicitor.[431] The reasonable costs of obtaining a certificate and registering it are recoverable[432] and provision is made for the payment of interest on the judgment debt.[433] Once registered the judgment is of the same force and effect as if the judgment had been given by the registering court.[434]

9.5.3.2.4 It is expressly provided that (i) the court must set aside registration if registration is contrary to the provisions of Schedule 6 and (ii) the court may set aside registration if it is satisfied that the matter in dispute in the proceedings in which the judgment was given had previously been the subject of a judgment by another court having jurisdiction in the matter.[435] The court may stay proceedings for enforcement if it is satisfied that any person against whom enforcement is sought is entitled and intends to apply to have the judgment quashed or set aside in the country of origin.[436]

9.5.3.3 Non-money judgments: Schedule 7

9.5.3.3.1 Prior to the entry into force of the 1982 Act, it was not possible to enforce in England non-money judgments granted by the courts of Scotland and Northern Ireland. Since the Brussels Convention made provision for the recognition and enforcement of judgments irrespective of whether they are for a sum of money it was appropriate to reform the internal law of the United Kingdom. Schedule 7 to the 1982 Act sets out the procedure for the enforcement of non-money judgments (which are defined as provisions "for any relief or remedy not requiring payment of a sum of money"[437]). The procedure is broadly similar to that provided by Schedule 6.

9.5.3.3.2 The person seeking enforcement of a non-money judgment in England must

427. Civil Jurisdiction and Judgments Act 1982, Schedule 6, para. 4.
428. Civil Jurisdiction and Judgments Act 1982, Schedule 6, para. 3.
429. Civil Jurisdiction and Judgments Act 1982, Schedule 6, para. 5.
430. RSC, Order 71, r. 37(1).
431. RSC, Order 71, r. 37(2).
432. Civil Jurisdiction and Judgments Act 1982, Schedule 6, para. 7.
433. Civil Jurisdiction and Judgments Act 1982, Schedule 6, para. 8.
434. Civil Jurisdiction and Judgments Act 1982, Schedule 6, para. 6.
435. Civil Jurisdiction and Judgments Act 1982, Schedule 6, para. 10.
436. Civil Jurisdiction and Judgments Act 1982, Schedule 6, para. 9.
437. Civil Jurisdiction and Judgments Act 1982, Schedule 7, para. 1.

obtain a certified copy of the judgment from the court of the country of origin.[438] The certified copy, which cannot be issued if certain conditions are satisfied,[439] must include both any money provisions and any provisions which relate to matters which fall outside the scope of section 18 of the 1982 Act.[440] The application must be made to the High Court and must be accompanied by the certified copy of the judgment and a certificate in the prescribed form stating that the judgment is enforceable and that no appeal may be brought or is pending.[441] An application for registration of a non-money judgment may be made *ex parte*, but the court hearing the application may direct the issue of a summons.[442] Once registered in the High Court a non-money judgment has the same force and effect as if the judgment had been given by the English court.[443] The reasonable costs of obtaining a certified copy of the judgment and registering it are recoverable.[444]

9.5.3.3 Registration must be refused if compliance with the judgment would involve a breach of English law[445] and registration must be set aside if registration is contrary to Schedule 7.[446] The court may set aside registration if the subject matter of the proceedings which led to the judgment in question had previously been the subject of a judgment by another court having jurisdiction in the matter.[447] The court may stay proceedings for enforcement if it is satisfied that any person against whom enforcement is sought is entitled and intends to apply to have the judgment quashed or set aside in the country of origin.[448]

9.6 JUDGMENTS AGAINST STATES AND EUROPEAN COMMUNITY JUDGMENTS

9.6.1 Recognition of judgments given against the United Kingdom

9.6.1.1 The regime for the recognition of judgments given against the United Kingdom is contained in the State Immunity Act 1978. Section 18 provides for the recognition of judgments given against the United Kingdom by the courts of other States which are also party to the 1972 European Convention on State Immunity. In order for such a judgment to be entitled to recognition in England it must be final and it must have been given in proceedings in which the United Kingdom was not entitled to immunity by virtue of provisions corresponding to those of sections 2 to 11.[449]

9.6.1.2 There are, however, various defences to recognition. First, an English court may refuse to recognise a foreign judgment given against the United Kingdom if:

438. Civil Jurisdiction and Judgments Act 1982, Schedule 7, para. 2.
439. Civil Jurisdiction and Judgments Act 1982, Schedule 7, para. 3. The substance of this paragraph is the same as paragraph 3 of Schedule 6.
440. Civil Jurisdiction and Judgments Act 1982, Schedule 7, para. 4.
441. Civil Jurisdiction and Judgments Act 1982, Schedule 7, para. 5; RSC, Order 71, r. 38(2).
442. RSC, Order 71, r. 38(1).
443. Civil Jurisdiction and Judgments Act 1982, Schedule 7, para. 6.
444. Civil Jurisdiction and Judgments Act 1982, Schedule 7, para. 7.
445. Civil Jurisdiction and Judgments Act 1982, Schedule 7, para. 5(5).
446. Civil Jurisdiction and Judgments Act 1982, Schedule 7, para. 9.
447. Civil Jurisdiction and Judgments Act 1982, Schedule 7, para. 9.
448. Civil Jurisdiction and Judgments Act 1982, Schedule 7, para. 8.
449. State Immunity Act 1978, s. 18(1).

(i) to accord recognition would be manifestly contrary to public policy; or
(ii) any party to the original proceedings did not have an adequate opportunity to present his case; or
(iii) the judgment was given in circumstances in which the provisions corresponding to section 12 of the 1978 Act[450] were not complied with and the United Kingdom neither entered an appearance nor applied to have the judgment set aside.[451]

9.6.1.3 Secondly, an English court must refuse recognition if:

(i) proceedings between the same parties on the same issues are pending in the United Kingdom or in another State which is party to the 1972 Convention (as long as those proceedings were instituted first); or
(ii) there is an earlier inconsistent judgment of the courts of the United Kingdom or of another State which is party to the 1972 Convention; or
(iii) the foreign judgment concerns an interest of the United Kingdom in property and either an English court would not have regarded itself as having jurisdiction in such circumstances or an English court, applying English conflicts rules, would have arrived at a decision different from that of the foreign court.[452]

9.6.2 Recognition and enforcement of judgments given against other States

The 1978 Act does not deal with foreign judgments given against foreign States. Section 31(1) of the Civil Jurisdiction and Judgments Act 1982 provides:

A judgment given by a court of an overseas country against a State other than the United Kingdom or the State to which that court belongs shall be recognised and enforced in the United Kingdom, if and only if—
(a) it would be so recognised and enforced if it had not been given against a State; and
(b) that court would have had jurisdiction in the matter if it had applied rules corresponding to those applicable to such matters in the United Kingdom in accordance with sections 2 to 11 of the State Immunity Act 1978.[453]

This provision does not apply to judgments which are given in proceedings under international conventions and which are entitled to recognition or enforcement under the Foreign Judgments (Reciprocal Enforcement) Act 1933.[454]

9.6.3 European Community judgments

The European Communities (Enforcement of Community Judgments) Order 1972[455] provides the framework for the recognition and enforcement in the United Kingdom of judgments given by the Court of Justice of the European Communities and decisions of other institutions which impose monetary obligations on parties other than States. In practice, the recognition or enforcement of judgments or decisions in the United

450. See para. 2.3.6.
451. State Immunity Act 1978, s. 19(1).
452. State Immunity Act 1978, s. 19(2).
453. For a discussion of the scope of State Immunity Act 1978, ss. 2 to 11, see para. 2.3.4.
454. Civil Jurisdiction and Judgments Act 1982, s. 31(3).
455. SI 1972 No. 1590.

Kingdom under the 1972 Order is most likely to arise in relation to decisions of the Commission imposing fines or penalties, normally for breach of EC competition rules. A judgment or decision to which the 1972 Order relates is registered in the High Court and takes effect in the same way as a decision of the High Court.[456]

456. For the relevant procedure for enforcement see RSC, Order 71, rr. 15–24.

PART II

OBLIGATIONS

CHAPTER 10

CHOICE OF LAW IN CONTRACT: INTRODUCTION

10.0.1 The English choice of law rules relating to contractual obligations have recently undergone a revolution. For most practical purposes the period of common law development came to an abrupt halt on 1 April 1991, when the Rome Convention on the Law Applicable to Contractual Obligations was brought into force by the Contracts (Applicable Law) Act 1990 (Chapter 10).

10.0.2 The Rome Convention contains a number of general rules for determining the law applicable to contractual obligations—whether or not the parties have made a choice of law—as well as general provisions dealing with particular aspects of contractual obligations (Chapter 11). However, not all contracts are governed by these general rules. The Convention includes specific choice of law rules for certain types of contract and rules which are to be found outside the Convention apply to contracts which are excluded from its scope (Chapter 12).

10.0.3 There are not yet any reported instances of the English courts being called upon to consider the operation of the Convention. However, many of the issues which arise under the Convention are the same as—or similar to—issues considered by the courts in the context of the common law rules. Accordingly, in the chapters dealing with choice of law in contract some cases decided under the common law are used to illustrate the way in which the Convention is intended to work. Two points should be stressed, however.

(i) In some respects the similarity between the common law rules and the provisions of the Convention is more apparent than real; there are dangers in attempting to reason from the common law cases to a solution under the Convention.

(ii) It must be remembered that precedents decided in the context of the common law have no direct authority when considering questions of interpretation which arise under the Convention.

10.1 THE COMMON LAW

10.1.1 The development of choice of law rules in matters relating to contract has been described as "one of the great achievements of the English judiciary during the last 140 years".[1] The doctrine of the "proper law" of the contract reflects the doctrine of party

1. Mann, "The Proper Law of the Contract—an Obituary" (1991) 107 LQR 353. See also Nussbaum, *Principles of Private International Law* (1943) p. 168.

autonomy, the underlying basis of English contract law itself. The influence of the common law rules in other jurisdictions has been considerable, the English private international law of contracts "being recognised and followed in practically the whole world".[2]

10.1.2 At common law parties are free to choose the law governing their legal relationship. Furthermore, it would seem that, in practice, the choice need not have any connection with the contract. In *Vita Food Products Inc* v. *Unus Shipping Co Ltd*[3] the Privy Council upheld a choice of English law even though all the relevant factors were connected with Canada or the United States. In this case goods were shipped in Newfoundland under bills of lading which were expressed to be governed by English law. While in the course of carriage to New York the goods were damaged and the plaintiff sought to recover in proceedings in Nova Scotia. Neither party was English, nor was the ship. The only connection with England was that the vessel was insured through London brokers. The defendant sought to rely on an exclusion clause in the contract, which was valid by English law but void under the law of Newfoundland. The question was whether the court should uphold a choice of law which was unconnected with the transaction. The Privy Council decided that connection with the chosen law was not as a matter of principle essential. Lord Wright expressed the view that "where there is an express statement by the parties of their intention to select the law of the contract, it is difficult to see what qualifications are possible, provided the intention expressed is *bona fide* and legal, and provided there is no reason for avoiding the choice on the ground of public policy".[4] The precise scope of the proviso which limits the parties' freedom of choice has never been properly determined. It has been suggested that "too much has been made of Lord Wright's remark which reads like a 'throw-away' line".[5] In any event there is no reported case in which an English court has refused to uphold an express choice of law on the basis that it was *mala fide*, illegal or contrary to public policy.[6]

10.1.3 If the parties have not expressly chosen the governing law, the proper law of the contract is "the system of law by reference to which the contract was made or that with which the transaction has its closest and most real connection".[7] This formulation distinguishes implied choice ("the system of law by reference to which the contract was made") from cases in which the parties have made no choice (in which case the contract is governed by the objective proper law—that is, the law of the country "with which the transaction has its closest and most real connection").[8]

10.1.4 The combined effect of the decision in *Vita Food Products Inc* v. *Unus Shipping Co Ltd* and the *Bonython* formula is to produce a tripartite hierarchy of rules for determining the proper law of a contract.

(i) If the parties have made an express choice, the will of the parties is decisive (as

2. Mann, "The Proper Law of the Contract—an Obituary" (1991) 107 LQR 353.
3. [1939] AC 277.
4. [1939] AC 277, 290.
5. Collier, *The Conflict of Laws* (1987) p. 147.
6. See, however, *Golden Acres Ltd* v. *Queensland Estates Pty Ltd* [1969] Qd R 378. Kelly, "International Contracts and Party Autonomy" (1970) 19 ICLQ 701.
7. Lord Simonds in *Bonython* v. *Commonwealth of Australia* [1951] AC 201, 219.
8. Morris & Cheshire, "The Proper Law of a Contract in the Conflict of Laws" (1940) 56 LQR 320; Mann, "The Proper Law of the Contract" (1950) 3 ILQ 60; Morris, "The Proper Law of the Contract: A Rejoinder" (1950) 3 ILQ 197; Mann, "The Proper Law of the Contract: A Reply" (1950) 3 ILQ 597; Cohn, "The Objectivist Practice on the Proper Law of Contract" (1957) 6 ICLQ 373.

long as the choice is *bona fide*, legal and not contrary to public policy).

(ii) If there is no express choice, the parties may have impliedly chosen the proper law. The court may imply a choice of law from the nature of the contract (such as use of a Lloyd's form[9]) or from an arbitration clause[10] or a jurisdiction agreement.[11]

(iii) In the absence of express or implied choice, the objective proper law governs the contract.

In the early stages of development the English courts used to approach cases where there was no choice from the point of view of presumptions, such as the place of contracting, the place of performance or the flag of the ship. However, these presumptions lost favour and the courts adopted an approach based on a wide-ranging enquiry into all the relevant factors.

10.1.5 Although it was suggested by Lord Wilberforce that the second and third categories "merge into each other"[12] the conceptual distinction is clear:

> So long as the object of the court's inquiry is the intention of the parties, the language, terminology, form and terms of the contract will very often constitute a useful guide, bearing in mind that the search is for the system of law which they intended (or assumed) would govern their contract. However, once that search has been abandoned, the determination of the parties' intention (or assumption) with any degree of realism being impossible, resort must perforce be had to a purely objective test (as distinct from one based upon an "objectively" determined intention). Application of this purely objective test involves *geographical location* of the *transaction*. It is then actual or contemplated factual activity, rather than inference from the form, etc, of the contract which is most relevant.[13]

10.2 THE CONTRACTS (APPLICABLE LAW) ACT 1990[14]

10.2.1 Background and commencement

10.2.1.1 The goal of harmonising the private international law rules of the various Member States of the EC can be traced back to the late 1960s. The Brussels Convention of 1968 established uniform jurisdictional rules for the Member States; it does not, however, affect the choice of law process. Within the Community the idea took hold that the general goal of achieving legal certainty and predictability in commercial matters could not be achieved simply by the jurisdictional rules contained in the Brussels Convention—which in many cases give the plaintiff a choice as to the forum in

9. *Amin Rasheed Shipping Corporation* v. *Kuwait Insurance Co* [1984] AC 50.

10. *James Miller & Partners Ltd* v. *Whitworth Street Estates (Manchester) Ltd* [1970] AC 583; *Compagnie Tunisienne de Navigation SA* v. *Compagnie d'Armement Maritime SA* [1971] AC 572.

11. *The Komninos S* [1991] 1 Lloyd's Rep 370.

12. *Amin Rasheed Shipping Corporation* v. *Kuwait Insurance Co* [1984] AC 50, 69.

13. Carter, "Contracts in English Private International Law" (1986) 57 BYIL 1, 21–22. (Emphasis in original.)

14. In addition to the works referred to in para. 1.4 see: Diamond, "Conflict of Laws in the EEC" [1979] CLP 155; Hartley, "Beyond the Proper Law" (1979) 4 ELRev 236; Jaffey, "The English Proper Law Doctrine and the EEC Convention" (1984) 33 ICLQ 531; Lando, "The EEC Convention on the Law Applicable to Contractual Obligations" (1987) 24 CMLRev 159; Merkin, "Contracts (Applicable Law) Act 1990" [1991] JBL 205; Morse, "The EEC Convention on the Law Applicable to Contractual Obligations" (1982) 2 YBEL 107; North, "The EEC Convention on the Law Applicable to Contractual Obligations" [1980] JBL 382; Williams, "The EEC Convention on the Law Applicable to Contractual Obligations" (1986) 35 ICLQ 1; Young, "The Contracts (Applicable Law) Act 1990" [1991] LMCLQ 314.

which to pursue the defendant. If different countries apply different choice of law rules the outcome of a particular dispute may turn on whether proceedings are brought in one country rather than another.

10.2.1.2 Work on unification of choice of law rules started in the 1970s. Although the original draft convention dealt with both contractual and non-contractual obligations, those elements of the enterprise which concerned non-contractual obligations were dropped because of the wide divergences between the laws of the Member States. The Convention on the Law Applicable to Contractual Obligations was finally opened for signature in Rome in 1980. The Convention provided that it was to enter into force three months after the seventh ratification.[15] The Convention was ratified in the early 1980s by six States (Belgium, Denmark, France, Germany, Italy and Luxembourg) and implemented into domestic law by Germany and Denmark in advance of the Convention's coming into force. The United Kingdom's ratification, on 1 January 1991, was the seventh ratification, thereby triggering the entry into force of the Convention. The Contracts (Applicable Law) Act 1990, which implements the Rome Convention in the United Kingdom, came into force on 1 April 1991, "a day which many lawyers and traders will remember with sadness and resignation".[16] The Convention is accompanied by two Protocols on interpretation. Although the United Kingdom has ratified both Protocols, few of the other Contracting States have done so and there is no immediate prospect of their coming into force.

10.2.1.3 The Convention allows Contracting States to enter reservations on two provisions. Article 22(1) provides:

> Any Contracting State may, at the time of signature, ratification, acceptance or approval, reserve the right not to apply:
> (a) the provisions of Article 7(1);
> (b) the provisions of Article 10(1)(e).

The United Kingdom made these reservations and the Contracts (Applicable Law) Act 1990 provides that, although the Convention shall have the force of law in the United Kingdom,[17] Articles 7(1) and 10(1)(e) shall not.[18]

10.2.2 Opposition to the Rome Convention

10.2.2.1 The Rome Convention and Contracts (Applicable Law) Act 1990 have not been without their critics. One commentator has described the Convention as "one of the most unnecessary, useless and, indeed, unfortunate attempts at unification or harmonisation of the law that has ever been undertaken".[19] When the Bill first appeared it provoked correspondence in *The Times*.[20]

10.2.2.2 It is thought by some that the adoption of the Convention was a wholly unnecessary new departure: the common law rules have not led to any dissatisfaction or to a demand for reform[21]; it is debatable whether the unification of choice of law rules is

15. Article 29.
16. Mann, "The Proper Law of the Contract—an Obituary" (1991) 107 LQR 353.
17. Contracts (Applicable Law) Act 1990, s. 2(1).
18. Contracts (Applicable Law) Act 1990, s. 2(2).
19. Mann, (1983) 32 ICLQ 265.
20. See the letter written by Mann (*The Times*, 14 December 1989) and the reply by North (*The Times*, 19 December 1989).
21. Mann, "The Proper Law of the Contract—an Obituary" (1991) 107 LQR 353.

really necessary to prevent forum shopping since, when compared with procedural considerations, choice of law rules do not seem to figure largely in the equation when a plaintiff is deciding whether to proceed in one jurisdiction or another[22]; the laws of the various Contracting States prior to the entry into force of the Convention were broadly similar.[23] In any event, the application of the Convention itself will not always lead to identical results being achieved in different Contracting States.

10.2.2.3 By ratifying the Convention the United Kingdom broke an important link with all those English-speaking countries whose conflict of laws is derived from and influenced by English case law. In the debate on the Bill in the House of Lords Lord Goff wondered whether the attractiveness of the Commercial Court in London for the settling of international commercial disputes might be compromised by the application of the Convention to cases with no EC element. Why should England of all countries apply a European test to contracts between parties both of whom come from outside Europe?[24]

10.2.2.4 It is argued that the common law rules, "grown by experience and developed by judicial wisdom", are innately superior to "statutory tests drawn up by a committee of theorists speaking different languages and trained in different legal systems".[25] As for the way in which the Convention is drafted it is suggested that it contains "much obfuscating verbosity".[26] Furthermore, it may be questioned whether it is possible in twenty articles of a convention to deal adequately with all the complexities of this branch of private international law.[27]

10.2.2.5 The process whereby the Convention was introduced into English law—without interested parties having been consulted—is criticised: "The remarkable fact is that, contrary to the usual practice, the Act was passed after about nine years since the signature of the Convention without any consultation with lawyers or traders, an omission which is inexplicable if one rejects the cynical thought that a negative reaction would have been a foregone conclusion."[28]

10.2.2.6 The Protocols to the Convention make provision for the reference of questions of interpretation to the Court of Justice, "a tribunal which has proved to be singularly unsuited for the decision of matters of practical and commercial implications".[29]

10.3 INTERPRETATION OF THE ROME CONVENTION

10.3.1 The jurisdiction of the Court of Justice

10.3.1.1 At one point it appeared as though the whole project for unification of choice of law rules in contract was going to founder on the issue of the jurisdiction of the Court

22. Collins, "Contractual Obligations—the EEC Preliminary Draft Convention on Private International Law" (1976) 25 ICLQ 35, 36.
23. See the account in the Giuliano–Lagarde Report, OJ 1980 C282/15–20.
24. Hansard, HL Vol 515, col 1482. See also Lord Wilberforce, Hansard, HL Vol 515, col 1477–1478.
25. Mann, *The Times*, 14 December 1989.
26. Mann, "The Proper Law of the Contract—an Obituary" (1991) 107 LQR 353, 354.
27. Carter, "Contracts in English Private International Law" (1986) 57 BYIL 1, 32.
28. Mann, "The Proper Law of the Contract—an Obituary" (1991) 107 LQR 353, 355.
29. Mann, "The Proper Law of the Contract—an Obituary" (1991) 107 LQR 353, 354.

of Justice.[30] Two problems surrounded the issue of references to the Court of Justice: one of principle, the other more practical.

(i) Whereas the Brussels Convention of 1968 is one of the conventions to which EC Member States are required to accede by virtue of Article 220 of the Treaty of Rome, the Rome Convention is not. For this reason, the jurisdiction of the Court of Justice might be thought to be objectionable in principle. The point of principle is all the more relevant in view of the fact that the Rome Convention is universal in character—that is to say, it applies to contracts which have no connection with the Member States of the Community.

(ii) On a more practical level, a reference to the Court of Justice significantly slows the pace of litigation. The jurisdiction of the Court of Justice was of particular concern for the United Kingdom, since the relative attractiveness of London as a forum for the resolution of international commercial disputes might be seriously undermined if in certain situations the court were required to make a reference to Luxembourg.

10.3.1.2 The solution to the problems of interpretation was achieved by the conclusion of the two Protocols on interpretation on 19 December 1988. The First Protocol (referred to by the 1990 Act as the Brussels Protocol) defines the circumstances in which references may be made to the Court of Justice; the Second Protocol provides that the Court of Justice "shall, with respect to the Rome Convention, have the jurisdiction conferred upon it by the first Protocol".[31] The Second Protocol comes into force after ratification by all the Contracting States[32]; the First Protocol, however, comes into force if (i) the Second Protocol has entered into force and (ii) it has been ratified by seven Contracting States.[33] This structure is designed to provide a mechanism whereby references may be made by the courts of some Contracting States in advance of others. As long as the jurisdiction of the Court of Justice has been unanimously accepted by the Contracting States (by ratification of the Second Protocol) references may be made by the courts of those Contracting States which have ratified the First Protocol (as long as there are at least seven ratifications): "the purpose of the, so to speak, optional nature of one of the two Protocols was not to establish a permanent situation in advance, but merely to allow the system to get started so as to encourage the later accession of such States as might have declined to join [...] it".[34] Neither Protocol is yet in force.[35]

10.3.1.3 The First Protocol makes no provision for compulsory references. Article 2 states that a preliminary ruling on a question concerning interpretation may be made to the Court of Justice by (a) "the House of Lords and other courts from which no other appeal is possible" and (b) "the courts of the Contracting States when acting as appeal courts". The instruments on which references may be made include the Rome Convention, the First Protocol itself and any convention of accession to the Rome Convention by a State which became a Member State of the EC after the Rome Convention was opened for signature.[36]

30. See Tizzano Report, OJ 1990 C219/1.
31. Article 1.
32. Article 3.
33. Article 6.
34. Tizzano Report, OJ 1990 C219/11, para. 29.
35. Contracts (Applicable Law) Act 1990 (Commencement No. 1) Order, SI 1991 No. 707.
36. Greece acceded to the Rome Convention in 1984; Spain and Portugal acceded in 1992.

10.3.1.4 Article 3 of the First Protocol makes provision for references to be made to the Court of Justice by the competent authority of a Contracting State in respect of a matter which has been decided by a court falling within the scope of Article 2. This provision is identical in substance to Article 4 of the Luxembourg Protocol of 1971, which confers jurisdiction on the Court of Justice with regard to preliminary references under the Brussels Convention.[37] Since the entry into force of the Luxembourg Protocol in 1975, the power to refer under Article 4 has not be utilised.

10.3.2 Interpretation in cases where there is no reference

10.3.2.1 It seems likely that references to the Court of Justice will be relatively infrequent even once the Protocols have come into force. Accordingly, the relevant principles of interpretation in cases where there is no reference to the Court of Justice will be of considerable importance. The Convention itself and the 1990 Act set out the principles which should guide an English court when questions of interpretation arise.

10.3.2.2 Article 18 provides:

> In the interpretation and application of the preceding uniform rules, regard shall be had to their international character and to the desirability of achieving uniformity in their interpretation and application.

Although decisions of the courts of other countries are not formally a source of law, consideration of the jurisprudence of other Contracting States will be appropriate in cases coming before the English courts. In addition, Article 33 provides that all the different language versions of the Convention are equally authentic.

10.3.2.3 Section 3 of the 1990 Act lists important aids to interpretation in cases where no reference is made to the Court of Justice:

> (1) Any question as to the meaning or effect of any provision of the Conventions shall, if not referred to the European Court in accordance with the Brussels Protocol, be determined in accordance with the principles laid down by, and any relevant decision of, the European Court.
> (2) Judicial notice shall be taken of any decision of, or expression of opinion by, the European Court on any such question.
> (3) Without prejudice to any practice of the courts as to the matters which may be considered apart from this subsection—
> (a) the report on the Rome Convention by Professor Mario Giuliano and Professor Paul Lagarde which is reproduced in the Official Journal of the Communities of 31st October 1980[38] may be considered in ascertaining the meaning or effect of any provision of that Convention; and
> (b) any report on the Brussels Protocol which is reproduced in the Official Journal of the Communities may be considered in ascertaining the meaning or effect of any provision of that Protocol.[39]

This section adopts the same approach to interpretation as that taken by section 3 of the Civil Jurisdiction and Judgments Act 1982 in relation to the Brussels Convention.[40]

37. See para. 3.2.1.1.
38. Giuliano–Lagarde Report, OJ 1980 C282/1.
39. The official report on the Brussels Protocol is the Tizzano Report, OJ 1990 C219/1.
40. See para. 3.2.1.

10.4 THE SCOPE OF THE CONVENTION

The Convention is limited in its material and its temporal scope. As regards contractual obligations not governed by the Convention the common law choice of law rules continue to apply.[41]

10.4.1 Material scope

10.4.1.1 Choice of law relating to contractual obligations

10.4.1.1.1 Article 1 sets out the Convention's material scope. The first paragraph, which determines the outer limits of the Convention, provides:

> The rules of this Convention shall apply to contractual obligations in any situation involving a choice between the laws of different countries.

This superficially simple provision raises a number of potentially difficult questions of interpretation.

10.4.1.1.2 When can it be said that a situation involves "a choice between the laws of different countries"? The Giuliano–Lagarde Report indicates that the Convention applies both to "situations which involve one or more elements foreign to the internal social system of a country (for example, the fact that one or all the parties to the contract are foreign nationals or persons habitually resident abroad, the fact that the contract was made abroad, the fact that one or more of the obligations of the parties are to be performed in a foreign country, etc.)" and "in all cases where the dispute would give rise to a conflict between two or more legal systems."[42]

10.4.1.1.3 Article 1(1) also raises a difficult question of characterisation, since no indication is given as to the law which is to determine whether a particular obligation is "contractual". The Giuliano–Lagarde Report notes merely that property rights and intellectual property are not covered by these provisions.[43] Is the scope of the Convention to be determined by reference to an autonomous definition of "contractual" or is it for the *lex fori* to decide whether a particular set of facts involves "contractual obligations"? If the scope of the Convention were determined by the *lex fori*, this would be likely to lead to lack of uniformity. Accordingly, the better view is that the scope of the Convention must be interpreted by Community law. This is the approach generally adopted by the Court of Justice when considering the meaning of key concepts in the Brussels Convention.[44] On the assumption that the material scope of the Convention is to be interpreted from a Community perspective, it follows that an obligation may properly be regarded as contractual for the purposes of the Convention, even though under the law of the forum the obligation would be classified differently. So, for the purpose of the Convention, gifts and promises to give should be regarded as involving contractual obligations.[45]

41. See para. 10.1. For a detailed discussion of the common law rules see Cheshire & North, *Private International Law* (11th ed, 1987) pp. 447–503; Dicey & Morris, *The Conflict of Laws* (11th ed, 1987) Chapters 32 and 33.
42. OJ 1980 C282/10.
43. OJ 1980 C282/10.
44. See para. 3.2.1.2.
45. Giuliano–Lagarde Report, OJ 1980 C282/10. See, for example, *Re Bonacina* [1912] 2 Ch 394.

10.4.1.1.4 Do the provisions of the Convention have to be applied by the English courts even if not raised by the parties to the dispute? The traditional English approach is to regard questions of foreign law as questions of fact which must be pleaded and proved in the same way as other facts. If the relevant foreign law is not pleaded or proved to the court's satisfaction, English law is applied.[46] It has been suggested that, in order that the United Kingdom should comply with the international obligations assumed on ratification of the Convention, judges should be willing to apply the Convention of their own motion where necessary and to request the parties to provide evidence and to plead the applicable law under the Convention in the appropriate manner.[47] The entry into force of the Contracts (Applicable Law) Act 1990 does not, however, require such a profound break with the past. Questions of "evidence and procedure" are excluded from the scope of the Convention by Article 1(2)(h). Furthermore, failure by the parties to plead foreign law in the context of English proceedings may be interpreted by the court as an implied agreement in favour of the law of forum—which is valid by virtue of Article 3(2) of the Convention.[48]

10.4.1.2 Exceptions

The material scope of the Convention, as defined by the first paragraph of Article 1, is limited by the second, third and fourth paragraphs:

2. [The rules in this Convention] shall not apply to:
   (a) questions involving the status or legal capacity of natural persons, without prejudice to Article 11;
   (b) contractual obligations relating to:
   — wills and succession,
   — rights in property arising out of a matrimonial relationship,
   — rights and duties arising out of a family relationship, parentage, marriage or affinity, including maintenance obligations in respect of children who are not legitimate;
   (c) obligations arising under bills of exchange, cheques and promissory notes and other negotiable instruments to the extent that the obligations under such other negotiable instruments arise out of their negotiable character;
   (d) arbitration agreements and agreements on the choice of court;
   (e) questions governed by the law of companies and other bodies corporate or unincorporate such as the creation, by registration or otherwise, legal capacity, internal organisation or winding up of companies and other bodies corporate or unincorporate and the personal liability of officers and members as such for the obligations of the company or body;
   (f) the question whether an agent is able to bind a principal, or an organ to bind a company or body corporate or unincorporate, to a third party;
   (g) the constitution of trusts and the relationship between settlors, trustees and beneficiaries;
   (h) evidence and procedure, without prejudice to Article 14.
3. The rules of this Convention do not apply to contracts of insurance which cover risks situated in the territories of the Member States of the European Economic Community. In order to determine whether a risk is situated in these territories the court shall apply its internal law.
4. The preceding paragraph does not apply to contracts of re-insurance.

46. See para. 23.1.
47. Kaye, *The New Private International Law of Contract of the European Community* (1993) p. 98.
48. Cf. Cheshire & North, *Private International Law* (12th ed, 1992) p. 479.

These various exclusions to the Convention are motivated by different reasons: as regards some of the excluded matters the choice of law rules in the Convention would be inappropriate; some excluded matters are not regarded as being essentially contractual by some of the Contracting States; other specific matters were excluded because of legal developments in other contexts.

10.4.1.2.1 STATUS AND FAMILY LAW MATTERS

The terminology of subparagraphs (a) and (b) corresponds to the equivalent provisions of Article 1 of the Brussels and Lugano Conventions.[49] Their purpose is to exclude all questions of family law and status from the scope of the Convention (subject to the limited exception in Article 11).[50]

10.4.1.2.2 INSURANCE CONTRACTS

10.4.1.2.2.1 Contracts of reinsurance fall within the scope of the Convention, as do contracts of insurance where the risk is situated outside the territories of the Member States of the EC; only contracts of insurance where the risk is situated within the EC are excluded. This exclusion results from the fact that when the Convention was being negotiated work was being undertaken within the Community with a view to harmonising various aspects of insurance law.[51]

10.4.1.2.2.2 For the purposes of Article 1(3) it is for the *lex fori* to determine where a risk is situated. As far as English law is concerned, section 96A(3) of the Insurance Companies Act 1982 provides a *prima facie* rule that a risk is located at the assured's domicile (in the case of individuals) or at the place of business to which the policy relates (in the case of companies). There are, however, exceptions: as regards insured buildings, the risk is located where the building is located; as regards vehicles, the risk is located where the vehicle is registered; as regards short-term travel policies, the risk is located where the policy is taken out.

10.4.1.2.2.3 The effect of Article 1(3) is that the Convention does not apply to most everyday insurance contracts (such as contracts for life insurance, property insurance and motor insurance) entered into by individuals who are habitually resident within one of the Member States or by corporations who carry on business in the Community. Where, for example, an English resident takes out fire insurance in respect of a villa in the south of France, the Convention does not apply to the contract of insurance; the Convention would apply, however, if the property were situated in the Bahamas.

10.4.1.2.3 JURISDICTION AND ARBITRATION AGREEMENTS

10.4.1.2.3.1 Although the United Kingdom delegation was keen that the Convention should apply to jurisdiction and arbitration agreements, the majority favoured their exclusion. Many jurisdiction clauses are regulated by Article 17 of the Brussels Convention or the equivalent provision of the Lugano Convention[52]; the New York Convention of 1958 (which has been ratified by all the Contracting States except

49. See para. 3.3.3.1.
50. Contractual capacity is discussed further at para. 11.4.4.
51. For further discussion of contracts of insurance see para. 12.8.
52. See para. 5.3.

Portugal) applies to arbitration agreements.[53] It was thought appropriate to exclude jurisdiction clauses on the basis that "[t]he outstanding points, notably those relating to consent, do not arise in practice, having regard to the fact that Article 17 provides that these agreements shall be in writing".[54] As regards arbitration agreements, it was thought that "any increase in the number of conventions in this area should be avoided".[55] There are, however, cogent arguments in favour of the inclusion of dispute resolution agreements within the scope of the Convention.

(i) Although Article 17 and the New York Convention deal with formal validity, they do not regulate questions of material validity.
(ii) As a result of amendments it is no longer true that Article 17 requires jurisdiction agreements in favour of the courts of a Contracting State to be in writing.[56]
(iii) Article 17 does not apply to an agreement in favour of the courts of a non-contracting State.

10.4.1.2.3.2 The effect of the exclusion is that if choice of law questions arise in English proceedings in relation to an international contract which contains a jurisdiction or arbitration clause, the law governing the clause is to be determined by reference to the common law choice of law rules and the law governing the rest of the contract falls to be determined by the Convention. It is likely in practice that, notwithstanding the fact that different choice of law regimes apply to different aspects of the same contract, the proper law of the clause will be the same as the law applicable to the contract as a whole. Nevertheless, the application of two different sets of choice of law rules might lead to the jurisdiction or arbitration agreement being governed by law of country X and the contract as a whole being governed by the law of country Y.

10.4.1.2.4 NEGOTIABLE INSTRUMENTS

10.4.1.2.4.1 Choice of law questions concerning bills of exchange, cheques and promissory notes are excluded from the scope of the Convention; they are governed by the Bills of Exchange Act 1882.[57] As regards negotiable instruments which are not bills of exchange, cheques or promissory notes, the rules laid down by the Convention do not apply to those obligations which arise out of their negotiable character; the Convention rules do apply, however, to those obligations which do not arise out of their negotiable character. The effect of Article 1(2)(c) is that where a negotiable instrument is used as a method of payment (for example, in the context of a contract for the sale of goods) although the obligations arising out of the instrument fall outside the scope of the Convention, the underlying contract does not.

10.4.1.2.4.2 As regards a negotiable instrument which is not a bill of exchange, a cheque or a promissory note it is important to distinguish two different transactions: sale and negotiation. Whereas the sale of a negotiable instrument falls within the Convention's scope,[58] its negotiation does not. Whether a document is characterised as

53. See para. 18.2.
54. Giuliano–Lagarde Report, OJ 1980 C282/11.
55. Giuliano–Lagarde Report, OJ 1980 C282/12.
56. See para. 5.3.3.1.
57. See para. 12.9.
58. Giuliano–Lagarde Report, OJ 1980 C282/11.

a negotiable instrument is a matter for the law of the forum (including its conflicts rules).[59] Transactions which are related to negotiable instruments, but which are not themselves negotiable instruments (such as letters of credit) plainly fall within the scope of the Convention.

10.4.1.2.5 AGENCY

To the extent that such relations are contractual, choice of law questions arising out of the relationship between, on the one hand, the principal and the agent and, on the other, between the agent and the third party are within the scope of the Convention. The agency exception applies only to the legal relationship between the principal and the third party.[60]

10.4.1.2.6 QUESTIONS GOVERNED BY COMPANY LAW

Acts which are necessary for the creation of a company or firm and to the regulation of its internal organisation and its winding up are all outside the scope of the Convention. However, preliminary contracts whose sole purpose is to create obligations between interested parties with a view to forming a company or firm are regulated by the choice of law rules contained in the Convention.[61] For example, where two persons enter a joint venture to stage a musical and the medium through which the joint venture is realised is a company established by the parties, the original joint venture agreement falls within the scope of the Convention, although the liability of the organs of the company is a matter which is excluded.

10.4.1.2.7 EVIDENCE AND PROCEDURE

As a general principle, questions of procedure are for the *lex fori*, regardless of the law which governs the substantive issues disputed by the parties. Subject to Article 10(1)(c),[62] the Convention adheres to this traditional analysis. Article 14(1), however, provides:

> The law governing the contract under this Convention applies to the extent that it contains, in the law of contract, rules which raise presumptions of law or determine the burden of proof.

The effect of Article 14(1) is not to allow general procedural rules which form part of the *lex causae* to encroach upon the procedural law of the forum. Rather its purpose is to include within the applicable law those rules—specific to contractual obligations—which are in reality rules of substance, even though phrased in terms of presumptions and the burden of proof.

Article 14(2) provides that a contract may be proved in any manner permitted by the *lex fori* or in any manner permitted by the law which renders the contract formally valid under Article 9.

59. Giuliano–Lagarde Report, OJ 1980 C282/11. For further discussion see para. 12.9.1.2.
60. Giuliano–Lagarde Report, OJ 1980 C282/13. For further discussion of agency, see para. 12.7.
61. Giuliano–Lagarde Report, OJ 1980 C282/12.
62. See paras. 11.4.7.2 and 11.4.7.3.

10.4.2 Territorial scope

10.4.2.1 Universal application

Article 2 provides: "Any law specified by this Convention shall be applied whether or not it is the law of a Contracting State."

In the course of the debate of the Bill Lord Wilberforce and Lord Goff unsuccessfully tried to have the Act amended so that it applied only "as between any parties to a contract who, at the time of conclusion of the contract, have their habitual residence, or in the case of bodies corporate or unincorporate, their central administration in a Contracting State".[63] In relation to those matters which fall within the material scope of the Convention the choice of law rules set out in the Convention are to be applied in England regardless of the domicile, residence or nationality of the parties and regardless of whether the contract is connected in any way with any Contracting State.

10.4.2.2 "Internal" conflicts

As the United Kingdom is made up of three different legal systems—England, Scotland and Northern Ireland—choice of law questions may arise as between these different countries. Notwithstanding Article 19(2) of the Convention, which provides that a Contracting State which is made up of several territorial units, each with their own law of contract, is not required to apply the Convention rules to purely internal conflicts, the 1990 Act states that the Convention shall apply "in the case of conflicts between the laws of different parts of the United Kingdom".[64]

10.4.3 Temporal scope

Article 17 provides that the Convention is to apply only "to contracts made after the date on which this Convention has entered into force with respect to that State". Accordingly, the common law choice of law rules continue to apply in relation to any contractual obligation entered into prior to 1 April 1991.

10.5 EXCLUSION OF THE DOCTRINE OF RENVOI

The doctrine of renvoi has no role to play in the field of choice of law in contract. Accordingly, where the choice of law rules contained in the Convention or (where relevant) under the common law indicate that the law of a particular country is to be applied, the domestic rules of law of that country are exclusively relevant; that country's rules of private international law are excluded. The decision of the House of Lords in *Amin Rasheed Shipping Corporation* v. *Kuwait Insurance Co*[65] confirmed that, at common law, the doctrine of renvoi has no application in cases involving international contracts. Article 15 of the Convention adopts the same position:

> The application of the law of any country specified by this Convention means the application of the rules of law in force in that country other than its rules of private international law.

63. Hansard, HL Vol 515, col 1474.
64. Contracts (Applicable Law) Act 1990, s. 2(3).
65. [1984] AC 50. See the speech of Lord Diplock, [1984] AC 50, 61–62.

CHAPTER 11

CHOICE OF LAW IN CONTRACT: GENERAL CHOICE OF LAW RULES

For the purposes of this chapter general choice of law rules—the vast majority of which are to be found in the Rome Convention on the Law Applicable to Contractual Obligations—can be divided into three groups.

(i) Articles 3 and 4 are the core provisions of the Convention. Article 3 identifies the applicable law in cases where the parties have chosen the law to govern their contractual relations, whether expressly or impliedly (para. 11.1). Article 4 contains the provisions for ascertaining the applicable law in situations where the parties have not made a choice (para. 11.2).

(ii) Although the applicable law is the law which plays the predominant role in regulating the rights and obligations of the parties, there are circumstances in which the applicable law yields to the mandatory rules of the forum or of another country (para. 11.3).

(iii) Not all aspects of a contract are necessarily governed by the same law. It is important to have regard to the way in which the various choice of law rules apply to specific aspects of the contract (such as material and formal validity, interpretation, performance, the quantification of contractual damages) (para. 11.4).

11.1 THE APPLICABLE LAW IN CASES OF CHOICE

11.1.1 Introduction

11.1.1.1 The principle of party autonomy

11.1.1.1.1 Article 3(1) embodies the principle of party autonomy: "A contract shall be governed by the law chosen by the parties. The choice must be express or demonstrated with reasonable certainty by the terms of the contract or the circumstances of the case." There is nothing in the Convention which says that there needs to be any connection between the law chosen and the contract or the parties. Even a choice made in bad faith (for example, with the express purpose of evading statutory provisions which would otherwise govern the contract) is valid. However, where the parties make an evasive choice, it is more than likely that the chosen law will be subject to the mandatory rules of the law which the parties have sought to evade.[1]

11.1.1.1.2 Whether the parties' choice is limited to domestic systems of law is not

1. See para. 11.3.

clear. What, for example, would be the effect of a choice of "internationally accepted principles of law governing contractual obligations"[2]? It has been suggested that a choice of the *lex mercatoria* would be regarded by the court as falling outside the range of choice available to the parties.[3] However, in cases where the parties have agreed to refer disputes to arbitration there are strong arguments in favour of upholding the parties' choice of law—whether the choice refers to a national system of law, to public international law or to the *lex mercatoria*.[4]

11.1.1.2 The existence and validity of choice

In cases where it is alleged that the parties have made a choice of law—whether express or implied—that choice will be effective only if it is valid by the applicable law. Questions of the existence and validity of a choice of law are governed by the general principles which apply to the existence and validity of any other contractual agreement. Article 3(4) provides that "the existence and validity of the consent of the parties as to the choice of the applicable law shall be determined in accordance with the provisions of Articles 8, 9 and 11". Article 8 applies to material validity; Article 9 to formal validity; and Article 11 to questions of capacity.[5]

11.1.1.3 Choice and incorporation

11.1.1.3.1 It is important to distinguish a choice of law from the incorporation of foreign legal provisions into a contract. Where, for example, parties choose French law to govern their contract as a whole, the chosen law determines the rights and obligations of the parties and applies as "a living and changing body of law".[6] Accordingly, the parties take the risk that between the conclusion of the contract and its performance the chosen law will change in such a way as to alter their rights and obligations.[7]

11.1.1.3.2 Incorporation operates in a different way. It is perfectly possible for a contract which is governed by the law of country X to incorporate rules of law from country Y. This is not, however, a case of the applicable law being split. Provisions of a foreign law which are incorporated into the text of the contract, whether by reference or verbatim, take effect as written terms which must be interpreted by the applicable law. So, for example, a contract which is governed by English law may provide that in case of breach the liability of the parties is to be governed by specific provisions of the French Civil Code. In this case, the incorporated provisions have to be construed as English contractual terms.[8] Moreover, the rights and obligations of the parties are fixed at the date of incorporation; rules which are incorporated are not affected by any change in the law of which they form a part between the conclusion of the contract and its performance. Whether a particular contractual clause amounts to a choice of law or the incorporation of specific provisions is a question of construction.

2. *Deutsche Schachtbau-und Tiefbohrgesellschaft mbH* v. *R'As al-Khaimah National Oil Co* [1990] 1 AC 295 (HL).
3. Cheshire & North, *Private International Law* (12th ed, 1992) p. 482.
4. See para. 17.3.
5. See paras. 11.4.2–11.4.4.
6. Wolff, "The Choice of Law by the Parties in International Contracts" (1937) 49 Jur Rev 110, 124.
7. *Re Chesterman's Trusts* [1923] 2 Ch 466.
8. *GE Dobell & Co* v. *Steamship Rossmore Co Ltd* [1895] 2 QB 408.

11.1.2 Express choice

11.1.2.1 Whether a contractual clause constitutes an express choice is a matter of construction. Most cases are entirely straightforward, since the parties simply agree that the contract is to be governed by the law of a particular country. Problems may arise, however, in cases where the parties seek to determine the applicable law indirectly. In *Compagnie Tunisienne de Navigation SA* v. *Compagnie d'Armement Maritime SA*[9] the defendant, a French shipowner, and the plaintiff, a Tunisian company, entered a contract for the shipment of oil between Algerian ports. Clause 13 of the contract provided that the contract was to be governed by the "the laws of the Flag of the Vessel carrying the goods".

11.1.2.2 The defendant owned four ships and through a subsidiary company controlled a fifth, all of which flew the French flag. Although the printed form which the parties used for the agreement was designed for a single voyage charterparty, it was envisaged that performance of the contract would require at least a dozen voyages. The printed form was, therefore, adapted to suit the contract in question. Ships of five different flags were used in the first six voyages. After the sixth voyage war broke out in the Middle East and the defendant ceased to perform the contract. The plaintiff contended that the contract was governed by English law and that the defendant was in breach. It was the defendant's argument that the contract was governed by French law, under which the contract was frustrated. One of the issues facing the House of Lords was the effect of clause 13.

11.1.2.3 The minority thought that clause 13 was meaningless and should be regarded "as having failed in its purpose to determine the proper law of the contract".[10] The majority, however, decided that, since the parties had envisaged that the shipowner would primarily use ships flying the French flag, clause 13 was operative as a choice of French law. Lord Diplock was motivated by a desire to give effect to what he understood to be the obvious intentions of the parties:

> [I]n commerce business men frequently find it convenient to use printed forms of contract with which they are familiar to record their agreements about transactions for which the printed clauses are not literally apt, as they were drafted for use as contracts about transactions which have somewhat different characteristics. If the law is to give effect to their intentions . . . the court must construe the words of the printed form not exclusively literally but, if necessary, analogistically. . . . By clause 13 when used for a single voyage charter the parties clearly intended to choose the system of law with which the contract had its connection through the nationality of the carrying vessel. Had the parties contemplated that the contract would be performed exclusively by vessels owned or controlled by the French company there could be no question but that the parties intended to choose French law as the proper law of the contract. Is the court to treat the clause as meaningless simply because, notwithstanding that they did contemplate that vessels owned by the French company would be used primarily to perform the contract, they also contemplated that there might be exceptional occasions on which chartered vessels might be used? It does not seem to me that from the business point of view this could make any significant difference so far as choice of proper law was concerned.[11]

11.1.2.4 Although the *Compagnie Tunisienne* case was decided under the common law, the question of what constitutes a choice can arise under Article 3(1) of the

9. [1971] AC 572.
10. Lord Reid, [1971] AC 572, 583.
11. [1971] AC 572, 608–609.

Convention. Whether a contractual term is an express choice of law is a question of construction to be determined in each case in the light of the relevant circumstances.

11.1.3 "Implied" choice

It is extremely important to distinguish cases of implied choice, which fall within Article 3(1), from cases in which the parties have failed to make a choice, which are governed by Article 4. The Giuliano–Lagarde Report indicates that "the Convention recognises the possibility that the court may, in the light of all the facts, find that the parties have made a real choice of law although this is not expressly stated in the contract".[12] The Report gives six examples where it might be possible to discern a genuine choice, notwithstanding the fact that the choice is not express:

> For example, the contract may be in a standard form which is known to be governed by a particular system of law even though there is no express statement to this effect, such as a Lloyd's policy of marine insurance. In other cases, a previous course of dealing between the parties under contracts containing an express choice of law may leave the court in no doubt that the contract in question is to be governed by the law previously chosen where the choice of law clause has been omitted in circumstances which do not indicate a deliberate change of policy by the parties. In some cases the choice of a particular forum may show in no uncertain manner that the parties intend the contract to be governed by the law of that forum, but this must always be subject to the other terms of the contract and all the circumstances of the case. Similarly references in a contract to specific Articles of the French Civil Code may leave the court in no doubt that the parties have deliberately chosen French law, although there is no expressly stated choice of law. Other matters that may impel the court to the conclusion that a real choice of law has been made might include an express choice of law in related transactions between the same parties, or the choice of a place where disputes are to be settled by arbitration in circumstances indicating that the arbitrator should apply the law of that place.[13]

Each of the six factors referred to may incline the court to conclude that the parties have made a real choice. However, none of the factors are in themselves decisive; much depends on the surrounding circumstances.

A choice of law is effective under Article 3(1), notwithstanding the fact that it is not express, if it is "demonstrated with reasonable certainty by the terms of the contract or the circumstances of the case". In this respect the approach of the Convention is somewhat similar to the proper law doctrine formulated by the English courts.

11.1.3.1 Standard forms

11.1.3.1.1 The fact that the parties have used a standard form in the English language does not necessarily imply a choice of English law. Some forms are in worldwide use and it would not be appropriate to imply a choice in all cases.[14] In *Amin Rasheed Shipping Corporation* v. *Kuwait Insurance Co*[15] the plaintiff, a Liberian company resident in Dubai, owned a vessel which was insured with the defendant, a Kuwaiti insurance company. The policy, which was issued in Kuwait, was based on the Lloyd's SG form (as set out in Schedule 1 to the Marine Insurance Act 1906) but did not contain a choice of law clause. When a dispute arose under the contract the plaintiff sought to bring

12. OJ 1980 C282/17.
13. OJ 1980 C282/17.
14. Stone, "The Proper Law of a Marine Insurance Policy" [1984] LMCLQ 438.
15. [1984] AC 50. Collier, [1983] CLJ 214.

proceedings in England under what is now RSC, Order 11, rule 1(1)(d)(iii).[16] The first issue facing the court was whether the contract was by implication governed by English law.

11.1.3.1.2 The majority of the House of Lords thought that English law was the proper law of the contract by virtue of the choice of the parties. Having referred to a number of "the more esoteric provisions of the policy of which the legal effect is undiscoverable except by reference to the Marine Insurance Act 1906" Lord Diplock ventured the opinion that "[e]xcept by reference to the English statute and to judicial exegesis of the code that it enacts it is not possible to interpret the policy so as to determine what [the parties'] mutual rights and obligations are".[17] On this basis it was concluded that the parties had impliedly chosen English law as the proper law of the contract. Lord Wilberforce, on the other hand, took the view that there was "no basis for inferring, as between the parties to this contract, an intention that the contract should be governed either by English law or by the law of Kuwait".[18] Accordingly, the proper law was the system of law with which the contract had its closest and most real connection. Lord Wilberforce concluded, albeit "[w]ith no great confidence",[19] that the proper law of the contract was English.

11.1.3.1.3 In this case, the result did not depend on whether the situation was regarded as involving an implied choice or an absence of choice; in either event the proper law was English. The fact that this will not always be the case is illustrated by the decision of the House of Lords in *James Miller & Partners Ltd* v. *Whitworth Street Estates (Manchester) Ltd*.[20] This case concerned a contract—between an English company and a Scottish company—which was concluded on a RIBA standard form (which included an arbitration clause). The subject matter of the contract was the conversion of premises in Scotland into a bonded warehouse. A dispute arose, arbitration proceedings were commenced in Scotland and litigation ensued in which one of the questions facing the court was whether the contract was governed by English or Scots law. The argument in favour of English law was that the RIBA contract was in English form and that there was in common use at the time a Scottish form of contract drawn up by a different professional body. This argument persuaded two members of the House of Lords; Lord Hodson—with whom Viscount Dilhorne agreed—thought that the proper law was "determined by the use of the English form, the selection of which shows the intention of the parties to be bound by English law".[21] Although Lord Guest had "no doubt that the parties never chose English law as the proper law of the contract or evinced any intention to be bound by this law",[22] his Lordship thought that English law governed the contract as the objective proper law. The remaining two members of the House of Lords—Lord Reid and Lord Wilberforce—agreed with Lord Guest that the parties had not chosen English law, either expressly or impliedly, but

16. See para. 6.3.3.4.
17. [1984] AC 50, 64.
18. [1984] AC 50, 69.
19. [1984] AC 50, 71.
20. [1970] AC 583.
21. [1970] AC 583, 606.
22. [1970] AC 583, 607–608.

concluded that Scots law was the law with which the contract had its closest and most real connection.[23]

11.1.3.2 *Previous course of dealing*

In certain circumstances it will be reasonable to imply a choice of law in cases where, although the particular contract between the parties does not contain a choice of law clause, earlier similar transactions between the parties have included an express choice. However, the court should not be too ready to imply a choice of law on the basis of a previous course of dealing. The absence of a choice of law clause in a particular written contract may result from the fact that the parties were unable to reach an agreement. Even if the parties have contracted with each other previously, the absence of a choice of law may signify a change in policy by one of the parties. Furthermore, it cannot be implied from the fact that parties have repeatedly contracted for the sale of apples on a standard form which includes an express choice of law that the same parties intend that a contract for the sale of pears which does not include a choice of law should be governed by the same law.

11.1.3.3 *Jurisdiction clause*

11.1.3.3.1 Whether a jurisdiction clause is to be treated as an implied choice of law is a difficult issue. Essentially, it is a question of interpretation, having regard to all the circumstances of the case. In *The Komninos S*,[24] for example, the plaintiff was the owner of a cargo of steel coils which was shipped on a vessel owned by the defendant. The cargo was loaded in Greece for carriage to Italy. The bills of lading were in the English language and contained the following clause: "In case any controversies arise with respect to the construction of the foregoing terms the English text alone is to be conclusive. All dispute[s] to be referred to British courts."

11.1.3.3.2 None of the parties to the dispute was English nor connected with England; the contract was made in Greece between Greek shippers and Greek managers on behalf of the Cypriot owners of a Panamanian vessel to carry steel from Greece to Italy for freight payable in Greece in Greek currency. When the cargo was discharged in Italy it was discovered that the coils had corroded during the voyage. The plaintiff commenced proceedings in England, alleging that the ship was unseaworthy and that the defendant had been negligent. The first issue was whether the bills of lading were governed by English law or Greek law. If Greek law applied, the plaintiff's action was *prima facie* time barred. The plaintiff, however, sought to rely on the jurisdiction clause as an implied choice of English law. At first instance, Leggatt J held that there had been no choice and that the bills of lading were governed by Greek law, being the law with which the transaction had its closest and most real connection. It was the judge's view that the very strong factual connections with Greece predominated over the equivocal reference to the British courts.[25] This decision was reversed on appeal. The Court of

23. Viscount Dilhorne also indicated that, had the parties not impliedly chosen English law, the proper law would have been Scots law as the law of the country with which the transaction had its closest and most real connection: [1970] AC 583, 611.
24. [1991] 1 Lloyd's Rep 370.
25. [1990] 1 Lloyd's Rep 541, 544.

Appeal decided, first, that the reference to British courts operated as a choice of English forum.[26] Secondly, in relation to the impact of the jurisdiction clause on the choice of law question, Bingham LJ (with whom Nourse and Lloyd LJJ agreed) thought that it was appropriate to "infer that the parties intended their contracts to be governed by the law of the forum where disputes were to be tried unless there were strong indications that they did not intend or may not have intended this result".[27] Even though the contract had its closest and most real connection with Greek law, there was no indication to displace the *prima facie* inference from the jurisdiction clause.

11.1.3.3.3 Whether the same result would be reached under the Convention is a matter for conjecture. It has been suggested that for the purposes of Article 3(1) the court should require stronger evidence of the parties' intention than is required under the common law.[28] Furthermore, it is clear that the methodology of the Court of Appeal in *The Komninos S* would not be appropriate in cases falling within the scope of the Convention. The terms of Article 3(1) do not entitle the court to assume that a jurisdiction clause is to be regarded as an implied choice of law unless there are strong indications to the contrary. The onus must be on the person seeking to rely on a jurisdiction clause to demonstrate "with reasonable certainty" that a real choice was made by the parties.

11.1.3.4 Reference to provisions of domestic law

The Report indicates that a choice may be inferred from reference to specific provisions of a system of domestic law. However, it is important to distinguish choice of law from the incorporation of provisions of law into the contract.[29] The important point to make in the present context is to note that where provisions of law have been incorporated into a contract it does not follow that the contract as a whole is to be governed by that law. Much depends on the circumstances of the case. Where, for example, an Englishman and a Scotsman enter into a contract for the sale of goods, but agree that in the event of breach damages are to be determined by specific provisions of the French Civil Code, it would be wrong to assume that reference to the French Civil Code indicates an intention that French law should be the applicable law. Indeed, if anything, the reference to a provision of French law without a choice of French law suggests that the parties do not intend French law to be the applicable law. It must always be remembered that, for the purposes of Article 3(1), the choice must be "demonstrated with reasonable certainty".

11.1.3.5 Related transactions between the same parties

At common law it has often been held that, where transactions are related, an express choice of law in one contract allows a choice of law to be implied into another contract on the basis that the parties must have intended or assumed that the transactions would be governed by the same law. Where, for example, a charterparty is governed by English

26. [1991] 1 Lloyd's Rep 370, 374.
27. [1991] 1 Lloyd's Rep 370, 376.
28. Morse, "The EEC Convention on the Law Applicable to Contractual Obligations" (1982) 2 YBEL 107, 117.
29. See para. 11.1.1.3.

law it may be legitimate to imply that bills of lading are also governed by English law, even though no specific intention can be gleaned from the terms of the bills of lading themselves.[30] Similarly, in cases involving a contract of guarantee, the court may imply that the law governing the primary obligation—by virtue of the parties' choice—should govern the contract of guarantee by implication.[31]

11.1.3.6 Arbitration clauses[32]

11.1.3.6.1 At common law "an arbitration clause is generally intended by the parties to operate as a choice of the proper law of the contract ... unless there are compelling indications to the contrary in the other terms of the contract or the surrounding circumstances of the transaction".[33] Although "there is no inflexible or conclusive rule to the effect that an agreement to refer disputes to arbitration in a particular country carries with it the additional agreement or necessarily indicates a clear intention that the law governing the matters in dispute is to be the law of that country,"[34] it would appear that, at common law, "[t]he mere fact that there are systems of law with which the transaction has a closer connection is not sufficient to rebut the implication".[35]

11.1.3.6.2 It is doubtful whether the common law approach should be adopted under the Convention. In the discussion of the potential effect of an arbitration clause under Article 3(1) the Giuliano–Lagarde Report states that where the parties have agreed to an arbitration clause and have selected the seat of arbitration, a choice of law may be implied from the selection of the seat of arbitration "in circumstances indicating that the arbitrator should apply the law of that place".[36] Accordingly, it would be wrong to presume that the parties have impliedly chosen the law of country X simply from the fact that the parties have agreed to refer any disputes to arbitration in country X.

11.1.3.7 Concluding remarks

11.1.3.7.1 The cases decided at common law illustrate the problems which the English courts have experienced in attempting to draw a clear dividing line between an implied choice, on the one hand, and an absence of choice, on the other. Because there are no hard and fast rules as to when a choice of law should be implied, many of the problems which have arisen in the common law will continue to plague the courts in cases falling within the scope of the Convention. It cannot be assumed, however, that the application of the Convention leads to the same solutions as those arrived at by the English courts under the common law rules.

30. *The Njegos* [1936] P 90; *The Freights Queen* [1977] 2 Lloyd's Rep 140.

31. *Broken Hill Proprietary Co Ltd* v. *Xanakis* [1982] 2 Lloyd's Rep 304; *Mitsubishi Corporation* v. *Alafouzos* [1988] 1 Lloyd's Rep 191. See also *Turkiye Is Bankasi AS* v. *Bank of China* [1993] 1 Lloyd's Rep 132.

32. For a discussion of the position at common law see Thomas, "Arbitration Agreements as a Signpost of the Proper Law" [1984] LMCLQ 141.

33. Lord Diplock in *Compagnie Tunisienne de Navigation SA* v. *Compagnie d'Armement Maritime SA* [1971] AC 572, 609.

34. Lord Morris in *Compagnie Tunisienne de Navigation SA* v. *Compagnie d'Armement Maritime SA* [1971] AC 572, 588.

35. Lord Diplock in *Compagnie Tunisienne de Navigation SA* v. *Compagnie d'Armement Maritime SA* [1971] AC 572, 609.

36. OJ 1980 C282/17.

11.1.3.7.2 In view of these difficulties the usefulness of the concept of an implied choice of law may be questioned:

> Surely the only situation where it is clear what the parties' *actual* intentions are is where they have expressly provided for the governing law by a choice of law clause. The whole notion of inferring an *actual* intent is based, at best, upon making assumptions which may or may not be correct, and, at worst, upon a form of dishonesty. It would be better to apply a purely objective test in all cases where there is no express choice of law clause.[37]

11.1.4 Splitting the applicable law

11.1.4.1 While no contractual obligation can be governed simultaneously by the laws of more than one country, there is no obvious reason why all aspects of a contract should be governed by the same law. Splitting the applicable law can take a number of different forms:

(i) it is possible to apply different laws to different aspects of the same obligation (for example, formation and performance[38]);
(ii) different terms of one contract may be governed by different laws (for example, an index-linking clause may be made subject to a different law from the rest of the contract[39]);
(iii) different groups of obligations may be governed by different laws (for example, a contract which is both a sale of goods and a distributorship agreement may be governed by the law of the seller as regards the sales aspects and by the law of the buyer/distributor as far as the distributorship aspects are concerned[40]);
(iv) the obligations of each party may be governed by a different law (for example, in a contract of sale the obligations of the seller may be governed by the law of one country and the obligations of the buyer by the law of another).[41]

11.1.4.2 The ideology of party autonomy inevitably leads to acceptance of the notion that parties to a contract may split the applicable law. The final sentence of Article 3(1) provides: "By their choice the parties can select the law applicable to the whole or a part only of the contract." Accordingly, the parties may choose different laws for different parts or aspects of a single contract or may choose a law for part of a contract—leaving the remainder to be governed by the law resulting from the application of Article 4.

11.1.4.3 The extent to which Article 3(1) allows splitting of the applicable law is not entirely free from doubt. The Giuliano–Lagarde Report states that "the choice must be logically consistent, ie it must relate to elements in the contract which can be governed by different laws without giving rise to contradictions".[42] From a practical perspective, splitting the applicable law is most likely in cases involving a single contract which consists in reality of several contracts or parts which are separable and independent of

37. Cheshire & North, *Private International Law* (11th ed, 1987) p. 461. (Emphasis in original.) This comment on the common law is equally applicable to the Convention.
38. This is a true example of *dépeçage*.
39. Giuliano–Lagarde Report, OJ 1980 C282/17.
40. Lando, "The EEC Convention on the Law Applicable to Contractual Obligations" (1987) 24 CMLRev 159, 168.
41. For a general discussion see McLachlan, "Splitting the Proper Law in Private International Law" (1990) 61 BYIL 311.
42. OJ 1980 C282/17.

each other from a legal and economic point of view. In this context, the application of different laws to different parts does not present significant problems. However, the Report questions whether it would be appropriate to uphold a choice of law clause which purported to subject the obligations of each of the contracting parties to the laws of different countries.[43] As one commentator notes: "The harmony between the obligations of the parties to a bilateral contract is disturbed if different laws are to be applied to the two obligations."[44] Where the choices of the parties cannot be logically reconciled, Article 4 of the Convention is applicable.[45]

11.1.5 Changing the chosen law[46]

11.1.5.1 The Convention provides flexibility as to when the choice of law can be made. Article 3(2) provides:

> The parties may at any time agree to subject the contract to a law other than that which previously governed it, whether as a result of an earlier choice under this Article or of other provisions of this Convention. Any variation by the parties of the law to be applied made after the conclusion of the contract shall not prejudice its formal validity under Article 9 or adversely affect the rights of third parties.

By virtue of this provision the parties may, having included a choice of law clause in their contract, subsequently decide to change the applicable law by a new agreement. Alternatively, in a situation where the contract is silent as to the governing law, the parties may agree on the applicable law at some later stage. Article 3(2) is a natural extension of the general principle of party autonomy; if parties are free to decide on the applicable law, there is no reason why they should not be able to change it.

11.1.5.2 Article 3(2) is not, however, without its difficulties—although some of the problems may be more theoretical than practical. In particular, the question arises as to which law governs the validity of the agreement varying the chosen law. Arguments can be advanced for three different possibilities.

- (i) As a matter of principle, the original applicable law should govern the validity of the variation.[47]
- (ii) It can be argued, on the basis of Article 8(1),[48] that the validity of the variation should be governed by the law which would apply if the variation were valid.[49]
- (iii) It has been argued that the terms of Article 3(2) itself treat the validity of the variation as a question to be determined by the *lex fori*.[50]

According to the second and third views parties would be permitted to change the applicable law irrespective of whether the original governing law permits them to do so.

43. OJ 1980 C282/17.
44. Lando, "The EEC Convention on the Law Applicable to Contractual Obligations" (1987) 24 CMLRev 159, 169.
45. Giuliano–Lagarde Report, OJ 1980 C282/17.
46. For a discussion of post-contractual choice of law at common law see Briggs, "The Validity of 'Floating' Choice of Law and Jurisdiction Clauses" [1986] LMCLQ 508; Beck, "Floating Choice of Law Clauses" [1987] LMCLQ 523; Pierce, "Post-Formation Choice of Law in Contract" (1987) 50 MLR 176.
47. Wolff, *Private International Law* (2nd ed, 1950) p. 426.
48. See para. 11.4.2.
49. Morse, "The EEC Convention on the Law Applicable to Contractual Obligations" (1982) 2 YBEL 107, 121.
50. Diamond, "Conflict of Laws in the EEC" [1979] CLP 155, 165.

It is clear that arguments of simplicity point in favour of the application of the *lex fori*. Nevertheless, whichever solution is adopted, some problems are likely to remain. What, for example, is the solution to the problem posed by a contract which is void under the law which applies to it at its inception, but is valid according to the new applicable law after the variation? It should be noted that if a contract is formally valid at its inception a subsequent variation of the applicable law cannot have the effect of rendering the contract formally invalid, nor can a change in the applicable law adversely affect the rights of third parties.

11.1.5.3 Finally, the status of a "floating" choice of law clause under Article 3 should be considered. What is the effect of a clause which provides that a contract shall, at the option of one of the parties, be governed by the law of country X or the law of country Y? At common law such a clause, if governed by English law, is ineffective.[51] In view of the fact that the Convention seeks to give full expression to the freedom of the parties, there is no obvious reason why a floating choice of law should be regarded as ineffective under Article 3. If the parties can agree to the applicable law at any time, a contractual agreement that one party may determine the applicable law at a future point would appear to fall within the scope of Article 3(2). Until such time as a final determination is made by the party authorised to make the choice, the contract is governed by the law designated by Article 4.

11.1.6 Mandatory rules

Although there are no restrictions on the law which the parties may choose, some provisions of the chosen law may be overridden by mandatory rules of the laws of other countries or may be disapplied on grounds of public policy.[52]

11.2 THE APPLICABLE LAW IN THE ABSENCE OF CHOICE

11.2.1 Introductory remarks

Article 4 provides:

> 1. To the extent that the law applicable to the contract has not been chosen in accordance with Article 3, the contract shall be governed by the law of the country with which it is most closely connected. Nevertheless, a severable part of the contract which has a closer connection with another country may by way of exception be governed by the law of that other country.
>
> 2. Subject to the provisions of paragraph 5 of this Article, it shall be presumed that the contract is most closely connected with the country where the party who is to effect the performance which is characteristic of the contract has, at the time of conclusion of the contract, his habitual residence, or, in the case of a body corporate or unincorporate, its central administration. However, if the contract is entered into in the course of that party's trade or profession, that country shall be the country in which the principal place of business is situated or, where under the terms of the contract the performance is to be effected through a place of business other than the principal place of business, the country in which that other place of business is situated.
>
> . . .

51. *Armar Shipping Co Ltd* v. *Caisse Algérienne d'Assurance et de Réassurance* [1981] 1 WLR 207.
52. See para. 11.3.

5. Paragraph 2 shall not apply if the characteristic performance cannot be determined, and the presumptions in paragraph [...] 2 ... shall be disregarded if it appears from the circumstances as a whole that the contract is more closely connected with another country.

Article 4 is one of the most controversial features of the Convention; it has even been described as "almost bizarre".[53] The basic idea is not, however, controversial; in the absence of choice by the parties a contract should be governed by the law of the country with which it is most closely connected. What is controversial is the way in which Article 4 raises presumptions to assist in finding the closest connection.[54]

11.2.2 Closest connection

Although the rule set out in the first sentence of Article 4(1) is similar to the objective proper law doctrine there are three important differences which should be noted.

(i) It is clear that the relevant connecting factors for determining the law which has the closest connection with the contract for the purposes of Article 4 are connections with countries. Under the objective proper law doctrine there is some ambiguity as to whether the relevant connecting factors are connections with countries, as geographical units, or with systems of law (or with both).

(ii) Under the common law all factors are taken into account in order to determine the proper law—not only connections relating to the contract, but also the connections of the parties, such as where the parties are resident. By contrast, Article 4(1) refers only to connections relating to the contract itself.

(iii) Under the common law doctrine the court is not entitled to consider events occurring after the conclusion of the contract.[55] The position under Article 4 is intended to be different. The Giuliano–Lagarde Report states that in order to determine the country with which the contract is most closely connected "it is also possible to take account of factors which supervened after the conclusion of the contract".[56] However, subsequent factors should be taken into account only as evidence of the strength of connections existing as at the date of the conclusion of the contract and not as independent factors in their own right.[57]

11.2.3 The presumption in paragraph 2

The effect of paragraphs 2 to 4 is that where the parties have not made a choice—whether express or implied—the contract is presumed to be most closely connected with the law of a particular country. The connecting factor which is used to identify the particular country depends on the nature of the parties and the type of contract in question. Paragraph 2 applies to all contracts falling within the scope of

53. Mann, "The Proper Law of the Contract—an Obituary" (1991) 107 LQR 353, 354.
54. See, for example, Morse, "The EEC Convention on the Law Applicable to Contractual Obligations" (1982) 2 YBEL 107, 126–131.
55. *James Miller & Partners Ltd* v. *Whitworth Street Estates (Manchester) Ltd* [1970] AC 583.
56. OJ 1980 C282/20.
57. Kaye, *The New Private International Law of Contract of the European Community* (1993) pp. 173–174.

Article 4 other than contracts relating to rights in immovable property and contracts for the carriage of goods.[58]

11.2.3.1 Introduction

11.2.3.1.1 The application of the presumption in Article 4(2) depends on two factors: (i) identification of the person who is to effect the performance which is characteristic of the contract (the "characteristic performer"); and (ii) identification of the connecting factor which localises the contract. The connecting factor, which is a territorial connection between a country and the "characteristic performer", will be one of four possibilities, depending on the circumstances of the case: habitual residence, central administration, principal place of business, or a place of business other than the principal place of business.

11.2.3.1.2 The Giuliano–Lagarde Report seeks to justify the use of the doctrine of characteristic performance—which originated in Switzerland, rather than in any of the Contracting States—in the following terms:

> The submission of the contract, in the absence of choice by the parties, to the law appropriate to the characteristic performance defines the connecting factor of the contract from the inside, and not from the outside by elements unrelated to the essence of the obligation such as the nationality of the contracting parties or the place where the contract was concluded. In addition it is possible to relate the concept of characteristic performance to an even more general idea, namely the idea that his performance refers to the function which the legal relationship involved fulfils in the economic and social life of any country. The concept of characteristic performance essentially links the contract to the social and economic environment of which it will form a part.[59]

Not everyone finds this passage entirely convincing; few would dispute that it "borders on the metaphysical".[60] Moreover, Article 4 does not necessarily forge a link between the "characteristic performance" and "the economic and social environment" of which the contract forms a part, since the presumption in Article 4(2) points to the place where the person who is to effect the characteristic performance is habitually resident rather than to the law of the place where the characteristic obligation is to be performed.

11.2.3.2 Characteristic performance

11.2.3.2.1 The central problem with paragraph 2 is the concept of "characteristic performance". The authors of the Giuliano–Lagarde Report make two general points. (i) In a unilateral contract the characteristic performance is easy to identify. Where, for example, A promises to pay B £500 if B walks to York it is obvious that B is the person who is to effect the characteristic performance. (ii) In a simple bilateral contract (such as a contract for the sale of goods or services) the characteristic performance is the performance for which payment is due.[61] So, in a contract of sale the seller is the characteristic performer; in a contract for the provision of services the person who

58. Article 4(3) deals with contracts relating to a right in or a right to use immovable property (see para. 12.4) and Article 4(4) with contracts for the carriage of goods (see para. 12.3). Article 5 applies to consumer contracts (para. 12.1) and Article 6 to individual contracts of employment (para. 12.2).

59. OJ 1980 C282/20.

60. Morse, "The EEC Convention on the Law Applicable to Contractual Obligations" (1982) 2 YBEL 107, 131.

61. OJ 1980 C282/20.

provides the services is the one who effects the characteristic performance. Why, in a contract of sale, should the seller's law be given preference over the law of the buyer? The answer given by the Report is that the obligations of the seller are generally more complex and therefore more regulated by law than those of the buyer. In addition, since it is generally the seller who frames the contract, a justification for the application of the seller's law is that "mass bargaining, like mass production, brings down the cost and the price".[62]

11.2.3.2.2 The notion of characteristic performance—which has been described as "a mysterious, almost mystical concept"[63]—may be criticised from a number of perspectives. At the most fundamental level it has been suggested that the basic notion is unsound:

> The attempt to see ontological qualities in aspects of a contractual relationship is doomed to failure. It is self-deception to believe that the characteristic performance is a criterion for the "objective localisation" of the contract, in the sense of a universally valid manner of connecting the contract that coincides with its essence. The essence of a given type of contract is not something that is present within it and can—by following simple(!) rules—be discovered. What we are actually concerned with here is not the determination of a real state of affairs but the attribution of values. It is not a matter of describing the intrinsic and immutable qualities of the contract, but of evaluating its various aspects in relation to one another.[64]

11.2.3.2.3 The doctrine—which favours the seller over the buyer and the person who provides services over the person who pays for them—is said to be no more than "a reflection of the prejudices of Helvetian hotel-keepers and cuckoo-clock makers, prejudices that will not be shared in countries that export tourists and import cuckoo-clocks".[65]

11.2.3.2.4 As a general doctrine for determining the applicable law, the notion of characteristic performance is subject to a number of limitations. The presumption clearly does not apply in certain relatively straightforward situations—notably in cases where the parties undertake reciprocal obligations of a similar type. For example, it will generally not be possible to identify the characteristic performance of a contract under the terms of which two or more enterprises agree to enter a joint venture. Similarly, the presumption does not apply to contracts of exchange. Furthermore, in a complex commercial agreement which imposes a range of obligations on both parties, it may well be impossible to determine the performance which is characteristic of the contract as a whole. In this type of case, the court may either seek to find the closest connection without the aid of the presumption in Article 4(2) or sever the contract and to apply different laws to different parts of the contract.[66]

11.2.3.2.5 Because the presumption in Article 4(2) obviously applies to some types of contract and equally clearly does not apply to others, the Convention creates problems of classification. For example, the distinction between exchange and sale, a controversy which can be traced back to Roman law,[67] is fundamental for the operation of the

62. Lando, "The EEC Convention on the Law Applicable to Contractual Obligations" (1987) 24 CMLRev 159, 202.
63. Diamond, "Conflict of Laws in the EEC" [1979] CLP 155, 168.
64. D'Oliveira, " 'Characteristic Obligation' in the Draft EEC Obligation Convention" (1977) 25 Am J Comp L 303, 308.
65. D'Oliveira, " 'Characteristic Obligation' in the Draft EEC Obligation Convention" (1977) 25 Am J Comp L 303, 328.
66. See the discussion of splitting the applicable law at para. 11.2.3.7.
67. See Smith, "Exchange or Sale?" (1974) 48 Tulane LR 1029.

Convention—since the presumption in Article 4(2) applies to sales but not to contracts of exchange. It is not always easy, however, to distinguish a sale from an exchange. In the context of countertrade,[68] for example, if the countertrade takes the form of reciprocal sales, the presumption in Article 4(2) applies to each separate sale; if the countertrade takes the form of barter the presumption in Article 4(2) cannot apply. To determine whether or not the presumption in Article 4(2) can be applied the court has, first, to classify the contract as being either a contract of sale or a contract of exchange. Traditional methodology in private international law indicates that the process of classification is to be undertaken by reference only to the conceptions of the *lex fori*. If this approach is applied in the context of Article 4(2) there is the danger that the Convention will not be applied consistently throughout the Contracting States.

11.2.3.2.6 Similar problems arise in the context of contracts which involve the performance of money obligations. If the characteristic performance is that in return for which payment is due, what is the characteristic performance of a bilateral contract where the obligation of each party is to pay? In a loan agreement, for example, there may be legitimate disagreement over whether the essence of the obligation is the provision of the loan or the obligation to repay.[69] According to the Swiss doctrine on which Article 4(2) is based, where there are two performances involving the payment of money, the characteristic performer is the party carrying the greater risk.[70] So, in a contract for the loan of money, the lender is the characteristic performer; in relation to a contract of insurance it is the insurer who is to effect the characteristic performance. Currency transactions pose equivalent difficulties. Depending on the particular circumstances an obligation to provide a certain number of units of a foreign currency may be regarded as an obligation to provide a commodity (in which case performance of that obligation would *prima facie* be characteristic of the contract) or as a monetary obligation (in which case its performance could not be so regarded).[71]

11.2.3.2.7 Because the characteristic performance is defined as that in return for which payment is due there is some uncertainty surrounding the operation of Article 4(2) in relation to contracts such as a distributorship agreement, where the distributor undertakes to market the manufacturer's goods, or a publisher's contract, where the publisher undertakes to print, bind and market the author's work. Notwithstanding the fact that the manufacturer and the author do not pay money to the distributor and the publisher, it may be supposed that, since the performance of the distributor and the publisher—who are remunerated by selling the product to the public—is the economic purpose of the contract, it is their performance which is characteristic.[72] The position cannot, however, be regarded as entirely free from doubt.

68. For a discussion of the various forms of countertrade and its growing practical importance see Schmitthoff, "Countertrade" [1985] JBL 115.

69. Morse, "The EEC Convention on the Law Applicable to Contractual Obligations" (1982) 2 YBEL 107, 131.

70. D'Oliveira, " 'Characteristic Obligation' in the Draft EEC Obligation Convention" (1977) 25 Am J Comp L 303, 314.

71. See Mann, *The Legal Aspect of Money* (5th ed, 1992) pp. 190–196.

72. Lando, "The EEC Convention on the Law Applicable to Contractual Obligations" (1987) 24 CMLRev 159, 204.

11.2.3.3 The connecting factor

There is nothing in the Convention or the Giuliano–Lagarde Report which sheds light on the meaning to be attached to the concepts "habitual residence", "central administration", "place of business" and "principal place of business". There are, however, English authorities which discuss some of the concepts employed in Article 4(2). Although these decisions may provide some assistance in the interpretation of Article 4(2) they need to be approached with considerable caution. It cannot be assumed that a concept such as "habitual residence" should have the same meaning in different contexts. Furthermore, since the Convention is an international instrument, national courts are required to have regard to the desirability of achieving uniformity in the interpretation and application of the Convention's provisions.[73]

11.2.3.3.1 HABITUAL RESIDENCE

11.2.3.3.1.1 A number of statutes which are derived from international conventions in the field of family law use "habitual residence" as a connecting factor.[74] Although the meaning of "habitual residence" has been considered by the English courts relatively infrequently,[75] there are some recent authorities decided in the context of Article 3 of the Hague Convention of the Civil Aspects of International Abduction (which is set out in Schedule 1 to the Child Abduction and Custody Act 1985).[76]

11.2.3.3.1.2 Three important propositions emerge from the English cases. (i) Habitual residence refers to a person's abode in a particular place or country which he has adopted voluntarily and for settled purposes as part of the regular order of his life for the time being, whether of short or long duration.[77] It goes without saying that a person may be regarded as habitually resident in a country even though at the particular time the person is not physically present there. Even long and repeated absences will often not negative habitual residence. (ii) Habitual residence is primarily a question of fact to be decided by reference to all the circumstances of any particular case.[78] (iii) It has been said that:

> [T]here is a significant difference between a person ceasing to be habitually resident in country A, and his subsequently becoming habitually resident in country B. A person may cease to be habitually resident in country A in a single day if he or she leaves it with a settled intention not to return to it but to take up long-term residence in country B instead. Such a person cannot, however, become habitually resident in country B in a single day. An appreciable period of time and a settled intention will be necessary to enable him or her to become so. During that appreciable period of time the person will have ceased to be habitually resident in country A but not yet have become habitually resident in country B.[79]

73. Article 18.

74. See, for example, Matrimonial Causes Act 1973, Domicile and Matrimonial Proceedings Act 1974, Child Abduction and Custody Act 1985, Family Law Act 1986.

75. *Cruse* v. *Chittum* [1974] 2 All ER 940 (discussed by Hall, "Cruse v. Chittum: Habitual Residence Judicially Explored" (1975) 24 ICLQ 1); *R* v. *Barnet LBC ex parte Shah* [1983] 2 AC 309; *Kapur* v. *Kapur* [1984] FLR 920.

76. *Re J (A Minor) (Abduction: Custody Rights)* [1990] 2 AC 562; *V* v. *B (A Minor) (Abduction)* [1991] 1 FLR 266.

77. See Lord Scarman in *R* v. *Barnet LBC ex parte Shah* [1983] 2 AC 309, 343.

78. Lord Brandon in *Re J (A Minor) (Abduction: Custody Rights)* [1990] 2 AC 562, 578.

79. Lord Brandon in *Re J (A Minor) (Abduction: Custody Rights)* [1990] 2 AC 562, 578–579.

11.2.3.3.1.3 According to these principles, it would appear that a person may not be habitually resident in any country or may be habitually resident in more than one country at the same time.[80] If a person cannot be regarded as habitually resident anywhere, the presumption in Article 4(2) cannot be applied and the applicable law has to be determined without the assistance of any presumption. Where an individual is habitually resident in two different countries at the same time the position under the Convention is less clear. The choice is between applying the presumption in favour of the country with which the characteristic performer is more (or most) closely connected or ignoring paragraph 2 and relying entirely on paragraph 1.

11.2.3.3.2 CENTRAL ADMINISTRATION

Central administration is not a connecting factor which has traditionally been used widely in English private international law. However, the place where "central management and control" is exercised is used for determining the residence of companies, primarily for the purpose of tax legislation; in addition section 42 of the Civil Jurisdiction and Judgments Act 1982 uses "central management and control" as one of the connecting factors for determining the domicile of corporations for the purposes of the Brussels and Lugano Conventions.[81] To determine the place where central management and control is exercised, it is important to look at the actual facts, rather than the company's constitution.[82] The same approach is appropriate when considering the location of the central administration of a company (or other body) for the purposes of Article 4(2).

Potential problems may arise in cases where the administration of a company is divided between different centres. In such a case, it may be concluded that the company has no central administration or has more than one central administration. These problems mirror those that arise in cases where an individual is not habitually resident in any country or is regarded as being habitually resident in more than one country.

11.2.3.3.3 PLACE OF BUSINESS

In the context of Part XXIII of the Companies Act 1985 the courts have interpreted the words "place of business" broadly.[83] In *South India Shipping Corporation Ltd* v. *Export-Import Bank of Korea*[84] the Court of Appeal held that the defendant bank had a place of business in England notwithstanding the fact that it contracted no banking business from its premises in London. In the context of the Brussels and Lugano Conventions the term "place of business" is understood in a broad sense; in particular, it covers "any entity such as a branch or agency with no legal personality".[85]

80. A person may be domiciled in more than one country for the purposes of the Brussels and Lugano Conventions: *Daniel* v. *Foster*, 1989 SLT 90 (Sh Ct) (a decision under the Modified Convention).

81. See para. 4.1.2.

82. *Unit Construction Co Ltd* v. *Bullock (Inspector of Taxes)* [1960] AC 351.

83. Companies Act 1985, s. 691. See para. 6.1.2.4.

84. [1985] 1 WLR 585.

85. Almeida Cruz–Desantes Real–Jenard Report, OJ 1990 C198/45, n. 1.

11.2.3.3.4 PRINCIPAL PLACE OF BUSINESS

11.2.3.3.4.1 A party to a contract may have only one principal place of business. The Convention does not indicate the criteria which should be applied in deciding which of several places of business is to be regarded as the principal one. The choice is essentially between the administrative centre, where important business decisions are taken, and the main business centre, where most business is transacted. Under English law the principal place of business is not necessarily the place where most of the business is carried out.[86] In *The Polzeath*[87] the issue facing the court was whether a company's principal place of business was in England for the purposes of section 1 of the Merchant Shipping Act 1894. The Court of Appeal decided that:

> [I]n considering what is the principal place of business of [a] company, one has to consider the centre from which instructions are given, and from which control is exercised on behalf of the company over the employees of and the business of the company, and where control is exercised, and the centre from which the company is managed without any further control except such control as every company or the directors of a company are liable to by the larger body which they represent, the shareholders of the company in general meeting.[88]

11.2.3.3.4.2 *The Rewia*[89] concerned the interpretation of a bill of lading which provided that any dispute arising under it "shall be decided in the country where the carrier has its principal place of business". The vessel in which the goods were carried was owned by the defendant, a one-ship Liberian company. The shareholders of the defendant company were German banks, the directors of the company were German residents and the board of directors met in Germany. The operation and management of the ship was, however, delegated entirely to a Hong Kong company. When a dispute arose under the bill of lading, proceedings were commenced in England and one of the issues facing the court was to determine whether the defendant's principal place of business was in Liberia (the place of registration), Germany (the place where decisions concerning the company were taken) or Hong Kong (where the company carried on its economic activity).

11.2.3.3.4.3 At first instance Sheen J took the view that the defendant's principal place of business was in Hong Kong on the basis that "principal" means "main" and that Hong Kong was the place where most of the defendant's business was conducted.[90] This decision was reversed on appeal. The Court of Appeal decided that "principal" means "chief" or "most important", with the consequence that the defendant's principal place of business was located where the "most important decisions would be taken".[91] According to this test the principal place of business was Germany. Furthermore, this conclusion was not negatived by the fact that there was no building or establishment in Germany which could be identified as the company's place of business.

11.2.3.3.4.4 The extent to which the approach adopted in these cases is equally applicable to Article 4(2) is questionable. The test formulated by the Court of Appeal in *The Polzeath* and applied in *The Rewia* tends to equate the principal place of business

86. Leggatt LJ in *The Rewia* [1991] 2 Lloyd's Rep 325, 334.
87. [1916] P 241.
88. Swinfen Eady LJ, [1916] P 241, 245. See also *Palmer* v. *Caledonian Railway Co* [1892] 1 QB 823.
89. [1991] 2 Lloyd's Rep 325.
90. [1991] 1 Lloyd's Rep 69.
91. Leggatt LJ, [1991] 2 Lloyd's Rep 325, 335.

with the central administration. The structure of Article 4(2) suggests that a distinction should be drawn between a company's central administration and its principal place of business. Accordingly, the test proposed at first instance by Sheen J in *The Rewia* is more likely to give effect to the purpose of Article 4(2).

11.2.3.4 The presumption

11.2.3.4.1 It should be stressed that in the context of Article 4(2) it is not the place of performance which is important, but the territorial connections of the "characteristic performer". The territorial connection depends on (i) whether the characteristic performer is an individual or a body corporate or unincorporate and (ii) whether the characteristic performer enters into the contract in the course of his trade or profession.

11.2.3.4.2 If the characteristic performer is an individual and he enters the contract otherwise than in the course of his trade or profession, the presumption points to the country where the characteristic performer is habitually resident. So, if an English holidaymaker sells his caravan while on holiday in France, it will be presumed that the contract of sale is most closely connected with England—since the seller is habitually resident in England and the contract is concluded otherwise than in course of the seller's trade or profession. It is irrelevant whether the buyer enters the contract as part of his trade or profession. Where the characteristic performer is not an individual and the contract is entered into otherwise than in that party's trade or profession, the contract is presumed to be most closely connected with the country in which the central administration of the characteristic performer is located.

11.2.3.4.3 It is to be expected that in the commercial sphere most contracts—whether involving individuals or firms—will be in entered into in the course of the trade or profession of the characteristic performer. Accordingly, the general rule set out in the first part of Article 4(2) is likely to yield to the exception in the majority of cases. Where the characteristic performer enters the contract in the course of his trade or profession the factor which localises the contract is either the principal place of business of the characteristic performer or, if the characteristic performance is to be effected through a place of business other than the principal place of business, the place where the other place of business is located. The connecting factor indicated by Article 4(2) (whether habitual residence, central administration, principal place of business or other place of business) is determined at the time when the contract is concluded, not at the date of performance.

11.2.3.4.4 Article 4(2) is a tortuously drafted provision, which is not without its difficulties. Its operation can, however, be illustrated by a couple of examples.

(i) A, a company with its central administration in London, but its principal place of business in Dublin, contracts to provide services to B, a French company. If the contract is concluded in the course of A's trade or profession, the presumption points to Irish law; if the contract is not concluded in the course of A's trade or profession, the presumption points to English law.

(ii) A is a company with its central administration in London, but its principal place of business in Dublin. A also has a branch office in France. A contracts to provide services to B, a French company. The contract stipulates that the services will be provided through the French branch office. If the contract is concluded in the course of A's trade or profession, the presumption points to

French law, but if the contract is concluded otherwise than in the course of A's trade or profession, the presumption in Article 4(2) points to English law.

It should be noted that where performance is effected through a place of business other than the principal place of business this is only significant to the extent that the contract stipulates that performance is to be effected through that place. The fact that performance is effected through a place of business other than the principal place of business is, in itself, irrelevant.

11.2.3.5 The presumption does not apply

In certain cases it may be impossible to establish the characteristic performance of a contract. In such a case Article 4(5) indicates that the test laid down in the first paragraph of Article 4 must be applied; the applicable law is the law of the country with which the contract is most closely connected. The determination of the applicable law in these circumstances involves a consideration and weighing of a wide variety of relevant factors.

11.2.3.6 Rebuttal of the presumption

11.2.3.6.1 More problematical is the second part of Article 4(5) which provides for the rebuttal of the presumption where the contract is more closely connected with the law of another country. One of the most criticised aspects of the Convention is the relationship between paragraph 1, paragraph 2 and paragraph 5. For example, it has been said that Article 4 "introduces three steps into a search for the applicable law which can be just as easily satisfied by one step and by posing one question, namely, the question posed in Article 4(1)".[92] It cannot be denied that there are potential problems surrounding the application of Article 4(5). Indeed, the Giuliano–Lagarde Report admits that Article 4(5) leaves the judge a margin of discretion as to whether a set of circumstances exists in each specific case justifying the non-application of the presumption.[93] Nevertheless, the argument that, in cases where the parties have not made a choice of law, paragraphs 2 to 5 of Article 4 are effectively redundant misses the point.

11.2.3.6.2 The purpose of choice of law rules in contract is not merely to guide the courts in determining the applicable law in cases which are litigated before them. Parties who have failed to make a choice of law may nevertheless legitimately expect to be able to determine the applicable law for themselves by reference to the relevant choice of law rules. A pure test of closest connection is perfectly adequate for cases in which it is obvious that the contract is more closely connected with one country rather than another. In this type of situation the presumption in Article 4(2) does little to assist the choice of law process. However, in cases where the relevant connecting factors are evenly divided between two or more different countries, a pure test of closest

92. Morse, "The EEC Convention on the Law Applicable to Contractual Obligations" (1982) 2 YBEL 107, 129–130. See also Collins, "Contractual Obligations—the EEC Preliminary Draft Convention on Private International Law" (1976) 25 ICLQ 35, 49.
93. OJ 1980 C282/22.

connection generates considerable uncertainty, since it may be very difficult to assess which factor or factors might be regarded by the court as crucial in tipping the balance one way or the other. The value of the presumption in Article 4(2) is clearly revealed in those cases in which the distribution of connecting factors produces a "dead heat" between the laws of two or more countries; in this type of case "the tie is broken by the presumption".[94] Whatever system of choice of law rules is adopted difficult borderline cases will almost inevitably occur. Those who criticise the approach adopted by the drafters of the Convention fail to recognise that the presumption in paragraph 2 can provide a consistent and predictable solution to most difficult cases.

11.2.3.6.3 Whether the English courts will allow the presumption to perform its intended function remains to be seen. There is no doubt that if paragraph 5 is allowed to dominate paragraph 2, the presumption will become redundant. However, in the interests of certainty and predictability the presumption should be displaced only in clear cases, not in cases where the relevant connecting factors are evenly distributed between two or more countries.

11.2.3.7 Scission

Article 4(1) provides for different laws to be applied to different parts of a single contract. This may arise in two different ways.

(i) Different laws may apply to different parts of a contract as a consequence of the interaction of Articles 3 and 4. Article 3 allows the parties to choose the law to govern their contractual relations. If the parties choose the applicable law in relation to only part of the contract, Article 4 determines the law which governs the remainder of the contract. In this situation the law which has the closest connection with the contract for the purposes of Article 4 may be different from the law chosen by the parties.

(ii) Article 4(1) provides that, even in cases where the parties have not made a choice and Article 3 is wholly irrelevant, a severable part of the contract may be governed by a law which is different from that which governs the main part of the contract. So, where the main contract is most closely connected with the law of country X and a severable part of the contract is more closely connected with country Y, the law of country Y may be applied to that severable part. The Giuliano–Lagarde Report makes it clear that courts should effect severance only "by way of exception, for part of a contract which is independent and separable, in terms of the contract and not of the dispute" and should have recourse to severance "as seldom as possible".[95]

11.2.4 Mandatory rules

In cases where the parties have failed to make a choice for the purposes of Article 3(1), specific rules which form part of the applicable law—as determined by the principles

94. Diamond, "Conflict of Laws in the EEC" [1979] CLP 155, 167.
95. OJ 1980 C282/23.

set out in Article 4—may be overridden by mandatory rules of the laws of other countries or may be disapplied on grounds of public policy.[96]

11.3 MANDATORY RULES AND PUBLIC POLICY

11.3.1 Introduction

11.3.1.1 The Convention imposes no restrictions on the law which can be chosen by the parties to a contract; the choice of a law which is wholly unconnected with the transaction is perfectly valid. However, in certain circumstances specific rules which are part of the law chosen by the parties may yield to the mandatory rules of another law. Similarly, in cases where the parties have not made a choice of law and the applicable law is determined by Article 4, the applicable law may be overridden by the mandatory rules of another law.[97]

11.3.1.2 From a policy point of view almost all mandatory rules which have an impact on contractual relations fall into one of two categories.[98]

(i) Many legal systems include rules which are intended to protect the weaker party. Classic examples of mandatory rules of this type include consumer legislation (such as legislation dealing with product liability, the right to cancel a contract, maximum interest rates, the right to be given certain information, the requirement that goods should be of a reasonable quality) and employment protection legislation (such as rules relating to hours of work, minimum wages, the right to strike, remedies for unfair dismissal and compensation for industrial injuries).

(ii) Legal systems also include rules intended to promote the social and economic policies of the State. Important examples of rules of this type include exchange control legislation, price control legislation, rules on cartels, monopolies and mergers and legislation relating to import and export controls.

Although mandatory rules are most likely to be statutory in origin, it is perfectly possible for a common law rule to be mandatory for the purposes of the Convention.[99]

11.3.1.3 The Convention draws a distinction between two different types of mandatory rule, an aspect of the Convention which is, to some extent, disguised in the English language version, but which is clear from both the French and German texts.[100] Article 3(3) defines mandatory rules as "rules ... which cannot be derogated from by contract". Article 7 defines a narrower category of rules which not only are mandatory in the sense of Article 3(3) (ie cannot be derogated from by contract) but also "must be applied whatever the law applicable to the contract". In the French version of the Convention rules of the first type are referred to as *dispositions impératives*, whereas rules of the second type are called *lois de police*. By comparison the English text is rather

96. See para. 11.3.

97. There are also specific provisions dealing with consumer contracts (see para. 12.1.2.2) and individual contracts of employment (para. 12.2.3).

98. Hartley, "Beyond the Proper Law" (1979) 4 ELRev 236, 238–239.

99. Giuliano–Lagarde Report, OJ 1980 C282/27.

100. See Plender, *The European Contracts Convention* (1991) p. 101.

inelegant. Since it is vital to distinguish these two different categories of rules, mandatory rules which must be applied whatever the law applicable to the contract—the narrower category—are referred to as "overriding rules".

11.3.1.4 Mandatory rules are provisions which the parties cannot by agreement exclude in a purely domestic contract which does not include among its terms a choice of law. There are numerous examples of rules of this type in English law. For example, it is an implied condition in a sale that the seller has a right to sell the goods; in the case of an agreement to sell it is an implied condition that the seller will have such a right at the time when the property is to pass.[101] These implied conditions cannot be excluded or restricted by reference to any contract term.[102] Similarly, in a lease of a dwelling-house for a term of less than seven years the landlord's implied covenant to keep the structure and exterior in repair[103] cannot be limited by the terms of the lease.[104] "Overriding rules", however, are rules which are not only mandatory but which the parties cannot avoid by the selection of a foreign law, even though a foreign element is present.[105]

11.3.1.5 Whether a particular rule of law is mandatory or "overriding" (or neither) is a question of construction, which can only be answered by reference to the law of which the particular rule forms a part. Although in certain circumstances it may be perfectly clear whether a rule is mandatory, in others the position will be obscure. English rules are particularly difficult to classify; the terminology and conceptual structure of the Convention in relation to mandatory rules is alien to English law and it is unusual for English legislation to include any indication as to whether or not a particular rule of law is mandatory.[106] The problems surrounding the classification of common law rules are even more pronounced.

11.3.2 The application of mandatory rules

11.3.2.1 Article 3(3), the purpose of which is to prevent the evasion of domestic rules which would in the normal course of events govern the parties' contractual obligations, provides:

> The fact that the parties have chosen a foreign law, whether or not accompanied by the choice of a foreign tribunal, shall not, where all the other elements relevant to the situation at the time of the choice are connected with one country only, prejudice the application of rules of the law of that country which cannot be derogated from by contract, hereinafter called "mandatory rules".

11.3.2.2 This provision is concerned with the situation where parties have concluded an agreement which is to all intents and purposes a domestic contract, but have chosen the law of a foreign country to govern the contract. In this type of case the choice of a foreign law does not prejudice the application of the mandatory rules of the law of the country with which all the relevant factors are connected. Article 3(3) does not, however, invalidate the choice of law; the choice is still operative as regards the contract

101. Sale of Goods Act 1979, s. 12(1).
102. Unfair Contract Terms Act 1977, s. 6(1)(a).
103. Landlord and Tenant Act 1985, s. 11(1)(a) and s. 13(1).
104. Landlord and Tenant Act 1985, s. 12(1).
105. Plender, *The European Contracts Convention* (1991) p. 101.
106. In *Chiron Corporation* v. *Organon Teknika Ltd (No. 2)* [1993] FSR 567, for example, the Court of Appeal held that section 44(1) of the Patents Act 1977—which renders void various terms of "a contract for the supply of a patented product or of a licence to work a patented invention, or of a contract relating to any such supply or licence"—applies to contracts which are governed by the law of a foreign country.

as a whole. The effect of Article 3(3) is to supersede the chosen law only to the extent that mandatory rules of another legal system are applicable.

11.3.2.3 Although the basic purpose of Article 3(3) is to counteract an evasive choice of law in a domestic contract, the test applied by Article 3(3) is based on objective criteria ("elements relevant to the situation"), rather than the subjective intentions of the parties. Nevertheless, a major problem of interpretation surrounds the meaning of the word "relevant". The Giuliano–Lagarde Report sheds no light on this potentially difficult question. What, for example, is the position where two English parties include a choice of foreign law in a contract for the sale of goods which are manufactured by the seller at a factory in a foreign country? Is the fact that the goods are made abroad a "relevant" element? All the factors relating to the contract are connected with England and from the point of view of the applicable law whether the goods are made in England or abroad would not seem to be relevant. However, Article 3(3) refers to elements which are relevant to the "situation", rather than to the contract. In this regard Article 3(3) appears to leave considerable latitude to the courts.

11.3.2.4 Another issue is whether Article 3(3) requires the application of the mandatory rules of the country with which all the factors relevant to the situation are connected or whether a discretion is conferred on the courts. As a matter of common sense, Article 3(3) should be interpreted in such a way that the forum gives effect to foreign mandatory rules only to the extent that they would be applied by the court of the country with which all the relevant elements are connected.[107]

11.3.3 The application of "overriding rules"

The application of "overriding rules" may arise both in cases where the parties have chosen a law and in cases where the applicable law is determined by Article 4.

11.3.3.1 "Overriding rules" under Article 7(1)

Article 7(1) provides:

> When applying under this Convention the law of a country, effect may be given to the mandatory rules of the law of another country with which the situation has a close connection, if and in so far as, under the law of the latter country, those rules must be applied whatever the law applicable to the contract. In considering whether to give effect to these mandatory rules, regard shall be had to their nature and purpose and to the consequences of their application or non-application.

Article 7(1), which owes something to governmental interest analysis both in its phrasing and its substance, has no obvious counterpart in the common law. When the draft convention was being considered Article 7(1) came in for considerable criticism[108] and when the final version of the Convention was being negotiated the United Kingdom

107. Morse, "The EEC Convention on the Law Applicable to Contractual Obligations" (1982) 2 YBEL 107, 123.

108. See, for example, Collins, "Contractual Obligations—the EEC Preliminary Draft Convention on Private International Law" (1976) 25 ICLQ 35, 49–51.

delegates expressed fears that this provision would give rise to uncertainty.[109] Notwithstanding the fact that certain commentators hoped that Article 7(1) would be implemented in the United Kingdom,[110] the United Kingdom entered a reservation on Article 7(1) (as permitted by Article 22(1)(a)) and this provision does not have the force of law in England.[111]

11.3.3.2 "Overriding rules" of the forum: Article 7(2)

11.3.3.2.1 Article 7(2) provides:

> Nothing in this Convention shall restrict the application of the rules of the law of the forum in a situation where they are mandatory irrespective of the law otherwise applicable to the contract.

Whereas Article 3(3) is concerned with domestic rules which cannot be excluded by contractual agreement, Article 7 is directed at overriding rules—rules which not only are mandatory, in the sense that they cannot be derogated from by contract in the domestic context, but which must be applied regardless of the applicable law. The Giuliano–Lagarde Report suggests that overriding rules within the scope of Article 7(2) are likely to be "rules on cartels, competition and restrictive practices, consumer protection and certain rules concerning carriage".[112] In English law, the Unfair Contract Terms Act 1977, the Employment Protection (Consolidation) Act 1978 and the Carriage of Goods by Sea Act 1971 include examples of overriding rules.[113]

11.3.3.2.2 The operation of Article 7(2) can be illustrated by considering the Unfair Contract Terms Act 1977. The primary purpose of the 1977 Act is to regulate clauses which limit or exclude contractual liability. Many of the controls contained in the Act are directed at consumer contracts. Nevertheless, some provisions apply to ordinary commercial contracts as well as to consumer contracts. The scope of the controls contained in the 1977 Act is clearly defined by sections 26 and 27. The limits imposed by the Act do not apply to international supply contracts which are governed by English law.[114] Furthermore, sections 2 to 7 of the 1977 Act do not apply in cases where the applicable law is English law "only by choice of the parties".[115] Conversely, in certain circumstances the Act applies, notwithstanding the fact that the applicable law is the law of a country outside the United Kingdom. Section 27(2), which defines the extent to which the Act contains overriding rules within the meaning of Article 7(2) of the Convention, provides:

> This Act has effect notwithstanding any contract term which applies or purports to apply the law of some country outside the United Kingdom, where (either or both) —
> (a) the term appears to the court, or arbitrator ... to have been imposed wholly or mainly for the purpose of enabling the party imposing it to evade the operation of this Act; or

109. Giuliano–Lagarde Report, OJ 1980 C282/28.
110. Carter, "Contracts in English Private International Law" (1986) 57 BYIL 1, 20.
111. Contracts (Applicable Law) Act 1990, s. 2(2). Germany, Ireland and Luxembourg also entered a reservation on Article 7(1).
112. OJ 1980 C282/28.
113. Aspects of these statutes are discussed in the context of the specific contracts in question. See para. 12.1 (consumer contacts); para. 12.2 (individual employment contracts); para. 12.3 (contracts for the carriage of goods).
114. Unfair Contract Terms Act 1977, s. 26.
115. Unfair Contract Terms Act 1977, s. 27(1).

(b) in the making of the contract one of the parties dealt as consumer, and he was then habitually resident in the United Kingdom, and the essential steps necessary for the making of the contract were taken there, whether by him or by others on his behalf.

11.3.3.2.3 Where, for example, an English traveller buys a train ticket from a foreign railway operator for transportation between two foreign cities, a clause in the contract which excludes the railway operator's liability for death or personal injury will be void in England by virtue of Article 7(2) if the traveller takes all the essential steps necessary for the making of the contract in England, even though the contract contains an express choice of law in favour of a foreign law under which the contractual exclusion is valid.[116] Section 27(2) states that the 1977 Act (which includes a provision which renders void any contract term which seeks to exclude or restrict liability for death or personal injury resulting from negligence[117]) is overriding in these circumstances.

11.3.4 Public policy: Article 16

11.3.4.1 According to the traditional common law approach to cases involving contractual obligations, questions of public policy may generally be placed in one of two categories.[118] (i) The doctrine of public policy may be invoked if the nature or content of the foreign rule is so unacceptably repugnant that it could never be applied in England. For example, a contract for the sale of slaves or a contract to bribe a public official would not be enforced in England. (ii) The second category of case is not so much focused on the content of a foreign rule, but on the undesirability of an English court being seen to act in a particular way: "The main thrust of public policy here is not to achieve the rejection of an intrinsically repugnant foreign rule, but rather to protect the public or national interest or image of the United Kingdom."[119] So, in *Foster* v. *Driscoll*[120] the Court of Appeal refused to enforce a contract for the introduction of alcohol into the United States of America during prohibition, and in *Regazzoni* v. *K C Sethia (1944) Ltd*[121] a contract designed to circumvent Indian export controls was refused enforcement by the House of Lords on grounds of public policy. These cases are an illustration of "[t]he overriding principle ... that an English court will decline to take action which would be liable to be significantly detrimental to the national or international interests of the United Kingdom, and this is so regardless of the identity of the *lex causae*".[122]

11.3.4.2 Article 16 provides:

The application of a rule of the law of any country specified by this Convention may be refused only if such application is manifestly incompatible with the public policy ("ordre public") of the forum.

116. By virtue of Article 5(4) this contract is not a consumer contract for the purposes of Article 5 of the Convention. See para. 12.1.1.1.

117. Unfair Contract Terms Act 1977, s. 2(1).

118. See Carter, "Rejection of Foreign Law: Some Private International Law Inhibitions" (1984) 55 BYIL 111, 123–125.

119. Carter, "Rejection of Foreign Law: Some Private International Law Inhibitions" (1984) 55 BYIL 111, 124.

120. [1929] 1 KB 470.

121. [1958] AC 301.

122. Carter, "Rejection of Foreign Law: Some Private International Law Inhibitions" (1984) 55 BYIL 111, 125. For further discussion see para. 11.4.10.

As a general rule, international conventions in the field of private international law make some allowances for the fact that different countries apply different standards to certain fundamental questions. Article 16 provides for the non-application of a foreign rule which conflicts with the public policy of the forum. Article 16 is different in its operation from Article 7(2). Whereas Article 7(2) is positive, in the sense that it provides that certain "overriding rules" of the forum displace the applicable law, the effect of Article 16 is negative in that it involves the exclusion by the forum of a particular rule of the applicable law. Nevertheless, in certain circumstances it may be difficult to determine whether an agreement is null and void because it violates the public policy of the forum (Article 16) or because an overriding rule of the forum makes it unenforceable (Article 7(2)). The result, however, is the same.[123]

11.3.4.3 Article 16 is intended to be very narrow in scope; the application of the foreign rule must be manifestly contrary to the public policy of the forum. Moreover, the fact that the content of a foreign rule is contrary to English public policy is not in itself a ground on which Article 16 may be invoked. The effect of Article 16 is that the court may refuse to apply a foreign rule of law only where the result of the application of the foreign rule of law is contrary to English public policy: "It may therefore happen that a foreign law, which might in the abstract be held to be contrary to the public policy of the forum, could nevertheless be applied, if the actual result of its being applied does not in itself offend the public policy of the forum."[124]

11.3.4.4 For example, if a Swiss citizen, domiciled in France and resident in England, enters into an agreement with a French resident in France, by which the former undertakes not to compete with the latter in England, the contract is void in this country (irrespective of its validity under the applicable law), if it is contrary to the English principles on restraint of trade which are a matter of public policy. If, however, the contract provides that the former will not compete with the latter in France there would be no basis on which enforcement of the contract could be refused on public policy grounds, since the enforcement of an agreement not to compete in a foreign country does not conflict with English public policy.

11.4 PARTICULAR ASPECTS OF THE CONTRACT

11.4.1 Preliminary remarks

The applicable law plays the most significant role in determining the rights and obligations of the parties to a contract. The applicable law is one of the systems of rules by which the formal validity is tested[125] and the putative applicable law governs questions of material validity.[126] In addition, Article 10(1) provides a list of matters which are governed by the applicable law:

123. Lando, "The EEC Convention on the Law Applicable to Contractual Obligations" (1987) 24 CMLRev 159, 208.
124. Giuliano–Lagarde Report, OJ 1980 C282/38.
125. Article 9.
126. Article 8.

The law applicable to a contract by virtue of Articles 3 to 6 and 12 of this Convention shall govern in particular:

(a) interpretation;
(b) performance;
(c) within the limits of the powers conferred on the court by its procedural law, the consequences of breach, including the assessment of damages in so far as it is governed by rules of law;
(d) the various ways of extinguishing obligations, and prescription and limitation of actions;
(e) the consequences of nullity of the contract.

A number of general points should be made about this provision before examining the particular issues. (i) The list in Article 10(1) is illustrative rather than exhaustive.[127] (ii) The United Kingdom has made a reservation on paragraph (e) on the basis that the effects of nullity are classified under English law as concerning restitution or quasi-contract rather than contract. (iii) There are some matters which are not governed by the applicable law at all or are not exclusively governed by the applicable law.

11.4.2 Material validity: Article 8

11.4.2.1 Introduction

11.4.2.1.1 Under the common law, the formation of a contract is governed by the putative proper law—that is, the law which would be the proper law of the contract if the contract was validly concluded.[128] The rationale for the application of the putative proper law is that "it is (or will be) the law governing validity, quite regardless of whether this is (or will be) because it represents the parties' choice or because it is the law of the country of closest and most real connection".[129] According to this approach, a disputed choice of law clause is relevant for determining the law which will govern the validity of the clause itself and, if valid, the validity of the contract as a whole.

11.4.2.1.2 Article 8 of the Convention adopts a similar principle in paragraph 1, but provides an exception in the second paragraph:

1. The existence and validity of a contract, or of any term of a contract, shall be determined by the law which would govern it under this Convention if the contract or term were valid.

2. Nevertheless a party may rely upon the law of the country in which he has his habitual residence to establish that he did not consent if it appears from the circumstances that it would not be reasonable to determine the effect of his conduct in accordance with the law specified in the preceding paragraph.

The Convention draws a distinction between formal and material validity: Article 8 deals with material validity; Article 9 provides rules concerning formal validity. Article 8 "is intended to cover all aspects of formation of the contract other than general validity", including "the existence and validity of the parties' consent as to choice of the applicable law".[130] The issues which fall within the scope of Article 8 include: whether

127. Giuliano–Lagarde Report, OJ 1980 C282/32.

128. *Marc Rich & Co AG* v. *Societa Italiana Impianti PA* [1989] 1 Lloyd's Rep 548, 552. See also *The Parouth* [1982] 2 Lloyd's Rep 351.

129. Carter, "Contracts in English Private International Law" (1986) 57 BYIL 1, 26. Cf. Collins, "Choice of Forum and the Exercise of Judicial Discretion—the Resolution of an Anglo-American Conflict" (1973) 22 ICLQ 332, 339–340. For further consideration of the position at common law see Libling, "Formation of International Contracts" (1979) 42 MLR 169; Briggs, "The Formation of International Contracts" [1990] LMCLQ 192.

130. Giuliano–Lagarde Report, OJ 1980 C282/28.

the parties have reached agreement; whether an agreement is unenforceable for want of consideration; whether a contract is void for mistake; whether a contract is void for illegality; whether a contract is voidable for duress, misrepresentation or undue influence.

11.4.2.2 The general principle

11.4.2.2.1 Article 8(1) provides a simple—perhaps even simplistic—solution to potentially difficult questions. The general principle contained in Article 8(1) is that all questions of existence and validity (excluding questions of formal validity) are governed by the putative applicable law—that is, the law which would apply if the contract were valid. Where, for example, a seller fails to deliver goods under an alleged contract of sale and, as a defence to the buyer's action for breach, claims that the contract is void for mistake, the question of whether the contract is void is to be determined by the putative applicable law as determined by the principles set out in Article 4, the presumption being that the seller's law will apply.

11.4.2.2.2 The position is more complex in cases where the dispute over the existence of the contract also involves a dispute concerning the existence of a choice of law. Suppose that a buyer offers to buy specific goods from the seller on terms which include a choice of law clause in favour of the buyer's law; before the seller replies, the buyer purports to withdraw the offer; notwithstanding the purported revocation, the seller accepts the offer. Under the buyer's law the revocation is effective; under the seller's law it is not. Is there a valid contract? The first point to consider is whether a contractual choice of law exists. The combined effect of Article 3 and Article 8(1) is that the buyer's law, as the putative applicable law, governs the existence and validity of the term in question. Under the buyer's law, however, the revocation is effective and, therefore, the choice of law clause fails to come into existence. Accordingly, the existence of the contract as a whole has to be determined on the basis that the parties made no choice. In these circumstances, as a result of Article 8(1) and Article 4, the putative applicable law will normally be the seller's law, since the seller is the "characteristic performer". According to the seller's law the purported revocation of the buyer's offer is ineffective; therefore the contract is validly created.

11.4.2.2.3 Opinion on the merits of Article 8(1) is divided. In terms of pure logic the approach adopted by Article 8(1) is questionable; on this basis it is thought by some to be "wrong and misguided".[131] Although Article 8(1) involves "bootstraps" reasoning, it is not obvious that any other solution would achieve uniformity across the Contracting States. At least Article 8(1) "cuts the knot by an arbitrary but convenient solution".[132]

11.4.2.3 The problem of consent

11.4.2.3.1 Without the exception contained in paragraph 2, Article 8(1) could lead to potentially absurd and unjust results in cases where one of the parties claims that he did not consent. Suppose that a French seller offers goods to an English buyer and expressly provides that the contract of sale is to be governed by Ruritanian law, according to which silence equals acceptance. The application of Article 8(1) to this situation leads to

131. Briggs, "The Formation of International Contracts" [1990] LMCLQ 192, 193.
132. Diamond, "Conflict of Laws in the EEC" [1979] CLP 155, 162.

the conclusion that there is a binding contract, notwithstanding the fact that the buyer has done nothing positive to indicate his acceptance and that no contract comes into existence under either the seller's or the buyer's law. In this type of situation Article 8(2) allows the offeree to rely on the law of his habitual residence. If, according to the law of the offeree's habitual residence, silence does not constitute acceptance, the court may decide that no contract has been concluded.

11.4.2.3.2 A number of further points should be noted.

(i) Article 8(2) refers to "conduct", and does not relate solely to silence.

(ii) Article 8(2) uses the term "party" and, therefore, can be relied upon either by the offeror or the offeree.

(iii) Although Article 8(2) may invalidate an agreement which would be valid under its putative applicable law, it cannot have the effect of validating an agreement which would be invalid under its putative applicable law.

(iv) Article 8(2) confers a discretion on the court, which must consider whether it is reasonable to allow the party in question to rely on the law of his habitual residence in order to establish his lack of consent.

(v) There is a question surrounding the use of the words "habitual residence". Since a company does not have a habitual residence, it may be argued that Article 8(2) applies only to individuals. This interpretation would, however, hardly be consistent with the policy of the provision. Where the question of consent is raised by a corporation, it would seem reasonable to enable that party to rely on Article 8(2) and to interpret the words "habitual residence" as referring either to the place of the company's central administration or to its principal place of business.

11.4.3 Formal validity: Article 9

11.4.3.1 What are questions of form?

11.4.3.1.1 Although Article 9 does not define what is meant by formal validity, the Giuliano–Lagarde Report states that matters of form should be understood to include "every external manifestation required on the part of a person expressing the will to be legally bound, and in the absence of which such expression of will would not be regarded as fully effective".[133] The requirement under English law that a contract for the sale of land or an interest in land must be made in writing in order to be valid[134] is a classic example of a formal requirement.

11.4.3.1.2 More problematical are the requirements laid down by the Statute of Frauds 1677 in relation to contracts of guarantee. Section 4 of the Statute of Frauds provides that "noe action shall be brought... whereby to charge the defendant upon any speciale promise to answere for the debt, default or miscarriages of another person ... unlesse the agreement upon which such action shall be brought or some memorandum or note thereof shall be in writeing and signed by the partie to be charged therewith or by some other person thereunto by him lawfully authorised". In *Leroux* v. *Brown*[135] it was held that section 4 was a procedural rule which rendered unenforceable a contract

133. OJ 1980 C282/29.
134. Law of Property (Miscellaneous Provisions) Act 1989, s. 2.
135. (1852) 12 CB 801.

which was concluded in France and governed by French law. Although this decision has been widely criticised,[136] it has not been overruled.

11.4.3.1.3 The decision in *Leroux* v. *Brown* is an example of the tendency of the English courts to characterise as procedural, matters which continental courts would classify as questions of form. In view of Article 18[137] the concepts employed in the Convention cannot be approached from an entirely domestic point of view. Notwithstanding the decision in *Leroux* v. *Brown* and the fact that matters of procedure are excluded from the scope of the Convention,[138] section 4 of the Statute of Frauds should be regarded as laying down formal requirements for the purposes of Article 9. Any other interpretation would be inconsistent with the approach adopted by the Giuliano–Lagarde Report.

11.4.3.2 Choice of law rules

11.4.3.2.1 The Convention adopts a liberal attitude to questions of form. Accordingly, it should be unusual for an international contract to be rendered formally invalid by the Convention. The key provisions are set out in the first four paragraphs of Article 9[139] which draw a distinction between cases involving the conclusion of a contract by parties who are in the same country and cases where the parties are in different countries. The test for determining whether parties to a contract are in the same country or different countries would seem to be a purely factual one.[140] The habitual residence or place of business of the parties is not relevant. The Convention does not indicate what is meant by the conclusion of a contract for the purposes of Article 9. If the terms of a contract are negotiated and agreed by telephone, but subsequently the parties sign a written agreement at a meeting in an airport departure lounge is the contract concluded when the terms are orally agreed or when the written memorandum is signed?

11.4.3.2.2 Article 9(1) provides:

> A contract concluded between persons who are in the same country is formally valid if it satisfies the formal requirements of the law which governs it under this Convention or of the law of the country where it is concluded.

This rule is effectively the same as the common law rule which applied before the Convention's entry into force.[141]

11.4.3.2.3 Paragraph 2, which deals with the situation where the parties are not in the same country at the time of the conclusion of the contract, provides:

> A contract concluded between persons who are in different countries is formally valid if it satisfies the formal requirements of the law which governs it under this Convention or of the law of one of those countries.

Accordingly, if an English seller and a French buyer enter a contract by correspondence according to the terms of which German law is the applicable law, the contract is formally valid if it satisfies the formal requirements of German, English or French law.

11.4.3.2.4 Article 9(3) states that "[w]here a contract is concluded by an agent, the

136. See, for example, Cheshire & North, *Private International Law* (12th ed, 1993) p. 76.
137. See para. 10.3.2.
138. Article 1(2)(h).
139. Paragraph 5 is discussed at para. 12.1.2.3; paragraph 6 is discussed at para. 12.4.2.
140. See Giuliano–Lagarde Report, OJ 1980 C282/30–31.
141. Giuliano–Lagarde Report, OJ 1980 C282/30.

country in which the agent acts is the relevant country for the purposes of paragraphs 1 and 2". Article 9(3) should be construed liberally so as to include the situation where an organ of a company concludes a contract on the company's behalf.

11.4.3.2.5 Finally, attention should be drawn to paragraph 4 which provides that the rules contained in the first two paragraphs of Article 9 also apply for determining the formal validity of a unilateral act:

> An act intended to have legal effect relating to an existing or contemplated contract is formally valid if it satisfies the formal requirements of the law which under this Convention governs or would govern the contract or of the law of the country where the act was done.

So, an offer will be valid if it satisfies the formal requirements of the law of the place where the offer is made or the putative applicable law.

11.4.4 Capacity

As regards individuals, it is expressly provided by Article 1(1)(a) that, subject to Article 11, questions of contractual capacity do not fall within the scope of the Convention. Accordingly, in those cases in which Article 11 does not apply the common law conflicts rules continue to be relevant. In relation to corporations questions of capacity are entirely outside the Convention's scope.[142]

11.4.4.1 Individuals

11.4.4.1.1 GENERAL PRINCIPLES

11.4.4.1.1.1 The common law rules relating to contractual capacity are not entirely free from doubt. Many of the older cases are regarded as being unsatisfactory[143] and there are few recent authorities which clarify the position. It has been suggested that a contract should be regarded as valid so far as capacity is concerned if each party has capacity either under the system of law with which the contract has its closest and most real connection or under the law of that party's domicile and residence.[144] Although the pedigree of this rule is not beyond question, it can be defended from the point of view of principle.

11.4.4.1.1.2 Since capacity is to some extent an extension of legal status, there is a natural connection between an individual's personal law and his contractual capacity. If, however, an individual is regarded as having capacity—and therefore is deemed not to need protection—under the law of the country with which he is closely connected (in this context, the country of his domicile and residence) there is no good reason why another country should seek to invalidate the contract on the ground that the individual in question does not have capacity by the law of that country. So, if an English resident, aged twenty, buys goods abroad, the fact that the purchaser has capacity by English law should be sufficient to ensure that the contract is valid so far as capacity is concerned.

142. Article 1(2)(e).

143. For example, *Simonin* v. *Mallac* (1860) 2 Sw & Tr 67 which seems to favour the law of the place of contracting.

144. Dicey & Morris, *The Conflict of Laws* (12th ed, 1993) p. 1271 (Rule 181).

Absence of capacity by the law of the place of contracting in these circumstances should not be relevant.

11.4.4.1.1.3 There are, however, strong arguments for not referring questions of capacity to an individual's personal law alone. If, for example, an English resident, aged seventeen, contracts to buy a motor-car from a foreign seller, the contract would not be valid if contractual capacity were regarded as being a matter solely for the personal law. On the assumption that the contract is more closely connected with the seller's law, should the seller be expected to take the risk that the buyer does not have capacity by his personal law? As a general rule an individual ought to be regarded as having the necessary capacity if he has capacity by the putative proper law.

11.4.4.1.1.4 It is important to stress that the proper law in this context should mean the law with which the contract has its closest and most real connection and not the proper law chosen by the parties (whether expressly or impliedly). Some of the cases do not make this clear. In *Bodley Head Ltd* v. *Flegon*[145] the Russian novelist, Alexander Solzhenitsyn, signed a power of attorney in Moscow authorising a Swiss lawyer to deal outside Russia with the former's literary works. The power of attorney, which was in the German language, contained the following jurisdiction and choice of law clause: "In regard to disputes arising out of this mandate, the donor of the power recognises the courts at the place of business of the attorney as competent, and Swiss law as applicable."

11.4.4.1.1.5 The plaintiff acquired the right to produce an English language version of one of Solzhenitsyn's works in England. When the defendant proposed producing a rival English language version of the work, the plaintiff sought an injunction restraining the defendant from producing this work on the basis that the copyright was vested in the plaintiff. It was clear that to the extent that the plaintiff had rights in Solzhenitsyn's works they were derived from the power of attorney concluded between the author and the Swiss lawyer. It was the defendant's contention that the power of attorney was invalid on the basis that Solzhenitsyn did not have capacity under Russian law. Brightman J concluded that the author's capacity was to be tested by Swiss law, on the basis that agency in favour of the Swiss lawyer was constituted in Switzerland and was intended to be governed by Swiss law and that the agency contract had no relevant connection with Russia.[146]

11.4.4.1.1.6 To the extent that this decision supports the contention that, as regards capacity under the common law, the putative proper law of the contract should be determined by reference to the law which the parties expressly or impliedly choose, rather than by reference to the law of the country with which the contract has its closest and most real connection it cannot be supported in principle. If, for the purpose of capacity rules, the proper law were to be determined subjectively rather than objectively, this would enable an individual who does not have capacity by his personal law to confer capacity on himself merely by the choice of a law under which no such incapacity exists—thereby nullifying the protective effect of the individual's personal law.

145. [1972] 1 WLR 680.
146. [1972] 1 WLR 680, 689.

11.4.4.1.2 ARTICLE 11

Article 11 provides:

In a contract concluded between persons who are in the same country, a natural person who would have capacity under the law of that country may invoke his incapacity resulting from another law only if the other party to the contract was aware of this incapacity at the time of the conclusion of the contract or was not aware thereof as a result of negligence.

The purpose behind Article 11 is "to protect a party who in good faith believed himself to be contracting with a person of full capacity and who, after the contract has been entered into, is confronted by the incapacity of the other contracting party".[147] Article 11 has no application to situations where the parties are in different countries when the contract is concluded. Where parties are in the same country, the effect of Article 11 will be generally to validate the contract where both parties have capacity under the law of the place of contracting. The burden of proof lies on the incapacitated party to show that the other party knew of his incapacity or should have known of it.[148] If the person raising the incapacity cannot satisfy the burden of proof, that person will be regarded as having the necessary capacity if he has capacity under the law of the place of contracting.

11.4.4.2 Corporations

The contractual capacity of a corporation is governed both by the law governing the constitution of the company and the law governing the transaction in question.[149]

(i) A corporation does not have capacity to enter transactions unless authorised to do so by its constitution; an *ultra vires* act is invalid.
(ii) If the company does not have capacity by the law governing the transaction, the transaction will be invalid. For the purposes of this rule it would seem that, as regards contractual obligations, the *lex causae* must be determined by reference to common law principles, rather than the provisions of the Convention.

11.4.5 Performance

11.4.5.1 The applicable law

11.4.5.1.1 Article 10(1)(b) provides that "performance" is to be governed by the applicable law. The Giuliano–Lagarde Report lists various matters which fall within the scope of subparagraph (b):

the diligence with which the obligation must be performed; conditions relating to the place and time of performance; the extent to which the obligation can be performed by a person other than the party liable; the conditions as to performance of the obligation both in general and in relation to certain categories of obligation (joint and several obligations, alternative obligations, divisible and indivisible obligations, pecuniary obligations); where performance consists of the payment of

147. Giuliano–Lagarde Report, OJ 1980 C282/34.
148. Giuliano–Lagarde Report, OJ 1980 C282/34.
149. Dicey & Morris, *The Conflict of Laws* (12th ed, 1993) p. 1111 (Rule 156).

a sum of money, the conditions relating to the discharge of the debtor who made the payment, the appropriation of the payment, the receipt, etc.[150]

11.4.5.1.2 The approach of the Convention reflects the position under the common law. For example, in *Jacobs, Marcus & Co* v. *Crédit Lyonnais*[151] the defendant contracted to sell to the plaintiff goods which were to be shipped by a French company from Algeria to London. Before all the goods had been delivered hostilities broke out in Algeria, as a consequence of which the defendant failed to perform the remainder of the contract. The plaintiff commenced proceedings for breach of contract in England. Notwithstanding the fact that English law governed the contract, the defendant sought to rely on the law of the place of performance, under the terms of which the defendant was not in breach, since the outbreak of hostilities would be treated as *force majeure*. Under English law, however, the defendant was liable in damages since the events in question did not have the effect of frustrating the contract. In the course of his judgment Bowen LJ said:

> If a contract made in England by English subjects or residents, and upon which payment is to be made in England, has to be performed in part abroad, it might not be unreasonable to assume that the mode in which any part of it has to be performed abroad was intended to be in accordance with the law of the foreign country, and to construe the contract as incorporating silently to that extent all provisions of a foreign law which would regulate the method of performance, and which were not inconsistent with the English contract. But it cannot be gathered from such a contract as the present that the parties desired to go further and to discharge the defendants from performance whenever circumstances arose which would, according to the foreign law, excuse them.[152]

The issue of the liability of the defendant for failure to perform the contract is not concerned with the mode or manner of performance, but with the substance of the defendant's obligation, and therefore is governed by the applicable law.

11.4.5.2 Performance and manner of performance

11.4.5.2.1 Although performance is governed by the applicable law, when it comes to the manner of performance attention should be paid to the law of the place of performance. Article 10(2) provides:

> In relation to the manner of performance and the steps to be taken in the event of defective performance regard shall be had to the law of the country in which performance takes place.

11.4.5.2.2 As regards the relationship between Article 10(1)(b) and Article 10(2) two issues emerge. (i) What is meant by the "manner of performance" of an obligation? According to the Giuliano–Lagarde Report, although this question has to be answered by reference to the *lex fori*, the following matters should normally be regarded as concerned with the manner of performance: "the rules governing public holidays, the manner in which goods are to be examined, and the steps to be taken if they are refused".[153] (ii) As regards the significance which should be attached to the law of the place of performance the Report gives the following guidance:

150. OJ 1980 C282/32–33.
151. (1884) 12 QBD 589.
152. (1884) 12 QBD 589, 604.
153. OJ 1980 C282/33.

Article 10(2) says that a court may have regard to the law of the place of performance. This means that the court may consider whether such law has any relevance to the manner in which the contract should be performed and has a discretion whether to apply it in whole or in part so as to do justice between the parties.[154]

The operation of Article 10(2) may be illustrated by a simple example. In the case where, under a contract governed by English law, a carrier undertakes to deliver goods to the buyer in France "during normal business hours" it would be reasonable to have regard to French law—as the law of the place of performance—in order to decide what significance to give the words "normal business hours".

11.4.5.2.3 There is perhaps a risk that judges may be encouraged by the Giuliano-Lagarde Report, which seems to leave the court considerable discretion in working out the relationship between Article 10(1)(b) and Article 10(2), to think that the substance of the obligation—as defined by the applicable law—may be modified by the law of the place of performance. Although there may arise borderline cases where the dividing line between performance and mode of performance is difficult to draw, the role of Article 10(2) should be limited since the law of the place of performance should not be allowed to affect the substance of the parties' obligations.

11.4.6 Interpretation

The substantive obligations of the parties to a contract are governed by the applicable law. It follows that a contract should be interpreted by reference to its applicable law. Article 10(1)(a) of the Convention provides that "interpretation" is governed by the applicable law. The position under the Convention accords with the common law.[155] So, where a contract of sale states that the purchase price is to be paid in "dollars" or "francs", the canons of construction of the applicable law determine the money of account.[156]

11.4.7 Consequences of breach

11.4.7.1 One of the fundamental distinctions in private international law is the distinction between substance and procedure. Whereas substantive questions are governed by the *lex causae*, questions of procedure are governed by the *lex fori*. According to English principles of classification, rules relating to remoteness of damage and heads of damage are substantive, but rules governing the quantification of damage are procedural.[157] So, at common law, whether the plaintiff is entitled to recover damages for inconvenience and distress is a matter for the proper law of the contract, but if this head of damage is available under the proper law, the level of compensation which is recoverable depends on the procedural law of the forum.

11.4.7.2 Although Article 1(2)(h) states that "evidence and procedure" are excluded from the scope of the Convention, Article 10(1)(c) provides that the applicable law

154. OJ 1980 C282/33.
155. *St Pierre* v. *South American Stores (Gath & Chaves) Ltd* [1936] 1 KB 382.
156. For further discussion of foreign currency obligations, see para. 14.2.2.
157. *D'Almeida Araujo Lda* v. *Sir Frederick Becker & Co Ltd* [1953] 2 QB 329.

governs "within the limits of the powers conferred on the court by its procedural law, the consequences of breach, including the assessment of damages in so far as it is governed by rules of law". The expression "consequences of breach" refers to "the consequences which the law or the contract attaches to the breach of a contractual obligation, whether it is a matter of the liability of the party to whom the breach is attributable or of a claim to terminate the contract for breach".[158] The Giuliano–Lagarde Report also notes that any requirement for service of notice on the party to assume his liability comes within the scope of this provision.[159]

11.4.7.3 As regards the assessment of damages the Giuliano–Lagarde Report sets out the background to Article 10(1)(c):

> According to some delegations the assessment of the amount of damages is a question of fact and should not be covered by the Convention. To determine the amount of damages the court is obliged to take account of economic and social conditions in its country; there are some cases in which the amount of damages is fixed by a jury; some countries use methods of calculation which might not be accepted in others. Other delegations countered these arguments, however, by pointing out that in several legal systems there are rules for determining the amount of damages; some international conventions fix limits as to the amount of compensation (for example, conventions relating to carriage); the amount of damages in case of non-performance is often prescribed in the contract and grave difficulties would be created for the parties if these amounts had to be determined later by the court hearing the action. By way of compromise the Group finally decided to refer in subparagraph (c) solely to rules of law in matters of assessment of damages, given that questions of fact will always be a matter for the court hearing the action.[160]

11.4.7.4 The solution adopted by the Convention is, therefore, different from the position at common law. To the extent that quantification of damage is regulated by rules of law, the applicable law governs. This is, however, subject to the limits of the procedural law of the forum: "if the applicable law provides for the payment of damages by instalments and the procedural law of the forum is not suited to the task of supervising such payments ... the judge of the forum could require a single lump sum payment instead".[161]

11.4.8 Discharge

11.4.8.1 By virtue of Article 10(1)(d) the applicable law governs "the various ways of extinguishing obligations, and prescription and limitation of actions". At common law, the proper law of the contract governs the question of whether a debtor is discharged by performance,[162] by bankruptcy,[163] by legislation,[164] by outbreak of war,[165] by a moratorium,[166] or by subsequent impossibility.[167] In this respect Article 10(1)(d) follows the common law.

11.4.8.2 Traditionally, the common law regarded English limitation periods as

158. Giuliano–Lagarde Report, OJ 1980 C282/33.
159. OJ 1980 C282/33.
160. OJ 1980 C282/33.
161. Plender, *The European Contracts Convention* (1991) p. 175.
162. *Jacobs, Marcus & Co* v. *Crédit Lyonnais* (1884) 12 QBD 589.
163. *Ellis* v. *M'Henry* (1871) LR 6 CP 228.
164. *Mount Albert Borough Council* v. *Australasian Temperance & General Mutual Life Assurance Society Ltd* [1938] AC 224.
165. *Re Anglo-Austrian Bank* [1920] 1 Ch 69.
166. *Re Claim by Helbert Wagg & Co Ltd* [1956] Ch 323.
167. *Jacobs, Marcus & Co* v. *Crédit Lyonnais* (1884) 12 QBD 589.

procedural rather than substantive. Accordingly, at common law a claim arising under a contract which was time barred under the applicable law could nevertheless be brought in England as long as the English limitation period had not expired. Since Article 10(1)(d) treats defences based on limitation as substantive rather than procedural, whether a claim is barred by lapse of time is governed by the applicable law rather than the *lex fori*. It should be remembered, however, that by virtue of Article 16 of the Convention the application of a rule of the governing law may be refused on grounds of public policy. Accordingly, notwithstanding Article 10(1)(d) there may be circumstances in which, relying on Article 16, an English court may refuse to apply a foreign limitation period.

11.4.8.3 In cases not falling within the Convention the common law has been replaced by the Foreign Limitation Periods Act 1984, section 1 of which provides that the limitation rules of the *lex causae* are to be applied in litigation which takes place in England.[168]

11.4.9 Nullity

Article 10(1)(e) states that the applicable law also governs "the consequences of nullity of the contract". This provision does not, however, have the force of law in England,[169] the United Kingdom having entered a reservation as permitted by Article 22 of the Convention. Under English law the consequences of nullity are regarded as forming part of the law of restitution, rather than the law of contract. Where, however, an obligation to restore a benefit arises in connection with a contract, the proper law of the contract will generally be the proper law of the obligation for the purposes of English private international law.[170] For nearly all practical purposes Article 10(1)(e) and the common law rules lead to the same results.[171]

11.4.10 Illegality[172]

Whereas at common law the English courts formulated a number of principles relating to problems of illegality, there are no specific provisions of the Convention on this question as such. In considering the problems of illegality it is important to distinguish cases involving initial illegality (where the contract is illegal at its inception) from cases of subsequent illegality (where the contract is valid and legal at its inception, but is rendered illegal by a subsequent change in the law).

There are various different laws which may potentially be relevant to questions of illegality: the applicable law, the law of the place of performance (*lex loci solutionis*) and the *lex fori*.

168. See Chapter 15.
169. Contracts (Applicable Law) Act 1990, s. 2(2).
170. See para. 12.10.
171. For an exception (albeit arising out of a rather unlikely set of hypothetical facts) see North, "The EEC Convention on the Law Applicable to Contractual Obligations (1980): Its History and Main Features" in *Contract Conflicts* (1982) 3, 17.
172. Mann, "Proper Law and Illegality in Private International Law" (1937) 18 BYIL 97.

11.4.10.1 Initial illegality

11.4.10.1.1 If a contract is void on grounds of illegality by the putative applicable law, it will not be enforceable in England.[173] In this situation it is irrelevant whether the parties knew of the illegality at the time when the contract was concluded.

It is not contrary to English public policy to enforce a contract which is valid by its applicable law, but is contrary to the public policy of the *lex loci solutionis*.[174] Nevertheless, the English courts have taken the view that where contracting parties intend the doing, or the procuring of the doing by a third party, of an act in a friendly foreign country which is illegal by its law the contract is contrary to public policy.[175] For example, in *Foster* v. *Driscoll*[176] a number of English residents entered a partnership agreement for the shipment of whisky across the Atlantic, the purpose of which was to smuggle the whisky into the United States. At the time the import of alcohol into the United States was illegal. The majority of the Court of Appeal refused to enforce the contract on the ground of public policy. Sankey LJ thought that a contract should be held invalid "on account of illegality if the real object and intention of the parties necessitates them joining in an endeavour to perform in a foreign and friendly country some act which is illegal by the law of such country notwithstanding the fact that there may be, in a certain event, alternative modes or places of performing which permits the contract to be performed legally".[177] Although in *Foster* v. *Driscoll* the applicable law was English law, it is generally assumed that, since the decision depended on English public policy, the contract would have been refused enforcement had the applicable law been the law of a foreign country.

11.4.10.1.2 There seems little doubt that a case such as *Foster* v. *Driscoll*—in which English law is the applicable law—would be decided in the same way under the Convention. More problematical is the case where a contract—which is governed by a foreign law under which it is valid—involves the performance of acts which are illegal under the *lex loci solutionis*. Article 16 of the Convention allows a court to refuse to apply a rule of law on the basis that it is manifestly incompatible with the public policy of the forum.[178] Article 16 is, however, focused on an individual rule of law which is regarded by the forum as offensive. Accordingly, the illegality cases do not fit very satisfactorily within the framework created by Article 16, unless it is possible to regard as a "rule of law" for the purposes of Article 16 "the notional, unexpressed rule of the applicable law, according to which the contract is not illegal or invalid".[179]

173. Article 8(1).
174. *Lemeda Trading Co Ltd* v. *African Middle East Petroleum Co Ltd* [1988] QB 448. Collier, [1988] CLJ 169.
175. *De Wutz* v. *Hendricks* (1824) 2 Bing 314; *Foster* v. *Driscoll* [1929] 1 KB 470; *Regazzoni* v. *KC Sethia (1944) Ltd* [1958] AC 301 (Mann, "Illegality and the Conflict of Laws" (1958) 21 MLR 130; Jennings, [1958] CLJ 17).
176. [1929] 1 KB 470.
177. [1929] 1 KB 470, 521–522.
178. See para. 11.3.4.
179. Kaye, *The New Private International Law of Contract of the European Community* (1993) p. 347.

11.4.10.2 Subsequent illegality

11.4.10.2.1 As regards subsequent illegality, there are four factual situations which need to be distinguished. The first three situations are relatively straightforward and uncontroversial; the fourth is the one which is potentially more problematical.

(i) If, after a contract is concluded, it becomes illegal under the applicable law for one or more of the parties to perform their obligations, the contract is unenforceable in England to the extent that it is unenforceable under its applicable law. This follows from the rule that the discharge of contractual obligations is governed by the applicable law.[180]

(ii) It is a rule of English domestic law that a contract which becomes impossible to perform by the *lex loci solutionis* is frustrated.[181] So, in relation to a contract which is governed by English law, if performance becomes illegal under the *lex loci solutionis* after the conclusion of the contract, the contracting party who, under the terms of the contract is required to perform in that place, is discharged.[182]

(iii) Where a contract is illegal neither by its applicable law nor by the *lex loci solutionis*, illegality by the law of a third country is irrelevant.[183]

(iv) What is the correct solution under the Convention in the situation where, following the conclusion of the contract, performance becomes illegal by the *lex loci solutionis*, but by the foreign applicable law illegality by the *lex loci solutionis* does not frustrate the contract? As regards those Contracting States which have not made a reservation on Article 7(1), this provision would appear to provide the framework for the resolution of the problem. Article 7(1)[184] provides that a court may apply "overriding rules"[185] which form part of the law of a third country, that is a country which is not the forum and whose law is not the applicable law. The basic condition which must be satisfied is that the situation must have a close connection with the third country in question. In deciding whether or not to apply the overriding rules of a third country the court must have regard to their nature and purpose and to the consequences of their application or non-application. In a situation where a contract is enforceable by the applicable law, but performance is illegal by the *lex loci solutionis* the forum may apply Article 7(1) and refuse enforcement on the basis that the place of performance is a country with which the situation has a close connection and a rule which renders performance illegal is an overriding rule.

11.4.10.2.2 Since Article 7(1) does not have the force of law in the United Kingdom, an English court must approach the problem from a different perspective. Although a variety of theories are possible, there are only three plausible solutions once Article 7(1)

180. Article 10(1)(d).
181. *Ralli Brothers* v. *Compania Naviera Sota y Aznar* [1920] 2 KB 287.
182. Article 10(1)(d).
183. As in *Kleinwort, Sons & Co* v. *Ungarische Baumwolle Industrie Aktiengesellschaft* [1939] 2 KB 678.
184. For the text see para. 11.3.3.1.
185. "Overriding rules" are mandatory rules which apply regardless of the law applicable to the contract. See paras. 11.3.1.3–11.3.1.5.

is taken out of the equation: first, the contract is enforceable in England because it is enforceable under its applicable law; secondly, the contract is unenforceable in England on the ground of public policy (Article 16); thirdly, the applicable law is overridden by an "overriding rule" of the *lex fori* (Article 7(2)).

11.4.10.2.3 Of these three possibilities, the first is immediately the most attractive, since questions of performance and discharge fall within the scope of the applicable law.[186] However, at common law there are many cases in which the courts have approved (*obiter*) the rule (known as "the first exception to Rule 184") that "[a] contract (whether lawful by its proper law or not) is, in general, invalid in so far as the performance of it is unlawful by the law of the country where the contract is to be performed".[187] For example, in *Libyan Arab Foreign Bank* v. *Bankers Trust Co* Staughton J thought that there was no need to cite authority to support the proposition that performance of a contract is excused if "it necessarily involves doing an act which is unlawful by the law of the place where the act has to be done".[188] In the context of the Convention it might be argued that the "first exception to Rule 184" is either a rule of public policy for the purposes of Article 16 or an "overriding rule" of the forum within the meaning of Article 7(2). There are, however, various objections to the application of either Article 7(2) or Article 16 to this situation. The pedigree of the first exception to Rule 184 is somewhat questionable: "in spite of the judicial approval frequently and emphatically, though invariably *obiter*, given to the exception it may be confidently asserted that it does not form part of the conflict of laws at all, but is a rule of the English law of contracts, an aspect of the English doctrine of frustration".[189] On this basis it can hardly be argued that the first exception to Rule 184 is an overriding rule for the purposes of Article 7(2). Even if the exception is an accurate statement of English law prior to the entry into force of the Contracts (Applicable Law) Act 1990, the fact that, at common law, performance is excused if it involves the commission of an act which is illegal under the *lex loci solutionis* does not necessarily mean that it would be manifestly contrary to public policy—within the meaning of Article 16 of the Convention—to enforce a foreign contract in these circumstances.

11.4.10.2.4 It is to be hoped that the English courts will not look sympathetically on any attempts to invoke the first exception to Rule 184 in cases to be decided under the Convention. If performance is to be made in England and such performance is contrary to English public policy there may be good reasons for denying enforcement on the basis of Article 16. However, where the only connection with England is that the proceedings are brought here, the correct solution is that the applicable law should govern. Accordingly, subsequent illegality by the *lex loci solutionis* should be regarded as discharging the defendant's obligations only to the extent that those obligations are discharged under the applicable law.[190]

186. Article 10(1).
187. Dicey & Morris, *The Conflict of Laws* (11th ed, 1987) p. 1218 (Rule 184, Exception 1). This principle, which originated in the 1908 edition of the work, was approved by the Court of Appeal in *Ralli Brothers* v. *Compania Naviera Sota y Aznar* [1920] 2 KB 287.
188. [1989] QB 720, 743.
189. Mann, "The Proper Law of Contracts Concluded by International Persons" (1959) 35 BYIL 34, 47.
190. See Reynolds, "Illegality by Lex Loci Solutionis" (1992) 108 LQR 553.

CHAPTER 12

CHOICE OF LAW IN CONTRACT: SPECIFIC CONTRACTS

Some of the choice of law rules which apply to specific types of contract are contained in the Rome Convention on the Law Applicable to Contractual Obligations. For example, in relation to consumer contracts, individual employment contracts, contracts relating to immovables and contracts for the carriage of goods, the Convention lays down specific rules for determining the applicable law in cases where the parties have not made a choice of law. In relation to those contracts which fall within the scope of the Convention, it is important to note that the general rules discussed in the previous chapter apply to those issues which are not specifically addressed by the special rules set out in this chapter. So, for example, in relation to a single voyage charterparty which does not include a choice of law, the applicable law is determined by paragraphs 1, 4 and 5 of Article 4; all other aspects of the contract are governed by the general choice of law rules outlined in Chapter 11. Other types of contract—such as bills of exchange and certain contracts of insurance—are excluded entirely from the scope of the Convention. As regards these contracts, the relevant choice of law rules must be found in the common law and in various statutory provisions.

12.1 CERTAIN CONSUMER CONTRACTS

Article 5 of the Convention includes a number of specific choice of law rules which apply only to consumer contracts. The basic purpose of these rules is to ensure that the consumer is not deprived of consumer protection legislation. In cases where a consumer contract includes a choice of law, this cannot have the effect of depriving the consumer of the protection of the mandatory rules of the law of the country where he is habitually resident. Where the contract does not include a choice of law, it is provided that the law of the consumer's habitual residence should govern.

12.1.1 The scope of Article 5

Article 5 is somewhat tortuously drafted. To be governed by the special provisions of the Convention which apply to consumer contracts, the transaction must fall within the general scope of Article 5 (which is defined by paragraphs 1, 4 and 5) and the contract must have been concluded in one of the circumstances outlined in paragraph 2.

12.1.1.1 General scope

12.1.1.1.1 Article 5 provides:

> 1. This Article applies to a contract the object of which is the supply of goods or services to a person ("the consumer") for a purpose which can be regarded as being outside his trade or profession, or a contract for the provision of credit for that object.
>
> ...
>
> 4. This Article shall not apply to:
> (a) a contract of carriage;
> (b) a contract for the supply of services where the services are to be supplied to the consumer exclusively in a country other than that in which he has his habitual residence.
>
> 5. Notwithstanding the provisions of paragraph 4, this Article shall apply to a contract which, for an inclusive price, provides for a combination of travel and accommodation.

The first paragraph of Article 5 defines the outermost limits of the special provisions dealing with consumer contracts. The Giuliano–Lagarde Report suggests that Article 5 "should be interpreted in the light of its purpose which is to protect the weaker party and in accordance with other international instruments with the same purpose such as the Judgments Convention".[1]

12.1.1.1.2 If goods or services are supplied to a person for use in his trade or profession, the contract cannot be a consumer contract. Where a person acts partly within and partly outside his trade or profession, the situation only falls within the scope of Article 5 if he acts primarily outside his trade or profession.[2] Article 5 does not apply, however, where the supplier of goods, services or credit reasonably supposes that the other party is acting in the course of his trade or profession: "Thus if the receiver of goods or services holds himself out as a professional, eg by ordering goods which might well be used in his trade or profession on his professional paper the good faith of the other party is protected and the case will not be governed by Article 5."[3] Although the wording of Article 5 does not regard the characteristics of the supplier as relevant, the Giuliano–Lagarde Report notes that "in the opinion of the majority of the delegations it will, normally, only apply where the person who supplies goods or services or provides credit acts in the course of his trade or profession".[4]

12.1.1.1.3 Whereas the Brussels and Lugano Conventions contain separate regimes for consumer contracts and insurance contracts, there are no special provisions in the Rome Convention dealing with contracts of insurance which fall within its scope. Where a person, otherwise than in the course of his trade or profession, enters a contract of insurance which covers risks not situated within the territories of the Member States of the EC, the contract falls within the scope of Article 5 of the Convention.

12.1.1.1.4 Paragraphs 4 and 5 lead to a number of arbitrary distinctions. If an English resident purchases an air ticket to fly from London to Paris and takes a room in a Parisian hotel, the contract of carriage is excluded from the scope of Article 5 by paragraph 4(a) and the contract with the hotel is excluded by paragraph 4(b) because "the services are to be supplied to the consumer exclusively in a country other than that in which he has his habitual residence". If, however, the same consumer purchases a

1. OJ 1980 C282/23. For a discussion of Article 13 of the Brussels and Lugano Convention, see para. 5.7.2.1.
2. Giuliano–Lagarde Report, OJ 1980 C282/23.
3. Giuliano–Lagarde Report, OJ 1980 C282/23.
4. OJ 1990 C282/23.

package holiday, involving a flight from London to Paris and accommodation in a Parisian hotel, the contract falls within the scope of the consumer contract provisions by virtue of paragraph 5.

12.1.1.1.5 The Giuliano–Lagarde Report seeks to justify the exclusion of various contracts by paragraph 4 in the following terms:

> The exclusion of contracts of carriage is justified by the fact that the special protective measures for which provision is made in Article 5 are not appropriate for governing contracts of this type. Similarly, in the case of contracts relating to the supply of services (for example, accommodation in a hotel, or a language course) which are supplied exclusively outside the State in which the consumer is resident, the latter cannot reasonably expect the law of his State of origin to be applied in derogation from the general rules of Articles 3 and 4. In the cases referred to under (b) the contract is more closely connected with the State in which the other contracting party is resident, even if the latter has performed one of the acts described in paragraph 2 (advertising, for example) in the State in which the consumer is resident.[5]

Perhaps not surprisingly, some commentators do not find this explanation entirely convincing.[6]

12.1.1.2 The qualifying conditions

A contract whereby goods, services or credit are provided to a person otherwise than in the course of his trade or profession is not subject to the consumer contract rules unless one of the three qualifying conditions laid down by Article 5(2) is met.

(i) The consumer contract rules apply if the contract was preceded by a specific invitation addressed to the consumer or advertising in the country of the consumer's habitual residence and the consumer took in that country all the steps necessary on his part for the conclusion of the contract.

(ii) The second condition is satisfied if the other party or his agent received the consumer's order in the country of the consumer's habitual residence.

(iii) The third condition is intended to bring within the scope of the consumer contract provisions an activity which is referred to as border-crossing excursion-selling (for example, where a store-owner in country X arranges one-day bus trips for consumers in a neighbouring country Y with the main purpose of inducing the consumers to buy in his store[7]). The third condition is satisfied if the contract is for the sale of goods and the consumer travelled from the country of his habitual residence to another country and there gave his order, provided that the consumer's journey was arranged by the seller for the purpose of inducing the consumer to buy.

12.1.2 Three special rules

12.1.2.1 The applicable law in the absence of choice

Article 5(3) provides that if one of the qualifying conditions is satisfied, "a contract to which this Article applies shall, in the absence of choice in accordance with Article 3, be

5. OJ 1980 C282/24–25.
6. See, for example, Morse, "Consumer Contracts, Employment Contracts and the Rome Convention" (1992) 41 ICLQ 1, 4–6.
7. Giuliano–Lagarde Report, OJ 1980 C282/24.

governed by the law of the country in which the consumer has his habitual residence". It should be noted that Article 5(3) is unlike Article 4(2) in the sense that it does not raise a rebuttable presumption that the contract is more closely connected with the country where the consumer is habitually resident. Article 5(3) is a rigid rule, the effect of which is that a consumer receives the benefit of the consumer protection legislation of the place where he is habitually resident.

12.1.2.2 The application of mandatory rules in cases where the parties have chosen a law

12.1.2.2.1 Article 5(2) provides that, as long as one of the qualifying conditions is satisfied, a choice of law made by the parties shall not have the result of depriving the consumer of the protection afforded to him by the mandatory rules of the law of the country in which he has his habitual residence. The purpose of Article 5(2) is to ensure that, even where the contract contains a choice of law within the terms of Article 3(1), that choice cannot have the effect of depriving the consumer of the benefit of the mandatory rules which would have applied had the parties not made a choice. So, if an English consumer receives an advertising catalogue from a French seller inviting him to purchase the seller's goods, the consumer is able to rely on the Unfair Contract Terms Act 1977, the provisions of which cannot be derogated from by contract, notwithstanding the fact that the contract is concluded on the seller's standard terms and conditions which include a French choice of law and terms which purport to exclude the seller's liability for any damage caused by the goods.

12.1.2.2.2 An interesting question arises in this case if the applicable law under Article 3(1) is more generous to the consumer than the law of the place where the consumer is habitually resident. Can the consumer rely on the chosen law in these circumstances? The proper solution would appear to be that the applicable law should be applied where it provides a greater degree of protection than the law which would have applied in the absence of choice. Paragraph 2 talks in terms of the consumer being "deprived" of the benefit of the mandatory rules of the law of the country where he is habitually resident. There can be no "deprivation" if the standards of the chosen law are higher than those of the law of the country where the consumer is habitually resident. Article 5(2) does no more than lay down a minimum standard.[8]

12.1.2.3 Formal validity

Article 9(5) provides that, as long as one of the qualifying conditions in Article 5(2) is satisfied, the formal validity of a consumer contract within the scope of Article 5 is governed by the law of the country in which the consumer has his habitual residence.

12.1.3 "Overriding rules"[9] of the forum

12.1.3.1 Consumer contracts which are governed by Article 5 are also subject to the general choice of law rules in the Convention relating to mandatory rules. Accordingly,

8. See Morse, "Consumer Contracts, Employment Contracts and the Rome Convention" (1992) 41 ICLQ 1, 8–9.

9. For consideration of the distinction between mandatory rules and "overriding rules" see para. 11.3.1.

the applicable law may be modified by the "overriding rules" of the forum.[10] Section 27(2) of the Unfair Contract Terms Act 1977 indicates that the controls of the Act apply regardless of a choice of the law of a foreign country by the parties if either (a) the choice of law was imposed "wholly or mainly for the purpose of enabling the party imposing it to evade the operation of this Act" or (b) "one of the parties dealt as consumer, and he was then habitually resident in the United Kingdom, and the essential steps necessary for the making of the contract were taken there, whether by him or by others on his behalf".[11]

12.1.3.2 In the consumer context, section 27(2) of the 1977 Act has—to a significant extent—been superseded by the Convention. If a contract falls within the scope of Article 5, the consumer receives the protection of the mandatory rules which form part of the law of the country where he is habitually resident, whether or not the contract includes a choice of law.[12] Furthermore, if a contract contains a choice of the law of a foreign country and all the factors relevant to the situation are connected with England, the mandatory rules of English law are applicable by virtue of Article 3(3) of the Convention.[13]

12.1.3.3 However, even in the consumer context, section 27(2) of the 1977 Act may be relevant in two situations.

(i) If a contract includes a choice of the law of a foreign country, the court may, relying on Article 7(2), apply the Unfair Contract Terms Act 1977 if it appears that the purpose of the choice of law was to evade the operation of the Act, even though not all the factors relevant to the situation are connected with England.[14]

(ii) As regards those consumer contracts which do not fall within the scope of Article 5 of the Convention (either because the subject matter is excluded by paragraph 4 or because none of the qualifying conditions in paragraph 2 is satisfied) section 27(2)(b) directs that the controls of the Act are to apply, notwithstanding the fact that the contract contains a choice of foreign law, if a contracting party—who is habitually resident in the United Kingdom—dealt as consumer and the essential steps necessary for the making of the contract were taken in the United Kingdom.[15]

12.2 INDIVIDUAL EMPLOYMENT CONTRACTS

12.2.1 What is an individual employment contract?

12.2.1.1 The Giuliano–Lagarde Report gives little guidance as to the scope of the special provisions concerning individual employment contracts contained in Article 6. It is made clear, however, that Article 6 "covers the case of void contracts and also *de facto*

10. Article 7(2).
11. See Mann, "Unfair Contract Terms Act 1977 and the Conflict of Laws" (1978) 27 ICLQ 661.
12. Article 5(2) and (3).
13. For a discussion of Article 3(3) see para. 11.3.2.
14. If all the factors relevant to the case are connected with England, English mandatory rules (which by definition include "overriding rules") would apply by virtue of Article 3(3).
15. For an example of the application of this provision see para. 11.3.3.2.

employment relationships in particular those characterised by failure to respect the contract imposed by law for the protection of employees".[16]

12.2.1.2 Neither the Convention nor the Report indicates the way in which the court should approach the interpretation of the concept "individual employment contract". Should the court seek to arrive at an autonomous definition or should contracts be characterised by reference to the *lex fori* or the *lex causae*? Although it is sensible to seek to give an autonomous meaning to many of the concepts employed in the Convention, this is not the case as regards contracts of employment since this "could well have the result that a particular State's employment law would have to be applied to a particular contract even though that State would regard the contract as being, say, one of agency rather than one of employment".[17] It has been convincingly argued that, notwithstanding objections based on logic, the approach which is most likely to promote uniformity in the application of the Convention is to determine whether or not a contract is an individual employment contract for the purposes of Article 6 by reference to the *lex causae*.[18]

12.2.2 The applicable law in cases where the parties have not made a choice of law

12.2.2.1 The common law

12.2.2.1.1 The leading authority on the proper law of a contract of employment is the decision of the Court of Appeal in *Sayers* v. *International Drilling Co NV*.[19] In this case the plaintiff, an English resident, entered into a contract of employment with the defendant, a Dutch company. The contract stated that, although the work was expected to be done in Nigeria, the defendant had the right to change the venue of work. Under the terms of the contract the plaintiff agreed that in the event of his suffering injury or disability at work he would accept the benefits payable under the "voluntary death and disability compensation program" maintained by the defendant as his "exclusive remedy in lieu of all other claims, rights, demands or actions, whether at common law or under the statutes of the United Kingdom". The contract did not contain an express choice of law. The plaintiff was injured while working on one of the defendant's oil rigs situated off the Nigerian coast. In the plaintiff's action against the defendant in England a preliminary issue arose as to the law governing the contract. Whereas the exclusion of liability in the contract was valid under Dutch law, under English law it was void.[20]

12.2.2.1.2 The majority of the Court of Appeal decided that the contract of employment was governed by Dutch law. Among the various factors considered by Salmon LJ one of the most important was the fact that the employer was based in the Netherlands: "Since the Dutch employers were engaging people of various nationalities in different parts of the world to work abroad together it certainly gives the greatest business efficacy to such contracts to presume that the parties must have intended to

16. Giuliano–Lagarde Report, OJ 1980 C282/25–26.
17. Morse, "Consumer Contracts, Employment Contracts and the Rome Convention" (1992) 41 ICLQ 1, 13.
18. Morse, "Consumer Contracts, Employment Contracts and the Rome Convention" (1992) 41 ICLQ 1, 13.
19. [1971] 1 WLR 1176. Smith, "International Employment Contracts—Contracting Out" (1972) 21 ICLQ 164.
20. By virtue of Law Reform (Personal Injuries) Act 1948, s. 1(3).

adhere to the law of Holland, or, put in a different way, that that system of law has the closest and most real connection with the contract."[21]

12.2.2.2 Article 6(2)

12.2.2.2.1 As regards individual employment contracts concluded on or after 1 April 1991 the choice of law rules contained in the Convention apply. If the parties fail to make a choice of law, the applicable law is not determined by Article 4, but by Article 6(2) which provides:

Notwithstanding the provisions of Article 4, a contract of employment shall, in the absence of choice in accordance with Article 3, be governed:

(a) by the law of the country in which the employee habitually carries out his work in performance of the contract, even if he is temporarily employed in another country; or
(b) if the employee does not habitually carry out his work in any one country, by the law of the country in which the place of business through which he was engaged is situated;

unless it appears from the circumstances as a whole that the contract is more closely connected with another country, in which case the contract shall be governed by the law of that country.

12.2.2.2.2 The basic structure of Article 6(2) is similar to that which is found in Article 4. Subparagraphs (a) and (b) define connecting factors (the place where the employee habitually works or the place through which the employee was engaged) which localise the contract. However, these connecting factors may be overridden if the contract is more closely connected with another country. Although Article 6(2) does not use the language of presumptions, the effect of subparagraphs (a) and (b) is to raise a rebuttable presumption that an employment contract is most closely connected with the place where the employee habitually works or the place through which the employee was engaged.

12.2.2.2.3 Article 6(2) raises a number of difficulties of interpretation, not least the relationship between subparagraphs (a) and (b), on the one hand, and between subparagraphs (a) and (b) and the final proviso, on the other. Some of these problems can be illustrated by reference to *Sayers* v. *International Drilling Co NV*.[22]

(i) How is the test in Article 6(2)(a) to be applied? In *Sayers* v. *International Drilling Co NV* the plaintiff was employed to work on a oil rig in Nigerian territorial waters, but the contract provided that the defendant had the right to change the venue of work. Could it be said that the employee habitually worked in Nigeria?
(ii) Questions of interpretation arise concerning the place of business through which the employee was engaged for the purposes of Article 6(2)(b). In *Sayers* v. *International Drilling Co NV* the plaintiff was recruited in England by an agent acting on behalf of a Dutch company. If the agent operates from a place of business in the country where the employee is recruited, subparagraph (b) may point to the law of the country where the agent's place of business is located, rather than to the law of the country where the principal's place of business is situated. If, however, the agent does not operate from a place of

21. [1971] 1 WLR 1176, 1184.
22. [1971] 1 WLR 1176. See Morse, "The EEC Convention on the Law applicable to Contractual Obligations" (1982) 2 YBEL 107, 141–142.

business, subparagraph (b) must be regarded as pointing to the country where the principal's place of business is located.

(iii) In what circumstances do the connecting factors in subparagraphs (a) and (b) yield to the test of closest connection? These problems mirror those surrounding the relationship between paragraphs 2 and 5 of Article 4.[23] In *Sayers* v. *International Drilling Co NV* the majority of the Court of Appeal laid particular emphasis on the fact that the employer's administrative centre was located in the Netherlands. Would this be sufficient to justify the conclusion that the contract was most closely connected with the Netherlands?

There are no simple answers to these questions, which will have to be considered by national courts (and perhaps in due course by the Court of Justice).

12.2.3 The application of mandatory rules in cases where the parties have made a choice of law

12.2.3.1 Article 6(1) provides:

> Notwithstanding the provisions of Article 3, in a contract of employment a choice of law made by the parties shall not have the result of depriving the employee of the protection afforded to him by the mandatory rules of the law which would be applicable under paragraph 2 in the absence of choice.

Article 6(1) is inspired by the same philosophy as Article 5(2)—an intention to protect the weaker party by ensuring that a choice of law does not prejudice the application of protective legislation which would apply in the absence of choice. If, for example, a French resident is employed by a German subsidiary of a New York corporation to work in different countries in the Middle East under a contract which is expressly governed by New York law, Article 6(1) requires the application of any relevant mandatory rules of the law of the country which would have applied in the absence of choice (which would probably be German law by virtue of Article 6(2)(b)) even though the contract is governed by New York law. As the Giuliano–Lagarde Report indicates, for the purpose of Article 6(2) mandatory rules "consist not only of the provisions relating to the contract of employment itself, but also provisions such as those concerning industrial safety and hygiene which are regarded in certain Member States as being provisions of public law".[24]

12.2.3.2 In deciding whether a mandatory rule should be applied by virtue of Article 6(2) it is important to have regard to the legal system of which the rule forms a part. The point has been made that it is often the case that employment protection legislation only applies if the relevant employment is in the enacting country, whatever law may be applicable to the contract of employment.[25] It would be absurd for a court in which a dispute is litigated to give effect to foreign legislation which according to its own terms is not applicable. If the applicable law gives the employee more extensive protection than the law which would be applicable in the absence of choice, the wording of the

23. See para. 11.2.3.6.
24. OJ 1980 C282/25.
25. Morse, "The EEC Convention on the Law Applicable to Contractual Obligations" (1982) 2 YBEL 107, 139.

Convention indicates that the employee obtains the benefit of the law which is more favourable.[26]

12.2.4 "Overriding rules"[27] of the forum

12.2.4.1 Whether or not parties have chosen a law, Article 7(2) provides for the application of the overriding rules of the forum. The Employment Protection (Consolidation) Act 1978 includes rules which determine the Act's scope of application and which indicate the extent to which the Act's provisions are overriding. The general rule under section 140(1) is that any provision in any agreement shall be void in so far as it purports either to exclude or limit the operation of the 1978 Act or to preclude any person from presenting a complaint to, or bringing any proceedings before, an industrial tribunal. So, for example, a contract term which purported to restrict an employee's rights in connection with pregnancy and confinement[28] would be overridden by section 140(1)(a), even if the contract were governed by a foreign law under which the term in question was valid. The general principle in section 140(1) is, however, subject to restrictions. (i) There are various matters which may be excluded by agreement.[29] (ii) Various provisions of the 1978 Act (such as the provisions relating to unfair dismissal) do not in any event apply to employment outside Great Britain even if the contract of employment is governed by English law.[30]

12.2.4.2 Legislation in the United Kingdom rarely indicates whether particular provisions are or are not overriding. For example, section 1(3) of the Law Reform (Personal Injuries) Act 1948 simply provides:

> Any provision contained in a contract of service or apprenticeship, or in an agreement collateral thereto (including a contract or agreement entered into before the commencement of this Act), shall be void in so far as it would have the effect of excluding or limiting any liability of the employer in respect of personal injuries caused to the person employed or apprenticed by the negligence of persons in common employment with him.

Although it is clear that this provision is a mandatory rule—in the sense that it cannot be excluded by agreement in a domestic contract—the extent to which section 1(3) is to be regarded as a rule which is capable of overriding the law chosen by the parties in an international contract is not obvious from the terms of the legislation itself. As a general principle, legislation of this type is not regarded as having extraterritorial effect. So, on the one hand, where an employee is injured by the negligence of a fellow employee in England, the effect of section 1(3) of the 1948 Act is to override an exclusion clause in the contract of employment even if the clause is valid under the applicable law.[31] If, on the other hand, injuries result from negligence committed in a foreign country it seems that section 1(3) is not to be regarded as an overriding rule for the purposes of Article 7(2).[32]

26. Allwood, "Characteristic Performance and Labour Disputes under the Brussels Convention: Pandora's Box" (1987) 7 YBEL 131, 154.
27. For consideration of the distinction between mandatory rules and "overriding rules" see paras. 11.3.1.3–11.3.1.5.
28. Employment Protection (Consolidation) Act 1978, s. 33.
29. Employment Protection (Consolidation) Act 1978, s. 140(2).
30. Employment Protection (Consolidation) Act 1978, s. 141.
31. This result follows from the analysis of the Court of Session in *Brodin* v. *A/R Seljan* 1973 SLT 198.
32. *Sayers* v. *International Drilling Co NV* [1971] 1 WLR 1176.

12.3 CARRIAGE OF GOODS

There are two specific aspects of the choice of law rules relating to contracts for the carriage of goods which need to be considered: (i) the determination of the applicable law in cases where the parties have not made a choice; and (ii) the impact of mandatory rules.

12.3.1 The applicable law

12.3.1.1 In cases of choice—whether express or implied—the general choice of law rules contained in Article 3 for determining the applicable law are relevant. However, in cases where the parties have not made a choice Article 4(4) provides:

> A contract for the carriage of goods shall not be subject to the presumption in paragraph 2. In such a contract if the country in which, at the time the contract is concluded, the carrier has his principal place of business is also the country in which the place of loading or the place of discharge or the principal place of business of the consignor is situated, it shall be presumed that the contract is most closely connected with that country. In applying this paragraph single voyage charterparties and other contracts the main purpose of which is the carriage of goods shall be treated as contracts for the carriage of goods.

12.3.1.2 Whereas the general rule in paragraph 2 is to localise the contract by reference to a single factor, the presumption in paragraph 4 requires the coincidence of the carrier's principal place of business[33] and another factor, which may be the place of loading, the place of discharge or the consignor's principal place of business. Various concepts employed in Article 4(4) are explained by the Giuliano–Lagarde Report: the carrier is "the party to the contract who undertakes to carry the goods, whether or not he performs the carriage himself"[34]; the consignor "refers in general to any person who consigns goods to the carrier"[35]; the place of loading and the place of discharge are the places of loading and unloading which are "agreed at the time when the contract is concluded"[36]; the wording of paragraph 4 is intended to make it clear that "charterparties may be considered to be contracts for the carriage of goods in so far as that is their substance".[37]

12.3.1.3 There are, of course, situations where the presumption in paragraph 4 cannot be applied (for example, where the carrier's principal place of business is in country X, the ports of loading and discharge are in country Y and the consignor's principal place of business is in country Z). In this situation reliance must be placed exclusively on the general rule contained in Article 4(1) which provides that "the contract shall be governed by the law of the country with which it is most closely connected". Furthermore, it should be noted that the presumption in paragraph 4 may be "disregarded if it appears from the circumstances as a whole that the contract is more closely connected with another country".[38]

33. For a discussion of "principal place of business" see para. 11.2.3.3.4.
34. OJ 1980 C282/22.
35. OJ 1980 C282/21–22. For a general discussion of the problems surrounding the identification of the consignor see Cashmore, "Who are Consignors and Consignees for the Purposes of a Contract of Carriage?" [1990] JBL 377.
36. OJ 1980 C282/22.
37. OJ 1980 C282/22.
38. Article 4(5). See para. 11.2.3.6.

12.3.1.4 Although the use of presumptions in Article 4 has been the subject of criticism, it is not difficult to find examples where the approach adopted by the Convention produces a greater degree of certainty and predictability than the common law rules. The value of the presumption in Article 4(4) is to provide clear guidance as to the applicable law in cases where the relevant connecting factors are evenly divided between two or more different countries. In a case such as *The Assunzione*[39]—in which a ship belonging to Italian owners was chartered for the carriage of goods from France to Italy—Italian law would be presumed to be the law with which the contract is most closely connected. By taking the carrier's principal place of business as the main connecting factor, it is relatively easy to localise the contract by reference to one of the other three factors. While the result may be no less arbitrary than the solution provided by the common law rules, the advantage of the Convention is that the solution is easier to predict.

12.3.2 "Overriding rules"[40] of the forum

12.3.2.1 Article 7(2) states that the Convention "shall not restrict the application of the rules of the law of the forum in a situation in which they are mandatory irrespective of the law otherwise applicable to the contract". The Carriage of Goods by Sea Act 1971, which provides that the Hague-Visby Rules have the force of law in the United Kingdom, is a clear example of legislation which enacts rules which are to be regarded as overriding for the purposes of Article 7(2). Although decided before the entry into force of the Contracts (Applicable Law) Act 1990, *The Hollandia*[41] illustrates the overriding effect of the 1971 Act. In this case the plaintiff shipped goods from Scotland to the West Indies on a vessel owned by the defendant. The contract included a jurisdiction clause in favour of the Dutch courts and a choice of Dutch law. The contract also contained an exclusion clause which purported to limit the defendant's liability to £250. When the goods were unloaded in the West Indies it was discovered that they were damaged. The plaintiff estimated the damage to be in the region of £22,000. When the plaintiff started proceedings in England, the defendant contested the jurisdiction of the court on the basis of the Dutch jurisdiction clause. Dutch law—the law chosen by the parties—included the unamended Hague Rules under which the exclusion clause was effective. The defendant's liability under the Hague-Visby Rules was £11,000.

12.3.2.2 Article III, paragraph 8 of the Hague-Visby Rules provides:

> Any clause, covenant, or agreement in a contract of carriage relieving the carrier or the ship from liability for loss or damage to, or in connection with, goods arising from negligence, fault, or failure in the duties and obligations provided in this article or lessening such liability otherwise than as provided in these Rules, shall be null and void and of no effect ...

The question facing the court was whether the Carriage of Goods by Sea Act 1971 rendered the jurisdiction clause null and void in England. The scope of the 1971 Act had been the subject of a vigorous academic dispute. According to one view, the 1971 Act

39. [1954] P 150.
40. For consideration of the distinction between mandatory rules and "overriding rules" see paras. 11.3.1.3–11.3.1.5.
41. [1983] 1 AC 565. Jaffey, "Statutes and Choice of Law" (1984) 100 LQR 198; and the reply by Mann, (1984) 100 LQR 369.

applies only where the law governing the transaction is English law.[42] Conversely, it had been argued that the 1971 Act is an overriding statute, which has to be applied regardless of any foreign choice of law clause in the contract.[43] The House of Lords accepted the second view; since the jurisdiction clause—if upheld—would have the effect of lessening the defendant's liability in a way which was not permitted by the Hague-Visby Rules that clause was null and void.

12.4 CONTRACTS RELATING TO IMMOVABLES

It is important to distinguish contractual and proprietary questions. Although a contract for the sale of immovables is governed by its applicable law, the transfer or conveyance of land is governed by the law of the country in which the land is situated (*lex situs*).[44]

12.4.1 The applicable law

12.4.1.1 Parties to a contract for the sale of immovable property situated in country X are free to agree that the contract should be governed by the law of country Y. Such a choice is valid under Article 3(1). However, where the parties have not chosen the applicable law—either expressly or impliedly—the *lex situs* normally governs. Article 4(3) provides:

> Notwithstanding the provisions of paragraph 2 of this Article, to the extent that the subject matter of the contract is a right in immovable property or a right to use immovable property it shall be presumed that the contract is most closely connected with the country where the immovable property is situated.

12.4.1.2 The presumption is, of course, subject to Article 4(5), which provides that the presumption in favour of the *lex situs* may be rebutted in cases where the contract is more closely connected with the law of another country: "For example, this presumption could be rebutted if two persons resident in Belgium were to make a contract for renting a holiday home on the island of Elba (Italy). It might be thought in such a case that the contract was more closely connected with the country of the contracting parties' residence, not with Italy."[45]

12.4.1.3 One of the major questions of interpretation surrounding Article 4(3) concerns the phrase "a right in immovable property or a right to use immovable property". Although the Giuliano–Lagarde Report does not address the issue directly, it is clear that contracts for the construction or repair of immovable property are not within Article 4(3); the subject matter of such contracts is the construction or repair, rather than the property.[46] The central question is whether the scope of Article 4(3) should be determined by the *lex fori*, the *lex situs* or by an independent definition. The problems concerning Article 4(3) are similar to those which arise out of Article 16(1) of the Brussels and Lugano Conventions which, in cases where the proceedings "have as

42. Mann, "Statutes and the Conflict of Laws" (1972–73) 46 BYIL 117. Also, by the same author: "Uniform Laws and the Conflict of Laws" (1979) 95 LQR 346; "Uniform Statutes in English Law" (1983) 99 LQR 376, 392–398.
43. Morris, "The Scope of the Carriage of Goods by Sea Act 1971" (1979) 95 LQR 61.
44. *Lord Nelson* v. *Earl Bridport* (1845) 8 Beav 527.
45. Giuliano–Lagarde Report, OJ 1980 C282/21.
46. OJ 1980 C282/21.

their object rights *in rem* in immovable property, or tenancies of immovable property", allocates exclusive jurisdiction to the courts of the Contracting State where the property is situated. The Schlosser Report, which accompanied the 1978 Accession Convention suggests that the question of whether an action concerns a right *in rem* should be determined by the *lex situs*.[47] This view has not, however, been adopted by the Court of Justice which has formulated an autonomous definition.[48]

12.4.2 Formal validity

The general rules set out in the first two paragraphs of Article 9 apply equally to contracts relating to immovable property.[49] So, where the contracting parties are in the same country, the contract is formally valid if it satisfies the formal requirements of the applicable law or of the law of the place of contracting; if one party is in country X and the other in country Y, the contract is formally valid if it satisfies the formal requirements of the applicable law, the law of country X or the law of country Y. These general rules are, however, subject to Article 9(6) which provides:

> Notwithstanding paragraphs 1 to 4 of this Article, a contract the subject matter of which is a right in immovable property or a right to use immovable property shall be subject to the mandatory requirements of form of the law of the country where the property is situated if by that law those requirements are imposed irrespective of the country where the contract is concluded and irrespective of the law governing the contract.

The effect of Article 9(6) is that "if the law of the country where the property is situated lays down mandatory rules determining formal validity, these must be applied to the contract".[50] Mandatory rules in this context means overriding formal rules which must be applied even when the contract has been entered into abroad and is governed by a foreign law. It is thought that such rules are probably rather rare.[51]

12.4.3 Capacity

Subject to Article 11, questions of capacity are excluded from the scope of the Convention.[52] The common law capacity rules are considered in the context of general choice of law rules.[53] These general rules should be equally applicable to contracts for the sale of immovable property. However, in *Bank of Africa Ltd* v. *Cohen* Buckley LJ indicated that "a person's capacity to make a contract with regard to an immovable is governed by the *lex situs*".[54] This decision is unsatisfactory.[55] Although there may be sound reasons of principle for the application of the *lex situs* to questions relating to capacity to transfer land, capacity to undertake contractual obligations should be governed by general principles—regardless of the subject matter of the contract.

47. OJ 1979 C59/121, para. 168(c).
48. Case C-115/88 *Reichert* v. *Dresdner Bank* [1990] ECR I-27. See para. 5.1.1.2.
49. See para. 11.4.3.
50. Giuliano–Lagarde Report, OJ 1980 C282/32.
51. Giuliano–Lagarde Report, OJ 1980 C282/32.
52. Article 1(2)(a).
53. See para. 11.4.4.
54. [1909] 2 Ch 129, 143.
55. Dicey & Morris, *The Conflict of Laws* (12th ed, 1993) p. 962; Cheshire & North, *Private International Law* (12th ed, 1992) p. 788.

12.5 THE SALE OF TANGIBLE MOVABLES

Subject to mandatory rules which may be applicable by virtue of Article 3(3) and/or Article 7, a contract of sale is governed by the law chosen by the parties[56] or—in the absence of choice—by the law of the country with which it is most closely connected.[57] If S, whose principal place of business is in England, agrees to sell goods to B, a French company, the contract of sale will, in the absence of an agreement on choice of law, be presumed to be most closely connected with England. It cannot be assumed, however, that the law which governs the contractual obligations of the parties, also governs questions of title to the goods. As a general rule the choice of law rules in the Convention do not apply to property rights.[58]

12.5.1 The transfer of tangible movables

12.5.1.1 What, for example, is the position where S, having contracted to sell goods to B1, fails to deliver them and instead ships them abroad where he sells them to B2? Although there are many cases in which B1's entitlement to damages for breach of contract will be a satisfactory remedy, where the subject matter of the contract of sale is unique or where the goods which are the subject matter of the contract are in short supply damages may not be enough. Which law governs the question of whether B1 or B2 has title to the property in question?

12.5.1.2 Where the location (or *situs*) of the chattel remains constant, the basic principle is that "with regard to the transfer of goods, the law applicable must be the law of the country where the movable is situate. Business could not be carried on if that were not so".[59] So, if S, having contracted to sell goods in Ruritania to B1, transfers them to B2 in circumstances in which B2 becomes the owner of the goods under Ruritanian law, the court will respect B2's title, regardless of the law applicable to the contract of sale between S and B1.

12.5.1.3 Where the *situs* of the chattels in question does not remain constant, the position is more complex. The starting-point for English law is *Cammell* v. *Sewell*,[60] a case in which the plaintiff bought some timber in Russia (country X) and shipped it to England. When the ship was wrecked off the coast of Norway, the master sold the timber to the defendant in Norway (country Y). Under Norwegian law the defendant acquired a good title to the goods. When the defendant subsequently brought the timber to England, the plaintiff claimed to be the owner of it. The court held that the defendant's title, validly acquired in Norway, prevailed over the plaintiff's earlier title.

12.5.1.4 The decision in *Cammell* v. *Sewell* stands for two uncontroversial principles. (i) Title to goods acquired in country X will be recognised in England if the goods are subsequently moved to country Y, until some new title validity acquired in country Y overrides the title acquired in country X. (ii) If—after the goods have been transported to country Y—a new title is acquired under the law of country Y which has the effect of

56. Article 3(1).
57. Article 4.
58. Giuliano–Lagarde Report, OJ 1980 C282/10.
59. Maugham J in *Re Anziani* [1930] 1 Ch 407, 420.
60. (1860) 5 H & N 728.

overriding prior titles, the title previously acquired under the law of country X is displaced.[61]

12.5.1.5 These principles were considered and confirmed in *Winkworth* v. *Christie, Manson & Woods Ltd.*[62] Works of art belonging to the plaintiff were stolen from the plaintiff's home in England and sold to the second defendant in Italy under an Italian contract. The second defendant sent the works to England to be auctioned by the first defendant in London. The plaintiff sought to establish title to the stolen works. Under Italian law, but not English law, the sale in Italy gave the second defendant good title. Slade J held that the title acquired by the second defendant in Italy had the effect of overriding the plaintiff's prior title, notwithstanding the fact that the goods were returned to the original *situs*. While this result may seem harsh on the owner of goods which have been stolen, the law cannot satisfy the competing claims of the original owner and the purchaser of the stolen goods, both of whom are innocent. Ultimately, the solution adopted is based on practicality and convenience:

> Security of title is as important to an innocent purchaser as it is to an innocent owner whose goods have been stolen from him. Commercial convenience may be said imperatively to demand that proprietary rights to movables shall generally be determined by the *lex situs* under the rules of private international law.[63]

12.5.2 Retention of title agreements[64]

12.5.2.1 Particular problems may arise from retention of title clauses in international contracts. When a seller seeks to retain title in goods until the buyer has paid for them in full, which law determines whether or not the retention of title clause effectively reserves title to the seller? It is important to have regard to the applicable law, which determines whether the agreement is valid, and the *lex situs*, which is relevant to the question of whether the agreement is an effective reservation of title. There are no English authorities dealing directly with these issues, but there are a few cases decided in Scotland[65] and Ireland.[66]

12.5.2.2 The *lex situs* of the goods at the time the contract is made should determine whether, as between the buyer and the seller, a reservation of title agreement is effective to reserve title to the seller. The fact that the retention of title agreement does not have proprietary effect under the applicable law should be irrelevant. What, however, is the position where the applicable law provides that the reservation of title agreement is invalid (either because the applicable law does not recognise such reservation or because under the applicable law there is no valid contract)? Notwithstanding the fact that "the notion that a reservation of title clause may be enforceable even if contained in

61. For a discussion of various more complex problems see Dicey & Morris, *The Conflict of Laws* (12th ed, 1993) pp. 972–976.

62. [1980] Ch 496.

63. Slade J, [1980] Ch 496, 512.

64. Davis, "Conditional Sales and Chattel Mortgages in the Conflict of Laws" (1964) 13 ICLQ 53; Chesterman, "Choice of Law Aspects of Liens and Similar Claims in International Sale of Goods" (1973) 22 ICLQ 213; North, "Reform, But Not Revolution: General Course on Private International Law" [1990] I Hag Rec 9, 265–273; Morse, "Retention of Title in English Private International Law" [1993] JBL 168.

65. See, in particular, *Hammer & Sohne* v. *HWT Realisations Ltd*, 1985 SLT (Sh Ct) 21; *Zahnrad Fabrik Passau GmbH* v. *Terex Ltd*, 1986 SLT 84; *Armour* v. *Thyssen Edelstahlwerke AG*, 1986 SLT 94, affirmed 1989 SLT 182, reversed [1991] 2 AC 339.

66. *Re Interview Ltd* [1975] IR 382; *Kruppstaal AG* v. *Quitmann Products Ltd* [1982] ILRM 551.

an invalid contract does, to some extent, jar on common sense",[67] the view has been expressed that "it is for the *lex situs* to decide whether title has passed to the buyer or has been validly reserved by the seller and the law applicable to the contract is relevant only to the extent that the *lex situs* takes account of it in determining whether title has or has not so passed".[68]

12.5.2.3 The *lex situs* should also govern questions of title in cases where the buyer of goods, which are subject to a retention of title clause, sells them to a third party.[69] If under the *lex situs* the third party acquires good title to the goods, the fact that the seller reserved title as against the buyer does not give the seller a proprietary claim against the third party. The seller is left with contractual remedies—which are almost certainly worthless—against the buyer. When the *situs* of goods changes, which is typically the case in international contracts, two questions should be considered: (i) whether the retention of title is effective under the law of the *situs* of the goods at the time of the conclusion of the contract; (ii) on the assumption that the retention of title is effective at the outset, whether "the law of the new *situs* accepts and/or overrides the title reserved under the law of the first *situs*".[70]

12.6 VOLUNTARY ASSIGNMENT OF INTANGIBLES[71]

12.6.1 Introduction

12.6.1.1 The problems surrounding the assignment of intangibles are, in certain respects, similar to those which concern the transfer of other types of property. An assignment of a debt, for example, involves contractual elements (as between the assignor and the assignee) and proprietary elements (as between the debtor and the assignee). An assignment does not merely create personal rights between the assignor and the assignee, but affects third parties.

12.6.1.2 In cases involving the voluntary assignment of intangible property the effect of Article 12 of the Convention is to divide choice of law questions into those which relate solely to the validity of the assignment itself (the assignor–assignee relationship) and those which are dependent on the validity of the original transaction by which the debt came into existence (the assignee–debtor relationship). Article 12, which largely replaces the uncertain and unsatisfactory common law rules, provides:

1. The mutual obligations of assignor and assignee under a voluntary assignment of a right against another person ("the debtor") shall be governed by the law which under this Convention applies to the contract between the assignor and the assignee.
2. The law governing the right to which the assignment relates shall determine its assignability, the relationship between the assignee and the debtor, the conditions under which the assignment can be invoked against the debtor and any question whether the debtor's obligations have been discharged.

67. Morse, "Retention of Title in English Private International Law" [1993] JBL 168, 174.
68. Dicey & Morris, *The Conflict of Laws* (12th ed, 1993) p. 1334.
69. *Re Interview Ltd* [1975] IR 382.
70. North, "Reform, But Not Revolution: General Course on Private International Law" [1990] I Hag Rec 9, 269.
71. Moshinsky, "The Assignment of Debts in the Conflict of Laws" (1992) 108 LQR 591.

12.6.2 The assignor–assignee relationship

12.6.2.1 The contract between the assignor and the assignee

12.6.2.1.1 The first paragraph simply confirms the fact that the general principles contained in the Convention apply to the assignment of an intangible movable (such as a debt) and adds nothing of substance to the Convention. If the parties have chosen the applicable law the chosen law governs.[72] In the absence of choice the assignment is governed by the law of the country with which it is most closely connected; it will be presumed that the assignment is most closely connected with the assignor's law; the presumption may, however, be rebutted.[73] The formal validity of an assignment is governed by the rules in Article 9, the material validity of an assignment is determined by reference to Article 8 and so on.

12.6.2.1.2 Questions of capacity are excluded from the scope of the Convention by Article 1(2)(a) and must be referred to common law rules. The common law authorities are not very satisfactory. In *Republica de Guatemala* v. *Nunez*,[74] for example, the majority of the Court of Appeal took the view that capacity to take under an assignment of an intangible movable is governed either by the law of the relevant person's domicile or by the law of the place of acting.[75] (Since on the facts of the case the place of acting and the domicile of the assignee were the same, the Court of Appeal was not required to decide between them.) To the extent that this decision represents the current state of the law, logic dictates that the same rule should apply to capacity to make an assignment. However, the approach adopted in *Republica de Guatemala* v. *Nunez* does not find favour with modern commentators; it has been suggested that questions of capacity to assign an intangible movable should be governed by the proper law of the assignment.[76] The proper law of the assignment will usually be the same as the law which, by virtue of Article 12(1) of the Convention, governs the assignment.

12.6.2.2 The transfer of property from the assignor to the assignee

It seems unlikely that Article 12(1) refers to the proprietary effects of an assignment as well as to its contractual aspects.[77] The Giuliano–Lagarde Report makes it clear that the Convention is not intended to apply to "property rights and intellectual property".[78] Accordingly, where intangible property is assigned by contract, the Convention determines the law governing the contractual rights and obligations of the parties, but the property aspects of the transaction are governed by rules to be found outside the Convention. At common law, whether an assignment is effective to transfer title to the assignee is determined by the law under which the right was created.[79] So, if the owner of the United Kingdom copyright of a book printed and published in England purports to assign the copyright under an oral contract governed by the law of a foreign country, by virtue of section 90(3) of the Copyright, Designs and Patents Act 1988 the transaction is

72. Article 3(1).
73. Article 4.
74. [1927] 1 KB 669.
75. See also *Lee* v. *Abdy* (1886) 17 QBD 309.
76. Cheshire & North, *Private International Law* (12th ed, 1992) p. 815.
77. Moshinsky, "The Assignment of Debts in the Conflict of Laws" (1992) 108 LQR 591, 615–616.
78. Giuliano–Lagarde Report, OJ 1980 C282/10.
79. *Campbell Connelly & Co Ltd* v. *Noble* [1963] 1 WLR 252.

not effective as an assignment, regardless of the validity of the contract under the applicable law.[80]

12.6.3 The assignee–debtor relationship

The second paragraph establishes that the law governing the right which is assigned governs other issues, notably whether the right in question is assignable, the relationship between the assignee and the debtor and the discharge of the debtor's obligations. Article 12(2) does not directly identify the law which governs the relationship between the assignee and the debtor; the matter is referred to the conflicts rules of the forum. As far as English private international law is concerned, the law governing the right to which the assignment relates is the law governing the transaction creating the debt.[81] The rationale of this rule is that the debtor should not be adversely affected (or made better off) by an assignment, except to the extent provided by the law under which the original obligation was assumed.[82] Where the debt arises out of a contract which falls within the material scope of the Convention, the law governing the debt will be the law applicable to the contract (as determined by Articles 3 and 4).

As regards priorities Article 12(2) provides that "the law governing the right to which the assignment relates" applies. So, where a debt has been assigned more than once, the effect of Article 12(2) is that the question of priorities between the competing assignees is governed by the law applicable to the transaction creating the debt.[83]

12.7 AGENCY

12.7.1 Introduction

In cases involving agency it is important to distinguish two different contractual relationships: (i) the contract of agency between the principal and the agent and (ii) the contract between the principal and the third party. Both of these contracts fall within the scope of the Convention. As regards the contract between the principal and the agent, the applicable law in the absence of choice is the law of the country with which the contract is most closely connected. Since the agent is the party who effects the characteristic performance of the contract, it will be presumed that the contract is most closely connected with the country in which the agent is habitually resident or where he has his principal place of business.[84] The legal relationship between the principal and the third party is governed by the law applicable to the contract concluded between the agent and the third party. As regards this contract the general choice of law rules apply (subject to one modification to the rules relating to formal validity). If, for example, the third party contracts to sell goods to the principal, in the absence of choice, the contract of sale will normally be governed by the third party's law. The Convention does not, however, apply to the question of whether the agent has the authority to bind the

80. Dicey & Morris, *The Conflict of Laws* (12th ed, 1993) p. 983.
81. *Trendtex Trading Corporation* v. *Crédit Suisse* [1982] AC 679.
82. Moshinsky, "The Assignment of Debts in the Conflict of Laws" (1992) 108 LQR 591, 619.
83. This is also the position at common law: *Kelly* v. *Selwyn* [1905] 2 Ch 117.
84. Article 4(2).

principal or whether an organ of a company can bind the company.[85] These questions continue to be governed by the common law.

12.7.2 Formal validity

As a general rule, a contract is formally valid if it satisfies the formal requirements of the applicable law or of the law of the place where the contract is concluded.[86] If, at the time of the conclusion of the contract, the parties are in different countries, the contract is formally valid if it satisfies the formal requirements of the applicable law or the law of one of those countries.[87]

Where a contract is concluded by an agent on behalf of a principal, the country in which the principal is to be found is irrelevant; the country in which the agent acts is the relevant country.[88] So, if the agent and the third party are in the same country at the time of the conclusion of the contract, the contract between the principal and the third party is formally valid if it is valid by the applicable law or the law of the place where the contract is concluded. If, however, the agent is in country X and the third party is in country Y at the time when the contract is concluded, formal validity may be conferred by any one of three potentially different laws: the applicable law, the law of country X or the law of country Y.

12.7.3 Is the principal bound?

Since the Convention does not determine the question as to whether an agent has authority to bind the principal, this issue must be referred to the common law. It is well established that, as a general rule, the proper law of the contract between the agent and the third party determines the rights and liabilities of the principal as regards third parties.[89] So, if an English resident appoints an agent in France to assist in the purchase of a villa on the Côte d'Azur the question of whether the principal is contractually bound to the third party will be referred to French law. However, once it is established that the principal is so bound, the contract is governed by the applicable law as determined by the Convention.

12.8 INSURANCE AND REINSURANCE[90]

12.8.1 Introduction

12.8.1.1 At common law, the proper law of a contract of insurance is determined by the application of general principles. For example, a choice of law is effective whether express or implied.[91] In the absence of choice, a contract of insurance is governed by the

85. Article 1(2)(f); Giuliano–Lagarde Report, OJ 1980 C282/13.
86. Article 9(1).
87. Article 9(2).
88. Article 9(3).
89. Cheshire & North, *Private International Law* (12th ed, 1992) p. 473; Dicey & Morris, *The Conflict of Laws* (12th ed, 1993) p. 1458 (Rule 199).
90. Smulders & Glazener, "Harmonisation in the Field of Insurance Law through the Introduction of Community Rules of Conflict" (1992) 29 CMLRev 775.
91. For example, in *Amin Rasheed Shipping Corporation* v. *Kuwait Insurance Co* [1984] AC 50 the House

law of the country with which it has its closest and most real connection. In certain cases, especially those involving life insurance, a contract is regarded as having its closest and most real connection with "the country in which the insurer carries on its business and, if it carries on its business in two or more countries, ... the country in which its head office is situated."[92] In other cases, especially those involving a multiplicity of parties from different countries, the objective proper law is the place in which the machinery for setting the contract in motion was located.[93]

12.8.1.2 These common law choice of law rules have been displaced by the Convention and by the choice of law regimes established by specific EC legislation. Contracts of insurance where the risk is situated outside the territory of the EC[94] and contracts of reinsurance fall within the scope of the Convention.[95] If the contract includes a choice of law, the chosen law is the applicable law.[96] If the parties have not made a choice, the applicable law is determined by the general principles contained in Article 4.[97] In a contract of insurance the insurer is the party who is to effect the characteristic performance under the contract for the purposes of the presumption in Article 4(2); in a contract of reinsurance, the reinsurer is the "characteristic performer".[98] In principle, therefore, it is perfectly possible for the law governing the contract of reinsurance to be different from that governing the original contract of insurance.[99] It must be remembered, however, that the presumption in Article 4(2) may be rebutted if the contract is more closely connected with a country other than that in which the principal place of business of the characteristic performer is located.[100] Whether the parties have made a choice of law or not, specific aspects of the applicable law may be overridden by the mandatory rules of other laws.[101]

12.8.1.3 Harmonisation of choice of law rules with regard to insurance contracts relating to risks situated in the territory of the EC has been effected by Article 7 of the Second Non-life Directive[102] and Article 4 of the Second Life Directive.[103] These provisions are implemented in the United Kingdom by the Insurance Companies Act 1982[104] and the Friendly Societies Act 1992.[105]

---

of Lords held that parties to a contract of marine insurance had impliedly chosen English law as the proper law of the contract by adopting a statutory Lloyd's policy.

92. Dicey & Morris, *The Conflict of Laws* (11th ed, 1987) pp. 1289–1290 (Rule 193(2)). This rule is taken from *Greer* v. *Poole* (1880) 5 QBD 272; *Pick* v. *Manufacturers' Life Insurance Co* [1958] 2 Lloyd's Rep 93; and *Rossano* v. *Manufacturers' Life Insurance Co* [1963] 2 QB 352.

93. See Merkin, "The Proper Law of Insurance and Reinsurance Contracts" in Rose (ed), *New Foundations for Insurance Law* (1987) 61–79.

94. On the question of where a risk is situated see para. 10.4.1.2.2.2.

95. Article 1(3) and (4).

96. Article 3(1). See para. 11.1.

97. See para. 11.2.

98. See para. 11.2.3.2.

99. This is the position at common law: *Royal Exchange Assurance Corporation* v. *Sjoforsakrings Aktiebslaget Vega* [1902] 2 KB 384; *Armadora Occidental SA* v. *Horace Mann Insurance Co* [1977] 1 WLR 1098; *Citadel Insurance Co* v. *Atlantic Union Insurance Co SA* [1982] 2 Lloyd's Rep 543.

100. Article 4(5).

101. Article 3(3); Article 7. See para. 11.3.

102. Directive 88/357 EEC, OJ 1988 L172/1.

103. Directive 90/619 EEC, OJ 1990 L330/50. Subsequent directives in these fields have not made any changes to the choice of law regimes.

104. Insurance Companies Act 1982, s. 94B and Schedule 3A.

105. Friendly Societies Act 1992, s. 101 and Schedule 20.

12.8.2 Insurance Companies Act 1982

Schedule 3A to the 1982 Act draws a distinction between general (non-life) policies (Part I) and long-term (life) policies (Part II).

12.8.2.1 General policies

As regards general policies it is important to distinguish large industrial and commercial risks[106] from other risks. In relation to the former the parties may choose any law.[107] A choice is not effective unless it is expressed or demonstrated with reasonable certainty by the terms of the contract or the circumstances of the case.[108] In relation to risks which are not large industrial and commercial risks a complex series of choice of law rules must be applied.

(i) If the Member State where the policy holder has his habitual residence or its central administration coincides with the location of the risk, the law of that Member State applies.[109] So, a contract whereby a German company insures a car registered in Germany will normally be governed by German law. However, if the law of that Member State allows it, the parties may choose the law of another country.[110] The rationale for this rule is that there is no need to protect the policy-holder against a choice of law which deprives him of the protection of his own law if under his own law such a choice is permitted.

(ii) If the policy-holder does not have his habitual residence or its central administration within the Member State where the risk is situated, the parties may choose either the law of the Member State where the risk is situated or the law of the country where the policy-holder has his habitual residence or its central administration.[111] So, if an English resident insures immovable property in France, the parties may choose English or French law. Furthermore, the parties may take advantage of any freedom of choice that is granted by either English or French law.[112]

(iii) Where the policy-holder carries on a business (which is defined as including a trade or profession[113]) and the contract of insurance covers two or more risks relating to the business situated in different Member States, the parties may choose the law of any of the States in which the risk is situated or the law of the Member State in which the policy-holder has his habitual residence or its central administration. So, if an English company, under one contract of insurance, insures buildings in France, Germany and Italy, the parties may choose French, German, Italian or English law. In addition, the parties may take advantage of any freedom of choice that is granted by French, German, Italian or English law.[114]

106. Classified under classes 4, 5, 6, 7, 11 and 12 of Part I of Schedule 2 to the 1982 Act.
107. Schedule 3A, para. 1(6).
108. Schedule 3A, para. 2(1). This formula is the one used in Article 3(1) of the Convention.
109. Schedule 3A, para. 1(1).
110. Schedule 3A, para. 1(1).
111. Schedule 3A, para. 1(2).
112. Schedule 3A, para. 1(4).
113. Schedule 3A, para. 1(3).
114. Schedule 3A, para. 1(4).

(iv) Where a contract of insurance is limited to events occurring in a Member State other than the Member State in which the risk is situated the parties may choose to apply the law of the former State.[115] So, where, for example, an English motorist takes out a policy of insurance to cover accidents in Belgium, the parties may choose Belgian law.

(v) In cases where the policy-holder does not have his habitual residence or its central administration in the Member State in which the risk is situated and the parties have not made a valid choice of law, the contract is governed by the law of the country with which it is most closely connected,[116] which is rebuttably presumed to be the Member State in which the risk is situated.[117]

(vi) The applicable law may be subject to the mandatory rules of the laws of other Member States.[118] In cases where the parties have made a choice in favour of the law of Member State X, but all the elements relevant to the situation are connected with Member State Y, the parties' choice of law shall not prejudice the application of the mandatory rules of the law of Member State Y.[119] Furthermore, the court is free to apply the "overriding rules" of the forum.[120]

12.8.2.2 Long-term policies

In relation to long-term policies, the general principle is that the applicable law is the law of the Member State of the commitment (that is, the Member State where the policy-holder has his habitual residence or its central administration).[121] There are three qualifications to the general rule.

(i) The parties may choose the law of another country if so permitted by the law of the Member State of the commitment (that is, the law which would apply in the absence of choice).[122]

(ii) If the policy-holder is an individual and has his habitual residence in a Member State other than that of which he is a national, the parties may choose the law of the Member State of which the policy-holder is a national.[123]

(iii) The applicable law is subject to the "overriding rules" of the forum.[124]

12.8.3 The Friendly Societies Act 1992

The Friendly Societies Act 1992 governs contracts of insurance made by a friendly society, the effecting of which constitutes long-term business or general business and

115. Schedule 3A, para. 1(5).
116. Schedule 3A, para. 2(2).
117. Schedule 3A, para. 2(4).
118. For a general discussion of mandatory rules see para. 11.3.
119. Schedule 3A, para. 3(1). This provision is very similar to Article 3(3) of the Convention. See para. 11.3.2.
120. Schedule 3A, para. 3(1). This provision is the equivalent of Article 7(2) of the Convention. See para. 11.3.3.2.
121. Schedule 3A, para. 6.
122. Schedule 3A, para. 6.
123. Schedule 3A, para. 7.
124. Schedule 3A, para. 8.

which covers risks situated in the United Kingdom or in another Member State.[125] The relevant choice of law rules are set out in Schedule 20 to the 1992 Act: Part I contains rules which relate to general business; Part II applies to long-term business. The rules to be found in Schedule 20 are to a large extent the same as those contained in Schedule 3A to the Insurance Companies Act 1982.

12.9 NEGOTIABLE INSTRUMENTS

12.9.1 Introduction

12.9.1.1 What is a negotiable instrument?

12.9.1.1.1 A negotiable instrument is an instrument which, by statute or mercantile usage, may be transferred by delivery and indorsement (if the instrument is payable to order) or by delivery (if the instrument is payable to bearer) to a *bona fide* purchaser for value in such circumstances that the purchaser takes free from defects in title of prior parties. The most common types of negotiable instruments are bills of exchange, cheques and promissory notes.

12.9.1.1.2 A bill of exchange is "an unconditional order in writing, addressed by one person to another, signed by the person giving it, requiring the person to whom it is addressed to pay on demand or at a fixed or determinable future time a sum certain of money to or to the order of a specified person, or to bearer".[126] The person who draws the bill is the drawer; the drawer is the person who directs the intended paymaster. The person to whom the bill is addressed, the person on whom the bill is drawn, is the drawee. Where a bill is payable at some future date the drawee does not incur liability on the bill unless and until he has accepted it. So, except in cases where the bill is payable on demand, the drawee is also the acceptor. The person in whose favour the bill is drawn is the payee. Where a bill of exchange is payable to order, it may be transferred by indorsement and delivery. The payee indorses the bill by placing his signature on the back and delivering it to the indorsee (who becomes the holder of the bill). A bill of exchange may be transferred from one holder to another many times before the final holder presents it for payment. Primary liability to pay the holder at the time when the bill matures rests on the acceptor; the liability of the drawer and subsequent indorsers is similar to that of a surety.

12.9.1.1.3 A cheque is "a bill of exchange drawn on a banker payable on demand".[127] A promissory note is "an unconditional promise in writing made by one person to another signed by the maker, engaging to pay, on demand or at a fixed or determinable future time, a sum certain in money, to, or to the order of, a specified person or to bearer".[128] A promissory note is a promise to pay, not an order to pay; accordingly, there is no acceptor. The person who makes the promise, the maker of the note, incurs primary liability for payment of the note and is in a position similar to that of the

125. Friendly Societies Act 1992, s. 101. The 1992 Act applies only to registered or incorporated friendly societies; it does not apply to foreign societies or other analogous bodies created under the law of a foreign country: Friendly Societies Act 1992, s. 116.
126. Bills of Exchange Act 1882, s. 3(1).
127. Bills of Exchange Act 1882, s. 73.
128. Bills of Exchange Act 1882, s. 83(1).

acceptor of a bill of exchange.[129] If the note is payable to order, the payee may transfer it to a third party by indorsement and delivery. (If the note is payable to bearer, transfer is effected simply by delivery.) The first indorser of a promissory note is in the same position as a drawer of an accepted bill payable to drawer's order.[130] So, the holder of a promissory note should present the note to the maker for payment; if the note is dishonoured, the first and subsequent indorsers may be liable on the note as sureties.

12.9.1.1.4 There are certain types of document—such as bills of lading—which are loosely described as negotiable. A bill of lading is similar to a negotiable instrument in the sense that it operates as a document of title in relation to the goods referred to in the bill and the transfer of the bill of lading effects a transfer of title to the goods in question. However, from a technical point of view a bill of lading is not a negotiable instrument, since the principle *nemo dat quod non habet* is strictly applied; that is to say, a transferee of a bill of lading cannot acquire a better title than the transferor. This is not the position when a bill of exchange or other negotiable instrument is transferred. The essence of negotiability is not simply the fact that title may be transferred by indorsement or delivery of the instrument; if an instrument is negotiable, the transferor of the instrument may, in certain circumstances, give to the transferee a better title than that enjoyed by the transferor.

12.9.1.2 Which law governs whether a particular instrument is negotiable?

12.9.1.2.1 According to English domestic law an instrument is regarded as negotiable either if legislation provides that it is negotiable or if it is regarded as negotiable by custom of the mercantile world in England.[131] However, in cases with a foreign element, whether or not a particular instrument is negotiable is tested by the law specified by the conflicts rules of the forum.[132]

12.9.1.2.2 When considering the law which should govern the issue of negotiability there are two possible solutions: (i) the law where the instrument is created or (ii) the law of the place where the instrument is "negotiated". The advantage of the first solution is that the character of an instrument is determined once and for all at the moment of creation. English law has, however, adopted the second solution; whether an instrument is negotiable is governed by the law of the place where it is "negotiated". Accordingly, an instrument which is not negotiable at the time of its creation may nevertheless be negotiated in another country if the law of that country regards the instrument as negotiable. Similarly, an instrument which is negotiable in the place where it was created cannot be negotiated in England unless it is negotiable by legislation or by custom of the mercantile world in England. In *Picker* v. *London and County Banking Co*[133] bonds, which had been issued by the Prussian government, were stolen in England from the plaintiff (without their coupon sheets) and deposited in the defendant bank as security for an overdraft. Under Prussian law and custom the bonds were negotiable without the coupon sheets, whereas by English law and custom they

129. Bills of Exchange Act 1882, s. 89(2).
130. Bills of Exchange Act 1882, s. 89(2).
131. *Goodwin* v. *Robarts* (1876) 1 App Cas 476.
132. See Giuliano–Lagarde Report, OJ 1980 C282/11.
133. (1887) 18 QBD 515.

were not. Accordingly, even though the bank had acted in good faith, they were not entitled—as against the plaintiff—to retain the bonds.

12.9.1.3 The Contracts (Applicable Law) Act 1990

For the most part negotiable instruments are excluded from the choice of law rules contained in the Convention. The Convention has no application at all to the most important types of negotiable instruments: "obligations arising under bills of exchange, cheques and promissory notes" are entirely excluded from the Convention's scope; as regards other negotiable instruments the Convention does not apply "to the extent that the obligations under such other negotiable instruments arise out of their negotiable character".[134]

12.9.2 Choice of law rules

Because of the ease with which a negotiable instrument may be transferred, it is only to be expected that choice of law questions will arise; a bill of exchange may be drawn in one country, accepted in another country, indorsed in a third, and payable in a fourth. For choice of law purposes the basic approach of English law is to treat a negotiable instrument, not as a single transaction, but as a series of separate contracts. Accordingly, the acceptance of a bill of exchange may be governed by the law of one country and the indorsement of the bill by the law of another.

The Bills of Exchange Act 1882—which applies not only to bills of exchange, but also to cheques and promissory notes—includes detailed provisions dealing with choice of law questions. The Act provides that where "a bill drawn in one country is negotiated, accepted, or payable in another, the rights, duties, and liabilities of the parties thereto" shall be determined by the choice of law rules contained in section 72. The foreign elements which are relevant for the purposes of section 72 relate to the places where the bill is drawn, negotiated and accepted and where it is payable; the domicile, residence or nationality of the parties is wholly irrelevant. Where, for example, an English resident makes a promissory note in France in favour of a German national, the note being payable in France, section 72 has no application—unless the note is negotiated in another country.

Section 72 does not provide a comprehensive set of rules governing all choice of law issues. In particular, the law governing contractual capacity and the transfer of the instrument are outside the scope of section 72.

12.9.2.1 Questions of form

12.9.2.1.1 Section 72(1) provides:

The validity of a bill as regards requisites in form is determined by the law of the place of issue, and the validity as regards requisites in form of the supervening contracts, such as acceptance, or

134. Article 1(2)(c). See para. 10.4.1.2.4.

indorsement, or acceptance supra protest, is determined by the law of the place where such contract was made.

Provided that—

(a) Where a bill is issued out of the United Kingdom it is not invalid by reason only that it is not stamped in accordance with the law of the place of issue:

(b) Where a bill, issued out of the United Kingdom, conforms as regard requisites in form, to the law of the United Kingdom, it may, for the purpose of enforcing payment thereof, be treated as valid as between all persons who negotiate, hold, or become parties to it in the United Kingdom.

With respect to questions of formal validity, each separate contract relating to a bill of exchange (issue, acceptance, indorsement) is determined by the law of the place where that contract is concluded. It will be rare for there to be any problem in determining the place where a bill of exchange is issued, accepted or indorsed: a bill is issued at the place where it is delivered, complete in form, to a person who takes it as holder[135]; a bill is accepted where the acceptance is completed by either delivery or notification[136]; where a bill is transferred by indorsement and delivery, the indorsement is completed by delivery, so the contract of indorsement is made where delivery takes place.[137]

12.9.2.1.2 The provisos to subsection (1) are designed to facilitate the negotiation of foreign bills in England. Although English law has removed stamping requirements, there are some legal systems which continue to impose them. The effect of proviso (a) is to render valid in England an unstamped bill which has been issued abroad. This proviso does not, however, remedy any defects of form other than failure to comply with the stamping requirements of the law of the place of contracting.

12.9.2.1.3 The second proviso enables a foreign bill to be negotiated in England even though it is not formally valid under the law of the place where it was issued. The condition which must be satisfied for this proviso to operate is that the bill complies with the formal requirements of the law of the United Kingdom. Nevertheless, there are restrictions on the proviso's area of impact: (i) both the parties to the proceedings must have become parties to the bill in the United Kingdom; (ii) the proviso may be relied upon only where the plaintiff is seeking to enforce payment of the bill.[138]

12.9.2.2 Interpretation

12.9.2.2.1 Section 72(2) provides:

Subject to the provisions of this Act, the interpretation of the drawing, indorsement, acceptance, or acceptance supra protest of a bill, is determined by the law of the place where such contract is made.

Provided that where an inland bill[139] is indorsed in a foreign country the indorsement shall as regards the payer be interpreted according to the law of the United Kingdom.

135. Bills of Exchange Act 1882, s. 21.
136. Bills of Exchange Act 1882, s. 2.
137. Bills of Exchange Act 1882, s. 2.
138. *Guaranty Trust Co of New York* v. *Hannay & Co* [1918] 1 KB 43.
139. An inland bill is defined by section 4 of the 1882 Act:

(1) An inland bill is a bill which is or on the face of it purports to be (a) both drawn and payable within the British Islands, or (b) drawn within the British Islands upon some other person resident therein. Any other bill is a foreign bill. For the purposes of this Act "British Islands" means any part of the United Kingdom of Great Britain and Ireland, the islands of Man, Guernsey, Jersey, Alderney and Sark, and the islands adjacent to any of them being part of the dominions of Her Majesty.

(2) Unless the contrary appears on the face of the bill the holder may treat it as an inland bill.

12.9.2.2.2 What meaning is to be ascribed to the word "interpretation"? In the context of this subsection "interpretation" should be regarded as covering not only the way in which words or expressions are construed, but also their legal effect.[140] For example, the law of the place of contracting determines whether a party who signs a bill and adds the words "bon pour aval par les tirés" assumes the obligations of a guarantor or those of an indorser.[141]

The law of the place of contract should also govern questions of material or essential validity (such as whether consideration is a requirement for an enforceable contract).[142] Accordingly, the material validity of a contract of indorsement should be governed by the law of the place where the indorsement is completed by delivery.

12.9.2.2.3 It would be a natural extension of section 72 to apply the law of the place of contracting to questions of performance and discharge—such as whether payment has been effectively made or whether the bill has been validly cancelled. It also follows from a broad interpretation of section 72(2) that questions concerning illegality should be governed by the law of the place where the relevant contract was made. So, if a bill is indorsed in Ruritania, in circumstances where such indorsement is illegal under Ruritanian law, the indorsement is void and cannot be enforced in England. However, it would seem from *Moulis* v. *Owen*[143] and *Re Banque des Marchands de Moscou (Koupetschesky) (No. 2)*,[144] that a contract on a bill, cheque or note will not be enforced in England if it is illegal by the law of the place of performance of the obligation or if the consideration for the contract was a transaction which is illegal by its governing law.[145]

12.9.2.2.4 The effect of the proviso to subsection (2)—which in substance preserves the rule laid down in *Lebel* v. *Tucker*[146]—is that if a bill is drawn, accepted and payable in England, but is indorsed in a foreign country, in an action by the holder of the bill against the acceptor, the "interpretation" of the indorsement is governed by English law. So, if the indorsement is valid by English law, but invalid by the law of the place where the bill was indorsed, the holder may nevertheless maintain an action in England against the acceptor. It is important, however, to draw attention to the limits of the proviso, which applies only where the action is brought by or against the payer (that is, the drawee or acceptor of a bill or the maker of a promissory note). The proviso does not apply in a situation where a dispute arises between two parties as to which of them is entitled as holder to payment under a bill of exchange.[147]

12.9.2.2.5 There are questions surrounding the word "indorsement" in cases involving the interaction of a contract of aval and English law. An aval, who is a surety for one of the parties to a bill of exchange (normally the acceptor), undertakes the obligations of a surety simply by adding his signature to the bill, accompanied by the words "bon pour aval par les tirés". Although many legal systems recognise the contract of aval, no such institution exists in English law. Indeed, no effect will be given in

140. *Alcock* v. *Smith* [1892] 1 Ch 238.
141. *Banco Atlantico SA* v. *British Bank of the Middle East* [1990] 2 Lloyd's Rep 504.
142. Chalmers and Guest, *Bills of Exchange, Cheques and Promissory Notes* (14th ed, 1991) p. 570.
143. [1907] 1 KB 746.
144. [1954] 1 WLR 1108.
145. Chalmers and Guest, *Bills of Exchange, Cheques and Promissory Notes* (14th ed, 1991) p. 576.
146. (1867) LR 3 QB 77.
147. *Alcock* v. *Smith* [1892] 1 Ch 238.

England to a contract of aval governed by English law.[148] The question arises, however, as to whether the court will recognise and give effect to a contract of aval governed by the law of a foreign country under which such an agreement is valid.

12.9.2.2.6 In *G & H Montage GmbH* v. *Irvani*[149] the Court of Appeal held that a contract of aval is enforceable in England as long as it is enforceable where the contract is made. Mustill LJ thought that section 72(2) was not applicable to a claim by a drawer/payee on an aval, but that by analogy, the conflicts rule at common law should reflect section 72(2). According to this approach, the validity and effect of a contract of aval should be governed by the law of the place of contracting. Purchas LJ, who reached the same result by a different route, thought that a contract of aval could be regarded as an indorsement for the purposes of section 72(2). The third judgment, which was given by Woolf LJ, is not free from ambiguity, but seems to provide support for both lines of reasoning.

12.9.2.3 Presentment

12.9.2.3.1 Enforcement of a bill of exchange is effected by the holder of the bill presenting it to the drawee for payment. Under English law, if the drawee dishonours the bill, section 48 of the 1882 Act requires the holder of the bill to notify promptly the drawer and any prior indorser by giving them notice of dishonour. In the case of a foreign bill (that is, a bill which is not an inland bill[150]) section 51(2) imposes the additional requirement of formally establishing dishonour by non-acceptance or non-payment by protesting the bill. (It should be noted that, even if a contract of aval can be regarded as an indorsement within section 72(2), an aval cannot be regarded as an indorser for the purposes of section 48 and section 51(2). Where a bill is presented and dishonoured in England, an aval's liability cannot be discharged on the basis that notice was not given to the aval or that the bill was not protested within the relevant period.[151]) Compliance with the necessary procedure—notifying the other parties and, in the case of foreign bills, protesting the bill—is of vital importance in terms of the remedies available to the holder of the bill. Where the correct procedures have been followed, the holder is able to seek payment from prior indorsers and the drawer of the bill, who are collectively sureties for the drawee.

12.9.2.3.2 Where a bill drawn in one country is negotiated, accepted or payable in another the duties of the holder in a case of dishonour are governed by section 72(3) which provides:

> The duties of the holder with respect to presentment for acceptance or payment and the necessity for or sufficiency of a protest or notice of dishonour, or otherwise, are determined by the law of the place where the act is done or the bill is dishonoured.

12.9.2.3.3 The meaning of this subsection is not immediately clear; it refers to three events (presentment, protest and notice of dishonour) and two applicable laws (the law of the place where the act is done and the law of the place where the bill is dishonoured).

148. See *Steele* v. *M'Kinlay* (1880) 5 App Cas 754; *Jenkins & Sons* v. *Coomber* [1898] 2 QB 168.
149. [1990] 1 WLR 667. Forsyth, "The Recognition of an Aval by English Courts" (1992) 41 ICLQ 858.
150. See n. 139.
151. *G & H Montage GmbH* v. *Irvani* [1990] 1 WLR 667.

How are these two systems to be distributed between the three events?[152] The most convincing interpretation is that subsection (3) contains, in effect, two rules.

(i) The duties of the holder with respect to presentment for acceptance and payment are determined by the law of the place where the act is done. Although there is much to be said for the view that the question of whether the holder has a duty to present the bill should be governed by the law of the place where such act is to be done,[153] it has been held that the existence or non-existence of the duty to present is not within the scope of section 72(3).[154] This question would, therefore, appear to be governed by the proper law of the acceptor's contract. The distinction between the mode of presentment and the necessity for presentment is not one which has appealed to commentators.[155]

(ii) The necessity for or sufficiency of a protest of dishonour is determined by the law of the place where the bill is dishonoured.[156]

12.9.2.4 The date of payment

Section 72(5) provides:

Where a bill is drawn in one country and is payable in another, the due date thereof is determined according to the law of the place where it is payable.

This principle that the due date is determined by the law of the place where it is payable is also applicable in cases where the bill is drawn and payable in the same country.

12.9.2.5 Contractual capacity

Section 22 of the 1882 Act would appear to provide that questions of capacity are governed by the general law:

(1) Capacity to incur liability as a party to a bill is coextensive with capacity to contract.

(2) Where a bill is drawn or indorsed by an infant, minor or corporation having no capacity or power to incur liability on a bill, the drawing or indorsement entitles the holder to receive payment of the bill, and to enforce it against any other party thereto.

The general conflicts rules concerning contractual capacity are not free from ambiguity.[157] Nevertheless, as a general rule, a person should be regarded as having contractual capacity if he has capacity either by the law of the country where he is domiciled and resident or by the law of the country with which the contract has its

152. The question is posed by Cheshire & North, *Private International Law* (12th ed, 1992) p. 527.

153. This gloss on subsection (3) has been suggested by Dicey & Morris, *The Conflict of Laws* (12th ed, 1993) p. 1439.

154. *Banku Polskiego* v. *Mulder (KJ) & Co* [1941] 2 KB 266.

155. See, for example, Chalmers and Guest, *Bills of Exchange, Cheques and Promissory Notes* (14th ed, 1991) p. 586.

156. Chalmers and Guest, *Bills of Exchange, Cheques and Promissory Notes* (14th ed, 1991) pp. 585–586.

157. See para. 11.4.4.

closest and most real connection.[158] Notwithstanding the terms of section 22(1), the application of the law of the place of contracting to capacity to incur liability as a party to a bill is favoured by some commentators.[159]

12.9.2.6 Transfer of the instrument

There is no doubt that the law of the place where the transfer is made determines whether property in a bill passes to the transferee. In the case of a negotiable instrument the place where the transfer is made necessarily coincides with the place where the subject matter of the transfer is located. The only question is whether the basis of this rule is section 72(2) of the 1882 Act or the general principle that the transfer of chattels is governed by the *lex situs* of the subject matter of the transfer. The English cases on this question are inconsistent.[160] However, from the point of view of principle, the general rule which applies to the transfer of tangible movables should also govern the transfer of a negotiable instrument. An exception to this arises in the case where the transferee's title depends on the formal validity of an indorsement of the bill, in which case section 72(1) applies.[161]

12.10 QUASI-CONTRACT AND RESTITUTION[162]

The Rome Convention deals only with contractual obligations; claims based on tort or unjust enrichment do not fall within the Convention's scope. In view of the relatively recent emergence of restitution as an organising category in English law it is hardly surprising that the conflicts problems surrounding unjust enrichment have received little attention in England.

12.10.1 Classification

12.10.1.1 In any situation which raises choice of law questions the nature of the issue facing the court must be classified before the appropriate choice of law rule can be identified. This process of classification has to be effected according to the organising framework of the *lex fori*. However, for the purposes of private international law, the organising framework does not have to correspond to the divisions of domestic law. So, for example, in the field of property, the private international law distinction between movables and immovables does not mirror precisely the division between real and personal property in English law. Similarly, the English courts have traditionally classified as contractual, situations which would not give rise to contractual obligations

158. Dicey & Morris, *The Conflict of Laws* (12th ed, 1993) p. 1271 (Rule 181).

159. Morris, *The Conflict of Laws* (4th ed, 1993) p. 328; Chalmers and Guest, *Bills of Exchange, Cheques and Promissory Notes* (14th ed, 1991) p. 570.

160. *Alcock* v. *Smith* [1892] 1 Ch 238; *Embiricos* v. *Anglo-Austrian Bank* [1905] 1 KB 677; *Koechlin et Cie* v. *Kestenbaum Brothers* [1927] 1 KB 889. These cases are discussed by Chalmers and Guest, *Bills of Exchange, Cheques and Promissory Notes* (14th ed, 1991) pp. 582–584; Cheshire & North, *Private International Law* (12th ed, 1992) pp. 821–823; Dicey & Morris, *The Conflict of Laws* (12th ed, 1993) pp. 1435–1438.

161. *Koechlin et Cie* v. *Kestenbaum Brothers* [1927] 1 KB 889.

162. Bennett, "Choice of Law Rules in Claims of Unjust Enrichment" (1990) 39 ICLQ 136; Blaikie, "Unjust Enrichment in the Conflict of Laws" [1984] Jur Rev 112; Gutteridge & Lipstein, "Conflicts of Law in Matters of Unjustifiable Enrichment" [1939–41] CLJ 80.

under English domestic law.[163] There is, therefore, no theoretical difficulty in classifying a legal question arising out of a set of facts as being concerned with restitution for the purposes of English private international law, notwithstanding the fact that this classification might not be appropriate in an entirely domestic context.

12.10.1.2 To some extent, the choice of law problem in unjust enrichment cases can be made to disappear by treating issues relating to unjust enrichment as procedural. If a case which raises questions of restitution is regarded as being concerned with remedies, the court may apply its own law on the basis that questions of procedure are entirely within the province of the *lex fori*. Nevertheless, the classification of enrichment claims as procedural is an unsatisfactory solution: first, because right and remedy are two sides of the same coin; secondly, the classification of an issue as procedural leaves unresolved the question as to the system of law which should govern the cause of action. It is, therefore, essential that unjust enrichment should be regarded, for choice of law purposes, as a substantive category.

12.10.2 Choice of law rules

In restitution cases, the choice is between the application of the *lex fori*, the law of the place of enrichment or the proper law of the obligation. The third possibility is the one which seems to have found favour in England. As a general principle "the obligation to restore the benefit of an enrichment obtained at another person's expense is governed by the proper law of the obligation".[164] The proper law is the law of the country with which the obligation is most closely connected.[165] It will generally be the case that where the obligation arises in connection with a contract, the proper law of the obligation will be the (putative) proper law of the contract. Where, for example, a contract is voidable for duress under its proper law, any subsequent claim to restitution is governed by the proper law of the contract.[166] However, the proper law doctrine cannot be stated as a series of hard and fast rules; the operation of the test of closest connection depends on the circumstances of the case.[167]

163. See, for example, *Re Bonacina* [1912] 2 Ch 394.
164. Dicey & Morris, *The Conflict of Laws* (12th ed, 1993) p. 1471 (Rule 201(1)).
165. Evans J in *Arab Monetary Fund* v. *Hashim* [1993] 1 Lloyd's Rep 543, 566.
166. *Dimskal Shipping Co SA* v. *International Transport Workers Federation (No. 2)* [1992] 2 AC 152.
167. See, for example, *Re Jogia (A Bankrupt)* [1988] 1 WLR 484.

CHAPTER 13

CHOICE OF LAW IN TORT

In the context of cases with a foreign element it is vitally important to determine the place where a tort is committed (para. 13.1). In litigation concerning a tort which has allegedly been committed in England, the choice of law rule is simple. Although it is possible to imagine cases in which it might be appropriate to apply a foreign law to a tort which has been committed in England (for example, in certain circumstances where both parties are foreigners), in cases involving torts committed within the jurisdiction English law is the applicable law.[1] Where, however, the alleged tort has been committed abroad difficult choice of law issues may arise (paras. 13.2–13.3). Even more problematical are the difficulties surrounding the interaction of choice of law rules in contract and choice of law rules in tort (para. 13.4). In view of the present state of English law in this area it is hardly surprising that in recent years there have been proposals for reform (para. 13.5).

13.1 THE PLACE OF THE TORT

Before turning to consider the issues surrounding choice of law in tort and English law's response to them, the initial question must be addressed: what is the test for identifying the place where the tort was committed?

13.1.1 Introduction

13.1.1.1 Before 1 January 1987 the court could assume jurisdiction under RSC, Order 11, rule 1(1) in tort cases where the action begun by the writ was "founded on a tort committed within the jurisdiction". The current Rules of the Supreme Court provide that the court may give leave for service of a writ out of the jurisdiction if "the claim is founded on a tort and the damage was sustained, or resulted from an act committed, within the jurisdiction".[2] Similarly, under Article 5(3) of the Brussels and Lugano Conventions "in matters relating to tort, delict or quasi-delict" jurisdiction is based on where "the harmful event occurred". Accordingly, for jurisdictional purposes the determination of the place where the tort was committed is not the central issue. In the context of choice of law, however, the identification of the place of the tort is of crucial importance. Whereas the court applies English law to torts committed within the

1. *Szalatnay-Stacho* v. *Fink* [1947] KB 1; *Metall und Rohstoff A G* v. *Donaldson Lufkin & Jenrette Inc* [1990] 1 QB 391.
2. RSC, Order 11, r. 1(1)(f). See para. 6.3.3.6.

jurisdiction, if the tort was committed in a country other than England the law of the place where the tort is committed (*lex loci delicti*) plays a role in determining the rights and obligations of the parties.

13.1.1.2 It is important at this stage to distinguish cases in which the tortfeasor's wrongful act and the victim's loss occur in the same country (single locality cases) from situations where the constituent elements of the tort are divided between two or more countries (multiple locality cases). There is obviously no problem in determining the place of the tort in single locality cases. If a German driver negligently causes injury to an English resident in a motor accident in Scotland, there can be no doubt that the tort is committed in Scotland. The problem surrounding the question of where a tort is committed only really surfaces in multiple locality cases. If a company discharges effluent into the Rhine in France as a consequence of which damage is caused to nurseries in the Netherlands which are irrigated by water from the Rhine, where is the tort committed?[3]

13.1.2 Various theories

13.1.2.1 The place of acting and the place of result

The natural starting-point for consideration of the place of the tort is the place where the alleged tortfeasor performed the act or acts which form the basis of the plaintiff's complaint. There are, however, problems with this approach. (i) A tort does not generally comprise merely the defendant's wrongful act; a fundamental feature of most torts is the requirement that damage is suffered by the plaintiff. Negligently driving a motor vehicle is not in itself a tortious act; no tort is committed unless the act of negligence causes damage. (ii) It is unrealistic in certain circumstances to treat the place of acting as the place where the tort was committed, especially when there may be considerable distance—both in time and space—between the defendant's act and the harm suffered by the plaintiff.

Of course, similar objections apply to the attempt to localise torts by reference to the place where the damage is sustained. Reliance on the place of result, no less than reliance on the place of acting, lays emphasis on only one of the constituent elements which—as a general rule—have to be proved if tortious liability is to be established. The use of the place of result as the connecting factor for determining the place of the tort is also defective as regards torts such as libel in relation to which proof of damage is not a necessary element.

13.1.2.2 The substance of the tort

Essentially, the problems surrounding the use of the place of acting and the place of result to determine the place of the tort centre on their mechanical nature and lack of flexibility. Accordingly, a more open-textured approach has found favour; the place of

3. In Case 21/76 *Handelskwekerij GJ Bier BV* v. *Mines de Potasse d'Alsace SA* [1976] ECR 1735 the issue was where the harmful event occurred for the purposes of jurisdiction under Article 5(3) of the Brussels Convention, rather than where the tort was committed. See para. 5.5.4.

the tort should be the place where in substance the tort was committed. While this test has the advantage of flexibility it has the disadvantage of being uncertain.

13.1.3 The test formulated by the English courts

13.1.3.1 The use of authorities

There are relatively few reported English cases involving questions of choice of law in tort, and even fewer in which there has been any uncertainty as to the place where the tort was committed. The question therefore arises as to whether cases decided under RSC, Order 11, rule 1(1) prior to 1 January 1987 (and under other procedural rules) can be used as authorities for determining the place of the tort for choice of law purposes. Although in recent cases the courts have rejected the argument that decisions under the old version of RSC, Order 11 are not relevant in the context of choice of law,[4] a certain degree of caution has to be exercised when considering some of the older authorities.

13.1.3.2 Evolution of the common law

13.1.3.2.1 Some of the cases decided earlier this century favour the place of acting theory. In *George Monro Ltd* v. *American Cyanamid & Chemical Corporation*,[5] for example, Du Parcq LJ said:

> Looking at the substance of the matter without regard to any technical consideration, the question is: Where was the wrongful act, from which the damage flows, in fact done? The question is not where was the damage suffered, even though damage may be the gist of the action.[6]

13.1.3.2.2 The turning point in the evolution of the common law came in the decision of the Privy Council in *Distillers Co (Biochemicals) Ltd* v. *Thompson*.[7] In this case the defendant, an English company, manufactured and sold a quantity of Distaval (a drug, the principal ingredient of which was thalidomide) to an Australian company. The defendant did not warn the Australian company of the damage which could be sustained to a foetus if a pregnant woman took the drug and, when the Australian company sold the drug on the Australian market, no warning was given to individual purchasers. The plaintiff's mother purchased Distaval in New South Wales and, as a result of her mother having taken the drug during the pregnancy, the plaintiff was born with defective eyesight and without arms. When proceedings were started against the defendant in the plaintiff's name in New South Wales the question arose as to whether the court had jurisdiction on the basis that the plaintiff's "cause of action . . . arose within the jurisdiction".

13.1.3.2.3 The Privy Council concluded that the cause of action arose in New South Wales. In rejecting the place of result theory as a general test Lord Pearson said: "The right approach is, when the tort is complete, to look back over the series of events

4. See Staughton J in *Armagas Ltd* v. *Mundogas SA* [1985] 1 Lloyd's Rep 1, 24 (reversed on other grounds [1986] AC 717); Slade LJ in *Metall und Rohstoff AG* v. *Donaldson Lufkin & Jenrette Inc* [1990] 1 QB 391, 446.

5. [1944] 1 KB 432.

6. [1944] 1 KB 432, 441. See, also, the judgment of Goddard LJ [1944] 1 KB 432, 439 and the judgment of Winn J in *Cordova Land Co Ltd* v. *Victor Brothers Inc* [1966] 1 WLR 793, 798–799.

7. [1971] AC 458.

constituting it and ask the question, where in substance did this cause of action arise?"[8] The problem in multiple locality cases is "the problem of deciding where in substance the wrongdoing occurred".[9]

13.1.3.2.4 It is clear that New South Wales was regarded by the Privy Council as being both the place of acting and the place of result[10] and any discussion of the problems posed by multiple locality cases is *obiter*. Nevertheless, in subsequent cases the short dictum taken from Lord Pearson's opinion has been applied as the general principle for identifying the place of the tort in multiple locality cases.[11] Although in some of the cases it seems to have been assumed that the principle formulated by Du Parcq LJ in *George Monro Ltd* v. *American Cyanamid & Chemical Corporation* and Lord Pearson's test in *Distillers Co (Biochemicals) Ltd* v. *Thompson* are substantially to the same effect,[12] there are real differences between them. Whereas the traditional test, which involves a search for where the wrongful act was done, is based on the place of acting theory, the modern test is more flexible in that it simply requires the court to determine where in substance the tort was committed. There is no necessary connection between the place of acting and the place where the cause of action may be regarded as having arisen.

13.1.3.3 Specific torts

How is the test to be applied in the case of specific torts? In *Diamond* v. *Bank of London & Montreal Ltd* Lord Denning MR indicated that there is no simple answer: "each tort has to be considered on its own to see where it is committed".[13] In seeking to determine where in substance the cause of action arose, the court applies exclusively English law.[14]

13.1.3.3.1 NEGLIGENCE

13.1.3.3.1.1 Apart from the cases involving misrepresentation, the negligence cases which have come before the English courts have involved dangerous goods which have been made in one country and then sold in another country without a warning. Unfortunately, the cases are not entirely consistent. In *George Monro Ltd* v. *American Cyanamid & Chemical Corporation*[15] the goods were manufactured and sold to the plaintiff in the United States of America. Although it was obvious that the goods were purchased by the plaintiff for resale in England, the Court of Appeal indicated that the alleged tort occurred in America. On the other hand, in *Castree* v. *ER Squibb & Sons Ltd*[16] the plaintiff was injured by machinery which was manufactured in Germany, but sold by the defendant in England through an English agent. The Court of Appeal decided that the substantial wrongdoing alleged to have been committed by the

8. [1971] AC 458, 468.
9. Lord Pearson, [1971] AC 458, 469.
10. [1971] AC 458, 469.
11. *Castree* v. *ER Squibb & Sons Ltd* [1980] 1 WLR 1248 (Carter, (1981) 52 BYIL 319); *Multinational Gas & Petrochemical Co* v. *Multinational Gas & Petrochemical Services Ltd* [1983] Ch 258; *Metall und Rohstoff AG* v. *Donaldson Lufkin & Jenrette Inc* [1990] 1 QB 391.
12. See, for example, the judgment of Ackner LJ in *Castree* v. *ER Squibb & Sons Ltd* [1980] 1 WLR 1248, 1251 and the judgment of Dillon LJ in *Multinational Gas & Petrochemical Co* v. *Multinational Gas & Petrochemical Services Ltd* [1983] Ch 258, 284.
13. [1979] QB 333, 346.
14. *Metall und Rohstoff AG* v. *Donaldson Lufkin & Jenrette Inc* [1990] 1 QB 391.
15. [1944] KB 432.
16. [1980] 1 WLR 1248.

defendant was putting a defective machine on the English market with no warning as to its defects.[17]

13.1.3.3.1.2 The difference between these two cases is that in the former, although the goods were used in England, they were sold in America, whereas in the latter the goods were both sold and used in England. It would seem to follow that, in this type of case, the tort is to be regarded as having been committed not where the goods are manufactured, but where the goods are sold without a warning. The result in *Distillers Co (Biochemicals) Ltd* v. *Thompson*[18] does not, however, conform to this analysis. In this case the drugs were sold in England for resale in Australia, but the Privy Council took the view that the cause of action arose in Australia (where the goods were put on the market) rather than England (where the goods were originally sold by the manufacturer without a warning).

13.1.3.3.1.3 Although it is dangerous to draw too general a conclusion from a relatively small amount of material, what appears to emerge from these cases is the idea that no single factor can answer the question "where in substance did the cause of action arise?". Although the modern test evolved from the place of acting theory, a test based on the substance of the tort does not require the court to identify a place where the defendant did something—or failed to do something. It is certainly not inconsistent with the modern approach for the court, in appropriate circumstances, to regard a tort as having been committed at the place where the plaintiff suffers harm.[19]

13.1.3.3.2 MISREPRESENTATION

13.1.3.3.2.1 In *Cordova Land Co Ltd* v. *Victor Brothers Inc*[20] Winn J decided that where a misrepresentation was made in the United States, but relied upon in England, the tort could not be regarded as having been committed in England. However, this decision pre-dated the adoption of the test based on the substance of the tort; the more recent authorities show that, as a general rule, in cases involving misstatement or misrepresentation the tort is regarded as having been committed at the place where the statement or representation is received and acted upon.

13.1.3.3.2.2 For example, in *Diamond* v. *Bank of London & Montreal Ltd*[21] the plaintiff, an English commodity broker, negotiated a contract with an American broker under which the plaintiff would buy (on behalf of clients) one million tonnes of sugar from one of the American broker's clients. In accordance with usual practice, the seller was required to provide confirmation by a bank of the availability of the commodity. Although an appropriate reference was provided by the defendant, a bank based in the Bahamas, the contract was never concluded—because the sugar did not exist. When the plaintiff started proceedings against the defendant, claiming damages for the loss suffered as a result of the defendant's misrepresentation regarding the availability of the commodity, the defendant contested the jurisdiction of the court on the ground that the alleged tort had not been committed in England. All three members of the Court of

17. Ackner LJ, [1980] 1 WLR 1248, 1252.
18. [1971] AC 458.
19. See *Metall und Rohstoff AG* v. *Donaldson Lufkin & Jenrette Inc* [1990] 1 QB 391 (albeit in the context of the tort of inducing breach of contract).
20. [1966] 1 WLR 793. Carter, (1965–66) 41 BYIL 440.
21. [1979] QB 333.

Appeal agreed that the place of the tort was England, where the representation had been received and acted upon.

13.1.3.3.2.3 This decision was followed in *The Albaforth*.[22] In this case the plaintiff had chartered a ship to a Liberian company, whose obligations under the charter were guaranteed by a Connecticut company. Before entering the charter the plaintiff had sought a report on the creditworthiness of the guarantor and the defendant, an American bank, had provided a reference in glowing terms. The major part of the hire under the charter was never paid. Proceedings were commenced against the defendant in England, the plaintiff alleging that the charter had been concluded on the basis of the defendant's negligent advice as to the financial standing of the guarantor. The Court of Appeal took the view that the alleged tort had been committed in England; since the plaintiff had received and relied upon the reference in England, England was the place where in substance the cause of action arose.

13.1.3.3.3 ECONOMIC TORTS

13.1.3.3.3.1 In *Metall und Rohstoff AG* v. *Donaldson Lufkin & Jenrette Inc*[23] the plaintiff, a Swiss company which bought and sold aluminium, employed London brokers in relation to their transactions on the London Metal Exchange. One of the London brokers was a subsidiary company of the second defendant; the second defendant was a subsidiary of the first defendant. Both of the defendants were incorporated in Delaware with their principal offices in New York. It was alleged that the defendants were guilty of inducing the London broker to break its contract with the plaintiff. Although the first and second defendants had operated largely in New York, the plaintiff suffered damage in England—in that sums which were owed were not credited to the plaintiff's account in London.

13.1.3.3.3.2 Slade LJ, giving the judgment of the Court of Appeal, explained the basis on which the alleged tort of inducing breach of contract should be regarded as having been committed in England:

> If the acts of inducement alleged are viewed in isolation, the torts alleged here, would in our judgment, be properly regarded as, in substance, torts committed in New York. ... But, if, as we have concluded, the question is where as a matter of substance the torts were committed, the matter must be looked at more broadly, taking account of the breaches (particularly the effective breaches) induced and the resulting damage. On this approach we conclude that as a matter of substance the torts were committed in London.[24]

13.1.3.3.3.3 It would, however, be dangerous to conclude from this decision that the Court of Appeal has laid down a rule that economic torts are to be regarded as having been committed at the place where the economic loss is suffered by the plaintiff. Much depends on the circumstances of the individual case. In *Dimskal Shipping Co SA* v. *International Transport Workers Federation (No. 2)*[25] the judge assumed, in a case involving allegations of interference with contractual rights, that the place of the tort was where the acts of interference were committed.

22. [1984] 2 Lloyd's Rep 91. Carter, (1984) 55 BYIL 347. See also *Armagas Ltd* v. *Mundogas SA* [1986] AC 717 (a case involving allegations of fraud).

23. [1990] 1 QB 391.

24. [1990] 1 QB 391, 449.

25. [1989] 1 Lloyd's Rep 166, 177; reversed on other grounds [1990] 1 Lloyd's Rep 319 (CA); [1992] 2 AC 152 (HL).

13.1.3.3.4 LIBEL

It is well settled that the tort of defamation is generally deemed to have been committed where the publication takes place, even though the allegedly defamatory words were uttered elsewhere.[26] Accordingly, a defamation may be regarded as having occurred in various places if the words are published in more than one place.

13.1.3.4 The Law Commission's proposals

13.1.3.4.1 In 1984 the English and Scottish Law Commissions produced a working paper on the problems concerning choice of law in tort.[27] This was followed by a report in 1990.[28] The major part of the Law Commissions' endeavour was focused specifically on the choice of law rules themselves. However, the Law Commissions also considered the rules for determining the place of the tort.

13.1.3.4.2 In the Working Paper it was suggested that the following principles should be applied:

(i) in cases involving personal injury, the place of the tort should be regarded as the place where the injury was suffered;

(ii) in cases where the plaintiff is seeking to recover damages for the wrongful death of another, the place of the tort should be regarded as the place where the deceased suffered the injury which led to the death;

(iii) in other cases, the place of the tort should be regarded as the place where the substance of the tort occurred.[29]

This approach was modified in the Report because it was thought that trying to identify the place of the tort in multiple locality cases is somewhat metaphysical. The Report states:

> Instead of stating the general rule that the law of the place of the tort or delict applies, and then identifying that place for certain types of tort or delict, we recommend a new formulation ... under which the applicable law is identified directly without involving the fictional place of the tort or delict.[30]

13.1.3.4.3 So, for example, in relation to cases involving property damage, the applicable law would be law of the place where the property was located when damaged. Although the formulation is different the effect of the Law Commissions' proposal is the same as selecting the place of result as the place of the tort and designating the *lex loci delicti* as the applicable law.

26. *Bata* v. *Bata* [1948] WN 366; *Church of Scientology of California* v. *Commissioner of Metropolitan Police* (1976) 120 Sol J 690.
27. *Choice of Law in Tort and Delict*, Law Com WP No. 87.
28. *Choice of Law in Tort and Delict*, Law Com No. 193.
29. Law Com WP No. 87, pp. 32–33, para. 4.90.
30. Law Com No. 193, p. 11, para. 3.6.

13.2 APPROACHES TO CHOICE OF LAW IN TORT

13.2.1 Introduction

Looked at from the most general perspective there are three possible approaches to choice of law in tort: (i) the application of the law of the forum (*lex fori*); (ii) the application of the law of the place where the tort was committed (*lex loci delicti*); (iii) the application of the law which has the most real and substantial connection with the situation (the proper law of the tort). Of course, it is quite possible for a system of private international law to involve a combination of these different laws.

13.2.1.1 Lex fori

13.2.1.1.1 A general choice of law rule which requires the application of the *lex fori* to foreign torts cannot be supported from the point of view of principle or policy. At the most basic level the choice of law process is concerned with conflicts justice and the suggestion that the law of the forum is the law which is most suitable is effectively a denial of the validity of choice of law principles as part of the system for resolving disputes with a foreign element. Although attempts may be made to justify the application of the *lex fori* on the grounds that the court knows its own law and that proof of foreign law may present difficulties, reasoning along these lines is no more than a counsel of despair. The choice of law process is premised on the assumption that courts will apply the law of a foreign country where it is appropriate to do so. Of course, if the appropriate foreign law is not pleaded or cannot be proved, the court has to fall back on the *lex fori*.[31] This is not, however, an argument in favour of the application of the law of the forum as the basic choice of law rule.

13.2.1.1.2 The rejection of the *lex fori* as the generally applicable law does not mean that the law of the forum is wholly irrelevant in cases involving choice of law in tort. As with all areas of private international law, a court will not apply a foreign rule which conflicts with the forum's conceptions of justice or with public policy. This sentiment, in a relatively extreme form, finds its expression in some of the reported cases. For example, it has been suggested that "it would be too much to expect the court of the forum to entertain an action for what is not a wrong by the law of the forum. The court of the forum must in fundamentals be true to its own law."[32]

13.2.1.2 Lex loci delicti

If the *lex fori* is not acceptable as the applicable law, the *lex loci delicti* immediately suggests itself as the applicable law. It seems intuitively sensible that liability for a road accident in France should be determined by French law. It is, therefore, not altogether surprising that many systems of private international law have started from the point that, in principle, the law governing a tort should be the *lex loci delicti*. However, it is not very difficult to see the shortcomings of the rigid application of the *lex loci delicti* in tort cases: the place of the tort may be more or less fortuitous; a tort committed in country X may be more closely connected with country Y. For example, in the situation where A

31. Chapter 23.
32. Lord Justice-Clerk (Thomson) in *M'Elroy* v. *M'Allister* 1949 SC 110, 117.

and B, having set off together on a car journey from country X, are involved in a road accident in country Y in which B is injured as a result of A's negligence, the application of the *lex loci delicti* by the courts of country X might seem unjust if B is denied recovery under the law of country Y, but not under the law of country X. It should be stressed, however, that this example should not be regarded as lending support to the application of the law of the forum as such. In this type of case, to the extent that the *lex fori* is to be regarded as the appropriate law it is because it is the law of the country with which the situation is most closely connected.

13.2.1.3 Alternative approaches

Dissatisfaction with the results achieved by the rigid application of the *lex loci delicti* provoked a revolution in thinking about the choice of law process in the United States. This revolution arose in the context of inter-state road traffic accidents. The issue surfaced first on the other side of the Atlantic because the United States is a technologically advanced, wealthy and highly mobile society, which is made up of a large number of relatively small law districts. The combination of these factors means that there is a high incidence of road accidents involving parties from different states. Although opposition to the inflexible application of the *lex loci delicti* has become almost universal, there is considerable disagreement as to what precisely should replace the traditional rule.[33] Two doctrines have, however, gained a measure of acceptance: the proper law doctrine and governmental interest analysis.

13.2.2 Alternative approaches to choice of law in tort

One of the criticisms aimed at traditional choice of law thinking is that it is centred on what are, somewhat pejoratively, referred to as "jurisdiction-selecting" rules—that is, rules which identify the country whose law is to govern the particular issue before the court. A choice of law rule which stipulates that foreign torts are governed by the *lex loci delicti* does not involve an investigation of the substantive rules which are relevant or the result which will be reached. The alternative approaches stress that the choice of law process should be about choosing rules rather than choosing countries. Emphasis on the content of substantive rules themselves may show that what at first glance appears to be a conflict is in fact a "false conflict".[34]

13.2.2.1 The proper law of the tort

13.2.2.1.1 The notion of the proper law of the tort originates in an article by Morris in the *Harvard Law Review*.[35] Morris took as his starting-point the observation that the proper law doctrine is a perfectly acceptable basis on which to resolve choice of law questions in contract. Of course, in tort cases there can be no question of an express or implied choice of law by the parties. However, under the contract doctrine if the parties do not make a choice the court will select the law of the country with which the contract

33. See Nygh, "Some Thoughts on the Proper Law of a Tort" (1977) 26 ICLQ 932.
34. See para. 13.2.2.2.2.
35. "The Proper Law of a Tort" (1951) 64 Harv LR 881. This article was foreshadowed by an earlier note: Morris, "Torts in the Conflict of Laws" (1949) 12 MLR 248.

has its closest and most real connection. By analogy, why should a tort not be governed by the law of the country with which it has its closest and most real connection?

13.2.2.1.2 The advantage of the proper law doctrine in the tort context is that it breaks free from the straitjacket of a one-dimensional choice of law rule. The rigid application of the *lex loci delicti* (or the *lex fori*) is inappropriate in that, given the very large number of different questions which can arise in tort litigation, it is "extraordinarily unlikely"[36] that all these questions can be satisfactorily answered by the mechanical application of the same choice of law rule. A proper law approach would not only "furnish much needed flexibility",[37] it would also "enable the problems to be broken down into smaller groups and thus facilitate a more adequate analysis of the social factors involved".[38]

13.2.2.1.3 Of course, it would be naïve to suggest that the proper law doctrine does not give rise to certain problems.[39] In a sense the proper law doctrine is not a choice of law rule at all; it is a method, which involves a weighing of connecting factors to determine the law with which the tort has its closest and most real connection. Since the process of weighing is a somewhat subjective one, the doctrine necessarily involves a measure of uncertainty and can be used to justify the application of the law of the forum or the avoidance of an unpopular rule which forms part of the law which would otherwise be applicable. There are, however, three reasons why the problems associated with uncertainty should not be exaggerated.

(i) Over a period of time the English courts were successful in injecting a high degree of certainty in contract cases and there is, therefore, no reason in principle why a similar process could not be achieved in the context of tort.

(ii) As Morris himself pointed out, "in many, perhaps most, situations there would be no need to look beyond the law of the place of wrong, so long as there is no doubt where that place is".[40]

(iii) Certainty and predictability (which are clearly at a premium in contract cases where business people may legitimately wish to make rational decisions on the basis of a body of settled rules) are less obviously necessary in tort cases. In most cases, a tort is something which was not planned (at least, not by the plaintiff).

13.2.2.2 Governmental interest analysis[41]

13.2.2.2.1 Governmental interest analysis is inspired by the same factors which prompted Morris to advocate the application of the proper law doctrine to tort cases.

36. Morris, "The Proper Law of a Tort" (1951) 64 Harv LR 881, 893.
37. "The Proper Law of a Tort" (1951) 64 Harv LR 881, 884.
38. "The Proper Law of a Tort" (1951) 64 Harv LR 881, 892.
39. See, for example, Ehrenzweig, "The Not So 'Proper' Law of a Tort: Pandora's Box" (1968) 17 ICLQ 1; Carter, "Torts in English Private International Law" (1981) 52 BYIL 9, 18–20.
40. "The Proper Law of the Tort" (1951) 64 Harv LR 881, 884–885.
41. The most influential proponent of governmental interest analysis is Brainerd Currie, who developed the theory in a series of articles, the most important of which are reprinted in his *Selected Essays on the Conflict of Laws* (1963). Some of the seeds of interest analysis were sown by Cavers, "A Critique of the Choice of Law Problem" (1933) 47 Harv LR 173. See also Cavers, "Contemporary Conflicts Law in American Perspective" [1970] III Hag Rec 75.

Whereas Morris's approach is within the framework of a traditional "grouping of contacts" or "centre of gravity" framework, governmental interest analysis approaches the choice of law process more overtly from the perspective of policy, rather than factual connections.

13.2.2.2.2 One of the key features of classic interest analysis is the primacy given to the *lex fori*. Currie's approach starts from the position that "[n]ormally, even in cases involving foreign elements, the court should be expected, as a matter of course, to apply the rule of decision found in the law of the forum".[42] When it is argued that a foreign law ought to be applied the court should determine the governmental policy expressed by the law of the forum and the policy expressed by the foreign law. Whether a country has a legitimate interest in the application of its law to a specific case depends on the policy behind the law and the reasonableness of asserting that policy to a specific set of facts. If the court finds that the forum country has no interest in the application of its policy, but that the foreign country has—an example of a "false conflict"—the court should apply the foreign law. If, conversely, the forum has an interest in the application of its policy, and the foreign country does not—another "false conflict"—the court should apply the law of the forum. More difficult is the problem presented by the "true conflict", where two or more countries are legitimately interested in the application of their policies. Currie's solution was the application of the law of the forum in any case where the forum has an interest in the application of its policy.[43] This solution does not, of course, deal with the problem where the forum is "disinterested" and the conflict is between the laws of two foreign countries. An alternative approach to "true conflicts" is to require the court to weigh the relative strengths of the interests of the countries involved and to apply the law of the country which has the greatest interest. For example, the comparative impairment theory requires the application of the law of the country whose policy will be most impaired in general scope and impact by its non-application.[44]

13.2.3 Alternative approaches in practice

There can be no doubt that in the United States governmental interest analysis has been instrumental in introducing a more elastic approach to choice of law questions in tort cases. No longer do the courts relentlessly apply the *lex loci delicti* to inter-state torts. Nevertheless, although governmental interest analysis has found its way into countless judicial decisions in numerous American jurisdictions, there are questions concerning the extent to which the courts of any state have fully embraced Currie's theory.[45]

13.2.3.1 Babcock v. Jackson: an easy starting-point

13.2.3.1.1 In *Babcock* v. *Jackson*[46] the parties, both of whom lived in New York, set off in the defendant's car for a week-end trip to Canada. While in Ontario the parties were

42. Currie, "Notes on Methods and Objectives in the Conflict of Laws" in *Selected Essays on the Conflict of Laws* (1963) 177, 183.
43. Currie, "Notes on Methods and Objectives in the Conflict of Laws" in *Selected Essays on the Conflict of Laws* (1963) 177, 184.
44. Baxter, "Choice of Law and the Federal System" (1963) 16 Stan LR 1.
45. See Juenger, "Conflict of Laws: A Critique of Interest Analysis" (1984) 32 Am J Comp L 1, 13–25.
46. [1963] 2 Lloyd's Rep 286 (New York Court of Appeals). Morris, "The Proper Law of the Tort Again" (1963) 79 LQR 484.

involved in a road accident—resulting from the defendant's negligence—in which the plaintiff was injured. The plaintiff sued the defendant for damages in New York. Although the defendant was liable under New York law for the plaintiff's injuries, under the law of Ontario the defendant had a defence based on a so-called guest-statute which provided that a driver could not be civilly liable to his gratuitous passengers. Fuld J, who gave the decision of the majority of the New York Court of Appeals, posed the question facing the court in the following terms: "Shall the law of the place of the tort *invariably* govern the availability of relief for the tort or shall the applicable choice of law rule also reflect a consideration of other factors which are relevant to the purposes served by the enforcement or denial of the remedy?"[47]

13.2.3.1.2 *Babcock* v. *Jackson* is generally regarded as supporting both the proper law doctrine and government interest analysis. Fuld J justified the application of New York law not only on the basis that the "centre of gravity" doctrine was the appropriate approach for accommodating the competing interests in inter-state tort cases, but also because a comparison of the relative contacts and interests of New York and Ontario made it clear that the concern of New York was unquestionably the greater and more direct and that the interest of Ontario was at best minimal.[48] Of course, the two lines of reasoning pointed in the same direction.

13.2.3.1.3 The application of governmental interest analysis in *Babcock* v. *Jackson* exposed a "false conflict": the policy of New York law in imposing liability on the defendant was advanced by the application of New York law; the policy of the Ontario law—to prevent the fraudulent assertion of claims by passengers in collusion with drivers against Ontario insurance companies—did not require the application of the guest-statute when both parties were New York residents and the defendant was insured with a New York insurance company. The revelation of this type of "false conflict" is one of the alleged strengths of governmental interest analysis.

13.2.3.1.4 The application of governmental interest analysis and the proper law doctrine also reveals that the same law is not necessarily appropriate to govern all the legal issues arising out of a claim in tort. Although the question of the possible exclusion of a driver's liability to a non-paying passenger was referred to the law of the country in which both parties were resident, had the relevant issue in *Babcock* v. *Jackson* concerned the standard of care imposed on drivers of motor vehicles the application of New York law would not have been appropriate. As Fuld J pointed out: "Where the defendant's exercise of due care in the operation of his automobile is in issue, the jurisdiction in which the allegedly wrongful conduct occurred will usually have a predominant, if not exclusive, concern."[49]

13.2.3.2 Subsequent developments: harder cases

13.2.3.2.1 *Babcock* v. *Jackson* was in many respects an easy case. Apart from those who favour the inflexible application of the *lex loci delicti* to all tort questions, there can be hardly anyone who believes that the result achieved by the New York Court of Appeals is unsatisfactory. If ever there was a case where the application of the *lex loci delicti* was inappropriate *Babcock* v. *Jackson* was that case. However, not all cases are so simple

47. [1963] 2 Lloyd's Rep 286, 287. (Emphasis in original.)
48. [1963] 2 Lloyd's Rep 286, 289–290.
49. [1963] 2 Lloyd's Rep 286, 290.

and "*Babcock* spawned an unruly progeny in which variations in the issues and in the facts of the parties' relationship and its connection with New York led to a perplexed and divided court".[50]

13.2.3.2.2 Although interest analysis has found favour with the courts of New York and other American jurisdictions, its application becomes more and more difficult when the various connecting factors are not so obviously linked with one jurisdiction as was the case in *Babcock* v. *Jackson* itself. In *Tooker* v. *Lopez*[51] the parties were New York residents, but the accident occurred in Michigan, where the driver and the passenger were studying at college. The New York Court of Appeals confirmed the application of governmental interest analysis to the problems posed by inter-state torts and held that, even though the nexus between the driver and the passenger had been formed in Michigan rather than in New York, Michigan had no interest in whether or not a New York plaintiff is able to recover against a New York defendant where the car is insured in New York. The fact that the passenger and driver were in Michigan for an extended period of time was regarded as being irrelevant.

13.2.3.2.3 In *Babcock* v. *Jackson* and *Tooker* v. *Lopez*, since both parties had a significant connection with the forum, the conflict which the court had to resolve was between the *lex loci delicti* and *lex fori*. Difficulties increase when the parties do not come from the same law district. In *Reich* v. *Purcell*[52] the forum was largely "disinterested" and to the extent that there was a conflict it was between the laws of two other jurisdictions. The basic facts were quite simple: the deceased and the plaintiffs were domiciled in Ohio; the defendant was domiciled in California; the accident took place in Missouri; and the trial took place in California. Under the law of Missouri there was a statutory maximum of $25,000 for damages for wrongful death. Under the laws of California and Ohio there was no such limitation. Ohio had an interest in the application of its law, since this would ensure that the plaintiffs recovered in full; *prima facie* Missouri also had an interest in the application of its law, since the accident took place in Missouri. The Supreme Court of California concluded, however, that *Reich* v. *Purcell* was really another case of a "false conflict". Although Missouri has a predominant interest with conduct within its borders, the issue in this case—the limitation of damages for wrongful death—had nothing to do with conduct as such. The court concluded that the place of the wrong has little or no interest in the level of the plaintiff's compensation if none of the parties reside there. Ohio, on the other hand, had a legitimate interest in promoting the economic welfare of the plaintiffs. Accordingly, the court refused to apply the limitation imposed by the *lex loci delicti*.

13.2.3.2.4 In each of the cases considered so far, the line of reasoning adopted by the court led to the conclusion that there was a "false conflict". To what extent can interest analysis yield satisfactory results in cases of "true conflict"? *Bernhard* v. *Harrah's Club*[53] concerned a motor accident in California. The plaintiff, a Californian resident, was injured when his car was struck by another car, which was being driven by another Californian resident. The driver who caused the accident was intoxicated, having been drinking in the defendant's bar in Nevada. Under Californian law the defendant was liable on the ground that he had served drinks to an intoxicated person who had

50. Cavers, "Contemporary Conflicts Law in American Perspective" [1970] III Hag Rec 75, 173.
51. 24 NY 2d 569; 249 NE 2d 394 (1969).
52. 67 Cal 2d 551; 432 P 2d 727 (1967).
53. 16 Cal 3d 313; 546 P 2d 719 (1976).

subsequently injured another. Under the law of Nevada no liability was imposed on the defendant. Although the accident occurred in California, the alleged wrongful act was the serving of alcohol to an intoxicated person and, therefore, Nevada was the place of the tort.

13.2.3.2.5 The Supreme Court of California thought that in this case both California and Nevada had an interest in the application of its law: California has an interest in the protection of Californian residents; Nevada has an interest in the protection of Nevada bar owners. The "true conflict" presents governmental interest analysis with one of its sternest challenges: how is the court to determine the relative importance of competing governmental policies? The court applied Californian law, not simply on the basis that it was the *lex fori*, but on the ground that the policy of the Californian law would be impaired more by the non-application of Californian law than the policy of Nevada law would have been impaired by the non-application of Nevada law.

13.2.4 Problems with governmental interest analysis

There are various possible reservations surrounding governmental interest analysis as a means of solving choice of law problems.

13.2.4.1 At the most fundamental level, there are those who question the whole enterprise. Some argue that the doctrine is misconceived on the basis that the purpose of civil litigation is to do justice between the parties before the court.[54] The purpose of choice of law rules is not to promote or reconcile the interests, supposed or actual, legitimate or otherwise, of foreign countries, but to identify the law which is most likely to achieve justice between the parties. According to this view, governmental interest analysis focuses on a wholly irrelevant issue—namely, governmental policy. Others question whether it is really possible to ascribe public purposes or governmental interests to private law rules. Many would concede that the process is, at times, highly artificial.

13.2.4.2 Even if the basic notion is accepted, there are practical problems in its application. It is frequently difficult to discover the purposes or policies of specific rules of law. In view of the fact that many legal rules represent a compromise between competing policies, is it possible to discern an intelligible purpose behind each rule of law? Statutory rules generally are enacted for a purpose—which often, though by no means always, can be identified. For example, there is no real ambiguity over the policy underlying section 2 of the Unfair Contract Terms Act 1977, which renders invalid any contractual term or non-contractual notice which purports to exclude liability for death or personal injury. However, the purpose of a statutory rule may be controversial and common law rules—which have evolved over a period of decades or even centuries—do not always have obvious purposes. Consequently, the application of governmental interest analysis does not encourage predictability. Fuld J who led the charge in *Babcock* v. *Jackson* admitted in a later case that the application of interest analysis had led to a body of decisions which "lack consistency".[55]

13.2.4.3 The results of the application of interest analysis are not free from criticism.

54. Carter, "Torts in English Private International Law" (1981) 52 BYIL 9, 21; Jaffey, "Choice of Law in Tort: A Justice-Based Approach" (1982) 2 LS 98.

55. *Neumeier* v. *Kuehner*, 31 NY 2d 121; 286 NE 2d 454 (1972).

In particular, interest analysis tends towards the application of the law of the forum.[56] It seems almost inevitable that in cases of "true conflict" the forum is likely to value the perceived policies of its own law more highly than the policies of the laws of other countries. It is not, therefore, surprising that governmental interest analysis is viewed by some with a measure of scepticism: "Since the forum must have some contacts with the defendant to take the case, and interests are easily conjured up, the state of litigation will rarely be 'disinterested'. Why then should it be necessary even to consider the multifarious policies of other states and nations? The elaborate conceptual scheme of interest analysis could easily be replaced by a simple rule of non-choice."[57] By placing so much emphasis on the law of the forum interest analysis undervalues traditional choice of law methodologies, one of the aims of which is to achieve uniformity of result and to discourage forum shopping. Interest analysis promotes a state of affairs in which the result of a dispute depends on who sues whom where. Interest analysis is also discriminatory in the sense that it is premised on the idea that laws are passed primarily for the benefit of local residents.

13.2.4.4 Even if it is accepted that governmental interest analysis has something to offer in the federal context of the United States, it may be questioned whether it is suitable for export.[58] In the United States there is a substantial degree of similarity between the legal systems of the various states. It is, therefore, relatively easy for those involved in the legal process to understand the policies behind the rules of a neighbouring state. The same cannot be said in the European context, where there are fundamental differences between neighbouring legal systems. In international cases experts are unable to agree on the content of foreign legal rules, let alone on the policies which underlie those rules.

13.3 THE ENGLISH CASES

13.3.1 Background to the English choice of law rules

13.3.1.1 The rules on choice of law in tort constitute one of the most unnecessarily complex aspects of English private international law. When the negotiations which ultimately led to the Rome Convention on the Law Applicable to Contractual Obligations were commenced it was intended that the Convention should cover both contractual and non-contractual obligations. However, because of fundamental differences in approach between the various participating States the final text dealt only with contractual obligations. Accordingly, where proceedings involving questions of choice of law in tort are brought in England the relevant choice of law rules are those which have been formulated at common law over the last hundred years or so. An understanding of the current state of this branch of English private international law is dependent—at least to a certain extent—on an understanding its historical development.

56. In *Tooker* v. *Lopez*, 24 NY 2d 12; 449 NE 2d 394 (1969) Judge Breitel dissented on the basis that the decision of the majority revealed unacceptable forum-bias.

57. Juenger, "Conflict of Laws: A Critique of Interest Analysis" (1984) 32 Am J Comp L 1, 43–44.

58. See, for example, Vitta, "The Impact in Europe of the American 'Conflicts Revolution' " (1982) 30 Am J Comp L 1; Fawcett, "Is American Governmental Interest Analysis the Solution to English Tort Choice of Law Problems?" (1982) 31 ICLQ 150.

13.3.1.2 The obvious starting-point is *Phillips* v. *Eyre*.[59] In this case the plaintiff brought an action in England for false imprisonment. The defendant was the Governor of Jamaica and the events which gave rise to the alleged tort had occurred in Jamaica. In the course of his judgment Willes J said:

> As a general rule, in order to found a suit in England for a wrong alleged to have been committed abroad, two conditions must be fulfilled. First, the wrong must be of such a character that it would have been actionable if committed in England.... Secondly, the act must not have been justifiable by the law of the place where it was done.[60]

13.3.1.3 The first limb of this test was derived from *The Halley*,[61] a case decided a couple of years earlier by the Privy Council concerning a collision between two ships in Belgian territorial waters. The collision resulted from the negligence of the pilot of the defendant's ship. The plaintiff's action was rejected on the basis that, under English law, the defendant was not vicariously liable for the pilot's negligence.

13.3.1.4 The precise verbal formulation of the second part of Willes J's rule can be explained by the facts in *Phillips* v. *Eyre*.[62] At common law there was no doubt that the defendant's action constituted a tort. However, the imprisonment of the plaintiff had taken place within the context of the defendant's efforts to put down a rebellion on the island of Jamaica and, subsequently, the local Parliament had passed legislation which retrospectively legitimated the defendant's actions. So, although the defendant's action was tortious at the time of commission, his action was "justifiable" in view of the subsequent legislation.

13.3.1.5 There are various ambiguities in *Phillips* v. *Eyre*, one of which may be dealt with at this stage. From the terms of Willes J's judgment it is far from clear that the double-limbed rule was intended as a choice of law rule at all. In subsequent cases it was argued (and by some judges accepted) that the *Phillips* v. *Eyre* rule was either a jurisdiction rule or that the first part of the rule was a jurisdiction rule and the second part was a choice of law rule. This particular uncertainty has, however, been resolved by the decision in *Boys* v. *Chaplin*,[63] in which the House of Lords confirmed that the decision in *Phillips* v. *Eyre* laid down a double-barrelled choice of law rule.

13.3.2 Boys v. Chaplin: outline

13.3.2.1 *Boys* v. *Chaplin*[64] involved a road accident in Malta in which the plaintiff was injured; the accident resulted from the defendant's negligence. Both parties were members of the British forces serving in Malta. The plaintiff started proceedings against the defendant in England with a view to recovering damages for negligence. Under

59. (1870) LR 6 QB 1.
60. (1870) LR 6 QB 1, 28–29.
61. (1868) LR 2 PC 193.
62. (1870) LR 6 QB 1.
63. [1971] AC 356.
64. [1971] AC 356. Carter, (1970) 44 BYIL 222; Graveson, "Towards a Modern Applicable Law in Tort" (1969) 85 LQR 505; Karsten, "Chaplin v. Boys: Another Analysis" (1970) 19 ICLQ 35; Lazar, "Phillips v. Eyre Revisited" (1969) 32 MLR 638; McGregor, "The International Accident Problem" (1970) 33 MLR 1; North & Webb, "The Effect of Chaplin v. Boys" (1970) 19 ICLQ 24; Shapira, "A Transatlantic Inspiration: The 'Proper Law of the Tort' Doctrine" (1970) 33 MLR 27. See also Fawcett, "Policy Considerations in Tort Choice of Law" (1984) 47 MLR 650.

Maltese law the defendant was liable for special damages, but damages for pain and suffering were not recoverable. Under English law the defendant was liable both for special damages (£53) and for damages for pain and suffering (£2,250). The key question, therefore, was whether the plaintiff was entitled to recover damages for pain and suffering.

13.3.2.2 At the various stages of the litigation a total of nine judges considered the case. Of those nine judges, eight (including all five members of the House of Lords) thought that the plaintiff was entitled to recover both special damages and damages for pain and suffering. Only one judge—Diplock LJ who dissented from the decision of the majority of the Court of Appeal—took the view that the defendant's liability was limited by the *lex loci delicti* and, therefore, that the plaintiff was entitled to recover only £53. Among the eight judges who found in the plaintiff's favour there were fundamental disagreements as to the proper analysis and the basis on which English law should be applied to the key question.

13.3.2.3 Lord Denning MR in the Court of Appeal held that the *lex fori* governed the defendant's liability on the basis that English law was the proper law of the tort. The idea that English private international law should embrace the proper law doctrine as the general choice of law rule in tort cases was clearly rejected by the House of Lords.[65]

13.3.2.4 Four judges—Milmo J at first instance, Lord Upjohn in the Court of Appeal and, in the House of Lords, Lord Donovan and Lord Pearson—applied English law on the basis of the decision of the Court of Appeal's interpretation of the second limb of the *Phillips* v. *Eyre* test in *Machado* v. *Fontes*.[66] In this case the plaintiff alleged that he had been libelled by the defendant in Brazil. While it was clear that the defendant's action was a tort under English law, under Brazilian law libel, although a criminal offence, did not give rise to civil liability. The Court of Appeal took the view that the plaintiff was entitled to recover damages in England, since not only did the defendant's conduct amount to a tort in English law, it was not "justifiable" (because it was criminal) under the law where the act took place. Accordingly, English law alone determined questions of the defendant's civil liability.

Machado v. *Fontes* was, however, overruled by a majority of the House of Lords in *Boys* v. *Chaplin*.[67] Lord Wilberforce, Lord Hodson and Lord Guest favoured the reinterpretation of the general rule in *Phillips* v. *Eyre* and adopted the Scottish approach.[68] According to the majority, for the purposes of the second limb of the rule "justifiable" should not be equated with "innocent"; as regards a foreign tort, liability cannot be established unless the defendant's conduct gives rise to civil liability (whether contractual or non-contractual) according to the *lex loci delicti*.

13.3.2.5 Lord Guest, who was part of the majority which overruled *Machado* v. *Fontes*, decided for the plaintiff on the basis that the question whether damages could be recovered for pain and suffering was governed by English law as the *lex fori*. This was also the basis on which Lord Donovan favoured the application of English law. The rule that matters of procedure are governed by the *lex fori* is entirely uncontroversial. However, a differently constituted majority—comprising Lord Hodson, Lord

65. Lord Denning MR did not, however, interpret the House of Lords' decision in this way in *Sayers* v. *International Drilling Co NV* [1971] 1 WLR 1176.
66. [1897] 2 QB 231.
67. [1971] AC 356.
68. See *MacKinnon* v. *Iberia Shipping Co Ltd*, 1955 SC 20; *M'Elroy* v. *M'Allister* 1949 SC 110.

Wilberforce and Lord Pearson—accepted that whether damages could be recovered for pain and suffering was a matter of substantive law.

13.3.2.6 Lord Hodson and Lord Wilberforce, who were part of the majority which opted for a reinterpretation of the second limb of the *Phillips* v. *Eyre* rule, proposed that there should be an exception to that rule. The exception favoured by Lord Hodson and Lord Wilberforce derives its intellectual inspiration from the proper law doctrine and American governmental interest analysis. Lord Pearson, who was part of the minority who favoured the retention of *Machado* v. *Fontes*, also thought that in certain circumstances a qualification of the general rule might be appropriate.

13.3.2.7 It is obvious that the identification of the true *ratio decidendi* of *Boys* v. *Chaplin* is not without its difficulties.[69] However, in *Church of Scientology of California* v. *Commissioner of Metropolitan Police*[70] the Court of Appeal took the view that Lord Wilberforce's speech provides the most authoritative guidance as to what was decided by the House of Lords; in *Armagas Ltd* v. *Mundogas SA*, Goff LJ thought that "the applicable principle in respect of foreign torts is as stated by Lord Wilberforce in his speech in *Boys* v. *Chaplin*".[71] In subsequent cases it seems that litigants and judges alike have gratefully accepted this view which allows them "to go, and to go alone, to the speech of Lord Wilberforce".[72]

13.3.3 Lord Wilberforce's speech and its application

It would be wrong to think that, even on the assumption that Lord Wilberforce's speech represents the *ratio* of *Boys* v. *Chaplin*, all potential problems disappear from view. Although one commentator "confidently expect[ed] a spate of litigation on this subject to work out the answers to the innumerable possibilities opened up by the House of Lords' decision",[73] the dearth of authority following *Boys* v. *Chaplin* means that many of the questions raised by Lord Wilberforce's speech remain unresolved.

13.3.3.1 The general rule

13.3.3.1.1 The major part of Lord Wilberforce's speech is a reappraisal of the rule in *Phillips* v. *Eyre*. Lord Wilberforce was content to accept "the orthodox judicial view that the first part of the rule is laying down, not a test of jurisdiction, but what we now call a rule of choice of law".[74] As regards the first part of the rule, "actionability as a tort under and in accordance with English law is required".[75] As regards the second part of the rule Lord Wilberforce thought that "a person should not be permitted to claim in England in respect of a matter for which civil liability does not exist, or is excluded, under the law of the place where the wrong was committed".[76] Accordingly, the choice

69. Briggs, "What Did Boys v. Chaplin Decide?" (1984) 12 Anglo-Am LR 237. See the comments of Hodgson J in *Coupland* v. *Arabian Gulf Oil Co* [1983] 1 WLR 1136, 1145.
70. (1976) 120 Sol J 690.
71. [1986] AC 717, 740.
72. Hodgson J in *Coupland* v. *Arabian Gulf Oil Co* [1983] 1 WLR 1136, 1146. See also *Dimskal Shipping Co SA* v. *International Transport Workers Federation (No. 2)* [1992] 2 AC 152; *Johnson* v. *Coventry Churchill International Ltd* [1992] 3 All ER 14.
73. Pearl, [1969] CLJ 201, 204.
74. [1971] AC 356, 385.
75. [1971] AC 356, 387.
76. [1971] AC 356, 389.

of law rule favoured by Lord Wilberforce, as a general rule, is a rule of double actionability which requires actionability as a tort according to English law, subject to the condition that civil liability in respect of the relevant claim exists as between the actual parties under the law of the foreign country where the act was done.[77]

13.3.3.1.2 In order for the plaintiff to succeed under the general rule there can be no doubt that it must be established that the defendant is actually liable under English law. However, it has been argued that as regards the second limb of the rule the same degree of specificity is not required and that it is sufficient merely that there should be actionability in principle under the *lex loci delicti*. This issue was discussed, albeit *obiter*, by the Court of Appeal in *Armagas Ltd* v. *Mundogas SA*.[78] In this case it was "submitted that for the purpose of the 'double actionability test' as laid down in *Boys* v. *Chaplin* ... the question was not which party would be likely to succeed in the foreign court, but rather whether the conduct complained of was actionable in the foreign court, in the sense that it was not demurrable".[79] This argument was rejected on the basis that Lord Wilberforce's speech in *Boys* v. *Chaplin* makes it clear that for the purposes of the second limb of the double actionability rule "it is the relevant claim as between the actual parties that must be looked at, and not whether such a claim could in theory be actionable".[80]

13.3.3.1.3 The requirement that actual liability should be established under both the *lex loci delicti* and the *lex fori* may prove to be important in any case where there are substantive differences between the two laws. So, in the case of a road accident abroad, the plaintiff's claim will not succeed unless it can be shown that the defendant's act would constitute negligence if committed in England even if under the *lex loci delicti* the defendant would be strictly liable.[81] Similarly, the requirement of double actionability is not satisfied in a case where the *lex fori* and the *lex loci delicti* do not precisely overlap as a consequence of different conceptual structures (for example, where the *lex fori* and the *lex loci delicti* provide different heads of damage for the same type of loss[82]) or different institutional arrangements. Where, for example, a Chief Constable is sued in relation to a tort committed by an English police officer in Germany liability is likely to be denied under the general rule on the basis that, although in English law the effect of section 48(1) of the Police Act 1964 is to impose vicarious liability on the Chief Constable, under German law vicarious liability for the torts of police officers attaches to the State by virtue of Article 34 of the Basic Law.[83] To have a chance of success in this type of situation the plaintiff has to invoke the exception to the general rule.

13.3.3.1.4 In relation to the general rule what significance should be attached to defences under the *lex loci delicti*? What, for example, is the solution in a case where the defence of contributory negligence operates as a complete defence under the *lex loci delicti*? If defences are regarded as procedural, the extent of the defence under the *lex*

77. [1971] AC 356, 389.
78. [1986] AC 717. The choice of law point was not raised in the appeal to the House of Lords.
79. Dunn LJ, [1986] AC 717, 752.
80. Dunn LJ, [1986] AC 717, 753.
81. For a discussion of the problems of applying the double actionability rule to cases falling within the scope of the Consumer Protection Act 1987 see Morse, "Products Liability in the Conflict of Laws" [1989] CLP 167.
82. *M'Elroy* v. *M'Allister* 1949 SC 110.
83. *Church of Scientology of California* v. *Commissioner of Metropolitan Police* (1976) 120 Sol J 690. Collins, "Vicarious Liability and the Conflict of Laws" (1977) 26 ICLQ 480.

loci delicti can be ignored on the ground that procedural matters are governed by the *lex fori*. The better view is that defences are to be regarded as substantive. Accordingly, a complete defence under the *lex loci delicti* defeats the plaintiff's claim in England. The alternative view has, however, been adopted in some Commonwealth cases.[84] A defence based on limitation is also substantive under the Foreign Limitation Periods Act 1984. Accordingly, if the limitation period under the *lex loci delicti* has expired, the plaintiff's claim will fail under the second limb of the general rule laid down in *Boys* v. *Chaplin*.[85]

13.3.3.1.5 Under the interpretation of *Phillips* v. *Eyre* adopted by the Court of Appeal in *Machado* v. *Fontes*[86] it was clear that English law was the applicable law. In view of the fact that in *Machado* v. *Fontes* the plaintiff was allowed to recover notwithstanding the fact that the defendant's actions did not give rise to civil liability under the *lex loci delicti* the position could hardly have been any different. After *Boys* v. *Chaplin* the question may still be posed as to the applicable law under the general rule.[87] However, the question has no significance; if the requirement of double actionability is satisfied it can make no difference as to whether English law or the *lex loci delicti* is applied, since by definition they are in substance identical. Nevertheless, once the plaintiff has satisfied both limbs of the general rule, it is natural for an English court to assume that the action proceeds on the basis of English law.[88]

13.3.3.2 The exception

13.3.3.2.1 The general rule can cause injustice since the requirement of double actionability gives the plaintiff the worst of both worlds.[89] If, for example, the plaintiff is injured in an accident abroad by a person employed by A but, at the time of the accident, working for B, the plaintiff is not able to recover under the general rule against either A or B, if A is vicariously liable under the *lex fori* and B is vicariously liable under the *lex loci delicti*. Similarly, if there are two heads of damage (A and C) under the *lex fori* and two heads of damage (B and C) under the *lex loci delicti*, the double actionability rule allows the plaintiff to recover only C, the lowest common denominator. *Boys* v. *Chaplin* was a case of this type; according to the general rule propounded by Lord Wilberforce the plaintiff was entitled to special damages of only £53, since under Maltese law damages for pain and suffering were not recoverable. As Lord Wilberforce noted, the question of whether there should be an exception to the general rule highlights two conflicting pressures: "the first in favour of certainty and simplicity in the law, the second in favour of flexibility in the interest of individual justice".[90] Both Lord Wilberforce and Lord Hodson thought that the requirements of justice may in certain circumstances outweigh the arguments in favour of certainty. In cases where the double

84. See, for example, *Kolsky* v. *Mayne Nickless Ltd* [1970] 3 NSWR 511.
85. *Arab Monetary Fund* v. *Hashim* [1993] 1 Lloyd's Rep 543. The English court may, however, disapply a foreign limitation rule on the basis of public policy: Foreign Limitation Periods Act 1984, s. 2(2). See para. 15.1.2.
86. [1897] 2 QB 231.
87. See Cheshire & North, *Private International Law* (12th ed, 1993) p. 545.
88. See, for example, Goff LJ in *Coupland* v. *Arabian Gulf Oil Co* [1983] 1 WLR 1136, 1154.
89. For a graphic example, see *M'Elroy* v. *M'Allister* 1949 SC 110.
90. [1971] AC 356, 389.

actionability rule has the effect of limiting or excluding liability the possibility of applying an exception to the general rule should be considered.[91]

13.3.3.2.2 The exception to the general rule has been formulated in the following terms: "a particular issue between the parties may be governed by the law of the country which, with respect to that issue, has the most significant relationship with the occurrence and the parties".[92] Although this formulation "has not received the seal of explicit judicial approval",[93] in recent cases neither litigants nor members of the judiciary have sought to challenge its accuracy.[94] Before looking more closely at the exception it is important to stress that the exception "will not be invoked in every case or even, probably, in many cases. The general rule must apply unless clear and satisfying grounds are shown why it should be departed from and what solution, derived from what other rule, should be preferred."[95] The exception will not be applied unless, in the light of all the circumstances, justice requires that the exception should be applied in preference to the general rule.[96]

13.3.3.2.3 Although it is usual to refer to the law which is applicable under the exception to the general rule as the proper law of the tort, it is far from clear that the law to be applied by way of exception to the general rule is to be determined by reference to a traditional "centre of gravity" or "grouping of contacts" approach. Lord Wilberforce indicated his support for the methodology adopted in *Babcock* v. *Jackson*[97] (in which Fuld J relied not only on the proper law doctrine, which is based on a search for the law of the place which has the most dominant contacts with the matter in dispute, but also on governmental interest analysis, which seeks to apply the law of the place which, from the point of view of policy, has the greatest concern with the specific issue raised in the litigation[98]) and much of his speech is couched in terms of interest analysis. Lord Wilberforce thought that:

> [T]he necessary flexibility can be obtained from that principle which represents at least a common denominator of the United States decisions, namely, through segregation of the relevant issue and consideration whether, in relation to that issue, the relevant foreign rule ought, as a matter of policy ... to be applied. For this purpose it is necessary to identify the policy of the rule, to inquire to what situations, with what contacts, it was intended to apply; whether not to apply it, in the circumstances of the instant case, would serve any interest which the rule was devised to meet.[99]

In *Boys* v. *Chaplin* Lord Wilberforce considered that it was appropriate to apply the exception to the general rule: neither party had significant connections with Malta; there was no reason to think that the Maltese State had any interest in applying the rule denying damages for pain and suffering to persons not resident in Malta or in denying the application of the English rule allowing recovery.[100] Accordingly, Lord Wilberforce

91. *Boys* v. *Chaplin* [1971] AC 356, 391; *Johnson* v. *Coventry Churchill International Ltd* [1992] 3 All ER 14.
92. Dicey & Morris, *The Conflict of Laws* (12th ed, 1993) p. 1488 (Rule 203(2)).
93. Slade LJ in *Metall und Rohstoff AG* v. *Donaldson Lufkin & Jenrette Inc* [1990] 1 QB 391, 440.
94. See, for example, *Johnson* v. *Coventry Churchill International Ltd* [1992] 3 All ER 14.
95. Lord Wilberforce in *Boys* v. *Chaplin* [1971] AC 356, 391.
96. Judge Kay QC in *Johnson* v. *Coventry Churchill International Ltd* [1992] 3 All ER 14, 26.
97. [1963] 2 Lloyd's Rep 286.
98. See para. 13.2.3.1.
99. [1971] AC 356, 391.
100. [1971] AC 356, 392.

was prepared to segregate the availability of damages for pain and suffering from other questions arising in the case and to apply English law to this particular issue.

13.3.3.2.4 The methodology proposed by Lord Wilberforce has been adopted in subsequent cases. In *Johnson* v. *Coventry Churchill International Ltd*[101] the plaintiff, an English carpenter, was employed by the defendant, an English company, to work in Germany. While working on a construction site in Stuttgart the plaintiff fell and suffered personal injuries. The plaintiff commenced proceedings in England, alleging that the injuries were caused by the defendant's negligent failure to provide a safe system of work. Although under English law the defendant's default would have amounted to a tort had the events occurred in England, the defendant was not civilly liable under German law.[102]

Judge Kay QC approached the question of whether the exception to the general rule should be applied in two stages: (i) the judge thought that "there is nothing in the policy underlying the foreign rule that was ever intended to have any application to the case of an English citizen working for an English employer"[103]; (ii) England was "the country with the most significant relationship with the occurrence and the parties".[104] The important connections were with England: the plaintiff was English; the defendant was an English company; the contract giving rise to the defendant's duty was made in England and was governed by English law; the intended duration of the plaintiff's period of employment in Germany was only 13 weeks; and the failure to act that led to the accident could be traced back to decisions made in England. In this case—as in *Boys* v. *Chaplin* itself—both traditional proper law thinking and interest analysis pointed to the application of the *lex fori*. The cases do not, however, shed light on the problems which would arise in a situation where the application of the proper law doctrine and interest analysis do not lead to identical results.

13.3.3.2.5 In *Babcock* v. *Jackson*[105] the New York Court of Appeals departed from the traditional choice of law rule in order to apply New York law. The effect of invoking the exception to the general rule in *Boys* v. *Chaplin*[106] was to justify the application of English law and there is no reported decision in which an English court has considered the application of a law other than the *lex fori* by way of exception to the general rule. It is not entirely surprising that this pattern should be found in the cases; not only do jurisdiction rules tend to channel litigation towards the forum which is most closely connected with the dispute, courts are also naturally inclined towards the application of the law of the forum. One of the justifications of the position prior to the decision of the House of Lords in *Boys* v. *Chaplin* was that it enabled an English court "to give judgment according to its own ideas of justice".[107]

There is no clear guidance in *Boys* v. *Chaplin* as to whether the exception to the general rule can be invoked otherwise than to justify the exclusion of the *lex loci delicti* in favour of the *lex fori*. The answer to this problem depends on the extent to which the

101. [1992] 3 All ER 14. Rogerson, [1992] CLJ 439.
102. Germany has a system of social security payments for persons injured at work and section 636 of the German Social Security Act exempts the employer from liability except in cases where the employee's injury is the result of a wilful breach of duty.
103. [1992] 3 All ER 14, 24.
104. [1992] 3 All ER 14, 25.
105. [1963] 2 Lloyd's Rep 286.
106. [1971] AC 356.
107. Lord Pearson, [1971] AC 356, 400.

approach adopted by Lord Wilberforce in *Boys* v. *Chaplin* can be divorced from the specific factual context of that decision. There is nothing in Lord Wilberforce's speech which indicates that the exception is inapplicable in cases where the proper law is the law of some country other than the forum and there is no reason in principle why, in appropriate cases, the exception should not lead to the application of the *lex loci delicti* or even the law of a third country.

13.3.3.2.6 In *Boys* v. *Chaplin*[108] all five members of the House of Lords confirmed the decision of the Privy Council in *The Halley*[109]—from which the first limb of the *Phillips* v. *Eyre* rule was derived. This has led some commentators to question whether the exception can operate to displace the *lex fori*.[110] If, however, the exception does not operate to displace both limbs of the general rule, there would be no difference at all between the general rule and the exception in cases where the *lex loci delicti* is also the proper law of the tort. Since the exception is an exception *to the general rule* it seems reasonable to suppose that the proper law—be it the *lex fori*, the *lex loci delicti* or the law of a third country—displaces both limbs of the test and that the proper law alone governs the particular issue.[111] Nevertheless, an English court will not allow the *lex fori* to be displaced entirely in favour of a foreign proper law in cases where the cause of action relied upon by the plaintiff is not only unknown to English law but also contrary to English public policy. To the extent that the first limb of the general rule is justifiable it is that it protects the public policy of the forum.[112] Of course, the rule derived from *The Halley* does much more than protect the public policy of the forum since it excludes any liability imposed by the *lex loci delicti* which is not precisely replicated under the *lex fori*.

13.3.3.2.7 The only judicial guidance as to whether the exception is applicable in cases where the parties come from different countries is to be found in dicta in *Boys* v. *Chaplin*. Lord Wilberforce, having indicated that the general rule would be applicable if both parties were Maltese residents, expressed the view that "if the defendant were a Maltese resident the same result might follow".[113] Lord Hodson also thought that the application of the general rule would have led to a just result "if both the parties were Maltese residents or even if the defendant were a Maltese resident".[114] What would have been the position, however, if the plaintiff had been a Maltese resident and the driver an English resident? In view of the fact that Lord Wilberforce stressed that the general rule should be applied unless clear and satisfying grounds are shown why it should be departed from, it seems likely that the exception would not be applicable in this situation.

13.3.3.2.8 It has been convincingly argued that the various patterns of reasoning adopted in *Boys* v. *Chaplin* are explicable, at least in part, by the judges' desire to reach a particular result.[115] Notwithstanding the numerous different approaches taken at the various stages of the litigation only one of the nine judges who were involved in the case thought that the plaintiff was not entitled to recover damages for pain and suffering. Would the court consider the exception if the application of the proper law were less

108. [1971] AC 356.
109. (1868) LR 2 PC 193.
110. Cheshire & North, *Private International Law* (12th ed, 1992) p. 548.
111. See Dicey & Morris, *The Conflict of Laws* (12th ed, 1993) p. 1497.
112. See Carter, "Torts in English Private International Law" (1981) 52 BYIL 9, 12–14.
113. [1971] AC 356, 392.
114. [1971] AC 356, 379.
115. Fawcett, "Policy Considerations in Tort Choice of Law" (1984) 47 MLR 650.

advantageous to the plaintiff than the application of the general rule?[116] The logic of the decision in *Boys* v. *Chaplin* requires the application of the exception to the general rule whenever justice requires it. Justice cannot be viewed entirely from the point of view of the plaintiff. The justification for the proper law is that, as the law of the country which has the most significant relationship with the occurrence and the parties, it is the law by reference to which the rights and obligations of the parties can most appropriately be determined. This justification does not turn on whether the plaintiff is advantaged or disadvantaged by the proper law's application.

13.3.3.3 Quantification: substance and procedure

13.3.3.3.1 It is a well established principle that matters of procedure are governed by the *lex fori*. The quantification of damages in tort is a procedural matter which therefore falls to be determined by English law regardless of the applicable law. Since there is no case in which an English court has applied the exception to the general rule in favour of a law other than the *lex fori*, there is no authority on how the court should approach the quantification of damages under a head of damage which is unknown to English law.

13.3.3.3.2 In *Boys* v. *Chaplin* there was disagreement in the House of Lords as to whether the availability of particular heads of damage is also a procedural matter. While Lord Guest and Lord Donovan thought that the question as to whether the plaintiff could recover damages for pain and suffering was a matter for the *lex fori* alone, the other three members of the House of Lords—Lord Hodson, Lord Wilberforce and Lord Pearson—decided that the availability of heads of damage is substantive and therefore governed by the applicable law. It would seem to follow that the limitation of damages by the imposition of a statutory ceiling is also a substantive issue.[117]

13.4 THE INTERACTION OF CONTRACT AND TORT CHOICE OF LAW RULES

13.4.1 Introduction

13.4.1.1 The nature of the problem

13.4.1.1.1 There are various situations in the conflict of laws where mixed questions of contract and tort arise. The simplest situation is where a foreign contract is relied upon by the defendant as a defence to a tort which is alleged to have been committed in England. In *Galaxias Steamship Co Ltd* v. *Panagos Christofis*[118] the defendants worked on a ship which was owned by the plaintiff. The parties were Greek and the contract of employment between the plaintiff and the defendants was governed by Greek law. When the ship was docked in England, the plaintiff paid off the defendants, having purported to terminate their contract of employment. The defendants failed to leave the

116. Cheshire & North, *Private International Law* (12th ed, 1993) p. 548.

117. *Choice of Law in Tort and Delict*, Law Com No. 193, p. 22, para. 3.39. It may be noted, however, that the Australian High Court decided, by a majority of 4:3, that such matters are procedural: *Stevens* v. *Head* (1993) 67 ALJR 343. See Opeskin, "Statutory Caps on Damages in Australian Conflict of Laws" (1993) 109 LQR 533.

118. (1948) 81 Ll L Rep 499. This case is discussed by North, "Contract as a Tort Defence in the Conflict of Laws" (1977) 26 ICLQ 914, 915–916.

ship and the plaintiff sued them for trespass. The defendants sought to rely on the contract of employment as a defence, alleging that they were still entitled under the contract to remain on board. For the plaintiff to establish the tort of trespass, it had to be shown that the defendants' presence was unlawful. If the contract gave the defendants the right to remain on board, no tort could be established. It is clear in this case that the rights of the parties under the contract had to be determined by reference to Greek law as the law governing the contract. Since under Greek law the plaintiff had validly discharged the defendants, the defendants' presence on the ship was unlawful and the plaintiff's claim in trespass succeeded.

13.4.1.1.2 *Galaxias Steamship Co Ltd* v. *Panagos Christofis* is a straightforward case where the contract issue and the tort issue can be clearly segregated and different laws can be applied to each issue. More problematical are cases which involve the interrelationship between contract and tort choice of law rules. The most important and difficult questions surround the potential impact of a contractual exemption clause on a tort claim. These issues arise most frequently in the context of cases in which an employee suffers personal injury as a result of an accident at work.

13.4.1.2 Contract or tort?

13.4.1.2.1 Under English law where a set of facts constitutes both a breach of contract and a tort a plaintiff may choose to base his claim either on contract or on tort. In *Matthews* v. *Kuwait Bechtel Corporation*[119] the plaintiff had been injured while working for the defendant in Kuwait. The contract of employment was governed by English law. As the defendant had no place of business in England, the plaintiff sought leave to serve the defendant out of the jurisdiction under what is now RSC, Order 11, rule 1(1)(d)(iii). The defendant argued that the plaintiff's claim was in tort and that, since the alleged tort had been committed abroad, the plaintiff was unable to satisfy any of the heads under RSC, Order 11. The Court of Appeal concluded that the acts alleged by the plaintiff gave rise to a claim for damages either in tort or for breach of contract. Accordingly, the plaintiff could choose to frame his action in contract and take advantage of the rule which allows the English court to assume jurisdiction in a case involving a contract governed by English law.

13.4.1.2.2 This approach was confirmed in *Coupland* v. *Arabian Gulf Oil Co*,[120] in which the plaintiff was injured while working for the defendant in Libya. Whereas the plaintiff in *Matthews* v. *Kuwait Bechtel Corporation* framed his action in contract, in *Coupland* v. *Arabian Gulf Oil Co* the plaintiff commenced proceedings in England claiming damages in tort. The defendant argued (i) that the plaintiff's claim was in contract, rather than tort, (ii) that the contract of employment was governed by Libyan law, and (iii) that under Libyan law the defendant was not liable for breach of contract. The Court of Appeal rejected the first limb of this argument: "The plaintiff can advance his claim, as he wishes, either in contract or in tort; and no doubt he will, acting on advice, advance the claim on the basis which is most advantageous to him."[121]

13.4.1.2.3 The position is somewhat different in cases in which jurisdiction is

119. [1959] 2 QB 57. Webber, "Servant Suing Master for Negligence, in Contract" (1959) 22 MLR 521; Jolowicz, [1959] CLJ 163.
120. [1983] 1 WLR 1136.
121. Goff LJ, [1983] 1 WLR 1136, 1153.

determined by Title II of the Brussels and Lugano Conventions. For the purposes of Article 5, the question whether proceedings concern "matters relating to a contract" or "matters relating to tort" is to be answered by reference to Community law, rather than to the *lex fori.*[122] So, a court may not assume jurisdiction under Article 5(1) if the proceedings involve "matters relating to tort" as defined by the Court of Justice. However, the classification of proceedings for jurisdiction purposes does not determine the classification for choice of law purposes. An English court may, for example, assume jurisdiction under Article 5(1)—on the basis that the proceedings concern "matters relating to a contract" within the meaning of the Conventions—but apply the rule in *Boys* v. *Chaplin* on the ground that, as far as English law is concerned, the claim is in tort.

13.4.1.3 The position if the plaintiff advances the claim in contract

If the plaintiff chooses to advance his claim in contract, the matter is governed exclusively by contract choice of law rules. Where the contract is concluded on or after 1 April 1991, the applicable law is to be determined by the Contracts (Applicable Law) Act 1990, which implements the Rome Convention on the Law Applicable to Contractual Obligations.[123] If the contract contains a clause which purports to limit or exclude the defendant's liability under the contract, the validity of such a clause is determined in accordance with the applicable law.[124] If a contractual term is invalid under the applicable law, the defendant is unable to rely on it. If, on the other hand, the contractual term is valid according to the applicable law, as a general rule, the plaintiff's claim in contract will be limited or defeated. It must, however, be remembered that under the Convention there are circumstances in which the applicable law is superseded or overridden by the mandatory rules of other legal systems.[125] In the context of employment contracts, Article 6(2) of the Convention provides that, where the contract contains a choice of law, that choice shall not deprive the employee of the benefit of the mandatory rules of the law which would have applied in the absence of choice. Furthermore, Article 7(2) of the Rome Convention provides that the applicable law yields to the "overriding rules" of the law of the forum. Accordingly, the fact that a contractual exclusion of liability is valid by the applicable law does not necessarily mean that a claim by the plaintiff in contract will fail.[126]

13.4.2 The position if the plaintiff advances the claim in tort

13.4.2.1 Preliminary remarks

If the plaintiff advances his claim in tort, the main practical issue to be considered is the effect of any term of the contract which purports to limit or exclude the defendant's

122. Case C-26/91 *Jakob Handte & Co GmbH* v. *Société Traitements Mécano-chimiques des Surfaces* [1993] ILPr 5; Case 189/87 *Kalfelis* v. *Bankhaus Schröder, Münchmeyer, Hengst & Co* [1988] ECR 5565. See para. 5.5.2.
123. See Chapters 10 and 11. For specific rules relating to contracts of employment see para. 12.2.
124. Rome Convention, Article 8(1).
125. See para. 11.3.
126. See paras. 12.2.3–12.2.4.

liability. There are a number of different laws which are potentially relevant: the *lex fori*, the *lex loci delicti*, the law of the country which—with respect to that issue—has the most real and substantial relationship with the occurrence and the parties (the proper law of the tort); and the law applicable to the contract. The decided cases in this area are not entirely consistent and the analysis of the courts has not always been convincing.

13.4.2.2 The basic approach

It is widely accepted that Lord Wilberforce's speech in *Boys* v. *Chaplin* represents the current state of English law on the subject of choice of law in tort.[127] The general double actionability rule requires the plaintiff to establish that the defendant's conduct is both actionable as a tort under English law and gives rise to civil liability under the *lex loci delicti*. By way of an exception to this general rule, a specific issue may be governed by the proper law of the tort.

When a contractual defence is relevant to an action which is framed in tort, if the general rule is applicable, there are three legal systems to consider: the *lex fori*, the *lex loci delicti* and the law applicable to the contract. When the exception to the general rule is relevant, as regards the particular issue to which the exception applies, there are two legal systems to consider: the proper law of the tort and the law applicable to the contract. What precisely is the relationship between these various legal systems? There are broadly speaking two approaches: the "simple analysis" and the "developed analysis".

13.4.2.2.1 THE SIMPLE ANALYSIS

13.4.2.2.1.1 According to the simple analysis the claim in tort and the contractual defence are treated independently. The effect of this approach is that a contractual defence which is valid according to the law applicable to the contract operates to limit or bar the claim in tort. This seems to be the view taken by members of the Court of Appeal in *Sayers* v. *International Drilling Co NV*[128] and *Coupland* v. *Arabian Gulf Oil Co.*[129] These cases are, however, not very satisfactory as authorities.

13.4.2.2.1.2 *Sayers* v. *International Drilling Co NV* involved an appeal on a very narrow issue. Salmon LJ indicated that only one point was raised in the appeal: "was the judge right in coming to the conclusion that the proper law of the contract of employment was Dutch law?"[130] Neither Salmon LJ nor Stamp LJ, both of whom concluded that the law governing the contract was Dutch law, expressly addressed the problems posed by the potential interaction of contract and tort choice of law rules. Nevertheless, it is clear that the plaintiff's action was in tort[131] and it is implicit in the judgments of Salmon and Stamp LJJ that if the exclusion of liability was valid according to the law governing the contract the plaintiff's action was bound to fail.

127. See paras. 13.3.2–13.3.3.

128. [1971] 1 WLR 1176. Carter, (1971) 45 BYIL 404; Smith, "International Employment Contracts—Contracting Out" (1972) 21 ICLQ 164.

129. [1983] 1 WLR 1136. Carter, (1983) 54 BYIL 301.

130. [1971] 1 WLR 1176.

131. Lord Denning MR states that "the claim by the plaintiff is a claim founded in tort": [1971] 1 WLR 1176, 1180. Salmon LJ describes the plaintiff's action as an action "for damages for negligence": [1971] 1 WLR 1176, 1182.

13.4.2.2.1.3 In *Coupland* v. *Arabian Gulf Oil Co* it was argued by the defendant that the contract of employment, which was governed by Libyan law, had to be considered in the context of the plaintiff's claim in tort. Hodgson J rejected this argument on the basis that the defendant had failed to show that the contract contained any defence to the plaintiff's claim in tort.[132] When the matter came before the Court of Appeal Robert Goff LJ indicated that "the contract is only relevant to the claim in tort in so far as it does, on its true construction in accordance with the proper law of the contract, have the effect of excluding or restricting the tortious claim".[133] However, this apparent endorsement of the view that the effect on a claim in tort of a contractual defence, valid under its applicable law, should be governed by the law applicable to the contract rather than the law applicable to the tort was *obiter*, since on the facts of the case there was no contractual defence available to the defendants.

13.4.2.2.2 THE DEVELOPED ANALYSIS

The simple analysis has been convincingly criticised. For the purposes of the double actionability rule the important issue is the availability of a contractual defence as a defence to the tort in accordance with the law governing the tort, rather than the law governing the contract:

> It should be asked ... whether a valid exemption clause provides a good defence to a tort claim under the law of the place of the wrong and under the law of the forum. If the answer, in either case, is yes, then *prima facie* the plaintiff will lose because the requirement of double actionability is not satisfied. The question whether the exemption clause is valid is, however, a contractual issue to be determined by the proper law of the contract. If the clause is invalid under that law, then there will be no tort defence available.[134]

There are a number of cases which either support or are consistent with this analysis, rather than the simple analysis.

13.4.2.2.3 FURTHER PRELIMINARY CHOICE OF LAW QUESTIONS

13.4.2.2.3.1 Although it is clear that the validity of the contractual term on which the defendant seeks to rely as a defence to the plaintiff's claim in tort is to be considered under the law applicable to the contract, there is the question as to which choice of law rules are to be used to determine the law applicable to the contract: the conflicts rules of the forum or the conflicts rules of the law governing the tort. The purist view is that the conflicts rules of the law governing the tort are relevant,[135] since to know whether an exemption clause will be given effect to under the law governing the tort, it is important to know whether under that country's law (including its choice of law rules) the clause is valid.[136] The pragmatic view is that "it must be for the *lex fori* to determine the validity of the contractual exemption clause according to its proper law".[137]

13.4.2.2.3.2 As a general proposition, the doctrine of renvoi has no role to play in the

132. [1983] 1 WLR 1136, 1151.
133. [1983] 1 WLR 1136, 1153.
134. North, "Reform, But Not Revolution: General Course on Private International Law" [1990] I Hag Rec 9, 230. See also Morse, "Tort, Employment Contracts and the Conflict of Laws" (1984) 33 ICLQ 449, 459.
135. North, "Contract as a Tort Defence in the Conflict of Laws" (1977) 26 ICLQ 914, 927.
136. North, "Reform, But Not Revolution: General Course on Private International Law" [1990] I Hag Rec 9, 231.
137. Collins, "Interaction between Contract and Tort in the Conflict of Laws" (1967) 16 ICLQ 103, 115.

field of contract[138] and such authorities as there are suggest that the doctrine has no role to play in the field of tort either.[139] Although it is perhaps unlikely that the issue will arise frequently (if ever) in practice, it is suggested that the validity of a contractual exclusion clause under its applicable law is to be determined by the application of the conflicts rules of the forum. There can be little doubt that the pragmatic view is more convenient and simpler to apply.[140]

13.4.2.2.3.3 Exceptionally, a tort issue will be governed by the proper law of the tort rather than by the *lex fori* and the *lex loci delicti*. It has been suggested that, where there is a pre-existing contractual relationship between the parties, the contract might be relevant for the purpose of determining the law applicable to the tort.[141] If this suggestion is accepted there will be a tendency for the law applicable to the tort to follow the law governing the contract. The decided cases point in different directions. On the one hand, in *Sayers* v. *International Drilling Co NV*[142] Lord Denning MR thought that English law was the law applicable to the contract, but that Dutch law was the law of the country with which the parties and the acts done had the most significant connection.[143] On the other hand, in *Johnson* v. *Coventry Churchill International Ltd*[144] the fact that the contract of employment between the parties was concluded in England and was governed by English law was one of the factors which the judge took into account in deciding that English law was the proper law of the tort.

13.4.2.3 The application of the developed analysis

13.4.2.3.1 The simple analysis yields simple solutions. According to the simple analysis, if the contractual term on which the defendant seeks to rely as a defence is valid under the law applicable to the contract the plaintiff's action is limited or defeated, as the case may be, both in tort and in contract—unless the mandatory rules of another legal system override the law applicable to the contract. According to the developed analysis, however, when a contractual defence is raised in the context of an action which is framed in tort, the basic issues which the court should consider are (i) the availability of a contractual term as a defence to an action in tort under the relevant legal systems (the *lex fori* and the *lex loci delicti* if the double actionability rule applies or the proper law of the tort if the exception applies) and (ii) the validity of the contractual term according to the law applicable to the contract. If the contractual term is valid by the law governing the contract and is available as a defence under the law applicable to the tort the plaintiff obviously cannot recover in tort. If, however, under the law governing the tort the

138. *Amin Rasheed Shipping Corporation* v. *Kuwait Insurance Co* [1984] AC 50; Rome Convention, Article 15.

139. See *Church of Scientology of California* v. *Commissioner of Metropolitan Police* (1976) 120 Sol J 690. The English and Scottish Law Commissions think that the doctrine of renvoi should not operate in the relation to tort: *Choice of Law in Tort and Delict*, Law Com No. 193, p. 28, para. 3.56.

140. North, "Reform, But Not Revolution: General Course on Private International Law" [1990] I Hag Rec 9, 231.

141. Morse, "Tort, Employment Contracts and the Conflict of Laws" (1984) 33 ICLQ 449, 460.

142. [1971] 1 WLR 1176.

143. Two points should be noted about Lord Denning MR's judgment. (i) The majority thought that Dutch law was the law applicable to the contract. (ii) Lord Denning MR's interpretation of *Boys* v. *Chaplin* [1971] AC 356 was highly unorthodox and in the light of subsequent cases must be regarded as wrong.

144. [1992] 3 All ER 14.

contractual defence is not available, there is no reason in principle why the plaintiff should not be able to recover in tort, notwithstanding the validity of the contractual term under the law governing the contract.

13.4.2.3.2 In *Brodin* v. *A/R Seljan*[145] the plaintiff's husband was a seaman who died as a consequence of injuries sustained in an accident on board a fishing vessel owned by the defendant, a Norwegian company. The plaintiff's husband was employed by the defendant under a contract of employment which was expressly governed by Norwegian law. The accident took place in Scottish waters. When the plaintiff sued the defendant in Scotland claiming damages for negligence the defendant sought to rely on a term in the contract of employment which exempted the defendant from liability for negligence. Under Scots law the contractual exclusion of liability was void by virtue of section 1(3) of the Law Reform (Personal Injuries) Act 1948. The court held that the defendant was liable in tort on the basis that the law governing the tort (Scots law was both the *lex fori* and *lex loci delicti*) prevailed over the law governing the contract (Norwegian law).

13.4.2.3.3 Of course, *Brodin* v. *A/R Seljan* does not directly raise the issue of the relationship between *Boys* v. *Chaplin* and contract choice of law rules since the tort had been committed within the territorial jurisdiction of the court. Nevertheless, the case does raise the question of the relationship between tortious and contractual liability where the contract and the tort are not subject to the same law and the analysis employed in *Brodin* v. *A/R Seljan* is an appropriate one to adopt in cases involving foreign torts. Accordingly, the result should be the same in a case where the tort is committed abroad and under both the *lex fori* and the *lex loci delicti* the contractual term is not available as a defence. Suppose, for example, that on the same basic facts as those which arose in *Brodin* v. *A/R Seljan* the plaintiff commences proceedings against the defendant in England, rather than Scotland. From the point of view of the English court the case concerns a foreign tort—the place of the tort being Scotland—and therefore the rule in *Boys* v. *Chaplin* is applicable. Both limbs of the double actionability rule are satisfied: (i) since the contractual exclusion is not available as a defence in tort under English law the defendant is guilty of an act, which if done in England, would be a tort; (ii) as *Brodin* v. *A/R Seljan* shows, the defendant's conduct is also actionable under Scots law. The defendant is, therefore, liable in tort, even though the exclusion clause is valid according to the law governing the contract.

13.4.2.3.4 In reality, this is the analysis which should have been considered in *Sayers* v. *International Drilling Co NV*.[146] The proper application of *Boys* v. *Chaplin* to the facts of *Sayers* v. *International Drilling Co NV* should lead to the imposition of tortious liability.[147] If the claim is framed in tort the double actionability rule is satisfied since the act of negligence in Nigeria would be actionable had it occurred in England—as a result of section 1(3) of the Law Reform (Personal Injuries) Act 1948—and, there being no evidence of Nigerian law, it can only be assumed that Nigerian law is the same as English law. (In *Sayers* v. *International Drilling Co NV*, even though the plaintiff's claim was in

145. 1973 SLT 198. Thompson, "International Employment Contracts—The Scottish Approach" (1974) 23 ICLQ 458.

146. [1971] 1 WLR 1176.

147. See Collins, "Exemption Clauses, Employment Contracts and the Conflict of Laws" (1972) 21 ICLQ 320, 332–333.

tort, none of the judges in the Court of Appeal considered Nigerian law, notwithstanding the fact that Nigeria was the place of the tort.)

13.4.2.3.5 Where the contractual term is available as a defence under the *lex fori*, but not under the *lex loci delicti* (or vice versa), as a general rule, the plaintiff's claim in tort will fail. In *Canadian Pacific Railway Co* v. *Parent*,[148] a case decided by the Privy Council on appeal from the Supreme Court of Canada, the plaintiff's husband was killed as a result of an accident on a train in Ontario. The accident was caused by the negligence of employees of the defendant, the railway owner. At the time of the accident the plaintiff's husband was travelling at a reduced fare and the contract between the plaintiff's husband and the defendant provided that, in relation to a person travelling at less than full fare, the defendant was not liable for that person's death or personal injury, whether caused by negligence or otherwise. The plaintiff started proceedings against the defendant in Quebec claiming damages for negligence. Although the defendant had no defence to the action under the *lex fori*, the claim failed; under the *lex loci delicti* the terms of the contract were effective to bar the plaintiff's claim in tort and, therefore, the plaintiff was unable to satisfy the second limb of the rule in *Phillips* v. *Eyre*.

13.4.2.3.6 This result is consistent with the approach suggested for dealing with cases involving a mixture of contract and tort. However, in this type of case—where the operation of the general tort choice of law rule prevents recovery—it is appropriate to consider the possible application of the exception to the general rule. If, under the proper law of the tort, the contractual term is not available as a defence, liability in tort may be ėstablished (just as in *Brodin* v. *A/R Seljan*).

13.4.2.3.7 If the contractual term is invalid by the law governing the contract, the plaintiff can maintain an action in contract. It is also reasonable to suppose that the plaintiff may succeed in tort in these circumstances. There is no obvious reason why the forum should give any effect to a contractual term which is invalid by its applicable law.

13.5 REFORM OF THE ENGLISH CHOICE OF LAW RULES

13.5.1 Perhaps not altogether surprisingly the rule in *Phillips* v. *Eyre* has been subjected to extensive criticism. For example, it has been said that the rule "has nothing to recommend it because it is capable of producing quite arbitrary decisions and it is a mixture of parochialism and a vehicle for being, in some cases, unduly generous to the plaintiff and, in others, unduly harsh".[149] Although the current state of English law is not without its supporters,[150] it is widely thought that the law is defective and in need of reform. The case for reform is based on the fact that the present law is uncertain and

148. [1917] AC 195.

149. Walsh J in *Grehan* v. *Medical Inc* [1988] ECC 6, 20 (Irish Supreme Court). This case is critically discussed by North, "Reform, But Not Revolution: General Course on Private International Law" [1990] I Hag Rec 9, 232–235.

150. For a spirited defence of the common law see Carter, "Choice of Law in Tort and Delict" (1991) 107 LQR 405.

anomalous—in that the *lex fori* is allowed to play a prominent role—and leads to injustice.[151]

13.5.2 The central feature of the reform proposed by the English and Scottish Law Commissions is the abolition of the first limb of the rule of *Phillips* v. *Eyre*.[152] If the proposals were adopted, a tort would, as a general rule, be governed by the law of the place of the wrong. However, in order to avoid injustice in particular cases, the law of the place of wrong would be displaced in certain circumstances by the proper law of the tort. Different rules are proposed in relation to conduct in the United Kingdom and on the high seas.[153]

13.5.3 The main substance of the choice of law regime proposed by the Law Commissions is to be found in clause 2 of the draft Bill which accompanies the report. The three general rules are to be found in subclauses (1) to (3).

(i) An action in respect of injury caused to an individual or in respect of the death of an individual resulting from personal injury is governed by the law of the country where the individual was when he sustained the injury.

(ii) The applicable law in relation to an action in respect of damage to property is the law of the country in which the property was situated when it was damaged.

(iii) As regards other tortious matters, the applicable law is the law of the country where the most significant elements of the events constituting the subject matter of the proceedings took place. If, however, there is no single country in which the most significant elements in the sequence of events occurred, the applicable law is the law of the country with which the subject matter of the proceedings has the most real and substantial connection.

13.5.4 Clause 2(4), which contains the exception to the general rules, requires the court to make a comparison between (a) the significance, in all the circumstances, of factors which connect the subject matter of the proceedings with the country whose law would apply under the general rules, and (b) the significance, in those circumstances, of any factors constituting a real and substantial connection between the subject matter of the proceedings and another country. If it appears from this comparison that it would be substantially more appropriate for the questions to which the proceedings give rise to be determined according to the law of the "other country" than according to the law designated by the general rules, the law of the "other country" shall be the applicable law.

13.5.5 Although the drafting of clause 2 may leave something to be desired, its purpose is reasonably clear. The obvious point of difficulty is the relationship between the general rules and the exception. Clause 2(4) is intended to impose a threshold which should maintain the exceptional nature of the exception. For the application of the proper law it is not sufficient merely that the subject matter of the proceedings should be more closely connected with a country other than the place where the wrong was

151. *Choice of Law in Tort and Delict*, Law Com No. 193, pp. 7–8, paras. 2.6–2.9.

152. For consideration of the proposals see North, "Torts in the Dismal Swamp: Choice of Law Revisited" (1991) 42 NILQ 183. For a discussion of the earlier working paper see Fawcett, "Law Commission Working Paper No. 97: Choice of Law in Tort and Delict" (1985) 48 MLR 439.

153. Draft Tort and Delict (Applicable Law) Bill, clause 3.

committed. Clause 2(4) makes it clear that the proper law exception applies only if the application of the proper law is "substantially more appropriate" than the application of the law designated by the general rules.

CHAPTER 14

FOREIGN CURRENCY OBLIGATIONS AND JUDGMENTS IN A FOREIGN CURRENCY

Legal issues concerning foreign currency obligations frequently arise in international litigation. The courts have had to formulate principles to deal not only with the problems resulting from the currency depreciation (para. 14.1), but also with questions concerning the identification of the money in which debts are expressed and damages are to be computed (the money of account) and the money in which debts are to be discharged (the money of payment) (para. 14.2). There is also the question as to the currency in which judgments are to be expressed (para. 14.3). Finally, the effects of exchange control legislation—which in many parts of the world has become an important aspect of modern economic policy—have to be considered (para. 14.4).

14.1 NOMINALISM

14.1.1 The general principle

14.1.1.1 Nominalism is a fundamental principle which is recognised by almost every legal system.[1] The effect of the nominalistic principle is that "[a] debt expressed in the currency of any country involves an obligation to pay the nominal amount of the debt in whatever currency is legal tender at the time of payment according to the law of the country in whose currency the debt is expressed".[2] The law of the currency is referred to as the *lex monetae*. In English law the principle of nominalism can be traced back to the early seventeenth century[3] and it seems never to have been seriously questioned since. Accordingly, if in 1910 A borrows a sum of money from B and undertakes to repay 50,000 French francs in 1925, A can discharge the obligation by payment of whatever constitutes 50,000 French francs in 1925 even if the value of the French franc has fallen against sterling between the date of the contract and the date of payment. It is for French law—as the *lex monetae*—to define what constitutes a French franc.

14.1.1.2 In this century particular problems have arisen as a consequence of extreme changes in the relative value of different currencies: "nominalism puts the risk of depreciation on the creditor and the risk of appreciation (or revaluation) on the debtor and neither part can be heard to complain about unexpected losses".[4] Notwithstanding the hardship caused to creditors in individual cases the English courts have resolutely

1. See Mann, *The Legal Aspect of Money* (5th ed, 1992) pp. 86–142.
2. Dicey & Morris, *The Conflict of Laws* (12th ed, 1993) p. 1550 (Rule 204(1)).
3. *Gilbert* v. *Brett (The Case of Mixt Moneys)* (1604) Davis 18.
4. Mann, *The Legal Aspect of Money* (5th ed, 1992) p. 277.

continued to apply the nominalistic principle. *Re Chesterman's Trusts*,[5] for example, concerned trust property which had been mortgaged to secure the repayment of sums expressed in German reichsmarks. There were two mortgages, the first dated 1906 and the second 1911. After the death of one of the beneficiaries, the issue arose as to the creditor's entitlements under the mortgages. At the time of the transactions the creditor could have insisted on payment in gold. After 1914, however, German law provided that obligations to pay in gold could not be enforced, with the result that the debtors were free under German law to make payment by way of paper notes. At the time of the commencement of litigation in 1922, the value in sterling of the nominal debt owing under the two mortgages had fallen to less than £5. At first instance it was decided that the creditors were entitled to no more than the nominal amount of the loan and that the debtors could satisfy the obligation under the mortgages "by repayment in whatever may be the legal tender or legal currency at the time of repayment in the foreign country whose money is the subject matter of the loan".[6] This decision was confirmed by the Court of Appeal on the basis that "an obligation to pay so many German reichsmarks is simply one to pay so many units of German currency. The form in which such a payment is to be made must... be regulated by German municipal law, and what would or would not be a legal tender must depend upon the law on that subject in force at the time of the tender."[7]

14.1.1.3 The absolute character of the principle of nominalism has a number of consequences.

(i) A creditor cannot seek to avoid the *lex monetae* on grounds of public policy.[8]
(ii) Foreign currency obligations cannot become impossible to perform. If the currency in which the debt is expressed ceases to exist, the currency which replaces it defines the relationship between the old and the new currencies.[9]
(iii) The principle of nominalism applies regardless of the law governing the contract and the place of payment.[10]

14.1.2 The importance of the law governing the obligation

As the case of *Re Chesterman's Trusts* reveals the nominalistic principle may operate in a way which is very harsh on one of the parties. Where the currency in which a debt is expressed depreciates in a dramatic and unforeseen way, the creditor recovers in economic terms much less than was envisaged at the time of contracting. It is at this stage that it is important to distinguish between the law of the currency (*lex monetae*) and the law which governs the substance of the obligation (*lex causae*). In a situation where money is owed under a contract the *lex causae* is the law applicable to the contract.

Although the effect of the principle of nominalism is that the definition of the

5. [1923] 2 Ch 466.
6. Russell J, [1923] 2 Ch 466, 473.
7. Warrington LJ, [1923] 2 Ch 466, 483.
8. Mann, *The Legal Aspect of Money* (5th ed, 1992) p. 278.
9. *Franklin* v. *Westminster Bank* (1931), reproduced in Mann, *The Legal Aspect of Money* (5th ed, 1992) pp. 561–564.
10. See Mann, *The Legal Aspect of Money* (5th ed, 1992) p. 279.

currency in which the obligation is expressed is within the exclusive province of the *lex monetae*, it must be remembered that, under general principles, the applicable law governs those aspects which relate to the substance of the obligation, including its performance, the consequences of breach and its extinction.[11] Accordingly, questions such as whether damages can be recovered for late payment or whether a debt may be revalorised fall within the scope of the *lex causae*. In this way the law governing the obligation may operate to mitigate some of the effects of the nominalistic principle.

14.1.2.1 Ravalorisation under the law applicable to the transaction

14.1.2.1.1 During the period 1919 to 1923 Germany experienced inflation at a quite unprecedented level; by 1923 the mark stood at one-billionth of its 1914 value. Although, for a time, the German courts continued to apply the nominalistic principle, as the effects of hyperinflation became more and more serious, it was decided that the revalorisation of debts was, in certain circumstances, permissible. The peg on which the courts chose to hang this particular doctrine was paragraph 242 of the German Civil Code, which provides simply that "[t]he debtor is bound to effect performance according to the requirements of good faith, giving consideration to common usage". According to the doctrine of revalorisation, in a case concerning the repayment of a loan the debtor's obligation is regarded as being not to repay the same amount of money, but to repay in money of the same value. The doctrine is applied on a case by case basis, the principle of good faith determining the degree of inflation which is required before a creditor can have his claim revalorised.[12]

14.1.2.1.2 In a number of cases which have come before the English courts a creditor has sought to rely on the German doctrine of revalorisation in order to avoid the implications of the principle of nominalism. In *Anderson* v. *Equitable Assurance Society of the United States*,[13] for example, the plaintiff's husband had taken out an insurance policy with the defendant's Hamburg branch in 1887. The policy was denominated in marks, but it was expressly provided that the contract was governed by English law. After the death of her husband in 1922 the plaintiff claimed the sums due under the policy and sought to rely on the German decisions which allowed for revalorisation. The Court of Appeal regarded the German law on revalorisation to be wholly irrelevant. Since the contract was governed by English law the relevant question was whether English law provided for revalorisation in these circumstances. As it did not, the plaintiff had to the bear the loss flowing from the decline in value of the German currency between 1887 and 1922.

14.1.2.1.3 Conversely, in relation to a contract which is governed by German law, the court should apply the doctrine of revalorisation—where appropriate—as part of the law applicable to the obligation in question.[14] Since questions of revalorisation are governed by the law applicable to the obligation, the operation of German revalorisation principles does not depend on German law being the *lex monetae*. So, if Russian roubles are owed under a German contract, the court has to admit

11. Rome Convention, Article 10(1). See paras. 11.4.5–11.4.8 and 11.4.10.
12. For the development of the German doctrine see Von Mehren & Gordley, *The Civil Law System* (2nd ed, 1977) pp. 1066–1099.
13. (1926) 134 LT 557.
14. As in *Kornatzki* v. *Oppenheimer* [1937] 4 All ER 133.

revalorisation in accordance with the rules of German law, even though revalorisation is unknown to the law of Russia.[15]

14.1.2.2 Damages for late payment

14.1.2.2.1 What is the position where a debtor repays a debt after the date of maturity and the value of the currency in which the debt was expressed has fallen against other currencies between the date of maturity and the date of actual repayment? Where, for example, a French debtor makes late payment of a franc debt to an English creditor, can the English creditor recover damages for currency exchange losses if the franc depreciates against sterling between the date of maturity and the date of actual repayment?

14.1.2.2.2 The availability of damages for the detention of a debt or for breach of a contractual obligation to pay a sum on a particular date is a question which is to be determined by the law applicable to the obligation.[16] Where the contract is governed by English law the creditor may recover damages for delayed payment of a debt expressed in a foreign currency as long as the loss suffered as a consequence of exchange rate fluctuations between the date of maturity and the date of payment was reasonably foreseeable.[17] A claim for currency exchange losses is a claim for special damages which must be specifically proved; if the creditor cannot prove the loss or cannot rebut any defence of remoteness, the claim must fail.[18]

14.1.2.2.3 The general principles of foreseeability do not apply in respect of a claim for liquidated damages. In *President of India* v. *Lips Maritime Co*[19] the defendant chartered a ship from the plaintiff and failed to pay demurrage due under the charter. Demurrage, which was calculated at the rate of $6,000 per day, was payable in sterling at the rate of exchange prevailing on 1 July 1980. Although discharge of the ship was concluded in October 1980, the dispute concerning demurrage was not finally determined by arbitration until February 1983. Between December 1980 and February 1983 sterling had depreciated against the US dollar and the award included damages for the currency exchange losses which resulted from the depreciation of sterling.

14.1.2.2.4 On an appeal under the Arbitration Act 1979 on a point of law the House of Lords set aside the award. It was held that "[t]here is no such thing as a cause of action in damages for late payment of damages. The only remedy which the law affords for delay is the discretionary award of interest pursuant to statute."[20] Accordingly, the plaintiff was not entitled to recover damages for currency exchange losses between the date when the cause of action arose and the date when the arbitrator made the award. This decision, which has been described as "remarkable" and "unfortunate",[21] has been

15. Mann, *The Legal Aspect of Money* (5th ed, 1992) p. 281.
16. *Société des Hôtels Le Touquet* v. *Cummings* [1922] 1 KB 451.
17. *Ozalid Group (Export) Ltd* v. *African Continental Bank Ltd* [1979] 2 Lloyd's Rep 231; *International Minerals & Chemical Corporation* v. *Karl O Helm AG* [1986] 1 Lloyd's Rep 81.
18. *President of India* v. *La Pintada Compania Navigacion SA* [1985] AC 104.
19. [1988] AC 395. Mann, "Recovering Currency Exchange Losses" (1988) 104 LQR 3; Michel, "Damages and the Late Payer" [1987] LMCLQ 414.
20. Lord Brandon, [1988] AC 395, 425.
21. Mann, *The Legal Aspect of Money* (5th ed, 1992) p. 293.

convincingly criticised—particularly on the basis that the distinction between a debt, on the one hand, and liquidated damages, on the other, is wholly artificial.[22]

14.1.3 Avoiding the effects of nominalism: gold clauses

In times of economic instability a creditor may seek to escape the impact of currency fluctuations by linking the debtor's obligation to the value of gold, a commodity which has historically retained its value. In considering gold clauses, which are of much less practical significance than was once the case, a distinction must be drawn between gold-coin clauses and gold-value clauses.

14.1.3.1 Gold-coin clauses and gold-value clauses

14.1.3.1.1 Where a contract includes a clause requiring the debtor to make payment in gold coins this will not normally have the effect of protecting the creditor against depreciation of the currency in which the debt is expressed. This results from two general principles: (i) it is for the *lex monetae* to determine what is legal tender; (ii) as regards the mode of performance regard must be had to the law of the place of performance (*lex loci solutionis*). Since it is at times of currency depreciation that legislation is passed providing that debts expressed in gold are to be repaid in paper notes the protection offered by a gold-coin clause tends to be somewhat illusory. For example, where in 1917 the defendant issues bonds to the plaintiff and undertakes to repay the capital in "gold dollars" in New York in 1937, on the assumption that the clause is a gold-coin clause governed by English law, the plaintiff cannot insist on the payment of the debt in gold coins if, in 1933, before the debt is repaid, the US legislature passes legislation outlawing gold clauses and providing that all dollar obligations, whether undertaken before or after the entry into force of the legislation, are dischargeable "upon payment, dollar for dollar, in any coin or currency which at the time of payment is legal tender for public or private debts".[23] The reasoning behind this conclusion is that a gold-coin clause does not concern the substance of the obligation, but the mode of performance. Accordingly, the creditor must be content with payment of paper notes representing the nominal value of the debt.

14.1.3.1.2 By contrast, a gold-value clause requires the debtor to pay a sum equal to the value of gold of a particular weight and fineness. Whereas a gold-coin clause seeks to determine the method of payment (and is therefore subject to the vagaries of the *lex loci solutionis*) a gold-value clause fixes the substance of the debtor's obligation. For example, in *Feist* v. *Société Intercommunale Belge d'Eléctricité*[24] a Belgian company issued bonds in 1928 for the payment of £100 in 1963 and of interest at 5.5 per cent per annum "in sterling gold coin of the United Kingdom of or equal to the standard weight and fineness existing on 1 September 1928". The question arose as to the extent of the

22. See Mann, *The Legal Aspect of Money* (5th ed, 1992) p. 294, n. 102.

23. This was the conclusion of Branson J in *R* v. *International Trustee for the Protection of Bondholders Aktiengesellschaft* [1936] WN 325. The House of Lords held, however, that the clause was governed by New York law rather than English law: [1937] AC 500.

24. [1934] AC 161.

liability arising under this obligation following the devaluation of sterling in 1931. The House of Lords held that the bond was in the form of a gold-value clause and therefore the debtor's obligation was to be discharged by payment in depreciated pounds of a sum sufficient to purchase 100 gold pounds. So, although the nominal amount of the debt remained constant (£100) the amount of currency required to discharge the obligation varied. (Had the clause been interpreted as a gold-coin clause the obligation could have been discharged by payment of paper notes representing the nominal value of the debt.[25])

14.1.3.2 The role of the applicable law

It is well established that it is for the law applicable to the obligation to determine not only the question of interpretation (whether the contractual term is a gold-coin or a gold-value clause), but also the clause's validity and effect.[26] Where the law governing the obligation is English law it is presumed—following *Feist* v. *Société Intercommunale Belge d'Eléctricité*[27]—that a clause which refers to payment in gold of a specified sum in coins of a particular weight and fineness is a gold-value clause. Such a clause imposes on the debtor an obligation to pay in the legal tender of the currency in question an amount which, on the day of payment, will be sufficient to buy coins representing the nominal value of the debt. The debtor is not, however, required to discharge the obligation by paying gold coins.[28]

14.2 THE MONEY OF ACCOUNT AND THE MONEY OF PAYMENT

14.2.1 Introduction

14.2.1.1 A fundamental aspect of the law affecting currency obligations is the distinction between the money of account and the money of payment. This is the distinction between the substance of the obligation and the method of payment. In the words of Lord Denning MR in *Woodhouse AC Israel Cocoa Ltd SA* v. *Nigerian Produce Marketing Co Ltd*: "The *money of account* is the currency in which an obligation is to be measured. It tells the debtor *how much* he has to pay. The *money of payment* is the currency in which the obligation is to be discharged. It tells the debtor *by what means* he is to pay."[29] In other words, the money of account determines the quantum of the debt; the money of payment is merely the instrument of payment.[30]

14.2.1.2 There is no necessary connection between the money of account and the currency of the country whose law governs the obligation in question. For example, in a contract governed by English law, the debtor may undertake to pay the creditor 100 Canadian dollars. If there is any doubt as to the identity of the money of account (for example, where a contract between an American seller and a Canadian buyer states the price in "dollars" but fails to indicate whether Canadian or US dollars are intended) this

25. This had been the view taken by Farwell J, at first instance, and by the Court of Appeal: [1933] Ch 684.
26. *Feist* v. *Société Intercommunale Belge d'Eléctricité* [1934] AC 161.
27. [1934] AC 161.
28. *New Brunswick Railway Co* v. *British & French Trust Corporation Ltd* [1939] AC 1.
29. [1971] 2 QB 23, 54. (Emphasis in original.)
30. See Mann, *The Legal Aspect of Money* (5th ed, 1992) p. 207.

issue has to be determined in accordance with the canons of construction of the *lex causae*. Similarly, there is no necessary connection between the money of account and the money of payment. For example, an obligation may be expressed as "10,000 lire payable in pounds sterling". In this case the money of account is Italian lire and the money of payment is sterling. Wherever the money of payment is not also the money of account there has to be a conversion from one currency into another thereby giving rise to problems if the exchange rate applicable under the *lex causae* is different from that applicable under the *lex loci solutionis*.[31]

14.2.2 Determining the money of account

14.2.2.1 Debts

14.2.2.1.1 At common law it is a clear principle that where the money of account is not expressly indicated by the parties, it is for the *lex causae* to determine which currency is the money of account. In *Bonython* v. *Commonwealth of Australia*[32] the question facing the Privy Council concerned the determination of the money of account in relation to an obligation to pay "pounds sterling" at Brisbane, Melbourne, Sydney or London. Lord Simonds rejected any suggestion that the law of the place of payment was relevant in deciding this question: "the substance of the obligation must be determined by the proper law of the contract".[33] The same result is achieved in relation to contractual obligations governed by the Rome Convention on the Law Applicable to Contractual Obligations; Article 10(1)(a) provides that the applicable law governs "interpretation".

14.2.2.1.2 The general approach to the determination of the money of account under English law has been described in the following terms:

> As in connection with all other problems of construction so it is here necessary to have regard to all the circumstances of the case and so to deduce the true intention of the parties. The nature of the transaction, the nationality, residence and domicile of the parties, the valuation of the respective currencies at the time when the contract was made, the place where the contract was made and where it was to be performed, all these and similar facts will have to be looked at and weighed.[34]

This approach is reflected by the decision in *Bonython* v. *Commonwealth of Australia* where the money of account was taken to be the currency of the country with which the contract had its closest and most real connection.

14.2.2.1.3 In relation to obligations governed by English law the courts have applied various presumptions to assist in ascertaining the money of account.

(i) There is a natural assumption that the parties intend the money of account to be the currency of the place of payment (since this avoids the need for

31. See para. 14.2.3.
32. [1951] AC 201.
33. [1951] AC 201, 219. In two earlier cases—*Adelaide Electric Supply Co Ltd* v. *Prudential Assurance Co Ltd* [1934] AC 122, a decision of the House of Lords, and *Auckland Corporation* v. *Alliance Assurance Co Ltd* [1937] AC 587, an appeal to the Privy Council—Lord Wright appears to have been of the opinion that the law of the place of performance determined the money of account. Lord Wright's position—which is clearly unsound in principle—has been subjected to exhaustive analysis by Mann (*The Legal Aspect of Money* (5th ed, 1992) pp. 242–246) and, in the light of *Bonython* v. *Commonwealth of Australia* [1951] AC 201, cannot be regarded as reflecting the current state of the law.
34. Mann, *The Legal Aspect of Money* (5th ed, 1992) p. 230.

exchange from the money of account to the money of payment).[35]

(ii) In *Bonython* v. *Commonwealth of Australia* Lord Simonds thought that "[t]he Government of a self-governing country, using the terms appropriate to its own monetary system, must be presumed to refer to that system whether or not those terms are apt to refer to another system also".[36] This presumption is not restricted to government contracts; it is also relevant in cases where one of the contracting parties is a public authority (such as a local corporation).

(iii) In a contract which is governed by English law "the word 'pound' *prima facie* means an English pound".[37]

14.2.2.1.4 These presumptions are not, however, hard and fast rules.[38] Indeed, it has been suggested that "general principles cannot be laid down, each case requiring an examination of its particular facts".[39] It would be impossible for the presumptions to operate as rules, since in certain circumstances the presumptions are inconclusive (for example, where an obligation to pay a sum of "dollars" may be discharged either in San Francisco or Vancouver[40]) and in others the presumptions may conflict. For example, in *National Mutual Life Association of Australasia Ltd* v. *Attorney-General for New Zealand*[41] the Government of New Zealand undertook to discharge a monetary obligation in Melbourne (Australia) "free of exchange". The obligation was expressed in "pounds" and the question arose as to whether the money of account was Australian or New Zealand pounds. It was held that, notwithstanding the fact that the defendant was the Government of New Zealand, the money of account was Australian pounds. What was important was not only that the place of performance was Australia, but also the fact that the debt was stated to be repayable "free of exchange", thereby indicating that the parties intended to avoid having to convert one currency into another.

14.2.2.2 Damages

14.2.2.2.1 It is generally accepted that it is for the *lex causae* to identify the money of account in which damages are to be determined. As regards contractual obligations this question is governed by Article 10(1)(c) of the Rome Convention which provides that the applicable law shall govern "the consequences of breach including the assessment of damages in so far as it is governed by rules of law". This does not, of course, mean that damages will be assessed in the currency of the country whose law governs the obligation. Where a contract is not governed by English law it is for the foreign applicable law to determine the currency in which damages are to be assessed.

Although in many cases concerning contracts governed by English law it is appropriate for the court to award damages in sterling, situations arise in which not only is it inappropriate to give judgment in sterling but there is more than one eligible foreign currency. In this type of case the determination of the currency in which damages are to

35. See, for example, *Adelaide Electric Supply Co Ltd* v. *Prudential Assurance Co Ltd* [1934] AC 122; *Auckland Corporation* v. *Alliance Assurance Co Ltd* [1937] AC 587.
36. [1951] AC 201, 222.
37. Romer LJ in *Broken Hill Proprietary Co Ltd* v. *Latham* [1933] Ch 373, 409.
38. For example, in *Bonython* v. *Commonwealth of Australia* [1951] AC 201 it was held that "pounds sterling" referred to Australian pounds.
39. Mann, *The Legal Aspect of Money* (5th ed, 1992) p. 234.
40. This was the sort of issue which arose in *Bonython* v. *Commonwealth of Australia* [1951] AC 201.
41. [1956] AC 369.

be awarded depends on "general principles of the law of contract and on rules of conflict of laws".[42] Whether the claim is for damages in contract, tort or restitution, if the applicable law is English law, damages will be assessed in the currency which best expresses the plaintiff's loss. This flexible principle emerges from the decision of the House of Lords in the combined appeals in *The Despina R* and *Services Europe Atlantique Sud (SEAS)* v. *Stockholms Rederiaktiebolag Svea*.[43]

14.2.2.2.2 In *Services Europe Atlantique Sud (SEAS)* v. *Stockholms Rederiaktiebolag Svea* the plaintiff, a French company, chartered a vessel from the defendant for the shipment of a cargo of onions to Brazil. Although the charterparty was governed by English law, the hire of the vessel was denominated in US dollars. The vessel's refrigeration failed as a consequence of which the cargo was damaged. The receivers of the cargo claimed damages from the plaintiff and this claim was settled by the payment of 456,250 Brazilian cruzeiros. The plaintiff made this payment by purchasing the necessary Brazilian cruzeiros with French francs. When the plaintiff sought indemnity from the defendant the question arose as to the currency in which the plaintiff's loss should be identified. This issue was of considerable importance since the Brazilian cruzeiro had depreciated against the French franc between the settlement of the claim in Brazil and the commencement of proceedings in England. In theory, there were three possible solutions: (i) the currency of the contract (US dollars); (ii) the currency of the plaintiff's immediate loss (Brazilian cruzeiros); or (iii) the currency in which the plaintiff's loss was felt (French francs).

14.2.2.2.3 In deciding in which currency damages should be awarded, the court should start by looking at the contract:

> If the proper law is English, the first step must be to see whether, expressly or by implication, the contract provides an answer to the currency question. This may lead to selection of the "currency of the contract". If from the terms of the contract it appears that the parties have accepted a currency as the currency of account and payment in respect of all transactions arising under the contract, then it would be proper to give judgment for damages in that currency.... But there may be cases in which, although obligations under the contract are to be met in a specified currency, or currencies, the right conclusion may be that there is no intention shown that damages for breach of contract should be given in that currency or currencies.[44]

In the present case, although the hire was expressed in US dollars, this in itself was not sufficient to justify a conclusion that the parties had agreed that damages should be payable in that currency.

14.2.2.2.4 In the absence of an agreement on the currency in which damages are to be given "the plaintiff should be compensated for the expense or loss in the currency which most truly expresses his loss".[45] The currency which most truly expresses the plaintiff's loss is not necessarily that in which it first arose.[46] Lord Wilberforce indicated that to determine the currency which most truly expresses the plaintiff's loss "the court must ask what is the currency, payment in which will as nearly as possible compensate the

42. Lord Wilberforce, [1979] AC 685, 700.

43. [1979] AC 685. Bowles & Whelan, "Judgments in Foreign Currencies: Extension of the Miliangos Rule" (1979) 42 MLR 452. For a summary of the principles laid down by the House of Lords see the judgment of Brandon J in *The Federal Huron* [1985] 3 All ER 378.

44. Lord Wilberforce, [1979] AC 685, 700.

45. This principle—which was formulated by Lord Denning MR in the Court of Appeal [1979] QB 491, 514—was adopted by Lord Wilberforce [1979] AC 685, 701.

46. Lord Wilberforce, [1979] AC 685, 701.

plaintiff in accordance with the principle of restitution, and whether the parties must be taken reasonably to have had this in contemplation".[47]

14.2.2.2.5 In the present case it was clear that the currency which best expressed the plaintiff's loss was the French franc. What was important in this case was not the loss suffered by the receivers of the cargo, but the loss suffered by the plaintiffs. Although the receivers' loss was in Brazilian cruzeiros, the plaintiff's loss was "the discharge of the receivers' claim, together with the legal and other expenses they incurred. They discharged all of these by providing francs—until they provided the francs to meet the receivers' claim they suffered no loss."[48]

14.2.2.2.6 The basic approach adopted in *Services Europe Atlantique Sud (SEAS)* v. *Stockholms Rederiaktiebolag Svea* is equally applicable to tort claims (although in tort cases there can be no question of the parties having expressly or impliedly chosen a money of account). *The Despina R* involved a claim based on negligence arising out of a collision between two Greek ships off Shanghai. The plaintiff's vessel was taken, first, to Shanghai where temporary repairs were carried out, then, to Japan where further repairs were carried out and, finally, to California for permanent repairs. The plaintiff's claim against the defendant was for recovery of the expenses incurred in China (in renmimbi yuan), in Japan (in yen) and in California (in US dollars). Since, as regards all these disbursements, the bank account used by the plaintiff was a US dollar account in New York, all the expenses incurred in currencies other than US dollars were met by transferring US dollars from this account.

14.2.2.2.7 The choice facing the court was whether the plaintiff's loss should be expressed in the "expenditure currency" (the currency in which the expense or loss was immediately sustained) or in the "plaintiff's currency" (the currency in which the loss was effectively borne by the plaintiff). Lord Wilberforce decided that damages should be assessed in US dollars:

> a plaintiff, who normally conducts his business through a particular currency, and who, when other currencies are immediately involved, uses his own currency to obtain those currencies, can reasonably say that the loss he sustains is to be measured not by the immediate currencies in which the loss first emerges but by the amount of his own currency, which in the normal course of operation, he uses to obtain those currencies. This is the currency in which his loss is felt, and is the currency which it is reasonably foreseeable he will have to spend.[49]

14.2.2.2.8 Two qualifications to the general principles formulated by the House of Lords in *Services Europe Atlantique Sud (SEAS)* v. *Stockholms Rederiaktiebolag Svea* and *The Despina R* should be noted. First, the burden is on the plaintiff to prove that he conducts his operations in a particular currency and that the loss was felt in that currency. If the plaintiff is unable to prove this, damages will be expressed in the currency or currencies in which the loss immediately arose. In the case of delivery of damaged goods, for example, the ordinary measure of damages leads to the *prima facie* result that the currency of loss is the currency of the place of discharge.[50] Secondly, Lord Wilberforce stressed that it would not be appropriate to lay down "a hard and fast rule that in all cases where a plaintiff suffers a loss or damage in a foreign currency the right

47. [1979] AC 685, 701.
48. Lord Wilberforce, [1979] AC 685, 702.
49. [1979] AC 685, 697.
50. Bingham J in *The Kefalonia Wind* [1986] 1 Lloyd's Rep 273, 291.

currency to take for the purposes of his claim is 'the plaintiff's currency'".[51] The principle underlying the flexible approach advocated by the House of Lords is that the plaintiff should be properly compensated for his loss; a decision as to the currency in which the loss was felt is equivalent to a finding as to the currency which most appropriately or justly reflects the recoverable loss.[52]

14.2.2.2.9 Where damages are assessed in a foreign currency under the foregoing principles the plaintiff has to stand the risk of any fluctuations in the value of that currency which take place after the date on which the cause of action accrued.[53] The object of an award in damages is to put the plaintiff in the position he would have been in had the defendant performed his obligation, not to indemnify the plaintiff against the fall in the value of the currency in which he operates. In *The Texaco Melbourne*[54] the defendant failed to deliver a cargo of fuel oil to the plaintiff in Ghana. The plaintiff had intended to sell the cargo to buyers in Ghana and the expectation was that the sale would have fetched 11.6 million Ghanaian cedis. Between the defendant's failure to deliver and the commencement of proceedings in England the cedi fell spectacularly against the US dollar. The plaintiff claimed that damages should be assessed in dollars, applying the dollar/cedi rate at the date of breach. The Court of Appeal held that, since the currency in which the plaintiff carried on business was the cedi, the currency in which the loss was felt and which most truly expressed that loss was also the cedi.

14.2.3 Discharging foreign currency obligations

14.2.3.1 As regards the identification of the money of payment, the relevant framework in relation to contractual obligations is that provided by the Rome Convention. Article 10(2) provides that in relation to the manner of performance "regard shall be had to the law of the country in which performance takes place". If, for example, the applicable law provides that all debts must be discharged in the money of account, but the law of the place of performance insists that all debts be discharged in the local currency, the effect of Article 10(2) is to enable the court to treat discharge of the debt in the local currency of the place of payment as good discharge.

14.2.3.2 Although Article 10(2) allows the court to have regard to the *lex loci solutionis* Article 10(1) makes it clear that the applicable law governs questions relating to the substance of the obligation.[55] If, for example, a contract which is not governed by English law provides for payment of a sum of money in England, the court may have regard to English law but the application of English rules on the discharge of foreign currency obligations may not be allowed to alter the substance of the obligation.

14.2.3.3 Under English law "when someone is under an obligation to pay another a sum of money expressed in a foreign currency but to pay it in this country, the person under the obligation has an option ... either to produce the appropriate amount in the foreign currency in question or to pay the equivalent in sterling at the rate of exchange prevailing at the due date".[56] The creditor cannot insist on payment in sterling.

51. [1979] AC 685, 698.
52. Brandon J in *The Federal Huron* [1985] 3 All ER 378, 381.
53. Leggatt LJ in *The Texaco Melbourne* [1993] 1 Lloyd's Rep 471, 477.
54. [1993] 1 Lloyd's Rep 471. The House of Lords dismissed the plaintiff's appeal: *Lloyd's List*, 5 March 1994.
55. This analysis of the Rome Convention is consistent with the generally accepted position under the common law: *Report on Foreign Money Liabilities*, Law Com No. 124 (1983) p. 4, para. 2.2.
56. Mocatta J in *Barclays Bank International Ltd* v. *Levin Brothers (Bradford) Ltd* [1977] QB 270, 277.

Although the matter is not free from doubt, it appears that the parties may effectively exclude the debtor's right to discharge a foreign currency obligation in sterling.[57]

14.2.3.4 The significance of the distinction between performance (which is governed by the applicable law) and manner of performance (in relation to which regard may be had to the *lex loci solutionis*) emerges in the situation where the discharge of a foreign currency obligation involves payment in a currency other than the money of account. Whether payment is to be effected in England or abroad, the exchange rate to be applied should be determined by the law applicable to the obligation, rather than by the law of the place of payment.[58] Where the obligation is governed by English law if the debtor chooses to discharge in England a foreign currency obligation in sterling the rate of exchange is that at which "units of the foreign legal tender can, on the day when the money is paid, be bought in London in a recognised and accessible market, irrespective of any official rate of exchange between that currency and sterling".[59] Of course, if the debtor tenders the appropriate amount in the foreign currency[60] potential problems concerning exchange rates can be avoided.

14.2.3.5 The general principle that the applicable law should govern questions of substance may need some qualification in cases where the transaction required by the terms of the contract is illegal in the place of performance. Where a contract envisages the performance of an illegal act in a friendly foreign country, it is possible that the court may refuse to enforce the contract on the basis of public policy.[61]

14.3 JUDGMENTS IN A FOREIGN CURRENCY

14.3.1 Background

Until relatively recently all English judgments had to be expressed in sterling and, where the claim concerned foreign currency obligations, the sum of sterling was calculated by converting the foreign currency at the date of the breach or wrong, rather than the date of judgment or the date of payment. In 1961 the "sterling-breach date" rule was confirmed by the House of Lords in *Re United Railways of Havana and Regla Warehouses Ltd.*[62] In the 1970s, however, the rule came under tremendous pressure as a

57. Support for this proposition may be derived from the judgments of Bankes LJ in *Anderson* v. *Equitable Assurance Society of the United States of America* (1926) 134 LT 557 and Somervell LJ in *Heisler* v. *Anglo-Dal Ltd* [1954] 1 WLR 1273, 1278. If this is not already the law, the Law Commission proposes that English law should give effect to a contractual agreement giving the debtor the right to pay in foreign currency alone: *Foreign Money Liabilities*, Law Com No. 124 (1983) pp. 31–32, paras. 3.16–3.17.

None of the authorities deal with the situation where the parties have expressly agreed that payment should be made in England in a particular currency which is not the money of account (for example, in a situation where the debt is expressed as "1,000 Canadian dollars to be paid in London in French francs"). There is no obvious reason why the creditor should not be able to insist on the obligation being discharged in the agreed money of payment.

58. *Report on Foreign Money Liabilities*, Law Com No. 124 (1983) p. 4, n. 15. Although the report discusses the common law, the position under the Rome Convention is the same. See also Mann, *The Legal Aspect of Money* (5th ed, 1992) pp. 326–327.

59. Dicey & Morris, *The Conflict of Laws* (12th ed, 1993) p. 1579 (Rule 208). See, for example, *George Veflings Rederi A/S* v. *President of India* [1979] 1 WLR 59.

60. See, for example, *Marrache* v. *Ashton* [1943] AC 311.

61. Rome Convention, Article 16; *Foster* v. *Driscoll* [1929] 1 KB 470. For further discussion of the problems posed by illegality see para. 11.4.10.

62. [1961] AC 1007.

result of fluctuations in the value of different currencies—in particular the decline in the value of sterling as against stronger currencies. It is not difficult to see how the sterling-breach date rule could operate in a way which was unfair to a foreign plaintiff. If between the date of the breach and the date of judgment sterling declines in value against the currency in which the plaintiff's loss was suffered a judgment in sterling converted at the rate of exchange prevailing at the date of the breach works to the advantage of the English defendant. The sterling-breach date rule had long been the subject of academic criticism and in a number of cases in the 1970s the rule in *Re United Railways of Havana and Regla Warehouses Ltd* was challenged, particularly by Lord Denning MR. In *Jugoslavenska Oceanska Plovidba* v. *Castel Investment Co Inc*[63] it was held that arbitrators in England were able to make an award in foreign currency and in *Schorsch Meier GmbH* v. *Hennin*[64] the Court of Appeal went further in suggesting that the rule that an English court could express a money judgment only in sterling should be discarded. These developments made it imperative that the House of Lords should reconsider the sterling-breach date rule.

14.3.2 The *Miliangos* case

14.3.2.1 In *Miliangos* v. *George Frank (Textiles) Ltd*[65] the House of Lords utilised the 1966 Practice Direction[66] and reversed the decision in *Re United Railways of Havana and Regla Warehouses Ltd*. The case concerned a contract, governed by Swiss law, under the terms of which the defendant owed the plaintiff a liquidated sum expressed in Swiss francs. The defendant failed to make the payment due under the contract and the plaintiff sought to recover the sum in proceedings in England. Between the date of the defendant's breach and the judgment sterling had depreciated against the Swiss franc. If the debt was converted at the exchange rate prevailing at the date of judgment the plaintiff would recover 50 per cent more than if conversion were effected at the rate at the date of breach.

14.3.2.2 The majority of the House of Lords took the view that the court was able to give judgment in an amount expressed in a foreign currency. If the defendant chooses to satisfy the judgment voluntarily he may do so by payment of the relevant amount of the currency in which the judgment is expressed or the equivalent sum in sterling converted at the rate prevailing at the date of payment. If, however, the defendant fails to deliver the foreign currency "the date for its conversion into sterling should be the date when the plaintiff is given leave to levy execution for a sum expressed in sterling".[67] There are exceptions to the general rule in various statutory regimes.[68]

14.3.2.3 Although the House of Lords stressed that its decision was limited to the facts of the case—which was concerned with a contractual obligation of a money

63. [1974] QB 292. Lipstein, [1974] CLJ 11.
64. [1975] QB 416. Lipstein, [1975] CLJ 215.
65. [1976] AC 443. Carter, (1974–75) 47 BYIL 369; Isaacs, "Foreign Currency Claims and the English Courts" [1977] LMCLQ 356; Powles, "Foreign Currency Judgments" [1979] LMCLQ 485. For an American view of the decision see Becker, "The Currency of Judgment" (1977) 25 Am J Comp L 152.
66. *Practice Statement (Judicial Precedent)* [1966] 1 WLR 1234.
67. Lord Cross, [1976] AC 443, 497–498. See also, Lord Wilberforce, [1976] AC 443, 468–469 and Lord Fraser, [1976] AC 443, 501.
68. See Dicey & Morris, *The Conflict of Laws* (12th ed, 1993) p. 1583, n. 32.

character to pay foreign currency arising under a contract governed by the law of a foreign country, where the money of account and the money of payment were the currency of a country other than the United Kingdom[69]—subsequent cases have, however, revealed that the rule that judgments may be given in a foreign currency is one of general application.

(i) The *Miliangos* rule is a procedural rule which must be applied by the court regardless of the law applicable to the obligation in question.

(ii) The rule is not limited to claims for a liquidated debt in a foreign currency. Judgment in a foreign currency may be given where the plaintiff's claim is for an unliquidated sum, regardless of whether the claim is for breach of contract,[70] for tort[71] or for restitution.[72]

(iii) As a matter of principle, the court should be able to grant a judgment in a foreign currency at the behest of either the plaintiff or the defendant. If this were not the case a defendant might be unfairly prejudiced. Where sterling appreciates as against the foreign currency in which the debt is expressed between the date of breach and the date of judgment, a judgment in sterling converted at the date of breach would overcompensate the plaintiff.

14.4 PROBLEMS ARISING OUT OF EXCHANGE CONTROL LEGISLATION

14.4.1 General principles

14.4.1.1 The regulation of exchange control is used by many governments as a tool of economic policy. Exchange control normally takes the form of regulating the export of currency.[73] The courts give effect to the exchange control legislation of a foreign country in a number of situations.

Where the exchange control regulations of the foreign country form part of the law which governs the contract, if the contract is rendered invalid by the foreign regulations, it is invalid in England. Similarly, where under the applicable law the effect of the exchange controls is to discharge the contractual obligation, the court will regard the debtor as discharged. This is the position at common law[74] and the same principles apply under Article 10(1)(d) of the Rome Convention.[75] For example, in *Re Claim by Helbert Wagg & Co Ltd*[76] the defendant, a German company, owed a sum of money payable in sterling to the plaintiff, an English company, under a contract governed by German law. After the conclusion of the contract Germany enacted exchange control legislation which had the effect of enabling the defendant to pay the sum owed in German currency

69. Lord Wilberforce, [1976] AC 443, 467–468.
70. *Services Europe Atlantique Sud (SEAS)* v. *Stockholms Rederiaktiebolag Svea* [1979] AC 685.
71. *The Despina R* [1979] AC 685.
72. *BP Exploration Co (Libya) Ltd* v. *Hunt (No. 2)* [1979] 1 WLR 783.
73. There has been no exchange control in the United Kingdom since 1979 and the Exchange Control Act 1947 was repealed in 1987.
74. See, for example, *De Beéche* v. *South American Stores (Gath & Chaves) Ltd* [1935] AC 148; *Re Banque des Marchands de Moscou (Koupetschesky) (No. 2)* [1954] 1 WLR 1108; *Zivonstenska Banka National Corporation* v. *Frankman* [1950] AC 57.
75. See para. 11.4.8.
76. [1956] Ch 323.

to a government agency in Berlin. Under German law payment in this way discharged the obligation. When the plaintiff sought to recover the sum owing under the contract in England the claim was rejected. Upjohn J decided that the court "must recognise the right of every foreign State to protect its economy by measures of foreign exchange control and by altering the value of its currency. Effect must be given to those measures where the law of the foreign State is the proper law of the contract".[77]

14.4.1.2 As a general rule, the mere fact that the contract infringes the exchange control regulations of a country whose law does not govern the parties' obligations does not affect the validity and enforcement of the contract in England. However, Article 16 of the Rome Convention provides that the court may refuse to apply "a rule of the law of any country specified by this Convention" if the application of the rule "is manifestly incompatible with the public policy ... of the forum". In *Foster* v. *Driscoll*[78]—a case decided at common law—the Court of Appeal decided that the court should refuse to enforce a contract "if the real object and intention of the parties necessitates them joining in an endeavour to perform in a foreign and friendly country some act which is illegal by the law of such country".[79] This rule was extended by the House of Lords in *Reggazoni* v. *KC Sethia (1944) Ltd*[80]—another case which pre-dates the entry into force of the Convention—to a situation where the main purpose of the contract necessarily involves the commission of an illegal act in a friendly, foreign State. The basis of this doctrine is said to be public policy. Although it is generally accepted that Article 16 is not to be interpreted widely, it would nevertheless seem sufficiently wide to justify an English court in refusing to enforce a contract to smuggle currency out of a foreign country in breach of that country's exchange control legislation—irrespective of the legality of the contract under its applicable law.

14.4.1.3 Where the parties enter a contract which is illegal to perform under the *lex loci solutionis*, if the contract is governed by English law the court will not enforce it.[81] If, however, the contract is governed neither by English law nor by the *lex loci solutionis* the position is not entirely free from ambiguity. The principled view is that if the contract is enforceable under the applicable law, it should be enforceable in England; if the contract is discharged under the applicable law, it should be regarded as discharged in England. It is hoped that following the entry into force of the Rome Convention in the United Kingdom the principled view will prevail.[82] However, the common law cases suggest, albeit *obiter*, that it is contrary to English public policy to enforce a contractual obligation, the performance of which is illegal by the law of the place of performance, irrespective of the law governing the contract.[83] Accordingly, for the moment the position may be regarded as uncertain.

14.4.1.4 There are also cases where foreign exchange controls will be disregarded in England.

77. [1956] Ch 323, 351.
78. [1929] 1 KB 470.
79. Sankey LJ, [1929] 1 KB 470, 521.
80. [1958] AC 301.
81. *Ralli Brothers* v. *Compania Naviera Sota y Aznar* [1920] 2 KB 287.
82. Reynolds, "Illegality by Lex Loci Solutionis" (1992) 108 LQR 553.
83. See para. 11.4.10.2.

(i) Where, under a contract governed by English law, a sum of money is payable in England, the court will not have regard to the exchange control legislation of foreign countries.[84]

(ii) It should be noted that, as a matter of public policy, an English court will not enforce foreign exchange control legislation, irrespective of the law governing the contract, if the foreign law is in reality an instrument of oppression or discrimination.[85]

14.4.1.5 Finally, it should be noted that if exchange control legislation were reintroduced in the United Kingdom, such legislation would almost certainly be, according to its proper interpretation, an "overriding rule"[86] within the meaning of Article 7(2) of the Rome Convention, as a result of which it would be applicable regardless of the law governing the contract.[87]

14.4.2 "Exchange contracts"

By virtue of the Bretton Woods Agreement there are special rules applicable to "exchange contracts". The relevant provision of the Bretton Woods Agreement[88] is Article VIII(2)(b) which provides:

> Exchange contracts which involve a currency of any member and which are contrary to the exchange control regulations of any member maintained or imposed consistently with this Agreement shall be unenforceable in the territories.

14.4.2.1 What is an "exchange contract"?

There are two possible approaches to the interpretation of the words "exchange contract". (i) The broad approach is that a contract which in any way affects a country's exchange resources is to be regarded as an exchange contract. (ii) The narrow view is that exchange contracts are contracts to exchange the currency of one country for that of another. It has been strongly argued that only the broad interpretation can achieve the overriding purposes of the Bretton Woods Agreement[89] and, for a time, it appeared that the English courts would adopt the liberal view.[90] However, it is now firmly established that—as far as English law is concerned—the narrow interpretation is the

84. *Toprak Mahsulleri Ofisi* v. *Finagrain Compagnie Commerciale Agricole et Financière SA* [1979] 2 Lloyd's Rep 98. See, however, para. 14.4.2.

85. *Re Claim of Helbert Wagg & Co Ltd* [1956] Ch 323.

86. For the definition of "overriding rules" see para. 11.3.1.

87. *Boissevain* v. *Weil* [1950] AC 327 (in which the English courts dismissed a claim by a plaintiff to recover foreign currency which had been loaned to the defendant in Monaco during the Second World War on the ground that the loan was illegal under English wartime restrictions) would be decided in the same way under the Rome Convention on the ground that English wartime restrictions were overriding rules within the scope of Article 7(2).

88. The Agreement was made part of English law by the Bretton Woods Agreements Order in Council 1946, SR & O 1946 No. 36 (made under the Bretton Woods Agreements Act 1945).

89. Mann, "The Private International Law of Exchange Control Under the International Monetary Fund Agreement" (1953) 2 ICLQ 97, 102.

90. *Sharif* v. *Azad* [1967] 1 QB 605. Mann, "The Bretton Woods Agreement in the English Courts" (1967) 16 ICLQ 539.

proper one. In *Wilson, Smithett & Cope Ltd* v. *Terruzzi*[91] the Court of Appeal decided that exchange contracts are contracts which involve the exchange of one currency for another, including such contracts which are disguised as something else. Although the decision was deplored[92] it was approved by the House of Lords in *United City Merchants (Investments) Ltd.* v. *Royal Bank of Canada.*[93]

14.4.2.2 The effect of Article VIII(2)(b)

Article VIII(2)(b) is an overriding rule—in the sense that it is applicable regardless of the law governing the contract[94]—which falls within the scope of Article 7(2) of the Rome Convention. In cases where Article VIII(2)(b) is applicable, as a general rule, it is not open to the court to disregard the foreign exchange control legislation on grounds of public policy.[95] Where Article VIII(2)(b) arises the court, having identified any monetary transaction—whether concealed or not—which constitutes a relevant exchange contract, must refuse to enforce the monetary transaction or any linked transaction or contract which, if enforced, would give effect to the monetary transaction.[96] In *Mansouri* v. *Singh*[97] the Court of Appeal decided that where parties to an exchange contract, which is unenforceable under Article VIII(2)(b), are also parties to a cheque—in circumstances in which it is intended and contemplated that the cheque will be used to give effect to and carry out obligations under the exchange contract—the court is obliged to refuse to enforce payment of the cheque. However, the Court of Appeal reserved its position on whether the same result would have been reached had the question concerned payment under a cheque to an innocent third party to whom the cheque had been negotiated. In this type of case, the court might take the view that the obligation under the cheque should not be regarded as giving effect to the exchange contract.[98]

91. [1976] QB 683. Corbett, "Exchange Contracts and the International Sale of Goods" [1977] LMCLQ 310; Crawford, (1976–77) 48 BYIL 337; Lipstein, [1976] CLJ 203.

92. Gold, " 'Exchange Contracts', Exchange Control and the IMF Articles of Agreement: Some Animadversions on Wilson, Smithett & Cope Ltd v. Terruzzi" (1984) 33 ICLQ 777; Merrills, "Interpretation of the Bretton Woods Agreement" (1977) 26 ICLQ 218.

93. [1983] 1 AC 168. Collier, [1983] CLJ 49; Crawford, (1982) 53 BYIL 288; Mann, "Documentary Credits and Bretton Woods" (1982) 98 LQR 526.

94. *United City Merchants (Investments) Ltd* v. *Royal Bank of Canada* [1983] 1 AC 168.

95. Mann, *The Legal Aspect of Money* (5th ed, 1992) pp. 368–369.

96. Neill LJ in *Mansouri* v. *Singh* [1986] 1 WLR 1393, 1403.

97. [1986] 1 WLR 1393. Crawford, (1986–86) 57 BYIL 421.

98. Neill LJ in *Mansouri* v. *Singh* [1986] 1 WLR 1393, 1404.

CHAPTER 15

FOREIGN LIMITATION PERIODS

15.1 THE FOREIGN LIMITATION PERIODS ACT 1984[1]

The Foreign Limitation Periods Act 1984, which implemented the recommendations of the Law Commission,[2] came into force on 1 October 1985. The Act has no application to proceedings commenced before that date[3] and the Act's provisions cannot have the effect of reviving a claim which was already time barred under the old law at the time of the Act's entry into force.[4] The 1984 Act applies to proceedings by or against the Crown[5] and to arbitrations.[6]

15.1.1 The general principle

15.1.1.1 The 1984 Act provides that questions of limitation are to be governed by the *lex causae* (which may or may not be English law). Section 1 states:

(1) Subject to the following provisions of this Act, where in any action or proceedings in a court in England and Wales the law of any other country falls (in accordance with rules of private international law applicable by any such court) to be taken into account in the determination of any matter—

(a) the law of that other country relating to limitation shall apply in respect of that matter for the purposes of the action or proceedings; and

(b) except where that matter falls within subsection (2) below, the law of England and Wales relating to limitation shall not so apply.

(2) A matter falls within this subsection if it is a matter in the determination of which both the law of England and Wales and the law of some other country fall to be taken into account.

(3) The law of England and Wales shall determine for the purposes of any law applicable by virtue of subsection (1)(a) above whether, and the time at which, proceedings have been commenced in respect of any matter; and, accordingly, section 35 of the Limitation Act 1980 (new claims in pending proceedings) shall apply in relation to time limits applicable by virtue of subsection (1)(a) above as it applies in relation to time limits under that Act.

(4) A court in England and Wales, in exercising in pursuance of subsection (1)(a) above any discretion conferred by the law of any other country, shall so far as practicable exercise that discretion in the manner in which it is exercised in comparable cases by the courts of that other country.

1. Carter, "The Foreign Limitation Periods Act 1984" (1985) 101 LQR 68; Stone, "Time Limitation in the English Conflict of Laws" [1985] LMCLQ 497.
2. *Classification of Limitation in Private International Law*, Law Com No. 114 (1982).
3. Foreign Limitation Periods Act 1984, s. 7(3)(a).
4. Foreign Limitation Periods Act 1984, s. 7(3)(b). For a discussion of the position at common law see Dicey & Morris, *The Conflict of Laws* (12th ed, 1993) pp. 185–186.
5. Foreign Limitation Periods Act 1984, s. 6.
6. Foreign Limitation Periods Act 1984, s. 5.

(5) In this section "law", in relation to any country, shall not include rules of private international law applicable by the courts of that country or, in the case of England and Wales, this Act.

15.1.1.2 The effect of section 1 is that the applicable law determines whether or not the action is time barred (although English law determines the moment at which any action is commenced[7]). If the claim is time barred under the applicable law, but the foreign law confers on the court the power to extend the limitation period, the task of the English court is to approach the question in the same way as would the foreign court.[8] The doctrine of renvoi is excluded.[9]

15.1.1.3 In including section 1(2) in the 1984 Act the legislature clearly had in mind the double actionability rule which governs questions of choice of law in relation to torts committed abroad.[10] The double actionability rule requires that in order for a foreign tort to be actionable in England the defendant's action must constitute a tort in English law and must give rise to civil liability under the law of the place where the tort is committed (*lex loci delicti*).[11] The effect of section 1(2) is that the plaintiff's action may be time barred by either English law (as the *lex fori*) or the *lex loci delicti*.[12] Accordingly, the plaintiff must commence the action before the expiry of whichever is the shorter period.[13]

15.1.1.4 Section 1(1)(a) refers to "the law . . . relating to limitation". This is defined by section 4 of the 1984 Act:

(1) Subject to subsection (3) below, references in this Act to the law of any country (including England and Wales) relating to limitation shall, in relation to any matter, be construed as references to so much of the relevant law of that country as (in any manner) makes provision with respect to a limitation period applicable to the bringing of proceedings in respect of that matter in the courts of that country and shall include—

(a) references to so much of that law as relates to, and to the effect of, the application, extension, reduction or interruption of that period; and

(b) a reference, where under that law there is no limitation period which is so applicable, to the rule that such proceedings may be brought within an indefinite period.

(2) In subsection (1) above "relevant law", in relation to any country, means the procedural and substantive law applicable, apart from any rules of private international law, by the courts of that country.

(3) References in this Act to the law of England and Wales relating to limitation shall not include the rules by virtue of which a court may, in the exercise of any discretion, refuse equitable relief on the grounds of acquiescence or otherwise; but, in applying those rules to a case in relation to which the law of any country outside England and Wales is applicable by virtue of section 1(1)(a) above (not being a law that provides for a limitation period that has expired), a court in England and Wales shall have regard, in particular, to the provisions of the law that is so applicable.

15.1.1.5 Section 4(3) preserves the equitable doctrine of laches, under which an English court may refuse to grant equitable relief on account of the plaintiff's delay. There is, however, a check on the court's discretion; when exercising its discretion, the court must have regard to the relevant foreign limitation period.

7. Foreign Limitation Periods Act 1984, s. 1(3).
8. Foreign Limitation Periods Act 1984, s. 1(4).
9. Foreign Limitation Periods Act 1984, ss. 1(5) and 4(2).
10. Slade LJ in *Metall und Rohstoff AG* v. *Donaldson Lufkin & Jenrette Inc* [1990] 1 QB 391, 438.
11. See para. 13.3.3.
12. *Société Commerciale de Réassurance* v. *ERAS International Ltd* [1992] 1 Lloyd's Rep. 570, 604.
13. *Arab Monetary Fund* v. *Hashim* [1993] 1 Lloyd's Rep 543.

15.1.2 Public policy and undue hardship

The general approach in section 1 is subject to the possibility of the English court deciding to disapply the foreign limitation period on the ground of public policy. Section 2 of the 1984 Act provides:

(1) In any case in which the application of section 1 above would to any extent conflict (whether under subsection (2) below or otherwise) with public policy, that section shall not apply to the extent that its application would so conflict.

(2) The application of section 1 above in relation to any action or proceedings shall conflict with public policy to the extent that its application would cause undue hardship to a person who is, or might be made, a party to the action or proceedings.

(3) Where, under a law applicable by virtue of section 1(1)(a) above for the purposes of any action or proceedings, a limitation period is or may be extended or interrupted in respect of the absence of a party to the action or proceedings from any specified jurisdiction or country, so much of that law as provides for the extension or interruption shall be disregarded for those purposes.

15.1.2.1 Undue hardship: section 2(2)

15.1.2.1.1 In order for the court to have to resort to section 2(2) the application of section 1 must cause undue hardship to one of the parties. Although it seems likely that section 2(2) will be invoked most frequently by a plaintiff whose claim is statute barred under the applicable law, the section "applies equally whether the application of a long limitation period deprives the defendant of his defence, or a short period the plaintiff of his claim".[14]

15.1.2.1.2 Section 27 of the Arbitration Act 1950 provides that contractual time limits for the commencement of arbitration may be extended by the court in cases where their application would cause "undue hardship".[15] In *Liberian Shipping Corporation "Pegasus"* v. *A King & Sons Ltd* Lord Denning MR said, in relation to this statutory provision: " 'Undue' simply means excessive. That is greater hardship than the circumstances warrant. Even though a claimant has been at fault himself, it is an undue hardship on him if the consequences are out of proportion to his fault."[16] This passage has been cited with approval in the context of cases concerning the operation of section 2 of the 1984 Act.[17] It would, however, be wrong to import into section 2 a balancing exercise of factors affecting both the plaintiff and defendant by analogy with the approach applied to section 27 of the Arbitration Act 1950.[18] In deciding whether a plaintiff whose claim is time barred under the applicable law has suffered undue hardship within the meaning of section 2, the court must look at the circumstances of the plaintiff and decide whether he has suffered hardship of an undue or excessive character.[19]

15.1.2.1.3 Section 2 is intended to have a narrow application.[20] The courts must be careful not to nullify the policy of section 1 by disapplying under section 2(2) the limitation rules which form part of the applicable law simply on the basis that the foreign

14. Evans J in *Arab Monetary Fund* v. *Hashim* [1993] 1 Lloyd's Rep 543, 592.
15. See para. 16.2.3.1.3.3.
16. [1967] 2 QB 86, 98.
17. *Jones* v. *Trollope Colls Cementation Overseas Ltd*, *The Times*, 26 January 1990; *Arab Monetary Fund* v. *Hashim* [1993] 1 Lloyd's Rep 543.
18. As in *The Aspen Trader* [1981] 1 Lloyd's Rep 273.
19. Farquharson LJ in *Jones* v. *Trollope Colls Cementation Overseas Ltd*, *The Times*, 26 January 1990.
20. Evans J in *Arab Monetary Fund* v. *Hashim* [1993] 1 Lloyd's Rep 543, 592.

limitation period is shorter than the English period. Whenever a limitation defence succeeds, in one sense the plaintiff suffers hardship by virtue of the fact that the claim is defeated. However, unless the applicable limitation period is remarkably short, it cannot be said that plaintiff suffers undue hardship merely by reason of the fact that the foreign limitation rule is applied. In each case there must be some additional factors which make the hardship excessive in the particular circumstances.

15.1.2.1.4 In *Jones* v. *Trollope Colls Cementation Overseas Ltd*,[21] for example, the plaintiff, who had been injured in a road accident in Pakistan, started proceedings in England against the driver's employer. Not long after the accident the plaintiff had been flown to Germany, where she spent seven months in hospital. Although the proceedings in England were commenced within the three year limitation period, the claim was time barred under the law of Pakistan, where the limitation period was one year. The Court of Appeal held that the application of section 1 would cause undue hardship to the plaintiff and therefore disapplied the foreign limitation under section 2(2). Of particular significance was the fact that before starting proceedings in England the plaintiff had been in correspondence with a representative of the defendant who had made statements suggesting that her claim would be settled by the defendant's insurers. Similarly, in *The Komninos S*[22] it was decided that undue hardship would be caused to the plaintiff if the defendant were allowed to rely on a foreign limitation period when, at an earlier stage of the proceedings, the defendant had agreed to an extension of time (albeit an extension which was ineffective under the applicable law).

15.1.2.2 Public policy

Although the first two subsections of section 2 are "difficult to construe together", it would seem that "undue hardship is an example of a conflict with public policy and that there are other potential grounds of conflict".[23] In practice, however, there are likely to be few situations in which a foreign limitation period which allegedly conflicts with English public policy would not cause undue hardship to one of the parties.

15.1.2.3 The effects of disapplying the foreign limitation period under section 2

It was argued in *The Komninos S*[24] that in a situation where the foreign limitation period is disapplied, the position is governed by the common law, with the consequence that, if the foreign limitation period is regarded as substantive, the plaintiff's claim is barred. This argument was rejected by the Court of Appeal; once a foreign limitation period has been disapplied by virtue of section 2, it has no role to play and cannot form part of the applicable law which governs the substantive rights of the parties.[25] So, in cases where the foreign limitation period is disapplied under section 2 which limitation rules, if any, should the English court apply? Although in *The Komninos S* the Court of Appeal declined to decide whether no limitation period applies, or whether English limitation

21. *The Times*, 26 January 1990.
22. [1991] 1 Lloyd's Rep 370.
23. Farquharson LJ in *Jones* v. *Trollope Colls Cementation Overseas Ltd*, *The Times*, 26 January 1990 (Lexis transcript).
24. [1991] 1 Lloyd's Rep 370.
25. [1991] 1 Lloyd's Rep 370, 377. See also Evans J in *Arab Monetary Fund* v. *Hashim* [1993] 1 Lloyd's Rep 543, 593.

rules apply, the latter alternative was the one which was thought to be clearly preferable.[26]

15.2 THE ROME CONVENTION

As regards contractual obligations falling within the scope of the Rome Convention on the Law Applicable to Contractual Obligations section 1 the 1984 Act has been superseded by Article 10(1)(d) of the Convention which states that the applicable law shall govern "the various ways of extinguishing obligations, and prescription and limitation of actions".[27] In its effect Article 10(1)(d) is no different from section 1(1) of the 1984 Act.

Whereas section 2 of the 1984 Act allows the English court to disapply a foreign limitation rule on grounds of public policy (which includes cases of undue hardship), Article 16 of the Convention provides that the courts may refuse to apply a foreign rule the application of which is manifestly incompatible with the public policy of the forum. It is clear that Article 16 is meant to be invoked only exceptionally.

26. [1991] 1 Lloyd's Rep 370, 377.
27. See para. 11.4.8.

PART III

ARBITRATION

CHAPTER 16

ARBITRATION: INTRODUCTION

16.1 WHAT IS ARBITRATION?

16.1.1 There are various general characteristics of arbitration which distinguish it from litigation. Perhaps the most fundamental aspect of the arbitral process is that it is built on the foundation of the agreement of the parties. Whereas the jurisdiction of the courts is derived directly from the law, the jurisdiction of an arbitrator is derived from the arbitration agreement itself. Furthermore, unlike litigation which is public, arbitration is essentially a private mechanism for the resolution of disputes. This, indeed, is one of its attractions.[1] Although it is sometimes asserted that the essence of arbitration is to enable parties to a dispute to obtain a speedy and cheap decision without having recourse to the courts,[2] in the international context commercial arbitration is rarely cheap and can be a very lengthy process.

16.1.2 There are, however, certain ways in which arbitration resembles litigation. An award is not a negotiated settlement; it is a decision which is reached by the application of rules of law. In this respect arbitration is clearly distinguishable from mediation and conciliation. Moreover, from a procedural point of view there is a common principle to both litigation and arbitration; it is fundamental that the parties should have a right to a fair hearing.

16.1.3 The undertaking to arbitrate involves three major commitments: (i) an immediate irrevocable obligation to refer a dispute to arbitration; (ii) an obligation to settle the dispute by means of arbitration in preference and prior to any other type of legal proceedings; and (iii) an obligation to honour the award of the arbitrator.[3]

16.2 OUTLINE OF ENGLISH ARBITRATION LAW

16.2.1 What is arbitration law?

The focus of arbitration law is the relationship between the courts and the arbitral process. In the final analysis, the effectiveness of arbitration as a dispute resolution mechanism depends on the coercive powers which the State entrusts to its courts. In the

1. See Kerr, "International Arbitration v. Litigation" [1980] JBL 164.
2. For example, see the opinion of Advocate-General Reischl in Case 102/81 *Nordsee Deutsche Hochseefischerei GmbH* v. *Reederei Mond Hochseefischerei AG & Co KG* [1982] ECR 1095, 1122.
3. Fox, "States and the Undertaking to Arbitrate" (1988) 37 ICLQ 1.

absence of voluntary compliance by the parties, it is the exercise of the coercive powers of the State which determines whether the acts of arbitrators are effective or ineffective.[4] The fundamental question therefore is not whether the court should play a role in the arbitral process but what the limits of that role should be. Arbitration law defines the nature and extent of the court's powers in relation to the arbitral process.

16.2.2 The sources of English arbitration law

English arbitration law is a complex combination of statute and case law. The Arbitration Act 1950, a consolidation of a number of earlier statutes, contains a detailed framework of powers which the courts may exercise in relation to the arbitral process. The 1950 Act has itself been supplemented by the Arbitration Act 1975 (which implements the New York Convention of 1958) and the Arbitration Act 1979 (which regulates the right of appeal to the court on a point of law). These statutes have been described as "incoherent and fragmentary".[5] There are many questions on which the statutes are silent; these are regulated by the common law. Furthermore, there are numerous statutory provisions whose effect can only be explained by reference to the decided cases.

16.2.3 The powers of the court

In relation to disputes which the parties have agreed to refer to arbitration the court serves two functions; on the one hand, the court provides assistance and support and, on the other, it supervises and controls. The control exercised by the court over the arbitral process is the price which has to be paid for the court's support. The State cannot reasonably be expected to allow a court of law to exercise its coercive powers to compel enforcement of an award unless it is satisfied that the arbitral procedure and the resulting award meet certain minimum standards. If, for example, the arbitral procedure has not complied with the basic requirements of due process, the State is justified in refusing to allow its sovereign powers to be used to obtain enforcement of the award.[6]

16.2.3.1 Assistance and support

16.2.3.1.1 ENFORCING THE AGREEMENT TO ARBITRATE[7]

Where proceedings are brought in England in breach of the terms of an arbitration agreement the proceedings will generally be stayed, thereby forcing the claimant to have recourse to the agreed method of dispute resolution. In international cases, if certain conditions are satisfied, the grant of a stay of proceedings is mandatory.

16.2.3.1.2 THE CONSTITUTION OF THE ARBITRAL TRIBUNAL

Often the arbitration agreement provides, either directly or indirectly, the mechanism for the appointment of the arbitrator or arbitrators. For example, an *ad hoc* arbitration clause may provide for a sole arbitrator to be appointed by agreement of the parties;

4. Kerr, "Arbitration and the Courts: the UNCITRAL Model Law" (1985) 34 ICLQ 1.
5. Mustill, "Transnational Arbitration in English Law" [1984] CLP 133, 136.
6. Craig, "Uses and Abuses of Appeal from Awards" (1988) 4 Arb Int 174, 182.
7. See Chapter 18.

alternatively, the agreement may make provision for a tribunal of three, with each party appointing one arbitrator and these two arbitrators appointing the third. A well drafted clause also nominates an appointing authority (such as the President of the LCIA) so that the tribunal can be established in cases of a failure to appoint or disagreement. If the parties agree to institutional arbitration the rules of the institution provide a comprehensive scheme which ensures that the tribunal will be properly constituted. However, in cases where the arbitration agreement does not include a watertight set of provisions for the proper constitution of the tribunal, the court may be called upon to appoint an arbitrator under section 10 of the 1950 Act.

16.2.3.1.3 EXTENDING TIME LIMITS

16.2.3.1.3.1 A civil claim may be barred by lapse of time under the Limitation Act 1980. The statutory period of limitation applies to arbitrations in the same way as to court actions.[8] For the purposes of the 1980 Act an arbitration is commenced when one party serves on the other a notice which calls upon the other party to appoint an arbitrator or to agree to the appointment of an arbitrator or to submit the dispute to a person designated by the arbitration agreement.[9] The notice, which must also contain some information about the dispute, must be served in one of the methods prescribed by the legislation[10] or by some other agreed method (such as post or telex).

16.2.3.1.3.2 Many arbitration clauses stipulate time limits which are much shorter than the statutory limitation period, which in most cases is six years.[11] Such clauses normally provide that a claim which is not brought within the stipulated time—for example, fourteen days or three months—is barred.[12] If the time limit for making a claim is allowed to elapse, the arbitrator ceases to have jurisdiction over the matter.

16.2.3.1.3.3 The 1950 Act empowers the court to extend time limits in cases of undue hardship.[13] Section 27 provides:

> Where the terms of an agreement to refer future disputes to arbitration provide that any claims to which the agreement applies shall be barred unless notice to appoint an arbitrator is given or an arbitrator is appointed or some other step to commence arbitration proceedings is taken within a time fixed by the agreement, and a dispute arises to which the agreement applies, the High Court, if it is of the opinion that in the circumstances of the case undue hardship[14] would otherwise be

8. Limitation Act 1980, s. 34(1).
9. Limitation Act 1980, s. 34(3).
10. Limitation Act 1980, s. 34(4).
11. Limitation Act 1980, s. 5.
12. The courts have drawn a distinction between (i) clauses which bar the claim and (ii) clauses which bar the right to arbitration. In the second category of case, once the time limit has expired the arbitrator has no jurisdiction, but the claim is not barred and may be pursued by litigation. See Mustill & Boyd, *Commercial Arbitration* (2nd ed, 1989) pp. 202–204.
13. Thomas, "Power of Court to Extend Time For Commencing Arbitration Proceedings" [1981] LMCLQ 529.
14. The words "undue hardship" are not defined by Act. The following principles were laid down by Brandon LJ in *The Aspen Trader* [1981] 1 Lloyd's Rep 273, 279 and approved by the House of Lords in *Comdel Commodities Ltd* v. *Siporex Trade SA (No. 2)* [1991] 1 AC 148. (i) The words "undue hardship" should not be construed too narrowly. (ii) "Undue hardship" means excessive hardship and, where the hardship is the fault of the claimant, it means hardship the consequence of which is out of proportion to such fault. (iii) In deciding whether to extend time, the court should look at all the relevant circumstances of the case. (iv) In particular the following matters should be considered: the length of the delay; the amount at stake; whether the delay was due to the fault of the claimant or to circumstances outside his control; if it was due to the claimant's fault, the degree of fault; whether the claimant was misled by the respondent; whether the respondent has been prejudiced by the delay and, if so, the degree of such prejudice.

caused, and notwithstanding that the time so fixed has expired, may, on such terms, if any, as the justice of the case may require, but without prejudice to the provisions of any enactment limiting the time for the commencement of arbitration proceedings, extend the time for such period as it thinks proper.

The power in section 27 applies not only in cases where the arbitration clause imposes an absolute time limit, but also in cases where the agreement confers a discretion on the arbitrator to extend the contractual period in which a claim must be brought.[15]

16.2.3.1.4 THE CONDUCT OF PROCEEDINGS

16.2.3.1.4.1 The court has various powers in relation to the conduct of proceedings. Specific powers in relation to arbitration are contained in section 12(6) of the 1950 Act, which provides:

The High Court shall have, for the purpose of and in relation to a reference, the same power of making orders in respect of—

(a) security for costs;

. .

(c) the giving of evidence by affidavit;

(d) examination on oath of any witness before an officer of the High Court or any other person, and the issue of a commission or request for the examination of a witness out of the jurisdiction;

(e) the preservation, interim custody, or sale of any goods which are the subject matter of the reference;

(f) securing the amount in dispute in the reference;

(g) the detention, preservation or inspection of any property or thing which is the subject of the reference or as to which any question may arise therein, and authorising for any of the purposes aforesaid any persons to enter upon or into any land or building in the possession of any party to the reference, or authorising any samples to be taken or any observation to be made or experiment to be tried which may be necessary or expedient for the purpose of obtaining full information or evidence; and

(h) interim injunctions or the appointment of a receiver;

as it has for the purpose of and in relation to an action or matter in the High Court:

Provided that nothing in this subsection shall be taken to prejudice any power which may be vested in an arbitrator or umpire of making orders with respect to any of the matters aforesaid.

16.2.3.1.4.2 One of the most important aspects of the court's support of the arbitral process is the power to grant interim measures under section 12(6)(h). The proviso to section 12 makes it clear, however, that the powers of the arbitrator co-exist with those enjoyed by the court. Where the parties have adopted institutional arbitration rules, those rules invariably confer on the arbitrator the necessary power to order provisional measures. For example, Article 26(1) of the UNCITRAL Arbitration Rules provides:

At the request of either party, the arbitral tribunal may take any interim measures it deems necessary in respect of the subject matter of the dispute, including measures for the conservation of the goods forming the subject matter in dispute, such as ordering their deposit with a third person or the sale of perishable goods.

16.2.3.1.4.3 Although, by virtue of section 12(1) of the 1950 Act, an arbitration agreement is deemed to contain a provision imposing an obligation on the parties to

15. *Comdel Commodities Ltd* v. *Siporex Trade SA (No. 2)* [1991] 1 AC 148.

submit to be examined by the arbitrator, to produce documents, and "to do all such other things which during the proceedings on the reference the arbitrator ... may require", the arbitrator's lack of formal coercive powers prevents him from granting some of the most potent interim measures. For instance, since an arbitrator may not direct orders to third parties, he cannot effectively make a Mareva-type order freezing a bank account. Moreover, if the assistance of the court is required as a result of the failure by one of the parties to comply with the arbitrator's order the element of surprise is lost. Accordingly, there are many situations where an application to the court for interim measures is either the only available course of action or is the most effective one to pursue.

In addition to the specific powers contained in section 12(6) of the 1950 Act, general powers are conferred by section 37(1) of the Supreme Court Act 1981.[16]

16.2.3.1.5 ENFORCEMENT OF THE AWARD

Many awards are complied with by the losing party voluntarily. Where, however, the losing party fails to honour an award, the successful party will have to apply to the court for enforcement. The court's powers in relation to domestic awards exist both at common law and under section 26 of the 1950 Act. As regards foreign awards, the position is regulated by common law and statute (most notably, the 1975 Act).[17]

16.2.3.2 Supervision and control

The supervisory role of the court is based on the common law and on a number of statutory powers. The function of control is exercised by denying effect to an arbitration agreement, by removing an arbitrator, by setting aside the award or by reviewing the award on procedural or substantive grounds.

16.2.3.2.1 THE PROBLEM OF DELAY[18]

16.2.3.2.1.1 In the context of litigation, the court may dismiss an action for want of prosecution in cases where the plaintiff is guilty of excessive delay. However, at common law, the court does not have similar powers in relation to arbitration proceedings. Furthermore, an arbitrator has no inherent power to dismiss arbitration proceedings for want of prosecution. In *Bremer Vulkan Schiffbau und Maschinenfabrik* v. *South India Shipping Corporation Ltd*[19] the House of Lords rejected the argument that the court could bring an arbitration to an end merely on the basis of the claimant's delay. According to the analysis of Lord Diplock, an arbitration involves more than one agreement; a distinction has to be drawn between (i) the main agreement under which the parties agree to refer future disputes to arbitration and (ii) the secondary contract to arbitrate which arises when a particular dispute is referred to arbitration. In principle,

16. For the text of this provision see para. 21.1.1.2.
17. See Chapter 20.
18. For a comprehensive account of the development of English law in this area see Owsia, "Consensual Abandonment of Contract: Innovatory Developments under English Law in the Eighties Concerning Arbitration References" (1991) 8 J Int Arb (4) 55. For a discussion of the ways in which a respondent may slow down an arbitration see Harris, "Abuse of the Arbitration Process—Delaying Tactics and Disruptions" (1992) 9 J Int Arb (2) 87.
19. [1981] AC 909.

both the arbitration agreement and the secondary contract to arbitrate may be brought to an end in the same way as any other contract—for example, by repudiatory breach, by frustration or by consensual abandonment.

16.2.3.2.1.2 Where a claimant, who is guilty of inordinate delay, seeks to revive an arbitration which has been allowed to go to sleep, it would seem reasonable to treat the secondary contract to arbitrate as having come to an end. However, in the *Bremer Vulkan* case Lord Diplock took the view that an arbitration agreement does not simply impose an obligation on the claimant to prosecute the claim: "the obligation is ... mutual; it obliges each party to co-operate with the other in taking appropriate steps to keep the procedure in the arbitration moving, whether he happens to be the claimant or the respondent in the particular dispute".[20] On the basis of this analysis if the claimant is not in breach of any order made by the arbitrator and the respondent has done nothing to accelerate the procedure, delay by the claimant cannot be treated as a repudiatory breach.

16.2.3.2.1.3 Although the decision in the *Bremer Vulkan* case was "immediately and universally regarded as wrong",[21] it was upheld by the House of Lords two years later in *Paal Wilson & Co A/S* v. *Partenreederei Hannah Blumenthal*[22]—a case in which it was held that the secondary contract to arbitrate cannot be regarded as discharged by frustration simply on account of the claimant's delay. A second opportunity to reconsider the law was presented by *Food Corporation of India* v. *Antclizo Shipping Corporation*.[23] In this case it was argued that, in the situation where the claimant fails to prosecute the claim with reasonable dispatch, the secondary contract to arbitrate should be regarded as having been brought to an end by the agreement of the parties. Of course, if there is an express agreement the position is clear. However, since such an agreement is rare, the important issue is to identify the circumstances in which it is possible to imply or infer an agreement to terminate a reference. It would seem that an agreement to abandon may be inferred only if one party acts in such a way that his conduct, objectively considered, constitutes an offer and the other party, believing that the conduct of the first represents his actual intention, accepts that offer. In the absence of special circumstances, mere silence and inaction cannot give rise to an agreement to abandon.[24] Nevertheless, it may be possible to infer such an agreement where the period of silence is so long that all possibilities other than an inferred agreement to abandon are plainly excluded, or at least that an agreement to abandon is the most probable inference.[25]

16.2.3.2.1.4 Since the common law has proved singularly incapable of dealing with stale arbitrations, Parliament has twice sought to deal with the practical problems of delay.

(i) Under section 5(2) of the 1979 Act the court may specifically confer on an arbitrator power "to continue with the reference in default of appearance or of any other act by one of the parties in like manner as a judge of the High Court might

20. [1981] AC 909, 983.
21. Mann, "The Antclizo, Missed Opportunities by the English House of Lords" (1988) 4 Arb Int 158.
22. [1983] 1 AC 854; Lewis, "When Arbitration Proceedings Become Stale" [1983] LMCLQ 289.
23. [1988] 1 WLR 603; Davenport, "Stale Arbitrations" [1985] LMCLQ 293.
24. *Food Corporation of India* v. *Antclizo Shipping Corporation* [1988] 1 WLR 603; *Allied Marine Transport Ltd* v. *Vale do Rio Doce Navegaçao SA* [1985] 1 WLR 925.
25. *Unisys International Services Ltd* v. *Eastern Counties Newspapers Ltd* [1991] 1 Lloyd's Rep 538.

continue with proceedings in that court when a party fails to comply with an order of that court or a requirement of rules of court". This provision, which in any event is not ideally suited to cases of delay on the part of the claimant, has not been a great success. It seems that the procedure, which is cumbersome, has been little used in practice.[26]

(ii) Following the recommendations of the Mustill Committee,[27] the 1950 Act was amended to give arbitrators the power to dismiss a claim for want of prosecution. Section 13A of the 1950 Act, which came into force on 1 January 1992, provides:

> (1) Unless a contrary intention is expressed in the arbitration agreement, the arbitrator or umpire shall have power to make an award dismissing any claim in any dispute referred to him if it appears to him that the conditions mentioned in subsection (2) are satisfied.
> (2) The conditions are—
> (a) that there has been inordinate and inexcusable delay on the part of the claimant in pursuing the claim; and
> (b) that the delay—
> (i) will give rise to a substantial risk that it is not possible to have a fair resolution of the issues in that claim; or
> (ii) has caused, or is likely to cause or to have caused, serious prejudice to the respondent.[28]

Section 13A entitles an arbitrator to dismiss a claim for want of prosecution on the basis of inexcusable delay, whether before or after the section's entry into force.[29]

16.2.3.2.2 INTERVENTION DURING THE CONDUCT OF AN ARBITRATION

16.2.3.2.2.1 The court may decide that the arbitration agreement shall cease to have effect in cases where the dispute involves the question whether one of the parties has been guilty of fraud.[30] More generally, the court may order that the arbitration agreement shall cease to have effect with respect to a dispute which has been referred to arbitration.[31] This general power is "likely to be reserved for cases where the arbitration has gone irreparably wrong".[32]

16.2.3.2.2.2 As for the removal of an arbitrator the 1950 Act contains a number of important provisions. Section 24(1) provides that the court may grant an injunction to restrain arbitration proceedings or give leave for a party to revoke the authority of an arbitrator on the ground that the arbitrator "is not or may not be impartial"; it is not a ground for refusing the application that the applicant "at the time when he made the agreement knew, or ought to have known, that the arbitrator, by reason of his relation towards any other party to the agreement or of his connection with the subject referred, might not be capable of impartiality". Furthermore, the court may remove an arbitrator who has "misconducted himself or the proceedings"[33] or "who fails to use all reasonable

26. See, however, *Sumitomo Heavy Industries Ltd* v. *Oil & Natural Gas Commission* [1994] 1 Lloyd's Rep 45; *Waverley SF Ltd* v. *Carnand Metalbox Engineering Plc* [1994] 1 Lloyd's Rep 38.

27. Departmental Advisory Committee on Arbitration Law, *A Report on the UNCITRAL Model Law on International Commercial Arbitration* (1989). Thomas, "Arbitral Delay and the Recommendations of the Departmental Advisory Committee" [1990] JBL 110.

28. For a criticism of the drafting of section 13A see Miller, "Another Blunder Hits the Statute Book" (1992) 142 NLJ 1421.

29. *L'Office Cherifien des Phosphates* v. *Yamashita-Shinnihon Steamship Co Ltd* [1994] 2 WLR 39.

30. Arbitration Act 1950, s. 24(2).

31. Arbitration Act 1950, s. 25(2)(b).

32. Mustill & Boyd, *Commercial Arbitration* (2nd ed, 1989) p. 500. See, for example, *Pratt* v. *Swanmore Builders Ltd* [1980] 2 Lloyd's Rep 504.

33. Arbitration Act 1950, s. 23(1).

dispatch in entering on and proceeding with the reference and making an award".[34] Section 25 confers powers on the court to appoint a replacement in cases where an arbitrator has been removed or his authority has been revoked.

16.2.3.2.3 COSTS AND FEES

The legislation gives the court a degree of control over the costs of an arbitration and the arbitrator's fees. Although costs are normally within the discretion of the arbitrator,[35] costs directed by an award to be paid are "taxable in the High Court".[36] Furthermore, in certain circumstances, the court may, on application by one of the parties, order that the arbitrator's fees "shall be taxed by the taxing officer" and that the arbitrator should receive only "such sum as may be found reasonable on taxation".[37]

16.2.3.2.4 RECOURSE AGAINST THE AWARD[38]

16.2.3.2.4.1 There are three different types of recourse against an arbitral award.

(i) It may be possible to appeal to the courts on the merits.

(ii) A party to an arbitration may apply to have the award set aside on the basis of some procedural or other irregularity. If an award is set aside, it is a nullity; it is as if the award had never been made. If only part of the award is set aside, only that part is a nullity; the rest remains valid.

(iii) As an alternative to setting aside, the court may remit the award to the arbitrator for further consideration. Remission, which is a less draconian remedy than setting aside, may be appropriate in a case where the parties have referred a number of issues to the arbitrator, but the award does not determine all of them. If only part of an award is remitted, the arbitrator may reconsider only the part of the award which has been remitted.

16.2.3.2.4.2 Under English law all three forms of recourse are potentially available. Whereas the right of appeal on a point of law may be excluded by the agreement of the parties, the supervisory jurisdiction of the court to set aside or remit an award may not. The 1979 Act regulates the right of appeal to the court on a point of law.[39] The jurisdiction to set aside an award is conferred by the 1950 Act. Section 22(1) of the 1950 Act provides:

> In all cases of reference to arbitration the High Court or a judge thereof may from time to time remit the matters referred, or any of them, to the reconsideration of the arbitrator or umpire.

The power of the court to set aside an arbitrator's award is to be found in section 23(2):

> Where an arbitrator or umpire has misconducted himself or the proceedings, or an arbitration or award has been improperly procured, the High Court may set the award aside.

16.2.3.2.4.3 There is considerable overlap between the grounds on which an award

34. Arbitration Act 1950, s. 13(3).
35. Arbitration Act 1950, s. 18(1).
36. Arbitration Act 1950, s. 18(2).
37. Arbitration Act 1950, s. 19(1).
38. For some comparative observations see Davidson, "The Relationship between Arbitration and the Courts in Scotland and England" (1993) 12 CJQ 372; Kerameus, "Waiver of Setting Aside Procedures in International Arbitration" (1993) 41 Am J Comp L 73.
39. This issue is discussed in Chapter 19.

may be remitted or set aside; the court has a broad discretion in deciding whether or not to intervene and, if intervention is justified, what action is most appropriate. Where an application is made to the court to set aside an award, the court may decide to remit the award instead. As a general rule, if the court decides to intervene it is more likely to remit than to set aside. Setting aside is fairly rare and tends to be limited to cases of serious irregularity.

16.2.3.2.4.4 Most cases in which the court decides to exercise its power to remit or set aside fall into one of four categories: (i) the award is bad on its face (for example, where the award does not resolve the disputed issues); (ii) the arbitrator has admitted a mistake and wishes the mistake to be corrected; (iii) fresh evidence has arisen after the making of the award; (iv) the arbitrator has "misconducted" himself. Misconduct includes the rare situations where there is fraud, corruption, bribery or bias, but also—more commonly—some form of technical error in the conduct or procedure of the arbitration. Most cases of misconduct involve either a failure to conduct the reference in accordance with the terms of the arbitration agreement (for example, where the arbitrator acts without jurisdiction) or a breach of public policy or a departure from the principles of natural justice.

16.2.3.2.4.5 These four categories are not, however, exhaustive. For example:

> [T]he remission jurisdiction extends beyond the four traditional grounds to any case where, notwithstanding that the arbitrators have acted with complete propriety, due to mishap or misunderstanding, some aspect of the dispute which has been the subject of the reference has not been considered and adjudicated upon as fully or in a manner which the parties were entitled to expect and it would be inequitable to allow the award to take effect without some further consideration by the arbitrator.[40]

16.2.3.2.4.6 The court's power to intervene in cases of misconduct cannot be used as an excuse for backdoor tampering with the merits of an arbitration. The purpose of the power to remit or set aside is to guarantee the fundamental integrity of the arbitral process.[41] Accordingly, the power to remit "cannot be used merely to enable the arbitrator to correct errors of judgment, whether on fact or law, or to have second thoughts, even if they would be better thoughts".[42] The only way in which errors of law can be corrected is by an appeal under the 1979 Act; a simple error of law does not entitle the court to remit or set aside the award for misconduct.[43]

16.3 VARIOUS TYPES OF ARBITRATION

16.3.1 Domestic and international

16.3.1.1 Arbitration, like litigation, may be entirely domestic or it may involve a foreign element. Where all the elements relevant to an arbitration are connected with England English law governs the validity of the agreement, the procedure to be followed, the availability of interlocutory orders, the form of the award, the grounds on which the award may be challenged and the enforcement of the award. However, many arbitrations which take place in England have connections with other countries.

40. Lord Donaldson MR in *King* v. *Thomas McKenna Ltd* [1991] 2 QB 480, 492.
41. See, for example, *Bank Mellat* v. *GAA Development & Construction Co* [1988] 2 Lloyd's Rep 44.
42. Lord Donaldson MR in *King* v. *Thomas McKenna Ltd* [1991] 2 QB 480, 492.
43. *President of India* v. *Jadranska Slobodna Plovidba* [1992] 2 Lloyd's Rep 274.

16.3.1.2 There are three types of non-domestic arbitration arising from contractual obligations: (i) arbitration between States (or other international persons); (ii) arbitration between parties subject respectively to the jurisdiction of different States; and (iii) arbitration between States and private persons of foreign nationality or residence.[44] Only an arbitration within the first of these categories is truly international—in the sense that it is divorced from any municipal law and is submitted to public international law. The second and third categories are international in the sense that they are connected with more than one country; they are, however, normally governed, not by public international law, but by municipal law. (Although, as a general rule, an arbitration between a State and a private individual or corporation is subject to municipal law, arbitration under the auspices of the International Centre for the Resolution of Investment Disputes (ICSID) is wholly independent from municipal arbitration law—except as regards questions of enforcement.[45])

16.3.1.3 While under the laws of some countries the same legal rules apply to all arbitrations, many legal systems seek to distinguish domestic from international arbitrations with a view to relaxing the degree of control exercised by the courts in international cases. There are two areas in which English law draws such a distinction.

(i) Where proceedings are commenced in England in breach of an arbitration agreement, the court has a discretion to stay the proceedings in domestic cases, but a stay is mandatory in international cases.[46]
(ii) Whereas in domestic cases the right of appeal can be excluded only by agreement after the commencement of the arbitration, greater latitude is given to the parties in international cases.[47]

16.3.2 *Ad hoc* and institutional

16.3.2.1 The words "*ad hoc*" in relation to arbitration signify a situation where the parties conclude an agreement which provides a framework for the resolution of their disputes by arbitration without any assistance from an arbitration institution. A clause providing for *ad hoc* arbitration may set out in detail the procedures to be followed at all the various stages. It is not uncommon, however, for the parties to incorporate a set of arbitration rules—such as the UNCITRAL Arbitration Rules—into the arbitration agreement. The model arbitration clause suggested by the UNCITRAL Arbitration Rules is in the following form:

> Any dispute, controversy or claim arising out of this contract, or the breach, termination or invalidity thereof, shall be settled by arbitration in accordance with the UNCITRAL Arbitration Rules as at present in force.

The effect of this clause is to import into the arbitration agreement all the procedural elements contained in the Rules. If the parties choose *ad hoc* arbitration but decide not to use a set of arbitration rules there is a greater danger that it will be necessary to have resort to the court to supplement the arbitration agreement.

44. Mann, "State Contracts and International Arbitration" (1967) 42 BYIL 1.
45. See para. 20.5.4.
46. Arbitration Act 1950, s. 4 and Arbitration Act 1975, s. 1. For further discussion see Chapter 18.
47. See Chapter 19.

16.3.2.2 Institutional arbitration refers to an arbitration which is carried out under the auspices of an institution which administers the progress of the arbitration. There are some seventy such arbitration institutions around the world. Some of the more important are the International Chamber of Commerce (ICC),[48] the London Court of International Arbitration (LCIA),[49] the American Arbitration Association (AAA), the Stockholm Chamber of Commerce (SCC) and the Netherlands Arbitration Institute (NAI).[50] Generally, an institutional arbitration takes place according to the rules of the institution in question. So, where parties adopt the standard arbitration clause suggested by the ICC, the parties agree to an arbitration administered by the ICC and conducted according to the ICC Rules.

16.3.2.3 The institution has a number of functions: (i) it assists in the constitution of the tribunal if the parties do not specify in their agreement how the tribunal is to be appointed; (ii) it provides a mechanism for the challenge and replacement of arbitrators; and (iii) it provides the necessary back-up during the arbitration proceedings (such as the communication of documents). Furthermore, the fact that an award is obtained under the auspices of a well known institution adds international respectability to the award and reduces the chances of the losing party defaulting or resisting enforcement. There are, however, certain drawbacks to institutional arbitration. It can be very expensive since the institution requires payment for its services; these costs are in addition to the general costs of an arbitration (the arbitrator's fees and expenses, costs of hiring rooms, travelling costs, legal fees etc).

16.3.3 Specialised arbitrations

16.3.3.1 Arbitration in trade and commodity fields has developed along its own lines. There are many trade associations which have their own arbitration rules—such as the Federation of Oils, Seeds and Fats Association (FOSFA) and the Grain and Food Trade Association (GAFTA). Standard contracts entered into by members of these associations often incorporate the association's rules.

(i) Trade and commodity arbitrations are often of the "look and sniff"[51] variety. Many commodity disputes concern questions such as whether goods which have been sold by sample conform to the sample. In this type of case the task of the arbitrator involves factual rather than legal questions.

(ii) The arbitration rules of some trade associations provide that each party shall appoint an arbitrator, and that a third arbitrator shall be appointed only in case of disagreement between the party-appointed arbitrators. In this type of case the final award is made either by a tribunal of two, or by the third arbitrator, but not by a tribunal of three.

48. For detailed and comprehensive account of ICC arbitration see Craig, Park & Paulsson, *International Chamber of Commerce Arbitration* (2nd ed, 1990).

49. See Kerr, "The London Court of International Arbitration 1892–1992" (1992) 8 Arb Int 317; Lebedev, "The LCIA Rules for International Commercial Arbitration" (1992) 8 Arb Int 321.

50. For the arbitration rules of these institutions see Redfern & Hunter, *Law and Practice of International Commercial Arbitration* (2nd ed, 1991) pp. 541–553 (AAA), pp. 571–594 (ICC), pp. 619–629 (LCIA), pp. 645–677 (NAI), pp. 678–687 (SCC).

51. Donaldson J in *Faure, Fairclough Ltd* v. *Premier Oil & Cake Mills Ltd* [1968] 1 Lloyd's Rep 237, 238.

(iii) The arbitration rules of a trade association may exclude lawyers from the arbitral process.

16.3.3.2 Practice in the field of trade and commodity arbitration is not static, however, and trade associations regularly update their arbitration rules. It has been observed that:

> The modern trend is towards arbitrations which are conducted in accordance with generally accepted notions of openness and impartiality, rather than in accordance with a particular trade practice. Recent developments are directed towards affording the parties the opportunity to choose their own arbitral tribunal, rather than having it chosen for them by a trade association; towards a right for the parties to be represented by lawyers or advisers of their choice, rather than this being a matter of discretion; and towards the parties being able to insist upon an arbitral tribunal which may readily be seen to be independent and impartial.[52]

16.4 TRENDS IN COMMERCIAL ARBITRATION

16.4.1 Encouragement

The general trends in the second half of this century have been to encourage and facilitate international arbitration and to make it more effective. English law has encouraged arbitration in two ways.

(i) The court's supervisory role has been reduced. Since the entry into force of the 1979 Act the right of appeal to the court on a point of law can be excluded by the agreement of the parties.[53]

(ii) Enforcement of arbitration agreements and awards has been made much easier by the New York Convention of 1958, which was implemented in England by the 1975 Act.[54]

If a successful claimant is not confident of being able to enforce an award abroad arbitration in the non-domestic context remains a relatively unattractive prospect. As soon as enforcement abroad becomes readily available, arbitration becomes a more realistic alternative to the resolution of international disputes by litigation. Furthermore, the integrity of arbitral process is protected if courts are required to uphold the agreement of the parties to refer their disputes to arbitration.

16.4.2 Harmonisation

Arbitration law is rooted in national legal systems which enjoy different cultures and traditions. Even in those cases where arbitration involves parties from different countries, the arbitral process is nevertheless regulated by national legal systems, both as regards the conduct of the arbitration and the enforcement of the award. The second half of this century has seen developments—achieved largely through the work of the United Nations—aimed at bringing national arbitration laws closer together.

52. Redfern & Hunter, *Law and Practice of International Commercial Arbitration* (2nd ed, 1991) p. 53.
53. See para. 19.5.
54. See paras. 18.2 and 20.2.

16.4.2.1 The Geneva Protocol 1923 and the Geneva Convention 1927

Many legal systems have traditionally been suspicious of and hostile to arbitration. In the 1920s the international community took the first steps towards promoting international arbitration. These developments were accomplished with the backing of the League of Nations. The Geneva Protocol of 1923 was designed to promote the enforcement of arbitration clauses—which at that time were prohibited by many national laws—by imposing an obligation on national courts to refer to arbitration disputes in respect of which an arbitration agreement had been concluded. The Geneva Convention of 1927 sought to facilitate the enforcement of foreign awards. These conventions were no more than a limited success; they fell a long way short of guaranteeing the international enforcement of arbitral agreements and awards.

16.4.2.2 The New York Convention 1958

The New York Convention of 1958 is the most important development in international commercial arbitration this century. The 1958 Convention has been ratified by more than eighty States, including all the Member States of the EC with the exception of Portugal.[55] The Convention, which is a significant improvement on the earlier international instruments in the field of arbitration, is designed to achieve two things: (i) to ensure the respect of arbitration agreements by requiring national courts to decline jurisdiction over the merits of a dispute where the parties have agreed to arbitration[56]; and (ii) to provide a simple mechanism for the enforcement of foreign arbitral awards.[57]

16.4.2.3 UNCITRAL Arbitration Rules[58]

16.4.2.3.1 The institution of arbitration has traditionally been seen by the developing world as one of the tools employed by former colonial governments and western corporations to secure advantages over their contracting partners. States and corporations in the Third World have, therefore, tended to regard arbitration with a degree of mistrust:

> African countries rightfully feel threatened by the overwhelming power of certain multinational corporations whose financial resources far surpass their own and whose tentacles extend into many different countries. Whether such fears are well grounded or not, they obviously still produce feelings of insecurity and dependence and a deep suspicion of a hidden agenda essentially for the benefit of big business. Without sufficient information on how the arbitral process benefits them immediately, African lawyers and their governments are understandably unwilling to get too involved in a process which they perceive as largely benefiting the trading entities of the west.[59]

55. For a comprehensive study of the Convention see Van den Berg, *The New York Arbitration Convention of 1958* (1981). See also Pisar, "The United Nations Convention on Foreign Arbitral Awards" [1959] JBL 219.
56. See para. 18.2.
57. See para. 20.2.
58. Dietz, "Introduction: Development of the UNCITRAL Arbitration Rules" (1979) 27 Am J Comp L 449; Sanders, "Procedures and Practices under the UNCITRAL Rules" (1979) 27 Am J Comp L 453. Redfern & Hunter, *Law and Practice of International Commercial Arbitration* (2nd ed, 1991) contains both a commentary on the rules (pp. 476–501) and the full text (pp. 688–703).
59. Sempasa, "Obstacles to International Commercial Arbitration in African Countries" (1992) 41 ICLQ 387, 393.

16.4.2.3.2 To a certain extent the image of arbitration has been given a boost in the developing world by the UNCITRAL Arbitration Rules, which were unanimously approved by the General Assembly of the United Nations in 1976. The Rules have been successful in promoting arbitration in parts of the world which have traditionally been hostile to arbitration as a mechanism for resolving commercial disputes. The fact that the UNCITRAL Arbitration Rules have the seal of approval from the United Nations gives them an international respectability not enjoyed by the institutional rules of all arbitration institutions.

16.4.2.3.3 Although the Rules were originally designed for use in *ad hoc* arbitrations, their influence on institutional arbitration has been considerable. The arbitration rules of some arbitration institutions are very closely modelled on the UNCITRAL Arbitration Rules. Furthermore, some arbitration institutions (such as the LCIA) are prepared to administer arbitrations conducted under the UNCITRAL Arbitration Rules.

16.4.2.4 The UNCITRAL Model Law

16.4.2.4.1 The New York Convention of 1958 provides a framework for the enforcement of arbitration agreements and awards; it does not regulate in a general way the relationship between the arbitral process and national courts. So, the court's powers to grant interim relief or to set aside an award are derived entirely from municipal law.

16.4.2.4.2 International commercial arbitration is hindered by differences in national arbitration laws. For example, the setting aside of an award in the country where the arbitration was conducted is a ground on which enforcement of the award may be refused under the New York Convention.[60] Accordingly, an award which would be regarded as acceptable by most legal systems is nevertheless vulnerable to the idiosyncrasies of the municipal law of the country where the award is made.

16.4.2.4.3 There were various ways in which the international community might have sought to deal with the problems posed by the lack of uniformity in the field of arbitration law. The most ambitious solution would have been for the United Nations to draft a uniform law. However, this option was regarded as impracticable on the basis that, even if international agreement could be reached on a text, a convention which gave no flexibility would be unlikely to receive very many ratifications. The alternative approach, which was the one adopted by UNCITRAL, was to encourage harmonisation in the field of arbitration by the adoption of a Model Law. In 1985 a resolution of the General Assembly of the United Nations was passed recommending the UNCITRAL Model Law on Arbitration to Member States. There are three main policy objectives in the Model Law: (i) to allow the parties freedom to choose the procedure for the resolution of the dispute; (ii) to ensure fairness in arbitration proceedings; and (iii) to provide a legal framework which ensures that an arbitration can be completed notwithstanding disagreement by the parties. Countries which decide to adopt the Model Law are free to adapt it to suit their own requirements. The Model Law is, however, drafted in such a way that it can be adopted in its entirety without amendment.

60. Article V(1)(e); Arbitration Act 1975, s. 5(2)(f).

Already a number of countries have enacted the Model Law, either without change or with minor modifications. Although it seems unlikely that the Model Law will be embraced by any of the major arbitration centres, the Model Law has set the agenda for the reform of arbitration law even in those countries which prefer to follow their own traditions.

16.4.2.4.4 In 1989 the Departmental Advisory Committee on Arbitration (the Mustill Committee) concluded that the Model Law should not be adopted in England.[61] The Model Law was rejected for three main reasons: (i) the undesirability of introducing multiple regimes into the law of arbitration; (ii) the desirability of preserving a limited right of appeal against a decision of an arbitrator on a point of law, as currently provided by the 1979 Act; and most importantly (iii) the fact that England already has an extremely sophisticated and highly developed body of arbitration law, based on statute, case law, writings and usages, which is familiar to practitioners and which would have to be discarded to accommodate the Model Law.

16.4.2.4.5 The Committee did, however, recommend that English arbitration law should be amended in certain respects and that its form should be altered. In particular, English law "should be set out in a logical order, and expressed in language which is sufficiently clear and free from technicalities to be readily comprehensible to the layman" and "consideration should be given to ensuring that any such new statute should, so far as possible, have the same structure and language as the Model Law, so as to enhance its accessibility to those who are familiar with the Model Law".[62]

16.4.2.4.6 Following the recommendations of the Committee, the task of promoting a new Arbitration Act was commenced by a private group of arbitration practitioners, acting in consultation with the Department of Trade and Industry and the Chairman of the Departmental Advisory Committee. The project has since been adopted by the Department of Trade and Industry, the intention being that the reform proposals should proceed as a government measure. There is, however, no realistic prospect of a new Arbitration Act hitting the statute book before 1995 at the very earliest.

61. For a discussion of the Committee's report see Reymond, "The Report of the Mustill Committee: A Foreign View" (1990) 106 LQR 431. The Model Law has, however, been adopted in Scotland: Law Reform (Miscellaneous Provisions) (Scotland) Act 1990, s. 66 and Schedule 7. For an analysis of the Model Law and its impact in Scotland see Davidson, *International Commercial Arbitration: Scotland and the UNCITRAL Model Law* (1991) and "International Commercial Arbitration in Scotland" [1992] LMCLQ 376.

62. Departmental Advisory Committee on Arbitration Law, *A Report on the UNCITRAL Model Law on International Commercial Arbitration* (1989) p. 34, para. 108(7).

CHAPTER 17

ARBITRATION: THE APPLICABLE LAW AND JURISDICTION

In considering the applicable law it is important to distinguish the law governing the arbitration agreement (para. 17.1), the law governing the arbitration (referred to as the curial law or *lex arbitri*) (para. 17.2) and the law governing the merits of the dispute (referred to as the *lex causae* or applicable law) (para. 17.3). It is perfectly possible for different laws to govern these different elements. As regards the *lex causae*, there is the further question of whether under English law a dispute which is referred to arbitration may be resolved by reference to a set of rules other than the rules of a national legal system. This question arises in a number of different guises: for example, may an arbitrator resolve a dispute *ex aequo et bono* or as *aimable compositeur*? or may a dispute be determined by reference to general principles of international trade law or to the *lex mercatoria*? There are also issues concerning the impact of EC law on the arbitral process (para. 17.4).

Two issues concerning jurisdiction have to be addressed (para. 17.5). First, it has to be asked whether the defendant is amenable to the jurisdiction of the court. Secondly, on the assumption that the defendant is amenable to English jurisdiction, the extent to which the court may exercise its powers in a case with one or more foreign elements has to be considered.

17.1 THE LAW GOVERNING THE ARBITRATION AGREEMENT[1]

17.1.1 Under the doctrine of separability the agreement to arbitrate is separate from the contract of which it forms a part.[2] While it is to be expected that the proper law of the arbitration agreement will normally be the same as the law applicable to the contract as a whole, it is possible for the arbitration agreement to be governed by the law of country X, but for the substantive obligations of the parties under the contract to be governed by the law of country Y. Arbitration agreements are excluded from the material scope of the Rome Convention on the Law Applicable to Contractual Obligations.[3] So, in cases where the subject matter of the contract is within the Convention's scope, the law applicable to the contract as a whole is to be determined by the choice of law rules in the Convention, but the proper law of the arbitration agreement is determined by the common law doctrine as formulated by the English courts prior to the Convention's entry into force.

1. See Thomas, "Proper Law of Arbitration Agreements" [1984] LMCLQ 304.
2. See para. 18.1.2.
3. Article 1(2)(d).

17.1.2 If the parties have expressly or impliedly chosen a law, the arbitration agreement is governed by the chosen law. If the parties have not made a choice, the agreement is governed by the law of the country with which the agreement has its closest and most real connection.[4] Where the parties have not expressly chosen a law it is presumed, as a general rule, that the proper law of the arbitration agreement is the law of the country in which the arbitration has its seat.[5] If the parties do not choose the seat of arbitration, no presumption can be made. In this case the proper law of the arbitration agreement has to be determined by reference to the relevant connecting factors.[5a]

17.1.3 The proper law governs the validity and effect of the arbitration agreement, the consequences which flow from its breach and the remedies which are available. The proper law also governs questions relating to the jurisdiction of the arbitrator and the scope of the arbitration agreement.[6] In *International Tank & Pipe SAK* v. *Kuwait Aviation Fuelling Co KSC*[7] it was held that section 27 of the 1950 Act, which allows the court to extend contractual time limits for the commencement of arbitral proceedings, applies in cases where the arbitration agreement is governed by English law; section 27 is, in effect, an implied statutory term. Accordingly, if English law is the proper law of the arbitration agreement, the court may exercise the powers conferred by section 27 even if the parties have agreed to arbitration abroad. Conversely, if the proper law of the arbitration agreement is the law of another country, the court has no power to extend contractual time limits, even if the agreement makes provision for disputes to be referred to arbitration in England.[8]

17.1.4 An arbitration agreement must be interpreted according to the canons of construction of its proper law.[9] The proper law determines whether the agreement has been brought to an end whether by repudiation, frustration or voluntary termination.[10] Equally, the proper law covers such questions as whether the agreement is void, voidable or illegal.[11]

17.1.5 Where the existence of the contract containing an arbitration clause or the arbitration agreement itself is contested on the basis of some factor which makes the arbitration agreement void *ab initio*, there is, strictly speaking, no proper law, only a putative proper law—that is, the law which would govern if there were a valid agreement. In these circumstances the putative proper law is determined subjectively, full weight being given to the (disputed) arbitration clause itself.[12] Even if one of the

4. See para. 10.1.

5. *Hamlyn & Co* v. *Talisker Distillery* [1894] AC 202; *Deutsche Schachtbau- und Tiefbohrgesellschaft mbH* v. *R'As al-Khaimah National Oil Co* [1990] 1 AC 295 (HL). The common law principle is consistent with the general scheme of the New York Convention: Van den Berg, *The New York Arbitration Convention of 1958* (1981) pp. 126–127.

5a. See *The Star Texas* [1993] 2 Lloyd's Rep 445.

6. *Nova (Jersey) Knit Ltd* v. *Kammgarn Spinnerei* [1977] 1 WLR 713. See Thomas, "Proper Law of Arbitration Agreements" [1984] LMCLQ 304, 309.

7. [1975] QB 224.

8. *The Castle Alpha* [1989] 2 Lloyd's Rep 383. It has, however, been suggested that section 27 might be interpreted as being both substantive and procedural, with the consequence that it would be applicable not only where the proper law of the arbitration agreement is English, but also where English law is the curial law: Dicey & Morris, *The Conflict of Laws* (12th ed, 1993) p. 579.

9. *AB Bofors-Uva CAV Ltd* v. *AB Skandia Transport* [1982] 1 Lloyd's Rep 410.

10. *Black-Clawson International Ltd* v. *Papierwerke Waldhof-Aschaffenburg AG* [1981] 2 Lloyd's Rep 446.

11. *Dalmia Dairy Industries Ltd* v. *National Bank of Pakistan* [1978] 2 Lloyd's Rep 223.

12. *The Parouth* [1982] 2 Lloyd's Rep 351; *Marc Rich & Co AG* v. *Societa Italiana Impianti PA* [1989] 1 Lloyd's Rep 548.

parties denies having agreed to a clause providing for disputes to be referred to arbitration in England, the existence and validity of the arbitration agreement is governed by English law as the putative proper law. While the logic of the analysis adopted by the English courts may be questionable, the principle seems to be firmly established.[13]

17.2 THE CURIAL LAW[14]

17.2.1 Introduction: the "delocalisation" theory

17.2.1.1 Arbitration depends for its existence on the agreement of the parties; if there is no arbitration agreement there can be no arbitration. In recent years much attention has been directed towards seeking to establish the independence of the arbitral process from national courts. By emphasising the principle of party autonomy and the contractual foundation of arbitration certain commentators have suggested that, at least at the international level, arbitration may be liberated from the control of municipal law. The theory has been propounded that, in international cases, an arbitration agreement creates an exclusive and self-sufficient legal regime, as a result of which the arbitral process is to be regarded as being detached from the system of municipal law of the country where the arbitration is conducted. As a result of this theory, international arbitration is described as "delocalised" (or "denationalised" or "anational").[15] The theory is largely based on a practical consideration which flows from the fact that the municipal laws of some countries are outmoded and overzealous in their desire to control the arbitral process. If international arbitration can be "delocalised", it may be possible to escape the peculiarities of the law of the seat of arbitration.

17.2.1.2 There are, of course, strong arguments against the theory of "delocalisation". In particular, the viability of arbitration as a mechanism for resolving international commercial disputes depends upon confidence that the system operates fairly. This confidence is fostered by the fact that the municipal legal systems which give binding force to arbitration can also be relied upon to guarantee its integrity.[16]

17.2.1.3 The theory of "delocalisation" has made little headway in England.[17] Recognition that the agreement of the parties provides the foundation of the arbitral process cannot hide the fact that a State's jurisdiction over its territory provides a justification for the supervision of the arbitral process and the enforcement of awards by the courts.[18] The traditional view is that—except in truly international cases, where both parties are States or other international persons—all arbitrations are subject to a municipal system of law:

13. For different approaches to this question see Briggs, "The Formation of International Contracts" [1990] LMCLQ 192; Plender, *The European Contracts Convention* (1991) pp. 68–70.

14. Thomas, "The Curial Law of Arbitration Proceedings" [1984] LMCLQ 491.

15. See Paulsson, "Arbitration Unbound: Award Detached from the Law of its Country of Origin" (1981) 30 ICLQ 358; Park, "The Lex Loci Arbitri and International Commercial Arbitration" (1983) 32 ICLQ 21; Paulsson, "Delocalisation of International Commercial Arbitration: When and Why it Matters" (1983) 32 ICLQ 53.

16. Park, "National Law and Commercial Justice: Safeguarding Procedural Integrity in International Arbitration" (1989) 63 Tulane LR 647, 658.

17. See Mustill, "Transnational Arbitration in English Law" [1984] CLP 133.

18. Fox, "States and the Undertaking to Arbitrate" (1988) 37 ICLQ 1.

Although, where international aspects of some kind arise, it is not uncommon and, on the whole, harmless to speak, somewhat colloquially, of international arbitration, the phrase is a misnomer. In the legal sense no international commercial arbitration exists. Just as, notwithstanding its notoriously misleading name, every system of private international law is a system of national law, every arbitration is a national arbitration, that is to say, subject to a specific system of national law.[19]

This view has been clearly endorsed by the English courts. In *Amin Rasheed Shipping Corporation* v. *Kuwait Insurance Co*[20] Lord Diplock made it clear that, as far as English law is concerned, all contracts depend for their existence on a system of law:

... contracts are incapable of existing in a legal vacuum. They are mere pieces of paper devoid of all legal effect unless they were made by reference to some system of private law which defines the obligations assumed by the parties to the contract by their use of particular forms of words and prescribes the remedies enforceable in a court of justice for failure to perform any of those obligations.[21]

17.2.1.4 The implications of this analysis in the field of arbitration were spelled out in *Bank Mellat* v. *Helliniki Techniki SA*,[22] a case concerning the court's jurisdiction to make an order for security for costs in relation to an ICC arbitration which was being conducted in England. It had been argued by the defendant that the effect of the ICC Rules was to exclude all applications to the local courts other than for interim or conservatory measures. In the course of his judgment Kerr LJ said:

Despite suggestions to the contrary by some learned writers under other systems, our jurisprudence does not recognise the concept of arbitral procedures floating in the transnational firmament, unconnected with any municipal system of law.[23]

English law is premised on the notion that arbitration must rely for its existence in the legal order upon some law—whether international or municipal—which renders the process valid and effective.

17.2.2 Internal and external procedures

17.2.2.1 The curial law regulates the procedural aspects of the arbitral process. For example, the curial law governs the procedures under which the court exercises powers of supervision and support:

The law governing the arbitration comprises the rules governing interim measures (eg court orders for the preservation or storage of goods), the rules empowering the exercise by the court of supportive measures to assist an arbitration which has run into difficulties (eg filling a vacancy in the composition of the tribunal if there is no other mechanism) and rules providing for the exercise by the court of its supervisory jurisdiction over arbitrations (eg removing an arbitrator for misconduct).[24]

The curial law also governs the validity and effect of the submission (though the validity of the arbitration agreement is governed by its proper law), the constitution of the

19. Mann, "Lex Facit Arbitrum" in Sanders (ed), *International Arbitration: Liber Amicorum for Martin Domke* (1967) 157, 159. See also, Smit, "A-National Arbitration" (1989) 63 Tulane LR 629.
20. [1984] AC 50. Mann, "England Rejects 'Delocalised' Contracts and Arbitration" (1984) 33 ICLQ 193.
21. [1984] AC 50, 65.
22. [1984] QB 291.
23. [1984] QB 291, 301. See also *Naviera Amazonica Peruana SA* v. *Compania Internacional de Seguros del Peru* [1988] 1 Lloyd's Rep 116.
24. Steyn J in *Paul Smith Ltd* v. *H & S International Holding Inc* [1991] 2 Lloyd's Rep 127, 130.

tribunal, the conduct of the arbitration, the powers of the arbitrator (including the question of whether an arbitrator can decide the case *ex aequo et bono* or as *aimable compositeur*), and the making, publication, interpretation, annulment and revision of the award.[25]

17.2.2.2 Although it is common to think of the law governing the procedural aspects of an arbitration as a unified whole, in reality the curial law includes two distinct elements: the rules which govern the internal conduct of the arbitration and those which regulate the external supervision of the arbitration. Although, as a general rule, the internal conduct of an arbitration and its external supervision are governed by the same law, it is possible for the parties to split the curial law.[26]

17.2.3 Choice of law principles and the seat of arbitration

17.2.3.1 Contracting parties who enter an arbitration agreement are free to select the curial law.[27] The principle of party autonomy means that parties may agree that the law of country X should be the curial law, but that the law of country Y should govern the merits of the case. If the parties do not choose the curial law, the governing law is the law of the seat of arbitration (*lex loci arbitri*).[28] In the absence of choice "the inference that the parties when contracting to arbitrate in a particular place consented to having the arbitral process governed by the law of that place is irresistible".[29] Where, for example, the parties agree to arbitration in Scotland without specifying the governing law, Scots law is the curial law—with the consequence that the parties may not have recourse to the appeals procedure laid down by the English legislation—even if the law governing the merits of the dispute is English law. The right to appeal to the court on a point of law is a question of procedure governed by the curial law, not a question of substance governed by the *lex causae*.

17.2.3.2 There is, however, no requirement that the curial law must be fixed at the moment that the arbitration agreement is concluded. The court will uphold an arbitration clause which provides that disputes should be referred to arbitration "in Beijing or London in defendant's option"; in these circumstances, the curial law will be Chinese or English law depending on whether the defendant chooses Beijing or London as the seat of arbitration.[29a]

17.2.3.3 Parties to an arbitration agreement are also entitled to fix the seat of arbitration, which is the place where, from a legal point of view, the arbitration is centred. A well drafted arbitration clause normally includes an express reference to the intended seat. However, if the parties choose the curial law without expressly designating the seat, the seat is to be implied from the choice of the curial law.[30] So, if the

25. Mann, "State Contracts and International Arbitration" (1967) 42 BYIL 1, 6; Redfern & Hunter, "Law and Practice of International Commercial Arbitration" (2nd ed, 1991) p. 79.

26. *Union of India* v. *McDonnell Douglas Corporation* [1993] 2 Lloyd's Rep 48.

27. *James Miller & Partners Ltd* v. *Whitworth Street Estates (Manchester) Ltd* [1970] AC 583; *Naviera Amazonica Peruana SA* v. *Compania Internacional de Seguros del Peru* [1988] 1 Lloyd's Rep 116.

28. *James Miller & Partners Ltd* v. *Whitworth Street Estates (Manchester) Ltd* [1970] AC 583; *Naviera Amazonica Peruana SA* v. *Compania Internacional de Seguros del Peru* [1988] 1 Lloyd's Rep 116.

29. Lord Mustill in *Channel Tunnel Group Ltd* v. *Balfour Beatty Construction Ltd* [1993] AC 334, 357–358.

29a. *The Star Texas* [1993] 2 Lloyd's Rep 445.

30. *Naviera Amazonica Peruana SA* v. *Compania Internacional de Seguros del Peru* [1988] 1 Lloyd's Rep 116. Hunter, [1988] LMCLQ 23; Mann, "Lex Arbitri and Locus Arbitri" (1988) 104 LQR 348; Marshall, [1988] JBL 405.

parties choose English law as the curial law it is implied that the parties intend that England should be the seat of arbitration.

17.2.4 Severing the link between the curial law and the seat of arbitration

17.2.4.1 As a result of the foregoing principles, the law of the seat of arbitration is normally the curial law. As a matter of legal principle, however, since parties to an agreement are free to select both the curial law and the seat of arbitration, it is clear that "[t]here is ... no reason in theory which precludes parties to agree that an arbitration shall be held at a place or in a country X but subject to the procedural laws of Y".[31]

17.2.4.2 It is clear that—at least as regards external supervision—immense practical difficulties may flow if the link between the curial law and the seat of arbitration is broken. Accordingly, the court will interpret an arbitration clause as having such an effect only if the words of the agreement cannot be interpreted in any other way. In *Union of India* v. *McDonnell Douglas Inc*[32] the parties agreed that "[t]he seat of the arbitration proceedings shall be London" but that "[t]he arbitration shall be conducted in accordance with the procedure provided in the Indian Arbitration Act 1940". Saville J interpreted the parties' agreement as effectively splitting the curial law: English law—as the law of the seat of arbitration—governed external supervision; Indian law governed the internal conduct of the arbitration, although only to the extent that such law was not inconsistent with the implied choice of English law as the curial law. By drawing a distinction between the internal conduct of the arbitration and its external supervision—and holding that the choice of London as the seat of arbitration operated as an implied choice of English law as the law governing external supervision of the arbitration—Saville J avoided having to consider the implications of a situation where in relation to an arbitration to be conducted in country X the parties expressly agree that external supervision of the arbitration should be governed by the law of country Y.[33]

17.2.4.3 From a practical point of view "there is no useful reason to agree to arbitrate in one country under the arbitration law of another country".[34] The potential problems of conducting an arbitration in country X in accordance with the curial law of country Y can easily be avoided—since there is no requirement that hearings should be conducted at the legal seat of arbitration.[35] This is spelt out in many institutional rules; Article 7(2) of the LCIA Arbitration Rules, for example, provides that "[t]he Tribunal may hold hearings and meetings anywhere convenient". If the most convenient geographical location for the hearings is country X, but the parties want the arbitration to be governed by the law of country Y, instead of fixing the seat in country X and choosing the law of country Y as the curial law, the parties should choose country Y as the seat and conduct the hearings in country X.[36]

31. Kerr LJ in *Naviera Amazonica Peruana SA* v. *Compania Internacional de Seguros del Peru* [1988] 1 Lloyd's Rep 116, 120.

32. [1993] 2 Lloyd's Rep 48.

33. For further consideration of this issue see para. 17.5.2.

34. Van den Berg, "Non-Domestic Arbitral Awards under the 1958 New York Convention" (1986) 2 Arb Int 191, 201.

35. Kerr LJ in *Naviera Amazonica Peruana SA* v. *Compania Internacional de Seguros del Peru* [1988] 1 Lloyd's Rep 116, 120–121.

36. Redfern & Hunter, *Law and Practice of International Commercial Arbitration* (2nd ed, 1991), pp. 93–94.

17.2.5 The internal conduct of an arbitration

17.2.5.1 The sources of the rules

17.2.5.1.1 The arbitration agreement, which is the foundation of the arbitrator's authority, may expressly determine many aspects of the arbitral process (such as the place where the arbitration is to be conducted and the procedure to be adopted).

17.2.5.1.2 Parties may expressly incorporate into the arbitration agreement a set of arbitration rules—whether institutional or *ad hoc*—which play a major role in shaping the way in which the arbitration is conducted.[37] Articles 15 to 30 of the UNCITRAL Arbitration Rules, for example, indicate the general shape which the proceedings should take. Article 15(1) provides:

> Subject to these Rules, the arbitral tribunal may conduct the arbitration in such manner as it considers appropriate, provided that the parties are treated with equality and that at any stage of the proceedings each party is given full opportunity of presenting his case.

17.2.5.1.3 The other relevant rules govern the following matters: Article 16 (place of arbitration); Article 17 (language); Articles 18 to 20 (statement of claim and statement of defence); Article 21 (pleas as to the jurisdiction of the arbitral tribunal); Article 22 (further written statements); Article 23 (periods of time); Articles 24 and 25 (evidence and hearings); Article 26 (interim measures of protection); Article 27 (experts); Article 28 (default); Article 29 (closure of hearings); Article 30 (waiver of rules). These rules tend to be very general. For example, Article 23, which deals with time limits, merely states:

> The periods of time fixed by the arbitral tribunal for the communication of written statements (including the statement of claim and statement of defence) should not exceed forty-five days. However, the arbitral tribunal may extend the time-limits if it concludes that an extension is justified.

17.2.5.1.4 Even though arbitration rules such as the ICC Rules are "designed to cover every aspect of arbitrations conducted under their terms, from the inception of the arbitration to the issue of a final award",[38] the details of the procedure (such as the extent of to which there is to be discovery of documents, the relative importance of written submissions and oral hearings) have to be worked out by the arbitrator in each individual case. Although an arbitrator has considerable discretion in determining the procedure to be employed, he must normally respect the express wishes of the parties.

17.2.5.1.5 Instead of adopting institutional rules, the parties may choose the law of a foreign country. English law gives the contracting parties freedom to determine the rules governing the internal conduct of an arbitration; whether that procedure is provided by the parties, by incorporating into their agreement a set of rules such as the UNCITRAL Arbitration Rules, or lifted completely from the procedural law of some existing sovereign State, would not appear to make any difference in principle.[39] So, in an English arbitration, a reference to German procedural rules should operate as a contractual incorporation in the same manner as the rules of an institutional arbitral body might be incorporated.[40] In *Union of India* v. *McDonnell Douglas Inc*[41] an

37. See, for example, *Paul Smith Ltd* v. *H & S International Holding Inc* [1991] 2 Lloyd's Rep 127.
38. Kerr LJ in *Bank Mellat* v. *Helliniki Techniki SA* [1984] QB 291, 304.
39. *Russell on Arbitration* (20th ed, 1982) p. 245.
40. Thomas, "The Curial Law of Arbitration Proceedings" [1984] LMCLQ 491, 497–498.
41. [1993] 2 Lloyd's Rep 48.

arbitration agreement was interpreted as including both an express choice of Indian law to govern the internal conduct of the arbitration and, by virtue of the choice of London as the seat of arbitration, an implied choice of English law as regards external supervision.

17.2.5.1.6 To the extent that the rules governing the internal conduct of the arbitration are not agreed by the parties, the law of the seat applies. For example, in relation to an arbitration conducted in England, where there is no express agreement by the parties to the contrary, an arbitrator is bound by the same rules of evidence as courts of law.[42]

17.2.5.2 Conflicts between the curial law and the agreement of the parties

17.2.5.2.1 The parties' freedom to determine the arbitral procedure "exists only if and to such extent as it is granted by the law of the arbitration tribunal's seat".[43] So, in *Union of India* v. *McDonnell Douglas Inc*,[44] although the court upheld a choice of Indian law as the law governing the internal conduct of an arbitration in England, Indian law was applicable only to the extent that it was not inconsistent with the application of English law as the curial law. There are, however, very few mandatory rules in English arbitration law.[45]

17.2.5.2.2 The arbitrator is under a duty to respect the terms of the arbitration agreement (including the arbitration rules adopted by the parties) and to observe the law which governs the arbitration. It is possible, however, for there to be conflict between the terms of the arbitration agreement and the law of the seat. For example, if an arbitration were conducted in Germany under English procedural law, it would not be appropriate for the arbitrator to examine witnesses on oath, even though such a power is conferred by section 12(2) of the 1950 Act, since under German law an arbitrator is not authorised to administer oaths to witnesses.[46] In cases where the agreement of the parties conflicts with the mandatory requirements of the law of the seat the arbitrator should give precedence to the latter.[47]

17.3 THE LAW APPLICABLE TO THE MERITS OF THE DISPUTE[48]

17.3.1 Types of choice of law clause[49]

In situations where the contracting parties include a choice of law clause in their agreement, but do not agree to arbitration, the clause normally involves the choice of the law of a particular country. The parties may choose the law of one of the parties or the law of a third country. Clauses in arbitration agreements which seek to determine the body of rules to govern the substantive rights and obligations of the parties may be much more complex. Parties to an arbitration agreement may decide to refer to one or more of the following:

42. *East & West India Dock Co* v. *Kirk* (1887) 12 App Cas 738.
43. Mann, "English Procedural Law and Foreign Arbitrations" (1970) 19 ICLQ 693, 695.
44. [1993] 2 Lloyd's Rep 48.
45. Mustill, "Transnational Arbitration in English Law" [1984] CLP 133, 148.
46. German Code of Civil Procedure, para. 1035.
47. For discussion of the enforcement problems which arise in this situation see para. 20.2.3.6.
48. Lew, *Applicable Law in International Commercial Arbitration* (1978).
49. See Redfern & Hunter, *Law and Practice of International Commercial Arbitration* (2nd ed, 1991) pp. 101–122; Lalive, "Contracts between a State or a State Agency and a Foreign Company" (1964) 13 ICLQ 987, 992; Böckstiegel, "States in the International Arbitral Process" (1986) 2 Arb Int 22, 28–29.

(i) the law of a particular country;
(ii) public international law;
(iii) the rules of law common to two or more countries or common to the law of a country and public international law[50];
(iv) international trade law (also referred to as "transnational law" or the *lex mercatoria*);
(v) equity and good conscience (arbitration *ex aequo et bono*, *aimable composition*).

17.3.2 Legal introduction

17.3.2.1 A judge in England is required to apply the law of the forum; this includes not only domestic law, but also the rules of English private international law. Where the parties have chosen the applicable law, the court will respect that choice (subject to the possible application of mandatory rules of a law or laws not chosen by the parties); where the parties have failed to make a choice, the court will, as a general rule, apply the law of the country with which the contract is most closely connected.[51] Arbitrators are in a position which is analogous to that of a judge, in the sense that they are required to decide the dispute which has been referred to them in a judicial manner. However, their position is different since the immediate source of their jurisdiction is the agreement of the parties. This raises the question of how an arbitrator should approach the choice of law process.

17.3.2.2 The basic principle is that the curial law determines the law which the arbitrator must apply.[52] In many continental countries, the arbitrator is free, in the absence of a choice of law by the parties, to apply those rules of law which he considers appropriate.[53] Furthermore, in many countries, the law expressly provides that the parties may authorise an arbitrator to act *ex aequo et bono* or as *aimable compositeur*.[54] Traditionally, the position in England is thought to be different. There is no specific legislation dealing with the law to be applied by an arbitrator to the merits of the dispute. The relevant principle, at common law, was stated by Scrutton LJ in *Czarnikow* v. *Roth, Schmidt & Co* in the following terms: "Arbitrators, unless expressly otherwise authorised, have to apply the laws of England."[55] Accordingly, where English law is the curial law, an arbitrator should apply English conflicts rules to determine the applicable law: "Just as the judge has to apply the private international law of the forum, so the arbitrator has to apply the private international law of the arbitration tribunal's seat, the *lex arbitri*. Any other solution would involve the conclusion that it is open to the

50. See Rubino-Sammartano, "The Channel Tunnel and the Tronc Commun Doctrine" (1993) 10 J Int Arb (3) 59.
51. For a discussion of choice of law in contract see Chapters 10 to 12.
52. *Norske Atlas Insurance Co Ltd* v. *London General Insurance Co Ltd* (1927) 28 Ll L Rep 104; *Union Nationale des Coopératives Agricoles de Céréales* v. *Robert Catterall & Co Ltd* [1959] 2 QB 44.
53. See, for example, Article 1496 of the French New Code of Civil Procedure and Article 1054(2) of the Dutch Code of Civil Procedure.
54. See, for example, Article 1497 of the French New Code of Civil Procedure; Article 1054(3) of the Dutch Code of Civil Procedure; Article 187(2) of the Swiss Private International Law Act.
55. [1922] 2 KB 478, 488.

arbitrator to disregard the law."[56] While the principle that arbitrators are bound by the conflicts rules of the seat of arbitration seems clear, the traditional interpretation of *Czarnikow* v. *Roth, Schmidt & Co* goes further in suggesting that, where the curial law is English law, an arbitrator is required to decide disputes in accordance with a recognised system of rules, whether a national legal system or, in certain contexts (for example, where one or more of the parties is a State), public international law.[57]

17.3.2.3 What, however, is the position where the parties have agreed that their rights and obligations should be governed by a system of rules or principles which is neither the law of a particular country nor public international law? What is the effect in English law of a clause which requires the arbitrator to apply the *lex mercatoria* or which authorises the arbitrator to decide as *aimable compositeur* or *ex aequo et bono*? The traditional view states that in such circumstances the arbitration agreement should not be enforced and any award which results from such an agreement should be liable to be varied, set aside or remitted by the court.

17.3.2.4 The traditional view has never been properly tested; no other possibility has been envisaged and the question has never been expressly discussed by the courts.[58] Moreover, in recent years the courts have indicated a willingness to adopt a less strict approach to equity clauses and clauses whereby the parties choose to have their rights and obligations determined by general principles.

17.3.3 Choice of law of a particular country

If the subject matter of the dispute falls within the scope of the Rome Convention on the Law Applicable to Contractual Obligations, an English arbitrator must apply the choice of law rules contained in the Convention. Under the Convention parties to a contract are free to choose the law of any country to govern their contractual relations—even if that law has no connection, meaningful or otherwise, with the contract or the parties. So, if the parties agree that their rights and obligations are to be governed by the law of country X that choice is effective and will be respected by the arbitrator.[59] Reported arbitral awards show that arbitrators invariably apply the law selected by the parties; while some do so without referring to any choice of law rules, others justify upholding the parties' choice by reference to the choice of law rules of the curial law.[60]

17.3.4 The applicable law in the absence of express choice

17.3.4.1 Under Dutch law, if the parties to an arbitration agreement fail to make a choice of law "the arbitral tribunal shall make its award in accordance with the rules of law which it considers appropriate".[61] This rule has much to recommend it. In the

56. Mann, "Lex Facit Arbitrum" in Sanders (ed), *International Arbitration: Liber Amicorum for Martin Domke* (1967) 157, 167. See also Thomas, "Commercial Arbitration—Justice According to Law" (1983) 2 CJQ 166; Jaffey, "Arbitration of Commercial Contracts: the Law to be Applied by the Arbitrators" in Perrott & Pogany (eds), *Current Problems in International Trade Law* (1987) 129–151.

57. *Orion Compania Espanola de Seguros* v. *Belfort Maatschappij voor Algemene Verzekgringeen* [1962] 2 Lloyd's Rep 257, 264.

58. Jaffey, "Arbitration of Commercial Contracts: the Law to be Applied by the Arbitrators" in Perrott & Pogany (eds), *Current Problems in International Trade Law* (1987) 129, 131.

59. Rome Convention, Article 3(1).

60. Lando, "The Law Applicable to the Merits of the Dispute" (1986) 2 Arb Int 104, 107.

61. Article 1054(2) of the Code of Civil Procedure.

absence of express choice by the parties it may legitimately be presumed that, since the parties must have envisaged that their contract would be governed by some law, they must have intended the arbitrator to apply the law which he thinks is appropriate.[62] There is, unfortunately, no equivalent statutory provision in English law.

17.3.4.2 If the parties do not make an express choice of law, there are two possibilities under the Rome Convention: implied choice and no choice.

(i) In cases where the parties have failed to make an express choice of law, an arbitration clause is, at common law, generally to be regarded as an implied choice of the law of the seat of arbitration. So, if parties agree to arbitration in England, the presumption at common law is that the parties intend that the merits of the dispute are to be governed by English law.[63] This is not, however, an immutable rule.[64] Under the Rome Convention, which applies to contracts concluded on or after 1 April 1991, a choice of law, if not express, must be "demonstrated with reasonable certainty by the terms of the contract or the circumstances of the case".[65] Whether or not an arbitration clause is to be regarded as a choice of law depends on the context.[66]

(ii) In the absence of a choice of law by the parties a contract is governed by the law of the country with which it is most closely connected.[67] In determining the closest connection there is a presumption in favour of the law of the place of business of the party who is to effect the characteristic performance under the contract.[68] This presumption may be rebutted if the contract is shown to be more closely connected with another law.[69]

17.3.4.3 It follows that, in a situation where English law is the curial law, the approach taken by the arbitrator in the *Sapphire* arbitration[70] would not be legitimate. This arbitration concerned a dispute arising under a contract between a Canadian oil company and the National Iranian Oil Company. The arbitrator, having taken the view that he was not bound to conform to the conflicts rules of the seat of arbitration, decided as follows:

> It is quite clear ... that the parties intended to exclude the application of Iranian law. But they have not chosen another positive legal system and this omission is on all the evidence deliberate. All the connecting factors ... point to the fact that the parties therefore intended to submit the interpretation and performance of their contract to principles of law generally recognised by civilised nations. ... The arbitrator will therefore apply these principles, in taking account, when necessary, of the decisions taken by international tribunals.[71]

17.3.4.4 It should be stressed, however, that the principle in *Czarnikow* v. *Roth, Schmidt & Co* that arbitrators are required to apply the law of England (including

62. Jaffey, "Arbitration of Commercial Contracts: the Law to be Applied by the Arbitrators" in Perrott & Pogany (eds), *Current Problems in International Trade Law* (1987) 129, 136.
63. *Hamlyn & Co* v. *Talisker Distillery* [1894] AC 202. See Thomas, "Arbitration Agreements as a Signpost of the Proper Law" [1984] LMCLQ 141.
64. *Compagnie d'Armement Maritime SA* v. *Compagnie Tunisienne de Navigation SA* [1971] AC 572.
65. Rome Convention, Article 3(1).
66. For further consideration of this point see para. 11.1.3.6.
67. Rome Convention, Article 4(1).
68. Rome Convention, Article 4(2).
69. Rome Convention, Article 4(5). See para. 11.2.
70. Part of the award is reproduced as an appendix to Lalive, "Contracts Between a State or a State Agency and a Foreign Company" (1964) 13 ICLQ 987, 1011–1021.
71. (1964) 13 ICLQ 987, 1015.

English private international law) does not apply where an arbitrator is "expressly otherwise authorised".[72] Where the parties have not made an express choice of law, but have agreed to arbitration in accordance with arbitration rules which confer a discretion on the arbitrator to select the *lex causae* by reference to the choice of law rules which he considers appropriate, the arbitrator is not required to apply the conflict rules of the curial law. After all, under English private international law, the parties are free to choose the law to govern their contract; what is wrong with allowing them to empower the arbitrator to make a choice for them?[73]

17.3.4.5 If the parties choose institutional arbitration rules or the UNCITRAL Arbitration Rules the choice of law provisions contained in the rules are effectively incorporated into the arbitration agreement. Article 33(1) of the UNCITRAL Arbitration Rules, for example, provides:

> The arbitral tribunal shall apply the law designated by the parties as applicable to the substance of the dispute. Failing such designation by the parties, the arbitral tribunal shall apply the law determined by the conflict of laws rules which it considers applicable.

17.3.4.6 Where an arbitration takes place in England under the UNCITRAL Arbitration Rules the cautious arbitrator would select the law in accordance with the rules laid down in the Rome Convention. However, by incorporating the UNCITRAL Arbitration Rules into their agreement, the parties have agreed to delegate the task of choice to the arbitrator. The court should be prepared to uphold the arbitrator's decision whether the arbitrator selects as the *lex causae* the law which is the applicable law according to the provisions of the Rome Convention or the law of another country.

17.3.4.7 More problematical is the situation where the arbitrator decides that the parties' rights are to be governed by a non-national set of rules (such as the *lex mercatoria*). *Deutsche Schachtbau- und Tiefbohrgesellschaft mbH* v. *R'As al-Khaimah National Oil Co*[74] involved an ICC arbitration conducted in Switzerland. Article 13(3) of the ICC Rules provides:

> The parties shall be free to determine the law to be applied by the arbitrator to the merits of the dispute. In the absence of any indication by the parties as to the applicable law, the arbitrator shall apply the law designated as the proper law by the rules of conflict which he deems appropriate.

The arbitrators, in reliance on this provision, took the view that the rights and obligations of the parties were to be governed by "internationally accepted principles of law governing contractual relations". In the context of proceedings in England to enforce the award, Donaldson MR said:

> By choosing to arbitrate under the rules of the ICC and, in particular, article 13(3) the parties have left [the] proper law to be decided by the arbitrators and have not in terms confined the choice to national systems of law. I can see no basis for concluding that the arbitrators' choice of proper law—a common denominator of principles underlying the laws of the various nations governing contractual relations—is outwith the scope of the choice which the parties left to the arbitrators.[75]

72. Scrutton LJ in *Czarnikow* v. *Roth, Schmidt & Co* [1922] 2 KB 478, 488.
73. Jaffey, "Arbitration of Commercial Contracts: the Law to be Applied by the Arbitrators" in Perrott & Pogany (eds), *Current Problems in International Trade Law* (1987) 129, 133.
74. [1990] 1 AC 295 (HL).
75. [1990] 1 AC 295, 316.

17.3.4.8 In the *Deutsche Schachtbau* case the arbitration had been conducted abroad. Nevertheless, there is no reason why the court should take a less liberal approach to arbitrations conducted in England in accordance with arbitration rules—whether institutional or *ad hoc*—which allow the arbitrator discretion in the choice of law process. It should be immaterial whether the parties expressly choose the applicable law or adopt a formula which allows a third party to choose the applicable law on their behalf. As Donaldson MR noted in the *Deutsche Schachtbau* case "there is a vital distinction between an agreement to agree in the future and an agreement to accept terms to be determined by a third party. The former cannot and the latter can form the basis for a legally enforceable agreement."[76] It must be remembered, however, that the Rome Convention contains provisions relating to mandatory rules which must be respected.[77]

17.3.5 Public international law

A contract concluded by two States (or other international persons) is normally governed by public international law rather than by the municipal law of any country. Furthermore, a contract between a State and a national corporation may include a clause to the effect that the contract should be governed by public international law. It is generally agreed that, in these situations, the court should respect clauses whereby parties choose public international law as the applicable law and should respect arbitral awards which are based on them.[78]

17.3.6 Arbitration *extra legem*

17.3.6.1 Introduction

17.3.6.1.1 According to the traditional analysis, if the seat of arbitration is England arbitration *extra legem*—whether in the form of *aimable composition* or arbitration *ex aequo et bono*—is legally void. This conclusion is based on the idea that, if parties agree to arbitration by reference to standards other than the law of a particular country or public international law, the agreement negates the intention to create legal relations; if there is no intention to create legal relations there can be no contract and no enforceable award. There are various arguments against this traditional analysis.

(i) Some of the authorities which are cited in support of the traditional approach are not as convincing as it is sometimes suggested. *Czarnikow* v. *Roth, Schmidt & Co*,[79] which is regarded by many as one of the leading cases, is limited authority; it decided that, prior to the 1979 Act, parties could not by agreement exclude the supervisory jurisdiction of the court. The question as to whether parties can authorise an arbitrator to rule otherwise than by reference to English law (including English private international law) was not directly in issue.

76. [1990] 1 AC 295, 315–316.
77. Articles 3(3), 5(2), 6(1), 7 and 16. See paras. 11.3 and 17.3.8.
78. *Orion Compania Espanola de Seguros* v. *Belfort Maatschappij voor Algemene Verzekgringeen* [1962] 2 Lloyd's Rep 257.
79. [1922] 2 KB 478.

(ii) The traditional analysis is based on a non sequitur: "The fact that the parties wish the award to be arrived at otherwise than by recourse to rules of law does not mean that they intend to deny legal force to the undertaking to arbitrate [or] the resulting award, merely that the arbitrator may apply non-legal criteria in reaching his decision."[80]

(iii) From a policy perspective, one might question whether the traditional opposition to arbitration *extra legem* is justified. The laws of many continental countries provide that parties may empower the arbitrator to decide the dispute according to equity or good conscience and to depart from strict legal rules.[81] Institutional arbitration rules also accept this possibility, albeit subject to the limitations of the curial law. Article 33(2) of the UNCITRAL Arbitration Rules, for example, provides:

> The arbitral tribunal shall decide as *aimable compositeur* or *ex aequo et bono* only if the parties have expressly authorised the arbitral tribunal to do so and if the law applicable to the arbitral procedure permits such arbitration.

17.3.6.1.2 There is no basis on which an English court can refuse to recognise a foreign award where the arbitrator has decided *ex aequo et bono* or as *aimable compositeur*—as long as the award is valid under the law of the country governing the arbitration. In *Norske Atlas Insurance Co Ltd* v. *London General Insurance Co*, for example, a Norwegian award was enforced in England notwithstanding the fact that the parties had provided that the arbitrators "must not necessarily judge according to the strict law but as a general rule ought chiefly to consider the principles of practical business".[82] If there is no reason to refuse to enforce a foreign award in these circumstances, English law should also accept the validity of an award made in England in cases where the parties agreed to arbitration *extra legem*.

17.3.6.1.3 Parties to a contract are generally free to decide whether or not to enforce their legal rights. A and B may settle a dispute by agreement, and—as long as mandatory rules of law are not infringed—such an agreement is not regarded as posing a threat to the legal order. Arbitration *extra legem* is no more of a threat; within the limits laid down by mandatory rules and general principles of natural justice, "nothing of any particular consequence turns on the question whether or not the award is in tune with contemporary commercial law. In this regard an arbitration award may be likened to a settlement in litigation."[83] Although, as a general principle, commercial arbitrators should act in accordance with legal principles, it is equally supportable that arbitrators should have the power to decide *extra legem* when that is the express wish of the contracting parties.[84]

80. Goode, "The Adaptation of English Law to International Commercial Arbitration" (1992) 8 Arb Int 1, 7.
81. See n. 54.
82. MacKinnon J, (1927) 28 Ll L Rep 104, 107.
83. Thomas, "Commercial Arbitration—Justice According to Law?" (1983) 2 CJQ 166, 181–182.
84. Schmitthoff, "Arbitration: The Supervisory Jurisdiction of the Courts" [1967] JBL 318; Goode, "The Adaptation of English Law to International Commercial Arbitration" (1992) 8 Arb Int 1.

17.3.6.2 Equity and good conscience: aimable composition and arbitration ex aequo et bono[85]

17.3.6.2.1 Although strictly speaking the French and Latin expressions are not really coterminous, the terms "*aimable composition*" and arbitration "*ex aequo et bono*" are generally used interchangeably. In each case an arbitrator may, to some extent, dispense with rules of law. An *aimable compositeur* is not, however, a mediator or conciliator; he may not, for example, modify the terms of the contract.[86] The importance of the distinction between arbitrators who decide according to rules of law and those who decide as *aimables compositeurs* can be exaggerated; under both systems arbitrators are bound by relevant mandatory procedural and substantive rules and by public policy. It has been said that "the difference between the two systems is certainly not as great as many, especially those who are accustomed to the English concept of arbitration, are inclined to think".[87]

17.3.6.2.2 Since, in English law, the general principle is that arbitrators are bound by the conflicts rules of the curial law, there can be no question of an arbitrator acting as *aimable compositeur* if the parties do not expressly authorise him to do so. The fact that arbitrators are bound to apply the law does not, however, provide a simple answer where the parties have expressly agreed that their relationship should be governed otherwise than by the rules of a national legal system or the rules of public international law.

17.3.6.2.3 English law does not formally recognise arbitration *extra legem*. Arbitration is a legal procedure and arbitrators are required to apply the relevant legal rules and principles. It has been suggested, however, that, notwithstanding the formal position, the reality is rather different: "English arbitration is as successful as it is because arbitrators do act *ex aequo et bono* and behave as good and reliable *aimables compositeurs*.... [I]n this country names are more important than substance, and ... you can alter anything here, provided you retain the old name, thereby maintaining the pleasant illusion that no change has been made."[88] This observation is supported by the more recent English cases concerning equity clauses; the former view that arbitrators must always apply the law has been supplanted, to some extent at least, by more liberal attitudes.[89]

17.3.6.2.4 In *Eagle Star Insurance Co Ltd* v. *Yuval Insurance Co Ltd*[90] the Court of Appeal accepted that an agreement which authorised arbitrators to settle disputes "according to an equitable rather than strictly legal interpretation of the provisions of this Agreement" was not contrary to public policy; Robert Goff LJ thought that an equity clause in this form entitles the arbitrators "to view the matter more leniently"[91] than a court would do. In *Home & Overseas Insurance Co Ltd* v. *Mentor Insurance Co*

85. Rubino-Sammartano, "Aimable Compositeur (Joint Mandate to Settle) and Ex Bono et Aequo (Discretional Authority to Mitigate Strict Law)" (1992) 9 J Int Arb (1) 5.
86. Park, "National Law and Commercial Justice: Safeguarding Procedural Integrity in International Arbitration" (1989) 63 Tulane LR 647, 648 n. 1.
87. Sanders, "Trends in the Field of International Commercial Arbitration" [1975] II Hag Rec 205, 238.
88. Lord Tangley, "International Arbitration Today" (1966) 15 ICLQ 719, 722.
89. Evans J in *Overseas Union Insurance Ltd* v. *AA Mutual International Insurance Co Ltd* [1988] 2 Lloyd's Rep 63, 72.
90. [1978] 1 Lloyd's Rep 357. Mann, "Arbitration Extra Legem?" (1978) 94 LQR 486.
91. [1978] 1 Lloyd's Rep 357, 363.

(UK) Ltd[92] the parties had entered an arbitration agreement under the terms of which the arbitrators were to interpret the contract, which was governed by English law, as "an honourable engagement ... with a view to effecting the general purpose of [the contract] in a reasonable manner rather than in accordance with a literal interpretation of the language". The Court of Appeal upheld the award, notwithstanding the fact that the curial law was English law and the award was made in England.

17.3.6.2.5 In *Home & Overseas Insurance Co Ltd* v. *Mentor Insurance Co (UK) Ltd*[93] Parker LJ made it clear that in his view "a clause which purported to free arbitrators to decide without regard to the law, and according, for example, to their own notions of what would be fair, would not be a valid arbitration clause".[94] However, Lloyd LJ, in the same case, took a different view: "It is implicit in the decision of the Court of Appeal in the *Eagle Star* case that arbitrators appointed under a clause which entitles them to look to the general purpose of the contract, rather than the literal interpretation of the language, may properly reach a result which would not be the same, or not necessarily the same, as a court would reach in the absence of the clause."[95] It is difficult to see how an objection to arbitration *ex aequo et bono* and *aimable composition* can be logically maintained once it is accepted that arbitrators may legitimately reach a conclusion which would not be that reached by a court of law on the same facts.

17.3.6.2.6 Nevertheless, the present status of arbitration *extra legem* in English law must be regarded as uncertain.[96] In the types of contract which form the staple of English arbitration practice equity clauses are not very common[97] and, to the extent that they are to be found in English arbitrations, they are generally outside the control of the courts. Accordingly, the courts have little experience of dealing with them. There can be no doubt that the trend in the case law is towards a greater tolerance towards arbitration *extra legem*: "If the English courts will enforce a foreign award where the contract is governed by 'a system of law which is not that of England or any other State or is a serious modification of such a law,' why should it not enforce an English award in like circumstances?"[98] This trend is to be welcomed; if the parties have agreed to *aimable composition* or arbitration *ex aequo et bono* in England the court should uphold their agreement by enforcing the agreement to arbitrate and any ensuing award.

17.3.7 The *lex mercatoria*[99]

17.3.7.1 Although the parties to an international contract may expressly choose the law of a particular country to govern the agreement, there are contexts in which a choice of

92. [1990] 1 WLR 153.
93. [1990] 1 WLR 153.
94. [1990] 1 WLR 153, 161.
95. [1990] 1 WLR 153, 164.
96. On the question of the validity of an award in circumstances where the parties have authorised the arbitrator to act as *aimable compositeur* or *ex aequo et bono* see Kodwo Bentil, "Commercial Arbitrators Authorised not to Apply Strict Rules of Law and Judicial Review" [1992] JBL 26.
97. Mustill & Boyd, *Commercial Arbitration* (2nd ed, 1989) p. 75.
98. Lloyd LJ in *Home & Overseas Insurance Co Ltd* v. *Mentor Insurance Co (UK) Ltd* [1990] 1 WLR 153, 166
99. For a discussion by one of the leading proponents of the *lex mercatoria* see Goldman, "The Applicable Law: General Principles of Law—The Lex Mercatoria" in Lew (ed), *Contemporary Problems in International Arbitration* (1987) 113 *et seq*. Carbonneau (ed), *Lex Mercatoria and Arbitration: A Discussion of the New Law Merchant* (1990) contains "a broad spectrum of opinions on what the expression *lex mercatoria* actually means, as well as upon the concept's theoretical soundness and practical utility" (Mustill, (1992) 8 Arb Int 215, 215–216).

this type may not seem appropriate. For example, in investment contracts between a State and a foreign corporation, if the contract is governed by the law of the host State, the foreign corporation runs the risk that the host State will change the law in a way which benefits the State and is detrimental to the other contracting party. The host State is, however, equally unlikely to be willing to submit to the law of a foreign country. In this situation, the corporation needs a choice of law clause which avoids the tangles of nationalisation and unilateral action by the host State.[100] Even in a contract between two private persons neither party may wish to submit to the law of the other or to the law of a country with which neither party is closely connected.

17.3.7.2 In these situations the parties may choose to submit to the *lex mercatoria*, the new law merchant, by using one of a number of different formulas—such as general principles of law, principles of law recognised by civilised nations or principles of law applied by international tribunals.[101] While the meaning of such formulas may not always be self-evident, it is clear that by adopting one of them the parties are seeking to avoid the idiosyncrasies of the laws of particular countries.

17.3.7.3 The *lex mercatoria* is said to be made up of public international law, principles derived from uniform laws, general principles recognised by the commercial nations, rules of international organisations, customs and usages, clauses in standard form contracts and reported awards.[102] The subject of the *lex mercatoria* provokes strong feelings. Some argue that it is the panacea for the problems posed by transnational commercial transactions; others, for whom the *lex mercatoria* is like the Emperor's new clothes, regard the whole notion with a high degree of scepticism.

17.3.7.4 Notwithstanding the claims made by proponents of the theory, it has been suggested that—even if the methodological problems surrounding the identification or creation of rules which go to make up the *lex mercatoria* are put to one side—the *lex mercatoria* is far from being a self-sufficient system of rules. One critic of the new law merchant, having listed twenty rules and principles which are said to constitute the *lex mercatoria* in its present form, suggests that "[t]his list, incomplete as it may be, seems a rather a modest haul for twenty-five years of international arbitration".[103] Others go further: "It is not even possible to supply more than a meagre inventory, loaded with vagueness and charged with logical and analytical legal error."[104]

17.3.7.5 Whatever may be the arguments for or against the theory, the *lex mercatoria* seems to fulfil a need—in the sense that some members of the international business community indicate, by choosing the *lex mercatoria*, a desire not to submit transnational legal disputes to national laws. Are the arguments against the *lex mercatoria* so compelling that businessmen and women should be refused the opportunity of selecting the *lex mercatoria* as the system of rules to govern their contracts?

100. Highet, "The Enigma of the Lex Mercatoria" (1989) 63 Tulane LR 613, 628.

101. Delaume, "Comparative Analysis as a Basis of Law in State Contracts: the Myth of the Lex Mercatoria" (1989) 63 Tulane LR 574, 583. See also the examples given by Rivkin, "Enforceability of Arbitral Awards based on Lex Mercatoria" (1993) 9 Arb Int 67, 68–72.

102. Lando, "The Lex Mercatoria in International Commercial Arbitration" (1985) 34 ICLQ 745, 748–751. See also Goldstajn, "The New Law Merchant" [1961] JBL 12.

103. Mustill, "The New Lex Mercatoria: The First Twenty-Five Years" (1988) 4 Arb Int 86, 114.

104. Highet, "The Enigma of the Lex Mercatoria" (1989) 63 Tulane LR 613, 623.

(i) Parties to a contract may choose the law of a country which is wholly unconnected with the contract. If, for example, an English company and a German company can expressly choose Peruvian law to govern their contract, why not the *lex mercatoria*?

(ii) Even the proponents of the *lex mercatoria* concede that any choice by the parties—be it the choice of an unconnected law or of the *lex mercatoria*—should not be allowed to prejudice the application of relevant mandatory rules of law.

(iii) Parties who choose the *lex mercatoria* should be deemed to be aware of its merits and demerits.

On the basis of these considerations there is no obvious reason of principle why national legal systems should seek to deny the validity of a choice of the *lex mercatoria* in an arbitration agreement.

17.3.7.6 In *Deutsche Schachtbau- und Tiefbohrgesellschaft mbH* v. *R'As al-Khaimah National Oil Co*[105] the Court of Appeal accepted that a foreign award was enforceable under the 1975 Act even though the arbitrators determined that the substantive obligations of the parties were governed by "internationally accepted principles of law governing contractual relations". The Court of Appeal rejected the argument that it was contrary to public policy to enforce an award which is based not on any particular national law, but on unspecified, and possibly ill-defined, internationally accepted principles of law. Of course, the decision to authorise enforcement of a foreign award where the dispute was decided by reference to general principles of law—rather than to a national law or public international law—does not necessarily entail the consequence that the court should uphold an English arbitration agreement or award in similar circumstances. Furthermore, in the *Deutsche Schachtbau* case the arbitrators had largely decided the dispute on questions of fact rather than law; in the award itself the arbitrators admitted that "the choice of the law to be applied to the agreement is of little significance, if any, under the prevailing circumstances".[106] Accordingly, the courts have yet to rule directly on the validity or otherwise of a clause which subjects the rights and obligations of the parties to the *lex mercatoria* or any other similar non-national body of rules. The Court of Appeal's discussion of the *lex mercatoria* in the *Deutsche Schachtbau* case does, however, indicate the way in which the wind is blowing.

17.3.7.7 Finally, it is important that the issue of the *lex mercatoria* should be kept in proportion. The majority of international commercial agreements which provide for the resolution of disputes by arbitration contain choice of law clauses which adhere to traditional conflicts methodology. In practice, the appeal of the *lex mercatoria* has been limited largely to economic development agreements between States and foreign investors; however, even in this limited field, "departures from conflicts methodology are not as widespread as the abundant literature on the point might suggest, and there are signs that previous enthusiasm for the *lex mercatoria* may have waned and may be subject to serious reconsideration".[107]

105. [1990] 1 AC 295. Hunter, "Lex Mercatoria" [1987] LMCLQ 277.

106. ICC No. 3572, cited by Mustill, "The New Lex Mercatoria: The First Twenty-Five Years" (1988) 4 Arb Int 86, 107.

107. Delaume, "Comparative Analysis as a Basis of Law in State Contracts: the Myth of the Lex Mercatoria" (1989) 63 Tulane LR 575, 578.

17.3.8 The impact of mandatory rules[108]

17.3.8.1 Mandatory rules comprise rules of law that cannot be derogated from by contract, including rules which a legal system regards as being of such importance that they must be applied irrespective of the applicable law. Mandatory rules include competition laws, exchange control legislation, environmental protection laws, and laws designed to protect the weaker party in consumer and employment contracts.

17.3.8.2 It is widely acknowledged that whatever methodology is employed for determining the applicable law, an arbitrator is required to have regard to mandatory rules—even if the parties have chosen the *lex mercatoria* or have authorised the arbitrator to decide the dispute *extra legem*. Failure by the arbitrator to have regard to relevant mandatory rules may result in the award either being set aside by the court with supervisory jurisdiction over the arbitration or being unenforceable in other countries on the ground of public policy.

17.3.8.3 It goes without saying that the mandatory rules of the *lex causae* must be applied; the real problem concerns the applicability of rules of law which are not part of the *lex causae*. To what extent are arbitrators required to apply mandatory rules which are part of the law of the seat or the law of another country? Although it has been suggested that, as a general rule, an arbitrator "must consider any strong principle of public policy of a country closely connected with the contract",[109] it would seem that where English law is the curial law an arbitrator must apply the relevant English conflicts rules which relate to the application of mandatory rules of law.[110] From the point of view of English law two provisions of the Rome Convention are relevant.[111]

17.3.8.4 The effect of Article 3(3) is that, if all the elements relevant to the situation are connected with England, but the parties to the arbitration agreement have chosen a law other than English law to govern the contract, this choice cannot prejudice the application of English mandatory rules. Failure by an arbitrator to apply English mandatory rules would provide a ground for an appeal under the 1979 Act. Since the arbitration agreement would be regarded as domestic, the parties' right to exclude the possibility of appeal on a point of law would be limited.[112]

17.3.8.5 Article 7 makes provision for the application of "overriding rules". Since Article 7(1) has not been implemented in the United Kingdom, it is reasonable to suppose that, in an arbitration conducted in England, the arbitrator is not permitted to have regard to the overriding rules of another country with which the situation has a close connection—despite the fact that failure to do so may render the award unenforceable in that country. Article 7(2) makes it clear that the overriding rules of the forum are always applicable. Although, strictly speaking, arbitrators "do not have a forum",[113] the traditional English view that arbitrators are bound by the same conflicts rules as the courts, leads to the conclusion that, as regards arbitrations conducted in England, arbitrators are required to apply English overriding rules, irrespective of the applicable law.

108. Mayer, "Mandatory Rules of Law in International Arbitration" (1986) 2 Arb Int 274.
109. Lando, "The Lex Mercatoria in International Commercial Arbitration" (1985) 34 ICLQ 747, 766–767.
110. See para. 11.3.
111. For a discussion of the difference between mandatory rules and "overriding rules" see para. 11.3.1.
112. Arbitration Act 1979, s. 3(6).
113. Mayer, "Mandatory Rules of Law in International Arbitration" (1986) 2 Arb Int 274, 283.

17.3.8.6 From the point of view of principle, however, the automatic application of English mandatory rules to an arbitration whose seat is located in England is of questionable validity. Although it is reasonable for an arbitrator to be bound by the mandatory rules of the seat in those cases where the arbitrator can be seen simply as a substitute for the local courts, in international situations the arbitrator takes the place of all the courts which might have had jurisdiction to determine the dispute in the absence of the arbitration agreement. It is perfectly possible that, had the parties not agreed to arbitration, the dispute could not have been litigated in the country chosen as the seat of arbitration. Logically, it would follow that, except in cases where the dispute has a close connection with the seat of arbitration, an arbitrator should not be regarded as being under a legal obligation to apply the "overriding rules" of the law of the seat, but should be limited only by international public policy.[114]

17.3.9 Remedies in cases where the arbitrator fails to apply the conflicts rules of the forum

17.3.9.1 Appeals on a point of law and exclusion agreements

When considering the remedies which are potentially available in cases where the arbitrator fails to apply English conflicts rules, it is important to know whether or not the parties have entered an agreement which effectively excludes the right of appeal to the court on a point of law. As a general principle, when an arbitrator makes an error of law, there exists a right of appeal to the court. Although, traditionally, English arbitration law has placed legality above the finality of arbitration proceedings, the court's supervisory jurisdiction on points of law is severely limited by the 1979 Act, which allows parties to an arbitration agreement to exclude the right of appeal. In domestic cases such an agreement is effective only if concluded after the commencement of the arbitration. However, in cases with a foreign element the parties may generally exclude the right of appeal by means of an agreement concluded prior to the dispute arising. (As regards contracts in the field of insurance, admiralty matters and commodities, an exclusion agreement is valid only if concluded after the commencement of the arbitration.) Even where the right of appeal has not been excluded, an appeal may be brought only with the leave of the court.[115]

17.3.9.2 Where there is no valid exclusion agreement

Where the parties have not entered an exclusion agreement and have not authorised the arbitrator to depart from the law, it must be assumed that, if English law is the curial law, the arbitrator is bound by English conflicts rules. If the arbitrator fails to apply English conflicts rules there is a right of appeal to the court with leave. If the court gives leave and finds that the arbitrator made a mistake as to the applicable law, the court may vary

114. Redfern & Hunter, *Law and Practice of International Commercial Arbitration* (2nd ed, 1991) pp. 444–446.

115. For further consideration of the right to appeal and exclusion agreements see Chapter 19.

or set aside the award or remit it to the arbitrator for reconsideration.[116] For example, in a case where the parties have not chosen the applicable law, if the arbitrator misapplies Article 4 of the Rome Convention, the arbitrator's error of law may be corrected by the court under the 1979 Act. If, however, the parties have expressly authorised the arbitrator to determine the dispute by standards other than a national system of law the court should not intervene, notwithstanding the fact that the right of appeal has not been excluded. Indeed, this is a classic situation where it would be inappropriate for the court to give leave to appeal under the 1979 Act.

17.3.9.3 Where there is a valid exclusion agreement

17.3.9.3.1 Where the parties have entered a valid exclusion agreement, one must distinguish cases in which the arbitrator honestly seeks to carry out the mandate of the parties according to the terms of their agreement but makes an error of law from situations where the arbitrator acts without jurisdiction by wholly disregarding the agreement of the parties. In individual cases it may be difficult to draw the dividing line between mere error of law and excess of jurisdiction.

17.3.9.3.2 The court's power under section 23 of the 1950 Act to set aside an award for misconduct may not be exercised where the only misconduct alleged is merely an error of law in a reasoned award. A simple mistake by an arbitrator in his assessment of the parties' substantive rights and obligations under a contract cannot amount to an excess of jurisdiction—regardless of whether the parties' substantive rights are governed by English or foreign law.[117] The only way to challenge an error of English law is to seek leave to appeal under the 1979 Act.[118] Accordingly, in those cases where the parties have excluded the right of appeal to the court on a point of law, there is no mechanism whereby simple errors of law can be corrected. In this situation, English law adopts the position that the finality of the award should prevail over its legality.

17.3.9.3.3 The position may, however, be different in those cases where the arbitrator wilfully disregards the terms of the arbitration agreement (for example, where the arbitrator decides *ex aequo et bono* notwithstanding the fact that the parties have agreed that the merits of the dispute should be governed by the law of a particular country).[119] An arbitrator who wilfully fails to carry out the parties' mandate—for example, by deliberately ignoring or rejecting the relevant rules of law (including the relevant conflicts rules)—is guilty of misconduct and in such a case the award may be set aside under section 23 of the 1950 Act: "if [two] merchants agree that the arbitrator will apply English law, and he explicitly applies provisions of the Swiss *Code des obligations*, such a decision normally falls outside the arbitrator's jurisdiction".[120] The fact that the parties have entered an exclusion agreement does not deprive the court of its supervisory jurisdiction in these circumstances: "An exclusion agreement merely operates to erase the right to seek leave to appeal, it does not further annul the obligation of an

116. Arbitration Act 1979, s. 1(2).

117. Steyn J in *Bank Mellat* v. *GAA Development & Construction Ltd* [1988] 2 Lloyd's Rep 44, 52.

118. *President of India* v. *Jadranska Slobodna Plovidba* [1992] 2 Lloyd's Rep 274.

119. Jaffey, "Arbitration of Commercial Contracts: the Law to be Applied by the Arbitrators" in Perrott & Pogany (eds), *Current Problems in International Trade Law* (1987) 129, 138.

120. Park, "National Law and Commercial Justice: Safeguarding Procedural Integrity in International Arbitration" (1989) 63 Tulane LR 647, 675.

arbitrator to decide according to law. A valid exclusion agreement is not a licence to decide *extra legem*."[121]

17.3.9.3.4 This still leaves the question of whether the court is entitled to set aside an award in cases where the parties have concluded a valid exclusion agreement and the arbitrator has decided *ex aequo et bono* or applied the *lex mercatoria* having been expressly authorised by the parties to do so. There is no clear reason—based either on precedent or principle—for the court to refuse to uphold the award in such cases.[122]

17.4 ARBITRATION AND EC LAW

17.4.1 It is important that EC law should be applied uniformly throughout the territories of the Member States. Accordingly, it is clear that arbitrators are bound by Community law: "Community law must be observed in its entirety throughout the territory of all the Member States; parties to a contract are not, therefore, free to create exceptions to it."[123] Moreover, in certain circumstances arbitrators should raise a point of EC law of their own motion—even if the point is neglected by the parties: "If [EC] law, by way of direct application, confers a right on one of the parties to the arbitration but the party does not claim that right and does not rely on [EC] law in support of it, the arbitrator need not raise the point *ex officio*. ... On the other hand, if the EEC Treaty declares a contract or agreement to be void but this invalidity is ignored by the parties in proceedings before the arbitrator, the arbitrator should take notice of this point *ex officio* and should not adjudicate on a contract which is null and void under [EC] law."[124]

17.4.2 In the context of legal proceedings, the uniform application of Community law is, to a considerable extent, achieved by Article 177 of the Treaty of Rome which provides a mechanism whereby national courts may refer questions of Community law to the Court of Justice for a preliminary ruling. Although Article 177 provides that a reference for a preliminary ruling may be made by a "court or tribunal of a Member State" the Court of Justice has decided that commercial arbitrators are not entitled to make use of the procedure provided by Article 177. In *Vaassen* v. *Management of the Beambtenfonds voor het Mijnbedrijf*[125] the Court of Justice accepted a reference from a Dutch *Scheidsgerecht* (literally "arbitral tribunal"). The Dutch tribunal was a body constituted in accordance with Dutch law to hear disputes relating to a miners' pension fund. This case was, however, distinguished in *Nordsee Deutsche Hochseefischerei GmbH* v. *Reederei Mond Hochseefischerei AG & Co KG*,[126] in which, following the reference of a dispute under a shipbuilding contract to arbitration, the arbitrators wished to seek a ruling from the Court of Justice on the question of whether the agreement contravened EC law. The Court of Justice decided that commercial

121. Thomas, "Commercial Arbitration—Justice According to Law" (1983) 2 CJQ 166, 170.

122. See paras. 17.3.6–17.3.7.

123. Case 102/81 *Nordsee Deutsche Hochseefischerei GmbH* v. *Reederei Mond Hochseefischerei AG & Co KG* [1982] ECR 1095, 1111 (para. 14).

124. Schmitthoff, "Arbitration and EEC Law" (1987) 24 CMLRev 143, 146.

125. Case 61/65 [1966] ECR 261.

126. Case 102/81 [1982] ECR 1095. Friend, "EEC Law, Preliminary Rulings and Arbitrators" (1983) 99 LQR 356.

arbitrators—whose jurisdiction derives from the agreement of the parties rather than the law of the country where the arbitration has its seat—are not a "tribunal" for the purposes of Article 177.

17.4.3 This decision has not escaped criticism. It has been suggested that it would have been more in keeping with contemporary legal thinking if the Court of Justice had recognised arbitration as an integral part of modern systems for the administration of justice and accepted a direct reference from commercial arbitrators.[127] Moreover, it is somewhat paradoxical for the Court of Justice to have asserted, on the one hand, that arbitrators have an obligation to respect Community law yet, on the other hand, to preclude arbitrators from making a preliminary ruling which could ensure its correct and full respect in a dispute.[128]

17.4.4 There are, however, channels through which points of law which arise in arbitration proceedings may be referred to the Court of Justice. It seems that there is no reason why a national court should not make a reference to the Court of Justice in the context of legal proceedings which involve an arbitration agreement, arbitration proceedings or an award. For example, questions of Community law may arise in the context of proceedings to enforce an award under the New York Convention of 1958. One of the grounds on which enforcement may be refused under the Convention is public policy. Since Community law is part of national law, in proceedings for the enforcement of an award which potentially infringes the public policy of the EC, a reference to the Court of Justice may be appropriate.[129]

17.4.5 English arbitration law is unusual in that it provides a mechanism for appeals to be made to the court on points of law. Where the right of appeal has not been excluded by the agreement of the parties, a party to the arbitration may apply to the court for leave to bring an appeal under the 1979 Act. It has been held that, in appropriate circumstances, where leave to appeal has been given, the court may make a reference to the Court of Justice on a point of Community law.[130] However, where a point of Community law arises and leave to appeal is sought under the 1979 Act, leave should not be given automatically (thereby presenting an opportunity for a reference under Article 177 to the Court of Justice); for leave to be given under the 1979 Act, the point of law which the case raises should be capable of serious argument.[131]

17.4.6 It would be fair to say that channelling references through national courts is cumbersome and does not guarantee the uniform application of Community law. Since arbitrators do not have direct access to the Court of Justice and, in international cases, the opportunities to appeal to national courts on points of law are severely limited (indeed, in most Member States they are wholly excluded), it seems highly likely that Community law is being enforced somewhat imperfectly in the context of disputes which are referred to arbitration.[132] There can be little doubt that the uniform interpretation and application of Community law is not as well protected in commercial arbitration as it is in national courts.[133]

127. Schmitthoff, "Arbitration and EEC Law" (1987) 24 CMLR 143, 153.
128. Bebr, "Arbitration Tribunals and Article 177 of the EEC Treaty" (1985) 22 CMLRev 489, 497–498.
129. McClellan, "Commercial Arbitration and European Community Law" (1989) 5 Arb Int 68, 79.
130. *Bulk Oil (Zug) Ltd* v. *Sun International Ltd* [1984] 1 WLR 147. Leigh & Velik, (1984) 9 ELRev 128.
131. Ackner LJ in *Bulk Oil (Zug) Ltd* v. *Sun International Ltd* [1984] 1 WLR 147, 154.
132. Weigand, "Evading EC Competition Law by Resorting to Arbitration?" (1993) 9 Arb Int 249.
133. Brown, "Commercial Arbitration and the European Economic Community" (1985) 2 J Int Arb (1) 21, 27.

17.5 JURISDICTION

When considering the jurisdiction of the English courts, there are various matters to consider. First, there is the issue of whether or not the court has jurisdiction *in personam* over the defendant. This issue can be broken down into two questions. (i) To what extent—if at all—is jurisdiction determined by the Brussels and Lugano Conventions? (ii) If the matter is not determined by the Conventions, what are the bases on which the court may assume jurisdiction under the traditional rules?

Secondly, in those circumstances in which the court has jurisdiction *in personam* over the defendant, the court must decide which—if any—of its statutory or common law powers may be exercised. Where the defendant is, in principle, amenable to the jurisdiction of the court (for example, where the defendant is domiciled in England) it cannot be assumed that the court has jurisdiction to exercise all its powers in relation to an arbitration to which the defendant is a party. To determine whether the court may exercise its powers under English law one must "ascertain the connecting factor prescribed by the rules of conflict of laws in order to find which country's laws are to be applied to a dispute of the kind which has arisen".[134] So, for example, where two English companies enter a contract which provides for disputes to be referred to arbitration in Geneva, the fact that the parties are amenable to English jurisdiction does not mean that the court has the power to set aside the resulting Swiss award under section 23 of the 1950 Act.[135]

17.5.1 Jurisdiction *in personam*

17.5.1.1 The scope of the Brussels and Lugano Conventions

17.5.1.1.1 The jurisdiction of the English courts in civil and commercial matters is regulated, in part, by the Brussels and Lugano Conventions.[136] The Conventions lay down not only jurisdiction rules which must be applied in cases where the defendant is domiciled in a Contracting State but also bases of jurisdiction which must be applied regardless of the domicile of the defendant. In cases where jurisdiction is not determined by the rules in Title II, Article 4 provides that the jurisdiction of the courts of a Contracting State shall be "determined by the law of that State".

17.5.1.1.2 Although Article 1 provides that the material scope of the Conventions extends to "civil and commercial matters" it is also provided that "arbitration" is excluded. Following the decision of the Court of Justice in *Marc Rich & Co AG* v. *Societa Italiana Impianti PA*[137] it seems clear that the jurisdiction rules contained in the Conventions do not apply to proceedings relating to arbitration or to proceedings in which the existence of an arbitration agreement is contested. The only issue on which uncertainty still exists is whether proceedings relating to the recognition and enforcement of a foreign judgment given in defiance of an arbitration agreement fall within the scope of the Conventions.[138] Accordingly, the traditional rules determine whether the court has jurisdiction to assist in the constitution of the tribunal, to grant

134. Staughton LJ in *Channel Tunnel Group Ltd* v. *Balfour Beatty Construction Ltd* [1992] QB 656, 671.
135. See para. 17.5.2.1.
136. See Chapters 4 and 5.
137. Case C-190/89 [1991] ECR I-3855. Briggs (1991) 11 YBEL 527.
138. See para. 3.3.3.4.

interim measures in support of an arbitration, to set aside an award or to order enforcement of an award.

17.5.1.2 Traditional rules: general principles[139]

17.5.1.2.1 The general principles which apply to all actions *in personam* are equally relevant to legal proceedings which relate to arbitration. In the context of commercial litigation the court has jurisdiction over a defendant in three situations:

(i) where the defendant is present within the jurisdiction;
(ii) where the defendant has submitted to the jurisdiction of the court;
(iii) where the defendant is served out of the jurisdiction with the leave of the court under RSC, Order 11, rule 1(1).

17.5.1.2.2 Where jurisdiction is established on the basis of the defendant's presence, the defendant may seek a stay of proceedings on the basis of *forum non conveniens*. If the defendant cannot be served in the jurisdiction and declines to submit, the plaintiff needs the leave of the court to serve out of the jurisdiction. There are many circumstances in which the general rules contained in RSC, Order 11 are potentially relevant.[140] Where, for example, the scope of the arbitrator's jurisdiction turns on the interpretation of an arbitration clause which is governed by English law, the court may assume jurisdiction over proceedings challenging the arbitrator's jurisdiction under RSC, Order 11, rule 1(1)(d)(iii). Similarly, where a party to an arbitration agreement which was concluded in England seeks a declaration that the agreement has been discharged by consent, the court may assume jurisdiction under RSC, Order 11, rule 1(1)(d)(i). Of course, where the plaintiff seeks to rely on RSC, Order 11, rule 1(1), the court must be satisfied that England is the *forum conveniens*.

17.5.1.2.3 In addition, RSC, Order 73, rule 7(1) provides that service out of the jurisdiction of any originating summons or notice of originating motion under the Acts of 1950 or 1979 is permissible with the leave of the court provided that either (i) the arbitration to which the summons or motion relates is governed by English law or (ii) the arbitration has been, is being, or is to be held within the jurisdiction. Where leave is sought under RSC, Order 73, rule 7(1) the plaintiff must establish that England is the *forum conveniens*.

17.5.1.2.4 The cases concerning the exercise of discretion under RSC, Order 73 are not entirely consistent. In *Marc Rich & Co AG* v. *Societa Italiana Impianti PA* Hirst J took the view that the relevant criteria for determining whether or not England is the most appropriate forum are those laid down by the House of Lords in *Spiliada Maritime Corporation* v. *Cansulex Ltd*[141] in the context of RSC, Order 11.[142] However, in *The John C Helmsing*,[143] a case concerning an application for the appointment of an arbitrator by the court under section 10(3) of the 1950 Act, the Court of Appeal indicated that special

139. See Chapter 6.
140. The jurisdictional bases which are most likely to be important in practice are contained in RSC, Order 11, r. 1(1)(a), (b), (c) and (d).
141. [1987] AC 460.
142. [1989] 1 Lloyd's Rep 548, 553.
143. [1990] 2 Lloyd's Rep 290.

considerations must be taken into account when the plaintiff seeks leave under RSC, Order 73. In particular:

the court must bear in mind, in exercising its jurisdiction under Order 73, rule 7 ... that the plaintiff has *ex hypothesi* bound himself to refer differences to arbitration and cannot therefore pursue his substantive claim against the defendant in legal proceedings abroad. He may also be bound to pursue the arbitration reference here ... If, therefore, the court exercises discretion so as to prevent the plaintiff achieving a properly constituted arbitration tribunal, it may leave him with no means of pursuing his claim anywhere, this being a notable distinction with the position under Order 11.[144]

When a situation appears to fall within the scope of both rules leave should be sought under RSC, Order 73, rule 7 which is "very much more specific and therefore more apt".[145]

17.5.1.3 Enforcement proceedings

(i) RSC, Order 73, rule 7(1A) provides that "[s]ervice out of the jurisdiction of an originating summons for leave to enforce an award is permissible with the leave of the court whether or not the arbitration is governed by English law".
(ii) RSC, Order 11, rule 1(1)(m) provides that service of a writ out of the jurisdiction is permissible with the leave of the court if, in the action begun by the writ, "the claim is brought to enforce any ... arbitral award".

Whether the award has been made in England or abroad, leave is required under both rules. It is reasonable to suppose that, in deciding whether or not to give leave, the same criteria are applied by the courts in both categories of application. The presence of the defendant's assets is not sufficient to give the court jurisdiction in enforcement proceedings. Neither, however, is the presence of assets within the jurisdiction a precondition for leave to be given.[146]

17.5.2 The scope of the court's powers

17.5.2.1 Typical cases

17.5.2.1.1 In the paradigm case—where an arbitration is conducted in England in accordance with English procedural law—the court has jurisdiction to exercise the full range of powers conferred by the Arbitration Acts, irrespective of the fact that the arbitration involves foreign elements. The statutory jurisdiction of the court under the Arbitration Acts cannot be excluded by agreement of the parties—except to the extent that such exclusion is permitted by the legislation itself.[147]

17.5.2.1.2 Many of the powers conferred by the Acts are discretionary, however, and the fact that the arbitration is international may provide a good reason for not exercising one or more of the powers. For example, section 12(6)(a) of the 1950 Act confers on the

144. Bingham LJ in *The John C Helmsing* [1990] 2 Lloyd's Rep 290, 293.
145. Bingham LJ in *The John C Helmsing* [1990] 2 Lloyd's Rep 290, 293.
146. Steyn J in *Rosseel NV* v. *Oriental Commercial & Shipping Co (UK) Ltd* [1991] 2 Lloyd's Rep 625, 629.
147. See Chapter 19.

court the power to make an order in respect of security for costs.[148] When deciding whether to order security for the costs of an international arbitration conducted in England, it is a relevant consideration weighing against making the order that the parties have expressly or impliedly agreed[149] or mutually indicated that there should be no application to the court for security (for example, by incorporating the ICC Rules).[150] The court will generally not order security if both parties are foreign, the dispute relates to a contract which was to be performed abroad and the only connection between the arbitration and England is that the parties chose England as the seat of arbitration. However, even if the parties are foreign and the performance of the contract has nothing to do with England, the court is not unwilling to make an order under section 12(6)(a) if the parties have agreed to arbitration in England under English arbitration rules and English law is the substantive law governing the dispute.[151]

17.5.2.1.3 In the converse situation—where an arbitration is conducted abroad under the curial law of a foreign country—the court does not normally have jurisdiction to exercise the powers conferred by the legislation. As Lord Mustill noted in *Channel Tunnel Group Ltd* v. *Balfour Beatty Ltd* there is no obvious reason "why Parliament should have had the least concern to regulate the conduct of an arbitration carried on abroad pursuant to a foreign arbitral law".[152] For example, the court cannot order interim measures under section 12(6)(h) of the 1950 Act in relation to an arbitration which is to be conducted in Brussels under the procedural law of Belgium.[153] Nevertheless, there are some statutory provisions of general application which are not limited to arbitrations governed by English law.

(i) The duty of the court in non-domestic cases to stay proceedings brought in England in breach of the terms of an arbitration agreement is universal—in the sense that it arises regardless of whether the seat of arbitration is in England or abroad and irrespective of the law governing the arbitration agreement or the arbitration.[154]

(ii) The various regimes for the recognition and enforcement in England of foreign awards depend on the court having jurisdiction over the defendant in relation to the proceedings[155]; there is no requirement that the arbitration itself should have had any factual or legal connection with the forum.

(iii) The power to grant interim injunctions under section 37(1) of the Supreme Court Act 1981 may be exercised in support of a foreign arbitration. This power exists notwithstanding the fact that the English proceedings are brought in breach of an arbitration agreement to refer all disputes to arbitration abroad and the court proceedings in England are stayed under section 1(1) of the 1975 Act.[156] The jurisdiction of the court under section 37(1)

148. See para. 16.2.3.1.4.1.
149. *Mavani* v. *Ralli Bros Ltd* [1973] 1 WLR 468.
150. *Bank Mellat* v. *Helliniki Techniki SA* [1984] QB 291.
151. *K/S A/S Bani* v. *Korea Shipbuilding & Engineering Corporation* [1987] 2 Lloyd's Rep 445.
152. [1993] AC 334, 359.
153. *Channel Tunnel Group Ltd* v. *Balfour Beatty Construction Ltd* [1993] AC 334.
154. See para. 18.2.
155. See para. 17.5.1.3.
156. *Channel Tunnel Group Ltd* v. *Balfour Beatty Construction Ltd* [1993] AC 334. Collins, "The End of the Siskina?" (1993) 109 342; Reymond, "The Channel Tunnel Case and the Law of International Commercial Arbitration" (1993) 109 LQR 337.

depends simply on there being a cause of action which is justiciable in the English courts.[157] Where section 37(1) confers a power on the court to grant interim measures, the exercise of the power depends on the exercise of the court's discretion. When the court is asked to order, by way of interim relief, a remedy of the same kind as will be sought from the arbitrator, the court must be careful not to usurp the arbitrator's functions; the court must have regard to "the duty of the court to respect the choice of tribunal which both parties have made, and not to take out of the hands of the arbitrators . . . a power of decision which the parties have entrusted to them alone".[158] Notwithstanding that the court can and should in the right case provide reinforcement for the arbitral process by granting interim relief, it will be most unusual for the court to intervene in support of a foreign arbitration, since the court with supervisory jurisdiction over the arbitration is normally the natural forum for obtaining relief of this type.

17.5.2.2 Potential problems

17.5.2.2.1 It will be most rare for an arbitration clause to be construed as providing for an arbitration to be conducted in country X under the supervisory jurisdiction of the courts of country Y.[159] When the link between the curial law and the seat of arbitration is broken by the express choice of the parties, the following question has to be considered: are the court's powers of supervision and support derived from the will of the parties or the mere fact that the arbitration is conducted within the jurisdiction? Although there is no reported case in which an English court has been required to answer this question, in a number of cases the issue has been addressed.

17.5.2.2.2 Such authority as there is supports a strictly territorial view of the court's powers. In *Dalmia Cement Ltd* v. *National Bank of Pakistan* Kerr J thought that "most of the provisions of Part I [of the 1950 Act] can only sensibly be applied to English arbitrations and to awards made in England. This is because the provisions are designed to deal with arbitrations whose procedural law is English and the English courts cannot render amenable to their process the conduct of arbitrations or arbitrators outside the jurisdiction."[160] This view was reiterated in *Naviera Amazonica Peruana SA* v. *Compania Internacional de Seguros del Peru*:

> At any rate under the principles of English law, which rest upon the territorially limited jurisdiction of our courts, an agreement to arbitrate in X subject to English procedural law would not empower our courts to exercise jurisdiction over the arbitration in X.[161]

17.5.2.2.3 The territorial approach also leads to the view that the court has jurisdiction over an arbitration which is conducted in England even if the parties have purported to subject the arbitration to the supervisory jurisdiction of a foreign court.[162]

157. See paras. 21.3.1.1 and 21.3.2.2.
158. Lord Mustill in *Channel Tunnel Group Ltd* v. *Balfour Beatty Construction Ltd* [1993] AC 334, 367–368.
159. See paras. 17.2.3–17.2.4.
160. [1975] 1 QB 9, 21.
161. Kerr LJ, [1988] 1 Lloyd's Rep 116, 120. See also *Channel Tunnel Group Ltd* v. *Balfour Beatty Construction Ltd* [1992] QB 656 (CA).
162. *Union of India* v. *McDonnell Douglas Inc* [1993] 2 Lloyd's Rep 48.

The rationale for the position adopted by the courts is the generally accepted view that the general supervisory jurisdiction of the court cannot be excluded by agreement:

It has never ... been suggested that parties may validly contract out of the power to set aside or remit an award for misconduct; and if an express agreement cannot accomplish this, it is hard to see how it could be achieved indirectly by the choice of a foreign curial law.[163]

17.5.2.2.4 However, to the extent that the court's powers of supervision are discretionary the fact that the parties intend that the arbitration should be subject to the supervisory jurisdiction of a foreign court might discourage the court from interfering, notwithstanding the fact that the seat of arbitration is in England.[164] In addition, an agreement to subject an English arbitration to the supervisory jurisdiction of a foreign court might be regarded as a valid exclusion agreement for the purposes of the 1979 Act.

17.5.2.2.5 Fortunately, the problems posed by an agreement to arbitrate in country X under the supervision of the courts of country Y are not very likely to loom large in practice. Nevertheless, the approach advocated by the English courts raises interesting theoretical considerations, since it reveals the limits of the principle of party autonomy in arbitration.[165] Since arbitration is founded on the parties' agreement it is to be expected that the principle of party autonomy should be regarded as having a particular importance in the field of arbitration. Taken to its logical conclusion the principle of party autonomy gives the parties freedom to select for themselves the rules which should govern all aspects of the arbitral process. Within this framework the freedom to conduct an arbitration in country X according to the law of country Y is unexceptional. Indeed, the theory that parties might sever the link between the curial law and the seat of arbitration is the inspiration behind Article V(1)(d) of the New York Convention which provides that an award may be refused enforcement if it has been set aside "by a competent authority of the country in which, *or under the law of which* it was made".[166]

17.5.2.2.6 The position taken by the English courts imposes limitations on the parties' freedom of choice. Parties to an arbitration agreement are free to choose the rules to govern the internal conduct of an arbitration—subject to the mandatory procedural rules of the law of the seat—and may select the seat of arbitration, thereby indirectly choosing the law which governs external supervision. However, the supposed freedom to choose a law to govern external supervision which is not the law of the seat is illusory.

163. Mustill & Boyd, *Commercial Arbitration* (2nd ed, 1989) p. 90.
164. Saville J in *Union of India* v. *McDonnell Douglas Inc* [1993] 2 Lloyd's Rep 48, 51.
165. See para. 17.2.1.
166. Emphasis added.

CHAPTER 18

THE AGREEMENT TO ARBITRATE

18.1 INTRODUCTION

18.1.1 What is an arbitration agreement?

Arbitration is a consensual process based on an arbitration agreement. Such agreements may take the form of a submission agreement entered into after the dispute has arisen or an arbitration clause which refers to arbitration disputes which may arise in the future in relation to a particular legal relationship. A variation of the standard arbitration agreement is the *Scott* v. *Avery*[1] clause, which may take the form of either a contractual term which provides that a reference to arbitration and the making of an award shall be a condition precedent to the commencement of any litigation or a provision to the effect that the defendant's only contractual obligation is to pay such sum as the arbitrator shall award.[2] Under English law submission agreements and arbitration clauses (including *Scott* v. *Avery* clauses) are equally valid. Under English law there are no formal requirements which have to be satisfied for a valid arbitration agreement. However, in practice an oral agreement is difficult to enforce and the powers conferred on the courts by the 1950 Act are only exercisable in relation to a written agreement.[3]

18.1.2 The doctrine of separability

18.1.2.1 A submission agreement—under which the parties agree to refer a dispute to arbitration—is obviously a discrete contract. Similarly, as a general rule an arbitration clause in a contract constitutes a self-contained contract, collateral or ancillary to the principal contract of which it forms a part.[4] This is the doctrine of separability (or severability).

18.1.2.2 Since many contractual claims are referred to arbitration following the termination of the contract it would, in practical terms, seriously detract from the usefulness of arbitration as a method of dispute resolution if an arbitration clause applied only to pre-termination disputes. It is well established that an arbitration clause in a contract remains enforceable—as an autonomous contract—even though the

1. (1856) 5 HL Cas 811.
2. Thomas, "Scott v. Avery Agreements" [1991] LMCLQ 508.
3. Arbitration Act 1950, s. 32.
4. Lord Diplock in *Bremer Vulkan Schiffbau und Maschinenfabrik* v. *South India Shipping Corporation Ltd* [1981] AC 909, 980.

principal contract has been terminated whether by repudiation,[5] frustration,[6] rescission,[7] or supervening illegality.[8]

18.1.2.3 In cases where the main contract is void *ab initio*, the traditional view was that "an arbitrator does not have jurisdiction, nor can the arbitration agreement be construed to give him jurisdiction to rule upon the initial existence of the contract".[9] The rationale for the principle was that "if one party to the alleged contract is contending that it is void *ab initio* (because, for example, the making of such a contract is illegal), the arbitration clause cannot operate, for on this view the clause itself also is void".[10]

18.1.2.4 The traditional view has, however, been discarded in favour of a more liberal approach to the doctrine of separability.[11] In *Harbour Assurance Co (UK) Ltd* v. *Kansa General International Insurance Co Ltd*[12] the Court of Appeal decided that questions concerning the initial validity of a contract may be within the arbitrator's jurisdiction. Notwithstanding the orthodox understanding of some earlier cases,[13] it was held there was no binding authority for the proposition that an arbitrator cannot have jurisdiction to determine whether a contract is void *ab initio*—even where it is alleged that the contract is void as a result of illegality. Accordingly, in cases where the arbitration clause is drafted sufficiently broadly, questions of initial validity (including questions of initial illegality) are not beyond the scope of the arbitrator's jurisdiction. Furthermore, it is implicit in the decision of the Court of Appeal in *Harbour Assurance Co (UK) Ltd* v. *Kansa General International Insurance Co Ltd* that, as long as the clause is drafted appropriately, questions of fraud may also be within the arbitrator's jurisdiction.[14] So, the question of whether a contract is voidable for fraudulent misrepresentation is just as much capable of being referred to arbitration as an issue of avoidance for innocent misrepresentation.[15]

18.1.2.5 There are, however, limits to the doctrine of separability. In English law an arbitrator does not have jurisdiction in cases where (i) the arbitration clause itself is invalid under its proper law or (ii) the arbitration clause never comes into existence (for example, where there was no consensus between the parties on the contract of which the arbitration agreement forms a part).

5. *Heyman* v. *Darwins Ltd* [1942] AC 356.
6. *Kruse* v. *Questier & Co Ltd* [1953] 1 QB 669; *Government of Gibraltar* v. *Kenney* [1956] 2 QB 410.
7. *Mackender* v. *Feldia AG* [1967] 2 QB 590. This case concerned a jurisdiction clause, but the principle applies equally to an arbitration clause.
8. *Prodexport State Co for Foreign Trade* v. *ED & F Man Ltd* [1973] 1 QB 389.
9. May LJ in *Ashville Investments Ltd* v. *Elmer Contractors Ltd* [1989] QB 488, 494.
10. Viscount Simon LC in *Heyman* v. *Darwins Ltd* [1942] AC 356, 366. See *Dalmia Dairy Industries Ltd* v. *National Bank of Pakistan* [1978] 2 Lloyd's Rep 223, 286.
11. See the judgments of Steyn J in *Paul Smith Ltd* v. *H & S International Holdings Inc* [1991] 2 Lloyd's Rep 127) and *Harbour Assurance Co (UK) Ltd* v. *Kansa General International Insurance Co Ltd* [1992] 1 Lloyd's Rep 81. See also Hill, "The Scope of the Doctrine of Separability" [1992] LMCLQ 306.
12. [1993] QB 701.
13. *Smith, Coney & Barrett* v. *Becker, Gray & Co* [1916] 2 Ch 86; *David Taylor & Son Ltd* v. *Barnett Trading Co* [1953] 1 WLR 562.
14. See the judgment of Ralph Gibson LJ, [1993] QB 701, 712.
15. Steyn J in *Harbour Assurance Co (UK) Ltd* v. *Kansa General International Insurance Co Ltd* [1992] 1 Lloyd's Rep 81, 91. See also Mustill & Boyd, *Commercial Arbitration* (2nd ed, 1989) p. 116.

18.1.3 Validity and scope of the arbitration agreement

18.1.3.1 The arbitrator's jurisdiction is derived from the arbitration agreement. If the arbitration agreement is for any reason invalid, or if the dispute falls outside the scope of the arbitration agreement, the arbitrator has no jurisdiction. The validity and scope of an arbitration clause are to be determined by its proper law.[16] The proper law of the arbitration agreement governs whether the parties consented to the arbitration clause and determines the meaning to be given to various words and phrases which are commonly found in arbitration clauses (for example, "disputes", "differences", "arising out of", "in relation to", "with regard to").[17]

18.1.3.2 English law is very liberal in allowing either party to apply to the court for a ruling on the arbitrator's jurisdiction at almost any time.[18]

(i) Even before the arbitration has been commenced, a party to the alleged agreement may seek a declaration from the court that the arbitration clause is invalid.
(ii) During the course of the reference one of the parties may apply for a stay of the arbitration proceedings on the basis that the arbitrator has no jurisdiction.
(iii) Once the award has been made, one of the parties may apply to have the award set aside on the basis of the arbitrator's lack of jurisdiction.
(iv) Where the successful party seeks to enforce the award in a country other than that in which the arbitration was conducted enforcement may be resisted on the basis either that the arbitration agreement was "not valid under the law to which the parties [have] subjected it or, failing any indication thereon, under the law of the country where the award was made"[19] or that "the award deals with a difference not contemplated by or not falling within the terms of the submission to arbitration or contains decisions on matters beyond the scope of the submission to arbitration".[20]

18.1.4 The enforcement of domestic arbitration agreements

18.1.4.1 If a court accepts jurisdiction over the substance of a dispute which the parties agreed to refer to arbitration, the institution of arbitration is undermined. There can be no objection to the court's assumption of jurisdiction if the parties to an arbitration agreement subsequently choose to litigate their dispute; where one party to an arbitration agreement starts court proceedings the defendant may choose to waive the arbitration clause and to fight the action on the merits. However, in cases where court proceedings are commenced in breach of the terms of an arbitration agreement the defendant should be able to rely on agreement and ask the court to decline jurisdiction.

16. See para. 17.1.

17. See Mustill & Boyd, *Commercial Arbitration* (2nd ed, 1989) pp. 117–121; *Russell on Arbitration* (20th ed, 1982) pp. 82–92. For an analysis of the meaning of "disputes" see *Hayter* v. *Nelson* [1990] 2 Lloyd's Rep 265.

18. See, for example, *Metal Scrap Trade Corporation Ltd* v. *Kate Shipping Co Ltd* [1988] 1 WLR 767, reversed on other grounds by the House of Lords: [1990] 1 WLR 115.

19. New York Convention, Article V(1)(a); Arbitration Act 1975, s. 5(2)(b). The word in parentheses appears in the text of the New York Convention, but not in the 1975 Act.

20. New York Convention, Article V(1)(c); Arbitration Act 1975, s. 5(2)(d).

Whereas judges used to view arbitration agreements as tending to oust the jurisdiction of the courts, it is now appreciated that a less interventionist approach is appropriate: "there is no good reason why the courts should strive to take matters out of the hands of the tribunal into which the parties have by agreement undertaken to place them".[21]

18.1.4.2 In a case involving a domestic arbitration agreement, if litigation is brought in breach of the terms of the agreement, the court has a discretion whether or not to stay proceedings under section 4(1) of the 1950 Act which provides:

If any party to an arbitration agreement, or any person claiming through or under him, commences any legal proceedings in any court against any other party to the agreement, or any person claiming through or under him, in respect of any matter agreed to be referred, any party to those legal proceedings may at any time after appearance, and before delivering any pleadings or taking any other steps in the proceedings, apply to that court to stay the proceedings and that court or a judge thereof, if satisfied that there is no sufficient reason why the matter should not be referred in accordance with the agreement, and that the applicant was, at the time when the proceedings were commenced, and still remains, ready and willing to do all things necessary to the proper conduct of the arbitration, may make an order staying the proceedings.

Although a stay under this provision is discretionary, in recent years the presumption in favour of granting a stay has become almost overwhelming. In cases with a foreign element, however, there is no discretion; if the necessary conditions are satisfied a stay is mandatory.[22]

18.2 THE ENFORCEMENT OF ARBITRATION AGREEMENTS UNDER THE ARBITRATION ACT 1975

18.2.1 The statutory framework

18.2.1.1 One of the aims of the New York Convention on the Recognition and Enforcement of Foreign Arbitral Awards was to ensure the respect of arbitration agreements and to prevent a party who had entered an arbitration agreement from being able to opt for litigation instead. The 1975 Act implements the Convention in the United Kingdom. It should be noted, however, that there are some differences between the Convention and the implementing legislation. Where the Act and the Convention are in conflict the provisions of the Act prevail.

18.2.1.2 Section 1(1) of the 1975 Act provides:

If any party to an arbitration agreement to which this section applies, or any person claiming through or under him, commences any legal proceedings in any court against any other party to the agreement, or any person claiming through or under him, in respect of any matter agreed to be referred, any party to the proceedings may at any time after appearance, and before delivering any pleadings or taking any other steps in the proceedings, apply to the court to stay the proceedings; and the court, unless satisfied that the arbitration agreement is null and void, inoperative or incapable of being performed or that there is not in fact any dispute between the parties with regard to the matter agreed to be referred, shall make an order staying the proceedings.

The territorial scope of section 1 is clear; it applies to any court proceedings in England concerning a dispute arising out of an agreement to arbitrate irrespective of the seat of

21. Saville J in *Hayter* v. *Nelson* [1990] 2 Lloyd's Rep 265, 269.
22. See para. 18.2.

arbitration.[23] The duty to stay proceedings arises regardless of whether the parties agreed to refer disputes to arbitration in England, Scotland, France or any other place in the world.

18.2.2 Conditions for the grant of a stay under section 1[24]

In order for the court to be under a duty to grant a stay of proceedings under section 1 a number of conditions must be satisfied:

(i) the arbitration agreement must be within the scope of the section;
(ii) the dispute must also fall within the scope of the arbitration agreement;
(iii) the defendant must apply for a stay before making an appearance in the court proceedings;
(iv) the arbitration agreement must not be null and void, inoperative or incapable of being performed; and
(v) there must be a dispute between the parties.

18.2.2.1 An arbitration agreement within the scope of section 1

Section 1 does not apply to all arbitration agreements. To fall within the scope of section 1(1) three conditions must be satisfied: there must be a foreign element; the arbitration agreement must be in writing; and the subject matter of the dispute must be arbitrable.

18.2.2.1.1 FOREIGN ELEMENT

18.2.2.1.1.1 In order for the duty to stay to arise the case must include a foreign element. Section 1 applies to "any arbitration agreement which is not a domestic arbitration agreement".[25] For the purposes of section 1 a "domestic arbitration agreement" is

> an arbitration agreement which does not provide, expressly or by implication, for arbitration in a State other than the United Kingdom and to which neither
> (a) an individual who is a national of, or habitually resident in, any State other than the United Kingdom; nor
> (b) a body corporate which is incorporated in, or whose central management and control is exercised in, any State other than the United Kingdom;
> is a party at the time the proceedings are commenced.[26]

18.2.2.1.1.2 The effect of this subsection is that if there is any non-United Kingdom element—in terms of the place of arbitration or the nationality, habitual residence, place of incorporation or central management and control of one or more of the parties—the agreement is not a domestic arbitration agreement. It follows from the definition in the Act that an arbitration agreement which has connections with more

23. Staughton LJ in *Channel Tunnel Group Ltd* v. *Balfour Beatty Construction Ltd* [1992] QB 656, 671.
24. See Thomas, "International Commercial Arbitration Agreements and the Enforcement of Foreign Arbitral Awards—A Commentary on the Arbitration Act 1975" [1981] LMCLQ 17, 19–30.
25. Arbitration Act 1975, s. 1(2).
26. Arbitration Act 1975, s. 1(4).

than one part of the United Kingdom may be a domestic arbitration agreement, in which case the court has discretion whether or not to grant a stay under section 4(1) of the 1950 Act. So, where a Scottish company and a person habitually resident in Northern Ireland enter into an arbitration agreement which provides for arbitration in London, the court is not required to grant a stay of proceedings.

18.2.2.1.1.3 There are potential problems which flow from the fact that the concept "domestic arbitration agreement" is defined negatively. What is the nature of an arbitration agreement involving United Kingdom citizens or corporations and providing for arbitration under the ICC Rules, but silent as to where the arbitration is to take place?[27] Since in this type of case the place of arbitration will not be determined until after the arbitration has been commenced it may be unclear as to whether the case involves a foreign element at the time when one of the parties invokes the jurisdiction of the court. Unless the incorporation of the ICC Rules is to be regarded *ipso facto* as an implied agreement to arbitrate in a foreign country (which must be doubtful), the terms of the legislation indicate that in these circumstances the arbitration agreement must be regarded as domestic since by failing to provide for arbitration in any particular place, the agreement cannot be regarded as providing, expressly or impliedly, for arbitration in a State other than the United Kingdom. The position would, however, be different if the parties expressly chose the law of a foreign country as the curial law. The express choice of the law of country X as the law to govern the arbitration operates as an implied choice of country X as the seat of arbitration.[28]

18.2.2.1.2 IN WRITING

18.2.2.1.2.1 An arbitration agreement does not fall within the scope of the 1975 Act unless it is "an agreement in writing (including an agreement contained in an exchange of letters or telegrams) to submit to arbitration present or future differences . . ."[29] The provision of the Convention on which this definition is based is Article II(2) which provides: "The term 'agreement in writing' shall include an arbitral clause in a contract or an arbitration agreement, signed by the parties or contained in an exchange of letters or telegrams."

18.2.2.1.2.2 It is clear that an oral agreement falls outside the scope of both the Convention and the 1975 Act. It is equally clear that there are three types of arbitration agreement which fall within the scope of both the Convention and the 1975 Act: (i) an arbitral clause in a contract which is signed by the parties; (ii) a submission agreement which is signed by the parties; (iii) an arbitration agreement contained in an exchange of letters or telegrams. Technological advances suggest that the words "an exchange of letters or telegrams" should not be interpreted literally. In *Arab African Energy Corporation Ltd* v. *Olieprodukten Nederland BV*[30] it was held that an exchange of telexes containing the words "English law—arbitration, if any, London according to ICC Rules" satisfied the formal requirements imposed by the Act. Presumably an exchange of facsimile messages would also be regarded as sufficient.

18.2.2.1.2.3 To the extent that problems of interpretation arise they result from the

27. The question is posed (but not answered) by Lew, "The Arbitration Act 1975" (1975) 24 ICLQ 870, 872.
28. *Naviera Amazonica Peruana SA* v. *Compania Internacional de Seguros del Peru* [1988] 1 Lloyd's Rep 116.
29. Arbitration Act 1975, s. 7(1).
30. [1983] 2 Lloyd's Rep 419.

fact that, whereas the Convention provides that, as regards an arbitration clause in a contract, the contract must be signed by the parties, the 1975 Act does not refer to signatures at all. The purpose of Article II(2) of the Convention was to exclude "an arbitration agreement which is proposed in writing and accepted orally or tacitly".[31] An agreement in this form constitutes neither an agreement contained in a contract signed by the parties nor an exchange of letters or telegrams.

18.2.2.1.2.4 The English courts have not, however, interpreted the implementing legislation in a manner which is consistent with the objectives of the Convention. In *Zambia Steel & Building Supplies Ltd* v. *James Clark & Eaton Ltd*[32] the Court of Appeal decided that an oral acceptance of a written proposal to arbitrate qualified as an agreement in writing within the meaning of the Act. In this case the defendant, an English company, provided the plaintiff, a Zambian company, with a written price quotation for goods "made on our terms of business". The defendant's standard terms—which were set out on the back of the price quotation—included an arbitration clause which provided for arbitration in England. The plaintiff ordered goods from the defendant and orally assented to the defendant's terms. When the plaintiff, claiming that the goods were damaged on delivery, started proceedings in England, the defendant sought a stay under section 1 of the 1975 Act. O'Conner LJ decided that "if it is established that a document with an arbitration clause in writing forms part of a contract between the parties, the assent by one party orally to the contract is sufficient".[33] Ralph Gibson LJ adopted a similar view: "If the term containing the agreement to submit is incorporated in a document and it is proved that the party is bound by an agreement which includes the terms of that document, then no further proof of the agreement to submit ... is required."[34]

18.2.2.1.2.5 The decision has been legitimately criticised on the basis that the Court of Appeal went beyond anything contemplated by the Convention.[35] Article II(2) is intended as a uniform rule which lays down both a minimum and a maximum requirement; accordingly, "a court may not require more, but also may not accept less than is provided by Article II(2) for the form of the arbitration agreement".[36]

18.2.2.1.2.6 This is not to say that the result in *Zambia Steel & Building Supplies Ltd.* v. *James Clark & Eaton Ltd* was inappropriate. One of the purposes of the Convention is to encourage the enforcement of arbitration agreements; to achieve this aim the Convention lays down limited circumstances in which the participating States are obliged to enforce such agreements. Article VII(1)—the so-called "more favourable right" clause—provides that, in relation to the enforcement of awards, the enforcement regime in the Convention is not exclusive; a party may take advantage of any more liberal provisions of the law of the country where enforcement is sought. Since the omission of an express mention of arbitration agreements in Article VII(1) should be regarded as unintentional,[37] the same principle should apply to the enforcement of

31. Van den Berg, *The New York Arbitration Convention of 1958* (1981) p. 196.
32. [1986] 2 Lloyd's Rep 225.
33. [1986] 2 Lloyd's Rep 225, 229.
34. [1986] 2 Lloyd's Rep 225, 235.
35. Mann, "An 'Agreement in Writing' to Arbitrate" (1987) 3 Arb Int 171, 172. Not all commentators are unhappy with the decision: Samuel, "The Effect of the Place of Arbitration on the Enforcement of the Agreement to Arbitrate" (1992) 8 Arb Int 257, 271.
36. Van den Berg, *The New York Arbitration Convention of 1958* (1981) p. 179.
37. Van den Berg, *The New York Arbitration Convention of 1958* (1981) p. 86.

arbitration agreements. This line of reasoning leads to the notion that where an arbitration agreement does not satisfy the requirements for a mandatory stay, a party to the agreement is not precluded from applying for and, in appropriate circumstances, obtaining a stay of proceedings under the court's inherent jurisdiction.[38]

18.2.2.1.3 CAPABLE OF SETTLEMENT BY ARBITRATION

18.2.2.1.3.1 To fall within the scope of the 1975 Act it is not sufficient that the arbitration agreement should satisfy the relevant formal requirements; the dispute must also be one which is "capable of settlement by arbitration".[39] Neither the Convention nor the 1975 Act indicates the system of law by reference to which the question of arbitrability is to be tested and there is no English authority directly on this point. There are various possibilities: (i) the law of the seat of arbitration; (ii) the proper law of the arbitration agreement (as determined by the conflicts rules of the forum); (iii) the law of the forum in which the litigation has been brought. As a matter of principle it would appear that the first two laws are relevant: "If the arbitration agreement covers matters incapable of being settled by arbitration, under the law of the agreement or under the law of the place of arbitration, the agreement is ineffective since it will be unenforceable."[40] Although the law of the forum has no obvious claim to be applied, its application finds favour in some quarters.[41]

18.2.2.1.3.2 Under English law there are very few restrictions on the type of dispute which is arbitrable. It has been suggested that "any dispute or claim concerning legal rights which can be the subject of an enforceable award, is capable of being settled by arbitration".[42] There are, however, certain practical limitations on the matters which can be the subject of a binding award. Arbitrators do not enjoy the coercive powers of the State and have no authority over persons who are not parties to the arbitration agreement. So, for example, an arbitrator may not make an award *in rem* in a shipping dispute nor make an award winding up a company. Although questions of EC law in general are arbitrable,[43] an arbitrator may not make an award exempting a contract from competition rules under Article 85(3) of the Treaty of Rome and any matter which would give rise to penal sanctions under EC regulations is not capable of being resolved by arbitration in England.[44]

18.2.2.2 Scope of the clause

For the defendant to be entitled to a stay the dispute must fall within the scope of the arbitration clause.[45] In some contracts the arbitration clause does not adequately cover all potential disputes between the parties. For example, if parties agree that disputes which concern the "correctness of documents for goods shipped" shall be referred to

38. See para. 18.3.
39. Arbitration Act 1975, s. 7(1).
40. Redfern & Hunter, *Law and Practice of International Commercial Arbitration* (2nd ed, 1991) p. 137.
41. Van den Berg, *The New York Arbitration Convention of 1958* (1981) p. 152.
42. Mustill & Boyd, *Commercial Arbitration* (2nd ed, 1989) p. 149.
43. See, for example, *Bulk Oil (Zug) Ltd* v. *Sun International Ltd* [1984] 1 WLR 147. For further discussion of arbitration and EC law see para. 17.4.
44. Redfern & Hunter, *Law and Practice of International Commercial Arbitration* (2nd ed, 1991) p. 138, n. 43.
45. See para. 18.1.3.

arbitration, a claim for damages for non-delivery of shipping documents does not fall within the jurisdiction of the arbitrator.[46] Similarly, a clause referring to arbitration "disputes arising under" a contract may not be wide enough to cover disputes as to misrepresentation or negligent misstatements.[47] On the other hand, a clause providing for the arbitration of "[a]ll claims or questions arising out of or in connection with" a contract may be wide enough to encompass a claim in tort brought by one contracting party against the other.[48]

18.2.2.3 Before appearance

18.2.2.3.1 Where one of the parties commences court proceedings, a defendant who wishes to force the plaintiff to refer the dispute to arbitration must apply for a stay "at any time after appearance, and before delivering any pleadings or taking any other steps in the proceedings".[49] A defendant who submits to the jurisdiction of the court is treated as having waived the right to rely on the arbitration clause.

18.2.2.3.2 A party to litigation is regarded as having taken a step in the proceedings if (i) he does some act which indicates an intention to abandon the right to a stay[50] and (ii) the act in question has the effect of invoking the jurisdiction of the court (such as obtaining an order for discovery, or issuing a summons for further and better particulars).[51] However, in *Metal Scrap Trade Corporation* v. *Kate Shipping Co Ltd*[52] it was accepted by the House of Lords that a party who fails in an application for a declaration that an alleged arbitration agreement does not exist is not deprived of the right to apply for a stay of proceedings.

The court does not have the power to impose arbitration when both parties are content to have the dispute adjudicated by the court. Accordingly, the court may not stay the proceedings of its own motion.

18.2.2.4 Null and void, inoperative or incapable of being performed

If the arbitration agreement is "null and void, inoperative or incapable of being performed" the defendant has no right to a stay.

18.2.2.4.1 NULL AND VOID

18.2.2.4.1.1 The words "null and void" denote an arbitration agreement which is affected by some invalidity from the outset. The 1975 Act does not indicate the law by which the validity or invalidity of the clause is to be tested. The various possibilities include the curial law, the *lex fori* and the (putative) proper law of the arbitration agreement. In principle, whether an arbitration agreement is null and void should be governed by its proper law. According to this view there is an obvious relationship

46. *May & Hassell Ltd* v. *Vsesojuznoje Objedinenije "Exportles"* (1940) 66 Ll L Rep 103.
47. *Fillite (Runcorn) Ltd* v. *Aqua-Lift (a firm)* (1989) 45 BLR 27.
48. *Lonrho Ltd* v. *Shell Petroleum Co Ltd*, *The Times*, 1 February 1978.
49. If the defendant acknowledges service of the writ without challenging the jurisdiction of the court, this is regarded as an appearance for the purposes of section 1(1): RSC, Order 12, r. 10.
50. *Eagle Star Insurance Co Ltd* v. *Yuval Insurance Co Ltd* [1978] 1 Lloyd's Rep 357.
51. See *Chappell* v. *North* [1891] 2 QB 252.
52. [1990] 1 WLR 115.

between the doctrine of separability and the rule that a stay will be refused if the arbitration agreement is null and void.[53]

18.2.2.4.1.2 Where the arbitration agreement is governed by English law a stay will be refused in the following situations: (i) there is no consensus between the parties either on the arbitration agreement itself or on the main contract of which the arbitration clause forms a part; (ii) the arbitration agreement itself is void *ab initio*. The fact that the contract of which the arbitration clause forms a part is void *ab initio* (whether for illegality or some other reason) is not, however, a basis for refusing a stay, since a suitably drafted arbitration clause is capable of surviving the initial invalidity of the contract.[54] As for the burden of proof, once the defendant has proved the existence of what appears to be a relevant arbitration agreement, then the burden shifts to the plaintiff to prove that the agreement is in fact null and void.[55]

18.2.2.4.1.3 Although as a general principle the validity of an arbitration clause is to be determined exclusively by its proper law, the court will not give effect to an arbitration agreement which conflicts with mandatory rules of English law—regardless of the agreement's validity under its proper law. *AB Bofors-Uva CAV Ltd* v. *AB Skandia Transport*[56] concerned an arbitration agreement which was governed by Swedish law and provided for arbitration in Sweden. When the plaintiff started litigation in England the defendant applied for a stay under section 1 of the 1975 Act. The court refused to grant a stay on the ground that the arbitration clause was invalid. It was held that the clause infringed the CMR Convention—which is incorporated into English law by the Carriage of Goods by Road Act 1965—because it did not expressly provide that the arbitrators should apply the CMR Convention.

18.2.2.4.2 INOPERATIVE OR INCAPABLE OF BEING PERFORMED

18.2.2.4.2.1 In principle, the question of whether an arbitration agreement has become inoperative or incapable of being performed should also be governed by the proper law of the arbitration agreement. However, it has been noted that in practice the English court is likely to determine these matters for itself, uninfluenced by foreign law.[57] An arbitration agreement may be regarded as inoperative when it ceases to have effect. For example, the court may order that an arbitration agreement ceases to have effect on the basis that the dispute involves the question whether a contracting party has been guilty of fraud.[58] At common law an arbitration agreement may be brought to an end in the same way as any other contract (for example, by frustration).

18.2.2.4.2.2 Only rarely will an arbitration clause be regarded as incapable of being performed; indeed, there appears to be no reported case in which an English court has refused a stay on this basis. It is clear that the financial position of the parties is not a relevant factor in deciding whether a stay should be granted. In *The Rena K*[59] the

53. See para. 18.1.2.
54. *Harbour Assurance Co (UK) Ltd* v. *Kansa General International Insurance Co Ltd* [1993] QB 701.
55. *Overseas Union Insurance Ltd* v. *AA Mutual International Insurance Co Ltd* [1988] 2 Lloyd's Rep 63, 70.
56. [1982] 1 Lloyd's Rep 410.
57. Dicey & Morris, *The Conflict of Laws* (12th ed, 1993) p. 598.
58. Arbitration Act 1950, s. 24(2).
59. [1979] QB 377.

plaintiff resisted the application for a stay on the basis that if an award was made against him he would not be able to honour it. Brandon J thought that this consideration was wholly irrelevant:

> [T]he words "incapable of being performed" should be construed as referring only to the question of whether an arbitration agreement is capable of being performed up to the stage when it results in an award; and should not be construed as extending to the question whether, once an award has been made, the party against whom it is made will be capable of satisfying it.[60]

18.2.2.4.2.3 In *Paczy* v. *Haendler & Nattermann GmbH*[61] the Court of Appeal took the view that the fact that the plaintiff in the litigation is unable to afford the deposit for the costs of arbitration does not justify the refusal of a stay. Furthermore, the fact that if a stay is granted the claim will necessarily be dismissed (for example, as a result of the fact that the agreed time limits have not been complied with) does not render the arbitration agreement incapable of being performed.[62]

18.2.2.4.2.4 Nevertheless, an arbitration agreement is incapable of being performed if the arbitration cannot be set in motion. Accordingly, an application for a stay under section 1 might be refused in a case where the arbitrator refuses to act and the court is unable to replace him or where the mechanism for constituting the arbitral tribunal breaks down completely and the court is unable to rectify the situation.

18.2.2.5 Dispute

18.2.2.5.1 The 1975 Act provides that the court's duty to stay the proceedings does not arise if "there is not in fact any dispute between the parties with regard to the matter agreed to be referred".[63] As this phrase has no counterpart in the text of the Convention which the 1975 Act purports to implement it is legitimate to question whether the addition of a further condition to those set out in the Convention is permissible under international law.[64]

18.2.2.5.2 The question of whether or not there is a dispute for the purposes of section 1 arises most frequently in practice in cases where, following an application by the plaintiff for summary judgment under RSC, Order 14 (on the ground that the defendant "has no defence to a claim"[65]), the defendant applies for a stay under section 1 of the 1975 Act.[66] The orthodox view on the relationship between RSC, Order 14 and section 1 is that an order for summary judgment and the refusal of a stay are opposite sides of the same coin; if the plaintiff can show that there is no defence to the claim, there is no dispute between the parties. The jurisdiction under RSC, Order 14 "has proved to be very useful in practice, especially in times when interest rates are high, for protecting creditors with valid claims from being forced into an unfavourable settlement by the

60. [1979] QB 377, 393.
61. [1981] 1 Lloyd's Rep 302.
62. *The Merak* [1965] P 223.
63. This phrase has an interesting history: it was inserted into the Arbitration Clauses (Protocol) Act 1924 by section 8 of the Arbitration (Foreign Awards) Act 1930; when the arbitration legislation was consolidated the phrase appeared in section 4(2) of the Arbitration Act 1950; section 4(2) of the 1950 Act was in turn repealed by the 1975 Act, but the phrase was included in the text of section 1(1).
64. Reymond, "The Channel Tunnel Case and the Law of International Arbitration" (1993) 109 LQR 337, 340.
65. RSC, Order 14, r. 1(1).
66. See, for example, *Paul Smith Ltd* v. *H & S International Holdings Ltd* [1991] 2 Lloyd's Rep 127.

prospect that they will have to wait until the end of an arbitration in order to collect their money".[67]

18.2.2.5.3 The traditional test for deciding whether there is a dispute for the purposes of section 1 was formulated by Kerr LJ in *SL Sethia Liners Ltd* v. *State Trading Corporation of India Ltd*:

> If the court is satisfied that the plaintiffs are clearly right in law, and that the defendants have no arguable defence, then it will not avail the defendants to have raised a point of law which the court can see is in fact bad. In those circumstances the defendants cannot be heard to say that there was a dispute to be referred to arbitration. But if the court concludes that the plaintiffs are not clearly entitled to judgment because the case raises problems which should be argued and considered fully, then it will give leave to defend, and it is therefore then bound to refer the matter to arbitration under section 1 of the 1975 Act.[68]

18.2.2.5.4 In more recent cases, however, the courts have suggested a less sympathetic attitude to applications under RSC, Order 14 might be appropriate in cases where the defendant seeks a stay under section 1 of the 1975 Act. In *Home and Overseas Insurance Co Ltd* v. *Mentor Insurance Co (UK) Ltd* Parker LJ warned of the dangers of allowing an application for summary judgment to become a means of circumventing an arbitration clause:

> The purpose of Order 14 is to enable a plaintiff to obtain a quick judgment where there is plainly no defence to the claim. If the defendant's only suggested defence is a point of law and the court can see at once that the point is misconceived the plaintiff is entitled to judgment. If at first sight the point appears to be arguable but with a relatively short argument can be shown to be plainly unsustainable the plaintiff is also entitled to judgment. But Order 14 proceedings should not . . . be allowed to become a means for obtaining, in effect, an immediate trial of an action, which will be the case if the court lends itself to determining on Order 14 applications points of law which may take hours or even days and the citation of many authorities before the court is in a position to arrive at the final decision.[69]

18.2.2.5.5 In *Hayter* v. *Nelson*[70] Saville J went further:

> [W]hen considering an application for summary judgment, a factor to be taken into account is the existence of an arbitration agreement between the parties; so that only in the simplest and clearest cases, ie where it is readily and immediately demonstrable that the respondent has no good grounds for disputing the claim, should that party be deprived of his contractual right to arbitrate. In the context of the 1975 Act, this means that only in such cases can the court be satisfied that there is not in any fact any dispute between the parties with regard to the matter agreed to be referred.[71]

18.2.2.5.6 It is important to stress that, in cases where the parties have entered an arbitration agreement, it is primarily the arbitrator's function to decide whether or not there is a good defence to the claimant's claims; if the court abrogates for itself the task of deciding whether or not the claim is disputable it is failing to give effect to the parties' agreement. While the policy behind RSC, Order 14 is to prevent delays in cases where the defendant has no defence,[72] an application for summary judgment in cases where the

67. Lord Mustill in *Channel Tunnel Group Ltd* v. *Balfour Beatty Ltd* [1993] AC 334, 356.
68. [1985] 1 WLR 1398, 1401.
69. [1990] 1 WLR 153, 158–159. Although this discussion was in the context of an application to stay under section 4(1) of the Arbitration Act 1950, the same approach applies *a fortiori* in cases where the application to stay is made under section 1 of the 1975 Act.
70. [1990] 2 Lloyd's Rep 265.
71. [1990] 2 Lloyd's Rep 265, 271.
72. Robert Goff LJ in *European Asian Bank AG* v. *Punjab & Sind Bank (No. 2)* [1983] 1 WLR 642, 654.

parties have agreed to arbitration may have the effect of drawing the court into deciding a question which is within the jurisdiction of the arbitrator.

18.2.2.5.7 The conflict between the traditional view and the more recent cases relates to the strictness of the test to be applied. The traditional approach entitles the court to investigate the defence; on the basis of *Hayter* v. *Nelson* it may be appropriate to grant a stay under section 1 even though it would have emerged, on closer investigation, that there would have been insufficient material on which to give leave to defend under RSC, Order 14. Although recent cases have expressed a distinct preference for the analysis adopted in *Hayter* v. *Nelson*,[73] it has not yet been necessary for the divergence in the authorities to be settled by the appellate courts. In *The John C Helmsing*[74] Bingham LJ, while favouring *Hayter* v. *Nelson* in principle, thought that the weight of authority was on the side of *Sethia Liners Ltd* v. *State Trading Corporation of India Ltd*. Nevertheless, in *Channel Tunnel Group Ltd* v. *Balfour Beatty Construction Ltd*[75] the House of Lords gave support to the more modern approach. Besides indicating that "care should be taken not to confuse a situation in which the defendant disputes the claim on grounds which the plaintiff is very likely indeed to overcome, with the situation in which the defendant is not really raising a dispute at all".[76] Lord Mustill endorsed "the powerful warnings against encroachment on the parties' agreement to have their commercial differences decided by their chosen tribunals, and on the international policy exemplified in the English legislation that this consent should be honoured by the courts given by Parker LJ in *Home and Overseas Insurance Co Ltd* v. *Mentor Insurance Co (UK) Ltd* and Saville J in *Hayter* v. *Nelson*".[77]

18.2.3 The effect of a stay under section 1

18.2.3.1 If the conditions for a grant of a stay are satisfied the court has no discretion; a stay must be granted. Lord Mustill's decision in *Channel Tunnel Group Ltd* v. *Balfour Beatty Construction Ltd*[78] to grant a stay of proceedings in the exercise of the court's inherent jurisdiction, notwithstanding the conclusion that the conditions laid down by section 1 were satisfied, is surprising and cannot be supported in principle.

18.2.3.2 When a stay is granted under section 1 the court has no general power to impose conditions.[79] However, the grant of a stay does not fetter in any way the power of the court to order protective measures.[80] The court may, for example, grant an injunction (assuming that the court has the necessary jurisdiction) under either section 12(6)(h) of the 1950 Act or section 37(1) of the Supreme Court Act 1981.[81] Similarly, where the court stays proceedings *in rem* under section 1 the court may, in appropriate circumstances, refuse to order the release of a ship which has been properly arrested, or make release conditional on the provision of equivalent security.[82]

73. *Paul Smith Ltd* v. *H & S International Holdings Inc* [1991] 2 Lloyd's Rep 127; *The John C Helmsing* [1990] 2 Lloyd's Rep 290.
74. [1990] 2 Lloyd's Rep 290, 296.
75. [1993] AC 334.
76. [1993] AC 334, 356.
77. [1993] AC 334, 356 (citations omitted).
78. [1993] AC 334, 352.
79. *The Rena K* [1979] QB 377.
80. *Channel Tunnel Group Ltd* v. *Balfour Beatty Construction Ltd* [1993] AC 334.
81. See paras. 21.3.2.1 and 21.3.2.2.
82. Civil Jurisdiction and Judgments Act 1982, s. 26. See para. 21.2.

18.3 INHERENT JURISDICTION

18.3.1 Where litigation is commenced in England in breach of the terms of an arbitration agreement, the vast majority of international cases fall within the scope of section 1 of the 1975 Act. As long as the necessary conditions are satisfied, a stay must be granted. There may, however, be situations where one of the conditions imposed by section 1 is not satisfied (where, for example, the arbitration agreement does not satisfy the relevant formal requirements) or where an application for a stay is made "in a case which comes close to section 1 of the Act of 1975, and yet falls short either because of some special feature of the dispute resolution clause, or because for some reason an agreement to arbitrate cannot immediately, or effectively, be applied to the dispute in question".[83]

18.3.2 In *Channel Tunnel Group Ltd* v. *Balfour Beatty Construction Ltd*[84] the House of Lords confirmed that the court has an inherent power to stay proceedings brought before it in breach of agreement to decide disputes in some other way (whether by a jurisdiction agreement or some other form of dispute resolution agreement).[85] The inherent power of the court is, however, "truly a residual one principally confined to dealing with cases not contemplated by the statutory provisions".[86]

18.3.3 The power of the court to stay proceedings under its inherent jurisdiction is discretionary rather than mandatory. There is, however, a clear presumption that contracting parties are to be held to their agreements unless they can show good reasons for departing from them. Accordingly, in those limited cases where the court's inherent jurisdiction is relevant, a stay will normally be granted.

83. Lord Mustill in *Channel Tunnel Group Ltd* v. *Balfour Beatty Construction Ltd* [1993] AC 334, 352.
84. [1993] AC 334, 352.
85. See also *Roussel-Uclaf* v. *GD Searle & Co Ltd* [1978] 1 Lloyd's Rep 225; *Etri Fans Ltd* v. *NMB (UK) Ltd* [1987] 1 WLR 1110.
86. Woolf LJ in *Etri Fans Ltd* v. *NMB (UK) Ltd* [1987] 1 WLR 1110, 1114.

CHAPTER 19

APPEALS UNDER THE ARBITRATION ACT 1979

19.1 PRELIMINARY REMARKS

19.1.1 Although appeals in arbitration are rare, they are not unknown. Parties may, for example, expressly agree to a two-tier procedure which provides for an appeal on the merits against the decision of the arbitral tribunal. More importantly, some institutional arbitration rules provide for an internal appeal procedure.[1] This form of procedure is not common outside the sphere of commodities arbitration.

19.1.2 Most legal systems provide for judicial review of the arbitral process in order to prevent "improper conduct, breaches of the principle of natural justice, or decisions which clearly transcend any standard of objective reasonableness".[2] English law is unusual in also providing a mechanism for the parties to appeal from the decision of the arbitrator to the court on a point of law. The justification of the approach adopted by English law is the principle of legality; if awards were not subject to the supervision of the court on points of law "the result might be that in time codes of law would come to be administered in various trades differing substantially from the English mercantile law".[3]

19.1.3 In the entirely domestic context, the control of the courts of the seat of arbitration on points of law may have something to commend it, since in this situation arbitration is effectively a substitute for litigation in the local courts. However, in the international context, it is necessary for the law to strike a balance between control by the courts of the seat of arbitration and the independence of the arbitral process. It can be presumed that parties who choose to refer their dispute to arbitration are aware of the strengths and weaknesses of the process and are prepared to take the risk that the arbitrator will make mistakes of law—just as they take the risk of errors of fact.

19.1.4 Before the entry into force of the 1979 Act a party to an arbitration who wished to appeal on a point of law could require the arbitrator to state a case for the opinion of the High Court—as long as the dispute involved a genuine question of law. In the post-war years "those who wished to delay the evil day when they had to meet their commitments came to realise that the special case procedure could be manipulated to produce very considerable delay".[4] The existence of an appeal procedure which was open to abuse did little to encourage the international business community to regard England as an appropriate seat for international commercial arbitration. Indeed, the

1. For example, rule 8 of the GAFTA Arbitration Rules provides for an appeal to be made from the decision of the arbitrator to the Board of GAFTA.
2. Kerr, "Arbitration and the Courts: The UNCITRAL Model Law" (1985) 34 ICLQ 1, 15.
3. Atkin LJ in *Czarnikow* v. *Roth, Schmidt & Co* [1922] 2 KB 478, 491.
4. Donaldson, "Commercial Arbitration—1979 And After" [1983] CLP 1, 3.

very existence of a right of appeal to the court on a point of law—which is not found in continental legal systems—undermines the finality of the arbitrator's decision. The 1979 Act radically altered the position; the old forms of appeal were abolished[5] and a new limited right of appeal was introduced.[6]

19.1.5 The operation of the 1979 Act depends on three principles:

(i) a right of appeal exists unless it is excluded by agreement of the parties;
(ii) although there are certain situations where an agreement excluding the right of appeal is valid only if entered into after the commencement of the arbitration, as a general rule, an exclusion agreement in the arbitration clause itself is effective in international cases;
(iii) even where the right of appeal exists (because it has not been properly excluded) an appeal is only possible if the court gives leave, and such leave will be given in limited circumstances.

19.1.6 There are two possible avenues for the bringing of an appeal. Section 2, which is of very limited significance, provides that an application may be made to the court to determine a question of law arising in the course of the reference. An application may be made only with the consent of the arbitrator, or with the consent of all the other parties. Perhaps not surprisingly section 2 is little used in practice.

19.1.7 Much more important is section 1, which provides as follows:

(2) Subject to subsection (3) below, an appeal shall lie to the High Court on any question of law arising out of an award made on an arbitration agreement; and on the determination of such an appeal the High Court may by order—
(a) confirm, vary or set aside the award; or
(b) remit the award to the reconsideration of the arbitrator or umpire together with the court's opinion on the question of law which was the subject of the appeal;
and where the award is remitted under paragraph (b) above the arbitrator or umpire shall, unless the order otherwise directs, make his award within three months after the date of the order.

(3) An appeal under this section may be brought by any of the parties to the reference—
(a) with the consent of all the parties to the reference; or
(b) subject to section 3 below, with the leave of the court.

(4) The High Court shall not grant leave under subsection (3)(b) above unless it considers that, having regard to all the circumstances, the determination of the question of law concerned could substantially affect the rights of one or more of the parties to the arbitration agreement; and the court may make any leave which it gives conditional upon the applicant complying with such conditions as it considers appropriate.

(5) Subject to subsection (6) below, if an award is made and, on an application made by any parties to the reference,—
(a) with the consent of all the other parties to the reference; or
(b) subject to section 3 below, with the leave of the court,
it appears to the High Court that the award does not sufficiently set out the reasons for the award, the court may order the arbitrator or umpire concerned to state the reasons for his award in sufficient detail to enable the court, should an appeal be brought under this section, to consider any question of law arising out of the award.

(6) In any case where an award is made without any reason being given, the High Court shall not make an order under subsection (5) above unless it is satisfied—
(a) that before the award was made one of the parties to the reference gave notice to the arbitrator or umpire concerned that a reasoned award would be required; or

5. Arbitration Act 1979, s. 1(1).
6. Donaldson, "Commercial Arbitration—1979 And After" [1983] CLP 1; Marshall, "The Arbitration Act 1979" [1979] JBL 241; Thomas, "An Appraisal of the Arbitration Act 1979" [1981] LMCLQ 199.

(b) that there is some special reason why such a notice was not given.

(6A) Unless the High Court gives leave, no appeal shall lie to the Court of Appeal from a decision of the High Court—

(a) to grant or refuse leave under subsection (3)(b) or 5(b) above; or

(b) to make or not to make an order under subsection (5) above.

(7) No appeal shall lie to the Court of Appeal from a decision of the High Court on an appeal under this section unless—

(a) the High Court or the Court of Appeal gives leave; and

(b) it is certified by the High Court that the question of law to which its decision relates either is one of general public importance or is one which for some other special reason should be considered by the Court of Appeal.

(8) Where the award of an arbitrator or umpire is varied on appeal, the award as varied shall have effect (except for the purposes of this section) as if it were the award of the arbitrator or umpire.

19.2 WHAT IS AN AWARD?

19.2.1 It is very common for a dispute which is referred to arbitration to involve a number of different questions of law and fact. To give a very simple example: A sells goods to B; B, having paid for the goods, alleges that they are defective. There are two issues: are the goods defective (liability)? if the goods are defective, what is the extent of A's liability (quantum)? It may well be appropriate for the arbitrator to make an interim or partial award on the first question. If the arbitrator finds for the respondent on the first question, there is no need to consider the second issue—and accordingly time, effort and costs are saved. Even if the arbitrator finds for the claimant, it may be unnecessary to continue with the reference, since once the issue of liability is determined, the parties may come to an agreement on the question of quantum.

19.2.2 Section 14 of the 1950 Act confers on arbitrators the power to make interim or partial awards:

> Unless a contrary intention is expressed therein, every arbitration agreement shall, where such a provision is applicable to the reference, be deemed to contain a provision that the arbitrator or umpire may, if he thinks fit, make an interim award, and any reference in this Part of this Act to an award includes a reference to an interim award.

The powers of the court to correct errors of law exist in relation to both interim and final awards. An interim award should, however, be distinguished from the exercise of a discretion relating to a procedural step in the arbitration—which is not reviewable under the 1979 Act. If the arbitrator is asked to make an interim award and he decides to do so, the interim award may be reviewed under the 1979 Act; conversely, if the arbitrator chooses not to make an award and simply informs the parties of the decision, this decision cannot be reviewed.[7] Nevertheless, if the arbitrator embodies his decision not to make an interim award in a reasoned document which he describes as an "Interim Final Award" the decision constitutes an interim award for the purposes of section 14 of the 1950 Act and is, therefore, reviewable under the 1979 Act.[8]

7. *The Angelic Grace* [1980] 1 Lloyd's Rep 288.
8. *The Trade Fortitude* [1992] 1 Lloyd's Rep 169.

19.3 LEAVE OF THE COURT FOR THE PURPOSE OF AN APPEAL TO THE HIGH COURT

19.3.1 In those cases where the right of appeal exists the court still controls access to judicial review on a point of law through the requirement of leave. According to the terms of the 1979 Act itself there appears to be only one substantive requirement which must be satisfied in order for leave to be given, namely that "the determination of the question of law concerned could substantially affect the rights of one or more of the parties to the arbitration agreement".[9] If this requirement is not met, the court has no jurisdiction to give leave. However, even if this requirement is satisfied, there still remains the question of discretion. In *The Nema*[10] and *The Antaios*[11] the House of Lords laid down strict guidelines which must be satisfied if leave to appeal under section 1 is to be given. As a result of the "new philosophy of arbitration"[12] which emerges from the 1979 Act and its interpretation by the House of Lords, "there is always a presumption in favour of finality and that, where there is nothing to rebut it, the application [for leave] should be unceremoniously refused".[13]

19.3.2 The guidelines laid down by the House of Lords require various distinctions to be drawn. A distinction has to be made between three different types of legal issue.[14]

(i) As regards pure questions of law (other than questions of construction) leave to appeal should not be given unless the error of law appears from a mere perusal of the award: "Being left in the frame of mind that the arbitrator may or may not have been right—being left in real doubt in that sense—is not sufficient."[15]

(ii) In relation to mixed questions of law and fact (for example, whether the facts found by the arbitrator satisfy the legal test for frustration) leave should not normally be given unless it appears "on perusal of the award that the arbitrator misdirected himself in law or that his decision was such that no reasonable arbitrator could reach".[16]

(iii) The most difficult cases involve questions of construction (notably, the interpretation of contractual terms). In this context the case law of the House of Lords has drawn a further distinction between standard-form contracts and so-called "one-off" contracts. In relation to "one-off" clauses leave should not be given unless either the award is obviously wrong upon a mere perusal[17] or there are conflicting decisions on the question of law raised by the application—in which case the decision of the court would be useful for the development of English law. A more liberal approach is taken in cases involving the interpretation of standard terms. However, even in a case that

9. Arbitration Act 1979, s. 1(4).
10. *Pioneer Shipping Ltd* v. *BTP Tioxide Ltd* [1982] AC 724. Lewis, "Leave to Appeal under the Arbitration Act 1979" [1982] LMCLQ 271.
11. *Antaios Compania Naviera SA* v. *Salen Rederierna AB* [1985] AC 191. Thomas, "The Antaios: The Nema Guidelines Reconsidered" [1985] JBL 200.
12. Mustill & Boyd, *Commercial Arbitration* (2nd ed, 1989) p. 604.
13. Lord Donaldson MR in *Ipswich BC* v. *Fisons Plc* [1990] Ch 709, 724.
14. See Mann, "Private Arbitration and Public Policy" (1985) 4 CJQ 257, 260.
15. Lord Donaldson MR in *Ipswich BC* v. *Fisons Plc* [1990] Ch 709, 724.
16. Lord Diplock in *The Nema* [1982] AC 724, 744.
17. Lord Diplock in *The Nema* [1982] AC 724, 742.

turns on the construction of a standard term leave to appeal should not be given unless the judge considers that a strong *prima facie* case has been made out that the arbitrator has been wrong in his construction.[18]

19.3.3 As a result of these guidelines, applications for leave to appeal under the 1979 Act can be placed on a spectrum. At one end is the case where parties agreed to refer a dispute concerning the construction of a "one-off" contract to arbitration and the arbitrator possibly made an error of law. In such a case leave will be refused almost as a matter of course. At the opposite end is the case where the dispute concerns the interpretation of a widely used standard-form contract on a point on which there are conflicting decisions. Between these two extreme points it is not always easy to predict whether or not leave will be given by the High Court. This is not altogether surprising in view of the range of relevant factors which the court must consider:

> [W]hether the situation is "one-off" or repeat; whether, in the former case, it is of limited interest or raises an important point of principle; whether the dispute depends upon the interpretation of contracts or clauses in general use in a particular trade; whether determination of the point of law by the court would add significantly to the clarity and certainty of English commercial law; whether the circumstances in which the reference was made suggest that the parties attached importance to the speed and finality of the decision; whether it is clear, probable or merely possible that the arbitrator has gone wrong in law, noting, however, that the degree of certainty of error required var[ies] according to the first two factors mentioned and has been expressed in a wide variety of judicial expressions.[19]

In the final analysis, each case turns on its individual facts.

19.4 APPEALS TO THE COURT OF APPEAL

After an application has been decided by the High Court under section 1(2), there are two different types of appeal which may be brought before the Court of Appeal: (i) an appeal under section 1(6A) against the decision of the High Court on the question of leave; (ii) an appeal under section 1(7) on the substantive question raised by the appeal.

19.4.1 Appeals under section 1(6A)

The decision of the High Court whether to give or refuse leave to appeal can be reviewed by the Court of Appeal under section 1(6A). The right of appeal to the Court of Appeal under this provision depends, however, on the judge giving leave to appeal against his decision on the original application for leave to appeal against the award. Leave should only be granted where the judge considers that the existing guidelines for giving leave to appeal against the award need "some amplification, elucidation or adaptation to changing practices".[20]

18. Lord Diplock in *The Antaios* [1985] AC 191, 203.
19. Goode, "The Adaptation of English Law and International Commercial Arbitration" (1992) 8 Arb Int 1, 8.
20. Lord Diplock in *The Antaios* [1985] AC 191, 205.

19.4.2 Appeals under section 1(7)

Where, having given leave to appeal, the High Court makes a decision on the substantive issue raised by the appeal, an appeal against that decision may then be brought before the Court of Appeal under section 1(7). There are, however, hurdles which the appellant must overcome before an appeal can be brought under section 1(7): (i) the High Court must certify that the question of law is of general public importance; and (ii) leave must be given—either by the High Court or the Court of Appeal.

19.4.2.1 The requirement of a certificate under section 1(7)(b)

If the High Court refuses to grant a certificate as required by section 1(7)(b) there is no right of appeal to the Court of Appeal against this refusal.[21] Furthermore, the High Court has no jurisdiction to entertain a renewed application for a certificate under section 1(7) when an application for such a certificate has already been refused. Section 1(7) is based on a once and for all process; legal developments subsequent to the original rejection of the application for a certificate—which might cast doubt on the correctness of the decision of the High Court on the point of law raised by the appeal—are to be ignored.[22]

19.4.2.2 Leave

19.4.2.2.1 If the High Court refuses to give leave under section 1(7) the party seeking to challenge the decision of the judge at first instance may seek leave to appeal from the Court of Appeal. The test for giving leave under section 1(7) of the 1979 Act has been considered most recently by the Court of Appeal in *Geogas SA* v. *Trammo Gas Ltd.*[23] It was argued, on the basis of *The Roachbank*[24] that, to give leave under section 1(7), the Court of Appeal had to be satisfied either that there were two conflicting decisions of the High Court—not merely conflicting dicta—or that there was at least a strong *prima facie* case for saying that the judge's decision was wrong. This was rejected by the majority; the relevant test is whether the question of law certified by the judge is worthy of consideration by the Court of Appeal. In deciding whether or not to give leave the Court of Appeal must assess:

(i) whether there is sufficient doubt about the judge's decision;
(ii) whether the decision of the Court of Appeal would add significantly to the clarity and certainty of English commercial law; and
(iii) whether there is some other reason why the Court of Appeal should consider the question of law.

19.4.2.2.2 In the view of the majority the key element of the procedure under section 1 of the 1979 Act is the transition from the private to the public domain when leave is given under section 1(3)(b) to appeal to the High Court on a point of law. Once the case has entered the public domain it is important that the final decision should be legally correct. The imposition of additional hurdles between the High Court and the Court of

21. *Arnold* v. *National Westminster Bank Plc* [1989] Ch 63.
22. *National Westminster Bank Plc* v. *Arthur Young McLelland Moores & Co (No. 2)* [1991] 1 WLR 1256.
23. [1991] 2 QB 139.
24. [1988] 2 Lloyd's Rep 337.

Appeal flies in the face of one of the main justifications for retaining any right of appeal on points of law—namely, to provide a source of raw material for the development of English commercial law:

> Unless the parties have consented, the application of the *Nema* guidelines on appeal to the High Court will already have decimated the number of awards that are the subject of appeal to the High Court. Once there, it would be unfortunate if in this important branch of the law litigants and practitioners should have to be content mainly with a body of decisions at first instance that had been immunised against supervision, testing, direction and enhancement by the usual appellate process.[25]

19.4.2.2.3 When an application for leave is made to the Court of Appeal, the Court of Appeal's decision—either to give or refuse leave—is final. Since a decision to give or refuse leave is not an order of the Court of Appeal within the meaning of section 3 of the Appellate Jurisdiction Act 1876, the House of Lords has no jurisdiction to entertain an appeal against such a decision.[26] However, if leave is given the decision of the Court of Appeal on the question of law raised by the appeal may be appealed to the House of Lords in the same way as any other decision of the Court of Appeal.

19.5 EXCLUSION AGREEMENTS

Sections 3 and 4 of the 1979 Act regulate the circumstances in which the right of appeal can be excluded. If the parties do not seek to exclude the right of appeal, an appeal under section 1 is possible—as long as the court is prepared to give leave.

19.5.1 What is an exclusion agreement?

19.5.1.1 The mechanism whereby the parties may exclude the right of appeal is by an "exclusion agreement", which must be "an agreement in writing".[27] In order for an agreement to qualify as an exclusion agreement for the purposes of the 1979 Act it does not have to be expressly referred to as such. The arbitration rules of the major arbitral institutions are drafted in such a way as to effect an exclusion of the parties' right of appeal. So, for example, the first paragraph of Article 24 of the ICC Rules states that "[t]he arbitral award shall be final" and paragraph 2 provides:

> By submitting the dispute to arbitration by the International Chamber of Commerce, the parties shall be deemed to have undertaken to carry out the resulting award without delay and to have waived their right to any form of appeal insofar as such waiver can validly be made.

19.5.1.2 An agreement to refer disputes to arbitration under the ICC Rules is interpreted as excluding the jurisdiction of the court on points of law.[28] An agreement to refer disputes under the LCIA Arbitration Rules should be interpreted as having the same effect.[29] The position as regards an *ad hoc* arbitration conducted under the UNCITRAL Arbitration Rules is less clear. Where parties decide to refer disputes to

25. Leggatt LJ in *Geogas SA* v. *Trammo Gas Ltd* [1991] 2 QB 139, 163.
26. *Geogas SA* v. *Trammo Gas Ltd* [1991] 1 WLR 776.
27. Arbitration Act 1979, s. 3(1).
28. *Arab African Energy Corporation Ltd* v. *Olieprodukten Nederland BV* [1983] 2 Lloyd's Rep 419; *Marine Contractors Ltd* v. *Shell Petroleum Development Co of Nigeria Ltd* [1984] 2 Lloyd's Rep 77.
29. See Article 16(8) of the LCIA Arbitration Rules.

arbitration in England under the UNCITRAL Arbitration Rules and wish to exclude the right of appeal it is sensible to include an exclusion agreement in the contract. An exclusion agreement might be in the following form: "The award of the arbitrators shall be final and binding on the parties and shall not be subject to appeal under section 1 of the Arbitration Act 1979."

19.5.2 When can the right of appeal be excluded?

19.5.2.1 Domestic and non-domestic arbitration agreements

The first distinction to be drawn is between domestic arbitration agreements and non-domestic arbitration agreements. Section 3(7) defines a "domestic arbitration agreement" as:

> [A]n arbitration agreement which does not provide, expressly or by implication, for arbitration in a State other than the United Kingdom and to which neither
> (a) an individual who is a national of, or habitually resident in, any State other than the United Kingdom, nor
> (b) a body corporate which is incorporated in, or whose central management and control is exercised in, any State other than the United Kingdom,
> is a party at the time the arbitration agreement is entered into.

The definition, cast in negative form, means that if there is a territorial connection between one of the parties to the agreement and a State other than the United Kingdom the agreement is a non-domestic agreement.

19.5.2.2 Exclusion agreements in cases involving domestic arbitration agreements

As regards a domestic arbitration agreement within the meaning of section 3(7) the right of appeal can be effectively excluded only by an agreement between the parties entered into after the commencement of the arbitration.[30] Furthermore, the parties to a domestic arbitration agreement may not exclude the powers conferred on the courts by section 24(3) of the 1950 Act in cases of fraud.[31]

19.5.2.3 Exclusion agreements in cases involving non-domestic arbitration agreements

In relation to non-domestic arbitration agreements the general principles are that (i) the parties are free to exclude the right of appeal to the court on a point of law and (ii) an exclusion agreement which forms part of an arbitration agreement (such as an arbitration clause in a contract) is valid.

19.5.2.4 Exclusion agreements in special category cases involving non-domestic arbitration agreements

19.5.2.4.1 Section 4 limits the circumstances in which an exclusion agreement is effective:

> (1)... [I]f an arbitration award or a question of law arising in the course of a reference relates, in whole or in part, to—

30. Arbitration Act 1979, s. 3(6).
31. Arbitration Act 1979, s. 3(3).

(a) a question or claim falling within the Admiralty jurisdiction of the High Court,[32] or
(b) a dispute arising out of a contract of insurance, or
(c) a dispute arising out of a commodity contract,[33]

an exclusion agreement shall have no effect in relation to the award or question unless either—

(i) the exclusion agreement is entered into after the commencement of the arbitration in which the award is made or, as the case may be, in which the question of law arises, or
(ii) the award or question relates to a contract which is expressed to be governed by a law other than the law of England and Wales.

There are no cases in which it is impossible to exclude the right of appeal. If the arbitration does not involve one of the special categories (Admiralty matters, insurance or commodity contracts) an exclusion is effective, whether it forms part of the contractual arbitration clause or a submission agreement after the dispute has arisen.

19.5.2.4.2 In cases falling within the special categories the exclusion agreement is effective if one of two conditions is satisfied.

(i) If the agreement is concluded after the commencement of arbitration the agreement is effective. A charterparty arbitration clause which includes an exclusion agreement, for example, does not satisfy this first condition.
(ii) In cases falling within the scope of the special categories an exclusion agreement is effective if the arbitration clause expressly provides that the law of a foreign country is to govern the merits of the case. If, for example, in a commodity contract which includes an arbitration clause referring disputes to arbitration in England, the parties expressly agree that the law of Bermuda is to govern the substance of the contract, any exclusion agreement in the original contract is effective—even though the law of Bermuda is largely the same as English law.[34]

19.5.2.4.3 It is clear from the wording of section 4(1)(ii) that, in the context of disputes falling within one of the special categories, anything less than an express choice of a foreign law is not sufficient to confer efficacy on an exclusion agreement which is concluded before the commencement of the arbitration. So, in a case falling within the special categories, where the parties agree to arbitration in England but fail to specify the applicable law, the right of appeal can be excluded only by an agreement concluded after the arbitration has been commenced.

19.5.2.4.4 Where the parties have agreed to arbitration in England, the application of English choice of law principles normally leads to English law being the applicable law.[35] If the arbitrator misapplies English conflicts rules or, having correctly applied English private international law, makes an error of English municipal law, the right of appeal under the 1979 Act is not effectively excluded by an agreement in the original contract. If the parties have not expressly made a choice of law and the arbitrator concludes that the law applicable to the merits of the dispute is the law of a foreign country, there is a right of appeal on points of English private international law. If, however,

32. See para. 8.1.
33. "Commodity contract" is defined by Arbitration Act 1979, s. 4(2). To fall within the scope of the definition the contract must be for the sale of goods on a commodity market or exchange specified by the Secretary of State. For a list of specified commodity markets and exchanges see Arbitration (Commodity Contracts) Order 1979, SI 1979 No. 754.
34. See Mustill & Boyd, *Commercial Arbitration* (2nd ed, 1989) p. 633, n. 19.
35. See para. 11.1.3.6.

notwithstanding the choice of England as the seat of arbitration, the correct application of English conflicts rules leads to the conclusion that the law of a foreign country is the applicable law,[36] there can be no right of appeal on the substance of the foreign law, since from the point of view of English law foreign law is only a question of fact.[37]

19.5.2.5 The effect of a valid exclusion agreement

Where the parties have made a valid exclusion agreement, section 3(1) provides:

(a) the High Court shall not, under section 1(3)(b) above, grant leave to appeal with respect to a question of law arising out of an award, and
(b) the High Court shall not, under section 1(5)(b) above, grant leave to make an application with respect to an award, and
(c) no application may be made under section 2(1)(a) above in respect to a question of law.

Section 3(3) provides that, in the non-domestic context, the parties may exclude the power of the courts to intervene in cases involving fraud under section 24(3) of the 1950 Act.

19.5.2.6 The future

19.5.2.6.1 It was originally envisaged that the restrictions imposed by the 1979 Act as regards cases falling within the scope of section 4(1) would last for between two and ten years. The restrictions are, however, still in force,[38] though not surprisingly they have been the subject of criticism. There are essentially three justifications for the rules relating to Admiralty matters, insurance and commodity contracts:

(i) appeals to the courts within the scope of the special categories have contributed significantly to the development of English law and progress would be impeded without these appeals;
(ii) if opting out were permitted in advance of a dispute, exclusion agreements would be routinely incorporated in standard-form contracts with the result that the inexperienced might unwittingly surrender their right of appeal to the court on a point of law;
(iii) the availability of the right of appeal induces consistency in awards, thereby enabling the legal professions to advise their clients and allowing the business community to know where they stand.

19.5.2.6.2 Whether these reasons still provide a satisfactory justification today may be questioned. The first reason, in particular, is highly controversial. For example, it is estimated that 90 per cent. of maritime arbitrations in England involve at least one foreigner and that 25 per cent. involve foreigners on both sides: "It is difficult to understand why foreigners in the shipping, commodities and insurance industries should be singled out to underwrite the cost of developing English jurisprudence."[39]

36. As in *Compagnie d'Armement Maritime SA* v. *Compagnie Tunisienne de Navigation SA* [1971] AC 572.
37. See para. 23.1.
38. The special categories in section 4 of the 1979 Act are being reviewed by the Departmental Advisory Committee on Arbitration. For the text of the Committee's memorandum see (1993) 9 Arb. Int. 405.
39. See Cohen, "Excluding Appeals to the Courts in Maritime Arbitration" [1992] LMCLQ 1, 2.

CHAPTER 20

THE ENFORCEMENT OF ARBITRAL AWARDS

20.1 PRELIMINARY ISSUES

20.1.1 The relationship between enforcement and setting aside

20.1.1.1 If the arbitrator decides in favour of the claimant, the respondent may seek to challenge the award in two different ways. (i) The respondent may take the initiative and apply to the courts of the country of origin to have the award set aside. (ii) The respondent may wait and let the claimant take the initiative; if the claimant seeks to enforce the award the respondent may challenge the award in the context of the enforcement proceedings. If the claimant seeks to enforce the award in a country other than the country of origin the rules governing the enforcement of foreign awards apply.

20.1.1.2 If an award has been set aside in the country of origin, if the successful party seeks to enforce the award in another country, enforcement will normally be refused.[1] Whereas setting aside operates *erga omnes*, the result reached by the courts in enforcement proceedings is strictly territorial. So, where the courts of country Y refuse to enforce an award made in country X (for example, on the ground that the respondent was not given proper notice of the arbitration proceedings), the decision of the courts of country Y does not preclude enforcement of the award in country Z.

20.1.2 The enforcement of domestic awards

20.1.2.1 An award is unlike a judgment in the sense that it is not self-executing. If the debtor fails to comply voluntarily with the award, the creditor who wishes to enforce the award has to invoke the jurisdiction of the court. Where the award is made in England, the creditor may seek enforcement in one of two ways. (i) The creditor may bring an action on the award—based on the debtor's breach of the implied obligation to comply with the terms of the award. If the award is upheld, the court essentially translates the award into a judgment for the amount awarded by the arbitrator. (ii) The creditor may make an application to the court under section 26 of the 1950 Act, subsection (1) of which provides:

> An award on an arbitration agreement may, by leave of the High Court or a judge thereof, be enforced in the same manner as a judgment or order to the same effect, and where leave is so given, judgment may be entered in terms of the award.

1. New York Convention, Article V(1)(e); Arbitration Act 1975, s. 5(2)(f).

20.1.2.2 If the court gives leave to enforce, the award may be enforced in the same manner as a judgment. Since section 26 makes provision for a summary procedure the court may refuse leave to enforce where the case raises a question of law which cannot be disposed of without trial. However, unless there is real ground for doubting the validity of the award leave to enforce under section 26 is given.[2] If the court refuses leave to enforce, the creditor's only means of enforcement is by an action on the award. In order to save time and expense, where leave to enforce is refused, the court may order that the proceedings should continue as if they had been commenced by writ.[3]

20.1.3 The enforcement of foreign arbitral awards

20.1.3.1 International commercial arbitration could not function effectively without an adequate mechanism for the enforcement of awards in countries other than the country where the award is made:

> The effectiveness of international arbitration depends ultimately on the question whether the award can be enforced against the losing party. That is not to say that most arbitrations lead to enforcement proceedings before the courts of some State. Quite the contrary, awards are complied with voluntarily in a large number of cases. But this large degree of voluntary compliance is, for a significant part, probably due to the fact that effective international enforcement measures are generally available to the winning party.[4]

In this regard the New York Convention of 1958, which was implemented in the United Kingdom by the 1975 Act, is of prime importance.

20.1.3.2 The 1975 Act is not, however, the only legal regime for the enforcement of foreign awards. Under English law a foreign award may be enforced at common law or may be entitled to enforcement under other statutory provisions. To a considerable extent the other legal regimes for enforcement are preserved by the 1975 Act.

20.1.3.3 A foreign award may be enforced in England under one (or more) of the following regimes:

(i) the 1975 Act;
(ii) the common law;
(iii) Part II of the 1950 Act (which implements the Geneva Protocol of 1923 and the Geneva Convention of 1927);
(iv) Part II of the Civil Jurisdiction and Judgments Act 1982 (as regards awards made in another part of the United Kingdom);
(v) Part I of the Foreign Judgments (Reciprocal Enforcement) Act 1933;
(vi) Part II of the Administration of Justice Act 1920;
(vii) the Arbitration (International Investment Disputes) Act 1966 (which implements the Washington Convention of 1965).

The relationship between these various regimes is rather complex: some of them are mutually exclusive; in certain circumstances a creditor will have a choice as to which set of rules to rely upon.

2. *Middlemiss & Gould* v. *Hartlepool Corporation* [1972] 1 WLR 1643.
3. RSC, Order 28, r. 8.
4. Van den Berg, "Recent Enforcement Problems under the New York and ICSID Conventions" (1989) 5 Arb Int 2.

20.2 RECOGNITION AND ENFORCEMENT OF FOREIGN AWARDS UNDER THE ARBITRATION ACT 1975[5]

To be entitled to recognition or enforcement under the 1975 Act an award must be a Convention award within the scope of the 1975 Act and the person seeking to rely on the award must produce various documents. Even if these conditions are satisfied recognition or enforcement may be refused if the party against whom the award is invoked can establish a ground for refusing enforcement.

Section 3(2) of the 1975 Act provides that if the award "would be enforceable under this Act" it "shall be treated as binding for all purposes on the persons as between whom it was made, and may accordingly be relied on by any of those persons by way of defence, set off or otherwise in any legal proceedings in the United Kingdom". So, not only may a successful claimant seek to enforce a Convention award in England under the 1975 Act, but also a successful respondent may rely on a Convention award as a defence to subsequent legal proceedings in England on the same cause of action.

20.2.1 The scope of the Arbitration Act 1975

20.2.1.1 The arbitration agreement

The 1975 Act applies to the recognition and enforcement of awards made "in pursuance of an arbitration agreement".[6] For the purposes of the 1975 Act an arbitration agreement is "an agreement in writing (including an agreement contained in an exchange of letters or telegrams) to submit to arbitration present or future differences capable of settlement by arbitration".[7] An award which is based on an arbitration agreement which does not satisfy this definition is not entitled to recognition or enforcement under the 1975 Act.[8]

20.2.1.2 Territorial scope

20.2.1.2.1 INTRODUCTION

20.2.1.2.1.1 The Convention provides that it shall apply both to the recognition and enforcement of "arbitral awards made in the territory of a State other than the State where the recognition and enforcement of such awards are sought" (foreign awards) and to "arbitral awards not considered as domestic awards in the State where their recognition and enforcement are sought" (non-domestic awards).[9] The second category is intended to confer on the courts of country X a discretion to include within the Convention's scope an award which is made in country X under the procedural law of

5. See Lew, "The Arbitration Act 1975" (1975) 24 ICLQ 870; Thomas, "International Commercial Arbitration Agreements and the Enforcement of Foreign Arbitral Awards—A Commentary on the Arbitration Act 1975" [1981] LMCLQ 17, 30–39. The leading work on the New York Convention is Van den Berg, *The New York Convention of 1958* (1981).

6. Arbitration Act 1975, ss. 2 and 7(1).

7. Arbitration Act 1975, s. 7(1). See para. 18.2.2.1.

8. In these circumstances the award might be entitled to recognition or enforcement at common law. See para. 20.3.

9. Article I(1).

country Y.[10] So, if an arbitration is conducted in France under German procedural law, the French courts may regard the award as being entitled to recognition and enforcement in France under the terms of the Convention.

20.2.1.2.1.2 From a practical perspective it is only the enforcement of foreign awards under the Convention which is of importance; the reference to non-domestic awards in the Convention is a dead letter.[11] The 1975 Act provides for the enforcement of awards "made ... in the territory of a State, other than the United Kingdom, which is party to the New York Convention".[12] The 1975 Act does not provide for the enforcement of non-domestic awards (that is, awards made in England under the curial law of a foreign country). The Act does not apply to the enforcement in England of awards made in Scotland or Northern Ireland. For an award to fall within the scope of the 1975 Act there is no requirement that the arbitration should be international; an award made in Paris in an arbitration involving two French traders is a Convention award.[13] More than eighty States have ratified the Convention; among the members of the EC and EFTA the only States which have not are Iceland and Portugal.[14] Since nearly all the major arbitration centres are located in States which have ratified the Convention the vast majority of foreign awards are Convention awards for the purposes of the 1975 Act.

20.2.1.2.2 WHERE IS AN AWARD MADE?

20.2.1.2.2.1 Normally, the award is signed or deemed to have been signed by the arbitrator at the seat of arbitration. For example, Article 16(4) of the UNCITRAL Arbitration Rules requires that the award "shall be made at the place of arbitration"; Article 22 of the ICC Rules states that the award "shall be deemed to be made at the place of the arbitration proceedings and on the date when it is signed by the arbitrator".

20.2.1.2.2.2 Problems may arise if the arbitration is conducted in country X, but the award is signed in country Y. The view adopted by academic commentators is that an award is made in the country where the arbitration took place. This view, which is based on the notion that "[t]he rendering of the award forms part of the arbitral procedure",[15] was, however, rejected by the House of Lords in *Hiscox* v. *Outhwaite*.[16] In this case, although the arbitration had been conducted in England, with hearings having taken place in London, the arbitrator signed and dated the award in Paris. The plaintiff applied for leave to appeal against the award under section 1 of the 1979 Act and for remission under section 22 of the 1950 Act. The defendant, however, sought to enforce the award in England, arguing that the award was "made" in France and therefore that the award was entitled to enforcement in England as a Convention award within the scope of the 1975 Act.

10. Van den Berg, *The New York Arbitration Convention of 1958* (1981) pp. 22–28; Van den Berg, "Non-Domestic Arbitral Awards under the 1958 New York Convention" (1986) 2 Arb Int 191, 200–201. See also Pryles, "Foreign Awards and the New York Convention" (1993) 9 Arb Int 259.

11. Van den Berg, *The New York Arbitration Convention of 1958* (1981) p. 28.

12. Arbitration Act 1975, ss. 2 and 7(1).

13. Van den Berg, *The New York Arbitration Convention of 1958* (1981) p. 17.

14. For a list of ratifications see Redfern & Hunter, *Law and Practice of International Commercial Arbitration* (2nd ed, 1991) pp. 813–819.

15. Sanders, "Trends in the Field of International Commercial Arbitration" [1975] II Hag Rec 205, 274. See also Mann, "Where is an Award 'Made'?" (1985) 1 Arb Int 107, 108; Van den Berg, *The New York Arbitration Convention of 1958* (1981) pp. 294–295.

16. [1992] 1 AC 562.

20.2.1.2.2.3 The House of Lords accepted the defendant's argument that the award was "made" in France—and therefore was a Convention award for the purposes of the 1975 Act.[17] Lord Oliver said:

> An award, whilst it is no doubt the final culmination of a continuing process, is not itself a continuing process. It is simply a written instrument and I can see no context for departing from what I apprehend to be the ordinary, common and natural construction of the word "made". A document is made when and where it is perfected. An award is perfected when it is signed.[18]

20.2.1.2.2.4 This conclusion has been described as "truly startling"[19] and it is hardly surprising that the decision has been vigorously criticised.[20] While the view that an award is made at the seat of arbitration attributes a somewhat strained meaning to the word "made", the interpretation favoured by the House of Lords has profound implications and may lead to bizarre results. For example, if parties agree to arbitration in a State which has ratified the Convention, but the arbitrator signs the award in a State which has not, the legitimate expectations of the parties will be confounded, since the award will not be entitled to enforcement in England under the 1975 Act.[21]

20.2.1.3 Temporal scope

The relevant time for deciding whether an award was made in the territory of a State which is a party to the Convention is the time when enforcement proceedings are commenced in England. *Minister of Public Works of the Government of the State of Kuwait* v. *Sir Frederick Snow & Partners*[22] concerned an application to enforce an award made in Kuwait. It was held that the award was entitled to enforcement in England under the 1975 Act; although Kuwait was not a party to the Convention at the time the award was made, it had become a party before enforcement of the award was sought in England.

20.2.2 Conditions for obtaining enforcement

20.2.2.1 The relevant documents

Section 4 of the 1975 Act provides:

> The party seeking to enforce a Convention award must produce—
> (a) the duly authenticated original award or a duly certified copy of it; and
> (b) the original arbitration agreement or a duly certified copy of it; and
> (c) where the award or agreement is in a foreign language, a translation of it certified by an official or sworn translator or by a diplomatic or consular agent.

17. It was also held that the court retained its supervisory jurisdiction over English arbitrations, even if the award happens to be made in a foreign country. Accordingly, enforcement of the award was suspended under section 5(5) of the Arbitration Act 1975 (see para. 20.2.4) pending the outcome of the plaintiff's applications.
18. [1992] 1 AC 562, 594.
19. Thomas, "Reflections on Recent Judicial Development of the Concept of a Convention Award" (1992) 11 CJQ 352, 358.
20. Davidson, "Where Is An Arbitral Award Made?—Hiscox v. Outhwaite" (1992) 41 ICLQ 637; Reymond, "Where Is An Arbitral Award Made?" (1992) 108 LQR 1; Mann, "Foreign Awards" (1992) 108 LQR 6.
21. For further examples of the possible implications of the House of Lords' decision see paras. 20.2.3.3 and 20.2.3.7.2.
22. [1984] AC 426. Crawford, (1984) 55 BYIL 336.

The effect of section 4 is to require the original arbitration agreement to have been in writing if enforcement is to be obtained. Once the party seeking enforcement has produced the documents required by section 4, the award is *prima facie* entitled to enforcement; the onus shifts to the party against whom the award is invoked to satisfy the court that there is a good reason for refusing enforcement.

20.2.2.2 Procedural steps

20.2.2.2.1 Section 3(1)(a) of the 1975 Act provides that a Convention award shall be enforceable in England in the same way as an English award—namely, "either by action or in the same manner as the award of an arbitrator is enforceable by virtue of section 26 of the 1950 Act".

The summary procedure for obtaining leave to enforce is commenced by the creditor making an application for leave to enforce the award; the application may be made by originating summons or *ex parte*. If the application is made *ex parte* the court may nevertheless direct a summons to be issued.[23] The court will direct the issue of a summons if the right to enforce an award as a judgment is not clearly made out.[24] In any case where a summons is issued it must be served on the defendant; if the defendant is not otherwise amenable to the jurisdiction of the court, leave to serve out of the jurisdiction is required.[25] If leave to enforce is given *ex parte* the order giving leave to enforce may be served out of the jurisdiction without leave.[26] The order must, however, inform the debtor of his right to apply to have the order set aside.[27] Moreover, the award may not be enforced until after the expiration of the period during which the debtor may apply to have the order set aside or, if the debtor makes an application during that period, until after the application has been finally disposed of.[28]

20.2.2.2.2 There may be difficulties in obtaining enforcement in England under section 26 in the international context. In *Dalmia Cement Ltd* v. *National Bank of Pakistan*[29] Kerr J held that awards which in their operative parts directed payment "in India" could not be summarily enforced under section 26 because the court could not give judgment in such terms. However, in *Bank Mellat* v. *GAA Development & Construction Co*[30] a statement in the reasons (rather than in the operative parts of the award) that the respondent should "pay the awarded sum in Switzerland" did not prevent enforcement of the award under section 26.

Where the creditor seeks enforcement by way of action on the award, the action is commenced by writ. If the debtor is not otherwise amenable to the jurisdiction of the court, the creditor has to obtain leave of the court to serve the writ out of the jurisdiction.[31]

23. RSC, Order 73, r. 10(1).
24. Mustill & Boyd, *Commercial Arbitration* (2nd ed, 1989) p. 420.
25. RSC, Order 73, r. 7(1A).
26. RSC, Order 73, r. 10(5).
27. RSC, Order 73, r. 10(7).
28. RSC, Order 73, r. 10(6).
29. [1975] QB 9.
30. [1988] 2 Lloyd's Rep 44.
31. RSC, Order 11, r. 1(1)(m). See para. 17.5.1.3.

20.2.3 Grounds for refusing enforcement

20.2.3.1 The statutory framework

20.2.3.1.1 The grounds on which enforcement of a Convention award may be refused are set out in subsections (2) to (4) of section 5.[32] Subsection (2)—which is supplemented by subsection (4)—lists six grounds on which enforcement may be refused: the party against whom the award is invoked lacked capacity; the arbitration agreement on which the award was based was invalid; the arbitration proceedings did not comply with principles of natural justice; the arbitrator lacked jurisdiction; there was a failure to comply with the applicable procedural rules; the award is not binding or has been set aside in the country of origin. In addition, subsection (3) provides two further grounds on which enforcement may be refused: the award is contrary to public policy; the subject matter of the dispute was not arbitrable.

20.2.3.1.2 The grounds for refusal listed in subsection (2) must be proved by "the person against whom the award is invoked". By contrast, the two defences enumerated in subsection (3) may be raised by the court of its own motion. In practice, however, if the grounds for refusal in subsection (3) are invoked it is invariably by the party seeking to resist enforcement.

It would seem from the English text of the Convention—which is substantially reproduced in the 1975 Act—that "even if the party against whom the award is invoked proves the existence of one of the grounds for refusal of enforcement, the court still has a certain discretion to overrule the defence and to grant enforcement of the award".[33] There is, however, no indication in either the Convention or the 1975 Act as to how such discretion might be exercised. Although enforcement of the award should normally be refused if one of the grounds is made out, it has been suggested it would be appropriate to order enforcement "where the respondent can be deemed to be estopped from invoking the ground for refusal".[34]

20.2.3.1.3 Conversely, as regards cases falling within the scope of the 1975 Act, the grounds set out in section 5 are exhaustive.[35] Section 5(1) provides that "[e]nforcement of a Convention award shall not be refused except in the cases mentioned in this section". If none of the grounds for refusing enforcement under the 1975 Act is established, enforcement cannot be refused for a reason outside the Act.[36] However, if the person against whom the award is invoked has brought proceedings in the country of origin with a view to having the award set aside the court may, in certain circumstances, stay the enforcement proceedings under section 5(5).

20.2.3.2 Lack of capacity: section 5(2)(a)

20.2.3.2.1 Section 5(2)(a) provides that enforcement of an award may be refused if "a party to the arbitration agreement was (under the law applicable to him) under some

32. The relationship between section 5 of the 1975 Act and the equivalent provisions of the New York Convention of 1958 is as follows: Article V(1)(a) = s. 5(2)(a) and (b); Article V(1)(b) = s. 5(2)(c); Article V(1)(c) = s. 5(2)(d) and s. 5(4); Article V(1)(d) = s. 5(2)(e); Article V(1)(e) = s. 5(2)(f); Article V(2) = s. 5(3); Article VI = s. 5(5).

33. Van den Berg, *The New York Arbitration Convention of 1958* (1981) p. 267.

34. Van den Berg, *The New York Arbitration Convention of 1958* (1981) p. 267.

35. Van den Berg, *The New York Arbitration Convention of 1958* (1981) p. 265.

36. *Rosseel NV* v. *Oriental Commercial & Shipping Co (UK) Ltd* [1991] 2 Lloyd's Rep 625.

incapacity". The precursor of Article V(1)(a) (on which section 5(2)(a) is based) was Article 2(1)(b) of the Geneva Convention of 1927 which provides that enforcement of an award shall be refused if the person against whom enforcement is sought "being under a legal incapacity, ... was not properly represented". Although it has been suggested that it would be reasonable for Article V(1)(a) of the Convention to be interpreted in the same sense,[37] this suggestion fails to take into account the fact that Article V(1)(a) is aimed not at the improper representation of a party in the arbitral proceedings (which must be very unusual), but at the invalidity of the arbitration agreement on the basis of the incapacity of one of the parties (which is more likely).

20.2.3.2.2 Article V(1)(a) and section 5(2)(a) state simply that where the incapacity of one of the parties to the arbitration agreement is raised, the relevant law is "the law applicable to" the party in question. In the absence of any indication in the Convention to the contrary, it is assumed that the applicable law in this context is to be determined by reference to the conflicts rules of the country in which the proceedings for enforcement are brought. While English law in this area is not free from doubt, it is generally accepted that an individual is regarded as having contractual capacity if he has capacity either under the law of the country where he is domiciled and resident or under the law with which the contract has its closest and most real connection.[38] As regards corporations, capacity is to be judged by reference to the law under which the company in question is incorporated. Where one of the parties is a State or a state entity the law of that State determines whether that party has the necessary capacity.

20.2.3.3 Invalidity of the arbitration agreement: section 5(2)(b)

20.2.3.3.1 If the arbitration agreement is invalid, any resulting award is not entitled to enforcement. Section 5(2)(b) contains two principles:

(i) enforcement of an award may be refused if "the arbitration agreement was not valid under the law to which the parties subjected it";
(ii) where the parties gave no indication on which law should govern the arbitration agreement, enforcement of an award may be refused if the arbitration agreement was not valid "under the law of the country where the award was made".

The second principle is premised on the notion that, where the parties have failed to choose the applicable law, an arbitration agreement is governed by the law of the seat of arbitration.[39]

20.2.3.3.2 The second principle in section 5(2)(b) makes sense only if the "the law of the country where the award was made" is understood to mean the law of the seat of arbitration[40]; that law is relevant only because it is the proper law of the arbitration agreement. Unfortunately, as far as English law is concerned, the decision of the House of Lords in *Hiscox* v. *Outhwaite*[41] stands in the way of this rational interpretation. In the

37. Contini, "The United Nations Convention on the Recognition and Enforcement of Foreign Arbitral Awards" (1959) 8 Am J Comp L 283, 301.
38. See para. 11.4.4.
39. Pisar, "The United Nations Convention on Foreign Arbitral Awards" [1959] JBL 219, 221. See para. 17.2.
40. Sanders, "Trends in the Field of International Commercial Arbitration" [1975] II Hag Rec 205, 275.
41. [1992] 1 AC 562. See para. 20.2.1.2.2.

context of section 7(1) of the 1975 Act it was held that an award is "made" where it is signed by the arbitrator—rather than where the arbitration has its seat. This interpretation, if applied to section 5(2)(b), could lead to bizarre results, since the place where the award is signed may be quite fortuitous and have no meaningful connection with the parties, the arbitration agreement or the seat of arbitration.

20.2.3.3.3 The implications of *Hiscox* v. *Outhwaite* may, however, be avoided. Section 5(2) confers a discretion on the court even in cases where a ground for refusing enforcement is established. If the arbitration agreement is invalid under the law of the country where the award was signed the court should exercise its discretion in favour of upholding an award—unless, of course, the arbitration agreement is also invalid under the law of the seat of arbitration.

20.2.3.4 Procedural unfairness: section 5(2)(c)

20.2.3.4.1 Section 5(2)(c) provides the party against whom an award is invoked with a defence to enforcement in cases where the arbitration was conducted in a manner which is not consistent with principles of natural justice. The due process defence contained in section 5(2)(c) has three alternative elements: enforcement of an award may be refused if the person against whom the award is invoked can prove (i) that "he was not given proper notice of the appointment of the arbitrator"; or (ii) that "he was not given proper notice of ... the arbitration proceedings"; or (iii) that he was "otherwise unable to present his case". It has been suggested that the defence in section 5(2)(c) should be successful only in cases where the violation of due process is very serious.[42]

20.2.3.4.2 Section 5(2)(c) enables the courts in which enforcement is sought to provide a check on the procedural requirements of the curial law. The fact that the procedural rules of the law of the seat of arbitration were complied with is not sufficient to deprive the party against whom the award is invoked of the possibility of resisting enforcement of the award under section 5(2)(c). It is for the court in which enforcement is sought to determine—according to its own standards of fairness—whether the party resisting enforcement was given proper notice of the appointment of the arbitrator and the proceedings and whether the party resisting enforcement was able to present his case. To a large extent, the defence under section 5(2)(c) involves questions of fact.

20.2.3.4.3 Where parties agree to arbitrate under institutional arbitration rules the arbitrator generally has a broad discretion over the internal conduct of the arbitration. Article 5(2) of the LCIA Arbitration Rules, for example, provides:

> In the absence of procedural rules agreed by the parties or contained herein, the Tribunal shall have the widest discretion allowed under such law as may be applicable to ensure the just, expeditious, economical, and final determination of the dispute.

Except in the most unusual cases, the mere fact that the arbitrator adopts one procedural model rather than another does not justify the court in refusing enforcement under section 5(2)(c). So, for example, where the arbitrator declines to hear oral evidence this cannot without more entitle the court to refuse enforcement on the ground that one of the parties was given insufficient opportunity to present his case.[43] A person seeking to resist the enforcement of a foreign award may, however, rely on

42. Van den Berg, *The New York Arbitration Convention of 1958* (1981) p. 310.
43. *Dalmia Dairy Industries Ltd* v. *National Bank of Pakistan* [1978] 2 Lloyd's Rep 223.

section 5(2)(c) in cases where the tribunal failed to treat the parties equally[44] or where the arbitral tribunal did not act in a judicial manner.[45] The defence in section 5(2)(c) should also be available in cases where the procedural model adopted by the arbitrator unfairly prejudices one party—for example, if the arbitrator conducts a documents-only arbitration in a situation where the evidence of one of the parties consists mainly of oral testimony.

20.2.3.4.4 Finally, it should be recalled that the 1975 Act does not require the court to refuse enforcement simply because the party against whom the award is invoked establishes one of the grounds in section 5(2). Where the party resisting enforcement satisfies the court that there was a breach of the principles of natural justice, it may nevertheless be legitimate for the court to uphold the award if it is obvious that the decision of the arbitrator would have been the same even if the irregularity had not occurred.[46]

20.2.3.5 Excess of jurisdiction: section 5(2)(d) and section 5(4)

20.2.3.5.1 The arbitrator's jurisdiction is determined by the terms of the arbitration agreement. If the arbitrator exceeds his jurisdiction, the award is a nullity and may be set aside by the court with supervisory jurisdiction over the arbitration. Section 5(2)(d) provides that enforcement of a Convention award may be refused if "the award deals with a difference not contemplated by or not falling within the terms of the submission to arbitration, or contains decisions on matters beyond the scope of the submission to arbitration". Whether the arbitrator had the necessary jurisdiction over the dispute dealt with in the award is essentially a question of construction of the arbitration agreement. Accordingly, the scope of the defence is to be determined by reference to the proper law of the arbitration agreement.

20.2.3.5.2 The operation of the defence in section 5(2)(d) can be illustrated by cases decided at common law and under Part II of the 1950 Act. In *Kianta Osekeyhtio* v. *Britain & Overseas Trading Co Ltd*[47] a Finnish timber merchant contracted to sell a quantity of pit-props to an English buyer. The contract, which was governed by Finnish law, included an arbitration clause making provision for the reference of disputes to arbitrators in Finland. When the buyer refused to take delivery of part of the last shipment, the parties entered a compromise agreement, which did not include the arbitration clause. When a dispute arose under the compromise agreement the seller commenced arbitration proceedings in Finland. An award was made in the seller's favour, the buyer having taken no part in the proceedings. The seller then sought to enforce the award in England and the question facing the court was whether the arbitration clause in the original contract of sale conferred jurisdiction on the arbitrators in relation to a dispute under the compromise agreement. The Court of Appeal held that, since under Finnish law (which was not different from English law in any material respect) the arbitration clause in the original agreement did not confer

44. *Re Enoch and Zaretzky, Bock & Co's Arbitration* [1910] 1 KB 327 (a case decided at common law).
45. This would follow from the decision of the Court of Appeal in *Adams* v. *Cape Industries Plc* [1990] Ch 433. See para. 9.2.7.1.2.
46. Van den Berg, *The New York Arbitration Convention of 1958* (1981) pp. 301–302.
47. [1954] 1 Lloyd's Rep 247.

jurisdiction on the arbitrators to decide a dispute arising under the compromise agreement, enforcement of the award in England should be refused.

20.2.3.5.3 A different question concerning the arbitrator's jurisdiction arose in *Dalmia Dairy Industries Ltd* v. *National Bank of Pakistan*.[48] In this case two arbitrations had been conducted in Geneva under the ICC Rules. The parties to the contract, which was governed by Indian law, were an Indian company and a bank registered in Pakistan. While the arbitrations were being conducted hostilities broke out between Pakistan and India. When the plaintiff applied to enforce the awards in England, one of the grounds on which the defendant sought to resist enforcement was that the arbitrator had no jurisdiction. The essence of the defendant's argument was that, although the arbitration agreement was valid under Indian law at the time of the conclusion of the contract, it was rendered illegal and void by the armed conflict between India and Pakistan. The Court of Appeal held that, since in the particular circumstances of the case the arbitration clause was not illegal under Indian law, the awards could not be refused enforcement on the basis that the arbitrator no longer had jurisdiction. However, had the effect of Indian law been to render the arbitration clause void, the awards would have been unenforceable on the ground that the arbitrator lacked jurisdiction.

20.2.3.5.4 Where it is possible to distinguish those matters in relation to which the arbitrator did have jurisdiction from those in relation to which he did not, the court may grant partial enforcement of the award to the extent that it deals with matters falling within the arbitrator's jurisdiction. Section 5(4) provides:

> A Convention award which contains decisions on matters not submitted to arbitration may be enforced to the extent that it contains decisions on matters submitted to arbitration which can be separated from those on matters not so submitted.

20.2.3.6 Failure to comply with the relevant procedural rules: section 5(2)(e)

20.2.3.6.1 Section 5(2)(e) contains two rules:

(i) enforcement of an award may be refused if "the composition of the arbitral authority or the arbitral procedure was not in accordance with the agreement of the parties";
(ii) failing an agreement on these matters, enforcement of an award may be refused if the composition of the arbitral authority or the arbitral procedure was not in accordance with "the law of the country where the arbitration took place".

The second of these rules does not give rise to any problems. In the absence of agreement by the parties, procedural matters such as the mechanism for the appointment of the tribunal or the rules regulating the internal conduct of the arbitration are governed by the law of the seat. Failure by the arbitrator to comply with the applicable procedural rules is likely to be a ground for setting aside the award by the court with supervisory jurisdiction over the arbitration besides providing a basis for refusing enforcement.

48. [1978] 2 Lloyd's Rep 223.

20.2.3.6.2 As regards the operation of the first rule two situations should be distinguished. If there is no conflict between the procedure chosen by the parties and the procedural rules of the law of the seat, it is obvious that the arbitrator should comply with the terms of the parties' agreement, since failure to do so provides a basis for enforcement of the award being refused. However, if the parties agree on a procedure which is at variance with mandatory procedural rules of the law of the seat the arbitrator would appear to be placed in an insoluble dilemma. If, on the one hand, the procedure agreed by the parties is followed, the award is liable to be set aside by the court with supervisory jurisdiction over the arbitration (as a consequence of which the award will be unenforceable abroad by virtue of section 5(2)(f)). If, on the other hand, the arbitrator ignores the agreement of the parties and complies with the mandatory rules of the law of the seat, enforcement of the award may be refused under section 5(2)(e).

20.2.3.6.3 As a matter of policy, if the arbitrator departs from the procedure chosen by the parties in order to comply with mandatory rules of the law of the seat the award should not be denied enforcement.[49] The discretion conferred by section 5(2) on the court in which enforcement is sought should be exercised in favour of upholding the award in a situation where the arbitrator complies with the mandatory rules of the law of the seat rather than the agreement of the parties. This approach is supported—to some extent—by the *travaux préparatoires* of the Convention. The Italian representative on the Working Party expressed the view that the text of Article V(1)(d) (which is implemented by section 5(2)(e) of the 1975 Act) "should not be interpreted to mean that parties could agree to disregard all national laws and determine some special procedure applicable to their case alone".[50]

20.2.3.7 Invalid award: section 5(2)(f)

20.2.3.7.1 NOT BINDING

20.2.3.7.1.1 The Geneva Convention of 1927—the forerunner of the 1958 Convention—provides that a foreign award is not enforceable unless it has "become final in the country in which it was made".[51] Because the burden is placed on the party seeking to rely on an award to show that the award is "final", in practice, enforcement of a foreign award under the Geneva Convention depends on the party seeking to rely on the award obtaining a so-called double *exequatur*—that is, an order for enforcement from the courts of the country of origin and an order for enforcement from the court of the country in which enforcement is sought.

20.2.3.7.1.2 Under the first part of section 5(2)(f) an award may be refused enforcement if it "has not yet become binding on the parties". By using the term "binding" rather than "final" the drafters of the Convention intended to avoid the complications generated by the Geneva Convention. So, for the purposes of section 5(2)(f) in order for an award to be "binding" it does not have to be final in the absolute

49. Van den Berg, "Recent Enforcement Problems under the New York and ICSID Conventions" (1989) 5 Arb Int 2, 9–10.

50. Cited by Contini, "The United Nations Convention on the Recognition and Enforcement of Foreign Arbitral Awards" (1959) 8 Am J Comp L 283, 301.

51. Article I(d); Arbitration Act 1950, s. 37(1)(d).

sense; an award is "binding" if it has obligatory force between the parties under the curial law and it is no longer open to a genuine appeal on the merits to a second arbitral instance or to a court. Only if there is still the possibility of a genuine appeal in full should an award be regarded as not "binding".[52]

20.2.3.7.1.3 According to this interpretation, where an arbitration is conducted under the GAFTA Arbitration Rules, which provide that if any party is "dissatisfied with an arbitration award, a right of appeal shall lie to a Board of Appeal",[53] the award only becomes "binding" for the purposes of the 1975 Act if either an appeal has been heard or the time limit for bringing an appeal has expired. On the other hand, the possibility of an appeal under the 1979 Act is not sufficient to deprive an English award of its "binding" nature for the purposes of the Convention.[54] *A fortiori*, an award is not to be regarded as not "binding" simply because there is the possibility of an action for setting aside the award in the country of origin.[55]

20.2.3.7.2 SET ASIDE OR SUSPENDED

20.2.3.7.2.1 The second limb of the defence in section 5(2)(f) provides that enforcement may be refused if the award "has been set aside or suspended by a competent authority of the country in which, or under the law of which, it was made". On the basis of this provision, where an award is made under an arbitration agreement providing for arbitration in France, if the French courts set aside the award, the award may be refused enforcement in England.

20.2.3.7.2.2 In some legal systems an application to set aside an award suspends the award by operation of law; in others, on an application to set aside the court of the country of origin may make an order suspending the award. If a party seeks to enforce a foreign award in England, and the person against whom the award is invoked applies to have the award set aside before the courts of the country of origin, may the English courts order enforcement, notwithstanding the fact that as a result of the application in the country of origin the award is suspended in the country of origin? Although the answer to this question is not free from doubt, it has been argued that enforcement may be refused only if the party resisting enforcement proves that suspension of the award has been ordered by the court in the country of origin.[56] According to this view, the automatic suspension of the award by operation of law in the country of origin is not sufficient.

20.2.3.7.2.3 There are two factual situations which need further consideration. (i) Section 5(2)(f) is intended to deal with the rare situations where the parties—by express agreement—sever the link between the curial law and the seat of arbitration. In a case where parties agree to refer disputes to arbitration in country X under the curial law of country Y enforcement of the award may be refused in England if the award is set aside

52. Van den Berg, *The New York Arbitration Convention of 1958* (1981) p. 345.
53. GAFTA Arbitration Rules, r. 8.2.
54. Van den Berg, *The New York Arbitration Convention of 1958* (1981) p. 345.
55. This was the view of the Supreme Court of Sweden in *AB Götaverken* v. *General National Maritime Transport Co*, reported in (1981) 6 YB Comm Arb 237; cited by Tupman, "Staying Enforcement of Arbitral Awards under the New York Convention" (1987) 3 Arb Int 209, 213.
56. Van den Berg, *The New York Arbitration Convention of 1958* (1981) p. 352.

in country X or in country Y. (ii) The decision in *Hiscox* v. *Outhwaite*[57]—in which the House of Lords held that an award is "made" where it is signed—could have unfortunate implications. If this interpretation of "made" were applied in the context of section 5(2)(f), where an arbitration is conducted in country X, but the award is signed in country Y, the setting aside of the award by the courts in country Y would provide a ground on which enforcement of the award could be refused. It goes without saying that this possibility is not something which was envisaged by the drafters of the Convention, who considered that an award should—as a matter of law—be regarded as having been made at the seat of arbitration. The reference in section 5(2)(f) of the 1975 Act to "the country in which ... [the award] was made" is meant to indicate the country in which the seat of arbitration was located.[58]

20.2.3.7.2.4 Nevertheless, the implications of *Hiscox* v. *Outhwaite* may be avoided by the exercise of the court's discretion under section 5(2); the court may, in the exercise of its discretion, order enforcement in a case where the award has been set aside in the country where the award was signed, but not in the country where the arbitration had its seat.

20.2.3.8 Non-arbitrability

Section 5(3) provides that enforcement of an award "may also be refused if the award is in respect of a matter which is not capable of settlement by arbitration". The 1975 Act does not state the law by reference to which the arbitrability of the dispute is to be referred. The provision of the Convention on which section 5(3) is based indicates that enforcement may be refused if the subject matter of the dispute is not capable of settlement by arbitration under the law of the country in which enforcement is sought.[59] Under English law there are very few restrictions as to the type of dispute which may be referred to arbitration.[60]

Two further points should be noted:

(i) if the dispute is not arbitrable under the proper law of the arbitration agreement, the arbitration agreement is invalid and enforcement of the award may be refused under section 5(2)(a);

(ii) if the dispute is not arbitrable under the law of the seat the award is likely to be set aside—as a consequence of which enforcement may be refused under section 5(2)(f).

20.2.3.9 Public policy

Section 5(3) also provides that the court may refuse to enforce an award "if it would be contrary to public policy" to do so. The defence of public policy applies not only in cases falling within the scope of the 1975 Act but also in cases relating to the enforcement of awards at common law and under Part II of the 1950 Act. Since EC law is part of national law, for the purposes of section 5(3) of the 1975 Act, public policy should include Community public policy. So, for example, where an arbitrator upholds and

57. [1992] 1 AC 562.
58. Sanders, "Trends in the Field of International Commercial Arbitration" [1975] II Hag Rec 205, 274.
59. Article V(2).
60. See para. 18.2.2.1.3.2.

enforces a contract which is blatantly in breach of the terms of Article 85 of the Treaty of Rome, the award should be refused enforcement.[61]

Nevertheless, the scope of public policy should be narrowly circumscribed; enforcement should not be refused on the ground of public policy unless "enforcement would violate the forum State's most basic notions of morality and justice".[62] In *Deutsche Schachtbau- und Tiefbohrgesellschaft mbH* v. *R'As al-Khaimah National Oil Co*[63] Donaldson MR thought that an award should not be refused enforcement on the ground of public policy unless "there is some element of illegality or that the enforcement would be clearly contrary to the public good or, possibly, that enforcement would be wholly offensive to the ordinary reasonable and fully informed members of the public on whose behalf the powers of the State are exercised".[64]

20.2.3.9.1 AWARDS BASED ON THE LEX MERCATORIA OR ARBITRATION EXTRA LEGEM

It is not contrary to public policy to enforce a foreign award in cases where the arbitrator decided the merits of the dispute on the basis of "some system of 'law' which is not that of England or any other State or is a serious modification of such a law".[65] In *Norske Atlas Insurance Co Ltd v London General Insurance Co Ltd* the court ordered enforcement in England of a Norwegian award, notwithstanding the fact that the parties had expressly provided that the arbitrators "must not necessarily judge according to the strict law but as a general rule ought chiefly to consider the principles of practical business".[66] If the parties to the agreement intended to create legally enforceable rights and obligations and if the resulting agreement is sufficiently certain to constitute a legally enforceable contract the award is *prima facie* enforceable.[67] The mere fact that the arbitrator decided the dispute according to "internationally accepted principles of law governing contractual relations" does not render the award unenforceable on grounds of public policy.[68]

20.2.3.9.2 ILLEGALITY AND COMITY

20.2.3.9.2.1 *Dalmia Dairy Industries Ltd* v. *National Bank of Pakistan*[69]—a case decided at common law—involved two awards made following arbitrations conducted in

61. See the decision of the German Bundesfinanzhof (Decision of 27 February 1969, (1969) 22 NJW 978–980; cited by Bebr, "Arbitration Tribunals and Article 177 of the EEC Treat;" (1985) 22 CMLRev 489, 498 n. 16) in which the court refused to allow the enforcement of an award on the ground that the award settled a dispute in a way which was contrary to Article 85(1) of the EEC Treaty.

62. *Parsons & Whittemore Overseas Co Inc* v. *Société Générale de l'Industrie du Papier*, 508 F 2d 969 (2d Cir, 1974).

63. [1990] 1 AC 295.

64. [1990] 1 AC 295, 316.

65. Donaldson MR in *Deutsche Schachtbau- und Tiefbohrgesellschaft mbH* v. *R'As al-Khaimah National Oil Co* [1990] 1 AC 295, 315.

66. MacKinnon J, (1927) 28 Ll L Rep 104, 107.

67. Donaldson MR in *Deutsche Schachtbau- und Tiefbohrgesellschaft mbH* v. *R'As al-Khaimah National Oil Co* [1990] 1 AC 295, 316.

68. *Deutsche Schachtbau- und Tiefbohrgesellschaft mbH* v. *R'As al-Khaimah National Oil Co* [1990] 1 AC 295. For further discussion of this case see para. 17.3.7. See also Rivkin, "Enforceability of Arbitral Awards Based on Lex Mercatoria" (1993) 9 Arb Int 67.

69. [1978] 2 Lloyd's Rep 223.

Geneva under the ICC Rules. The awards directed the defendant to make certain payments in India. The defendant raised two points of public policy: (i) it was argued that enforcement of the award would be contrary to public policy on the basis that in order to comply with the award the defendant, a bank registered in Pakistan, would have to perform acts which were unlawful under the law of Pakistan, namely the transfer of foreign exchange from Pakistan to India; (ii) the defendant argued that it was contrary to public policy to enforce an award between persons who are nationals of foreign States who are at war with each other.

20.2.3.9.2.2 The first point was rejected on the basis of *Kleinwort, Sons & Co* v. *Ungarische Baumwolle Industrie Aktiengesellschaft*.[70] On the facts of the case "the act required to be done, both under the contract and under the awards, was to make a payment in India, not in Pakistan, and by Indian law the payment was lawful".[71] However, what emerges from this decision is an implicit acceptance that had the award been in terms such that the debtor was required to perform an obligation which was illegal by the law of the place of performance, the court would have refused to enforce the award on the basis of public policy. This is the significance of the observation by Donaldson MR in the *Deutsche Schachtbau* case to the effect that the public policy defence may succeed if "there is some element of illegality".[72]

20.2.3.9.2.3 On the second point the Court of Appeal rejected the idea that "it would be harmful to this country's international relations with friendly countries if it were to allow the machinery of its courts to be used to enforce a judgment, or an arbitral award, in favour of a national of one foreign State, friendly to the United Kingdom, against the national of another foreign State, also friendly to the United Kingdom, where the two foreign States are enemies of one another".[73] Again, there is an implicit acceptance that if enforcement of an award would involve breach of comity, the defence of public policy may be invoked.

20.2.3.10 No review of the merits

In cases falling within the scope of the 1975 Act the list of grounds for refusing recognition is exhaustive.[74] Accordingly, as a general rule, there can be no review of a Convention award on the merits by the court in which enforcement is sought—even if the arbitrator has manifestly erred on questions of fact or law. However, as a result of the decision of the House of Lords in *Hiscox* v. *Outhwaite*[75] there would appear to be an exception to this principle. In the situation where the court is both the court in which enforcement is sought and the court with supervisory jurisdiction over the arbitration—as is the case where an arbitration is conducted in England under English

70. [1939] 2 KB 678.
71. Kerr J, [1978] 2 Lloyd's Rep 223, 267.
72. [1990] 1 AC 295, 316.
73. [1978] 2 Lloyd's Rep 223, 300.
74. *Rosseel NV* v. *Oriental Commercial & Shipping Co (UK) Ltd* [1991] 2 Lloyd's Rep 625.
75. [1992] 1 AC 562.

law, but the award is signed in France—the court has jurisdiction to entertain an appeal on points of law under the 1979 Act, even though the award is regarded as a Convention award within the meaning of the 1975 Act. The exception only arises, however, because of the House of Lords' surprising conclusion that the award was made in France—where the award was signed—rather than England, which was the seat of arbitration.[76]

20.2.4 Discretion to stay enforcement proceedings

20.2.4.1 Section 5(2)(f) enables the court to refuse enforcement if the award has been set aside in the country of origin. Section 5(5) deals with the situation where proceedings to have the award set aside have been commenced in the country of origin, but before those proceedings are resolved an application is made to enforce the award in England. Section 5(5), which confers a discretion on the court in which enforcement is sought, provides:

> Where an application for the setting aside or suspension of a Convention award has been made to such a competent authority as is mentioned in subsection (2)(f) of this section, the court before which enforcement of the award is sought may, if it thinks fit, adjourn the proceedings and may, on the application of the party seeking to enforce the award, order the other party to give security.

The rationale of section 5(5) is clear. If, after an award has been made in country X, the creditor applies for enforcement in country Y and the debtor applies to have the award set aside in country X, it would be unfortunate if the courts of country Y ordered enforcement, only for the courts of country X to set aside the award.

20.2.4.2 There is some disagreement as to the correct approach which should be adopted to the question of discretion under section 5(5). At one extreme it has been suggested that enforcement should invariably be postponed when an application for setting aside the award has been made, particularly when security for the award is provided by the respondent in the context of the enforcement proceedings.[77] This suggestion cannot, however, be supported; if the courts invariably stay enforcement proceedings, they present the unsuccessful respondent with a simple means of frustrating the claimant's legitimate interests by slowing down the enforcement process.

20.2.4.3 Experience shows that the chances of the respondent being successful in his application to have the award set aside in the country of origin are likely to be small. Since the delay caused by the stay will prejudice the claimant by depriving him of the spoils of victory, as a general rule, a stay should be refused. A stay is only appropriate if the respondent offers "some summary proof that the award is tainted by a defect which is likely to cause its setting aside in the country of origin".[78]

20.2.4.4 The court of the country in which enforcement is sought also has a discretion as to whether the respondent should provide security (for example, in the form of a bank guarantee) to secure the amount of the award and accruing interest. The view has been expressed that "it is difficult to think of any circumstances in which security would not be warranted".[79] This view has not, however, commended itself to the Court of Appeal: "If, for example, the challenge to the validity of an award is manifestly well-founded, it

76. For further consideration of this decision see para. 20.2.1.2.2.
77. Deshpande, "Enforcement of Foreign Awards in India, UK and USA" (1987) 4 J Int Arb (1) 41, 53.
78. Van den Berg, *The New York Arbitration Convention of 1958* (1981) pp. 353–354.
79. Tupman, "Staying Enforcement of Arbitral Awards under the New York Convention" (1987) 3 Arb Int 209, 223.

would be quite wrong to order security until that is demonstrated in a foreign court."[80] In *Soleh Boneh International Ltd* v. *Government of the Republic of Uganda* the Court of Appeal decided that there are two important factors which should be considered in the context of an application for a stay of enforcement proceedings under section 5(5):

> The first is the strength of the argument that the award is invalid, as perceived on a brief consideration of the court which is asked to enforce the award while proceedings to set it aside are pending elsewhere. If the award is manifestly invalid, there should be an adjournment and no order for security; if it is manifestly valid, there should either be an order for immediate enforcement, or else an order for substantial security. In between there will be various degrees of plausibility in the argument for invalidity and the judge must be guided by his preliminary conclusion on the point. The second point is that the court must consider the ease or difficulty of enforcement of the award, and whether it will be rendered more difficult, for example, by movement of assets or by improvident trading, if enforcement is delayed.[81]

20.3 RECOGNITION AND ENFORCEMENT OF FOREIGN AWARDS AT COMMON LAW

20.3.1 The relationship between the Arbitration Act 1975 and the common law

A foreign award which is not entitled to recognition or enforcement under the 1975 Act (for example, because the award is not a Convention award) may nevertheless be entitled to recognition or enforcement in England under the common law. It was the aim of the Convention to facilitate the international recognition and enforcement of awards, not to provide an exclusive and comprehensive code. Accordingly, Article VII(1) of the Convention (the "more favourable right" clause) provides that the provisions of the Convention shall not "deprive any interested party of any right he may have to avail himself of an arbitral award in the manner and to the extent allowed by the law or the treaties of the country where such award is sought to be relied upon". This provision is implemented by section 6 of the 1975 Act.

20.3.2 Methods of enforcement

A foreign award which is entitled to enforcement at common law may be enforced in the same manner as a domestic award. The party seeking to rely on the award is not restricted to bringing an action on the award; a foreign award may be enforced by obtaining leave to enforce under section 26 of the 1950 Act.[82] Nevertheless, two limitations on the scope of section 26 should be noted in this context.

(i) Section 26 is not available where, according to the terms of the award which the plaintiff is seeking to enforce, the defendant is obliged to make payment in a foreign country.[83]

(ii) It is to be expected that the more frequently used method of enforcing a foreign award at common law is by means of an action on the award.

80. Staughton LJ in *Soleh Boneh International Ltd* v. *Government of the Republic of Uganda* [1993] 2 Lloyd's Rep 208, 212.

81. Staughton LJ, [1993] 2 Lloyd's Rep 208, 212.

82. See the judgment of Kerr J in *Dalmia Cement Ltd* v. *National Bank of Pakistan* [1975] QB 9, 20–23. Collier, [1975] CLJ 44.

83. *Dalmia Cement Ltd* v. *National Bank of Pakistan* [1975] QB 9. See para. 20.2.2.2.2.

Indeed, even where summary enforcement under section 26 is, in principle, available, the court may refuse to give leave to enforce: "In many, and perhaps most, cases of non-convention awards there may well be circumstances which would lead the court to the conclusion that the summary method of enforcement under section 26 is not an appropriate remedy if this is challenged."[84]

20.3.3 Conditions for enforcement at common law

20.3.3.1 A Convention award is presumed to be entitled to enforcement, the burden being placed on the party seeking to challenge the award to establish a ground for refusing enforcement. At common law, however, there are conditions which must be satisfied by the person seeking to rely on the award before enforcement of a foreign award can be considered.

20.3.3.2 In order for a foreign award to be entitled to recognition or enforcement in England at common law, the person seeking to enforce the award must prove (i) "that there was a submission"; (ii) "that the arbitration was conducted in pursuance of the submission"; and (iii) "that the award is a valid award, made pursuant to the provisions of the submission, and valid according to the *lex fori* of the place where the arbitration was carried out and where the award was made".[85] In addition, the award must be final and conclusive according to the law governing the arbitration proceedings.[86] The requirement that the award should be in accordance with an agreement to arbitrate which is valid by its proper law does not seem to give rise to problems in practice; the requirements that the award should be valid and final according to the law governing the arbitration proceedings may be illustrated by examples.

20.3.3.3 If the award is invalid under the law governing the arbitration proceedings, it cannot be enforced in England at common law. In *Bankers & Shippers Insurance Co of New York* v. *Liverpool Marine & General Insurance Co Ltd*[87] the parties entered a contract which included an agreement providing for arbitration in New York. A dispute arose and the claimant appointed an arbitrator. On the respondent's failure to appoint, the claimant, relying on the terms of the arbitration agreement, appointed a second arbitrator. The arbitral tribunal made an award in the claimant's favour. When the claimant sought enforcement in England the respondent resisted on the basis that the award was invalid under the curial law. It was established that, under New York law, where the respondent failed to appoint an arbitrator, the arbitration could proceed only if allowed to do so by an order of the court; failure to obtain an order of the court rendered the award invalid. Accordingly, the House of Lords refused to enforce the award in England.

20.3.3.4 As with the validity of an award, the finality of an award is, in principle, a question to be determined by the law governing the arbitration proceedings. There is, however, an important qualification; although it is for the law governing the arbitration proceedings to determine the effects of the award, the issue as to whether the award is

84. Kerr J in *Dalmia Cement Ltd* v. *National Bank of Pakistan* [1975] QB 9, 23.

85. *Norske Atlas Insurance Company Ltd* v. *London General Insurance Co Ltd* (1927) 28 Ll L Rep 104, 106–107.

86. *Dalmia Dairy Industries Ltd* v. *National Bank of Pakistan* [1978] 2 Lloyd's Rep 223.

87. (1926) 24 Ll L Rep 85.

final is a question of classification—which is to be determined by English law. Although the question whether the award is final in the country of origin depends on the law of that country, the law of the country of origin is directed to showing whether it is final as that word is understood in English.[88]

20.3.3.5 The requirement of finality must not be confused with enforceability. The importance of this distinction is illustrated by *Union Nationale des Coopératives Agricoles de Céréales* v. *Robert Catterall & Co Ltd*,[89] a case concerning proceedings for the enforcement of a Danish award. It was established that there was no time limit under Danish law for raising objections to the validity of an award and that execution of a Danish award in Denmark depended on a judgment having been obtained from the court based on the award. When enforcement proceedings were commenced in England, the plaintiff had not obtained a judgment on the award in Denmark. Even though it was clear that the award was not enforceable in Denmark, the Court of Appeal concluded that the award was final and, therefore, entitled to enforcement in England. As a general principle, an award is "valid, final and binding unless and until it is set aside by any procedure available for this purpose".[90]

20.3.4 Defences at common law

Even if the person seeking to rely on a foreign award shows that the award is valid and final, the party against whom the award is invoked may nevertheless resist enforcement by establishing a valid defence. The authorities concerning defences to the enforcement of foreign awards at common law are few and far between. The relevant principles are, however, reasonably clear.

20.3.4.1 Matters which are not defences

(i) Although there is no authority directly on the point, it is universally accepted that the court cannot refuse to enforce a foreign award on the ground that the arbitral tribunal made an error of law or fact. In this respect foreign awards are to be treated in the same way as foreign judgments—in relation to which there can be no review of the merits by the court in which enforcement is sought.[91]

(ii) An allegation of misconduct, which may found a claim for setting aside an award before the courts of the country of origin, is no defence to the enforcement of a foreign award at common law.[92]

(iii) It was once thought, on the basis of *Merrifield, Ziegler & Co* v. *Liverpool Cotton Association*,[93] that the court would not enforce a foreign award unless it

88. Lord Evershed MR in *Union Nationale des Coopératives Agricoles de Céréales* v. *Robert Catterall & Co Ltd* [1959] 2 QB 44, 53. Although this decision was made in the context of Part II of the Arbitration Act 1950, the principle is equally applicable in cases governed by the common law.

89. [1959] 2 QB 44.

90. Kerr J in *Dalmia Dairy Industries Ltd* v. *National Bank of Pakistan* [1978] 2 Lloyd's Rep 223, 247.

91. *Godard* v. *Gray* (1870) LR 6 QB 139.

92. See Kerr J in *Dalmia Dairy Industries Ltd* v. *National Bank of Pakistan* [1978] 2 Lloyd's Rep 223.

93. (1911) 105 LT 97. This case has been described as "extremely difficult to understand" (*Russell on Arbitration* (20th ed, 1982) pp. 379–380).

was actually enforceable in the country of origin. If correct, this rule would lead to the result that in most cases the plaintiff would have to obtain a judgment on the award in the country of origin before seeking enforcement in England. However, in *Union Nationale des Coopératives Agricoles de Céréales* v. *Robert Catterall & Co Ltd*[94] it was established that enforcement depends on the validity and finality of the foreign award, rather than its enforceability. In subsequent cases the rule in *Union Nationale des Coopératives Agricoles de Céréales* v. *Robert Catterall & Co Ltd* has been regarded as laying down the relevant principle.[95]

20.3.4.2 Valid defences

20.3.4.2.1 EXCESS OF JURISDICTION

Enforcement of a foreign award will be refused if the arbitral tribunal had no jurisdiction to make the award. The defence of excess of jurisdiction at common law corresponds to section 5(2)(d) of the 1975 Act.[96] The jurisdiction of the arbitrator is to be determined by reference to the arbitration agreement, construed in accordance with its proper law.[97]

For the purposes of section 5(2)(d) of the 1975 Act if the party seeking to rely on a Convention award produces the documents required by section 4, the burden is on the party against whom the award is invoked to show that the arbitrator did not have the necessary jurisdiction. At common law (and under Part II of the 1950 Act) the position is as follows: it is for the party who is setting up the award to prove that the arbitrator acted within the terms of the authority which was given to him; but, if the party who is setting up the award produces a document which appears to be regular and made with jurisdiction, the onus passes to the other party to prove that the award is defective in that it has dealt with matters beyond the scope of the arbitration agreement.[98]

20.3.4.2.2 BREACH OF THE PRINCIPLES OF NATURAL JUSTICE

The natural justice defence at common law broadly corresponds with the ground for refusing enforcement to a Convention award provided by section 5(2)(c) of the 1975 Act.[99] In *Dalmia Dairy Industries Ltd* v. *National Bank of Pakistan*[100] the issue of natural justice was raised in relation to arbitrations conducted under the ICC Rules. The arbitrator had followed the usual practice in ICC arbitration and, in his discretion, declined to hear any oral evidence. The defendant's contention that this involved a breach of the principles of natural justice—thereby rendering the awards unenforceable—was rejected.

94. [1959] 2 QB 44 (a case decided under Part II of the 1950 Act).
95. See, for example, Kerr J in *Dalmia Dairy Industries Ltd* v. *National Bank of Pakistan* [1978] 2 Lloyd's Rep 223, 249–250.
96. See para. 20.2.3.5.
97. *Kianta Osekeyhtio* v. *Britain & Overseas Trading Co Ltd* [1954] 1 Lloyd's Rep 247; *Dalmia Dairy Industries Ltd* v. *National Bank of Pakistan* [1978] 2 Lloyd's Rep 223.
98. *Kianta Osekeyhtio* v. *Britain & Overseas Trading Co Ltd* [1954] 1 Lloyd's Rep 247, 250–251.
99. See para. 20.2.3.4.
100. [1978] 2 Lloyd's Rep 223.

20.3.4.2.3 PUBLIC POLICY

The courts may refuse to enforce a foreign award where to do so would be contrary to public policy.[101]

20.3.4.2.4 FRAUD

It may be assumed that, at common law, the person against whom an award is invoked may seek to resist the enforcement of a foreign award on the ground that the award was procured by fraud. Although there is no clear authority on this point—the only reference to the issue being a dictum in a decision of the Privy Council[102]—it is reasonable to suppose that if a foreign judgment may be refused enforcement on the basis of fraud, the same should be true in relation to a foreign award. However, if an analogy is to be drawn between foreign judgments and foreign awards, there are limitations on the availability of the defence of fraud. Where, for example, a party has sought to challenge an award on the basis of fraud in the country of origin, it should not be possible to raise the defence in the context of enforcement proceedings in England, if the courts of the country of origin decide that the allegation of fraud is not made out.[103]

20.4 RECOGNITION AND ENFORCEMENT OF FOREIGN AWARDS UNDER PART II OF THE ARBITRATION ACT 1950

20.4.1 The relationship between Part II of the 1950 Act and other regimes

20.4.1.1 The first international attempts to facilitate the mutual recognition and enforcement of awards date from the 1920s. The Arbitration (Foreign Awards) Act 1930 was passed to give effect to the Geneva Convention on the Execution of Foreign Arbitral Awards of 1927. The 1930 Act was re-enacted in Part II of the 1950 Act. The recognition and enforcement of awards under this statutory scheme is unnecessarily complex.

20.4.1.2 The 1975 Act leaves Part II of the 1950 Act in place, but very significantly cuts down its scope. Part II of the 1950 Act now plays only a residual role since an award which is a Convention award within the scope of the 1975 Act is not entitled to recognition and enforcement under Part II of the 1950 Act. To this extent the earlier enactment is superseded by the 1975 Act.[104] Part II of the 1950 Act is relevant only as regards "foreign awards" (as defined by section 35 of the 1950 Act) which are not Convention awards within the scope of the 1975 Act. In view of the number of States which have ratified the New York Convention, Part II of the 1950 Act is primarily of historical interest.

Part II of the 1950 Act, where applicable, is not exclusive; a creditor may seek enforcement at common law, rather than under the statutory scheme.[105]

101. The defence of public policy has already been considered in the context of recognition and enforcement under the Arbitration Act 1975. For a discussion of the relevant English case law, both at common law and under the Arbitration Act 1975, see para. 20.2.3.9.

102. Viscount Cave in *Oppenheim & Co* v. *Mahomed Haneef* [1922] 1 AC 482, 487.

103. This proposition is consistent with the decision of the Court of Appeal in *House of Spring Gardens Ltd* v. *Waite* [1991] QB 241 (discussed at para. 9.2.7.2.1.2).

104. Arbitration Act 1975, s. 2.

105. Arbitration Act 1950, s. 40.

20.4.2 Conditions for recognition and enforcement

20.4.2.1 In order for an award to be entitled to recognition and enforcement in England under Part II of the 1950 Act it must be a "foreign award" within the meaning of section 35(1) of the 1950 Act (but not a Convention award within the scope of the 1975 Act). An award is a "foreign award" if three conditions are satisfied:

(a) the award must have been made in a State to which the 1927 Convention has been declared to apply, but which has not ratified the 1958 Convention[106];
(b) the award must have been made under an arbitration agreement which is not governed by English law and to which the Geneva Protocol on Arbitration Clauses of 1923 is applicable[107];
(c) the arbitration agreement under which the award was made must be between parties who are subject to the jurisdiction of different States which have been declared to be parties to the 1927 Convention.[108]

20.4.2.2 A "foreign award" must satisfy the criteria laid down by section 37(1), which provides:

In order that a foreign award may be enforceable under this Part of this Act it must have—
(a) been made in pursuance of an agreement for arbitration which was valid under the law by which it was governed;
(b) been made by the tribunal provided for in the agreement or constituted in manner agreed upon by the parties;
(c) been made in conformity with the law governing the arbitration procedure;
(d) become final in the country where it was made;
(e) been in respect of a matter which may lawfully be referred to arbitration under the law of England;
and the enforcement thereof must not be contrary to the public policy or the law of England.

20.4.2.3 The party seeking to enforce a "foreign award" must produce the documents specified by section 38(1) (or where appropriate a certified translation[109]):

(a) the original award or a copy thereof duly authenticated in manner required by the law of the country in which it was made; and
(b) evidence proving that the award has become final; and
(c) such evidence as may be necessary to prove that the award is a foreign award and that the conditions mentioned in paragraphs (a), (b) and (c) of subsection (1) of the last foregoing section are satisfied.

Subject to the defences listed in section 37(2), an award which satisfies all these conditions may be enforced in the same way as a domestic award—by action on the award or by an application under section 26 of the 1950 Act.[110]

106. Arbitration Act 1950, s. 35(1)(c); Arbitration Act 1975, s. 2. There is only a handful of States, none of them important arbitration centres, which satisfy this condition. For a list of the countries to which Part II of the 1950 Act has been declared to apply by Order in Council see Mustill & Boyd, *Commercial Arbitration* (2nd ed, 1989) pp. 670–671.
107. Arbitration Act 1950, s. 35(1)(a).
108. Arbitration Act 1950, s. 35(1)(b). For a list of parties to the 1927 Convention for the purposes of Part II of the 1950 Act see Mustill & Boyd, *Commercial Arbitration* (2nd ed, 1989) pp. 670–671.
109. Arbitration Act 1950, s. 38(2).
110. Arbitration Act 1950, s. 36(1).

20.4.3 Defences to enforcement

The defences to enforcement under Part II of the 1950 Act are listed in section 37(2) which provides:

> Subject to the provisions of this subsection, a foreign award shall not be enforceable under this Part of this Act if the court dealing with the case is satisfied that—
> (a) the award has been annulled in the country in which it was made; or
> (b) the party against whom it is sought to enforce the award was not given notice of the arbitration proceedings in sufficient time to enable him to present his case, or was under some legal incapacity and was not properly represented; or
> (c) the award does not deal with all the questions referred or contains decisions on matters beyond the scope of the agreement for arbitration:
> Provided that, if the award does not deal with all the questions referred, the court may, if it thinks fit, either postpone the enforcement of the award or order its enforcement subject to the giving of such security by the person seeking to enforce it as the court may think fit.

20.5 OTHER REGIMES FOR THE RECOGNITION AND ENFORCEMENT OF FOREIGN ARBITRAL AWARDS

20.5.1 Part II of the Civil Jurisdiction and Judgments Act 1982

20.5.1.1 Part II of the Civil Jurisdiction and Judgments Act 1982 provides a simple mechanism for the recognition and enforcement of judgments given by the courts of one part of the United Kingdom in other parts of the United Kingdom.[111] By virtue of the definition of "judgment" for the purposes of Part II of the 1982 Act the same regime applies to awards.

20.5.1.2 Section 18(2) of the Civil Jurisdiction and Judgments Act 1982 provides:

> In this section "judgment" means any of the following (references to the giving of a judgment being construed accordingly)—...
> (e) an arbitration award which has become enforceable in the part of the United Kingdom in which it was given in the same manner as a judgment given by a court of law in that part.

An award made in Scotland or Northern Ireland for a sum of money may be enforced in England under Schedule 6 to the 1982 Act and non-money awards may be enforced under Schedule 7.[112] In order to enforce an award made in Scotland or Northern Ireland under Part II of the 1982 Act the party seeking to set up the award must obtain a certificate from the court which gave the judgment or made the order by virtue of which the award has become enforceable.[113] When a certificate has been issued it can then be registered in England.[114] The effect of registration is that the award has the same force as if the English court had given leave to enforce under section 26 of the 1950 Act.[115]

20.5.1.3 Sections 18 and 19 of the 1982 Act provide that the court may not refuse to recognise or enforce a judgment given by the courts of Scotland or Northern Ireland

111. See para. 9.5.
112. See para. 9.5.3.
113. Civil Jurisdiction and Judgments Act 1982, Sched. 6, para. 2(2)(e); Sched. 7, para. 2(2)(e).
114. Civil Jurisdiction and Judgments Act 1982, Sched. 6, para. 5; Sched. 7, para. 5.
115. Civil Jurisdiction and Judgments Act 1982, Sched. 6, para. 6; Sched. 7, para. 6.

solely on the ground that the court of origin did not have jurisdiction under English private international law rules. The position is different as regards awards made in Scotland or Northern Ireland. It is provided in this context that if the court of origin did not have jurisdiction to make the judgment or order by virtue of which the award has become enforceable the award may be refused enforcement in England.[116] This basis of refusing recognition and enforcement is in addition to other defences which may be available.[117]

20.5.1.4 In relation to awards the regime provided by Part II of the 1982 Act is not exclusive in those cases falling within its scope. The party seeking to set up the award may seek to enforce the award by an action on the award or by an application for leave to enforce under section 26 of the 1950 Act.[118]

20.5.2 Part II of the Administration of Justice Act 1920

Certain judgments may be registered under Part II of the Administration of Justice Act 1920, in consequence of which they become enforceable in England as if they were judgments of the High Court.[119] For the purposes of Part II of the 1920 Act "judgment" is defined as extending to awards which have become enforceable in the same manner as a judgment given by a court.[120]

20.5.3 Part I of the Foreign Judgments (Reciprocal Enforcement) Act 1933

20.5.3.1 A similar regime to that existing under Part II of the Administration of Justice Act 1920 was established under the Foreign Judgments (Reciprocal Enforcement) Act 1933. Indeed, the original intention was that the 1933 Act should supersede the earlier legislation. The basic condition for enforcement under the 1933 Act is the same as that which must be satisfied under Part II of the 1920 Act—in pursuance of the law in force in the place where it was made the award must have become enforceable in the same manner as a judgment given by a court in that place. In practice, this means that the award must have been accorded judicial recognition in the foreign country by some process analogous to that created by section 26 of the 1950 Act. The grounds for setting aside registration under section 4(1) of the 1933 Act apply to awards just as they do to foreign judgments.

20.5.3.2 An arbitration award made in a country other than the United Kingdom which is a party to the Geneva Convention on the International Carriage of Goods by Road (which is given effect by the Carriage of Goods by Road Act 1965) is enforceable under the 1933 Act if two conditions are satisfied: (i) the award is enforceable in the country where the award was made; and (ii) the arbitration agreement provided that the arbitrator should apply the CMR Convention. When deciding whether the second condition is satisfied it is not sufficient that the substantive rights and obligations of the parties are governed by a national law which has incorporated the CMR Convention;

116. Civil Jurisdiction and Judgments Act 1982, s. 19(3)(b).
117. See para. 9.5.2.
118. Civil Jurisdiction and Judgments Act 1982, s. 18(8).
119. See para. 9.3.1.
120. Administration of Justice Act 1920, s. 12(1).

the arbitration agreement must expressly provide that the tribunal shall apply the CMR Convention.[121]

20.5.3.3 A judgment falling within the scope of the 1933 Act may not be enforced except under the statutory provisions; a judgment creditor cannot rely on the common law.[122] The Act is not exclusive, however, as regards awards falling within its scope.[123]

20.5.4 Arbitration (International Investment Disputes) Act 1966

20.5.4.1 The Arbitration (International Investment Disputes) Act 1966 was passed to give effect to the United Kingdom's treaty obligations under the Washington Convention of 1965 for the settlement of investment disputes between States and nationals of other States. The 1965 Convention set up the International Centre for Settlement of Investment Disputes (ICSID). The purpose of the Washington Convention was to promote private investment in developing countries by providing a mechanism for the settlement of disputes between States and foreign investors.[124]

20.5.4.2 ICSID helps to promote dispute resolution by arbitration or conciliation, depending on the choice of the parties. Although the jurisdiction of the Centre is dependent on the consent of the parties (effected by means of a suitable clause in the principal contract or a submission agreement after the dispute has arisen), there are additional conditions which have to be satisfied if arbitration under ICSID is to take place: (i) the dispute must be between a Contracting State and a national of another Contracting State; (ii) the difference between the parties must be a legal dispute arising out of investment.[125]

20.5.4.3 Compared to other arbitration institutions very few awards have been rendered under the auspices of ICSID.[126] An ICSID award may be registered in the High Court.[127] Once registered such an award has the same effect as a judgment of the High Court.[128] There are no grounds on which an award which has been registered can be refused; enforcement may not be refused even on grounds of public policy. However, either party to a dispute arbitrated under ICSID may seek annulment of an award under the internal appeal procedure set out in the ICSID Convention, which provides that requests for annulment shall be heard by an *ad hoc* committee appointed by the President of the World Bank.[129]

20.5.5 Recognition of awards made by the Iran–US Claims Tribunal

20.5.5.1 The Iran–US Claims Tribunal was established pursuant to the Algiers Declaration of 1981. The purpose of the Tribunal was to settle claims between, on the

121. *AB Bofors-Uva CAV Ltd* v. *AB Skandia Transport* [1982] 1 Lloyd's Rep 410.
122. Foreign Judgments (Reciprocal Enforcement) Act 1933, s. 6.
123. Foreign Judgments (Reciprocal Enforcement) Act 1933, s. 10A.
124. See, generally, Sutherland, "The World Bank Convention on the Settlement of Investment Disputes" (1979) 28 ICLQ 367.
125. See Amerasinghe, "Jurisdiction Ratione Personae under the Convention on the Settlement of Investment Disputes Between States and Nationals of Other States" (1974–75) 47 BYIL 227.
126. For a discussion of the seven cases decided by the mid-1980s see Tupman, "Case Studies in the Jurisdiction of the International Centre for Settlement of Investment Disputes" (1986) 35 ICLQ 813.
127. Arbitration (International Investment Disputes) Act 1966, s. 1.
128. Arbitration (International Investment Disputes) Act 1966, s. 2(1).
129. See Craig, "Uses and Abuses of Appeal from Awards" (1988) 4 Arb Int 174, 209–214.

one hand, US nationals and corporations and, on the other, the State of Iran and Iranian state corporations. The Tribunal was established in The Hague and the procedure adopted by the Tribunal was that laid down in the UNCITRAL Arbitration Rules. Awards are satisfied out of a specially established fund and are binding on the parties.

20.5.5.2 In *Dallal* v. *Bank Mellat*[130] the plaintiff, whose claim had been rejected by the Tribunal, started proceedings in England on the same cause of action. The defendant sought to raise the Tribunal's award as a defence and the question arose as to whether the award was entitled to recognition in England so as to bar the plaintiff's claim. Hobhouse J held that the award was not entitled to recognition under the common law or the 1975 Act, since it was established that the "arbitration agreement"—on which the jurisdiction of the Tribunal was based—was void under its proper law (which was regarded as being Dutch law). Nevertheless, it was held that the award was entitled to recognition. This result was arrived at by treating the award as arising out of a "statutory" arbitration established under public international law; the competence of the Tribunal was derived from international law and that competence was recognised in England. Although the reasoning adopted by Hobhouse J may be less than entirely convincing, it is highly desirable that awards of the Tribunal should be entitled to recognition in England.

20.6 AWARDS, JUDGMENTS AND THE CAUSE OF ACTION

There are three different questions concerning the relationship between judgments, awards and the cause of action.

(i) What is the solution in a case where there is a conflict between a foreign judgment and an award?
(ii) Does a foreign award, which has been the subject of a foreign judgment on the award, remain enforceable in England as an award?
(iii) Does a foreign award extinguish the cause of action?

20.6.1 Conflicting judgments and awards

20.6.1.1 Potential problems arise in connection with the interaction of the 1975 Act and the Brussels and Lugano Conventions. What is the position where an award made in one country conflicts with a judgment granted in another country? In considering this question it is important to distinguish foreign awards from English awards and to distinguish judgments granted by the courts of a Brussels or Lugano Contracting State from judgments granted by the courts of a non-contracting State.

20.6.1.2 Section 32 of the Civil Jurisdiction and Judgments Act 1982 provides that a foreign judgment shall be refused recognition and enforcement if the bringing of the foreign proceedings was "contrary to an agreement under which the dispute in question

130. [1986] 1 QB 441. Crawford, (1986) 57 BYIL 410; Ellis, "Arbitration Still Bound" (1986) 102 LQR 500; Kunzlik, [1986] CLJ 377.

was to be settled otherwise than by proceedings in the courts of that country".[131] So, where there is a conflict between a foreign award which is entitled to enforcement in England and a foreign judgment given in defiance of the arbitration agreement, the foreign judgment does not call into question the enforceability of the award.

20.6.1.3 There is some doubt as to whether the result is the same where a judgment is granted by a court of a Brussels or Lugano Contracting State in defiance of an arbitration clause. Can a Belgian award be enforced in England under the 1975 Act in a situation where, notwithstanding an agreement of the parties to refer the dispute to arbitration in Belgium, an Italian court renders a judgment declaring the arbitration agreement to be null and void? The key issue is whether the Italian judgment concerns "arbitration" for the purposes of Article 1(4) of the Brussels Convention. If the judgment falls outside the scope of the Brussels Convention and the court does not share the view of the Italian courts that the arbitration agreement is invalid, recognition of the judgment may be refused under section 32 of the 1982 Act and the award is enforceable under the 1975 Act. If, however, the proceedings relating to the judgment do not concern "arbitration", both the award and the judgment are *prima facie* entitled to recognition (under the 1975 Act and the 1982 Act respectively). In this situation, it would appear that the later treaty (the Brussels Convention) takes precedence over the earlier one (the New York Convention).[132] This conclusion, which follows inexorably from the premise that a judgment given in defiance of an arbitration agreement falls within the material scope of the Brussels and Lugano Conventions, might legitimately be regarded as supporting the broader interpretation of Article 1(4) according to which the recognition of a judgment given in defiance of an arbitration clause should be regarded as a matter falling outside the Conventions' scope.[133]

20.6.1.4 The same basic problems arise in the situation where an English award conflicts with a judgment given by the courts of a Contracting State. If section 32 of the Civil Jurisdiction and Judgments Act 1982 is not applicable—because the judgment falls within the material scope of Title I—the only possible basis on which recognition and enforcement of the judgment might be resisted is Article 27(3) which provides that a judgment shall not be recognised "if the judgment is irreconcilable with a judgment given in a dispute between the parties in the State in which recognition is sought". Since it is highly unlikely that an award can be regarded as a "judgment" for the purposes of Article 27(3), the view that proceedings relating a judgment given in defiance of an arbitration agreement should be regarded as falling within the scope of the Brussels and Lugano Conventions could lead to a situation in which the court is required to give preference to a foreign judgment over an award made by arbitrators in England, notwithstanding the fact that the arbitration agreement and the award are valid under English law. For these reasons, proceedings relating to a judgment given in defiance of an arbitration agreement should be regarded as falling outside the scope of Title I of the Brussels and Lugano Conventions.

131. See para. 9.2.7.5.
132. Davidson, "Civil Jurisdiction and Arbitration" 1992 SLT 267, 270.
133. See para. 3.3.3.4.5.

20.6.2 The effect of a foreign judgment on the award

20.6.2.1 Enforcement under Part II of the Civil Jurisdiction and Judgments Act 1982, Part II of the Administration of Justice Act 1920 and the Foreign Judgments (Reciprocal Enforcement) Act 1933 is dependent on the award having become enforceable under the law of the seat. However, none of these statutory regimes provide an exclusive code for the enforcement of foreign awards falling within their scope. Accordingly, in principle, an award which is enforceable under one of these regimes may, in appropriate circumstances, be enforceable at common law or as a Convention award under the 1975 Act. For a foreign award to be entitled to enforcement in England either at common law or under the 1975 Act there is no requirement that the award should be enforceable by the law governing the arbitration proceedings.[134] Under the 1975 Act the requirement is simply that the award should be "binding".[135]

20.6.2.2 In those cases where a foreign award has become enforceable abroad it is important to distinguish two different situations: (i) the award may have become enforceable by a summary procedure (for example, by deposit of the award with the court); (ii) the award may have been converted into a judgment by a procedure analogous to an action on the award at common law.

20.6.2.3 In the first category of case, if the appropriate conditions are satisfied, there can be no doubt that the award remains enforceable as such in England. In the second category, however, the question is whether the foreign judgment and/or the foreign award is entitled to enforcement in England. There is clear authority for the proposition that in cases where there has been a foreign judgment on a foreign award the judgment is entitled to enforcement in England according to general principles.[136] Furthermore, as a result of the abolition of the non-merger rule in relation to foreign judgments,[137] it is possible that, provided that the judgment satisfies the relevant condition, it is the judgment alone—and not the award—which is entitled to enforcement.[138]

20.6.2.4 However, as a matter of principle, the merger of the award with the judgment in the country of origin should not be regarded as having extraterritorial effect and the award should remain enforceable in these circumstances: "The fact that leave for enforcement has the effect of absorbing the award in the country of origin is a technical aspect for the purposes of enforcement within that country. The award can therefore be deemed to remain a cause of action for enforcement in other countries."[139] Indeed, in *Marc Rich & Co AG* v. *Societa Italiana Impianti PA* Advocate-General Darmon went further and suggested that "the 'merger' of the award must be regarded as limited to the territory of the court which delivered the judgment and *only* the award must be taken into account for the purpose of recognition and enforcement in other States".[140]

134. *Union Nationale des Coopératives Agricoles des Céréales* v. *Robert Catterall & Co Ltd* [1959] 2 QB 44.
135. See para. 20.2.3.7.1.
136. *East India Trading Co Inc* v. *Carmel Exporters and Importers Ltd* [1952] 2 QB 439.
137. Civil Jurisdiction and Judgments Act 1982, s. 34.
138. Dicey & Morris, *The Conflict of Laws* (12th ed, 1993) pp. 606–607.
139. Van den Berg, *The New York Arbitration Convention of 1958* (1981) p. 347.
140. Case C-190/89 [1991] ECR I-3855, 3883 (para. 69). (Emphasis added.)

20.6.3 The effect of a foreign arbitral award on the cause of action

Under the common law rules which applied before the entry into force of the Civil Jurisdiction and Judgments Act 1982 a foreign judgment was not effective to extinguish the original cause of action. As a result a plaintiff who had obtained a judgment abroad was not prevented from suing on the original cause of action in England. The doctrine of non-merger was laid to rest by section 34 of 1982 Act.[141]

Since section 34 refers only to foreign judgments the question arises as to whether the doctrine of non-merger applies to foreign awards. There is no judicial authority on this point, but common sense suggests that the original cause of action should be regarded as merging with the award:

> [T]here is no reason of policy or principle why the obsolete and anomalous rule of non-merger in relation to foreign judgments should be extended to foreign awards. Indeed the consensual and contractual character of arbitration means that parties to an arbitration agreement impliedly promise to perform a valid award, and it should follow also that they impliedly promise not to take any action inconsistent with their submission to arbitration. Bringing an action on the original cause of action would be wholly inconsistent with the obligation under the submission and the subsequent award.[142]

141. See para. 9.1.3.1.

142. Dicey & Morris, *The Conflict of Laws* (12th ed, 1993) pp. 605–606. See also Mustill & Boyd, *Commercial Arbitration* (2nd ed, 1989) p. 415.

PART IV

PROCEDURAL MATTERS

CHAPTER 21

PROVISIONAL MEASURES[1]

In any legal system it is inevitable that there will be delays between the commencement of proceedings by the plaintiff and the final determination of the action. Delays in litigation may lead to the plaintiff's efforts to vindicate his rights being frustrated if the defendant is allowed either to thwart the legal process (for example, by destroying evidence) or to deprive the successful plaintiff of the fruits of success (for example, by dissipating his assets and making himself judgment-proof). The same dangers exist in the context of disputes which the parties have agreed to refer to arbitration. Accordingly, the courts have developed a range of provisional measures, the purpose of which is to ensure that, as far as possible, the rights of the parties are not irreparably harmed pending the final judgment or award (para. 21.1). In recent years the jurisdiction of the courts to grant provisional measures has been clarified and extended (paras. 21.2–21.3). Provisional measures may be granted in relation to acts or things within the jurisdiction or abroad. Although the courts must exercise caution when considering the grant of provisional measures with extraterritorial effect, the courts have become increasingly aware of the importance (as well as the dangers) of granting such measures (para. 21.4). Notwithstanding developments on both the domestic and international planes, the cross-border enforcement of provisional measures remains fraught with difficulty (para. 21.5).

21.1 DIFFERENT TYPES OF PROVISIONAL MEASURE

21.1.1 Introduction

21.1.1.1 Although the classification of provisional measures is not free from controversy, they can, broadly speaking, be divided into three categories.

(i) Some measures are designed to maintain the status quo pending the final decision on the merits. In English law the court may grant interlocutory injunctions (which, in appropriate circumstances, may be obtained on an *ex parte* application) with a view to ensuring that justice can be done when the dispute is ultimately determined. So, for example, a plaintiff employer may apply for an injunction to prevent the defendant contractor from ceasing work on a construction project.[2] Similarly, the court may make an order "for the

1. Collins, "Provisional and Protective Measures in International Litigation" [1992] III Hag Rec 9.
2. *Channel Tunnel Group Ltd* v. *Balfour Beatty Construction Ltd* [1993] AC 334.

detention, custody or preservation of any property which is the subject matter of the cause or matter".[3]

(ii) The court may take measures which are designed to secure the ultimate judgment or award by preventing the defendant from disposing of assets pending the final determination of the proceedings. The objective of ensuring compliance with the final judgment or award may be achieved in one of two ways. Perhaps the most simple and effective provisional measure in this context is a court order which allows the plaintiff to attach property within the court's jurisdiction. In matters falling within the jurisdiction of the Admiralty Court the plaintiff may, in certain circumstances, bring proceedings *in rem* by serving a writ on the *res* (normally a ship) within the jurisdiction.[4] Where proceedings are commenced *in rem* the plaintiff is also entitled to arrest the *res*. In practice, either the *res* is sold and the judgment or award is enforced out of the proceeds of sale or the owner puts up security for the claim to obtain the release of the *res* or, if it has not yet been arrested, to prevent the plaintiff from arresting it. In any event the plaintiff obtains security for his claim.

In cases not falling within the jurisdiction of the Admiralty Court, there is no equivalent to the action *in rem*. Indeed, the presence of the defendant's assets in England does not, in itself, entitle the court to assume jurisdiction over the plaintiff's claim.[5] Modern technological conditions—particularly the development of systems for the electronic transfer of funds—make it increasingly difficult for a party who obtains a judgment or an award in his favour to execute the judgment or award against the assets of the losing party. Legal and practical problems surrounding enforcement have led to the development in England of new provisional measures. The courts have developed the Mareva[6] injunction, which enables a plaintiff to obtain an order freezing the defendant's assets.

(iii) Provisional measures include procedural orders of an investigative nature. In *CFEM Façades SA* v. *Bovis Construction Ltd*,[7] for example, the court was faced with an application to enforce a French order appointing experts to inspect a building in London and to take evidence from potential witnesses. The most significant development in this area in English law has been the birth of the Anton Piller[8] order which enables the plaintiff to enter the defendant's premises with a view to collecting evidence.

21.1.1.2 While there are statutory provisions and procedural rules concerned with specific measures, section 37(1) of the Supreme Court Act 1981 provides the foundation of the court's broad discretionary jurisdiction to grant provisional measures:

The High Court may by order (whether interlocutory or final) grant an injunction or appoint a receiver in all cases in which it appears to the court to be just and convenient to do so.

3. RSC, Order 29, r. 2(1). The power granted by this rule is only exercisable *inter partes*.
4. See paras. 8.1.1–8.1.2.
5. *Siskina (Owners of cargo lately laden on board)* v. *Distos Compania Naviera SA* [1979] AC 210.
6. *Mareva Compania Naviera SA* v. *International Bulk Carriers SA* [1975] 2 Lloyd's Rep 509. *Nippon Yusen Kaisha* v. *Karageorgis* [1975] 1 WLR 1093 was, however, the first English case in which Mareva-type relief was granted.
7. [1992] ILPr 561.
8. Named after the seminal case *Anton Piller KG* v. *Manufacturing Processes Ltd* [1976] Ch 55.

The extreme generality of section 37(1) means that the principles according to which provisional measures are granted must be gleaned from the cases.

21.1.2 Interlocutory injunctions

21.1.2.1 Any consideration of the law relating to interlocutory injunctions must take as its starting-point the decision of the House of Lords in *American Cyanamid Co* v. *Ethicon Ltd.*[9] It should be stressed, however, that this decision should be regarded as no more that a set of useful guidelines.[10] The decision contains no principle of universal application and it must always be remembered that the ultimate test as to whether an injunction should be granted is whether it is just and convenient to do so. The guidelines in *American Cyanamid Co* v. *Ethicon Ltd* indicate that in deciding whether or not to grant an interlocutory injunction the court should have regard to a number of questions.

(i) As a general rule, the court should be satisfied that there is a serious question to be tried.

(ii) The court should consider the balance of convenience. This means, for example, that an injunction should normally be refused if the plaintiff, if successful, will be adequately compensated by an award of damages. However, as Lord Diplock noted: "Where other factors appear to be evenly balanced it is a counsel of prudence to take such measures as are calculated to preserve the status quo."[11]

(iii) Unless the court exercises restraint, an application for provisional measures may draw the court into a mini-trial on the merits at the interlocutory stage. As a general rule, therefore, the court should not be concerned with the relative strength of the parties' arguments (subject, of course, to the requirement that there should be a serious question to be tried). However, where it is clear that the plaintiff's claim is unanswerable on the facts or that the case involves a simple point of law (for example, concerning the interpretation of a statutory or contractual provision) which will obviously be resolved in the plaintiff's favour the court will generally grant the relief sought. Where the case will be effectively determined by the decision to grant, or to refuse to grant, the measure sought by the plaintiff the court has no choice but to look at the merits of the claim.

21.1.2.2 It is important to draw attention to the limits of the guidelines in *American Cyanamid Co* v. *Ethicon Ltd.* For example, the guidelines are inappropriate in cases where there is no prospect of a trial. Similarly, it would seem that the guidelines do not apply to mandatory interlocutory injunctions[12]; the court will seldom grant a mandatory injunction at the interlocutory stage. Finally, it should be noted that special principles have been worked out by the courts in relation to Mareva injunctions and Anton Piller orders.

9. [1975] AC 396.
10. *Cambridge Nutrition Ltd* v. *British Broadcasting Corporation* [1990] 3 All ER 523.
11. *American Cyanamid Co* v. *Ethicon Ltd* [1975] AC 396, 408.
12. *Leisure Data* v. *Bell* [1988] FSR 367.

21.1.3 Mareva injunctions

21.1.3.1 Background

21.1.3.1.1 Perhaps the most important function of provisional measures in the context of international litigation is to secure the ultimate judgment by preventing the defendant from disposing of his assets before the final determination of the proceedings. From the point of view of the plaintiff what is needed is a mechanism whereby the defendant is, first, required to disclose the extent and location of his assets and, then, prevented from dealing with his assets to the extent which is necessary to ensure that, as far as possible, any judgment obtained by the plaintiff can be satisfied. From the point of view of the defendant, however, it is important that remedies which are made available to the plaintiff are not so extensive that they may be used as an instrument of oppression.

21.1.3.1.2 Civil law countries have developed a mechanism—which in France is known as the *saisie conservatoire*—whereby at the very outset of proceedings the assets of a defendant may be seized so that there will be property against which the plaintiff, if successful, will be able to levy execution. Often, in practice, the defendant provides security for the plaintiff's claim to obtain the release of his assets. Although, until relatively recently, there was no equivalent institution in English law, in the 1970s the Mareva injunction was born.

21.1.3.1.3 The purpose of a Mareva injunction is "to prevent parties to actions frustrating [the court's] orders by moving assets out of the jurisdiction, or dissipating assets in one way or another, with a view to making themselves proof against a future judgment".[13] This purpose is achieved by the court making an order which freezes the defendant's assets (often a credit balance in a bank account) so that if the plaintiff succeeds in the action, there will be property of the defendant out of which the judgment can be satisfied.[14] A Mareva injunction may be granted by the court either before or after the granting of the judgment on the merits of the dispute.

21.1.3.2 Obtaining a Mareva injunction

21.1.3.2.1 An application for a Mareva injunction is normally made at the interlocutory stage. Because speed and the element of surprise are important the plaintiff's application is usually made *ex parte*. Notwithstanding the generality of section 37(1), where the relief sought is a freezing order as regards assets within the jurisdiction, a Mareva injunction will not be granted unless the plaintiff shows that there is at least a good arguable case that he will succeed at the trial and the court considers that, on the whole of the evidence then before it, the refusal of a Mareva injunction would involve a real risk that a judgment or award in favour of the plaintiff would remain unsatisfied.[15] Furthermore, where the plaintiff is seeking an order freezing assets within the jurisdiction, it must be shown that the defendant has assets within the jurisdiction.

21.1.3.2.2 Originally, Mareva injunctions were subject to three limitations: they were granted only against persons resident outside the jurisdiction; they were granted only against persons who had property within the jurisdiction; and they were granted only to

13. Lord Donaldson MR in *Jet West Ltd* v. *Haddican* [1992] 1 WLR 487, 489.
14. Brandon J in *The Rena K* [1979] QB 377, 407.
15. *Ninemia Maritime Corporation* v. *Trave Schiffahrtsgesellschaft mbH und Co KG* [1983] 1 WLR 1412.

restrain the removal of property from the jurisdiction.[16] None of these limitations apply today.

(i) The factual context which gave birth to the Mareva injunction was an action in England against a foreign defendant who had assets in England.[17] On the basis of the early cases, it was uncertain whether it was a requirement for the exercise of the Mareva jurisdiction that the defendant should be either a foreign company or a foreign resident. Cases decided in 1980 indicated that a Mareva injunction could also be granted against an English resident.[18] The approach adopted by the courts was endorsed by section 37(3) of the 1981 Act, which provides:

> The power of the High Court under subsection (1) to grant an interlocutory injunction restraining a party to any proceedings from removing from the jurisdiction of the High Court, or otherwise dealing with, assets located within that jurisdiction shall be exercisable in cases where that party is, as well as in cases where he is not, domiciled, resident or present within that jurisdiction.

(ii) Until recently it was generally assumed that the scope of the Mareva jurisdiction was limited to assets within the jurisdiction.[19] The practice of the courts has changed in this regard; in appropriate circumstances a Mareva injunction affecting assets abroad may be granted.[20]

(iii) Originally, a Mareva injunction was an order restraining the defendant from removing assets from the jurisdiction of the court. Subsequently, in *Rahman (Prince Abdul) bin Turki al Sudairy* v. *Abu-Taha*[21] Lord Denning MR expressed the opinion that a Mareva injunction could be obtained if the plaintiff established that there was a danger that the defendant would dispose of his assets within the jurisdiction. Although this dictum was for a time doubted, section 37(3) refers to "removing from the jurisdiction of the High Court, or otherwise dealing with, assets". If any doubt persisted after the entry into force of the 1981 Act *Ninemia Maritime Corporation* v. *Trave Schiffahrtsgesellschaft mbH und Co KG*[22] clearly established that a Mareva injunction could be granted where there is a risk that the defendant will either dissipate his assets within the jurisdiction or remove them from the jurisdiction.

21.1.3.2.3 Mareva injunctions "confer on one party to litigation draconian powers to interfere with the defendant's life and privacy without the party so interfered with being heard at all".[23] Because the defendant is unable to take part at this initial stage, the courts impose two requirements on the plaintiff.

(i) A plaintiff applying for an *ex parte* order must disclose to the court all matters relevant to the exercise of the court's discretion whether or not to grant relief before giving the defendant the opportunity to be heard.[24]

16. See Neill LJ in *Derby & Co Ltd* v. *Weldon (Nos. 3 & 4)* [1990] Ch 65, 89.
17. *Nippon Yusen Kaisha* v. *Karageorgis* [1975] 1 WLR 1093; *Mareva Compania Naviera SA* v. *International Bulk Carriers* [1975] 2 Lloyd's Rep 509.
18. *Chartered Bank* v. *Daklouche* [1980] 1 WLR 107; *Barclay-Johnson* v. *Yuill* [1980] 1 WLR 1259; *Rahman (Prince Abdul) bin Turki al Sudairy* v. *Abu-Taha* [1980] 1 WLR 1258.
19. *Ashtiani* v. *Kashi* [1987] QB 888.
20. See para. 21.4.
21. [1980] 1 WLR 1258, 1273.
22. [1983] 1 WLR 1412.
23. Browne-Wilkinson V-C in *Tate Access Floors Inc* v. *Boswell* [1991] Ch 512, 533.
24. For a summary of the relevant principles see the judgment of Ralph Gibson LJ in *Brink's-Mat Ltd* v. *Elcombe* [1988] 1 WLR 1350.

(ii) The plaintiff will normally be required to give an undertaking in damages in the event of the main action being unsuccessful.[25]

21.1.3.3 The effect of a Mareva injunction

21.1.3.3.1 INJUNCTIONS OPERATE IN PERSONAM

21.1.3.3.1.1 A Mareva injunction may be granted against the totality of the defendant's assets or a defendant may be restrained from dealing with assets "save insofar as the unencumbered value of such assets exceeds" a specified sum. A Mareva injunction is not, however, a proprietary remedy; it is not intended to give security for the plaintiff's claim in advance of judgment, but merely to prevent the defendant from defeating the plaintiff's chances of recovery.[26] A Mareva injunction operates *in personam*[27] and does not attach to the defendant's property as such. Accordingly, a plaintiff who obtains a Mareva injunction does not thereby obtain priority over other creditors.[28] The effect of a Mareva injunction is that the person to whom it is addressed is in contempt of court if he fails to comply with the terms of the injunction. Depending on the seriousness of the contempt, penalties may range from an immediate prison sentence[29] or a fine to an order simply requiring the party who is in breach of the terms of the injunction to restore to the frozen assets any sums which have been unlawfully dissipated.[30]

21.1.3.3.1.2 The courts must strike a balance between the interests of the parties and should not allow a Mareva injunction to act oppressively against the defendant. If a Mareva injunction is granted at the *ex parte* stage, the defendant may at any time apply for the variation or discharge of the injunction either on the basis that the original terms of the injunction are oppressive or on the basis of a material change of circumstances. When deciding the extent to which the defendant should be prevented from dealing with his assets the courts must bear in mind that "[i]t is not the purpose of a Mareva injunction to prevent a defendant acting as he would have acted in the absence of a claim against him".[31] This means that, as regards an individual, the defendant must be given access to sufficient funds for usual living expenses (which may amount to a considerable total).[32] So, "[w]hile a defendant who is a natural person can and should be enjoined from indulging in a spending spree undertaken with the intention of dissipating or reducing his assets before the day of judgment, he cannot be required to reduce his ordinary standard of living with a view to putting by sums to satisfy a judgment which may or may not be given in the future".[33] Similarly, a Mareva injunction ought not to

25. *Securities and Investment Board* v. *Lloyd-Wright* [1993] 4 All ER 210.

26. *Hitachi Shipbuilding and Engineering Co Ltd* v. *Viafiel Compania Naviera SA* [1981] 2 Lloyd's Rep 498; *Polly Peck International Plc* v. *Nadir* [1992] 2 Lloyd's Rep 238.

27. Lord Denning MR expressed the view that Mareva injunctions operated *in rem*: *Z Ltd* v. *A-Z & AA-LL* [1982] QB 558, 573. It has since been decided that this observation was made *per incuriam*: see Lord Ackner in *Attorney General* v. *Times Newspapers Ltd* [1992] 1 AC 191, 215.

28. *Cretanor Maritime Co Ltd* v. *Irish Marine Management Ltd* [1978] 1 WLR 966; *Iraqi Ministry of Defence* v. *Arcepey Shipping Co* [1981] QB 65; *K/S A/S Admiral Shipping* v. *Portlink Ferries Ltd* [1984] 2 Lloyd's Rep 166.

29. *Pospischal* v. *Phillips*, *The Times*, 20 January 1988.

30. *TDK Tape Distributor UK Ltd* v. *Videochoice Ltd* [1986] 1 WLR 141.

31. Lord Donaldson MR in *Polly Peck International Plc* v. *Nadir* [1992] 2 Lloyd's Rep 238, 249.

32. *Babanaft International Co SA* v. *Bassatne* [1990] Ch 13.

33. Lord Donaldson MR in *Polly Peck International Plc* v. *Nadir* [1992] 2 Lloyd's Rep 238, 249.

interfere with the defendant's ordinary course of business. No defendant, whether a natural or legal person, should be prevented from carrying on his business in the ordinary way or from meeting his debts or other obligations as they come due prior to judgment being given in the action.[34] This principle makes the grant of a Mareva injunction against a bank—or, at any rate, a bank carrying on a normal banking business—very difficult, since a bank must be able to repay its depositors in accordance with the terms on which the deposits are held.

21.1.3.3.2 THIRD PARTIES

A Mareva injunction may affect third parties. It is usual to serve notice of a Mareva injunction on third parties, such as banks, who hold the defendant's assets. A person who has notice of the injunction and who knowingly aids and abets the defendant to deal with his assets in breach of the terms of the injunction is guilty of a contempt of court.[35]

21.1.3.3.3 MAREVA INJUNCTIONS AND THE PROVISION OF SECURITY

Whereas in an action *in rem* the arrest (or threat of arrest) of the *res* ensures that the plaintiff obtains security for the claim, a Mareva injunction, which operates *in personam*, is not a form of attachment of assets. Nevertheless, it has been argued that, notwithstanding the courts' attempt to balance the interests of the parties, the Mareva jurisdiction involves the unequal treatment of defendants in the sense that it denies the defendant the right to be heard at the initial stage, thereby giving the plaintiff a powerful leverage against the defendant.[36] Although a Mareva injunction does not in itself provide security for the plaintiff's claim, it may lead to this result. Once a Mareva injunction has been granted (particularly one which prevents the defendant from disposing of any of his assets within the jurisdiction), it may well be in the defendant's interest to put up security (for example, by way of a third party guarantee or bond) in order to obtain the discharge of the injunction.

21.1.3.4 Ancillary and related orders

21.1.3.4.1 DISCLOSURE ORDERS

21.1.3.4.1.1 If the defendant's assets are to be frozen, the plaintiff must first locate them. In international disputes the availability of a disclosure order, ancillary to Mareva relief, is an extremely valuable weapon in the plaintiff's armoury. Furthermore, disclosure of the extent and whereabouts of the defendant's assets is essential for the smooth operation of the Mareva jurisdiction:

> The defendant may have more than one asset within the jurisdiction—for example, he may have a number of bank accounts. The plaintiff does not know how much, if anything, is in any of them; nor does each of the defendant's bankers know what is in the other accounts. Without information about the state of each account it is difficult, if not impossible, to operate the Mareva jurisdiction properly: for example, if each banker prevents the drawing from his account to the limit of the sum claimed, the defendant will be treated oppressively, and the plaintiff may be held liable on his undertaking in damages. ... Furthermore, the very generality of the order creates

34. *Iraqi Ministry of Defence* v. *Arcepey Shipping Co* [1981] QB 65; *Avant Petroleum Inc* v. *Gatoil Overseas Inc* [1986] 2 Lloyd's Rep 236; *Polly Peck International Plc* v. *Nadir* [1992] 2 Lloyd's Rep 238.
35. *Seaward* v. *Paterson* [1897] 1 Ch 545; *Z Ltd* v. *A-Z & AA-LL* [1982] QB 558.
36. Zuckerman, "Interlocutory Remedies in Quest of Procedural Fairness" (1993) 56 MLR 325, 335.

difficulty for the defendant's bankers, who may for example be unaware of the existence of other assets of the defendant within the jurisdiction; indeed, if a more specific order is possible, it may give much needed protection for the defendant's bankers, who are after all simply the innocent holders of one form of the defendant's assets.[37]

21.1.3.4.1.2 The court has "the power to make such ancillary orders as appear to the court to be just and convenient, to ensure that the exercise of the Mareva jurisdiction is effective to achieve its purpose".[38] Such orders include disclosure orders requiring the defendant to provide information relating to the extent and whereabouts of his assets. Indeed, the court may insist that the defendant orders his bank to disclose information about his account; the fact that a foreign bank will not, or may not, comply with a request for disclosure of documents relating to the account of one of its clients is not, by itself, a ground for refusing to make the order.[39] As a general rule where the court makes a disclosure order ancillary to a Mareva injunction the discovery order should not go beyond the ambit of the injunction.[40]

21.1.3.4.1.3 Although the court may make an order affecting both assets within and outside the jurisdiction,[41] in practice where a disclosure order reveals the existence of assets abroad, there are many circumstances in which it is more effective for the plaintiff to bring attachment proceedings in the country or countries where the assets are located, rather than seek the grant of a worldwide Mareva injunction in England.[42] Often it is only by taking action in the country where the assets are located that the plaintiff can obtain an order which is binding on parties other than the defendant.[43]

21.1.3.4.1.4 After the court has given judgment in the plaintiff's favour the court also has the power to make a disclosure order against the judgment debtor under RSC, Order 48, rule 1. This type of order is quite distinct from a disclosure order which is ancillary to a Mareva injunction. A disclosure order may be made under RSC, Order 48 without the plaintiff having to establish the preconditions which are required for the grant of a Mareva injunction. So, a post-judgment disclosure order under RSC, Order 48 can be made without the plaintiff having to show that there is a risk of removal or dissipation of the defendant's assets.

21.1.3.4.2 RECEIVERSHIP ORDERS

The court's jurisdiction to appoint a receiver is derived from the same statutory source as its jurisdiction to grant an interlocutory injunction.[44] The parties to the proceedings are required to relinquish control of the assets specified in the order to the receiver, who is an officer of the court. Any person who, with knowledge of the appointment of the

37. Robert Goff J in *A* v. *C* [1981] QB 956, 959–960.
38. Ackner LJ in *AJ Bekhor & Co Ltd* v. *Bilton* [1981] QB 923, 940. See also *Allied Arab Bank Ltd* v. *Hajjar* [1988] QB 787.
39. *Bank of Crete SA* v. *Koskotas* [1991] 2 Lloyd's Rep 587.
40. *AJ Bekhor & Co Ltd* v. *Bilton* [1981] QB 923; Neill LJ in *Derby & Co Ltd* v. *Weldon (Nos. 3 & 4)* [1990] Ch 65, 94. Neill LJ did, however, leave the door open to the possibility that "in certain circumstances a discovery order can be made with a wider ambit than the Mareva injunction to which it is ancillary": [1990] Ch 65, 94.
41. See para. 21.4.
42. Collins, "Fraudulent Conduct in International Law" [1989] CLP 255, 274.
43. See para. 21.5.
44. Supreme Court Act 1981, s. 37(1). For the text of this provision see para. 21.1.1.2.

receiver, attempts to deal with the assets which are the subject matter of the receivership order may be liable for contempt of court. The appointment of a receiver and the grant of a Mareva injunction are separate remedies. Depending on the circumstances, the court may decide to grant one remedy or the other—or to grant both.[45]

21.1.4 Anton Piller orders

21.1.4.1 There are certain circumstances in which there is a serious danger that the defendant may dispose of or destroy property which is relevant to the plaintiff's claim. For example, where the defendant has made copies of a recording in breach of the plaintiff's intellectual property rights the illegal copies are important evidence which is liable to be destroyed by the defendant once legal proceedings are started. A remedy in the context of an *inter partes* application is not likely to be effective, since the element of surprise is lost.

21.1.4.2 An Anton Piller order, which is made by the court *ex parte*, requires the defendant to permit the plaintiff (or his representatives) to enter the defendant's premises in order to search for and remove items such as documents, other evidence or specified property. Such an order will not be made unless the plaintiff has an extremely strong *prima facie* case, the potential or actual damage to the plaintiff's interests is very serious, there is clear evidence that the defendant has in his possession property which is incriminating and there is a serious possibility that the property in question will be disposed of or destroyed before an application *inter partes* can be made.[46] As in cases involving applications for a Mareva injunction, the plaintiff is required to give an undertaking in damages. While the usefulness of Anton Piller orders to the plaintiff can hardly be doubted, there are some indications that Anton Piller orders have been granted too readily and operated oppressively.[47]

21.2 JURISDICTION TO GRANT PROVISIONAL MEASURES: PROCEEDINGS IN REM

21.2.1 In cases where the plaintiff starts proceedings in the Admiralty Court *in rem*, the plaintiff is entitled to have the *res* arrested.[48] The plaintiff issues both a writ *in rem*, which the plaintiff may serve, and a warrant for arrest, which must be served by the Admiralty Marshal.[49] The writ and warrant are often served at approximately the same time, but either may be served first. The owner of the *res* may obtain the consent of the plaintiff to release the *res*—or to refrain from arresting it—by giving bail (which is given to the court) to the plaintiff's satisfaction. Normally, however, the plaintiff will not require bail, but will be satisfied with a guarantee or undertaking given out of court, typically by a bank or insurance company.

21.2.2 The original purpose of the system for the provision of security for the plaintiff's claim in actions *in rem* was to ensure that the plaintiff—if successful—could

45. *Derby & Co Ltd* v. *Weldon (Nos. 3 & 4)* [1990] Ch 65.
46. *Anton Piller KG* v. *Manufacturing Processes Ltd* [1976] Ch 55.
47. *Columbia Picture Industries* v. *Robinson* [1987] Ch 38; *Universal Thermosensors Ltd* v. *Hibben* [1992] 1 WLR 840.
48. For a discussion of the circumstances in which proceedings may be brought *in rem* see para. 8.1.2.
49. RSC, Order 75, rr. 5 and 10.

enforce the judgment against assets in England. What, however, is the position where the dispute is to be resolved by the courts of another country or by arbitrators? Is the plaintiff entitled to obtain security in England for his claim in a situation where the English court is not the proper forum for the determination of the substantive dispute? Before the entry into force of section 26 of the Civil Jurisdiction and Judgments Act 1982 the view adopted by the courts was that the purpose of the jurisdiction *in rem* was to provide security in respect of the action *in rem*, not to provide security in some other proceedings—for example, arbitration proceedings.[50] Section 26 of the 1982 Act, however, provides:

> (1) Where in England and Wales ... a court stays or dismisses Admiralty proceedings on the ground that the dispute in question should be submitted to arbitration or to the determination of the courts of another part of the United Kingdom or of an overseas country, the court may, if in those proceedings property has been arrested or bail or other security has been given to prevent or to obtain the release from arrest—
>
> (a) order that the property arrested be retained as security for the satisfaction of an award or judgment which—
>
> (i) is given in respect of the dispute in the arbitration or legal proceedings in favour of which those proceedings are stayed or dismissed; and
>
> (ii) is enforceable in England and Wales ... ; or
>
> (b) order that the stay or dismissal of those proceedings be conditional on the provision of equivalent security for the satisfaction of any such award or judgment.
>
> (2) Where a court makes an order under subsection (1), it may attach such conditions to the order as it thinks fit, in particular conditions with respect to the institution or prosecution of the relevant arbitration or legal proceedings.
>
> (3) Subject to any provision made by rules of court and to any necessary modifications, the same law and practice shall apply in relation to property retained in pursuance of an order made by a court under subsection (1) as would apply if it were held for the purposes of proceedings in that court.

21.2.3 The effect of this section is both to clarify the law and to sweep away the unnecessarily complex rules formulated by the courts.[51] The position under section 26 is that a court which stays or dismisses an action *in rem*, may order the retention of the *res* which has been arrested or may order that the stay or dismissal of proceedings be conditional on the provision of security for the award or judgment. It is important to note, however, that the jurisdiction under section 26 is linked to the court's jurisdiction over the *res*. Section 26 should not apply in cases where the court is incompetent from the outset (for example, where the action commenced *in rem* is not within the jurisdiction of the Admiralty Court as defined by the Supreme Court Act 1981).[52] Where the court does not have jurisdiction over the claim, the proper course is for the court to dismiss the action and order the unconditional release of any security obtained by reason of the arrest.

21.2.4 The power to order the retention of arrested property or other security may be exercised when the stay of proceedings is granted (i) on the basis of Article 21 of the Brussels Convention[53] or the equivalent provision of the Lugano Convention or (ii) under the court's inherent jurisdiction (for example, where a stay is granted on the basis

50. See Robert Goff LJ in *The Andria now renamed Vasso* [1984] QB 477, 490.
51. See *The Andria now renamed Vasso* [1984] QB 477; *The Tuyuti* [1984] QB 838.
52. Hobhouse J in *The Nordglimt* [1988] 1 QB 183, 204.
53. Hobhouse J in *The Nordglimt* [1988] 1 QB 183, 204.

of the doctrine of *forum non conveniens*[54] or on the basis of a jurisdiction agreement in favour of the courts of another country[55]) or (iii) on the ground that the matter should be referred to arbitration whether in England or abroad.[56] It has been held, however, that the court cannot attach conditions to the grant of a mandatory stay under section 1 of the Arbitration Act 1975.[57] Accordingly, where the parties have agreed—in a non-domestic case—to refer their dispute to arbitration the court may order retention of the security under section 26(1)(a) but may not make an order under section 26(1)(b). It seems likely that the position is the same in cases where, by virtue of the provisions of the Conventions, the defendant is entitled to a mandatory stay of the English proceedings.

21.2.5 Under the old version of the Rules of the Supreme Court the plaintiff was required to make full and frank disclosure of material facts at the time of the application for arrest[58]; failure to do so could lead to the court making an unconditional order for the release of the *res* and the discharge of any security obtained by reason of the arrest.[59] However, the Rules of the Supreme Court were amended in 1986; under the new rules a warrant of arrest is issued as of right consequent upon the issuing of the writ *in rem* and upon compliance with the affidavit requirements of RSC, Order 75, rule 5.[60]

21.2.6 Where a stay has been granted without the ship having been arrested, the court may lift the stay temporarily in order that arrest may be effected and an order made under section 26.[61] Furthermore, section 26 applies whether or not the arbitration or foreign proceedings have already been commenced.[62] It follows that if arbitration has been commenced a claimant who has not obtained security in the arbitration proceedings may quite properly issue a writ *in rem* for the sole purpose of obtaining security.[63]

21.2.7 The final point concerns the question of discretion. The effect of section 26 is that the court may (i) order the retention of the property which has been arrested or (ii) release the property, but require the provision of equivalent security, or (iii) release the property without requiring equivalent security.[64] How should the court exercise its discretion? As a general rule the court will only exercise its discretion to release the *res* on the provision of "sufficient security to cover the amount of the claim with interest and costs on the basis of the plaintiff's reasonably arguable best case".[65] Where, for example, the court is of the view that the plaintiff's claim is "certain or nearly certain"[66] to fail or the claim is "likely to fail"[67] or will "probably"[68] fail, the proper course of action is to release the *res* free from conditions. Where, however, the plaintiff has "an arguable

54. *The Emre II* [1989] 2 Lloyd's Rep 182.
55. *The Havhelt* [1993] 1 Lloyd's Rep 523.
56. See, for example, *The Jalamatsya* [1987] 2 Lloyd's Rep 164.
57. *The World Star* [1986] 2 Lloyd's Rep 274.
58. *The Andria now renamed Vasso* [1984] QB 477.
59. *The Kherson* [1992] 2 Lloyd's Rep 261. This case was wrongly decided under the old rules, notwithstanding the fact that the new rules had entered into force.
60. Scott LJ in *The Varna* [1993] 2 Lloyd's Rep 253, 257.
61. *The Silver Athens (No. 2)* [1986] 2 Lloyd's Rep 583.
62. *The Nordglimt* [1988] 1 QB 183.
63. Sheen J in *The Jalamatsya* [1987] 2 Lloyd's Rep 164, 165.
64. *The Bazias 3, The Bazias 4* [1993] QB 673.
65. *The Moschanthy* [1971] 1 Lloyd's Rep 37; *The Bazias 3, The Bazias 4* [1993] QB 673.
66. Brandon J in *The Moschanthy* [1971] 1 Lloyd's Rep 37, 43.
67. Saville J in *The Havhelt* [1993] 1 Lloyd's Rep 523, 525.
68. Saville J in *The Havhelt* [1993] 1 Lloyd's Rep 523, 526.

claim on fact or law"[69] security should not be released. The fact that, because the *res* is heavily mortgaged, it seems unlikely that the plaintiff will recover anything from the value of the *res* is not a basis on which the court should exercise its discretion to order the unconditional release of the *res*.[70] Where the court has little evidence on the likelihood of the plaintiff's claim being successful in arbitration proceedings or in proceedings abroad, the court may, by virtue of the powers conferred by section 26(2), order that, as a condition of the *res* being retained, the plaintiff must provide security for the losses which the owner of the *res* is likely to sustain as a result of the *res* not being released.[71]

21.3 JURISDICTION TO GRANT PROVISIONAL MEASURES: PROCEEDINGS IN PERSONAM

Where England is the forum for the trial of the plaintiff's claim, the court has jurisdiction to grant the full range of provisional measures available under English law in relation to those proceedings. So, if a plaintiff brings proceedings in England against a defendant domiciled in England or if the defendant is served out of the jurisdiction under RSC, Order 11, rule 1 the court may, where appropriate, grant interim relief.[72] More problematical are cases (i) where the court has no jurisdiction over the plaintiff's claim and (ii) where, although the defendant is amenable to the court's jurisdiction, either no proceedings have been brought in England or English proceedings have been stayed.

21.3.1 Jurisdiction to grant provisional measures in aid of foreign proceedings

21.3.1.1 The position at common law

21.3.1.1.1 In *Siskina (Owners of cargo lately laden on board)* v. *Distos Compania Naviera SA*[73] the plaintiff was the owner of a cargo being carried on a ship owned by the defendant, a Panamanian company. During the voyage the defendant diverted the vessel to Cyprus, where the cargo was off-loaded. The ship subsequently sank and the insurance money—which was the defendant's only asset—was paid into the broker's account in England. The plaintiff, who suffered loss as a result of delay and the deterioration of the cargo, issued a writ claiming (i) damages and (ii) a Mareva injunction to prevent the insurance money being dissipated or removed from the jurisdiction. As the defendant could not be served with the writ in England the plaintiff applied for leave to serve the writ out of the jurisdiction under what is now RSC, Order 11, rule 1(1)(b)—which provides that leave to serve out may be granted where "an injunction is sought ordering the defendant to do or refrain from doing anything within the jurisdiction . . .". The House of Lords, in reliance on the principle that an injunction may be granted only in support of the invasion of a legal or equitable right which is

69. Brandon J in *The Moschanthy* [1971] 1 Lloyd's Rep 37, 43.
70. *The Havhelt* [1993] 1 Lloyd's Rep 523.
71. *The Havhelt* [1993] 1 Lloyd's Rep 523.
72. If service out of the jurisdiction is required, the plaintiff can rely on RSC, Order 11, r. 1(1)(b).
73. [1979] AC 210. Lipstein, [1978] CLJ 241.

enforceable in England,[74] held that since the court had no jurisdiction over the plaintiff's substantive claim there was no jurisdiction to grant the injunction—notwithstanding the fact that the plaintiff's application appeared to fall within the literal wording of the paragraph relied on.

21.3.1.1.2 The effect of the *Siskina* doctrine is that an application for an injunction cannot stand alone as a basis of jurisdiction under RSC, Order 11; provisional measures can be granted only in support of a claim in relation to which the court has jurisdiction—whether on the basis of the defendant's presence or submission or on the basis of one of the grounds of jurisdiction set out in RSC, Order 11, rule 1(1) (other than paragraph (b)).[75]

21.3.1.1.3 The scope of the decision in the *Siskina* case has been considered on numerous subsequent occasions. It has, for example, been decided that the principle that an injunction may be granted only in relation to the invasion of a legal or equitable right means that an injunction cannot be granted in support of a contemplated action if the cause of action has not already accrued—even if the cause of action is imminent and is, in practical terms, inevitable.[76] The greatest attention has, however, been directed at the practical significance of the principle that the availability of provisional measures depends upon the court having jurisdiction over the claim. The question is whether the *Siskina* doctrine precludes the court from granting provisional measures under section 37(1) of the 1981 Act if the substance of the claim is not to be determined by proceedings in England[77] or whether an interlocutory injunction (such as a Mareva injunction) may be granted as long as the defendant is amenable to the *in personam* jurisdiction of the court, it being irrelevant whether the final relief is given by the English court or by another tribunal.[78]

21.3.1.1.4 In *Channel Tunnel Group Ltd* v. *Balfour Beatty Construction Ltd*[79] the House of Lords decided that the *Siskina* doctrine is simply that "the right to an interlocutory injunction cannot exist in isolation, but is always incidental to and dependent on the enforcement of a substantive right, which usually although not invariably takes the shape of a cause of action. If the underlying right itself is not subject to the jurisdiction of the English court, then the court should never exercise its power under section 37(1) by way of interim relief."[80] It follows that "the court has power to grant interlocutory relief based on a cause of action recognised by English law against a defendant duly served where such relief is ancillary to a final order whether to be granted by the English court or by some other court or arbitral body".[81] So, where the plaintiff is pursuing his claim against the defendant in a foreign forum, if the defendant

74. *North London Railway Co* v. *Great Northern Railway Co* (1883) 11 QBD 30.

75. This common law principle is subject to the provisions of the Civil Jurisdiction and Judgments Act 1982. See para. 21.3.1.2.

76. *The Veracruz I* [1992] 1 Lloyd's Rep 353 (Marshall, "The Conditional or Anticipatory Mareva Injunction" [1992] LMCLQ 161; Collins, "The Legacy of The Siskina" (1992) 108 LQR 175); *Zucker* v. *Tyndalls Holdings Plc* [1992] 1 WLR 1127 (Wilde, "Jurisdiction to Grant Interlocutory (Mareva) Injunctions" [1993] LMCLQ 309).

77. See, for example, Collins, "The Legacy of The Siskina"(1992) 108 LQR 175, 180; Hogan, "The Judgments Convention and Mareva Injunctions in the United Kingdom and Ireland" (1989) 14 ELRev 191.

78. See Rose, "The Mareva Injunction—Attachment in Personam" [1981] LMCLQ 1, 5–6; Hoyle, *Mareva Injunctions and Related Orders* (2nd ed, 1989) pp. 172–173.

79. [1993] AC 334. Collins, "The End of The Siskina?" (1993) 109 LQR 342.

80. Lord Mustill, [1993] AC 334, 362.

81. Lord Browne-Wilkinson, [1993] AC 334, 343.

can be served in England (for example, on the basis of presence within the jurisdiction) the court may grant provisional measures in aid of those foreign proceedings under section 37(1). The fact that the defendant is entitled to a stay—for example, on the basis that another court is clearly a more appropriate forum—does not deprive the English court of the power to grant provisional measures.

21.3.1.1.5 What of the situation which arose in the *Siskina* case itself? As the law currently stands, if the defendant is out of the jurisdiction (and the case does not fall within the scope of section 25 of the Civil Jurisdiction and Judgments Act 1982) the court has no jurisdiction under section 37(1). Nevertheless, it should be noted that in recent cases some doubts have been expressed as to the correctness of the *Siskina* doctrine.[82] It is possible that English law is moving towards the position where "an interlocutory injunction may be available in England if justice requires it even if the defendant is outside the jurisdiction and the case is not within section 25 of the Civil Jurisdiction and Judgments Act 1982".[83]

21.3.1.2 Section 25 of the Civil Jurisdiction and Judgments Act 1982[84]

21.3.1.2.1 JURISDICTION UNDER SECTION 25

21.3.1.2.1.1 Article 24 of the Brussels and Lugano Conventions provides:

> Application may be made to the courts of a Contracting State for such provisional, including protective, measures as may be available under the law of that State, even if, under this Convention, the courts of another Contracting State have jurisdiction as to the substance of the matter.

Measures falling within the scope of Article 24 are "measures which, in matters coming within the ambit of the Convention, are intended to maintain a legal or factual situation in order to safeguard rights".[85]

21.3.1.2.1.2 Because of the decision of the House of Lords in the *Siskina* case Article 24 does not in itself give the English court jurisdiction to grant a Mareva injunction in support of foreign proceedings unless the court also has jurisdiction over the plaintiff's claim.[86] Section 25 of the Civil Jurisdiction and Judgments Act 1982, however, reverses the effect of the *Siskina* doctrine as regards cases involving proceedings in the courts of other Contracting States or other parts of the United Kingdom, the subject matter of which falls within the scope of Article 1 of the Brussels Convention:

> (1) The High Court in England and Wales ... shall have power to grant interim relief where—
> (a) proceedings have been or are to be commenced in a Brussels or Lugano Contracting State other than the United Kingdom or in a part of the United Kingdom other than that in which the High Court in question exercises jurisdiction; and
> (b) they are or will be proceedings whose subject matter is within the scope of the 1968

82. See the observations of Lord Goff and Lord Mackay in *South Carolina Insurance Co* v. *Assurantie Maatschappij "De Zeven Provincien" NV* [1987] AC 24 and of Lord Browne-Wilkinson in *Channel Tunnel Group Ltd* v. *Balfour Beatty Construction Ltd* [1993] AC 334.

83. Collins, "The End of The Siskina?" (1993) 109 LQR 342, 343.

84. Hogan, "The Judgments Convention and Mareva Injunctions in the United Kingdom and Ireland" (1989) 14 ELRev 191.

85. Case C-261/90 *Reichert* v. *Dresdner Bank (No. 2)* [1992] ILPr 404, 426 (para. 34).

86. Kerr LJ in *Babanaft International Co SA* v. *Bassatne* [1990] Ch 13, 30.

Convention as determined by Article 1 (whether or not that or any other Convention has effect in relation to those proceedings).

(2) On an application for any interim relief under subsection (1) the court may refuse to grant that relief if, in the opinion of the court, the fact that the court has no jurisdiction apart from this section in relation to the subject matter of the proceedings in question makes it inexpedient for the court to grant it.

Subsection (3) provides for the extension of section 25 to non-contracting States by Order in Council. There is, as yet, no delegated legislation under this provision.

21.3.1.2.1.3 For the purposes of section 25 it is irrelevant whether the English court has jurisdiction over the claim or whether the foreign court assumed jurisdiction on one of the bases set out in Title II. The court may grant interim measures in support of proceedings in a Contracting State where the foreign proceedings are entirely domestic or where the foreign proceedings were commenced before the entry into force of the Convention in the United Kingdom.[87] Furthermore, if the substantive proceedings are taking place—or are to take place—in the courts of a Contracting State, the English court may grant provisional measures under section 25 of the 1982 Act in support of those proceedings whether or not the defendant can be served with the originating summons in England and whether or not the defendant is domiciled in a Contracting State. *Republic of Haiti* v. *Duvalier*[88] concerned proceedings brought by the Republic against Baby Doc Duvalier for the recovery of sums in excess of $120 million which the Republic claimed the defendant had embezzled while in office. Having brought the claim in France, where the defendant had become domiciled, the Republic obtained a Mareva injunction in England to restrain the defendant from dealing with his assets worldwide. One of the grounds of the appeal was that there was no method of effecting service on the defendant, notwithstanding the fact that the requirements of section 25(1) were met. The Court of Appeal upheld the plaintiff's contention that, since the defendant was domiciled in a Contracting State, the writ[89] could be served out of the jurisdiction without leave of the court under RSC, Order 11, rule 1(2).[90] If the defendant is not domiciled in a Contracting State the plaintiff may serve the originating summons out of the jurisdiction with leave of the court under RSC, Order 11, rule 1(1)(b).[91]

21.3.1.2.2 PROVISIONAL MEASURES AND ARTICLE 21

Article 21 of the Brussels and Lugano Conventions provides that where there are parallel proceedings between the same parties involving the same cause of action before the courts of two or more Contracting States any court other than the court first seised must decline jurisdiction or stay its proceedings.[92] In *Republic of Haiti* v. *Duvalier*[93] it was argued that because the substantive proceedings had been brought in France, the effect of Article 21 of the Brussels Convention was to deprive the English court of

87. *Alltrans Inc* v. *Interdom Holdings Ltd* [1991] 4 All ER 458.
88. [1990] 1 QB 202.
89. The action ought properly to have been started by originating summons; see Staughton LJ, [1990] 1 QB 202, 212. However, the rules relating to service out of the jurisdiction under RSC, Order 11, r. 1 also apply to an originating summons: RSC, Order 11, r. 9(1).
90. For the text of RSC, Order 11, r. 1(2) see para. 4.3.1.1.
91. *X* v. *Y* [1990] 1 QB 220.
92. See para. 5.9.
93. [1990] 1 QB 202.

jurisdiction to grant provisional measures under section 25(1) of the 1982 Act in support of those proceedings. The Court of Appeal had no hesitation in rejecting this argument: "Either a claim for interim relief does not involve or concern any cause of action, or it is based on a new and distinct cause of action created by section 25."[94] It would make nonsense of Article 24 and the implementing legislation if, for the purposes of Article 21, the main proceedings in France and the application for a Mareva injunction in England in aid of those proceedings were regarded as "involving the same cause of action".

21.3.1.2.3 POST-JUDGMENT PROVISIONAL MEASURES AND ARTICLE 16(5)

21.3.1.2.3.1 In those cases falling with the scope of the Conventions a potential jurisdictional problem arises as regards post-judgment measures. Article 16(5) provides that, in proceedings concerned with the enforcement of judgments, the courts of the Contracting State in which the judgment is to be enforced shall have exclusive jurisdiction.[95] It has been argued that the effect of Article 16(5) is that where a plaintiff intends to enforce a judgment in another Contracting State the English court is precluded from granting a post-judgment Mareva injunction in respect of the judgment debtor's assets.[96] This argument is in part based on the framework of the Conventions as a whole which treat post-judgment protective measures as part of the enforcement process.[97]

21.3.1.2.3.2 The only discussion in the reported English cases rejects this interpretation of the effect of Article 16(5). In *Babanaft International Co SA* v. *Bassatne* Kerr LJ did not think that

> a "holding order" in the form of a post-judgment Mareva injunction, covering assets of a defendant in the territory of an [EC] State pending proceedings for the enforcement of the judgment in accordance with the applicable provisions of the European Judgments Convention and the national law of that State, would constitute an infringement of Article 16(5). It seems illogical, at any rate from an English point of view, that a post-judgment provisional protective order should fall outside the scope of Article 24. The better view would be that after judgment "the substance of the matter" referred to in Article 24 consists of the "proceedings concerned with the enforcement of judgments" referred to in Article 16(5).[98]

According to this analysis, although the proceedings concerned with the enforcement of judgments are within the exclusive jurisdiction of the State where the assets are, there is no reason why Article 24 should not be available, pending enforcement of the judgment, to entitle the court to grant a Mareva injunction over foreign assets. The same analysis may be applied to the grant of an independent post-judgment disclosure order under RSC, Order 48, rule 1 in support of foreign enforcement proceedings.[99] It has been argued, however, that a disclosure order which is not ancillary to a Mareva injunction cannot properly be regarded as a "provisional, including protective measure" within the meaning of Article 24.[100]

94. Staughton LJ, [1990] 1 QB 202, 211.
95. See para. 5.1.5.
96. See Hogan, "The Judgments Convention and Mareva Injunctions in the United Kingdom and Ireland" (1989) 14 ELRev 191, 197–200.
97. See, in particular, Article 39.
98. [1990] Ch 13, 35.
99. Dicey & Morris, *The Conflict of Laws* (12th ed, 1993) p. 393.
100. Kaye, "Property Restraint and Disclosure Orders in the English Courts: Extraterritorial Developments" (1989) 10 *Company Lawyer* 227, 230.

21.3.1.2.4 DISCRETION?

21.3.1.2.4.1 In *Republic of Haiti* v. *Duvalier* Staughton LJ suggested that the effect of Article 24 is to require each Contracting State to make available, in aid of the courts of other Contracting States, such provisional and protective measures as its own domestic law would afford if its courts were trying the substantive action.[101] This conclusion has been castigated as "almost certainly wrong as a matter of law".[102] The better view is that the effect of Article 24 and section 25 is to confer a discretion on the court as to whether or not to grant provisional measures. Nevertheless, it is reasonable to suppose that, in the exercise of its discretion, the court will grant the same provisional measures in support of proceedings in other Contracting States as it would if dealing with the substantive dispute itself.

21.3.1.2.4.2 There is, however, one situation where it would appear that the court is required by the Brussels and Lugano Conventions to order protective measures in favour of a judgment creditor. Where the plaintiff obtains leave to enforce a foreign judgment in a Contracting State under Title III, the defendant may appeal against the enforcement order under Article 37. In this situation Article 39 provides that "no measures of enforcement may be taken other than protective measures taken against the property of the party against whom enforcement has been sought". In *Capelloni* v. *Pelkmans*[103] the Court of Justice held that a plaintiff who has obtained an enforcement order, the effect of which is suspended pending the defendant's appeal under Article 37, is entitled under Article 39 to protective measures from the courts of the State where enforcement is sought.[104]

21.3.1.3 Jurisdiction to grant provisional measures in cases involving an exclusive jurisdiction clause

21.3.1.3.1 In English law injunctions are equitable remedies and, therefore, discretionary. In a situation where the court may, in principle, grant a Mareva injunction in the plaintiff's favour, what significance, if any, should the court attach to an agreement by the parties to refer the dispute to the court of another country when exercising its discretion under section 37(1) of the 1981 Act?

21.3.1.3.2 It is clear that in cases covered by the Brussels and Lugano Conventions the existence of a jurisdiction clause in favour of another Contracting State does not affect the jurisdiction of the English court to grant provisional or protective measures. Where, for example, the French courts have exclusive jurisdiction by virtue of Article 17, the English court may, by virtue of Article 24 and section 25 of the 1982 Act, grant provisional measures.[105] Any other interpretation would be wholly inconsistent with the framework established by the Conventions.

21.3.1.3.3 In cases not falling within the scope of Article 24 and section 25 of the 1982 Act the court should be equally willing to grant provisional measures notwithstanding

101. [1990] 1 QB 202, 212.
102. Collins, "Provisional and Protective Measures in International Litigation" [1992] III Hag Rec 9, 56.
103. Case 119/84 [1985] ECR 3147.
104. For further consideration of this point see para. 9.4.4.4.3. Hogan, "The Judgments Convention and Mareva Injunction in the United Kingdom and Ireland" (1989) 14 ELRev 191, 200–204.
105. Collins, "Provisional Measures, the Conflict of Laws and the Brussels Convention" (1981) 1 YBEL 249, 258.

the fact that the parties have agreed to the exclusive jurisdiction of a foreign court. Of course, the grant of such measures depends on the court having the necessary jurisdiction; if the defendant cannot be served with the originating process there is no basis on which the court can grant interim relief.[106] Where the parties have agreed to refer their disputes to the exclusive jurisdiction of the courts of a particular country, the English court should, as a general rule, hold the parties to their bargain as regards the substantive dispute between them. However, unless there are very clear words to the contrary in the agreement itself, an application for provisional or protective measures should not be regarded as falling within the scope of the jurisdiction agreement.[107] So, in a case where an Englishman and a New Yorker enter a contract which contains an exclusive jurisdiction clause in favour of the courts of New York, if the New Yorker starts proceedings in England and applies for a Mareva injunction freezing the Englishman's assets, the court should not be deterred from granting interim relief by the fact that the defendant may apply for—and will in all probability be entitled to—a stay of the substantive proceedings.[108] The same approach should be adopted in cases where the plaintiff starts an action *in rem* in England notwithstanding the existence of a jurisdiction clause in favour of the courts of another country. Although the English proceedings *in rem* will normally be stayed on account of the jurisdiction clause, the court may order the retention of the *res* which has been arrested or order that the stay or dismissal of proceedings be conditional on the provision of security.[109]

21.3.2 Jurisdiction to grant provisional measures in support of arbitration proceedings

Where the parties have agreed to arbitration there are two possible bases on which the court may grant provisional measures in support of existing or anticipated arbitration proceedings: section 12(1)(h) of the Arbitration Act 1950 and section 37(1) of the Supreme Court Act 1981.

21.3.2.1 Section 12(6)(h) of the Arbitration Act 1950

21.3.2.1.1 Under section 12(6)(h) the High Court has, in relation to an arbitration, the same powers to grant interim injunctions as it has in relation to an action in the High Court. Where the parties have agreed to arbitration in England the court may grant an interim injunction under section 12(6)(h),[110] even if the parties have no connection with England and the court proceedings are otherwise stayed: "by agreeing to arbitrate in England the parties will, in the absence of any express or implied agreement to the contrary, be deemed to have subjected themselves to the English rules of procedure as those of the forum they have selected, including the jurisdictions conferred on the English courts by section 12(6)".[111]

106. *Siskina (Owners of cargo lately laden on board)* v. *Distos Compania Naviera SA* [1979] AC 210; *Channel Tunnel Group Ltd* v. *Balfour Beatty Construction Ltd* [1993] AC 334.
107. See the judgment of Lord Denning MR in *The Lisboa* [1980] 2 Lloyd's Rep 546, 548–549.
108. This analysis is consistent with the approach of the House of Lords in *Channel Tunnel Group Ltd* v. *Balfour Beatty Construction Ltd* [1993] AC 334.
109. Civil Jurisdiction and Judgments Act 1982, s. 26(1). See para. 21.2.
110. *The Rena K* [1979] QB 377.
111. Kerr LJ in *Bank Mellat* v. *Helliniki Techniki SA* [1984] QB 291, 302.

21.3.2.1.2 The jurisdiction question is more complex when parties have agreed to arbitration abroad. In *Channel Tunnel Group Ltd* v. *Balfour Beatty Construction Ltd*[112] the Court of Appeal decided (*obiter*) that section 12(6)(h) has no application where the parties have agreed to arbitration abroad—regardless of the curial law of the arbitration. Staughton LJ thought that "an express choice of English law as the curial law does not confer jurisdiction under section 12(6)(h), if the arbitration has a foreign seat; nor would a choice of foreign law have taken away jurisdiction if the seat of the arbitration was in England".[113] The House of Lords confirmed that the powers conferred by section 12(6) are limited to arbitrations conducted in England.[114]

21.3.2.2 Section 37(1) of the Supreme Court Act 1981

Although the territorial scope of section 12(6)(h) is limited to arbitrations in England, the jurisdiction of the court under section 37(1) is broader. The court has jurisdiction under section 37(1) to grant interim measures in support of existing or anticipated arbitration proceedings—whether in England or abroad—as long as the defendant is amenable to the *in personam* jurisdiction of the court. In *Channel Tunnel Group Ltd* v. *Balfour Beatty Construction Ltd*[115] the defendant was an English company working for the plaintiff on the Channel tunnel project. The contract between the parties contained a two-stage dispute resolution procedure, the second stage of which involved arbitration in Belgium. When the defendant informed the plaintiff that unless certain conditions were met all work relating to the tunnel's cooling system would be suspended, the plaintiff started proceedings in England and applied for a mandatory injunction to restrain the defendant from suspending the work. The House of Lords relied on the principle that "the court has power to grant interlocutory relief based on a cause of action recognised by English law against a defendant duly served where such relief is ancillary to a final order whether to be granted by the English court or by some other court or arbitral body".[116] Accordingly, since the defendant had been duly served, the court had jurisdiction to grant the injunction sought by the plaintiff, notwithstanding the fact that the defendant was entitled to a stay of the English proceedings and that the final relief, if any, would be given by the arbitrators in Belgium. However, the House of Lords did not want to pre-empt the arbitrators' decision; since the relief claimed from the court overlapped with that available from the arbitrators, the plaintiff's application for interim relief was refused.

112. [1992] QB 656.
113. Staughton LJ, [1992] QB 656, 676. See also Kerr LJ in *Naviera Amazonica Peruana SA* v. *Compania Internacional de Seguros del Peru* [1988] 1 Lloyd's Rep 116, 120.
114. Lord Mustill, [1993] AC 334, 359. See para. 17.5.2.1.
115. [1993] AC 334. Reymond, "The Channel Tunnel Case and the Law of International Arbitration" (1993) 109 LQR 337; Collins, "The End of The Siskina?" (1993) 109 LQR 342.
116. Lord Browne-Wilkinson, [1993] AC 334, 343.

21.4 EXTRATERRITORIAL PROVISIONAL MEASURES[117]

21.4.1 Introduction

21.4.1.1 Since equitable remedies operate *in personam*, there is no theoretical reason why, as long as the defendant is amenable to the court's jurisdiction, provisional measures granted by the court should be limited to acts performed or assets situated within the jurisdiction. In principle, an act committed by the defendant anywhere in the world in breach of the terms of an injunction or other equitable remedy is a contempt which may be punished by the court. So, the court has power under section 37(1) to appoint a receiver over assets not within the court's jurisdiction[118] even though the appointment may not prove effective without assistance from the appropriate foreign court.[119] Similarly, the court may make an Anton Piller order in respect of foreign premises.[120] In *Cook Industries Inc* v. *Galliher*[121] the court ordered a foreign defendant to disclose the contents of a flat in his name situated in France and to permit the flat to be inspected by a French *avocat*. However, the decision in *Protector Alarms Ltd* v. *Maxim Alarms Ltd*[122]—in which the court declined to make an Anton Piller order in respect of Scottish premises on the basis that it would be better for the plaintiff to seek an equivalent order from the local courts—suggested that Anton Piller orders ought not to be made against foreign defendants in respect of foreign premises.

21.4.1.2 In *Altertext Inc* v. *Advanced Data Communications Ltd* Scott J indicated that "Anton Piller orders to be executed in respect of foreign premises ought not to be granted ... except against defendants over whom the court has unquestionable jurisdiction".[123] So, in a case where the plaintiff seeks an Anton Piller order and the only basis on which the court may assume jurisdiction over the defendant is one of the heads of RSC, Order 11, rule 1(1) "the Anton Piller order ought not to be executed until the foreign defendant has been given the opportunity to apply to set aside the Order 11 leave. ... It would be wrong ... for the court to assume jurisdiction over a foreign defendant on an *ex parte* application, and then to require a mandatory order of an Anton Piller character to be executed by the foreign defendant before he has had an opportunity to challenge the court's assumption of jurisdiction over him."[124]

21.4.1.3 For a number of years the English courts granted Mareva injunctions (and ancillary orders) only in relation to assets located within the jurisdiction. In *Ashtiani* v. *Kashi*[125] the Court of Appeal, in refusing to grant an injunction restraining the defendant from dealing with his foreign assets, attached some weight to section 37(3) of the 1981 Act which refers to the power to grant injunctions restraining a party from dealing with assets located "within the jurisdiction of the High Court". However,

117. Capper, "Worldwide Mareva Injunctions" (1991) 54 MLR 329; Collins, "The Territorial Reach of Mareva Injunctions" (1989) 105 LQR 262; Rogers, "The Extraterritorial Reach of the Mareva Injunction" [1991] LMCLQ 231.

118. *Duder* v. *Amsterdamsch Trustees Kantoor* [1902] 2 Ch 132.

119. *In Re Maudslay, Sons & Field* [1900] 1 Ch 602.

120. McLachlan, "Transnational Applications of Mareva Injunctions and Anton Piller Orders" (1987) 36 ICLQ 669, 678–679.

121. [1979] Ch 439.

122. [1978] FSR 442.

123. [1985] 1 WLR 457, 463.

124. Scott J, [1985] 1 WLR 457, 462–463.

125. [1987] QB 888.

following the decision *Ashtiani* v. *Kashi* the pressure on the courts to change their practice became considerable. As Lord Donaldson MR noted in *Derby & Co Ltd* v. *Weldon (Nos. 3 & 4)*:

> We live in a time of rapidly growing commercial and financial sophistication and it behoves the courts to adapt their practices to meet the current wiles of those defendants who are prepared to devote as much energy to making themselves immune from the courts' orders as to resisting the making of such orders on the merits of their case.[126]

21.4.1.4 Furthermore, following the decision in *Ashtiani* v. *Kashi* there was an evolution of the practice of the courts in related areas. In *Interpool Ltd* v. *Galani*[127] it was held that an order for the disclosure of assets after judgment under RSC, Order 48 could extend to assets located outside the jurisdiction and in *Maclaine Watson & Co Ltd* v. *International Tin Council (No. 2)*[128] the defendants were ordered to make full disclosure of the location of their assets both within and outside the jurisdiction, even though the plaintiffs could not rely on RSC, Order 48.

21.4.1.5 In *Babanaft International Co SA* v. *Bassatne*[129] the Court of Appeal took the view that the earlier decision in *Ashtiani* v. *Kashi* was to be regarded as merely a reflection of the way in which the jurisdiction to grant Mareva injunctions had been developed in England up to that point.[130] There is, therefore, nothing to preclude the court from granting a Mareva injunction against a defendant which extends to assets outside the jurisdiction; the purpose of section 37(3) is not to limit the geographical scope of the court's power but to prevent discrimination against defendants who are not domiciled, resident or present within the jurisdiction.

21.4.1.6 The possibility of granting an extraterritorial or worldwide Mareva injunction was confirmed in a number of cases decided towards the end of the 1980s,[131] notably *Republic of Haiti* v. *Duvalier*,[132] *Derby & Co Ltd* v. *Weldon*,[133] *Derby & Co Ltd* v. *Weldon (Nos. 3 & 4)*[134] and *Derby & Co Ltd* v. *Weldon (No. 6)*.[135] As a result of these cases it can be definitively stated that:

> [t]he jurisdiction of the court to grant a Mareva injunction against a person depends not on territorial jurisdiction of the English court over assets within its jurisdiction, but on the unlimited jurisdiction of the English court *in personam* against any person, whether an individual or a corporation, who is, under English procedure, properly made a party to proceedings pending before the English court.[136]

Although the problems surrounding extraterritorial provisional measures are not limited to Mareva injunctions, it is in relation to the Mareva jurisdiction that issues concerning the exercise of discretion to grant measures which have extraterritorial effect have arisen most frequently.

126. [1990] Ch 65, 77.
127. [1988] QB 738.
128. [1989] Ch 286.
129. [1990] Ch 13.
130. See the judgment of Neill LJ (who was a member of the Court of Appeal in both *Ashtiani* v. *Kashi* [1987] QB 888 and *Babanaft International Co SA* v. *Bassatne* [1990] Ch 13).
131. For a brief discussion see Andrews, [1989] CLJ 199.
132. [1990] 1 QB 202.
133. [1990] Ch 48.
134. [1990] Ch 65.
135. [1990] 1 WLR 1139. Capper, "The Worldwide Mareva Marches On" [1991] LMCLQ 26.
136. Dillon LJ in *Derby & Co Ltd* v. *Weldon (No. 6)* [1990] 1 WLR 1139, 1149.

21.4.2 Extraterritorial Mareva injunctions

21.4.2.1 The necessary conditions

21.4.2.1.1 The most fundamental conditions for the grant of an extraterritorial Mareva injunction are the same as those which apply to any Mareva injunction: the plaintiff must have a good arguable case on the merits and the court must consider that the refusal of a Mareva injunction would involve a real risk that a judgment (or award) in favour of the plaintiff would remain unsatisfied.[137] There is, however, no requirement that the defendant should have any assets within the jurisdiction. In *Derby & Co Ltd* v. *Weldon (Nos. 3 & 4)* Lord Donaldson MR suggested that "[t]he existence of sufficient assets within the jurisdiction is an excellent reason for confining the [Mareva] jurisdiction to such assets, but other considerations apart, the fewer the assets within the jurisdiction the greater the necessity for taking protective measures in relation to those outside it".[138]

21.4.2.1.2 However, "[t]he mere fact that the plaintiff shows a good arguable case and a real risk of disposal or hiding of English assets—the requisites for an internal Mareva—clearly cannot by itself be sufficient to justify an extraterritorial Mareva either worldwide or at all".[139] Before the court will grant an extraterritorial Mareva injunction it must be satisfied that the defendant has insufficient English assets to satisfy the plaintiff's claim, if successful, and that there is a high risk that the defendant will dispose of his foreign assets. Furthermore, since equity does not act in vain, the court will not grant an extraterritorial Mareva injunction if "there is doubt about whether the order will be obeyed and if, should that occur, no real sanction would exist".[140] What is a "real sanction" for the purposes of this principle? In *Derby & Co Ltd* v. *Weldon (Nos. 3 & 4)* the Court of Appeal decided that the fact that, in the case of disobedience, the court could bar the defendant's right to defend was a sufficient sanction on the basis that if the court barred the right to defend the defendant "would become a fugitive from a final judgment given against it without its explanations having been heard and which might well be enforced against it by other courts".[141] The requirement that there should be a sanction for disobedience does not mean that the court should be satisfied that an extraterritorial Mareva injunction will be recognised abroad or otherwise be made binding.[142]

21.4.2.1.3 In the context of internal Mareva injunctions, the effect of the injunction is to prevent the removal of the assets from the jurisdiction or their dissipation within the jurisdiction. In cases concerning an application for a Mareva injunction in respect of foreign assets, the question arises as to whether the court may go further and order the transfer of assets from one country to another. In *Derby & Co Ltd* v. *Weldon (No. 6)* the Court of Appeal decided that, having regard to the fact that the object of a Mareva injunction (and any ancillary orders) is to ensure as far as possible that any judgment obtained by the plaintiff will be satisfied, a Mareva injunction in respect of foreign assets

137. *Ninemia Maritime Corporation* v. *Trave Schiffahrtsgesellschaft mbH und Co KG* [1983] 1 WLR 1412.
138. [1990] Ch 65, 79.
139. Parker LJ in *Derby & Co Ltd* v. *Weldon* [1990] Ch 48, 56.
140. Lord Donaldson MR in *Derby & Co Ltd* v. *Weldon (Nos. 3 & 4)* [1990] Ch 65, 81. For the application of this principle see *Derby & Co Ltd* v. *Weldon (No. 6)* [1990] 1 WLR 1139.
141. Lord Donaldson MR, [1990] Ch 65, 81.
142. *Derby & Co Ltd* v. *Weldon (Nos. 3 & 4)* [1990] Ch 65; *Derby & Co Ltd* v. *Weldon (No. 6)* [1990] 1 WLR 1139. Kaye, "Extraterritorial Mareva Orders and the Relevance of Enforceability" (1990) 9 CJQ 12.

is not necessarily limited to ordering that the assets should be frozen; there is no reason why in principle a Mareva injunction should not be extended to ordering the transfer of assets to a jurisdiction in which the court's judgment will be recognised and from a jurisdiction in which that judgment will not be recognised.[143]

21.4.2.2 Factors relevant to the exercise of discretion

21.4.2.2.1 In *Babanaft International Co SA* v. *Bassatne* Kerr LJ noted that "some situations, which are nowadays by no means uncommon, cry out—as a matter of justice to plaintiffs—for disclosure orders and Mareva type injunctions covering foreign assets of defendants even before judgment."[144] Nevertheless, with regard to extraterritorial orders, the courts are conscious that they are operating in a new area and that orders affecting foreign assets should be considered with care. Although the courts have the power to grant an injunction affecting the assets which are not located within the jurisdiction, they are prepared to exercise that power only in exceptional circumstances.[145] As regards Mareva injunctions ordering the transfer of foreign assets from one country to another, special care is required in view of the questions of comity which arise. In *Derby & Co Ltd* v. *Weldon (No. 6)* Staughton LJ sounded the following note of caution: "If it ever became common practice for English courts not merely to assume jurisdiction over defendants abroad under RSC, Order 11, but also to order them to transfer assets here so that any eventual judgment could be more readily enforced, that would in my view justifiably be regarded as unacceptable chauvinism by the international community."[146]

21.4.2.2.2 A plaintiff may make an application for an extraterritorial Mareva injunction at any stage—from before the issue of the writ to the period between judgment and satisfaction of the judgment. Although the court's powers are, in principle, the same both before and after judgment "as a matter of discretion, such orders will in practice no doubt be made more readily after judgment".[147] Where an injunction is granted after judgment it should normally be limited in duration. The plaintiff should be encouraged to proceed swiftly with proper methods of execution since "perpetual injunctions restraining a defendant from dealing with his assets until the crack of doom are undesirable".[148] Although the court will be more inclined to grant Mareva relief in cases where the plaintiff's claim is proprietary rather than personal,[149] the court should not, as a general rule, grant an extraterritorial Mareva injunction in cases where the plaintiff is seeking to enforce a foreign judgment or award in England.[150]

143. Dillon LJ, [1990] 1 WLR 1139, 1151.
144. [1990] Ch 13, 33.
145. Members of the Court of Appeal have used various phrases to describe the exceptional nature of a Mareva injunction covering a defendant's assets outside the jurisdiction. Such injunctions will be granted "in extreme situations" (Kerr LJ in *Babanaft International Co SA* v. *Bassatne* [1990] Ch 13, 37); "it will only be in an exceptional case that the court will make such an order" (May LJ in *Derby & Co Ltd* v. *Weldon* [1990] Ch 48, 55); "cases where it will be appropriate to grant such an injunction will be rare—if not very rare indeed" (Staughton LJ in *Republic of Haiti* v. *Duvalier* [1990] 1 QB 202, 215); a worldwide pre-judgment Mareva injunction will be granted "only in an unusual case" (Butler-Sloss LJ in *Derby & Co Ltd* v. *Weldon (Nos. 3 & 4)* [1990] Ch 65, 96).
146. [1990] 1 WLR 1139, 1153.
147. Kerr LJ in *Babanaft International Co SA* v. *Bassatne* [1990] Ch 13, 37.
148. Staughton LJ in *Republic of Haiti* v. *Duvalier* [1990] 1 QB 202, 213–214.
149. *Republic of Haiti* v. *Duvalier* [1990] 1 QB 202.
150. *Rosseel NV* v. *Oriental Commercial Shipping (UK) Ltd* [1990] 1 WLR 1387.

More generally, it has been suggested that "apart from the very exceptional case, the proper attitude of the English courts ... is to confine themselves to their own territorial area, save in cases in which they are the court or tribunal which determines the rights of the parties".[151] According to this view, where the court has jurisdiction to grant provisional measures under section 25(1) of the 1982 Act in support of substantive proceedings in another Contracting State, the court should normally restrict its orders to assets within the jurisdiction.[152]

21.4.2.3 Practice

In *ALG Incorporated* v. *Uganda Airlines Corporation*[153] Judge Southwell QC listed the following considerations which ought to be taken into account in cases where the plaintiff makes an application for a worldwide Mareva injunction.

(i) Evidence in support of Mareva applications should be limited to evidence necessary to give a fair statement of relevant facts. More attention should be given to providing a clear and fair affidavit than to flooding the court with a large number of exhibits which may be largely irrelevant and may conceal the real issue.

(ii) In all applications for Mareva injunctions—but especially in relation to applications for a worldwide Mareva injunction—the papers should be delivered to the court sufficiently long before the hearing to enable the judge to read and digest them all before the hearing, whether *ex parte* or *inter partes*.

(iii) In cases where an extraterritorial Mareva injunction would inevitably cause problems for a legitimate business carried on by the defendant worldwide, the plaintiff should be required to produce a skeleton argument as part of the application. The skeleton argument should be delivered to the court with the other papers and should set out the precise grounds on which the case is said (a) to meet the requirements of the issue of a Mareva injunction and (b) to give rise to specified exceptional circumstances justifying the grant of a worldwide injunction.

21.4.2.4 The protection of the defendant and third parties

In *Derby & Co Ltd* v. *Weldon* Parker LJ said that "there is every justification for a worldwide Mareva, so long as, by undertaking or proviso or a combination of both, (a) oppression of the defendants by way of exposure to a multiplicity of proceedings is avoided, (b) the defendants are protected against the misuse of information gained from the ordinary order for disclosure in aid of the Mareva, and (c) the position of third parties is protected".[154]

151. Lord Donaldson MR in *Rosseel NV* v. *Oriental Commercial Shipping (UK) Ltd* [1990] 1 WLR 1387, 1389.

152. *Republic of Haiti* v. *Duvalier* [1990] 1 QB 202 is an example of a case where, although the substantive proceedings were abroad, the English court granted a worldwide Mareva injunction.

153. *The Times*, 31 July 1992.

154. [1990] Ch 48, 57.

21.4.2.4.1 PROTECTING THE DEFENDANT AGAINST A MULTIPLICITY OF PROCEEDINGS AND THE MISUSE OF INFORMATION

In *Babanaft International Co SA* v. *Bassatne*[155] Neill and Nicholls LJJ thought that a plaintiff should be required to undertake that information disclosed under an extraterritorial disclosure order would not be used abroad (for example, as the basis for legal proceedings in a foreign country) without the consent of the defendant or the leave of the court. Kerr LJ, however, indicated that such undertakings should not be required. In subsequent cases, the Court of Appeal has followed the view of the majority.[156] In view of the fact that an order restraining the defendant from dealing with any of his assets overseas and requiring him to disclose details of all his assets wherever located is a draconian order a worldwide pre-judgment Mareva injunction should normally include an undertaking by the plaintiff not to take any action in a foreign jurisdiction in respect of the defendant's assets without the leave of the court.

(i) It is not sufficient merely that the plaintiff makes the relevant undertaking: "before making a disclosure order in respect of foreign assets, the court normally will need to be satisfied that, by reason of the plaintiff's continuing connection with this country or otherwise, the court has over the plaintiff a degree of control sufficient to ensure compliance with any orders it may make regarding the use of information".[157]

(ii) It is not appropriate to require such undertakings from a foreign State which "has complied scrupulously with its undertaking in the past".[158]

21.4.2.4.2 THE PROTECTION OF THIRD PARTIES: THE BABANAFT PROVISO[159]

21.4.2.4.2.1 Although an injunction operates *in personam*—against the person to whom it is addressed—it may have an indirect effect on third parties. It is well established that a person who is not a party to the injunction may nevertheless be in contempt of court if he knowingly does acts which assist the defendant in breaking the terms of the injunction. When a third party has knowledge of a Mareva injunction he must do what he reasonably can to preserve the assets affected. If he knowingly assists in any way in their disposal or in prohibited dealing with them, he will be in contempt of court. In *Z Ltd* v. *A-Z & AA-LL*,[160] for example, the plaintiff had obtained Mareva injunctions against a number of defendants. A bank, which held assets of one of the defendants against whom the injunction had been granted, had been served with a copy of the injunction (and therefore had notice of it) even though the defendant had not been served. It was held that the bank would be in contempt by disposing of the defendant's assets after having received notice of the injunction, even though the defendant, not having been served, could not at that time be in contempt for failing to comply with the terms of the injunction.

155. [1990] Ch 13.
156. *Republic of Haiti* v. *Duvalier* [1990] 1 QB 202; *Derby & Co Ltd* v. *Weldon* [1990] Ch 48; *Derby & Co Ltd* v. *Weldon (Nos. 3 & 4)* [1990] Ch 65.
157. Nicholls LJ in *Babanaft International Co SA* v. *Bassatne* [1990] Ch 13, 47.
158. Staughton LJ in *Republic of Haiti* v. *Duvalier* [1990] 1 QB 202, 217.
159. Malek & Lewis, "Worldwide Mareva Injunctions: the Position of International Banks" [1990] LMCLQ 88.
160. [1982] QB 558.

21.4.2.4.2.2 In *Babanaft International Co SA* v. *Bassatne*, when the Court of Appeal first decided that, in appropriate circumstances, the court could restrain by injunction a defendant from dealing with foreign assets, it was clear that an extraterritorial Mareva injunction posed novel problems for third parties. Although a whole range of individuals and corporations might be affected by a Mareva injunction, there is no doubt that banks are in the most vulnerable position; Mareva injunctions are often directed to all the defendant's assets, many of which will be held in accounts in various banks in numerous countries. If these banks have branches in London, they are *prima facie* within the contempt jurisdiction of the English courts.

21.4.2.4.2.3 In *Babanaft International Co SA* v. *Bassatne* the members of the Court of Appeal agreed that a worldwide Mareva injunction should not expose third parties to unreasonable risks of liability for contempt of court; subsequent cases have confirmed the principle that a worldwide Mareva injunction should contain appropriate provisions for the protection of third parties.[161] The crucial question, however, concerns the form which such protective provisions should take. In *Babanaft International Co SA* v. *Bassatne*, whereas Neill and Nicholls LJJ took the view that the injunction should be binding only on the defendant, Kerr LJ would have preferred a proviso which would not affect third parties "unless and to the extent that [the injunction] is enforced by the courts of the States in which any of the defendants' assets are located".[162] This aspect of Kerr LJ's judgment is the seed from which has grown what has become known as the *Babanaft* proviso.

21.4.2.4.2.4 The appropriate level of protection for third parties was the subject of further consideration by the Court of Appeal in *Republic of Haiti* v. *Duvalier*[163] and *Derby & Co Ltd* v. *Weldon*.[164] In *Republic of Haiti* v. *Duvalier* Staughton LJ proposed a refinement of the *Babanaft* proviso, so that only corporations—and not individuals—should be protected in respect of their actions abroad. This modification was followed in *Derby & Co Ltd* v. *Weldon*. In *Derby & Co Ltd* v. *Weldon (Nos. 3 & 4)* Lord Donaldson MR suggested the rejection of the distinction between corporations and individuals and a reformulation of the *Babanaft* proviso—which was endorsed by the other members of the Court of Appeal—in the following terms:

> Provided that, in so far as this order purports to have any extraterritorial effect, no person shall be affected thereby or concerned with the terms thereof until it shall be declared enforceable or be enforced by a foreign court and then shall only affect them to the extent of such declaration or enforcement unless they are: (a) a person to whom this order is addressed or an officer of or agent appointed by a power of attorney of such a person or (b) persons who are subject to the jurisdiction of this court and (i) have been given written notice of this order at their residence or place of business within the jurisdiction, and (ii) are able to prevent acts or omissions outside the jurisdiction of this court which assist in the breach of the terms of this order.[165]

21.4.2.4.2.5 Although the precise form of the proviso may vary from case to case, it seems that the basic shape of the *Babanaft* proviso has now been fixed. The effect of the proviso in its latest form can be broken down into a number of elements.

161. *Ghoth* v. *Ghoth* [1992] 2 All ER 920.
162. [1990] Ch 13, 37.
163. [1990] 1 QB 202.
164. [1990] Ch 48.
165. [1990] Ch 65, 84.

(i) As a general rule a third party will not be affected by a Mareva injunction in respect of acts performed abroad unless and until the courts of the country where the assets are located have recognised or enforced the injunction. Even in such a case the third party is affected only to the extent decided by the foreign court. In practice, in only very limited circumstances will an English Mareva injunction be entitled to recognition or enforcement abroad.[166]

(ii) As an exception to the general rule, a third party may be affected by a Mareva injunction in respect of actions undertaken abroad, notwithstanding the fact that the injunction is not entitled to recognition in the country where the assets are located. In order for the exception to apply three conditions must be satisfied. First, the third party in question must be subject to English jurisdiction. Secondly, the third party must have been given written notice in England of the injunction. There can be no question of a third party being exposed to the risk of contempt until he has received notice of the injunction. Thirdly, an extraterritorial Mareva injunction affects a third party only if the individual or establishment in England is able to prevent acts or omissions outside the jurisdiction of the court.

This third condition raises very difficult questions, particularly with regard to banks. In what circumstances, for example, can a bank in England be regarded as having the necessary control over branches in other countries? As regards an English bank with branches abroad the effect of the *Babanaft* proviso is that the English bank will be liable for contempt if foreign branches allow the defendant to make withdrawals from accounts held at the foreign branches.[167] As regards foreign banks with branches in England, the effect of the *Babanaft* proviso is that, as a general rule, activities conducted abroad will not incur liability for contempt in England even though, by virtue of its presence in England, the bank is subject to English jurisdiction:

> [I]t will only be in exceptional cases (eg where the account abroad is under its control) in which [the English branch] will be "able to prevent acts or omissions outside the jurisdiction". The mere fact that a foreign bank with a branch in London is part of one juridical entity should not mean, for this purpose, that the foreign bank is in contempt because of the acts of one of its branches outside England.[168]

21.4.2.5 The dangers of extraterritorial Mareva injunctions

Although the worldwide Mareva injunction has taken root in England, it would be foolish to think that the practice of the courts is entirely free from dangers and problems. Attention may be drawn to three issues.[169]

(i) Even though the elaborate structure of the *Babanaft* proviso is designed to lessen the invasive impact of a worldwide Mareva injunction, the grant of an extraterritorial order may come very close to an unwarranted interference with the jurisdiction of the courts of the country where the assets are situated.

166. See para. 21.5.
167. *Securities and Investments Board* v. *Pantell SA* [1990] Ch 426.
168. Collins, "Provisional and Protective Measures in International Litigation" [1992] III Hag Rec 9, 120.
169. See Browne-Wilkinson, "Territorial Jurisdiction and the New Technologies" (1991) 25 Israel LR 145, 152–153.

(ii) The theoretical justification for the grant of extraterritorial orders—namely, that the order acts only *in personam*—is not entirely convincing, especially in cases where the court appoints a receiver who is entitled to take possession of the assets. The worldwide Mareva injunction "smacks too much of the arrogance of a former imperial power sending a gun-boat where there is trouble abroad".[170]

(iii) An extraterritorial Mareva injunction is not effective against defendants who are not resident in England. The sanction for disobedience is normally simply that the defendant is barred from defending the substantive proceedings. The sanction will probably prove to be illusory, since if the defendant is not allowed to defend the proceedings it is likely that the courts of foreign countries where the defendant's assets are located will refuse to recognise or enforce the final judgment of the English court.[171]

Ultimately, the answers to these concerns can only be found in international co-operation. However, it is not easy to see how significant advances can be made. The Brussels and Lugano Conventions show how difficult it is to achieve an effective system for the reciprocal enforcement of provisional measures.

21.5 ENFORCEMENT OF FOREIGN PROVISIONAL MEASURES

21.5.1 Introduction

21.5.1.1 The swift and easy transfer of assets across frontiers means that a plaintiff may seek protective measures in a country where the defendant's assets are no longer located. If the court makes an order—notwithstanding the fact that the assets are elsewhere—the question arises as to whether the order should be entitled to enforcement in countries where the assets are to be found. The question of the enforcement of foreign provisional measures has not yet loomed large in English practice. For reasons of practical convenience, a plaintiff will often apply for provisional measures in the country where those measures are intended to take effect. Moreover, until recently there could be no question of seeking enforcement of foreign provisional measures in England. The only foreign judgments which may entitled to enforcement at common law or under the statutory regimes which are based on the common law[172] are judgments for a fixed sum of money.

21.5.1.2 In theory, the position within the system established by the Brussels and Lugano Conventions is different from that which exists at common law. The enforcement provisions in Title III do not distinguish between judgments on interlocutory matters and final judgments or between money judgments and judgments in specie.[173] In practice, however, many provisional measures given in Contracting States are not entitled to enforcement in England under Title III. In addition, protective measures (other than orders for the making of an interim payment) granted by the

170. Browne-Wilkinson, "Territorial Jurisdiction and the New Technologies" (1991) 25 Israel LR 145, 153.
171. Cf. Lord Donaldson MR in *Derby & Co Ltd* v. *Weldon (Nos. 3 & 4)* [1990] Ch 65, 81.
172. Administration of Justice Act 1920; Foreign Judgments (Reciprocal Enforcement) Act 1933.
173. Case 143/78 *de Cavel* v. *de Cavel* [1979] ECR 1055, 1066–1067 (paras. 8–9).

courts of Scotland and Northern Ireland are not enforceable in England under Part II of the 1982 Act.[174]

21.5.2 Title III and provisional measures[175]

21.5.2.1 Procedural orders

The general scope of Title III is limited to judgments given in Contracting States in civil and commercial matters (as defined by Article 1) which govern the legal relationships of the parties.[176] Procedural orders, for example, the purpose of which is simply to arrange the further conduct of the proceedings—rather than to regulate the parties' substantive rights—do not fall within Title III. Accordingly, a foreign court order which appoints experts to examine a building in London and to take evidence from witnesses is not entitled to enforcement in England.[177]

21.5.2.2 Measures granted ex parte

An important aspect of many provisional measures is the element of surprise. In the context of English proceedings, an application for a Mareva injunction or an Anton Piller order will normally be made *ex parte*. The case law of the Court of Justice establishes, however, that Title III does not apply to "judicial decisions authorising provisional or protective measures, which are delivered without the party against which they are directed having been summoned to appear and which are intended to be enforced without prior service".[178] Accordingly, it is clear that a provisional measure which has been granted on the basis of an *ex parte* application is not entitled to enforcement under Title III. Even if, after a provisional measure has been granted in a Contracting State following an *ex parte* application, the defendant is given a reasonable opportunity under the law of the State of origin to apply to have the measure set aside, the measure remains unenforceable in England.[179] It follows from these decisions that in a case in which speed and surprise are of the essence, a plaintiff who wishes to obtain provisional measures in more than one Contracting State has little choice but to make the necessary applications in all the jurisdictions in which such measures are required.

174. Civil Jurisdiction and Judgments Act 1982, s. 18(5)(d).
175. See para. 9.4.1.2.
176. Schlosser Report, OJ 1979 C59/126–127, paras. 184–187.
177. *CFEM Façades SA* v. *Bovis Construction Ltd* [1992] ILPr 561.
178. Case 125/79 *Denilauer* v. *Snc Couchet Frères* [1980] ECR 1553, 1571 (para. 18).
179. *EMI Records Ltd* v. *Modern Music Karl-Ulrich Walterbach GmbH* [1992] QB 115.

CHAPTER 22

ANTISUIT INJUNCTIONS[1]

There are many situations in which the courts of more than one country have jurisdiction over a particular dispute between the parties. Under traditional English jurisdiction rules where, for example, A sues B in a foreign country and B sues A on the same cause of action in England, A may apply for a stay of the English proceedings on the basis that the foreign court is the more appropriate forum.[2] What is the position if England is the more appropriate forum? May the plaintiff in the English proceedings obtain an antisuit injunction—that is, an injunction requiring a litigant not to commence or to discontinue proceedings in a foreign court? Because antisuit injunctions raise delicate questions of comity, the court will not restrain a litigant from proceeding abroad simply on the basis that England is the *forum conveniens* (para. 22.1). An antisuit injunction will not normally be granted unless proceedings in the foreign forum are "vexatious or oppressive" or if the bringing of the proceedings infringes a legal or equitable right of the defendant in the foreign proceedings (for example, where proceedings are brought in breach of a dispute resolution agreement concluded between the parties) (para. 22.2). Special factors should be considered in cases where the foreign proceedings have been brought in the courts of a Brussels or Lugano Contracting State (para. 22.3).

22.1 PRELIMINARY REMARKS

22.1.1 Can an English court limit the jurisdiction of foreign courts? Although an English court may not directly order a foreign court to do or not to do something a litigant may apply to the English court for an antisuit injunction. In theory an antisuit injunction does not interfere with the foreign court because it operates *in personam*; if an English court makes an order against a person who is amenable to the jurisdiction of the court[3] failure by the defendant to comply with the order amounts to contempt for which the defendant may be punished, but it does not have an impact on the foreign proceedings as such. Of course, proceedings continue only as long as the parties take the necessary procedural steps. In reality, therefore, the grant of an antisuit injunction

1. Hartley, "Comity and the Use of Antisuit Injunctions in International Litigation" (1987) 35 Am J Comp L 487.
2. See para. 6.4 (in particular para. 6.4.4.2).
3. On the question of the court's jurisdiction to grant injunctions see para. 21.3.

interferes indirectly with the foreign court's jurisdiction and runs counter to the idea of comity.[4] Nevertheless, antisuit injunctions can play an important role in international litigation.

22.1.2 If the courts were not able, in appropriate circumstances, to grant antisuit injunctions there would arise situations in which a litigant in foreign proceedings would suffer injustice. There are certain cases which cry out for a remedy—for example, where the plaintiff, having agreed to the exclusive jurisdiction of the English courts, oppressively pursues the defendant in a number of foreign jurisdictions. It is important, however, to stress that it is rare for the grant of an antisuit injunction to be appropriate: "Injunctive relief with extraterritorial effect . . . must be an exceptional remedy. It ought only to be granted in exceptional circumstances. It is, after all, inconsistent with normal relations between friendly sovereign States, and it is subversive of the best interests of the international trade system".[5]

22.1.3 If England is the *forum conveniens* is the plaintiff entitled to an injunction restraining the defendant from litigating abroad? In the early 1980s there emerged the idea that the same basic test should be applied to applications for a stay of English proceedings and applications for an antisuit injunction.[6] However, as the test for the grant of a stay of English proceedings became more liberal, it became clear that, if the English courts were to avoid interfering excessively in the affairs of foreign countries, a stricter test would have to be formulated in the context of applications for an injunction restraining the defendant from litigating abroad. If the rules for the grant of an antisuit injunction were the mirror image of the *Spiliada* test the position would be as follows:

> To justify the grant of an injunction, the defendant must show: (a) that the English court is the natural forum for the trial of the action, to whose jurisdiction the parties are amenable; *and* (b) that justice does not require that the action should nevertheless be allowed to proceed in the foreign court.[7]

22.1.4 For a litigant to be prevented from pursuing proceedings abroad simply on the basis that the English court regards itself as the natural forum would be wholly inconsistent with the principle of comity. Although it is clear that among the forms of injunction which the court has power to grant is an injunction granted to one party to an action to restrain the other party from beginning or from continuing proceedings in a foreign court, the court should exercise this jurisdiction with caution "because it involves indirect interference with the process of the foreign court concerned".[8] Accordingly, the test to be applied to an application for an antisuit injunction is not the same as the test which applies to an application for a stay of English proceedings.[9]

4. Hartley, "Comity and the Use of Antisuit Injunctions in International Litigation" (1987) 35 Am J Comp L 487, 506.
5. Steyn J in *ED & F Man (Sugar) Ltd* v. *Haryanto (No. 2)* [1991] 1 Lloyd's Rep 161, 168.
6. *Castanho* v. *Brown & Root (UK) Ltd* [1981] AC 557. Briggs, "No Interference with Foreign Court" (1982) 31 ICLQ 189; Morgan, "Discretion to Stay Jurisdiction" (1982) 31 ICLQ 582.
7. Lord Goff in *Société Nationale Industrielle Aérospatiale* v. *Lee Kui Jak* [1987] AC 871, 895.
8. Lord Brandon in *South Carolina Insurance Co* v. *Assurantie Maatschappij "De Zeven Provincien" NV* [1987] AC 24, 40. Carter, (1986) 57 BYIL 434; Forsyth, [1988] CLJ 177.
9. *Société Nationale Industrielle Aérospatiale* v. *Lee Kui Jak* [1987] AC 871, 895.

22.2 THE BASES ON WHICH AN INJUNCTION MAY BE GRANTED

Although the modern view is that the court's discretion to grant injunctive relief should not be regarded as being limited to a fixed number of categories,[10] in the context of antisuit injunctions the circumstances in which the court will consider granting relief generally fall into two situations: (i) "where one party to an action has behaved, or threatens to behave, in a manner which is unconscionable" and (ii) "where one party to an action can show that the other party has either invaded, or threatens to invade, a legal or equitable right of the former for the enforcement of which the latter is amenable to the jurisdiction of the court".[11]

22.2.1 Unconscionable conduct

22.2.1.1 In *South Carolina Insurance Co* v. *Assurantie Maatschappij "De Zeven Provincien" NV* Lord Brandon said that, although it was probably not wise to attempt to provide an exhaustive definition of "unconscionable conduct", that term clearly includes "conduct which is oppressive or vexatious".[12] This formula was applied in *Société Nationale Internationale Aérospatiale* v. *Lee Kui Jak.*[13] Lord Goff said:

> [W]here a remedy for a particular wrong is available both in the English ... court and in a foreign court, the English ... court will, generally speaking, only restrain the plaintiff from pursuing proceedings in the foreign court if such pursuit would be vexatious or oppressive. This presupposes that, as a general rule, the English ... court must conclude that it provides the natural forum for the trial of the action; and further, since the court is concerned with the ends of justice, that account must be taken not only of injustice to the defendant if the plaintiff is allowed to pursue the foreign proceedings, but also of injustice to the plaintiff if he is not allowed to do so. So the court will not grant an injunction if, by doing so, it will deprive him of advantages in the foreign forum of which it would be unjust to deprive him.[14]

22.2.1.2 Whereas under the doctrine of *forum non conveniens* the defendant merely has to establish that another forum is more appropriate, where an antisuit injunction is sought from an English court, it be must shown not only that the foreign forum is not the natural forum, but also that England is the natural forum. Furthermore, it must be shown that to allow the foreign proceedings to continue would cause positive injustice. In most cases, this will be established by showing that the foreign proceedings would be vexatious or oppressive.

22.2.1.3 There are, of course, problems with a test which is formulated in such a general way. In particular, how is the dividing line between seeking a legitimate advantage, on the one hand, and acting in a vexatious or oppressive manner, on the other, to be drawn? It is not enough that acts should be "vexatious or oppressive" in the

10. See the speeches of Lord Goff and Lord Mackay in *South Carolina Insurance Co* v. *Assurantie Maatschappij "De Zeven Provincien" NV* [1987] AC 24; *Société Nationale Industrielle Aérospatiale* v. *Lee Kui Jak* [1987] AC 871.

11. Lord Brandon in *South Carolina Insurance Co* v. *Assurantie Maatschappij "De Zeven Provincien" NV* [1987] AC 24, 40.

12. [1987] AC 24, 41.

13. [1987] AC 871. Briggs, "Restraint of Foreign Proceedings" [1987] LMCLQ 391; Carter, (1988) 59 BYIL 342; Forsyth, [1988] CLJ 177; Kunzlik, [1987] CLJ 406.

14. [1987] AC 871, 896.

ordinary domestic sense in which actions might be summarily struck out under the Rules of the Supreme Court; something more is required.[15]

22.2.1.4 The mere fact that the law applied by the foreign forum is different from English law does not mean that the foreign proceedings are inherently oppressive.[16] Where the question is simply one of justice between litigants the court should be slow to intervene unless it is satisfied that justice can be achieved only by granting an injunction. The power to restrain a litigant in foreign proceedings by injunction is "to be exercised with great caution so as to avoid even the appearance of interference with another court".[17]

22.2.1.5 *Société Nationale Internationale Aérospatiale* v. *Lee Kui Jak*[18] concerned proceedings brought following a helicopter crash in Brunei in which the plaintiff's husband was killed. The helicopter had been manufactured by a French company and operated by a Malaysian company. The plaintiff started proceedings against both companies in Brunei and against the French company in Texas. The French company applied to the Brunei courts for an injunction restraining the plaintiff from continuing with the proceedings in Texas. The basis of the application was that, whereas in the context of the Brunei proceedings the French company—if found liable—could claim indemnity from the Malaysian company, there was no such possibility in Texas. Furthermore, there was no advantage to the plaintiff in pursuing the Texas proceedings, since the French company had given undertakings which ensured that any potential advantages to the plaintiff in the Texas proceedings would also be available in the Brunei proceedings. The Privy Council decided that, in these circumstances, the proceedings in Texas were oppressive and that the grant of an injunction was appropriate.

22.2.1.6 Where foreign proceedings have not yet been commenced and are not contemplated the court will be extremely unwilling to grant an antisuit injunction. In *ED & F Man (Sugar) Ltd* v. *Haryanto (No. 2)*[19] the parties had entered two contracts for the sale of sugar, both of which were governed by English law. After protracted arbitration and legal proceedings the parties made a settlement agreement. Subsequently, the defendant obtained a judgment from the Indonesian courts to the effect that the original contracts and the settlement agreement were illegal and of no effect. In the context of proceedings in England to enforce the settlement agreement, the plaintiff also sought a general worldwide ban on the defendant's relying on the Indonesian judgment, whether by way of offence or defence. The injunction sought by the plaintiff was not, however, aimed at specific foreign proceedings; indeed, it was not even known whether the defendant was contemplating further proceedings abroad. The Court of Appeal upheld Steyn J's refusal to grant the injunction on the basis that the grant of an injunction would be "an illegitimate interference (albeit indirectly) with the processes of the courts worldwide".[20]

22.2.1.7 Where, however, private litigation gives rise to a conflict of national policy, the court may be more prepared to grant an antisuit injunction. For example, certain

15. *Arab Monetary Fund* v. *Hashim (No. 6)*, *Financial Times*, 24 July 1992.
16. *Barclays Bank Plc* v. *Homan*, *The Times*, 13 October 1992.
17. Lord Denning MR in *The Lisboa* [1980] 2 Lloyd's Rep 546, 549.
18. [1987] AC 871.
19. [1991] 1 Lloyd's Rep 429.
20. [1991] 1 Lloyd's Rep 161, 168.

types of foreign proceedings—notably anti-trust suits in the United States under the Sherman and Clayton Acts—are oppressive in English eyes. In *Midland Bank Plc* v. *Laker Airways Ltd*[21] the Court of Appeal granted an injunction to restrain a plaintiff from pursuing an anti-trust suit in the United States; in view of the oppressive nature of the United States procedures, it was unconscionable and unjust for the plaintiff to invoke the United States jurisdiction under the Sherman and Clayton Acts against the defendant, an English company, whose dealings with the plaintiff had taken place entirely in England and who had not submitted to the jurisdiction of the United States courts.

22.2.2 Infringement of a legal or equitable right

22.2.2.1 If A invades or threatens to invade a legal or equitable right of B for the enforcement of which A is amenable to the jurisdiction of the court, the court may grant an injunction restraining A.[22] Accordingly, the court may grant an antisuit injunction when a litigant has a legal or equitable right not to be sued in a foreign court on the cause of action in question. A right not to be sued abroad may be contractual (for example, where there is an arbitration clause or a clause conferring exclusive jurisdiction on the English courts) or arise by virtue of an equitable defence to the claim (such as estoppel, election, waiver, or laches).[23]

22.2.2.2 In practice, the possibility of a litigant obtaining an antisuit injunction to protect a legal or equitable right arises most frequently where foreign proceedings have been brought in breach of an arbitration clause or an exclusive jurisdiction clause. How should the courts exercise their discretion in these circumstances? Although, where the parties have agreed to litigate in a particular forum, whether in England or abroad, the court will normally hold the parties to their bargain, it does not necessarily follow that the court should restrain a litigant from pursuing foreign proceedings brought in breach of a dispute resolution clause as readily as it would stay English proceedings which are brought in breach of a foreign jurisdiction clause. In the context of an application for an antisuit injunction the question of comity is more prominent.

22.2.2.3 Although the courts have appeared willing to grant an antisuit injunction where the foreign proceedings have been brought in breach of the agreed dispute resolution clause, the court has not sought to justify the grant of an injunction solely on the basis of the parties' agreement. In *Tracomin SA* v. *Sudan Oil Seeds (No. 2)*[24] the defendant, a Sudanese company, had contracted to sell groundnuts to the plaintiff, a Swiss company. The contract provided for arbitration in London. When a dispute as to the quality of the groundnuts arose, the plaintiff started proceedings in Switzerland. In the Swiss proceedings the court assumed jurisdiction, holding that the arbitration clause was of no effect. The defendant then started arbitration in England and sought an injunction to restrain the plaintiff from pursuing the litigation in Switzerland. The Court

21. [1986] QB 689. Crawford, (1986) 57 BYIL 414.
22. Lord Brandon in *South Carolina Insurance Co* v. *Assurantie Maatschappij "De Zeven Provincien" NV* [1987] AC 24, 40.
23. *British Airways Board* v. *Laker Airways Ltd* [1985] AC 58. Collier, [1984] CLJ 253; Davenport, "Restraining Foreign Proceedings" [1984] LMCLQ 563.
24. [1983] 1 WLR 1026.

of Appeal thought that an injunction should be granted; it was important not only to enforce the parties' agreement as to arbitration but also to avoid (i) a multiplicity of proceedings in different countries, with the possible risk of conflicting decisions, and (ii) the "unseemly spectacle"[25] of the arbitrators effectively having to decide whether they agreed with the conclusion of the Swiss court.

22.2.2.4 In *Sohio Supply Co* v. *Gatoil (USA) Inc*[26] the contract between the parties was governed by English law and contained a clause which provided that disputes arising under the contract were subject to "the jurisdiction of the English court without recourse to arbitration". The plaintiff started proceedings in England; the defendant started proceedings in Texas; the plaintiff applied for an injunction to restrain the defendant from proceeding in the Texas court. Staughton LJ justified the grant of an antisuit injunction on three grounds: (i) the parties had agreed to the exclusive jurisdiction of the English courts; (ii) in the Texas proceedings the defendant was applying for a declaration of non-liability; (iii) it is inherently undesirable that there should be concurrent proceedings in different jurisdictions.

22.2.2.5 There are circumstances in which it is inappropriate for the court to grant an antisuit injunction notwithstanding the fact that the parties have agreed to the exclusive jurisdiction of the English courts and one of the parties has commenced proceedings abroad. A distinction should be drawn between proceedings concerning the substantive issues and proceedings relating to provisional or protective measures. Where the litigation abroad concerns the merits of the dispute there are good reasons why the defendant should seek an antisuit injunction from the English court. The position is different, however, where the foreign proceedings are concerned only with provisional measures or security. Where, for example, a cargo owner, who has agreed to the exclusive jurisdiction of the English courts, has a claim against a one-ship company, if the exclusive jurisdiction agreement entitles the shipowner to an injunction preventing the cargo owner from taking protective measures in a foreign forum where the ship is located, this is tantamount to depriving the cargo owner of any effective remedy.[27] There are two possible ways of approaching this type of problem. The simple solution is to interpret the exclusive jurisdiction clause as relating only to substantive proceedings and not to proceedings concerned with provisional measures, security or enforcement.[28] Alternatively, even if the jurisdiction agreement extends to all types of proceedings, as a matter of discretion, an antisuit injunction should not be granted where the foreign proceedings do not involve the substance of the dispute.[29]

22.2.2.6 It should also be noted that a judgment given by a court of a foreign country is not entitled to recognition and enforcement if the bringing of the proceedings in the foreign court was contrary to an arbitration clause or jurisdiction agreement.[30] In cases where the defendant's assets are located in England this provision effectively deprives the plaintiff of any benefit of litigating abroad in breach of the terms of a dispute resolution clause.

25. Donaldson MR, [1983] 1 WLR 1026, 1037.
26. [1989] 1 Lloyd's Rep 588.
27. Lord Denning MR in *The Lisboa* [1980] 2 Lloyd's Rep 546, 548–549.
28. See, for example, Lord Denning MR in *The Lisboa* [1980] 2 Lloyd's Rep 546, 548.
29. *The Lisboa* [1980] 2 Lloyd's Rep 546.
30. Civil Jurisdiction and Judgments Act 1982, s. 32(1). For further discussion see para. 9.2.7.5.

22.3 THE BRUSSELS AND LUGANO CONVENTIONS

22.3.1 It may be presumed that, where proceedings concerning civil and commercial matters are brought in the courts of another Contracting State, the court retains its general equitable jurisdiction to grant an antisuit injunction to restrain a litigant in those foreign proceedings. The key question relates to discretion: when might it be appropriate to grant such an injunction?

22.3.2 The Conventions are designed to provide a uniform code for the allocation of jurisdiction in civil and commercial matters between the Contracting States. Where jurisdiction is conferred on the courts of another Contracting State by the terms of Title II it is hard to imagine circumstances in which an antisuit injunction would be appropriate. Furthermore, Article 21 of the Conventions provides that where proceedings between the same parties concerning the same cause of action are brought in the courts of more than one Contracting State any court other than the court first seised must stay its proceedings or decline jurisdiction.[31] Where, for example, the plaintiff exercises the option conferred by Title II to sue a defendant for breach of contract in the courts for the place of performance of the obligation in question there should be no question of the English court restraining the plaintiff from proceeding in the courts which have jurisdiction under Article 5(1) rather than in the courts with jurisdiction under Article 2.

22.3.3 The uniform code in Title II is subject to Article 4, according to which proceedings may be brought against a defendant who is not domiciled in a Contracting State under traditional rules if jurisdiction is not allocated by the provisions of Title II.[32] It does not follow from Article 4, however, that the court should be willing to grant an antisuit injunction in cases where the court of a Contracting State assumes jurisdiction on a basis of jurisdiction outside Title II.

22.3.4 It must be remembered that, because Title III provides for the free movement of judgments in civil and commercial matters regardless of the basis on which the court of the State of origin assumed jurisdiction,[33] the aim of the Conventions to reduce the chances of the courts of different Contracting States rendering irreconcilable judgments can be achieved only if Article 21 is given a broad interpretation. In *Overseas Union Insurance Ltd* v. *New Hampshire Insurance Co*[34] the Court of Justice decided that Article 21 is one of the provisions of Title II which applies regardless of the parties' domicile and regardless of the basis on which the court first seised assumed jurisdiction. In the course of its judgment the Court of Justice stressed that "in no case is the court second seised in a better position than the court first seised to determine whether the latter has jurisdiction".[35] It follows, therefore, that as regards proceedings which fall within the scope of Article 1 the English court should not even consider the grant of an antisuit injunction in cases where proceedings are brought in the courts of another Contracting State.

31. See para. 5.9.
32. See para. 4.2.2.
33. See para. 9.4.1.3.
34. Case C-351/89 [1991] ECR I-3317.
35. Case C-351/89 *Overseas Union Insurance Ltd* v. *New Hampshire Insurance Co* [1991] ECR I-3317, 3350 (para. 23).

22.3.5 The Court of Appeal adopted a completely different approach in *Continental Bank NA* v. *Akakos Compania Naviera SA*.[36] In this case proceedings were brought in Greece against a bank in breach of an English jurisdiction agreement which, in the eyes of the English court, satisfied the conditions laid down by Article 17. The bank subsequently brought proceedings in England and applied for an injunction to restrain the Greek plaintiffs from continuing with the Greek proceedings. The Greek plaintiffs, relying on Article 21 of the Brussels Convention, applied for a stay of the English proceedings on the basis that the Greek court was the court first seised. Having decided that the jurisdiction clause was valid under Article 17, the Court of Appeal concluded not only that Article 17 takes precedence over Article 21 (and, therefore, that there was no duty to stay the English proceedings) but also that the grant of an antisuit injunction was appropriate on the basis that the continuance of the Greek proceedings amounted to conduct which was vexatious and oppressive.

22.3.6 This decision is not compatible with the framework and spirit of the Brussels Convention. The fallacy on which the Court of Appeal's decision is based is the proposition that Article 17 takes precedence over Article 21; there is nothing in Title II to suggest that this is the case.[37] In the situation which arose in *Continental Bank NA* v. *Akakos Compania Naviera SA* if the Greek court assumes jurisdiction it can only be on the basis that Article 17 does not confer exclusive jurisdiction on the English courts (for example, because the agreement does not satisfy the formal requirements of Article 17 or because the dispute does not fall within the scope of the clause). In these circumstances it hardly seems appropriate for the English court to review the decision of the Greek court as to the effect of the jurisdiction clause. If the defendant in proceedings brought in another Contracting State wishes to challenge the assumption of jurisdiction the appropriate forum is the Contracting State in question rather than England. The grant of an antisuit injunction by the English court adds insult to injury and is inconsistent with the principles on which the Convention is founded.

36. *The Times*, 26 November 1993.

37. The matter was, however, left open by the Court of Justice in Case C-351/89 *Overseas Union Insurance Ltd* v. *New Hampshire Insurance Co* [1991] ECR I-3317. See para. 5.9.2.3.3.

CHAPTER 23

PROOF OF FOREIGN LAW[1]

The fact that, in a case with a foreign element, English conflicts rules indicate that the applicable law is the law of a foreign country does not necessarily mean that the foreign law will be applied. As a general rule foreign law is treated as a question of fact which must be pleaded and proved by the party seeking to rely on it (para. 23.1). There are, however, certain situations where foreign law does not have to be proved (para. 23.2). Where foreign law is disputed the court has to rely on expert evidence (para. 23.3). Although foreign law is treated as a question of fact, appeals on question of foreign law are regarded differently from appeals on other questions of fact (para. 23.4).

23.1 FOREIGN LAW: A QUESTION OF FACT

23.1.1 There are many cases in which English choice of law rules point towards the law of a foreign country as the *lex causae*. Whereas the court has judicial notice of English law (which includes EC law[2] and public international law[3]), there is no similar principle as regards the law of foreign countries. Foreign law is treated as a fact, which must be pleaded and proved by appropriate evidence; it is for the party seeking to establish the foreign law to plead the relevant rules of law and prove them. If the foreign law is not pleaded, or cannot be proved to the satisfaction of the court, English law is applied by default.[4] So, where a plaintiff sues a defendant in England in relation to a tort which was committed abroad, if neither party pleads the *lex loci delicti* the defendant's liability is determined by English law. It is sometimes said that the court assumes that foreign law is the same as English law unless it is proved to be different.[5] It has been suggested, however, that the terminology of presumption should be abandoned.[6] It is better simply to say that, since English law is the only law of which the court has judicial notice, if the foreign law is not proved, the court has no choice but to apply English law.

23.1.2 Although foreign law is treated as a fact, in those cases where a judge sits with a jury, the foreign law has to be proved to the satisfaction of the judge, rather than the jury. Section 69(5) of the Supreme Court Act 1981 provides:

1. Fentiman, "Foreign Law in English Courts" (1992) 108 LQR 142.
2. European Communities Act 1972, s. 3.
3. *Trendtex Trading Corporation* v. *Central Bank of Nigeria* [1977] QB 529.
4. *Dynamit AG* v. *Rio Tinto Co* [1918] AC 260; *Guaranty Trust Co of New York* v. *Hannay & Co* [1918] 2 KB 623; *Callwood* v. *Callwood* [1960] AC 659 (Carter, (1960) 36 BYIL 408).
5. See, for example, the judgment of Purchas LJ in *Bumper Development Corporation* v. *Commissioner of Police of the Metropolis* [1991] 1 WLR 1362, 1368.
6. See Dicey & Morris, *The Conflict of Laws* (12th ed, 1993) p. 238.

Where . . . it is necessary to ascertain the law of any other country which is applicable to the facts of the case, any question as to the effect of the evidence given with respect to that law shall, instead of being submitted to the jury, be decided by the judge alone.

23.1.3 The operation of the principle that the court may not, of its own motion, consider or apply foreign law has been questioned in relation to those cases falling within the scope of the Contracts (Applicable Law) Act 1990, which implements the Rome Convention on the Law Applicable to Contractual Obligations. Article 1(1) provides that the rules of the Convention "shall apply to contractual obligations in any situation involving a choice between the laws of different countries" and Article 2 states that any law specified by the Convention "shall be applied". On the basis of these provisions it may be argued that in certain circumstances the court should apply rules of foreign law, even if not pleaded or proved by either of the parties. On the other hand, Article 1(2)(h) excludes "evidence and procedure" from the Convention's scope. It is difficult to see how questions relating to the proof of foreign law can be regarded otherwise than as relating to "evidence and procedure", and therefore as being outside the scope of the Convention. In any event, Article 3(2) provides that the parties may agree to subject a contract to a law other than that which previously governed it (whether as a result of an earlier choice or as a result of other provisions of the Convention which determine the applicable law in the absence of choice by the parties). Where in English proceedings the parties choose not to plead the applicable law, the parties' conduct may legitimately be interpreted as an implied agreement to subject the contract to English law.

23.2 CASES IN WHICH FOREIGN LAW DOES NOT HAVE TO BE PROVED

23.2.1 In certain rather limited circumstances a court may have judicial notice of a law other than English law. Generally speaking, for the purpose of English private international law, the laws of Scotland and Northern Ireland are treated in the same way as the laws of politically foreign countries, such as France and Germany. So, where litigation arising out of a contract governed by Scots law comes before the English High Court, since the judge does not have judicial notice of the applicable law, a party wishing to enforce his rights under the applicable law has to plead and prove the relevant Scottish rules. However, the House of Lords, which has jurisdiction to hear appeals from England and Wales, Scotland and Northern Ireland, has judicial notice of the laws of all parts of the United Kingdom when hearing an appeal from the courts of one of the parts. It may also be presumed that the Judicial Committee of the Privy Council has judicial notice of the laws of those countries in relation to which it exercises appellate jurisdiction.

23.2.2 There may be circumstances in which the court has judicial notice of a rule of foreign law as a notorious fact. For example, the English courts have taken judicial notice of the fact that roulette is not unlawful in Monte Carlo.[7]

7. *Saxby* v. *Fulton* [1909] 2 KB 208.

23.2.3 The parties may dispense with the aid of witnesses and request the court to decide a question of foreign law without proof. The court is not, however, obliged to accede to the parties' request. Except in cases where the substantive issue turns on the interpretation of a foreign statute, the court is reluctant to decide questions of foreign law without having had the benefit of expert evidence.[8]

23.2.4 Statute may expressly provide that the court shall have judicial notice of the laws of a foreign country.[9]

23.3 MODE OF PROOF

23.3.1 The requirement of evidence

Foreign law has to be proved in the same manner as other facts. If the foreign law is admitted, no proof is necessary.[10] Where, however, the foreign law is disputed, evidence is required. It is clear that it is not sufficient for the party pleading the foreign law simply to place before the court the relevant primary and secondary sources of law (statutes, decided cases and commentaries), leaving the judge to draw his own conclusions.[11] What is required is the evidence of qualified experts in the foreign law.[12] When it comes to questions of foreign law the judge "has not organs to know and to deal with the text of that law, and therefore requires the assistance of a lawyer who knows how to interpret it".[13] The principle which requires the parties to prove the foreign law means that if an expert refers only to part of a foreign legal text the judge may not refer to other parts which have not been put in evidence.[14] Moreover, a judge is not entitled to conduct his own researches into the foreign law.[15] If the evidence put before the court is not satisfactory the judge is not entitled "to search for himself into the sources of knowledge from which witnesses have drawn, and produce for himself the fact which is required to be proved as part of the case before him".[16] While the court may allow evidence to be given by affidavit or in other written form, it is usual for experts to be required to give their evidence orally, with the consequence that they may be subjected to cross-examination.

23.3.2 Uncontradicted evidence

Where the evidence of an expert is uncontradicted, the court will not generally reject it.[17] However, the court is not required to accept the uncontradicted evidence of an

8. Dicey & Morris, *The Conflict of Laws* (12th ed, 1993) p. 228, citing *Beatty* v. *Beatty* [1924] 1 KB 807.
9. For example, section 22(2) of the Maintenance Orders Act 1950 provides that in certain circumstances the court of one part of the United Kingdom shall have judicial notice of the laws of the other parts.
10. *Prowse* v. *European & American Steam Shipping Co* (1860) 13 Moo PC 484; *Moulis* v. *Owen* [1907] 1 KB 746.
11. *Buerger* v. *New York Life Assurance Co* (1927) 96 LJKB 930.
12. See Lord Wright in *Lazard Brothers & Co* v. *Midland Bank Ltd* [1933] AC 289, 298.
13. Lord Brougham in the *Sussex Peerage Case* (1844) 11 Cl & Fin 85, 115.
14. *Bumper Development Corporation* v. *Commissioner of Police of the Metropolis* [1991] 1 WLR 1362.
15. *Bumper Development Corporation* v. *Commissioner of Police of the Metropolis* [1991] 1 WLR 1362.
16. Lord Chelmsford in *Duchess Di Sora* v. *Phillips* (1863) 10 HL Cas 624, 640.
17. *Buerger* v. *New York Life Assurance Co* (1927) 96 LJKB 930; *Koechlin & Cie* v. *Kestenbaum Brothers* [1927] 1 KB 889; *Re Banque des Marchands de Moscou (Koupetschesky)* [1958] Ch 182; *Sharif* v. *Azad* [1967] 1 QB 605.

expert and there are examples where such evidence has been rejected on the basis that it was obviously wrong: "The witness, however expert in the foreign law, cannot prevent the court using its common sense; and the court can reject his evidence if he says something patently absurd, or something inconsistent with the rest of his evidence—including the correct translation, for instance, of a foreign statute which *ex hypothesi* has been proved and therefore is before the court."[18]

23.3.3 Conflicting evidence

Where the evidence of the experts conflicts, the court is required to determine which version of the foreign law is correct. Of course, the court is not restricted to adopting wholesale the views of one expert or another; the judge may accept the views of one expert on some points and those of another expert on others.[19] If the evidence of several expert witnesses conflicts as to the effect of foreign sources, the court is entitled and, indeed, bound to look at those sources in order to decide between conflicting testimony.[20] In *Lord Nelson* v. *Earl Bridport*[21] Lord Langdale MR said:

> Though a knowledge of foreign law is not to be imputed to the judge, you may impute to him such a knowledge of the general art of reasoning, as will enable him, with the assistance of the bar, to discover where fallacies are probably concealed, and in what cases he ought to require testimony more or less strict. If the utmost strictness were required in every case, justice might often have to stand still; and I am not disposed to say, that there may not be cases in which the judge may, without impropriety take upon himself to construe the words of a foreign law, and determine their application to the case in question, especially if there should be a variance or want of clearness in the testimony.[22]

23.3.4 Who is an expert?

There is no statutory definition of an expert. Nevertheless, in order to be an expert a person does not have to be qualified to practise law in the relevant foreign jurisdiction. Section 4(1) of the Civil Evidence Act 1972 provides:

> It is hereby declared that in civil proceedings a person who is suitably qualified to do so on account of his knowledge or experience is competent to give expert evidence as to the law of any country or territory outside the United Kingdom or of any part of the United Kingdom other than England and Wales, irrespective of whether he has acted or is entitled to act as a legal practitioner there.

This provision is thought to be declaratory of the pre-existing common law. While some of the older cases suggest that even a bank manager,[23] a former colonial governor,[24] or a diplomatic official,[25] may be suitably qualified to give expert evidence on questions of

18. Scott LJ in *A/S Tallinna Laevauhisus* v. *Estonian State Steamship Line* (1947) 80 L Ll Rep 99, 108.
19. As in *Dubai Bank Ltd* v. *Galadari (No. 5)*, *The Times*, 26 June 1990.
20. *Bumper Development Corporation* v. *Commissioner of Police of the Metropolis* [1991] 1 WLR 1362, 1369.
21. (1845) 8 Beav 527. See also *Concha* v. *Murrieta* (1889) 40 ChD 543.
22. (1845) 8 Beav 527, 537.
23. *De Beéche* v. *South American Stores (Gath & Chaves) Ltd* [1935] AC 148.
24. *Cooper-King* v. *Cooper-King* [1900] P 65.
25. *In the Goods of Dost Aly Khan* (1880) 6 PD 6.

foreign law with which they are familiar by virtue of their profession or calling, the modern practice is to use as expert witnesses legal practitioners and academic lawyers who have specialised in the foreign legal system.

23.3.5 Decisions on points of foreign law in subsequent cases

23.3.5.1 At common law, a decision on a point of foreign law is not binding in subsequent cases. This is a logical consequence of the doctrine which states that in English proceedings foreign law is a question of fact. In *Lazard Brothers & Co* v. *Midland Bank Ltd* Lord Wright indicated that the court may not take judicial cognisance of the law of a foreign country "even though the foreign law has already been proved before it in another case".[26] The common law rule is that the court must act upon the evidence before it in the actual case.

23.3.5.2 The strict common law position has, however, been modified by section 4(2) of the Civil Evidence Act 1972 which provides:

> Where any question as to the law of any country or territory outside the United Kingdom, or any part of the United Kingdom other than England and Wales, with respect to any matter has been determined (whether before or after the passing of this Act) in any such proceedings as are mentioned in subsection (4) below, then in any civil proceedings (not being a court which can take judicial notice of the law of that country, territory or part with respect to that matter):
> (a) any finding made or decision given on that question in the first-mentioned proceedings shall, if reported or recorded in citable form, be admissible in evidence for the purpose of proving the law of that country, territory or part with respect to that matter; and
> (b) if that finding or decision, as so reported or recorded, is adduced for that purpose, the law of that country, territory or part with respect to that matter shall be taken to be in accordance with that finding or decision unless the contrary is proved:
> Provided that paragraph (b) above shall not apply in the case of a finding or decision which conflicts with another finding or decision on the same question adduced by virtue of this subsection in the same proceedings.

23.3.5.3 The proceedings, whether civil or criminal, to which subsection (2) applies are listed in subsection (4):

> (a) proceedings at first instance in any of the following courts, namely the High Court, the Crown Court, . . .;
> (b) appeals arising out of any such proceedings as are mentioned in paragraph (a) above;
> (c) proceedings in the Judicial Committee of the Privy Council on appeal (whether to Her Majesty in Council or to the Judicial Committee as such) from any decision of any court outside the United Kingdom.

The effect of these provisions is that, whereas normally it is for the party pleading the foreign law to prove it, once a particular question of foreign law has been decided by an English court, the English judgment is evidence of the foreign law unless it can be proved to be wrong. Section 4(2) does not, however, create a system of binding precedent in cases involving questions of foreign law, since the existence of an English decision on a point of foreign law raises no more than a presumption.[27]

26. [1933] AC 289, 297–298.
27. The procedure to be followed when reliance is to be placed on the Civil Evidence Act 1972 is set out in RSC, Order 38, r. 7.

23.3.6 Seeking outside help

23.3.6.1 Under the Evidence (Colonial Statutes) Act 1907 copies of legislation of a "British possession" may be admitted as evidence without having to be proved by expert evidence. This Act is still in force in relation to numerous Commonwealth countries.[28] Under the British Law Ascertainment Act 1859 the court may state a case for an opinion of a court of any part of Her Majesty's dominions. The opinion of the foreign court is binding (unless the court which states the case has appellate jurisdiction over the court which gives the opinion). There are very few reported instances in which this procedure has been used and it would appear that, for most practical purposes, the 1859 Act has become a dead letter.

23.3.6.2 Attention may also be drawn to the European Convention on Information on Foreign Law of 1968. This Convention, which came into force on 17 December 1969, is designed to assist courts in obtaining information on foreign law in civil and commercial matters. The Convention has been ratified by all the EC Member States, except for Ireland. Although the Convention has not been implemented by legislation in the United Kingdom, it has been argued that in an appropriate case the court may be able to take advantage of the Convention's provisions for mutual judicial assistance, either under its powers to issue a letter of request for the taking of evidence abroad[29] or under the court's inherent jurisdiction.[30]

23.4 APPEALS

As a general rule the appellate courts are unwilling to overturn findings of fact made by courts of first instance. Where questions of foreign law are involved the appellate courts are more ready to interfere on the basis that a question of foreign law is "a question of fact of a peculiar kind".[31] The appellate court will examine the evidence of foreign law which was before the lower court and decide for itself whether that evidence justifies the conclusion to which the lower court came.[32] The appellate court "must not by uncritical acceptance of a trial judge's conclusions of fact shirk its function of considering the evidence afresh and forming its own view of the cogency of the rival contentions, whilst of course always remembering that the trial judge had the undoubted initial advantage of having seen and heard the witnesses".[33]

28. See O'Malley & Layton, *European Civil Practice* (1989) p. 238, n. 79.
29. RSC, Order 39, r. 13.
30. O'Malley & Layton, *European Civil Practice* (1989) p. 239.
31. Megaw LJ in *Dalmia Dairy Industries Ltd* v. *National Bank of Pakistan* [1978] 2 Lloyd's Rep 223, 286.
32. Cairns J in *Parkasho* v. *Singh* [1968] P 233, 250.
33. Megaw LJ in *Dalmia Dairy Industries Ltd* v. *National Bank of Pakistan* [1978] 2 Lloyd's Rep 223, 286.

APPENDICES

CIVIL JURISDICTION AND JUDGMENTS ACT 1982 (c 27)

An Act to make further provision about the jurisdiction of courts and tribunals in the United Kingdom and certain other territories and about the recognition and enforcement of judgments given in the United Kingdom or elsewhere; to provide for the modification of certain provisions relating to legal aid; and for connected purposes.

[13th July 1982]

PART I. IMPLEMENTATION OF THE CONVENTIONS: MAIN IMPLEMENTING PROVISIONS

Interpretation of references to the Conventions and Contracting States

1.—(1) In this Act—

"the 1968 Convention" means the Convention on jurisdiction and the enforcement of judgments in civil and commercial matters (including the Protocol annexed to that Convention), signed at Brussels on 27th September 1968;

"the 1971 Protocol" means the Protocol on the interpretation of the 1968 Convention by the European Court, signed at Luxembourg on 3rd June 1971;

"the Accession Convention" means the Convention on the accession to the 1968 Convention and the 1971 Protocol of Denmark, the Republic of Ireland and the United Kingdom, signed at Luxembourg on 9th October 1978;

"the 1982 Accession Convention" means the Convention on the accession of the Hellenic Republic to the 1968 Convention and the 1971 Protocol, with the adjustments made to them by the Accession Convention, signed at Luxembourg on 25th October 1982;

"the 1989 Accession Convention" means the Convention on the accession of the Kingdom of Spain and the Portuguese Republic to the 1968 Convention and the 1971 Protocol, with the adjustments made to them by the Accession Convention and the 1982 Accession Convention, signed at Donostia—San Sebastian on 26th May 1989;

"the Brussels Conventions" means the 1968 Convention, the 1971 Protocol, the Accession Convention, the 1982 Accession Convention and the 1989 Accession Convention;

"the Lugano Convention" means the Convention on jurisdiction and the enforcement of judgments in civil and commercial matters (including the Protocols annexed to that Convention) opened for signature at Lugano on 16th September 1988 and signed by the United Kingdom on 18th September 1989.

(2) In this Act, unless the context otherwise requires—

(a) references to, or to any provision of, the 1968 Convention or the 1971 Protocol are references to that Convention, Protocol or provision as amended by the Accession Convention, the 1982 Accession Convention and the 1989 Accession Convention; and

(b) any reference in any provision to a numbered Article without more is a reference—

(i) to the Article so numbered of the 1968 Convention, in so far as the provision applies in relation to that Convention, and

(ii) to the Article so numbered of the Lugano Convention, in so far as the provision applies in relation to that Convention,

and any reference to a sub-division of a numbered Article shall be construed accordingly.

(3) In this Act—

"Contracting State", without more, in any provision means—

(a) in the application of the provision in relation to the Brussels Conventions, a Brussels Contracting State; and

(b) in the application of the provision in relation to the Lugano Convention, a Lugano Contracting State;

"Brussels Contracting State" means—

(a) one of the original parties to the 1968 Convention (Belgium, the Federal Republic of Germany, France, Italy, Luxembourg and the Netherlands); or

(b) one of the parties acceding to that Convention under the Accession Convention (Denmark, the Republic of Ireland and the United Kingdom), or under the 1982 Accession Convention (the Hellenic Republic), or under the 1989 Accession Convention (Spain and Portugal),

being a state in respect of which the Accession Convention has entered into force in accordance with Article 39 of that Convention, or being a state in respect of which the 1982 Accession Convention has entered into force in accordance with Article 15 of that Convention, or being a state in respect of which the 1989 Accession Convention has entered into force in accordance with Article 32 of that Convention, as the case might be.

"Lugano Contracting State" means one of the original parties to the Lugano Convention, that is to say—

Austria, Belgium, Denmark, Finland, France, the Federal Republic of Germany, the Hellenic Republic, Iceland, the Republic of Ireland, Italy, Luxembourg, the Netherlands, Norway, Portugal, Spain, Sweden, Switzerland and the United Kingdom,

being a State in relation to which that Convention has taken effect in accordance with paragraph 3 or 4 of Article 61.

The Brussels Conventions to have the force of law

2.—(1) The Brussels Conventions shall have the force of law in the United Kingdom, and judicial notice shall be taken of them.

(2) For convenience of reference there are set out in Schedules 1, 2, 3, 3A and 3B respectively the English texts of—

(a) the 1968 Convention as amended by Titles II and III of the Accession Convention, by Titles II and III of the 1982 Accession Convention and by Titles II and III of, and Annex I(d) to, the 1989 Accession Convention;

(b) the 1971 Protocol as amended by Title IV of the Accession Convention, by Title IV of the 1982 Accession Convention and by Title IV of the 1989 Accession Convention;

(c) Titles V and VI of the Accession Convention (transitional and final provisions) as amended by Title V of the 1989 Accession Convention;

(d) Titles V and VI of the 1982 Accession Convention (transitional and final provisions); and

(e) Titles VI and VII of the 1989 Accession Convention (transitional and final provisions),

being texts prepared from the authentic English texts referred to in Articles 37 and 41 of the Accession Convention, in Article 17 of the 1982 Accession Convention and in Article 34 of the 1989 Accession Convention.

Interpretation of the Brussels Conventions

3.—(1) Any question as to the meaning or effect of any provision of the Brussels Conventions shall, if not referred to the European Court in accordance with the 1971 Protocol, be determined in accordance with the principles laid down by and any relevant decision of the European Court.

(2) Judicial notice shall be taken of any decision of, or expression of opinion by, the European Court on any such question.

(3) Without prejudice to the generality of subsection (1), the following reports (which are reproduced in the Official Journal of the Communities), namely—

(a) the reports by Mr. P. Jenard on the 1968 Convention and the 1971 Protocol; and

(b) the report by Professor Peter Schlosser on the Accession Convention; and

(c) the report by Professor Demetrios I. Evrigenis and Professor K. D. Kerameus on the 1982 Accession Convention; and

(d) the report by Mr. Martinho de Almeida Cruz, Mr. Manuel Desantes Real and Mr. P. Jenard on the 1989 Accession Convention,

may be considered in ascertaining the meaning or effect of any provision of the Brussels Conventions and shall be given such weight as is appropriate in the circumstances.

The Lugano Convention to have the force of law

3A.—(1) The Lugano Convention shall have the force of law in the United Kingdom, and judicial notice shall be taken of it.

(2) For convenience of reference there is set out in Schedule 3C the English text of the Lugano Convention.

Interpretation of the Lugano Convention

3B.—(1) In determining any question as to the meaning or effect of a provision of the Lugano Convention, a court in the United Kingdom shall, in accordance with Protocol No. 2 to that Convention, take account of any principles laid down in any relevant decision delivered by a court of any other Lugano Contracting State concerning provisions of the Convention.

(2) Without prejudice to any practice of the courts as to the matters which may be considered apart from this section, the report on the Lugano Convention by Mr. P. Jenard and Mr. G. Möller (which is reproduced in the Official Journal of the Communities of 28th July 1990) may be considered in ascertaining the meaning or effect of any provision of the Convention and shall be given such weight as is appropriate in the circumstances.

Enforcement of judgments other than maintenance orders

4.—(1) A judgment, other than a maintenance order, which is the subject of an application under Article 31 of the 1968 Convention or of the Lugano Convention for its enforcement in any part of the United Kingdom shall, to the extent that its enforcement is authorised by the appropriate court, be registered in the prescribed manner in that court.

In this subsection "the appropriate court" means the court to which the application is made in pursuance of Article 32 (that is to say, the High Court or the Court of Session).

(2) Where a judgment is registered under this section, the reasonable costs or expenses of and incidental to its registration shall be recoverable as if they were sums recoverable under the judgment.

(3) A judgment registered under this section shall, for the purposes of its enforcement, be of the same force and effect, the registering court shall have in relation to its enforcement the same powers, and proceedings for or with respect to its enforcement may be taken, as if the judgment had been originally given by the registering court and had (where relevant) been entered.

(4) Subsection (3) is subject to Article 39 (restriction on enforcement where appeal pending or time for appeal unexpired), to section 7 and to any provision made by rules of court as to the manner in which and conditions subject to which a judgment registered under this section may be enforced.

. . .

Appeals under Article 37, second paragraph and Article 41

6.—(1) The single further appeal on a point of law referred to in the 1968 Convention and the Lugano Convention in Article 37, second paragraph and Article 41 in relation to the recognition or enforcement of a judgment other than a maintenance order lies—

(a) in England and Wales or Northern Ireland, to the Court of Appeal or to the House of Lords in accordance with Part II of the Administration of Justice Act 1969 (appeals direct from the High Court to the House of Lords);

(b) in Scotland, to the Inner House of the Court of Session.

(2) Paragraph (a) of subsection (1) has effect notwithstanding section 15(2) of the Administration of Justice Act 1969 (exclusion of direct appeal to the House of Lords in cases where no appeal to that House lies from a decision of the Court of Appeal).

. . .

Interest on registered judgments

7.—(1) Subject to subsection (4), where in connection with an application for registration of a judgment under section 4 or 5 the applicant shows—

(a) that the judgment provides for the payment of a sum of money; and

(b) that in accordance with the law of the Contracting State in which the judgment was given interest on that sum is recoverable under the judgment from a particular date or time,

the rate of interest and the date or time from which it is so recoverable shall be registered with the judgment and, subject to any provision made under subsection (2), the debt resulting, apart from section 4(2), from the registration of the judgment shall carry interest in accordance with the registered particulars.

(2) Provision may be made by rules of court as to the manner in which and the periods by reference to which any interest payable by virtue of subsection (1) is to be calculated and paid, including provision for such interest to cease to accrue as from a prescribed date.

(3) Costs or expenses recoverable by virtue of section 4(2) shall carry interest as if they were the subject of an order for the payment of costs or expenses made by the registering court on the date of registration.

...

(5) Except as mentioned in subsection (4), debts under judgments registered under section 4 or 5 shall carry interest only as provided by this section.

...

Provisions supplementary to Title VII of 1968 Convention

9.—(1) The provisions of Title VII of the 1968 Convention and, apart from Article 54B, of Title VII of the Lugano Convention (relationship between the Convention in question and other conventions to which Contracting States are or may become parties) shall have effect in relation to—

(a) any statutory provision, whenever passed or made, implementing any such other convention in the United Kingdom; and

(b) any rule of law so far as it has the effect of so implementing any such other convention,

as they have effect in relation to that other convention itself.

(1A) Any question arising as to whether it is the Lugano Convention or any of the Brussels Conventions which applies in the circumstances of a particular case falls to be determined in accordance with the provisions of Article 54B of the Lugano Convention.

(2) Her Majesty may by Order in Council declare a provision of a convention entered into by the United Kingdom to be a provision whereby the United Kingdom assumed an obligation of a kind provided for in Article 59 (which allows a Contracting State to agree with a third State to withhold recognition in certain cases from a judgment given by a court in another Contracting State which took jurisdiction on one of the grounds mentioned in the second paragraph of Article 3).

Allocation within UK of jurisdiction with respect to trusts and consumer contracts

10.—(1) The provisions of this section have effect for the purpose of allocating within the United Kingdom jurisdiction in certain proceedings in respect of which the 1968 Convention or the Lugano Convention confers jurisdiction on the courts of the United Kingdom generally and to which section 16 does not apply.

(2) Any proceedings which by virtue of Article 5(6) (trusts) are brought in the United Kingdom shall be brought in the courts of the part of the United Kingdom in which the trust is domiciled.

(3) Any proceedings which by virtue of the first paragraph of Article 14 (consumer contracts) are brought in the United Kingdom by a consumer on the ground that he is himself domiciled there shall be brought in the courts of the part of the United Kingdom in which he is domiciled.

Proof and admissibility of certain judgments and related documents

11.—(1) For the purposes of the 1968 Convention and the Lugano Convention—

(a) a document, duly authenticated, which purports to be a copy of a judgment given by a court of a Contracting State other than the United Kingdom shall without further proof be deemed to be a true copy, unless the contrary is shown; and

(b) the original or a copy of any such document as is mentioned in Article 46(2) or 47 (supporting documents to be produced by a party seeking recognition or enforcement of a judgment) shall be evidence, and in Scotland sufficient evidence, of any matter to which it relates.

(2) A document purporting to be a copy of a judgment given by any such court as is mentioned in subsection (1)(a) is duly authenticated for the purposes of this section if it purports—

(a) to bear the seal of that court; or

(b) to be certified by any person in his capacity as a judge or officer of that court to be a true copy of a judgment given by that court.

(3) Nothing in this section shall prejudice the admission in evidence of any document which is admissible apart from this section.

...

PART II. JURISDICTION AND RECOGNITION AND ENFORCEMENT OF JUDGMENTS WITHIN UNITED KINGDOM

Allocation within UK of jurisdiction in certain civil proceedings

16.—(1) The provisions set out in Schedule 4 (which contains a modified version of Title II of the 1968 Convention) shall have effect for determining, for each part of the United Kingdom, whether the courts of law of that part, or any particular court of law in that part, have or has jurisdiction in proceedings where—

(a) the subject-matter of the proceedings is within the scope of the 1968 Convention as determined by Article 1 (whether or not that or any other Convention has effect in relation to the proceedings); and

(b) the defendant or defender is domiciled in the United Kingdom or the proceedings are of a kind mentioned in Article 16 of the 1968 Convention (exclusive jurisdiction regardless of domicile).

(2) In Schedule 4 modifications of Title II of the 1968 Convention are indicated as follows—

(a) modifications by way of omission are indicated by dots; and

(b) within each Article words resulting from modifications by way of addition or substitution are printed in heavy type.

(3) In determining any question as to the meaning or effect of any provision contained in Schedule 4—

(a) regard shall be had to any relevant principles laid down by the European Court in connection with Title II of the 1968 Convention and to any relevant decision of that court as to the meaning or effect of any provision of that Title; and

(b) without prejudice to the generality of paragraph (a), the reports mentioned in section 3(3) may be considered and shall, so far as relevant, be given such weight as is appropriate in the circumstances.

(4) The provisions of this section and Schedule 4 shall have effect subject to the 1968 Convention and the Lugano Convention and to the provisions of section 17.

...

Exclusion of certain proceedings from Schedule 4

17.—(1) Schedule 4 shall not apply to proceedings of any description listed in Schedule 5 or to proceedings in Scotland under any enactment which confers jurisdiction on a Scottish court in respect of a specific subject-matter on specific grounds.

...

Enforcement of UK judgments in other parts of UK

18.—(1) In relation to any judgment to which this section applies—

(a) Schedule 6 shall have effect for the purpose of enabling any money provisions contained in the judgment to be enforced in a part of the United Kingdom other than the part in which the judgment was given; and

(b) Schedule 7 shall have effect for the purpose of enabling any non-money provisions so contained to be so enforced.

(2) In this section "judgment" means any of the following (references to the giving of a judgment being construed accordingly)—

(a) any judgment or order (by whatever name called) given or made by a court of law in the United Kingdom;

(b) any judgment or order not within paragraph (a) which has been entered in England and Wales or Northern Ireland in the High Court or a county court;

(c) any document which in Scotland has been registered for execution in the Books of Council and Session or in the sheriff court books kept for any sheriffdom;

(d) any award or order made by a tribunal in any part of the United Kingdom which is enforceable in that part without an order of a court of law;

(e) an arbitration award which has become enforceable in the part of the United Kingdom in which it was given in the same manner as a judgment given by a court of law in that part;

and, subject to the following provisions of this section, this section applies to all such judgments.

(3) Subject to subsection (4), this section does not apply to—

(a) a judgment given in proceedings in a magistrates' court in England and Wales or Northern Ireland;

(b) a judgment given in proceedings other than civil proceedings;

(ba) a judgment given in the exercise of jurisdiction in relation to insolvency law, within the meaning of section 426 of the Insolvency Act 1986;

(c) a judgment given in proceedings relating to—

(i), (ii) ...

(iii) the obtaining of title to administer the estate of a deceased person.

(4) This section applies, whatever the nature of the proceedings in which it is made, to—

(a) a decree issued under section 13 of the Court of Exchequer (Scotland) Act 1856 (recovery of certain rentcharges and penalties by process of the Court of Session);

(b) an order which is enforceable in the same manner as a judgment of the High Court in England and Wales by virtue of section 16 of the Contempt of Court Act 1981 or section 140 of the Supreme Court Act 1981 (which relate to fines for contempt of court and forfeiture of recognisances).

(5) This section does not apply to so much of any judgment as—

...

(d) is a provisional (including protective) measure other than an order for the making of an interim payment;

and except where otherwise stated references to a judgment to which this section applies are to such a judgment exclusive of any such provisions.

...

(7) This section does not apply to a judgment of a court outside the United Kingdom which falls to be treated for the purposes of its enforcement as a judgment of a court of law in the United Kingdom by virtue of registration under Part II of the Administration of Justice Act 1920, Part I of the Foreign Judgments (Reciprocal Enforcement) Act 1933, Part I of the Maintenance Orders (Reciprocal Enforcement) Act 1972 or section 4 or 5 of this Act.

(8) A judgment to which this section applies, other than a judgment within paragraph (e) of subsection (2), shall not be enforced in another part of the United Kingdom except by way of registration under Schedule 6 or 7.

Recognition of UK judgments in other parts of UK

19.—(1) A judgment to which this section applies given in one part of the United Kingdom shall not be refused recognition in another part of the United Kingdom solely on the ground that, in relation to that judgment, the court which gave it was not a court of competent jurisdiction according to the rules of private international law in force in that other part.

(2) Subject to subsection (3), this section applies to any judgment to which section 18 applies.

(3) This section does not apply to—
- (a) the documents mentioned in paragraph (c) of the definition of "judgment" in section 18(2);
- (b) the awards and orders mentioned in paragraphs (d) and (e) of that definition;
- (c) the decrees and orders referred to in section 18(4).

...

PART IV. MISCELLANEOUS PROVISIONS: PROVISIONS RELATING TO JURISDICTION

...

Interim relief in England and Wales and Northern Ireland in the absence of substantive proceedings

25.—(1) The High Court in England and Wales or Northern Ireland shall have power to grant interim relief where—
- (a) proceedings have been or are to be commenced in a Brussels or Lugano Contracting State other than the United Kingdom or in a part of the United Kingdom other than that in which the High Court in question exercises jurisdiction; and
- (b) they are or will be proceedings whose subject-matter is within the scope of the 1968 Convention as determined by Article 1 (whether or not that or any other Convention has effect in relation to the proceedings).

(2) On an application for any interim relief under subsection (1) the court may refuse to grant that relief if, in the opinion of the court, the fact that the court has no jurisdiction apart from this section in relation to the subject-matter of the proceedings in question makes it inexpedient for the court to grant it.

(3) Her Majesty may by Order in Council extend the power to grant interim relief conferred by subsection (1) so as to make it exercisable in relation to proceedings of any of the following descriptions, namely—
- (a) proceedings commenced or to be commenced otherwise than in a Brussels or Lugano Contracting State;
- (b) proceedings whose subject-matter is not within the scope of the 1968 Convention as determined by Article 1;
- (c) arbitration proceedings.

(4) An Order in Council under subsection (3)—
- (a) may confer power to grant only specified descriptions of interim relief;
- (b) may make different provision for different classes of proceedings, for proceedings pending in different countries or courts outside the United Kingdom or in different parts of the United Kingdom, and for other different circumstances; and
- (c) may impose conditions or restrictions on the exercise of any power conferred by the Order.

(5) An Order in Council under subsection (3) which confers power to grant interim relief in relation to arbitration proceedings may provide for the repeal of any provision of section 12(6) of the Arbitration Act 1950 or section 21(1) of the Arbitration Act (Northern Ireland) 1937 to the extent that it is superseded by the provisions of the Order.

(6) Any Order in Council under subsection (3) shall be subject to annulment in pursuance of a resolution of either House of Parliament.

(7) In this section "interim relief", in relation to the High Court in England and Wales or Northern Ireland, means interim relief of any kind which that court has power to grant in proceedings relating to matters within its jurisdiction, other than—
- (a) a warrant for the arrest of property; or
- (b) provision for obtaining evidence.

Security in Admiralty proceedings in England and Wales or Northern Ireland in case of stay, etc.

26.—(1) Where in England and Wales or Northern Ireland a court stays or dismisses Admiralty proceedings on the ground that the dispute in question should be submitted to arbitration or to the determination of the courts of another part of the United Kingdom or of an overseas country, the court may, if in those proceedings property has been arrested or bail or other security has been given to prevent or obtain release from arrest—

- (a) order that the property arrested be retained as security for the satisfaction of any award or judgment which—
  - (i) is given in respect of the dispute in the arbitration or legal proceedings in favour of which those proceedings are stayed or dismissed; and
  - (ii) is enforceable in England and Wales or, as the case may be, in Northern Ireland; or
- (b) order that the stay or dismissal of those proceedings be conditional on the provision of equivalent security for the satisfaction of any such award or judgment.

(2) Where a court makes an order under subsection (1), it may attach such conditions to the order as it thinks fit, in particular conditions with respect to the institution or prosecution of the relevant arbitration or legal proceedings.

(3) Subject to any provision made by rules of court and to any necessary modifications, the same law and practice shall apply in relation to property retained in pursuance of an order made by a court under subsection (1) as would apply if it were held for the purposes of proceedings in that court.

. . .

Proceedings in England and Wales or Northern Ireland for torts to immovable property

30.—(1) The jurisdiction of any court in England and Wales or Northern Ireland to entertain proceedings for trespass to, or any other tort affecting, immovable property shall extend to cases in which the property in question is situated outside that part of the United Kingdom unless the proceedings are principally concerned with a question of the title to, or the right to possession of, that property.

(2) Subsection (1) has effect subject to the 1968 Convention and the Lugano Convention and to the provisions set out in Schedule 4.

Overseas judgments given against states, etc.

31.—(1) A judgment given by a court of an overseas country against a state other than the United Kingdom or the state to which that court belongs shall be recognised and enforced in the United Kingdom if, and only if—

- (a) it would be so recognised and enforced if it had not been given against a state; and
- (b) that court would have had jurisdiction in the matter if it had applied rules corresponding to those applicable to such matters in the United Kingdom in accordance with sections 2 to 11 of the State Immunity Act 1978.

(2) References in subsection (1) to a judgment given against a state include references to judgments of any of the following descriptions given in relation to a state—

- (a) judgments against the government, or a department of the government, of the state but not (except as mentioned in paragraph (c)) judgments against an entity which is distinct from the executive organs of government;
- (b) judgments against the sovereign or head of state in his public capacity;
- (c) judgments against any such separate entity as is mentioned in paragraph (a) given in proceedings relating to anything done by it in the exercise of the sovereign authority of the state.

(3) Nothing in subsection (1) shall affect the recognition or enforcement in the United Kingdom of a judgment to which Part I of the Foreign Judgments (Reciprocal Enforcement) Act 1933 applies by virtue of section 4 of the Carriage of Goods by Road Act 1965, section 17(4) of the Nuclear Installations Act 1965, section 13(3) of the Merchant Shipping (Oil Pollution) Act 1971, section 6 of the International Transport Conventions Act 1983 or section 5 of the Carriage of Passengers by Road Act 1974.

(4) Sections 12, 13 and 14(3) and (4) of the State Immunity Act 1978 (service of process and procedural privileges) shall apply to proceedings for the recognition or enforcement in the United Kingdom of a judgment given by a court of an overseas country (whether or not that judgment is within subsection (1) of this section) as they apply to other proceedings.

(5) In this section "state", in the case of a federal state, includes any of its constituent territories.

Overseas judgments given in proceedings brought in breach of agreement for settlement of disputes

32.—(1) Subject to the following provisions of this section, a judgment given by a court of an overseas country in any proceedings shall not be recognised or enforced in the United Kingdom if—

(a) the bringing of those proceedings in that court was contrary to an agreement under which the dispute in question was to be settled otherwise than by proceedings in the courts of that country; and
(b) those proceedings were not brought in that court by, or with the agreement of, the person against whom the judgment was given; and
(c) that person did not counterclaim in the proceedings or otherwise submit to the jurisdiction of that court.

(2) Subsection (1) does not apply where the agreement referred to in paragraph (a) of that subsection was illegal, void or unenforceable or was incapable of being performed for reasons not attributable to the fault of the party bringing the proceedings in which the judgment was given.

(3) In determining whether a judgment given by a court of an overseas country should be recognised or enforced in the United Kingdom, a court in the United Kingdom shall not be bound by any decision of the overseas court relating to any of the matters mentioned in subsection (1) or (2).

(4) Nothing in subsection (1) shall affect the recognition or enforcement in the United Kingdom of—

(a) a judgment which is required to be recognised or enforced there under the 1968 Convention or the Lugano Convention;
(b) a judgment to which Part I of the Foreign Judgments (Reciprocal Enforcement) Act 1933 applies by virtue of section 4 of the Carriage of Goods by Road Act 1965, section 17(4) of the Nuclear Installations Act 1965, section 13(3) of the Merchant Shipping (Oil Pollution) Act 1971, section 6 of the International Transport Conventions Act 1983, section 5 of the Carriage of Passengers by Road Act 1974 or section 6(4) of the Merchant Shipping Act 1974.

Certain steps not to amount to submission to jurisdiction of overseas court

33.—(1) For the purposes of determining whether a judgment given by a court of an overseas country should be recognised or enforced in England and Wales or Northern Ireland, the person against whom the judgment was given shall not be regarded as having submitted to the jurisdiction of the court by reason only of the fact that he appeared (conditionally or otherwise) in the proceedings for all or any one or more of the following purposes, namely—

(a) to contest the jurisdiction of the court;
(b) to ask the court to dismiss or stay the proceedings on the ground that the dispute in question should be submitted to arbitration or to the determination of the courts of another country;
(c) to protect, or obtain the release of, property seized or threatened with seizure in the proceedings.

(2) Nothing in this section shall affect the recognition or enforcement in England and Wales or Northern Ireland of a judgment which is required to be recognised or enforced there under the 1968 Convention or the Lugano Convention.

Certain judgments a bar to further proceedings on the same cause of action

34.—No proceedings may be brought by a person in England and Wales or Northern Ireland on a cause of action in respect of which a judgment has been given in his favour in proceedings between the same parties, or their privies, in a court in another part of the United Kingdom or in a court of an overseas country, unless that judgment is not enforceable or entitled to recognition in England and Wales or, as the case may be, in Northern Ireland.

...

PART V. SUPPLEMENTARY AND GENERAL PROVISIONS: DOMICILE

Domicile of individuals

41.—(1) Subject to Article 52 (which contains provisions for determining whether a party is domiciled in a Contracting State), the following provisions of this section determine, for the purposes of the 1968 Convention, the Lugano Convention and this Act, whether an individual is domiciled in the United Kingdom or in a particular part of, or place in, the United Kingdom or in a state other than a Contracting State.

(2) An individual is domiciled in the United Kingdom if and only if—

(a) he is resident in the United Kingdom; and

(b) the nature and circumstances of his residence indicate that he has a substantial connection with the United Kingdom.

(3) Subject to subsection (5), an individual is domiciled in a particular part of the United Kingdom if and only if—

(a) he is resident in that part; and

(b) the nature and circumstances of his residence indicate that he has a substantial connection with that part.

(4) An individual is domiciled in a particular place in the United Kingdom if and only if he—

(a) is domiciled in the part of the United Kingdom in which that place is situated; and

(b) is resident in that place.

(5) An individual who is domiciled in the United Kingdom but in whose case the requirements of subsection (3)(b) are not satisfied in relation to any particular part of the United Kingdom shall be treated as domiciled in the part of the United Kingdom in which he is resident.

(6) In the case of an individual who—

(a) is resident in the United Kingdom, or in a particular part of the United Kingdom; and

(b) has been so resident for the last three months or more,

the requirements of subsection (2)(b) or, as the case may be, subsection (3)(b) shall be presumed to be fulfilled unless the contrary is proved.

(7) An individual is domiciled in a state other than a Contracting State if and only if—

(a) he is resident in that state; and

(b) the nature and circumstances of his residence indicate that he has a substantial connection with that state.

Domicile and seat of corporation or association

42.—(1) For the purposes of this Act the seat of a corporation or association (as determined by this section) shall be treated as its domicile.

(2) The following provisions of this section determine where a corporation or association has its seat—

(a) for the purpose of Article 53 (which for the purposes of the 1968 Convention or, as the case may be, the Lugano Convention equates the domicile of such a body with its seat); and

(b) for the purposes of this Act other than the provisions mentioned in section 43(1)(b) and (c).

(3) A corporation or association has its seat in the United Kingdom if and only if—

(a) it was incorporated or formed under the law of a part of the United Kingdom and has its registered office or some other official address in the United Kingdom; or

(b) its central management and control is exercised in the United Kingdom.

(4) A corporation or association has its seat in a particular part of the United Kingdom if and only if it has its seat in the United Kingdom and—

(a) it has its registered office or some other official address in that part; or

(b) its central management and control is exercised in that part; or
(c) it has a place of business in that part.

(5) A corporation or association has its seat in a particular place in the United Kingdom if and only if it has its seat in the part of the United Kingdom in which that place is situated and—

(a) it has its registered office or some other official address in that place; or
(b) its central management and control is exercised in that place; or
(c) it has a place of business in that place.

(6) Subject to subsection (7), a corporation or association has its seat in a state other than the United Kingdom if and only if—

(a) it was incorporated or formed under the law of that state and has its registered office or some other official address there; or
(b) its central management and control is exercised in that state.

(7) A corporation or association shall not be regarded as having its seat in a Contracting State other than the United Kingdom if it is shown that the courts of that state would not regard it as having its seat there.

(8) In this section—

"business" includes any activity carried on by a corporation or association, and "place of business" shall be construed accordingly;

"official address", in relation to a corporation or association, means an address which it is required by law to register, notify or maintain for the purpose of receiving notices or other communications.

Seat of corporation or association for purposes of Article 16(2) and related provisions

43.—(1) The following provisions of this section determine where a corporation or association has its seat for the purposes of—

(a) Article 16(2) of the 1968 Convention or of the Lugano Convention (which confers exclusive jurisdiction over proceedings relating to the formation or dissolution of such bodies, or to the decisions of their organs);
(b) Articles 5A and 16(2) in Schedule 4; . . .

(2) A corporation or association has its seat in the United Kingdom if and only if—

(a) it was incorporated or formed under the law of a part of the United Kingdom; or
(b) its central management and control is exercised in the United Kingdom.

(3) A corporation or association has its seat in a particular part of the United Kingdom if and only if it has its seat in the United Kingdom and—

(a) subject to subsection (5), it was incorporated or formed under the law of that part; or
(b) being incorporated or formed under the law of a state other than the United Kingdom, its central management and control is exercised in that part.

(4) A corporation or association has its seat in a particular place in Scotland if and only if it has its seat in Scotland and—

(a) it has its registered office or some other official address in that place; or
(b) it has no registered office or other official address in Scotland, but its central management and control is exercised in that place.

(5) A corporation or association incorporated or formed under—

(a) an enactment forming part of the law of more than one part of the United Kingdom; or
(b) an instrument having effect in the domestic law of more than one part of the United Kingdom,

shall, if it has a registered office, be taken to have its seat in the part of the United Kingdom in which that office is situated, and not in any other part of the United Kingdom.

(6) Subject to subsection (7), a corporation or association has its seat in a Contracting State other than the United Kingdom if and only if—

(a) it was incorporated or formed under the law of that state; or
(b) its central management and control is exercised in that state.

(7) A corporation or association shall not be regarded as having its seat in a Contracting State other than the United Kingdom if—

(a) it has its seat in the United Kingdom by virtue of subsection (2)(a); or

(b) it is shown that the courts of that other state would not regard it for the purposes of Article 16(2) as having its seat there.

(8) In this section "official address" has the same meaning as in section 42.

Persons deemed to be domiciled in the United Kingdom for certain purposes

44.—(1) This section applies to—

(a) proceedings within Section 3 of Title II of the 1968 Convention or Section 3 of Title II of the Lugano Convention (insurance contracts), and

(b) proceedings within Section 4 of Title II of either of those Conventions (consumer contracts).

(2) A person who, for the purposes of proceedings to which this section applies arising out of the operations of a branch, agency or other establishment in the United Kingdom, is deemed for the purposes of the 1968 Convention or, as the case may be, of the Lugano Convention to be domiciled in the United Kingdom by virtue of—

(a) Article 8, second paragraph (insurers); or

(b) Article 13, second paragraph (suppliers of goods, services or credit to consumers),

shall, for the purposes of those proceedings, be treated for the purposes of this Act as so domiciled and as domiciled in the part of the United Kingdom in which the branch, agency or establishment in question is situated.

Domicile of trusts

45.—(1) The following provisions of this section determine, for the purposes of the 1968 Convention the Lugano Convention and this Act, where a trust is domiciled.

(2) A trust is domiciled in the United Kingdom if and only if it is by virtue of subsection (3) domiciled in a part of the United Kingdom.

(3) A trust is domiciled in a part of the United Kingdom if and only if the system of law of that part is the system of law with which the trust has its closest and most real connection.

Domicile and seat of the Crown

46.—(1) For the purposes of this Act the seat of the Crown (as determined by this section) shall be treated as its domicile.

(2) The following provisions of this section determine where the Crown has its seat—

(a) for the purposes of the 1968 Convention and the Lugano Convention (in each of which Article 53 equates the domicile of a legal person with its seat); and

(b) for the purposes of this Act.

(3) Subject to the provisions of any Order in Council for the time being in force under subsection (4)—

(a) the Crown in right of Her Majesty's government in the United Kingdom has its seat in every part of, and every place in, the United Kingdom; and

(b) the Crown in right of Her Majesty's government in Northern Ireland has its seat in, and in every place in, Northern Ireland.

(4) Her Majesty may by Order in Council provide that, in the case of proceedings of any specified description against the Crown in right of Her Majesty's government in the United Kingdom, the Crown shall be treated for the purposes of the 1968 Convention the Lugano Convention and this Act as having its seat in, and in every place in, a specified part of the United Kingdom and not in any other part of the United Kingdom.

(5) An Order in Council under subsection (4) may frame a description of proceedings in any way, and in particular may do so by reference to the government department or officer of the Crown against which or against whom they fall to be instituted.

(6) Any Order in Council made under this section shall be subject to annulment in pursuance of a resolution of either House of Parliament.

(7) Nothing in this section applies to the Crown otherwise than in right of Her Majesty's government in the United Kingdom or Her Majesty's government in Northern Ireland.

...

Saving for powers to stay, sist, strike out or dismiss proceedings

49. Nothing in this Act shall prevent any court in the United Kingdom from staying, sisting, striking out or dismissing any proceedings before it, on the ground of forum non conveniens or otherwise, where to do so is not inconsistent with the 1968 Convention or, as the case may be, the Lugano Convention.

Interpretation: general

50. In this Act, unless the context otherwise requires—

"the Accession Convention", "the 1982 Accession Convention" and "the 1989 Accession Convention" have the meaning given by section 1(1);

"Article" and references to sub-divisions of numbered Articles are to be construed in accordance with section 1(2)(b);

"association" means an unincorporated body of persons;

"Brussels Contracting State" has the meaning given by section 1(3);

"the Brussels Conventions" has the meaning given by section 1(1);

"Contracting State" has the meaning given by section 1(3);

"the 1968 Convention" has the meaning given by section 1(1), and references to that Convention and to provisions of it are to be construed in accordance with section 1(2)(a);

. . .

"corporation" means a body corporate, and includes a partnership subsisting under the law of Scotland;

"court", without more, includes a tribunal;

"court of law", in relation to the United Kingdom, means any of the following courts, namely—

(a) the House of Lords,

(b) in England and Wales or Northern Ireland, the Court of Appeal, the High Court, the Crown Court, a county court and a magistrates' court,

(c) in Scotland, the Court of Session and a sheriff court;

"the Crown" is to be construed in accordance with section 51(2);

"enactment" includes an enactment comprised in Northern Ireland legislation;

"judgment", subject to sections 15(1) and 18(2) and to paragraph 1 of Schedules 6 and 7, means any judgment or order (by whatever name called) given or made by a court in any civil proceedings;

"Lugano Contracting State" has the meaning given by section 1(3);

"the Lugano Convention" has the meaning given by section 1(1);

"magistrates' court", in relation to Northern Ireland, means a court of summary jurisdiction;

"modifications" includes additions, omissions and alterations;

"overseas country" means any country or territory outside the United Kingdom;

"part of the United Kingdom" means England and Wales, Scotland or Northern Ireland;

"the 1971 Protocol" has the meaning given by section 1(1), and references to that Protocol and to provisions of it are to be construed in accordance with section 1(2)(a);

. . .

"statutory provision" means any provision contained in an Act, or in any Northern Ireland legislation, or in—

(a) subordinate legislation (as defined in section 21(1) of the Interpretation Act 1978); or

(b) any instrument of a legislative character made under any Northern Ireland legislation;

"tribunal"—

(a) means a tribunal of any description other than a court of law;

(b) in relation to an overseas country, includes, as regards matters relating to maintenance within the meaning of the 1968 Convention, any authority having power to give, enforce, vary or revoke a maintenance order.

Application to Crown

51.—(1) This Act binds the Crown.

(2) In this section and elsewhere in this Act references to the Crown do not include references

to Her Majesty in Her private capacity or to Her Majesty in right of Her Duchy of Lancaster or to the Duke of Cornwall.

...

SCHEDULES

SCHEDULE 1. TEXT OF 1968 CONVENTION, AS AMENDED

CONVENTION ON JURISDICTION AND THE ENFORCEMENT OF JUDGMENTS IN CIVIL AND COMMERCIAL MATTERS

PREAMBLE

THE HIGH CONTRACTING PARTIES TO THE TREATY ESTABLISHING THE EUROPEAN ECONOMIC COMMUNITY,

Desiring to implement the provisions of Article 220 of that Treaty by virtue of which they undertook to secure the simplification of formalities governing the reciprocal recognition and enforcement of judgments of courts or tribunals;

Anxious to strengthen in the Community the legal protection of persons therein established;

Considering that it is necessary for this purpose to determine the international jurisdiction of their courts, to facilitate recognition and to introduce an expeditious procedure for securing the enforcement of judgments, authentic instruments and court settlements;

Have decided to conclude this Convention and to this end have designated as their Plenipotentiaries:

(Designations of Plenipotentiaries of the original six Contracting States)

Who, meeting within the Council, having exchanged their Full Powers, found in good and due form,

Have agreed as follows:

TITLE I. SCOPE

Article 1

This Convention shall apply in civil and commercial matters whatever the nature of the court or tribunal. It shall not extend, in particular, to revenue, customs or administrative matters.

The Convention shall not apply to:

1. the status or legal capacity of natural persons, rights in property arising out of a matrimonial relationship, wills and succession;
2. bankruptcy, proceedings relating to the winding-up of insolvent companies or other legal persons, judicial arrangements, compositions and analogous proceedings;
3. social security;
4. arbitration.

TITLE II. JURISDICTION

Section 1. General Provisions

Article 2

Subject to the provisions of this Convention, persons domiciled in a Contracting State shall, whatever their nationality, be sued in the courts of that State.

Persons who are not nationals of the State in which they are domiciled shall be governed by the rules of jurisdiction applicable to nationals of that State.

Article 3

Persons domiciled in a Contracting State may be sued in the courts of another Contracting State only by virtue of the rules set out in Sections 2 to 6 of this Title.

In particular the following provisions shall not be applicable as against them:

— in Belgium: Article 15 of the civil code (Code civil—Burgerlijk Wetboek) and Article 638 of the judicial code (Code judiciaire—Gerechtelijk Wetboek),

— in Denmark: Article 248(2) and (3) of the law on civil procedure (Lov om rettens pleje)

— in the Federal Republic of Germany: Article 23 of the code of civil procedure (Zivilprozeßordnung),

— in Greece: Article 40 of the code of civil procedure (Κώδικας πολιτικής δικονομίας),

— in France: Articles 14 and 15 of the civil code (Code civil),

— in Ireland: the rules which enable jurisdiction to be founded on the document instituting the proceedings having been served on the defendant during his temporary presence in Ireland,

— in Italy: Articles 2 and 4, nos 1 and 2 of the code of civil procedure (Codice di procedura civile),

— in Luxembourg: Articles 14 and 15 of the civil code (Code civil),

— in the Netherlands: Articles 126(3) and 127 of the code of civil procedure (Wetboek van Burgerlijke Rechtsvordering),

— in Portugal: Article 65(1)(c), Article 65(2) and Article 65A(c) of the code of civil procedure (Código de Processo Civil) and Article 11 of the code of labour procedure (Código de Processo de Trabalho),

— in the United Kingdom: the rules which enable jurisdiction to be founded on:

(a) the document instituting the proceedings having been served on the defendant during his temporary presence in the United Kingdom; or

(b) the presence within the United Kingdom of property belonging to the defendant; or

(c) the seizure by the plaintiff of property situated in the United Kingdom.

Article 4

If the defendant is not domiciled in a Contracting State, the jurisdiction of the courts of each Contracting State shall, subject to the provisions of Article 16, be determined by the law of that State.

As against such a defendant, any person domiciled in a Contracting State may, whatever his nationality, avail himself in that State of the rules of jurisdiction there in force, and in particular those specified in the second paragraph of Article 3, in the same way as the nationals of that State.

Section 2. Special Jurisdiction

Article 5

A person domiciled in a Contracting State may, in another Contracting State, be sued:

1. in matters relating to a contract, in the courts for the place of performance of the obligation in question; in matters relating to individual contracts of employment, this place is that where the employee habitually carries out his work, or if the employee does not habitually carry out his work in any one country, the employer may also be sued in the courts for the place where the business which engaged the employee was or is now situated;
2. in matters relating to maintenance, in the courts for the place where the maintenance creditor is domiciled or habitually resident or, if the matter is ancillary to proceedings concerning the status of a person, in the court which, according to its own law, has jurisdiction to entertain those proceedings, unless that jurisdiction is based solely on the nationality of one of the parties;

3. in matters relating to tort, delict or quasi-delict, in the courts for the place where the harmful event occurred;
4. as regards a civil claim for damages or restitution which is based on an act giving rise to criminal proceedings, in the court seised of those proceedings, to the extent that that court has jurisdiction under its own law to entertain civil proceedings;
5. as regards a dispute arising out of the operations of a branch, agency or other establishment, in the courts for the place in which the branch, agency or other establishment is situated;
6. as settlor, trustee or beneficiary of a trust created by the operation of a statute, or by a written instrument, or created orally and evidenced in writing, in the courts of the Contracting State in which the trust is domiciled;
7. as regards a dispute concerning the payment of remuneration claimed in respect of the salvage of a cargo or freight, in the court under the authority of which the cargo or freight in question:
   (a) has been arrested to secure such payment, or
   (b) could have been so arrested, but bail or other security has been given;
   provided that this provision shall apply only if it is claimed that the defendant has an interest in the cargo or freight or had such an interest at the time of salvage.

Article 6

A person domiciled in a Contracting State may also be sued:

1. where he is one of a number of defendants, in the courts for the place where any one of them is domiciled;
2. as a third party in an action on a warranty or guarantee or in any other third party proceedings, in the court seised of the original proceedings, unless these were instituted solely with the object of removing him from the jurisdiction of the court which would be competent in his case;
3. on a counterclaim arising from the same contract or facts on which the original claim was based, in the court in which the original claim is pending;
4. in matters relating to a contract, if the action may be combined with an action against the same defendant in matters relating to rights in rem in immovable property, in the court of the Contracting State in which the property is situated.

Article 6A

Where by virtue of this Convention a court of a Contracting State has jurisdiction in actions relating to liability from the use or operation of a ship, that court, or any other court substituted for this purpose by the internal law of that State, shall also have jurisdiction over claims for limitation of such liability.

Section 3. Jurisdiction in Matters Relating to Insurance

Article 7

In matters relating to insurance, jurisdiction shall be determined by this Section, without prejudice to the provisions of Articles 4 and 5(5).

Article 8

An insurer domiciled in a Contracting State may be sued:

1. in the courts of the State where he is domiciled, or
2. in another Contracting State, in the courts for the place where the policy-holder is domiciled, or
3. if he is a co-insurer, in the courts of a Contracting State in which proceedings are brought against the leading insurer.

An insurer who is not domiciled in a Contracting State but has a branch, agency or other establishment in one of the Contracting States shall, in disputes arising out of the operations of the branch, agency or establishment, be deemed to be domiciled in that State.

Article 9

In respect of liability insurance or insurance of immovable property, the insurer may in addition be sued in the courts for the place where the harmful event occurred. The same applies if movable and immovable property are covered by the same insurance policy and both are adversely affected by the same contingency.

Article 10

In respect of liability insurance, the insurer may also, if the law of the court permits it, be joined in proceedings which the injured party has brought against the insured.

The provisions of Articles 7, 8 and 9 shall apply to actions brought by the injured party directly against the insurer, where such direct actions are permitted.

If the law governing such direct actions provides that the policy-holder or the insured may be joined as a party to the action, the same court shall have jurisdiction over them.

Article 11

Without prejudice to the provisions of the third paragraph of Article 10, an insurer may bring proceedings only in the courts of the Contracting State in which the defendant is domiciled, irrespective of whether he is the policy-holder, the insured or a beneficiary.

The provisions of this Section shall not affect the right to bring a counterclaim in the court in which, in accordance with this Section, the original claim is pending.

Article 12

The provisions of this Section may be departed from only by an agreement on jurisdiction:

1. which is entered into after the dispute has arisen, or
2. which allows the policy-holder, the insured or a beneficiary to bring proceedings in courts other than those indicated in this Section, or
3. which is concluded between a policy-holder and an insurer, both of whom are domiciled in the same Contracting State, and which has the effect of conferring jurisdiction on the courts of that State even if the harmful event were to occur abroad, provided that such an agreement is not contrary to the law of that State, or
4. which is concluded with a policy-holder who is not domiciled in a Contracting State, except in so far as the insurance is compulsory or relates to immovable property in a Contracting State, or
5. which relates to a contract of insurance in so far as it covers one or more of the risks set out in Article 12A.

Article 12A

The following are the risks referred to in Article 12(5):

1. any loss of or damage to:
   (a) sea-going ships, installations situated off-shore or on the high seas, or aircraft, arising from perils which relate to their use for commercial purposes,
   (b) goods in transit other than passengers' baggage where the transit consists of or includes carriage by such ships or aircraft;
2. any liability, other than for bodily injury to passengers or loss of or damage to their baggage:
   (a) arising out of the use or operation of ships, installations or aircraft as referred to in

(1)(a) above in so far as the law of the Contracting State in which such aircraft are registered does not prohibit agreements on jurisdiction regarding insurance of such risks,

(b) for loss or damage caused by goods in transit as described in (1)(b) above;

3. any financial loss connected with the use or operation of ships, installations or aircraft as referred to in (1)(a) above, in particular loss of freight or charter-hire;
4. any risk or interest connected with any of those referred to in (1) to (3) above.

Section 4. Jurisdiction over Consumer Contracts

Article 13

In proceedings concerning a contract concluded by a person for a purpose which can be regarded as being outside his trade or profession, hereinafter called "the consumer", jurisdiction shall be determined by this Section, without prejudice to the provisions of Article 4 and Article 5(5), if it is:

1. a contract for the sale of goods on instalment credit terms; or
2. a contract for a loan repayable by instalments, or for any other form of credit, made to finance the sale of goods; or
3. any other contract for the supply of goods or a contract for the supply of services, and
   (a) in the State of the consumer's domicile the conclusion of the contract was preceded by a specific invitation addressed to him or by advertising, and
   (b) the consumer took in that State the steps necessary for the conclusion of the contract.

Where a consumer enters into a contract with a party who is not domiciled in a Contracting State but has a branch, agency or other establishment in one of the Contracting States, that party shall, in disputes arising out of the operations of the branch, agency or establishment, be deemed to be domiciled in that State.

This Section shall not apply to contracts of transport.

Article 14

A consumer may bring proceedings against the other party to a contract either in the courts of the Contracting State in which that party is domiciled or in the courts of the Contracting State in which he is himself domiciled.

Proceedings may be brought against a consumer by the other party to the contract only in the courts of the Contracting State in which the consumer is domiciled.

These provisions shall not affect the right to bring a counterclaim in the court in which, in accordance with this Section, the original claim is pending.

Article 15

The provisions of this Section may be departed from only by an agreement:

1. which is entered into after the dispute has arisen; or
2. which allows the consumer to bring proceedings in courts other than those indicated in this Section; or
3. which is entered into by the consumer and the other party to the contract, both of whom are at the time of conclusion of the contract domiciled or habitually resident in the same Contracting State, and which confers jurisdiction on the courts of that State, provided that such an agreement is not contrary to the law of that State.

Section 5. Exclusive Jurisdiction

Article 16

The following courts shall have exclusive jurisdiction, regardless of domicile:

1. (a) in proceedings which have as their object rights in rem in immovable property or tenancies of immovable property, the courts of the Contracting State in which the property is situated;

(b) however, in proceedings which have as their object tenancies of immovable property concluded for temporary private use for a maximum period of six consecutive months, the courts of the Contracting State in which the defendant is domiciled shall also have jurisdiction, provided that the landlord and the tenant are natural persons and are domiciled in the same Contracting State;

2. in proceedings which have as their object the validity of the constitution, the nullity or the dissolution of companies or other legal persons or associations of natural or legal persons, or the decisions of their organs, the courts of the Contracting State in which the company, legal person or association has its seat;
3. in proceedings which have as their object the validity of entries in public registers, the courts of the Contracting State in which the register is kept;
4. in proceedings concerned with the registration or validity of patents, trade marks, designs, or other similar rights required to be deposited or registered, the courts of the Contracting State in which the deposit or registration has been applied for, has taken place or is under the terms of an international convention deemed to have taken place;
5. in proceedings concerned with the enforcement of judgments, the courts of the Contracting State in which the judgment has been or is to be enforced.

Section 6. Prorogation of Jurisdiction

Article 17

1. If the parties, one or more of whom is domiciled in a Contracting State, have agreed that a court or the courts of a Contracting State are to have jurisdiction to settle any disputes which have arisen or which may arise in connection with a particular legal relationship, that court or those courts shall have exclusive jurisdiction. Such an agreement conferring jurisdiction shall be either—

(a) in writing or evidenced in writing or,
(b) in a form which accords with practices which the parties have established between themselves, or
(c) in international trade or commerce, in a form which accords with a usage of which the parties are or ought to have been aware and which in such trade or commerce is widely known to, and regularly observed by, parties to contracts of the type involved in the particular trade or commerce concerned.

Where such an agreement is concluded by parties, none of whom is domiciled in a Contracting State, the courts of other Contracting States shall have no jurisdiction over their disputes unless the court or courts chosen have declined jurisdiction.

2. The court or courts of a Contracting State on which a trust instrument has conferred jurisdiction shall have exclusive jurisdiction in any proceedings brought against a settlor, trustee or beneficiary, if relations between these persons or their rights or obligations under the trust are involved.

3. Agreements or provisions of a trust instrument conferring jurisdiction shall have no legal force if they are contrary to the provisions of Articles 12 or 15, or if the courts whose jurisdiction they purport to exclude have exclusive jurisdiction by virtue of Article 16.

4. If an agreement conferring jurisdiction was concluded for the benefit of only one of the parties, that party shall retain the right to bring proceedings in any other court which has jurisdiction by virtue of this Convention.

5. In matters relating to individual contracts of employment an agreement conferring jurisdiction shall have legal force only if it is entered into after the dispute has arisen or if the employee invokes it to seise courts other than those for the defendant's domicile or those specified in Article 5(1).

Article 18

Apart from jurisdiction derived from other provisions of this Convention, a court of a Contracting State before whom a defendant enters an appearance shall have jurisdiction. This rule shall not apply where appearance was entered solely to contest the jurisdiction, or where another court has exclusive jurisdiction by virtue of Article 16.

Section 7. Examination as to Jurisdiction and Admissibility

Article 19

Where a court of a Contracting State is seised of a claim which is principally concerned with a matter over which the courts of another Contracting State have exclusive jurisdiction by virtue of Article 16, it shall declare of its own motion that is has no jurisdiction.

Article 20

Where a defendant domiciled in one Contracting State is sued in a court of another Contracting State and does not enter an appearance, the court shall declare of its own motion that it has no jurisdiction unless its jurisdiction is derived from the provisions of this Convention.

The court shall stay the proceedings so long as it is not shown that the defendant has been able to receive the document instituting the proceedings or an equivalent document in sufficient time to enable him to arrange for his defence, or that all necessary steps have been taken to this end.

The provisions of the foregoing paragraph shall be replaced by those of Article 15 of the Hague Convention of 15 November 1965 on the service abroad of judicial and extrajudicial documents in civil or commercial matters, if the document instituting the proceedings or notice thereof had to be transmitted abroad in accordance with that Convention.

Section 8. Lis Pendens—Related Actions

Article 21

Where proceedings involving the same cause of action and between the same parties are brought in the courts of different Contracting States, any court other than the court first seised shall of its own motion stay its proceedings until such time as the jurisdiction of the court first seised is established.

Where the jurisdiction of the court first seised is established, any court other than the court first seised shall decline jurisdiction in favour of that court.

Article 22

Where related actions are brought in the courts of different Contracting States, any court other than the court first seised may, while the actions are pending at first instance, stay its proceedings.

A court other than the court first seised may also, on the application of one of the parties, decline jurisdiction if the law of that court permits the consolidation of related actions and the court first seised has jurisdiction over both actions.

For the purposes of this Article, actions are deemed to be related where they are so closely connected that it is expedient to hear and determine them together to avoid the risk of irreconcilable judgments resulting from separate proceedings.

Article 23

Where actions come within the exclusive jurisdiction of several courts, any court other than the court first seised shall decline jurisdiction in favour of that court.

Section 9. Provisional, Including Protective, Measures

Article 24

Application may be made to the courts of a Contracting State for such provisional, including protective, measures as may be available under the law of that State, even if, under this Convention, the courts of another Contracting State have jurisdiction as to the substance of the matter.

TITLE III. RECOGNITION AND ENFORCEMENT

Article 25

For the purposes of this Convention, "judgment" means any judgment given by a court or tribunal of a Contracting State, whatever the judgment may be called, including a decree, order, decision or writ of execution, as well as the determination of costs or expenses by an officer of the court.

Section 1. Recognition

Article 26

A judgment given in a Contracting State shall be recognised in the other Contracting States without any special procedure being required.

Any interested party who raises the recognition of a judgment as the principal issue in a dispute may, in accordance with the procedures provided for in Sections 2 and 3 of this Title, apply for a decision that the judgment be recognised.

If the outcome of proceedings in a court of a Contracting State depends on the determination of an incidental question of recognition that court shall have jurisdiction over that question.

Article 27

A judgment shall not be recognised:

1. if such recognition is contrary to public policy in the State in which recognition is sought;
2. where it was given in default of appearance, if the defendant was not duly served with the document which instituted the proceedings or with an equivalent document in sufficient time to enable him to arrange for his defence;
3. if the judgment is irreconcilable with a judgment given in a dispute between the same parties in the State in which recognition is sought;
4. if the court of the State of origin, in order to arrive at its judgment, has decided a preliminary question concerning the status or legal capacity of natural persons, rights in property arising out of a matrimonial relationship, wills or succession in a way that conflicts with a rule of the private international law of the State in which the recognition is sought, unless the same result would have been reached by the application of the rules of private international law of that State;
5. if the judgment is irreconcilable with an earlier judgment given in a non-contracting State involving the same cause of action and between the same parties, provided that this latter judgment fulfils the conditions necessary for its recognition in the State addressed.

Article 28

Moreover, a judgment shall not be recognised if it conflicts with the provisions of Sections 3, 4 or 5 of Title II, or in a case provided for in Article 59.

In its examination of the grounds of jurisdiction referred to in the foregoing paragraph, the court or authority applied to shall be bound by the findings of fact on which the court of the State of origin based its jurisdiction.

Subject to the provisions of the first paragraph, the jurisdiction of the court of the State of origin may not be reviewed; the test of public policy referred to in Article 27(1) may not be applied to the rules relating to jurisdiction.

Article 29

Under no circumstances may a foreign judgment be reviewed as to its substance.

Article 30

A court of a Contracting State in which recognition is sought of a judgment given in another Contracting State may stay the proceedings if an ordinary appeal against the judgment has been lodged.

A court of a Contracting State in which recognition is sought of a judgment given in Ireland or the United Kingdom may stay the proceedings if enforcement is suspended in the State of origin, by reason of an appeal.

Section 2. Enforcement

Article 31

A judgment given in a Contracting State and enforceable in that State shall be enforced in another Contracting State when, on the application of any interested party, it has been declared enforceable there.

However, in the United Kingdom, such a judgment shall be enforced in England and Wales, in Scotland, or in Northern Ireland when, on the application of any interested party, it has been registered for enforcement in that part of the United Kingdom.

Article 32

1. The application shall be submitted:
— in Belgium, to the tribunal de première instance or rechtbank van eerste aanleg,
— in Denmark, to the byret,
— in the Federal Republic of Germany, to the presiding judge of a chamber of the Landgericht,
— in Greece, to the μονομελές πρωτοδικείο,
— in Spain, to the Juzgado de Primera Instancia,
— in France, to the presiding judge of the tribunal de grande instance,
— in Ireland, to the High Court,
— in Italy, to the corte d'appello,
— in Luxembourg, to the presiding judge of the tribunal d'arrondissement,
— in the Netherlands, to the presiding judge of the arrondissementsrechtbank,
— in Portugal, to the Tribunal Judicial de Círculo,
— in the United Kingdom:
(a) in England and Wales, to the High Court of Justice, or in the case of a maintenance judgment to the Magistrates' Court on transmission by the Secretary of State;
(b) in Scotland, to the Court of Session, or in the case of a maintenance judgment to the Sheriff Court on transmission by the Secretary of State;
(c) in Northern Ireland, to the High Court of Justice, or in the case of a maintenance judgment to the Magistrates' Court on transmission by the Secretary of State.

2. The jurisdiction of local courts shall be determined by reference to the place of domicile of the party against whom enforcement is sought. If he is not domiciled in the State in which enforcement is sought, it shall be determined by reference to the place of enforcement.

Article 33

The procedure for making the application shall be governed by the law of the State in which enforcement is sought.

The applicant must give an address for service of process within the area of jurisdiction of the court applied to. However, if the law of the State in which enforcement is sought does not provide for the furnishing of such an address, the applicant shall appoint a representative ad litem.

The documents referred to in Articles 46 and 47 shall be attached to the application.

Article 34

The court applied to shall give its decision without delay; the party against whom enforcement is sought shall not at this stage of the proceedings be entitled to make any submissions on the application.

The application may be refused only for one of the reasons specified in Articles 27 and 28.

Under no circumstances may the foreign judgment be reviewed as to its substance.

Article 35

The appropriate officer of the court shall without delay bring the decision given on the application to the notice of the applicant in accordance with the procedure laid down by the law of the State in which enforcement is sought.

Article 36

If enforcement is authorised, the party against whom enforcement is sought may appeal against the decision within one month of service thereof.

If that party is domiciled in a Contracting State other than that in which the decision authorising enforcement was given, the time for appealing shall be two months and shall run from the date of service, either on him in person or at his residence. No extension of time may be granted on account of distance.

Article 37

1. An appeal against the decision authorising enforcement shall be lodged in accordance with the rules governing procedure in contentious matters:
   - in Belgium, with the tribunal de première instance or rechtbank van eerste aanleg,
   - in Denmark, with the landsret,
   - in the Federal Republic of Germany, with the Oberlandesgericht,
   - in Greece, with the ἐφετείο,
   - in Spain, with the Audiencia Provincial,
   - in France, with the cour d'appel,
   - in Ireland, with the High Court,
   - in Italy, with the corte d'appello,
   - in Luxembourg, with the Cour supérieure de justice sitting as a court of civil appeal,
   - in the Netherlands, with the arrondissementsrechtbank,
   - in Portugal, with the Tribunal da Relação,
   - in the United Kingdom:
     (a) in England and Wales, with the High Court of Justice, or in the case of a maintenance judgment with the Magistrates' Court;
     (b) in Scotland, with the Court of Session, or in the case of a maintenance judgment with the Sheriff Court;
     (c) in Northern Ireland, with the High Court of Justice, or in the case of a maintenance judgment with the Magistrates' Court.
2. The judgment given on the appeal may be contested only:
   - in Belgium, Greece, Spain, France, Italy, Luxembourg and in the Netherlands, by an appeal in cassation,
   - in Denmark, by an appeal to the højesteret, with the leave of the Minister of Justice,
   - in the Federal Republic of Germany, by a Rechtsbeschwerde,
   - in Ireland, by an appeal on a point of law to the Supreme Court,
   - in Portugal, by an appeal on a point of law,
   - in the United Kingdom, by a single further appeal on a point of law.

Article 38

The court with which the appeal under Article 37(1) is lodged may, on the application of the appellant, stay the proceedings if an ordinary appeal has been lodged against the judgment in the State of origin or if the time for such an appeal has not yet expired; in the latter case, the court may specify the time within which such an appeal is to be lodged.

Where the judgment was given in Ireland or the United Kingdom, any form of appeal available in the State of origin shall be treated as an ordinary appeal for the purposes of the first paragraph.

The court may also make enforcement conditional on the provision of such security as it shall determine.

Article 39

During the time specified for an appeal pursuant to Article 36 and until any such appeal has been determined, no measures of enforcement may be taken other than protective measures taken against the property of the party against whom enforcement is sought.

The decision authorising enforcement shall carry with it the power to proceed to any such protective measures.

Article 40

1. If the application for enforcement is refused, the applicant may appeal:
— in Belgium, to the cour d'appel or hof van beroep,
— in Denmark, to the landsret,
— in the Federal Republic of Germany, to the Oberlandesgericht,
— in Greece, to the ἐφετεῖο,
— in Spain, to the Audiencia Provincial,
— in France, to the cour d'appel,
— in Ireland, to the High Court,
— in Italy, to the corte d'appello,
— in Luxembourg, to the Cour supérieure de justice sitting as a court of civil appeal,
— in the Netherlands, to the gerechtshof,
— in Portugal, to the Tribunal da Relação,
— in the United Kingdom:
(a) in England and Wales, to the High Court of Justice, or in the case of a maintenance judgment to the Magistrates' Court;
(b) in Scotland, to the Court of Session, or in the case of a maintenance judgment to the Sheriff Court;
(c) in Northern Ireland, to the High Court of Justice, or in the case of a maintenance judgment to the Magistrates' Court.

2. The party against whom enforcement is sought shall be summoned to appear before the appellate court. If he fails to appear, the provisions of the second and third paragraphs of Article 20 shall apply even where he is not domiciled in any of the Contracting States.

Article 41

A judgment given on an appeal provided for in Article 40 may be contested only:
— in Belgium, Greece, Spain, France, Italy, Luxembourg and in the Netherlands, by an appeal in cassation,
— in Denmark, by an appeal to the højesteret, with the leave of the Minister of Justice,
— in the Federal Republic of Germany, by a Rechtsbeschwerde,
— in Ireland, by an appeal on a point of law to the Supreme Court,
— in Portugal, by an appeal on a point of law,
— in the United Kingdom, by a single further appeal on a point of law.

Article 42

Where a foreign judgment has been given in respect of several matters and enforcement cannot be authorised for all of them, the court shall authorise enforcement for one or more of them.

An applicant may request partial enforcement of a judgment.

Article 43

A foreign judgment which orders a periodic payment by way of a penalty shall be enforceable in the State in which enforcement is sought only if the amount of the payment has been finally determined by the courts of the State of origin.

Article 44

An applicant who, in the State of origin has benefited from complete or partial legal aid or exemption from costs or expenses, shall be entitled, in the procedures provided for in Articles 32 to 35, to benefit from the most favourable legal aid or the most extensive exemption from costs or expenses provided for by the law of the State addressed.

However, an applicant who requests the enforcement of a decision given by an administrative authority in Denmark in respect of a maintenance order may, in the State addressed, claim the benefits referred to in the first paragraph if he presents a statement from the Danish Ministry of Justice to the effect that he fulfils the economic requirements to qualify for the grant of complete or partial legal aid or exemption from costs or expenses.

Article 45

No security, bond or deposit, however described, shall be required of a party who in one Contracting State applies for enforcement of a judgment given in another Contracting State on the ground that he is a foreign national or that he is not domiciled or resident in the State in which the enforcement is sought.

Section 3. Common Provisions

Article 46

A party seeking recognition or applying for enforcement of a judgment shall produce:

1. a copy of the judgment which satisfies the conditions necessary to establish its authenticity;
2. in the case of a judgment given in default, the original or a certified true copy of the document which establishes that the party in default was served with the document instituting the proceedings or with an equivalent document.

Article 47

A party applying for enforcement shall also produce:

1. documents which establish that, according to the law of the State of origin the judgment is enforceable and has been served;
2. where appropriate, a document showing that the applicant is in receipt of legal aid in the State of origin.

Article 48

If the documents specified in Article 46(2) and Article 47(2) are not produced, the court may specify a time for their production, accept equivalent documents or, if it considers that it has sufficient information before it, dispense with their production.

If the court so requires, a translation of the documents shall be produced; the translation shall be certified by a person qualified to do so in one of the Contracting States.

Article 49

No legalisation or other similar formality shall be required in respect of the documents referred to in Articles 46 or 47 or the second paragraph of Article 48, or in respect of a document appointing a representative ad litem.

TITLE IV. AUTHENTIC INSTRUMENTS AND COURT SETTLEMENTS

Article 50

A document which has been formally drawn up or registered as an authentic instrument and is enforceable in one Contracting State shall, in another Contracting State, be declared enforceable there, on application made in accordance with the procedures provided for in Article 31 et seq. The application may be refused only if enforcement of the instrument is contrary to public policy in the State addressed.

The instrument produced must satisfy the conditions necessary to establish its authenticity in the State of origin.

The provisions of Section 3 of Title III shall apply as appropriate.

Article 51

A settlement which has been approved by a court in the course of proceedings and is enforceable in the State in which it was concluded shall be enforceable in the State addressed under the same conditions as authentic instruments.

TITLE V. GENERAL PROVISIONS

Article 52

In order to determine whether a party is domiciled in the Contracting State whose courts are seised of a matter, the court shall apply its internal law.

If a party is not domiciled in the State whose courts are seised of the matter, then, in order to determine whether the party is domiciled in another Contracting State, the court shall apply the law of that State.

Article 53

For the purposes of this Convention, the seat of a company or other legal person or association of natural or legal persons shall be treated as its domicile. However, in order to determine that seat, the court shall apply its rules of private international law.

In order to determine whether a trust is domiciled in the Contracting State whose courts are seised of the matter, the court shall apply its rules of private international law.

TITLE VI. TRANSITIONAL PROVISIONS

Article 54

The provisions of the Convention shall apply only to legal proceedings instituted and to documents formally drawn up or registered as authentic instruments after its entry into force in the State of origin and, where recognition or enforcement of a judgment or authentic instrument is sought, in the State addressed.

However, judgments given after the date of entry into force of this Convention between the State of origin and the State addressed in proceedings instituted before that date shall be recognised and enforced in accordance with the provisions of Title III if jurisdiction was founded upon rules which accorded with those provided for either in Title II of this Convention or in a convention concluded between the State of origin and the State addressed which was in force when the proceedings were instituted.

TITLE VII. RELATIONSHIP TO OTHER CONVENTIONS

Article 55

Subject to the provisions of the second subparagraph of Article 54, and of Article 56, this Convention shall, for the States which are parties to it, supersede the following conventions concluded between two or more of them:

- the Convention between Belgium and France on jurisdiction and the validity and enforcement of judgments, arbitration awards and authentic instruments, signed at Paris on 8 July 1899,
- the Convention between Belgium and the Netherlands on jurisdiction, bankruptcy, and the validity and enforcement of judgments, arbitration awards and authentic instruments, signed at Brussels on 28 March 1925,

— the Convention between France and Italy on the enforcement of judgments in civil and commercial matters, signed at Rome on 3 June 1930,
— the Convention between the United Kingdom and the French Republic providing for the reciprocal enforcement of judgments in civil and commercial matters, with Protocol, signed at Paris on 18 January 1934,
— the Convention between the United Kingdom and the Kingdom of Belgium providing for the reciprocal enforcement of judgments in civil and commercial matters, with Protocol, signed at Brussels on 2 May 1934,
— the Convention between Germany and Italy on the recognition and enforcement of judgments in civil and commercial matters, signed at Rome on 9 March 1936,
— the Convention between the Federal Republic of Germany and the Kingdom of Belgium on the mutual recognition and enforcement of judgments, arbitration awards and authentic instruments in civil and commercial matters, signed at Bonn on 30 June 1958,
— the Convention between the Kingdom of the Netherlands and the Italian Republic on the recognition and enforcement of judgments in civil and commercial matters, signed at Rome on 17 April 1959,
— the Convention between the United Kingdom and the Federal Republic of Germany for the reciprocal recognition and enforcement of judgments in civil and commercial matters, signed at Bonn on 14 July 1960,
— the Convention between the Kingdom of Greece and the Federal Republic of Germany for the reciprocal recognition and enforcement of judgments, settlements and authentic instruments in civil and commercial matters, signed at Athens on 4 November 1961,
— the Convention between the Kingdom of Belgium and the Italian Republic on the recognition and enforcement of judgments and other enforceable instruments in civil and commercial matters, signed at Rome on 6 April 1962,
— the Convention between the Kingdom of the Netherlands and the Federal Republic of Germany on the mutual recognition and enforcement of judgments and other enforceable instruments in civil and commercial matters, signed at The Hague on 30 August 1962,
— the Convention between the United Kingdom and the Republic of Italy for the reciprocal recognition and enforcement of judgments in civil and commercial matters, signed at Rome on 7 February 1964, with amending Protocol signed at Rome on 14 July 1970,
— the Convention between the United Kingdom and the Kingdom of the Netherlands providing for the reciprocal recognition and enforcement of judgments in civil matters, signed at The Hague on 17 November 1967,
— the Convention between Spain and France on the recognition and enforcement of judgments and arbitration awards in civil and commercial matters, signed at Paris on 28 May 1969,
— the Convention between Spain and Italy regarding legal aid and the recognition and enforcement of judgments in civil and commercial matters, signed at Madrid on 22 May 1973,
— the Convention between Spain and the Federal Republic of Germany on the recognition and enforcement of judgments, settlements and enforceable authentic instruments in civil and commercial matters, signed at Bonn on 14 November 1983,

and, in so far as it is in force:

— the Treaty between Belgium, the Netherlands and Luxembourg on jurisdiction, bankruptcy, and the validity and enforcement of judgments, arbitration awards and authentic instruments, signed at Brussels on 24 November 1961.

Article 56

The Treaty and the conventions referred to in Article 55 shall continue to have effect in relation to matters to which this Convention does not apply.

They shall continue to have effect in respect of judgments given and documents formally drawn up or registered as authentic instruments before the entry into force of this Convention.

Article 57

1. This Convention shall not affect any conventions to which the Contracting States are or will be parties and which, in relation to particular matters, govern jurisdiction or the recognition or enforcement of judgments.

2. With a view to its uniform interpretation, paragraph 1 shall be applied in the following manner:

(a) this Convention shall not prevent a court of a Contracting State which is a party to a convention on a particular matter from assuming jurisdiction in accordance with that convention, even where the defendant is domiciled in another Contracting State which is not a party to that convention. The court hearing the action shall, in any event, apply Article 20 of this Convention;

(b) judgments given in a Contracting State by a court in the exercise of jurisdiction provided for in a convention on a particular matter shall be recognised and enforced in the other Contracting States in accordance with this Convention.

Where a convention on a particular matter to which both the State of origin and the State addressed are parties lays down conditions for the recognition or enforcement of judgments, those conditions shall apply. In any event, the provisions of this Convention which concern the procedure for recognition and enforcement of judgments may be applied.

3. This Convention shall not affect the application of provisions which, in relation to particular matters, govern jurisdiction or the recognition or enforcement of judgments and which are or will be contained in acts of the institutions of the European Communities or in national laws harmonised in implementation of such acts.

Article 58

Until such time as the Convention on jurisdiction and the enforcement of judgments in civil and commercial matters, signed at Lugano on 16 September 1988, takes effect with regard to France and the Swiss Confederation, this Convention shall not affect the rights granted to Swiss nationals by the Convention between France and the Swiss Confederation on jurisdiction and the enforcement of judgments in civil matters, signed at Paris on 15 June 1869.

Article 59

This Convention shall not prevent a Contracting State from assuming, in a convention on the recognition and enforcement of judgments, an obligation towards a third State not to recognise judgments given in another Contracting State against defendants domiciled or habitually resident in the third State where, in cases provided for in Article 4, the judgment could only be founded on a ground of jurisdiction specified in the second paragraph of Article 3.

However, a Contracting State may not assume an obligation towards a third State not to recognise a judgment given in another Contracting State by a court basing its jurisdiction on the presence within that State of property belonging to the defendant, or the seizure by the plaintiff of property situated there:

1. if the action is brought to assert or declare proprietary or possessory rights in that property, seeks to obtain authority to dispose of it, or arises from another issue relating to such property, or
2. if the property constitutes the security for a debt which is the subject-matter of the action.

TITLE VIII. FINAL PROVISIONS

Article 60

[Deleted]

Article 61

This Convention shall be ratified by the signatory States. The instruments of ratification shall be deposited with the Secretary-General of the Council of the European Communities.

Article 62

This Convention shall enter into force on the first day of the third month following the deposit of the instrument of ratification by the last signatory State to take this step.

Article 63

The Contracting States recognise that any State which becomes a member of the European Economic Community shall be required to accept this Convention as a basis for the negotiations between the Contracting States and that State necessary to ensure the implementation of the last paragraph of Article 220 of the Treaty establishing the European Economic Community.

The necessary adjustments may be the subject of a special convention between the Contracting States of the one part and the new Member States of the other part.

Article 64

The Secretary-General of the Council of the European Communities shall notify the signatory States of—

(a) the deposit of each instrument of ratification;
(b) the date of entry into force of this Convention;
(c) [Deleted]
(d) any declaration received pursuant to Article IV of the Protocol;
(e) any communication made pursuant to Article VI of the Protocol.

Article 65

The Protocol annexed to this Convention by common accord of the Contracting States shall form an integral part thereof.

Article 66

This Convention is concluded for an unlimited period.

Article 67

Any Contracting State may request the revision of this Convention. In this event, a revision conference shall be convened by the President of the Council of the European Communities.

Article 68

This Convention, drawn up in a single original in the Dutch, French, German and Italian languages, all four texts being equally authentic, shall be deposited in the archives of the Secretariat of the Council of the European Communities. The Secretary-General shall transmit a certified copy to the Government of each signatory State.

(Signatures of Plenipotentiaries of the original six Contracting States)

ANNEXED PROTOCOL

The High Contracting Parties have agreed upon the following provisions, which shall be annexed to the Convention.

Article I

Any person domiciled in Luxembourg who is sued in a court of another Contracting State pursuant to Article 5(1) may refuse to submit to the jurisdiction of that court. If the defendant does not enter an appearance the court shall declare of its own motion that it has no jurisdiction.

An agreement conferring jurisdiction, within the meaning of Article 17, shall be valid with respect to a person domiciled in Luxembourg only if that person has expressly and specifically so agreed.

Article II

Without prejudice to any more favourable provisions of national laws, persons domiciled in a Contracting State who are being prosecuted in the criminal courts of another Contracting State of which they are not nationals for an offence which was not intentionally committed may be defended by persons qualified to do so, even if they do not appear in person.

However, the court seised of the matter may order appearance in person; in the case of failure to appear, a judgment given in the civil action without the person concerned having had the opportunity to arrange for his defence need not be recognised or enforced in the other Contracting States.

Article III

In proceedings for the issue of an order for enforcement, no charge, duty or fee calculated by reference to the value of the matter in issue may be levied in the State in which enforcement is sought.

Article IV

Judicial and extrajudicial documents drawn up in one Contracting State which have to be served on persons in another Contracting State shall be transmitted in accordance with the procedures laid down in the conventions and agreements concluded between the Contracting States.

Unless the State in which service is to take place objects by declaration to the Secretary-General of the Council of the European Communities, such documents may also be sent by the appropriate public officers of the State in which the document has been drawn up directly to the appropriate public officers of the State in which the addressee is to be found. In this case the officer of the State of origin shall send a copy of the document to the officer of the State applied to who is competent to forward it to the addressee. The document shall be forwarded in the manner specified by the law of the State applied to. The forwarding shall be recorded by a certificate sent directly to the officer of the State of origin.

Article V

The jurisdiction specified in Articles 6(2) and 10 in actions on a warranty or guarantee or in any other third party proceedings may not be resorted to in the Federal Republic of Germany. In that State, any person domiciled in another Contracting State may be sued in the courts in pursuance of Articles 68, 72, 73 and 74 of the code of civil procedure (Zivilprozeßordnung) concerning third-party notices.

Judgments given in the other Contracting States by virtue of Article 6(2) or Article 10 shall be recognised and enforced in the Federal Republic of Germany in accordance with Title III. Any effects which judgments given in that State may have on third parties by application of Articles 68, 72, 73 and 74 of the code of civil procedure (Zivilprozeßordnung) shall also be recognised in the other Contracting States.

Article Va

In matters relating to maintenance, the expression "court" includes the Danish administrative authorities.

Article Vb

In proceedings involving a dispute between the master and a member of the crew of a sea-going ship registered in Denmark, in Greece, in Ireland or in Portugal, concerning remuneration or other conditions of service, a court in a Contracting State shall establish whether the diplomatic or consular officer responsible for the ship has been notified of the dispute. It shall stay the proceedings so long as he has not been notified. It shall of its own motion decline jurisdiction if the officer, having been duly notified, has exercised the powers accorded to him in the matter by a consular convention, or in the absence of such a convention has, within the time allowed, raised any objection to the exercise of such jurisdiction.

Article Vc

Articles 52 and 53 of this Convention shall, when applied by Article 69(5) of the Convention for the European patent for the common market, signed at Luxembourg on 15 December 1975, to the provisions relating to "residence" in the English text of that Convention, operate as if "residence" in that text were the same as "domicile" in Articles 52 and 53.

Article Vd

Without prejudice to the jurisdiction of the European Patent Office under the Convention on the grant of European patents, signed at Munich on 5 October 1973, the courts of each Contracting State shall have exclusive jurisdiction, regardless of domicile, in proceedings concerned with the registration or validity of any European patent granted for that State which is not a Community patent by virtue of the provisions of Article 86 of the Convention for the European patent for the common market, signed at Luxembourg on 15 December 1975.

Article VI

The Contracting States shall communicate to the Secretary-General of the Council of the European Communities the text of any provisions of their laws which amend either those articles of their laws mentioned in the Convention or the lists of courts specified in Section 2 of Title III of the Convention.

(Signatures of Plenipotentiaries of the original six Contracting States)

SCHEDULE 2. TEXT OF THE 1971 PROTOCOL, AS AMENDED

Article 1

The Court of Justice of the European Communities shall have jurisdiction to give rulings on the interpretation of the Convention on jurisdiction and the enforcement of judgments in civil and commercial matters and of the Protocol annexed to that Convention, signed at Brussels on 27 September 1968, and also on the interpretation of the present Protocol.

The Court of Justice of the European Communities shall also have jurisdiction to give rulings on the interpretation of the Convention on the accession of the Kingdom of Denmark, Ireland and the United Kingdom of Great Britain and Northern Ireland to the Convention of 27 September 1968 and to this Protocol. The Court of Justice of the European Communities shall also have jurisdiction to give rulings on the interpretation of the Convention on the accession of the Hellenic Republic to the Convention of 27 September 1968 and to this Protocol, as adjusted by the 1978 Convention.

The Court of Justice of the European Communities shall also have jurisdiction to give rulings on the interpretation of the Convention on the accession of the Kingdom of Spain and the Portuguese Republic to the Convention of 27 September 1968 and to this Protocol, as adjusted by the 1978 Convention and the 1982 Convention.

Article 2

The following courts may request the Court of Justice to give preliminary rulings on questions of interpretation:

1. — in Belgium: la Cour de Cassation—het Hof van Cassatie and le Conseil d'Etat—de Raad van State,
   — in Denmark: højesteret,
   — in the Federal Republic of Germany: die obersten Gerichtshöfe des Bundes,

— in Greece: the ανώτατα δικαστήρια,
— in Spain: el Tribunal Supremo,
— in France: la Cour de Cassation and le Conseil d'Etat,
— in Ireland: the Supreme Court,
— in Italy: la Corte Suprema di Cassazione,
— in Luxembourg: la Cour supérieure de Justice when sitting as Cour de Cassation,
— in the Netherlands: de Hoge Raad,
— in Portugal: o Supremo Tribunal de Justiça and o Supremo Tribunal Administrativo,
— in the United Kingdom: the House of Lords and courts to which application has been made under the second paragraph of Article 37 or under Article 41 of the Convention;

2. the courts of the Contracting States when they are sitting in an appellate capacity;
3. in the cases provided for in Article 37 of the Convention, the courts referred to in that Article.

Article 3

1. Where a question of interpretation of the Convention or of one of the other instruments referred to in Article 1 is raised in a case pending before one of the courts listed in Article 2(1), that court shall, if it considers that a decision on the question is necessary to enable it to give judgment, request the Court of Justice to give a ruling thereon.

2. Where such a question is raised before any court referred to in Article 2(2) or (3), that court may, under the conditions laid down in paragraph 1, request the Court of Justice to give a ruling thereon.

Article 4

1. The competent authority of a Contracting State may request the Court of Justice to give a ruling on a question of interpretation of the Convention or of one of the other instruments referred to in Article 1 if judgments given by courts of that State conflict with the interpretation given either by the Court of Justice or in a judgment of one of the courts of another Contracting State referred to in Article 2(1) or (2). The provisions of this paragraph shall apply only to judgments which have become res judicata.

2. The interpretation given by the Court of Justice in response to such a request shall not affect the judgments which gave rise to the request for interpretation.

3. The Procurators-General of the Courts of Cassation of the Contracting States, or any other authority designated by a Contracting State, shall be entitled to request the Court of Justice for a ruling on interpretation in accordance with paragraph 1.

4. The Registrar of the Court of Justice shall give notice of the request to the Contracting States, to the Commission and to the Council of the European Communities; they shall then be entitled within two months of the notification to submit statements of case or written observations to the Court.

5. No fees shall be levied or any costs or expenses awarded in respect of the proceedings provided for in this Article.

Article 5

1. Except where this Protocol otherwise provides, the provisions of the Treaty establishing the European Economic Community and those of the Protocol on the Statute of the Court of Justice annexed thereto, which are applicable when the Court is requested to give a preliminary ruling, shall also apply to any proceedings for the interpretation of the Convention and the other instruments referred to in Article 1.

2. The Rules of Procedure of the Court of Justice shall, if necessary, be adjusted and supplemented in accordance with Article 188 of the Treaty establishing the European Economic Community.

Article 6

[Deleted]

Article 7

This Protocol shall be ratified by the signatory States. The instruments of ratification shall be deposited with the Secretary-General of the Council of the European Communities.

Article 8

This Protocol shall enter into force on the first day of the third month following the deposit of the instrument of ratification by the last signatory State to take this step; provided that it shall at the earliest enter into force at the same time as the Convention of 27 September 1968 on jurisdiction and the enforcement of judgments in civil and commercial matters.

Article 9

The Contracting States recognise that any State which becomes a member of the European Economic Community, and to which Article 63 of the Convention on jurisdiction and the enforcement of judgments in civil and commercial matters applies, must accept the provisions of this Protocol, subject to such adjustments as may be required.

Article 10

The Secretary-General of the Council of the European Communities shall notify the signatory States of:

(a) the deposit of each instrument of ratification;
(b) the date of entry into force of this Protocol;
(c) any designation received pursuant to Article 4(3);
(d) [Deleted]

Article 11

The Contracting States shall communicate to the Secretary-General of the Council of the European Communities the texts of any provisions of their laws which necessitate an amendment to the list of courts in Article 2(1).

Article 12

This Protocol is concluded for an unlimited period.

Article 13

Any Contracting State may request the revision of this Protocol. In this event, a revision conference shall be convened by the President of the Council of the European Communities.

Article 14

This Protocol, drawn up in a single original in the Dutch, French, German and Italian languages, all four texts being equally authentic, shall be deposited in the archives of the Secretariat of the Council of the European Communities. The Secretary-General shall transmit a certified copy to the Government of each signatory State.

. . .

SCHEDULE 3C. TEXT OF THE LUGANO CONVENTION[1]

CONVENTION ON JURISDICTION AND THE ENFORCEMENT OF JUDGMENTS IN CIVIL AND COMMERCIAL MATTERS

PREAMBLE

The High Contracting Parties to this Convention,

Anxious to strengthen in their territories the legal protection of persons therein established,

Considering that it is necessary for this purpose to determine the international jurisdiction of their courts, to facilitate recognition and to introduce an expeditious procedure for securing the enforcement of judgments, authentic instruments and court settlements,

Aware of the links between them, which have been sanctioned in the economic field by the free trade agreements concluded between the European Economic Community and the States members of the European Free Trade Association,

Taking into account the Brussels Convention of 27 September 1968 on jurisdiction and the enforcement of judgments in civil and commercial matters, as amended by the Accession Conventions under the successive enlargements of the European Communities,

Persuaded that the extension of the principles of that Convention to the States parties to this instrument will strengthen legal and economic co-operation in Europe,

Desiring to ensure as uniform an interpretation as possible of this instrument,

Have in this spirit decided to conclude this Convention and

Have agreed as follows:

...

TITLE II. JURISDICTION

Section 1. General Provisions

...

Article 3

...

In particular the following provisions shall not be applicable as against them:

- in Belgium: Article 15 of the civil code (Code civil—Burgerlijk Wetboek) and Article 638 of the judicial code (Code judiciaire—Gerechtelijk Wetboek),
- in Denmark: Article 246(2) and (3) of the law on civil procedure (Lov om rettens pleje),
- in the Federal Republic of Germany: Article 23 of the code of civil procedure (Zivilprozeßordnung),
- in Greece: Article 40 of the code of civil procedure (Κώδικας πολιτικής δικονομίας),
- in France: Articles 14 and 15 of the civil code (Code civil),
- in Ireland: the rules which enable jurisdiction to be founded on the document instituting the proceedings having been served on the defendant during his temporary presence in Ireland,
- in Iceland: Article 77 of the Civil Proceedings Act (lög um meδferδ einkamála í héraδi),
- in Italy: Articles 2 and 4, Nos 1 and 2 of the code of civil procedure (Codice di procedura civile),

1. Most of the provisions of the Lugano Convention are identical to the equivalent provisions of the Brussels Convention, the text of which is to be found in Schedule 1 to the 1982 Act. Only those provisions of the Lugano Convention which are different from the provisions of the Brussels Convention are reproduced in this Appendix.

— in Luxembourg: Articles 14 and 15 of the civil code (Code civil),
— in the Netherlands: Articles 126(3) and 127 of the code of civil procedure (Wetboek van Burgerlijke Rechtsvordering),
— in Norway: Section 32 of the Civil Proceedings Act (tvistemålsloven),
— in Austria: Article 99 of the Law on Court Jurisdiction (Jurisdiktionsnorm),
— in Portugal: Articles 65(1)(c), 65(2) and 65A(c) of the code of civil procedure (Código de Processo Civil) and Article 11 of the code of labour procedure (Código de Processo de Trabalho),
— in Switzerland: le for du lieu du séquestre/Gerichtsstand des Arrestortes/foro del luogo del sequestro within the meaning of Article 4 of the loi fédérale sur le droit international privé/Bundesgesetz über das internationale Privatrecht/legge federale sul diritto internazionale privato,
— in Finland: the second, third and fourth sentences of Section 1 of Chapter 10 of the Code of Judicial Procedure (oikeudenkäymiskaari/rättegångsbalken),
— in Sweden: the first sentence of Section 3 of Chapter 10 of the Code of Judicial Procedure (Rättegångsbalken),
— in the United Kingdom: the rules which enable jurisdiction to be founded on:
  (a) the document instituting the proceedings having been served on the defendant during his temporary presence in the United Kingdom; or
  (b) the presence within the United Kingdom of property belonging to the defendant; or
  (c) the seizure by the plaintiff of property situated in the United Kingdom.

. . .

Section 2. Special Jurisdiction

Article 5

A person domiciled in a Contracting State may, in another Contracting State, be sued:

1. in matters relating to a contract, in the courts for the place of performance of the obligation in question; in matters relating to individual contracts of employment, this place is that where the employee habitually carries out his work, or if the employee does not habitually carry out his work in any one country, this place shall be the place of business through which he was engaged;

. . .

Section 3. Jurisdiction in Matters Relating to Insurance

. . .

Article 12

The provisions of this Section may be departed from only by an agreement on jurisdiction—

. . .

. . .

3. which is concluded between a policy-holder and an insurer, both of whom are at the time of the conclusion of the contract domiciled or habitually resident in the same Contracting State, and which has the effect of conferring jurisdiction on the courts of that State even if the harmful event were to occur abroad, provided that such an agreement is not contrary to the law of that State, or . . .

Section 5. Exclusive Jurisdiction

Article 16

The following courts shall have exclusive jurisdiction, regardless of domicile:

1. . . .

(b) however, in proceedings which have as their object tenancies of immovable property concluded for temporary private use for a maximum period of six consecutive months, the courts of the Contracting State in which the defendant is domiciled shall also have jurisdiction, provided that the tenant is a natural person and neither party is domiciled in the Contracting State in which the property is situated;

. . .

Section 6. Prorogation of Jurisdiction

Article 17

. . .

. . .

. . .

. . .

5. In matters relating to individual contracts of employment an agreement conferring jurisdiction shall have legal force only if it is entered into after the dispute has arisen.

TITLE III. RECOGNITION AND ENFORCEMENT

. . .

Section 1. Recognition

Article 28

. . .

A judgment may furthermore be refused recognition in any case provided for in Article 54B(3) or 57(4).

. . .

. . .

Section 2. Enforcement

. . .

Article 32

1. The application shall be submitted:
- — in Belgium, to the tribunal de première instance or rechtbank van eerste aanleg,
- — in Denmark, to the byret,
- — in the Federal Republic of Germany, to the presiding judge of a chamber of the Landgericht,
- — in Greece, to the μονομελές πρωτοδικείο,
- — in Spain, to the Juzgado de Primera Instancia,
- — in France, to the presiding judge of the tribunal de grande instance,
- — in Ireland, to the High Court,
- — in Iceland, to the héraδsdómari,
- — in Italy, to the corte d'appello,
- — in Luxembourg, to the presiding judge of the tribunal d'arrondissement,
- — in the Netherlands, to the presiding judge of the arrondissementsrechtbank,
- — in Norway, to the herredsrett or byrett as namsrett,
- — in Austria, to the Landesgericht or the Kreisgericht,
- — in Portugal, to the Tribunal Judicial de Círculo,
- — in Switzerland:

(a) in respect of judgments ordering the payment of a sum of money, to the juge de la mainlevée/Rechtsöffnungsrichter/giudice competente a pronunciare sul rigetto dell'opposizione, within the framework of the procedure governed by Articles 80 and 81 of the loi fédérale sur la poursuite pour dettes et la faillite/Bundesgesetz über Schuldbetreibung und Konkurs/legge federale sulla esecuzione e sul fallimento;
(b) in respect of judgments ordering a performance other than the payment of a sum of money, to the juge cantonal d'exequatur compétent/zuständiger kantonaler Vollstreckungsrichter/giudice cantonale competente a pronunciare l'exequatur,

— in Finland, to the ulosotonhaltija/överexekutor,
— in Sweden, to the Svea hovrätt,
— in the United Kingdom:
(a) in England and Wales, to the High Court of Justice, or in the case of a maintenance judgment to the Magistrates' Court on transmission by the Secretary of State;
(b) in Scotland, to the Court of Session, or in the case of a maintenance judgment to the Sheriff Court on transmission by the Secretary of State;
(c) in Northern Ireland, to the High Court of Justice, or in the case of a maintenance judgment to the Magistrates' Court on transmission by the Secretary of State.

. . .

Article 37

1. An appeal against the decision authorising enforcement shall be lodged in accordance with the rules governing procedure in contentious matters:
— in Belgium, with the tribunal de première instance or rechtbank van eerste aanleg,
— in Denmark, with the landsret,
— in the Federal Republic of Germany, with the Oberlandesgericht,
— in Greece, with the ἐφετεῖο,
— in Spain, with the Audiencia Provincial,
— in France, with the cour d'appel,
— in Ireland, with the High Court,
— in Iceland, with the héraδsdómari,
— in Italy, with the corte d'appello,
— in Luxembourg, with the Cour supérieure de justice sitting as a court of civil appeal,
— in the Netherlands, with the arrondissementsrechtbank,
— in Norway, with the lagmannsrett,
— in Austria, with the Landesgericht or the Kreisgericht,
— in Portugal, with the Tribunal da Relação,
— in Switzerland, with the tribunal cantonal/Kantonsgericht/tribunale cantonale,
— in Finland, with the hovioikeus/hovrätt,
— in Sweden, with the Svea hovrätt,
— in the United Kingdom:
(a) in England and Wales, with the High Court of Justice, or in the case of a maintenance judgment with the Magistrates' Court;
(b) in Scotland, with the Court of Session, or in the case of a maintenance judgment with the Sheriff Court;
(c) in Northern Ireland, with the High Court of Justice, or in the case of a maintenance judgment with the Magistrates' Court.

2. The judgment given on the appeal may be contested only:
— in Belgium, Greece, Spain, France, Italy, Luxembourg and in the Netherlands, by an appeal in cassation,
— in Denmark, by an appeal to the højesteret, with the leave of the Minister of Justice,
— in the Federal Republic of Germany, by a Rechtsbeschwerde,
— in Ireland, by an appeal on a point of law to the Supreme Court,
— in Iceland, by an appeal to the Hæstiréttur,
— in Norway, by an appeal (kjæremål or anke) to the Hoyesteretts Kjæremålsutvalg or Hoyesterett,
— in Austria, in the case of an appeal, by a Revisionsrekurs and, in the case of opposition proceedings, by a Berufung with the possibility of a Revision,

— in Portugal, by an appeal on a point of law,
— in Switzerland, by a recours de droit public devant le tribunal fédéral/staatsrechtliche Beschwerde beim Bundesgericht/ricorso di diritto pubblico davanti al tribunale federale,
— in Finland, by an appeal to the korkein oikeus/högsta domstolen,
— in Sweden, by an appeal to the högsta domstolen,
— in the United Kingdom, by a single further appeal on a point of law.

...

Article 40

1. If the application for enforcement is refused, the applicant may appeal:
— in Belgium, to the cour d'appel or hof van beroep,
— in Denmark, to the landsret,
— in the Federal Republic of Germany, to the Oberlandesgericht,
— in Greece, to the ἐφετείο,
— in Spain, to the Audiencia Provincial,
— in France, to the cour d'appel,
— in Ireland, to the High Court,
— in Iceland, to the héraδsdómari,
— in Italy, to the corte d'appello,
— in Luxembourg, to the Cour supérieure de justice sitting as a court of civil appeal,
— in the Netherlands, to the gerechtshof,
— in Norway, to the lagmannsrett,
— in Austria, to the Landesgericht or the Kreisgericht,
— in Portugal, to the Tribunal da Relação,
— in Switzerland, to the tribunal cantonal/Kantonsgericht/tribunale cantonale,
— in Finland, to the hovioikeus/hovrätt,
— in Sweden, to the Svea hovrätt,
— in the United Kingdom:
(a) in England and Wales, to the High Court of Justice, or in the case of a maintenance judgment to the Magistrates' Court;
(b) in Scotland, to the Court of Session, or in the case of a maintenance judgment to the Sheriff Court;
(c) in Northern Ireland, to the High Court of Justice or in the case of a maintenance judgment to the Magistrates' Court.

...

Article 41

A judgment given on an appeal provided for in Article 40 may be contested only:
— in Belgium, Greece, Spain, France, Italy, Luxembourg and in the Netherlands, by an appeal in cassation,
— in Denmark, by an appeal to the højesteret, with the leave of the Minister of Justice,
— in the Federal Republic of Germany, by a Rechtsbeschwerde,
— in Ireland, by an appeal on a point of law to the Supreme Court,
— in Iceland, by an appeal to the Hæstiréttur,
— in Norway, by an appeal (kjæremål or anke) to the Hoyesteretts kjæremålsutvalg or Hoyesterett,
— in Austria, by a Revisionsrekurs,
— in Portugal, by an appeal on a point of law,
— in Switzerland, by a recours de droit public devant le tribunal fédéral/staatsrechtliche Beschwerde beim Bundesgericht/ricorso di diritto pubblico davanti al tribunale federale,
— in Finland, by an appeal to the korkein oikeus/högsta domstolen,
— in Sweden, by an appeal to the högsta domstolen,
— in the United Kingdom, by a single further appeal on a point of law.

Article 44

...

However, an applicant who requests the enforcement of a decision given by an administrative authority in Denmark or in Iceland in respect of a maintenance order may, in the State addressed, claim the benefits referred to in the first paragraph if he presents a statement from, respectively, the Danish Ministry of Justice or the Icelandic Ministry of Justice to the effect that he fulfils the economic requirements to qualify for the grant of complete or partial legal aid or exemption from costs or expenses.

...

TITLE VI. TRANSITIONAL PROVISIONS

Article 54

...

...

If the parties to a dispute concerning a contract had agreed in writing before the entry into force of this Convention that the contract was to be governed by the law of Ireland or of a part of the United Kingdom, the courts of Ireland or of that part of the United Kingdom shall retain the right to exercise jurisdiction in the dispute.

Article 54A

For a period of three years from the entry into force of this Convention for Denmark, Greece, Ireland, Iceland, Norway, Finland and Sweden, respectively, jurisdiction in maritime matters shall be determined in these States not only in accordance with the provisions of Title II, but also in accordance with the provisions of paragraphs 1 to 7 following. However, upon the entry into force of the International Convention relating to the arrest of sea-going ships, signed at Brussels on 10 May 1952, for one of these States, these provisions shall cease to have effect for that State.

1. A person who is domiciled in a Contracting State may be sued in the courts of one of the States mentioned above in respect of a maritime claim if the ship to which the claim relates or any other ship owned by him has been arrested by judicial process within the territory of the latter State to secure the claim, or could have been so arrested there but bail or other security has been given, and either:
   (a) the claimant is domiciled in the latter State; or
   (b) the claim arose in the latter State; or
   (c) the claim concerns the voyage during which the arrest was made or could have been made; or
   (d) the claim arises out of a collision or out of damage caused by a ship to another ship or to goods or persons on board either ship, either by the execution or non-execution of a manoeuvre or by the non-observance of regulations; or
   (e) the claim is for salvage; or
   (f) the claim is in respect of a mortgage or hypothecation of the ship arrested.
2. A claimant may arrest either the particular ship to which the maritime claim relates, or any other ship which is owned by the person who was, at the time when the maritime claim arose, the owner of the particular ship. However, only the particular ship to which the maritime claim relates may be arrested in respect of the maritime claims set out in 5.(o), (p) or (q) of this Article.
3. Ships shall be deemed to be in the same ownership when all the shares therein are owned by the same person or persons.
4. When in the case of a charter by demise of a ship the charterer alone is liable in respect of a maritime claim relating to that ship, the claimant may arrest that ship or any other ship owned by the charterer, but no other ship owned by the owner may be arrested in respect of such claim. The same shall apply to any case in which a person other than the owner of a ship is liable in respect of a maritime claim relating to that ship.
5. The expression "maritime claim" means a claim arising out of one or more of the following:
   (a) damage caused by any ship either in collision or otherwise;
   (b) loss of life or personal injury caused by any ship or occurring in connection with the operation of any ship;
   (c) salvage;

(d) agreement relating to the use or hire of any ship whether by charterparty or otherwise;
(e) agreement relating to the carriage of goods in any ship whether by charterparty or otherwise;
(f) loss of or damage to goods including baggage carried in any ship;
(g) general average;
(h) bottomry;
(i) towage;
(j) pilotage;
(k) goods or materials wherever supplied to a ship for her operation or maintenance;
(l) construction, repair or equipment of any ship or dock charges and dues;
(m) wages of masters, officers or crew;
(n) master's disbursements, including disbursements made by shippers, charterers or agents on behalf of a ship or her owner;
(o) dispute as to the title to or ownership of any ship;
(p) disputes between co-owners of any ship as to the ownership, possession, employment or earnings of that ship;
(q) the mortgage or hypothecation of any ship.

6. In Denmark, the expression "arrest" shall be deemed, as regards the maritime claims referred to in 5.(o) and (p) of this Article, to include a "forbud", where that is the only procedure allowed in respect of such a claim under Articles 646 to 653 of the law on civil procedure (lov om rettens pleje).

7. In Iceland, the expression "arrest" shall be deemed, as regards the maritime claims referred to in 5.(o) and (p) of this Article, to include a "lögbann", where that is the only procedure allowed in respect of such a claim under Chapter III of the law on arrest and injunction (lög um kyrrsetningu og lögbann).

TITLE VII. RELATIONSHIP TO THE BRUSSELS CONVENTION AND TO OTHER CONVENTIONS

Article 54B

1. This Convention shall not prejudice the application by the Member States of the European Communities of the Convention on Jurisdiction and the Enforcement of Judgments in Civil and Commercial Matters, signed at Brussels on 27 September 1968 and of the Protocol on interpretation of that Convention by the Court of Justice, signed at Luxembourg on 3 June 1971, as amended by the Conventions of Accession to the said Convention and the said Protocol by the States acceding to the European Communities, all of these Conventions and the Protocol being hereinafter referred to as the "Brussels Convention".

2. However, this Convention shall in any event be applied:
(a) in matters of jurisdiction, where the defendant is domiciled in the territory of a Contracting State which is not a member of the European Communities, or where Article 16 or 17 of this Convention confers a jurisdiction on the courts of such a Contracting State;
(b) in relation to a lis pendens or to related actions as provided for in Articles 21 and 22, when proceedings are instituted in a Contracting State which is not a member of the European Communities and in a Contracting State which is a member of the European Communities;
(c) in matters of recognition and enforcement, where either the State of origin or the State addressed is not a member of the European Communities.

3. In addition to the grounds provided for in Title III recognition or enforcement may be refused if the ground of jurisdiction on which the judgment has been based differs from that resulting from this Convention and recognition or enforcement is sought against a party who is domiciled in a Contracting State which is not a member of the European Communities, unless the judgment may otherwise be recognised or enforced under any rule of law in the State addressed.

Article 55

Subject to the provisions of the second paragraph of Article 54 and of Article 56, this Convention shall, for the States which are parties to it, supersede the following conventions concluded between two or more of them:

- the Convention between the Swiss Confederation and France on jurisdiction and enforcement of judgments in civil matters, signed at Paris on 15 June 1869,
- the Treaty between the Swiss Confederation and Spain on the mutual enforcement of judgments in civil or commercial matters, signed at Madrid on 19 November 1896,
- the Convention between the Swiss Confederation and the German Reich on the recognition and enforcement of judgments and arbitration awards, signed at Berne on 2 November 1929,
- the Convention between Denmark, Finland, Iceland, Norway and Sweden on the recognition and enforcement of judgments, signed at Copenhagen on 16 March 1932,
- the Convention between the Swiss Confederation and Italy on the recognition and enforcement of judgments, signed at Rome on 3 January 1933,
- the Convention between Sweden and the Swiss Confederation on the recognition and enforcement of judgments and arbitral awards, signed at Stockholm on 15 January 1936,
- the Convention between the Kingdom of Belgium and Austria on the reciprocal recognition and enforcement of judgments and authentic instruments relating to maintenance obligations, signed at Vienna on 25 October 1957,
- the Convention between the Swiss Confederation and Belgium on the recognition and enforcement of judgments and arbitration awards, signed at Berne on 29th April 1959,
- the Convention between the Federal Republic of Germany and Austria on the reciprocal recognition and enforcement of judgments, settlements, and authentic instruments in civil and commercial matters, signed at Vienna on 6 June 1959,
- the Convention between the Kingdom of Belgium and Austria on the reciprocal recognition and enforcement of judgments, arbitral awards and authentic instruments in civil and commercial matters, signed at Vienna on 16 June 1959,
- the Convention between Austria and the Swiss Confederation on the recognition and enforcement of judgments, signed at Berne on 16 December 1960,
- the Convention between Norway and the United Kingdom providing for the reciprocal recognition and enforcement of judgments in civil matters, signed at London on 12 June 1961,
- the Convention between the United Kingdom and Austria providing for the reciprocal recognition and enforcement of judgments in civil and commercial matters, signed at Vienna on 14 July 1961, with amending Protocol signed at London on 6 March 1970,
- the Convention between the Kingdom of the Netherlands and Austria on the reciprocal recognition and enforcement of judgments and authentic instruments in civil and commercial matters, signed at The Hague on 6 February 1963,
- the Convention between France and Austria on the recognition and enforcement of judgments and authentic instruments in civil and commercial matters, signed at Vienna on 15 July 1966,
- the Convention between Luxembourg and Austria on the recognition and enforcement of judgments and authentic instruments in civil and commercial matters, signed at Luxembourg on 29 July 1971,
- the Convention between Italy and Austria on the recognition and enforcement of judgments in civil and commercial matters, of judicial settlements and of authentic instruments, signed at Rome on 16 November 1971,
- the Convention between Norway and the Federal Republic of Germany on the recognition and enforcement of judgments and enforceable documents, in civil and commercial matters, signed at Oslo on 17 June 1977,
- the Convention between Denmark, Finland, Iceland, Norway and Sweden on the recognition and enforcement of judgments in civil matters, signed at Copenhagen on 11 October 1977,
- the Convention between Austria and Sweden on the recognition and enforcement of judgments in civil matters, signed at Stockholm on 16 September 1982,
- the Convention between Austria and Spain on the recognition and enforcement of judgments, settlements and enforceable authentic instruments in civil and commercial matters, signed at Vienna on 17 February 1984,

— the Convention between Norway and Austria on the recognition and enforcement of judgments in civil matters, signed at Vienna on 21 May 1984, and
— the Convention between Finland and Austria on the recognition and enforcement of judgments in civil matters, signed at Vienna on 17 November 1986.

. . .

Article 57

. . .

2. This Convention shall not prevent a court of a Contracting State which is party to a convention referred to in the first paragraph from assuming jurisdiction in accordance with that convention, even where the defendant is domiciled in a Contracting State which is not a party to that convention. The court hearing the action shall, in any event, apply Article 20 of this Convention.

3. Judgments given in a Contracting State by a court in the exercise of jurisdiction provided for in a convention referred to in the first paragraph shall be recognised and enforced in the other Contracting States in accordance with Title III of this Convention.

4. In addition to the grounds provided for in Title III, recognition or enforcement may be refused if the State addressed is not a contracting party to a convention referred to in the first paragraph and the person against whom recognition or enforcement is sought is domiciled in that State, unless the judgment may otherwise be recognised or enforced under any rule of law in the State addressed.

5. Where a convention referred to in the first paragraph to which both the State of origin and the State addressed are parties lays down conditions for the recognition or enforcement of judgments, those conditions shall apply. In any event, the provisions of this Convention which concern the procedures for recognition and enforcement of judgments may be applied.

Article 58

(None)

. . .

TITLE VIII. FINAL PROVISIONS

Article 60

The following may be parties to this Convention:

(a) States which, at the time of the opening of this Convention for signature, are members of the European Communities or of the European Free Trade Association;
(b) States which, after the opening of this Convention for signature, become members of the European Communities or of the European Free Trade Association;
(c) States invited to accede in accordance with Article 62(1)(b).

Article 61

1. This Convention shall be opened for signature by the States members of the European Communities or of the European Free Trade Association.

2. The Convention shall be submitted for ratification by the signatory States. The instruments of ratification shall be deposited with the Swiss Federal Council.

3. The Convention shall enter into force on the first day of the third month following the date on which two States, of which one is a member of the European Communities and the other a member of the European Free Trade Association, deposit their instruments of ratification.

4. The Convention shall take effect in relation to any other signatory State on the first day of the third month following the deposit of its instrument of ratification.

Article 62

1. After entering into force this Convention shall be open to accession by:

(a) the States referred to in Article 60(b);

(b) other States which have been invited to accede upon a request made by one of the Contracting States to the depositary State. The depositary State shall invite the State concerned to accede only if, after having communicated the contents of the communications that this State intends to make in accordance with Article 63, it has obtained the unanimous agreement of the signatory States and the Contracting States referred to in Article 60(a) and (b).

2. If an acceding State wishes to furnish details for the purposes of Protocol No. 1, negotiations shall be entered into to that end. A negotiating conference shall be convened by the Swiss Federal Council.

3. In respect of an acceding State, the Convention shall take effect on the first day of the third month following the deposit of its instrument of accession.

4. However, in respect of an acceding State referred to in paragraph 1(a) or (b), the Convention shall take effect only in relations between the acceding State and the Contracting States which have not made any objections to the accession before the first day of the third month following the deposit of the instrument of accession.

Article 63

Each acceding State shall, when depositing its instrument of accession, communicate the information required for the application of Articles 3, 32, 37, 40, 41 and 55 of this Convention and furnish, if need be, the details prescribed during the negotiations for the purposes of Protocol No. 1.

Article 64

1. This Convention is concluded for an initial period of five years from the date of its entry into force in accordance with Article 61(3), even in the case of States which ratify it or accede to it after that date.

2. At the end of the initial five-year period, the Convention shall be automatically renewed from year to year.

3. Upon the expiry of the initial five-year period, any Contracting State may, at any time, denounce the Convention by sending a notification to the Swiss Federal Council.

4. The denunciation shall take effect at the end of the calendar year following the expiry of a period of six months from the date of receipt by the Swiss Federal Council of the notification of denunciation.

Article 65

The following are annexed to this Convention:

— a Protocol No. 1, on certain questions of jurisdiction, procedure and enforcement,

— a Protocol No. 2, on the uniform interpretation of the Convention,

— a Protocol No. 3, on the application of Article 57.

These Protocols shall form an integral part of the Convention.

Article 66

Any Contracting State may request the revision of this Convention. To that end, the Swiss Federal Council shall issue invitations to a revision conference within a period of six months from the date of the request for revision.

Article 67

The Swiss Federal Council shall notify the States represented at the Diplomatic Conference of Lugano and the States who have later acceded to the Convention of:

(a) the deposit of each instrument of ratification or accession;

(b) the dates of entry into force of this Convention in respect of the Contracting States;

(c) any denunciation received pursuant to Article 64;

(d) any declaration received pursuant to Article Ia of Protocol No. 1;

(e) any declaration received pursuant to Article Ib of Protocol No. 1;
(f) any declaration received pursuant to Article IV of Protocol No. 1;
(g) any communication made pursuant to Article VI of Protocol No. 1.

Article 68

This Convention, drawn up in a single original in the Danish, Dutch, English, Finnish, French, German, Greek, Icelandic, Irish, Italian, Norwegian, Portuguese, Spanish and Swedish languages, all fourteen texts being equally authentic, shall be deposited in the archives of the Swiss Federal Council. The Swiss Federal Council shall transmit a certified copy to the Government of each State represented at the Diplomatic Conference of Lugano and to the Government of each acceding State.

PROTOCOL NO. 1[2]. ON CERTAIN QUESTIONS OF JURISDICTION, PROCEDURE AND ENFORCEMENT

The High Contracting Parties have agreed upon the following provisions, which shall be annexed to the Convention:

. . .

Article Ia

1. Switzerland reserves the right to declare, at the time of depositing its instrument of ratification, that a judgment given in another Contracting State shall be neither recognised nor enforced in Switzerland if the following conditions are met:

(a) the jurisdiction of the court which has given the judgment is based only on Article 5(1) of this Convention; and
(b) the defendant was domiciled in Switzerland at the time of the introduction of the proceedings; for the purposes of this Article, a company or other legal person is considered to be domiciled in Switzerland if it has its registered seat and the effective centre of activities in Switzerland; and
(c) the defendant raises an objection to the recognition or enforcement of the judgment in Switzerland, provided that he has not waived the benefit of the declaration foreseen under this paragraph.

2. This reservation shall not apply to the extent that at the time recognition or enforcement is sought a derogation has been granted from Article 59 of the Swiss Federal Constitution. The Swiss Government shall communicate such derogations to the signatory States and the acceding States.

3. This reservation shall cease to have effect on 31 December 1999. It may be withdrawn at any time.

Article Ib

Any Contracting State may, by declaration made at the time of signing or of deposit of its instrument of ratification or of accession, reserve the right, notwithstanding the provisions of Article 28, not to recognise and enforce judgments given in the other Contracting States if the jurisdiction of the court of the State of origin is based, pursuant to Article 16(1)(b), exclusively on

2. The only provisions of Protocol No. 1 to the Lugano Convention reproduced in this Appendix are those which are different from the equivalent provisions of, or have no counterpart in, the Protocol to the Brussels Convention.

the domicile of the defendant in the State of origin, and the property is situated in the territory of the State which entered the reservation.

...

Article IV

...

Unless the State in which service is to take place objects by declaration to the Swiss Federal Council, such documents may also be sent by the appropriate public officers of the State in which the document has been drawn up directly to the appropriate public officers of the State in which the addressee is to be found. In this case the officer of the State of origin shall send a copy of the document to the officer of the State applied to who is competent to forward it to the addressee. The document shall be forwarded in the manner specified by the law of the State applied to. The forwarding shall be recorded by a certificate sent directly to the officer of the State of origin.

Article V

The jurisdiction specified in Articles 6(2) and 10 in actions on a warranty or guarantee or in any other third party proceedings may not be resorted to in the Federal Republic of Germany, in Spain, in Austria and in Switzerland. Any person domiciled in another Contracting State may be sued in the courts:

- of the Federal Republic of Germany, pursuant to Articles 68, 72, 73 and 74 of the code of civil procedure (Zivilprozeßordnung) concerning third-party notices,
- of Spain, pursuant to Article 1482 of the civil code,
- of Austria, pursuant to Article 21 of the code of civil procedure (Zivilprozeßordnung) concerning third-party notices,
- of Switzerland, pursuant to the appropriate provisions concerning third-party notices of the cantonal codes of civil procedure.

Judgments given in the other Contracting States by virtue of Article 6(2) or Article 10 shall be recognised and enforced in the Federal Republic of Germany, in Spain, in Austria and in Switzerland in accordance with Title III. Any effects which judgments given in these States may have on third parties by application of the provisions in the preceding paragraph shall also be recognised in the other Contracting States.

Article Va

In matters relating to maintenance, the expression "court" includes the Danish, Icelandic and Norwegian administrative authorities.

In civil and commercial matters, the expression "court" includes the Finnish ulosotonhaltija/överexekutor.

Article Vb

In proceedings involving a dispute between the master and a member of the crew of a sea-going ship registered in Denmark, in Greece, in Ireland, in Iceland, in Norway, in Portugal or in Sweden concerning remuneration or other conditions of service, a court in a Contracting State shall establish whether the diplomatic or consular officer responsible for the ship has been notified of the dispute. It shall stay the proceedings so long as he has not been notified. It shall of its own motion decline jurisdiction if the officer, having been duly notified, has exercised the powers accorded to him in the matter by a consular convention, or in the absence of such a convention has, within the time allowed, raised any objection to the exercise of such jurisdiction.

Article Vc

(None)

...

Article VI

The Contracting States shall communicate to the Swiss Federal Council the text of any provisions of their laws which amend either those provisions of their laws mentioned in the Convention or the lists of courts specified in Section 2 of Title III.

PROTOCOL NO. 2. ON THE UNIFORM INTERPRETATION OF THE CONVENTION

PREAMBLE

The High Contracting Parties,

Having regard to Article 65 of this Convention,

Considering the substantial link between this Convention and the Brussels Convention,

Considering that the Court of Justice of the European Communities by virtue of the Protocol of 3 June 1971 has jurisdiction to give rulings on the interpretation of the provisions of the Brussels Convention,

Being aware of the rulings delivered by the Court of Justice of the European Communities on the interpretation of the Brussels Convention up to the time of signature of this Convention,

Considering that the negotiations which led to the conclusion of the Convention were based on the Brussels Convention in the light of these rulings,

Desiring to prevent, in full deference to the independence of the courts, divergent interpretations and to arrive at as uniform an interpretation as possible of the provisions of the Convention, and of these provisions and those of the Brussels Convention which are substantially reproduced in this Convention,

Have agreed as follows:

Article 1

The courts of each Contracting State shall, when applying and interpreting the provisions of the Convention, pay due account to the principles laid down by any relevant decision delivered by courts of the other Contracting States concerning provisions of this Convention.

Article 2

1. The Contracting Parties agree to set up a system of exchange of information concerning judgments delivered pursuant to this Convention as well as relevant judgments under the Brussels Convention. This system shall comprise:
   - — transmission to a central body by the competent authorities of judgments delivered by courts of last instance and the Court of Justice of the European Communities as well as judgments of particular importance which have become final and have been delivered pursuant to this Convention or the Brussels Convention,
   - — classification of these judgments by the central body including, as far as necessary, the drawing-up and publication of translations and abstracts,
   - — communication by the central body of the relevant documents to the competent national authorities of all signatories and acceding States to the Convention and to the Commission of the European Communities.
2. The central body is the Registrar of the Court of Justice of the European Communities.

Article 3

1. A Standing Committee shall be set up for the purposes of this Protocol.
2. The Committee shall be composed of representatives appointed by each signatory and acceding State.

3. The European Communities (Commission, Court of Justice and General Secretariat of the Council) and the European Free Trade Association may attend the meetings as observers.

Article 4

1. At the request of a Contracting Party, the depositary of the Convention shall convene meetings of the Committee for the purpose of exchanging views on the functioning of the Convention and in particular on:

— the development of the case-law as communicated under the first paragraph first indent of Article 2,

— the application of Article 57 of the Convention.

2. The Committee, in the light of these exchanges, may also examine the appropriateness of starting on particular topics a revision of the Convention and make recommendations.

PROTOCOL NO. 3. ON THE APPLICATION OF ARTICLE 57

The High Contracting Parties have agreed as follows:

1. For the purposes of the Convention, provisions which, in relation to particular matters, govern jurisdiction or the recognition or enforcement of judgments and which are, or will be, contained in acts of the institutions of the European Communities shall be treated in the same way as the conventions referred to in paragraph 1 of Article 57.

2. If one Contracting State is of the opinion that a provision contained in an act of the institutions of the European Communities is incompatible with the Convention, the Contracting States shall promptly consider amending the Convention pursuant to Article 66, without prejudice to the procedure established by Protocol No. 2.

SCHEDULE 4. TITLE II OF THE 1968 CONVENTION AS MODIFIED FOR ALLOCATION OF JURISDICTION WITHIN U.K.

TITLE II. JURISDICTION

Section 1. General Provisions

Article 2

Subject to the provisions of this Title, persons domiciled in a **part of the United Kingdom** shall . . . be sued in the courts of that **part**.

. . .

Article 3

Persons domiciled in a **part of the United Kingdom** may be sued in the courts of **another part of the United Kingdom** only by virtue of the rules set out in Sections 2, **4, 5 and** 6 of this Title.

. . .

Section 2. Special Jurisdiction

Article 5

A person domiciled in a **part of the United Kingdom** may, in another **part of the United Kingdom**, be sued:

1. in matters relating to a contract, in the courts for the place of performance of the obligation in question; in matters relating to individual contracts of employment, this place is that where the employee habitually carries out his work, or if the employee does not habitually carry out his work in any one country, the employer may also be sued in the courts for the place where the business which engaged the employee was or is now situated;

2. in matters relating to maintenance, in the courts for the place where the maintenance creditor is domiciled or habitually resident or, if the matter is ancillary to proceedings concerning the status of a person, in the court which, according to its own law, has jurisdiction to entertain those proceedings, unless that jurisdiction is based solely on the nationality of one of the parties;
3. in matters relating to tort, delict or quasi-delict, in the courts for the place where the harmful event occurred **or in the case of a threatened wrong is likely to occur**;
4. as regards a civil claim for damages or restitution which is based on an act giving rise to criminal proceedings, in the court seised of those proceedings, to the extent that that court has jurisdiction under its own law to entertain civil proceedings;
5. as regards a dispute arising out of the operations of a branch, agency or other establishment, in the courts for the place in which the branch, agency or other establishment is situated;
6. in his capacity as a settlor, trustee or beneficiary of a trust created by the operation of a statute, or by a written instrument, or created orally and evidenced in writing, in the courts of the **part of the United Kingdom** in which the trust is domiciled;
7. as regards a dispute concerning the payment of remuneration claimed in respect of the salvage of a cargo or freight, in the court under the authority of which the cargo or freight in question:
   (a) has been arrested to secure such payment, or
   (b) could have been so arrested, but bail or other security has been given;
   provided that this provision shall apply only it if its claimed that the defendant has an interest in the cargo or freight or had such an interest at the time of salvage;
8. **in proceedings—**
   (a) concerning a debt secured on immovable property; or
   (b) which are brought to assert, declare or determine proprietary or possessory rights, or rights of security, in or over movable property, or to obtain authority to dispose of movable property,
   in the courts of the part of the United Kingdom in which the property is situated.

Article 5A

Proceedings which have as their object a decision of an organ of a company or other legal person or association of natural or legal persons may, without prejudice to the other provisions of this Title, be brought in the courts of the part of the United Kingdom in which that company, legal person or association has its seat.

Article 6

A person domiciled in a **part of the United Kingdom** may, in another **part of the United Kingdom**, also be sued:

1. where he is one of a number of defendants, in the courts for the place where any one of them is domiciled;
2. as a third party in an action on a warranty or guarantee or in any other third party proceedings, in the court seised of the original proceedings, unless these were instituted solely with the object of removing him from the jurisdiction of the court which would be competent in his case;
3. on a counterclaim arising from the same contract or facts on which the original claim was based, in the court in which the original claim is pending;
4. in matters relating to a contract, if the action may be combined with an action against the same defendant in matters relating to rights in rem in immovable property, in the court of the **part of the United Kingdom** in which the property is situated.

Article 6A

Where by virtue of this **Title** a court of a **part of the United Kingdom** has jurisdiction in actions relating to liability arising from the use or operation of a ship, that court, or any other court substituted for this purpose by the internal law of that **part**, shall also have jurisdiction over claims for limitation of such liability.

. . .

Section 4. Jurisdiction over Consumer Contracts

Article 13

In proceedings concerning a contract concluded by a person for a purpose which can be regarded as being outside his trade or profession, hereinafter called "the consumer", jurisdiction shall be determined by this Section, without prejudice to the provisions of Articles ... 5(5) **and (8)(b)**, if it is:

1. a contract for the sale of goods on instalment credit terms, or
2. a contract for a loan repayable by instalments, or for any other form of credit, made to finance the sale of goods, or
3. any other contract for the supply of goods or a contract for the supply of services and ... the consumer took in the **part of the United Kingdom in which he is domiciled** the steps necessary for the conclusion of the contract.

...

This Section shall not apply to contracts of transport **or insurance**.

Article 14

A consumer may bring proceedings against the other party to a contract either in the courts of the **part of the United Kingdom** in which that party is domiciled or in the courts of the **part of the United Kingdom** in which he is himself domiciled.

Proceedings may be brought against a consumer by the other party to the contract only in the courts of the **part of the United Kingdom** in which the consumer is domiciled.

These provisions shall not affect the right to bring a counterclaim in the court in which, in accordance with this Section, the original claim is pending.

Article 15

The provisions of this Section may be departed from only by an agreement:

1. which is entered into after the dispute has arisen, or
2. which allows the consumer to bring proceedings in courts other than those indicated in this Section, or
3. which is entered into by the consumer and the other party to the contract, both of whom are at the time of conclusion of the contract domiciled or habitually resident in the same **part of the United Kingdom**, and which confers jurisdiction on the courts of that **part**, provided that such an agreement is not contrary to the law of that **part**.

Section 5. Exclusive Jurisdiction

Article 16

The following courts shall have exclusive jurisdiction, regardless of domicile:

1. (a) in proceedings which have as their object rights in rem in immovable property or tenancies of immovable property, the courts of the **part of the United Kingdom** in which the property is situated;
   (b) however, in proceedings which have as their object tenancies of immovable property concluded for temporary private use for a maximum period of six consecutive months, the courts of the **part of the United Kingdom** in which the defendant is domiciled shall also have jurisdiction, provided that the landlord and the tenant are natural persons and are domiciled in the same **part of the United Kingdom**;

2. in proceedings which have as their object the validity of the constitution, the nullity or the dissolution of companies or other legal persons or associations of natural or legal persons ... the courts of the **part of the United Kingdom** in which the company, legal person or association has its seat;
3. in proceedings which have as their object the validity of entries in public registers, the courts of the **part of the United Kingdom** in which the register is kept;

...

5. in proceedings concerned with the enforcement of judgments, the courts of the **part of the United Kingdom** in which the judgment has been or is to be enforced.

Section 6. Prorogation of jurisdiction

Article 17

If the parties ... have agreed that a court or the courts of a **part of the United Kingdom** are to have jurisdiction to settle any disputes which have arisen or which may arise in connection with a particular legal relationship, **and, apart from this Schedule, the agreement would be effective to confer jurisdiction under the law of that part**, that court or those courts shall have ... jurisdiction

...

The court or courts of a **part of the United Kingdom** on which a trust instrument has conferred jurisdiction shall have ... jurisdiction in any proceedings brought against a settlor, trustee or beneficiary, if relations between these persons or their rights or obligations under the trust are involved.

Agreements or provisions of a trust instrument conferring jurisdiction shall have no legal force if they are contrary to the provisions of Article ... 15, or if the courts whose jurisdiction they purport to exclude have exclusive jurisdiction by virtue of Article 16.

...

In matters relating to individual contracts of employment an agreement conferring jurisdiction shall have legal force only if it is entered into after the dispute has arisen or if the employee invokes it to seise courts other than those for the defendant's domicile or those specified in Article 5(1).

Article 18

Apart from jurisdiction derived from other provisions of this **Title**, a court of a **part of the United Kingdom** before whom a defendant enters an appearance shall have jurisdiction. This rule shall not apply where appearance was entered solely to contest the jurisdiction, or where another court has exclusive jurisdiction by virtue of Article 16.

Section 7. Examination as to Jurisdiction and Admissibility

Article 19

Where a court of a **part of the United Kingdom** is seised of a claim which is principally concerned with a matter over which the courts of another **part of the United Kingdom** have exclusive jurisdiction by virtue of Article 16, it shall declare of its own motion that it has no jurisdiction.

Article 20

Where a defendant domiciled in one **part of the United Kingdom** is sued in a court of another **part of the United Kingdom** and does not enter an appearance, the court shall declare of its own motion that it has no jurisdiction unless its jurisdiction is derived from the provisions of this **Title**.

The court shall stay the proceedings so long as it is not shown that the defendant has been able to receive the document instituting the proceedings or an equivalent document in sufficient time to enable him to arrange for his defence, or that all necessary steps have been taken to this end.

...

Section 9. Provisional, Including Protective, Measures

Article 24

Application may be made to the courts of a **part of the United Kingdom** for such provisional, including protective, measures as may be available under the law of that **part**, even if, under this **Title**, the courts of another **part of the United Kingdom** have jurisdiction as to the substance of the matter.

SCHEDULE 5. PROCEEDINGS EXCLUDED FROM SCHEDULE 4

Proceedings under the Companies Acts

1. Proceedings for the winding up of a company under the Insolvency Act 1986 or the Insolvency (Northern Ireland) Order 1989, or proceedings relating to a company as respects which jurisdiction is conferred on the court having winding up jurisdiction under either of those Acts.

Patents, trade marks, designs and similar rights

2. Proceedings concerned with the registration or validity of patents, trade marks, designs or other similar rights required to be deposited or registered.

Protection of Trading Interests Act 1980

3. Proceedings under section 6 of the Protection of Trading Interests Act 1980 (recovery of sums paid or obtained pursuant to a judgment for multiple damages).

Appeals etc. from tribunals

4. Proceedings on appeal from, or for review of, decisions of tribunals.

. . .

Proceedings under certain conventions, etc.

6. Proceedings brought in any court in pursuance of—

(a) any statutory provision which, in the case of any convention to which Article 57 applies (conventions relating to specific matters which override the general rules in the 1968 Convention), implements the convention or makes provision with respect to jurisdiction in any field to which the convention relates; and

(b) any rule of law so far as it has the effect of implementing any such convention.

. . .

Register of aircraft mortgages

8. Proceedings for the rectification of the register of aircraft mortgages kept by the Civil Aviation Authority.

Continental Shelf Act 1964

9. Proceedings brought in any court in pursuance of an order under section 23 of the Oil and Gas (Enterprise) Act 1982.

Financial Services Act 1986

10. Proceedings such as are mentioned in section 188 of the Financial Services Act 1986.

SCHEDULE 6. ENFORCEMENT OF U.K. JUDGMENTS (MONEY PROVISIONS)

Preliminary

1. In this Schedule—

"judgment" means any judgment to which section 18 applies and references to the giving of a judgment shall be construed accordingly;

"money provision" means a provision for the payment of one or more sums of money;

"prescribed" means prescribed by rules of court.

Certificates in respect of judgments

2.—(1) Any interested party who wishes to secure the enforcement in another part of the United Kingdom of any money provisions contained in a judgment may apply for a certificate under this Schedule.

(2) The application shall be made in the prescribed manner to the proper officer of the original court, that is to say—

(a) in relation to a judgment within paragraph (a) of the definition of "judgment" in section 18(2), the court by which the judgment or order was given or made;

(b) in relation to a judgment within paragraph (b) of that definition, the court in which the judgment or order is entered;

(c) in relation to a judgment within paragraph (c) of that definition, the court in whose books the document is registered;

(d) in relation to a judgment within paragraph (d) of that definition, the tribunal by which the award or order was made;

(e) in relation to a judgment within paragraph (e) of that definition, the court which gave the judgment or made the order by virtue of which the award has become enforceable as mentioned in that paragraph.

3. A certificate shall not be issued under this Schedule in respect of a judgment unless under the law of the part of the United Kingdom in which the judgment was given—

(a) either—

(i) the time for bringing an appeal against the judgment has expired, no such appeal having been brought within that time; or

(ii) such an appeal having been brought within that time, that appeal has been finally disposed of; and

(b) enforcement of the judgment is not for the time being stayed or suspended, and the time available for its enforcement has not expired.

4.—(1) Subject to paragraph 3, on an application under paragraph 2 the proper officer shall issue to the applicant a certificate in the prescribed form—

(a) stating the sum or aggregate of the sums (including any costs or expenses) payable under the money provisions contained in the judgment, the rate of interest, if any, payable thereon and the date or time from which any such interest began to accrue;

(b) stating that the conditions specified in paragraph 3(a) and (b) are satisfied in relation to the judgment; and

(c) containing such other particulars as may be prescribed.

(2) More than one certificate may be issued under this Schedule (simultaneously or at different times) in respect of the same judgment.

Registration of certificates

5.—(1) Where a certificate has been issued under this Schedule in any part of the United Kingdom, any interested party may, within six months from the date of its issue, apply in the prescribed manner to the proper officer of the superior court in any other part of the United Kingdom for the certificate to be registered in that court.

(2) In this paragraph "superior court" means, in relation to England and Wales or Northern Ireland, the High Court and, in relation to Scotland, the Court of Session.

(3) Where an application is duly made under this paragraph to the proper officer of a superior court, he shall register the certificate in that court in the prescribed manner.

General effect of registration

6.—(1) A certificate registered under this Schedule shall, for the purposes of its enforcement, be of the same force and effect, the registering court shall have in relation to its enforcement the same powers, and proceedings for or with respect to its enforcement may be taken, as if the certificate had been a judgment originally given in the registering court and had (where relevant) been entered.

(2) Sub-paragraph (1) is subject to the following provisions of this Schedule and to any provision made by rules of court as to the manner in which and the conditions subject to which a certificate registered under this Schedule may be enforced.

Costs or expenses

7. Where a certificate is registered under this Schedule, the reasonable costs or expenses of and incidental to the obtaining of the certificate and its registration shall be recoverable as if they were costs or expenses stated in the certificate to be payable under a money provision contained in the original judgment.

Interest

8.—(1) Subject to any provision made under sub-paragraph (2), the debt resulting, apart from paragraph 7, from the registration of the certificate shall carry interest at the rate, if any, stated in the certificate from the date or time so stated.

(2) Provision may be made by rules of court as to the manner in which and the periods by reference to which any interest payable by virtue of sub-paragraph (1) is to be calculated and paid, including provision for such interest to cease to accrue as from a prescribed date.

(3) All such sums as are recoverable by virtue of paragraph 7 carry interest as if they were the subject of an order for costs or expenses made by the registering court on the date of registration of the certificate.

(4) Except as provided by this paragraph sums payable by virtue of the registration of a certificate under this Schedule shall not carry interest.

Stay or sisting of enforcement in certain cases

9. Where a certificate in respect of a judgment has been registered under this Schedule, the registering court may, if it is satisfied that any person against whom it is sought to enforce the certificate is entitled and intends to apply under the law of the part of the United Kingdom in which the judgment was given for any remedy which would result in the setting aside or quashing of the judgment, stay (or, in Scotland, sist) proceedings for the enforcement of the certificate, on such terms as it thinks fit, for such period as appears to the court to be reasonably sufficient to enable the application to be disposed of.

Cases in which registration of a certificate must or may be set aside

10. Where a certificate has been registered under this Schedule, the registering court—

(a) shall set aside the registration if, on an application made by any interested party, it is satisfied that the registration was contrary to the provisions of this Schedule;

(b) may set aside the registration if, on an application so made, it is satisfied that the matter in dispute in the proceedings in which the judgment in question was given had previously been the subject of a judgment by another court or tribunal having jurisdiction in the matter.

SCHEDULE 7. ENFORCEMENT OF U.K. JUDGMENTS (NON-MONEY PROVISIONS)

Preliminary

1. In this Schedule—

"judgment" means any judgment to which section 18 applies and references to the giving of a judgment shall be construed accordingly;

"non-money provision" means a provision for any relief or remedy not requiring payment of a sum of money;

"prescribed" means prescribed by rules of court.

Certified copies of judgments

2.—(1) Any interested party who wishes to secure the enforcement in another part of the United Kingdom of any non-money provisions contained in a judgment may apply for a certified copy of the judgment.

(2) The application shall be made in the prescribed manner to the proper officer of the original court, that is to say—

(a) in relation to a judgment within paragraph (a) of the definition of "judgment" in section 18(2), the court by which the judgment or order was given or made;

(b) in relation to a judgment within paragraph (b) of that definition, the court in which the judgment or order is entered;

(c) in relation to a judgment within paragraph (c) of that definition, the court in whose books the document is registered;

(d) in relation to a judgment within paragraph (d) of that definition, the tribunal by which the award or order was made;

(e) in relation to a judgment within paragraph (e) of that definition, the court which gave the judgment or made the order by virtue of which the award has become enforceable as mentioned in that paragraph.

3. A certified copy of a judgment shall not be issued under this Schedule unless under the law of the part of the United Kingdom in which the judgment was given—

(a) either—

(i) the time for bringing an appeal against the judgment has expired, no such appeal having been brought within that time; or

(ii) such an appeal having been brought within that time, that appeal has been finally disposed of; and

(b) enforcement of the judgment is not for the time being stayed or suspended, and the time available for its enforcement has not expired.

4.—(1) Subject to paragraph 3, on an application under paragraph 2 the proper officer shall issue to the applicant—

(a) a certified copy of the judgment (including any money provisions or excepted provisions which it may contain); and

(b) a certificate stating that the conditions specified in paragraph 3(a) and (b) are satisfied in relation to the judgment.

(2) In sub-paragraph (1)(a) "excepted provision" means any provision of a judgment which is excepted from the application of section 18 by subsection (5) of that section.

(3) There may be issued under this Schedule (simultaneously or at different times)—

(a) more than one certified copy of the same judgment; and

(b) more than one certificate in respect of the same judgment.

Registration of judgments

5.—(1) Where a certified copy of a judgment has been issued under this Schedule in any part of the United Kingdom, any interested party may apply in the prescribed manner to the superior court in any other part of the United Kingdom for the judgment to be registered in that court.

(2) In this paragraph "superior court" means, in relation to England and Wales or Northern Ireland, the High Court and, in relation to Scotland, the Court of Session.

(3) An application under this paragraph for the registration of a judgment must be accompanied by—

(a) a certified copy of the judgment issued under this Schedule; and

(b) a certificate issued under paragraph 4(1)(b) in respect of the judgment not more than six months before the date of the application.

(4) Subject to sub-paragraph (5), where an application under this paragraph is duly made to a superior court, the court shall order the whole of the judgment as set out in the certified copy to be registered in that court in the prescribed manner.

(5) A judgment shall not be registered under this Schedule by the superior court in any part of the United Kingdom if compliance with the non-money provisions contained in the judgment would involve a breach of the law of that part of the United Kingdom.

General effect of registration

6.—(1) The non-money provisions contained in a judgment registered under this Schedule shall, for the purposes of their enforcement, be of the same force and effect, the registering court shall have in relation to their enforcement the same powers, and proceedings for or with respect to their enforcement may be taken, as if the judgment containing them had been originally given in the registering court and had (where relevant) been entered.

(2) Sub-paragraph (1) is subject to the following provisions of this Schedule and to any provision made by rules of court as to the manner in which and the conditions subject to which the non-money provisions contained in a judgment registered under this Schedule may be enforced.

Costs or expenses

7.—(1) Where a judgment is registered under this Schedule, the reasonable costs or expenses of and incidental to—

(a) the obtaining of the certified copy of the judgment and of the necessary certificate under paragraph 4(1)(b) in respect of it; and

(b) the registration of the judgment,

shall be recoverable as if on the date of registration there had also been registered in the registering court a certificate under Schedule 6 in respect of the judgment and as if those costs or expenses were costs or expenses stated in that certificate to be payable under a money provision contained in the judgment.

(2) All such sums as are recoverable by virtue of sub-paragraph (1) shall carry interest as if they were the subject of an order for costs or expenses made by the registering court on the date of registration of the judgment.

Stay or sisting of enforcement in certain cases

8. Where a judgment has been registered under this Schedule, the registering court may, if it is satisfied that any person against whom it is sought to enforce the judgment is entitled and intends to apply under the law of the part of the United Kingdom in which the judgment was given for any remedy which would result in the setting aside or quashing of the judgment, stay (or, in Scotland, sist) proceedings for the enforcement of the judgment, on such terms as it thinks fit, for such period as appears to the court to be reasonably sufficient to enable the application to be disposed of.

Cases in which registered judgment must or may be set aside

9. Where a judgment has been registered under this Schedule, the registering court—

(a) shall set aside the registration if, on an application made by any interested party, it is satisfied that the registration was contrary to the provisions of this Schedule;

(b) may set aside the registration if, on an application so made, it is satisfied that the matter in dispute in the proceedings in which the judgment was given had previously been the subject of a judgment by another court or tribunal having jurisdiction in the matter.

APPENDIX 2

SUPREME COURT ACT 1981 (c 54)

An Act to consolidate with amendments the Supreme Court of Judicature (Consolidation) Act 1925 and other enactments relating to the Supreme Court in England and Wales and the administration of justice therein; to repeal certain obsolete or unnecessary enactments so relating; to amend Part VIII of the Mental Health Act 1959, the Courts-Martial (Appeals) Act 1968, the Arbitration Act 1979 and the law relating to county courts; and for connected purposes.

[28th July 1981]

PART II. JURISDICTION

THE HIGH COURT

Admiralty jurisdiction

Admiralty jurisdiction of High Court

20.—(1) The Admiralty jurisdiction of the High Court shall be as follows, that is to say—

(a) jurisdiction to hear and determine any of the questions and claims mentioned in subsection (2);

(b) jurisdiction in relation to any of the proceedings mentioned in subsection (3);

(c) any other Admiralty jurisdiction which it had immediately before the commencement of this Act; and

(d) any jurisdiction connected with ships or aircraft which is vested in the High Court apart from this section and is for the time being by rules of court made or coming into force after the commencement of this Act assigned to the Queen's Bench Division and directed by the rules to be exercised by the Admiralty Court.

(2) The questions and claims referred to in subsection (1)(a) are—

(a) any claim to the possession or ownership of a ship or to the ownership of any share therein;

(b) any question arising between the co-owners of a ship as to possession, employment or earnings of that ship;

(c) any claim in respect of a mortgage of or charge on a ship or any share therein;

(d) any claim for damage received by a ship;

(e) any claim for damage done by a ship;

(f) any claim for loss of life or personal injury sustained in consequence of any defect in a ship or in her apparel or equipment, or in consequence of the wrongful act, neglect or default of—

(i) the owners, charterers or persons in possession or control of a ship; or

(ii) the master or crew of a ship, or any other person for whose wrongful acts, neglects or defaults the owners, charterers or persons in possession or control of a ship are responsible, being an act, neglect or default in the navigation or management of the ship, in the loading, carriage or discharge of goods on, in or from the ship, or in the embarkation, carriage or disembarkation of persons on, in or from the ship;

(g) any claim for loss of or damage to goods carried in a ship;

(h) any claim arising out of any agreement relating to the carriage of goods in a ship or to the use or hire of a ship;

(j) any claim in the nature of salvage (including any claim arising by virtue of the application, by or under section 87 of the Civil Aviation Act 1982, of the law relating to salvage to aircraft and their apparel and cargo);

(k) any claim in the nature of towage in respect of a ship or an aircraft;

(l) any claim in the nature of pilotage in respect of a ship or an aircraft;

(m) any claim in respect of goods or materials supplied to a ship for her operation or maintenance;

(n) any claim in respect of the construction, repair or equipment of a ship or in respect of dock charges or dues;

(o) any claim by a master or member of the crew of a ship for wages (including any sum allotted out of wages or adjudged by a superintendent to be due by way of wages);

(p) any claim by a master, shipper, charterer or agent in respect of disbursements made on account of a ship;

(q) any claim arising out of an act which is or is claimed to be a general average act;

(r) any claim arising out of bottomry;

(s) any claim for the forfeiture or condemnation of a ship or of goods which are being or have been carried, or have been attempted to be carried, in a ship, or for the restoration of a ship or any such goods after seizure, or for droits of Admiralty.

(3) The proceedings referred to in subsection (1)(b) are—

(a) any application to the High Court under the Merchant Shipping Acts 1894 to 1979 other than an application under section 55 of the Merchant Shipping Act 1894 for the appointment of a person to act as a substitute for a person incapable of acting;

(b) any action to enforce a claim for damage, loss of life or personal injury arising out of—

(i) a collision between ships; or

(ii) the carrying out of or omission to carry out a manoeuvre in the case of one or more of two or more ships; or

(iii) non-compliance, on the part of one or more of two or more ships, with the collision regulations;

(c) any action by shipowners or other persons under the Merchant Shipping Acts 1894 to 1979 for the limitation of the amount of their liability in connection with a ship or other property.

(4) The jurisdiction of the High Court under subsection (2)(b) includes power to settle any account outstanding and unsettled between the parties in relation to the ship, and to direct that the ship, or any share thereof, shall be sold, and to make such other order as the court thinks fit.

(5) Subsection (2)(e) extends to—

(a) any claim in respect of a liability incurred under the Merchant Shipping (Oil Pollution) Act 1971; and

(b) any claim in respect of a liability falling on the International Oil Pollution Compensation Fund, or on the International Oil Pollution Compensation Fund 1984, under Part I of the Merchant Shipping Act 1974.

(6) The reference in subsection (2)(j) to claims in the nature of salvage includes a reference to such claims for services rendered in saving life from a ship or an aircraft or in preserving cargo, apparel or wreck as, under sections 544 to 546 of the Merchant Shipping Act 1894, or any Order in Council made under section 87 of the Civil Aviation Act 1982, are authorised to be made in connection with a ship or an aircraft.

(7) The preceding provisions of this section apply—

(a) in relation to all ships or aircraft, whether British or not and whether registered or not and wherever the residence or domicile of their owners may be;

(b) in relation to all claims, wherever arising (including, in the case of cargo or wreck salvage, claims in respect of cargo or wreck found on land); and

(c) so far as they relate to mortgages and charges, to all mortgages or charges, whether registered or not and whether legal or equitable, including mortgages and charges created under foreign law:

Provided that nothing in this subsection shall be construed as extending the cases in which money or property is recoverable under any of the provisions of the Merchant Shipping Acts 1894 to 1979.

Mode of exercise of Admiralty jurisdiction

21.—(1) Subject to section 22, an action in personam may be brought in the High Court in all cases within the Admiralty jurisdiction of that court.

(2) In the case of any such claim as is mentioned in section 20(2)(a), (c) or (s) or any such question as is mentioned in section 20(2)(b), an action in rem may be brought in the High Court against the ship or property in connection with which the claim or question arises.

(3) In any case in which there is a maritime lien or other charge on any ship, aircraft or other property for the amount claimed, an action in rem may be brought in the High Court against that ship, aircraft or property.

(4) In the case of any such claim as is mentioned in section 20(2)(e) to (r), where—

(a) the claim arises in connection with a ship; and

(b) the person who would be liable on the claim in an action in personam ("the relevant person") was, when the cause of action arose, the owner or charterer of, or in possession or in control of, the ship,

an action in rem may (whether or not the claim gives rise to a maritime lien on that ship) be brought in the High Court against—

(i) that ship, if at the time when the action is brought the relevant person is either the beneficial owner of that ship as respects all the shares in it or the charterer of it under a charter by demise; or

(ii) any other ship of which, at the time when the action is brought, the relevant person is the beneficial owner as respects all the shares in it.

(5) In the case of a claim in the nature of towage or pilotage in respect of an aircraft, an action in rem may be brought in the High Court against that aircraft if, at the time when the action is brought, it is beneficially owned by the person who would be liable on the claim in an action in personam.

(6) Where, in the exercise of its Admiralty jurisdiction, the High Court orders any ship, aircraft or other property to be sold, the court shall have jurisdiction to hear and determine any question arising as to the title to the proceeds of sale.

(7) In determining for the purposes of subsections (4) and (5) whether a person would be liable on a claim in an action in personam it shall be assumed that he has his habitual residence or a place of business within England or Wales.

(8) Where, as regards any such claim as is mentioned in section 20(2)(e) to (r), a ship has been served with a writ or arrested in an action in rem brought to enforce that claim, no other ship may be served with a writ or arrested in that or any other action in rem brought to enforce that claim; but this subsection does not prevent the issue, in respect of any one such claim, of a writ naming more than one ship or of two or more writs each naming a different ship.

Restrictions on entertainment of actions in personam in collision and other similar cases

22.—(1) This section applies to any claim for damage, loss of life or personal injury arising out of—

(a) a collision between ships; or

(b) the carrying out of, or omission to carry out, a manoeuvre in the case of one or more of two or more ships; or

(c) non-compliance, on the part of one or more of two or more ships, with the collision regulations.

(2) The High Court shall not entertain any action in personam to enforce a claim to which this section applies unless—

(a) the defendant has his habitual residence or a place of business within England or Wales; or
(b) the cause of action arose within inland waters of England or Wales or within the limits of a port of England or Wales; or
(c) an action arising out of the same incident or series of incidents is proceeding in the court or has been heard and determined in the court.

In this subsection—

"inland waters" includes any part of the sea adjacent to the coast of the United Kingdom certified by the Secretary of State to be waters falling by international law to be treated as within the territorial sovereignty of Her Majesty apart from the operation of that law in relation to territorial waters;

"port" means any port, harbour, river, estuary, haven, dock, canal or other place so long as a person or body of persons is empowered by or under an Act to make charges in respect of ships entering it or using the facilities therein, and "limits of a port" means the limits thereof as fixed by or under the Act in question or, as the case may be, by the relevant charter or custom;

"charges" means any charges with the exception of light dues, local light dues and any other charges in respect of lighthouses, buoys or beacons and of charges in respect of pilotage.

(3) The High Court shall not entertain any action in personam to enforce a claim to which this section applies until any proceedings previously brought by the plaintiff in any court outside England and Wales against the same defendant in respect of the same incident or series of incidents have been discontinued or otherwise come to an end.

(4) Subsections (2) and (3) shall apply to counterclaims (except counterclaims in proceedings arising out of the same incident or series of incidents) as they apply to actions, the references to the plaintiff and the defendant being for this purpose read as references to the plaintiff on the counterclaim and the defendant to the counterclaim respectively.

(5) Subsections (2) and (3) shall not apply to any action or counterclaim if the defendant thereto submits or has agreed to submit to the jurisdiction of the court.

(6) Subject to the provisions of subsection (3), the High Court shall have jurisdiction to entertain an action in personam to enforce a claim to which this section applies whenever any of the conditions specified in subsection (2)(a) to (c) is satisfied, and the rules of court relating to the service of process outside the jurisdiction shall make such provision as may appear to the rule-making authority to be appropriate having regard to the provisions of this subsection.

(7) Nothing in this section shall prevent an action which is brought in accordance with the provisions of this section in the High Court being transferred, in accordance with the enactments in that behalf, to some other court.

(8) For the avoidance of doubt it is hereby declared that this section applies in relation to the jurisdiction of the High Court not being Admiralty jurisdiction, as well as in relation to its Admiralty jurisdiction.

High Court not to have jurisdiction in cases within Rhine Convention

23. The High Court shall not have jurisdiction to determine any claim or question certified by the Secretary of State to be a claim or question which, under the Rhine Navigation Convention, falls to be determined in accordance with the provisions of that Convention; and any proceedings to enforce such a claim which are commenced in the High Court shall be set aside.

Supplementary provisions as to Admiralty jurisdiction

24.—(1) In sections 20 to 23 and this section, unless the context otherwise requires—

"collision regulations" means regulations under section 418 of the Merchant Shipping Act 1894, or any such rules as are mentioned in section 421(1) of that Act, or any rules made under section 421(2) of that Act;

"goods" includes baggage;

"master" has the same meaning as in the Merchant Shipping Act 1894, and accordingly includes every person (except a pilot) having command or charge of a ship;

"the Rhine Navigation Convention" means the Convention of the 7th October 1868 as revised by any subsequent Convention;

"ship" includes any description of vessel used in navigation and (except in the definition of "port" in section 22(2) and in subsection (2)(c) of this section) includes, subject to section 2(3) of the Hovercraft Act 1968, a hovercraft;

"towage" and "pilotage", in relation to an aircraft, mean towage and pilotage while the aircraft is waterborne.

(2) Nothing in sections 20 to 23 shall—

(a) be construed as limiting the jurisdiction of the High Court to refuse to entertain an action for wages by the master or a member of the crew of a ship, not being a British ship;

(b) affect the provisions of section 552 of the Merchant Shipping Act 1894 (power of a receiver of wreck to detain a ship in respect of a salvage claim); or

(c) authorise proceedings in rem in respect of any claim against the Crown, or the arrest, detention or sale of any of Her Majesty's ships or Her Majesty's aircraft, or, subject to section 2(3) of the Hovercraft Act 1968, Her Majesty's hovercraft, or of any cargo or other property belonging to the Crown.

(3) In this section—

"Her Majesty's ships" and "Her Majesty's aircraft" have the meanings given by section 38(2) of the Crown Proceedings Act 1947;

"Her Majesty's hovercraft" means hovercraft belonging to the Crown in right of Her Majesty's Government in the United Kingdom or Her Majesty's Government in Northern Ireland.

CONTRACTS (APPLICABLE LAW) ACT 1990 (c 36)

An Act to make provision as to the law applicable to contractual obligations in the case of conflict of laws.

[26th July 1990]

Meaning of "the Conventions"

1. In this Act—

(a) "the Rome Convention" means the Convention on the law applicable to contractual obligations opened for signature in Rome on 19th June 1980 and signed by the United Kingdom on 7th December 1981;

(b) "the Luxembourg Convention" means the Convention on the accession of the Hellenic Republic to the Rome Convention signed by the United Kingdom in Luxembourg on 10th April 1984; and

(c) "the Brussels Protocol" means the first Protocol on the interpretation of the Rome Convention by the European Court signed by the United Kingdom in Brussels on 19th December 1988;

and the Rome Convention, the Luxembourg Convention and the Brussels Protocol are together referred to as "the Conventions".

Conventions to have force of law

2.—(1) Subject to subsections (2) and (3) below, the Conventions shall have the force of law in the United Kingdom.

(1A) The internal law for the purposes of Article 1(3) of the Rome Convention is whichever of the following are applicable, namely—

(a) the provisions of Schedule 3A to the Insurance Companies Act 1982 (law applicable to certain contracts of insurance with insurance companies), and

(b) the provisions of Schedule 20 to the Friendly Societies Act 1992 as applied by subsections (1)(a) and (2)(a) of section 101 of that Act (law applicable to certain contracts of insurance with friendly societies).

(2) Articles 7(1) and 10(1)(e) of the Rome Convention shall not have the force of law in the United Kingdom.

(3) Notwithstanding Article 19(2) of the Rome Convention, the Conventions shall apply in the case of conflicts between the laws of different parts of the United Kingdom.

(4) For ease of reference there are set out in Schedules 1, 2 and 3 to this Act respectively the English texts of—

(a) the Rome Convention;

(b) the Luxembourg Convention; and

(c) the Brussels Protocol.

Interpretation of Conventions

3.—(1) Any question as to the meaning or effect of any provision of the Conventions shall, if not referred to the European Court in accordance with the Brussels Protocol, be determined in accordance with the principles laid down by, and any relevant decision of, the European Court.

(2) Judicial notice shall be taken of any decision of, or expression of opinion by, the European Court on any such question.

(3) Without prejudice to any practice of the courts as to the matters which may be considered apart from this subsection—

(a) the report on the Rome Convention by Professor Mario Giuliano and Professor Paul Lagarde which is reproduced in the Official Journal of the Communities of 31st October 1980 may be considered in ascertaining the meaning or effect of any provision of that Convention; and

(b) any report on the Brussels Protocol which is reproduced in the Official Journal of the Communities may be considered in ascertaining the meaning or effect of any provision of that Protocol.

Revision of Conventions etc.

4.—(1) If at any time it appears to Her Majesty in Council that Her Majesty's Government in the United Kingdom—

(a) have agreed to a revision of any of the Conventions (including, in particular, any revision connected with the accession to the Rome Convention of any state); or

(b) have given notification in accordance with Article 22(3) of the Rome Convention that either or both of the provisions mentioned in section 2(2) above shall have the force of law in the United Kingdom,

Her Majesty may by Order in Council make such consequential modifications of this Act or any other statutory provision, whenever passed or made, as Her Majesty considers appropriate.

(2) An Order in Council under subsection (1) above shall not be made unless a draft of the Order has been laid before Parliament and approved by a resolution of each House.

(3) In subsection (1) above—

"modifications" includes additions, omissions and alterations;

"revision" means an omission from, addition to or alteration of any of the Conventions and includes replacement of any of the Conventions to any extent by another convention, protocol or other description of international agreement; and

"statutory provision" means any provision contained in an Act, or in any Northern Ireland legislation, or in—

(a) subordinate legislation (as defined in section 21(1) of the Interpretation Act 1978); or

(b) any instrument of a legislative character made under any Northern Ireland legislation.

Consequential amendments

5. The enactments specified in Schedule 4 to this Act shall have effect subject to the amendments specified in that Schedule.

Application to Crown

6. This Act binds the Crown.

...

SCHEDULES

SCHEDULE 1. THE ROME CONVENTION

THE HIGH CONTRACTING PARTIES TO THE TREATY ESTABLISHING THE EUROPEAN ECONOMIC COMMUNITY,

Anxious to continue in the field of private international law the work of unification of law which has already been done with the Community, in particular in the field of jurisdiction and enforcement of judgments,

Wishing to establish uniform rules concerning the law applicable to contractual obligations,

Have agreed as follows:

TITLE I. SCOPE OF THE CONVENTION

Article 1. Scope of the Convention

1. The rules of this Convention shall apply to contractual obligations in any situation involving a choice between the laws of different countries.

2. They shall not apply to:

(a) questions involving the status or legal capacity of natural persons, without prejudice to Article 11;

(b) contractual obligations relating to:
- wills and succession,
- rights in property arising out of a matrimonial relationship,
- rights and duties arising out of a family relationship, parentage, marriage or affinity, including maintenance obligations in respect of children who are not legitimate;

(c) obligations arising under bills of exchange, cheques and promissory notes and other negotiable instruments to the extent that the obligations under such other negotiable instruments arise out of their negotiable character;

(d) arbitration agreements and agreements on the choice of court;

(e) questions governed by the law of companies and other bodies corporate or unincorporate such as the creation, by registration or otherwise, legal capacity, internal organisation or winding up of companies and other bodies corporate or unincorporate and the personal liability of officers and members as such for the obligations of the company or body;

(f) the question whether an agent is able to bind a principal, or an organ to bind a company or body corporate or unincorporate, to a third party;

(g) the constitution of trusts and the relationship between settlors, trustees and beneficiaries;

(h) evidence and procedure, without prejudice to Article 14.

3. The rules of this Convention do not apply to contracts of insurance which cover risks situated in the territories of the Member States of the European Economic Community. In order to determine whether a risk is situated in these territories the court shall apply its internal law.

4. The preceding paragraph does not apply to contracts of re-insurance.

Article 2. Application of law of non-contracting States

Any law specified by this Convention shall be applied whether or not it is the law of a Contracting State.

TITLE II. UNIFORM RULES

Article 3. Freedom of choice

1. A contract shall be governed by the law chosen by the parties. The choice must be express or demonstrated with reasonable certainty by the terms of the contract or the circumstances of the case. By their choice the parties can select the law applicable to the whole or a part only of the contract.

2. The parties may at any time agree to subject the contract to a law other than that which previously governed it, whether as a result of an earlier choice under this Article or of other provisions of this Convention. Any variation by the parties of the law to be applied made after the conclusion of the contract shall not prejudice its formal validity under Article 9 or adversely affect the rights of third parties.

3. The fact that the parties have chosen a foreign law, whether or not accompanied by the choice of a foreign tribunal, shall not, where all the other elements relevant to the situation at the time of the choice are connected with one country only, prejudice the application of rules of the law of that country which cannot be derogated from by contract, hereinafter called "mandatory rules".

4. The existence and validity of the consent of the parties as to the choice of the applicable law shall be determined in accordance with the provisions of Articles 8, 9 and 11.

Article 4. Applicable law in the absence of choice

1. To the extent that the law applicable to the contract has not been chosen in accordance with Article 3, the contract shall be governed by the law of the country with which it is most closely connected. Nevertheless, a severable part of the contract which has a closer connection with another country may by way of exception be governed by the law of that other country.

2. Subject to the provisions of paragraph 5 of this Article, it shall be presumed that the contract is most closely connected with the country where the party who is to effect the performance which is characteristic of the contract has, at the time of conclusion of the contract, his habitual residence, or, in the case of a body corporate or unincorporate, its central administration. However, if the contract is entered into in the course of that party's trade or profession, that country shall be the country in which the principal place of business is situated or, where under the terms of the contract the performance is to be effected through a place of business other than the principal place of business, the country in which that other place of business is situated.

3. Notwithstanding the provisions of paragraph 2 of this Article, to the extent that the subject matter of the contract is a right in immovable property or a right to use immovable property it shall be presumed that the contract is most closely connected with the country where the immovable property is situated.

4. A contract for the carriage of goods shall not be subject to the presumption in paragraph 2. In such a contract if the country in which, at the time the contract is concluded, the carrier has his principal place of business is also the country in which the place of loading or the place of discharge or the principal place of business of the consignor is situated, it shall be presumed that the contract is most closely connected with that country. In applying this paragraph single voyage charter-parties and other contracts the main purpose of which is the carriage of goods shall be treated as contracts for the carriage of goods.

5. Paragraph 2 shall not apply if the characteristic performance cannot be determined, and the presumptions in paragraphs 2, 3 and 4 shall be disregarded if it appears from the circumstances as a whole that the contract is more closely connected with another country.

Article 5. Certain consumer contracts

1. This Article applies to a contract the object of which is the supply of goods or services to a person ("the consumer") for a purpose which can be regarded as being outside his trade or profession, or a contract for the provision of credit for that object.

2. Notwithstanding the provisions of Article 3, a choice of law made by the parties shall not have the result of depriving the consumer of the protection afforded to him by the mandatory rules of the law of the country in which he has his habitual residence:

— if in that country the conclusion of the contract was preceded by a specific invitation addressed to him or by advertising, and he had taken in that country all the steps necessary on his part for the conclusion of the contract, or

— if the other party or his agent received the consumer's order in that country, or
— if the contract is for the sale of goods and the consumer travelled from that country to another country and there gave his order, provided that the consumer's journey was arranged by the seller for the purpose of inducing the consumer to buy.

3. Notwithstanding the provisions of Article 4, a contract to which this Article applies shall, in the absence of choice in accordance with Article 3, be governed by the law of the country in which the consumer has his habitual residence if it is entered into in the circumstances described in paragraph 2 of this Article.

4. This Article shall not apply to:

(a) a contract of carriage;
(b) a contract for the supply of services where the services are to be supplied to the consumer exclusively in a country other than that in which he has his habitual residence.

5. Notwithstanding the provisions of paragraph 4, this Article shall apply to a contract which, for an inclusive price, provides for a combination of travel and accommodation.

Article 6. Individual employment contracts

1. Notwithstanding the provisions of Article 3, in a contract of employment a choice of law made by the parties shall not have the result of depriving the employee of the protection afforded to him by the mandatory rules of the law which would be applicable under paragraph 2 in the absence of choice.

2. Notwithstanding the provisions of Article 4, a contract of employment shall, in the absence of choice in accordance with Article 3, be governed:

(a) by the law of the country in which the employee habitually carries out his work in performance of the contract, even if he is temporarily employed in another country; or
(b) if the employee does not habitually carry out his work in any one country, by the law of the country in which the place of business through which he was engaged is situated;

unless it appears from the circumstances as a whole that the contract is more closely connected with another country, in which case the contract shall be governed by the law of that country.

Article 7. Mandatory rules

1. When applying under this Convention the law of a country, effect may be given to the mandatory rules of the law of another country with which the situation has a close connection, if and in so far as, under the law of the latter country, those rules must be applied whatever the law applicable to the contract. In considering whether to give effect to these mandatory rules, regard shall be had to their nature and purpose and to the consequences of their application or non-application.

2. Nothing in this Convention shall restrict the application of the rules of the law of the forum in a situation where they are mandatory irrespective of the law otherwise applicable to the contract.

Article 8. Material validity

1. The existence and validity of a contract, or of any term of a contract, shall be determined by the law which would govern it under this Convention if the contract or term were valid.

2. Nevertheless a party may rely upon the law of the country in which he has his habitual residence to establish that he did not consent if it appears from the circumstances that it would not be reasonable to determine the effect of his conduct in accordance with the law specified in the preceding paragraph.

Article 9. Formal validity

1. A contract concluded between persons who are in the same country is formally valid if it satisfies the formal requirements of the law which governs it under this Convention or of the law of the country where it is concluded.

2. A contract concluded between persons who are in different countries is formally valid if it satisfies the formal requirements of the law which governs it under this Convention or of the law of one of those countries.

3. Where a contract is concluded by an agent, the country in which the agent acts is the relevant country for the purposes of paragraphs 1 and 2.

4. An act intended to have legal effect relating to an existing or contemplated contract is formally valid if it satisfies the formal requirements of the law which under this Convention governs or would govern the contract or of the law of the country where the act was done.

5. The provisions of the preceding paragraphs shall not apply to a contract to which Article 5 applies, concluded in the circumstances described in paragraph 2 of Article 5. The formal validity of such a contract is governed by the law of the country in which the consumer has his habitual residence.

6. Notwithstanding paragraphs 1 to 4 of this Article, a contract the subject matter of which is a right in immovable property or a right to use immovable property shall be subject to the mandatory requirements of form of the law of the country where the property is situated if by that law those requirements are imposed irrespective of the country where the contract is concluded and irrespective of the law governing the contract.

Article 10. Scope of the applicable law

1. The law applicable to a contract by virtue of Articles 3 to 6 and 12 of this Convention shall govern in particular:

(a) interpretation;
(b) performance;
(c) within the limits of the powers conferred on the court by its procedural law, the consequences of breach, including the assessment of damages in so far as it is governed by rules of law;
(d) the various ways of extinguishing obligations, and prescription and limitation of actions;
(e) the consequences of nullity of the contract.

2. In relation to the manner of performance and the steps to be taken in the event of defective performance regard shall be had to the law of the country in which performance takes place.

Article 11. Incapacity

In a contract concluded between persons who are in the same country, a natural person who would have capacity under the law of that country may invoke his incapacity resulting from another law only if the other party to the contract was aware of this incapacity at the time of the conclusion of the contract or was not aware thereof as a result of negligence.

Article 12. Voluntary assignment

1. The mutual obligations of assignor and assignee under a voluntary assignment of a right against another person ("the debtor") shall be governed by the law which under this Convention applies to the contract between the assignor and assignee.

2. The law governing the right to which the assignment relates shall determine its assignability, the relationship between the assignee and the debtor, the conditions under which the assignment can be invoked against the debtor and any question whether the debtor's obligations have been discharged.

Article 13. Subrogation

1. Where a person ("the creditor") has a contractual claim upon another ("the debtor"), and a third person has a duty to satisfy the creditor, or has in fact satisfied the creditor in discharge of

that duty, the law which governs the third person's duty to satisfy the creditor shall determine whether the third person is entitled to exercise against the debtor the rights which the creditor had against the debtor under the law governing their relationship and, if so, whether he may do so in full or only to a limited extent.

2. The same rule applies where several persons are subject to the same contractual claim and one of them has satisfied the creditor.

Article 14. Burden of proof, etc.

1. The law governing the contract under this Convention applies to the extent that it contains, in the law of contract, rules which raise presumptions of law or determine the burden of proof.

2. A contract or an act intended to have legal effect may be proved by any mode of proof recognised by the law of the forum or by any of the laws referred to in Article 9 under which that contract or act is formally valid, provided that such mode of proof can be administered by the forum.

Article 15. Exclusion of renvoi

The application of the law of any country specified by this Convention means the application of the rules of law in force in that country other than its rules of private international law.

Article 16. "Ordre public"

The application of a rule of the law of any country specified by this Convention may be refused only if such application is manifestly incompatible with the public policy ("ordre public") of the forum.

Article 17. No retrospective effect

This Convention shall apply in a Contracting State to contracts made after the date on which this Convention has entered into force with respect to that State.

Article 18. Uniform interpretation

In the interpretation and application of the preceding uniform rules, regard shall be had to their international character and to the desirability of achieving uniformity in their interpretation and application.

Article 19. States with more than one legal system

1. Where a State comprises several territorial units each of which has its own rules of law in respect of contractual obligations, each territorial unit shall be considered as a country for the purposes of identifying the law applicable under this Convention.

2. A State within which different territorial units have their own rules of law in respect of contractual obligations shall not be bound to apply this Convention to conflicts solely between the laws of such units.

Article 20. Precedence of Community Law

This Convention shall not affect the application of provisions which, in relation to particular matters, lay down choice of law rules relating to contractual obligations and which are or will be contained in acts of the institutions of the European Communities or in national laws harmonised in implementation of such acts.

Article 21. Relationship with other conventions

This Convention shall not prejudice the application of international conventions to which a Contracting State is, or becomes, a party.

Article 22. Reservations

1. Any Contracting State may, at the time of signature, ratification, acceptance or approval, reserve the right not to apply:
   (a) the provisions of Article 7(1);
   (b) the provisions of Article 10(1)(e).

2. Any Contracting State may also, when notifying an extension of the Convention in accordance with Article 27(2), make one or more of these reservations, with its effect limited to all or some of the territories mentioned in the extension.

3. Any Contracting State may at any time withdraw a reservation which it has made; the reservation shall cease to have effect on the first day of the third calendar month after notification of the withdrawal.

TITLE III. FINAL PROVISIONS

Article 23

1. If, after the date on which this Convention has entered into force for a Contracting State, that State wishes to adopt any new choice of law rule in regard to any particular category of contract within the scope of this Convention, it shall communicate its intention to the other signatory States through the Secretary-General of the Council of the European Communities.

2. Any signatory State may, within six months from the date of the communication made to the Secretary-General, request him to arrange consultations between signatory States in order to reach agreement.

3. If no signatory State has requested consultations within this period or if within two years following the communications made to the Secretary-General no agreement is reached in the course of consultations, the Contracting State concerned may amend its law in the manner indicated. The measures taken by that State shall be brought to the knowledge of the other signatory States through the Secretary-General of the Council of the European Communities.

Article 24

1. If, after the date on which this Convention has entered into force with respect to a Contracting State, that State wishes to become a party to a multilateral convention whose principal aim or one of whose principal aims is to lay down rules of private international law concerning any of the matters governed by this Convention, the procedure set out in Article 23 shall apply. However, the period of two years, referred to in paragraph 3 of that Article, shall be reduced to one year.

2. The procedure referred to in the preceding paragraph need not be followed if a Contracting State or one of the European Communities is already a party to the multilateral convention, or if its object is to revise a convention to which the State concerned is already a party, or if it is a convention concluded within the framework of the Treaties establishing the European Communities.

Article 25

If a Contracting State considers that the unification achieved by this Convention is prejudiced by the conclusion of agreements not covered by Article 24(1), that State may request the Secretary-General of the Council of the European Communities to arrange consultations between the signatory States of this Convention.

Article 26

Any Contracting State may request the revision of this Convention. In this event a revision conference shall be convened by the President of the Council of the European Communities.

Article 27

1. This Convention shall apply to the European territories of the Contracting States, including Greenland, and to the entire territory of the French Republic.

2. Notwithstanding paragraph 1:

(a) this Convention shall not apply to the Faroe Islands, unless the Kingdom of Denmark makes a declaration to the contrary;

(b) this Convention shall not apply to any European territory situated outside the United Kingdom for the international relations of which the United Kingdom is responsible, unless the United Kingdom makes a declaration to the contrary in respect of any such territory;

(c) this Convention shall apply to the Netherlands Antilles, if the Kingdom of the Netherlands makes a declaration to that effect.

3. Such declarations may be made at any time by notifying the Secretary-General of the Council of the European Communities.

4. Proceedings brought in the United Kingdom on appeal from courts in one of the territories referred to in paragraph 2(b) shall be deemed to be proceedings taking place in those courts.

Article 28

1. This Convention shall be open from 19 June 1980 for signature by the States party to the Treaty establishing the European Economic Community.

2. This Convention shall be subject to ratification, acceptance or approval by the signatory States. The instruments of ratification, acceptance or approval shall be deposited with the Secretary-General of the Council of the European Communities.

Article 29

1. This Convention shall enter into force on the first day of the third month following the deposit of the seventh instrument of ratification, acceptance or approval.

2. This Convention shall enter into force for each signatory State ratifying, accepting or approving at a later date on the first day of the third month following the deposit of its instrument of ratification, acceptance or approval.

Article 30

1. This Convention shall remain in force for 10 years from the date of its entry into force in accordance with Article 29(1), even for States for which it enters into force at a later date.

2. If there has been no denunciation it shall be renewed tacitly every five years.

3. A Contracting State which wishes to denounce shall, not less than six months before the expiration of the period of 10 or five years, as the case may be, give notice to the Secretary-General of the Council of the European Communities. Denunciation may be limited to any territory to which the Convention has been extended by a declaration under Article 27(2).

4. The denunciation shall have effect only in relation to the State which has notified it. The Convention will remain in force as between all other Contracting States.

Article 31

The Secretary-General of the Council of the European Communities shall notify the States party to the Treaty establishing the European Economic Community of:

(a) the signatures;

(b) the deposit of each instrument of ratification, acceptance or approval;

(c) the date of entry into force of this Convention;
(d) communications made in pursuance of Articles 23, 24, 25, 26, 27 and 30;
(e) the reservations and withdrawals of reservations referred to in Article 22.

Article 32

The Protocol annexed to this Convention shall form an integral part thereof.

Article 33

This Convention, drawn up in a single original in the Danish, Dutch, English, French, German, Irish and Italian languages, these texts being equally authentic, shall be deposited in the archives of the Secretariat of the Council of the European Communities. The Secretary-General shall transmit a certified copy thereof to the Government of each signatory state.

PROTOCOL

The High Contracting Parties have agreed upon the following provision which shall be annexed to the Convention:

Notwithstanding the provisions of the Convention, Denmark may retain the rules contained in Søloven (Statute on Maritime Law) paragraph 169 concerning the applicable law in matters relating to carriage of goods by sea and may revise these rules without following the procedure prescribed in Article 23 of the Convention.

. . .

SCHEDULE 3. THE BRUSSELS PROTOCOL

The High Contracting Parties to the Treaty establishing the European Economic Community,

Having regard to the Joint Declaration annexed to the Convention on the law applicable to contractual obligations, opened for signature in Rome on 19 June 1980,

Have decided to conclude a Protocol conferring jurisdiction on the Court of Justice of the European Communities to interpret that Convention, and to this end have designated as their Plenipotentiaries:

(Designation of plenipotentiaries)

Who, meeting within the Council of the European Communities, having exchanged their full powers, found in good and due form,

Have agreed as follows:

Article 1

The Court of Justice of the European Communities shall have jurisdiction to give rulings on the interpretation of—

(a) the Convention on the law applicable to contractual obligations, opened for signature in Rome on 19 June 1980, hereinafter referred to as "the Rome Convention";
(b) the Convention on accession to the Rome Convention by the States which have become Members of the European Communities since the date on which it was opened for signature;
(c) this Protocol.

Article 2

Any of the courts referred to below may request the Court of Justice to give a preliminary ruling on a question raised in a case pending before it and concerning interpretation of the provisions contained in the instruments referred to in Article 1 if that court considers that a decision on the question is necessary to enable it to give judgment:

(a) — in Belgium:
la Cour de cassation (het Hof van Cassatie) and le Conseil d'Etat (de Raad van State),
— in Denmark:
Højesteret,
— in the Federal Republic of Germany:
die obersten Gerichschöfe des Bundes,
— in Greece:
τα ανώτατα δικαστήρια,
— in Spain:
el Tribunal Supremo,
— in France:
la Cour de cassation and le Conseil d'Etat,
— in Ireland:
— the Supreme Court,
— in Italy:
la Corte suprema di cassazione and il Consiglio di Stato,
— in Luxembourg:
la Cour Supérieure de Justice, when sitting as Cour de cassation,
— in the Netherlands:
de Hoge Raad,
— in Portugal:
o Supremo Tribunal de Justiça and o Supremo Tribunal Administrativo,
— in the United Kingdom:
the House of Lords and other courts from which no further appeal is possible;

(b) the courts of the Contracting States when acting as appeal courts.

Article 3

1. The competent authority of a Contracting State may request the Court of Justice to give a ruling on a question of interpretation of the provisions contained in the instruments referred to in Article 1 if judgments given by courts of that State conflict with the interpretation given either by the Court of Justice or in a judgment of one of the courts of another Contracting State referred to in Article 2. The provisions of this paragraph shall apply only to judgments which have become res judicata.

2. The interpretation given by the Court of Justice in response to such a request shall not affect the judgments which gave rise to the request for interpretation.

3. The Procurators-General of the Supreme Courts of Appeal of the Contracting States, or any other authority designated by a Contracting State, shall be entitled to request the Court of Justice for a ruling on interpretation in accordance with paragraph 1.

4. The Registrar of the Court of Justice shall give notice of the request to the Contracting States, to the Commission and to the Council of the European Communities; they shall then be entitled within two months of the notification to submit statements of case or written observations to the Court.

5. No fees shall be levied or any costs or expenses awarded in respect of the proceedings provided for in this Article.

Article 4

1. Except where this Protocol otherwise provides, the provisions of the Treaty establishing the European Economic Community and those of the Protocol on the Statute of the Court of Justice annexed thereto, which are applicable when the Court is requested to give a preliminary ruling, shall also apply to any proceedings for the interpretation of the instruments referred to in Article 1.

2. The Rules of Procedure of the Court of Justice shall, if necessary, be adjusted and supplemented in accordance with Article 188 of the Treaty establishing the European Economic Community.

Article 5

This Protocol shall be subject to ratification by the Signatory States. The instruments of ratification shall be deposited with the Secretary-General of the Council of the European Communities.

Article 6

1. To enter into force, this Protocol must be ratified by seven States in respect of which the Rome Convention is in force. This Protocol shall enter into force on the first day of the third month following the deposit of the instrument of ratification by the last such State to take this step. If, however, the Second Protocol conferring on the Court of Justice of the European Communities certain powers to interpret the Convention on the law applicable to contractual obligations, opened for signature in Rome on 19 June 1980, concluded in Brussels on 19 December 1988, enters into force on a later date, this Protocol shall enter into force on the date of entry into force of the Second Protocol.

2. Any ratification subsequent to the entry into force of this Protocol shall take effect on the first day of the third month following the deposit of the instrument of ratification provided that the ratification, acceptance or approval of the Rome Convention by the State in question has become effective.

Article 7

The Secretary-General of the Council of the European Communities shall notify the Signatory States of:

(a) the deposit of each instrument of ratification;
(b) the date of entry into force of this Protocol;
(c) any designation communicated pursuant to Article 3(3);
(d) any communication made pursuant to Article 8.

Article 8

The Contracting States shall communicate to the Secretary-General of the Council of the European Communities the texts of any provisions of their laws which necessitate an amendment to the list of courts in Article 2(a).

Article 9

This Protocol shall have effect for as long as the Rome Convention remains in force under the conditions laid down in Article 30 of that Convention.

Article 10

Any Contracting State may request the revision of this Protocol. In this event, a revision conference shall be convened by the President of the Council of the European Communities.

Article 11

This Protocol, drawn up in a single original in the Danish, Dutch, English, French, German, Greek, Irish, Italian, Portuguese and Spanish languages, all 10 texts being equally authentic, shall be deposited in the archives of the General Secretariat of the Council of the European Communities. The Secretary-General shall transmit a certified copy to the Government of each Signatory State.

SCHEDULE 4. CONSEQUENTIAL AMENDMENTS

This Schedule amends the Equal Pay Act 1970, s. 1(11), the Equal Pay Act (Northern Ireland) 1970, s. 1(12), the Consumer Credit Act 1974, ss. 43(2)(c), 145(3)(c), (4)(b), the Patents Act 1977, s. 82(5), (6), the Unfair Contract Terms Act 1977, s. 27(1), the Aviation Security Act 1982, s. 19(5), and the Income and Corporation Taxes Act 1988, s. 347B(1)(a).

APPENDIX 4

ARBITRATION ACT 1975 (c 3)

An Act to give effect to the New York Convention on the Recognition and Enforcement of Foreign Arbitral Awards.

[25th February 1975]

Effect of arbitration agreement on court proceedings

Staying court proceedings where party proves arbitration agreement

1.—(1) If any party to an arbitration agreement to which this section applies, or any person claiming through or under him, commences any legal proceedings in any court against any other party to the agreement, or any person claiming through or under him, in respect of any matter agreed to be referred, any party to the proceedings may at any time after appearance, and before delivering any pleadings or taking any other steps in the proceedings, apply to the court to stay the proceedings; and the court, unless satisfied that the arbitration agreement is null and void, inoperative or incapable of being performed or that there is not in fact any dispute between the parties with regard to the matter agreed to be referred, shall make an order staying the proceedings.

(2) This section applies to any arbitration agreement which is not a domestic arbitration agreement; ...

...

(4) In this section "domestic arbitration agreement" means an arbitration agreement which does not provide, expressly or by implication, for arbitration in a State other than the United Kingdom and to which neither—

(a) an individual who is a national of, or habitually resident in, any State other than the United Kingdom; nor

(b) a body corporate which is incorporated in, or whose central management and control is exercised in, any State other than the United Kingdom;

is a party at the time the proceedings are commenced.

Enforcement of Convention awards

Replacement of former provisions

2. Sections 3 to 6 of this Act shall have effect with respect to the enforcement of Convention awards; and where a Convention award would, but for this section, be also a foreign award within the meaning of Part II of the Arbitration Act 1950, that Part shall not apply to it.

Effect of Convention awards

3.—(1) A Convention award shall, subject to the following provisions of this Act, be enforceable—

(a) in England and Wales, either by action or in the same manner as the award of an arbitrator is enforceable by virtue of section 26 of the Arbitration Act 1950;

...

(2) Any Convention award which would be enforceable under this Act shall be treated as binding for all purposes on the persons as between whom it was made, and may accordingly be relied on by any of those persons by way of defence, set off or otherwise in any legal proceedings in the United Kingdom; and any reference in this Act to enforcing a Convention award shall be construed as including references to relying on such an award.

Evidence

4. The party seeking to enforce a Convention award must produce—

(a) the duly authenticated original award or a duly certified copy of it; and

(b) the original arbitration agreement or a duly certified copy of it; and

(c) where the award or agreement is in a foreign language, a translation of it certified by an official or sworn translator or by a diplomatic or consular agent.

Refusal of enforcement

5.—(1) Enforcement of a Convention award shall not be refused except in the cases mentioned in this section.

(2) Enforcement of a Convention award may be refused if the person against whom it is invoked proves—

(a) that a party to the arbitration agreement was (under the law applicable to him) under some incapacity; or

(b) that the arbitration agreement was not valid under the law to which the parties subjected it or, failing any indication thereon, under the law of the country where the award was made; or

(c) that he was not given proper notice of the appointment of the arbitrator or of the arbitration proceedings or was otherwise unable to present his case; or

(d) (subject to subsection (4) of this section) that the award deals with a difference not contemplated by or not falling within the terms of the submission to arbitration or contains decisions on matters beyond the scope of the submission to arbitration; or

(e) that the composition of the arbitral authority or the arbitral procedure was not in accordance with the agreement of the parties or, failing such agreement, with the law of the country where the arbitration took place; or

(f) that the award has not yet become binding on the parties, or has been set aside or suspended by a competent authority of the country in which, or under the law of which, it was made.

(3) Enforcement of a Convention award may also be refused if the award is in respect of a matter which is not capable of settlement by arbitration, or if it would be contrary to public policy to enforce the award.

(4) A Convention award which contains decisions on matters not submitted to arbitration may be enforced to the extent that it contains decisions on matters submitted to arbitration which can be separated from those on matters not so submitted.

(5) Where an application for the setting aside or suspension of a Convention award has been made to such a competent authority as is mentioned in subsection (2)(f) of this section, the court before which enforcement of the award is sought may, if it thinks fit, adjourn the proceedings and may, on the application of the party seeking to enforce the award, order the other party to give security.

Saving

6. Nothing in this Act shall prejudice any right to enforce or rely on an award otherwise than under this Act or Part II of the Arbitration Act 1950.

General

Interpretation

7.—(1) In this Act—

"arbitration agreement" means an agreement in writing (including an agreement contained in an exchange of letters or telegrams) to submit to arbitration present or future differences capable of settlement by arbitration;

"Convention award" means an award made in pursuance of an arbitration agreement in the territory of a State, other than the United Kingdom, which is a party to the New York Convention; and

"the New York Convention" means the Convention on the Recognition and Enforcement of Foreign Arbitral Awards adopted by the United Nations Conference on International Commercial Arbitration on 10th June 1958.

(2) If Her Majesty by Order in Council declares that any State specified in the Order is a party to the New York Convention the Order shall, while in force, be conclusive evidence that that State is a party to that Convention.

(3) An Order in Council under this section may be varied or revoked by a subsequent Order in Council.

. . .

ARBITRATION ACT 1979 (c 42)

An Act to amend the law relating to arbitrations and for purposes connected therewith.

[4th April 1979]

Judicial review of arbitration awards

1.—(1) In the Arbitration Act 1950 (in this Act referred to as "the principal Act") section 21 (statement of case for a decision of the High Court) shall cease to have effect and, without prejudice to the right of appeal conferred by subsection (2) below, the High Court shall not have jurisdiction to set aside or remit an award on an arbitration agreement on the ground of errors of fact or law on the face of the award.

(2) Subject to subsection (3) below, an appeal shall lie to the High Court on any question of law arising out of an award made on an arbitration agreement; and on the determination of such an appeal the High Court may by order—

(a) confirm, vary or set aside the award; or

(b) remit the award to the reconsideration of the arbitrator or umpire together with the court's opinion on the question of law which was the subject of the appeal;

and where the award is remitted under paragraph (b) above the arbitrator or umpire shall, unless the order otherwise directs, make his award within three months after the date of the order.

(3) An appeal under this section may be brought by any of the parties to the reference—

(a) with the consent of all the other parties to the reference; or

(b) subject to section 3 below, with the leave of the court.

(4) The High Court shall not grant leave under subsection (3)(b) above unless it considers that, having regard to all the circumstances, the determination of the question of law concerned could substantially affect the rights of one or more of the parties to the arbitration agreement; and the court may make any leave which it gives conditional upon the applicant complying with such conditions as it considers appropriate.

(5) Subject to subsection (6) below, if an award is made and, on an application made by any of the parties to the reference,—

(a) with the consent of all the other parties to the reference, or

(b) subject to section 3 below, with the leave of the court,

it appears to the High Court that the award does not or does not sufficiently set out the reasons for the award, the court may order the arbitrator or umpire concerned to state the reasons for his award in sufficient detail to enable the court, should an appeal be brought under this section, to consider any question of law arising out of the award.

(6) In any case where an award is made without any reason being given, the High Court shall not make an order under subsection (5) above unless it is satisfied—

(a) that before the award was made one of the parties to the reference gave notice to the arbitrator or umpire concerned that a reasoned award would be required; or

(b) that there is some special reason why such a notice was not given.

(6A) Unless the High Court gives leave, no appeal shall lie to the Court of Appeal from a decision of the High Court—

(a) to grant or refuse leave under subsection (3)(b) or (5)(b) above; or

(b) to make or not to make an order under subsection (5) above.

(7) No appeal shall lie to the Court of Appeal from a decision of the High Court on an appeal under this section unless—

(a) the High Court or the Court of Appeal gives leave; and

(b) it is certified by the High Court that the question of law to which its decision relates either is one of general public importance or is one which for some other special reason should be considered by the Court of Appeal.

(8) Where the award of an arbitrator or umpire is varied on appeal, the award as varied shall have effect (except for the purposes of this section) as if it were the award of the arbitrator or umpire.

Determination of preliminary point of law by court

2.—(1) Subject to subsection (2) and section 3 below, on an application to the High Court made by any of the parties to a reference—

(a) with the consent of an arbitrator who has entered on the reference or, if an umpire has entered on the reference, with his consent, or

(b) with the consent of all the other parties,

the High Court shall have jurisdiction to determine any question of law arising in the course of the reference.

(2) The High Court shall not entertain an application under subsection (1)(a) above with respect to any question of law unless it is satisfied that—

(a) the determination of the application might produce substantial savings in costs to the parties; and

(b) the question of law is one in respect of which leave to appeal would be likely to be given under section 1(3)(b) above.

(2A) Unless the High Court gives leave, no appeal shall lie to the Court of Appeal from a decision of the High Court to entertain or not to entertain an application under subsection (1)(a) above.

(3) A decision of the High Court under subsection (1) above shall be deemed to be a judgment of the court within the meaning of section 16 of the Supreme Court Act 1981 (appeals to the Court of Appeal), but no appeal shall lie from such a decision unless—

(a) the High Court or the Court of Appeal gives leave; and

(b) it is certified by the High Court that the question of law to which its decision relates either is one of general importance or is one which for some other special reason should be considered by the Court of Appeal.

Exclusion agreements affecting rights under sections 1 and 2

3.—(1) Subject to the following provisions of this section and section 4 below—

(a) the High Court shall not, under section 1(3)(b) above, grant leave to appeal with respect to a question of law arising out of an award, and

(b) the High Court shall not, under section 1(5)(b) above, grant leave to make an application with respect to an award, and

(c) no application may be made under section 2(1)(a) above with respect to a question of law,

if the parties to the reference in question have entered into an agreement in writing (in this section referred to as an "exclusion agreement") which excludes the right of appeal under section 1 above in relation to that award or, in a case falling within paragraph (c) above, in relation to an award to which the determination of the question of law is material.

(2) An exclusion agreement may be expressed so as to relate to a particular award, to awards under a particular reference or to any other description of awards, whether arising out of the same reference or not; and an agreement may be an exclusion agreement for the purposes of this section whether it is entered into before or after the passing of this Act and whether or not it forms part of an arbitration agreement.

(3) In any case where—

(a) an arbitration agreement, other than a domestic arbitration agreement, provides for disputes between the parties to be referred to arbitration, and
(b) a dispute to which the agreement relates involves the question whether a party has been guilty of fraud, and
(c) the parties have entered into an exclusion agreement which is applicable to any award made on the reference of that dispute,

then, except in so far as the exclusion agreement otherwise provides, the High Court shall not exercise its powers under section 24(2) of the principal Act (to take steps necessary to enable the question to be determined by the High Court) in relation to that dispute.

(4) Except as provided by subsection (1) above, sections 1 and 2 above shall have effect notwithstanding anything in any agreement purporting—

(a) to prohibit or restrict access to the High Court; or
(b) to restrict the jurisdiction of that court; or
(c) to prohibit or restrict the making of a reasoned award.

(5) An exclusion agreement shall be of no effect in relation to an award made on, or a question of law arising in the course of a reference under, a statutory arbitration, that is to say, such an arbitration as is referred to in subsection (1) of section 31 of the principal Act.

(6) An exclusion agreement shall be of no effect in relation to an award made on, or a question of law arising in the course of a reference under, an arbitration agreement which is a domestic arbitration agreement unless the exclusion agreement is entered into after the commencement of the arbitration in which the award is made or, as the case may be, in which the question of law arises.

(7) In this section "domestic arbitration agreement" means an arbitration agreement which does not provide, expressly or by implication, for arbitration in a State other than the United Kingdom and to which neither—

(a) an individual who is a national of, or habitually resident in, any State other than the United Kingdom, nor
(b) a body corporate which is incorporated in, or whose central management and control is exercised in, any State other than the United Kingdom,

is a party at the time the arbitration agreement is entered into.

Exclusion agreements not to apply in certain cases

4.—(1) Subject to subsection (3) below, if an arbitration award or a question of law arising in the course of a reference relates, in whole or in part, to—

(a) a question or claim falling within the Admiralty jurisdiction of the High Court, or
(b) a dispute arising out of a contract of insurance, or
(c) a dispute arising out of a commodity contract,

an exclusion agreement shall have no effect in relation to the award or question unless either—

(i) the exclusion agreement is entered into after the commencement of the arbitration in which the award is made or, as the case may be, in which the question of law arises, or
(ii) the award or question relates to a contract which is expressed to be governed by a law other than the law of England and Wales.

(2) In subsection (1)(c) above "commodity contract" means a contract—

(a) for the sale of goods regularly dealt with on a commodity market or exchange in England or Wales which is specified for the purposes of this section by an order made by the Secretary of State; and
(b) of a description so specified.

(3) The Secretary of State may by order provide that subsection (1) above—

(a) shall cease to have effect; or
(b) subject to such conditions as may be specified in the order, shall not apply to any exclusion agreement made in relation to an arbitration award of a description so specified;

and an order under this subsection may contain such supplementary, incidental and transitional provisions as appear to the Secretary of State to be necessary or expedient.

(4) The power to make an order under subsection (2) or subsection (3) above shall be exercisable by statutory instrument which shall be subject to annulment in pursuance of a resolution of either House of Parliament.

(5) In this section "exclusion agreement" has the same meaning as in section 3 above.

Interlocutory orders

5.—(1) If any party to a reference under an arbitration agreement fails within the time specified in the order or, if no time is so specified, within a reasonable time to comply with an order made by the arbitrator or umpire in the course of the reference, then, on the application of the arbitrator or umpire or of any party to the reference, the High Court may make an order extending the powers of the arbitrator or umpire as mentioned in subsection (2) below.

(2) If an order is made by the High Court under this section, the arbitrator or umpire shall have power, to the extent and subject to any conditions specified in that order, to continue with the reference in default of appearance or of any other act by one of the parties in like manner as a judge of the High Court might continue with proceedings in that court where a party fails to comply with an order of that court or a requirement of rules of court.

(3) Section 4(5) of the Administration of Justice Act 1970 (jurisdiction of the High Court to be exercisable by the Court of Appeal in relation to judge-arbitrators and judge-umpires) shall not apply in relation to the power of the High Court to make an order under this section, but in the case of a reference to a judge-arbitrator or judge-umpire that power shall be exercisable as in the case of any other reference to arbitration and also by the judge-arbitrator or judge-umpire himself.

(4) Anything done by a judge-arbitrator or judge-umpire in the exercise of the power conferred by subsection (3) above shall be done by him in his capacity as judge of the High Court and have effect as if done by that court.

(5) The preceding provisions of this section have effect notwithstanding anything in any agreement but do not derogate from any powers conferred on an arbitrator or umpire, whether by an arbitration agreement or otherwise.

(6) In this section "judge-arbitrator" and "judge-umpire" have the same meaning as in Schedule 3 to the Administration of Justice Act 1970.

. . .

Application and interpretation of certain provisions of Part I of principal Act

7.—(1) References in the following provisions of Part I of the principal Act to that Part of that Act shall have effect as if the preceding provisions of this Act were included in that Part, namely,—

(a) section 14 (interim awards);
(b) section 28 (terms as to costs of orders);
(c) section 30 (Crown to be bound);
(d) section 31 (application to statutory arbitrations); and
(e) section 32 (meaning of "arbitration agreement").

(2) Subsections (2) and (3) of section 29 of the principal Act shall apply to determine when an arbitration is deemed to be commenced for the purposes of this Act.

(3) For the avoidance of doubt, it is hereby declared that the reference in subsection (1) of section 31 of the principal Act (statutory arbitrations) to arbitration under any other Act does not extend to arbitration under section 64 of the County Courts Act 1984 (cases in which proceedings are to be or may be referred to arbitration) and accordingly nothing in this Act or in Part I of the principal Act applies to arbitration under the said section 64.

INDEX

Acta jure, imperii and *gestiones* distinguished, 2.3.1.2–2.3.1.3
Actions *in personam*
  and provisional measures, 21.3
    jurisdiction in support of arbitration proceedings, 21.3.2
    question of foreign proceedings, 21.3.1
  question of jurisdiction, 1.2.1.1.2.1, 1.2.2.1
  simultaneous with action *in rem*, 8.0.2
Actions *in rem*, *see* Shipping
Administration, central, application in British law, 11.2.3.3.2
Administration of Justice Act 1920
  enforcement of arbitration awards, 20.5.2
  enforcement of foreign judgments, 9.3.1
Admiralty proceedings, *see* Shipping
Agency
  choice of law in contract, 12.7
  question of alternative fora, 5.5.5
  and Rome Convention, 10.4.1.2.5
Agent, location, and service of writ out of jurisdiction, 6.3.3.4.3
Aliens, enemy, inability to sue, 2.2
Alternative fora, *see* Fora, alternative
Antisuit injunctions, 22.1–22.3
  and Conventions, 22.3
  unconscionable conduct, 22.2
Anton Piller orders
  development, 21.1.1
  operation, 21.1.4
  question of use abroad, 21.4.1.1–21.4.1.2
Appearance, voluntary, question of submission, 6.2.3
Applicable law
  contract, 11.2
    and characteristic performance, 11.2.3.1–11.2.3.2
    choice of law
      carriage of goods, 12.3.1
      consumers, question of generosity, 12.1.2.2.2
      immovables, 12.4.1
      individual contracts of employment, 12.2.2.2
      and performance, 11.4.5
    contrasted with proper law, 11.2.2
    mandatory rules and public policy, 11.2.4, 11.3
    scission, 11.2.3.7
    splitting, 11.1.4
  court's discretion to allow litigation, 6.4.4.10
  and gold clauses, 14.1.3.2
Arab Monetary Fund v. *Hashim*, question of international corporations' legal capacity, 2.1.4.3
Arbitration, 1.1.7, 16.1–16.4, 17.1–17.5, 18.1–18.3, 19.1–19.5, 20.1–20.6
  agreements, *see* Arbitration agreements
  appeals under 1979 Act, 19.1–19.5
    awards, nature of, 19.2
    exclusion agreements, 19.5
    question of leave of court, 19.3
    to Court of Appeal, 19.4
  characteristics, 16.1
  curial law, 17.2
    choice of law principles and seat of arbitration, 17.2.3
    internal and external procedures, 17.2.2
    question of delocalisation theory, 17.2.1
    question of internal conduct, 17.2.5
    severing link with seat of arbitration, 17.2.4
  and EC law, 17.4
  enforcement of awards, 20.1–20.6
    and 1950 Act, 20.4
      conditions, 20.4.2
      defences, 20.4.3
      relationship with other regimes, 20.4.1
    and 1975 Act, 20.2
      conditions, 20.2.2
        documents, 20.2.2.1
        procedure, 20.2.2.2
      discretion to stay proceedings, 20.2.4
      grounds for refusal, 20.2.3
        agreement invalid, 20.2.3.3
        award invalid, 20.2.3.7
        excess of jurisdiction, 20.2.3.5
        lack of capacity, 20.2.3.2
        non-arbitrability, 20.2.3.8
        public policy, 20.2.3.9
        question of procedural rules, 20.2.3.6
        question of procedural unfairness, 20.2.3.4
        question of review of merits, 20.2.3.10
        statutory framework, 20.2.3.1
      relationship with common law, 20.3.1
      scope, 20.2.1
        question of arbitration agreement, 20.2.1.1
        temporal, 20.2.1.3
        territorial, 20.2.1.2
    and Administration of Justice Act 1920, 20.5.2
    and Arbitration (International Investment Disputes) Act 1966, 20.5.4

Arbitration—*cont.*
enforcement of awards—*cont.*
and Civil Jurisdiction and Judgments Act 1982, 20.5.1
and common law, 20.3
conditions, 20.3.3
defences, 20.3.4
breach of natural justice, 20.3.4.2.2
excess of jurisdiction, 20.3.4.2.1
fraud, 20.3.4.2.4
public policy, 20.3.4.2.3
defences, invalid, 20.3.4.1
methods, 20.3.2
relationship with 1975 Act, 20.3.1
domestic awards, 20.1.2
effect of foreign award on cause of action, 20.6.3
effect of foreign judgment on award, 20.6.2
foreign awards, 20.1.3
and Foreign Judgments (Reciprocal Enforcement) Act 1933, 20.5.3
and Iran–US Claims Tribunal, 20.5.5
question of conflicting judgments and awards, 20.6.1
relationship with setting aside, 20.1.1
English law, 16.2
nature of, 16.2.1
powers of the court, 16.2.3
assistance and support, 16.2.3.1
supervision and control, 16.2.3.2
sources, 16.2.2
and UNCITRAL Model Law, 16.4.2.4.4–16.4.2.4.6
and immunity from adjudicative jurisdiction, 2.3.4.2
jurisdiction, 17.5
jurisdiction *in personam*, 17.5.1
enforcement proceedings, 17.5.1.3
scope of court's powers, 17.5.2
traditional rules, 17.5.1.2
law applicable to merits of dispute, 17.3
and absence of express choice, 17.3.4
arbitration *extra legem*, 17.3.6
choice of law of particular country, 17.3.3
impact of mandatory rules, 17.3.8
legal introduction, 17.3.2
lex mercatoria, 17.3.7, 20.2.3.9.1
public international law, 17.3.5
remedies where arbitrator fails to apply conflicts rules/question of exclusion agreements, 17.3.9
types of choice of law clauses, 17.3.1
law covering agreement, 17.1
and scope of Conventions, 3.3.3.4
types
ad hoc, 16.3.2.1
domestic and international, 16.3.1
institutional, 16.3.2.2–16.3.2.3
specialised, 16.3.3
Arbitration Act 1950
and jurisdiction to grant provisional measures in support of arbitration proceedings, 21.3.2.1
See also Arbitration, enforcement of awards
Arbitration Act 1975, *see* Arbitration, enforcement of awards; Arbitration agreements, enforcement
Arbitration Act 1979, *see* Arbitration, appeals under 1979 Act
Arbitration agreements, 18.1–18.3
doctrine of separability, 18.1.2
domestic enforcement, 18.1.4
enforcement, and recognition and enforcement of foreign awards, 20.2
enforcement under 1975 Act, 18.2
statutory framework, 18.2.1
stay under
effect, 18.2.3
grant of, 18.2.2
requirements, 18.2.2
capable of settlement by arbitration, 18.2.2.1.3
dispute, 18.2.2.5
foreign element, 18.2.2.1.1
in writing, 18.2.2.1.2
question of validity of original agreement, 18.2.2.4
scope of clause, 18.2.2.2
scope of s.1
timing, 18.2.2.3
text of Act, App.4
inherent jurisdiction, 18.3
nature, 18.1.1
and Rome Convention, 10.4.1.2.3
validity and scope, 18.1.2–18.1.3
Arbitration clauses, and choice of law, 10.1.4, 11.1.3.6
Arbitration, commercial, 16.4
Arbitration *extra legem*, question of grounds for refusal to enforce arbitral award, 20.2.3.9.1
Arbitration (International Investment Disputes) Act 1966, and enforcement of arbitration awards, 20.5.4
Arrest Convention, and Brussels and Lugano Conventions, 8.2.1.3
Assignment
choice of law in contract, 12.6
assignee–debtor relationship, 12.6.3
assignor–assignee relationship, 12.6.2
Authentic instruments, and Brussels and Lugano Conventions, 9.4.5.1
Aval, contract of, question of indorsement, and choice of law, 12.9.2.2.5–12.9.2.2.6

Babanaft Proviso, and effect of Mareva injunctions, 21.4.2.4.2
Babcock v. *Jackson*, and choice of law in tort, 13.2.3.1
Bankruptcy, and scope of Conventions, 3.3.3.2
Boys v. *Chaplin*, and choice of law in tort, 13.3.2–13.3.3
Branch registration regime, for oversea companies, 6.1.2.2.3
Branches
definition of, 6.1.2.3
in England, and service of process on oversea company, 6.1.2.5
question of alternative fora, 5.5.5

Brussels Convention, 1.2.3, 3.1.1–3.1.9
and antisuit injunctions, 22.3
and choice of law in contract, applicable law for individual contracts of employment, 12.2.2.2
interpretation, 3.2.1
jurisdiction *in personam*, 4.1–4.4
and arbitration, 17.5.1.1
See also Jurisdiction *in personam*
jurisdiction rules, 5.0–5.10
alternative fora, Articles 5 and 6, 5.5–5.6
and consumer contracts, Article(s) 13–15, 5.7.2
domicile rule, Article 2, 5.4
exclusive jurisdiction, Article 16, 5.1
and insurance contracts, Article(s) 7–12A, 5.7.1
jurisdiction agreements, Article 17, 5.3
lis pendens, Article(s) 21–23, 5.9
provisional and protective measures, 5.8
submission, Article 18, 5.2
recognition and enforcement under, 9.4
enforcement, 9.4.4
recognition, 9.4.2, 9.4.3
relationship with national law, 9.4.6
scope, 9.4.1.1
relationship with other conventions, 3.4–3.5
scope, 3.3
civil and commercial, 3.3.2
exceptions, 3.3.3
and shipping, 8.2
See also Lugano Convention *and* Table of Conventions

Cambridgeshire factor, and question of *forum conveniens*, 6.4.4.4
Central banks, and question of state immunity, 2.3.5.5.2
Choice of law, 1.3
contract, 10.0–10.5
applicable law
changing chosen law, 11.1.5
splitting, 11.1.4
common law, 10.1
express choice, 11.1.2
implied choice, 11.1.3
mandatory rules, 11.1.6
Civil Jurisdiction and Judgments Act 1982
enforcement of arbitration awards, 20.5.1
and proceedings *in personam*, 21.3.1.2
question of discretion, 21.3.1.2.4
relationship with Conventions, 21.3.1.2.2, 21.3.1.2.3
s.25, jurisdiction and proceedings *in personam*, 21.3.1.2.1
s.32, as defence to recognition and enforcement of foreign judgments, 9.2.7.5
text, App.1
Collision Convention, and Brussels and Lugano Conventions, 8.2.1.3
Commercial activities, question of state immunity, 2.3.4.4, 2.3.5.4
Commodity arbitration
features, 16.3.3
restrictions regarding agreements excluding appeals, 19.5.2.6
Common law
and choice of law in contract, 10.1, 11.4.2.1
advantages, 10.2.2.2–10.2.2.4
applicable law for individual contracts of employment, 12.2.2.1
and choice of law in tort, 13.1.3.2
English cases, 13.3.1.1
recognition and enforcement of arbitration awards, 20.3
recognition and enforcement of foreign judgments
basic framework, 9.2.1
defences, 9.2.7
judgments *in rem*, 9.2.8
question of statutory regimes, 9.3
requirements, 9.2.2–9.2.6
role, 9.0.1
relationship with Administration of Justice Act 1920, 9.3.1
See also Arbitration, enforcement of awards
Companies, *see* Corporations
Companies Act, 1985
and service of process on oversea company, 6.1.2.5–6.1.2.6
terms defined, 6.1.2.3–6.1.2.4
Company law, and Rome Convention, 10.4.1.2.6
Conflicts, true or false, and choice of law in tort, 13.2.2.2.2, 13.2.3.1.3
Consent, and choice of law in contract, 11.4.2.3
Consumer contracts
domicile rule, 5.4.2
jurisdiction rules, 5.7
and Conventions, 5.7.2
Modified Convention, 7.2.4
question of choice of law, 12.1
qualifying conditions, 12.1.1.2
Contract
alternative fora, 5.5.2–5.5.3
obligation in question, 5.5.3.2
question of place of performance, 5.5.3.3
choice of law, 10.0–10.5, 11.1–11.4, 12.1–12.10
agency, 12.7
applicable law, 11.1–11.2
changing, 11.1.5
express choice, 11.1.2
mandatory rules, 11.1.6, 11.2.4
question of implied choice, 11.1.3
scission, 11.2.3.7
splitting, 11.1.4
capacity, 11.4.4
corporations, 11.4.4.2
individuals, 11.4.4.1
and negotiable instruments, 12.9.2.5
carriage of goods, 12.3
common law, 10.1
consequences of breach, 11.4.7
consumer contracts, 12.1
discharge, 11.4.8
formal validity, 11.4.3
rules, 11.4.3.2
illegality, 11.4.10
individual contracts of employment, 12.2
insurance and reinsurance, 12.8
interaction with tort rules, 13.4. *See also* Tort

Contract—*cont.*
  choice of law—*cont.*
    interpretation, 11.4.6
    mandatory rules, 11.3
      overriding rules, 11.3.3
    material validity, 11.4.2
      general principle, 11.4.2.2
    negotiable instruments, 12.9
    nullity, 11.4.9
    performance, 11.4.5
    and property
      immovable, 12.4
      intangible, 12.6
      tangible movable, 12.5
    quasi-contract and restitution, 12.10
  and service of writ out of jurisdiction, 6.3.3.4–6.3.3.5
Contracts (Applicable Law) Act 1990, 10.2
  and negotiable instruments, 12.9.1.3
  text, App.3
Corporations
  branches, agencies and other establishments, test, 5.5.5.1
  choice of law in contract, 11.4.2.3.2, 11.4.4.2
  domicile, 4.1.2–4.1.3
  and exclusive jurisdiction, 5.1.2
  and Modified Convention, 7.2.1.2
  question of place of business, 9.3.2.2.2.2
  question of presence, 6.1.2
    British companies, 6.1.2.1
    oversea companies, 6.1.2.2–6.1.2.6
  territorial connection, and jurisdiction of original court, 9.2.5.4
Corporations, foreign, question of legal capacity, 2.1.1, 2.1.3
Corporations, international, question of legal capacity, 2.1.4
Counterclaims, and alternative fora, 5.6.4
Countertrade, question of characteristic performance, 11.2.3.2.4
Court, leave of, for service out of jurisdiction, *see* Service, out of jurisdiction
Court settlements, and Brussels and Lugano Conventions, 9.4.5.2
Courts
  choice of
    in Contracting State, 5.3.2.2
    in non-contracting State, 5.3.2.3
Courts, English, jurisdiction clauses in favour of, 6.3.3.4.5
Courts first and second seised
  and *lis pendens*, 5.9.1.4
  relationship, 5.9.2.3
Courts, national, interpretation of Brussels Convention, 3.2.1.3
Curial law, *see* Arbitration

Damages
  and choice of law in tort, 13.1.3.4.2
  and determining money of account, 14.2.2.2
  and question of *forum conveniens*, 6.4.4.8
Damages, multiple, as defence, 9.2.7.6
Debts, determining money of account, 14.2.2.1
Defamation, question of choice of law, 13.1.3.3.4
Defendant, consent of, and jurisdiction *in personam*, 6.2
Defendants, multiple
  alternative fora for, 5.6.2
  question of *forum conveniens*, 6.4.4.3
  and service of writ out of jurisdiction, 6.3.3.3
Delict, matters relating to, 5.5.2, 5.5.4
Diplomatic immunity, and legal capacity, 2.4
Diplomatic relations, breakdown, effect on proceedings, 2.3.6.1.3–2.3.6.1.6
Dispute resolution clauses, 1.1.4
Domestic law, reference to provisions of, and implied choice of law, 11.1.3.4
Domicile
  application of Article 18, 5.1.2
  and choice of court in non-contracting State, 5.3.2.3.1
  and court's jurisdiction, 4.4.2–4.4.3
  effect on jurisdiction agreements, 5.3.2.2.4–5.3.2.2.5
  and jurisdiction *in personam* under Conventions, 4.1
  and jurisdiction of original court in foreign judgments, 9.2.5.6
  and jurisdiction rules, 4.2.1, 4.2.2, 5.0.1
  lis pendens and related actions, 5.9.1.2
  and Modified Convention, 7.1.1.3–7.1.1.4
  national law and formal requirements of Article 17, 5.3.3.5
  and service of writ out of jurisdiction, 6.3.3.1
  See also Individuals
Domicile rule, Article 2, 5.4
Domiciles, multiple, question of, 4.1.3
Double actionability
  and choice of law in tort, 13.3.3
  and foreign limitation periods, 15.1.1.3

EC law, and arbitration, 17.4
Economic torts, question of choice of law, 13.1.3.3.3
Embassies, question of legal capacity of staff, 2.4
Employment
  contracts of
    agreements conferring jurisdiction, 5.3.1.1
    individual
      choice of law, 12.2
        applicable law, 12.2.2
          common law, 12.2.2.1
        defined, 12.2.1
        mandatory rules, 12.2.3
        overriding rules, 12.2.4
      interaction between rules of contract and tort, 13.4.1.3
      jurisdiction rules, 5.5.3.4.2
    jurisdiction clauses, 5.3.8
    jurisdiction rules, 5.5.3.4
Enemy aliens, inability to sue, 2.2
Enforcement, partial, under Conventions, 9.4.1.2.4
Enforcement proceedings
  and exclusive jurisdiction, 5.1.5
  question of *lis pendens*, 5.9.1.3
England
  courts' interpretation of Brussels Convention, 3.2.1.3

England—*cont.*
discretion to stay proceedings in, 5.10
and disputes concerning foreign land, 5.10.3
and foreign jurisdiction clauses, 5.10.2
and question of *forum conveniens*, 5.10.1
domicile
of individuals, 4.1.1.1–4.1.1.2
multiple, 4.1.3.2
procedure regarding submission, 5.2.4
question of public policy, and applicable law, 6.4.4.10.3
See also Modified Convention; United Kingdom
Enrichment, question of choice of law in contract, 12.10.1.2
Entities, separate, enforcement against, 2.3.5.5
Establishments, other, question of alternative fora, 5.5.5
Estoppel, cause of action, 9.2.6
Estoppel, issue, 9.2.6
Estoppel *per rem judicatam*
and foreign judgments, 9.2.1.2–9.2.1.3
defence, 9.2.7.4
European Community, 3.3.3.2.1, 9.6.3
See also Brussels Convention; Lugano Convention; Rome Convention
European Court of Justice, 3.2.1.2.4, 3.2.3, 6.1.2.3.2–6.1.2.3.3
and interpretation of Conventions, 3.2.1.1, 3.2.2.3, 10.3.1–10.3.2
European Free Trade Association (EFTA)
and Conventions, 3.2.2.1.2, 3.2.2.2
See also Lugano Convention
Exchange contracts, and foreign currency, 14.4.2
Exchange control legislation
problems, 14.4
exchange contracts, 14.4.2

Family law, and scope of Conventions, 3.3.3.1, 9.4.3.7, 9.4.4.2.1
Federal states, question of territorial connection, and jurisdiction of original court in recognition and enforcement of foreign judgments, 9.2.5.5
Fora, alternative
Article 5, 5.5
for jurisdiction agreements, 5.3.5
question of choice between, 6.4.1
See also Forum
Foreign currency, 14.1–14.4
exchange control legislation, 14.4
judgments in, 14.3
Miliangos case, 14.3.2
money of account and money of payment, 14.2
determination, 14.2.2
damages, 14.2.2.2
debts, 14.2.2.1
discharge of obligations, 14.2.3
nominalism, 14.1
gold clauses, 14.1.3
question of law governing obligation, 14.1.2
and damages for late payment, 14.1.2.2
and revalorisation, 14.1.2.1
Foreign judgments
recognition and enforcement, 9.0–9.6
basic principles, 9.0.1
Foreign judgments—*cont.*
recognition and enforcement—*cont.*
common law, *see* Common law
in rem, 9.2.8
and jurisdiction, 1.2
question of merger, 9.1.3
scope, 9.1.1–9.1.2
Foreign Judgments (Reciprocal Enforcement) Act 1933
and enforcement of arbitration awards, 20.5.3
relationship with common law, 9.3.2
enforcement, 9.3.2.1
defences to, 9.3.2.2
recognition, 9.3.2.3
Foreign juristic entities, question of legal capacity, 2.1
Foreign law
and contract, 11.1.1.3.2
proof of, 23.1–23.4
appeals, 23.4
and conflict of evidence, 23.3.3
and experts, 23.3.4
and necessity, 23.2
requirement of evidence, 23.3.1
seeking outside help, 23.3.6
and subsequent use of decisions, 23.3.5
treatment, 23.1
uncontradicted evidence, 23.3.2
Foreign limitation periods, 15.1–15.2
and effects of disapplication, 15.1.2.3
and public policy, 15.1.2.2
and Rome Convention, 15.2
and undue hardship, 15.1.2.1
Foreign Limitation Periods Act 1984, 15.1
Forms, standard, use of, implications for choice of law, 11.1.3.1
Forum
and discretion to stay, 6.1.4
and service out of the jurisdiction, 6.3.1.1.2–6.3.1.1.4
Forum conveniens
choice of law rules, 6.4.4.12
court's discretion to allow litigation, 6.4
appeals against exercise of, 6.4.6
development of English law, 6.4.2
tests, 6.4.3–6.4.4
applicable law, 6.4.4.10
language, 6.4.4.11
and discretion to stay, 5.10.1, 6.1.4
and jurisdiction, 1.2.2.1, 1.3.5
and jurisdiction of original court, 9.2.5.3.3, 9.2.5.6
service on oversea company, 6.1.2.6.4
service under RSC Order 11, 6.3.1.1.1–6.3.1.1.2
procedure, 6.3.1.2
service of writ out of jurisdiction, 6.3.4
and shipping, 8.2.3.2
weighting of factors, 6.4.5
Forum non conveniens, *see Forum conveniens*
Fraud
and conduct of arbitration, 16.2.3.2.2.1
as defence, 9.2.7.2, 9.4.3.3.3, 20.3.4.2.4
and registration, 9.3.1.3, 9.3.2.2.4
restitution, and service of writ out of jurisdiction, 6.3.3.7

Friendly Societies Act 1992, and choice of law in insurance and reinsurance contracts, 12.8.3

Geneva Convention 1927, and harmonisation of commercial arbitration, 16.4.2.1
Geneva Protocol 1923, and harmonisation of commercial arbitration, 16.4.2.1
Gibraltar, and place of business registration regime, 6.1.2.2.4
Gold clauses, and involving foreign currency, 14.1.3
Goods, carriage of, and choice of law in contract, 12.3
Governmental interest analysis, and choice of law in tort, 13.2.2.2, 13.2.3.1.4, 13.2.4
Governments, foreign, question of legal capacity, 2.1.6
Guarantee, contracts of, and formal validity, 11.4.3.1.2–11.4.3.1.3

Hague-Visby Rules
  and choice of law in contract, 12.3.2
  effect on foreign jurisdiction clause, 5.3.4.3
Holiday lets, and jurisdiction rules, 5.1.1.3.2–5.1.1.3.5

Illegality, and choice of law in contract, 11.4.10
Immovables, *see* Property, immovable
Incorporation, and domestic law, 11.1.3.4
Individuals
  capacity and choice of law in contract, 11.4.4.1
  domicile, 4.1.1, 4.1.3
  residence, question of jurisdiction, 9.3.2.2.2.2
  service on, 6.1.1.1–6.1.1.2
  territorial connection, and jurisdiction of original court, 9.2.5.3
  See also Domicile
Injunctions, and service of writ out of jurisdiction, 6.3.3.2
Insolvency, and scope of Conventions, 3.3.3.2
Insurance Companies Act 1982, and choice of law in insurance and reinsurance contracts, 12.8.2
Insurance contracts
  and choice of law, 12.8
  domicile rule, 5.4.2
  jurisdiction rules, 5.7
    proceedings against insurers, 5.7.1.1
    proceedings against policy-holder, insured or beneficiary, 5.7.1.2
  Modified Convention, 7.2.4
  and restrictions under Arbitration Act 1979, 19.5.2.6
  and Rome Convention, 10.4.1.2.2
Intangibles, *see* Property, intangible
Intellectual property
  and adjudicative jurisdiction, 2.3.4.8
  and Conventions, 7.2.1.2, 10.4.1.1.3
  and exclusive jurisdiction, 5.1.4
  question of assignment, 12.6.2.2
Interlocutory injunctions, provisional measures, 21.1.2
Interlocutory orders, and judgments under Conventions, 9.4.1.2.2
International organisations, question of legal capacity, 2.5

Iran–US Claims Tribunal, and enforcement of arbitration awards, 20.5.5
Ireland, and Conventions, 9.4.3.8.2
Ireland, Northern
  and place of business registration regime, 6.1.2.2.4
  recognition and enforcement of foreign judgments, 9.2.7.5
  See also Modified Convention; United Kingdom
Irreconcilability, recognition and enforcement of foreign judgments, 9.3.2.2.6, 9.4.3.5–9.4.3.7

Judgments
  in foreign currency, *see* Foreign currency
  under Conventions, defined, 9.4.1.2
Judgments in default, 2.3.6.3
Judgments *in rem*
  recognition and enforcement, 9.2.8
    defences, 9.2.8.2
    enforcement, 9.2.8.3
    jurisdiction of original court, 9.2.8.1
Jurisdiction
  allocation within United Kingdom, 7.1–7.3
  arbitration, 17.5
  bases of, and Modified Convention, 7.2
  in cases involving foreign land, 6.6
  choice of law, principles, 1.3
  definitions, 1.2.1.1
  examination of, and exclusive jurisdiction, 5.1.6
  and recognition and enforcement of foreign judgments, 1.2
  relationship with merits of case when service out of jurisdiction, 6.3.2.2–6.3.2.5
  resisting enforcement, 9.3.2.2.2
  and service of writ out of, 6.3.3.4.2
Jurisdiction, adjudicative, and immunity, 2.3.4, 2.4.1.4
Jurisdiction agreements
  Article 17, 5.3
    alternative fora, 5.3.5
    material validity and interpretation, 5.3.4
    non-exclusive jurisdiction clauses, 5.3.6
  and choice of law in contract, 10.1.4
  and insurance contracts, 5.7.1.1.5, 5.7.1.3
  and Rome Convention, 10.4.1.2.3
  submission, 6.2.1
Jurisdiction clauses, 6.5
  English, 6.5.3
  in favour of English courts, 6.3.3.4.5
  foreign, 6.5.2
  and implied choice of law, 11.1.3.3
Jurisdiction clauses, foreign, and discretion to stay proceedings, 5.10.2
Jurisdiction, competent, and recognition and enforcement of foreign judgments, 9.2.5.1.1
Jurisdiction, enforcement, and state immunity, 2.3.5
Jurisdiction, exclusive
  Article 16, 5.1
    enforcement proceedings, 5.1.5
  question of rivalry, 5.9.4
Jurisdiction *in personam*
  and arbitration, 17.5.1
  and Conventions, 4.1–4.4, 5.0–5.10

Jurisdiction *in personam—cont.*
and Conventions—*cont.*
and exclusive jurisdiction, 5.1
procedural safeguards, 4.4
service of writ abroad, 4.3
structure, 4.2
presence
corporations, 6.1.2
individuals, 6.1.1
partnerships, 6.1.3
submission, 5.2, 6.2
traditional rules, 6.1–6.6
Justice, substantial, as defence, 9.2.7.1.2

Laches, and foreign limitation periods, 15.1.1.4–15.1.1.5
Land, and jurisdiction rules, 5.1.1.2.2–5.1.1.2.3
Land, foreign
disputes regarding, 5.10.3
and jurisdiction, 6.6
Language, as test for *forum conveniens*, 6.4.4.11
Law Commission, proposals regarding choice of law in tort, 13.1.3.4, 13.5.2–13.5.5
Legal aid, and Conventions, 9.4.4.6
Legal capacity, to sue or be sued, 2.1
Lex fori
and choice of law in tort, 13.2.1.1
compared with *lex loci delictii*, 13.2.3.2.3
Lex loci delictii
and choice of law in tort, 13.2.1.2
compared with *lex fori*, 13.2.3.2.3
Lex mercatoria, *see* Arbitration, law applicable to merits of dispute
Lex monetae, *see* Nominalism
Libel, question of choice of law, 13.1.3.3.4
Lis alibi pendens, question of *forum conveniens*, 6.4.4.2
Lis pendens
jurisdiction rules, 5.9
and Modified Convention, 7.3.1
Lloyd's form, and choice of law in contract, 10.1.4
Lugano Convention, 1.2.3, 3.1.10–3.1.14
alternative fora, Article 6, 5.6
and antisuit injunctions, 22.3
and consumer contracts, Article(s) 13–15, 5.7.2
direct jurisdiction rules, 5.0.1
domicile rule, Article 2, 5.4
exclusive jurisdiction, Article 16, 5.1
and insurance contracts, Article(s) 7–12A, 5.7.1
interpretation, 3.2.2
jurisdiction agreements, Article 17, 5.3
jurisdiction *in personam*, 4.1–4.4
and arbitration, 17.5.1.1
See also Jurisdiction *in personam*
lis pendens, Article(s) 21–23, 5.9
provisional and protective measures, 5.8
recognition and enforcement under, 9.4
enforcement, 9.4.4.3, 9.4.4.2
recognition, 9.4.2, 9.4.3
scope, 9.4.1.1
relationship with other conventions, 3.4–3.5
scope, 3.3
civil and commercial, 3.3.2
exceptions, 3.3.3
Lugano Convention—*cont.*
and shipping, 8.2
submission, Article 18, 5.2
Titles III and IV, relationship with national law, 9.4.6
See also Brussels Convention *and* Table of Conventions
Luxembourg Protocol
and European Court of Justice, 3.2.1.1
See also Brussels Convention *and* Table of Conventions

Mandatory rules, and contract law, 11.3
Mareva injunctions
and Article 24, 5.8.2
development, 21.1.1
operation, 21.1.3
development, 21.1.3.1
and disclosure orders, 21.1.3.4.1
effect, 21.1.3.3
in personam, 21.1.3.3.1
and security, 21.1.3.3.3
third parties, 21.1.3.3.2
obtaining, 21.1.3.2
and receivership orders, 21.1.3.4.2
use abroad, 21.4.1.5–21.4.1.6
conditions, 21.4.2.1
dangers, 21.4.2.5
exercise of discretion regarding, 21.4.2.2
practice, 21.4.2.3
protection of defendant and third parties, 21.4.2.4
Maritime liens, and Admiralty jurisdiction *in rem*, 8.1.2.2
Merger, of proceedings at home and abroad, 9.1.3
Miliangos case, and judgments in foreign currency, 14.3.2
Misrepresentation, and choice of law in tort, 13.1.3.3.2
Modified Convention
jurisdiction, 7.2
civil and commercial, 7.1
consumer contracts, 7.2.4
exclusive, 7.2.1
procedural matters and provisional measures, 7.2.5
prorogation, 7.2.2.1–7.2.2.2
special, 7.2.3
and staying proceedings, 7.3
discretion, 7.3.2
lis pendens, 7.3.1
Money of account, *see* Foreign currency
Money judgments, recognition and enforcement within United Kingdom, 9.5.3.2
Money of payment, *see* Foreign currency
Movables, tangible, *see* Property, tangible movable

National law, and formal requirements of Article 17, 5.3.3.5
Natural justice, as defence, 9.2.7.1, 20.3.4.2.2
Negligence, and choice of law in tort, 13.1.3.3.1
Negotiable instruments
choice of law in contract, 12.9
defined, 12.9.1.1

Negotiable instruments—*cont.*
choice of law in contract—*cont.*
question of governing law, 12.9.1.2
rules, 12.9.2
contractual capacity, 12.9.2.5
date of payment, 12.9.2.4
interpretation, 12.9.2.2
presentment, 12.9.2.3
questions of form, 12.9.2.1
transfer of the instrument, 12.9.2.6
and Rome Convention, 10.4.1.2.4
New York Convention 1958, and harmonisation of commercial arbitration, 16.4.2.2
Nominalism, question of judgments and obligations involving foreign currency, 14.1
Non-money judgments, recognition and enforcement within United Kingdom, 9.5.3.3
Nullity, and choice of law in contract, 11.4.9

Obligations, and contract, question of jurisdiction, 5.5.3.2
Organisations, and question of member State's immunity, 2.3.4.9
Oversea companies
question of presence in Britain, 6.1.2.2–6.1.2.6
service of process on, 6.1.2.5

Partnerships, rules regarding presence, 6.1.3
Party autonomy, principle regarding applicable law, 11.1.1.1
Performance
and choice of law in contract, 11.4.5
manner, 11.4.5.2
place of, and contract, question of jurisdiction, 5.5.3.3
Performance, characteristic, and applicable law, 11.2.3.4–11.2.3.5
Personal injury, and choice of law in tort, 13.1.3.4.2
Place of business
application in British law, 11.2.3.3.3–11.2.3.3.4
definition of, 6.1.2.4
in England, and service of process on oversea company, 6.1.2.6
registration regime for oversea companies, 6.1.2.2.3
Proceedings, stay of, question of appropriate forum, 6.1.4
Proper law
and choice of law in tort, 13.2.3.1.4, 13.2.2.1
contrasted with applicable law, 11.2.2
Property
and question of State's immunity, 2.3.4.7
scope of Rome Convention, 10.4.1.1.3
Property, immovable
choice of law in contract, 12.4
applicable law, 12.4.1
capacity, 12.4.3
formal validity, 12.4.2
contractual claims and rights *in rem*, and alternative fora, 5.6.5
and insurance contracts, jurisdiction rules, 5.7.1.1.2
tenancies, 5.1.1
in more than one Contracting State, 5.1.1.4
Property, intangible, assignment, choice of law in contract, 12.6
Property, tangible movable
choice of law in contract, 12.5
retention of title agreements, 12.5.2
transfer, 12.5.1
Protection of Trading Interests Act 1980, scope, 9.3.2.2.8
Protective measures, *see* Provisional measures
Provisional measures, 21.1–21.5
Anton Piller orders, *see* Anton Piller orders
different types, 21.1
extraterritorial, 21.4
foreign, enforcement, 21.5
interlocutory injunctions, 21.1.2
and interlocutory orders, 9.4.1.2.2.2–9.4.1.2.2.3
jurisdiction to grant
proceedings *in personam*, *see* Actions *in personam*
proceedings *in rem*, *see* Shipping
Mareva injunctions, *see* Mareva injunctions
Public authorities, and scope of Conventions, 3.3.2.4–3.3.2.5
Public policy
and application of contract law, 11.3
and arbitration, 17.3.8.2, 20.2.3.9
and choice of law, 1.3.5
and choice of law in contract, question of illegality, 11.4.10.1.1–11.4.10.1.2
as defence, 9.2.7.3, 9.4.3.3, 20.3.4.2.3
EC law and arbitration, 17.4.4
and foreign limitation periods, 15.1.2.1
question of, and enforcement of foreign judgments, 9.3.1.3, 9.3.2.2.5

Quasi-contract, and choice of law in contract, 12.10
Quasi-delict, *see* Delict

Registers, public, and exclusive jurisdiction, 5.1.3
Registration, improper, and Foreign Judgments (Reciprocal Enforcement) Act 1933, 9.3.2.2.1
Registration regimes, for oversea companies, 6.1.2.2.3
Reinsurance, and choice of law in contract, *see* Insurance
Renvoi, doctrine of, 10.5, 13.4.2.2.3.2
Res judicata, *see* Estoppel *per rem judicatam*
Residence, habitual, application in British law, 11.2.3.3.1
Restitution
and choice of law in contract, 12.10
and service of writ out of jurisdiction, 6.3.3.7
Road accidents, question of insurance, jurisdiction rules, 5.7.1.1.3
Rome Convention on the Law Applicable to Contractual Obligations
and choice of law, opposition, 10.2.2
and foreign limitation periods, 15.2
interpretation, 10.3
material scope, 10.4.1
temporal scope, 10.4.3
territorial scope, 10.4.2

Salvage
effect of Conventions, 8.2.4.1
and maritime liens, 8.1.2.4
Scotland
and Civil Jurisdiction and Judgments Act 1982, s.32, 9.2.7.5
See also Modified Convention; United Kingdom
Separability, doctrine of, and arbitration agreements, 18.1.2
Service
on defendant, and jurisdiction agreements, 6.2.1.2
means of
and British companies, 6.1.2.1
and individuals, 6.1.1
and oversea companies, 6.1.2.2.3
and partnerships, 6.1.3
out of jurisdiction, 6.3
procedure, 6.3.1.2–6.3.1.3
question of question to be tried, 6.3.2
and question of voluntary appearance, 6.2.3.2
Service, letter box, *see* Service, means of
Service, personal, *see* Service, means of
Service, postal, *see* Service, means of
Severability, doctrine of, *see* Arbitration agreements, doctrine of separability
Shareholders
and jurisdiction agreements, 5.3.2.1
writing as evidence, 5.3.3.1.2
Shipping, 8.0–8.2
actions *in rem*, 8.0.2, 8.1.2
and court first seised, 5.9.1.4.2
and *lis pendens*, 5.9.2.2.2–5.9.2.2.3
principles, 1.2.1.1.2.2
and provisional measures, 21.1.1.1, 21.2
Admiralty Marshal, and warrants for arrest, 8.1.4.1.3
and arbitration, 18.2.2.1.3.2, 18.2.3.2, 19.5.2.6
commencing proceedings, 8.1.4
and Conventions, 8.2
limitation of liability, 8.2.4.2
question of actions *in rem*, 8.2.1.2
salvage, 8.2.4.1
staying proceedings, 8.2.3
and enforcement of judgment, 2.3.5.4.2
and insurance contracts, 5.7.1.3.5.4, 5.7.1.3.5.2
proceedings *in personam*, *see* Actions *in personam*
question of State's immunity, 2.3.4.3
scope, 8.1.1.1–8.1.1.3
staying proceedings, 8.1.4.3
Social security, and scope of Conventions, 3.3.3.3
State immunity
question of legal capacity, 2.3
scope, 2.3.2.1, 2.3.5.3–2.3.5.5
and service of process, 2.3.6
State Immunity Act 1978, scheme, 2.3.3
States, service of process in proceedings against, 2.3.6
States, foreign, question of legal capacity, 2.1.5
Submission
Article 18, 5.2
jurisdiction *in personam*, 6.2
agreements to submit, 6.2.2
Submission—*cont.*
jurisdiction *in personam*—*cont.*
and jurisdiction agreements, 6.2.1
voluntary appearance, 6.2.3
and jurisdiction of original court, 9.2.5.2
and registration, 9.3.1.3, 9.3.2.2.2.1
and State's immunity from adjudicative jurisdiction, 2.3.4.1
Supreme Court Act 1981
jurisdiction
actions *in personam*, 8.1.3
actions *in rem*, 8.1.2
Admiralty, 8.1.1
and provisional measures, 21.3.2.2
text, App.2

Territories, not States, question of corporations' legal capacity, 2.1.3
Third parties
and alternative fora for proceedings, 5.6.3
and jurisdiction agreements, 5.3.3.4
and service of writ out of jurisdiction, 6.3.3.3.1–6.3.3.3.4
Time, and recognition and enforcement of foreign judgments under Conventions, 9.4.3.4.5
Time limits, and arbitration, 16.2.3.1.3
Tin Council case, question of international corporations' legal capacity, 2.1.4.2
Tort
choice of law, 13.1–13.5
approaches, 13.2
governmental interest analysis, 13.2.2.2, 13.2.4
lex fori, 13.2.1.1
lex loci delictii, 13.2.1.2
and proper law, 13.2.2.1
English rules, 13.1.3
background, 13.3.1
Boys v. *Chaplin*, 13.3.2
question of reform, 13.1.3.4, 13.5
interaction with contract rules, 13.4
and claims advanced in tort, 13.4.2
developed analysis, 13.4.2.2.2
simple analysis, 13.4.2.2.1
question of place, 13.1
matters relating to, 5.5.2, 5.5.4
and service of writ out of jurisdiction, 6.3.3.6
and State's immunity from adjudicative jurisdiction, 2.3.4.6
Trade arbitration, features, 16.3.3
Trade usages, and jurisdiction agreements, 5.3.3.3
Transactions, related, and implied choice of law, 11.1.3.5
Trusts, and special jurisdiction of Modified Convention, 7.2.3.1.1

UNCITRAL Arbitration Rules
and appeals under 1979 Act, 19.5.1.2
and choice of law, 17.3.4.5–17.3.4.6
and harmonisation of commercial arbitration, 16.4.2.3
model clause, 16.3.2.1
UNCITRAL Model Law, and harmonisation of commercial arbitration, 16.4.2.4

Undue hardship
  and arbitration, extending time limits, 16.2.3.1.3.3
  and foreign limitation periods, 15.1.2.1
Undue influence, as defence, 9.2.7.3.2–9.2.7.3.3
United Kingdom
  allocation of jurisdiction within, 7.1–7.3
  and choice of law in contract, 11.4.1
  corporate domicile, 4.1.2.2
  and enforcement of arbitration awards, 20.5.1
  individual domicile, 4.1.1.2, 4.1.3.2
  question of internal conflicts regarding Rome Convention, 10.4.2.2
  question of jurisdiction within, 1.2.4
  recognition and enforcement of judgments
    against other States, 9.6.2
    European Community, 9.6.3
  recognition and enforcement of judgments within, 9.5
    enforcement, 9.5.3
      money judgments, 9.5.3.2
      non-money judgments, 9.5.3.3
United Kingdom—*cont.*
  recognition and enforcement of judgments within—*cont.*
    recognition, 9.5.2
  recognition of internal foreign law, 23.2
  recognition of judgments against, 9.6.1
  reservation on Article 7(1), effect on illegality, 11.4.10.2.1–11.4.10.2.2
  service of writs within, 6.1.2.1
  See also England; Ireland, Northern; Modified Convention; Scotland
United States, approach to choice of law in tort, 13.2.1.3

Waiver, of diplomatic immunity, 2.4.1.4, 2.4.2.2
Wales, *see* England
War, and enemy aliens' inability to sue, 2.2.1
Writ, service abroad, 4.3
Writing, as evidence of jurisdiction agreement under Article 17, 5.3.3.1
Wrongs, threatened, and Modified Convention, 7.2.3.1.2